8502

P9-EEL-938

Short Story Criticism

Guide to Gale Literary Criticism Series

When you need to review criticism of literary works, these are the Gale series to use:

If the author's death date is:	You should turn to:

**After Dec. 31, 1959
(or author is still living)**

CONTEMPORARY LITERARY CRITICISM

for example: Jorge Luis Borges, Anthony Burgess,
William Faulkner, Mary Gordon,
Ernest Hemingway, Iris Murdoch

1900 through 1959

TWENTIETH-CENTURY LITERARY CRITICISM

for example: Willa Cather, F. Scott Fitzgerald,
Henry James, Mark Twain, Virginia Woolf

1800 through 1899

NINETEENTH-CENTURY LITERATURE CRITICISM

for example: Fedor Dostoevski, Nathaniel Hawthorne,
George Sand, William Wordsworth

1400 through 1799

LITERATURE CRITICISM FROM 1400 TO 1800
(excluding Shakespeare)

for example: Anne Bradstreet, Daniel Defoe,
Alexander Pope, François Rabelais,
Jonathan Swift, Phillis Wheatley

SHAKESPEAREAN CRITICISM

Shakespeare's plays and poetry

Antiquity through 1399

CLASSICAL AND MEDIEVAL LITERATURE CRITICISM

for example: Dante, Homer, Plato, Sophocles, Vergil,
the Beowulf Poet

Gale also publishes related criticism series:

CHILDREN'S LITERATURE REVIEW

This series covers authors of all eras who have written for the preschool through high school audience.

SHORT STORY CRITICISM

This series covers the major short fiction writers of all nationalities and periods of literary history.

POETRY CRITICISM

This series covers poets of all nationalities, movements, and periods of literary history.

Volume 7

Short Story Criticism

8502

Excerpts from Criticism of the
Works of Short Fiction Writers

Thomas Votteler
Editor

Bridget Travers
Associate Editor

Gale Research Inc. · *DETROIT* · *LONDON*

STAFF

Thomas Votteler, *Editor*

Cathy Falk, Marie Lazzari, Sean R. Pollock, Bridget Travers, *Associate Editors*

Elizabeth P. Henry, Dave Kmenta, James Poniewozik, Janet Witalec, *Assistant Editors*

Jeanne A. Gough, *Permissions & Production Manager*
Linda M. Pugliese, *Production Supervisor*
Maureen Puhl, Jennifer VanSickle, *Editorial Associates*
Donna Craft, Paul Lewon, Lorna M. Mabunda, Camille Robinson, *Editorial Assistants*

Victoria B. Cariappa, *Research Manager*
H. Nelson Fields, Judy L. Gale, Maureen Richards, *Editorial Associates*
Jennifer Brostrom, Paula Cutcher, Alan Hedblad, Robin Lupa, Mary Beth McElmeel, *Editorial Assistants*

Sandra C. Davis, *Permissions Supervisor (Text)*
Josephine M. Keene, Kimberly F. Smilay, *Permissions Associates*
Maria L. Franklin, Michele M. Lonoconus, Shalice Shah, Denise M. Singleton, Rebecca A. Stanko, *Permissions Assistants*

Patricia A. Seefelt, *Permissions Supervisor (Pictures)*
Margaret A. Chamberlain, *Permissions Associate*
Pamela A. Hayes, Keith Reed, *Permissions Assistants*

Mary Beth Trimper, *Production Manager*
Evi Seoud, *Assistant Production Manager*

Arthur Chartow, *Art Director*
C. J. Jonik, *Keyliner*

The paper used in this publication meets the minimum requirements of American National Standard for Information Sciences—Permanence Paper for Printed Library Materials, ANSI Z39.48-1984

Copyright © 1991 Gale Research Inc.
835 Penobscot Bldg.
Detroit, MI 48226-4094

Library of Congress Catalog Card Number 88-641014
ISBN 0-8103-2556-X
ISSN 0895-9439

Printed in the United States of America

Published simultaneously in the United Kingdom
by Gale Research International Limited
(An affiliated company of Gale Research Inc.)

Contents

Preface   vii

Acknowledgments   ix

Authors to be Featured in Forthcoming Volumes   xiii

Preface

Short Story Criticism (SSC) presents significant passages from criticism of the world's greatest short story writers and provides supplementary biographical and bibliographical materials to guide the interested reader to a greater understanding of the authors of short fiction. This series was developed in response to suggestions from librarians serving high school, college, and public library patrons, who had noted a considerable number of requests for critical material on short story writers. Although major short story writers are covered in such Gale literary criticism series as *Contemporary Literary Criticism (CLC), Twentieth-Century Literary Criticism (TCLC), Nineteenth-Century Literature Criticism (NCLC),* and *Literature Criticism from 1400 to 1800 (LC),* librarians perceived the need for a series devoted solely to writers of the short story genre.

Scope of the Work

SSC is designed to serve as an introduction to major short story writers of all eras and nationalities. For example, the present volume includes commentary on contemporary Argentinian author Julio Cortázar, nineteenth-century American writer Stephen Crane, contemporary Canadian writer Margaret Laurence, and early twentieth-century author Virginia Woolf.

Since these authors have inspired a great deal of relevant critical material, *SSC* is necessarily selective, and the editors have chosen the most important published criticism to aid readers and students in their research.

Approximately ten to fifteen authors are included in each volume, and each entry presents a historical survey of the critical response to that author's work. The length of an entry is intended to reflect the amount of critical attention the author has received from critics writing in English and from foreign critics in translation. Every attempt has been made to identify and include excerpts from the most significant essays on each author's work. In order to provide these important critical pieces, the editors will sometimes reprint essays that have appeared in previous volumes of Gale's Literary Criticism Series. Such duplication, however, never exceeds twenty percent of an *SSC* volume.

Organization of the Book

An *SSC* author entry consists of the following elements:

- The **author heading** cites the name under which the author most commonly wrote, followed by birth and death dates. If the author wrote consistently under a pseudonym, the pseudonym will be listed in the author heading and the author's actual name given in parentheses on the first line of the biographical and critical introduction.

- The **biographical and critical introduction** contains background information designed to introduce a reader to the author and the critical debates surrounding his or her work. Parenthetical material following the introduction provides references to other biographical and critical series published by Gale, including *CLC, TCLC, NCLC, Contemporary Authors,* and *Dictionary of Literary Biography.*

- A **portrait of the author** is included when available. Many entries also contain illustrations of materials pertinent to an author's career, including holographs of manuscript pages, title pages, dust jackets, letters, or representations of important people, places, and events in the author's life.

- The list of **principal works** is chronological by date of first publication and lists the most important works by the author. The first section comprises short story collections, novellas, and novella collections. The second section gives information on other major works by the author. For foreign authors, the editors have provided original foreign-language publication information and have selected what are considered the best and most complete English-language editions of their works.

- **Criticism** is arranged chronologically in each author entry to provide a useful perspective on changes in critical evaluation over the years. All short story, novella, and collection titles by the author featured in the entry are printed in boldface type to enable a reader to ascertain without difficulty the works discussed. Also for purposes of easier identification, the critic's name and the publication date of the essay are given at the beginning of each piece of criticism. Unsigned criticism is preceded by the title of the journal in which it appeared.

- Critical essays are prefaced with **explanatory notes** as an additional aid to students and readers using *SSC*. The explanatory notes provide several types of useful information, including: the reputation of a critic, the importance of a work of criticism, and the specific type of criticism (biographical, psychoanalytic, structuralist, etc.).

- A complete **bibliographical citation,** designed to help the interested reader locate the original essay or book, follows each piece of criticism.

- The **further reading list** appearing at the end of each author entry suggests additional materials on the author. In some cases it includes essays for which the editors could not obtain reprint rights.

New Features

Beginning with volume six, *SSC* contains two additional features designed to enhance the reader's understanding of short fiction writers and their works:

- Each *SSC* entry now includes, when available, **comments by the author** that illuminate his or her own works or the short story genre in general. These statements are set within boxes to distinguish them from the criticism.

- A **select bibliography of general sources on short fiction** is included as an appendix. Updated and amended with each new *SSC* volume, this listing of materials for further research provides readers with a selection of the best available general studies of the short story genre.

Other Features

A **cumulative author index** lists all the authors who have appeared in *SSC, CLC, TCLC, NCLC, LC,* and *Classical and Medieval Literature Criticism (CMLC),* as well as cross-references to other Gale series. Users will welcome this cumulated index as a useful tool for locating an author within the Literary Criticism Series.

A **cumulative nationality index** lists all authors featured in *SSC* by nationality, followed by the number of the *SSC* volume in which their entry appears.

A **cumulative title index** lists in alphabetical order all short story, novella, and collection titles contained in the *SSC* series. Titles of short story collections, separately published novellas, and novella collections are printed in italics, while titles of individual short stories are printed in roman type with quotation marks. Each title is followed by the author's name and the corresponding volume and page numbers where commentary on the work may be located. English-language translations of original foreign-language titles are cross-referenced to the foreign titles so that all references to discussion of a work are combined in one listing.

A Note to the Reader

When writing papers, students who quote directly from any volume in the Literary Criticism Series may use the following general forms to footnote reprinted criticism. The first example pertains to material drawn from periodicals, the second to material reprinted from books:

[1] Henry James, Jr., "Honoré de Balzac," *The Galaxy* 20 (December 1875), 814-36; excerpted and reprinted in *Short Story Criticism,* Vol. 5, ed. Thomas Votteler (Detroit: Gale Research, 1990), pp. 8-11.

[2] F. R. Leavis, *D. H. Lawrence: Novelist* (Alfred A. Knopf, 1956); excerpted and reprinted in *Short Story Criticism,* Vol. 4, ed. Thomas Votteler (Detroit: Gale Research, 1990), pp. 202-06.

Suggestions Are Welcome

Readers who wish to suggest authors to appear in future volumes, or who have other suggestions, are invited to contact the editors by writing to Gale Research, Inc., Literary Criticism Division, 835 Penobscot Building, Detroit, Mi., 48226-4094.

Acknowledgments

The editors wish to thank the copyright holders of the excerpted criticism included in this volume, the permissions managers of many book and magazine publishing companies for assisting us in securing reprint rights, and Anthony Bogucki for assistance with copyright research. We are also grateful to the staffs of the Detroit Public Library, the Library of Congress, the University of Detroit Library, Wayne State University Purdy/Kresge Library Complex, and the University of Michigan Libraries for making their resources available to us. Following is a list of the copyright holders who have granted us permission to reprint material in this volume of *SSC*. Every effort has been made to trace copyright, but if omissions have been made, please let us know.

COPYRIGHTED EXCERPTS IN *SSC* VOLUME 7, WERE REPRINTED FROM THE FOLLOWING PERIODICALS:

American Literature, v. 43, November, 1971; v. LI, November, 1979. Copyright © 1971, 1979 Duke University Press, Durham, NC. Both reprinted with permission of the publisher.—*Arizona Quarterly,* v. 38, Summer, 1982 for "Stephen Crane's 'The Upturned Face' as Expressionist Fiction" by Bill Christopherson. Copyright © 1982 by Arizona Board of Regents. Reprinted by permission of the publisher and the author.—*The Atlantic Monthly,* v. 225, March, 1970 for a review of "A Bird in the House" by Edward Weeks. Copyright 1970 by The Atlantic Monthly Company, Boston, MA. Reprinted by permission of the author.—*Book World—Chicago Tribune,* May 24, 1981 for "John Gardner's Wizardry Brings His Art of Life" by Peter Collier. Contents copyright © by the *Chicago Tribune.* Reprinted by permission of the author.—*The Canadian Forum,* v. XLIV, July, 1964 for "The Compassionate Eve" by Hilda Kirkwood. Reprinted by permission of the author.—*Canadian Literature,* n. 45, Summer, 1970 for "Jungle and Prairie" by George Woodcock; n. 112, Spring, 1987 for " 'Uncertain Flowering': An Overlooked Short Story by Margaret Laurence" by W. J. Keith. Both reprinted by permission of the respective authors.—*Chicago Tribune,* December 1, 1974 for "Gardner's Characters Give Fiction Back Its Intelligence" by Kelly Cherry. © copyrighted 1974, Chicago Tribune Company. All rights reserved. Reprinted by permission of the author.—*The Christian Science Monitor,* June 24, 1981 for "From Gardner, Short Studies Dimmed by Abstractions" by Bruce Allen. © 1981 The Christian Science Publishing Society. All rights reserved. Reprinted by permission of the author.—*CLA Journal,* v. XVIII, December, 1974. Copyright, 1974 by The College Language Association. Used by permission of The College Language Association.—*Dada/Surrealism,* n. 5, 1975. 1975 © Association for the Study of Dada and Surrealism.—*The Detroit News,* May 10, 1981. Copyright 1981, *The Detroit News,* a Gannett Corporation. Reprinted with the permission of the publisher.—*English Journal,* v. 54, April, 1965 for "Stephen Crane's 'The Bride Comes to Yellow Sky' " by A. M. Tibbetts. Copyright © 1965 by the National Council of Teachers of English. Reprinted by permission of the publisher and the author.—*English Studies,* Netherlands, v. 68, June, 1987. © 1987 by Swets & Zeitlinger B. V. Reprinted by permission of the publisher.—*English Studies in Canada,* v. XV, June, 1989 for " 'I Am Not Trying to Tell a Story': Three Short Fictions by Virginia Woolf" by Susan Dick. © Association of Canadian University Teachers of English 1989. Reprinted by permission of the publisher and the author.—*Hispania,* v. 56, December, 1973 for "Destructive and Ironically Redemptive Fantasy in Cortázar" by Lanin A. Gyurko. © 1973 The American Association of Teachers of Spanish and Portuguese, Inc. Reprinted by permission of the publisher and the author.—*The Hudson Review,* v. XVII, Winter, 1964-65. Copyright © 1965 by The Hudson Review, Inc. Reprinted by permission of the publisher.—*The International Fiction Review,* v. 12, Winter, 1985. © copyright 1985 International Fiction Association. Reprinted by permission of the publisher.—*Journal of American Culture,* v. 11, Winter, 1988. Copyright © 1988 by Ray B. Browne. Reprinted by permission of the publisher.—*Journal of Canadian Studies/Revue d'etudes canadiennes,* v. XI, November, 1976 for "The Long Trek Home: Margaret Laurence's Stories" by Patricia Morley. Reprinted by permission of the publisher and the author.—*The Journal of Narrative Technique,* v. 15, Winter, 1985. Copyright © 1985 by *The Journal of Narrative Technique.* Reprinted by permission of the publisher.—*Kentucky Romance Quarterly,* v. 30, 1983. © 1983 University Press of Kentucky. Reprinted by permission of the publisher.—*Latin American Literary Review,* v. XV, July-December, 1987. Reprinted by permission of the publisher.—*Los Angeles Times,* May 19, 1981. Copyright, 1981, *Los Angeles Times.* Reprinted by permission of the publisher.—*The Markham Review,* v. 3, May, 1973. Reprinted by permission of the publisher.—*The Massachusetts Review,* v. XIX, Summer, 1978. © 1978. Reprinted from *The Massachusetts Review,* The Massachusetts Review, Inc. by permission.—*Modern Fiction Studies,* v. 18, Autumn, 1972; v. 24, Winter, 1978. Copyright © 1972, 1978 by Purdue Research Foundation, West Lafayette, IN 47907. All rights reserved. Both reprinted with permission.—*Mosaic: A Journal for the Interdisciplinary Study of Literature,* v. XIV, Fall, 1981. © *Mosaic* 1981. Acknowledgment of previous publication is herewith made.—*National Review,* New York, v. XXVII, February 28, 1975. © 1975 by National Review, Inc., 150 East 35th Street, New York, NY 10016. Reprinted with permission of the publisher.—*New Mexico Quarterly,*

v. XXXVI, Summer, 1966 for "Julio Cortázar or The Slap in the Face" by Luis Harss with Barbara Dohmann. Copyright, 1966 by The University of New Mexico. Reprinted by permission of the authors.—*The New Republic,* v. 171, December 7, 1974. © 1974 The New Republic, Inc. Reprinted by permission of *The New Republic.*—*The New York Review of Books,* v. XXII, February 20, 1975. Copyright © 1975 Nyrev, Inc. Reprinted with permission from *The New York Review of Books.*—*The New York Times Book Review,* February 12, 1978. Copyright © 1978 by The New York Times Company./ April 19, 1970; December 15, 1974; November 9, 1980; May 17, 1981; February 23, 1986. Copyright © 1970, 1974, 1980, 1981, 1986 by The New York Times Company. All reprinted by permission of the publisher.—*Nineteenth-Century French Studies,* v. XIV, Spring-Summer, 1986. © 1986 by T. H. Goetz. Reprinted by permission of the publisher.—*Nottingham French Studies,* v. 27, November, 1988. Reprinted by permission of the publisher.—*Partisan Review,* v. XLII, 1975 for "The Name of the Game" by George Levine. Copyright © 1975 by *Partisan Review.* Reprinted by permission of the publisher and the author.—*Prairie Schooner,* v. 54, Winter, 1980-81. © 1980 by University of Nebraska Press./ v. XLIII, Summer, 1969. © 1969 by University of Nebraska Press. Reprinted from *Prairie Schooner* by permission of the University of Nebraska Press.—*Rendezvous,* v. 1, Spring, 1966. Copyright © 1966 *Rendezvous.* Reprinted by permission of the publisher.—*The Review of Contemporary Fiction,* v. III, Fall, 1983. Copyright, 1983, by John O'Brien. Reprinted by permission of the publisher.—*Revista Canadiense de Estudios Hispanicos,* v. XIII, Otoño, 1988 for "The Writer and Politics in Four Stories by Julio Cortázar" by Maurice Hemingway and Frank McQuade. Reprinted by permission of Carleton University and the authors.—*Revue des langues vivantes,* v. 40, 1974-75 for " 'The Mark on the Wall': Virginia Woolf's World in a Snailshell" by Jeanne Delbaere-Garant. Reprinted by permission of the author.—*Saturday Review,* v. XLVII, June 13, 1964. © 1964 *Saturday Review* magazine.—*Slavic and East-European Journal,* v. 15, 1971; v. 30, Summer, 1986; v. 31, Summer, 1987. © 1971, 1986, 1987 by AATSEEL of the U.S., Inc. All reprinted by permission of the publisher.—*The Southern Review,* Louisiana State University, v. X, April, 1974 for "Experiments in Another Country: Stephen Crane's City Sketches" by Alan Trachtenberg. Copyright, 1974, by the author. Reprinted by permission of the author.—*Studies in American Fiction,* v. 15, Autumn, 1987. Copyright © 1987 Northeastern University. Reprinted by permission of the publisher.—*Studies in English,* v. XXXVII, 1958 for "Style and Meaning in Stephen Crane: 'The Open Boat' " by James B. Colvert. Reprinted by permission of the publisher and the author.—*Studies in Short Fiction,* v. VIII, Winter, 1971; v. X, Spring, 1973; v. 19, Winter, 1982. Copyright 1971, 1973, 1982 by Newberry College. All reprinted by permission of the publisher.—*The Tamarack Review,* n. 55, 1970 for "A Familiar Landscape" by Henry Kreisel. Reprinted by permission of the author.—*The Times Literary Supplement,* n. 3848, December 12, 1975; n. 3988, September 8, 1978. © Times Supplements Ltd. (London) 1975, 1978. Both reproduced from *The Times Literary Supplement* by permission.—*Twentieth Century Literature,* v. 33, Spring, 1987. Copyright 1987, Hofstra University Press. Reprinted by permission of the publisher.—*The University of Windsor Review,* v. XVI, Fall-Winter, 1981 for "Cages and Escapes in Margaret Laurence's 'A Bird in the House' " by Arnold E. Davidson. Reprinted by permission of the publisher and the author.—*World Literature Today,* v. 56, Winter, 1982. Copyright 1982 by the University of Oklahoma Press. Reprinted by permission of the publisher.—*World Literature Written in English,* v. 11, April, 1972 for "The Short Stories of Margaret Laurence" by Clara Thomas. © copyright 1972 *WLWE-World Literature Written in English.* Reprinted by permission of the publisher and the author.

COPYRIGHTED EXCERPTS IN *SSC,* VOLUME 7, WERE REPRINTED FROM THE FOLLOWING BOOKS:

Andrews, William L. From *The Literary Career of Charles W. Chesnutt.* Louisiana State University Press, 1980. Copyright © 1980 by Louisiana State University Press. All rights reserved. Reprinted by permission of the publisher.—Banks, Joanne Trautman. From "Virginia Woolf and Katherine Mansfield," in *The English Short Story, 1880-1945: A Critical History.* Edited by Joseph M. Flora. Twayne, 1985. Copyright 1985 by Twayne Publishers. Reprinted with the permission of Twayne Publishers, a division of G. K. Hall & Co., Boston.—Belinsky, V. G. From "A Survey of Russian Literature in 1847: Part Two," in *Belinsky, Chernyshevsky, and Dobrolyubov: Selected Criticism.* Edited by Ralph E. Matlaw. E. P. Dutton & Co., 1962. Copyright 1962 by E. P. Dutton, Inc. All rights reserved. Reprinted by permission of the publisher, E. P. Dutton, a division of Penguin Books USA Inc.—Berryman, John. From *The Freedom of the Poet.* Farrar, Straus and Giroux, 1976. Copyright © 1940, 1968, 1976 by John Berryman. Reprinted by permission of Farrar, Straus and Giroux, Inc.—Buss, Helen M. From *Mother and Daughter Relationships in the Manawaka Works of Margaret Laurence.* University of Victoria, 1985. © 1985 by Helen M. Buss. Reprinted by permission of the author.—Capone, Giovanna. From " 'A Bird in the House': Margaret Laurence on Order and the Artist," in *Gaining Ground: European Critics on Canadian Literature, Vol. VI.* Edited by Robert Kroetsch and Reingard M. Nischik. NeWest Press, 1985. Copyright © 1985 Giovanna Capone. All rights reserved. Reprinted by permission of the author.—Cooley, John R. From *Savages and Naturals: Black Portraits by White Writers in Modern American Literature.* University of Delaware Press, 1982. © 1982 by Associated University Presses, Inc. Reprinted by permission of the publisher.—Crane, Stephen. From a letter to Lily Brandon on February 29, 1896 as quoted in Melvin Schoberlin's introduction to *The Sullivan County Sketches of Stephen Crane.* Edited by Melvin Schoberlin. Syracuse University Press, 1949. Copyright 1949 by Melvin Schoberlin. All rights reserved.—Crane, Stephen. From *Stephen Crane: Letters.* Edited by R. W. Stallman and Lillian Gilkes. New York University Press, 1960. Copyright © 1960 by New York University.—Dinesen, Isak. From *Daguerreotypes and Other Essays.* The University of Chicago Press, 1979. © 1979 by the Rungstedlund Foundation. All rights

by permission of Farrar, Straus and Giroux, Inc.—Woolf, Virginia. From *The Common Reader.* Harcourt Brace Jovanovich, 1925, L. & V. Woolf, 1925. Copyright 1925 by Harcourt Brace Jovanovich. Renewed 1953 by Leonard Woolf.—Woolf, Virginia. From *A Writer's Diary.* Edited by Leonard Woolf. Hogarth Press, 1953. Copyright, 1953, 1954 by Leonard Woolf.—Woolf, Virginia. From *A Reflection of the Other Person.* Edited by Nigel Nicolson and Joanne Trautmann. Hogarth Press, 1978. Letters copyright © 1978 by Quentin Bell and Angelica Garnett.

PHOTOGRAPHS AND ILLUSTRATIONS APPEARING IN *SSC,* VOLUME 7 WERE RECEIVED FROM THE FOLLOWING SOURCES:

Peter E. Beard: **p. 159;** Juncker-Jensen: **p. 165;** Thomas Dinesen: **p. 192;** Photograph by Joel Gardner: **p. 211;** Illustration by Herbert L. Fink: **p. 230;** McClelland and Stewart: **p. 243;** Photo Lenare: **p. 365;** © Gisele Freund: **p. 403.**

Authors to Be Featured in Forthcoming Volumes

James Baldwin, 1924-1987. (American novelist, essayist, dramatist, and short story writer)—Baldwin, who emerged in the 1960s as one of the civil rights movement's most eloquent spokesmen, is widely regarded as an important figure in contemporary American literature. In the short stories of his acclaimed collection, *Going to Meet the Man,* Baldwin vividly exposed some of the polarized racial and sexual attitudes prevalent in American society during the 1960s, while challenging readers to confront and resolve these issues.

Raymond Carver, 1938-1988. (American short story writer, poet, and editor)—Credited with helping to revive the popularity of short stories in the United States, Carver wrote minimalistic tales that often focus on working-class protagonists struggling to survive outside mainstream society. Collected in such books as *Will You Please Be Quiet, Please, What We Talk about When We Talk about Love, Cathedral,* and *Where I'm Calling From,* Carver's realistic stories are frequently infused with elements drawn from his own difficult life.

Kate Chopin, 1851-1904. (American short story writer, novelist, poet, and essayist)—A popular local colorist during her lifetime, Chopin is best known today for her psychological novel, *The Awakening.* She is also well regarded for such short stories as "Désirée's Baby" and "Story of an Hour," which, like *The Awakening,* incisively portray women who seek to subvert the restrictive mores of nineteenth-century Louisiana society.

Colette (Sidonie Gabrielle Colette), 1873-1954. (French novelist, short story writer, and journalist)—One of the most prolific French authors of the twentieth century, Colette focused in her writings upon some of the more unusual aspects of such traditional themes as human nature, sexual love, and the innocence of childhood. Her short story collections, including *Animal Dialogues, The Kepi,* and *Gigi, and Other Stories,* are often praised for their deft blending of sensuous detail, metaphorical language, and intense emotion.

Joseph Conrad, 1857-1924. (Polish-born English novelist, novella and short story writer, essayist, and autobiographer)—Conrad is a major writer of modern narrative fiction whose work is considered to have significantly affected the development of twentieth-century literature. His well-known novella *The Heart of Darkness* and his short story "The Secret Sharer" are often anthologized and are widely considered among the best works of their genres in the English language.

Gabriel García Márquez, b. 1928. (Colombian novelist, short story writer, journalist, critic, and scriptwriter)—A nobel laureate, García Márquez rose to international prominence during the "boom" of interest in Latin American literature during the 1960s. While best known for his acclaimed novel *One Hundred Years of Solitude,* García Márquez has also published several short fiction collections, including *Leaf Storm, and Other Stories, Big Mama's Funeral,* and *No One Writes to the Colonel, and Other Stories.* In these works, as in his novels, García Márquez blends fantasy and realism to examine the tumultuous history of South America.

Henry James, 1843-1916. (American novelist, novella and short story writer, essayist, biographer, autobiographer, and dramatist)—James is considered one of the greatest novelists in the English language for, among other reasons, his development of the point of view technique and his leadership in the advancement of Realism in American literature. In his stories and novellas, including "The Beast in the Jungle," *The Aspern Papers,* "The Lesson of the Master," and *The Turn of the Screw,* James successfully applied techniques and explored themes similar to those of his longer fiction.

Katherine Mansfield, 1888-1923. (New Zealand short story writer, critic, and poet)—During her brief career, Mansfield helped shape the modern short story form with her poetic, highly descriptive tales that emphasize mood over plot. Although she lived in London for most of her adult life, such acclaimed stories as "Prelude" and "A Doll's House" are set in her native New Zealand and evoke vivid images of her childhood.

Grace Paley, b. 1922. (American short story writer and essayist)—Critically acclaimed for her fiction collections *The Little Disturbances of Man, Enormous Changes at the Last Minute,* and *Later the Same Day,* Paley creates seriocomic stories noted for their authentic portrayals of working-class New Yorkers.

Leo Tolstoy, 1828-1910. (Russian novelist, dramatist, short story writer, and critic)—Among the most important figures in world literature, Tolstoy is revered for his novels *War and Peace* and *Anna Karenina.* His works of short fiction, including *The Death of Ivan Ilyich* and "God Sees the Truth, but Waits," set literary standards as well. In these and other tales, Tolstoy employed a simple narrative approach to mystical experience and philosophical truth, while creating multidimensional portraits of Tsarist Russian society.

Charles Waddell Chesnutt

1858-1932

American short story writer, novelist, essayist, journalist, and biographer.

Chesnutt was the first black American fiction writer to receive critical and popular attention from the predominantly white literary establishment and readership of his age. He is especially noted for short stories in which he conveyed implicit denunciations of slavery while appealing to readers of Plantation School fiction—fiction by white authors who wrote nostalgically of the antebellum South. Chesnutt also wrote overtly didactic short stories and novels with racial themes, advocating in particular the cause of mixed-race Americans, but the unpopularity of these preceptive works virtually ended Chesnutt's literary career.

Chesnutt was born in Cleveland, Ohio, to free parents of mixed racial heritage, and raised in Fayetteville, North Carolina. An excellent student, at the age of fourteen he became a pupil-teacher at the State Normal School for black students. He taught elsewhere in North and South Carolina before returning to Fayetteville in 1877 to become assistant principal, and then principal, at the State Normal School. Married in 1878, Chesnutt left teaching to pursue more profitable employment to support his growing family. He worked briefly as a reporter for a New York newspaper before settling his family in Cleveland in 1884, taking a job as a clerk and stenographer in the legal department of a railway company. Stimulated to study law, Chesnutt passed the Ohio bar exam in 1887 and founded a successful stenographic court reporting service. Although he was light-complected enough to "pass" in white society, Chesnutt never denied his black ancestry and furthermore was unwilling to accept the elitism of the nascent black and mulatto middle class that was then becoming established in the North. Subject to the inequities that befell those of mixed race, he was repudiated by many blacks as well as by whites.

Throughout his life Chesnutt considered pursuing a literary career, both as a means of making a living and with the aim of presenting racial issues from the point of view of a black person. After a few short stories and sketches appeared in local periodicals, his story "The Goophered Grapevine" was published in the *Atlantic Monthly* in 1887. Similar in structure to the Uncle Remus stories of Joel Chandler Harris, "The Goophered Grapevine" begins and ends with a frame narrative—commentary by the white narrator. A white northern couple who have moved to the South encounter Julius McAdoo, a former slave, who regales them with a "conjure tale," or supernatural folktale. An adept raconteur, McAdoo tells the story to entertain the northerners and to influence a decision they are contemplating. Claiming that the vineyard on the plantation that the couple wishes to buy is under a dangerous "goopher," or magic spell, McAdoo hopes to persuade them not to buy; this would allow McAdoo to continue living on the abandoned plantation and profiting from his illicit manufacture of wine. Although the northerners do

not believe the tale of magic, they enjoy the tale-telling, and offer McAdoo employment. Similarly, each subsequent conjure story influences the couple in a way that benefits McAdoo. Capitalizing on a vogue for southern local color fiction, Houghton Mifflin published *The Conjure Woman* in 1899. The success of the volume contributed to the decision to bring out a second collection, *The Wife of His Youth, and Other Stories of the Color Line,* that includes stories exploring the divided racial identity of mixed-blood Americans and the impassable racial barriers that prevent blacks from participating fully in the social, economic, and political life of the United States. This collection was less favorably received than Chesnutt's first, drawing criticism for focusing on racial issues that were commonly considered too sensitive for fictional exposition. Three subsequent novels, *The House behind the Cedars, The Marrow of Tradition,* and *The Colonel's Dream,* deal at length with such controversial themes as "passing" in white society, miscegenation, and proposed solutions to the racial problems of the South. The novels were unsuccessful financially and have been evaluated by critics as less accomplished artistically than the short stories. Chesnutt encountered increasing difficulties in finding publishers, and although he wrote several novels after *The Colonel's Dream,* these works remain unpublished. While he

1

continued to publish short stories in periodicals, as well as nonfiction essays addressing racial issues, he returned to his court reporting business in 1902 and devoted much of his time to it thereafter. His 1928 award of the Spingarn Medal by the National Association for the Advancement of Colored People was largely due to his literary achievements of several decades earlier. He died in 1932.

With Chesnutt's conjure stories, American readers were presented for the first time with authentic black folk culture. In these works, folktale motifs of magic and the traditional African folk figure of the trickster are cast against a background of the antebellum South. Often the stories are tragic, illustrating the injustice and cruelty of the slave system. The framing device rendered the protest elements of the stories less explicit and therefore, some critics contend, more acceptable to Chesnutt's white readers. The uncompromising racial themes of his second collection and his published novels are presented within no such propitiating format, and critics maintain that in his novels Chesnutt further sacrificed literary artistry to the urgency of his message. Nevertheless, these works are acclaimed for addressing the pressing social problems of race relations in the United States. As the first American author to explore the range of black experience in his fiction, Chesnutt stands at the forefront of an entire generation of black realist authors.

(For further information on Chesnutt's life and career, see *Twentieth-Century Literary Criticism,* Vols. 5, 39; *Black Literature Criticism,* Vol. 1; *Contemporary Authors,* Vols. 106, 125; and *Dictionary of Literary Biography,* Vols. 12, 50.)

PRINCIPAL WORKS

SHORT FICTION

The Conjure Woman　1899
The Wife of His Youth, and Other Stories of the Color Line
　1899
The Short Fiction of Charles W. Chesnutt　1974; revised
　edition, 1981

OTHER MAJOR WORKS

Frederick Douglass (biography)　1899
The House behind the Cedars (novel)　1900
The Marrow of Tradition (novel)　1901
The Colonel's Dream (novel)　1905

W. D. Howells (essay date 1900)

[*Howells was the chief progenitor of American Realism and one of the most influential American literary critics of the late nineteenth century. Through realism, a theory central to his fiction and criticism, Howells sought to disperse "the conventional acceptations by which men live on easy terms with themselves" so that they might "examine the grounds of their social and moral opinions." To accomplish this, according to Howells, the writer must strive to record detailed impressions of everyday life, endowing characters with believable motives and*
avoiding authorial comment in the narrative. In addition to perceptive criticism of the works of Henry James and Mark Twain, Howells reviewed three generations of international literature, promoting the works of Émile Zola, Bernard Shaw, Henrik Ibsen, Emily Dickinson, and other important authors. In the following essay, Howells reviews Chesnutt's two short story collections, The Conjure Woman *and* The Wife of His Youth, and Other Stories of the Color Line, *commenting on their literary and racial interest.*]

The critical reader of the story called **"The Wife of his Youth"** . . . must have noticed uncommon traits in what was altogether a remarkable piece of work. The first was the novelty of the material; for the writer dealt not only with people who were not white, but with people who were not black enough to contrast grotesquely with white people,—who in fact were of that near approach to the ordinary American in race and color which leaves, at the last degree, every one but the connoisseur in doubt whether they are Anglo-Saxon or Anglo-African. Quite as striking as this novelty of the material was the author's thorough mastery of it, and his unerring knowledge of the life he had chosen in its peculiar racial characteristics. But above all, the story was notable for the passionless handling of a phase of our common life which is tense with potential tragedy; for the attitude, almost ironical, in which the artist observes the play of contesting emotions in the drama under his eyes; and for his apparently reluctant, apparently helpless consent to let the spectator know his real feeling in the matter. Any one accustomed to study methods in fiction, to distinguish between good and bad art, to feel the joy which the delicate skill possible only from a love of truth can give, must have known a high pleasure in the quiet self-restraint of the performance; and such a reader would probably have decided that the social situation in the piece was studied wholly from the outside, by an observer with special opportunities for knowing it, who was, as it were, surprised into final sympathy.

Now, however, it is known that the author of this story is of negro blood,—diluted, indeed, in such measure that if he did not admit this descent few would imagine it, but still quite of that middle world which lies next, though wholly outside, our own. Since his first story appeared he has contributed several others to these pages, and he now makes a showing palpable to criticism in a volume called **The Wife of his Youth, and Other Stories of the Color Line;** a volume of Southern sketches called **The Conjure Woman;** and a short life of Frederick Douglass, in the Beacon Series of biographies. The last is a simple, solid, straight piece of work, not remarkable above many other biographical studies by people entirely white, and yet important as the work of a man not entirely white treating of a great man of his inalienable race. But the volumes of fiction *are* remarkable above many, above most short stories by people entirely white, and would be worthy of unusual notice if they were not the work of a man not entirely white.

It is not from their racial interest that we could first wish to speak of them, though that must have a very great and very just claim upon the critic. It is much more simply and directly, as works of art, that they make their appeal, and we must allow the force of this quite independently of the other interest. Yet it cannot always be allowed. There are times in each of the stories of the first volume when the simplicity lapses, and the effect is as of a weak and uninstructed touch. There are other times when the attitude, severely impartial and studiously aloof, accuses itself of a little pompousness. There are still other times when the literature is a little too ornate for beauty, and the diction is journalistic, reporteristic. But it is right to add that these are the exceptional times, and that for far the greatest part Mr. Chesnutt seems to know quite as well what he wants to do in a given case as Maupassant, or Tourguénief, or Mr. James, or Miss Jewett, or Miss Wilkins, in other given cases, and has done it with an art of kindred quiet and force. He belongs, in other words, to the good school, the only school, all aberrations from nature being so much truancy and anarchy. He sees his people very clearly, very justly, and he shows them as he sees them, leaving the reader to divine the depth of his feeling for them. He touches all the stops, and with equal delicacy in stories of real tragedy and comedy and pathos, so that it would be hard to say which is the finest in such admirably rendered effects as **"The Web of Circumstance," "The Bouquet,"** and **"Uncle Wellington's Wives."** In some others the comedy degenerates into satire, with a look in the reader's direction which the author's friend must deplore.

As these stories are of our own time and country, and as there is not a swash-buckler of the seventeenth century, or a sentimentalist of this, or a princess of an imaginary kingdom, in any of them, they will possibly not reach half a million readers in six months, but in twelve months possibly more readers will remember them than if they had reached the half million. They are new and fresh and strong, as life always is, and fable never is; and the stories of **The Conjure Woman** have a wild, indigenous poetry, the creation of sincere and original imagination, which is imparted with a tender humorousness and a very artistic reticence. As far as his race is concerned, or his sixteenth part of a race, it does not greatly matter whether Mr. Chesnutt invented their motives, or found them, as he feigns, among his distant cousins of the Southern cabins. In either case, the wonder of their beauty is the same; and whatever is primitive and sylvan or campestral in the reader's heart is touched by the spells thrown on the simple black lives in these enchanting tales. Character, the most precious thing in fiction, is as faithfully portrayed against the poetic background as in the setting of the **Stories of the Color Line.**

Yet these stories, after all, are Mr. Chesnutt's most important work, whether we consider them merely as realistic fiction, apart from their author, or as studies of that middle world of which he is naturally and voluntarily a citizen. We had known the nethermost world of the grotesque and comical negro and the terrible and tragic negro through the white observer on the outside, and black character in its lyrical moods we had known from such an inside witness as Mr. Paul Dunbar; but it had remained for Mr. Chesnutt to acquaint us with those regions where the paler shades dwell as hopelessly, with relation to ourselves, as the blackest negro. He has not shown the dwellers there as very different from ourselves. They have within their own circles the same social ambitions and prejudices; they intrigue and truckle and crawl, and are snobs, like ourselves, both of the snobs that snub and the snobs that are snubbed. We may choose to think them droll in their parody of pure white society, but perhaps it would

be wiser to recognize that they are like us because they are of our blood by more than a half, or three quarters, or nine tenths. It is not, in such cases, their negro blood that characterizes them; but it is their negro blood that excludes them, and that will imaginably fortify them and exalt them. Bound in that sad solidarity from which there is no hope of entrance into polite white society for them, they may create a civilization of their own, which need not lack the highest quality. They need not be ashamed of the race from which they have sprung, and whose exile they share; for in many of the arts it has already shown, during a single generation of freedom, gifts which slavery apparently only obscured. With Mr. Booker Washington the first American orator of our time, fresh upon the time of Frederick Douglass; with Mr. Dunbar among the truest of our poets; with Mr. Tanner, a black American, among the only three Americans from whom the French government ever bought a picture, Mr. Chesnutt may well be willing to own his color.

But that is his personal affair. Our own more universal interest in him arises from the more than promise he has given in a department of literature where Americans hold the foremost place. In this there is, happily, no color line; and if he has it in him to go forward on the way which he has traced for himself, to be true to life as he has known it, to deny himself the glories of the cheap success which awaits the charlatan in fiction, one of the places at the top is open to him. He has sounded a fresh note, boldly, not blatantly, and he has won the ear of the more intelligent public. (pp. 699-701)

> W. D. Howells, "Mr. Charles W. Chesnutt's Stories," in The Atlantic Monthly, *Vol. 85, No. 511, May, 1900, pp. 699-701.*

Richard E. Baldwin   (essay date 1971)

[*In the following essay, Baldwin maintains that Chesnutt explored serious racial themes in the dialect stories of* The Conjure Woman *more effectively and with greater artistry than in his later, avowedly didactic realistic fiction.*]

In **The Conjure Woman** Charles Chesnutt analyzes with balance and subtlety the paradoxes and tensions of American racial life. The penetrating insights of these stories he never matched in his realistic fiction. Here Chesnutt avoids stifling stereotypes while criticizing the myths of white supremacy and demonstrating the range and quality of black experience. Other early black writers sought to do the same, but not until *Uncle Tom's Children* [by Richard Wright] did any succeed as fully as did Chesnutt, for in **The Conjure Woman** he developed and exploited a finely balanced technique which solved the major artistic problems faced by early black writers.

The central problem was the audience. The reading public was predominantly white, and the audience that most early black writers cared most to reach was white, for it was to whites that they needed to tell the truth about the black experience in America. The need and the difficulty were one, for the problem of the black in America arose from the refusal of whites to perceive black experience accurately, and the artist's task was not simply to present the truth to white minds but to change those minds so that they could perceive the humanity of the black and the inhumanities which he suffered in America. The sentiments of white Americans could easily enough be touched, but the important and difficult task was changing their perceptions. Whites had to be trained to perceive black experience from the black point of view, for until the white man was so changed no serious black literature could receive a hearing because it would not be understood. The situation held dangers for the artist, since the task of reeducating America could not be completed quickly and the pressure of circumstances easily led writers to hasten the process by recourse to the melodramatic moral simplicity of propaganda.

Chesnutt began his career with a clear understanding of the problem and of the necessary response of the artist. In 1880, before he began writing fiction, he noted in his journal that "if I do write, I shall write for a purpose, a high, holy purpose. . . . The object of my writings would be not so much the elevation of the colored people as the elevation of the whites." A little later in the same entry, in an observation basic to the strategy of *The Conjure Woman*, he noted that in the struggle of the Negro to win "recognition and equality" it was "the province of literature to open the way for him to get it—to accustom the public mind to the idea [of Negro equality]; to lead people out, imperceptibly, unconsciously, step by step, to the desired state of feeling" toward Negroes.

Chesnutt aimed to modify white minds to feel the equality of the black man, and with the conjure tales he developed a perfect vehicle for his artistic needs. Chesnutt's genius shows in the certainty of touch involved in the choice of Uncle Julius as his central character. Choosing a character so close to widely current pejorative stereotypes was a stroke as significant as Wright's choice of Bigger Thomas, for only by confronting and thus destroying the stereotypes could the black artist hope to alter the public mind. Further, Uncle Julius resolves for Chesnutt the black artist's problem of creating a black character in a situation in which significant dramatic incident is possible. To demonstrate the equality of blacks and whites, a black character must be presented in dramatic conflict with whites in a situation which allows the black not only to survive but to succeed with dignity. The difficulty of imagining such situations was clearly formulated by William Couch, Jr., in an essay on "The Problem of Negro Character and Dramatic Incident" [*Phylon* XI, 1950]: "Serious dramatic situation necessitates consequential action committed by a protagonist with whom we can sympathize and admire. The assumptions of American culture, on the other hand, are not congenial to emphatic and uncompromising action on the part of a Negro. This is especially true when white interests are involved. Therefore, a dramatic situation, capable of producing a powerful effect, will usually suffer a distortion of that effect when the agent of action is a Negro character." In the face of this dilemma black artists have frequently relied on a conflict of virtuous blacks against vicious whites, thus accentuating the dilemma rather than resolving it.

Chesnutt's conjure stories, on the other hand, resolve this basic problem. The tales which Uncle Julius tells stand in the tradition of subterfuge, indirection, and subtle manipulation of whites developed by the slaves as a strategy for surviving in the face of oppression. Chesnutt's conjure sto-

ries turn the strategy of "puttin' on ol' massa" into effective dramatic action through parallels and tensions between the frames established by the white narrator and the tales told by Uncle Julius. In **"The Goophered Grapevine,"** Chesnutt's first conjure story, Julius's attempt to use the tale of the goophered grapevine to place a new "goopher" on the vineyard in order to keep the white man from depriving him of his livelihood provides the most obvious parallel between frame and tale. Julius emerges from this dramatic conflict with a qualified success, for while he loses the vineyard he gains a more stable livelihood in the white man's employment.

The limitations of his success are illuminated by another parallel between frame and tale, however. An important part of the tale centers on the experiences of Henry, a slave of Dugald McAdoo, antebellum owner of the vineyard. McAdoo purchased Henry after the success of the fatal conjure Aunt Peggy had placed on his vineyards had so increased his crop that he needed more help. Henry ate some of the grapes before he could be warned of the conjure, and his life was saved by an antidote which involved his anointing himself with sap from one of the vines. From that time on Henry's life followed the rhythms of the growing season; he became strong and supple in the spring and summer, then withered up during the winter months. McAdoo made a great deal of money exploiting Henry by selling him when he was strong and buying him back cheap when he weakened in the fall. During the winter months McAdoo coddled Henry to protect the valuable chattel. Although Henry enjoyed this comfortable life, he was more than ever at McAdoo's mercy, for his life depended on the life of the vineyards. When McAdoo's greed led him to follow foolish advice which killed the vines, Henry paid with his life for his master's folly.

Henry was about Uncle Julius's age when McAdoo purchased him, and the narrator's hiring of Julius ominously parallels that transaction. Julius had been a free entrepreneur, and although his new job may pay more than the vineyard could yield to him, it represents a new form of slavery in which Julius loses a significant measure of his freedom in return for security; Julius's love of grapes, like Henry's, places him in the power of the white man. Yet this judgment must in turn be qualified by the implied parallel between the narrator and McAdoo, for it is obvious that the narrator is in some ways a wiser man than his slave-owning predecessor, a fact which mutes the threatening potential of his hiring of Julius while the mutual service of each to the other emphasizes the ways in which the story demonstrates the inescapable connections between the lives of black and white, a central theme in much of Chesnutt's work.

"The Goophered Grapevine" gains additional richness through the complicated nature of Julius's motivation. While he wants very much to preserve his vineyard, he simultaneously wants to strike out at the racial superiority assumed by the narrator. The tale which he tells consistently presents white men bested by blacks or acting in ways whose folly is clearly perceived by the blacks. Both in the broad outline of his tale of the goophered grapevine and in numerous minor points, such as the inability of the best white doctors to cure the goopher that Aunt Peggy has placed on Henry, Uncle Julius asserts the humanity of the black and his equality with, or superiority to, whites. Julius thus has the pleasure of effectively calling the white man a fool to his face, yet he fails to make any impression because the narrator is too blinded by racism to be able to perceive what Julius is up to. Ironically, that failure, while it underscores the truth in Julius's point, is vital to his success at preserving his livelihood, since the narrator would not likely have hired Julius had he perceived the insults. The concluding frame thus generates multiple ironies which illuminate the complex tension between the black's need to deny and attack white supremacy and the hard fact that while whites are not superior beings they nevertheless have very real power.

Chesnutt's success in dealing with this tension in *The Conjure Woman* depends not only on the complex motivation of Uncle Julius but also on the two white characters of the frame, the Northern narrator and his wife Annie. The two white people are crucial to Chesnutt's rhetorical strategy for leading white America "imperceptibly, unconsciously, step by step, to the desired state of feeling" toward blacks. The narrator, a basically decent sort of man, takes a typical paternalistic attitude towards Uncle Julius and his tales. He accepts Julius's attempts at manipulating him yet remains blinded by his own sense of superiority. His understanding of black life has been molded more by Uncle Remus and the plantation school than by Uncle Julius. As Julius begins the tale of the goophered grapevine, for instance, the narrator observes that "As he became more and more absorbed in the narrative, his eyes assumed a dreamy expression, and he seemed to lose sight of his auditors, and to be living over again in monologue his life on the old plantation." This evocation of the plantation tradition reveals the narrator's blindness to Julius's revelations about slavery, for life on the McAdoo plantation had nothing of the dreamy quality of the idyls of Harris. The statement becomes richly ironic when the conclusion shows that Uncle Julius has had his eyes very much on his auditors and the demands of the present moment. It is the narrator whose eyes are closed, and in an adumbration of the Invisible Man motif he is "beaten" by a man he never sees.

The narrator's posture has immense rhetorical value for Chesnutt, for it enables him to present his stories with detachment from the point of view of any of his characters. The framing narrative voice is that of a typical white American liberal, an unconscious racist who seems free of bigotry. In his reactions to Julius's tale the narrator is not so dull as to miss all that the black is up to, yet he misses enough that he can report the tale of slavery with no sense of the range of its meaning, especially those portions directed against him. The narrator thus appears as a mixture of sensitivity and callousness, and he can be treated sympathetically while his blindness to Uncle Julius's character and to the implications of his tales provides ironic commentary on his own character and on America's racial absurdities.

Chesnutt's technique relies heavily on irony, and like any ironic technique it runs the risk that readers will miss the point. Annie, the narrator's wife, is developed as a contrasting character in order to reduce this danger. Her permanent convalescent state underscores the feminine sensibility which leads her to respond more deeply to Uncle Julius than does her husband. When Julius announces that the vineyard is goophered, for instance, the narrator ob-

serves that "He imparted this information with such solemn earnestness, and with such an air of confidential mystery, that I felt somewhat interested, while Annie was evidently much impressed, and drew closer to me." The narrator's attitude toward his wife frequently is as condescending as his attitude toward Julius, and after the tale is finished he notes that she "doubtfully, but seriously" asked, " 'Is that story true?' " His own reaction to the tale appears only in his assertion that he bought the vineyard in spite of the purported goopher. Annie's question, however, allows Chesnutt to imply the presence of metaphoric meanings through the absurd literalness of Uncle Julius's response that he can prove its truth by showing her Henry's grave. At such levels the tale obviously is not true, but the nature of the question and answer implies that other levels of meaning can be discovered by any who care to look for them.

Chesnutt seems not to have fully grasped the value of his white characters when he first wrote **"The Goophered Grapevine,"** for his second conjure story openly exploits the contrast, and when he prepared the first story for book publication he added to the opening frame several long sections which develop the narrator more fully. The opening frame of the second story, **"Po' Sandy,"** points out the difference between the narrator and Annie. When she rises eagerly to Julius's hint of a story, her husband comments that "some of these stories are quaintly humorous; others wildly extravagant, revealing the Oriental cast of the negro's imagination; while others, poured freely into the sympathetic ear of a Northern-bred woman, disclose many a tragic incident of the darker side of slavery." While the narrator has sufficient curiosity to listen to the tales with pleasure he has no patience for discovering meanings in them; rather than revelations about American life he sees only an "Oriental cast of the negro's imagination." Annie, on the other hand, instinctively leaps to at least some meanings. The resulting contrast helps Chesnutt bring a white audience to perceive events from the black point of view, for while the narrator reacts with a typical white obtuseness, Annie, by seeing through the surface of fantastic and supernatural machinery, points the reader to the vital human life behind.

Chesnutt uses this contrast most effectively in **"Po' Sandy."** Uncle Julius's tale tells of Sandy, a young slave devoted to his wife Tenie, a conjure woman. Mars Marrabo continually sends Sandy, an exceptionally good worker, to help out relatives on distant plantations, and when Sandy tires of this Tenie turns him into a tree to keep him near her. When Sandy disappears, the dogs track him to the tree, where they lose the trail. After the excitement of his disappearance passes, Tenie nightly returns Sandy to human form. But then Marrabo sends Tenie to nurse his daughter-in-law, and during her absence Sandy is cut down, and Tenie returns just in time to watch her husband sawn into lumber to build a new kitchen on the plantation. The kitchen remains haunted by Sandy's ghost, so it is eventually torn down and the lumber used to build a schoolhouse. The narrator now plans to tear down the school and use the lumber to build Annie a new kitchen.

After Julius finishes his tale, the following exchange between Annie and the narrator occurs:

> "What a system it was," she exclaimed, when Ju-

lius had finished, "under which such things were possible!"

"What things?" I asked, in amazement. "Are you seriously considering the possibility of a man's being turned into a tree?"

"Oh, no," she replied quickly, "not that"; and then she murmured absently, and with a dim look in her fine eyes, "Poor Tenie!"

The narrator as usual sees nothing but the surface of the tale, but with his insensitivity as a contrast Chesnutt needs no more than Annie's murmured "Poor Tenie" to alert us to the story of the pain caused by the inhuman violations of personal life and the brutalities endured by slaves. The narrator believes in the beauty of the Old South and the quaintness of Negro folktales, but through Annie we see the horrors of slavery.

Had Annie's role ended with "Poor Tenie!" the story would have verged on the sentimentality which so quickly destroys the effect of tales of pathos. But the sentimentality of the "dim look in her fine eyes" and the quiet murmur are the narrator's, not Chesnutt's. Annie has a sentimental streak, but Chesnutt nevertheless uses her to help effect a most unsentimental change of tone from the pathos and horror of the tale to the grotesquely incongruous, anticlimactic humor of the concluding frame. Through Annie's agency Chesnutt modulates the story from the grim brutalities of a man sawn into lumber to end on a note of gentle, ironic humor.

The humor of the conclusion is vital to the overall effect of the story, avoiding sentimentality and creating an impact more tautly complex than pathos. The humor of the frame relieves the pain of the tale itself, emphasizing the similar effect created by the incongruity between the horror experienced by the characters of the tales and the improbability of the conjure elements. The final effect has the complexity described by Ralph Ellison as the blues, the transcendence of pain "not by the consolation of philosophy, but by squeezing from it a near-tragic, near-comic lyricism" ["Richard Wright's Blues," in *Shadow and Act,* 1964]. At their best, Chesnutt's conjure stories require a response which sustains that type of tension between the tragic and the comic. The tension is most striking in **"Po' Sandy,"** yet Chesnutt's third conjure story, **"The Conjurer's Revenge,"** exploits it in an equally effective and perhaps more sophisticated way. In **"The Conjurer's Revenge"** the narrator needs a draught animal, and Julius hopes it will not be a mule; he hates to drive a mule for fear it may be a human being, and thereby hangs a tale. The tale tells how Primus, a slave, stole a shoat from a conjure man who revenged the theft by turning him into a mule. A large portion of the tale deals with Primus's escapades as a mule—eating tobacco in the field, guzzling a huge quantity of wine, attacking the man who had taken over his woman. When the conjure man neared death he got religion, and feeling guilty about Primus summoned him in order to return him to human form. He lived long enough to turn back all of Primus except for one foot, which remained clubbed.

When Uncle Julius finishes the tale it appears that he knows a man with a horse to sell. Shortly after the narrator buys the horse Uncle Julius sports a flashy new suit, apparently purchased with his share of the money paid for

the horse. Within three months, the animal dies of diseases brought on by old age, and while the entire affair makes fine comedy, the comedy has a harsh, vindictive quality unknown in the two earlier tales. The tale itself is a disconcerting mixture of the comic escapades of a man turned into a mule and the story of a slave who, to take the view of Primus's master, " 'had runned erway, en stay' 'tel he got ti'ed er de swamps, en den come back on him ter be fed. He tried ter 'count fer de shape er Primus' foot by sayin' Primus got his foot smash', er snake-bit, er sump'n, w'iles he wuz erway, en den stayed out in de woods whar he couldn' git it kyoed up straight, 'stidder comin' long home whar a doctor could 'a' 'tended ter it'." Either way this tale lacks the compelling quality of the tale of Po' Sandy, and Annie's reaction to it is negative: " 'That story does not appeal to me, Uncle Julius, and is not up to your usual mark. It isn't pathetic, it has no moral that I can discover, and I can't see why you should tell it. In fact, it seems to me like nonsense'."

There is a moral, although not the sort that would dim Annie's fine eyes. The moral is enunciated by the narrator when, after discovering that the fine looking animal he bought is half blind and thoroughly broken down, he exclaims, "But alas for the deceitfulness of appearances." The story underscores this point. Julius's tale is pointless by comparison with the earlier two, but his telling of the pointless tale was a deceitful appearance intentionally used to cover his own motives and set up the narrator for the sales pitch made at the end.

Chesnutt's concern reaches beyond the sales of horses and mules, though, and **"The Conjurer's Revenge"** provides a broad commentary on the American racial situation. The title suggests that Uncle Julius's intentional swindling of his employer amounts to revenge. As in the tale Primus felt the wrath of the conjure man because he stole a shoat, so in Chesnutt's story the narrator is bilked because Julius has had a valuable possession stolen—the dignity, freedom, and equality which are the components of his humanity—and works a goopher on the white man in revenge. The story focuses on "the deceitfulness of appearances" which lies at the heart of race relations, and in part on the deceitfulness of appearances in Chesnutt's earlier two stories. The earlier stories had glossed the moral turpitude of race relations by implicitly justifying Uncle Julius's behavior—in **"The Goophered Grapevine"** on grounds of practical necessity, in **"Po' Sandy"** on grounds of service to a communal group. **"The Conjurer's Revenge"** strips all romantic gloss from Southern life and presents the hard core of racial conflict, that mutual dehumanization which eliminates all moral compunctions from the black man's dealing with whites and which enables the white man to hide from himself the fact that the black man is a human being. If the white man becomes vulnerable to the deceitfulness of appearances, the appearances are his own creation, the self-delusions spawned by his denial of the black man's humanity. In this situation the black man quite naturally becomes a conjure man, using his wits to exploit and encourage the deceitful appearances which the white man has created. There is nothing moral or pathetic here, just a bald power struggle which is comically, tragically human, the deepest reality of American racial conflict.

Nearly ten years intervened between the publication of

"The Conjurer's Revenge" and the appearance of *The Conjure Woman* in 1898. None of the additional four stories appeared previously in periodicals; so the sequence in which they were written is unknown. Each of these later stories, while it follows the original frame-tale pattern, reveals Chesnutt reaching the limits of the form's usefulness. The later four stories lack the complex balance of the earlier three. In **"Sis' Becky's Pickaninny,"** for instance, the tight relation between frame and tale is lacking. By itself the tale fails to develop significant dramatic action, and unlike the tale in **"The Conjurer's Revenge"** it is not an integral part of a larger conception. **"Hot-Foot Hannibal,"** on the other hand, has a frame and a tale technically well matched. Here, however, Julius has no significant role in either tale or frame. The parallels between tale and frame thus remain mechanical, and Chesnutt's point seems to be simply to demonstrate by the parallel that blacks feel the same pains, joys, and sorrows as whites. **"Hot-Foot Hannibal"** comes closer than any other conjure tale to the special group pleading of the propagandist.

The weakness of **"Hot-Foot Hannibal"** appears clearly when it is compared with **"The Gray Wolf's Ha'nt."** Nothing in *The Conjure Woman* surpasses Uncle Julius's tale of the gray wolf's ha'nt. This story of love, jealousy, and murder among the slaves achieves tragic stature and has no taint of propaganda. The tale is perfect in itself, but it is badly marred by being forced into a trite and irrelevant frame. The tale deals with conflict within the slave community and lacks the interracial conflict on which vital parallels between tale and frame depended in the three earlier stories. The tale does not need a frame, and its strength indicates that the conjure story could have been developed into a vehicle for exploring black culture. Interracial conflict was essential to the vitality of the form as Chesnutt initially conceived it, however, and his willingness to place this magnificent story in an unsuitable frame suggests that he was uninterested in forms which did not deal with such conflict.

The remaining conjure story, **"Mars Jeems's Nightmare,"** suggests in fact that Chesnutt had reached the limits of the form even as a vehicle for exploring racial conflict. **"Mars Jeems's Nightmare,"** which focuses on racial conflict with the unrelenting rigor of **"The Conjurer's Revenge,"** is the only one of the later stories that creates something like the balanced tone, the intellectual strength, and the imaginative integrity of the early stories. The frame drama centers around Uncle Julius's grandson Tom, formerly employed by the narrator but fired for laziness and carelessness; Julius's aim in telling this tale is to get his grandson rehired. The tale tells how a vicious master is turned into a Negro and delivered into the hands of his own sadistic poor-white overseer until he is beaten into sympathy for his slaves. Moved by this tale Annie effects the desired change (in the concluding frame) by taking the boy back. Her act angers the narrator, but he lets the boy stay. Implicit in his acquiescence are the effects on him of the story of Mars Jeems's being turned into a slave. At the end of the tale the narrator acknowledges that the changing of a white man into a Negro was "powerful goopher," an ironic admission of the power of the tale on him and Annie, for it has in effect put them through the experience of Mars Jeems and has acted as a "powerful goopher" on them.

More than any other story, **"Mars Jeems's Nightmare"**

examines the psychology which gives Uncle Julius power over the narrator. At the beginning of the story Chesnutt has the narrator characterize Uncle Julius at length in a passage which reveals more about the narrator than about Uncle Julius:

> Toward my tract of land and the things that were on it—the creeks, the swamps, the hills, the meadows, the stones, the trees—he maintained a peculiar personal attitude, that might be called predial rather than proprietary. He had been accustomed, until long after middle life, to look upon himself as the property of another. When this relation was no longer possible, owing to the war, and to his master's death and the dispersion of the family, he had been unable to break off entirely the mental habits of a lifetime, but had attached himself to the old plantation, of which he seemed to consider himself an appurtenance. We found him useful in many ways and entertaining in others, and my wife and I took quite a fancy to him.

As an analysis of Uncle Julius this passage is accurate only in its assumption that the mental habits of a lifetime could not be cast off. It is dead wrong on the nature of those habits, however. The other stories in *The Conjure Woman* reveal how little Uncle Julius sees himself as another's property, while the tales reveal how little the slaves themselves had thought that way. The narrator's error reveals the patronizing attitude which blinds him to the reality of Uncle Julius's activities and which amounts to a wish to consign the freed slave to a new subservience.

The passage also reveals how the guilt created by this attempt to create a new slavery manifests itself in a sense of responsibility for blacks. Uncle Julius understands this psychological complex thoroughly enough to be able to exploit it cynically. At the conclusion of his tale about Mars Jeems he points the moral of the tale: "Dis yer tale goes ter show . . . dat w'ite folks w'at is so ha'd en stric', en doan make no 'lowance fer po' ign'ant niggers w'at ain' had no chanst ter l'arn, is li'ble ter hab bad dreams, ter say de leas', en dat dem w'at is kin' en good ter po' people is sho' ter prosper en git 'long in de worl'." This sententious moralizing reveals Uncle Julius's awareness of the white man's guilt and his willingness to exploit that sense of guilt unscrupulously. Uncle Julius has no interest in having his grandson educated; he asks only that allowance be made for him. Uncle Julius wants the patronizing whites to pay for their sense of superiority by supporting the blacks whose shiftlessness they have created by their attitudes and actions. In this story Uncle Julius emerges as an opportunist like Ellison's Bledsoe, and his relation to the narrator in many ways resembles that of Bledsoe to Norton. The situation Chesnutt draws is virtually hopeless, a vicious circle of mutual exploitation with no will on either side to break the cycle.

Although the situation **"Mars Jeems's Nightmare"** exposes is nightmarish, the story avoids pessimism and bitterness. While it does not achieve that lyrical tension between tragedy and comedy which made **"Po' Sandy"** a prose blues, **"Mars Jeems's Nightmare"** nevertheless does balance the hopelessness of the situation with the humor of Uncle Julius's manipulation of the whites and Annie's active complicity in his success. The balance vital to the conjure stories is also threatened from another quarter, however. From the beginning Chesnutt has been the ultimate conjure man, hoping that by "wukking de roots" of black culture he might be able to work a powerful goopher on white America and lead it to accept the equality of the black. The indirection of the conjure stories enabled him to pursue his goal with consummate artistry but without sufficient power to save America from bad dreams.

His desire to deal more directly with racial problems shows in **"Mars Jeems's Nightmare"** in its concern with an issue with broad social implications, the questions of employment and education for blacks and of white responsibility therefor. The indirection of the conjure story was ill adapted to such concerns, and **"Mars Jeems's Nightmare"** inevitably raises questions which the limits of the form prevent it from dealing with. The crucial relation of the drama—the relation between the narrator as employer and Tom as employee—is peripheral rather than central. We can never learn about Tom, the nature of his purported laziness and carelessness, the possible causes, or the possible ways of dealing with the situation. The point of the story, of course, is that the situation precludes either party from dealing directly with these issues, and the story quite properly does not attempt to examine them. Nevertheless, such questions arise simply because the frame drama and the point of Uncle Julius's tale both enter the realm of practical social problems where these questions exist and demand attention. The grim vision of **"Mars Jeems's Nightmare"** registers the hopelessness of America's racial life and reveals the limitations of the indirect approach to racism which the conjure story provided. On the one hand, the conjure story provided a subtle instrument which could portray with a terrifying accuracy and clarity the functioning of American racial life, but it offered no imaginative way out for either author or audience. The lesson of the white narrator—that whites are too blind to perceive the truth about race—may have suggested to Chesnutt that it was not enough to show race relations in action but that what was needed was an art which would outline explicitly the white misconceptions about blacks and the forces responsible for their formation and perpetuation. In any event, Chesnutt's concern shifted from working a subtle goopher on white minds to attacking specific social problems and clearly laying bare the mechanics and consequences of racism, and the conjure story ceased to be a useful vehicle. After *The Conjure Woman* was published Chesnutt gave full attention to the realistic fiction he had been working with throughout the 1890's.

If Americans were too blind for subtle methods, they were no more amenable to direct confrontation. White Americans would not allow themselves to perceive life from a black perspective, and Chesnutt's turn from the complex art of the conjure story was unavailing. Realism did give Chesnutt room to explore additional dimensions of racial life in America, but the ultimate irony is that his realistic fiction never achieved sharper insights than those of **"Mars Jeems's Nightmare"** and the early conjure stories, while losing their balance, control, and clarity. It is through the marvelously subtle conjure fiction, which transcends the nightmare of American racism in a near-tragic, near-comic lyricism, that Chesnutt works his most powerful goopher. (pp. 385-98)

Richard E. Baldwin, "The Art of 'The Conjure Woman'," in American Literature, *Vol. 43, No. 3, November, 1971, pp. 385-98.*

Melvin Dixon   (essay date 1974)

[*In the following excerpt, Dixon identifies the role of the black narrator of the conjure tales with that of the traditional folkloric figure of the trickster.*]

[*The Conjure Woman*] was published in 1899. At that time white Americans were lamenting the passing of the Old South and creating gross stereotypes of the benevolent planter and his docile child-like slaves.

Chesnutt used these same stereotypes in [*The Conjure Woman*], which is constructed in a sequence of seven short stories, each of which was published separately in the *Atlantic Monthly* magazine. The stories were later compiled into the present novel structure under the title *The Conjure Woman.* While each tale is independent of the others, together they become a series of verbal contests engaged in by the teller to accomplish many interrelated goals. Chesnutt, by compiling these tales into a single volume, has consciously created a folk novel that describes a series of adventures of equal importance. Thus, there is no single climax or denouement. However, there is a clear progression in the character of the teller, Julius. It is in his character that we find the unity of the novel.

The major plot of the *Conjure Woman* is Julius' retelling of local tales to his new white employer, John, a northerner, who has intruded upon his domain with his ailing wife to begin a grape and wine industry. Julius responds to this threat by tricking this newcomer in order to maintain his residence on the land as well as provide him with steady employment. Thus, the novel describes how Julius fulfills his own material and psychological needs by telling folktales which describe a similar trickery accomplished by conjuring and witchcraft used during slavery.

External to the drama in each tale is the dramatic character of Julius as teller. He becomes a symbolic conjure man as he attempts, through the medium of his folklore, to establish an identity of man and folk artist that slavery tried to suppress.

The attempt of American slavery to reduce black men to the status of children automatically relates the slave's stereotypical character to that of the traditional trickster. This trickster, according to Roger Abrahams' folk study, *Deep Down In the Jungle,* is a child figure who is not "immoral, he is rather, amoral, because he exists in the stage before morality has had a chance to inculcate itself upon his being." During slavery, blacks in America were considered beneath the moral code of white society. Because blacks were considered categorically unequal to whites, the white ruling class was never too seriously concerned with the slave's moral development. Thus, the slave, for all practical purposes was considered amoral and child-like in the white man's conception of him.

This historical characterization of the black slave is fertile ground for an elevation of the slave in fiction from oppressed man to the dubious stature of folk trickster. In Chesnutt's novel we find, moreover, this character progression on two levels. On the first level Julius is both trickster and teller of the plantation tales. Secondly, there is a trickster characterization in the author himself. Chesnutt as a black writer is writing about a white landowner's re-telling of the stories told him and his wife by the former slave Julius. The novelist here enters the psyche of the white listener as he retells the folktales of Julius. Furthermore, Chesnutt himself is aware that he is writing for a predominately white audience who have a strong nostalgia for the antebellum southern tradition. What the contemporary reader discovers, then, is a complexity of trickery in the narrative focus of *The Conjure Woman.* What this paper attempts is a study of the character Julius as teller and trickster for his small audience, and, on a larger scale, a study of Chesnutt as teller and trickster for his wider literary audience. Each person, the fictional trickster and the novelist, constructs an elaborate fictive world which, using the cultural framework outlined by Abrahams, is a "playground for playing out the aggressions [in which] he is able to achieve a kind of precarious masculine identity for himself and his group in a basically hostile environment." The identity struggles on each narrative level are both sexual and artistic.

In the first story the white narrator (I will distinguish Julius' story from his employer's overall narration by referring to Julius as the *teller* and his employer as the *narrator* throughout) describes himself as a northern businessman whose only interest is in establishing a grape culture in the old town of Patesville, North Carolina. He introduces Uncle Julius as a "venerable-looking colored man" with "a shrewdness in his eyes." When the narrator informs Julius of his intention to buy the property and start a grape culture Julius recites the solemn tale of the **"Goophered Grapevine."**

The grapevine, it seems, was bewitched by the conjure woman Aunt Peggy, who "lived doan 'mong' de free niggers on de Wim'l'ton Road, ed all de darkies fum Rockfish ter Beaver Crik wuz feared er her." She was commissioned by the owner Mars' Dugal' to conjure the vine in order to keep the slaves from stealing the grapes. One new slave, Henry, who did not know the vine was bewitched, ate some grapes. But before the conjure caused his death Aunt Peggy gave him some medicine which made him as seasonally strong and fertile as the grapevine. Henry's strength and youth would return in the spring and summer and his old age would return in the fall and winter as the vine itself prospered and withered. This cycle repeated itself for many years. Then one day the tree was poisoned and when it died old Henry died.

The tale seems simple enough when one dissects it from the creative verbal imagination of Julius as teller. But what is more important about the tale characteristically is the process of identification which takes place between the teller and the hero of the story.

We see Julius first through the eyes of the white landowner who spies him sitting on a log near his vineyard. "He held on his knees a hat full of grapes, over which he was smacking his lips with great gusto, and a pile of grapeskins near him indicated that the performance was no new thing." Furthermore, he is described physically as,

> . . . not entirely black, and this fact, together with
> the quality of his hair, which was about six inches
> long and very bushy, except on top of his head,
> where he was quite bald, suggested a strain of other
> than negro blood.

Similarly Henry, the hero of Julius' first tale, loves grapes. He, too, in Julius' description of him, was "er ole nigger, er de color er a gingy-cake, en ball ez a hoss-apple on de

top er his head. He wuz peart ole nigger, do, en could do a big day's wuk."

When this new slave appeared on the plantation "he smell de grapes en see de vimes, an atter dahk de fus thing he done wuz ter slip off ter de grapevimes 'dout sayin nuffin ter nobody." The rest of the **"Goophered Grapevine"** tale is the product of Julius' folkloric imagination; the important point being the character connection between the teller and the hero. This dual character, moreover, this double character accomplishes an important narrative focus as well as a unity of character in the novel. According to Abrahams:

> The conflict of the hero must be in some way echo
> the conflict of the narrator and his audience in
> order for the story to get the approbation of being
> heard, applauded, and remembered.

The conflict in the folktale between Henry and the master's grapevine mirrors the present conflict of the teller Julius with his new employer over the territoriality and ownership of the grapevine. That the echo of this conflict is heard and applauded is indicated by the employer's wife's question at the conclusion of the tale. She asks, rather seriously, "Is that story true?" To which Julius replies; "Its des ez true I'm a-settin' here, miss." This point is not to say that the employer's wife understands the story or its implications. It merely suggests a recognition and reception of the tale.

The folktale, however, is not without its moral. This moral becomes the major trick device Julius uses to get what he wants from his employer. The term moral used here may be misleading. It is used to mean the giving of advice in a serious and sometimes condescending way to illustrate a virtue one should live by. In this story Julius advises his new landowner:

> En I tell you w'at, marster, I wouldn' 'vise you to
> buy dis yer ole vimeya'd 'caze de goopher's on it yit,
> en dey ain' no tellin' w'en it's gwine ter crap out.

Nevertheless the landowner acquires the property. He tells us later that he discovered Julius' trick and ulterior motive.

> I found when I bought the vineyard, that Uncle Ju-
> lius had occupied a cabin on the place for many
> years, and derived a respectable revenue from the
> product of the neglected grapevines. This doubtless
> accounted for his advice to me not to buy the vine-
> yard, though whether it inspired the goopher story
> I am unable to state.

Here the narrator reveals his knowledge of Julius' trickery which is a point in his favor. But what the reader discovers as the novel progresses are the many levels on which Julius' trickery operates in order to fulfill his immediate material needs as well as his psychological need for a masculine and artistic self-esteem. Through the medium of the folktale he is able to vent his aggression against the institution of slavery which dehumanized him, and which now continues to emasculate him in his present relationship with his employer.

As the novel progresses Julius' trick of storytelling assumes gigantic proportions beyond the comprehension of the landowner or his wife. Thus, they are continually tricked, although the white narrator will never admit to being duped in his present retelling of the entire novel as its *persona*. This consistent duping of the employer is the curious way in which Julius assumes power over him and more control over his own life.

Furthermore, Julius, as teller in the oral tradition outlined by Abrahams, is "master of the situation he is narrating; he is the director of the lives of the heroes of the pieces and of the structure in which they are appearing." Julius' story telling ability represents his "ability to convince and thus illustrate his masculine power."

The assertion of a masculine identity, according to Abrahams, is one of the chief functions of the oral tradition among urban (and, for that matter, rural) blacks who have found themselves in a hostile and often matriarchal environment. In this oral tradition "the sexual power of words is, of course, patent. To recognize this, one need only to see a popular singer or an effective speaker at work and watch the effect of such language upon women."

But the power of the Afro-American oral tradition reaches further back in history to African traditions. Here the spoken word has divine power. Janheinz Jahn, in his important work, *Muntu,* calls this "magic power of the word," *Nommo*. In African tradition, Jahn states;

> Through Nommo, the word, man establishes his mastery over things . . . the word itself is force, . . . According to African philosophy, man has by force of his word, dominion over "things": he can change them, make them work for him, and command them. But to command things with words is to practice magic. And to practice magic is to write poetry.

For poetry we might well insert the word folklore. Therefore, in his oral tale Julius gains mastery over his employer by asserting his masculine and artistic power in the verbal dramatization of conflicts endured by his slave ancestors. Julius, then, is "Muntu, man who speaks and through the word conquers the world of things; directs it and uses it to change the world. His word is more powerful the more he speaks in the name of his people, living as well as dead." By the same token Julius achieves a divine power as artist-creator, which his employer recognizes as a certain "air of confidential mystery," in his ability to conjure up images that strike painful truths.

The other tales in *The Conjure Woman;* **"Po' Sandy,"** **"Mars Jeems's Nightmare,"** **"The Gray Wolf's Ha'nt,"** and **"Hot-Foot Hannibal,"** follow the same structure. Julius is either asked to deliver a tale, or, if the occasion arises in which his needs require that he assert himself over his employer, he volunteers one to mirror his present conflict. In each moral resolution of the tale Julius gains something new. Thus,

> any of the battles won, physical or verbal, are won by both the hero and the narrator. Yet he is in so much control of his small universe that he can be both protagonist and antagonist in this contest. He directs this battle as well as winning it. The glory is all his and the triumph is more than just a verbal one [Abrahams, *Deep Down in the Jungle*].

From the tale of **"The Goophered Grapevine"** Julius gains a job as coachman for his new landowner. In the second tale of **"Po' Sandy"** Julius gains a new meeting house for his church, the Sandy Run Colored Baptist Church. In

"Mars Jeems's Nightmare" Julius' friend, once fired, gets rehired by the employer's wife. (She comments: "he was hanging around the place all morning, and looking so down at the mouth, that I told him that if he would try to do better, we would give him one more chance.") Following the tale of the **"Conjurer's Revenge"** another of Julius' friends gets the opportunity to sell the employer an old horse. Half the profit from the sale goes to Julius, who is now seen "in a new suit of clothes, which [the employer] had seen displayed in the window of Mr. Solomon Cohen's store."

The pattern of personal gain is interrupted in the next tale of **"Sis' Becky's Pickaninny"** when Julius *gives* the employer's wife his good luck rabbit's foot. At this point in the novel Julius' trickery, which has heretofore been concerned with survival (the only value traditional trickster's hold sacred), now changes into the more obvious sexual quality that has subtly accompanied his tales and tricks throughout.

What Julius accomplishes in this tale is a subtle seduction of the wife. One will note in the above tales that the material benefits Julius gains at the conclusion of each tale come directly or indirectly from the employer's wife, usually without her husband's knowledge until it is too late to reverse her deed.

This symbolic seduction of the wife by the language and drama of Julius' speech is heightened in the present tale, **"Sis' Becky's Pickaninny."** The story grows out of a discussion of the superstitious value of the rabbit's foot. This rabbit's foot assumes the characteristics of a phallic symbol in the following interchange between narrator and trickster:

> The old man [Julius] did not seem inclined to go away, so I asked him to sit down. I had noticed, as he came up, *that he held some small object in his hand.* When he had taken his seat on the top step, *he kept fingering this object,*—what it was I could not make out.
>
> "What is that you have there, Julius?" I asked with mild curiosity.
>
> "Dis is my rabbit foot, suh."
>
> (emphasis mine).

The rabbit's foot is no regular foot. As Julius reminds us, "De fo-foot ain' got no power. It has ter be de hin'-foot, suh, de lef' hih'-foot er a grabeya'd rabbit, kilt by a cross-eyed nigger on a da'k night in de full er de moon." The association of the rabbit's foot with the night and graveyard gives the foot sensual as well as supernatural characteristics. And it is this phallic rabbit's foot that secretly charms the wife.

Julius now tells the tale of **"Sis' Becky's Pickaninny,"** which is the story of an implied incestuous relationship between a son and his mother. Their incest is implied by the physical intimacy of their life and the fact that:

> W'en little Mose growed up . . . He tu'nt out ter be a smart man, en l'arnt de blacksmif trade . . . En bimeby he bought his mammy en sot her free, en den he bought hisse'f, en tuk keer er Sis' Becky ez long ez de bofe libbed.

The perverse sexual intimacy between Sis' Becky and her

son mirrors the growing sexual attraction between Julius and his employer's wife. Even the employer, symbolically cuckolded by the masculine power Julius gains through his tale-telling, notices a significant change in his wife's character:

> My wife had listened to this story with greater interest than she had manifested in any subject for several days. I had watched her furtively from time to time during the recital, and had observed the play of her countenance. It had expressed in turn sympathy, indignation, pity, and at the end satisfaction.

Chesnutt's word choice here is significant enough to establish a sexual link. John, the employer, then responds to Julius, perhaps out of jealousy; "that is a very ingenious fairy tale." This line indicates a further attempt by the white narrator to subordinate the verbal creativity of the teller as well as his masculinity with the word "fairy" to mean not so much homosexual, but ephemeral and flitty. The wife, however, comes to Julius' defense. "Why John!" said [the wife] severely, "the story bears the stamp of truth, if ever a story did." Days later the symbolically cuckolded husband discovers the instrument that links the sexual flirtation between Julius and his wife.

> When I pulled the handkerchief out of her pocket, something else came with it and fell on the floor. I picked up the object and looked at it. It was Julius' rabbit foot.

Julius' trickery has progressed from the level of material gratification to the level of a metaphorical sexual union with the employer's wife. Recall the earlier note from Abrahams on the sexual power of words. Julius' triumph in this tale is a sexual one.

In the next tale, **"The Gray Wolf 's Ha'nt,"** we realize the extent to which John has been cuckolded and emasculated by Julius. Here John tries to entertain his wife by reading from his literary tradition in Western philosophy. At once the differences between the Afro-American and Anglo-American oral and literary traditions become obvious from the differences in language, style and feeling. John's recitation begins:

> The difficulty of dealing with transformations so many-sided as those which all existences have undergone, or are undergoing, is such as to make a complete and deductive interpretation almost hopeless.

The vocabulary of John's oral tradition, however, renders him impotent. It lacks the sensuality and the vitality of Julius' folk literature. And, more significantly, John has failed to please his wife.

> "John," interrupted my wife, "I wish you would stop reading that nonsense and see who that is coming up the lane."

> I closed my book with a sigh. I had never been able to interest my wife in the study of philosophy, even when presented in the simplest and most lucid form.

Julius enters; once again he triumphs. He symbolically seduces the wife with the drama of another folktale.

This story, **"The Gray Wolf 's Ha'nt,"** reveals the frustra-

tion of the love between the slaves, Dan and Mahaly. The tale's drama mirrors the present dull, frustrating and impotent relationship between Julius' employers, Annie and John. On a literal level the story functions to dissuade John from clearing the land on which Julius has a beehive that provides him with a monopoly on the honey produced from it. At the end of the tale Julius succeeds in delaying the clearing of the land for a year. However, on a more important figurative level, the story works to remind John and Annie of the sterility and frustration in their own relationship. This implication is made clearer in the last story, **"Hot-Foot Hannibal."**

This last tale is initiated by a lovers quarrel between a neighbor, Murchison and Mabel, a relation of the employer. The story concerns the misunderstanding between two slave lovers Chloe and Hannibal who, by their misjudgement of each other's fidelity, die in separate suicides. From the moral lesson within the tale Mabel reconciles her quarrel with Murchison and they reunite. This grand reconciliation of the sexes in a symbolic epithalamium or wedding festival unifies and consummates the sexual imagery used throughout the novel. The further implication of Mabel and Murchison's reunion is that John and Annie will be reconciled to each other in a more dynamic union than what had previously existed. Julius, nonetheless, will remain the trickster and teller to delight their lives and gain material comfort for himself.

The fact that Chesnutt's ***Conjure Woman*** was written when the United States was desperately trying to reconstruct itself from the Civil War and the racial polarity that precipitated it, reveals the hostile literary world Chesnutt had to contend with in the social realism of his novel. It was therefore necessary for Chesnutt as a black author to assume the *persona* of a white northerner in order to mask his real sentiments. In this way Chesnutt's survival as a writer was at stake. And, just as trickster Julius masked his moral lesson in the fictive world of his folklore to get what he wanted, so too did Chesnutt use the fictive medium of the novel to accomplish his professional goals.

According to Abrahams, this fictive process dealing with cultural and racial aggression works best folklorically. "The device of narrative," he writes, "permits free play of hostile actions on a fictitious level; it allows for the construction of a fictive playground in which these important conflicts, which both express and effect the dynamic unity of the group, can be fought." Thus, Chesnutt becomes a trickster in order to communicate his reaction against Reconstruction, the American literary environment, and conventional southern stereotypes through the fictive medium of the novel. Any other means would be prohibited, especially in the *Atlantic Monthly* of the late nineteenth century.

Chesnutt's technique of trickery is the same as Julius'. The author mirrors the problems of race in his contemporary society within the fictive world of Julius and John and Annie, as well as the more distant historical world of Julius' slavery, which for Chesnutt and other black writers of the time was the crux of American racial antagonism. Fiction, as literary technique, makes one way in which that oppression can be tolerable but also creative. In this way the cruelty and bitterness of race relations can be exposed and perhaps, remedied. This progression from history to fiction marks the beginning of social realism in fiction.

Critic Russell Ames points out that Chesnutt's trickery manifests itself in his seemingly sterotypical characters, who grow beyond their social sterotypes, as the novel itself progresses, into social realism. In Chesnutt's characters, he observes, "there was more than a 'fair' share of well-meaning liberal white southerners, of disreputable Negroes. His method was first to disarm his readers with conventional scenes and seeming sterotypes—for example, with idyllic relations with servants and aristocrats—and then in lightning flashes to reveal the underlying facts of injustice and rebellion" [see Further Reading list].

Thus, as Julius is both folk trickster and tale teller, so too is Chesnutt a trickster and teller in the larger scope of **Conjure Woman.** The conjuring effect of the novel attempts a liberation in the audience, and certainly in the lives of the characters themselves, from common sterotypes to real people, each struggling for survival, for reconciliation of the sexes, and reconciliation of the races. Nineteenth century America would tolerate this message only in the guise of folklore entertainment. But as Julius and Charles Chesnutt remind us through the medium of North Carolina black folklore:

> It's all in de tale, ma'm;
> . . . it's all in de tale.

> (pp. 186-97)

Melvin Dixon, "The Teller as Folk Trickster in Chesnutt's 'The Conjure Woman'," in CLA Journal, Vol. XVIII, No. 2, December, 1974, pp. 186-97.

J. Noel Heermance   (essay date 1974)

[*Heermance is an American educator and critic. In the following excerpt from his* Charles W. Chesnutt: America's First Great Black Novelist, *he surveys the principal themes of Chesnutt's short fiction.*]

By and large, Chesnutt's early stories [1885–1898] can be placed into two distinct categories: those written in a light, popular vein and those concerned with racial characters and racial themes. Most of the former stories are satirical and witty, often featuring white (i.e., raceless) characters in an urban, professional business world; and generally they were written for Chesnutt's own witty enjoyment and for his desire to establish a literary reputation on the national magazine scene. The latter, racial group itself rather clearly divided into two parts. Several stories are "racial" only in the sense that the characters are Black, i.e., they are less social-concern stories than they are universal, "human foible" stories that use Black characters as the specific situation from which the general foible is to be drawn (in the same way that Sarah Orne Jewett used New Hampshirites, Mary Noilles Murfree used Appalachian figures, and all the "local color" followers of William Dean Howells used specific situations from their own personal experiences from which to draw general morals on general human conduct). On the other hand, several of these racial stories were very clearly written around Black characters because the social comment in them is one that deals specifically with the Black man's position in America.

It is significant that Chesnutt's first published story was one of the social comment, racial stories. **"Uncle Peter's House,"** appearing in the *Cleveland News and Herald* in 1885, is a racial tragedy concerned with the bitter hardships and prejudice which the newly freed Black man faced in the South during Reconstruction; and, as such, the story has a great deal of social realism about it.

Having eventually overcome most of his social and economic obstacles, Peter was finally on the threshold of success and the construction of a new home. However, just as he was completing the chimmey, he accidentally fell from the roof, suffering fatal internal injuries. In his last moments, surrounded by his wife and son, he laments not having finished the house for them, is comforted with the real vision and song of "A mansion in hebben I see," and dies.

The story itself concludes on an optimistic note, as Peter's wife and son carry on towards the completion of the house. As the last paragraph tells us, the grove of elm trees which Peter planted before his death also "is thriving and will probably shade the yard nicely by the time the house is painted and the green blinds hung." Despite this optimistic, "romantic" note, however, the story achieves most of its power from the harshly realistic, historical elements in it.

There is, first of all, the fact that nobody in the area will sell Peter any land to build on, and the only one who finally does is a Northern turpentine man, who does so only because his trees have exhausted the soil and rendered it useless for any further commercial timber. Secondly, Chesnutt realistically depicts the average freedman's economic plight right after the war when Peter, because he has no capital, falls "an easy prey to the plausible eloquence of a big land owner, who persuaded him to buy a mule on time and rent a farm on shares." The net result . . . is that Peter ends his first season deeply in debt. (pp. 161-62)

Two other realistic elements are presented now. The first of these concerns Peter's oldest son and Southern justice. The son becomes involved in a brawl and is convicted, and Peter's sacrificing for a good lawyer may have been the only thing that kept the son from being hanged. Or, Chesnutt explains, there may have been other reasons here as well:

> . . . possibly, too, the jury were influenced by the consideration that to hang him would be an expense to the county while the ten years' penal term could be utilized for the public good in building the railroads which were at this time beginning to stretch across the State and bring it into closer communication with the rest of the world.

It will be no coincidence that Chesnutt will return to indict this convict lease system in far greater detail in his final two novels.

The final and most dramatic element deals with the local KKK group, whose violent night rides for "amusement" (the traditional rationalization for the KKK's postwar genesis in Tennessee) result in the burning down of Peter's house. Pointedly accompanying the "entertaining" bonfire is an incisive comment which Chesnutt puts in the mouth of one of the sheet wearers. As he sees it, "The idee of a nigger livin' in a two-story house is jes' ridic'lous," and this, of course, is the real reasoning behind the Klan's harassment and ultimate use of violence to maintain the Southern *status quo.* Significantly, Chesnutt goes into further detail as he extends the dramatic moment here to include all individuals in the South—white and Black—who would run afoul of the Klan's politics." "The bell tolls for thee too," he seems to be implying when he notes that a typical Klan "prank" was to attach "to the gate of a prominent citizen of opposite political opinions"

> a placard ornamented with what was intended as the picture of a coffin, and containing a notice to leave the country in thirty days, on pain of the consequence.

Again it will be no coincidence that such a note will form the grisly climax of Chesnutt's dramatic final novel, *The Colonel's Dream,* nineteen years later.

Other early stories in this vein were **"Aunt Lucy's Search,"** appearing in *Family Fiction* of April 16, 1887, and **"The Sheriff's Children,"** appearing in the *Independent* of November 7, 1889. The former is a tender and heroic tale of an old Black woman who spends her postbellum freedom searching for and touchingly finding all her children who were sold away from her during slavery. The latter is one of Chesnutt's most bitter stories, dealing with a white sheriff in a Southern town who sires a mulatto son, characteristically refuses to acknowledge him, and then is haunted by guilt and reproach when this son returns to the sheriff's town and ultimately chooses to bleed to death in his "father's" jail as his ultimate rejection of a world and father who could treat a human being in such an inhuman way.

Then there were those racial stories which were rooted in Black experience but whose meaning and tone tended towards understanding and often satirizing universal human experience. One of the earliest of these was the story of **"How Dasdy Came Through,"** appearing in *Family Fiction* of February 12, 1887. A warm, genial narrative of young love, it is also a satire of revivalist religions which feature the active, thrashing "passing through" of the repentant sinner "caught up" in the emotional ecstasy of religious salvation. The plot of the story revolves around the young girl Dasdy and her successful attempt to capture the heart of a young man in her church. Though they had been fond of each other initially, when another girl in the congregation seeks to lure him away from Dasdy, she in turn presses to win him back. The appeal of this new rival is the fine clothing which she wears each Sunday to church, so one Sunday Dasdy very calculatingly attaches herself to the same group of penitents as her rival and dramatically manages to tear to pieces her rival's Sunday finery in the middle of her "ecstatic" moment of sanctification. The irony, of course, is that Dasdy really did "come through" on the human level, as she managed to win her man back through the destruction of her rival's competitive appeal.

An earlier and somewhat perplexing story in this vein was Chesnutt's second published story, **"A Tight Boot,"** appearing in the January 30, 1886, issue of the *Cleveland News and Herald.* The story itself seems innocuous enough as a satire of people who falsely seek to appear greater than they are, yet one wonders how it was read by Cleveland readers of the period.

Chesnutt in 1883, the year he resigned his post at the State Normal School in Fayetteville, North Carolina.

Subtitled **"A Humorous Southern Story,"** it is about—and strongly satirizes—an antebellum slave who tries to act bigger than he is by wearing his master's boots to a fancy ball and then being caught and chastened when he can't get the tight boot off in the crucial moment of detection. On one level this merely looks like—and was probably intended to be—a reverse Cinderella story, with the moral being a Socratic "Know thyself and act with the honest perception of who you are." Thus, after his chastening experience, the protagonist, Bob, "was not known to indulge again in the luxury of wearing other men's boots."

For the 1886 Cleveland audience, however, this story must have seemed an example of the negative minstrel stereotype which Chesnutt had so consciously set himself to fight. Thus Bob is portrayed as a typically ignorant, buffoonish and "uppity" adjunct to the "comic Negro" stereotype which so delighted the minds of the condescending, patronizing whites of the period. Whatever the story's intended moral, we can only guess the actual effect which it had on its Cleveland readers. This is what makes it so perplexing.

Perhaps the best story in this racial-yet-universal vein is **"Po' Sandy,"** which appeared in *Atlantic Monthly* in May,

1888. It subsequently appeared as the second story in *The Conjure Woman,* and since its method and meaning are integrally part of that work, we will leave our discussion of it until our analysis of *The Conjure Woman* and the sort of artistry and perspective which it represents.

The second major type of story by Chesnutt during this apprentice period was that dealing with white characters; these also appeared in two related, yet different, veins.

First and less important were local color stories, usually in rural settings, which humorously satirized universal foibles. The best example is **"Tom's Warm Welcome,"** Chesnutt's fifth published story, which appeared in the November 27, 1886, issue of *Family Fiction.* **"An Idyll of North Carolina Sand-Hill Life"** is its subtitle, and it is essentially a tall tale and local color story told to our unnamed, first person narrator by Dugald McDugald about "ole Tom Macdonal'."

The story is humorous and well told. It deals with how "pore an no 'count" Tom is smitten by Jinnie Campbell; how he schemes to be present at a dance at her house to which he is decidedly not invited; and how he is completely put to rout by Jinnie's father, who keeps cheering Tom to partake in everything with "Don't be back'ard. You wa'nt invited to the dancin', but Lord bless me, you're jest as welcome as ef you had a 'been." The satire concludes with Tom suddenly inheriting a plantation "down in Sampson County," at which point his stock in the community immediately soars, he is allowed to marry Jinnie, and every family in the area makes it a point to "tuk 'im up then."

The second group of Chesnutt's "raceless" stories of this period were even more universal than the local color stories like **"Tom's Warm Welcome."** These were the satires written for magazines like *Puck,* usually dealing with urban business and professional situations.

The earliest story in this vein, ostensibly an article which appeared in the *Social Circle Journal* of November, 1886, under the pseudonym "Uncle Solomon," was a piece devoted to giving whimsical **"Advice to Young Men."** "Marriages are getting to be such common, every-year affairs in Cleveland," the writer begins,

> that I think it might be well to lay down a few rules for the guidance of young men who may be contemplating matrimony. The rules are based on experience—the experience of other people. I made up my mind to get married some years ago, but haven't had time yet.

Such is its tone and such are its gems of wisdom. Listed in a numerical hierarchy, number three is a fair sample:

> 3. Always marry for money. . . . Some men find music teachers a good investment; others have been successful with milliners and dressmakers; but perhaps the safest thing for a prudent man is a good laundress. . . . In fact I am now hesitating between a Euclid Avenue heiress and a washerwoman with a large business.

More sophisticated than this were the stories which Chesnutt began to write specifically for such magazines as *Tid-Bits* and *Puck.* The first of these was **"A Busy Day in a Lawyer's Office,"** appearing in *Tid-Bits* of January 15,

1887. Basically it is a general social satire of the contemporary scene, lawyers, women, and so on.

> "Ah! good-morning, madam," said the lawyer with a smile of recognition, placing a chair for his client. "How are you getting along with your last husband Mrs.——I forget your present name?"
>
> "Mrs. Rogg. Oh, we've quarrelled already, and I want a divorce."
>
> "Let me see," said the attorney reflectively, "this is the ——"
>
> "The fifth," replied the young woman. "You promised to make a reduction of ten per cent each time."

Of significant interest in this story is its echoing of literature which we earlier saw Chesnutt reading in his youth. As his Journal entry of August 25, 1874, notes "I have re-read *Pickwick Papers* by Dickens, and, it was not at all old to me. I enjoyed it very much." It comes as no surprise, then, to find that much of Chesnutt's social satire here is quite Dickensian in tone and technique:

> "Why, certainly," said Dr. Vaseline, rubbing his oily hands together.

Two months after this piece, *Tid-Bits* carried another in the same vein in its April 16, 1887, issue. **"A Soulless Corportion"** is the brief anecdotal account of a staid, imposing-looking woman who tries to collect two hundred dollars for an expensive, jewelry-filled suitcase lost in a collision. When the suitcase is subsequently found in a creek and its value doesn't exceed five dollars, the woman accepts fifteen dollars for water damage and says haughtily (undercut by dialect) as she leaves,

> "I wouldn't a thought a rich comp'ny like this would insult a lady that way. But all men ain't gentlemen; an' corporations ain't got no souls nohow."

The first *Puck* story, **"How a Good Man Went Wrong,"** appeared a year later in the November 28, 1888, issue. It was in this same "satire of the times" vein, its gentle humor all revolving around a note sent within a small town by District Messenger Service which inefficiently doesn't arrive until eighteen years later. The best of the *Puck* stories, however, didn't appear until April 24, 1889. Greatly transcending the other satires, it is an early example of Chesnutt's artistic, subtle complexity of structure and meaning, even as it seems to be merely a surface satire.

"The Origin of the Hatchet Story" is the whimsical yet pointed account of how an American archeologist grows up at first greatly impressed by George Washington's hatchet experience. Progressively he becomes more and more annoyed at it, until he actually comes to dislike George himself.

In later life an archeological trip takes him to Egypt, where he accidentally discovers a scroll which tells the 19th Dynasty story of Rameses III and his son, Rameses IV. Needless to say, Rameses IV is given a scimitar by his father and, in the latter's absence, begins "trying the temper of his new blade." The parallel of George Washington's story is almost exact, and our narrator's veneration for the name of Washington is ironically restored when he realizes that "The hated Hatchet Story was merely one of those myths which, floating down the stream of tradition, become attached in successive generations to popular heroes. . . . " This is the basis of the ironic satire of fablized patriotism.

What is perhaps more interesting to us here is the exact nature of "Rammy's mischievous activities" and the final, "touching" scene between father and son.

> First he neatly sliced off the ear of the Nubian eunuch who waited at the door of the royal presence chamber. Then, toddling to the apartments of his mama, he deftly sliced off the headdress of one of the ladies in waiting, taking quite a slice of the scalp along with it; and, proceeding to the palace kitchen, skillfully amputated the little finger of one of the cooks, whose hand happened to be in a position convenient for the experiment.

> Passing thence out into the courtyard, he came up, unperceived, behind a servant who was kneeling before a wooden bench, polishing the royal crown with a soft brick. His head was bent forward, exposing the back of his neck in such a manner that Rammy could not resist the temptation, and playfully raising his puny right arm, he severed the head from the servant's body with one stroke,—such was the keenness of his blade. Such was his embarrassment, however, to discover that he had slain his father's favorite Hebrew slave, Abednego.

> The situation was a painful one, and he did not have time to reflect upon it before he heard the footsteps of his royal father approaching. Yielding to the impulse of the moment, the royal infant hastily concealed himself in a large earthen water-jar which stood close by.

> When Rameses III saw the dead body of his favorite slave, his rage at first knew no bounds: "Who slew my Hebrew slave?" he cried.

> In a moment all the members of the household had gathered in the courtyard. They, one and all, had disclaimed any responsibility for the unfortunate death, when the head of young Rammy appeared above the rim of the water-jar, from which he lightly sprang and prostrated himself at his father's feet.

> "Sire," he said, "I can not tell a lie. I did it with my little scimitar."

> For a moment Rameses III was speechless with conflicting emotions. Then the trembling bystanders saw the great monarch's face soften, and heard him exclaim, in feeling tones:

> "Come to my arms, my son! I would rather you had killed a thousand Hebrew slaves than to have told a lie. I thank Isis that she has given me such a son."

Needless to say, there is an obvious social moral beneath this **"Hatchet Story"**; yet it is made so deftly and the satire's irony-within-irony structure is so delicately pointed that the moral never seems obtrusive at all. Thus, as well as a charmingly told, gentle satire, **"The Origin of the Hatchet Story"** is also an example of how the bastion of prejudice can be undermined through deeply felt yet delicately controlled art.

In his mature period [1889-1905], Chesnutt's writings seemed less diversified than in his earlier period, a situation which is understandable when we remember that he undertook writing as a profession in direct response to progressively worsening social conditions in America. In any case, all of his published work during this period, with the exception of his sophisticated bagatelle **"Baxter's Procrustes,"** is racial in subject matter and essentially serious and realistic in approach.

Having said this, however, we must immediately interject an important note of caution suggested by Arna Bontemps in a July 7, 1967 interview with this author at Fisk University. One of the great dangers of judging a Black writer's work during this period, Mr. Bontemps reminds us, is that generally we are dealing only with the published work of that writer. This, he asserts, can be a very misleading approach since the publishers of Black writers of the early 1900s often rejected a great deal of material which the writer thought important but which the publisher feared no one would buy.

Such is the case with Chesnutt. Interestingly enough, with the exception of his very first novel, *Mandy Oxendine,* an intriguing socially concerned novel which was completed in 1897, all of Chesnutt's rejected novels during this period were not racial novels at all, but were various kinds of "white" novels. *A Business Career* in 1898, *The Rainbow Chasers* in 1900, *Evelyn's Husband* in 1903: all were completely raceless novels that reflected Chesnutt's interest in the Howellsian, Jamesian novels of the period. With this said, however, we must now return to the various racially oriented, published works during the period, for these are Chesnutt's major works of this period.

As we have noted, Chesnutt's work of this period are all generally serious and realistic, and there are several reasons for this dominant tone. On the one hand, Chesnutt was no longer a fledging writer so eager to obtain recognition and the pleasure of being "published" that he would write the kind of frothy, light material which *Tid-Bits, Puck,* and the *Cleveland News* and *Herald* desired. And a mature artist now, he felt free to turn his attention to serious subjects which he felt mattered deeply to the world around him. He still retained his own unique interests and literary enjoyments, as his three unpublished "white" novels so dramatically attest; yet his social sense of commitment was more important in his life during this period. We have already noted that he consciously dedicated himself to a writing career in 1889 and that this commitment was made in direct response to his shock over the violence and brutality shown in the Wilmington Massacre of 1898, which heightened and intensified those social fears he had been feeling over the violent wave of disfranchisement sweeping the South since the early 1890s.

Even so, his first work of this period was one of great variety. His collection of short stories, entitled *The Wife of His Youth,* concerned itself with material and stories of "the Color Line." The major point for us, however, is not so much what kind of material was presented here, but how and in what ways that material was presented. Setting, characters, themes and tones: variety and range were found in all these areas.

The first and title story of the collection, **"The Wife of His Youth,"** is a sensitive, powerful drama of racial identity and the Socratic commitment to honest self-awareness and self-acceptance. It is the story of how a light-skinned, well-to-do, socially aspiring Black man in Groveland, a Mr. Ryder, is faced with the sudden choice between ad-

mitting or simply ignoring his past, slavery marriage to a
dark, ignorant slave girl who had shriveled into a quaint,
"amusing" figure: a woman whose past relationship to
Ryder would hardly be an asset to him with his present
"Blue Vein" social set.

Somehow, however, after "gazing thoughtfully at the reflection of his own face" in his bedroom mirror, Ryder
finds the deep courage to announce to all the gathered
members of his set that this woman is "the wife of his
youth." Both tender and compelling, it is a beautifully and
significantly conceived story which is structured and developed with great artistic effect.

The second story in the collection, **"Her Virginia
Mammy,"** is equally brilliant in its fusion of suspense and
deep tenderness. Directly following **"The Wife of His
Youth,"** it is essentially the former story's basic plot as
seen from a different point of view and resolved with the
completely opposite theme. For where the former story
stressed the need for deep, painful honesty, the later story
stresses the importance of sensitive—yet still painful and
courageous—dissemblance.

The plot of this story is one in which an old slave mother
searches after the war for her lost mulatto daughter and
finally finds her doing well as a dance teacher in a Northern city. The girl does not know that she is a mulatto;
knows only that she is an orphan; and is engaged to marry
a handsome, successful boy whom she deeply loves. All
that has kept her from agreeing to his persistent proposals
of marriage is her desire to discover her background; for
she wants to be sure that she comes from the same "quality" family that he represents as the descendent of a May-
flower arrivee, Connecticut governor, and so on.

When Mrs. Harper, the old slave woman, eventually finds
her daughter Clara, she is about to exclaim with joy and
"reclaim" her daughter with the truth of her parentage
when she, Mrs. Harper, suddenly realizes with great sensitivity that her daughter does not want to know that her
mother is Black—that her daughter's whole concept of
who she wants to be will be shattered. Half way through
her story about the past, therefore, Mrs. Harper sacrifices
all her future happiness for her daughter's, and without
directly lying, tells Clara of the high family breeding of her
father, without mentioning the fact that she is her mother:
at which point Clara assumes that Mrs. Harper was simply a family servant—her "Virginia Mammy." Irony, pathos, suspense, pain and love: all are here and all are beautifully fused together.

The third story in the collection, **"The Sheriff's Children"** . . . is different radically from the first two in all aspects of setting, characters, theme and tone. It is, in fact,
a very sobering experience.

The fourth story, in turn, differs from all three of its predecessors in tone, if not completely in theme and setting.
"A Matter of Principle" is a satire of the sort of "Blue
Vein" socialites whom we saw as background in **"The
Wife of His Youth."** These are cultured, educated mulattoes in Northern cities like Groveland (i.e., Cleveland)
who develop for themselves a whole social clique which
stresses as its first and greatest virtue the lightness of each
member's skin. As Chesnutt allows one of its members in
"The Wife of His Youth" to explain,

"I have no race prejudice . . . but we people of
mixed blood are ground between the upper and
nether millstone. Our fate lies between absorption
by the white race and extinction in the black. The
one doesn't want us yet, but may take us in time.
The other would welcome us, but it would be for
us a backward step."

The plot here is close to slapstick in its satire, all hinging
on a case of similar names and mistaken identity. But the
ironic moral is very clear: those who lead artificial lives
based on absurd criteria for basic values will find themselves disappointed and empty (handed) in the end.

Each of the other stories in the collection adds its own
unique quality to the book's overall dimension. **"The
Passing of Grandison"** is another farcical satire, this time
undermining the antebellum stereotype of the "contented
slave," as Grandison seemingly is a man who simply
doesn't want to escape from his masters, no matter how
many opportunities they give—and eventually thrust on—
him. In fact, he even drags himself back South after being
forcibly abducted into free Canada, which brings joy and
cheer to the hearts of his white owners, who "knew" all
along that this was the contented nature of all slaves—
until the next day dawns and they discover that Grandison
has returned only to lead his whole family to the freedom
that lies North.

Another "enjoyably meaningful" story is **"Uncle Wellington's Wives."** This is the saga of a middle-aged Southern
Black man who, once the war ends, finds himself free and
his ears full of exotic reports about the kind of money and
freedom which the North now offers. Furthermore,
though he is married to an industrious, loving woman
(whose work actually supports both of them, since Uncle
Wellington finds leisure more congenial to his nature), he
is told by a local lawyer friend that he is free of this slavery
marriage also if he wishes.

So off he goes North to a new town, a new situation, and
eventually a new wife. She is Irish, and her color represents the epitome of "social freedom" to Uncle Wellington, until his job and eventually his marriage begin to
bump over rocky terrain: at which point his new wife
leaves him (unwilling to support him in the leisurely manner to which he had been accustomed), and he finds the
North suddenly too hostile and cold to his taste. At this
point he returns home, penitent and prodigal, and is taken
back by his old wife on their original easy terms. "The
grass," Chesnutt fabliau-ishly suggests, "is not always gr-
eener."

After the fragile, tender story of **"The Bouquet,"** Chesnutt's most powerful story concludes the collection. This
is **"The Web of Circumstance,"** and it shows Chesnutt at
his best.

The story deals with a hard-working blacksmith in a small
Southern town. Ben Davis is a conscientious and industrious worker—the epitome of the American success figure—and his future looks very bright. However, he has
two things against him; one obvious, the other more deceptively lethal. On the one hand, he is Black and living
in the South, which means that should he ever get into
trouble with the law, even his industriousness would be of
no aid, for Southern "justice" of the period brings with it
a predilection towards Black guilt and overly long prison

sentences. The second albatross in Ben's future is his young mulatto helper, who secretly envies Ben's success and wishes to undercut it in any way possible.

The "way" that presents itself in the story comes in the form of a handsome buggy whip which a certain Colonel Thornton has and which Ben openly admires one day as he is shoeing Thornton's horse. Soon afterwards, the whip is missed by Thornton, and a subsequent search locates it hidden in Ben's shop. Enter Southern justice.

Needless to say, everyone in the all-white court considers Ben guilty almost by definition, including his lawyer, who thereupon conducts a very mediocre defense. Furthermore, Ben is convicted on the circumstantial evidence alone and is sentenced to five years in the penitentiary at hard labor largely because, as the judge declares in his pre-sentence oratorio, Ben is being punished as a racial example. Indeed, as the judge notes with a typical quantity of prejudging,

> "Your conduct is wholly without excuse, and I can only regard your crime as the result of a tendency to offenses of this nature, a tendency which is only too common among your people."

Significantly, Chesnutt as structural artist has two other prisoners sentenced by the judge just prior to Ben that day, and Chesnutt pointedly compares the sentences involved. The first case involves a young white man convicted of manslaughter, who is "admonished of the sanctity of human life" and then given a one-year sentence. The second is a young white clerk convicted of forgery. Having "connections" and a white skin, he receives a sentence of six months in the county jail and a fine of one hundred dollars. Ben then gets five years for the circumstantial "theft" of a riding whip.

Five years later Ben comes home to find the complete dissolution of his house, his family, his whole life. His wife has recently drowned, probably while drunk say the neighbors; and his son has just been lynched for shooting a white man. Even the rumors which the neighbors remember about Ben's "crime" are painful to him—ranging from horse stealing to murder; and he finds that all he once had is gone. The five years have produced a total tragedy.

Brooding over all this, with nascent plans for exacting revenge from Thornton via a huge bludgeon which he has just cut, Ben falls asleep in a field near Thornton's and is later awakened by a "sweet little child" solicitously murmuring over him. It is Thornton's daughter; and though for a brief instant Ben sees her as the potential object of his revenge, the tender innocence of the girl and her childlike concern for him immediately dispel this feeling. After all of the harsh voices and sounds of prison life, Chesnutt tells us, the girl's innocent concern for him is deeply soothing. As a result, "he lay there with half-closed eyes while the child brought leaves and flowers and laid them on his face and on his breast, and arranged them with little caressing taps."

Time passes, the girl is off at a distance picking more flowers for him, when Ben hears a horse coming along the path behind him. Realizing that it is probably Thornton, he springs to his feet, club in hand, momentarily undecided as to his course of action. "But either the instinct of the convict, beaten, driven, and debased, or the influence of the child, which was still strong upon him, impelled him, after the first momentary pause, to flee as though seeking safety." Unfortunately, however, his path away from Thornton leads him towards the little girl, and as Thornton "turned the corner of the path, what he saw was a desperate-looking negro, clad in filthy rags, and carrying in his hand a murderous bludgeon, running toward the child." Accordingly, "A sickening fear came over the father's heart, and drawing the ever-ready revolver, which according to Southern custom he carried always upon his person, he fired with unerring aim. Ben Davis ran a few yards farther, faltered, threw out his hands, and fell dead at the child's feet."

The poignancy, the anguish, the drama all end here. There is a space on the page and a hushed stillness in the reader's feelings before Chesnutt returns with a final paragraph—his final plea. As an artist, a sensitive man, and almost a prophet in some sense, he says his own requiem—and prayer—over Ben's crumpled form:

> Some time, we are told, when the cycle of years has rolled around, there is to be another golden age, when all men will dwell together in love and harmony, and when peace and righteousness shall prevail for a thousand years. God speed the day, and let not the shining thread of hope become so enmeshed in the web of circumstance that we lose sight of it; but give us here and there, and now and then, some little foretaste of this golden age, that we may the more patiently and hopefully await its coming!

It is, magnificently, the finest moment in the book—and is, as well, the natural culmination of the cosmic artist. (pp. 162-77)

Chesnutt published only three short stories over the final twenty-seven years of his life. In April, 1906, **"The Prophet Peter,"** in *Hathaway-Brown Magazine,* showed Chesnutt still at his artistic prime. Like several of Chesnutt's other stories, the story satirically deals with a Black character who hypocritically utilizes his religious position for personal gain. Peter is a revivalist minister who predicts the Day of Doom and then surreptitiously buys up his followers' land as they abandon all their possessions and await the Final Judgment.

Unlike several of Chesnutt's stories in this vein, the satire here is softened at the end by a very delicate, almost tender tone. After Prophet Peter returns, completely crazed, to the poor house where he had started, one of his followers rather touchingly speaks his epitaph, which ends the story.

> "Pete alluz were a fool," she would say, placidly,—"I lived with him long enough to know,—an' now he ain't got no sense at all." And then she would add, with a certain naive pride, "But he were a big prophet an' a healer one time, he shore were."
>
> (pp. 178-79)

"The Doll," written for the April, 1912 issue [of the *Crisis*], is a dramatic, powerful story of inner conflict between revenge and a certain moral-social responsibility to one's people. The protagonist is a Black barber with a thriving business in the city (a success symbol for his race to aspire to) who is one day suddenly tempted to slit the throat of a white Southern colonel whom he is shaving and whom he recognizes as the man who shot the barber's father back in the South. The debate rages back and forth in the barber's mind, until he finally decides that the upward movement of his race is more important than his own personal satisfaction through vengeance.

There are, at this point, two interrelated ironies which we learn. On the one hand we learn that the colonel *knew* who this barber was, and he sees the barber's decision as just another proof that Blacks "are born to serve and to submit. . . . They have no proper self-respect; they will neither resent an insult, nor defend a right, nor avenge a wrong." Immediately after this, however, as we are re-evaluating the story with this first irony in mind, that re-evaluation is itself reevaluated for us by the objective bystander Northern judge who has accompanied the colonel to the barber shop, knows all the circumstances, and comes deeply to admire the strength and determination which the barber's powerful self-control represents.

"Mr. Taylor's Funeral," three years later, shows Chesnutt reverting to the kind of genial satire of human foibles which he had written twenty-eight years earlier. A satire on the hypocritical abuses of religion, the plot deals with the way Mr. Taylor's funeral is used by both his wife and the good-looking pastor of her old church in order to strike up a budding romance of their own. It is fair, if undistinguished, satire.

With "Mr. Taylor's Funeral" completed, Chesnutt's portfolio of published works was also completed. He was fifty-seven at the time, involved in various business and social concerns such as the Cleveland branch of the NAACP, and perhaps this was reason enough to stop writing. It is to his great credit as an artist, however, that the strong fire for literary self-expression still blazed within him, so that we find him working on still another novel as late as 1928, when he was seventy years old. The *Quarry* is not one of his better works as it stands; yet once more it shows him concerned with realistic social matters in the world immediately around him, based as it is on an actual experience which occurred to the Chesnutts in their 1920 Cleveland home. More important, it shows just how strong the artist and social crusader were in him throughout the full length of his life. (pp. 179-80)

> *J. Noel Heermance, in his* Charles W. Chesnutt: America's First Great Black Novelist, *Archon Books, 1974, 258 p.*

Hartmut K. Selke (essay date 1977)

[*In the following excerpt, Selke offers an extended analysis of the short story "The Sheriff's Children," which contains what he identifies as Chesnutt's characteristic literary themes.*]

Charles Waddell Chesnutt vies with Paul Laurence Dunbar in being the first Afro-American author to be accepted by major American publishing houses and to win national recognition and fame. Both authors, in order to be published at all, had to come to terms with the literary forms and conventions of the Plantation Tradition whose chief exponents were Joel Chandler Harris, Thomas Nelson Page, James Lane Allen and Harry Stillwell Edwards. This literary convention stipulated that the black charac-

ters be presented as living contentedly in an Edenic South, that they be quaint, childlike and docile, tellers of exotic yarns for the entertainment of massa's children or for massa himself. It is this tradition which gave rise to the literary stereotypes of the "Contended Slave," the "Wretched Freeman," who, being deprived of the paternal care of his master, is unable to provide for himself, the "Comic Negro" and the "Local Color Negro."

Since the black writer, who wanted to break into print with his accounts of the black experience in America, had to adapt his work to the prevalent tastes of the day and to present his characters in a pastoral, harmonious setting, the only freedom left to him was that of choosing "the genre or the countergenre," as Robert Bone points out [see Further Reading list]. By pastoral genre is meant the "idyllic posture toward experience," by countergenre the "ironic posture."

Whereas Dunbar by and large conformed to the limitations of the idyllic posture, wearing, as it were, "the mask that grins and lies," [the line is from Dunbar's poem "We Wear the Mask," *Majors and Minors,* 1895] Chesnutt never did, even when he made use of the established forms, as for example in his "conjure" stories, in which he subtly undercut the submissive message apparently inherent in the very form. (p. 21)

Among the themes treated most often in Chesnutt's works are (1) the inhumanity of the system of chattel slavery, (2) the incongruities of the color line as drawn within the black society itself, (3) the dual themes of passing and the ordeal of the double identity and (4) the injustices that Southern blacks have to suffer even after Emancipation, particularly during the restoration of white supremacy after Reconstruction.

At first sight, "The Sheriff's Children" might seem to be a treatment of the theme of the tragic mulatto. However, this is only one and, as shall be demonstrated, not the dominant theme of the story.

"The Sheriff's Children" was first published in the New York weekly magazine *Independent* in November 1889. The *Independent* then catered to an educated, liberal white audience. The first readers of the story were unaware of its author's racial identity. Earlier that year Chesnutt had moved into his own, rather spacious home in Cleveland. Yet, the other stories published or written during that year evince the same sombre and combative note that characterizes "The Sheriff's Children." In "The Conjurer's Revenge' (June 1889) the narrator, Uncle Julius, denounces slavery with unwonted explicitness, calling the slavetraders stealers and sellers of men and thus seeming to invoke the Biblical punishment for the man-stealer.

"Dave's Neckliss" (October 1889) is also an Uncle Julius story, although not a "conjure" story in the narrow sense. Like "The Sheriff's Children," this gruesome story exposes "the baleful influence of human slavery." Indeed, the story bears close resemblance to "The Sheriff's Children": punished unjustly by an otherwise "kind" master (this fact is peculiarly insisted on in the story), Dave is driven to insanity and suicide. The "kind" master's recognition of his own guilt and his repentance come too late to undo the wrongs wrought by a system of chattel slavery. The third story, of which Chesnutt completed the first draft in 1889, was the often revised **"Rena Walden."** It deals with the problem of the tragic mulatto, which is also touched upon in **"The Sheriff's Children."**

Chesnutt's sombre outlook may be explained by the fact that at that time he was butting his head against the restrictions imposed by the tastes of the reading public and of magazine publishers. This went so far that he even toyed with the idea of migrating to Europe. In a letter written some six months after the publication of **"The Sheriff's Children"** he confided [in a letter to George Washington Cable]:

> If I should remain idle for two weeks, at the end of that time I should be ready to close out my affairs and move my family to Europe. The kind of stuff I could write, if I were not all the time oppressed by the fear that this line or this sentiment would offend somebody's prejudices, jar on somebody's American-trained sense of propriety, would, I believe, find a ready sale in England.

Ten years after its original publication, **"The Sheriff's Children"** reached a wider audience through its inclusion in *The Wife of His Youth and Other Stories of the Color Line.* Whereas in the first collection of stories the superficial white reader could easily be deluded by Chesnutt's apparent adherence to the conventional forms of the Plantation Tradition, this second volume, at least in some of the stories, more openly strikes a note of poignant protest against the Afro-American's social and psychological predicament in the South.

In a letter to his publisher, in which he discussed promotion strategies for the volume, Chesnutt wrote:

> The book was written with the distinct hope that it might have its influence in directing attention to certain aspects of the race question which are quite familiar to those on the unfortunate side of it; and I should be glad to have that view of it emphasized if in your opinion the book is strong enough to stand it; for a *sermon* that is labeled a sermon must be a good one to get a hearing.

Whereas the book was well received in the North, Southern critics, as was to be expected, did not fail to discover the elements of "crusade" and "sermon" and berated Chesnutt for his impropriety. One critic wrote: " **'The Sheriff's Children'** furnishes, perhaps, the most shocking instance of his reckless disregard of matters respected by more experienced writers" [Nancy Huston Banks, in a review in *The Bookman,* New York, X, February 1900]. Criticism seems to have been directed primarily against **"The Sheriff's Children"** with its bold treatment of the tabooed subject of miscegenation, and not against **"The Passing of Grandison,"** which effectively explodes the myth of the happy, docile slave, or against **"The Web of Circumstance,"** which undermines Booker T. Washington's accommodationist contention that the acquisition of skills and property would automatically ensure recognition for the Afro-American even in the South.

The story opens with a description of the sleepy village of Troy, county seat of Branson County in North Carolina, a district so isolated that the war seems to have passed it by, had it not been for the tribute of one generation of young men that the great conflict demanded. Some ten years after the war, the citizens of Branson County are

shocked to learn that Captain Walker, an old soldier, "had been foully murdered." A mulatto, a stranger in the area, is suspected of the crime and quickly apprehended. While the prisoner is awaiting judgment in the county jail, the citizens decide to lynch him. The sheriff is informed of the plan by a Negro and determines to do his duty and resist the lynch mob. He proceeds to the jail where he locks himself into the prisoner's cell. After having warded off the lynching party and having fired a shot in reply to a sniper's bullet, he is disarmed by the prisoner who then reveals his identity. The mulatto is Tom, the sheriff's son, his mother is a slave woman whom the sheriff had sold to a speculator. The son demands that the sheriff release him or else he will shoot him. At the very moment when Tom decides that he cannot trust his father and prepares to shoot him, the sheriff's daughter, Polly, who had worried about her father's long absence, comes up from behind and fires at the mulatto, wounding his arm. The sheriff dresses his son's wound, telling him that he will call a doctor on the following morning. He spends a restless night, passing his life and his failings in review and finally deciding to "atone for his crime against this son of his." When he goes to the jail on Sunday morning, he finds that his son has committed suicide by tearing off the bandage and bleeding to death.

Chesnutt's story may be read simply as a carefully wrought suspense story, which moves in steadily increasing crescendo from the opening description of the dull and somnolent community to the final twist at the end of the story. As the plot develops, the scene narrows: the first two pages are devoted to the county, the following six to the village of Troy and its inhabitants, the next seven focus on the sheriff's house as the sheriff is informed of the plot by Sam. The scene then moves to the captive's cell in the jail. The next shift back to the sheriff's house seems to suggest that there is a break in the development delineated above. [In a dissertation] William L. Andrews sees in this supposed break a flaw of plot development: "The story . . . lapses into argument and introspection which fail to sustain the tenseness of the action in the first half of the story." However, this lapse into introspection is no more than a further narrowing of the scene along the pattern of the rest of the story, only this time to the sheriff's consciousness. The constant narrowing of the scene from the "sequestered district" of Branson County to the "hamlet" of Troy, from there to a prison cell and finally to the sheriff's mind conveys a feeling of claustrophobia, of inescapability.

This gradual restriction of space has its parallel in the gradual resolution of the question of identity, which was posed at the beginning of the story. The question is first raised in the speculations "upon the identity of the murderer." But at that point in the story everything is vague, ill-defined. A "strange mulatto" is suspected of the crime. The second central character, the sheriff, is only introduced at the beginning in his function as a public officer whose duty it is to arrest the suspect.

This vagueness is carried over into the next scene. As the design to lynch the prisoner assumes shape, the townspeople remain anonymous: no names are mentioned. Naturally, a major function of this scene is to demonstrate the genesis and anonymity of mob violence. By their very speech the townspeople are characterized as dumb-witted backwoods people whose dull minds are helped along by illegally distilled whiskey and vague notions of "honor" to give birth to the dastardly plan.

The heavy hand of the omniscient narrator who edits and comments on his material makes itself felt particularly in this scene, driving home a point that does not stand in need of such commenting. The planned lynching is to the townspeople's minds "a becoming way in which to honor [Captain Walker's] memory." Their perverted notion of justice is reflected in the mocking solemnity of the narrator's language as he describes the plan: "By agreement the lynchers were to meet at Tyson's store at five o'clock in the afternoon, and proceed thence to the jail . . . ".

The following scene at the sheriff's house marks a first departure from the aura of anonymity which had characterized the first pages. The reader is informed of the sheriff's name and of his appearance. Sheriff Campbell is a "tall, muscular man," he has "keen, deep-set gray eyes" and "a masterful expression." His very stature and "attitude of a soldier" as well as his language bespeak his determination and his superiority over the rest of the townspeople. Additional information provided by the omniscient narrator corroborates this first impression. Campbell is a cultivated man, "far above the average of the community in wealth, education, and social position. . . . He had graduated at the State University at Chapel Hill, and had kept up some acquaintance with current literature and advanced thought."

The members of the lynch mob, too, are given a semblance of identity when the sheriff asks Sam who is coming. They are an array of self-styled doctors, majors and colonels: " 'Dere's Mistah McSwayne, en Doc' Cain, en Maje' McDonal,' en Kunnel Wright, en a heap er yuthers.' " But even this identity is fleeting, as well befits a mob setting out with this purpose in mind. It is wiped away by the sheriff who declares them all to be "strangers" to him because he "did not think it necessary to recognize anybody in particular on such an occasion; the question of identity sometimes comes up in the investigation of these extra-judicial executions."

The question of identity comes up again in the confrontation between Campbell and his prisoner after the lynch mob has withdrawn. It is no longer the detective story question as to who was the murderer, a question which persists only as a vague hope of extricating the prisoner from his hopeless situation. In the course of the story every suspicion against him is dispelled in the reader as well as in the sheriff: "he no longer doubted the prisoner's innocence."

Alone in his cell with the sheriff, the prisoner undergoes an almost miraculous transformation from a "cowering wretch" who provokes the sheriff's "contempt and loathing" to a "keeneyed, desperate man . . . a different being altogether from the groveling wretch" of only a few minutes before. This transformation is possible only because Tom, the prisoner, is exclusively seen through the sheriff's eyes. He is never presented, except in his own utterances, in his own right, but remains a reflection in his father's eyes. Before the prisoner had gained control of the situation, he had remained a mere abstraction to the sheriff, a well-defined quantity that fitted into a prefabricated category. It is this refusal to look upon the prisoner as an individual human being that prevents him from recognizing his son sooner than he does.

As Tom points out to him, they have the same features: "no man need look at us together twice to see that . . . ". It is obvious that the sheriff had never looked at his son. Instead he had seen "the negro" in him: "He had relied on the negro's cowardice and subordination in the presence of an armed white man as a matter of course." It is only this unwonted behavior that "caused the sheriff to look at him more closely." Even then, however, he does not recognize the prisoner, and it is only after the question "Who are you?" that the latter's identity is revealed to him.

This revelation initiates a new movement. It is the beginning of yet another question of identity. The confrontation with "this wayward spirit" who had come "back from the vanished past to haunt him" forces the sheriff to see himself as he truly is, to explore his own smug identity.

This new and central theme of the story is prepared by a change of the point of view. The first two thirds of the story bear the mark of the omniscient narrator whose presence as editorial commentator is constantly felt. This is particularly true of the three-page introduction which leads up to the action proper. Here the author even appears in the first person, explaining his materials to the reader: "At the period of which I write . . . ". In what follows, the omniscient narrator as editorializing agency is also felt, at times very directly, as in his remark that something "is immaterial to this narrative," at times less so, as in the choice of scenes which are presented in the dramatic mode. In the last third of the story these editorial interventions do not cease altogether—they are particularly obvious in the description of Polly's stealthy approach, unnoticed by both the protagonist and Tom, in the authorial comments on the sheriff's character and in the imperative addressed to the reader: "Let no one ask what his answer would have been"—but a new dimension is added. Starting with the sentence, "The sheriff mentally cursed his own carelessness for allowing him to be caught in such a predicament," all subsequent events are mainly seen and evaluated through Campbell's consciousness. From now on, to apply Henry James' words to the sheriff, "It is *his* vision, *his* conception, *his* interpretation . . . He therefore supremely matters; all the rest matters only as he feels it, treats it, meets it" [*The Art of the Novel: Critical Prefaces*, 1950].

This change of perspective is a necessary prerequisite for the soul-searching that is about to follow. The sheriff, who had hitherto appeared an impeccable character, now realizes that he "had yielded" to the temptations of an evil system when he had sold his son and his lover to a speculator. This also throws a new light on a remark made earlier in the story. Yielding to his environment, to the force of circumstances, even against his better judgment, seems to be the sheriff's particular weakness: "At first an ardent supporter of the Union, he had opposed the secession movement in his native State as long as opposition availed to stem the tide of public opinion. Yielding at last to the force of circumstances, he had entered the Confederate service rather late in the war . . . ".

This weakness also accounts for the sheriff's decision in favor of his sense of duty and against his human instincts, both when his own life is in danger and when he asks himself how he can extricate Tom from his predicament and make up for his own previous shortcomings: "It occurred to him, purely as a hypothesis, that he might permit his prisoner to escape; but his oath of office, his duty as sheriff, stood in the way of such a course, and the sheriff dismissed the idea from his mind."

It is only after the initial shock of the confrontation has worn off that the full impact of the experience becomes clear to the sheriff. "Alone with God," he again experiences "a kind of clarifying of the moral faculty . . . a state of mind in which one sees himself as God may be supposed to see him." Seeing himself as he is, the sheriff decides to atone for his sin. It is interesting to note that neither Tom nor himself see his sin in the fact of miscegenation itself, but rather in the fact that he has neglected his parental duties, his moral obligations in depriving his son of a true identity of his own: Tom has "no name, no father, no mother—in the true meaning of motherhood."

The tragedy of the story lies in the fact that the circumstances are such that the father's recognition of the son comes too late. The sheriff's personal tragedy is that his attempts at atonement are only half-hearted and incomplete and that he is finally deprived of the "opportunity for direct expiation."

As quoted above, Chesnutt had thought of *The Wife of His Youth* in terms of a sermon. **"The Sheriff's Children"** preaches a sermon in the sense that it induces the enlightened white reader, to whom it is addressed, to identify with the sheriff who is presented in very positive terms as a courageous, law-abiding, conscientious and educated man. The sheriff's qualities make his moral shortcomings appear in an even cruder light, and the reader, who had come to identify himself with him, is made to share in his fall and to experience a purging similar to that "clarifying of the moral faculty" that the sheriff feels. Chesnutt's is a fire-and-brimstone sermon which shows no way out of the moral dilemma. The attempt to make amends comes too late. Injustice has been done and it seems irremediable. The impact on the reader who is required to go to task with himself, is all the greater.

Yet, even after the sheriff's failings have been revealed, the sympathetic narrator speaks out in his behalf in an authorial comment: "But the baleful influence of human slavery poisoned the very fountains of life, and created new standards of right. The sheriff was conscientious; his conscience had merely been warped by his environment." Without denying any of the sheriff's guilt, he thus places it in a broader perspective, indicting a system to which Campbell has fallen prey. Again, the reader may be led to ask himself if the influence of the environment is truly a valid attenuating circumstance for Campbell and for himself.

By choosing the sheriff's point of view in the last third of the story, Chesnutt has diverted the reader's attention from Tom, the mulatto. The narrator does not perform the role of advocate for him, trying to explain his motives and soliciting compassion or understanding, as he had done in the case of the sheriff. Seen only from outside except in his own utterances, Tom's story remains untold, although the narrative offers some hints as to the dramatic potential of the theme.

[Gerald W.] Haslam detects one of the strong points of the story in the absence of this theme, which is indeed fraught with grave dangers: "By emphasizing the white father rather than the mulatto son, he [Chesnutt] partially avoided the melodramatic stereotypes which marred so much of his work" [see Further Reading list].

The theme which Chesnutt partially subdued in this story is that of the tragic mulatto, which came out of anti-slavery fiction, as Sterling A. Brown has shown [in introductory comments to the Chesnutt entry in *The Negro Caravan,* 1969]. The mulattoes in fiction "are the intransigent, the resentful, the mentally alert, the proofs of the Negro's possibilities." The theme harbors the danger of presenting the material in such a way that the Afro-American's humanity is measured in proportion to the "white" blood in his veins.

Upon the completion of his second draft of **"Rena Walden"** only a few months after the publication of **"The Sheriff's Children,"** Chesnutt wrote to Cable on the subject of mulattoes in fiction:

> There are a great many intelligent people who consider the class to which Rena and Wain belong as unnatural. . . . [a] gentleman remarked to me in substance that he considered a mulatto an insult to nature, a kind of monster that he looked upon with infinite distaste. . . . I fear there is too much of the same sentiment for mulattoes to make good magazine characters.

Chesnutt was doubtless prompted by these sentiments when he made the sheriff's moral dilemma the central concern of his story instead of choosing the equally available theme of the tragic mulatto. Tom's major function in **"The Sheriff's Children'"** seems to be that of the spark which sets off the crisis.

Yet, there is more to him. When Tom first appears in the story, he is ambiguously called "a strange mulatto," an epithet which is reminiscent of Chesnutt's letter. Tom is not only a stranger in his own land, unrecognized in all senses of the word and by everybody including his father, he is also an abomination in the eyes of the whites.

The dilemma of the double-consciousness as defined by W. E. B. DuBois is particularly obvious for the mulatto. DuBois wrote:

> One ever feels his twoness,—an American, a Negro; two souls, two thoughts, two unreconciled strivings; two warring ideals in one dark body, whose dogged strength alone keeps it from being torn asunder. The history of the American Negro is the history of this strife,—this longing to attain self-conscious manhood, to merge this double self into a better and truer self. In this merging he wishes neither of the older selves to be lost. . . . He would not bleach his Negro soul in a flood of white Americanism, for he knows that Negro blood has a message for the world. He simply wishes to make it possible for a man to be both a Negro and an American, without being cursed and spit upon by his fellows, without having the doors of Opportunity closed roughly in his face.

Tom is obviously an individual who does not possess this dogged strength and who is torn asunder by the magnitude of the conflict. He is a tortured, warped character who has come to turn his aggression against the race that the custom of the country makes him a part of, and thus finally against himself. His attitude toward his mother, who, to his mind, has become synonymous with the black race, is highly ambivalent. While he pities her and admires her for having "had enough womanhood to call her soul her own," he is at the same time ashamed of her blackness: "You gave me your own blood . . . and you gave me a black mother. . . . You gave me a white man's spirit, and you made me a slave, and crushed it out." Tom has sought to flee his blackness, as by acquiring an education, but has found that his blackness stays with him as "a badge of degradation."

Commenting on the inappropriately refined language used by Tom, Haslam asks himself "if Chesnutt has not, in this one respect, fallen again into his habit of trying to demonstrate that mulattoes are more white than Negro." Similarly, Bone feels that "the story does not wholly escape from the stereotype of the tragic mulatto" but is redeemed by its pervasive irony. Tom does indeed seem to conform to what Brown had called the present image of the tragic mulatto: "The mulatto is a victim of a divided inheritance; from his white blood come his intellectual strivings, his unwillingness to be a slave; from his Negro blood come his baser emotional urges, his indolence, his savagery." We should, however, ask ourselves if Chesnutt did not intend to criticize Tom for his own interpretation of his situation, for his inability to turn his talents and his education to some good purpose, for his self-pitying despair.

Tom, then, is vaguely related to [Albion] Tourgée's mulatto characters towards whom Chesnutt had no charitable feelings. In the above quoted letter to Cable he writes: "Judge Tourgée's cultivated white Negroes are always bewailing their fate and cursing the drop of black blood which 'taints'—I hate the word, it implies corruption—their otherwise pure race." The only difference seems to be that Tom, distorted beyond recognition by the force of circumstance, is more sordid, his fate more sordid than that of Tourgée's characters.

This makes him very different from the saintly figures created by younger authors, figures who die a Christlike death on the cross, as in W. E. B. DuBois' story "Jesus Christ in Texas" or in Langston Hughes' poem "Christ in Alabama." Rather, Tom dies by his own hand, and the pattern of Crucifixion and Resurrection is thoroughly perverted. Yet, there is an obvious parallel in the story. The action takes place at a weekend, starting with a death on Friday morning (one page) and ending with another on Sunday morning (one page). The bulk of the story is devoted to the abortive attempt to lynch the prisoner and to the sheriff's soul-searching, which might be likened to a descent into the "hell" of his own mind where he has to face and overcome his own sinful self. But the parallel is not sustained by the characters. The whole story is pervaded by murder, near parricide, fratricide and, finally, suicide. The father cannot save the son. Instead of a resurrection, we witness the confirmation of death, of hopelessness. The Biblical allusion might be even further pursued. The death of the old soldier might be assumed to represent the sacrifice made by the nation as a whole—we are told that Branson County was robbed of "the flower of its young manhood." The redemption of the nation, however, fails miserably, ending with the death of him for whom the sacrifice has ostensibly been made.

Tom's only triumph might be that he dies of his own free will and thus in a way asserts his manhood, but it is not much of a triumph. **"The Sheriff's Children"** is the first sign of an angry strain in Chesnutt, more often than not subdued by his gradualist, even accommodationist, philosophy. Tom, though not possessing any of the greatness, vaguely foreshadows a later Chesnutt character, Josh Green in *The Marrow of Tradition,* who would rather die like a man than live like a dog.

The choice of the title **"The Sheriff's Children"** seems to be at odds with the point of view used in the story, which clearly favors the sheriff as the central character. However, the relationship between the sheriff's children opens the way to a deeper, parabolical reading of the story. It is important for this parabolical meaning that they should have no knowledge of each other's existence, or, to put it more precisely, that Polly should have no knowledge of the existence of a black half-brother. Tom and Polly do not come fully alive in the story precisely because they are made to represent more than themselves alone. They are both the heirs of a father who, by virtue of his ambivalence—he is torn between allegiance to the Union and the Confederacy—, very much resembles Thomas Jefferson who managed to reconcile his authorship of the Declaration of Independence with his status of slaveholder and progenitor of mulatto children. Tom, the Afro-American, is as much an heir to the political and cultural heritage left by Campbell, the Founding Father, as is Polly, the Anglo-Saxon. But whereas nobody will dare question the legitimacy of the latter's claim, the former's is generally denied. The original sin is the father's failure to recognize his son as his heir, his having left him out of the masterplan. Polly acts out a tragic role by being instrumental in the destruction of somebody who is in reality her brother. (pp. 25-36)

Hartmut K. Selke, "Charles Waddell Chesnutt: 'The Sheriff's Children' (1889)," in The Black American Short Story in the 20th Century: A Collection of Critical Essays, *edited by Peter Bruck, B. R. Grüner Publishing Co., 1977, pp. 21-38.*

P. Jay Delmar   (essay date 1979)

[*In the following essay, Delmar examines "the theme of the mask"—"how both whites and blacks are constrained to hide their true personalities and, often, their true racial identities from themselves and each other"— in "The Sheriff's Children" and "The Passing of Grandison," and suggests that this theme unifies the stories in* The Wife of His Youth, and Other Stories of the Color Line.]

Ever since 1900 when W. D. Howells analyzed Charles W. Chesnutt's *The Wife of His Youth, and Other Stories of the Color Line* (1899) as a collection which revealed the "tragic position of persons of mixed blood" [see excerpt above dated 1900], other critics have been prone to follow suit, sometimes disparaging Chesnutt's work for stylistic weaknesses born of his desire to write propagandistic fiction. While such commentary is not incorrect, in two among the nine pieces in the collection—**"The Bouquet"** and **"The Passing of Grandison"**—the mulatto theme plays no part, and in two others—**"Cicely's Dream"** and **"The Web of Circumstance"**—it is relatively insignificant.

Some other device, then, must help to hold the collection together, for it is clear that these stories of one of the best turn-of-the-century Black American writers, a master of the techniques of short fiction, are in fact unified and are designed within cohesive frameworks. Dunbar's "We Wear the Mask" suggests a possible solution. The stories in Chesnutt's collection exploit the theme of the mask. They show how both whites and Blacks are constrained to hide their true personalities and, often, their true racial identities from themselves and each other.

Chesnutt's development of the mask theme is not, of course, a constant in *The Wife of His Youth.* Stories such as **"The Wife of His Youth," "Uncle Wellington's Wives,"** and **"A Matter of Principle"** suggest that all mask-wearing by Blacks is an evil to be avoided; every attempt to deny one's Blackness or one's real personality is shown to be destructive and is therefore condemned. Mr. Ryder of **"The Wife of His Youth"** and Uncle Wellington Braboy of **"Uncle Wellington's Wives"** find "happiness" when they reaffirm their Blackness and renounce their attempts to join white society, while Cicero Clayton's attempts to reject his heritage in **"A Matter of Principle"** meet with laughable failure. However, stories like **"Her Virginia Mammy"** and **"Cicely's Dream"** suggest that wearing a mask might be a good thing. In the first, Mrs. Harper secures a happy life for her long-lost daughter by not revealing their relationship, allowing the young woman to pass and to be blissfully ignorant of her true heritage. **"Cicely's Dream"** reveals the trauma that can result from a mask's being lifted, as Cicely loses the love of a man who, in a state of amnesia, thought he was a mulatto. Apparently, Chesnutt is demonstrating that matters of racial identity are not easy to solve and that the "obvious" virtue of racial pride—obvious to modern racial sensibilities, at least—was not always so obvious to the Blacks of former generations.

Not only a subject of certain stories, moreover, the "mask-theme" is used to solve structural problems within Chesnutt's tales. The stories themselves tend to be masked. Their ultimate meanings and denouements are often hidden from the reader, each piece working artistically through ironic or satiric structures which seek to delay the reader's perception of the last truth as long as possible. Many stories "mask" their plots, of course, using elements of foreshadowing to guide a reader along without giving the ending away too soon. In *The Wife of His Youth,* Chesnutt consistently uses the fewest possible foreshadowing elements, however, never allowing the reader to feel too sure of the ending before the climactic psychological moment. He seldom misses a chance to delude a reader with the glimpse of a false trail. In **"Cicely's Dream,"** for example, Chesnutt early suggests the possibility that Cicely's lover might be a white man and that her love for him may be doomed, but he does not confirm the facts until the last page. Instead, he continually stresses the uncertain nature of the relationship, allowing his reader to hope that the relationship might turn out well. **"The Web of Circumstance,"** one of the most powerful stories in the collection, has a tragic ending which Chesnutt carefully screens until the final moment, even suggesting just before the story's conclusion that it will end happily. And in **"The Bouquet,"** the central event in the piece, Mary Myrover's death, is anticipated by only one brief reference. Everywhere Chesnutt sets up mutually exclusive possibilities for

the development of his plots—Cicely could be happy, or she could be hurt—and consistently delays the reader's perception of the correct endings.

The third and sixth stories in *The Wife of His Youth,* **"The Sheriff's Children"** and **"The Passing of Grandison,"** illustrate the mask-theme and the mask-structure in Chesnutt's fiction, and the fact that they do so in markedly different ways makes them worthy of separate consideration here. **"The Sheriff's Children"** uses his mask theme negatively: hiding one's true soul leads to tragedy. **"The Passing of Grandison,"** on the other hand, like **"Her Virginia Mammy,"** apparently argues that mask-wearing can be a virtue if it is directed toward virtuous ends. **"The Sheriff's Children"** uses techniques of subtle foreshadowing to screen its conclusion. In **"The Passing of Grandison,"** however, Chesnutt succeeds with a bold, dangerous ploy. Though he uses almost no foreshadowing, he succeeds in a nearly complete masking of the story's surprise ending.

The two major figures of **"The Sheriff's Children,"** Sheriff Campbell and his mulatto son, are both plagued by crises of personal identity; their reactions to these crises both exploit the theme of the mask and exemplify Chesnutt's structural use of the mask concept. These achievements make a powerful story of one which might without them have degenerated into a naive, run-of-the-mill treatment of the long-lost son plot. Had Chesnutt made the revelation of the relationship between the Sheriff and the son whom he had abandoned as a child its focal point, his story would never have attained any particular significance. Chesnutt instead uses the Sheriff's parenthood as the starting point for an examination of its tragic results.

Campbell is a man who wears the mask of duty and morality. Ronald Walcott stated the case quite well when he argued that while Campbell appears to be free of the primitive impulses which seem to motivate his neighbors, he "possesses his own inhibiting personal code before which all else must pay obeisance, his Southern gentleman's concept of duty" [see Further Reading list]. The point is that the Sheriff is not free of primitive impulses; the concept of duty which he has adopted has only hidden them. In his youth, he had fathered a child with a Black woman; later, in a fit of anger, he had sold them down the river. As the crisis of the story unfolds with his "child" standing before him—a prisoner accused of murder whom an unruly mob wants to lynch—Campbell begins to see himself for the first time without a mask, reflected in his son's eyes: "He knew whose passions coursed beneath that swarthy skin and burned in the black eyes opposite his own. He saw in this mulatto what he himself might have become had not the safeguards of parental restraint and public opinion been thrown around him." Campbell had always lived by the code of the Southern aristocracy, one which sanctioned his behavior toward his lover and child. But he had never consciously realized that he was using the code to mask his instincts from himself. Whether the passions which coursed within him were noble or not, they were his, and he should have come to terms with them. When he learns who his prisoner is, Campbell begins to get an inkling of the existence of the mask which he has worn so long.

The prisoner, though, does not really come to grips with who and what he is. He feels trapped between two racial worlds. As Mr. Ryder says, in a story which satirizes this viewpoint, persons of mixed blood "are ground between the upper and the nether millstone." They may be accepted by either the white race or the black but the former does not want them, and acceptance by the latter would be a disgrace. Ryder would prefer acceptance into the white world, and, here with Chesnutt's apparent sympathy, Sheriff Campbell's son has also selected that goal. The prisoner cries that he is "despised and scorned and set aside by the people to whose race [he belongs] far more than to [his] mother's." The mulatto rejects his Blackness, but the rigidity of white society prohibits him from taking up the white man's mask. Essentially, the Sheriff's son feels robbed of his birthright; he has grown rebellious as a result of his inability to wear a mask which appears to him to be not a mask at all but rather his true spirit. He feels that he is being forced to wear a mask of Blackness.

Whatever the merits of Chesnutt's point about the proper sphere of the mulatto, it is clear that the Sheriff's mask of duty and the mulatto's mask of Blackness are evil forces; they cause the prisoner's death and the father's failure to atone for his past misdeeds. This outcome, tragic because both figures are basically noble men whose personalities reveal weaknesses which lead to their downfall, is a part of the story's mask-structure. Two elements of the work are crucial here—the Sheriff's daughter's wounding of the prisoner and his subsequent suicide—and both are well disguised.

The first event occurs after the prisoner asks the Sheriff at gunpoint to let him escape. Paralyzed by his sense of duty, the Sheriff cannot agree to what Chesnutt unmistakably feels is a proper course of action: "It may seem strange that a man who could sell his own child into slavery should hesitate at such a moment, when his life was trembling in the balance. But the baleful influence of human slavery poisoned the very fountains of life, and created new standards of right. The sheriff was conscientious; his conscience had merely been warped by his environment." In all justice and mercy, as Chesnutt suggests, Campbell should let his son go. Even if he were guilty of murder, his chances of escaping the lynch mob are minimal at best; should he somehow escape its rage, his chances of receiving a fair trial in Troy are even worse. Although Campbell is now beginning to understand these truths, he cannot break through the barriers thrown up by years of tradition. He hesitates, and his son declares that he must die.

A reader might expect such a tragic result of the Sheriff's personality since hesitation is often a mark of a tragic figure, and Chesnutt does carry Campbell to the brink of catastrophe: the prisoner "raised his arm to fire, when there was a flash—a report from the passage behind him." Just as he was about to pull the trigger, he was shot by the Sheriff's daughter. This type of masking is well known to viewers of Westerns. Whenever the hero is in danger of being bushwhacked, an unseen marksman brings the villain down. One's expectations are keyed to an "anticipated event" (the death of the hero), but the event which actually occurs (the death of the villain) is its exact opposite. Such a situation is intended to shock the viewer momentarily, and Chesnutt intends a similar effect here. Of course, the tactic can be abused. In the worst examples of grade-B Westerns, the viewer is given no hint that the hero will be saved. In better examples, though, some foreshad-

owing hints at the truth; the film might show the hero's sidekick riding to the rescue, then leave him until he fires the mysterious shot.

"The Sheriff's Children" provides such foreshadowing just before the girl wounds her half-brother: "So absorbed were the two men in their colloquy and their own tumultuous thoughts that neither of them had heard a light step come stealthily up the stairs, nor seen a slender form creep along the darkening passage toward the mulatto." Without this suggestion—which only makes sense after the reader learns that the Sheriff's daughter has shot the prisoner—the "actual event" would come as a complete surprise to the reader; the anticipated event (Campbell's death) makes sense, and nothing would cause the reader to doubt its probability. So great a surprise would shock the reader too much; it would tend to annoy, rather than satisfy. If the foreshadowing were too heavy, on the other hand, there would be no surprise at all. In this case that charge cannot be made. There are 162 words heavily charged with emotional energy between the foreshadowing element and the prisoner's wounding, so the foreshadowing itself does not receive too much emphasis when the reader first encounters it. Moreover, the foreshadowing passage does not necessarily suggest the shooting, since "slender forms" do not generally carry horse-pistols.

The second crucial situation in the story, the mulatto's suicide, is equally masked. After the prisoner is injured, the Sheriff bandages his arm and tells him to lie about his escape attempt if he is questioned further. These are acts of kindness which apparently bode well for the Sheriff and his son, and they are followed by almost four pages which reveal Campbell's ruminations on his past life. When the Sheriff finally decides to "atone for his crime against this son of his—against society—against God," the reader feels that the story might end on a positive note. Even though a tragic atmosphere has been already established, a happy conclusion is not completely unlikely because of the inherent nobility of the characters. The qualities which make a tragic fall tragic could also be used to avert the tragedy. Campbell is basically a good man, and his son is not inherently evil. However, Chesnutt soon lifts the mask and reveals the actual ending. The tragedy is not averted because the mulatto kills himself while his father, still hesitating, slowly arrives at the decision to aid him.

This turn is clearly plausible, and, even more important, Chesnutt foreshadows it while he establishes his false trail. First, the mulatto had spoken of death as something he did not fear when he denounced his existence as a non-white, non-Black man: "When I think about it seriously I do not care particularly for such a life. It is the animal in me, not the man, that flees the gallows." Secondly, after he is wounded the mulatto's attitude of defiant rebellion transforms itself into sullen dejection; he simply gives up. Finally, the Sheriff himself tells his son how to die. The injury is described as a "flesh wound," something normally not very serious. However, as Campbell warns his son after bandaging him, "I'll have a doctor come and dress the wound in the morning. . . . It will do very well until then, if you will keep quiet." If he does *not* keep quiet . . . the conclusion is left unsaid, but the prisoner knows what his father meant. During the night, the mulatto tears his bandage off and bleeds to death. The suicide does not come as a complete surprise to the reader, then; it does fit the tragic atmosphere of the story, and Chesnutt has shown it to be a reasonable occurrence without focusing upon it as an obvious ending.

"The Sheriff's Children" uses both mask-theme and mask-structure. The Sheriff and his son fail because they cannot accept their true identities or, perhaps in the case of the mulatto, because he cannot achieve recognition for what he perceives to be a true identity. And by the use of foreshadowing Chesnutt is able to hide the story's tragic outcome, increasing its emotional impact when readers finally recognize the truth. **"The Passing of Grandison"** also uses the mask-theme and structure, but in a different way. As Joel Taxel notes, Grandison wears a Sambo-mask throughout the story; he wears a false mask of Blackness, one which his master expects to see, in order to survive and to escape his bondage [see Further Reading list]. That is obvious—as soon as one has read the entire piece. Until the end, though, even astute readers cannot tell what is really going on because Chesnutt carefully disguises the fact that Grandison is indeed wearing a mask and that, in this case, the mask has a positive virtue. Even more significant, Chesnutt does so without using any foreshadowing to speak of. Instead, he plays Grandison's apparent characterization and the plot's apparent development against the reader's logical and more humane perception of the realities of slavery until he is ready to reveal the story's true meaning. Chesnutt, that is, so carefully manipulates irony and satire that the reader is not certain about whom or what is being satirized.

Four situations in the work reveal the nature of Chesnutt's use of the mask structure: (1) Grandison's selection for a trip north as a bodyservant to his master's son, a young man who wants to "steal" one of his father's slaves, (2) Grandison's reaction to Northern abolitionists, (3) his reaction to a trip to Canada, and (4) his return to his master's plantation. Colonel Owens allows Grandison to go north, for instance, only after being convinced that his slave is absolutely loyal and "abolitionist-proof" to boot. When he asks Grandison if he does not believe himself to be better off than the "free negroes" of his acquaintance, Grandison replies with an answer which confirms the Colonel's fondest opinions of slavery: "Well, I sh'd jes' reckon I is better off, suh, dan dem low-down free niggers, suh! Ef anybody ax 'em who dey b'long ter, dey has ter say nobody, er e'se lie erbout it. Anybody ax me who I b'longs ter, I ain' got no 'casion ter be shame' ter tell 'em, no, suh, 'deed I ain', suh!" Although all of this seems a bit much, there is no indication that Grandison does not mean exactly what he says. The satire seems to be directed at the Colonel, who believes that slavery is a sophisticated form of chivalry, but the reader does not yet know what to make of the Colonel's slave. When the elder Owens broaches the subject of Grandison's going north and indicates that he might run into some "cussed abolitionists" there, Grandison reacts with horror: " 'Dey won't try ter steal me, will dey, marster?' asked the negro, with sudden alarm." While the reader might believe that no sane slave could react this way, Chesnutt says nothing in the entire section to indicate that Grandison is not being truthful; the authorial commentary in the phrase "with sudden alarm," after all, is seemingly straightforward.

How different was an earlier case, though, when Colonel Owens's son Dick approached another slave, Tom, with

the idea of going north. Chesnutt says, "Now, if there was anything that Tom would have liked to make, it was a trip North. It was something he had long contemplated in the abstract, but had never been able to muster up sufficient courage to attempt in the concrete. He was prudent enough, however, to dissemble his feelings." Here Chesnutt through his commentary explicitly reveals that Tom's hope for "safety" in the north is merely a smokescreen and that he would fulfill Dick's desire to aid the escape of a slave the first chance he got. In fact, Dick's cautious father refuses to let Tom leave the plantation because he had not dissembled his feelings quite well enough on previous occasions. In his portrayal of Grandison, however, Chesnutt never gives any indication that the slave is anything other than the Sambo he appears to be.

Once Dick and Grandison arrive in the north, everything the slave does confirms the reader's suspicion that he is as foolish as he seems. At one point during their stay in Boston, Dick sees Grandison talking to a young white preacher; as soon as Grandison sees Dick, "he edged away from the preacher and hastened toward his master, with a very evident expression of relief upon his countenance." Grandison then proceeds to tell young Owens how the "abolitioners" have been bothering him, how he fears that he might be forced to hit one of them, and how he longs to return to Kentucky. Dick himself curses "the stupidity of a slave who could be free and would not," but he believes it to exist in Grandison. Here one may begin to think Grandison has come clear, even though Chesnutt's commentary is again straightforward. Grandison saw Dick approach the preacher and him; perhaps he is covering his tracks after all. As soon as Chesnutt opens the shade, however, he unmistakably closes it, blinding his reader as much about Grandison as ever. Dick leaves Grandison alone with a hundred dollars, after telling him that he could do whatever he pleased with it, but when he returns after an absence of two days he finds "the faithful Grandison at his post, and the hundred dollars intact." If Grandison had been dissembling before, why had he not taken advantage of this new opportunity? Chesnutt is still taking extraordinary pains to mask the true nature of Grandison's character. By illustrating Grandison's reacting to situations in ways which defy logic, Chesnutt is able to build up tension within an essentially comic framework, tension which will only be released when the mask itself is removed.

Desperate to lose Grandison, Dick takes him to Canada and, standing on the Canadian side of Niagara Falls, carefully describes that country as a place where a slave may simply walk away from his master without any fear of being caught or punished. Grandison's reaction?: "Let's go back ober de ribber, Mars Dick. I's feared I'll lose you ovuh heah, an' den I won' hab no marster, an' won't nebber be able to git back home no mo'." Nothing in this dialogue even hints that Grandison would really like to escape. His reaction is presented as straightforwardly as possible, even if it appears too stupid to be credible. When Dick leaves Grandison alone on the Canadian side and he still makes no attempt to escape, the reader almost gives him up. Finally, Dick resorts to having Grandison kidnapped in Canada since the slave refuses to accept freedom on his own. The reader's tension appears to be relieved; at least Grandison is free, and one's view of slavery as something to be escaped is reconfirmed.

Within three pages, however, the reader's confidence in his/her perceptions is destroyed. Chesnutt pulls the structural mask on tighter as he shows that even enforced freedom is too much for Grandison. As Chesnutt describes it, without any trace of irony directed toward Grandison, the prodigal returns to servitude and his old Kentucky home: "The colonel killed the fatted calf for Grandison, and for two or three weeks the returned wanderer's life was a slave's dream of pleasure. His fame spread throughout the county, and the colonel gave him a permanent place among the house servants, where he could always have him conveniently at hand to relate his adventures to admiring visitors." The reader is thoroughly puzzled, as Chesnutt intends. Has this Black author written a story extolling slavery? Is Grandison a real Sambo, and does Chesnutt see a virtue in such blatant Uncle Tom-ism?

As soon as Chesnutt has "masked" the reader into asking these questions, he pulls the mask off with a vengeance, and the reader's tension is finally, explosively, relieved. The next paragraph reveals that three weeks after Grandison's return from Canada, not only he but his new wife Betty, as well as his father, mother, sister, and two brothers—seven of his master's most prized possessions—are missing from the plantation. Now the reader knows the truth: Grandison had been dissembling all along. He had been "passing" all the time, passing to freedom and passing for Black—or for his master's view of what constituted Blackness. The careful reader now remembers the only true foreshadowing which Chesnutt had provided; when the Colonel had finished quizzing Grandison about his attitude toward abolition, he had mentioned that Dick might buy a wedding present for Betty when she and Grandison got married in the fall. Grandison had not made good any of his opportunities to escape simply because he refused to escape alone. He would not leave his family or his lover; he would carefully bide his time, and they would all escape, or they would all suffer, together. The mask of the Sambo has allowed Grandison to gain his "marster's" confidence; moreover, it has allowed him to marry Betty sooner than they had expected and thus to escape sooner than they had planned. Far from being a stupid, childish Uncle Tom, Grandison proves to be representative of the noblest qualities in human nature—self-sacrifice, courage, and an indomitable will.

The mask structure succeeds without significant foreshadowing in this case because the foreshadowing is already present in the reader's mind. Despite the fact that Chesnutt never gives any indication that Grandison is wearing a mask, the reader cannot completely believe that anyone could be so naive or that Chesnutt could write such a naive story. Even if the reader had never heard of Chesnutt, he/she would still experience a paradoxical reaction to the work until the structural and thematic masks are removed. The story's ending, then, does not completely surprise the reader any more than such a work with adequate foreshadowing as **"The Sheriff's Children,"** but it surprises one enough to produce a powerful emotional response. While the masks are at their tightest, readers "know" that Grandison is a fool and that Chesnutt is perhaps a fool as well, but this knowledge does not seem quite "right." The removal of the masks resolves this conflict, and the resolution in turn produces pleasure.

"The Sheriff's Children" and **"The Passing of Grandi-** son" demonstrate Chesnutt's use of the mask, doing so in essentially opposite ways. The remaining seven stories in *The Wife of His Youth* also use the mask structure and theme, providing artistic unity in the collection in a way not always recognized. Why the mask theme varies from story to story is explained by Chesnutt's biography. A mulatto himself, one who experienced first hand the sensation of being trapped between two worlds, Chesnutt vacillated between a desire to be considered white and a pride in being identified as Black. At various times he had been Mr. Ryder confirming his Blackness and the Sheriff's son renouncing it; he had been Uncle Wellington removing the mask because it was wrong, and he had been Grandison wearing a different mask because it led to right. The mask fascinated Chesnutt because he could not decide what to do with his own. The stories of *The Wife of His Youth,* in both theme and structure, amply reflect that fascination. (pp. 364-75)

P. Jay Delmar, "The Mask as Theme and Structure: Charles W. Chesnutt's 'The Sherrif's Children' and 'The Passing of Grandison'," in American Literature, *Vol. LI, No. 3, November, 1979, pp. 364-75.*

William L. Andrews   (essay date 1980)

[*Andrews is an American educator and critic. In the following excerpt, he examines the principal themes of Chesnutt's color-line fiction.*]

The problems of black people and the more specialized difficulties of mixed-blooded people in America's pervasively racist post-Civil War environment were the subjects which informed Chesnutt's entire literary career after the publication of *The Conjure Woman.* These were also the twin texts of his non-dialect short fiction, of which *The Wife of His Youth and Other Stories of the Color Line* was the epitome. In naming a motive behind the publication of his second short story collection, Chesnutt stated the question which, in actuality, all his race problem short stories were designed to address: "I should like to hope that the stories, while written to depict life as it is, in certain aspects that no one has ever before attempted to adequately describe, may throw a light upon the great problem on which the stories are strung; for the backbone of this volume is not a character, like Uncle Julius in *The Conjure Woman,* but a subject, as indicated in the title— *The Color Line.*" (p. 74)

To Chesnutt the color line problem in the United States affected three unofficially definable classes—the whites, the mixed bloods, and the blacks. Each group was victimized by the problem; each was faced with the option of perpetuating it or of working toward its resolution. "How then," Chesnutt asked on one occasion, "are we to go about the eradication of the prejudice?" His answer summarized the message of his color line stories: "It is a matter primarily of individual effort, of the exercise of moral force." Consequently, Chesnutt's first fictional studies of the race prejudice problem discuss particular instructive situations in which moral enlightenment and effort, not group social or political force, are the one thing needful to promote the progress of individuals beyond color inhibitions and caste limitation. In many of Chesnutt's color line stories black people are lectured through fictional "sermons" on those aspects of the traditional work ethic which could elevate the race as a whole, morally, socially, and economically. In those sermonic tales where the lesson is learned and successfully applied by the Afro-American characters, white people would see a favorable race advertisement. Some of the more specialized color line stories address the mixed blood class, of which Chesnutt was a part, urging that, as members of the Afro-American "talented tenth," they promote and exemplify the moral progress of the race. Finally, a few of the color line stories expose the moral decrepitude of the "reconstructing" South and suggest the moral basis on which social progress could take place.

Chesnutt's later novels widen his focus on the race problem in an attempt to establish the complex causal relationship between the spirit of caste and the total social, economic, and political situation of black people in the South. From this perspective one may regard Chesnutt's short stories about the color line as initial inquiries. These first investigations probe the effects of race consciousness on fundamental cultural patterns and socioeconomic institutions, such as courtship, marriage, child rearing, education, and the pursuit of happiness in a vocation or career. Repeatedly, the color line stories develop in such a way as to demonstrate the author's preoccupation more with a general problem than a particular character. The stories confront the reader with a kind of fictional case study contrived so as to typify a social problem stemming from American color consciousness. The stories go on to dramatize the effect of this problem on the thought and behavior of characters who are stylized enough to represent the three racial classes to whom the color line stories were addressed. The conclusions of the stories suggest how the problem can be prevented, alleviated, or solved through right moral choices available to blacks, mixed bloods, or whites, depending on which group the story is designed to appeal to.

Despite differences in audience, tone, and specific moral purpose, Chesnutt's color line stories were united in one respect: they were motivated by their creator's strong revisionist point of view toward the popular concept of "Negro character" as retailed in the white magazine press. Chesnutt saw the Afro-American stereotyped in American fiction as 1) "the bad Negro" (a law breaker or one who demands his rights too vociferously); 2) "the good Negro" (the faithful retainer); 3) "the modern 'white man's nigger' " (a fawning client, preacher, or politician); 4) "the wastrel type" (one who "squandered his substance in riotous living"); and 5) "the minstrel type" (one who "tried to keep the white folks in good humor by his capers and antics"). In his color line stories, therefore, Chesnutt set out to counterbalance the weight of opinion against the black man by introducing white readers to the "many thrifty, progressive, serious-minded Negroes with a sincere respect for their own type, with high aspirations for themselves and their children, whose ideals of character and citizenship were of the best" and who resented "race prejudice and social intolerance." At the same time a number of Chesnutt's stories took exception to the existing popular stereotypes by trying to revise public opinion about such figures as the "good" and "bad" Negroes and the "wastrel" and "minstrel" types. Undoubtedly Chesnutt wrote many of his conjure stories with a revisionist motive in mind and with a desire to undercut the minstrel

stereotype through the characterization of Uncle Julius. In his color line stories Chesnutt waged his campaign against racial stereotypes in popular magazine fiction on a broader front and with more partisan vigor. His antagonists in the plantation school of fiction had unjustly denigrated the freedman almost as much as they had falsely eulogized the slave, in Chesnutt's view. Chesnutt's response to this propaganda was to write his first plainly identifiable protest fiction. (pp. 75-7)

Chesnutt wrote a few frankly propagandistic stories designed to revise the myth of the incompetent, unimprovable southern black man. Chesnutt began his writing career with a tribute to the freedman in the Reconstruction South. **"Uncle Peter's House"** is basically a success story about an ex-slave who survives poverty, poor land, debts, and visitations by the Ku Klux Klan to buy his own land, build his own house, and thereby achieve social and economic respectability. Neither a comical old "uncle" in the Page-Harris tradition nor an aggressive New Negro who threatens the social or political status quo, Peter is a farmer, an ex-field hand who triumphs in the story through the tenacious application of the most familiar and mundane of virtues: temperance, industry, patience, perseverance, thrift, and faith in God. Following the basic tenets of the traditional American work ethic and enduring those injustices which he cannot alter, Peter, representative of the average southern freedman, quietly assumes a modest dignity in the story. His deathbed admonition to his son to finish the house he started suggests a conservative, middle-class moral legacy inherited by the New Negro from the old-time black man.

"The March of Progress" was another race advertisement for the southern freedman. Genteel white readers of the *Century* would have found a dearth of dramatic action in this little sketch. Its plot simply dramatizes the discussion of a problem facing a black schoolboard in Patesville, North Carolina, in the 1880s. Its characters, moreover, are mere types. But even so, the types are unfamiliar to magazine writing about southern blacks, and the discussion of the schoolboard on whether to rehire Henrietta Noble, their aging white schoolmarm from the North, or to replace her with Mr. Williams, a young, well-qualified, hometown mulatto, is presented with greater seriousness than could ordinarily be expected.

It does not take great acuteness to see that **"The March of Progress"** symbolizes in its main characters various points of view on the larger question of how blacks might bring about their own "progress" and advancement in the popular eye. The choice facing the schoolboard rests between promoting a member of the aspiring "talented tenth," whose personal ambitions embody those of the race, or denying him in favor of prior loyalties to white people who, in spite of social ostracism, labored for the freedman's welfare. Initially, the two spokesmen for "the solid element of the colored population" in Patesville back Williams, claiming that " 'self-preservation is the first law of nature,' " and that the race must "stand together" lest the "march of progress" leave it behind. But in the rejoinder of Old Abe, who represents "the humbler class" of blacks on the committee, the policy of self-help based on racial solidarity and self-interest gets its moral comeuppance. After reciting Miss Noble's many years of service as teacher, preacher, and nurse and her evident dependence on their support, Abe convinces the committee to rehire her. In reversing itself, the schoolboard demonstrates the magnanimity and ethical discernment of the southern ex-slave.

Chesnutt's melodramatic and inept conclusion to this tale, which allows Miss Noble to die conveniently so that Williams may obtain the post after all, is a major flaw in **"The March of Progress,"** but it should not deflect attention from the central issue around which the sketch is built. At issue is the meaning of the term "progress." Superficially Chesnutt seems to celebrate another instance of the black man's unprogressive loyalty to his white benefactors at his own expense. However, in deciding that moral responsibility precedes race allegiance and that compassion, not color consciousness, should govern their dealings as free men, the schoolboard attests to a maturity and wisdom in southern blacks that was unheard of in popular white magazine fiction about Afro-American life. In this respect, the story argued the case for the black man as a serious moral agent. Additionally the theme of **"The March of Progress"** previews a key didactic element in practically all Chesnutt's color line fiction, short or lengthy—the idea that true progress could not be defined in terms of *racial* ascension but only in terms of *moral* ascension over the stumbling block of race consciousness, whether black or white. (pp. 81-3)

"Aunt Mimy's Son" sketches the career of one southern black youth whose failure to resist the blandishments of the fast life in the North brings about a concomitant loss for the race as a whole. Mimy's son is a member of the new generation of free-born blacks whose migration from the South to the North was a matter of concern for both Chesnutt and his best-known black fiction-writing contemporary, Paul Laurence Dunbar. Chesnutt's fiction is more sanguine about life in the North for black people than Dunbar's is. As a transplanted southerner himself Chesnutt generally spoke positively of the greater economic opportunities afforded the Afro-American in the North. But to the juvenile readers of *Youth's Companion,* where **"Aunt Mimy's Son"** appeared [1 March 1900], Chesnutt still emphasized through the white narrator of this story that "the true secret of prosperity and progress—thrift and good conduct" had to be kept foremost in mind. Mimy's son is a promising New Negro when he leaves home, " 'just the kind of man who, with fair opportunities and some strength of character, might have been of some use in the world.' " But, as the doctor who attends him on his deathbed concludes, " 'he took a wrong turn somewhere, and dissipation and disease have simply used him up.' "

Dunbar's frequently sentimentalized descriptions of the misfortunes of wayward southern blacks in northern cities imply that the "wrong turn" for most blacks is the one which takes them out of Dixie and the friendly confines of the old plantation. Chesnutt, on the other hand, refused to blame either overweening black ambition (as the white plantation writers would have done) or even a color line in the North (as Dunbar did at least once) for the moral collapse and wasted potential of Mimy's son. Instead Chesnutt took the New Negro himself to task for a lack of "strength of character" and made the youth's personal inadequacies culpable, not his environment or the dream of success itself.

Such a simplistic and exclusively moralistic assessment of the Afro-American's possibility of success in the North was not totally characteristic of Chesnutt, however. **"Aunt Mimy's Son"** fit the requirements of *Youth's Companion,* but it was not Chesnutt's definitive statement on the migration question. In **"Uncle Wellington's Wives,"** a much more sophisticated study of the qualities necessary to the southern black man's successful assimilation into northern society, Chesnutt goes far deeper into the psychological, environmental, and educational influences which shape the prospects of the black immigrant. Unlike the plantation writers who harped dolefully on the freedman's congenital inability to handle the moral temptations and socioeconomic responsibilities of life in industrial America, Chesnutt made the tragicomedy of Uncle Wellington in "Groveland," Ohio, a vehicle for some positive advice to his black readers about the meaning of and preparation for Afro-American success in the North.

"Uncle Wellington's Wives" recounts the career of a middle-aged mulatto who, filled with propaganda about the good life in the North, leaves his wife of many years in the South and sets out to gain the "state of ideal equality and happiness" which he believes awaits the black man in Ohio. In exchange for his loyal, industrious, pragmatic black wife of the South, Wellington takes an inconstant and unreliable Irish woman for his bride, believing that such a marriage would be "the acme of [his] felicity" as a black man in the North. However, having attained his "ideal state of social equality" about which he has day-dreamed for so long, Wellington soon takes his own "wrong turn" toward the bottle once too often, which causes him to lose his well-paying job and eventually his white wife. The lesson to be learned from this experience comes from a black lawyer who calls Wellington's reversals " 'what you might have expected when you turned your back on your own people and married a white woman. You weren't content with being a slave to the white folks once, but you must try it again. Some people never know when they've got enough.' "

It is not an unfamiliar text in Chesnutt's fiction, this disparagement of white imitation and color envy, but rarely did Chesnutt label so clearly the negative effects of substituting color preferences for more substantial values in making choices. Rarer still in American fiction was the chimera of "social equality" so matter-of-factly confronted. A few writers had toyed with the problem of miscegenation in magazine fiction, but the writer who dramatized the problem dispassionately, almost comically, rather than melodramatically, who treated miscegenation unhysterically as simply another phenomenon of American color consciousness, was virtually unique in the 1890s. In making miscegenation one of the subjects of **"Uncle Wellington's Wives,"** Chesnutt seems to have wanted to assuage the worries of paranoid whites while repudiating wrong-headed black notions of "social equality" as the "acme" of the ambition and achievement of the black man in the North. As a realistic student of the American color line, Chesnutt does not deny the fact of miscegenation, but he also points out through the example of Wellington that only a foolish old man, an ignorant country bumpkin, considers a white wife the most desirable goal of an upwardly mobile black man. Chesnutt does not denounce racial intermarriage on abstract moral, social, or biological grounds in this story (or anywhere else in his fiction), but

"Uncle Wellington's Wives" does disclaim it when the motive for it springs from misguided black priorities and illusory ideals.

Intermarriage in "Uncle Wellington's Wives" is, therefore, a collateral issue, a function of the old freedman's erroneous concept of success and respectability for the black man in the cities of the northern United States. After having shown how not to define these middle-class ideals, Chesnutt goes on in "Uncle Wellington's Wives" to make his economic point. In the midst of his protagonist's disillusionment, the author steps into the story to deliver the following summation:

> He had believed that all men were equal in this favored locality, but he discovered more degrees of inequality than he had ever perceived at the South. A colored man might be as good as a white man in theory, but neither of them was of any special consequence without money, or talent, or position. Uncle Wellington found a great many privileges open to him at the North, but he had not been educated to the point where he could appreciate them or take advantage of them; and the enjoyment of many of them was expensive, and for that reason alone, as far beyond his reach as they had ever been.

The key thing in these remarks is Chesnutt's conclusion about why Wellington is at such a disadvantage in the liberal but more complicated northern city. The author blames neither race prejudice nor the often-alleged racial incapabilities of the black man. The racial factor matters much less than the individual's possession of "money, talent, or position." Untrained vocationally and unprepared intellectually, Wellington's "age and temperament," in his creator's judgment, impede his relocation and adjustment to new requirements and opportunities. "The spirit of enterprise and ambition into which he had been temporarily galvanized could not longer prevail against the inertia of old habits of life and thought." If he had been a younger man, argues Chesnutt, or one more predisposed to the "active, industrious" life, Wellington could have made the move with less hardship.

Since Wellington has not received this prior conditioning and preparation, he makes the wisest choice at the end of his northern sojourn by returning to Milly, his conservative, unillusioned black wife, the embodiment of the social and economic creed of Chesnutt's didactic color line stories. Like so many of the characters in his color line tales, Milly is another symbolic type, but she does represent a distinctly revisionist version of the conventional southern black "mammy" figure. Wellington's first wife does not belong among the overstuffed dictatresses of the white folks' kitchen. She does not spend her time entertaining white children and amusing adults. Milly is an independent worker, a laundry woman beholden to no white mistress. A foil to Wellington's vanity and improvidence, she works ceaselessly, practices thrift, disbelieves in pie in the sky, and manages her affairs without help. Like Uncle Peter, Wellington's anti-type, Milly adheres to the traditional middle-class work ethic, holding a sensible estimate of her social and economic possibilities in the South, and achieving a realistic success. When Wellington asks her, " 'how would you lack ter live at de Norf?' " she replies pragmatically, " 'I dunno nuffin' 'bout de Norf. . . . It's hard 'nuff ter git erlong heah, whar we knows all erbout it.' "

It is crucial to the message of "Uncle Wellington's Wives" that Wellington eventually stop chasing the rainbow of "social equality," symbolized by the remote and specious ideal of a white wife, and return to the wife of his youth, the repository of truly valuable assets. Through Wellington's chastened experience, misguided blacks were to learn that the important things in life are not the "privileges" of close association with white people which theoretically the black man may share in the North. Instead, what really matters are the tangible benefits of life—marital devotion, financial security, careful planning, and restraining good sense—symbolized in Wellington's relationship to Milly.

In those moral sketches and tales which reached their artistic culmination in the story of Uncle Wellington, Chesnutt outlined with care and dedication, if not with a high degree of subtlety, some of the prerequisites for Afro-American socioeconomic success in postwar America. Given his assumption that black assimilation into American life was basic to the kinds of success he was concerned about, Chesnutt created color line stories like the ones thus far surveyed to propagandize and champion the upward movement of blacks throughout America. Using the *exemplum* as his typical literary mode, Chesnutt upheld the aspiring black person as a dutiful, conscientious, reliable member of a progressive America. Negative object lessons like Aunt Mimy's son or Wellington, whose extravagant expectations and delusive goals show how not to climb the ladder of success, complemented Chesnutt's positive *exempla* in propagandizing the efficacy of the traditional conservative American work ethic for the black man. The American Dream could be made to work. The freedman had established a toehold in the South through prudent management of his economic affairs and social institutions. Now, beyond the Mason-Dixon line lay "larger opportunities for development" for "the younger and more aspiring element." The optimistic message of Chesnutt's *exempla* stressed, therefore, the imminent completion of the Afro-American's house of respectability, in the North particularly, so long as he persevered in conservative fashion, as Booker T. Washington taught, to create a sound economic base. "The principal trouble, in the matter of development for colored people, is not the trained man, but the untrained man," Chesnutt postulated once to an audience. "The trained, the educated man, the capable man, of whatever race, seems to be able to take care of himself, in whatever place." Advertising this black "capable man" as able to "take care of himself " whether in the North or the South is the fundamental purpose of fully one-third of Charles Chesnutt's color line short stories.

In a smaller group of color line stories, Chesnutt restrained his didactic predilection in favor of a more disinterested, journalistic tone befitting a social observer and commentator. The social phenomena observed in such stories as "The Bouquet" or "The Web of Circumstance" or "The Sheriff 's Children" bear witness to problems inherent in the Afro-American's situation in the postwar South which could not be alleviated simply by the more steadfast practice of the middle-class work ethic by blacks. Exacerbating the problem of Afro-American progress in the New South were white prejudices, suspicions, envy, and indifference toward blacks, all of which were rapidly becoming institutionalized in varying forms of racial discrimination. The more obvious and well-publicized aspect of the New South color line, that which stretched around the voting booth, Chesnutt did not take up in his earliest short stories of social analysis. Instead, he focused on manifestations of color bias in less politically sensitive areas of southern civil and social activity in order to point up the extent of the color line problem without embroiling it in the fires of political controversy. (pp. 87-93)

From the beginning of "The Bouquet" Chesnutt as narrator assumes the role of social commentator on southern affairs since the Civil War. His remarks run counter to the progressive image of the New South which had been popularly disseminated in the 1880s and 1890s and which had been sketched into the frame stories of *The Conjure Woman.* In these three color line stories, Chesnutt pictured the North Carolina he had known as a youth without the sanguinity of his midwestern businessman alter ego. "Down-east" North Carolina is characterized as underpopulated, agriculturally backward, socially conservative, politically reactionary, with few developed economic resources and little direct connection with the flow of ideas and events from the outside world.

In "The Bouquet" Chesnutt divided his attention between the delineation of the segregated pattern of small-town southern life and the recounting of a pathetic, almost sentimental tale of a black schoolgirl's adoring love for her beautiful white teacher, a flower of southern womanhood who wilts in death in the course of the story. The social analysis in the story is not detailed; examples of discrimination against blacks are mentioned without special highlighting from the author. Loss of caste for aristocrats who associate with blacks, segregation in church services, and resistance to black education in general are features of southern life and thought which provide the social background and influence the action of "The Bouquet." Occasionally Chesnutt dips into sarcasm at the expense of the schoolteacher's mother, one of the many unreconstructed aristocrats in his color line fiction, but he also speaks with tolerant comprehension of the causes of her bigoted behavior, leaving the reader to judge her as he wishes. At the end of the story, when Sophy Tucker is excluded from the funeral of her idolized teacher, Miss Myrover, Chesnutt draws the threads of his tale together in an emotionally charged denouement. The Old South racial credo expounded by Mrs. Myrover finds its social manifestation in the segregated funeral service which ostracizes Sophy, the unoffending representative of the New Negro generation in the story. Thus the partially enlightened noblesse oblige of Miss Myrover, ambivalently eulogized by Chesnutt, is undone by her benighted mother, whose survival past her daughter's death testifies to the frailty of New South progressivism and the vitality of the old caste spirit.

The Wilmington, North Carolina, *Messenger* winced at the indictment of "Wellington's" small-town cruelty in "The Bouquet" and denounced Chesnutt for distorting the social relations between the races in the contemporary South. On the other hand, William Dean Howells pronounced himself "touched" by the sentimental strategy of "The Bouquet" [see excerpt dated 1900]. A more distanced critical perspective, however, will find too little to recommend in it. The firmness of Chesnutt's moral convictions tends to force the literary issue. The characters in "The Bouquet" are type-ridden, particularly Sophy, the black schoolgirl, who is little more than a diminutive personification of the Afro-American as devoted, patient, long-suffering, and wholly self-forgetful. Such stereotypical characteristics do not make her an interesting figure, but in the situation in which she is placed, this extreme simplification of her nature does make her eminently pitiable. And this seems to be the author's paramount purpose in the story, to evoke pity from a situation of patent injustice. Because Sophy is an innocent child, not an "uppity" black adult, no justification can be mustered for Mrs. Myrover's prejudice or Wellington's segregation customs. What more trenchant comment on the effect of the color line could be posed for an American reading audience already primed by domestic childhood literature to sentimentalize and idealize children? Segregation is not pictured as a socioeconomic system in "The Bouquet." It is a moral blight which ultimately thwarts the love of little children. No wonder the *Atlantic* chose this story to run as an advertisement for *The Wife of His Youth.* It had a social timeliness and muted sensational appeal which at the same time was sugared to the tastes of genteel readers by use of a simple plot turning on matters of the heart toward an almost lachrymose conclusion. Thus "The Bouquet" shows one way Chesnutt tried early in his career to reconcile serious social comment and purpose with popular reader expectations. If the story seems more successful in arousing strong feelings than in dispassionately analyzing color line conditions, it foreshadows the uneasy yoking of melodramatic scene and social protest rhetoric which pervades Chesnutt's later and longer color line fiction.

While "The Bouquet" evidences Chesnutt's affinity for sentimentality in his protest-oriented stories, "The Web of Circumstance," the concluding story in *The Wife of His Youth,* reveals the influence of the "new realists" on Chesnutt's approach to the fiction of social analysis. Although most of Chesnutt's most memorable color line stories follow Howells' emphasis on the accurate portrayal of ordinary experience with special concern for the social and moral consequences of human choice, the themes of determinism and atavism which emerge from "The Web of Circumstance" imply Chesnutt's reading of naturalistic authors. The main character of his story, Ben Davis, initially resembles Nimbus Ware of Albion Tourgée's *Bricks without Straw* (1880). Both men are industrious, self-reliant, prosperous black men in the postwar South, the leaders of a potential black middle class. But both men's impolitic views about black self-determination and white reparations stir up white resentment. Nimbus Ware is removed from the scene by the Ku Klux Klan, in keeping with the realities of southern life during the Reconstruction period which Tourgée chronicled. Ben Davis, on the other hand, is separated from his property, his family, and finally his hope by the influence of less visible forces. Both Tourgée and Chesnutt denigrate "Southern justice" in these stories, but for Chesnutt a truthful dramatization of the black man's chances in the white man's courts could not proceed upon the assumption that old villains like the Klan remained the chief obstacles between the New Negro and his rights. In "The Web of Circumstance" Ben Davis is not up against a malign, identifiable foe. He is done in by a concatenation of random circumstances: the jealousy of his employee, the unfaithfulness of his wife, the ambition of a prosecutor, the race prejudice of a judge, the blind despair of his own subsequent criminal status, the degrading companionship of imprisoned, brutalized men, and final-

Cover illustration for The Conjure Woman, *Chesnutt's first book.*

ly, the misinterpretation of an unthinking act, which causes a white man to shoot him down.

The thread of circumstance which entangles Davis and his family in a web of powerlessness, poverty, and eventual destruction is supported in several crucial instances by color prejudice. The theft of the whip which leads to Davis' trial, wrongful conviction, and imprisonment appears to be motivated by intra-racial envy, but the "evidence" which convicts him and which governs the judge's unduly harsh sentence arises out of white fear of black upward mobility. For sounding hardly more radical than Booker T. Washington in his counsel to blacks that they support their own enterprises, accumulate capital, and acquire property, Davis is slandered as an anarchist, a nihilist, a communist, and a revolutionary by the prosecutor in his trial. After white killers and forgers receive mercy at the bench, Davis, whose "crime" is the avowed pursuit of black economic power in a white supremacist system, gets five years for stealing a whip.

Once his protagonist is incarcerated, the oppressive influence of environment becomes Chesnutt's major theme. "After five years of unrequited toil, and unspeakable hardship in convict camps,—five years of slaving by the side

of human brutes, and of nightly herding with them in vermin-haunted huts,—Ben Davis had become like them." When Davis returns home it is not to resume his leadership role among his people, as Nimbus Ware does after working on a prison crew in *Bricks without Straw*. Less hopeful than Tourgée about his hero's recuperative powers, Chesnutt presses the naturalistic implications of Davis' tragedy by surveying the fate of his family, all of them victims of the chain of events which they could control even less than Davis. Davis' ignominious death, the result of a combination of coincidence, misleading appearances, and automatic racial suppositions, brings Chesnutt to the end of this most pessimistic of his color line stories. Told with detached objectivity and an absence of the authorial interruptions which mar the pace of his other socioeconomic tales, **"The Web of Circumstance"** does not pile up the "scientific" detail of a Norris or a Dreiser. But as a record of the way in which economic, social, and psychological conditions can unite to throttle human aspirations and quash human dignity, the story stands firmly in the naturalistic tradition. The logic of events in the story may not seem always compellingly naturalistic, but then the story seems more concerned with using some of the premises of naturalism to make a social point than merely to demonstrate naturalistic conclusions for their own sake.

Like Hamlin Garland, Mary E. Wilkins Freeman, and the early Jack London, all of whom infused regionalism with a new critical realism, Chesnutt took a familiar regional character—the southern Negro—located in a familiar local color setting—the southern small town—and created a socioeconomic case study. He made **"The Web of Circumstance"** illustrate the impossibility of black assimilation into the forefront of southern economic life so long as racism continued to poison the social atmosphere. While reporting how color prejudice permeates the total environment of the black man, ready at the rise of fortuitous circumstance to crush his economic aspirations, Chesnutt implicitly admitted his own reservations to his much-declaimed faith in the middle-class work ethic. Yet he would not give voice to this nay-saying sentiment. On the contrary, as if realizing the despairing drift of his story, Chesnutt dropped the pose of the impartial reporter and practitioner of the new analytic realism at the end of **"The Web of Circumstance."** Instead, the story concludes with the following prayer, delivered by the author as he looks past Davis' tragedy toward a "golden age" of social "peace and righteousness": "Let not the shining thread of hope become so enmeshed in the web of circumstance that we lose sight of it; but give us here and there, and now and then, some little foretaste of this golden age, that we may patiently and hopefully await its coming!"

Through this exhortatory coda, urging patience, not despair in the face of Davis' tragic example, Chesnutt drew back from the dispiriting conclusions which a strictly naturalistic representation of the Afro-American's situation demanded. His idea of the writer's moral responsibility balked at the absolute detachment of the "scientific" realist. His color line fiction would never allow his reader to lose sight of "the shining thread of hope." In **"The Web of Circumstance,"** unfortunately, that thread of hope hangs by a rhetorical tack at the conclusion, detracting from the aesthetic integrity of the story as a work of new realism. This structural weakness seems to have impressed Chesnutt, for he never wrote another naturalistic short story. The aesthetic problem raised in **"The Web of Circumstance"**—reconciling the new realist's method to Chesnutt's moral aims—would return in Chesnutt's last novel. But in the interval, picturing the Afro-American situation as hopelessly determined precluded the possibility of choice and change, at least on the individual level, and such possibilities were what Chesnutt had designed his writing to encourage, not deny.

Because **"The Sheriff's Children"** allows for these possibilities within a southern context as oppressive and racist as that of **"The Web of Circumstance,"** its significance among Chesnutt's pioneering protest-oriented color line stories is central. Among his short fiction, **"The Sheriff's Children"** constitutes Chesnutt's boldest arraignment of the South, both Old and New, for its sins of omission and commission against black people. The bitterness of the mulatto protagonist in this story and his hopeless estimate of his situation in postwar America represents the extremest statement of the southern Afro-American's case that Chesnutt ever mustered in his color line fiction. Nevertheless, the focal question in this, Chesnutt's quintessential "problem" story, is not the abuses suffered by the black man in the New South, which is the theme of protest stories like **"The Bouquet"** or **"The Web of Circumstance."** What makes **"The Sheriff's Children"** both unique among Chesnutt's race problem stories and prophetic of his later problem novels is its redirection of the southern color question, so that the problem of the black man's presence in the South is laid before the southern white man, who, as **"The Sheriff's Children"** argues, must recognize his past complicity and present responsibility if "the problem" is ever to be solved.

"The Sheriff's Children" is set in Chesnutt's typical small town, the provincial hamlet of Troy, North Carolina, not much different from the Patesvilles and Wellingtons which are the loci of Chesnutt's most famous protest short stories and novels. Exemplifying the small-town South in the postbellum era, Troy is bereft of the romantic accoutrements of the Old South and untouched by the instruments of New South enterprise and progressivism. Time seems to stand still in the decaying pastoral world of Troy, as is usual in the typical southern town of Chesnutt's color line fiction. Within such a protective stasis, most of the townspeople exist in a world of their own myths and memories, to be roused only by the intrusion of dynamic forces from the outside. Reminiscent of the unromantic depiction of small-town folk in *Huckleberry Finn,* Chesnutt's gallery of background characters in his story is realistically sketched. The denizens of Troy are summoned before the reader as "bearded men in straw hats and blue homespun shirts, and butternut trousers of great amplitude of material and vagueness of outline; women in homespun frocks and slat-bonnets, with faces as expressionless as the dreary sandhills which gave them a meagre sustenance." These occupants of the southern deserted village set the mood of **"The Sheriff's Children."** The general ambience of lethargy and cultural stagnation which so oppressed Chesnutt while he labored in the Troys and Patesvilles of postwar North Carolina signifies in **"The Sheriff's Children"** the atrophy of the moral fiber of the New South.

In the midst of this "social corpse" of a town, Chesnutt elevates one man of awareness and distinction, Sheriff Campbell, scion of an aristocratic family, a former Con-federate officer, a man of some intellectual sophistication and progressive bent. His job it is to protect "a strange mulatto," suspected of murdering a white man, from a local lynch mob. The sheriff proves equal to the task. "I'm sheriff of this county; I know my duty, and I mean to do it," Campbell proclaims confidently, and through his victory of will over the mob of ex-rebels, the story reaches a preliminary climax. For once, the forces of law and decency prevail over those of racial enmity and violence in the South of Chesnutt's fiction. Under the moderating guardian care of one of the "best people" of the New South, a reconstructed aristocrat, civil rehabilitation under law appears to be progressing. True justice seems available to the Afro-American because the southern aristocracy has extended its sense of noblesse oblige to the freedman's legal rights.

This is all very well as far as it goes, but the point of **"The Sheriff's Children"** is to show that Campbell's duty-consciousness to the Afro-American in his custody has never gone far enough. Chesnutt as narrator hints as much when he states that Campbell "knew what his duty was, as sheriff, perhaps more clearly than he had apprehended it in other passages of his life." Tom, the mulatto, forces the "duty" issue to the forefront of the story when, after revealing to his captor that he is the sheriff's illegitimate slave-born son, he demands, " 'What father's duty have you ever performed for me?' " The answer the sheriff must give is morally damning. Many years before he had sired a son by one of his slaves and then sold them both to avoid the onus of moral and paternal responsibility. But, as it so often turns out in Chesnutt's fiction, the past will not stay past. **"The Sheriff's Children"** is but the first of many Chesnutt "parables" in which the individual and collective moral sins of the southern fathers haunt the New South like a dark incubus, like Tom the outraged and vengeful mulatto. The purpose of **"The Sheriff's Children"**—and of most of Chesnutt's later studies of the New South race problem—is to force the morally culpable white southerner, symbolized at his best in Campbell, to realize that he cannot easily "shake off the consequences of his sin" against the black man. Nor will official recognition of the Afro-American's legal rights "atone for [Campbell's] crime against this son of his—against society—against God." Only a moral enlightenment within the white man will suffice.

Chesnutt outlines the nature and effect of this kind of experience in describing the sheriff's agonized pondering over the appearance of this long-forgotten son of his youth. Foreshadowing the climactic moments of truth experienced by later morally myopic New South aristocrats in Chesnutt's fiction, Campbell's "moral faculty," for so long "warped by his environment," undergoes "a kind of clarifying." "Obscuring passions and prejudices" fade away for a moment and all his actions "stand out, in the clear light of truth, in their correct proportions and relations." At this second climactic moment in the story the sheriff finally sees "that he had owed some duty to this son of his,—that neither law nor custom could destroy a responsibility inherent in the nature of mankind." Through the eyes of a progenitor he remembers that he saw "in this mulatto what he himself might have become had not the safeguards of parental restraint and public opinion been thrown around him." Having recognized his hypocrisy beneath his progressive social exterior, the sheriff begins to feel "a great pity" instead of resentment toward his victimized son's desperate condition. He approaches the future unsure of what to do for his son, but with a new sensitivity toward his filial relationship, social obligation, and moral responsibility to the Afro-American.

Within **"The Sheriff 's Children"** lies the germ of practically all Chesnutt's major protest fiction. The seeds of naturalism, melodrama, and sensationalism which sprout from the muck raked up in his later race problem stories and novels are virtually all present in **"The Sheriff 's Children."** But they still do not supplant the basically moral preoccupation which is the hallmark of Chesnutt's literary approach to "the problem." In such experimental stories as **"The Bouquet"** or **"The Web of Circumstance,"** Chesnutt adapted himself to popular literary modes and employed them with relative success. But most often the themes, structural elements, and plot devices of his problem fiction were patterned on his own literary model, **"The Sheriff 's Children."** The moral consequences of miscegenation, the confrontation of aspiring New Negro and entrenched southern aristocracy, the struggle for social justice in the small-town New South—these are the problems which Chesnutt continued to brood over and to write about with increasing frequency after the republication of **"The Sheriff 's Children"** in *The Wife of His Youth.* The same technical approaches to the exposition of his literary case—the use of revised character types often in atypical roles, the focusing of the action on dramatized discussions of the problem and on melodramatic climaxes of individual moral decision—would reappear after **"The Sheriff 's Children"** in Chesnutt's best-known problem novels. Even the final mood of unrelieved tension in **"The Sheriff 's Children,"** originating from conflicting moral demands and private desires impossible fully to resolve or ignore, would become the concluding note of much of the author's most characteristic problem fiction. Thus for the first time in **"The Sheriff 's Children,"** Chesnutt combined the two predominant purposes of his color line fiction, analysis and exposure of the caste system in the small-town South together with a sympathetic portrayal of the mulatto as the human product and victim of that unjust system.

Between the publication of **"The Sheriff 's Children"** in 1889 and the appearance of his first two novels, *The House behind the Cedars* and *The Marrow of Tradition* at the turn of the century, Chesnutt wrote six stories centered on the moral conflicts and psychological strains peculiar to the experience of those who lived closest to the color line of Chesnutt's day. These stories did not stress the victimization of the mulatto by the white man's caste system, however, as **"The Sheriff 's Children"** had done and as the later novels would do. Instead, during the late 1890s Chesnutt wrote **"The Wife of His Youth," "A Matter of Principle," "Uncle Wellington's Wives," "Her Virginia Mammy," "Cicely's Dream,"** and **"The Sway-Backed House"** (probably in that order) to illustrate the effects of color consciousness in the mind of the mixed-blood, North and South, on his social prospects and moral development. The fact that five of these stories joined **"The Sheriff 's Children"** in Chesnutt's second collection of short stories indicates their significance, both to Chesnutt himself and his publishers, in the author's literary career. If, as Chesnutt wrote in retrospect in 1931, "substantially all" of his writing after *The Conjure Woman* dealt "with

the problems of mixed blood," these color line stories served to introduce Chesnutt's readers to his special province in literature. Through such unprecedented works as **"The Wife of His Youth"** and **"A Matter of Principle"** in particular, Chesnutt demonstrated that he was ready to break the ice in the American fiction of manners. He would be the first to introduce, with a tonal ambiguity reminiscent of a Henry James or an Edith Wharton, the upper crust of Afro-American society to the upper crust of the white American reading public.

In the pioneering color line stories of the late 1880s, **"The Sheriff 's Children"** and **"Rena Walden,"** Chesnutt drew on his personal knowledge of the mulatto predicament in the South, knowledge steeped in private pain and a degree of repressed bitterness. The apprehensive tone and distressing conclusions vis-à-vis the mulatto's fate in both stories reflect the feelings and outlook which had been inculcated in the author by his youthful years in North Carolina. However, by the late 1890s, Chesnutt's period of alienation and frustration in the South lay some fifteen years behind him. Having put down roots in Ohio's more hospitable soil, Chesnutt quite naturally began to tap the social ground of his new existence for a new fiction about the mixed-blood's situation and prospects. The friendlier environment lent itself to a more comic rendering of the mixed-blood's lot. On two occasions in the late 1890s Chesnutt returned to "Patesville" and the theme of **"Rena Walden"**—the marital options of a young, attractive mulatto woman—only to gloss over the question with superficial humor in **"The Sway-Backed House"** and ironic condescension in **"Cicely's Dream."** But in stories like **"Her Virginia Mammy," "A Matter of Principle,"** and **"The Wife of His Youth,"** which treated the social prejudices and color preoccupations of northern mulattoes in "Groveland," Ohio, Chesnutt's art and tone grew more complex as the subjects and issues of these stories engaged more of his own identification with and sympathy for the "paler shades" of the Afro-American "talented tenth."

Although **"The Sway-Backed House"** alludes obliquely to the presence of color prejudice among mulattoes and suggests how misleading such prejudice can be in the choice of a mate, the story, a slight one at best, is really much more a moral tale than a psychological analysis or social study of the mulatto situation. The same can be said for **"Cicely's Dream,"** probably the weakest story included in *The Wife of His Youth.* Like much of Chesnutt's most characteristic color line fiction, **"Cicely's Dream"** raises the touchy issue of interracial marriage in a nonjudgmental manner. But the story's contrived plot and somewhat puzzling tone and *raison d'etre* remind the reader that **"Cicely's Dream"** was conceived as an afterthought, as something needed to fatten a volume for publication. Certainly the unconvincing plot of **"Cicely's Dream"** testifies either to hasty composition or to the author's ill-considered reliance on the stock situations of romantic fiction. In **"Cicely's Dream"** Chesnutt belabors the mistaken-identity convention by depicting Arthur Carey, an amnesiac northern soldier, rescued and brought up as a "bright mulatto" by Cicely, a pretty mixed-blood recently freed by the Union army and in love with Carey. At the resolution of the story, Chesnutt safely skirts the possibility of miscegenation, but only by resorting to a melodramatic climax in which Carey is reunited with his former fiancée, coincidentally the teacher in the black school which Cicely attends. In the end, Cicely takes her place as "the other woman" in this uninspired tale of yet another love which conquers all. The question one is left with is, what does Chesnutt mean by this story of "a dream that went by contraries"?

The essential point of the story seems to be the futility of Cicely's attempt to keep Arthur Carey in a state of ignorance about his identity and his past. **"Cicely's Dream"** displays its author's divided attitude toward the determinative effects of environment. On the one hand, Chesnutt reiterates an environmentalist point made in **"The Sheriff's Children"** when the Yankee schoolmarm realizes that if "Cicely had been reared on Beacon Street, in the shadow of the State House dome, Cicely would have been very much like herself." On the other hand, by showing the eventual triumph of Carey's "imprisoned mind" in its struggle for "liberty" from the "dungeon" of amnesia and Cicely's patronage, Chesnutt celebrated the power of the human will to overcome environmental influences and impediments to the achievement of its rightful destiny. Whether, therefore, Cicely is to be laughed at or pitied in this story becomes, in this light, a problematic matter. Is Chesnutt satirizing Cicely for her white color preferences, symbolized in her dream of marriage to the light-skinned stranger? If so, the punishment of her error seems inordinate. Or is Cicely chastened because of her selfish decision against encouraging her beloved to attend school, learn about his past, and perhaps achieve self-awareness? Clearly, her well-meaning custody of Carey—"She had found him; he was hers"—places Cicely in the ironic position of "owning" a white man and enslaving him mentally, just as her own people had been so enslaved. Does **"Cicely's Dream"** deliberately exploit this curious and contrived turn of events to make a social comment, or is Chesnutt simply playing with a set of ironically reversed racial circumstances before opting for the standard romantic denouement? Because of this ambiguity the moral and social significance of Cicely's choices is blurred, not through conscious artistic design, it appears, but through authorial failure to reconcile the contradictory thematic drift of this oddly noncommittal racial romance.

Much more straightforward in its message and controversial in its social implication is **"Her Virginia Mammy."** Set in Groveland, Ohio, the story contains one of Chesnutt's most explicit pronouncements on the character and social motivations of the northern New Negro, the middle class and often light-complexioned "talented tenth." Solomon Sadler, a character who also appears in **"A Matter of Principle,"** offers Clara Hohlfelder, the heroine of the story, the following introduction to the dancing class she has engaged, a group composed of Afro-American "lawyers and doctors, teachers, telegraph operators, clerks, milliners and dressmakers, students of the local college and scientific school, and . . . even a member of the legislature."

> Of course, Miss Hohlfelder . . . the more advanced of us are not numerous enough to make the fine distinctions that are possible among white people; and of course as we rise in life we can't get entirely away from our brothers and our sisters and our cousins, who don't always keep abreast of us. We do, however, draw certain lines of character and manners and occupation. You see the sort of people we are. Of course we have no prejudice against color, and

> we regard all labor as honorable, provided a man does the best he can. But we must have standards that will give our people something to aspire to.

Speaking through Sadler, Chesnutt presents the social and racial sub-group with which he was identified and for which he often pleaded in his fiction as respectable and properly aspiring, somewhat self-conscious and perhaps invidiously discriminating, but not on the basis of color, only as a result of their adherence to prevailing social conventions. Stories like **"A Matter of Principle"** and **"The Wife of His Youth"** raise questions about the veracity of Sadler's statement that " 'we have no prejudices against color.' " But in **"Her Virginia Mammy,"** Chesnutt discloses no such moral reservations about the ambitiousness of the New Negro. The purpose of this story is, at least in its opening pages, to build a solid case for the mixed-blood as neither a grotesque nor naturally alien social entity, as neither pitiable nor indivisible from the mass of the aspiring American middle class. Clara Hohlfelder, a white woman of representative Middle West background, gets Chesnutt's message. When her lover comments that her light-skinned pupils must " 'find their position painful and more or less pathetic; to be so white and yet to be classed as black,' " she replies, " 'They don't accept our classification blindly. They do not acknowledge any inferiority; they think they are a great deal better than any but the best white people. . . . I hardly think of them as any different from other people. I feel perfectly at home among them.' "

Aside from the common ground of bourgeois ambitions and mores, Clara Hohlfelder's fellow-feeling among the mixed-bloods in her class seems traceable to her family past, which as **"Her Virginia Mammy"** broadly hints, contains a stream of maternal black blood. However, by showing the mixed-blood from the beginning as respectable, as neither socially, economically, nor morally repugnant, Chesnutt disallowed reader response to Clara Hohlfelder in terms of the knee-jerk pity and condescension which were ritualistically invoked in "tragic mulatto" fiction. While much popular literature considered the mulatto simplistically as an inescapably "tainted" and doomed figure—a stereotype which particularly incensed Chesnutt—**"Her Virginia Mammy"** suggests that Clara's mixed background, of which she is unaware, need not point her fate on any such predetermined downward course. " 'We are all worms of the dust,' " Chesnutt reminds his reader through the voice of Clara's suitor. " 'For the past we can claim no credit, for those who made it died with it. Our destiny lies in the future.' " Thus, at the end of the story, Chesnutt comes to a rare conclusion in the race fiction of his day, a conclusion which allows his mixed-blooded heroine to escape the potentially blighting influence of her past by marrying a white man.

Unfortunately, Chesnutt's means of arriving at this conclusion is aesthetically derivative and ethically questionable, despite its bold unconventionality. If the story undermines some of the stereotypes of mulatto character, it does not free itself from some of the plot clichés of sentimental "tragic mulatto" fiction. The plot of **"Her Virginia Mammy"** works up to the familiar moment of ethical choice in Chesnutt's fiction, this time one in which Clara's black mother must choose between admitting her daughter's mixed heritage or suppressing that information so that Clara may marry the white man who woos her. But both the problem and the mother's solution to it owe much to George W. Cable's " 'Tite Poulette" and *Madame Delphine*. The mother's solution, which anticipates the attitude toward miscegenation in *The House behind the Cedars,* is the deliberate concealment of one's racial background justified by the choice of legitimate self-interest over racial proscription. Thus **"Her Virginia Mammy"** became the first of several stories in which Chesnutt at first tacitly and then openly admitted the justifiability of crossing the color line and racial intermixture. However, by placing the choice of passing for white on Clara's mother, not on Clara herself, who at the end of the story continues to think herself white, Chesnutt finessed the sticky problem of overt deception and conscious decision to pass, a problem which became the central moral issue in *The House behind the Cedars*. By barring Clara Hohlfelder from potentially tragic self-knowledge, Chesnutt allowed her a rare reprieve from the racist traditions and codes which so often sentence the unoffending young in Chesnutt's fiction to tragedy. But in **"Her Virginia Mammy,"** even though Clara weds herself to the hopeful future, not the past, the felicity of this interracial couple is predicated on their ignorance—not on the kind of self-knowledge and difficult moral decision which are among the best features of Chesnutt's color line fiction.

"Her Virginia Mammy" can be appreciated as an unusual propaganda piece on behalf of mixed-bloods, especially in its attitude toward miscegenation. But there can be little question that without the publication of **"The Wife of His Youth"** and **"A Matter of Principle,"** the two stories that spotlighted the urban mulatto subculture for the first time in mainstream American fiction, Chesnutt's literary skill could not have caught, even briefly, public attention. In these two companion pieces Chesnutt exploited his experience as a mulatto in the urban North just as, in stories like **"The Sheriff's Children"** and **"Rena Walden,"** he had converted his knowledge of the mixed-blood's situation in the rural South into fiction. More specifically, the transition from **"Rena Walden"** to **"The Wife of His Youth"** showed Chesnutt simply transferring his abiding interest in the manners and social mores of the mulatto subculture from his southern to his northern environs, from Fayetteville (Patesville), North Carolina, to Cleveland (Groveland), Ohio. As a result, the most arresting and distinctive features of both **"The Wife of His Youth"** and **"A Matter of Principle"** became their revelation and delineation of "Blue Vein" society in the progressive midwestern city of Groveland.

The introductory section of **"The Wife of His Youth"** tells who the "Blue Veins" were.

> The original Blue Veins were a little society of colored persons organized in a certain Northern city shortly after the war. Its purpose was to establish and maintain correct social standards among a people whose social condition presented almost unlimited room for improvement. By accident, combined perhaps with some natural affinity, the society consisted of individuals who were, generally speaking, more white than black. Some envious outsider made the suggestion that no one was eligible for membership who was not white enough to show blue veins. The suggestion was readily adopted by those who were not of the favored few, and since that time the society, though possessing a longer and more pretentious name, had been known far

and wide as the "Blue Vein Society," and its members as the "Blue Veins."

That "longer and more pretentious name" alluded to was probably the Cleveland Social Circle, which was, in the words of Chesnutt's daughter, "a very exclusive organization" founded in 1869 by "a group of young colored people who wanted to promote social intercourse and cultural activities among the better-educated people of color." After becoming active members in this *"sine qua non* of social standing" sometime in the late 1880s, the Chesnutts found considerable satisfaction in their association with the club. Its little journal provided an outlet for Charles's early attempts at verse and the humorous sketch. Its membership, composed of self-respecting, middle-class mulattoes like himself, offered Chesnutt the sort of social welcome and cultural interchange that he had moved northward in hopes of finding. Most important to his literary career, however, was Chesnutt's ambivalent assessment of his group's exclusivism and its leadership role as a part of the Afro-American "talented tenth." "As to the usefulness of the society," Chesnutt remarks as narrator of **"The Wife of His Youth"**: "There were those who had been known to assail it violently as a glaring example of the very prejudice from which the colored race had suffered most; and later, when such critics had succeeded in getting on the inside, they had been heard to maintain with zeal and earnestness that the society was a lifeboat, an anchor, a bulwark and a shield,—a pillar of cloud by day and of fire by night, to guide their people through the social wilderness." Between these poles of opinion **"The Wife of His Youth"** and **"A Matter of Principle"** oscillate, suggestive of Chesnutt's own unsettled feelings about the aspiring mulatto's relationship to the rest of the race. Late in his life, Chesnutt confided privately, "I belonged to the 'Blue Vein Society', and the characters in 'The Wife of His Youth' and 'A Matter of Principle' were my personal friends. I shared their sentiments to a degree, though I could see the comic side of them." Able both to identify sympathetically with the Blue Veins' concerns while facetiously scoring their foibles, Chesnutt wrote **"A Matter of Principle"** and **"The Wife of His Youth"** with a balance of objectivity and "kindly irony," as he called it, which had not been equalled in American race fiction up to his day.

The irony of **"A Matter of Principle"** may be "kindly," but it is nonetheless tellingly administered at the expense of Cicero Clayton, a "prominent member" of the Blue Veins and a persistent exponent of "brotherhood" as the solution to the American race problem. The basis for the story's thematic irony lies in the contradiction between Clayton's espousal of the theory of "the brotherhood of man" and his practice of exclusivism and color consciousness in his own social relationships. Clayton's hypocritical example does not constitute, however, an attack by Chesnutt on the Blue Veins themselves. The purpose of **"A Matter of Principle"** seems to be the exposing of absurd excesses to which understandable mulatto social predilections and self-consciousness could be taken.

For instance, Chesnutt pointedly informs the reader at the outset of the story that "the fundamental article of Mr. Clayton's social creed was that he himself was not a negro." Later one sees how Clayton's preoccupation with this matter of his racial definition causes him to treat those he considers "negroes" with the same sort of color bigotry that he deplores among whites. Chesnutt himself was not opposed to the idea of the mulatto's claim to a special racial denotation for himself; he wanted mixed-bloods to be termed "colored people," not "Negroes." But for Clayton this somewhat academic approach to the complexities of racial status in America can not satisfy. The understandable resentment of an inappropriate racial classification has evolved in his mind into a self-deluding obsession. As Chesnutt notes in a narrative aside, Clayton has dwelt so much upon the blanket " 'social ostracism' " which arbitrarily covered all men of color that "he had not been able to escape entirely the tendency" of "even the clearest minds" to become "morbid."

The danger of "morbid" self-absorption after personally felt racial slights was something Chesnutt took seriously and guarded against, mainly by immersing himself in his business career and his literary work. **"A Matter of Principle"** allowed him the opportunity to warn other Afro-Americans like himself about the distorting and self-defeating effects of even understandable resentments like Clayton's. Moreover, Chesnutt refused to be morbid about what could have been a study in morbid racial psychology. He chose to make Clayton a familiarly comic figure, the tolerable, ordinary fellow who through an obsession loses his mental equipoise and falls into foolish traps of his own making. While Clayton's "principles" are all disposed toward brotherhood, his ruling passion impels him in the opposite direction, so that in the name of his principles he does some highly unprincipled things. He tries to marry his daughter to a prominent congressman on the theory that the latter is light-complexioned enough to comply with Clayton's principles. When he discovers that the congressman may be, in fact, "aggressively black," Clayton engineers an elaborate deception to escape contact with the unsavory "nigger," as his wife calls him—she too is a person of "principles." Ultimately Clayton's foolish discriminations backfire and his business assistant, the Mosca to Clayton's Volpone, manipulates Clayton into accepting him as an alternate husband. At the end of the story Clayton appears once again piously mouthing his brotherhood principles, proving he has learned nothing, reaffirming the depth of self-deception into which his obsessive color consciousness has led him.

In his exposure of the racist ramifications of Clayton's principles, Chesnutt produced a tale of considerable satiric vigor. Yet unlike most of his satiric sallies into the jerry-built structure of American racial opinion, the story of Cicero Clayton is not charged with moral outrage or designed to explode the myths of a cruel and unjust white-controlled caste system. Instead of the obtrusive social commentary and explicit asides to the reader, which became more and more prevalent in Chesnutt's later fiction of purpose, one finds in **"A Matter of Principle"** an author still content to observe calmly the comic deflation of racial pretensions which, though wrong-headed, are not pictured as malignant. The choice Clayton makes on the basis of his own colorphobia is appropriately rewarded in failure without the author's having to comment on the wages of Clayton's race opinions. The example is enough. Clayton's case serves as one of Chesnutt's most successful exposures of the ill effects of color consciousness precisely because the lesson is rendered dramatically, without rancor or moralizing and with only slight hints from the au-

thor of his own attitudes toward Clayton and the racial "philosophy" he espouses. For the most part Chesnutt writes in **"A Matter of Principle"** as the unperturbed ironist confident in his ability to discern the presence of false racial superiority behind whatever mask, and amusedly serene in his conviction that such pretense must betray itself. Such a narrative stance became increasingly difficult for Chesnutt to maintain in his later writing as he became more the literary polemicist and less the Horatian ironist. But in such stories as **"A Matter of Principle"** and **"The Wife of His Youth,"** a confidence and optimism preserves the emotional balance and the narrative control.

Perhaps the best rendered and controlled of Chesnutt's color line stories was the first of them to receive substantial notice among the critics, **"The Wife of His Youth."** As an introduction to the little-known mulatto bourgeoisie of the urban North, this story incorporated many of the virtues of local color writing, a genre in which Chesnutt had already proven his facility. Moreover, the story was not weakened artistically by the occasional lapses and excesses which mark many of Chesnutt's problem stories as beginning efforts. The ironic view of color line myths and realities which interlaces much of Chesnutt's short fiction too often binds the narrative package, so that the reader is prevented by the author's arch, disingenuous, or defensive asides from opening and fully appreciating it. But in **"The Wife of His Youth,"** Chesnutt confines himself to presenting the reader with a relatively clearly defined but difficult problem of choice without interrupting the suspense or diluting the climactic action with comments in the reader's direction. The author's attitude toward his protagonist and his problem lurks elusively within the dispassionate, quizzical tone of the narration. At the same time, a genuine sense of pathos envelops **"The Wife of His Youth,"** a pathos arising from the fact that the problem in the story—the conflicting claims of love and loyalty—is not so exclusively Afro-American that white readers could not empathize with the protagonist's situation.

The problem facing the hero, Mr. Ryder, is whether to marry a young, attractive, and cultivated woman of his own class, or to acknowledge the wife of his humble origins, the aging but devoted partner of his legally invalid but morally exacting antebellum marriage. Chesnutt posed the question to his readers as essentially a moral dilemma, not primarily a racial one. This management of the color dimension of the story with neither the exaggerated pathos of **"The Bouquet"** nor the broad ironies of **"A Matter of Principle"** demonstrated Chesnutt's mastery, at least in this instance, of the technical problem of tone which impinges upon much of his color line writing. When Chesnutt could reach a balance of his characteristic moods of pathos and irony, of sympathetic identification with the mixed-blood's social problems and detached appreciation of "the comic side" of them, then he could please the popular magazine market without deserting his own moral standards as a writer.

The thrust of events in **"The Wife of His Youth"** forces Ryder, "the dean of the Blue Veins," into a position in which his personal integrity and the Blue Veins' corporate claim to exemplary status and social respectability are tested. Although Ryder's "principles" are not so patently self-serving as those of his fellow Blue Vein Cicero Clayton, his philosophy of upward mobility, posited as the

Blue Veins' unofficial social creed, does contain some rather questionable points. Ryder professes that he has " 'no race prejudice,' " but his sentiments barely camouflage a feeling of superiority to darker and less economically advantaged Afro-Americans. Ryder predicates the goal of the Blue Veins, " 'absorption by the white race,' " largely on their patience and their remembering that association with blacks would be " 'a backward step.' " He justifies this policy of social climbing and class, if not caste, exclusivism with an appeal to social Darwinism—" 'Self-preservation is the first law of nature' "—a slogan whose moral viability Chesnutt challenges in **"The March of Progress."** The party given by Ryder at the conclusion of **"The Wife of His Youth"** is intended to give him the chance to announce his betrothal to a woman of culture and light color, an alliance which "would help to further the upward process of absorption he had been wishing and waiting for."

When the wife of his slave youth appears, Ryder, like so many of Chesnutt's protagonists, is compelled to reexamine his complacent racial policy on the grounds of morality, not expedience. Unlike **"The Sheriff 's Children"** and Chesnutt's later novels, **"The Wife of His Youth"** does not try to outline the internal argument confronting Ryder, nor does it risk melodrama by trying to dramatize his moment of moral clarification. One only sees the result of Ryder's decision when at the end of the story he calls the wife of his youth before his guests and identifies her as such, thus reaffirming his plantation marriage, his bond to the past. In choosing the wife of his humbler past, Ryder does not renounce nor does Chesnutt judge the idea of mulatto upward mobility and eventual "absorption" in the white mainstream. Ryder's decision simply affirms his often-claimed superiority in something more than his culture, his economic condition, and his skin color. In taking the "backward step" toward the uncouth black woman of his past, he actually takes a step forward morally, proving his worthiness by his honorable behavior, not by the lightness of his color. Like Silas Lapham, Ryder "rises" when he sacrifices a narrow notion of public success for a more private moral responsibility. Like the schoolboard members of **"The March of Progress"** and Wellington in **"Uncle Wellington's Wives,"** Ryder realizes that social progress for the Afro-American is an illusory and self-defeating goal unless it arises from moral advancement past the hindrance of color consciousness.

Thus Ryder, like Uncle Wellington, returns to his former wife, the personification of many virtues associated with the "old-time Negro"—devotion, sacrifice, fortitude, and unaffected dignity—to regain a truer standard of judgment than skin color on which to base relationships and obligations to others. In the marriage of the educated, aspiring, bourgeois Ryder to the uncultured but faithful and enduring woman of the rural South, Chesnutt indirectly stressed the need for an integration of the best characteristics of the "Old" and "New Negro," the rural, conservative freedman of the South and the urban, aggressive middle-class mulatto in the North. In place of the caste consciousness and "self-preservation" instincts which are the chief impediments to social progress in Chesnutt's color line stories, the author seemed to be calling for a bond of unity based on human sympathy between the small Afro-American group which had risen in American society and the large mass which had hardly been touched by the new

opportunities since emancipation. In this light, **"The Wife of His Youth"** could be read as Chesnutt's sermon to the northern "talented tenth" on the meaning of progress and on its moral responsibilities as the putative leaders of the rest of the race. (pp. 95-116)

[The] fundamental social issue in *The Wife of His Youth* and the unifying theme of the stories, whether northern-or southern-based, was the causes and effects of race mixing in America, both past and present. Boldly pictured in **"The Sheriff 's Children"** as the blot on the moral escutcheon of the Old South, sentimentally countenanced in **"Her Virginia Mammy,"** realistically acknowledged in **"Uncle Wellington's Wives,"** melodramatically blocked in **"Cicely's Dream,"** miscegenation took its place as the most dramatic and complex metaphor of interracial relations in America that Chesnutt could adapt to his purposes. The goal of *The Wife of His Youth* was not to remake American opinion about the morality of miscegenation. But racial assimilation, the shaping character influence and a major preoccupation of the mulatto in Chesnutt's view, *was* the necessary thematic ingredient to almost any attempt by Chesnutt to portray seriously his basic subject in *The Wife of His Youth,* life along the color line. Thus in examining the mulatto through the focusing medium of the miscegenation issue, Chesnutt remained faithful to his concept of realistic writing. However, the danger was that his white readers could too easily misread the medium as the message of *The Wife of His Youth.* It is no accident that **"The Wife of His Youth"** was so popular, whereas Chesnutt was never able to get such stories as **"Her Virginia Mammy"** or **"Uncle Wellington's Wives"** published in the magazines. The former story presents the mulatto in his own peculiar environment with a fidelity to local color description and an appeal to sentimental domestic interest that was almost certain to fascinate genteel readers and literary critics alike. But several of the stories in the collection produce the mulatto outside his segregated world—marrying a white woman in **"Uncle Wellington's Wives,"** playing the "other woman" in an interracial love triangle in **"Cicely's Dream,"** slandering white heroes in **"The Sheriff 's Children,"** and quietly passing his children for white in **"Her Virginia Mammy."** Furthermore, these stories seem to side with the mulatto; they seem to accept and even argue for his right to assert himself outside the sphere to which he had been relegated. William Dean Howells might insist that the mulattoes of Chesnutt's color line fiction accept the fact that there is "no hope of entrance into polite white society for them." But a reading of *The Wife of His Youth* might very well leave the impression that the mulatto was not content to accept more racial indignities, that in fact he felt and resented these indignities more acutely than had been pointed out hitherto in fiction. For an American reading audience which had seen its racial problems trivialized in popular fiction to yield the horselaugh, the nostalgic sigh, or the sentimental tear, Chesnutt's moral fervor and his disquieting attention to half-concealed racial tragedies must have made for an unsettling and unwelcome reading experience.

Readers of today have received more appreciatively the color line stories' moral seriousness and their heightened frankness in the characterization of the Afro-American and his social situation. Few will dispute the conclusion that in such stories as **"The Wife of His Youth,"** **"The Sheriff 's Children,"** and **"The Web of Circumstance,"**

Chesnutt widened the scope and added a weightier, more analytic mood to the short story concerned with Afro-American life in his own day. As a literary "pioneer of the color line" Chesnutt made a crucial break with conventional literary sensibility in judging many ignored aspects of Afro-American life worthy of literary treatment and revelatory of profound social and moral truths. In the rural South and the urban North, among the slave-born and the free-born, among the well-to-do and the less fortunate, the light- and dark-skinned, he found the materials for a distinctively Afro-American fiction. He crafted these materials with personal artistic distinction, so that on several occasions they reached an audience far broader than any Afro-American writer before him had been able to touch. The stories of *The Wife of His Youth* showed that audience that in the breadth of his literary interests and his perception of "the great problem" of the color line, Charles W. Chesnutt was a writer of national significance. (pp. 119-20)

> *William L. Andrews, in his* The Literary Career of Charles W. Chesnutt, *Louisiana State University Press, 1980, 292 p.*

Lorne Fienberg (essay date 1987)

[*In the following essay, Fienberg suggests that Chesnutt's depiction of dealings between the white northern landowners and the former slave in the* Conjure Woman *stories parallels the transitional nature of race relations in the postbellum South.*]

Charles W. Chesnutt's collection of tales of the Old South, *The Conjure Woman* (1899), begins appropriately at the "crossroads." In search of a rundown, abandoned plantation he hopes to buy, John, the narrator, finds himself lost and bewildered at the junction of two country roads. A shy negro child directs him down a sandy lane, surrounded by decay, rot, and overgrown briers, to the open space where only the ruined chimneys remain of the once splendid mansion. This is explicitly a setting on the margin, where the distinguishing feature is an "open space," the absence of the symbol of the ante-bellum slave society. John has come to North Carolina from Ohio, ostensibly out of solicitude for his wife's frail health but also to see if he can capitalize on the unsettled economic conditions and cheap labor of the Reconstruction South to make a profit in the cultivation of grapes. But if John determines to profit from a period of flux and uncertainty, he can just as easily become a victim of the marketplace, as in his relationship with Chesnutt's black storyteller, Uncle Julius.

Much more than John the Yankee, Uncle Julius, the freed man, finds himself at a crossroads, at a stage of his life when he is "betwixt and between." More than John, Uncle Julius must confront the significance of absence:

> He had been accustomed, until long after middle life, to look upon himself as the property of another. When this relation was no longer possible, owing to the war, and to his master's death . . . he had been unable to break off entirely the mental habits of a lifetime, but had attached himself to the old plantation, of which he seemed to consider himself an appurtenance.

The condition of "liminality" can, however, be "pure po-

tency," as Victor Turner explains, a state which necessarily confronts Uncle Julius with new relationships, social, economic, and racial, and "the power to transcend the limits of his previous status" [Turner, "Myth and Symbol," in *International Encyclopedia of the Social Sciences,* 1968]. As such, *The Conjure Woman* depicts a kind of rite of passage, made all the more striking because it is undertaken by an old man rather than a young. The narrative act and the economic contract that frames the tales provide Uncle Julius with opportunities to annul or invalidate some of the brutal conditions of his slave past. His plantation tales seem constantly to hold out to his listeners, John and Annie, the invitation to transcend the purely material standard of valuation. In the process, Uncle Julius can test his identity as a freed man, entering into a range of new social and economic relationships. But the framework of the tales also enforces the recognition that, if slavery is dead, Uncle Julius' survival as a black man, and in particular as a black performer, will involve a constant re-enactment of the "economics of slavery." It can further be determined that Uncle Julius' efforts to balance the artistic and economic imperatives of his situation mirror Chesnutt's own dilemma as a black writer seeking a white audience at the turn of the twentieth century.

Houston A. Baker, Jr.'s stimulating study *Blues, Ideology, and Afro-American Literature* (1984) places students of black expressive culture at the critical crossroads where they can view the juncture of creativity and commerce. His exploration of the "blues matrix" of Afro-American literature depicts the commodification of black expressiveness as "a crucial move in a repertoire of black survival motions in the United States. . . . Exchanging words for safety and profit is scarcely an alienating act. It is, instead, a defining act in expressive culture." But the minstrel's mask of accommodation is also the mask of subversion. Although the black artist sings the song his white audience expects, he can maintain his integrity by singing in a way that subtly reshapes the relationship between the listener and the song.

In *The Conjure Woman,* Uncle Julius dons the mask that establishes an ironic barrier between his tales and his listeners' ability to decipher their full intent. But the reader may find that W. E. B. DuBois' metaphor of the veil provides a more dynamic way to understand the tensions of the narrative frame and of the Reconstruction South Chesnutt is depicting. The barrier that separates John and Uncle Julius is real, but it is both opaque, allowing for the passage of light, and permeable, enabling a free play of shifting relationships and values. Moreover, the strategy of a black author creating a white narrator to frame the tales of a black teller establishes the "double consciousness" DuBois was to depict as the peculiar "gift" of life behind the veil. Only by viewing themselves through the eyes of a white "other" can Uncle Julius and Chesnutt achieve a "true" consciousness of their roles as black artists. By recreating through Julius the intimacy of the oral storytelling situation, Chesnutt, the writer, can compensate for the invisibility of his own white audience.

Early on in his literary apprenticeship, Chesnutt was able to identify in a journal entry both the object of his fiction and his audience:

> The object of my writing would be not so much the elevation of the colored people as the elevation of

the white—for I consider the unjust spirit of caste which is so insidious as to pervade a whole nation, and so powerful as to subject a whole race and all connected with it to scorn and social ostracism—I consider this a barrier to the moral progress of the American people; and I would be one of the first to head a determined, organized crusade against it.

In this purpose, Chesnutt shared the difficulties faced by other black writers of the period, such as Booker T. Washington and W. E. B. DuBois, who sought to engage a white audience, move them to a sympathy for black people, bring them to an understanding of their complicity in the oppression of blacks, and still not antagonize them. Moreover, although several black novelists in the nineteenth century, such as William Wells Brown, Martin Delany, and Harriet Wilson, found audiences for their works, Chesnutt's was the critical vulnerability of a black man writing without literary models and a literary tradition. In his early attempts to work within a distinctive tradition of black expressiveness, Chesnutt once proposed to publish "a collection of the ballads and hymns which the colored people sing with such fervor." But commerce impinges upon creativity because a writer must write what a publisher will publish (if he wishes to be successful). And so Chesnutt faced his vulnerability as a black artist by capitalizing on a popular white literary form, writing within it, and simultaneously subverting and reconstructing the form.

The subversive intent of *The Conjure Woman* has been remarked upon by several readers, but several aspects of Chesnutt's masking deserve elaboration. The collection does not even need to be opened before the duplicity begins. The cover of the first edition in 1899 baits a cunning trap for the unsuspecting white reader. Above the title, a reader confronts the jovial countenance of a smiling old darkie framed by two mischievous white rabbits. The comfortable reader may immediately identify old friends in Uncle Remus and Br'er Rabbit and approach Chesnutt's stories as accounts of the gracious life of the Old South cast in the mode of the popular plantation tales of Joel Chandler Harris and Thomas Nelson Page. There is a superficial resemblance between *The Conjure Woman* and the works of Harris and Page and between Chesnutt's narrator, Uncle Julius, and the garrulous uncles who tell nostalgic tales of the ante-bellum South in the works by the white authors. But Chesnutt uses the similarities to subvert both the familiar conventions of those popular works and the unsuspecting white reader's acquiescence in the slave system and the racial inequality those works affirm.

To appreciate Chesnutt's subversive moves in *The Conjure Woman,* it is helpful to consider briefly the narrative strategies and the framing device that unify a work such as Thomas Nelson Page's *In Ole Virginia* (1887). Conventionally in the plantation genre, the tales of the black teller are framed by the introductory remarks of a cultivated, well-educated, white narrator. The white narrator's frame creates the illusion of distance for the comfortable reader, a kind of *cordon sanitaire* which makes it safe to contemplate the words and deeds of social and racial inferiors. The white narrator is perfectly free to interrupt the black teller at any juncture of his tale to pass judgment or to point out to the reader the comical ignorance or superstition of the narration. Even his silences are significant, for they are silences of condescension that leave him firmly in control of the narrative situation. Put another way, the frame is a strategy of containment which returns the freed slave to a state of narrative bondage.

The most immediately striking aspect of Page's *In Ole Virginia* is the barrenness of the frame in all of the elements that will make Chesnutt's collection of stories so rich and complex. There is little pretext or context for tales such as "Marse Chan: A Story of Old Virginia." The genteel white narrator is on a leisurely ride down a sandy backroad in the Virginia of 1872 when he happens upon Uncle Sam, a relic of the plantation past. The narrator has nothing to gain by stopping to listen to a story, no real motive for listening, other than idleness and a superior indulgence of the whims of the teller. He demonstrates his superiority by having time to waste on Uncle Sam and by according only a trivial amusement value to his verbal wanderings. More significant, the teller has no motive for telling his tale. It is simply assumed that old darkies' tongues run on and that they will tell tales of the good old days of slavery at the drop of a hat.

Page's collection of stories introduces three apparently different black tellers, or at least three different names attached to one thinly developed character type. This serves to fragment the narrative authority of the black characters. All three address their white listener as "master," even though they are complete strangers, and even though the year is 1872 and there are no masters anymore. All three express their unfailing allegiance to the system that enslaved them. The crucial pronoun throughout the tale is "we," which refers to Southern blacks and whites alike: "We wuz rich den"; "we wuz de bes' of quality"; "we wuz boys togerr"; "ourn land." The oppositional third-person plural is reserved, predictably, for "dem Yankees."

The key to the value system of the tales is Sam's assertion "Dem was good ole times, marster," and the most pious wish in the collection is expressed by Uncle Billie at the beginning of "Meh Lady: A Story of the War": " 'Hit cyars me back so sometimes, I mos' furgit de ain' nuver been no war nor nuttin'.'" The chief function of the frame in *In Ole Virginia* would seem to be what Page must have felt to be a quite impressive irony, that the freed slaves yearned for the days of their captivity. The best defense of the system is the one that is placed into the mouth of one of the oppressed. As they are presented, these narrators are not victims but contented, childlike innocents, a group for whom mere separation from the land would be catastrophic.

At the end of each of Page's tales, the white narrator offers neither summation, moral, nor judgment. The tales bear their own message of genteel sentimentality about a more noble past that is irrecoverable except in memory. The black narrator tells precisely the tale the white Southern listener would wish to hear. Perhaps it is, finally, the radical lack of racial tension that most clearly signifies the work's value system. At the conclusion of "Marse Chan," the white listener offers no reflection on the story nor praise of its ingenuity; he would never think to accord the tale any intellectual or artistic value. Instead, he unthinkingly gives Uncle Sam two coins. This payment may at least be an acknowledgment of the commodity status of Uncle Sam's creation. More likely, the coins are a condescending form of charity, separate from the possibility that the black man's product has even a monetary or exchange value.

In contrast, both the narrative frame and the tales of Chesnutt's collection are permeated by the signs of the marketplace and by the concern for economic value. In *The Conjure Woman,* the reader is confronted by a setting quite different from the lush, verdant, and fertile plantations of Page's Virginia or Joel Chandler Harris' Georgia. These are the pine woods, sandy barrens, and swamps of Eastern Carolina where, in the height of the slave period, profit had to be wrested from a frequently unyielding soil. The soil produced not plantation aristocrats but a mean and grasping group of capitalists. The determinism of environment has shaped the masters of Uncle Julius' slave memory into crude embodiments of a profit motive the tales are calculated to expose and efface. At the time of his tellings, the plantations have vanished and so have the masters, but the singlemindedness of the profit motive is about to be passed on as a sad legacy to John the Yankee entrepreneur. Nor is Uncle Julius exempt from the same economic values his tales criticize. But the narrative contract that binds the two men is characterized by subtle shifts in the market—the "value" of each tale is contingent upon the time and situation of its telling—and by a dynamic struggle for power. The very opportunities to negotiate a contract, to test one's worth in the marketplace, to question the control of a white man, represent radical new freedoms for the freed slave and form a major part of his rite of passage. Such freedoms are fraught with peril, but Chesnutt is able to endow Uncle Julius with certain advantages.

At one level, of course, the relationship between Uncle Julius and John and Annie is rigidly economic. It need not concern Julius why John and Annie desire to hear his tales; what matters is that his words are commodities he can offer in exchange for employment for himself and his relatives and for the continued security of remaining on the land. But this view of Julius' tales as alienated objects which express nothing of his inner self is ever at odds with the strong ludic spirit of the collection.

Nearly every tale begins with a variant of the child's urgent request "tell us a story!" and thus situates itself in "a playground set off from the verbal marketplace," which Barbara Herrnstein Smith has styled "Storytime" [Smith, *On the Margins of Discourse: The Relation of Literature to Language,* 1978]. Readers of the plantation tales of Joel Chandler Harris will recognize this as the convention that initiates the narrative act in the Uncle Remus stories. There, of course, the listener really is a child, with a child's imagination and expectations of his teller. Chesnutt, however, upsets the economics of "Storytime" by introducing two adults who ask to be treated as if they were children.

The normal conditions of "Storytime" reflect subtle power relationships between children and grownups. In requesting a story, the child surrenders authority to a teller who commands the floor, who knows the tale, and who can manipulate its details and its listeners at will. The teller also has a reasonable certainty that the unsophisticated child will listen without passing judgment, as long as the story is interesting. But the listening child has powers as well: the power to demand a story that is engaging and imaginative; the right to bestow approval or disapproval at the conclusion. Children like stories that contain appropriate morals, but they only occasionally demand that a story be "true."

As listeners, John and Annie certainly are child-like. As strangers to North Carolina, they carry with them the unsophisticated naiveté of children anxious to learn the codes of a new culture. Uncle Julius' first use of the word "goopher" exposes the ignorance of his listeners and places them at a disadvantage (as he knows it will). It is also important that John and Annie find novelty in a convention of black expressiveness (often referred to as "puttin' on ol' massa") that is already outdated. Uncle Julius is trading in bits of local lore and superstition, artistic trinkets which have a value only because his listeners are outsiders. John and Annie also value the tales as a hedge against boredom and the strange (to them) Southern custom of doing things slowly and in due course. When a rain shower postpones an outing (**"The Grey Wolf's Ha'nt"**), or they must wait for the spring to be cleaned before filling their jugs (**"Mars Jeems's Nightmare"**), or if the mare simply refuses to cross a creek (**"Hot-Foot Hannibal"**), Uncle Julius can be counted upon to help them pass the time. In the process, however, they surrender to Uncle Julius a control of the narrative that subverts the conventional use of the framing device. Under the guise of "storytime," Julius can confront the issue of race oppression and the brutality of his slave past with a freedom precluded by normal discourse. Moreover, the black man discovers the unusual psychological power of commanding a captive white audience.

But this freedom constitutes a perilous reversal of roles because the "storytime" situation is a fraudulent one. John and Annie are well-educated and sophisticated adults. Although they maintain silence during Julius' tales, the silences mask a constant process of intellectual and moral judgment (as in the conclusions of each tale). Above all, theirs is the first move in the relationship—"treat us like children"—and that first move carries the implicit power—"we can reverse this anytime we want."

In such a situation, it is virtually impossible for Julius to fix the terms of his powers as a teller. Often, Uncle Julius takes refuge in deliberate stereotypes to veil his condemnation of the slave system. Early in **"Sis' Becky's Pickaninny,"** Julius describes Becky's child: "Dis yer little Mose wuz de cutes', blackes' shiny-eyedes' little nigger you eber laid eyes on." Julius characterizes Mose exactly as he knows the white folks would do it. The deception of the comfortable stereotype is made devastatingly clear in the next instant when the reader discovers that Sis' Becky is to be torn from her child and swapped for a race horse.

But it is the theme of metamorphosis pervading each of the seven tales that serves as the most cunning of Julius' strategies to control his audience and, simultaneously, to understand the mutability of his own position in Southern society. At one level, Julius' educated white listeners can take comfort in the security of the Ovidian literary tradition; by seeing the tales as mere fantasies or flights of imagination, John is able to cling to the delusion that the atrocities described are not "true." But this is cold comfort indeed when Julius is able to capitalize on John's discomfort with a new environment by investing it with magic, witchcraft, and sorcery. As an analogue to a Reconstruction Era of instability and flux, the very landscape becomes bewitched and mutable. For Julius himself, the recognition that things change and that people are transformed reminds him that he has been metamorphosed from a slave to a free man.

Metamorphosis further becomes Julius' primary strategy for veiling his critique of the pattern of human oppression by commodification during the slave era. The transformation of humans into objects through witchcraft parallels the reification of the slaves and their exploitation as goods to be sold and bartered. The linkage between metamorphosis and commodification is established in the first tale, **"The Goophered Grapevine."** It is a tale of characteristic economic exploitation in the antebellum South in which the villain is, ominously, a Yankee entrepreneur who attempts to teach the plantation owner Mars Dugall McAdoo how to wring some extra profit from his grapes. In the process he destroys the vineyard. But Mars Dugall is himself a master exploiter. He is gleeful that the superstitious slaves are willing to "buy" the power of Aunt Peggy's goopher that protects his vines. And although he does not for a second believe in the spell, when the bewitched Henry begins to turn into a grapevine, flourishing and withering in harmony with the rhythm of the planting season, McAdoo realizes that he can sell and repurchase his slave each year at a tremendous profit. As a slave, Henry's work has a minimal economic value, but he is a precious saleable commodity. Mars Dugall

"tuk good keer uv 'im dyoin' er de winter,—give 'im w'iskey ter rub his rheumatiz, en terbacker ter smoke, en all he want ter eat,—'caze a nigger w'at he could make a thousan' dollars a year off 'n did n' grow on eve'y huckleberry bush."

Henry is never seriously developed as a human character. When he falls victim to the Yankee's quack agronomy experiment along with the rest of the vines, his is a "human" loss that the reader can bear partly because of the wild fantasy of the metamorphosis and also in amazement at Mars Dugall's shrewd capitalism.

The issue of economic exploitation is critical to the aftermath of the tale, both because of what John misses and because of what he sees. He misses the lesson about the harmful effects of exploiting the land, and he fails to see the tie between the economic grasping in the tale and his own motives. He does, however, see Uncle Julius' ulterior motive, to prevent the purchase of the plantation and thus maintain his own private reserve of choice scuppernong vines.

Throughout the collection, John clings to a position of economic absolutism, while the reader comes to appreciate the links between metamorphosis, commodification, and the devaluing of human life. The process allows for some of Uncle Julius' finest effects as a teller. That his mat-

Chesnutt in his study at his home in Cleveland.

ter-of-fact, vernacular descriptions of human exploitation have led one contemporary critic to assert that "Julius remembers his years as a slave without apparent rancor," is evidence that the strategies of subversion run deep indeed.

Early in **"Po' Sandy,"** Uncle Julius offers an extended instance of his mastery of understatement:

> "Sandy wuz a monst'us good nigger, en could do so many things erbout a plantation, en alluz 'ten' ter his wuk so well, dat w'en Mars Marrabo's chilluns growed up en married off, dey all un 'em wanted dey daddy fer ter gin 'em Sandy fer a weddin' present. But Mars Marrabo knowed de res' would n' be satisfied ef he gin Sandy ter a'er one un 'em; so w'en dey wuz all done married, he fix it by 'lowin' one er his chilluns ter take Sandy fer a mont' er so, en den ernudder for a mont' er so, en so on dat erway tel dey had all had 'im de same lenk er time; en den dey would all take him roun' ag'in, 'cep'n' oncet in a w'ile w'en Mars Marrabo would len' 'im ter some er his yuther kinfolks 'roun' de country, w'en dey wuz short er han's; tel bimeby it go so Sandy did n' hardly knowed whar he wuz gwine ter stay fum one week's een' ter de yuther."

Julius begins with the white man's stereotyped image of the "good nigger," the one who works hard and tends to his business. He makes it seem the most natural thing on earth that such a human being could be given as a wedding present. For his part, Mars Marrabo is depicted as a kind and humane person, who values harmony in his family above all else, and whose generosity extends to lending his most valued possessions to others in their time of need. Meanwhile, Julius' narrative winds in a single dizzying sentence until a reader ceases to perceive that it is a human being who is passing from hand to hand around in circles until he does not know where his home is.

The reader should not be deceived by Julius' refusal to express his outrage. One time while Sandy is on his slave's progress, Mars Marrabo simply sells his wife to a speculator. That Sandy "soon seed dey want no use cryin' ober spilt merlasses" and that he instantly takes up with a new woman only begins to suggest how thoroughly the profit motive has dehumanized the slave system. Finally, it is Sandy who asks his new woman to use her conjuring powers to turn him into a tree, preferring actually to be an object than to suffer the perpetual uprooting the reified slave system sanctions. The process of commodification is completed when the tree (Sandy) is cut down and sent to the sawmill to be made into timber.

The conclusion of the narrative precipitates a lively discussion between John and Annie about Julius' intent in telling the tale. When Annie exclaims "what a system it was . . . under which such things were possible!" she demonstrates her ability to understand the social meaning latent in the transformation tale. John, meanwhile, finds only an "absurdly impossible yarn." When he learns that Uncle Julius hopes to preserve the remnants of Po' Sandy (an abandoned old schoolhouse) to use as a meeting place for his church, he is content that he has unmasked a trickster and that he need give no further thought to the tale's message. The repetition of the pattern in each of the tales accentuates the slave system's process of commodification. And John's repeated evaluation of Julius' self-interested motives reveals the shifting terms of the black man's struggle for economic survival. No longer an eco-

nomic object, he must become an economic subject, participating in the marketplace with whatever goods he can turn to profit.

Throughout the tales, the value of actual work seems at variance with exchange values. The majority of slaves in the tales, perhaps because they have nothing to gain from their labor, stereotypically do the least possible work they can get away with. Also, they need only look at the fates of the good workers—Henry, Po' Sandy, Sis' Becky—to appreciate the personal economy of laziness. The lazy worker survives from day-to-day fixed in one place; the good worker is sold, lent to relatives, exchanged for horses, or offered in payment of gambling debts. Slavery has taught the black man to hold labor in contempt; barter, exchange, and shrewd dealing are in the ascendant. With this lesson in mind, Uncle Julius tests the value of his tales in the verbal marketplace.

John, his listener or potential buyer, is, with characteristic entrepreneurial efficiency, able to reduce the value of all commodities—grapevines, mules, new suits of clothes, and artistic expression—to a single commercial absolute. With the blithe certitude that all men share his single-minded eye for material gain, he is able to discern for each tale, the financial advantage accruing to Uncle Julius, either from the manner or the matter of his tale. But the tension between commerce and creativity in Julius' expressive acts cannot be thus simply submerged. If one remembers that Thomas Nelson Page's "Marse Chan" concludes with the callous tossing of two coins, one can appreciate the recurring act of judgment and evaluation that follows each of Chesnutt's tales. To some extent, the sentimental and passionately sympathetic Annie provides the counterpoise to John's obtuse commercialism. But she is also capable of a childish petulance when the tale of Primus the mule in **"The Conjurer's Revenge"** fails to please:

> "That story does not appeal to me, Uncle Julius, and is not up to your usual mark. It isn't pathetic, it has no moral that I can discover, and I can't see why you should tell it. In fact, it seems to me like nonsense."

By acknowledging that Uncle Julius' tales characteristically have both an emotional and a moral dimension, Annie has clearly expanded the sphere of the evaluative process beyond commercial bounds. Even though Uncle Julius finally has his way in cajoling John into a lucrative horse trade, he is both "puzzled" and "pained" by the apparent failure of his creativity in other terms.

The most spirited and problematic debate over the "value" of Julius' tales occurs at the conclusion of **"Sis' Becky's Pickaninny."** This is, significantly, the only tale for which John is unable to determine a conspicuous monetary motive. The tale has had a strong emotional impact on Annie, who has been suffering from a mysterious illness, and the "play of her countenance . . . had expressed in turn sympathy, indignation, pity, and at the end lively satisfaction." Unable to discern an economic design he can understand, John attempts to mock the tale by playing the formalist critic. He praises the narrative as "a very ingenious tale," "especially the humming-bird episode" and "the mocking-bird digression." But what John intends ironically, Annie takes in earnest, urging him to see that beyond the stylistic features "the story is true to nature, and might have happened half a hundred times, and no doubt did happen, in those horrid days before the war." Such a timid assertion can scarcely be said to constitute a meaningful reversal of the "good ole times" that Thomas Nelson Page's darkies fondly recall. But by according the tale a *truth* value, she suggests a new status for Uncle Julius as historian and chronicler of his culture. Even more perplexing is the apparent therapeutic value of the tale, which seems to set Annie instantly on the road to recovery from her illness. *The Conjure Woman* makes no attempt to resolve this plurality of responses. Rather, the critical debate on the value, the moral, or even the truth of Uncle Julius' tales alerts the reader (if not John his listener) to the evils of an absolute financial standard of value the Yankee entrepreneur seems to share with his plantation predecessors.

At one level, the breaking down of an absolute standard of commodity or exchange value and a recognition of the "contingencies of value" constitute the lesson both Chesnutt and Uncle Julius offer to their white audiences. But they are just as certainly a part of the process of self-definition for the black artist who must balance the imperatives of commerce and creativity in the "liminal" culture of the Reconstruction South. For Uncle Julius, the telling of tales of his plantation past provides an opportunity for "taking stock of the cultural inventory," which is central to the liminal state. The evaluation of his tales and the intense scrutiny of his motives by a white audience are essential to his understanding of his own liminality.

In this sense, one may see that the barrier Chesnutt sets up between his white narrator and his black teller is both mask and veil. The mask enables him to tell the "truth" and offer a moral lesson in the guise of an innocuous minstrelsy. But the veil permits the dynamic interplay of relationships between black and white that alone can bring the black man to a consciousness of his position in American culture. [In his *The Souls of Black Folk*, 1903], W. E. B. DuBois, confronting similar cultural conditions to Chesnutt's, sums up the veil:

> After the Egyptian and Indian, the Greek and Roman, the Teuton and Mongolian, the Negro is a sort of seventh son, born with a veil, and gifted with second-sight in this American world—a world which yields him no true self-consciousness, but only lets him see himself through the revelation of the other world. It is a peculiar sensation, this double-consciousness, this sense of always looking at oneself through the eyes of others, of measuring one's soul by the tape of a world that looks on in amused contempt and pity. One ever feels his twoness,—an American, a Negro; two souls, two thoughts, two unreconciled strivings; two warring ideals in one dark body, whose dogged strength alone keeps it from being torn asunder.

Like DuBois's description of the veil and the "double-consciousness" of Black America, Houston A. Baker's metaphor of the "crossroads" challenges readers to explore works of black expressiveness always in motion, flux, and process, ever attempting to mediate between the antinomies of commerce and creativity. In *The Conjure Woman,* these tensions remain unresolved. Although the collection reflects Chesnutt's earlier intent to crusade for the moral regeneration of his white audience, Uncle Julius' efficacy as a moral instructor is both transitory and compromised. The tales can criticize the oppression of

Southern slave society, but the old values cannot be effaced. In fact, the obsession with commodity ominously resurfaces in new guises, and Uncle Julius, in offering his tales in the verbal marketplace, commits himself to the same values that once enslaved him. A list can be made of some of the things Julius "gains" in the course of the book, principally financial but also psychological in the power derived from turning the narrative tables. But these gains do not allow him to achieve a new fixed status in Southern society. Although he is no longer a slave, the economics of slavery remain his primary concern in life.

Similar conclusions can be drawn about Chesnutt's own status as a black artist in the literary marketplace. His subversion of the popular plantation tale formula enabled him to achieve his goal of publication for a white audience. But the moderate success of *The Conjure Woman* was never matched by his fictional works that followed, in which Chesnutt approached his racial themes without the elaborate narrative strategies of his first work. Even during the current "reconstruction" of American literature, which has come to value Chesnutt as a writer, the later works are still in search of readers. As black storytellers, both Chesnutt and Uncle Julius encounter the exhileration and the perils of a dynamic relationship with their white audiences. If entrance into the verbal marketplace brings neither teller the success or the fixed status he craves, it establishes the crucial lesson of the crossroads, that survival as an occupation cannot be taken too seriously. (pp. 161-72)

> *Lorne Fienberg, "Charles W. Chesnutt and Uncle Julius: Black Storytellers at the Crossroads," in* Studies in American Fiction, *Vol. 15, No. 2, Autumn, 1987, pp. 161-73.*

FURTHER READING

Ames, Russell. "Social Realism in Charles W. Chesnutt." *Phylon* XIII, No. 2 (1953): 199-206.

    Commends Chesnutt as "the first distinguished American Negro author of short stories and novels" and considers his work "the forerunner of a substantial body of fiction written by Negroes which has maintained an unusual level of social realism."

Andrews, William L. "A Reconsideration of *Charles Waddell Chesnutt: Pioneer of the Color Line*." *CLA Journal* XIX, No. 2 (December 1975): 136-51.

    Assessment of Chesnutt's life and career based on excerpted letters and journal entries reprinted in Helen M. Chesnutt's biography *Charles Waddell Chesnutt: Pioneer of the Color Line.*

————. "William Dean Howells and Charles W. Chesnutt: Criticism and Race Fiction in the Age of Booker T. Washington." *American Literature* XLVIII, No. 3 (November 1976): 327-39.

    Examines the influence of white literary critics such as Howells on Chesnutt's career and on the course of black literature predating the Harlem Renaissance.

Babb, Valerie. "Subversion and Repatriation in *The Conjure*

Woman." *The Southern Quarterly* XXV, No. 2 (Winter 1987): 66-75.

Contrasts Chesnutt's use of black dialect in his conjure stories with that of Joel Chandler Harris in his Uncle Remus stories. Babb notes that dialect is used in the Uncle Remus stories to reinforce a white supremacist order, while in Chesnutt's fiction the world view of the white northern landowner (who narrates the frame stories in standard English) is consistently subverted in the dialect narrative of former slave Julius McAdoo.

Bone, Robert. "Charles Chesnutt." In his *Down Home: A History of Afro-American Short Fiction from Its Beginnings to the End of the Harlem Renaissance,* pp. 74-105. New York: Capricorn Books, 1975.

Assesses Chesnutt's conjure stories as satiric works intended to oppose the pastoralism of Plantation School fiction.

Britt, David D. "Chesnutt's Conjure Tales: What You See Is What You Get." *CLA Journal* XV, No. 3 (March 1972): 269-83.

Maintains that the stories in *The Conjure Woman* are characterized by tension between the different perspectives from which the framing stories and the conjure stories are narrated.

Brown, Sterling. "A Century of Negro Portraiture in American Literature." *The Massachusetts Review* VII, No. 1 (Winter 1966): 73-96.

Briefly mentions Chesnutt's novels of social realism and attributes an underlying social purpose to the *Conjure Woman* stories.

Burnette, R. V. "Charles W. Chesnutt's *The Conjure Woman* Revisited." *CLA Journal* XXX, No. 4 (June 1987): 438-53.

Compares the texts of the conjure stories as they appeared in periodicals with revisions for book publication, focusing on changes in the character of Julius McAdoo.

Callahan, John F. "The Spoken in the Written Word: African-American Tales and the Middle Passage from *Uncle Remus: His Songs and Sayings* to *The Conjure Woman*." In his *In the African-American Grain: The Pursuit of Voice in Twentieth-Century Black Fiction,* pp. 25-61. Urbana: University of Illinois Press, 1978.

Considers the *Conjure Woman* stories as an African-American response to white appropriation of black folklore and the black oral tradition.

Chametzky, Jules. "Regional Literature and Ethnic Realities." *The Antioch Review* XXXI, No. 3 (Fall 1971): 385-96.

Maintains that Chesnutt's presentation in his short fiction of a black ethos, lifestyle, and values, was consistently misunderstood by the white literary establishment and his predominantly white readership, leading Chesnutt to write more overtly didactic novels.

Chesnutt, Helen M. *Charles Waddell Chesnutt: Pioneer of the Color Line.* Chapel Hill: University of North Carolina Press, 1952, 324 p.

Affectionate biography that reprints numerous passages from Chesnutt's journals and from correspondence to and from Chesnutt, quoting extensively from contemporary reviews of Chesnutt's published work.

Condit, John H. "Pulling a Chesnutt Out of the Fire: 'Hot-Foot Hannibal'." *CLA Journal* XXX, No. 4 (June 1987): 428-37.

Offers an analysis of the short story "Hot-Foot Hannibal."

Cooke, Michael G. "Self-Veiling: James Weldon Johnson, Charles Chesnutt, and Nella Larsen." In his *Afro-American Literature in the Twentieth Century: The Achievement of Intimacy,* pp. 43-70. New Haven: Yale University Press, 1984.

Includes discussion of "self-veiling": "pulling down a mask over [the] desire for independence and an unencumbered place" by the black narrator of the conjure tales, who both entertains and manipulates the white characters.

Delmar, P. Jay. "Charles W. Chesnutt's 'The Web of Circumstance' and Richard Wright's 'Long Black Song': The Tragedy of Property." *Studies in Short Fiction* 17, No. 2 (Spring 1980): 178-79.

Examines the presentation in both stories of the view that blacks are denied full participation in the white economic system.

———. "Elements of Tragedy in Charles W. Chesnutt's *The Conjure Woman*." *CLA Journal* XXIII, No. 4 (June 1980): 451-59.

Discusses tragic elements in a number of the *Conjure Woman* stories and analyzes "The Gray Wolf's Ha'nt" as a fully developed tragedy that is dependent on characterization and not the background of slavery to bring about the tragic action.

Elder, Arlene A. "Charles Waddell Chesnutt: Art or Assimilation?" In her *The "Hindered Hand": Cultural Implications of Early African-American Fiction,* pp. 147-215. Westport, Conn.: Greenwood Press, 1978.

Maintains that in *The Wife of His Youth, and Other Stories of the Color Line,* Chesnutt diverged from the folkloric basis of the *Conjure Woman* stories toward social realism in the portrayal of the social, economic, and political situation of black Americans.

Farnsworth, Robert. "Testing the Color Line—Dunbar and Chesnutt." In *The Black American Writer, Volume I: Fiction,* edited by C. W. E. Bigsby, pp. 111-24. Baltimore: Penguin Books, 1969.

Compares Chesnutt's and Paul Laurence Dunbar's approaches to racial issues in their fiction. Farnsworth maintains that Chesnutt more successfully addressed "the immediate problems of southern disfranchisement, Jim Crow legislation, and racial intermarriage."

———. "Charles Chesnutt and the Color Line." In *Minor American Novelists,* edited by Charles Alva Hoyt, pp. 28-40. Carbondale: Southern Illinois University Press, 1970.

Discusses Chesnutt's treatment of race relations in a chronological sketch of his literary career.

Ferguson, SallyAnn H. "Chesnutt's 'The Conjurer's Revenge': The Economics of Direct Confrontation." *Obsidian: Black Literature in Review* 7, Nos. 2 and 3 (Summer and Winter 1981): 37-42.

Examines economic themes in several of the *Conjure Woman* stories, noting that the collection as a whole demonstrates obstacles to black economic success in the antebellum South.

Fraiman, Susan. "Mother-Daughter Romance in Charles W.

Chesnutt's 'Her Virginia Mammy'." *Studies in Short Fiction* 22, No. 4 (Fall 1985): 443-48.

> Suggests that racial themes are secondary to themes of female identity and mother-daughter relationships in the short story "Her Virginia Mammy."

Gayle, Addison, Jr. "The Souls of Black Folk." In his *The Way of the New World: The Black Novel in America,* pp. 25-58. Garden City, N.Y.: Anchor Press, 1975.

> Defines advocacy of the special needs and rights of the mulatto as the major objective of Chesnutt's fiction.

Gibson, Donald B. "Charles W. Chesnutt: The Anatomy of a Dream." In his *The Politics of Literary Expression: A Study of Major Black Writers,* pp. 125-54. Westport, Conn.: Greenwood Press, 1981.

> Traces the development of Chesnutt's complex social and racial attitudes in his published fiction.

Gidden, Nancy Ann. " 'The Gray Wolf 's Ha'nt': Charles W. Chesnutt's Instructive Failure." *CLA Journal* XXVII, No. 4 (June 1984): 406-10.

> Suggests that "The Gray Wolf 's Ha'nt" fails to achieve the "delicate counterpoint of opposing views" usually accomplished in the conjure tales because of the incongruity between the comic function of the tale, which is related by Julius in order to obtain something of value from the northerners, and the tragic nature of the tale itself.

Giles, James R. "Chesnutt's Primus and Annie: A Contemporary View of *The Conjure Woman.*" *The Markham Review* 3, No. 3 (May 1972): 46-9.

> Suggests that Chesnutt introduced racial stereotypes—and in particular, demeaning characterizations of blacks—into the *Conjure Woman* stories to appease a racist white readership.

Gloster, Hugh M. "Negro Fiction to World War I." In his *Negro Voices in American Fiction,* pp. 23-100. Chapel Hill: University of North Carolina Press, 1948.

> Includes discussion of Chesnutt in a survey of black American writers of the period.

Gross, Seymour L. "Stereotype to Archetype: The Negro in American Literary Criticism." In *Images of the Negro in American Literature,* edited by Seymour L. Gross and John Edward Hardy, pp. 1-26. Chicago: University of Chicago Press, 1966.

> Considers Chesnutt's fiction a challenge to and refutation of limited and biased presentations of black characters in turn-of-the-century American literature.

Haslam, Gerald W. " 'The Sheriff 's Children': Chesnutt's Tragic Racial Parable." *Negro American Literature Forum* 2, No. 2 (Summer 1968): 21-6.

> Considers "The Sheriff 's Children" as a parable for ongoing racial crisis in the United States perpetuated by white moral degeneration.

Hemenway, Robert. "Gothic Sociology: Charles Chesnutt and the Gothic Mode." *Studies in the Literary Imagination* VII, No. 1 (Spring 1974): 101-19.

> Considers ways that the *Conjure Woman* stories both conform to and diverge from the Gothic mode.

———. " 'Baxter's Procrustes': Irony and Protest." *CLA Journal* XVIII, No. 2 (December 1974): 172-85.

> Examines the subtle protest elements of Chesnutt's short story "Baxter's Procrustes," which exposes certain ingrained, prejudicial habits of mind to ridicule but removes the action from the arena of racial confrontation by presenting conflict between all white characters.

Hovet, Theodore R. "Chesnutt's 'The Goophered Grapevine' as Social Criticism." *Negro American Literature Forum* 7, No. 3 (Fall 1973): 86-8.

> Suggests that Chesnutt's first published story, "The Goophered Grapevine," is primarily a work of social criticism designed to cast doubts on the soundness of the white northerners' value system and their response to the South.

Ikonné, Chidi. "Symptoms of a Phenomenon: Charles Waddell Chesnutt." In his *From Du Bois to Van Vechten: The Early New Negro Literature, 1903-1926,* pp. 45-8. Westport, Conn.: Greenwood Press, 1981.

> Suggests that Chesnutt's depiction of the lives of black people in the *Conjure Woman* stories "anticipates . . . the realism of the more typical New Negro writers' treatment of such material."

Jackson, Wendell. "Charles W. Chesnutt's Outrageous Fortune." *CLA Journal* XX, No. 2 (December 1976): 195-204.

> Examines the reaction of the white literary establishment to Chesnutt's fiction, noting that the didacticism of his novels lost Chesnutt the small conditional readership gained by the conjure stories.

Keller, Frances Richardson. *An American Crusade: The Life of Charles Waddell Chesnutt.* Provo, Utah: Brigham Young University Press, 1978, 304 p.

> Biography that includes discussion of the contemporary reception of Chesnutt's major fiction as well as commentary on his journalism and other nonfiction writing.

Lewis, Richard O. "Romanticism in the Fiction of Charles W. Chesnutt: The Influence of Dickens, Scott, Tourgée, and Douglass." *CLA Journal* XXVI, No. 2 (December 1982): 145-71.

> Suggests that Chesnutt's fiction is characteristic of Afro-American response to the late nineteenth-century shift from literary romanticism to realism.

Mason, Julian D., Jr. "Charles W. Chesnutt as Southern Author." *The Mississippi Quarterly* XX, No. 2 (Spring 1967): 77-89.

> Considers Chesnutt's place in American literature and within the southern literary tradition.

Morgan, Florence A. H. Review of *The Conjure Woman,* by Charles W. Chesnutt. *The Bookman,* New York IX, No. 3 (May 1899): 372-73.

> Assesses Chesnutt's first volume of short stories as "a collection of quaint tales, with an admirable Southern setting, replete with the humour and tragedy of slavery."

Ogunyemi, Chikwenye Okonjo. "The Africanness of *The Conjure Woman* and *Feather Woman of the Jungle.*" *Ariel* 8, No. 2 (April 1977): 17-30.

> Compares African themes in Chesnutt's *Conjure Woman* stories and Amos Tutuola's novel *Feather Woman of the Jungle.*

Shulman, Robert. "*The Conjure Woman:* Double Consciousness and the Genteel Tradition." In his *Social Criticism & Nineteenth-Century American Fictions,* pp. 50-65. Columbia: University of Missouri Press, 1987.

Examines ways that Chesnutt offered commentary on both the genteel tradition in American letters and the racism of American society by contrasting the sensibilities of the white northerners and the former slave in *The Conjure Woman.*

Sillen, Samuel. "Charles W. Chesnutt: A Pioneer Negro Novelist." *Masses & Mainstream* 6, No. 2 (February 1953): 8-14.

Review of *Charles Waddell Chesnutt: Pioneer of the Color Line,* by Helen M. Chesnutt that condemns the neglect of black writers by the white literary establishment.

Smith, Robert A. "A Note on the Folktales of Charles W. Chesnutt." *CLA Journal* V, No. 3 (March 1962): 229-32.

Considers traditional folkloric elements in Chesnutt's conjure stories.

Taxel, Joel. "Charles Waddell Chesnutt's Sambo: Myth and Reality." *Negro American Literature Forum* 9, No. 4 (Winter 1975): 105-08.

Examines Chesnutt's depiction of manipulation and trickery on the part of characters who outwardly conform to the archetype of the happy, docile slave.

Terry, Eugene. "The Shadow of Slavery in Charles Chesnutt's *The Conjure Woman.*" *Ethnic Groups* 4 (May 1982): 103-25.

Maintains that Chesnutt's purpose in writing the *Conjure Woman* stories was to discredit the benign presentation of slavery by white Plantation School authors.

Walcott, Ronald. "Chesnutt's 'The Sheriff's Children' as Parable." *Negro American Literature Forum* 7, No. 3 (Fall 1973): 83-5.

Considers this story of a white sheriff with a legitimate white and an illegitimate mulatto child emblematic of southern unwillingness to acknowledge responsibility for the plight of free blacks.

Whitt, Lena M. "Chesnutt's Chinquapin County." *The Southern Literary Journal* XIII, No. 2 (Spring 1981): 41-58.

Identifies Chesnutt's fictional Chinquapin County with North Carolina's Cumberland County and considers the area a microcosm of the moral and sociological problems facing the postbellum South.

Winkleman, Donald M. "Three American Authors as Semi-Folk Artists." *Journal of American Folklore* 78, No. 308 (April-June 1965): 130-35.

Includes discussion of Chesnutt's use of folktale techniques in the conjure stories.

Wintz, Cary D. "Race and Realism in the Fiction of Charles W. Chesnutt." *Ohio History* 81, No. 2 (Spring 1972): 122-30.

Explores the dualism between Chesnutt's desire to accurately present black experience in his fiction and his desire to win acceptance by the white literary establishment.

Julio Cortázar

1914-1984

(Also wrote under the pseudonym Julio Denís.) Argentine novelist, short story writer, poet, essayist, critic, translator, and dramatist.

Cortázar is one of the seminal figures of the "Boom," a surge of excellence and innovation in Latin American letters during the 1950s and 1960s. His novel *Rayuela* (*Hopscotch*) has been called Latin America's first great novel, and his myriad writings on art and the role of the artist have revitalized the essay; however, Cortázar has received his most prominent recognition as a short story writer. Influenced by Argentine author Jorge Luis Borges, Cortázar is considered to have enlarged literary tradition with a consistent inventiveness of style, language, and theme. Like Borges, Gabriel García Márquez, and other contemporary Latin American writers, Cortázar combined fantastic and often bizarre plots with commonplace events and characters. Much of Cortázar's fiction is a reaction to the Western tradition of rationalism and is an attempt to create new ways for literature to represent reality. To this end, he experimented with narrative identity, language, time, space, and form in such representative short fiction volumes as *Bestiario, A Change of Light, and Other Stories,* and *Historias de cronopios y de famas* (*Cronopios and Famas*).

Cortázar was born in Brussels, Belgium, in 1914, and in 1918 he moved with his parents to their native Argentina, where they settled in a suburb of Buenos Aires. An excellent student and reader, Cortázar began writing at a young age and completed a novel by the time he was nine years old. After earning a teaching degree, Cortázar taught high school from 1937 to 1944. During this time Cortázar began writing short stories, and, in 1938, under the pseudonym Julio Denís, he published *Presencia,* a book of sonnets evidencing the influence of French symbolist poet Stéphane Mallarmé.

In 1944 and 1945 Cortázar taught French literature at the University of Cuyo in Mendoza, Argentina; however, by 1946 he had resigned from his post after participating in demonstrations against Argentine president Juan Péron, and moved to Buenos Aires, where he began working for a publishing company. Also in 1946 Cortázar published his first short story, "Casa tomada" ("House Taken Over"), in *Los anales de Buenos Aires,* an influential literary magazine edited by Jorge Luis Borges. Between 1946 and 1948 Cortázar studied law and languages to earn a degree as a public translator. The arduous task of completing this three-year course in less than a year produced temporary neuroses that Cortázar relieved through writing fiction. One of Cortázar's phobias, a fear of eating insects hidden in his food, inspired the short story "Circe," a tale about a woman who feeds her suitors cockroaches in the guise of candies. Cortázar's characteristic mythological allusions, attacks on conventionality (which he later playfully developed in books of miscellany), and use of the labyrinth (a symbol of complexities and shifts in reality) first appeared in 1949 with the publication of his prose poem

Los reyes, a retelling of the classic myth of the Minotaur. In 1951 Cortázar published *Bestiario,* his first collection of short stories, and also received a scholarship to study in Paris, France, where he became a translator for UNESCO. In 1953, collaborating with his wife, Cortázar completed translations into Spanish of Edgar Allan Poe's prose works. Later that year he adopted France as his permanent residence. Throughout his life Cortázar traveled extensively—primarily between Argentina, Cuba, Nicaragua, and the United States—often lecturing for social reform in Latin America. Cortázar continued to publish writings in several genres and to work as a free-lance translator from the 1950s until his death in 1984.

Many of Cortázar's short stories are representations of a surreal, metaphysical, horror-filled world that prevailed upon his imagination. In these works, he often expressed a conflict between unreal and real events by allowing the fantastic to take control of the mundane in the lives of his characters. Significant in this transformation from the ordinary to the bizarre is the compliant acceptance of extraordinary events by Cortázar's characters. In "Carta a una señorita en Paris" ("Letter to a Young Lady in Paris"), for example, the narrator-protagonist, a man staying in the apartment of a friend who is out of town, begins inexplicably to vomit rabbits. He does not question this curious experience but is eventually driven to suicide when the rabbits overrun the apartment. Cortázar infused ambiguity into many of his tales. "La noche boca arriba" ("The Night Face Up") weaves the circumstances of a man injured in a motorcycle accident with his dreams of being chased, captured, and prepared for sacrifice by ancient Aztec Indians. The narrative alternates between what appears to be the terrifying dreamworld of the Aztecs and the man's experiences in the hospital, overlapping events in each, so that distinctions between dream and reality are obscured. In the end the protagonist cannot awaken from the Aztec world, yet when he is about to be sacrificed, he concludes that the Aztec world is real, while the modern world had been a dream.

Cortázar's fascination with the double, a character's other, or alter ego, and his related concept of "figures," or human constellations, which Evelyn Picon Garfield characterized as "magnetic fields . . . that allow people to communicate with each other across time and space," is evidenced in numerous short stories. In "Lejana" ("The Distances"), Alina Reyes, a wealthy South American woman, becomes obsessed with visions of a beggar woman living in Budapest whom Alina believes is her true self. Alina travels to Budapest, believing she will relieve the woman's suffering and her own by assuming her real identity as a beggar. After the women embrace on a bridge, Alina is left standing in the bitter cold as the beggar woman walks away in Alina's body. Another story, "Axolotl," depicts a character's transfiguration, displaying as well Cortázar's predilection toward employing unusual narrative perspectives. Through shifts in point of view and verb tense, the story's narrator-protagonist, a solitary man living in Paris, relates how he became obsessed with watching axolotls, a type of salamander indigenous to Mexico and the southwestern United States. As the narrator grows increasingly transfixed by the axolotls, he begins to sense an inextricable link with the creatures. Eventually he understands that he is becoming an axolotl himself and finally is physically transformed into one, looking out at the world from inside the aquarium tank, watching the man whom he had been, musing, "And in this final solitude to which he no longer comes, I console myself by thinking that perhaps he is going to write a story about us, that believing he's making up a story, he's going to write all this about axolotls."

Cortázar often employed motifs in his fiction based on games, children's play, and music as representations of humanity's search for an existence that surpasses limits imposed by logic and reason. With "El perseguidor" ("The Pursuer"), which Cortázar called a "miniature" of his highly acclaimed experimental novel *Hopscotch*, he not only incorporated the syncopated rhythms of jazz music to illustrate this search, but began to explore existential questions and focus on the inner lives of characters. Modeled upon jazz saxophonist Charlie Parker, the eponymous pursuer of the story is protagonist Johnny Carter, a character whose inability to articulate what he seeks is a source of anguish, while his talent for intuitive expression through music allows him to approach reality beyond ordinary existence that has been closed to most of humanity. In contrast, the narrator, a jazz critic and biographer, is entrenched in the analytical delineation of Johnny as he writes his biography—a book that is incapable of authenti-

cally portraying the artist's life. Cortázar commented in 1966: "Fantasy for its own sake had stopped interesting me. . . . I was a bit sick and tired of seeing how well my stories turned out. In 'The Pursuer' I wanted to stop inventing and stand on my own ground, to look at myself a bit. And looking at myself meant looking at my neighbor, at man."

Cortázar addressed complexities in the relationship between art and life in several works, including the metafictional piece "Las babas del diablo" ("Blow-Up"). From the first sentence the narrator, Roberto Michel, a translator and amateur photographer, struggles with the inadequacy of words to recount his story, stating that "it'll never be known how this has to be told, in the first person or in the second, using the third person plural or continually inventing modes that will serve for nothing." The action of the tale begins when Michel observes a woman whom he believes is attempting to seduce an adolescent boy and is intrigued by what he imagines might transpire between the two. Although he notices a parked car that he finds aesthetically displeasing in the background of the scene, he snaps a photograph, hoping to capture the essence of the encounter.

Michel develops and enlarges the photo and tacks it to a wall in his apartment, looking at it for inspiration when he translates. Several days later, however, he discerns that the photo has assumed life-like movement. Michel sees a man emerge from the parked car, which he had "carefully eliminated from the photo," and at this moment realizes the true nature of the episode: the woman was luring the boy for the man's purposes. In addition to the troubling implications of the subject matter, this story's convoluted narrative structure suggests, according to Terry J. Peavler, that " 'Blow-Up' is more a story about literature, a discourse about discourse, than a story about a photographer or his photograph."

Many of Cortázar's short stories reflect his concern for political and human rights while upholding his belief in open-ended art, in which, he states, it is the writer's responsibility "never to recede, for whatever reasons, along the path of creativity." Cortázar evidenced his political convictions in several works, including his early short story "Reunión" ("Meeting"), a fictional account of the Cuban revolution as told by Latin American revolutionary leader Che Guevara, and "Segund vez" ("Second Time Around"), in which Cortázar utilized the repressive political situation in Argentina during the 1970s, when citizens often disappeared under false arrests, as a backdrop for his delineation of a woman's experiences surrounding an official summons. According to Maurice Hemingway and Frank McQuade, the narrative voice, which changes from the first-person perspective of a bureaucrat to the third-person limited perspective of the woman, and then back to the bureaucrat's point of view in the last sentence, emphasizes the mysterious and omniscient nature of the summons, creating an Orwellian sense of institutionalized paranoia that extends the work beyond the Argentine government to encompass other Latin American totalitarian regimes.

In Cortázar's short fiction elements of the fantastic and commonplace; past, present, and future; reality and dream; the self and the other blend to suggest multiple layers of meaning that invite varied interpretations. Critics have suggested that Cortázar strove for this ambiguity as a means to express what may exist beyond humanity's rational perceptions. His stories are often characterized by humor despite their generally serious themes, and they are noted for Cortázar's technical innovations in point of view, language, and form. Jaime Alazraki commented: "Cortázar's stories are built with the rigorous precision and, at the same time, subtle naturalness of a cobweb. The text flows with the same perfection one finds in those fragile fabrics beautifully spun between two wires of a fence. . . . But there is nothing fragile in the texture of any of his stories." Along with his masterwork *Hopscotch*, Cortázar's short stories have established him as a leading voice in modern literature.

(For further information on Cortázar's life and career, see *Contemporary Literary Criticism*, Vols. 2, 3, 5, 10, 13, 15, 33, 34; *Contemporary Authors*, Vols. 21-24, rev. ed.; and *Contemporary Authors New Revision Series*, Vol. 12.)

PRINCIPAL WORKS

SHORT FICTION

Bestiario 1951
Final del juego 1956
Las armas secretas 1959
Historias de cronopios y de famas (short stories and other writings) 1962
 [*Cronopios and Famas*, 1969]
Cuentos 1964
Todos los fuegos el fuego 1966
 [*All Fires the Fire, and Other Stories*, 1973]
El perseguidor y otros cuentos 1967
End of the Game, and Other Stories 1967; also published as *Blow-Up, and Other Stories*, 1968
La vuelta al día en ochenta mundos. 2 vols. (short stories and other writings) 1967
 [*Around the Day in Eighty Worlds*, 1986]
Ceremonias 1968; contains *Final del juego* and *Las armas secretas*
Ultimo round (short stories and other writings) 1969
Relatos 1970; contains *Bestiario, Final del juego, Las armas secretas,* and *Todos los fuegos el fuego*
La isla a mediodía y otros relatos 1971
La casilla de los Morelli (short stories and other writings) 1973
Reunión 1973; contains *Bestiario, Final del juego, Las armas secretas, Todos los fuegos el fuego,* and *Historias de cronopios y de famas*
Octaedro 1974
Antología 1975
Vampiros multinacionales: una utopía realizable 1975
Los relatos. 4 vols. 1976-85
Alguien que anda por ahí y otros relatos 1977
Un tal Lucas 1979
 [*A Certain Lucas*, 1984]
A Change of Light, and Other Stories 1980; contains *Octaedro* and *Alguien que anda por ahí y otros relatos*
Queremos tanto a Glenda y otros realtos 1980
 [*We Love Glenda So Much, and Other Tales*, 1983]
Deshoras 1982
Nicaragua tan violentamente dulce (prose) 1983
 [*Nicaraguan Sketches*, 1989]

OTHER MAJOR WORKS

Presencia [as Julio Denís] (poetry) 1938
Los reyes (poetry) 1949
Los premios (novel) 1960
 [*The Winners*, 1965]
Rayuela (novel) 1963
 [*Hopscotch*, 1966]
62: Modelo para armar (novel) 1968
 [*62: A Model Kit*, 1972]
Pameos y meopas (poetry) 1971
Libro de Manuel (novel) 1973
 [*A Manual for Manuel*, 1978]
Salvo el crepúsculo (poetry) 1984

Luis Harss and Barbara Dohmann (essay date 1966)

[*Harss is a Chilean novelist, journalist, and lecturer whose studies in Latin American literature include* Into the Mainstream: Conversations with Latin American Writers *(1967), on which he collaborated with Barbara Dohmann. In the following excerpt, from an essay that was included in* Into the Mainstream, *Harss and Dohmann incorporate Cortázar's own comments into a discussion of fantastic and humorous elements in Cortázar's short fiction as well as his thematic concerns.*]

The years have shown, in our part of the world, as elsewhere, that those who live at odds with their land are often the ones that understand it best. Perhaps only they are in a position to hit the nail hard enough to drive it home. . . . World War II was something of a dividing line for us. It brought a drastic century to our doorstep at a time when we had already begun to part company with ourselves. This was particularly true of Argentina, a land of fallen idols. There the morning after dawned early. And with it were born the kiss of death and the slap in the face. (p. 105)

Cortázar is the evidence we needed that there is a powerful mutant strain in [Latin American] literature. It leads toward a mystic border line. "Where frontiers end, roads vanish," says Octavio Paz. And so it is with Cortázar. He works toward the outer limits of experience, thumbing his nose at the world. He is a brilliant wit, and a tireless innovator, who has given us a lot to ponder. The tendency in certain circles has been to accuse him of a lack of seriousness, probably with some justification, at least to the extent that he insists on pulling chairs out from under us all. Certainly there is an element of the practical joker in him. But it lives in close quarters with the visionary. How Cortázar became what he is, is a disconcertingly difficult question to answer. In his early days he was a sort of Borgesian aesthete, a qualifier to which he is not entirely invulnerable even today. But there was a change in midroad. For a while he leaned on the traditional props of the psychological novel. But that was a transitory stage. Whatever genre he touched, he seemed immune—or soon inured—to its conventions. He is a man of strong antibodies. Nowadays he has no use for what he considers easy effects: pedestrian dramatic situations, platitude or pathos. He travels along his own circuits. His importance is hard to assess. He wonders himself what it all amounts to. "I don't flatter myself that I'll be able to achieve anything transcendental," he says skeptically. But there is little doubt that he already has. (p. 107)

Cortázar has an intriguing background that makes him heir to an old dilemma. He was born in 1914, of Argentine parents—in Brussels. His ancestors were Basques, Frenchmen and Germans. He has spent a lot of his time welding opposites. From the age of four he was brought up in the outskirts of Buenos Aires, a city whose instincts and attitudes run deep in his work. No one has stronger emotional ties with his land than Cortázar. But intellectually he has lived beyond it, in a broader context. There has been agony in his constant inward migration between physical roots and spiritual affinities. The displaced persons in his books testify to the length and depth of a conflict that has never been satisfactorily settled. Yet in some way it has been put to fruitful use. (p. 108)

[Cortázar] was first heard from around 1941—the exact date is vague in his mind—with a small book of sonnets, published under the pseudonym of Julio Dénis, that he no longer cares to talk about. The sonnets were "very Mallarméan," he says succinctly. He had lofty aims at the time. There was a long silence, and then in 1949 he published *Los Reyes* (*The Kings*), a series of dialogues on the subject of the Cretan Minotaur, rather stately in style, abstract, intellectual, overrefined, reflecting his bookish addiction to classical mythology. There was nothing of particular note in those early works. But already in 1951, only two years after *Los Reyes,* he made what seems a complete about-face and came out with a stunning little volume called *Bestiario.* It was lean and luminous, and struck a keynote: the fantastic, suddenly revealing a master sorcerer. Cortázar had read his Poe, Hawthorne and Ambrose Bierce, as well as his Saki, Jacobs, H. G. Wells, Kipling, Lord Dunsany, E. M. Forster, and, closer to home, Lugones, the old master Quiroga, and, of course, Borges. He was a skillful storyteller—too skillful, perhaps. Five years later, in *Final del Juego* (*End of the Game,* 1956), he was still hard at work conjuring up his spells, a bit too scrupulously. Repeated exercises in an unchanging vein had given him an unfair advantage over himself, he says; he had begun to doubt his progress. There were already clear signs of a transition into new territory in his next collection of stories, *Las Armas Secretas* (*Secret Weapons,* 1959). Among them was **"El Perseguidor"** (**"The Pursuer"**), which marked a break in his work. It issued in what we might call his Arltian phase. Without sacrificing the imaginary, he had begun to draw live characters taken from real life, with their feet on the ground. His style had also become more muscular. He was beginning to shed aestheticism. Perhaps until then playing with literature had been his way of creating a fantasy world around himself to shield him against certain unpleasant realities. But now, more at home with himself, he took a closer look at the world. What he saw he described in 1960 in his first novel, *Los Premios* (*The Winners,* 1965). It was the somewhat defective and shapeless book of an author fumbling toward a subject and new forms to go with it. It was followed, in 1962, by *Historias de Cronopios y de Famas,* an assortment of loose notes, sketches, brief insights into hidden dimensions that demonstrate the author's fondness for fruitful improvisation. The Cronopios and Famas, playful poltergeists with coined names and strange habits, were blobs in a bubble world in some ways not unlike the real one. With this book Cortázar seemed to pause and

take a deep breath. What followed was a hurricane. It was called *Rayuela* (1963)—an "anti-novel" that shows every sign of having represented a major breakthrough for him. *Rayuela* is a therapeutic book, intended as a complete course of treatment against the empty dialectics of Western civilization and the rationalist tradition. It is an ambitious work, at once a philosophical manifesto, a revolt against literary language and the account of an extraordinary spiritual pilgrimage. (pp. 108-10)

"The attempt to find a center was, and still is, a personal problem of mine," he says. All his life he has been transferring it to his work without finding a concrete solution for it. Even the inexhaustible *Rayuela,* which provides a sort of unending catalog of available alternatives, in the end can offer only partial subterfuges. "*Rayuela,*" says Cortázar, "shows to what extent the attempt is doomed to failure, in the sense that it isn't that easy for one to unburden oneself of the whole Judaeo-Christian tradition one has inherited and been shaped by."

Yet the search for alternatives started early in Cortázar. Perhaps the search, in ersatz form, is implicit in all fantastic literature. This would be the Quirogan, the Borgesian, lesson. In this sense, Cortázar's fantastic stories, with their mysteriously disjunctive patterns, seem premonitory. There language, full of whispered hints, performs an almost ritual function. The stories are like incantations, psychic equivalents of magic formulas. One might compare them to charms that open doors, allowing the author a way out of himself. There is also what we might call a more practical side to them. Cortázar describes them as a sort of occupational therapy. "They're charms, they're a way out," he says, "but above all, they're exorcisms. Many of these stories, I can even single out a concrete example, are purgative, a sort of self-analysis." The case in point is **"Circe,"** where a woman makes repulsive sweets with cockroaches inside, which she offers to her boyfriends.

> When I wrote that story I was going through a time of exhaustion in Buenos Aires because I'd been studying to become a public translator and was taking a whole battery of exams, one on top of another. I wanted to have a profession, to be financially independent, already with the idea of eventually moving to France. So I packed all the work for my degree into eight or nine months. It was backbreaking. I was tired and I started to develop neurotic symptoms; nothing serious—I didn't have to see a doctor. But it was very unpleasant because I acquired a number of phobias which became more preposterous all the time. I noticed that when I ate I was constantly afraid of finding flies or bugs in my food, food I had prepared at home and which I trusted completely. But time and again I'd catch myself scratching with my fork before each mouthful. That gave me the idea for the story—the idea of something loathsome and inedible. And when I wrote the story, it really acted as an exorcism, because after I'd written it I was immediately cured. . . . I suppose other stories are in the same vein.

The stories leave a varied impression on the reader. Some are subtle word games—crossword puzzles. Others, like **"Omnibus"** (**"Busride"**), one of the most speculative—and therefore most suggestive, which is why it has been interpreted as everything from a parable on death to a political allegory—seem to go crashing through barriers into unknown realms, to dip into orders of experience that are normally closed to us.

"The truth," says Cortázar, "is that though these stories, seen, let's say, from the angle of *Rayuela,* may seem like games, while I was writing them and when I wrote them I didn't think of them that way at all. They were glimpses, dimensions, or hints of possibilities that terrified or fascinated me and that I had to exhaust by working them off in the story."

Some were written at a sitting, spun out with almost supernatural force and intensity, says Cortázar—and the reader senses this. They were produced in a state of grace, which the author invites us to share with him. He is "on to" something, and points the way. Dramatic congruity or psychological verisimilitude are not important to him. The experience imposes its own terms. What counts is that we be able to relive it—not as a vicarious experience, comfortably identifying with characters and situations, but in the flesh, as it were. We are in a closed circuit, armed with verbal formulas that, when invoked, will unleash the same sequence of events inside us as they did inside the author.

The source of a story's power, says Cortázar, is inner tension. The higher the tension, the better it transmits the author's pulsations.

> What the exact method for transmitting these pulsations is, I can't say, but in any case, it depends on the ruthless execution of the story. The tense wiring permits a maximum freedom of action. In other words, I've watched myself writing at top speed—all in one breath, literally beside myself, without having to correct much afterwards; but that speed had nothing to do with the preparation of the story. I'd been concentrating my forces, bending backward to tighten my bow, and that increased my impetus when I sat down to write the story. The tension isn't in the execution of the story, though of course it remains trapped in the tissue from where it is later transmitted to the reader. The tension as such precedes the story. Sometimes it takes six months of tension to produce a long story that comes out in a single night. I think that shows in some of my stories. The best are packed full of a sort of explosive charge.

"Structures," he calls them. Words are mere touchstones in these stories; one finds oneself reading between the lines. The language is disarmingly simple and straightforward. There are no verbal flourishes, no tortured effects. The tone is conversational. The surface is crystal clear. But intangible forces are building up underneath. The clarity is made of shadowy undercurrents that gradually fuse in a climax with cathartic aftereffects. The reader, swept along, spills over the brim, delivered of himself.

An experience of this sort, no longer projected through fantasy but seen in the context of real life, becomes the actual theme and subject of a story somewhat later in the highly speculative **"El Perseguidor,"** which in a sense makes Cortázar's previous work obsolete by rendering its preoccupations explicit, and perfectly down to earth. Here we have a Cortázar who may still be on the side of the angels, but with a foot on the ground. The setting of the story—made flagrant throughout—is Paris. When Cortázar wrote **"El Perseguidor,"** he had long liquidated his af-

fairs in Buenos Aires. He seems to be making this point in every line. But Cortázar points are turnstiles and tend to roll over on themselves and come up on the opposite side. And so to our surprise, in **"El Perseguidor"** we find ourselves in the numinous areas of Arltian low-life. We are introduced to an underworld character, Johnny Carter—alias Charlie Parker—a negro saxophonist, a man gifted by nature with metaphysical senses but of few intellectual resources, for whom music is not only a form of expression—a release into being—but an instrument in his search for an exit into godliness. Johnny, who walks the cemeteries of the earth, trying to revive the dead, hears echoes of divine voices in broken urns. He is a kind of blind seer—a star-chaser, a man with a thirst for the absolute. He feels his true self mortgaged in space and time, a hostage waiting to be ransomed from the bondage of individuality. His talent is his strength, but also his undoing. Because basically he is a poor lost soul, ignorant of his powers, who lives in anguish and torment without ever knowing why. He has intimations of eternity, but cannot shape or grasp them. He thrashes about hopelessly in the dark. The road leads downhill, through drug-addiction into final madness. (pp. 117-20)

Cortázar says of **"El Perseguidor"**:

> In everything I'd written until that moment, I'd been satisfied with inventing pure fantasies. In *Bestiario,* in *Final del Juego,* the mere fact of imagining a fantastic situation that resolved itself in a way that was aesthetically satisfactory to me—I've always been demanding in that area—was enough for me. *Bestiario* is the book of a man whose inquiries don't carry beyond literature. The stories of *Final del Juego* belong in the same cycle. But when I wrote **"El Perseguidor,"** I had reached a point where I felt I had to deal with something that was a lot closer to me. I wasn't sure of myself any more in that story. I took up an existential problem, a human problem which was later amplified in *Los Premios,* and above all in *Rayuela.* Fantasy for its own sake had stopped interesting me. By then I was fully aware of the dangerous perfection of the storyteller who reaches a certain level of achievement and stays on that same level forever, without moving on. I was a bit sick and tired of seeing how well my stories turned out. In **"El Perseguidor"** I wanted ed to stop inventing and stand on my own ground, to look at myself a bit. And looking at myself meant looking at my neighbor, at Man. I hadn't looked too closely at the human species until I wrote **"El Perseguidor."**

(p. 120)

Cortázar explains that certain forms of Surrealism may throw light on his methods. Modern French literature in general has left a deep mark on his work. Though as a young man he had so little sense of values, he says, that he could hardly distinguish between Montaigne and Pierre Loti, "I changed radically as a result of reading certain French writers—for instance, Cocteau. One day when I was about eighteen I read Cocteau's *Opium.* It was a flash of lightning that opened a new world to me." He threw out half his library and "plunged headfirst into the world Cocteau was showing me. Cocteau put me on to Picasso, Radiguet, the music of the Group of the Six, Diaghilev, all that world between 1915 and 1925, and Surrealism: Breton, Éluard, Crevel. The Surrealist movement has always fascinated me." Cortázar is one of those who think

Surrealism was one of the great moments in this century until it was ruined by the Surrealists themselves, among others, when it became a mere literary movement instead of an attitude toward life. Cortázar has also been a great reader of two of Surrealism's direct ancestors: Apollinaire, and above all, Alfred Jarry. "Jarry," he says, "was a man who realized perfectly that the gravest matters can be explored through humor. That was just what he tried to do with his 'pataphysique'—to touch bottom via black humor. I think that notion had a great influence on my way of looking at the world. I've always thought humor is one of the most serious things there are." The respect for humor as a valid means of investigation is the sign of a high civilization, he believes. It indicates an ability to go prospecting for buried treasure without reaching for big phrases. "The English know that better than anybody. Much of great English literature is based on humor." (pp. 126-27)

> [The book I want to write now] will probably have very few readers, because the ordinary bridges of language that the reader logically expects will have been reduced to a minimum. In *Rayuela* there are many bridges left. In that sense *Rayuela* is a hybrid product, a first attack. If I manage to write this other book, it will be a positive contribution in the sense that, having concluded the attack I mounted against conventional language in *Rayuela*, I'm going to try to create my own language. I've already started to work at it, and it's no easy task. The ideal would be to arrive at a language that would reject all the crutches (not only the obvious ones, but the other, the ones under cover) and other trappings of what is so cheerfully referred to as a literary style. I know it will be an anti-literary language, but it will be a language. The point is, I've always found it absurd to talk about transforming man if man doesn't simultaneously, or previously, transform his instruments of knowledge. How to transform oneself if one continues to use the same language Plato used? The essence of the problem hasn't changed; I mean the type of problems that were pondered in Athens in the fifth century before Christ are still basically the same today because our logical categories haven't changed. The question is: can one do something different, set out in another direction? Beyond logic, beyond Kantian categories, beyond the whole apparatus of Western thought—for instance, looking at the world as if it weren't an expression of Euclidean geometry—is it possible to push across a new border, to take a leap into something more authentic? Of course I don't know. But I think it is.

The problem is not only to replace a whole set of images of the world but, as Morelli [in *Rayuela*] says, to go beyond imagery itself, to discover a new stellar geometry that will open new mental galaxies. Here is where the "figures" come in.

Says Cortázar:

> The concept of "figures" will be of use to me instrumentally, because it provides me with a focus very different from the usual one in a novel or narrative that tends to individualize the characters and equip them with personal traits and psychologies. I'd like to write in such a way that my writing would be full of life in the deepest sense, full of action and meaning, but a life, action and meaning that would no longer rely exclusively on the interaction of individuals, but rather on a sort of super-action involving the "figures" formed by a constellation of characters. I realize it isn't at all easy to explain this. . . . But as time goes by, I feel this notion of "figures" more strongly everyday. In other words, I feel daily more connected with other elements in the universe, I am less of an egoist and I'm more aware of the constant interactions taking place between other things or beings and myself. I have an impression of all that moves on a plane responding to other laws, other structures that lie outside the world of individuality. I would like to write a book that would show how these figures constitute a sort of break with, or denial of individual reality, sometimes completely unknown to the characters themselves. One of the many problems that arise in this scheme, a problem already hinted at in *Rayuela*, is to know up to what point a character can serve a purpose that is fulfilling itself outside him, without his being in the least aware of it, without his realizing that he is one of the links in that super-action or super-structure.

In attempting to answer this question, Cortázar will have to bear arms against conventional notions of time and space. Having already denied us ordinary identification with characters and situations, Morelli, in *Rayuela*, goes a step farther. He points to the "error of postulating an absolute historical time" and suggests that the author should not "lean on circumstance." This is a principle Cortázar has begun to put into practice in a new collection of stories called *Todos Los Fuegos El Fuego (All Fires Are Fire)*. He can point to a story in this collection that ignores stereotyped time. "A single character lives in Buenos Aires today and in Paris in 1870. One day he's strolling in downtown Buenos Aires and at a certain moment, without any break in the continuity, suddenly he's in Paris. The only person who may be surprised is the reader," he adds. "Covered gallery—a sort of out-of-the-way territory I've always found very mysterious—symbolizes his passage from one place to the other. In France it's winter, in Argentina it's summer, but there's no clash in his mind. He finds it perfectly natural to live in two different worlds (but are they really two different worlds for him?)."

In a sense, this is the crucial point Cortázar has been trying to settle in all his work. (pp. 130-32)

The theme of the double, with its infinite variations, is a constant in Cortázar's work. It can take an oneiric form as in the story **"La noche boca arriba" ("On His Back under the Night")** where a man in his sleep retreads ancestral paths, or again in **"Lejana" ("Faraway Image")** where a woman on a honeymoon trip in Hungary meets herself coming the other way on a misty bridge, just as she had previously dreamed she would; or serve as the basis for a meditation on immortality as it does in the intellectually more stringent and exacting **"Una flor amarilla" ("A Yellow Flower")**. Doubles, says Cortázar, are like his "figures"—or, rather, reversing the equation, "the 'figures' are a sort of apex of the theme of the double, to the extent that they would tend to illustrate connections, concatenations existing between different elements that, from a logical standpoint, would seem to be entirely unrelated."

Cortázar's illustrations, always bifocal at least, sometimes take us to odd places, not only mentally, but also geographically. The mental fringes his characters inhabit are faithfully reflected in the marginal settings they frequent. (pp. 133-34)

"I like marginal situations of all kinds," he says. "I prefer back alleyways to main thoroughfares. I detest classic itineraries—at every level." An example of this attitude is his hobgoblinish *Historias de Cronopios y de Famas,* which is full of those serious jokes he is so fond of: instructions for mounting a staircase, for winding a clock; a sketch about a man who loses his head and learns to detect sounds, smells and colors with his sense of touch; a section called "Ocupaciones Raras" ("Strange Occupations"), which works its effects under the skin, on raw nerve ends. In *Cronopios* corpses grow nails, the bald drop their wigs. There is a warning against the dangers of zippers. The author is constantly emptying his pockets under the table. When the book appeared in Argentina, it was received with clacking dentures. Poets treated it with respect, says Cortázar, but the few critics who mentioned it were shocked. They deplored the fact that such a "serious writer" could stoop to such unimportance. "There," he says, "we touch on one of the worst things about Argentina: the stupid notion of importance. The idea of doing something just for the fun of it is practically nonexistent in our literature." Cortázar provides a cure for this ill. *Cronopios* came to him like a sudden twinge, a shot in the dark.

> In 1951, the year I came to Paris there was a concert one night in the Théâtre des Champs Elysées. Suddenly, sitting there, I thought of some characters that were going to be called Cronopios. They were somewhat extravagant creatures that I didn't see very clearly yet, kinds of microbes floating in the air, shapeless greenish blobs that gradually started to take on human traits. After that, in cafés, in the streets, in the subway, I started writing stories about the Cronopios and the Famas, and the Esperanzas, which came later. It was a pure game. . . . Another part of the book, "The Manual of Instructions," I wrote after I got married, when Aurora and I went to live in Italy for awhile. You have Aurora to blame for these texts. One day, mounting an endless staircase in a museum and out of breath, she said suddenly: 'The trouble is that this is a staircase for going down.' I loved that phrase. So I said to Aurora: 'One ought to write some instructions about how to go up and down a staircase.'
>
> (pp. 134-35)

He did.

Anything, even to fall back, rather than remain static, has been [Cortázar's] motto throughout his career. He allows himself no false reconciliation with himself or the world. "The world is full of people living in false bliss," he says. He will continue to trip himself up as he goes along. The important thing for him is to keep his inner dialogue going. Learning to speak to himself has been his way of trying to talk to others. He has just begun to find his voice.

> When all is said and done . . . I feel very much alone, and I think that's as it should be. In other words, I don't rely on Western tradition alone as a valid passport, and culturally I'm also totally disconnected from Eastern tradition, which I don't see any particular compensatory reason to lean on either. The truth is, each day I lose more confidence in myself, and I'm happy. I write worse and worse, from an aesthetic point of view. I'm glad, because

I think I'm approaching the point where perhaps I'll be able to start writing as I think one ought to write in our time. It may seem a kind of suicide, in a sense, but it's better to be a suicide than a zombie. It may be absurd for a writer to insist on discarding his work instruments. But I think those instruments are false. I want to wipe my slate clean, start from scratch.

(p. 139)

Luis Harss with Barbara Dohmann, "Julio Cortázar or The Slap in the Face," in New Mexico Quarterly, *Vol. XXXVI, No. 2, Summer, 1966, pp. 105-39.*

Roberto Gonzalez Echevarria   (essay date 1971)

[*Gonzalez Echevarria is a Cuban-born American educator, editor, and translator whose contributions to the study of Latin American literature include his* Alejo Carpentier: The Pilgrim at Home *(1977) and translation of several of Cortázar's short stories in* All Fires the Fire, and Other Stories *(1973). In the following excerpt, Gonzalez Echevarria examines Cortázar's mixture of real and fantastic elements in his short fiction, focusing on the story "La autopista del sur."*]

Borges said, evading my question about the new Latin American novel, that he had published Julio Cortázar's first short story ["**Casa tomada**"] in *Los Anales de Buenos Aires,* a magazine he edited in the forties. Borges' answer was a shrewd way of avoiding a topic he always shuns and a very Borgian way of pointing, not only to the link between Cortázar's work and his own, but also to what he probably considers Cortázar's forte—the short story.

Such an opinion, if indeed Borges' characteristically ambiguous answer could be construed as one, is probably contrary to that of most readers; for, although Cortázar has excelled in the short story genre his most resounding success to date is a novel *Hopscotch* (1963). And *Hopscotch* is not just the high point of Cortázar's literary production (from the point of view of sales and critical acclaim); it represents a turning point in Latin American prose fiction writing. (p. 130)

The Boom, as the success of the Latin American novel *après Hopscotch* has come to be known, now counts among its loudest echoes Asturias' Nobel Prize. This success cannot, of course, be attributed entirely to Cortázar. But it was *Hopscotch* that set off the chain reaction with record sales in the original, prizes for its English translation and a unprecedented critical response. (p. 131)

[In] spite of *Hopscotch,* Cortázar has been mainly a short story writer. He not only began his career as one (if one forgets his avowedly "Mallarmean" book of sonnets, *Presencia,* published in 1938 under the pseudonym Julio Denís), but has cultivated the genre assiduously. Aside from *Hopscotch, The Winners* (1960) and *62: Modelo para armar,* his three novels, and three ageneric books, *Los reyes* (1949), *La vuelta al día en ochenta mundos* (1967), and *El último round* (1970), Cortázar has published five volumes of short stories: *Bestiario* (1951), *Final del juego* (1956), *Las armas secretas* (1959), *Historias de cronopios y de famas* (1962) and *Todos los fuegos el fuego* (1966). There are, in addition, a few stories published elsewhere, translations of Poe's prose works and two essays on the short story genre—"Algunos aspectos del cuento," and "Del cuento breve y sus alrededores." It is also true, as Borges seemed to indicate, that if Cortázar has been an innovator almost *ad delirium* in the novel, in the short story he has remained largely faithful to a tradition, that of the River Plate area, which boasts names such as the Uruguayan master Horacio Quiroga and, of course, Jorge Luis Borges.

Some of Cortázar's early short stories are metaphysical *jeux d'esprit* in a very Borgian vein. In **"Continuity of Parks,"** for example, the characters of a novel, chasing one another through a forest, end up in the same room with the absorbed reader of the novel. In **"Night Face Up"**—a story in *Las armas secretas*—an injured motorcyclist suffers a Kafkaesque nightmare in which he is persecuted by Aztecs who want to kill him in a ritual sacrifice. At the end he realizes "that the marvelous dream had been the other, absurd as all dreams are—a dream in which he was going through the strange avenues of an astonishing city, with green and red lights that burned without fire or smoke, on an enormous metal insect that whirred away between his legs." Other stories from this early period are more 'regional' and are written in a streamlined *porteño* slang. **"Torito,"** for example, is the rambling recollections of an old boxer in his hospital bed. The story is full of pathos and ends on an anguished note. . . . (pp. 131-32)

But it is in **"Night Face Up"** that one finds the mixture of the real and the fantastic that will become the trademark of Cortázar's stories—a mixture that Severo Sarduy has compared to Magritte's portrait of a perfectly normal man in which a bird cage stands in place of the head. . . . It is precisely this particular way of conceiving the fantastic that will be studied here through an analysis of **"La autopisto del sur,"** the opening story of *Todos los fuegos el fuego.* This analysis is necessary because Cortázar himself has reacted somewhat negatively to the interpretation of his short fiction. . . . [He] suggests . . . that there is no break between the 'real' and 'fantastic' in his stories but instead a mode of presenting the 'real' that transfers it to the level of the 'unusual' (*insólito*). This perspective put forth by Cortázar may be, in the last analysis, the most fruitful one, not only for an understanding of his peculiar way of conceiving the real, but also for a more lucid understanding of his *métier*.

As in many of his short stories, Cortázar builds **"La autopista del sur"** upon a single situation; a set of circumstances within which the action and the characters are framed (more on this later). In **"La autopista del sur"** the situation is a traffic jam on the outskirts of Paris that begins on a Sunday afternoon and lasts days, months, and perhaps even years. The people caught in the jam are forced to organize communes to pool their supplies, trade services and help one another until they can reach Paris. The story focuses on one of these communes: there is a suicide, a natural death, a burial (in a trunk of a car), a desertion, a crime against the commune (drinking water without authorization) and a love affair between the protagonist, an engineer, and the girl driving the car next to his; life, in short, is resumed within a new order. The love affair between the engineer and the girl provides a tenuous plot line that does not monopolize the action. At the end of the story, when the traffic jam finally dissolves, the

bonds formed in time of fear and want are forgotten. . . . (pp. 132-33)

The plot, then, is not the whole story; the story is encased within a situation that is charged with potential meaning in itself. This technique is not, of course, original, and this is why Cortázar's definition is so valid and illuminating; it may finally lead us toward a structural understanding of the short story and away from vague criteria about length. (Even a great novel such as Cervantes' *Don Quijote* is largely built upon a single situation that is repeated over and over again, exploiting in each case its multiple potential meanings. For this reason it is relatively easy to lift episodes from Cervantes' novel without their losing meaning outside the context of the book). The situation, then, works as a sign, charged with multiple potential meanings that emerge in the telling of the story, the 'utterance' of that sign. This is obviously the case in **"Blow-up,"** in which the protagonist, a photographer, explores the various possible meanings that arise from a situation he has captured on film. . . . (p. 134)

The situation-sign that serves as point of departure for **"La autopista del sur"** is both a "slice of life" (*a recorte de la realidad* in the sense given this term by Cortázar) and a blatantly literary device. The vacation schedule of many Parisians, regardless of their trade, is uniform and as a result thousands leave and return to Paris at the same time (the return is called *La Rentrée* by the French). On certain days, in August particularly, when our story takes place, access to the city is practically impossible. Traffic jams such as the one portrayed in **"La autopista del sur"** have been known to last literally for days, especially on the *Autoroute du Sud,* which connects the city with the *Midi*. It is quite obvious that Cortázar, who has lived in Paris for many years, saw in such a jam a portion of reality he could frame and use as the mainspring for a story. On the other hand, the device of confining heterogeneous characters in an inclosure of some kind can be traced at least as far back as Boccaccio's *Decameron* or Brandt's *Ship of Fools*. In modern times it has been used very frequently both in literature and the cinema, and Cortázar himself used it as the main prop for his first novel, *The Winners* (where the inclosure, as in Brandt, is a ship) and also in **"Omnibus,"** a story in *Bestiario.* (pp. 134-35)

The inclosure has several functions. It may serve to isolate a group of characters in order to observe their responses under unusual circumstances, as in the [Luis Buñuel] film *Bus Stop*, where the emphasis lies upon the psychological and moral behavior of the characters. It may also, as in Golding's *Lord of the Flies*, present a perfectly rounded microcosm that is a scaled down model of a macrocosm, or a model for a possible one. Here the emphasis lies not so heavily on individual responses as on the model institutions created to regulate them. This has been the function served by the inclosure in utopias from More's to Skinner's *Walden Two*. Finally, the inclosure may be an allegory. (p. 135)

In **"La autopista del sur"** Cortázar exploits all these traditional functions of the inclosure: the commune is a microcosm, an isolated society that depends only on itself for survival, institutions and customs are created to regulate the interaction of the characters and, as shall be seen, it is also a sort of *theatrum mundi.*

But in Cortázar's story the nature of the device is particularly complex because there are, in fact, two inclosures—the traffic jam and the commune created by the characters. The aperture of which Cortázar speaks in his "Algunos aspectos del cuento" produces in **"La autopista del sur"** a double exposure—a picture where two distinct images are superimposed. This, it must be added, is the unifying device throughout *Todos los fuegos el fuego,* where Cortázar constantly portrays split worlds, images and mirror images that clash in **"El otro cielo," "La isla a mediodía,"** the title story itself and even on the covers of the book, where the title, the name of the author and the publishing house are printed in reverse on the back cover (and may be read, of course, if put before a mirror). . . . In **"La autopista del sur,"** however, the split worlds do not offer, as shall be seen, a direct commentary upon . . . general metaphysical problems. If the story does indeed refer to them, it does so only in a very devious way. (pp. 135-36)

It is quite obvious that Cortázar saw in *La Rentrée* a ready-made symbol for something that has been a major theme throughout his works—modern technological society and its very precarious balance. Confined in their useless metal cages, the people in the jam are obvious examples of alienated modern man. At the end, when the jam finally dissolves, each person returns to a mechanized existence controlled by machines. . . . The commune, on the other hand, is a primitive, tribal world of food-gathering, rituals and folklore. The people, deprived of all the trappings of modern civilization, return to a natural state where each depends on the other directly and where bonds of solidarity form; it is almost a perfect primitive Christian society.

It could very well be concluded then, particularly in view of the slightly melodramatic ending, that Cortázar offers in **"La autopista del sur"** an alternative to modern civilization; that the story is an indictment against modern life. In short, that the double exposure creates a dialectic between the modern and primitive worlds present in the two images. Yet, while this interpretation may be valid and justifiable, it seems to me that the 'topicality' of the story conceals a more profound reflection, not directly about man's condition, but about fiction.

The most salient characteristic of the traffic jam is its facility as metaphor. The commune, too, is not only a standard (and today standardized) alternative to technological society but consists of a series of literary *topoi*. There is the image of the river (in this case a motionless river). . . . Implicit in the entire story is also the image of the highway of life, so dear to the writers of romances of chivalry and of picaresque novels. In addition, there is the suggestion that the commune is organized by a mysterious supernatural being that keeps all the cars in close formation. . . . And the characters of the commune form, as a group, a sort of *theatrum mundi* or medieval dance of death: there is Youth—the two boys in the Simca—; Old Age—the old couple in the ID Citroen—; the Clergy—the nuns in the 2HP—; a Soldier—the soldier in the Volkswagen; and a couple of lovers, the engineer and the girl in the Dauphine. The dance of death motif is accentuated when someone throws a sickle into the middle of the commune, another symbol of medieval vintage. Cortázar's symbols are nearly always trite and obvious. The meaning of the board the characters of *Hopscotch* use to reach from one building to

another is not subtle. The photograph device in **"Blow-up"** is not only trite but obvious, as is the platitudinous escape-dream of Marini in **"La isla a mediodía"** (an island in the Aegean Sea that serves a similar function to that of the commune since it represents a primitive world.) This is not due to Cortázar's lack of imagination or subtlety. The triteness and the platitudinous meaning of his symbols and devices have a very specific purpose in his works: to focus attention not on the meaning of the literary sign but on the sign itself.

Some years ago—in 1947—Cortázar suggested in one of his first publications that the contrivance of an autonomous, self-sufficient fictional world was an absolute requirement in short-story writing. . . . (pp. 136-38)

The inclosure device is not merely one mode of short-story writing but an ontological characteristic of the genre; all fiction and short fiction in particular is a closed, autonomous world. Thus, the inclosures in **"La autopista del sur,"** while projecting the obvious meanings indicated above, as well as being a 'recorte de la realidad', are ultimately symbols of fiction itself. This is the reason why Cortázar utilizes literary signs that are so blatantly literary and also the reason for the platitudinous meanings of those signs.

This interpretation of the inclosures becomes clearer if one notices the relationship between the traffic jam and the commune at a formal level. Cortázar creates the commune before the reader, as when in the modern theater the actors themselves bring the properties onto the stage and then proceed with the representation of the play. In this respect the relationship between the commune and the traffic jam could be said to be homologous to that between the play within the play and the play itself. From the first page of the story, Cortázar begins to set off from the world outside what will become the autonomous commune. . . . Cortázar gives a meticulous phenomenological description of a self-contained world, of a complete cosmos. But the important thing is that he creates that fictitious world openly and arbitrarily, as if he were inviting the reader to analyse the elements of his fiction, the props of the set and the grease paint on the actors' faces.

The arbitrariness by which Cortázar constructs his fictional microcosm alludes to the arbitrariness of the real world. His 'utopia' points to a macrocosm that may be just as arbitrary and perhaps just as fictional. . . . In Cortázar's utopia everything has a place because he has arbitrarily created a grammar that will contain it; everything, including the characters, has a name because he has wrought a grammar that will accept it. Toward the end of **"La autopista del sur"** snow covers the ground—winter has set in on the people who had left for Paris on an August afternoon. But this is not a break with the syntax of Cortázar's new world. The perfectly normal man in Magritte's picture is as arbitrary in his normality as the bird cage in its abnormality. The two situation signs have become one; a fiction within a larger fiction, all fictions a fiction, all fires a fire. Cortázar's **"La autopista del sur"** falls within a very rich tradition of literature whose main preoccupation is literature. (pp. 138-40)

Roberto Gonzalez Echevarria, " 'La autopista del sur' and the Secret Weapons of Julio Cortázar's Short Narrative," in Studies in Short Fiction, *Vol. VIII, No. 1, Winter, 1971, pp. 130-40.*

Cortázar on the fantastic

Almost all the stories I have written belong to the genre called, for lack of a better name, fantastic. They oppose that false realism which upholds the belief that everything can be neatly described as was assumed by the philosophic and scientific optimism of the eighteenth century that is within a world ruled more or less harmoniously by a system of laws, of principles, of causal relations, of well-defined psychologies, of well-mapped geographies. In my case, the suspicion of another order, more secret and less communicable, and the fertile discovery of Alfred Jarry, for whom the true study of reality didn't rest on the laws but on the exceptions to those laws, were some of the guiding principles of my personal search for a literature beyond too naïve forms of realism.

> *From "Algunos aspectos del cuento," in* Casa de las Américas, *1962, as quoted by Jaime Alazraki, "The Fantastic of Surrealist Metaphors,"* Dada/Surrealism, *No. 5, 1975.*

Lanin A. Gyurko (essay date 1973)

[*In the excerpt below, Gyurko explores the diverse nature of fantasy in Cortázar's short fiction, positing that the real and the unreal are often combined in the minds of Cortázar's characters.*]

Many of the short stories of Julio Cortázar present situations that appear to be absurd or fantastic—a man vomits up live rabbits; an individual becomes converted into a Mexican salamander; the identity of a student is invaded and crushed by the reincarnated spirit of a dead Nazi soldier; a man slowly sinks into the ground without his family or his fiancée's being aware that he is disappearing before their eyes; phantasms take over a house, driving out the occupants; a dead man comes to Paris to visit the woman who jilted him to marry his brother; a tiger prowls through a country estate, dominating the lives of the strange family who lodge it. These stories of the bestial and the demonic may be interpreted on two different levels. One is the purely fantastic or supernatural, in which time is cyclical and the self has avatar identities. Metempsychoses occur not only between two human souls but between human and animal spirits. Demonic forces are conjured up, sometimes by a weird pagan ritual and at others by a type of extrasensory process or mental telepathy. Yet another, equally convincing tack of interpretation, and one that attests to the complexity of the short fiction of Cortázar, is to view him as a realist author and to interpret the bizarre experiences that plague the lives of his characters as due to the operation of their own disturbed consciousnesses. Their minds are invaded by subconscious impulses which they initially can suppress but

which finally increase in power and overwhelm them. Thus the world of the short stories of this modern Argentine author becomes one of delusions, hallucinations, and nightmares—powerful fantasies that at times have the strength to kill and that frequently destroy the minds of the afflicted characters. If seen as inhabiting a realm constantly invaded by the supernatural, Cortázar's characters are pawns of fate, suborned by demons that they struggle against but whom they are compelled to obey. But if viewed in realistic, psychological terms, in most instances Cortázar's characters destroy their own selves. Fate becomes an inner force, the relentless action of the obsessed and tormented consciousness.

Most all of Cortázar's characters are prone to absorption into fantasy worlds because they are narcissistic, socially alienated, and emotionally unstable. They have no strong or meaningful outer lives to counterbalance the awesome power of their delusions. These individuals are studies in deficiency. Many lack will, courage, professional role, social relationships, and, often, even a name. (p. 988)

Fantasy worlds are experienced with a conviction and an intensity that make them real for the characters. External reality, on the other hand, recedes to the level of the unreal. For the alienated airline steward Marini in **"La isla a mediodía,"** it is his real-life existence, a sterile routine of menial actions and inconsequential relationships, that is absurd. But his dream of a primitive life on the Greek island of Xiros that he only glimpses from the plane becomes a vision of salvation which is experienced with such an intensity that both Marini and the reader believe it to be a reality that the protagonist finally has found. (pp. 988-89)

Cortázar's narrative art is one of paradox, ambiguity, and ironic reversal. Throughout his short fiction there is a subtle blending of reality and illusion, nightmare and waking consciousness, man and beast, self and other, present and past, terror and humor, myth and fact, art (visual, verbal, musical) and life. Neither time nor space, psychic identity nor social role remain certain. In many stories reality is a mere façade that masks the demonic. In **"Omnibus,"** what seems to be an ordinary city bus turns out to be a vehicle driven by Death, a twentieth century equivalent of the bark of Charon. Clara, the terrified protagonist, journeys at the same time through the streets of Buenos Aires and through the depths of the Underworld. (p. 989)

The protean quality of Cortázar's world is particularly evident in the schizophrenic nature of many of his protagonists. The domineering Alina Reyes in **"Lejana,"** who fashions herself a queen, harbors masochistic impulses that take the form of a double, a beggar woman suffering in the snow and cold on a bridge in Budapest. Images of the beggar afflict Alina whenever she is about to feel happiness in her life in Buenos Aires. Although she marries a servile man, she has dreams of an anagram lover, Rod, Erod, or Rodo, who beats her. On the other hand, the self-effacing manner of the protagonist of **"Carta a una señorita en París"** conceals megalomanic impulses. This alienated individual, who is paranoic about disturbing the smallest object in the fashionable apartment of Andrée, secretly harbors destructive impulses that take the form of the hallucinatory rabbits that he believes he has vomited up and to which he ascribes the blame for the havoc that he himself is wreaking on the apartment. A Dr. Jekyll-Mr. Hyde existence characterizes Pierre Jolivet in **"Las armas** secretas." His original personality as a self-absorbed and sensitive student is corroded by a brutal and sadistic alternate identity of a reincarnated Nazi. The dead soldier returns through Pierre to take vengeance on Michèle, the girl whom he had violated and who had subsequently denounced him and brought about his death. The delicate Michèle, now the girl friend of Pierre, becomes the victim of a horrible cyclic time. (pp. 989-90)

The unstable identities of the characters are often given a structural expression within the stories. Some are narrated in constantly shifting panels of present and remote past, reality and nightmare. The protagonist of **"El otro cielo"** rotates between experiences within the bourgeoise world of Buenos Aires in the 1940's and adventures within his secret fantasy zone of Paris of 1870. His imaginative life is narrated with the same if not greater sense of authenticity as is his life in the real world. The story **"La noche boca arriba"** constantly oscillates between the twentieth century identity of the protagonist as a victim of a motorcycle accident and an oneiric self as an ancient Moteca Indian being pursued by Aztec warriors as a victim for blood sacrifice. The delirious mind of the guilt-stricken girl Wanda in **"Siestas"** confuses memory and nightmare, perception and hallucination. The molester with the hand of wax, initially a nightmare, finally materializes for the stricken girl, who has been driven insane. The hellworld created by the solipsistic consciousness is stylistically dramatized in many of Cortázar's narratives through a third-person indirect interior monologue or modified stream of consciousness technique. **"Bestiario," "Las armas secretas,"** and **"Siestas"** combine this technique with sentence-pyramiding at the climactic moment of the narrative. The bewilderment and terror of the characters are strikingly conveyed through use of this onrush of thoughts that endows the narratives with high dramatic tension.

Many of the narratives use the labyrinth as the symbol *par excellence* of the mind in crisis. . . . Sometimes the labyrinth takes the form of city streets, such as the Pasaje Güemes in **"El otro cielo,"** a street of Argentine low life that for the protagonist is the transitional zone between the stultifying reality of bourgeoise Buenos Aires and the imaginative world of the Galerie Vivienne in nineteenth-century France in which he initially finds liberation and enjoyment. But the labyrinthine fantasy zone also contains its monster, in the form of Laurent, the strangler of nine women, whose presence converts the zone into one of terror. The labyrinth of city streets and alleyways through which the terrified Wanda in **"Siestas"** flees finally becomes the maze of her anguished conscience, which also creates a monster. . . . (p. 990)

In addition to the labyrinth, another factor in many of the narratives that contributes to their air of unreality is that the protagonists are often artists—writers, photographers, musicians—or they are endowed with febrile imaginations easily influenced by artistic expression. Yet, ironically, the creative experience turns out to be a destructive one for most of the characters. The obsessed archeologist Somoza repeatedly attempts to duplicate the ancient **"Ídolo de las Cícladas"** in order to place himself in contact with the power of the goddess Haghesa. But his delusion that he has become her priest and his subsequent attempt to make a blood sacrifice of Morand in order to gain the latter's beautiful wife Thérèse, the real goddess for Somoza, result only in his death. . . .

A third factor that undergirds the unreality of Cortázar's stories and which emphasizes the fatalism of his vision is his use of classical myths. **"Silvia"** is a variation on the myth of Tantalus. The perplexed adult narrator is unable to grasp the alluring but forever elusive Silvia, the guardian angel created by the children and accepted nonchalantly by them but very seriously by the adult, who believes her to be a reality. (p. 991)

The preceding discussion has attempted to demonstrate the pervasiveness of fantasy in Cortázar's art and to provide the background for an analysis of the various types of fantasy, particularly as encountered within the Argentine author's short fiction. The fantasies of Cortázar's characters can be categorized into two major kinds, both predominantly negative: destructive and ironically redemptive. The destructive fantasies of the characters have their basis in fear, guilt, jealousy, or a thanatos instinct. Most of them initially are subconscious and are manifested in dreams and nightmares, but they rapidly become conscious and pervade the waking hours of the characters. These obsessive fantasies undermine the will and the integrity of the protagonists and often lead to their insanity, death, or both. Ironically redemptive fantasy can itself be divided into three types: premonitory, deceptive, and positive but unrealizable. Premonitory fantasy always adumbrates disaster or death. It is ironically redemptive in that although the characters are warned, often repeatedly, of their fate, they prefer to dismiss or to suppress these adumbrations. Instead they nurture another form of fantasy—their own illusions of self-exaltation. While destructive fantasies are afflictive from the start, deceptive fantasies initially seem to hold the promise of self-transcendence for the characters. For example, the hallucinatory bunnies give the protagonist of **"Carta a una señorita en Paris"** the opportunity to play god. Alina Reyes of **"Lejana"** believes that the meeting with her double will mark the confirmation of her exalted, regal and noble self. But both protagonists are finally driven insane by their fantasies that become monstrous and uncontrollable.

Deceptive fantasies, initially reinforcing the characters, turn destructive. Positive fantasies, which do not change, are visions of paradisiacal worlds, most often on the conscious level of reveries or daydreams. Marini in **"El otro cielo"** nurtures his dream of an island paradise; the narrator of **"Silvia"** is entranced by the vision of the beautiful and enticing dream girl. These positive fantasies act as a compensation for the identity or fulfillment that the characters are unable to find in the real world. Detaching themselves from emotional involvement with others and shunning a professional reality that they see as tedious, constricting, and incapable of being changed, they become passive rebels, withdrawing into their own solipsistic paradises of the imagination. Yet they cannot achieve salvation through submersion in their fantasy realms. The delight, wonder, exhilaration and sense of freedom that they experience are all fleeting. At the end they are defeated from without by an adverse and dominating reality that often leads to their brutal disillusionment. The adult in **"Silvia"** is prohibited by his age from re-entering the world of living poetry that is part of childhood; Marini is killed in an airplane crash before he ever can reach his island. (p. 992)

Destructive fantasies are most often the result of guilt feelings that work on the febrile imaginations of the characters. (p. 993)

Destructive fantasies are also a manifestation of the thanatos instinct that afflicts many of Cortázar's characters. The creative search that Johnny Carter in **"El perseguidor"** consciously undertakes for a higher plane of existence is a desperate reaction to a more powerful, subconscious urge to destroy himself. Johnny is haunted by fantasies of burial urns among which he searches for the one which contains the remains of his own self. His music is founded on these visions of death; it is both an expression of his anguish and a frustrated attempt to purge himself of it. Just after his vision of the urns he records one of his masterpieces, *Amorous*. But finally, as in many of Cortázar's stories, subconscious instincts become conscious and overpowering, and Johnny takes his own life. Ironically, his earthly pursuit for a transcendental state can be attained only by obliterating the self. . . .

In many of the stories of destructive fantasy, the nightmares and delusions of the characters are linked with a past that is primitive, savage, and demonic. The maniacal Somoza in **"El ídolo de las Cícladas"** deliberately conjures up the primitive spirit of blood sacrifice that is the goddess Haghesa. In **"Las armas secretas"** the brooding Pierre, continually frustrated in his desire to seduce his girl friend Michèle, seems involuntarily to conjure up the fiendish spirit of the Nazi. In both narratives fantasy provides the brutal power necessary to satisfy the lustful instincts that the characters' normal selves would be incapable of venting. (p. 994)

Like destructive fantasies, premonitions serve to underscore the determinism present in Cortázar's fictional world. Premonitory fantasies in some instances have a diabolical power of their own—Hélène in *62: Modelo para armar,* Alina in **"Lejana"** and the recluse in **"Relato con un fondo de agua"** experience visions that not only foreshadow their fate but that impel them toward actualization of it by their insistent and alluring quality. Alina Reyes has an intuition of her disastrous fate that she will not confide to her diary. Instead she suppresses the premonition and gives in to her delusions of grandeur. (p. 995)

It is ironic that many of Cortázar's protagonists who seek liberation through their fantasies are finally abased or enslaved by them. In **"Cefalea,"** the creation by Dr. Harbin's patients of the *mancuspias* is initially a form of imaginative therapy through which the patients, victims of recurrent and excruciating attacks of vertigo and migraine headaches, fill their degraded lives with purpose and take their minds off their horrible illnesses. At first the *mancuspias* are projections of health—a wish-fulfillment by the patients of the type of care that they do not receive from their neglectful attendants who finally desert them. Then, as their anxieties increase and their illnesses become worse, the patients attempt to purge themselves of fear and pain and even of death by projecting these states onto the animals. But they have less and less success in isolating the agonizing *mancuspias* from their own brains. Although the *mancuspias* originally have represented the salvation of the patients, they now become violent and cannibalistic and absorb all the attention of their creators, exhausting them, and, ironically, rendering them even more susceptible to the very diseases the patients had hoped to combat by dedicating themselves to the care of the bizarre animals. . . . The deluded Alina Reyes at the moment of unity with her double feels that she is liberating herself.

But at the end of her experience she remains imprisoned within the identity she has loathed, dominated by her masochistic impulses and also succumbing to madness, a state that she has predicted for herself.

The attempts made by these characters to gain the salvation through fantasy that they cannot achieve in the real world always collapse. Positive fantasies, like deceptive and destructive ones, are undergirded by irony and loss.

Fantasy in Cortázar is a complex, paradoxical phenomenon. Many times linked with the demonic, it also acts as a moral force, deflating vanity and destroying pretense. It often compels the characters to acknowledge or to confront a reality that they have refused to accept. (pp. 995-96)

Fantasy often represents truth. Although frequently seeming to be antithetical to the personality or life-style of the character, it often reflects his inner or subconscious life. In **"La caricia más profunda,"** the delusion that the protagonist suffers of slowly sinking into the ground while neither family nor friends note any change, is but the grotesque exaggeration of his strong feelings of social alienation. The failure of these outsiders to see his abnormal physical state is symbolic of their unwillingness to comprehend him psychologically. At the end of the story his fantasy becomes their reality. Although his fiancée previously could not see any difference in him, now she cannot see him at all as she stands above her suitor who has sunk entirely into the ground. Contrasting with the delusion of disappearance is the fantasy of materialization masterfully exemplified in **"Bestiario."** The perverted and predatory instincts of Nene become so powerful that they finally materialize into the tiger, a beast which is constantly kept fed not only by him but by the other members of the family who passively submit to his intimidation. Just as within the world of tense and distorted relationships of the Funes family it is normal for a tiger to be prowling, so also within the dehumanized life of the alienated protagonist of **"Axolotl"** it is no surprise to him that he finally becomes one of the monsters. . . .

Fantasy in Cortázar is both communal or contagious and intimate. Often the porous, unstable identities of the characters facilitate the transference of delusion. . . . In **"El ídolo de las Cícladas,"** the role of priest of Haghesa passes from Somoza to Morand. The deluded Somoza mouths a chant to Haghesa, strips down, and takes a hatchet in preparation for the killing of Morand. But after Morand kills Somoza with his own weapon, he too becomes absorbed by the spell of the goddess, bathes his hands in Somoza's blood, and crouches down in wait for his wife, licking the hatchet-blade. (p. 997)

Cortázar's art has a subtle ethical basis. The negative fate of almost all of his characters demonstrates the danger or the impossibility of giving oneself up to fantasy worlds which hold only the spectre of salvation. The fantasy consciousness many times is the result of characters who wish to gain fulfillment through exalting the self rather than through meaningful relationships with other human beings. But the fantasy paradise created by the narcissistic self either is unsustainable or it becomes converted into a hellworld. Many characters, like Alina Reyes, Johnny Carter, and Horacio Oliveira, are primarily interested not in unity with others but in unity with a higher form of the self through others. But their selfishness finally and ironically leads them only to a reductive selflessness. The grotesque extreme of the egotistical, fantasy dominated self is found in **"El río."** In a state between sleep and wakefulness, the husband believes that he is in his bedroom contemplating the sleeping body of his wife. In actuality he is in the Seine, looking at the drowned woman who has finally carried out her threat to commit suicide. The deluded husband even imagines that he is having physical relations with his wife. In death as in life, she is perceived only as a victim of his sadistic cruelty and monstrous egotism.

At times characters withdraw into self instead of communicating guilt or anguish to others. The fear of humiliation keeps them from confiding in one another. But, ironically, their fantasies increase in strength precisely because they are repressed instead of exorcised. Self-isolation instead of diminishing the problem renders the solipsistic self more vulnerable to defeat. (p. 998)

Cortázar's characters cannot gain redemption either within reality or within fantasy. . . .

Lured by the promise of freedom, happiness, and self-exaltation and fulfillment, the characters of Cortázar give themselves over to fantasy realms. Yet the inevitable result of this thrust within—into reverie, dream, and delusion—is disillusionment, insanity, and, sometimes even death. The most genuine relationship found in Cortázar, one grounded on a reality of sharing and of mutual concern, is that between Talita and Traveler in *Rayuela*. Both characters gain fulfillment, redeeming the self not through narcissistic expansion, as Alina Reyes, the protagonist of **"Carta"** and the narrator of **"El otro cielo"** attempt to do and fail, but through self-negation and selfless love. (p. 999)

> *Lanin A. Gyurko, "Destructive and Ironically Redemptive Fantasy in Cortázar," in* Hispania, *Vol. 56, No. 4, December, 1973, pp. 988-99.*

Gabriel Josipovici   (essay date 1978)

[*Josipovici is a French-born English contemporary literary theorist and a leading experimental fiction writer. In his highly respected critical work* The World and the Book: A Study of Modern Fiction *(1971), Josipovici urges readers to "remove the spectacles of habit" when reading unconventional literature. His fiction, which is characterized by fragmented dialogue, disjointed narrative, and interior monologue, also challenges preconceived ideas about the nature of art and reality. In the following excerpt from a review of* Cronopios and Famas, *Josipovici discusses the "uneasy tension between meaning and obscurity" in stories from this collection, faulting Cortázar for excessive self-consciousness in many of these pieces.*]

The volume [*Cronopios and famas*] consists of a hundred or so fragments, loosely bundled together under such titles as "The Instruction Manual", "Unusual Occupations", "Unstable Stuff", and "Cronopios and Famas". The first group includes instructions on "how to climb a staircase", "how to sing" ("begin by breaking all the mirrors in the house"), and "how to kill ants in Rome". The last group

deals with the cronopios, the famas and the esperanzas, though what these creatures are—if they are creatures at all—it is difficult to say. The very first fragment in that section begins:

> It happened that a fama was dancing respite and dancing catalan in front of a shop filled with cronopios and esperanzas. The esperanzas were the most irritated. They are always trying to see to it that the famas dance hopeful, not respite or catalan, since hopeful is the dance the cronopios and esperanzas know best.

This is clearly a headache for any translator, since Cortázar seems to be trying to disorientate us by retaining traditional syntax but refusing us the satisfaction of immediate access to meaning. The best pieces in this volume are able to maintain this uneasy tension between meaning and obscurity, leaving us at the end both puzzled and satisfied. Thus, in **"Scholar with a Hole in his Memory"** we read:

> Eminent scholar, Roman history in twenty-three volumes, sure candidate for Nobel prize, great enthusiasm in his country. Suddenly consternation: library creep and full-time hatchet man puts out scurrilous pamphlet denouncing omission of Caracalla. . . . Stupefied admirers consult together. . . . Incontrovertible evidence Caracalla missing, consternation, telephone disconnected, scholar cannot receive call from King Gustaf of Sweden, but that monarch is not even thinking of calling him, but rather another one who dials and dials the number in vain, cursing in a dead language.

Why the omission? we ask. And who is "the other one" who curses in a dead language? Caracalla himself? As in the best short prose pieces it is the very syntax and movement of the language which is the main protagonist, and the hole in the scholar's memory is echoed by the casual but inevitable shift from his story to that of "the other" and of the monarch with whom he cannot seem to communicate. There is no apparent connection between end and beginning, but the piece itself holds them together in a momentary tantalizing pose, before the whole thing disintegrates.

Yet even here there is something a little facile about the telegraphic style, and the ending is perhaps a little too casual. Unfortunately most of the pieces in this volume are much less good, and tend to be either nasty or fey: "What a wonderful pursuit: cut the leg off a spider, put it in an envelope, write on it *Minister of Foreign Affairs*, add the address, run down stairs, and drop the letter into the mailbox at the corner."

Novels have plots and poems have forms, so that even if you write badly or have little to say you can still produce an interesting novel or poem. With the short prose piece on the other hand you are entirely naked. This is why the genre has been so popular with writers dissatisfied with the existing forms, anxious to get as close to the truth as possible.

If you're not a Kafka or a Lichtenberg, however, the result can be grim. Cortázar, who has been living in Paris since 1952, tends when in doubt to fall back on tired surrealism or heavy allegory. But what makes the book so tedious to read is the immense self-consciousness of it all. Look at me, he seems to be saying. Aren't I clever? Aren't I profound? Compare with this Lichtenberg's "The thing that astonished him was that cats should have two holes cut in their coat exactly at the place where their eyes are". Not only is something acute being said here about teleology, but there is something light, off-hand, private even about the fragment. Similarly, when Kafka writes

> Many people prowl round Mount Sinai. Their speech is blurred, either they are garrulous or they shout or they are taciturn. But none of them comes straight down a broad, newly made, smooth road that does its own part in making ones strides long and swifter

we move from clear objectivity to a haunted subjectivity with the minimum of fuss; there is simply no room for the author to stand back and admire his handiwork: it is as much as he can do to get the words down. By contrast the ghost of Literature haunts Cortázar's book.

Gabriel Josipovici, "The Ghost of Literature,"
in The Times Literary Supplement, *No. 3988,*
September 8, 1978, p. 996.

Doris Sommer   (essay date 1979)

[*In the following excerpt, Sommer examines short stories collected in* Todos los fuegos el fuego *and* Octaedro, *noting what she contends is Cortázar's delineation of inescapable, meaningless patterns that condemn humanity to a tragic and absurd existence.*]

Julio Cortázar writes in a world limited by its absurdity and its indifference to human action. It is a world dominated by presentiment in which free will is treated either as a tragic misconception or as a comic error. Man's inability to manipulate or to give direction to his circumstances is certainly evocative of a similar theme in the stories of Jorge Luis Borges. The great difference between Cortázar's treatment and that of his acknowledged teacher is that the disciple's stories concentrate on the mundane, insignificant aspects of life, as José Lezama Lima points out, rather than on overtly philosophical and metaphysical musings. Related to that difference is probably the fact that Cortázar is not concerned with real mystery or suspense. Someone, the protagonist, the reader, or both, is painfully conscious of the inevitable outcome of each story. Chance exists in this mode of narration to mock intentional activity, as it does for Mallarmé, rather than as a means of escape from patterns determined by the absurd and irremediable circumstances of life.

A predictable objection to my basic premise is Cortázar's frequent use of play and dreams which have been interpreted as means of breaking the constraining patterns of life. I would like to address that objection before discussing Cortázar's narrative techniques in which I believe that pattern is primary.

In spite of his almost relentless experimentation with the "other reality", that of play and dream, Cortázar does not successfully relieve his obsession with the inevitable patterns of human life which make it tragic and absurd. The elements of play and dream, to which much of the ever-expanding field of Cortázar criticism is dedicated, do not appear to significantly alter the general atmosphere of doom and purposelessness in his stories. To illustrate these

rather sweeping but no less fundamental observations I will concentrate on his most recent books of short stories: *Todos los fuegos el fuego* of 1966 and *Octaedro* of 1974 in order to challenge those of Cortázar's critics who like to speculate about a generally optimistic development in his work. I hope convincingly to suggest that there is little evidence in Cortázar's latest work of his growing belief in man's ability to affect meaningful changes in his life. The only real exception to his generally cynical opus is a light-hearted experiment in a genre that merges fotonovela and political pamphlet: *Fantomas contra los vampiros multinacionales* of 1975. By contrast, it makes the theme of necessity and efficacy of human action even more conspicuously absent from Cortázar's more serious experiments in fiction.

It is undeniable that games and the spirit of play are salient features of Cortázar's fiction. It is questionable, however, whether these games afford the author and his protagonists the kind of freedom and open-endedness that is generally associated with play. . . . The games are played and they are inevitably lost. The purpose of play in Cortázar's fiction seems to be increased consciousness of our limitations and their tragic end rather than any possible freedom from them.

Alicia Borinsky discusses the notion of play in Cortázar's stories as an internal literary activity of an art that is turned in on itself and that investigates its own material and techniques. The analysis is interesting but not exhaustive, since formal considerations are not independent of content. It might have been pointed out that the experimentation with language and style reflect the ideas in Cortázar's work and that the constraints of communication fetter the artist in a web of convention just as his characters are limited by socially imposed patterns and conventions.

Several critics have either asserted or painstakingly proven that Cortázar is a spiritual son of André Breton and of his Surrealist movement in which chance and games are serious preoccupations. In her elaborately detailed study of Cortázar's artistic and intellectual relationship to the Surrealists, Evelyn Picon Garfield contrasts their optimistic self-abandonment, *disponibilidad,* to chance with Mallarmé's refusal to acknowledge it as a vehicle towards change or discovery. . . . Although the wealth of her evidence makes her general proposition irrefutable: that Cortázar should indeed be studied in the light of French Surrealism, her specific comments about his faith in chance do not seem well founded. Cortázar is probably much closer to Mallarmé's pessimism that to Breton's criticism.

Cortázar's masters of play and freedom from convention are the members of the family that lives on Humbolt Street from his 1962 *Historias de cronopios y de famas.* These model human beings who most closely approximate the poetic and liberated state of *cronopio* are marred, however, by a limitation that many readers seem to ignore; they are imitators. (pp. 71-3)

That is, even Cortázar's most unconventional characters are locked into colorless repetition. (p. 73)

Cortázar's less eccentric characters are also more tragic; their games and their attempts to escape the prescribed limitations of their meaningless lives are consistently thwarted. In **"Todos los fuegos el fuego"**, for example, both the gladiatorial and the amorous games are cruel in the extreme. They are designed to be lost by the victims of treachery. The only unforseen element in both halves of the double plot is the annihilation of the winners as well as the losers. Doom is forseen by them all, but it is naively thought by the proconsul, Roland and Sonia that doom can be limited and manipulated. They are the real participants of the games since their victims lack even apparent freedom, and Cortázar's players always lose.

"Manuscrito hallado en un bolsillo" is probably the most remarkable example of Cortázar's treatment of life as a game that is predictably and invariably lost. The narrator-protagonist begins his story by describing the procedure of a triangular flirtation which he has developed for excursions in the Parisian metro. . . . [But] the rules of the game are calculated to avert romance rather than engender it. The happiness achieved is an almost masochistic appreciation of the impossibility of love; it is the flirtation itself and the overwhelming probability that another meeting will not take place since it must be left to chance in an anonymous and complicated underground world. The game is repeated many times and always with the same disappointing but somehow comforting result. (pp. 73-4)

The negative version of this story, in both photographic and programatic senses, is the last in the volume *Octaedro* entitled **"Cuello de gatito negro"**. Again the plot develops from a flirtation in the subway, but the first sentence immediately indicates some differences. . . . The active agent of the underground seduction is now the woman; what's more, she is neither blond nor redhead but Mulatta. To further underline the differences, her flirtations seem consistently to culminate in sexual fulfilment, guilt, remorse, and the expulsion of her naked and transient lovers into the well lit corridor of her apartment building.

The reason for Cortázar's inversion of his tale of flirtation may very well be an intention to illustrate that no matter how different our games are, they are too easily converted into habits that constrain us increasingly and make a mockery of the myth that play is liberating. Dina, the Mulatta-seductress-in-spite-of-herself, intimates that the only way to break out of her maddening pattern is suicide. . . . She will not have been the first of Cortázar's protagonists to escape the absurdity of life through death. Johnny Carter, the jazz musician of **"El perseguidor"** ends by taking his own life, as does the desperate writer of **"Carta a una srta. en París"**; and there is some indication that Oliveira [in *Hopscotch*] ended the same way, although in his case insanity may have been the means of escape. Certainly death can be alluring for Cortázar and its lure frightens and fascinates him. His ambiguity is the theme of an ostensibly humorous piece about an aunt of the Humboldt Street family. The narrator contrasts her terror of falling and lying on her back with his own predilection for the position. . . . (pp. 74-5)

The lure and fear of internment is repeated in a short narrative from *La vuelta al día en ochenta mundos* entitled **"La caricia más profunda"** in which the young protagonist sinks helplessly and by stages into the earth.

Dreams seem to have as little efficacy as games in liberating Cortázar's characters. They are either frightening and obsessive or they represent another dimension of man's in-

ability to escape the closed circle of his existence. The daydreams that briefly convert themselves into reality for Marini in **"La isla a mediodía"** and for the protagonist of **"El otro cielo"** and inevitably in a return to stagnation. In the first case, defeat is unforseen by the victim of the world's circumstance and limitations. Most experienced readers of Cortázar, however, probably anticipated the catastrophe, not expecting the author to allow his character a long reprieve from absurdity. In the second case, the protagonist is always aware of the impermanence of his artificial paradise. Neither ignorance nor omniscience affect fate which is always synonymous with doom.

In **"Verano"** the dream is patently a nightmare caused presumably by the small disruption in Zulma's and Mariano's perfectly ordered existence. The wife had grown accustomed to the fastidious habits of her husband who defended them as weapons against emptiness, absurdity and death. . . . The night they were asked to babysit for Florencio's little girl brought them the horror of imagining that a wild horse was trying to force its way into their house. Cortázar merges their imaginative perception with the material evidence of hoof prints in the garden, and horror mounts. In the morning Mariano realizes that all is in order, that the horse never entered, in spite of the fact that the door was open, and that the clock still works accurately. Again he is comforted by the familiar routine of life.

Probably the most poignant exploration of dreams and obsession in Cortazar's work is his piece called **"Ahí, pero dónde, cómo"**. It is hardly a story but a meditation and an attempt to conjure the spirit of Paco, a friend who died thirty years earlier and who visits his dreams regularly. The narrator is certain that Paco exists, that he is not dead in the way that others who people dreams are dead. But where, how? That knowledge does not bring hope, it increases despair for even in dreams, even in that other realm which is real but inexplicable, destiny is a closed circle and its victims are helplessly limited to pre-ordained roles. . . . Writing this meditation is an attempt to break the circle of illness, death, helplessness and guilt; it is a confession, a short-lived alleviation, but it betrays no hope for change. (pp. 75-6)

Now that the issues of play and dream have been addressed, let us turn our attention to the two narrative techniques that seem to be the basis for most of Cortázar's stories. Both are expressions of his conviction that pattern and predictability are the tragic and absurd essences of life. The first technique, the more apparently fantastic one, is to introduce an absurd situation and to allow it to intensify over a considerable period of narrative time until it becomes unbearable or until it simply resolves itself with the same gratuitousness as it began. Several of the more evident examples of this technique are: **"Carta a una srta. en París"**, in which the writer's enjoyment of his absentee hostess's apartment is marred by his disconcerting habit of vomiting rabbits. The growing rabbits progressively destroy the apartment and its guest finds no recourse but suicide; **"La autopista del sur"** in which a traffic jam lasts for months and fosters relationships that are hastily destroyed as soon as movement is possible; **"La salud de los enfermos"** in which elaborate lies are invented to protect a mother from the news of her son's death; **"La caricia más profunda"** about the youth slowly sinking into earth;

"Manuscrito hallado en un bolsillo" which develops from the absurd game to which we are early introduced; and **"Liliana Llorando"**, the interior monologue of a dying man's concern and scenario for his wife's happiness. The last example is especially interesting because it is an illustration of a possible happy ending that is twisted into a defeat by the protagonist. His musings on the inevitable succession of events after his death are interrupted by his doctor's almost incredulous observation of the patient's signs of recovery. Liliana's husband is struck with remorse and a need to protect her new found happiness with another man.

Because of the essential emphasis on pattern rather than on unforseen development in the stories cited above (the change in the last example only emphasizes the narrator's stubborn adherence to pattern), the reader is hardly surprised by the progress of the action since neither the situation nor the characters change qualitatively. The change is quantitative as the original absurdity mounts and as the ever-present personal traits of the protagonists become more apparent.

One cannot help imagining that Kafka's "Metamorphosis" significantly informed this mode of Cortázar's narrative. Once the almost unbelievable premise of a salesman turned cockroach is accepted, the rest follows with a ruthless and inevitable logic that traps the protagonist as well as the reader. Cortázar has learned to trap us, or more accurately, to illustrate that we are trapped in a masterful and often more subtle way. His story which most closely approximates "Metamorphosis" is **"La caricia más profunda"**.

The other mode of making pattern and predictability the central aspects of Cortázar's stories is through the protagonist's rather than the reader's consciousness of the helplessness of his own situation. It is less amusing, more disquieting technique than the first described in which the reader is an omniscient, prophetic co-author of a barely believable tale. In this second mode, the reader is often as confused, perhaps more so, than the protagonist who generally understands the absurdity of his desire to act freely.

In **"La srta. Cora"**, **"La isla a mediodía"**, **"El otro cielo"**, **"Los pasos en las huellas"**, **"Verano"**, **"Ahí, pero dónde, cómo"** and specially in **"Instrucciones para John Howell"**, the protagonists are all desperately aware of their yearning to direct their lives. They choose to act professionally, freely, honorably, conventionally or unconventionally; each case ends in disaster. The apparent freedom of choice in each tale makes the characters tragic. They attempt to base action on judgement even when circumstances rule out the efficacy of deliberation. Rice, the almost-hero of **"John Howell"** cannot escape guilt and responsibility, even though he was aware of the stakes for which he played. Again, the spectre of Kafka looms in the background. The protagonist cannot realize his resolve to understand and to save the situation; he is forced to cede the stage to an actor who will commit the decreed murder. Both are guilty, the one for allowing it, the other for committing it. But neither one could possibly have averted the action. As several critics have pointed out, Howell is Rice's *doppelgänger,* his alter ego and mirror. It should be added that the notion of double characters serves to illustrate the inescapability of fate, since situations and circumstance, not personalities, dictate action. (pp. 77-8)

Another masterful example of Cortázar's use of the *dopplegänger* to emphasize the impossibility of free will is **"Los pasos en las huellas"**. It recounts the mixed success of Julio Fraga, a poet-professor, to re-create the life of Claudio Romero, an obscure but revered Argentine poet. Fraga's affectionate and respectful biography of Romero is acclaimed by critics and by government officials who offer him glamorous international posts. The acclaim and the offers are abruptly revoked when Fraga finally admits the truth he had long suspected: the biography is false; Romero was neither noble nor self-sacrificing but an embittered opportunist and social climber. The truth never surprises Fraga as it does everyone else. He had always known it intuitively. . . . The intuition came from his self-identification with his subject, his *dopplegänger.* (p. 79)

This type of vocabulary, of presentiment and inadmissable foreknowledge links many of Cortázar's stories to each other and inevitably to a theme of imminent and ineluctable doom. Anticipation of defeat in a demythified and mundane setting is an ever-present element in Cortázar's stories as it is in the narrative of Franz Kafka. Both writers seem to be reacting against the earlier wave of European novels which José Lezama Lima characterizes as Wagnerian: novels written by Proust, Joyce, Mann, and Hesse and somehow dedicated to the power of myth, subjective time and personalized worlds. For Cortázar as for Kafka, whom Lezama Lima does not indicate as a possible inspiration, myth does not and cannot re-organize and give meaning to an absurd world. The imagination does not inform material reality and when the protagonist is deceived into thinking otherwise, he is either the object of ridicule or of pity. Practically the only forces at work in organizing our lives are the patterns and circumstances to which we have been absurdly condemned. (pp. 79-80)

Doris Sommer, "Pattern and Predictability in the Stories of Julio Cortázar," in The Contemporary Latin American Short Story, *edited by Rose S. Minc, Senda Nueva de Ediciones, Inc., 1979, pp. 71-81.*

Joyce Carol Oates   (essay date 1980)

[*Oates is an American novelist, short story writer, and critic who is perhaps best known for her novel* them *(1969) and for several novels on Gothic themes written in the 1980s. Her fiction is noted for its exhaustive presentation of realistic detail as well as its striking inventiveness, especially in the delineation of abnormal psychological states. In the following excerpt from a review of* A Change of Light, and Other Stories, *Oates commends Cortázar's technical abilities and his evocation of authentic emotions and psychological states.*]

A Change of Light is Cortázar's eighth book of fiction to appear in English, and it is in many ways a change: of tone, of manner, of style, of emphasis, of "light" itself.

Here one does not find the lush and motile openness of *Hopscotch,* or the risky, funny, ceaselessly inventive predicaments of *End of the Game* (1967). The penchant for exploring obsessions—the more futile, the more fertile for the ravenous imagination—that was a thematic undercurrent in *All Fires the Fire* (1973) is given in these 20 stories an unexpected delicacy, a surprising Jamesian dignity, by the elegiac tone of Cortázar's language and a less hurried (and more dramatic) pace.

"You who read me," one of Cortázar's typical narrator-protagonists says, "will think that I'm inventing; it doesn't matter much, for a long time now people have credited my imagination for what I've really lived or vice versa." In **"The Faces of the Medal"** the narrator Javier—a man who "doesn't know how to cry"—attempts to free himself from nightmares of loss and impotence by "writing texts that try to be like nightmares . . . but, of course, they're only texts."

Throughout *A Change of Light* one is always aware that a story, an artifact, is being created. The political context is sometimes in the foreground, sometimes an ominous assumption, but at all times we are aware of the words that constitute the story as words, for the most part judiciously chosen. "He" frequently shifts to "I" and back again to "he" and then again to "I." The narrator may suddenly announce his own befuddlement. One of the more self-consciously literary of the stories, **"Footsteps in the Footprints,"** is prefaced, not altogether unfairly, by the author's terse summary, as a "rather tedious chronicle, more in the style of an exercise than in the exercise of a style, say that of a Henry James who might have sipped maté in some Buenos Aires or Mar del Plata courtyard in the twenties"; the least satisfactory story, **"The Ferry, or Another Trip to Venice,"** written in 1954, is "revised" here in a high-spirited gesture of defiance—the author, acknowledging the story's inferiority, is nevertheless intrigued by it and cannot let it go: "I like it, and it's so bad." (Cortázar, following the possibly infelicitous examples of Nabokov, is intermittently tempted to take himself very seriously indeed—as a literary phenomenon, a cultural figure whose every utterance, "bad" or not, is of value. Or is the pomposity really playful? Are the prefaces themselves jokes? Cortázar says: "Ever since I was young I've been tempted by the idea of rewriting literary texts that have moved me but the making of which seemed to me inferior to their internal possibilities. . . . What might have been attempted [however] through love would only be received as insolent pedantry." But even the most willfully self-conscious stories, even the "bad" story, are so finely written, sentence by sentence, and the author's melancholy intelligence so evident in every line, that the actual reading of *A Change of Light* is an invariable pleasure. And the incursions of fantasy, of improbability and nightmare, do not deflect from the stories' "realist" emotional authority: Several stories in this collection have the power to move us as Kafka's stories do.

In **"Summer"** . . . the pleasurable monotonous marriage of a quite ordinary couple is interrupted, perhaps fatally, by the overnight visit of a young daughter of a friend. The girl is innocent enough, a mere child, yet she appears to be accompanied by an enormous white horse who gallops snorting around the house, a ferocious white blur, a "rabid" creature, or anyway one maddened enough to want to enter a house. The white horse has stepped magnificently out of a dream recorded in Kafka's diary for 1914 (the year of Cortázar's birth, incidentally), and in this eerie parable of ritual monotony and ritual violence he acquires a new menacing authority: "In the window the horse rubbed his head against the large pane, not too forcefully, the white blotch appeared transparent in the darkness; they sensed the horse looking inside, as though searching for something. . . . He wants to come in, Zulma said feebly." In fact the horse does not enter the house, though the little girl—accidentally or deliberately—leaves the front door open for him. But the marriage has been altered, the "new day that had nothing new about it" has been irrevocably lost. Cortázar's most sympathetic people are those who believe in compulsions (which they call rituals or games) as a response to death and nothingness—"fixing things and times, establishing rituals and passages in opposition to chaos, which was full of holes and smudges." But no ritual can accommodate the snorting white horse, or even the overnight visit of a friend's child. (p. 9)

This collection's most compelling stories are unambiguous elegies. The narrator of **"Liliana Weeping"** imagines not only his own poignant death but a future for his wife that guarantees her survival; the narrator of **"The Faces of the Medal"** addresses a woman he has loved but to whom he cannot, inexplicably, make love—

> We didn't know what to do or what else to say, we didn't even know how to be silent . . . find each other in some look. It was as if Mireille were waiting for something from Javier that he was waiting for from Mireille, a question of initiatives or priorities, of the gestures of a man and the compliance of a woman, the immutability of sequences decided by others, received from without. . . . It would have been preferable to repeat together: we lose our life because of niceties; the poet would have pardoned us if we were also talking for ourselves.

And in the volume's title story two "lovers" are victims of their own self-absorbed fantasies about love: They are real enough people, but not so real as their obsessive dreams.

There are one or two stories here that seem out of place in the volume—fairly conventional "suspense" stories that dissolve to sheer plot, despite the fastidious writing. And no story is so irresistible, so immediately engaging as the classic **"Axolotl"** of *End of the Game*—my favorite Cortázar tale. But the risks of psychological realism, of genuine emotion, of the evocation of human beings enmeshed in plausible cobwebs of friendship and enmity make this volume all the more valuable. "I know that what I'm writing can't be written," one of Cortázar's narrators says in despair, and in any case, as the unhappy protagonist of **"Footsteps in the Footprints"** learns, one is always writing autobiography, however disguised; and the autobiography is always distorted. Perhaps writing is "social revenge" of a sort? Or an attempt, necessarily doomed, to compensate for the fact that one doesn't know how to cry? Nevertheless the writing is triumphant, and Cortázar's text survives tears or the lack of tears. It transcends both game and ritual to become art. (pp. 34-5)

> *Joyce Carol Oates, "Triumphant Tales of Obsession," in* The New York Times Book Review, *November 9, 1980, pp. 9, 34-5.*

Lois Parkinson Zamora   (essay date 1981)

[*In the excerpt below, Zamora analyzes multilayered spatial structures in Cortázar's short fiction, focusing on stories that feature artist-protagonists and illustrate the perception of language as an inadequate and even deceptive mode to express reality.*]

Spanish American writers have, over the past thirty years or so, produced a remarkable number of novels and short stories that are technically innovative in the most radical sense: in one work after another, there seems to exist an observable struggle to destroy the linear, stable, enclosed structures of traditional narration and to replace them with structures that can express the relativity, the mobility, the multiplicity of twentieth-century reality. (p. 45)

For Cortázar, the artist's responsibility—and compulsion—is to transcend limits, to cause *"una explosión que abre de par en par una realidad mucho más amplia"* ("an explosion that opens wide a much larger reality"). From his earliest work, *Los reyes* (*The Kings,* 1949), to his most recent fiction, **Queremos tanto a Glenda** (**We Love Glenda So Much,** 1980), Cortázar assaults the limitations of conventional modes of perception with spatial narrative structures. *Los reyes,* a series of dialogues (a "dramatic poem," as Cortázar calls it) explores the myth of Theseus, the Minotaur, and their labyrinthine activities. The labyrinth, which encompasses every spatial possibility and thus symbolizes for writers as different as Jorge Luis Borges, Alain Robbe-Grillet and John Barth the complexity and the relativity of our own contemporary experience, allows Cortázar to explore the shifting designs of reality. Ariadne speaks for Cortázar, and modern man: *"La entrada es lisa y fácil. Cuántas veces he llegado al punto en que la galería principal empieza a girar, a proponer el engaño sutilísimo"* ("The entrance is smooth and easy. How many times have I arrived at the point when the main passageway begins to turn, to deceive ever so subtly"). The labyrinth provides in this work both metaphor and method, symbol and structure, for Cortázar's spatial art.

Many of Cortázar's stories move back and forth through time and space, constantly juxtaposing—and superimposing—planes of experience. Temporal structure is not sequential but layered and unstable, the primitive world coexisting with our contemporary "civilized" world: narrative perspectives shift subtly between the chronological present and the timeless past which inhabits that present simultaneously. So subtle is the shift from one realm to the other that the reader often does not even perceive the discontinuity, and this is exactly Cortázar's aim: the realms exist simultaneously. **"Todos los fuegos el fuego,"** for example, juxtaposes the ancient ritual of gladiatorial combat to a contemporary conflict, a verbal battle between a woman and her cruel lover: both situations end with the expiatory death of the victim and the retributive death of the evil characters by the avenging force of fire, a force that levels the spatial and temporal distinctions between the two events. The title of the story suggests the symbolic fusion of various temporal and spatial levels by means of the annealing force of fire. In **"La noche boca arriba,"** a delirious man moves uncontrollably back and forth, upward and downward through time: the narration moves not only between past and present but between the conscious mind and the depths of the unconscious. Using imagery of light and darkness to suggest shifts in temporal and psychic perspectives, Cortázar encompasses temporal and spatial multiplicity in the structure of a single sen-

tence: the character exists at once in his modern hospital room and in an ancient cave among Aztec enemies. . . .

> He made one last effort, he sketched a gesture toward the bottle of water with his good hand and did not manage to reach it, his fingers closed again on a black emptiness, and the passageway went on endlessly, rock after rock, with momentary ruddy flares, and face up he choked out a dull moan because the roof was about to end, it rose, was opening like a mouth of shadow, and the acolytes straightened up, and from on high a waning moon fell on a face whose eyes wanted not to see it, were closing and opening desperately, trying to pass to the other side, to find again the bare, protecting ceiling of the ward.

The perfectly plain language of this sentence belies its synchronic complexity, undermining temporal linearity even as it moves inexorably through its temporal medium. The portrayal of objects gives way to the portrayal of perception, the bottle becoming a black emptiness, the hospital corridor a subterranean passage hewn out of dripping rock, the ceiling light a waning moon. The story ends with the coincidence of past and present, dream and reality, life and death.

Cortázar's evident Jungian orientation in these stories is perfectly consonant with his literary spatialism, for Jung's work with the subconscious levels of the mind made psychic time and space relative phenomena, just as Einstein had made physical time and space relative. In fact, Jung himself connected his own work on psychological synchronicity to physics, citing Einstein as his inspiration. . . . (pp. 46-8)

"Axolotl" is the most economically realized and the most startling of Cortázar's renditions of psychological synchronicity. In a few sentences, human reality converges on—and is subsumed by—the primordial world of the fish-like larva, axolotl; indeed, simultaneous levels of existence are suggested by the word axolotl, which means "two lives" in Nahuatl. The protagonist of the story, who sees the axolotls from the outside of an aquarium glass, soon finds that he has adopted their perspective and is looking through the glass of the aquarium from the inside. It is the ancient animals' desire "to abolish time and space" that magnetizes the man, drawing him involuntarily into their realm. Cortázar stresses the eyes of the axolotl, the *manera de ver* which the man-turned-fish assumes: their golden eyes, without irises, pupils or lids, devour the man outside the aquarium *"en un canibalismo de oro"* "in a cannibalism of gold"). As an axolotl, the mind that was only a moment ago on the other side of the glass realizes that he is incapable of communication, limited as he is to the "golden splendor" of his eyes. Experiencing the isolation inherent in the utterly unique point of view of the single pair of eyes even as he remembers another life, the protagonist, "an axolotl for good now," understands that in a world of spatial relativity, every perspective is by definition unique, irreducibly separate. Not only language but perception itself seems tragically limited. Nevertheless, the story ends with a reference to the possibility, however tenuous, that the narrative power of the storyteller might overcome the ontological isolation of the perceiving consciousness. The axolotl refers to the man whose point of view he used to occupy: *"Y en esta soledad final, a la que él no vuelve, me consuela pensar que acaso va a escribir sobre nosotros, creyendo imaginar un cuento va a escribir todo esto sobre los axolotl"* ("And in this final solitude to which he no longer comes, I console myself by thinking that perhaps he is going to write a story about us, that, believing he's making up a story, he's going to write all this about axolotls"). The narrator, imprisoned behind the aquarium glass which because it is transparent gives the illusion of spatial freedom but which crowds and confines nonetheless, expresses his hope that the language of art will free the self from bondage.

"Las babas del diablo," in turn, exposes the difficulties of embodying the spatial relativity of reality in either words or pictures, narration or photography. The relationship of the artist to the art object, the narrator to his experience, the photographer to his pictures, and ultimately the reader to the fiction are the subjects of Cortázar's story. The opening paragraph presents the difficulty of telling, of finding points of view or verb tenses or personal pronouns adequate to describe reality. . . .

> It'll never be known how this has to be told, in the first person or in the second, using the third person plural or continually inventing modes that will serve for nothing. If one might say: I will see the moon rose, or: we hurt me at the back of the eyes, and especially: you the blond woman was the clouds that race before my your his our yours their faces. What the hell.

Roberto Michel, translator and photographer, in fact never does settle on one stable narrative angle, but constantly shifts from a limited, first person point of view to an omniscient third person point of view: even within the third person narrative segments, parenthetical first person observations intrude, usually present tense observations within the past tense retrospective account. The spatially-structured narration juxtaposes fragments of time and space that are discontinuous and dissonant. With each shift of person and tense, the reader must adjust his relationships to the narration: when the initial "I" in the present tense fades into the "I" of the past tense description, the reader is placed in the odd position of having to serve as replacement for the initial first person narrator, of having to identify with the "author" of the account. As the narrative perspective shifts abruptly in tense and person, changing the relationship of the teller to the tale—as Roberto tries to distance himself from himself with words— so the reader must alter his own relationship to the story. The unsettling effect on the reader of the rejection of discursive, linear narration accurately reflects the unsettled quality of Roberto's mind.

Spatial relativity is thematic as well as structural in this story, for Roberto the photographer has no easier time finding a suitable artistic stance than does Roberto the storyteller. He carries a Contax camera, and it is indeed his contact with reality. He is rarely without it, for he says that it teaches one to be a good observer. Perhaps; but he begins to reveal his psychological dependence on the camera as he insists upon its value as a means of ordering and framing reality for him. In fact the lens, with the stable, enclosed reality which it creates, protects him from the open and relative spatial reality which his eyes perceive. Though he insists that he can see reality without a frame around it if he has to, in fact he relies completely on his camera to compose, freeze and frame what would other-

wise be "the keynote of distraction, the sight without a frame around it, light without the diaphragm aperture of 1/250 sec." Roberto goes out with his camera one windy November afternoon, confident that he will be able to take a photo that will "catch the revealing expression, one that would sum it all up. . . ." By the end of the story, Roberto and the reader realize that his photograph, which takes "time in cross section" and fixes space within a frame, is not at all satisfactory.

The scene upon which Roberto stumbles and which he decides to photograph is composed of an adolescent youth and an older, attractive woman; with supercilious amusement and detachment, Roberto is sure that he understands the illicit but commonplace nature of their incipient relationship. He complacently imagines "possible endings," "sets the scene," and feels "that malicious sensation of waiting for everything to happen." A passive voyeur behind his camera lens, he considers the spatial arrangement of his framed perspective and decides to shoot. . . . After Roberto takes his photograph, the boy runs in terror; the woman and a man, who has been sitting in the black car which Roberto has excluded from his frame, angrily approach Michel and demand his film. He refuses, and returns to his room, forgetting the incident until several days later.

Roberto develops the photograph of the scene, and begins to suspect that his little capsule of time and space may be

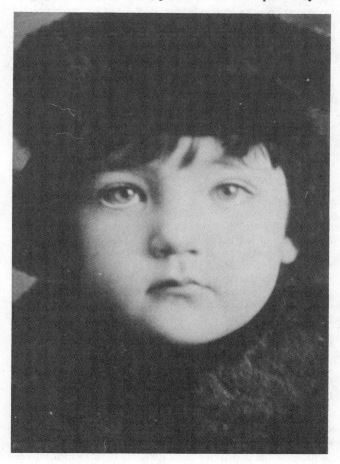

Cortázar at age two in Switzerland.

inadequate to reveal the truth about the three people his lens has recorded. He wants desperately to see beyond the surface of the photograph, beyond its single viewpoint, beyond the single angle of the shot. He realizes that he cannot be "only the lens of my camera, something fixed, rigid, incapable of intervention," an "impotent eye": he thus begins to expand the space of the photograph, to destroy the spatial limitations of the framed artifact in an attempt to escape from behind the ideal eye of the camera. He transcends his simple, stable point of view by blowing up—expanding and exploding—his enclosed, static version of reality. So intense is his desire to multiply his perspectives—to incorporate spatial and temporal relativity into his art—that the artifact is loosed from its temporal as well as its spatial stasis; temporal expansion becomes another dimension of spatial expansion; the photograph becomes a movie. Roberto is no longer a voyeur but a voyant, not passive but active. He understands that it is the *man* for whom the boy is intended, and that he must enter into the reality which the blow-up has revealed, and act.

The photograph expands—spatially and temporally—to include Roberto himself. He possesses his vision, but he is possessed by it as well. He realizes that he is the victim as well as the creator of his spatial structure, his blow-up. . . . He confronts the man, and in Christ-like fashion, becomes an expiatory figure, receiving the blow meant for the boy, allowing him to escape to "his precarious paradise." For at least a moment, artistic desire and artistic expression coincide: the attempt of Roberto's photograph, like much modern art—to present a moment that transcends our usual perception of time and space with its multiplicity of perspectives—is successful. (pp. 48-51)

"Las babas del diablo" is thus a consideration of the spatial relation of the artist to the art object, of point of view. In fact, we might consider Roberto's experience with his photograph to be a paradigm of the development of point of view in Western art since Giotto, as that development is set forth by Ortega y Gasset in "La Doctrina del Punto de Vista." Ortega traces the progression of the subject matter in paintings from things to sensations to ideas, and the progression of point of view from the external fixed location of the Renaissance artist, whose gaze penetrates the concave space between his eye and the horizon of the picture, to the subjective interior location within the consciousness of the modern artist. Thus, we might say that the history of art is the history of the *spatial* relationship between the object and the painter: the object has moved progressively closer to the painter's point of view until, with the Cubists and Surrealists it has moved inside his mind. Now, instead of putting himself outside of himself onto the canvas, the painter—and the viewer—have to do the opposite, to move into the mind. The eyes, instead of absorbing external phenomena, project the landscape of the mind onto the canvas.

Roberto begins like a Renaissance artist, concerning himself with the weight, texture and arrangement of the objects in his field of vision, giving each object equal importance in terms of perspective. After he blows up his photograph, he might be said to have an Impressionist moment, for he sees his photograph as the Impressionists portrayed objects: out of the corner of his eye, all surface, no point of focus at the depth of the picture. He berates himself because "it had never occurred to me that when we look at

a photo from the front, the eyes reproduce exactly the position and the vision of the lens . . . then it occurred to me that I had hung it exactly at the point of view of the lens." He moves to the side of his blow-up, thinking that a diagonal or lateral view "might even divulge different aspects." And like the Impressionists, he begins to invest his photograph with emotion, realizing the sensations inherent in his art. Then, in cubist or surrealist fashion, he abolishes altogether the frame of his art, destroying the boundaries between art and actuality, between object and subject: he moves, step by step, *into* his art and *beyond* it. . . . [Roberto] fractures the solid, framed, factual world of photography by studying its relation to consciousness: his spatial expansion projects the landscape of his mind, moving through space, suggesting the irreconcilable contradiction between real space and its illusionistic representation.

Roberto's blow-up, his expansion of reality, cannot be maintained, for his unbounded vision is not accompanied with unbounded powers of expression. The visual language of his blow-up, like the verbal language with which he struggles at his typewriter, is inadequate. As he opens his eyes after his terrifying participation in the expanded space of the blow-up, he sees only framed clouds and sky, "a very clean, clear rectangle tacked up with pins on the wall of my room." Ironically, all of reality is once again rigidly framed, even the constantly changing and ephemeral clouds. This frame, however, is a very different one from the kind which he so casually imposed upon reality by photographing it. Like the aquarium glass in **"Axolotl,"** the window is not an opening onto the world: Roberto's window does not carry him beyond the confined space of his room, but on the contrary, completes that confinement. The window, like Roberto's blow-up, is an unreal landscape, an artifice of the mind, offering no alternate or external reality even though it sustains the illusion of escape into a space beyond the self. Roberto understands to his dismay that reality is a prison we build ourselves, adding windows, like freedoms, when the claustrophobia threatens to overcome us; it is this recognition, not the events of the November afternoon *per se,* that so disturbs Roberto. (pp. 51-2)

In **"Las babas del diablo,"** structural irony reinforces the irony of the tacked up sky: this story about the momentary transcending of the rigidly framed artifact is itself a rigidly framed artifact. Just as Roberto sees the sky and the clouds within the parameters of his own window frame, so too he frames his story with literary definitions and disclaimers. He composes his verbal account of the November afternoon in the way he composed his picture on that same afternoon, fencing it off where it cannot expand in the unwonted fashion of his blow-up; it has been, after all, an unsettling enterprise, this destruction of the frame around his art by the expansion of spatial perspectives, this attempt to possess the world around him through the forms he has created. That Roberto fails to maintain his unbounded vision does not invalidate that vision, however, for it is continual aspiration rather than the finality of achievement which characterizes Cortázar's spatial esthetic. Cortázar's artist reminds us that human existence involves bondage within the mind's cage . . . , but that the artistic assault upon that cage, however short-lived, is necessary to sustain our fictions of freedom and our belief in worlds beyond the mind's enclosure.

The artist in **"El perseguidor"** is a jazz saxophonist, and it is with music, rather than pictures or words, that he attempts to open up the vast possibilities of time and space which he intuits. Johnny Carter, unlike Roberto Michel, does not begin with the misconception that art can—and should—stabilize and enclose the shifting perspectives of spatial reality. Nor does he make the mistake of assuming, as do Roberto and the narrator in **"Axolotl,"** that experience is ultimately recuperable in words. In fact, to his biographer, Bruno, Johnny says in his inarticulate but emphatic fashion that he hates words and hints at the "obscenity" of writing about it. It is jazz which provides for Johnny a means of transcending the limitations of time and space, the limitations of his single point of view, a means of freeing himself from the rational, logical, analytical tendency of Western thought. Johnny seeks to synthesize rather than analyze: he aims to transcend static form, to use the chaos of human experience as the substance of his vision. He conceives of art as created *from,* not *in spite of,* chaos. He is constantly aware of the creative work that the individual must perform within himself in order to find the *huecos* (holes), as he puts it, through which to project the spatial structure of his art.

The esthetic movement of Johnny's art is described in spatial terms: its motion is centrifugal, spinning upward and outward, sending flying fragments into space. His best music is produced in a dream-like state which is referred to as a spin: his style is *"como una explosión de la música . . . la costra de la costumbre se rajó en millones de pedazos"* ("like an explosion in music . . . the crust of habit splintered into a million pieces"). And this spatial expansion—another blow-up—seems limitless. . . . It is appropriate that jazz should be Johnny's artistic medium, for jazz is based not only on melodic sequence and synchronized rhythmic patterns, as is most classical and popular music, but on syncopation and superimposition of conflicting rhythms. Syncopation is the alteration of regular rhythm by placing the strongest emphasis on beats which are not usually accented: the rhythmic pulse that would normally be accented is not, and instead a counter-rhythm is established which upsets the listener's expectations. Syncopation thus distorts regular temporal progression, and deviates from standard sequential movement. The superimposition of conflicting rhythms, which is called polyrhythm, usually consists of simultaneously played phrases of different lengths: the superimposition of a three-beat rhythm on a four-beat rhythm is not unusual. . . . Thus, jazz creates a constantly changing structure of rhythmic relationships as one rhythmic strand is superimposed upon another. Furthermore, these rhythms are usually improvised so that spontaneous change is inherent in every performance. As with spatial structure in fiction, jazz structure depends on the apprehension of many unstable elements simultaneously. Johnny's desire to transcend linear time and sequential logic is possible through the improvised rhythmic montage of jazz.

The epigraphs of **"El perseguidor"** further reveal Johnny's spatial esthetic. The first epigraph is from the Revelation of John the Divine, II:x: *"Sé fiel hasta la muerte"* ("Be thou faithful unto death"). Johnny lives in the presence of death, dreaming of walking the cemeteries of the earth and finding burial urns in the fields. He renounces the limitations of death as he does the limitation of time and space,

considering death not an end but a metamorphosis, a means of regeneration. He has attempted suicide several times and knows that his drug addiction is slow death. Johnny rejects the notion of life which is opposed to death, of life which moves sequentially toward a given end; he embraces instead the intimations of eternity, the moments of mystic communion with the universe which his art provides. Through his music, Johnny attempts to embrace all things in their totality, to reveal a world beyond the reach of rational analysis, a world seen through the intuitive powers of the mind.

The epigraph is not the only reference to Revelation: Johnny refers to himself in terms of John's imagery, which describes one of the seven trumpet woes: *"El nombre de la estrella es Ajenjo"* ("The name of the star is called Wormwood"). Wormwood, or absinthe, is associated with bitterness and drunkenness: the star, "burning as it were a lamp," falls into the rivers and fountains, and "many men died of the waters." In apocalyptic writings, angels and stars are often linked: in this case, the star—an angelic being—unlocks the fearful judgment but remains under the control of God. Mixing his verb tenses as did Roberto Michel, Johnny identifies both with the victims of the star and with the star itself. . . . (pp. 53-5)

Like D. H. Lawrence, Johnny understands the imaginative power of the astrology in Revelation, the imaginative infusion of its symbols into his perception of space. As opposed to scientific astronomical space, where man can only move, Lawrence observed, "In the astrological heavens, that is to say, the ancient zodiacal heavens, the whole man is set free, once the imagination crosses the border"; to enter the astrological sky is to enter another world, measured by another spatial dimension, where "some prisoned self in us" emerges, where the self becomes "big and glittering and vast with a sumptuous vastness," and can say without hesitation, "I am the macrocosm." Such a comprehensive spatial vision is the source and focus of Johnny's esthetic impulse.

The affinity of the musician for myth is perhaps more completely understood in the general terms suggested by Claude Lévi-Strauss in his "Overture" to *Le cru et le cuit.* Here Lévi-Strauss compares the temporal structures of myth and music, asserting that both are languages which transcend articulate expression and yet require, like articulate speech, a temporal dimension in which to unfold. . . . Myth, like music, exists in tension between historical, enacted time and a "permanent constant" realm, between external, serial time and internal psycho-physiological time. This contradictory temporality of myth in general is heightened by Cortázar's particular choice of myth for his musician: apocalypse is after all a myth about history, about the movement of time toward its end—when, in the words of John of Patmos, "time shall cease."

The second epigraph of this story is Dylan Thomas' phrase: "O make me a mask." Johnny refers several times to Dylan Thomas in the story, and to his own search for a mask. A mask is necessary to accomplish Johnny's desire to transcend his single point in time, for Johnny believes that the artist must use his medium, not his individual personality, to create significant art. The mask which Johnny seeks will allow him to abandon his individualized and hence limited point of view, to extend his consciousness into space and surrender himself to the cosmos. Describing this phenomenon of esthetic impersonality, Leslie Fiedler observes: "In the mask of his life and the manifold masks of his work, the [artist] expresses for a whole society the ritual meaning of its inarticulate selves; the artist goes forth not to 'recreate the conscience of his race,' but to redeem its unconscious. We cannot get back into the primal garden of the unfallen Archetypes, but we can yield ourselves to the dreams and images that mean paradise regained." It is the self-effacement of the artist, his manifold masks, that allows Johnny to say with Lawrence, "I am the macrocosm."

There is in this story, as in **"Las babas del diablo,"** an overwhelming structural irony. The story is narrated by Bruno, a jazz critic whose reputation rests on a definitive verbal analysis of Johnny's jazz style, which he has just published. He is terrified that Johnny will say or do something to discredit his analysis, that he will "deny all the esthetic bases on which I've built the ultimate structure of his music." The critic wants to make controllable closed structures of both Johnny's life and art. Ironically, like Johnny, he is interested in death, not because it will open up possibilities but because it will close them off. He hopes Johnny will die so that his analysis will not be threatened by the change of interest in Johnny's art. . . . Thus, **"El perseguidor"** is not itself a spatial structure *per se,* for multiplicity and fluidity are threats to the narrator's analytic control; rather, spatial structure is treated thematically in the description of Johnny's esthetic medium and aspirations and in the simultaneous development of two opposing characters and two opposing attitudes toward the language of art.

As in **"Las babas del diablo,"** the artist's spatial structure is not tenable for long in a society where reason, rather than passionate transcendence, is the rule. The art critic, the voyeur, easily outlasts Johnny, the voyant. Johnny dies, the book on Johnny's art is published and receives great popular acclaim. Although the critic tells us he is sure that Johnny will continue searching after death, he is delighted not to have to attempt to understand that search: the story ends with the critic's proud statement that because of the immense success of his "ultimate analysis," he is already considering a new translation, into Swedish or Norwegian. . . . Johnny is justified in calling Bruno's language "filthy," but that his objections to language must themselves be expressed in words—with which he struggles ineptly—signals the futility of his protest. Cortázar thus seems to suggest that language is the artistic medium most likely to betray rather than render reality. Roberto Michel, in **"Las babas del diablo,"** is ultimately incarcerated at his typewriter, just as Johnny will inevitably be fixed within the frame of his biographer's dicta. As Wittgenstein considered his whole philosophy a battle against the bewitchment of intelligence by language, so these stories indicate that just such battle is the *sine qua non* of all true artistic expression. (pp. 55-7)

The fiction which I have discussed here is the product of an imagination which endows space with meaning, subjectively in the experience of everyday life and objectively in the esthetic structures which transform that experience into art. Cortázar's artist-protagonists occupy a single epistemological stance: each feels imprisoned within a hostile environment which he seeks to transcend by imagi-

native flight. Escape depends upon the mind's mediation, which promises to transform time and place into a timeless, limitless realm. The artist's vision, however, requires language, whether words or another artistic vocabulary, and language, when required to express the inexpressible, inevitably falls short, for it can evoke such a realm only in images which are temporal and in forms which are of necessity limited and specific. Thus, Roberto's animated blow-up becomes a self-reflexive window, Johnny's music is reduced to his critic's verbal summary. . . . By means of these characters and their experiences, Cortázar integrates into his fiction a rhetoric of self criticism, a commentary on the problematic endeavor of creating spatial structures in a time-bound world. In his characters' failures, Cortázar demonstrates his awareness of the limitations as well as the possibilities of the artist's shaping mind. These works serve not only as luminous examples of spatial structure but also as reminders that such structures lead back to a world of language where bondage is the rule, artistic transcendence the all too rare exception.

Cortázar's spatial structures challenge the limitations of his readers as well as of his linguistic medium. Roland Barthes suggests the nature of the challenge in his discussion of "readable" literature and "writeable" literature. "Readable" literature requires only a passive reader, for it is fixed in its context, and closed off within its frame. "Writeable" literature, on the other hand, requires an active perceiver, for its structure contains multiple perspectives, various semiotic strata, and allows for diverse and often divergent approaches: "writeable" texts necessarily resist definitive interpretation because they remain unfinished, awaiting re-writing with each re-reading. Certainly Cortázar's texts are "writeable" in these terms, for they resist clarification and defy definitive explication, offering themselves as examples of engagement with experience in its own right. The emphasis is always on the materials and processes of making rather than on the representation of character or situation, and that emphasis on creative activity extends into the reader's realm as well. Spatial structures, which aim to destroy the limitations of convention and to expand into the open realm of the "writeable" text, are indispensable to us in our attempt to understand the very relative nature of our location in space and time. (pp. 65-6)

Lois Parkinson Zamora, "Voyeur/Voyant: Julio Cortázar's Spatial Esthetic," in Mosaic: A Journal for the Interdisciplinary Study of Literature, *Vol. XIV, No. 4, Fall, 1981, pp. 45-68.*

Jaime Alazraki   (essay date 1983)

[*Alazraki is an Argentine-born American critic and educator who, in addition to writing several studies on Argentine author Jorge Luis Borges, has edited* The Final Island: The Fiction of Julio Cortázar *(1977), a collection of critical essays. Alazraki has stated that his emphasis in critical analysis is on form and that form is "the true realization of theme." In the following excerpt, Alazraki surveys developmental changes in Cortázar's short fiction despite similar subject matter and motifs in many short stories.*]

In [*We Love Glenda So Much*], one can recognize themes

and motifs found in previous collections. **"Orientation of Cats"** brings to mind Cortázar's fondness of cats purring and pawing throughout his writings. **"'We Love Glenda So Much"** reenacts the paroxismal admiration for an artist that borders on the collective hysteria treated earlier in **"The Maenads."** The unexpected twist that closes **"Story with Spiders"** reminds one of a similar situation and ending in **"Condemned Door."** Cortázar's attraction to subways as the scene of bizarre encounters and dramas, previously explored in **"Throat of a Black Kitten"** and **"Manuscript Found in a Pocket,"** is once again probed in **"Text in a Notebook."** **"Press Clippings"** deals with violence in terms reminiscent of his famous story **"Blow-Up."** His penchant for plots about triangular relationships—most memorably treated in **"The Idol of the Cyclades," "The Motive,"** and **"All Fires the Fire"**—is evinced here in **"Return Trip Tango."** The exquisite structure of **"Clone,"** based on that of Bach's *Musical Offering,* reveals a close affinity with *Hopscotch*'s intricate patterning, and at the level of theme, it restates Cortázar's fascination for groups as the framework of his novels: all of them resort to this constellational coterie for the development of situations and characters. **"Stories I Tell Myself"** pivots around that twilight zone where reality yields to dream, so characteristic of a good segment of his short fiction and so brilliantly captured in **"The Night Face Up."** **"Moebius Strip"** is more a motif than a "state of mind": Cortázar's intuition of an uncharted order where opposites coalesce and harmony follows.

That a writer writes and rewrites those few obsessions that form the backbone of his/her creation is neither new nor uncommon. One begins to be suspicious of a writer whose range of themes is unlimited since what determines the limits to his craft is the same limitation that underlies his human experience. . . . If a subject is too complex, it requires by necessity not one but several formulations, as if its intensity overflows the capacity of a single version and calls for new ones. Successive variations on a given theme aim at capturing new angles of the same face. If **"Blow-Up"** is an exploration of evil and violence, **"Press Clippings"** ventures into the same area, but the difference in treatment between the first story and the second is the same difference that separates Cortázar's art when he wrote *End of the Game* in 1959 and this last collection twenty years later.

Cortázar's handling of the short story has gone a long way. Although the stories of his first collection—*Bestiary* (1951)—display a rare perfection for an author who was making his first strides in the genre, his subsequent collections have been a relentless endeavor to push the medium's power to its utmost limits. Cortázar has refused to capitalize on what he calls, quoting Gide, the acquired "élan." Instead of relying on previous success, he has sought new roads, new challenges, new peaks to climb, reaching unsuspected heights. Since his beginning as a writer, he distrusted realism. He felt that realism and reality had little to do with each other. Realism had to do with convention, with an accepted code that acted as a surrogate of reality. One may say that all art forms are conventions seeking to represent reality; realism, on the other hand, posed as the embodiment of reality. Cortázar endorsed, instead, a motto written on one of Artaud's drawings: "Jamais réel et toujours vrai." He was subscribing, of course, to the surrealist effort "to discover and explore

the more real than real world behind the real." But if he recognized in its philosophy his own outlook on art, he never joined the verbal experimentalism of its magus and iconoclasts. His stories invariably present a world we recognize as our own, a world that seemingly does not depart from that of realism: the same routines, duties, ceremonies and institutionalized games; the same problems and situations, stereotypes and conflicts. Yet, his stories do not point at those surfaces we associate with realism, but rather at cracking them, at forcing them to yield to a hidden face. It is as if we mistakenly took the mask for the face, and the story proceeds to subtly remove that mask so that for a fleeting second the true face can be glimpsed. Another way to describe his approach is contained in a passage from Clarice Lispector's *Close to the Savage Heart* quoted as the epigraph for **"Moebius Strip"**: "Impossible to explain. She was leaving that zone where things have a fixed form and edges, where everything has a solid and immutable name. She was sinking deeper and deeper into the liquid, quiet, and unfathomable region where vague and cool mists like those of morning hovered." Although the passage fits more accurately the situation of the story where it has been inserted, it is also applicable to most of his stories. Most of them struggle to explain what "is impossible to explain" by means of language's conceptualizations, simply because language deals with those surfaces we habitually identify with reality. When language faces those cracks in its own makeup, it naturally closes them in the way skin heals its wounds. Why not peep through those cracks? How to make language enter that zone where things no longer "have a fixed form and edges," to become, instead, "a liquid and unfathomable region?" That is the province where most of his stories travel to. Of course the question is *how* to get there. If language, as the master tool of reason, has constructed the world we inhabit, it follows that to abandon the logic of language entails abandoning also the logic of our world. Confronted with this alternative, Cortázar broke with surrealism. In *Hopscotch,* one of the characters retorts: "The surrealists hung from words instead of brutally disengaging themselves from them. . . . Language means residence in reality, living in a reality. Even if it's true that the language we use betrays us, wanting to free it from its taboos isn't enough. We have to relive it, not reanimate it." Reliving language meant for him what it has always meant to literary art: converting the signs of its code into means of expression of a new code, that of literature. A notion or situation inconceivable in the language of communication—a person turned into an insect—becomes possible through the language of fiction. Fiction speaks where language remains silent. Furthermore, fiction dares to enter that *region* which is out of language's reach: a space irreducible to physical scales, a time outside the clock's domain, emotions not yet recorded in psychology manuals.

To explore that region, Cortázar resorted first to a fantastic event (a man who vomits rabbits, noises that evict homeowners from their house, a tiger roaming freely through the rooms of a middle-class home, etc.). I am referring to the stories collected in *Bestiary.* In all of them, the conflict presented through their plots comes to a resolution by means of this fantastic "crack" on the realist surface of the story. This is far from being fantastic fiction as understood in the nineteenth century, since their ultimate effect is not to assault the reader with those fears and horrors that have been defined as the attributes of the fantastic. In addition, the technique of mounting suspense gradually leading to a sudden break in our rational order—someone dead who is alive—characteristic of the fantastic tale, does not operate here. Instead, the fantastic event can appear at the very beginning of the story, purporting not to frighten or horrify the reader but rather to offer a metaphor. A metaphor is a sign, or group of signs, that stands for a meaning other than the normative one represented in that sign. The rabbits vomited by the character in **"Letter to a Young Lady in Paris"** stand for something else, pointing to a tenor contextualized in the story but never quite named or openly disclosed. Metaphors assist the poet in naming what conventional language cannot name, at least not quite in the same way. For Cortázar, these stories were a form of describing those perceptions which, coming from "an unfathomable region," defy conventional language. Their irrational images transcend realism to explore a territory loosely labeled as the fantastic.

Without totally abandoning this literary artifice, most of the stories in his next collection—*End of the Game* (1956)—respond to a different narrative strategy. The fantastic element reappears in the form of a classical Greek myth—**"The Maenads"** and **"The Idol of the Cyclades"**—through a metamorphosis of sorts (**"Axolotl"**), or by means of an unyielding silence (**"After Lunch"**), but the rest of them abandoned altogether the weird side manifested in the fantastic break. Not that the fantastic ceases to act in these stories; it does act, but in a different way. We have no longer uncanny metaphors, as in the first collection. The fantastic dimension of the story must be sought now at the level of its organization; not so much in its theme as in the way that theme has been treated. In each one of these stories there are two stories that have been craftily integrated. In **"Continuity of Parks,"** one story deals with an estate owner, and the other with two lovers plotting to murder the estate owner. In **"The River,"** there is a narrative about a middle-class couple and a second one about the wife's suicide. In **"After Dinner,"** there are two juxtaposed versions as to what happened during a friends' reunion. A similar juxtaposition of two versions of the same event occurs in **"The Friends."** There is a third juxtaposition; yet in **"The Motive,"** one triangular love affair, which ends in a killing, is understood and solved in the context of a second mirroring triangle. In **"Axolotl,"** the narrator's vision of the axolotl overlaps the axolotl's vision of the narrator. **"End of the Game"** has also this contrapuntal quality: the perception three girls have of an outsider collides with the outsider's perception of the three girls. This technique attains to virtuosity in **"The Night Face Up"** where the story of a motorcycle accident interlocks with the story of a Moteca Indian sacrificed by the Aztecs.

If there is a fantastic side to these stories, it does not depend on any fantastic event, but rather on the way the two stories or points of view have been amalgamated. There is nothing uncunning or particularly disturbing in each of the two stories if they are taken separately. But by coupling them in one single narrative where one bears a close adjacency with the other, the two stories can generate a meaning absent in each of the two individually. It goes without saying that braiding the two stories is not a haphazard or mechanical operation. It is precisely in this interweaving where Cortázar's art lies. By creating a net of intrinsic interrelations between the two stories, he has

forced them to say something denied to each one in isolation. There is nothing appealing or appalling in the story of a motorcyclist having an accident, being rushed to a hospital, and undergoing surgery. Nor is there anything unusual in the second story of a Moteca Indian fleeing hunting Aztecs during the "war of the blossom" and brought finally to a pyramid's altar to be sacrificed. Both stories are narrated in that compelling and liquid style that has become Cortázar's trademark, but what makes the story a narrative feat is the masterful articulation of the two stories in a single structure. By cunningly presenting the second story as a dream of the character in the first story, and by gradually reversing the condition of dream from the second to the first character, this short story achieves a magic that challenges causality. Its impact lies somewhere between the two stories: in that space or interstice that their interlacing has created. The fantastic aura that the story may have stems from that point of intersection where one tale is cleverly linked with the other: what was a dream becomes reality and what was reality becomes a dream. For the motorcyclist, the sacrificed Indian is a dream caused by his own delirium after the accident; for the Moteca Indian, the motorcyclist and his accident in a Paris street is a dream caused by his own delirium before the Aztec priest lowers his arm with a stone knife in his hand to open his chest. We readers shall never know who is the dream and who is the dreamer. There is here a reverberation of that old piece of wisdom uttered by Shakespeare—"Life is a dream." There is also an echo of that dilemma that has troubled generations of Chinese readers: Was it Chuang Tzu who dreamed that he was a butterfly or was he a butterfly dreaming that it was Chuang Tzu? A third reading points to the confrontation of two civilizations, one attempting to understand the other, one unfailingly appearing as a dream of the other. Jacques Soustelle expressed this idea in a lapidary and intense sentence: "The reality of one civilization is the dream of another." These interpretations and many others constitute a multiplicity of meanings embodied in the story and underline its nature of metaphor capable of manifold tenors. If in the previous collection only the fantastic event bears the metaphorical weight, in *End of the Game* the entire story has become, by virtue of its narrative organization, a metaphor. Cortázar has moved from reliance on fantastic events interpolated in the plots in *Bestiary,* to situations that depend no longer on *what happens* at the level of plot but on *how* the story has been structured in this second collection. In the first case, he resorted to a fantastic resolution; in the second, to a compositional solution. The second choice required, beyond any doubt, a greater skill in the handling of the genre.

In his next collection, *Las armas secretas* (*Secret Weapons*), 1959, he avoided cashing in on the accomplishments of his previous volumes. Instead, he left behind the fantastic metaphors of the first and the structural virtuosity of the second, to seek new possibilities, new questions, and new answers. Of that period, he said:

> When I wrote **"The Pursuer,"** I had reached a point where I felt I had to deal with something that was a lot closer to me. I wasn't sure of myself any more in that story. I took an existential problem, a human problem which was later amplified in *The Winners,* and above all in *Hopscotch.* Fantasy for its own sake had stopped interesting me. By then I was fully aware of the dangerous perfection of the

storyteller who reaches a certain level of achievement and stays on that same level forever, without
moving on. I was a bit sick and tired of seeing how
well my stories turned out. In **"The Pursuer"** I
wanted to stop inventing and stand on my own
ground, to look at myself a bit.

With **Secret Weapons,** Cortázar found new tones and in-
flections for his voice, new preoccupations and themes for
his fiction, and new forms of expression to tackle more effectively those new concerns. His stories became longer—
an average of 30 to 40 pages as opposed to the 3 to 10 page
story in the earlier collections—less focused on the exactly
structured plot and closer to the breadth of the novel, less
geared to situations and more concentrated on characters,
more vital and less dependent on plot. All this should suffice to prove the constant process of renovation in his art,
his tireless search for new forms and narrative modes, his
commitment to the short story as a genre capable of inexhaustible regeneration. What we have seen thus far brings
us also to the question of his most recent collection, **We
Love Glenda So Much,** and to its place in Cortázar's production as a short-story teller.

A good point of departure is his view of the short story
as a sister genre to poetry. In an essay devoted to the former and included in his book-collage **Ultimo round (Last
Round,** 1969), he stated that "there is no genetic difference
between the brief short story and poetry as we understand
it since Baudelaire." . . . Cortázar alludes to the nature
of literary artifact of the short story or poem: autonomous
and precise organisms capable of breathing on their own,
and of communicating their charge of experience thanks
to their sensitive and delicate machinery. The narratives
of this new collection share with earlier ones the same effort addressed to capturing an experience or perception or
feeling incommunicable by means of ordinary language.
They also share the condition of extended metaphors in
the sense that while they tell a well-crafted story, they also
open in the body of the narrative a double bottom, a second meaning awaiting to be detected in the same way that
a poem offers a message that goes beyond its immediate
text. We cannot have an exact translation for the rabbits
vomited by the narrator in **"A Letter to a Young Lady in
Paris,"** just as the ultimate message conveyed by the two
merged stories in **"The Night Face Up"** escapes a single
and rigid interpretation. In the end, the reader of these stories is confronted with a silence which represents its most
powerful message. In reading them, one has the distinct
feeling that the narrative has been woven around that silence, as its habitat, as the only way of transmitting its implications and resonances. The whistling wind one hears
in the nautilus shell is not the shell, but without its spiral
shape and its air-filled chambers there would not be that
sea whistle one hears. This is not a mystic silence; it is a
literary silence similar to the one elicited by poetry, hence
the brotherhood between the two genres Cortázar referred
to. The new in the stories from **Glenda** is the way that silence has of existing. Like poems, which convey their
meaning through the interplay of images and through the
music-filled lines of their linguistic patterns, these stories
too emit messages through narrative patterns of imagery,
rhythm and fictional diction.

The first three stories have in common an elliptic quality
that accentuates their kinship with poetry. What do cats
see when their look is lost in an invisible point? What does
a woman see when she looks at the images of a painting?
How to explain that the admiration for an artist could be
so strong as to destroy the very object of admiration? Is
there a point where a rapist and his victim could have reversed their times and turned the heinous crime into a
human experience? Are dreams and reality just different
manifestations of the same substance? How to answer
these questions without falling into the traps of common
sense and correct syllogisms? What **Glenda**'s stories seek
is not to provide answers but simply to explore questions,
and they do that in the same way a piece of music explores
an emotion and a poem encodes a charged silence. Yet the
medium of fiction is not music or verse. Its task is to tell
a story, but Cortázar tells it in the way a poem exudes poetry and a musician plays music. So much so that **"Clone"**
was patterned following the model of Bach's *Musical Offering,* and **"Orientation of Cats"** reads like a prose poem.
What approximates these stories to other art forms, however, is not their dress but their substance. Powerful short
stories loyal to their medium, they share with other art
forms the same matter that becomes music at one point,
painting, at another, and poetry, at a third: messages devoid of rational meaning.

What we have said thus far might give the impression that
Glenda's stories suffer from an excessively aesthetic pro-
clivity. This will be, of course, a wrong impression. They
are, quite the opposite, deeply rooted in the most immediate experiences of everyday life, but they avoid the triteness and the stereotype of its mechanics to focus on what
we suspect lies underneath that ocean of practicalities: not
what a truck driver does, but what he dreams; not what
a cat eats or breaks, but what she sees with her eyes lost
in some invisible sight; not a rape as reported by a newspaper, but as examined from within; not the entries of a couple's diary vacationing on an island, but the only entry
omitted in that hypothetical diary. Cortázar is a wizard
of those ellusive spaces, unrecorded experiences, unmea-
surable times. The butterflies caught in his fictional net are
either rara avis or extinguished species.

At the same time, and paradoxically, he is one of the most
courageous writers to have emerged from Latin America.
He comes from a country where military torture and murder have become the only laws. Argentina under the military rule has been turned into a prison, a slaughterhouse,
a swindled, deceived and frightened nation. . . . **"Press
Clippings"** is one of the most powerful literary texts written about that form of crime that Amnesty International
has called "political killings by governments." The 30,000
people who have "disappeared" in Argentina can no longer be dismissed: they are public information. We haven't
been able yet to measure the human suffering and horrors
implied in that abstract figure. Their story is beginning to
unfold painfully. How to deal with such an explosive subject without turning literature into a political pamphlet?
How to approach this horrible tragedy without trivializing
it? How to shout the horrors and stay at the same time
within the bounds of art? Julio Cortázar has performed
this tour de force with skill, verve, and integrity. In **"Press
Clippings"** we recognize all the marks of his craft: mastery
over his medium; the exactness, vivacity, and dignity of
his language; the text folding over itself to say the unsay-
able. At the same time, he has confronted with unusual
courage not only the murderers, but also himself as a
human consciousness witnessing those murders. Should

violence be met with violence? The story's answer is neither passionate nor legalistic, neither intellectual nor rhetorical. It is an existential one that chooses to elucidate the question rather than to provide answers. The narrator is swept away by violence, and she herself falls into its vortex before she can reflect: "How could I know how long it lasted, how could I understand that I too, I too even though I thought I was on the right side, I too, how could I accept that I too there on the other side from the cut-off hands and the common graves, I too on the other side from the girls tortured and shot that same Christmas night. . . ." Facing violence, the narrator is forced to act, and yet, by acting, she falls herself into the nightmare of violence. There are no blacks and whites: white turns black and vice versa. The reader is confronted with the inevitability of violence on the face of violence: evil cannot be witnessed impassively. At the same time, reacting to violence with violence puts us on the side of the criminal. The criminal has succeeded in turning us into criminals. Human values and human rights have disappeared, force has replaced laws and institutions, the stronger destroys the weaker and the weaker seeks to defend himself with the only weapon his oppressor understands: more violence. Savagery. Jungle. People turning into beasts.

Although Cortázar does not present a clear-cut answer, in poignantly enlightening the question, he has given his reader all the insights needed for a human response. This has always been art's task: not to dictate answers but to illuminate the question, not to solve the presented problem but to unveil its ins and outs. Catharsis still remains the only answer to which art accedes. To go any further amounts to distorting it and, consequently, to its denial. Cortázar understands too well this dangerous borderline. He knows that literature's power lies not in transgressing its boundaries, but in accepting them and pushing against them until those limits become the hidden source of its own strength and the secret fulcrum of its leverage. In *We Love Glenda So Much,* he put into practice his wisdom and craftsmanship as a storyteller. These stories prove, once again, that he can break his own record. It matters not if the story ponders on what a cat sees, or if it dares to venture into the hells of political killings; if it traces a literary counterpart to Bach's *Musical Offering,* or if it depicts the city subways as our modern purgatory. In all of them we sense the hand of a master telling us what perhaps we once knew and forgot. (pp. 94-9)

> *Jaime Alazraki, "From 'Bestiary' to 'Glenda':*
> *Pushing the Short Story to its Utmost Limits,"*
> *in* the Review of Contemporary Fiction, *Vol.*
> *III, No. 3, Fall, 1983, pp. 94-99.*

Harry L. Rosser   (essay date 1983)

[*In the following excerpt, Rosser interprets Cortázar's short story "Axolotl" as symbolic of the author's concepts of biological, spiritual, and literary realities, which Rosser compares with Swiss psychologist and psychiatrist Carl Gustav Jung's theories on the development of the self.*]

Cortázar believes that human beings can change and act upon their limitless potential for self-realization, for spiritual fulfillment, for a totality of life.

Cortázar uses the word "fantastic" in defining his fiction and his own special way of understanding reality. By "fantastic" he means the alternative to what he calls "false realism" or the view that "everything can be described and explained in line with the philosophical and scientific optimism of the eighteenth century, that is, within a world governed by a system of laws, of principles, of casual relations, of well-defined psychologies, of well-mapped geographies." He has emphasized that for him there exists "the suspicion of another order, more secret and less communicable" in which the true study of reality is found in the exceptions to the laws rather than in those laws themselves. For Cortázar, the approach to this order requires a loosening of the mind in order to make it a more receptive instrument of knowledge and to stimulate authentic transformations in man. This approach is evident in many of the short stories of this imaginative non-conformist.

Of the several stories that reflect Cortázar's fascination with fantastic incursions into the rational world of the self, **"Axolotl"** most memorably portrays a transformation experience and raises questions about the nature of that experience. While the story can be read as a direct narration of novelistic events, it lends itself to elucidation on another level as well. The purpose here is to offer an interpretation of Cortázar's narrative within the context of his unusual view of reality. (p. 419)

"Axolotl" is the autobiographical account of a lonely man, Cortázar's anonymous narrator-protagonist, who frequents the city zoo and one day wanders into an aquarium where he has never been before. There he feels a peculiar attraction toward a group of translucent, rose colored *axolotls,* a species of Mexican salamander with large golden eyes. He returns day after day to be drawn into hypnotic contemplation of the fishy creatures. He senses that they are endowed with a special intelligence and project an inexplicable power which he finds irresistable. He perceives that he has some remote link with the salamanders. Time and space disappear for him in the presence of these beings belonging to a different life.

Gradually a metamorphosis takes place as the man becomes convinced that he has been transformed into one of the tranquil salamanders looking at him from inside the aquarium. He feels alarmed but also strangely comforted. He senses that his human mind is inside the body of the amphibian. At the same time he feels a oneness with the other salamanders which glide about him inside the tank. The salamander element in the man has left him to establish a separate kind of existence. The expanded ego of the narrator goes from one side of the glass to the other. The salamander is no longer simply the object of the narrator's observation, it now becomes engaged in the act of observing.

The enigmatic communication between man and salamander, it becomes clear, cannot be sustained. A rupture of sorts occurs. Silence invades the atmosphere. By the end of the story, the narrator-protagonist is the salamander and comments on the man who had previously been the narrator. On one side of the glass the man, no longer the person he used to be, stops visiting the aquarium. On the other side remains the salamander, consoled by the possibility that the man will write a story about this unsettling experience.

Cortázar uses a variety of literary techniques in **"Axolotl."** The events of the story take place over a period of a few days during which the narrator-protagonist focuses on critical phases of the transformation process. There is no linear sequence or spatial constancy. There appears to be no plot development, an impression conveyed by a circular kind of narrative procedure. The central idea established in the first few lines of the story is regularly reiterated: "There was a time when I thought a great deal about the axolotls. I went to see them in the aquarium at the Jardin des Plantes and stayed for hours watching them, observing their immobility, their faint movements. Now I am an axolotl."

The opening paragraph is in itself a closed circle which, as one critic has pointed out, functions as the center of the larger circle of the story. For Antonio Pagés Larraya three distinct parts can be found in this cyclical structure. The first involves the protagonist's gradual approach to the fascinating but foreign world of the salamanders. He observes and describes them from outside the aquarium glass: "I saw from very close up the face of an axolotl immobile next to the glass." The second deals with the metamorphosis process: "No transition, no surprise," says the narrator, "I saw my face against the glass, I saw it on the outside of the tank, I saw it on the other side of the glass." At this point, the man believes himself to have metamorphosed into a salamander with his human mind intact—"buried alive," as he puts it, "condemned to move lucidly among unconscious creatures." In the third division, the feeling of horror stops as he becomes so immersed in his new world that he is able to sense what he could not perceive on the other side: ". . . a foot grazed my face, when I moved just a little to one side and saw an axolotl next to me who was looking at me. . . . "

It should be added that a fourth part to the story is found in its last paragraph, which functions as an epilogue. Here there is a definite separation between two worlds. The narrator-protagonist had achieved a kind of unity. There is now, however, a division between the man who became a salamander and the man whose visits to the aquarium have ceased. The salamander declares: "I am an axolotl for good now, and if I think like a man it's only because every axolotl thinks like a man inside his rosy stone semblance. I believe that all this succeeded in communicating something to him in those first days, when I was still he."

As in a number of Cortázar's stories, suspense in **"Axolotl"** is not dependent upon the element of surprise but upon the particular experience described and upon the atmosphere of tension in which that experience takes place. Cortázar has stated that it is of utmost importance to him to hold the attention of his reader-accomplices, as he likes to call them, and to widen their horizons. Thus he advocates a style that, in his words, "consists of those elements of form and expression that fit the thematic nature of the story in a precise fashion, elements that give it its most penetrating and original visual and auditory form, that make it unique, unforgettable, that fix it forever in its time, in its atmosphere and in its most primordial sense." **"Axolotl"** is typical of Cortázar in other ways: it introduces a protagonist in a situation characterized by a routine existence; it recounts the way in which an alien presence interrupts that routine; and it reveals—at least partially—the consequences of that intervention.

"Axolotl" is a story in which the line between reality and fantasy gradually blurs in the reader's mind. It is narrated from several different perspectives that shift unpredictably and whose sources are somewhat ambiguous. Intentional confusion is caused by the skillful use of personal pronouns, verbal suffixes, and several verb tenses that are associated with the varying points of view. (pp. 419-21)

The multiple perspectives established through the use of various pronouns and verbal suffixes is developed even further by a constant change in the temporal context. Several verb tenses appear in the same short paragraph or even in the same sentence: "The axolotls huddled on the wretched, narrow (only I can know how narrow and wretched) floor of stone and moss." The story begins in the past ("There was a time when I thought a great deal about the axolotls."), skips back and forth in time and then draws to a close in the present. The use of the present tense imbues the account with a sense of open-endedness. The last words of the salamander are: "And in this final solitude, to which he no longer comes, I console myself by thinking that perhaps he is going to write a story about us, that, believing he's making up a story, he's going to write all this about axolotls."

Taken together, these literary techniques underscore the multiplicity of reality which Cortázar is so intent upon conveying through his fiction. The constant interchange of perspectives and temporal planes that the techniques create undermines the reliability of rational thought. Cortázar's innovative methods are meant to revitalize language as well as people. "I've always found it absurd," he says, "to talk about transforming man if man doesn't simultaneously, or previously, transform his instruments of knowledge. How to transform oneself if oneself continues to use the same language Plato used?"

In **"Axolotl"** Cortázar has sought to express something for which there is no verbal concept within the realist mode of writing. He rejects writing on the basis of logical conceptualizations, for the mode he refers to as "fantastic" is not practiced from an intellectual standpoint. In fact, he has explained that, for the most part, writing just happens to him. It is a kind of literary exorcism. By his own admission it is a process by which he attempts to deal with the products of his own imagination which resist control and upset a carefully, albeit precariously, established way of life. On occasion it is as though he were a medium receiving a force over which he has no conscious control. The story under analysis, therefore, can be seen as a metaphor because it clearly has that mysterious quality of suggesting meaning beyond the mere anecdote of the narrative.

The meanings implied in the transformation may be numerous. The interpretation offered here is that the significance of the event described in **"Axolotl"** closely coincides with Carl Gustav Jung's views on the dynamics and development of the self. Indeed, the similarities are remarkable between Cortázar and the Swiss psychologist, particularly in regard to the concept of reality. "The distinctive thing about real facts," writes Jung, "is their individuality. Not to put too fine a point on it, one could say that the real picture consists of nothing but exceptions to the rule, and that, in consequence, absolute reality has predominantly the character of irregularity." What happens in **"Axolotl"** strongly suggests that Cortázar means to represent an ego-conscious personality striving for wholeness, or what Jung describes as "the ultimate integration of conscious and unconscious, or better, the assimilation of the ego to a wider personality."

Throughout the narrative it is suggested that Cortázar is actually portraying aspects of a process of self-realization. The solitary, routine existence in which the protagonist is mired is interrupted by an unexpected obsession for the salamanders. He is unable to think of anything else. Through the function of intuition he senses the attractive power of a collective image: "I knew that we were linked, that something infinitely lost and distant kept pulling us together." In Jungian terms the unconscious component of the self—that is, those personal psychic activities and contents which are "forgotten, repressed or subliminally perceived, thought, and felt"—erupts into consciousness. It does this on its own accord, requiring the ego somehow to assimilate the new content. Cortázar's protagonist describes psychic associations which suggest that the activity originates in the unconscious, not only on a personal but on a collective level as well. In the unconscious, as Jung explains, there is interaction between "the acquisitions of the personal existence" and "the inherited possibility of psychic functioning in general, namely, in the inherited brain structure." Being the base of the psyche of every individual, the collective unconscious is a kind of heritage passed on to all human beings, and maybe even to all animals as well.

With these concepts in mind, the salamander in Cortázar's story may be seen as an archetypal representation of basic drives and appetites which include the urge for self-fulfillment. Like the snake, the salamander is a symbol of what Jung calls "the undifferentiated instinctual world in man." Struggling for understanding, the protagonist makes mention of "a diaphanous interior mystery," "a secret will," "a mysterious humanity," "nonexistent consciousness," "the mystery," etc. which were all claiming him. Such references underscore the need for symbols to communicate something that cannot be fully expressed in rational terms.

The narrator-protagonist gives even more weight to the primordial image that amphibians convey by his persistent attention to the eyes of the salamanders: "Above all else, their eyes obsessed me," he reveals. They are referred to as "eyes of gold," "golden eyes," and "diminutive golden discs." Apart from the hypnotic effect that is suggested through the man's reaction to the eyes, they may be understood to have psychological meaning as well. The eye is traditionally considered to be a window to the soul. Like sparks and stars, it is an artistic motif associated with the illumination of consciousness. Indeed, consciousness has commonly been described in terms related to light. (pp. 421-23)

There is further and more telling evidence that the metamorphosis in this story has to do with a creative transformation, reflecting the archetypal experience of an inner rebirth. The protagonist overcomes his initial horror at feeling submerged in unconscious creatures. He conveys the idea of achieving a kind of complete unity, at least temporarily, in such statements as: "It would seem easy, almost obvious, to fall into mythology. I began seeing in the axolotls a metamorphosis which did not succeed in revoking a mysterious humanity . . . They were not human beings,

but I had found in no animal such a profound relation with myself." The man's consciousness had been struggling against the primitive unconsciousness of unmitigated instinctuality. (pp. 423-24)

It is understood that what the man in **"Axolotl"** has undergone is not only fantastic but primitive and symbolic as well. The more primordial the experience seems, the more it represents the potentiality of being. The contents of the unconscious can provide a more complete way of living and perceiving. The salamanders' eyes speak to the man "of the presence of a different life, of another way of seeing." Such subjective perception and introverted sensation have been discussed at length by Jung. He believes that primordial images, in their totality, constitute a "psychic mirror world" that represents the present contents of consciousness, not in their familiar form but in the way a million-year old consciousness might see them.

More primordial imagery can be found in **"Axolotl."** The narrator protagonist reiterates that to his way of thinking the salamanders are not human beings, but that they are not animals either. In comparing the two, he insists on the positive value of the animal. This is a recurring theme in Cortázar's fiction. "The intention is not to degrade man," as one critic has put it, "but to do away with certain ill-founded pretensions regarding the nature of mankind." The protagonist's sense of a superior perceptive faculty is alluded to at the end of the story. The transformed protagonist asserts that the salamander next to him "knew also, no communication possible, but very clearly knew." This observation seems to point to the idea of a world-soul which pervades all living creatures, enabling them to have a special sense of things, including those that are yet to be.

Jung's psychology of the unconscious provides for the specific kinds of instinctual patterns in human biology. The existence of these patterns, however, is difficult to establish through the empirical approach to knowledge. Cortázar deals with this very point in **"Axolotl."** He develops the idea that the ways for apprehending these patterns in man are characterized by an inherent duality. This kind of duality has been discussed by Jung, who explains that consciousness itself is a transformation of the original instinctual image while at the same time it is the transformer of that image. The man in Cortázar's story feels conflicts between conscious and unconscious contents, between knowledge and faith, and between spirit and nature. His psychic situation has disrupted him to the point where he admits, on the one hand, that he is frightened by a compulsive force within him. On the other hand, he implies that his consciousness has deepened and broadened, allowing him to deal with the instincts which he feared would make him a prisoner within the salamander.

Cortázar's protagonist, then, has been caught up in an unsettling development process which leads to a kind of synthesis of conscious and unconscious elements. As it is explained in the story "what was his obsession is now an axolotl." In other words, the narrator's momentous transformation signifies that he has become consciously aware of the effects of an instinctual side that he had neglected or suppressed. He has now integrated its valuable elements into his being. He no longer yields entirely to his rational conception of himself. He has discovered that he has a larger capacity for self-awareness. The details of what the hidden mind and spirit reveal to the narrator-protagonist are not disclosed specifically to the reader, but it is suggested that he has gained a deeper understanding of life. In relating to the amphibious creatures of the aquarium he acquires the insights, the means of comparison, that he needed for self-knowledge and for a sense of continuity as a living being. "Only the person who can consciously assent to the power of the inner voice becomes a personality," Jung has written. The man in **"Axolotl"** has heard that voice in the salamander and has gained the psychological advantage of a larger sense of life and of a reaffirmation of the spirit. He is now a changed, more complete being.

There may be disagreement over whether or not the transformation experience depicted in **"Axolotl"** has positive connotations. Some readers are of the opinion that Cortázar has told a story about a personal failure, about a defeat. The argument is that the salamander abandons the man, that a lack of communication ensues, and that at the end the man is left impoverished by the experience. "The 'I' is denied the possibility of living on two planes," concludes one critic. The interpretation that has been presented here views the transformation as positive. The conflicts over the matter arise from the enigmatic qualities of Cortázar's fiction, which reflects the inherent ambiguities of reality itself. Most likely, debate over the issue will go on. In any event, what is clear is that the readers of Cortázar's **"Axolotl"** are left with a heightened sense of awe regarding the potentialities of biological, spiritual and, most of all, literary realities. (pp. 424-25)

Harry L. Rosser, "The Voice of the Salamander: Cortázar's 'Axolotl' and the Transformation of the Self," in Kentucky Romance Quarterly, *Vol. 30, No. 4, 1983, pp. 419-27.*

Cortázar on short fiction

[A] novel is a long process or development, dealing with a number of subjects that evolve along the way. For instance, *A Manual for Manuel* has a lot to do with sex in Latin America. I try to go into that subject as far as I can and to deal with machismo and with notions of male superiority. This on top of the other things the book is about. So a novel is a rich experience, something that opens up many issues and lets them unfold. A short story is very different. I think of it as a kind of glass sphere in which you try to enclose a few perceptions, a few feelings. It must be complete within itself and brief enough to have a tight form. Sometimes when I am writing a novel I think of something that doesn't belong there but has a life of its own. So I stop and make a short story of it if I can. A short story is more like a poem than like a novel.

Cortázar in an interview in the New York Times Book Review, *1978.*

Carter Wheelock   (essay date 1985)

[*Wheelock is an American critic who specializes in Spanish-American literature and has written several studies on Argentine author Jorge Luis Borges. In the following excerpt, Wheelock places Cortázar's short fiction in the tradition of "new realism," contending that his short stories, which are informed by the writings of Borges and his concept of creating separate realities within works of literature, transcend normal reality to evoke "a heightened awareness of unreality."*]

Fifty-two years ago Jorge Luis Borges wrote an essay, "Narrative Art and Magic," in which he described a common narrative device—that of prefiguration by innuendo—to show how it produces in fiction the effect that he called "magical causality." Such foreshadowing by suggestion replaces objective reality with an inner reality belonging to the text alone . . . . His essay, long familiar to critics, is attracting second looks nowadays and getting increased attention in relation to literature outside of Spanish America. Clark Zlotchew, in a recent article, has linked it to later comments by Borges on the nature of unrealistic fiction to show a relationship to the French *nouveau roman,* in which he notes the frequent occurrence of the artifice called the *mise en abyme* or work within a work. Zlotchew quotes various critics to show their agreement that the *mise en abyme,* which has the effect of cutting the bonds that link the text to the real world, is there precisely for that purpose—to leave the work self-enclosed, without connection to anything but itself. He observes, citing words of novelist Alain Robbe-Grillet to this effect, that the question of verisimilitude (in the sense of likeness to reality) is of no interest to a writer of "new realism," whose affinity is for details that strike a false note.

Julio Cortázar (1914-1984) is second only to Borges in having set the tone and direction of the contemporary short story in Spanish America. I want to show how Borges's "magical causality" is produced in some of Cortázar's fiction by the procedure Borges describes, in order to get at the aesthetic concept underlying the self-encapsulating literature that has repudiated realism. The disconnection from everyday reality, I think we can agree, is more than that, being in its effect a disengagement from intellectual content of any kind, real or unreal. My purpose in trying to show a fundamental sameness in two writers generally considered quite different is to suggest the need of a different critical emphasis in regard to unrealistic fiction—an acknowledgment that its goal is to produce esthesia in the reader, not to avoid ordinary reality or to produce unreality for its own sake, and not to create some alternative metaphysical conception of the world. Neither can its distinction from what is called "the fantastic" be determined by the presence of some supposed insinuation of a social, political, philosophical, or other real-life value. (p. 3)

[Borges's] essay affirms, in effect, that a reader of fiction does not expect a literary work to hide its artifice, as in realism, or to mimic familiar truth. Verisimilitude consists, rather, in giving the reader something that completes his apprehension, no matter how distant from the laws of nature his mental contents may be. Borges does not imply that "prophesying" is the only means to this end, but he offers it as an example as if to say that it is the most fundamental. Before inserting the unreal into his narrative, the writer insinuates it casually as mere idea, through details that do not purport to be particularly significant. In this way he exposes the attributes of the thing to come, making it relevant as metaphor, so that when it materializes it comes as an appropriate, almost expected articulation. Its unreal character is no barrier to its acceptance on literary faith; the sudden literalization of what was conceived figuratively raises the whole textual environment above ordinary truth and imbues it with anagogic significance. The prefiguration is essential, for only by such means can the unreal be given the aura of the appropriate; mere unintelligibility or textual "insanity" has no aesthetic power. Most writers of nineteenth-century fantastic fiction seem not to have recognized this fact, which accounts for the "minor" status of so much fiction of the type.

Borges compares this kind of foreshadowing, and the resulting literary credibility of the unreal, to the rituals of primitive man—for example, to sympathetic magic, in which the tribe imitates in word and gesture what it hopes to see in nature. He thus implies that there is no generic difference between such ceremony and the writing or reading of fiction. In ritual and in literature a configuration of mind constitutes the "possession" of what is not present in reality, and this is satisfying in itself. The savage enjoys his dance whether it rains or not.

In another article I have related the foregoing to some of Borges's fiction, attempting to show that prophesying or prefiguration results in "prophecy" as textual transcendence—the realization that the work does not finally impart or signify anything except that it comprises art, which is artifice having an aesthetic effect; the only reality offered is the literature itself, self-enclosed and distinct from anything else: *ars, ars est*. Borges's fiction is by no means devoid of familiar truth, but it is there only as building material. The same can be said of Cortázar, despite the fact that he is often assigned the role of "realist" in his supposed commitment to existentialist moralizing and leftist ideology. Leaving aside obvious differences of style, structure, and specific content, it would be difficult to show that Borges and Cortázar differ in their conception of what a reader is supposed to get from a short story. Just as art is art no matter what its outer trappings may be, an artist by definition is unfaithful to common reality and has that disloyalty as his basic motivation.

Before his death in 1984, Cortázar produced both short stories and novels but is identified primarily with the former, notwithstanding the great success of his novel *Rayuela* (1963). His prose is all of the "new" kind, and most of his stories are unrealistic to the point of being called fantastic, although Jaime Alazraki has more aptly described them as "surrealist metaphor" [see Further Reading list]. A typical story is **"The Idol of the Cyclades,"** which in its execution is very similar to Borges's "El evangelio según Marcos" ("The Gospel According to Mark," *El informe de Brodie*, 1970), though it is less complex. The action might well be called psychosomatic; two characters, reverting to a primitive mode of thought, make a mental association which they project into reality, and this leads to an irrational ritualistic murder. In the summary that follows, the words in italic are emphasized for their significance as prefiguration. (pp. 4-5)

On a Greek island two archaeologists, Morand and Somoza, unearth a marble statuette thousands of years old.

It is the figure of a nude young woman, a relic of an ancient time when it was used in erotic bloodrites. Thérèse, Morand's wife, comes running along the beach to see the discovery, forgetting that she is carrying the toppiece of her bikini in her *hand,* and she is standing barebreasted by the excavation when Somoza's *hands* emerge holding the statue. Reproved by her husband, she covers her breasts with her *hands.* She resents the reproof, calling it a silly prejudice, and this causes a momentary alienation that has to be overcome later with an apology. That evening Morand and Thérèse are together in their tent while Somoza, alone in his, *caresses* the beautiful idol and strips off its "false clothes of time and oblivion." Somoza has the "absurd hope" of being able, some day, to relate to the statue as its ancient worshippers did; he wants to come to it "by other means than *hands* and eyes and science." Morand and Thérèse jokingly marvel, in private, at his *nonsensical* hope. Bribing an official, they take the statue out of the country, promising not to sell it for two years. Before leaving, Morand and Thérèse realize that Somoza has fallen in love with her, and this hurries their departure. Back in Paris, Somoza takes charge of the idol and keeps it in his apartment on a *pedestal,* where he continually *caresses* it and tries to duplicate it faithfully in plaster—finally with such success that Morand cannot tell the difference between *the original and Somoza's copy.* During this time Morand sees Somoza now and then, but Thérèse never does. In the climactic scene, Morand is in Somoza's apartment; for some reason he cannot explain to himself, he has asked Thérèse to meet him there later. Somoza tells Morand that he will never give him the statue although it belongs to both. He is acting very strangely and cannot explain his behavior; he says, "There are no words for it—at least, not our words," and he adopts a tone of voice that goes with "those explanations that get lost beyond intelligibility." *Caressing* the idol's breasts and sex organ, Somoza speaks of making a sacrifice—of smearing it with blood to make its eyes and mouth appear; then he takes off his clothes and picks up a stone hatchet. Morand says to him that all this *nonsense* is really about Thérèse. Backing away, he steps on some dirty rags which symbolize, for Morand, all the things that he, Somoza, and Thérèse ought to have said to each other; he senses that he cannot retreat farther. As Somoza attacks, Morand seizes the hatchet and kills him. He then dips his *hands* in Somoza's blood, takes off his clothes, and stands behind the door waiting, hatchet in *hand,* for Thérèse.

Most of the prefiguring elements in the narrative go almost unnoticed in the reading, seeming to be mere vocabulary or incidental detail. The actions done with hands begin to establish the metaphorical identity of Thérèse and the idol, as well as the association between her sexual attractiveness and the idol's primeval power. Hands are symbolic, at first, of possession and touching; Somoza's holding and caressing of the statue occurs throughout the text in often-abrupt proximity to mentions of Thérèse. Later, hands are associated with the statue's deadly influence; they receive the sacrificial blood and hold the murderous hatchet. Other links between the woman and the idol are made by coincidence: the idol is uncovered at the moment Thérèse stands uncovered, and Somoza's hands hold it while Thérèse's hands hold her breasts. Somoza's imagination—his absurd fantasy—is that he may reach the idol (Thérèse) with more than hands, eyes, and the detached view of science; his desire as an archaeologist to enter into the "nonsensical" thought mode of primitive man and commune with the idol is confused by suggestion with his yearning to "commune" with Morand's wife. Somoza's inner motives and mental associations are by no means made clear in the narrative, but subtle insinuation makes them the primary "reality" of the text. In the end, Morand will follow Somoza into a primeval way of thinking in which there is no difference between what is thought and what exists in reality; he will kill Thérèse because she and the idol are one. Somoza has coveted, caressed, and possessed *her*. As Somoza says, this is not in our words; the explanation gets lost in unintelligibility.

It would be easy to dismiss the whole business as a depiction of the workings of the mythic mind, which lacks an "as if " and conceives everything as "is." To do this would be to miss the value and meaning of the story. It is not lacking in psychological reality, and it mingles that reality with mythic "nonsense" in a way that reveals to us how close we still are to primitive thinking. When something of ours is coveted by another, it is somehow diminished in our estimation because our secure possession of it is undermined; it is as if the thing itself were disloyal, wanting to belong to the other. This is especially true if the coveted object is a person capable of being seduced. This psychological fact is adumbrated in the story when Thérèse and her husband are alienated by her resentment of his reproof as she stands bare breasted before Somoza. Besides this element of realism, there are traditional associations to reinforce the magic: the likeness between a cold, beautiful goddess and an unreachable woman, and the affinity between the idol's mystical power and a woman's power to inspire love or lust.

All of these prophetic details (I have by no means exhausted the list) converge on the periphery of the reader's consciousness, setting a context which "expects" the strange event to come. The reader senses that in some way the murder of Thérèse is not incredible. In the moment of reading, before analysis sets in, we cannot articulate that congruence, but we almost understand it; it has the quality of Borges's "aesthetic fact"—"the imminence of a revelation that does not materialize." The writer's prophesying has led us to a posture of mind where we are on the threshold of an idea that is outside our rational categories, like a whole number between one and two. Our effort to intellectualize the text results in a poor exegetical paraphrase of what only the text can say, because it does not "say" anything; it simply is. (pp. 5-6)

Alazraki has pointed out that Cortázar's brand of unrealism cannot be measured by nineteenth-century norms, including the structuralist criteria of Todorov. He does not violate reality, nor juxtapose the incongruent for shock effect, nor cause the reader to vacillate between reason and unreason. Instead, he insinuates another way of apprehending. Contemporary fiction has been preoccupied, in varying degree, with asserting its difference from what precedes it, and we can often detect notes of self-commentary woven into a text (Borges, of course, is famous for this). When Morand is in Somoza's apartment and sees how strangely he is acting, he at first concludes that Somoza has lost his reason, but then he decides that such a conclusion is "too easy." In other words, the primeval (unreal) mode of thought to which Somoza has surrendered, being coherent in itself, cannot be called insanity because it has itself as its only criterion. That way of thinking is to be identified with the text itself, for it is the very thing prophesied by the text and is therefore *in* it, essentially comprising it. The text as a corpus of language cannot be measured by outside norms, certainly not by those which divide the true from the false on an objective basis. The story was published in 1956, when the break with theoretical realism had just begun to manifest itself with vigor.

We can look now at what is surely one of the century's cleverest stories, **"Bestiario."** Cortázar, as third-person narrator of the story, reverses the rules of normal fiction. Normally, a reader is not prepared to accept as reality, right from the start, what the characters believe in; here the reader accepts literally what the characters take only metaphorically—if they can be said to "take" it at all. Usually, the fantastic is insinuated in the midst of reality; here the fantastic is openly affirmed while reality is evoked only by innuendo. Normally, analysis enables us to make a clear separation between language pointing to reality and that which points to fantasy; here the narrator so mixes the two that it is impossible to separate them. The story demonstrates that clear apprehension is possible in spite of the violation of language and logic. Again we are dealing with prefiguration, magical causality, and the credibility of what we can hardly conceive or articulate.

Cortázar puts two situations side by side, one unbelievable and clearly told, the other quite natural and evoked by innuendo. The natural and credible circumstance is that Nene, the irascible brother of Luis, has an incestuous lust for Luis's wife Rema, and his unwelcome attentions cause her constant unhappiness. The Funes family never alludes to this situation openly or otherwise. Luis, a scholar buried in his books, is half oblivious to the matter and does nothing about it except to swear in private. Luis and Rema have a boy, Nino; his visiting cousin, Isabel, loves her aunt Rema and suffers for her as her childish understanding of the situation grows. Isabel's mother had hesitated to send the girl to visit the Funes family because of what she referred to as the tiger that roamed the house. Here begins the incredible part. The family's daily life is complicated by the necessity of avoiding the tiger; one must never enter a room, particularly the dining room, without looking to see if the tiger is there. The family groundskeeper, Don Roberto, is the one who is most trusted to keep the family informed of the tiger's whereabouts and to come running with the dogs if the tiger gets troublesome. The story has little plot but tells the random activities of the children, which turn out to be prophetic by suggestion. At the climax, the child Isabel remarks casually that the tiger is in Nene's study, causing him to go into another room where the tiger really is. In the last lines Nene is screaming, Luis is yelling and pounding on the door, and Don Roberto is coming with the dogs, but Isabel is only looking tearfully at her beloved Rema, with Rema's grateful hand resting on her shoulder.

Only with difficulty, in contemplative reconstruction, does the reader conclude that there is no real tiger; the narrator has given material substance to the metaphor of Isabel's mother. Nene's lust for Rema is only *like* a roaming beast; the family's dread of acknowledging the painful reality is like a fear of being in the same room with something terrible; and Don Roberto with his dogs is only a symbol of the family's reticent shame and constant effort to suppress the truth. But this is afterthought; the immediate effect is bafflement. The reader cannot tell *how* Nene's encounter with the tiger is the same thing as the family's open acknowledgment of his offense, brought about by Isabel, because the text presents the two things as if they cannot be the same. For example, all the family members carefully avoid mentioning the unsavory situation but speak openly of the tiger that metaphorizes it. The family supposes that Isabel is ignorant of Nene's lust for Rema, but she too talks of the tiger. The caution against going into the dining room in particular, without first looking to see if it is safe, can be taken to mean that it is especially important to keep the problem of Nene out of sight in the one place where the whole family gathers at one time; this clearly shows the tiger's metaphorical character. How, then, can Isabel use the tiger as a reality to destroy Nene figuratively? The text does not make sense, and yet we know that Isabel in some way has delivered Rema from Nene's abuse by bringing his offense into the open. We reach this conclusion in spite of the language, transcending it with an intuition to which logic is irrelevant.

That intuition is made possible by prefiguration—the "logic" of the self-enclosed text. Apart from the fact that "tiger" is a common literary metaphor for terrible or inescapable truth, there are many prophesying details. I will mention only a few.

As in **"The Idol of the Cyclades,"** there is a symbolism of hands. It is Rema's soft, warm hands that inspire Isabel's affection. These loving hands are offended by Nene's when, as Rema is serving him coffee, he grasps her fingers instead of the cup, causing her to withdraw her hand. When Isabel is playing with an antfarm, she sees Rema's hand reflected in the glass; it seems as if the crawling ants are on her fingers, and Isabel asks her to take away her hand. We sense that the ants are associated in the girl's mind with Nene's touch, for she decides the antfarm is hideous and asks Rema to take it from the room—but Rema does not (we can interpret: she asks Rema to get rid of the problem with Nene, which she cannot do). The association of Nene with insects is carried further; he becomes, by suggestion, a praying mantis which Isabel promises to throw away because it disgusts Rema. Shortly after, Isabel "throws away" the disgusting Nene, and the last image in the story is that of Rema's hand on Isabel's shoulder.

The link between Nene and insects, the prominence of insects in the story (the children collect them), the title **"Bestiary,"** the tiger, and the bestial character of Nene all contribute to a oneness of final conception. (pp. 7-8)

The most pervasive prefiguration is the fact that in spite of the tiger's apparent reality, the family does not treat it as a real tiger. It is taken for granted, alluded to but not talked about or described even by the narrator; it is not feared or opposed but simply avoided, like something being ignored or suppressed. Anyone looking for Cortázar's commitment to existentialist moralizing can see here a statement about "authenticity"; the family's problem is one of timid withdrawal from the demand for communication. (p. 9)

I have several conclusions that I believe are valid to the extent that these stories are typical of Cortázar and of

"magical reality" or the "new realism," as I believe they are. In such fiction, the thing that is "disconnected from the real world" is simply the climactic event of the narrative—a result having no other cause than the one assigned by the text. That textually assigned cause is a prefiguring insinuation, not a statement that purports to replace one metaphysic with another. The cause can be discerned by analysis, but this is not necessary in order for the cause-and-effect relationship to comprise a coherence in the reader's mind. By being an autonomous text, the work implants in the reader's mind a sense of the mind's own autonomy; that is, it causes the reader to disengage himself from "commitment" to any of his mental contents, because they are all unreliable by any standard outside the mind itself. The text itself, as language and as intellectual content, is unworthy of "trust" and is transcended—by nothing. There is nothing for the mind to see or intuit except its own vacant posture; apart from this awareness of empty awareness, nothing is real.

This final result can perhaps be characterized as solipsism. "Solipsism" is a philosophical term defined most simply as the notion that the self can know nothing but its own modifications and states. This is not to say that in aesthetic apprehension the mind has no content, but that its ideational content cannot constitute "truth"; but neither can it be dispensed with, since the mind cannot stare directly at itself but must posit figments that reflect its outline. The literature of the "new realism" may not do anything new—in fact, it must deny that it does—but it asks for a new terminology. Instead of producing aesthesia as a "heightened awareness of reality," by traditional, nineteenth-century definition, it produces a heightened awareness of *unreality,* disconnecting the reader's consciousness from its own necessary "furniture." It strives to give the reader a state of sentience that is independent of what produced it. Implicit in such literature is a fundamental doubt about the adequacy of thought and language—a doubt that the mind can know any reality beyond itself.

By freely displaying their artifices, contemporary writers are encouraging the maturity and sophistication of the reader, like medical doctors who explain the theory of the treatment to the intelligent patient. There is no question that they have turned us back to a traditional conception of art as pure aesthesia—preintellectual experience or apprehension. Behind the metaphor "magical causality" lies a perfectly intelligible concept of literature as "language of independent value." That concept cannot refer to the literature as a body of words on the page, for this would imply what is to be denied—an objective value of "truth" apart from the reader's experience. "Magical causality" refers to the aesthetic state of mind that the text may evoke, apart from which a text has no value or meaning. The structures, styles, and artifices that can evoke aesthetic apprehension are many, but unreality is a part of them all. (pp. 9-10)

Carter Wheelock, "Borges, Cortázar, and the Aesthetic of the Vacant Mind," in The International Fiction Review, *Vol. 12, No. 1, Winter, 1985, pp. 3-10.*

John H. Turner   (essay date 1987)

[*In the excerpt below, Turner studies the role of mis-*

ogynistic attitudes and behavior among male characters in Cortázar's short stories "El río" and "Secret Weapons" and examines the potential effects of these attitudes on Cortázar's readers.]

Cortázar continually made the point that literature, even "fantastic" literature should, while avoiding cant and dogma, deal responsibly with its historical context. One of his clearest statements on the subject is to be found in the speech he gave in the gymnasium of Barnard College in 1979:

> In Latin America the same reader who is excited by finding in a story or a novel the description or the denunciation of things that he is living and suffering day by day, will also enjoy the reading of other texts which tear him away from his immediate surrounding to take him on a dizzying imaginary journey; but this enjoyment is based on the reader's feeling of confidence in the writer, since he knows that he is responsible, since he is sure that he is not trying to lull him to sleep or to distance him from a reality which both share and in which both struggle in their own way. So, when a reader reads my fantastic stories, he knows that I am not trying to tear him away from history and anaesthetize him with a literature of evasion and of renunciation; if he follows me along my most unreal and most experimental paths, it is because he knows that I have never tried to deceive him, to distance him from his own historical responsibility. (my own translation)

Cortázar insists on the writer's duty to be politically responsible, both in private life and in public statement, even when the subject matter of the latter is not overtly social or political. (p. 43)

In an address to students at Berkeley, Cortázar expressed his usual distaste for a narrowly aestheticist view of literary analysis by recourse to the metaphor of the sterility of the operating room: "Each time that it has been my lot," he says, "to be present in one of those operating rooms as spectator or patient I have left with a tremendous desire to drink wine in a bar or watch girls on buses." (my trans.) In the context of an address on the public responsibility of writers, the casual sexism of the remark about going out and looking at girls is slightly surprising. It is not my intention to use such a remark which was intended, successfully, to make students laugh, to accuse Cortázar of sexism, although few understood better than Cortázar, a student of Freud in this as in so many things, that in such unguarded moments as making a joke, the deepest prejudices of our culture often express themselves. But it is useful to remind ourselves at the outset that what authors say and what their works do need not be the same thing. Sexual attitudes, conscious and unconscious, are central to Cortázar's work and deserve careful attention.

A great many, perhaps the majority of Cortázar's fictions, are concerned in one way or another with sexuality, most particularly that of the male, which is the explicit focus of a large number of stories and a constant preoccupation in the novels. Cortázar offers, often by means of apparently "fantastic" adventures, a stream of evocations of male sexuality which are frighteningly "real" in the sense that they strike a familiar chord in the reader. Much of the appalling energy of these treatments derives from the constant association of eroticism with violence, with behavior

which in real life we call sexist or worse. In the context of Cortázar's Conscious Sixties liberated morality, the distorted and sometimes frankly sadistic attitudes portrayed are not condoned. In part, what Cortázar is doing, as he makes clear in several places, is deliberately violating taboos which he saw as preventing the liberation of literature and society from their disabling traditions. Some of these passages may be read as moral fables with clear condemnation of such attitudes, as I hope to demonstrate below; they certainly cannot be read as celebrations of sexism.

As Martha Paley Francescato made clear in her article called "The New Man (But Not the New Woman?)", Cortázar's central characters are primarily male [see Alazraki and Ivask in Further Reading list]. While there are noticeably more female protagonists in the last two collections of stories, **Queremos tanto a Glenda (We Love Glenda So Much)** and **Deshoras (Off-Hours)**, the focus, logical enough in a male author, and particularly in one who described his stories as exorcisms of personal demons, is primarily on the male's view of things . . . . The purpose of these pages is to consider the role of male sexuality as it is treated in two of Cortázar's stories which deal overtly with men's cruelty towards women, to see what the function of the apparent misogynism of his characters might be, and particularly the effect that such portrayals might have upon the reader.

One of the earliest of Cortázar's fictions to deal with sexual violence is **"El río" ("The River")** from the collection **Final del juego (End of the Game).** This extremely brief narrative, barely four pages long, involves one of those oscillations between two states of consciousness that are so frequent in Cortázar. In this case, a male narrator muses between sleep and waking about his wife's continual and, as far as he is concerned, empty threats to kill herself. The context is, as so often, a marriage perceived to have degenerated into a set of boring rituals, although in this case we only have the narrator's word for it; the monologue form admits no first-hand insight into the woman's feelings. The narrative paints a grimly clear picture of the man's sarcastic and patronizing insensitivity:

> You make me laugh, poor thing. Your tragic resolutions, that way of slamming the doors like an actress on a tour of the provinces, one asks oneself if you really believe in your threats, your repulsive attempts at blackmail, your endless pathetic scenes anointed with tears and adjectives and repetitions.

And the climax of the story superimposes an act of sexual domination on the woman's death by drowning in such a way that this male dominance becomes indistinguishable, for the reader, from the woman's death.

Two male critics [Antonio Planells and Saúl Sosnowski] have dealt briefly with the story without commenting upon the evident animus of the narrator's presentation of his wife's behavior. They treat the story principally from the point of view of form, referring to the two worlds, the world of what the man perceives as real, the tiresome but desired presence of the sexual object in his bed, and, on the other hand, the woman's hysterical threats to kill herself. Both seem to take the man's word for it that his wife is hysterical, though the text itself offers ample evidence of the man's extreme insensitivity toward her. [Planells] speaks of the bed as a "place of pleasure" when the very identification between the bed and the river implicit in the watery imagery of the latter half of the story suggests the bed as the locus of the woman's suffering and wish for death. Interestingly, though they both quote the last sentence of the story, pointing out the skill with which Cortázar interweaves the two realities, they both suppress (repress?) the extremely telling opening words of that sentence, which raise serious doubts about their readings. Here is the sentence in full:

> I have to dominate you slowly (and that, you know, I have always done with a ceremonial grace), without hurting you I am bending the reeds of your arms, I cling to your pleasure of clenched hands, of eyes wide open, now at the end your rhythm becomes deeper in slow movements of watered silk, of deep bubbles rising to my face, vaguely I caress the hair spilled on the pillow, in the green half darkness I look with surprise at my streaming hand, and before slipping down beside you I know that they have just taken you out of the water, too late, naturally, and that you are lying on the embankment stones surrounded by shoes and voices, naked face-up with your hair soaked and your eyes open.

The only lengthy study of **"El río"** that I am aware of also concentrates exclusively on form. The author [Roberto Hozven] describes in great detail the mechanics of the alternation between the two realities experienced in the man's "hypnagogic" state. Much of what he says is accurate enough, but it all seems to miss the point. The story moves us, not by the skill of its architecture alone but by the way that architecture involves the reader in the explosive emotions that are the material of the story. To concentrate so exclusively on mechanical details of the story while ignoring the human dilemma at its center is to engage in the very kind of literary activity that Cortázar found so stifling in the remarks quoted above. But, worse, such a focus leads to a fundamentally wrong conclusion about the story's human significance. Toward the end of the essay, the writer refers to "the amorous fusion of river with woman" which seems to imply a sexism as profound as that of the protagonist, and his conclusion reads in part:

> We see in this great little story an exacerbated critique of what Cortázar later, and much more explicitly, developed in the philosophy of his stories . . . ; the intuition of the annihilating disintegration that our productive societies exercise over the poor human. There is, in **"El río"** a glimpse of the "other way" which *Rayuela* explores discursively and irrationally. There are already present in this story this pretentious and marvellous aspiration towards contacts other than those of mere reason.

Whatever Cortázar's views of mankind as victim of modern society, his focus in this story, as in most places, is on human psychology, particularly on the human capacity for delusion and confusion about our victimization of fellow beings, and not at all on possible "other paths" to truth.

Evelyn Picon Garfield, in her treatment of the story [see Further Reading list], quotes the sentence referred to above in full and refers to the protagonist's "jeering at her warnings," and ends her commentary:

> By means of the state of dream-wakefulness that exists in the narrator's mind, Cortázar is able to

skillfully fuse two events. For in a description of dual meaning, the husband's sexual possession of his wife coincides with her drowning. In this way his desire as well as her warning seem to be fulfilled simultaneously.

I would go further: the selfish and even sadistic expression of desire ("you insist on fighting") is not only simultaneous with her death but actually seems to be identical to it. Just as we cannot ignore the centrality of the man's cruelty, it also seems to me impossible to avoid the clearly critical attitude of the narrator toward the protagonist. After all, on one level, the man is in the act of discovering, with a jolt that the reader comes to share, that he has totally misjudged the seriousness of her desperation and that he is copulating with her corpse.

The moral core of the story, impossible to ignore despite Cortázar's frequent denials of such moralizing intent, is the condemnation of the man's cruelly inhuman domination of the woman. The self-denouncing liberal awareness of what he does ("you're quite right but how can I help it?") only accentuates the nastiness. The beauty of the telling of such an ugly truth in the story of man's inhumanity toward woman is that it involves at least male readers as voyeurs (a woman reader of the story must react differently—certainly my female students have done so), fascinating us with a familiar taboo depicted with unusual frankness, only to shock us, as the protagonist is about to be shocked, with the ending. One might even argue that the understated, often even off-hand, endings of some of the most dramatic of Cortázar's narratives, have, as here, the effect of throwing the implied, expected horror at the reader, of setting up a situation in which the reader suffers, vicariously yet alone, the imagined fate of the protagonist. In this case, it is extremely difficult for an attentive and open-minded reader not to identify with the feelings so eloquently expressed and, at the same time, not to feel the clearly implicit condemnation of the attitudes evoked. Far from perpetuating such attitudes, it seems to me that this text subverts the cultural stereotype it deals with, not only by depicting it with such frightening lucidity but by forcing us to re-enact it and feel its inherent contradictions.

In a passage of one of the essays from ***Ultimo round (Last Round),*** Cortázar describes himself as writing his short stories as a kind of exorcism:

> Perhaps it is an exaggeration to affirm that all really successful stories and especially fantastic stories, are products of neuroses, nightmares, or hallucinations neutralized by objectification and the transfer of them to the world outside neurosis; at all events, in any memorable story one perceives this polarization, as if the author had wanted to separate himself as soon as possible and as absolutely as possible from his creature, exorcising it in the only way he could, by writing it.

A few lines further on, the therapeutic function of the act of writing becomes even clearer: "I saw myself obliged to write a story in order to avoid something much worse." Apparently the stories are expressions of wishes that would be dangerous to fulfill in real life. This amounts to a theory of writing as therapy, at least for the writer. But, in view of Cortázar's insistence on the collaboration between writer and reader, perhaps we can think about the therapeutic effects of some of these stories upon the reader. Cortázar's fiction has the effect of producing a kind of healthy confusion and, in the passage quoted from the speech at Barnard, Cortázar certainly seems to feel that his ideal "dizzying imaginary voyage" will affect, even change, the reader rather than merely distract him (or her?). It seems particularly significant that the story that Cortázar uses to illustrate his theory of literature as therapy is **"Secret Weapons,"** one of the collection of stories that marks, according to Cortázar, the transition from the "aesthetic period" of his writing to the "metaphysical period" where he says he was aware of exploring, as is clear from all five stories in the collection, psychological rather than purely literary ideas.

As in the case of **"El río,"** **"Secret Weapons"** deals with violent sexuality. This story must surely be one of the most powerful and unsettling of Cortázar's fictions. As in the other four stories that make up the collection, its protagonist has a contradictory and conflicted hold on reality. Pierre, along with Michéle, Luis, Madame Francinet, and Bruno (not to mention Johnny) are all trying to make sense of a world that they find bewildering, for various reasons. The "secret weapons" of the book's title might be seen as the usually unconscious forces with which these tormented souls do harm to themselves and others. (pp. 43-8)

The story is narrated in third person with an appearance of detached sympathy for the male point of view, although this point of view is at one point abandoned in a very revealing way. The narrator seems to reach out to the reader, as if taking him into his confidence, and, as it were, links arms for a few lines of first person plural:

> Where were we, he was going to see her as she is, naked and defenseless. We said that, we had gotten to the exact moment when he was seeing her sleep defenseless and naked, that is to say, there's no reason to imagine, even for a moment, that it's going to be necessary to. . . .

At this critical moment the three of us, narrator, reader, and protagonist are together seeing the same thing, we are sharing this experience. The identification between reader and character, everywhere implicit, is here made quite explicit. And we all share the moment of confusion, suspended between the two consciousnesses, seeing the defenseless woman and the "double-crossing bitch" as the same person and wondering whence comes the impulse to violence.

The barest outline of the story is this: Pierre (single, age 23) is in love with Michèle (single, age 24) who, for reasons she does not discuss, resists his clumsy sexual advances. Pierre's consciousness is gradually invaded and eventually taken over by that of the German soldier who had raped Michèle and been killed by her friends seven years before, during the Second World War. At the end of the story, the rape is apparently repeated and the narration stops at the moment her friends arrive. There are obvious parallels with several early stories, **"La noche boca arriba" ("The Night Face Up"), "Axolotl" ("Axolotl"), "Lejana" ("The Distances"),** for example, as well as **"El río,"** in which two states of consciousness converge or overlap. But the wealth of psychological detail in this story has suggested less technical critical approaches. Previous readers of the story have pointed out Pierre's extreme insecurity and have gone so far as to point to evidence within the story that the invading consciousness of

the German rapist is not a totally alien invasion of some sinister force into an innocent and completely undeserving victim. Just as in the early **"Casa tomada" ("House Taken Over")** the mysterious forces are not an unwarranted and totally capricious invasion of an idyll but rather the obverse of the extreme and even perverse passivity and indifference of the residents of the house, so here it is hard to avoid a sense of the association between the violence of the German's behavior and the latent aggressiveness evident in Pierre's extreme insecurity. This point is even made explicitly in the story. At one point Pierre asks his doctor (psychiatrist?) friend, Xavier, "Does it ever happen to you, all at once thinking about things completely different from what you've been thinking?", to which Xavier replies, "Completely different is a working hypothesis, that's all." The suggestion is clear: these manifestations of another consciousness are not alien; they are related to his own consciousness. When he asks his friend for some kind of "objectifier," needing to distinguish clearly between his own projections and something objective "out there," he is told that there is no such thing.

Pierre's attitude toward Michèle is contradictory and neurotic from the opening lines. He is tormented by self doubt. We are given some insight into the nature—and, if this were a real person, perhaps the origin—of his ambivalence very early in the story. He imagines Michèle rearranging things in his room and associates this trait unconsciously with feelings for his mother . . . . (pp. 49-50)

Since we are dealing in this story, in part, at least, with a man's oedipal feelings toward a woman who has been the victim of a previous rape and with a psychic confrontation with the original despoiler of the mother figure, the *coágulo,* which is what Cortázar calls the nexus of concern at the center of the sphere which is the story, has to do with unresolved oedipal attitudes toward women. Pierre identifies himself in the story with his mother's lover and repeats a pattern of association between sex felt as taboo, and death.

Oedipus is not the only myth evoked in the account of Pierre's self-preoccupation. Before long we see him standing in front of the mirror worrying over a lock of hair that Michèle has threatened to cut off. This narcissistic act, later mirrored when Pierre has become the German and looks at his changed hair style in a mirror in Michèle's house, leads to a vision of himself as tragic hero, victim of woman's wiles. The fear of the mother's meddling, confused as it is with sexual attraction, now becomes even more clearly a fear of castration, embodied in the myth of Samson and Delilah. (p. 50)

The way in which the narrator describes these tangled feelings is particularly telling: "Pierre tells himself that he's stupid for having thought that Michèle doesn't want to come to his room. He thinks it soundlessly, as if from far off. Thought at times seems to have to make its way through countless barriers, to resolve itself, to make itself known. It's idiotic to have imagined that Michèle doesn't want to come up to his room." This almost clinical exposition of mood swings and clashing symbols typical of male sexual confusion leads, as his self-doubt increases, to a classically conventional expression of misogyny: "Women won't be any different (*"serán siempre las mismas"*), in Enghien or Paris, young or full-blown." What might easily be taken as innocent passion contains within it the potential for the violent aggressiveness of rape.

Directly following the image of Samson, the mysterious double-barreled shotgun makes its first appearance. The sequence is not inappropriate because, whether Pierre sees it or not, the association of Michèle with Delilah has tragic implications for his own destiny (the end of the story will be traumatic whether Pierre is killed by Ronald or not). The feelings associated with the first vision of the shotgun, conjured up directly by the inhaling of cigarette smoke (an association that becomes clear later when we find out about the last cigarette smoked by the German soldier before his death), are curious: "He feels as though he has been pardoned for having done something stupid." What is perhaps "something stupid" in Pierre is obviously much more in the German, but perhaps the feeling of being pardoned comes from the sense of atonement. This unavoidable association between the mildly neurotic behavior of Pierre and the grossly criminal act of his "other" hangs over the whole story, making it, as one critic has already observed, a kind of Jekyll and Hyde story with almost clinical implications. The point about Jekyll and Hyde, of course, is that they are one person, just as in this story we may see the rapist as a figure from the unconscious of the neurotic, emotionally retarded young man.

A significant detail of the story is the song that Pierre finds himself singing in German, a language he hardly knows. The first time he finds the song going through his mind is at the moment when he kisses Michèle and draws blood, through what he calls clumsiness but which seems to the reader more like poorly understood feelings of fear and aggressiveness. It is a setting to music by Robert Schumann of one of the opening poems of Heine's *Buch der Lieder,* a collection which, in the words of one critic, "appear(s) to have been inspired by a devastating and enduring emotional catastrophe. . . . " However vaguely Pierre may recall the song, the reader cannot avoid the implication that Pierre is, or sees himself as, the victim of a despairing and tragic romantic passion. This passivity, backed by repressed aggressiveness is precisely what allows the invasion of the "alien" violence.

Such attempts to analyze the psychology of the protagonist of **"Secret Weapons"** do not exhaust the richness of detail that Cortázar gives us. But they provide a useful background against which to look at what happens to the reader. Our conscious minds are given a lot to work on, but what does the very close identification between reader and protagonist alluded to earlier imply about the actual experience of reading, rather than about the conscious thought processes that might occur subsequently? This text is not a treatise but a work of fiction which works on us in ways that need not be limited by logic. We are drawn into the experience of the story because it rings true. Our interest is maintained by the suspense caused by the gradual invasion of the elements of something totally mysterious. What had seemed familiar, even trivial or trite, is transformed into something much more threatening. The confusion and alarm experienced by the protagonist are shared vicariously by the reader, who is pulled into the vortex of emotions of the last few pages. As at the end of **"El río,"** the reader is left with the interrupted and unresolved tension of what we feel is about to happen. We assume that the rape has repeated itself although this is not

unequivocally stated, and we are left at the moment Ronald is arriving at the house. The narrator has made us witnesses to the confusions, fears, feelings of inadequacy of the protagonist and the invasion of his consciousness. It is as if we were taken somewhere and dumped, not brought back by a neat ending to the comfortable world where there are easy answers.

The story raises questions about sexual violence in such a way as to enthrall us but at the same time to focus our minds on an important issue, to establish a link between reader and writer, as Cortázar explains:

> I am speaking about awareness of that sometimes indefinable but always unequivocal link that binds literature, which does not negate or disguise the reality surrounding it, to those who recognize themselves in it as readers—this link that transports both reader and writer beyond themselves in the realm of consciousness, historical perspective, politics and aesthetics.

The particular "dizzying imaginary voyage" of **"Secret Weapons,"** far from providing an escape from the world that surrounds us, recreates an aspect of it in a way that unsettles the reader (at least the male reader). If the writing of the story is therapeutic for Cortázar, helping him to relieve himself of part of the burden that seems personally to have obsessed him, it may be that it acts in a similar way for readers, forcing us to share vicariously an intense experience which raises important emotional issues.

The claim that literature can edify while it entertains is as old as Western literature. Classical comedy had a function as social criticism; Aristotle thought tragedy could purge strong emotions. (pp. 51-3)

These days the debate is still going strong, in the forum and in academe . . . . Norman Holland has used the model of psychoanalysis to try to understand more systematically what happens when we read. He suggests that the primary process is identification; we project our world view onto an object that fosters such projection, validates it and reassures us. A recent article goes one step further when it suggests, still relying on the language and theories of psychoanalysis, that literature, like the psychotherapist, is capable of altering such projected images and returning them, subtly reformed, to the self. Such "introjects," or internalized viewpoints, become available to the self which is open to reorganization. The text may be seen as an object onto which we can project our feelings much as the analysand projects feelings onto the analyst, but the text, like the therapist, may also confront us, directly or by suggestion, with evidence of the falseness, partiality, or contradictory nature of those feelings. The text may, then, not merely passively receive our identifications but may also have the power to reorganize them, to question and perhaps help to correct misconceptions. In the words of the conclusion of the article, "Literature is seen to function, as critics have maintained from the beginning, not only to please but also to edify, in the most fundamental sense: to build or reform the self."

Although he did not use this terminology, Cortázar's view of readers and texts suggests a similar belief. While his *"lector hembra,"* or passive reader, looks to literature only to validate "her" world view (the readers of romance are always assumed to be women or are at least treated as if they were women), the accomplice reader is apparently open-minded enough to let the text work on him. Cortázar's texts do not suit the passive reader because, by undermining our faith in the conventions of literature by challenging and mocking them, by insisting upon their own unreliability, and by refusing to offer simplistic moral views, they refuse to accept passive identification, and project back at us an image that is less pliant to authority and more likely to look for complicated answers or different and better questions.

I believe that something like this occurs with the two texts I have discussed in these pages. In **"El río"** and **"Secret Weapons,"** the reader (at least the male reader) identifies with the male protagonist, but such identification cannot be validated because the texts are informed, not only by an aura of mystery and ambivalence, but also by violently contradictory images of male sexuality. Nor do I mean to suggest that this process occurs consciously. Without suggesting that the stories do not project a truth available to the conscious mind, I am more interested in what happens unconsciously. All readers of Cortázar are probably aware of the important trick played on the reader of **"Continuity of Parks."** Whatever we may consciously have thought about reader/text relations, we have also been forced to experience directly, to re-enact, a process of reading which draws us in and then pulls the rug out from under us. The story makes its most effective critique of the traditional relationship between book and reader not by what it says but by involving us directly in an experience: it undermines our temptation toward blind faith in literature. By identifying with these fascinatingly portrayed (in this case truth seems to equal beauty) but morally flawed male protagonists, we share their actions and the shocking experiences that befall them; one discovers he is making love to his wife's corpse, the other turns into his girl friend's rapist. I suspect that, whatever conscious messages may be derived from these stories, our unconscious view of male sexuality is shaken up in the act of reading them and that, if we read with our minds open, the experience is as therapeutic for the reader as Cortázar felt it was for the writer. (pp. 53-4)

John H. Turner, "Sexual Violence in Two Stories of Julio Cortázar: Reading as Psychotherapy?" in Latin American Literary Review, *Vol. XV, No. 30, July-December, 1987, pp. 43-56.*

Maurice Hemingway and Frank McQuade (essay date 1988)

[*In the following excerpt, Hemingway and McQuade demonstrate political commitment in some of Cortázar's short fiction, concluding that in such stories as "Segunda vez," "Grafitti," and "Recortes de prensa," Cortázar successfully interprets an open-ended artistic aesthetic with a far-reaching political message.*]

The main preoccupations of Cortázar's works are not overtly political; his fiction is always informed by a belief in the ambiguity of experience, the irrational forces within man, as well as a sheer delight in the imagination and what he called "lo lúdico." Yet from his visit to Cuba in 1962, at least, he was deeply committed to the socialist cause in Latin America, particularly in Argentina, Cuba, Chile and, latterly, in Nicaragua . . . . His prestige as a writer

was to be used in such activities as journalistic propaganda and his membership of the Russell Tribunal. [In January, 1975, Cortázar participated in the Russell Tribunal, which denounced repression and exploitation in Latin America.] But in his fiction itself he refused to accept the constraints of "dead socialist realism" or an unsophisticated proletarian readership. The writer's revolutionary role was to be revolutionary in his writing; he had the responsibility "never to recede, for whatever reasons, along the path of creativity." The "enrichment of reality through culture" contributes to the political process because it has "a clearly demonstrable effect on the revolutionary capability of the people." For this reason, Cortázar very rarely wrote on political subjects and when he did he almost never treated them in the reductionist way his critics would have preferred. (pp. 49-50)

It is hardly surprising that Cortázar should have reacted in this individualistic way to demands that he should have put his art at the service of propaganda. Central to his aesthetic was the notion that artistic creation is based "on the expansion rather than the limitation of reality," a notion expressed most famously in the appeal to the "lector cómplice." Clearly the denunciation or celebration of particular events or situations requires, if it is to be at all successful, the narrowing down of the possibilities of interpretation so that a very precise message is communicated to the (more or less passive) reader.

Cortázar, however, did on occasion write fiction with political content, the most obvious example being his novel *Libro de Manuel* (1973) . . . . There exists also a small corpus of short stories on political themes. Two of these, **"Reunión"** and **"Alguien que anda por ahí,"** which deal with the Cuban revolution, fall, in our view, on the one hand into sentimentalism and on the other into melodrama, precisely because they betray Cortázar's open-ended view of art in favour of political propaganda. But in another four, he manages, either with political allegories (**"Segunda vez"** and **"Grafitti"**), or explorations of the relationship between art and political protest (**"Apocalipsis de Solentiname"** and **"Recortes de prensa"**), to draw attention to his political concerns, while largely, though not entirely, avoiding these pitfalls.

Both **"Segunda vez"** and **"Grafitti"** were published and presumably written after the military coup in Argentina

Cortázar during his time as an amateur jazz musician, photographed in Paris, 1960.

in March 1976, and knowledge of this fact leans one towards precise interpretations. Unlike other stories mentioned above, however, they do not necessarily relate to an obvious political situation, such as the Cuban revolution, and they have resonances wider than their political implications. **"Segunda vez"** is set in Buenos Aires and deals with a girl, María Elena, who answers an official summons to a government department. In the waiting room all the people are there for the first time, except a young man, Carlos, who is on his second visit, and is the last one to go in before María Elena. She is eventually called in, but Carlos does not come out, and in the office she sees neither him nor any other exit. She fills in a form, answers questions, and is told to return three days later. She leaves, waits awhile for Carlos, but he never emerges.

This is an allegory which, despite the Argentine setting, can be interpreted with varying degrees of particularity: María Elena, Carlos and the others in the waiting room can represent (I) humanity, (II) the victims of faceless bureaucracy, (III) people living in Latin American totalitarian (or is it authoritarian?) regimes, and (IV) the *desaparecidos* of contemporary Argentina.

That this is not a realistic narrative is clear from the opposition established between two kinds of waiting—the unsuspecting waiting of María Elena and her companions, on the one hand, and the raised sacrificial knife of the unidentified officials, on the other. We cannot help seeing each group as standing for something else.

The opposition is built into the very narrative structure of the story. The first paragraph and a half are told in the first person by a Ministry official, but thereafter the story is told by a third-person narrator from María Elena's point of view, until the last sentence when the first-person narrator reappears. This gives the uneasy impression that the whole of the story has been told (impossibly) by the all-knowing bureaucrat. The tone of the narrative frame is set in the first clause . . . . The fact that we know the identity of neither the subject nor the object of the verb makes all the more sinister the casualness of the introductory colloquialism and the calculated deliberateness of the details which follow. (pp. 50-1)

The second paragraph, with its slick jokes, fills out the picture of the loutish officials' ambush, until halfway through we are taken back to the beginning with a reference to "el negro López" bringing coffee . . . . There follows a bridge passage which takes us from one point of view to another . . . . Although there is here a shift to María Elena's point of view, it is not at all clear on a first reading that the official is no longer the narrator, a confusion aided by the phrase "eso sí," which he had used in the first sentence. Moreover, the third-person narrator disguises his voice throughout by the flow between omniscient narrative, direct and indirect speech and *style indirect libre.* (pp. 51-2)

As the narrative proper begins, the emphasis moves from the official's ominous confidence to María Elena's ingenuousness. She is overawed by the "aire serio" of the summons and stares repeatedly at its green stamp, illegible signature and the place and date. Her submissiveness is shown by the way she responds obediently to the mysterious summons and winds up her watch in the bus to make sure she is not late. Yet she is puzzled . . . that the Minis-

try should be in such an unlikely place, that there is no national flag outside and that there is no elevator. Despite her sense that all is not quite as she might expect, the atmosphere in the street is presented as ordinary—houses, shops, trees, parked cars and the *piropo* she receives from the news vendor.

As so often in Cortázar, we enter into a different world through a more or less metaphorical door, in this case a suitably anonymous one, with no bell or nameplate. What María Elena sees, however, is again emphatically ordinary—a typical waiting-room scene, with its predictable embarrassment and boredom. The whole of this section deals with the second kind of waiting, quite different from that of the bureaucrats in the narrative frame. María Elena is shy and self-conscious: she blushes, does not dare sit down until invited, join in the conversation or ask why two summonses are necessary. Her companions are equally inoffensive and go out of their way to be affable. The contrast between the atmosphere in the waiting room and the sinister waiting in the first section is heightened by the slightly satirical way in which these new characters are treated. Satire is suggested first by the generic names they are given . . . , and we are only given Carlos's name because we need to identify with him enough to be concerned about his disappearance. Each of the characters is faintly comic. (p. 52)

The alternation between narrator's voice, *style indirect libre,* direct and indirect speech creates an ironic perspective on the characters' awkward earnestness because it is observed from a disconcerting variety of angles. However, the irony in this section is not malicious: it establishes the innocent ingenuousness of the characters and a misleading sense of the ordinariness of the situation.

The effect is to make all the more striking the contrast between the scene in the waiting room and the scene awaiting María Elena beyond the door which leads to the office. The clerks are not at all concerned with her as an individual . . . . Her human concern for Carlos is placed beside the mechanical impersonality of the clerks as they put her through the form-filling exercise . . . . Once again the effect is created by a mixing of discourse: the *style indirect libre* relating María Elena's thoughts about the forms and her questions about Carlos, and then what she reads on the forms (her voice or the narrator's?) and the official's instructions in direct speech. Before leaving, she has to answer another set of questions about her personal circumstances, as if the State is particularly concerned with keeping track of people's movements. She is then told she has to return, and, given the disappearance of Carlos, the story's title takes on sinister overtones as we are made aware of the unspecified fate awaiting María Elena when she visits the office for a second time. But she is still unsuspecting, and after waiting for a few minutes for Carlos, she comes to a naive conclusion . . . . Here, the shift from indirect speech to *style indirect libre* foregrounds her naivety. She came to the first interview unsuspectingly, and will come to the second like a lamb to the slaughter.

The story ends by returning abruptly to the narrative frame. As before, there is a bridge passage . . . . The reader is bound to assume that the words "ella no" at the beginning of the second sentence continue the *style indirect libre* of the previous sentence. But the word "claro" and the rest of the sentence, which are repetitions of phrases used by the official in the opening narrative frame, indicate whose voice this is and even suggest that he has been the narrator throughout. This is a chilling ending, especially since the unpleasant narrator does not even disclose his secret to the reader: it is inside information just like the fate of Carlos. The overbearing, oppressive nature of the bureaucrats is emphasized by the fact that the clerk has apparently told us of María Elena's every move and thought on the day of the interview, and this impossible omniscience adds to the uncomfortable feeling that Big Brother is watching, that the System sees and knows all.

As we have suggested, the obvious contrast between victims and victimizers establishes the allegorical status of **"Segunda vez."** However, in typically Cortazarian manner, there is more than one possible interpretation. The ruthlessness of the officials and the disappearance of Carlos suggest that this is a comment on the "dirty war" of contemporary Argentina. On the other hand, the Orwellian resonances of the story's ending suggest that the subject is the wider one of Latin American totalitarian regimes. Yet María Elena and her companions are unlikely terrorists or political activists. Of course, that may be the point: *desaparecidos* or victims of persecution quite often are. Even so, the obvious ingenuousness and vulnerability of the victims may prompt us to see this story as a warning of the horror of the bureaucratic monster, not only in Latin America. The obvious reminiscence here of Kafka's *The Trial* (K is apparently innocent and no charge against him is specified) invites a wider interpretation, that through a more or less precise political situation Cortázar is dramatizing the individual's sense of living in a threatening world, where undeserved suffering and inexplicable death await him. (pp. 53-5)

"Grafitti" also centres on the victims of a repressive system (the *voseo* suggests Argentina as the setting) and, as in the previous story, they are unlikely political offenders. This story deals with the activities of a graffiti artist in a police state where all forms of expression are prohibited. The man normally operates by night, but his drawings are invariably removed the following day. His interest in this activity increases when he finds other drawings next to his own, as if in answer to his expression, and he feels strangely certain that these are by a woman. Because of the drawings an unusual relationship of understanding and affection grows; the man worries about the girl taking such great risks, tries to meet her, and is terrified when he sees someone he takes to be her being caught making a drawing and being bundled into a police van. He knows well what tortures she will suffer in police detention, and a month later at dawn he draws another impassioned picture. When he returns to his drawing, he finds that the girl has responded with another drawing, from which seems to emerge a grotesquely disfigured face.

Throughout the story there are various hints of political repression, in, for example, the existence of a curfew, the presence of police vans, the prohibition of all forms of self-expression and the fact that people avoid showing open interest in the graffiti for fear of recrimination. But the situation is never made clear because the protagonists are not political animals. The graffiti itself are not political and consist only of such things as boats on the sea or abstract forms, lines and colours. The implication of such graffiti being removed and the pains taken by the authorities to

catch the offenders is that such repression is obtuse, brutal and uncompromising . . . . (p. 55)

As in **"Segunda vez,"** the brutality of the system is contrasted with the humanity of its victims. Far from being intimidated, however, the graffiti artist pursues his activity with even greater zest when he finds a kindred spirit, another person who merely wants to draw pictures. Hence the element of human interest intensifies . . . . (p. 56)

Again, as in **"Segunda vez,"** authority finally pounces: the girl is arrested, possibly never to be seen again. But at this point Cortázar moves on from **"Segunda vez,"** where he simply draws attention to the horror of the situation. The final twist when the girl replies to the man's new drawing with a horrifying self-portrait points to one positive response to political repression. His drawing is all joy, passion and hope . . . . Her reply is a reminder of how such feelings are rewarded in the system under which they live. Yet she appeals to him to carry on . . . . We are presumably not intended to take this at face value: that is, the story is not simply about graffiti, but is an allegory in which the graffiti stand not only for freedom of expression but also the specifically human characteristics which are threatened by totalitarianism. No matter how fierce the repression, the expression of joy, passion and hope must continue. Here the crucial role of art in the political struggle is hinted at. It is suggested that the authoritarian establishment is philistine, and hostile to creativity, imagination and human emotions. It follows then that any sincere art is *engagé* in so far as it flows from and expresses these qualities, and that the artist's role is not to be a propagandist but to be precisely an artist.

True to this principle, Cortázar writes this story with the ambiguity characteristic of his work, particularly in respect of the narrative technique. The story is told in the second person and describes the thoughts of the graffiti artist. We are bound to assume that he is either addressing himself or being addressed by a third person, a kind of omniscient narrator observing his mental processes. But at the end of the story there is a surprise revelation: the narrator is neither the man nor a third person, but the woman . . . . In other words, the whole narration belongs to the woman and what seems to have been the man's speculation about her turns out to be her speculations about him.

Cortázar had already used an identical technique in **"Reunión con un círculo rojo"** (*Alguien que anda por ahí*) in which a second-person narrator describes a man's thoughts as he sits in a restaurant and observes an Englishwoman whom he takes to be in some kind of danger. He delays his exit until she has left and follows her, only to find that she disappears into thin air. He returns to the restaurant to discover that he himself is the murder victim. We now realize that it is the woman who is telling the story, and that she, an earlier victim, is now a ghost who had intervened to try to lure the man away from the restaurant. Now, although the narrative technique is identical, its effect in the earlier work is simply to heighten the horror of what is essentially a ghost story. Like **"Grafitti,"** it deals with an attempt at communication which in this case fails because the protagonist, like the reader, sees the situation as a mirror image of what it really is. He thinks he is protecting the woman when in fact she is protecting him. The ghost disappears at the end thinking that she has saved the man, but she had not bargained on his returning to the restaurant to save her. Now she looks forward to their meeting when he is dead. In **"Grafitti"** the sinister element is not supernatural or criminal but political, and the meeting between the man and the woman is not finally a meeting of ghosts but of hearts. In the earlier story the surprise revelation is little more than a contrivance, whereas in the later one it creates poignancy as we learn that the woman has been describing her fate in such a nobly detached way and as we realize that, hiding herself away, she has been speculating about the graffiti artist's reactions to her. This then is an original and unusual setting for a kind of political *Romeo and Juliet*, and the reader feels a sense of loss, a sense that delicate human feelings, symbolized by the graffiti, have been violated by a régime of terror.

"Apocalipsis de Solentiname" (*Alquien que anda por ahí*) was written in 1976, three years before the Sandinista revolution, and deals with a vision of destruction vouchsafed to the narrator. The plot is simple. The narrator (Julio Cortázar himself) visits Ernesto Cardenal's community on the island of Solentiname. There he sees and photographs paintings by local peasant artists. Back in Paris, he projects the newly developed films onto a screen only to witness not a series of simple paintings, but a string of atrocities taking place in many Latin American locations.

The story's narrative pattern is common in Cortázar's work: an ordinary situation is invaded by the fantastic to create a reaction of "extrañamiento." Here the invasion is made all the more striking by the fact that the story appears to be autobiographical. Cortázar did in fact visit Solentiname in 1976 and the story was written soon after in Costa Rica and Cuba. In the story, on his arrival in Costa Rica, he faces the usual press conference and the predictable questions. He enters a recognizable geographical and historical situation (Nicaragua and the Sandinista struggle against Somoza) and meets real people such as Ernesto Cardenal. But this is an insidious trap, because the last and most important part of the story is clearly not autobiographical: the stereotyped, bland, middle-class intellectual, Claudine, is not, one assumes, Cortázar's real *compañera*, and his vision, again one assumes, did not really take place. Another stratagem to draw the reader into the narrative is the way the narrator presents himself through his engaging manner—his tone is rambling, familiar, lighthearted, irreverent, with touches of self-irony. Because there is virtually no distance between him and us we are much more likely to share his sense of "extrañamiento" when the inexplicable occurs.

What then is the point of the story? It clearly has to do with the paintings which Cortázar captures on film. At the press conference he is asked about the film *Blow-Up*, which inevitably brings to mind **"Las babas del diablo."** This is not an arbitrary association because **"Apocalipsis"** is an obvious echo of the earlier story. In **"Las babas del diablo"** Michel, the photographer, has a complacent attitude towards the representation of reality in his art, but when he blows up one particular photograph it escapes his control and reintegrates into itself those parts of reality the photographer has edited out. A second glance back at **"Las babas del diablo"** appears early in **"Apocalipsis"** when Cortázar marvels at reality emerging from nothing on a polaroid negative. He asks a friend what would hap-

pen if, after a family photo, Napoleon on horseback were suddenly to appear. This reference to Napoleon as an incongruous intrusion into a conventional image is picked up at the end of the story, after the vision, when the same question occurs to the narrator. He fundamentally regards the paintings in the same complacent way Michel regards the scene he photographs. He places them in a good light, ensures that each painting exactly fills the viewfinder and jokes that his photographs will be better ("más grandes y más brillantes") than the originals. (pp. 56-9)

As frequently happens in Cortázar's work, we move imperceptibly from this rational, unthreatening world into another by means of a bridge passage : . . . He begins to describe the scenes of violence which now appear on the screen with the same slightly detached wistfulness with which he has described the untransformed photographs, thus confusing the reader and increasing the sense of shock. The narrator, drink in hand, sees not a comfortable souvenir but a disturbing vision of the reality faced by the paintings' creators. A hint of this reality had been given earlier when at Sunday Mass the faithful comment on the story of Jesus' arrest in the Garden. They understand only too well the threat of sudden arrest. Yet the mannered rhetoric of this particular section, with its accumulation of appositional phrases, suggests that the situation is being viewed from outside. One feels that only someone who does not share these people's danger could treat it so melodramatically.

But ultimately the impact of the story derives from the contrast between the paintings as Cortázar photographs them and the images he sees on the screen. He describes the paintings of rustic scenes, which lack normal proportion or perspective . . . . They represent the prelapsarian innocence and vulnerability of their creators, which is forcefully contrasted with the brutal violence done to them in Cortázar's vision. Our view of the paintings makes us see the violence as a kind of Slaughter of the Innocents which in the Gospel narrative prefigures the Passion of Jesus, part of which has already been referred to in the story. Another point one might infer is that, although the details of the vision may themselves seem fantastic, Cortázar is drawing attention precisely to the fact that the violence and cruelty of the political establishments in Latin America do indeed pass belief.

Since the writer is anxious not to confine our perspective only to Nicaragua, the vision ranges all over Latin America. The story itself begins with an affirmation of Latin American solidarity when the narrator affectionately abbreviates the Latin American nationalities to diminutives, "ticos," "nicas" and "tinos," and declares that there is no difference between them. (pp. 59-60)

This is, then, an ambitious story. And here we are bound to express misgivings. In the first place, although on the surface Cortázar does not modify his style to suit the subject matter, and introduces a fantastic element into the apparently realistic narrative, this element is fundamentally gratuitous, as it is not part of the thematic structure. The reality Cortázar attempts to make us aware of (violence in Latin America) is empirical reality, not an irrational dimension which challenges the empirical. Perhaps, more importantly, Cortázar is forced into certain oversimplifications. In order to rally the troops, he postulates a Latin American homogeneity and solidarity which, stated as baldly as it is, does not convince. Moreover, the prelapsarian innocence of the "pueblo," which we see in the paintings and during the obviously postconciliar Mass, is perilously close to sentimentality. It seems as if, in the way he presents his material, Cortázar is proposing a model of the "hombre nuevo." It consists not only of the innocence referred to above, but also of the good-humoured camaraderie which flows from shared commitment to the revolutionary struggle, and a creativity and spirituality free from the constraints of institutional forms, whether cultural or ecclesiastical. Elsewhere Cortázar showed himself well aware that the search for the "hombre nuevo" is not as simple as is here suggested. (p. 60)

By contrast, **"Recortes de prensa"** (*Queremos tanto a Glenda*) combines both denunciation and an awareness of the complexity of the issues at stake. A first-person narrator, an Argentine writer, Naomi, living in Paris, visits another Argentine exile, a sculptor who has asked her to provide a text for a book of reproductions of his work. While she looks at the series of sculptures of various forms of torture, he reads a press cutting (the first "recorte" of the title) she has handed him. The cutting contains an account by an Argentine woman of the torture, murder and abduction of members of her family between 1975 and 1977. Having agreed to provide the text, Naomi leaves, and in the street she finds a small girl crying. The girl leads her to her house where they are confronted by a man torturing his wife who is bound and gagged on the bed. Naomi knocks the man unconscious with a stool, releases his wife, and between them the two women bind and gag the man and proceed to torture him. Next day, in a state of shock, Naomi records on paper what has happened, rings the sculptor to inform him of the previous day's events and tells him that her story is to be the text he has requested. A few days later she receives a letter from him enclosing a cutting from *France-Soir* (the second "recorte"). This describes a crime identical to the one Naomi has been party to, with photos of the very place. Yet it occurred not in Paris but in Marseilles. Naomi returns to the street where she had met the child but cannot find the house. She does, however, see the child who, she is told by a concierge, was found lost in the street. Naomi returns home to add a final section to her text.

This story is written in a certain defensive spirit. Naomi, despite her sex, is a thinly disguised Julio Cortázar: an exiled Argentine writer, she feels qualms of guilt about writing on non-political matters . . . . In other words, she feels, like the author, the force of the accusation of hermeticism. Both the discussion between the two exiles and the development of the story as a whole constitute a statement about the role of the artist in the political struggle.

One can identify three strands in the argument. The first is the simple point of making information available. As Cortázar tells us in a note, the first of the press cuttings is real and the source is given. The long list of accusations is carefully punctuated by the comments of Naomi and the sculptor to make it more digestible for the reader. The other two strands depend on the reactions of the two Argentines to the horrors exemplified by the cutting, and deal on the one hand with morality and on the other with aesthetics.

We can infer the moral point both from the conversation between Naomi and the sculptor and from the ensuing scene of torture. In expressing their disgust at the cruelty described, they distance themselves from it. Violence is an alien phenomenon . . . . (pp. 60-1)

[However], Naomi who derives a dubious pleasure from experiencing torture secondhand, is now inflicting it herself. The implication is that violence and even sadism are not just instruments of political repression but are universal human characteristics, and that it is less than honest to pretend otherwise. If this is so, then it is not only Naomi but also the reader who is implicated because his reaction to the description of the torture of the woman, with its sexual overtones, may well be, like Naomi's, a mixture of indignation and pleasure.

The aesthetic point follows from the moral point. The kind of writing which oversimplifies issues or indulges in sensationalism by inviting the reader to see situations in terms of "el buen lado" and "el otro lado" narrows rather than broadens our vision and consequently cannot serve any genuinely revolutionary purpose. The alternative is understatement, which leaves the question open because it does not delimit unduly the reader's response. Hence the series of understatements in the story and the one exception (the torture of the woman) mentioned above . . . . The first "recorte," cast as it is as a formal complaint, is at times chillingly understated, notably the comment that the dismembered body of the woman's daughter could not be handed over . . . . After helping to bind the man, Naomi forgets what happened next and attempts to convey the horror of the torture by referring to a story by Jack London in which the torture of a trapper by a group of Indian women is conveyed without ever being described. Finally, when she opens the letter from the sculptor, she inadvertently tears the press cutting so that the account of the torture is missing.

But at the heart of this story is the possibility of art contributing to the changing of reality. In the first section the writer and sculptor lament their inability to affect events . . . . [Yet], Naomi, as she looks at the sculptures, finds that they abolish time and space . . . . Naomi herself, when she leaves the flat, is transported in time and space, to Marseilles at, apparently, another moment. The sound of her steps on the pavement echoes the ticking of the clock . . . . [Words] suggest that she is entering a vague, unreal world. For a moment, perhaps . . . , we may take this to be a typically Cortazarian descent into Hell. The allusion to Jack London suggests the possible fictiveness of this event and . . . that this may be a nightmare provoked by a reading of either or both of the press cuttings. On the other hand, the fact that Naomi awakes next day fully dressed and with a bleeding knee (she had cut it on leaving the place of torture) does not easily allow us to explain away the event in psychological terms.

This fantastic event is apparently a metaphor of what art can do. When Naomi declares "yo estaba ahí, como sin estar", her words suggest that art, like the sculptures, can make present (in both senses of the word) what is distant in time and space. Moreover, it can achieve this in a way mere propaganda cannot, because of its ability to draw the perceiver into itself in the way proper to each art form and to convey ambiguities and complexities.

The question underlying the previous analyses is this: how did Cortázar, given his views on the open-endedness of art, rise to the challenge of dealing with political issues in which he was deeply involved?

To take **"Apocalipsis en Solentiname"** first, on the surface, Cortázar does not depart from the style to which he is committed, in so far as the irrational plays a major role. Yet, as we have suggested, this is gratuitous and the story is fundamentally a work of realism which almost descends into sentimentality. The reason is not hard to find. Cortázar in this story is working with recent personal experiences in Nicaragua and seems unwilling, or unable, to distance himself from them. Consequently, he cannot resist making a precise propagandist point, and the apparent narrative sophistication is simply a cover for the actual thematic over-simplification. (pp. 62-4)

Although the other three stories we have discussed can be related to an identifiable political situation, the treatment of the political subject matter and its implications is broader, and the irrational dimension and narrative ambiguity are integrated into each story's thematic structure. The issues these stories address are not short-term political goals on a collective level, but the defense of wider human values on an individual level which, for Cortázar at least, is the motive for his ideological commitment. One may deduce from this that for him the artist's role in the revolutionary struggle is prophetic, or that of the leaven in the lump: he contributes to the revolution by exploring and making present the liberation of the individual from all spiritual tyranny (including self-deception) so that, when the military and political objectives have been achieved, the real aims of the revolution will not have been forgotten. (p. 64)

Maurice Hemingway and Frank McQuade, "The Writer and Politics in Four Stories by Julio Cortázar," in Revista Canadiense de Estudios Hispanicos, *Vol. XIII, No. 1, Otoño, 1988, pp. 49-65.*

Terry J. Peavler   (essay date 1990)

[*In the following excerpt from two chapters of his critical biography* Julio Cortázar, *Peavler examines what he considers the realistic stories in Cortázar's canon, including "Segundo viaje," "Reunión," and "Grafitti," and provides an overview of Cortázar's four books of miscellany.*]

The boundary that separates Cortázar's realistic stories from the psychological, the mysterious, or even the fantastic, is often a fine one indeed. The realistic works, however, tend to be more specific in describing the immediate setting, and more importantly, deal with situations that readers have encountered, if not in their own lives, certainly through newspapers and television. The elegance and beauty that are often found in a Cortázar story are here frequently replaced by a sense of the sordid and ugly. (p. 82)

The realistic stories are spread throughout Cortázar's career, although it is clear that they became far more important to him later in life, for only three of the ten pieces were published before 1977. The first two, **"Torito"** (**"Little bull"**) and **"Los amigos"** (**"The friends"**) already represent the two predominant themes of the stories in this group: violence (usually hand in hand with politics) and boxing.

"Los amigos" has received scant critical attention. Only three characters are involved, and but two actually appear, a murderer and his victim. The third ordered the killing. Romero and Beltrán are old friends who used to frequent the race track together. Now they are involved either in a political organization or in organized crime, and their code names reflect their ranks: Número Uno (Number one), who gives the order, Número Dos (Number two), who is to be killed, and Número Tres (Number three), the hit man. Número Tres (Beltrán) waits in his automobile outside the restaurant that Número Dos (Romero) frequents and guns him down when he arrives. As Beltrán drives away from the scene he reflects on how the last thing Romero had seen was the face of an old friend from the race track. While it shows Cortázar's interest in the theme of organized violence, **"Los amigos"** is inferior to the majority of his stories from the period in which it was written.

"Torito," however, is a much different case and deals with a different theme, professional boxing. In fact the qualitative difference between the two stories may be in part due to the author's reluctance to write "compromised" literature on the one hand, and his unrestrained love for boxing and for great prizefighters on the other. His interest in the sport is reflected in his other writings, particularly in "El noble arte" ("The noble art") and "Descripción de un combate o a buen entendedor" ("Description of a fight, or to the well-initiated"). The first essay, in addition to showing his early interest in boxing, laments the fact that he witnessed both the birth of radio and the decline of boxing. One of his most vivid memories of his childhood was gathering around the radio to listen to the infamous fight between Luis Firpo and Jack Dempsey in 1923. Early in the context, Firpo sent Dempsey through the ropes, and in clear violation of the rules fans helped the groggy champion back into the ring where he went on to destroy the "Bull of the Pampas." The rule violation was overlooked, for the fight took place at the Polo Grounds in New York. Cortázar never forgot the fight, or its repercussions in Argentina . . . . In the same essay, he recalls how one rainy night in Paris, in 1952, he remembered the great fighters—Gene Tunney, Tony Canzoneri, the Argentines Julio Mocoroa and Justo Suárez, and, greatest of all, Sugar Ray Robinson—and how that reverie produced the story **"Torito."** In light of this affection for the sport, it is hardly surprising that the three boxing stories are arguably the best of the realistic group.

Torito himself is a former prizefighter, now hospitalized, perhaps punchdrunk, who recounts his career to an old friend. He reflects on his greatest fights: how he laughed at Tani after defeating him, how he destroyed a black fighter named Flores, but especially how he himself was badly beaten by a man he calls simply "el rubio" (the blonde). He sees the irony in his current predicament, lying flat on his back in a hospital . . . . (pp. 82-3)

Cortázar's love for his main character is unmistakable, and his affection for the sport is clearly reflected in his use of language: . . .

It was a war, old man, I was in a full crouch and from underneath I was darting in and out, punch for punch. And I go to the head, I swear that half-way through we were already teeing off on one another without a break. That time I didn't feel a thing, my manager was holding me by the head and saying kid don't leave yourself so wide open, go to the body, kid, keep your right up. I could hear him but as soon as we came out we started taking it to each other again, and right to the end when we were both worn out it was great. You know that night after the fight we got together in a bar, the whole gang was there and it was beautiful to see how the kid laughed, and he said to me you're unreal, kid, God you can fight, and I said to him I beat you but as far as I am concerned it was a draw, and everyone drank to us and it was a madhouse I can't begin to describe.

According to Luis Leal, **"Torito"** is as historically and factually accurate as **"The Pursuer."** The title character is modeled after Justo Suárez, his manager was Pepe Lectcure, the black fighter, Flores, was Bruce Flowers, and the blonde who ended Torito's career was Billy Petrolle. That Cortázar empathized with and identified with Torito is clear, even without his statement that "I was Justo Suárez for two hours." In fact, as Mercedes Rein has argued, **"Torito"** is one of the earliest of Cortázar's works to include a character who is of interest as a human being, not as a narrative function.

"Segundo viaje" ("Second trip"), perhaps also inspired by Justo Suárez, is an even better story, and indeed, one of Cortázar's best. It too is told by a first-person narrator, although this time he is not the protagonist but a close friend. The protagonist, Ciclón Molina, was an average club fighter who had nonetheless served as sparring partner for Mario Pradás. Pradás had a stellar career in Argentina, and then went north to the United States to fight for the world championship. After several brilliant tune-up bouts, Mario Pradás was destroyed by the champion, Tony Giardello. His career immediately went into decline, and, after a few bad fights, he died. Ciclón Molina, who idolized Pradás, soon began to show moments of greatness in his fights, and eventually he too went north to fight for the title, and to exact revenge from "Tony Giardello, hijo de puta" (Tony Giardello, that son of a bitch).

The narrator is now an old man telling the story of Ciclón to a much younger individual . . . . (pp. 84-5)

The scenes in which the narrator and his friends gather around early radio sets to listen to the fights are quite reminiscent of the moment, so vividly painted by Cortázar in "El noble arte," in which his family listened to the Firpo-Dempsey match . . . . (p. 85)

Unfortunately, this time things ended even more badly than with Firpo or Pradás: Ciclón Molina died the same night of the fight, from the effects of Giardello's devastating hook. Now his friend repeats his story over a drink in a bar, and tries to understand.

"La noche de Mantequilla" ("Butterball's Night") contains a double plot: an account of an actual world-title fight between middleweight Carlos Monzón, the Argentine champion, and José "Mantequilla" Nápoles, the Mexican challenger who also reigned as welterweight champion for many years, a bout that took place in Paris, and the story of a fictitious spectator who is involved in a dangerous political intrigue. The protagonist of the fictitious account, Estévez, is sent by Peralta to the fight to slip a packet of money and papers into the satchel of Walter, a man he does not know. Peralta's plan seems flawless, for surely no one will notice the subtle exchange that is to take place at the height of the championship action.

As in the other stories, Cortázar provides a marvelous description of the fight. Estévez accomplishes his mission without a hitch, but as he is leaving the arena he encounters Peralta and an associate. They drive him away and interrupt his enthusiastic account of the fight and the success of his errand with the news that the man with the satchel was not Walter. Walter had been seized by "them" and tortured until he revealed the entire plan. Peralta had been unable to reach Estévez in time to stop the transfer of papers! As Estévez speculates aloud on how to escape and save his wife and child, it dawns on him that he is like "Mantequilla" who lost the fight on a technical knockout when his corner threw in the towel. A live Estévez, who might be caught and broken by the enemy, is too much of a threat to Peralta, who takes out his pistol to remove that danger.

"Butterball's Night" is clearly a political story, but it is superior to many of Cortázar's "committed" works. The ending is a definite surprise, prepared by the author's astute withholding of information throughout the story and by his diversion of the reader's attention. The reader, like Estévez, becomes totally engrossed in the fight. Against the backdrop of an event that captured world attention and in which a great deal of nationalistic pride was at stake, a political activist (indeed two, counting Walter) loses his life on a remote country road, killed by members of the same cause he supports.

Cortázar was first inspired to write realistic stories on political themes by the Cuban revolution, which finally ousted Batista in 1959, and his style in the early political stories was undoubtedly influenced by Cuban writers. Although his first such work, **"Los amigos,"** is weak, his second, **"Reunión" ("Meeting"),** is excellent, and considered by some to be one of the author's masterpieces. The story resulted from debates Cortázar had with young Cuban revolutionaries, particularly members of the "Caimán Barbudo" (Bearded Crocodile) group, about what sort of things he should be writing: "it was going to be a friendly challenge that I wanted to make to them. An effort to show them that one can write a fantastic story—that is perhaps the most fantastic in the book—that has, at the same time, revolutionary content." The piece was published in the group's journal, but none of them ever commented on it.

If the story is indeed fantastic, it is only so through Cortázar's exuberant eyes. The events are real, even though they may still seem impossible thirty years later. In late November 1956, a dilapidated yacht, the *Granma,* left Mexico with eighty-two men on board. This group was the nucleus of the Cuban revolution, including Fidel Castro, his brother Raúl, Ernesto "Che" Guevara, and many other heroes of the revolution. They landed in Cuba in the wrong spot, in a swamp, and under adverse conditions. Apparently they were betrayed by one of their own, for Fulgencio Batista's fighter planes and soldiers descended to eradicate them. A few days later, only fifteen were still together, yet two years later they swept triumphantly into

Havana. **"Meeting"** tells the story of the first few days after the landing.

The narrator, only thinly disguised, is Che Guevara, an asthmatic Argentine doctor turned revolutionary. The landing groups have been scattered by the swamp and by the strafing airplanes, but are trying to make their way to the Sierra where they will reunite (hence the original title, **"Reunión"**). Surrounded by wounded and dead companions, and covered with blood and vomit, the protagonist thinks of his friend Luis (Fidel Castro) and remembers Mozart's "The Hunt." Eventually, against impossible odds, the men meet atop a hill. They crack jokes as always, although none of them expected ever to see the others again.

Within its own context, **"Meeting"** is highly realistic, with a wealth of descriptive detail that one does not expect from Cortázar. Many of the events and even the quotes are taken from Che Guevara's account of those dark days, as is the epigraph for the story. The following account, from Guevara's description of the intense battle during which he was wounded, is illustrative: . . . "Someone, on his knees, was screaming that we had to surrender and then a voice, that I later learned belonged to Camilo Cienfuegos, shouting: 'No one surrenders here . . . ' followed by a curse." In Cortázar, this passage becomes . . . "I especially remember that someone began shouting that we had to surrender, and then a voice that answered him between two bursts of a Thompson gun, the Lieutenant's voice, a roar above the shouting, a: 'No, fuck it, nobody surrenders here!' "

It would be a mistake, however, to assume that Cortázar blindly followed Guevara's description of what happened. Instead he selected a number of events that he evidently found particularly significant in Guevara's lengthy account of the days of the Sierra Maestra and molded them into a fine story. The narrator's combined recollections of Luis and the music of Mozart gives the text a poetic quality that is unusual in literature of this type. While the thinly-disguised Fidel Castro is perhaps overly idealized, he is still a flesh-and-blood human being, unlike the idol portrayed in many Cuban writings on the same subject. While Alfred Mac Adam is correct in his assessment that **"Meeting"** is an example of "compromised" literature, it is certainly much more than that, for it is also a highly successful work of art. Moreover, as Néstor García Canclini has pointed out, in this story friendship and brotherhood, just as poetry and jazz do elsewhere, provide the antidote to nihilism.

Cuba and her revolution also provide the backdrop for the much less satisfying **"Alguien que anda por ahí"** (**"Someone Walking Around"**). In this story, Jiménez, a counterrevolutionary, comes to Santiago to plant a bomb in a factory. He is dropped off by an electric launch and makes his way to a motel where he is met by a coconspirator, Alfonso. During the night he suddenly awakens to find a stranger, a man he previously noticed in the bar, in his room. The stranger says he is simply "someone walking around" who used to be an exile himself (presumably before the revolution). The stranger then chokes Jiménez to death.

While **"Someone Walking Around"** reflects Cortázar's continuing dedication to political commitment, it fails aesthetically. Its fatal flaw is that the controlling perspective is that of Jiménez, the counterrevolutionary. As he sneaks ashore and into the motel, as he plans his moves and glances furtively about for signs of danger, the tension builds quickly and effectively. Unfortunately, the reader's empathy for Jiménez also consequently builds. Moreover, in the early pages only subtle references to a bomb that is remote-controlled and to Stevenson's last fight (presumably Cuban heavyweight great Teófilo Stevenson, winner of several Olympic gold medals) reveal that Jiménez is plotting against Castro, not Batista. In keeping with Cortázar's political sympathies, the stranger should be the story's hero, but he appears only at the end, when he murders the man with whom the reader identifies.

Other stories, with a more generalized political backdrop, are more successful. After the military junta began the terror of the "desaparecidos" (the disappeared) in his native Argentina in the mid-1970s, Cortázar could find his political material much closer to home. In fact, **"Segunda vez"** (**"Second Time Around"**) and **"Apocalipsis en Solentiname"** (**"Apocalypse at Solentiname"**) were both suppressed by the junta's censors in the Argentine edition of *Alguien que anda por ahí.* (pp. 86-9)

[As in stories from *Alguien que anda por ahí*] Cortázar continued experimenting with perspective in his subsequent collection [*Queremos tanto a Glenda*], including the story **"Grafitti"** (**"Graffiti"**), another story of urban political violence. This piece, like **"Second Time Around,"** was based on the mood in Argentina during the military dictatorship that began in 1975. At first the identity of the narrator is unclear, for everything is told in second person . . . . (p. 90)

The anonymous narrator continues to tell the story of the also unknown "tú" ["you"] and his drawings, illegal graffiti sketched hastily on city walls to communicate the anguish of a city imprisoned by its own government. An unknown individual that "tú" recognizes as a woman through her work begins to paint sketches alongside his, thus forming a sort of dialogue through drawings. The graffiti incense the police, who step up their efforts to eradicate both the sketches and those who create them. After a particularly bold and dangerous drawing by "tú," he sees his correspondent arrested and beaten when she tries to answer. The walls of the neighborhood remain clean for days, but eventually "tú" again begins his clandestine activity, now painting the screams of the government's victims.

One night, a picture of a face, smashed and with one eyeball hanging from its socket, is drawn next to his sketch. The final sentences reveal that the narrator is the woman correspondent, who has finally been released by the government, although now completely broken . . . . (pp. 90-1)

Like Cortázar's other better stories of political commitment, **"Graffiti"** succeeds because of a poetic and often ambiguous presentation that saves it from the fate of stories that are more specific and declamatory. While there is a certain thematic sameness that unites Cortázar's stories on urban political violence with those of other writers—the endless sirens, unmarked police cars, lorries filled with policemen and soldiers, dry fear and sudden violence—his works are as a whole vastly superior to those of authors who write only to denounce, without acquiring or utilizing the tools of the master storyteller.

The Argentine situation inspired one more short story, **"Satarsa."** The title derives from a palindrome, "atar a la rata" (tie up the rat), which when attempted in the plural yields "atar a l[as ratas]." Cortázar himself explained the genesis of the story. While he was playing with the word "rata" he thought of the palindrome. Then, "Suddenly the idea of the 'rata' led to a series of ideas by way of the palindrome and those ideas were ideas of horror, ideas that reflected my feelings about the news from Argentina that I had been listening to or reading. Then I began to write palindromes. The story begins, as you know, with a character who does palindromes."

The character in question is Lozano, a refugee from what is apparently a civil strife (according to Alazraki, it is the 1976-83 brutal military repression known as the "guerra sucia"). He and his friends capture and sell live rats to sustain themselves and their families, hoping to save enough to be able to move on. Meanwhile they live in abject misery; Lozano's daughter's hand was eaten by rats, and an acquaintance was killed by the giant rodents. Lozano, the bravest and best of the rat hunters, devises a plan to burn hordes of them out of their cave, and capture enough to finance his family's escape to another country. The plan, although extremely risky, seems to work, and after a fierce battle against the rodents Lozano and his companions are on their way home with cages bulging with screaming rats. On the way, however, they are ambushed by a much more ominous pack of "rats," soldiers, who kill all of the refugees.

In some ways, **"Satarsa"** is a borderline fantastic story, for the vivid accounts of the wars waged against the rats, with men wrapping their legs in leather armor to protect themselves from the swarms of rodents, seem incredible. Moreover, just how, to whom, and why the rats are sold is never made clear. However, the sordid details, the specificity of the violence and degradation, and the interest and sympathy aroused by Lozano, who retains a certain nobility despite his plight, make the story quite realistic. In the fantastic stories, Cortázar tended to avoid this kind of detail, relying instead on powers of indirect suggestion, on events alone, or on phlegmatic remarks by the characters.

The final realistic story, **"Recortes de prensa" ("Press Clippings"),** again treats the theme of urban violence, but with a radical difference: here it is not institutionalized or perpetrated by the state, or even by an organization, but by individuals, and on a most personal, sordid level. The narrator, Noemí, a famous author living in Paris, is asked by a sculptor, who has done a series of works on the theme of violence, to write a text to accompany his work. While she is studying his sculptures, she shows him a press clipping that is an open letter, written by an Argentine woman living in Mexico, that describes how the woman's daughter and several other members of her family have been tortured and killed by the military junta. Noemí agrees to write the piece. Shortly after she leaves the sculptor's apartment, she finds a small girl crying in the street. The girl tells her that her father is "doing things" to her mother. Noemí follows the girl to a garden shack where she discovers that the father has the mother tied to a bed frame and is burning her with a cigarette. Noemí knocks the man unconscious with a stool and helps his victim tie him in

her place. Then Noemí, a sophisticated woman of the world who is repulsed by violence in all its forms, helps torture the man. (pp. 91-2)

"Press Clippings" is perhaps Cortázar's harshest story in terms of its realistic details. It is rendered all the more disturbing by its depiction of how even a cultured author and sworn enemy of violence can suddenly become a torturer. One cannot help but wonder if Cortázar had not come to fear that the monsters he so abhorred and denounced throughout Latin America might dwell within us all, and especially within Julio Cortázar himself.

The realistic stories, on the whole, are less satisfying aesthetically than the other types, although some, particularly those that deal with boxing, are nonetheless excellent. That Cortázar felt that the realistic stories formed a group apart from the others is made clear by his own grouping when he prepared the complete collection [*Los relatos*]: six of the ten are included in the final and briefest volume, *Ahí y ahora (There and Now).* The six, **"Graffiti," "Second Time Around," "Press Clippings," "Satarsa," "Someone Walking Around,"** and **"Butterball's Night,"** are joined by only three other works: the gripping portrayal of violence in Nicaragua **"Apocalypse at Solentiname,"** the grim depiction of blindly obedient youths who will serve tomorrow's juntas in **"La escuela de noche" ("The School by Night"),** and the horrifying view of urban, governmental violence in **"Pesadillas" ("Nightmares").** The content of these nine stories, combined with the ominous volume title *Ahí y ahora,* is clearly a warning to the world of what was happening in Latin America.

It is unquestionable that Cortázar eventually felt compelled to subordinate the quality of his art to his message. Having said that, however, one must also admit that the quality of even the most compromised stories is so high as to be envied by many well-known but lesser artists. Those stories that suffer from the weight of their message are few indeed, and many remain that combine seriousness and urgency of content with artistry of the highest imaginable quality. (p. 93)

• • •

Julio Cortázar published four additional important books, each of which almost defies description. Two, *La vuelta al día en ochenta mundos (Around the Day in Eighty Worlds)* and *Ultimo round* **(Final round),** are collections of miscellany, including essays, poems, short stories, vignettes, photographs, and drawings. The other two, *Historias de cronopios y de famas (Cronopios and Famas)* and *Un tal Lucas (A Certain Lucas),* are less varied, offering a mixture of fantasy, fiction, and essay.

Cronopios and famas was an important precursor to *Hopscotch,* for here. Cortázar declared war on conventionality, using as his primary weapons the illogical and a keen sense of humor. The first section, the "Instruction Manual," immediately attacks quotidian reality: . . .

> Drive the head like a reluctant bull through the transparent mass at the center of which we take a coffee with milk and open the newspaper to find out what has happened in whatever corner of that glass brick. Go ahead, deny up and down that the delicate act of turning the doorknob, that act which may transform everything, is done with the indif-

ferent vigor of a daily reflex. See you later, sweet-heart. Have a good day.

Included in this section are instructions on how to cry . . . how to climb a staircase . . . and how to perform a number of additional tasks that are so common as to be automatic.

Instructions for less usual activities are included as well, such as how to understand three famous painters and how to kill ants in Rome. The English version even has **"Instructions on How to Dissect a Ground Owl."**

Not only does Cortázar bring to our consciousness the complexity of many everyday tasks . . . he also alters our perception of everyday reality. When, for example, someone gives the gift of a watch: . . .

> They gift you with the job of having to wind it every day, an obligation to wind it, so that it goes on being a watch; they gift you with the obsession of looking into jewelry-shop windows to check the exact time, check the radio announcer, check the telephone service. They give you the gift of fear, someone will steal it from you, it'll fall on the street and get broken. They give you the gift of your trademark and the assurance that it's a trademark better than the others, they gift you with the impulse to compare your watch with other watches. They aren't giving you a watch, you are the gift, they're giving you yourself for the watch's birthday.

The second section, "Ocupaciones raras" ("Unusual Occupations"), contains a series of vignettes about a most peculiar family living on Humboldt Street (the author's old neighborhood) in Buenos Aires. Many of these, because of length, development, and structure, could properly be considered short stories, although they are rarely classified as such, even by the author.

The first, **"Simulacros" ("Simulacra"),** introduces the narrator's large, extended family and some of its peculiar habits. In this case, despite the narrator's assurances that the family lacks originality, they decide to build an executioner's platform, complete with instruments of torture and a gallows, in the yard behind their house. The construction is carefully planned to coincide with the full moon, and the girls in the family practice their howls. The project, once recognized, is most distressing to the neighbors, but because the building site is protected by a strong fence, they are helpless to intervene. When the gallows is finally erected, the family eats supper on the platform, watches the moon rise, and finally goes off to bed. The neighbors seem disappointed, perhaps because they had feared (and eagerly anticipated) that the instruments would actually be put to use. (pp. 116-18)

"Conducta en los velorios" ("Our Demeanor at Wakes") has, like **"Simulcra,"** the length and structure of a short story. When someone in the neighborhood dies, the Humboldt Street family first determines if the grief displayed by the family of the deceased is genuine or feigned. If it is genuine, the Humboldt Street family stays home, but if it is feigned, the entire clan descends on the wake, taking it over completely. The method is simple: members of the Humboldt Street family position themselves as close to the casket as possible and begin to weep until everyone present can see clearly that they are more grief-stricken than the

family of the deceased. This action shames the immediate family into a greater show of mourning. When the funeral cortége departs for the cemetery, the invaders usurp the first cars, often leaving members of the immediate family to catch a bus or a taxi. At the ceremony, they again occupy the seats reserved for closest relatives, and offer lengthy eulogies that totally eclipse the paltry offerings of the immediate relatives—if, indeed, the latter even dare to offer their previously prepared speeches once they have heard the oratory skills of the family from Humboldt Street. Then, the clan steals quietly away, leaving the stunned and thoroughly humiliated mourners to fight with their neighbors over control of the lowering of the coffin.

The third section, "Material plástico" ("Unstable Stuff"), is the least satisfying portion of the book. Here, Cortázar's flights of fancy occasionally become excessively obtuse, although one might argue that Cortázar made them deliberately so as an attack on social norms. Under the title **"Maravillosas ocupaciones" ("Marvelous Pursuits")** he includes cutting the leg off a spider and sending it to the Minister of Foreign Affairs, or building a mound of sugar on a table in a restaurant, then spitting on top of the mound so that the saliva slides down like a glacier. One particularly childlike and amusing vignette describes how a bear (the narrator) inhabits the plumbing system of a house, running through all the pipes and flues to keep them clean and in good working order.

The final section, which gives the volume its title, has had the greatest impact because of its delineation of three types of creatures—cronopios, famas, and esperanzas—types that soon became an important part of the vocabulary of Cortázar and his critics. A number of vignettes distinguish sharply between the cronopios and the famas, but the esperanzas are never developed to any recognizable degree. Famas are perfectly organized—when they travel, every detail is attended to, even down to lists of doctors on emergency call in the cities they visit. Cronopios cannot find vacancies in the hotels, their weather is miserable, they miss their trains, and they can find no taxis. Yet cronopios love to travel and are delighted by everything they see. Cronopios are happy, intuitive, instinctive creatures. Famas are logical and organized. Cronopios tend to be artists, while famas make good business leaders. Esperanzas are sedentary. The doors to their homes illustrate some of their differences. An esperanza has a plaque that reads, "Bienvenidos los que llegan a este hogar" ("Welcome all who come to this home"); the fama has no welcoming sign; the cronopio has five. The first four repeat the standard platitudes, "Welcome all who enter here," "The house is small but the heart is immense," "The presence of a guest is as soft as rest," "We are poor but still we have good will." The final plaque, however, reads, "Este cartel anula todos los anteriores. Rajá, perro" ("This placard cancels all of the others. Beat it"). Cortázar was proud to be a cronopio, a term he also used to flatter his friends and those he admired. (pp. 118-19)

The playfulness that dominates ***Cronopios and Famas*** is equally evident in ***A Certain Lucas.*** Lucas would certainly have to be a cronopio. When he goes shopping for matches for a friend, he finds himself entangled in everyone else's problems, stopping to help in each case. In a café he runs into a friend who insists that Lucas help him persuade the pharmacist to dispense medicine for the friend's sister; the

Cortázar in 1974 with other Argentines at a barbecue in Saignon, France. Although a resident of France for most of his adult life, Cortázar maintained connections with his homeland.

then requests some whiskey for the friends to drink, then asks for a wardrobe to make the room tidier and upon which to place the daisy, since there is no longer room on the table. Finally, when the nurses are finished moving and arranging furniture, Lucas throws the flower away, because he does not care much for daisies anyway.

A Certain Lucas is tripartite, with the first and final sections dealing with the personality and misadventures of the title character, while the second part is unrestricted. The tone is maintained throughout, however, and each section is comprised of a number of short vignettes, sketches, or commentaries. **"Love 77,"** for example, from part 2, describes love, presumably in 1977: . . . "And after doing everything they do, they get up, they bathe, they powder themselves, they perfume themselves, they comb their hair, they get dressed, and so, progressively, they go about going back to being what they aren't." Other pieces from this section, although humorous, have an equally serious underlying concern. **"Texturologías"** **("Texturologies"),** for example, parodies the nature of literary polemics. The debate is set off when Michel Pardal writes a review of José Lobizón's collection of poetry, *Goose Grease* (presumably all proper names and titles are invented by Cortázar). Pardal, writing in a French journal, attacks the work as a "poverty-stricken product of Latin American poetry." Another critic, writing in a U.S. journal, attacks Pardal and his lack of understanding of the process of creation, and is in turn denounced, in Russian, for her ideological intentions. A British scholar then takes the Russian critic to task for his primitive approach to criticism, only to be lambasted in turn by a Frenchman, for his ignorance of the work of Saussure. A Mexican scholar then writes a glowing commentary on the work of the Frenchman, and quotes from the poetry collection entitled *Goose Grease* to validate his position. Needless to say, any mention of the original, literary cause of the debate has been missing since the first attack on the initial article. Its reintroduction at the end is quite accidental and ironic.

"Texturologies" is a masterful parody of self-interested literary scholarship, playing upon the messianic rigidity and even bitterness with which ideological and methodological positions are argued while literature itself, the raison d'être of criticism, is totally ignored. Major journals are also playfully jibed. *Tel Quel* (Just as it is), for example, the famous journal of semiology, becomes *Quel Sel* (What salt). The Mexican critic seems particularly victimized. His acceptance of the French semiotician is blind, his vocabulary is even more pretentious, and he is the only scholar cited who defends another rather than advance his own position. Nonetheless, he is the only one to return to the literary work in question, even though he apparently does so unknowingly: . . .

> An admirable heuristic study, that of Gérard Depardiable, which might well be categorized as structurological because of its double ur-semiotic richness and its conjunctive rigor in a field so propitious for mere epiphonemes. I will let a poet premonitorially sum up these textological conquests that already foretell the parametainfracriticism of the future.

Cortázar also directs his barbs at Third World politics. **"Un pequeño paraíso" ("A Small Paradise")** tells of a

pharmacist's wife convinces him to take pictures of her daughter's birthday party; a man is injured in a fall and Lucas climbs into the ambulance with him, but at the hospital has to explain what he is doing there since he is not a relative; he is unable to find a taxi to return home, and gets on a bus going in the wrong direction. As he stands on the opposite end of town, waiting for another bus that he suspects may never come, he is approached by an old lady who needs a match . . . . (p. 120)

For the most part, *Lucas* is a collection of such misadventures. He disrupts concerts and is unceremoniously thrown out. He begins a lecture with an attempt to specify his theme, using the table in front of him in contrast to the world at large as an example of the need to be specific about one's topic, but the table and his comments upon it become the lecture. He goes to great lengths to create a special birthday cake for a friend, but at the party he smashes it into her face, without explanation, and is thrown out into the rainy street. He sends love notes clear across the city by snail messenger so that he can savor the delicious wait. When he is hospitalized and a friend sends him a daisy, he asks the nurses to bring a table to set it on, then suggests that the table needs some chairs for friends, country in which the inhabitants are injected with little goldfishes that swim in their bloodstreams and make them happy. The government provides these injections free of charge. However, because the fish gradually mature and die, the citizens must take special medicine to flush them out of their systems. The government charges twenty dollars for each ampule, which means that it collects millions of dollars a year from its poverty-stricken citizenry. But the people are happy.

In those sections dedicated to Lucas, the character is often a thinly veiled Cortázar. In **"Lucas, sus discusiones partidarias"** (**"Lucas, His Partisan Arguments"**) he defends difficult, avant-garde literature against the demands of message-oriented militants, a debate that reflects the polemics the author was involved in throughout his life. Lucas proposes that if writers must stop advancing into new frontiers, then others must stand pat as well. Writers will write only that which is easily understood, but then farmers must also give up their tractors for shovels. A comrade, choked with laughter, proposes such "defenestration" upon a unanimous vote. Lucas immediately votes no.

A Certain Lucas is a delightful book, with often serious undertones. As a whole it is less esoteric and seemingly more finished than *Cronopios and Famas.* As one might expect, it continues Cortázar's push into subjects traditionally considered untouchable. In **"Lucas, sus pudores"** (**"Lucas, His Modesty"**), for example, the protagonist is mortified by the noises he emits, despite all his efforts to be silent, when he is in the bathroom of a house full of people. He is equally chagrined by the odors he leaves behind for the next occupant. *Lucas* is particularly significant for being the last of Cortázar's truly funny books. Later works are much more somber, much more concerned with imparting a serious social message.

The two remaining major works are more difficult to describe. Saúl Sosnowski calls them "almanacs," while the author himself suggests both almanac and the term "sponge": . . . "Everything that follows imitates to the degree possible . . . the respiration of a sponge, with the coming and going of fishes of memory, explosive combinations of times and states and materials that seriousness, that all-too-heeded lady, would consider irreconcilable." Almanacs, sponges, collages (as the back cover suggests), or miscellanea, these two works, *Around the Day in Eighty Worlds,* and *Ultimo round* are among the most innovative and important of Cortázar's works. Each contains a wide variety of literary selections—essays, poems, stories, sketches, and vignettes—as well as photographs, drawings, and reproductions of art works.

The first, *Around the Day,* contains three pieces later included in the complete story collection: **"La caricia más profunda"** (**"The Most Profound Caress"**), **"Estación de la mano"** (**"Season of the Hand"**), and **"Con legítimo orgullo"** (**"With Justifiable Pride"**) . . . . (pp. 120-23)

"Encuentro con el mal" (**"Encounter with Evil"**) appears to contain another short story that may have been excluded from the complete collection only because it recounts a "real" episode from Cortázar's life. Here, it is intercalated within a piece on famous murderers. It is less about a confrontation with evil than with fear. The narrator (Cortázar himself?) is riding in a bus with a handful of

passengers when a man dressed totally in black gets on. He senses the fear that the ominous stranger inspires in all the passengers (or projects his own fear onto them). What the protagonist dreads happens; the man in black gets off at his stop, but as the narrator scurries off into the dark night he looks over his shoulder to discover that the figure has disappeared.

Another selection, **"Noches en los ministerios de Europa"** (**"Nights in Europe's Ministries"**), describes the eerie nocturnal reality of official government buildings into which, by means of side entrances, unknown translators, such as Cortázar himself, may enter without even showing identification papers. Within these strongholds of power to which almost everyone including the citizenry is denied access, foreign translators glide up and down corridors by night, translating documents, exploring, and even browsing through files and desks. (p. 123)

Two essays provide valuable insights into the reasons for Cortázar's success as a writer. "No hay peor sordo que el que" (There is no one more deaf than the one who) discusses the reasons for the failure of authors from the River Plate region. Cortázar believes that writers from the area place far too much emphasis on conveying information, on the message, with too little attention to style, arguments reminiscent of his running polemic with socialist critics. The following essay, "Hay que ser realmente idiota para" ("Only a Real Idiot") describes the author's unbridled and unabashed enthusiasm for the creative efforts of others, even when it is undeserved. He admits to being little more than a child in theaters and concert halls, one whose enthusiasm is not shared by wife or friends who are sufficiently intelligent and objective to recognize inferiority. These two essays, the first on the importance of style over content, the second concerning the author's ingenuous delight in art and the world about him, provide important keys to Cortázar's immense success as a creative artist. (p. 124)

Ultimo round is certainly not the author's last round, as the title suggests, nor was he in need of a comeback as a writer, for his international prestige was ever on the rise. However, the boxing analogies suggest that he was keenly aware that a writer, like a prize-fighter, may well deteriorate with time. All of his writings on boxing stress the importance of skill, training, and courage, certainly as important to the writer as to the athlete, and he frequently compared the two professions, even though the writer has no visible opponent. However, as William L. Siemens has pointed out, the description and the photographs that accompany the essay portray only one fighter, the fallen former champion.

Ultimo round is the most interesting and the most important of the potpourri books. In the first edition, even its physical nature was radically different, for the pages were cut horizontally, with one text on the top two-thirds and another on the bottom. The lower pages were in small print and normally contained documents and short texts, while the upper pages contained selections that Cortázar considered more significant. (pp. 124-25)

Like *Around the Day in Eighty Worlds, Ultimo round* contains a dizzying array of materials: poems, stories, letters, documents, essays, photographs and drawings. Most, but not all, are by Cortázar. (p. 125)

In one [story] **"Los testigos"** (**"The Witnesses"**; *Around the Day*), the narrator observes a fly that flies upside down. He sections off his apartment, gradually reducing the insect's available space, so that he can observe it close up. Once he has it well confined, he tells his friend Polanco (whom the reader will remember from *62: A Model Kit*) about his discovery, and asks him to verify it. Polanco refuses, on the basis that no one will believe him, for the fly is not upside down at all; the rest of the world has become inverted.

In an equally playful spirit, **"El tesoro de la juventud"** (**"The treasure of youth"**) describes how scientists improve the transportation system through a sort of reverse evolution: the propeller plane is found to be superior to the jet, the ship and the train superior to the propeller plane, and so forth, until the best means of locomotion of all, walking, is finally discovered. In **"De la grafología como ciencia aplicada"** (**"On Graphology as an Applied Science"**; *Around the Day*) Cortázar demonstrates the ramifications of graphology, basing his sketch on the premise that if one's handwriting can reveal everything about his or her character, then one only need learn to write exactly like Napoleon for the process to work in reverse. **"Datos para entender a los perqueos"** (**"Some Facts for Understanding the Perkians"**) describes how in the country of Perk they invented the wheel, but unlike that of the rest of the world, their version is imperfectly round, having a projection in one spot. These projections result in a sharp jolt with every turn of the wheel, or several jolts if the four wheels on a carriage are not aligned. This phenomenon has had quite notable effects on the Perkian culture, including its perceptions and language. (pp. 125-26)

Ultimo round seems to be simultaneously the author's most playful and most serious book. It is also his most important work in terms of the sensual and the erotic. In **"/que sepa abrir la puerta para ir a jugar"** (**"/May you learn to open the door to go out to play"**) he seriously proposes that the lack of erotica in Latin America is proof of underdevelopment. Advanced, confident cultures, such as those of France, England, and the United States, all have large quantities of erotica. The text, filled with references to and quotes from some of the major works of erotic literature, is accompanied by pictures of the scantily clad lower torso of a woman and by other suggestive illustrations.

The extremely sensual **"Tu más profunda piel"** (**"Your Most Profound Skin"**) is reminiscent of the love scenes from *A Manual for Manuel* and *62: A Model Kit*. The narrator, whose memories are triggered by the sensuous odor of tobacco, addresses his now-absent lover. Unlike the scenes in the novels, however, this description is purely sensual; the woman is willing and even eager to yield to the narrator's desires. (p. 127)

Less obvious, but equally sensual, is Cortázar's description of a girl, perched on the seat of a parked bicycle while engaged in conversation with friends, in **"Ciclismo en Grignan"** (**"Cycling in Grignan"**). The first-person narrator, enjoying a cup of coffee at a sidewalk café in Grignan, observes and is totally mesmerized by the interaction between the animated young woman's tightly clad buttocks and the leather-covered bicycle seat. Again, while reference is made to sexual intercourse . . . , unlike in the novels, here the act is not violent. In fact, the heightened eroti-

cism of *Ultimo round* is due primarily to the increased role played by the narrator's, and hence the reader's, imagination. (pp. 127-28)

Also significant in *Ultimo round,* although less important than the selections already discussed, are those pieces that, in true Cortazarian fashion, simply toy with the very bases of literature. **"Desayuno"** (**"Breakfast"**) tells the rather simple story of what happens in the narrator's home on a typical morning—but the nouns and pronouns are all wrong. The narrator says "Good morning, brother" to his mother. "Good morning, Doctor," she replies. He greets his father with "Good morning, nephew" and receives a "Good morning, lover" in return. Language is also undermined in **"La inmiscusión terrupta"** (**"Meddlance Tersplat"**), which is narrated in "giglish," the nonsense language invented by the characters of *Hopscotch*.

"Cortísimo metraje" (**"Short Feature"**) imitates a film that has been so severely cut that it reads like a sort of shorthand. Nonetheless, the reader is able to piece together the story of a man who picks up a young woman hitchhiker, then tries to rape her. The woman, however, shoots him with a pistol she had hidden, robs him, and steals his car. It is clear that she is a professional highway bandit.

Finally, **"Ya no quedan esperanzas de"** (**"There is no hope left that"**) is comprised of only the introductory clauses for sentences that the reader has to complete. This challenge echoes that offered by the series of poems . . . , which the reader is instructed to cut into segments (following the dotted lines, of course!), shuffle, and read. (p. 128)

These works, *Cronopios and Famas, A Certain Lucas, Around the Day in Eighty Worlds,* and *Ultimo round* . . . reflect Cortázar's fidelity to the principles he repeatedly defended in his debates with those critics who demanded of him more message and less play. His advice to writers is again clearly and succinctly stated in **"No te dejes"** (**"Don't Let Them"**; *Ultimo round; Around the Day*): do not let the capitalists buy you out; do not let those who share your views force you away from literature and into dogmatic "commitment"; maintain at all costs that delicate balance that allows your "commitment" to flower in your art. In summary, . . . "Bitter but necessary moral: Don't let them buy you out, [kid], but don't sell yourself either." These works in particular reveal the degree to which Cortázar was successful in pursuing those goals. (p. 129)

Terry J. Peavler, in his Julio Cortázar, *Twayne Publishers, 1990, 154 p.*

FURTHER READING

Alazraki, Jaime. "The Fantastic of Surrealist Metaphors." *Dada/Surrealism,* No. 5 (1975): 28-33.
     Examines the influence of surrealism and the fantastic on Cortázar's fiction.

Alazraki, Jaime, and Ivask, Ivar, eds. *The Final Island: The*

Fiction of Julio Cortázar. Norman, Okla.: University of Oklahoma Press, 1976, 199 p.

Collection of critical essays by well-known critics of Cortázar's fiction. The editors have also reprinted a short story and two essays by Cortázar.

Bennett, Maurice J. "A Dialogue of Gazes: Metamorphosis and Epiphany in Julio Cortázar's 'Axolotl'." *Studies in Short Fiction* 23, No. 1 (Winter 1986): 57-62.

Analysis of the protagonist's transformation in "Axolotl" as a complete blending of man and animal.

Bishop, Tom. "Cronopios and Famas." *Saturday Review* LII, No. 39 (27 September 1969): 26-7.

Appreciative review of *Cronopios and Famas* that stresses Cortázar's use of satiric humor.

Chanady, Amaryll B. "The Structure of the Fantastic in Cortázar's 'Cambio de luces'." In *The Scope of the Fantastic—Theory, Technique, Major Authors: Selected Essays from the First International Conference on the Fantastic in Literature and Film*, edited by Robert A. Collins and Howard D. Pearce, pp. 159-64. Westport, Conn.: Greenwood Press, 1985.

Discourse on the nature of the fantastic in literature, using Cortázar's short story "Cambio de luces" as example.

Garfield, Evelyn Picon. *Julio Cortázar*. New York: Frederick Ungar Publishing Co., 1975, 164 p.

Critical biography based chiefly upon interviews with Cortázar.

Gyurko, Lanin A. "Narcissistic and Ironic Paradise in Three Stories by Cortázar." *Hispanófila* 50 (1974): 19-42.

Posits that ironic destruction awaits protagonists in the short stories "Las puertas del cielo," "La isla a mediodía," and "El otro cielo," whose inward searches for self-fulfillment are narcissistic.

Hernández del Castillo, Ana. *Keats, Poe, and the Shaping of Cortázar's Mythopoesis*. Amsterdam: John Benjamins B. V., 1981, 135 p.

Studies the apparent influences of English poet John Keats and Edgar Allan Poe on Cortázar's fiction, focusing on Cortázar's reshaping of literary archetypes present in the works of these writers.

Jaeck, L. M. "The Engendering of Consciousness in Cortázar's 'Axolotl,' 'Casa tomada,' y 'Las babas del diablo'." *NS/Northsouth* V, No. 10 (1980): 103-20.

Deconstructionist analysis of Cortázar's short stories "Axolotl," "Casa tomada," and "Las babas del diablo."

Johnston, Craig P. "Irony and the Double in Short Fiction by Julio Cortázar and Severo Sarduy." *Journal of Spanish Studies: Twentieth Century* 5, No. 2 (Fall 1977): 111-22.

Analysis of Cortázar's short story "Historia" and Severo Sarduy's "Junto al Río de Cenizas de Rosa," noting specific functions of irony and the *Doppelgänger* that serve to create metafictional themes in these stories.

Krich, John. "A Great Man's Doodles." *New York Times Book Review* (4 May 1986): 9.

Review of *Around the Day in Eighty Worlds*, characterizing the work as representative of Cortázar's faults and strengths.

Neyenesch, John. "On This Side of the Glass: An Analysis of Julio Cortázar's 'Axolotl'." In *The Contemporary Latin American Short Story*, edited by Rose S. Minc, pp. 54-60. New York: Senda Nueva de Ediciones, 1979.

Discusses the immobility of several protagonists in Cortázar's short stories as a recurring motif suggestive of Western humanity's desire to escape reality.

Standish, Peter. "Cortázar's Latest Stories." *Revista de Estudios Hispanicos* XVI, No. 1 (1982): 45-65.

Explores thematic and technical elements within stories collected in *Alguien que anda por ahí* and *Octaedro*, discerning recurring characteristics evidenced in these collections and earlier works.

Valdés, Richard A. "Julio Cortázar's *Fantomas contra los vampiros multinacionales*: Literature or Propoganda?" In *The Contemporary Latin American Short Story*, edited by Rose S. Minc, pp. 82-7. New York: Senda Nueva de Ediciones, 1979.

Discerns artistic merit, personal dedication, and a commitment to social justice as Cortázar's aesthetic principles for literature with a political message, distinguishing *Fantomas contra los vampiros multinacionales* as a work that adheres to these principles.

Stephen Crane

1871-1900

(Full name: Stephen Townley Crane. Also wrote under the pseudonym Johnston Smith) American novelist, short story writer, poet, and journalist.

Crane was one of America's foremost Realistic writers, and his works have been credited with marking the beginning of modern American Naturalism. His Civil War novel *The Red Badge of Courage* is a classic of American literature that realistically depicts the psychological complexities of fear and courage on the battlefield. Influenced by William Dean Howells's theory of Realism, Crane utilized keen observations, as well as personal experience, to achieve a narrative vividness and sense of immediacy realized by few American writers before him. While *The Red Badge of Courage* is acknowledged as his masterpiece, Crane's novel *Maggie: A Girl of the Streets* is also acclaimed as an important work in the development of literary Naturalism, and his often-anthologized short stories "The Open Boat," "The Blue Hotel," and "The Bride Comes to Yellow Sky" are considered among the most skillfully crafted stories in American literature.

Born in Newark, New Jersey, Crane was the youngest in a family of fourteen children. His desire to write was inspired by his family: his father, a Methodist minister, and his mother, a devout woman dedicated to social concerns, were writers of religious articles, and two of his brothers were journalists. Crane began his higher education in 1888 at Hudson River Institute and later enrolled at Claverack College, a military school that nurtured his interest in Civil War studies and military training—knowledge he later used in *The Red Badge of Courage*. During two subsequent and respective semesters at Lafayette College and Syracuse University, Crane was distinguished more for his prowess on the baseball diamond and football field than for his ability in the classroom. During his college years, however, Crane also began his writing career. He worked as a "stringer" for his brother's news service, and it is thought that he wrote the preliminary sketch of *Maggie* while still at Syracuse.

In 1891, deciding that "humanity was a more interesting study" than the college curriculum, Crane quit school to work full time as a reporter with his brother and part time for the New York *Tribune*. In New York Crane lived a bohemian existence among the local artists in the city's Bowery district, and his firsthand knowledge of poverty during this period enabled him to realistically depict tenement life in his writings. In 1893, after several publishers had rejected his manuscript of *Maggie* on the grounds that his grim descriptions of slum realities would shock readers, Crane privately published this first novel under a pseudonym. According to Crane, *Maggie* "tries to show that environment is a tremendous thing in the world and frequently shapes lives regardless." Critics suggest that the novel was a major development in American literary Naturalism and that it introduced Crane's vision of life as warfare. Influenced by the social Darwinism popular at the time, Crane viewed individuals as victims of purposeless forces and be-

lieved that they encountered only hostility in their relationships with other individuals, society, nature, and God. Also prominent in his first novel is an ironic technique that exposes the hypocrisy of his characters' moral tenets when set against the sordid reality of slum life. Although it received the support of such literary figures as Hamlin Garland and William Dean Howells, *Maggie* was not a success. It was not until 1896, after Crane tempered the brutalities in a second edition, that the work received wide recognition.

Crane's second novel, *The Red Badge of Courage*, won him international fame following its publication in 1895. His vision of life as warfare is uniquely rendered in this short, essentially plotless novel. Often compared to Impressionist painting, *The Red Badge of Courage* is a series of vivid episodes in which a young soldier, Henry Fleming, confronts a gamut of emotions—fear, courage, pride, and humility—in an attempt to understand his battlefield experiences; in this respect, Fleming represents the "Everyman" of war. Critics have long debated whether *The Red Badge of Courage* should be considered a product of any specific literary movement or method. The work has been claimed by several schools and referred to as Realistic, Naturalistic, Symbolistic, and Impressionistic. A succinct estimate of this debate is offered by Edwin H. Cady, who writes: "The very secret of the novel's power inheres in the inviolably organic uniqueness with which Crane adapted all four methods to his need. *The Red Badge of Courage*'s method is all and none. There is no previous fiction like it." Shortly after the publication of *The Red Badge of Courage,* Crane published the poetry collection *The Black Riders, and Other Lines.* Although he is not widely recognized for his poetry, this volume of free verse foreshadowed the work of the Imagist poets with its concise, vivid images. During the mid-1890s Crane continued to work as a journalist, traveling throughout the American West and Mexico for a news syndicate, and later using his experiences as the basis for fictional works, including the stories in his early short fiction collections *The Little Regiment, and Other Episodes of the American Civil War* and *The Open Boat, and Other Tales of Adventure.* Returning to New York, Crane wrote *The Third Violet,* a story of bohemian life among the artists of the city. This novel is considered one of his least accomplished works, and some early critics believed that it was an indication of Crane's failing talent.

In 1897 Crane met Cora Taylor, proprietor of the dubiously named Hotel de Dream, a combination hotel, nightclub, and brothel. Together as common-law husband and wife they moved to England, where Crane formed literary friendships with Joseph Conrad, H. G. Wells, and Henry James. Shortly after this move, Crane left to report on the Spanish-American War for the New York *World,* an assignment he accepted, in part, to escape financial debts he and Cora had accrued. Although Crane was ill when he returned to England, he continued writing fiction in order to satisfy his artistic and financial needs. With *Active Service* he produced another work considered flawed by critics. This novel, based on his experiences as a correspondent during the Greco-Turkish War, is often described as an uneven and sprawling work. By 1900 Crane's health had rapidly deteriorated due to his own general disregard for his physical well-being. After several respiratory attacks, Crane died of tuberculosis at the age of twenty-eight.

Although Crane achieved the pinnacle of his success with the novel *The Red Badge of Courage,* many critics believe that he demonstrated his greatest literary strength as a short story writer. Such stories as "The Open Boat," "The Blue Hotel," "The Bride Comes to Yellow Sky," and "The Monster" are widely anthologized and are considered among his major achievements in the genre. "The Open Boat" is based on Crane's experience as a correspondent shipwrecked while on a filibustering expedition to supply Cuban revolutionaries in 1897. This Naturalistic story pits a handful of men stranded for days in a lifeboat against the destructive power of an indifferent, though violent, sea. Characteristically, Crane uses vivid imagery throughout this story to underscore both the beauty and terror of natural forces and to convey the antagonism between the survivors and the sea, which Crane viewed as indicative of the struggle of all humanity against nature. Despite the claims of critics who regard "The Open Boat" as merely a piece of creative journalism, many commentators consider Crane to be at his best in "The Open Boat" and agree with Robert Wooster Stallman's observation that although Crane transcribed "The Open Boat" from an actual event, "he converted every detail into symbol, designed

every image into a schemework of relationships, and manipulated the original facts and their sequence to form a patterned whole, a construct possessing a life of its own."

Crane's facility with the short story form is again displayed in the tragicomic story "The Blue Hotel." In this deceptively simple Western tale, an outsider, "the Swede," becomes an inevitable victim of his own preconceptions about the "Wild West"—expecting a lawless, uncivilized Western world, he creates in a quiet Nebraska town the unrest he is seeking and is killed in a brawl. Using a mixture of fantasy, realism, and parody in this work, Crane treats such themes as the nature of fear and courage and the role fear plays in acts of violence. In another Western story, "The Bride Comes to Yellow Sky," Crane parodies the "shoot 'em-up" Western myth. In this comic story Yellow Sky marshal Jack Potter arrives in town with his new bride and is confronted in the street by his old nemesis Scratchy Wilson, an aging cowboy who reverts to the role of tough gunfighter when drunk. Unarmed and with his wife beside him, Potter convinces Scratchy that he can no longer act out their ritual mock gunfight. Reluctantly, Scratchy lowers his gun and walks away disheartened. Eric Solomon observed: "The serious element of this comic tale comes from Scratchy Wilson's recommendation that, with Potter's shucking off his character of mythic marshal, Scratchy cannot retain his own particular dream role as mythic Western gunfighter." Solomon continued that in these and his other Western adventures tales, "Crane laughs at the formulae of the Western story; without commitment he still manages to employ the traditional evocative qualities of the form while engaged in the process of criticizing the form itself."

Like a number of Crane's short stories, "The Monster" is set in the fictitious town of Whilomville, New York, a site loosely based on Crane's childhood hometown of Port Jervis, New Jersey. In this tale Crane relates the story of Henry Johnson, a black coachman whose face is brutally and permanently misshapen by fire when he rescues his employer's son from a burning house. Henry's employer, Dr. Trescott, not only preserves Henry's life after the accident, but gratefully vows to take care of him as long as he lives. However, the people of Whilomville are terrified of Henry, whom they have transformed through gossip and half-truths into a horrific monster. Dr. Trescott's son, whom Henry rescued, and his companions play games at Henry's expense, and even Dr. Trescott's friends demand that he keep Henry elsewhere and then abuse the doctor when he refuses to comply. Several critics have assigned deep symbolic meanings to the characters in the story— Henry as Jesus Christ and Dr. Trescott as God, for example—though interpretations vary. However, most critics agree that although Henry is the ostensible monster in this tale because of his physical deformity, Crane's depiction of small-town hypocrisy and cruelty reveals society as the true monster.

Critics have long debated whether Crane's fiction should be considered a product of any specific literary movement or method. His work has been claimed by several schools and referred to as Realistic, Naturalistic, Symbolistic, and Impressionistic. Proponents of Realism view works like *Maggie: A Girl of the Streets, The Red Badge of Courage,* and "The Open Boat" as unromanticized accounts of urban slum life, the Civil War, and survival at sea in a lifeboat, respectively. Defenders of a Naturalistic reading contend that the actions and experiences of many of Crane's protagonists are shaped by social, biological, and psychological forces and that their "development" as characters is incidental to Crane's expert depiction of how these forces determine human existence. Stylistically, Crane's writings contain elements of both Impressionism and Symbolism. For example, some critics note that such works as *The Red Badge of Courage,* "The Open Boat," "The Blue Hotel," and "The Monster" are laden with symbols and images, while others explain that Crane's episodic narrative structures and consistent use of color imagery are indicative of an Impressionistic method. While commentators generally agree that for the most part Crane disregarded plot and character delineation in his work and was unable to sustain longer works of fiction, many critics contend that Crane's artistry lies in his ability to convey a personal vision based on what he termed his own "quality of personal honesty." In his short stories, as in most of his work, Crane utilized an incisive irony that suggests the disparity between an individual's perception of reality and reality as it actually exists. In so doing, according to most critics, Crane pioneered the development of literary Naturalism and other forms of fiction that subsequently supplanted the genteel Realism characteristic of late nineteenth-century American literature.

(For further information on Crane's life and career, see *Twentieth-Century Literary Criticism,* Vols. 11, 17, 32; *Contemporary Authors,* Vol. 109; *Dictionary of Literary Biography,* Vols. 12, 54, 78; and *Concise Dictionary of American Literary Biography: 1865-1917.*)

PRINCIPAL WORKS

SHORT FICTION

The Little Regiment, and Other Episodes of the American Civil War 1896
The Open Boat, and Other Tales of Adventure 1898
**The Monster, and Other Stories* 1899
Whilomville Stories 1900
Wounds in the Rain: A Collection of Stories Relating to the Spanish-American War of 1898 1900
**The Monster 1901
Last Words 1902
Men, Women, and Boats 1921
The Sullivan County Sketches 1949
Stephen Crane: An Omnibus (poetry, short stories, and novels) 1952
The Complete Short Stories and Sketches of Stephen Crane 1963
The New York City Sketches of Stephen Crane, and Related Pieces 1966
The Works of Stephen Crane. 10 vols. (poetry, short stories, novels, and journalism) 1969-72
The Western Writings of Stephen Crane 1979
Stephen Crane: Prose and Poetry (novels, novellas, short stories, sketches, journalism, and poetry) 1984

OTHER MAJOR WORKS

Maggie: A Girl of the Streets (A Story of New York) [as Johnston Smith] (novel) 1893; also published as *Maggie: A Girl of the Streets* [revised edition], 1896

The Black Riders, and Other Lines (poetry) 1895
The Red Badge of Courage: An Episode of the American Civil War (novel) 1895
George's Mother (novel) 1896
The Third Violet (novel) 1897
Active Service (novel) 1899
War Is Kind (poetry) 1899
†*The O'Ruddy* (novel) 1903
The Collected Poems of Stephen Crane (poetry) 1930
Stephen Crane: Letters (letters) 1960
The War Dispatches of Stephen Crane (journalism) 1964
The Complete Novels of Stephen Crane (novels) 1967

*Contains only "The Monster," "The Blue Hotel," and "His New Mittens."

**Contains "The Monster," "The Blue Hotel," "His New Mittens," "Twelve O'Clock," "Moonlight on the Snow," "Manacled," and "An Illusion in Red and White."

†This work was completed by Robert Barr.

H. G. Wells (essay date 1900)

[*Wells is best known today, along with Jules Verne, as the father of modern science fiction and as a utopian idealist who correctly foretold an era of chemical warfare, atomic weaponry, and world wars. His writing was shaped by the influence of Arnold Bennett, Frank Harris, Joseph Conrad, and other contemporaries, including Stephen Crane, with whom he exchanged criticism and opinions on the art of writing. Throughout much of his career, Wells wrote and lectured on the betterment of society through education and the advance of scientific innovation. A Fabian socialist and student of zoologist T. H. Huxley, Wells was, until his last bitter years, a believer in the gradual, inevitable moral and intellectual ascent of humanity. Much of his literary criticism was written during the 1890s at the* Saturday Review, *under the direction of Harris. In the following excerpt from an important early piece of criticism on Crane, Wells provides a personal reminiscence and appreciation of Crane's work, in which he laments the effects of early success on Crane and considers Crane's foray into journalism "the great blunder and misfortune of Crane's life," as it "utterly wrecked his health." Wells goes on to praise Crane's short fiction as "efforts in which his peculiar strength was displayed" and "The Open Boat" as "beyond all question, the crown of all his work."*]

The untimely death at thirty of Stephen Crane robs English literature of an interesting and significant figure, and the little world of those who write, of a stout friend and a pleasant comrade. For a year and more he had been ailing. The bitter hardships of his Cuban expedition had set its mark upon mind and body alike, and the slow darkling of the shadow upon him must have been evident to all who were not blinded by their confidence in what he was yet to do. Altogether, I knew Crane for less than a year, and I saw him for the last time hardly more than seven weeks ago. He was then in a hotel at Dover, lying still and comfortably wrapped about, before an open window and the calm and spacious sea. If you would figure him as I saw him, you must think of him as a face of a type very typically American, long and spare, with very straight hair and straight features and long, quiet hands and hollow eyes, moving slowly, smiling and speaking slowly, with that deliberate New Jersey manner he had, and lapsing from speech again into a quiet contemplation of his ancient enemy. For it was the sea that had taken his strength, the same sea that now shone, level waters beyond level waters, with here and there a minute, shining ship, warm and tranquil beneath the tranquil evening sky. (p. 233)

Though my personal acquaintance with Crane was so soon truncated, I have followed his work for all the four years it has been known in England. . . . His success in England began with *The Red Badge of Courage,* which did, indeed, more completely than any other book has done for many years, take the reading public by storm. Its freshness of method, its vigor of imagination, its force of color and its essential freedom from many traditions that dominate this side of the Atlantic, came—in spite of the previous shock of Mr. Kipling—with a positive effect of impact. It was a new thing, in a new school. (p. 234)

I do not propose to add anything here to the mass of criticism upon this remarkable book. Like everything else which has been abundantly praised, it has occasionally been praised "all wrong"; and I suppose that it must have been said hundreds of times that this book is a subjective study of the typical soldier in war. But Mr. George Wyndham, himself a soldier of experience, has pointed out in an admirable preface to a re-issue of this and other of Crane's war studies, that the hero of the *Red Badge* is, and is intended to be, altogether a more sensitive and imaginative person than the ordinary man. He is the idealist, the dreamer of boastful things brought suddenly to the test of danger and swift occasions and the presence of death. To this theme Crane returned several times, and particularly in a story called **"Death and the Child"** that was written after the Greek war. That story is considered by very many of Crane's admirers as absolutely his best. I have carefully re-read it in deference to opinions I am bound to respect, but I still find it inferior to the earlier work. The generalized application is, to my taste, a little too evidently underlined; there is just that touch of insistence that prevails so painfully at times in Victor Hugo's work, as of a writer not sure of his reader, not happy in his reader and seeking to drive his implication (of which also he is not quite sure) home. The child is not a natural child; there is no happy touch to make it personally alive; it is THE CHILD, something unfalteringly big; a large, pink, generalized thing, I cannot help but see it, after the fashion of a Vatican cherub. The fugitive runs panting to where, all innocent of the battle about it, it plays; and he falls down breathless to be asked, "Are you a man?" One sees the intention clearly enough; but in the later story it seems to me there is a new ingredient that is absent from the earlier stories, an ingredient imposed on Crane's natural genius from without—a concession to the demands of a criticism it had been wiser, if less modest, in him to disregard— criticism that missed this quality of generalization and demanded it, even though it had to be artificially and deliberately introduced.

Following hard upon the appearance of *The Red Badge of Courage* in England came reprints of two books, *Maggie* and *George's Mother,* that had already appeared in America six years earlier. Their reception gave Crane his first taste of the peculiarities of the new public he had come upon. These stories seem to me in no way inferior to the *Red Badge;* and at times there are passages, the lament of Maggie's mother at the end of *Maggie,* for example, that it would be hard to beat by any passage from the later book. But on all hands came discouragement or tepid praise. . . . Yet, they are absolutely essential to a just understanding of Crane. In these stories, and in these alone, he achieved tenderness and a compulsion of sympathy for other than vehement emotions. (pp. 235-36)

And upon the appearance of these books in England came what, in my present mood, I cannot but consider as the great blunder and misfortune of Crane's life. It is a trait of the public we writers serve, that to please it is to run the gravest risk of never writing again. Through a hundred channels and with a hundred varieties of seduction and compulsion, the public seeks to induce its favorite to do something else—to act, to lecture, to travel, to jump down volcanoes or perform in music halls, to do anything, rather than to possess his soul in peace and to pursue the work he was meant to do. Indeed, this modern public is as violently experimental with its writers as a little child with a kitten. It is animated, above all things, by an insatiable desire to plunge its victim into novel surroundings, and watch how he feels. And since Crane had demonstrated, beyond all cavil, that he could sit at home and, with nothing but his wonderful brain and his wonderful induction from recorded things, build up the truest and most convincing picture of war; since he was a fastidious and careful worker, intensely subjective in his mental habit; since he was a man of fragile physique and of that unreasonable courage that will wreck the strongest physique; and since, moreover, he was habitually a bad traveller, losing trains and luggage and missing connections even in the orderly circumstances of peace, it was clearly the most reasonable thing in the world to propose, it was received with the applause of two hemispheres as a most right and proper thing, that he should go as a war correspondent, first to Greece and then to Cuba. Thereby, and for nothing but disappointment and bitterness, he utterly wrecked his health. He came into comparison with men as entirely his masters in this work as he was the master of all men in his own; and I read even in the most punctual of his obituary notices the admission of his journalistic failure. I have read, too, that he brought back nothing from these expeditions. But, indeed, even not counting his death, he brought back much. On his way home from Cuba he was wrecked, and he wrote the story of the nights and days that followed the sinking of the ship with a simplicity and vigor that even he cannot rival elsewhere.

"The Open Boat" is to my mind, beyond all question, the crown of all his work. It has all the stark power of the earlier stories, with a new element of restraint; the color is as full and strong as ever, fuller and stronger, indeed; but those chromatic splashes that at times deafen and confuse in *The Red Badge,* those images that astonish rather than enlighten, are disciplined and controlled. "That and **'Flanagan',**" he told me, with a philosophical laugh, "was all I got out of Cuba." I cannot say whether they were worth the price, but I am convinced that these two things are as immortal as any work of any living man. And the way

"The Open Boat" begins, no stress, plain—even a little gray and flattish:

> None of them knew the color of the sky. Their eyes glanced level, and were fastened upon the waves that swept toward them. These waves were of the hue of slate, save for the tops, which were of foaming white, and all of the men knew the color of the sea. The horizon narrowed and widened, and dipped and rose, and at all times its edge was jagged with waves that seemed thrust up in points like rocks.
>
> Many a man ought to have a bath-tub larger than the boat which here rode upon the sea. These waves were most wrongfully and barbarously abrupt and tall, and each froth-top was a problem in smallboat navigation.
>
> The cook squatted in the bottom, and looked with both eyes at the six inches of gunwale which separated him from the ocean. His sleeves were rolled over his fat forearms, and the two flaps of his unbuttoned vest dangled as he bent to bail out the boat. Often he said, "Gawd! That was a narrow clip." As he remarked it, he invariably gazed eastward over the broken sea.
>
> The oiler, steering with one of the two oars in the boat, sometimes raised himself suddenly to keep clear of the water that swirled in over the stern. It was a thin little oar and it seemed often ready to snap.
>
> The correspondent, pulling at the other oar, watched the waves and wondered why he was there.

From that beginning, the story mounts and mounts over the waves, wave frothing after wave, each wave a threat, and the men toil and toil and toil again; by insensible degrees the day lights the waves to green and olive, and the foam grows dazzling. Then as the long day draws out, they come toward the land. (pp. 236-38)

"The Open Boat" gives its title to a volume containing, in addition to that and **"Flanagan,"** certain short pieces. One of these others, at least, is also to my mind a perfect thing, **"The Wise Men."** It tells of the race between two bartenders in the city of Mexico, and I cannot imagine how it could possibly have been better told. And in this volume, too, is that other masterpiece—the one I deny—**"Death and the Child."**

Now I do not know how Crane took the reception of this book, for he was not the man to babble of his wrongs; but I cannot conceive how it could have been anything but a grave disappointment to him. To use the silly phrase of the literary shopman, "the vogue of the short story" was already over; rubbish, pure rubbish, provided only it was lengthy, had resumed its former precedence again in the reviews, in the publishers' advertisements and on the library and book-sellers' counters. The book was taken as a trivial by-product, its author was exhorted to abandon this production of "brilliant fragments"—anything less than fifty thousand words is a fragment to the writer of literary columns—and to make that "sustained effort," that architectural undertaking, that alone impresses the commercial mind. Of course, the man who can call **"The Open Boat"** a brilliant fragment would reproach Rodin for not completing the edifice his brilliant fragments of statuary

are presumably intended to adorn, and would sigh, with the late Mr. Ruskin for the day when Mr. Whistler would "finish" his pictures. Moreover, he was strongly advised—just as they have advised Mr. Kipling—to embark upon a novel. And from other quarters, where a finer wisdom might have been displayed, he learned that the things he had written were not "short stories" at all; they were "sketches" perhaps, "anecdotes"—just as they call Mr. Kipling's short stories "anecdotes"; and it was insinuated that for him also the true, the ineffable "short story" was beyond his reach. I think it is indisputable that the quality of this reception, which a more self-satisfied or less sensitive man than Crane might have ignored, did react very unfavorably upon his work. They put him out of conceit with these brief intense efforts in which his peculiar strength was displayed. (pp. 239-40)

It would be absurd, here and now, to attempt to apportion any relativity of importance to Crane, to say that he was greater than A. or less important than B. That class-list business is, indeed, best left forever to the newspaper plebiscite and the library statistician; among artists, whose sole, just claim to recognition and whose sole title to immortality must necessarily be the possession of unique qualities, that is to say, of unclassifiable factors, these gradations are absurd. Suffice it that, even before his death, Crane's right to be counted in the hierarchy of those who have made a permanent addition to the great and growing fabric of English letters was not only assured, but conceded. To define his position in time, however, and in relation to periods and modes of writing will be a more reasonable undertaking; and it seems to me that, when at last the true proportions can be seen, Crane will be found to occupy a position singularly cardinal. He was a New Englander of Puritan lineage, and the son of a long tradition of literature. There had been many Cranes who wrote before him. He has shown me a shelf of books, for the most part the pious and theological works of various antecedent Stephen Cranes. He had been at some pains to gather together these alien products of his kin. For the most part they seemed little, insignificant books, and one opened them to read the beaten *clichés,* the battered outworn phrases, of a movement that has ebbed. Their very size and binding suggested a dying impulse, that very same impulse that in its prime had carried the magnificence of Milton's imagery and the pomp and splendors of Milton's prose. In Crane that impulse was altogether dead. He began stark—I find all through this brief notice I have been repeating that in a dozen disguises, "freedom from tradition," "absolute directness" and the like—as though he came into the world of letters without ever a predecessor. In style, in method and in all that is distinctively *not* found in his books, he is sharply defined, the expression in literary art of certain enormous repudiations. . . . Any richness of allusion, any melody or balance of phrase, the half quotation that refracts and softens and enriches the statement, the momentary digression that opens like a window upon beautiful or distant things, are not merely absent, but obviously and sedulously avoided. It is as if the racial thought and tradition had been razed from his mind and its site ploughed and salted. He is more than himself in this; he is the first expression of the opening mind of a new period, or, at least, the early emphatic phase of a new initiative—beginning, as a growing mind must needs begin, with the record of impressions, a record of a vigor and intensity beyond all precedent. (pp. 241-42)

H. G. Wells, "Stephen Crane: From an English Standpoint," *in* The North American Review, *Vol. 171, No. 2, August, 1900, pp. 233-42.*

Carl Van Doren (essay date 1945)

[*Van Doren is considered one of the most perceptive critics of the first half of the twentieth century. He worked for many years as a professor of English at Columbia University and served as literary editor and critic of the* Nation *and the* Century *magazines during the 1920s. A founder of the Literary Guild and author or editor of several American literary histories, Van Doren was also a critically acclaimed historian and biographer. In the following excerpt, Van Doren surveys Crane's career, positing that Crane "was not primarily a novelist" but "a story-teller without nonsense, a kind of poet among story-tellers."*]

Modern American literature, sounding its preliminary notes in the last decade of the nineteenth century, was the victim of opinions and events which obscured its promise and delayed its triumph. . . . The decade had enough striking books to set a new fashion, but they were by writers who were not a school and had no concerted program. (pp. v-vi)

Of these younger writers Crane, born in Newark in November 1871, was the most original and most precocious, as if he had, as William Dean Howells said, sprung into life fully armed. In school and at Lafayette College and Syracuse University Crane fell asleep over Dickens, called Tennyson swill, could not stand Stevenson, knew nothing of Henry James, thought Flaubert long-winded, preferred Tolstoy to any other contemporary. He cared little for reading, but he was a summer reporter while he was at school and college, and he looked directly and immediately at what he saw, with the least help from the forms or methods provided by literature. His two years at a military academy at Claverack may have disposed him to war as a subject, but when he left Syracuse in 1891 to be an irregular reporter for various newspapers in New York his first interest was in the city streets and slums. Like most writers of that New York decade he studied the Bowery, then the most famous centre of poverty and crime in America. Unlike any of the others, Crane produced—some time during the winter of 1891-2—a Bowery story which was neither jocose nor sentimental, but tragic and honest. . . . This plain story [*Maggie: A Girl of the Streets*] of a girl who is driven from home by a drunken mother, takes refuge with a lover, is deserted by him, and drowns herself in despair seemed naked and shocking to its few readers in 1893. They held that if a writer did choose such a theme he must sentimentalize or moralize it. Crane told the story bluntly, though somewhat naïvely and angularly. He would have thought it condescending and indecent to add alien comments to the pitiful plot.

He wrote another short Bowery novel, *George's Mother* (1896), less affecting and less felicitous than *Maggie,* and several sketches, of which the best was **"An Experiment in Misery"** (in *The Open Boat,* London, 1898) based on his own experience in a Bowery shelter. But hardly had *Maggie* been printed when Crane began reading whatever he could get hold of about the Civil War, and in March 1893 he wrote the first draft of his novel *The Red Badge of Courage,* which he rewrote and sold within a year to a newspaper syndicate as a serial. He knew nothing about war except what he had read or heard veterans tell. He was only twenty-two. Yet he had learned enough to visualize a battle in detail; he had the tact to limit himself to the sensations of a recruit his own age; he tolerated no heroics; and he was already master of a style that flashed like swords in the sun.

He might have followed the sale of the *Red Badge* with a quick cycle of Civil War stories if late in 1894 he had not been sent by the syndicate on a journey to the Far West and Mexico as a kind of roving correspondent free to write what he chose. . . . Crane took his intent eyes and individual vision with him wherever he went: Nebraska, Nevada, Arizona, Texas, Mexico. Somewhere in Nebraska he saw a hotel painted so ugly a blue that he afterwards chose it for the scene of ugly deeds. San Antonio delighted him, and was later to be the city from which Potter took his bride home to Yellow Sky. In a Mexican village Crane and his guide barely missed robbery and possibly murder at the hand of an ominous bandit. The night life of Mexico City gave Crane material for stories even sharper and harder than his stories of night life in New York.

Back in New York in May 1895, Crane found that his book of verse, *The Black Riders and Other Lines,* written at least two years before, had been published with little notice. In October, just before his twenty-fourth birthday, the *Red Badge* appeared as a book and brought him instantaneous renown. . . . The chronology of his actual writing is not exact, but the year after *The Black Riders* and the *Red Badge* he published a revised *Maggie, George's Mother,* and ***The Little Regiment and Other Episodes of the Civil War,*** and had written at least some of his Western and Mexican stories.

Of the Civil War episodes **"A Mystery of Heroism"** is pure, concentrated Crane. In the midst of a battle—"a tremendous scuffle, as if two animals of the size of islands were fighting"—Collins, of A Company, wishes he had a drink from a well which he can reach only by crossing an open meadow under the fire of an enemy battery. Because some of his companions laugh at his crazy idea, he resentfully insists on going.

> When Collins faced the meadow and walked away from the regiment, he was vaguely conscious that a chasm, the deep valley of all prides, was suddenly between him and his comrades. . . . He had been blindly led by quaint emotions, and laid himself under an obligation to walk squarely up to the face of death. But he was not sure that he wished to make a retraction, even if he could do so without shame. As a matter of truth, he was sure of very little. He was mainly surprised. . . . He wondered why he did not feel some keen agony of fear cutting his sense like a knife. . . . He was, then, a hero. He suffered that disappointment which we would all have if we discovered that we were ourselves capable of those deeds which we most admire in history and legend. This then, was a hero. After all, heroes were not much.

Later Collins feels wild fear and comes back in panic. To cap the mystery, and irony, of his heroism, the water he has brought is accidentally spilled. **"The Little Regiment"** turns on the characters of two brothers, sharply realized, who hide their strong affection for each other under apparent ridicule and contempt. Crane resisted the temptation, irresistible to almost any other story-teller, to be sentimental at the happy end. In **"Three Miraculous Soldiers"** Crane admitted women to his saga: in particular a girl who has hidden three Confederate fugitives in a barn and protects them from Union pursuers.

Though Crane was seldom at his best when there were women in his stories, this story is better than the more popular episode **"A Grey Sleeve,"** which runs painfully close to the traditional formula of the plucky Southern maiden and the Northern officer who must do his duty but nevertheless wins her involuntary love. Crane was not always pure Crane, and once in a while sagged into imitation. There is an alloy of Richard Harding Davis in **"A Grey Sleeve,"** as there is of contemporary historical romance in Crane's one Revolutionary story, **"Ol' Bennet and the Indians"** (in *Last Words*). He planned a Revolutionary novel of New Jersey, but never wrote it. The Civil War was as far back in time as his imagination went with any passionate knowledge.

At the end of 1896 Crane, sent to Florida to report filibustering activities, sailed from Jacksonville on a small steamer loaded with guns and cartridges for the insurrectionists in Cuba. The steamer sank early in the voyage, and Crane was one of the four men in the last boat to leave. **"The Open Boat,"** published the following June in a magazine, is as near reporting as Crane ever came in a story. There were the captain, the cook, the oiler, and the correspondent. They rowed fifty hours to land at Mosquito Inlet, where a wave broke the oiler's back. The narrative is true history, corrected by the captain's recollections, but it is also vivid art. "None of them knew the colour of the sky," the famous opening sentence says. "Their eyes glanced level, and were fastened upon the waves that swept toward them." The first words set the tone of the tense chronicle. They were men of one mind, united against the sea that might be death to them. It was a "subtle brotherhood. . . . The hurt captain . . . could never command a more ready and swiftly obedient crew than the motley three of the dinghy. . . . And after this devotion to the commander of the boat, there was this comradeship, that the correspondent, for instance, who had been taught to be cynical of men, knew even at the time was the best experience of his life." When it looked as if no one on shore would see and help them, the correspondent—that is, Crane—raged at fate. "If I am going to be drowned," he reflected, and reflected again in the same words to himself, "if I am going to be drowned, why, in the name of the seven mad gods who rule the sea, was I allowed to come thus far and contemplate sand and trees? Was I brought here merely to have my nose dragged away as I was about to nibble the sacred cheese of life?" The story is circumstantial, with a kind of iron humour, stinging intensity, and arresting images. "It is easier to steal eggs from under a hen than it was to change seats in the dinghy." "These two lights were the furniture of the world." "The welcome of the land to the men of the sea was warm and generous; but a still and dripping shape [the dead oiler] was carried slowly up the beach, and the land's welcome for it could be only the different and sinister hospitality of the grave."

Dropping his plans to write a play with Clyde Fitch, and leaving behind him a minor novel, *The Third Violet*, to be

Photograph of Crane in 1896, about which he wrote, "[It] is I think a very good portrait."

published in 1897, Crane was by March of that year in England on his way to Greece to report the war with Turkey. Harold Frederic welcomed him to London and introduced him, an observer said, as if he had invented the boy. Crane was slow in forming his impressions of London and he did not care for Paris. In Athens, with no language but English, he was handicapped in getting news, confused by the tumult of new experiences, and sick. Though he picked up material for a graphic short story and another minor novel, Crane knew that, as writer, he had wasted time in Greece. Cora Taylor, whom he had met in Jacksonville, came to Athens, nursed him through dysentery, and was married to him in August. He returned to England and took a house at Oxted in Surrey, where at Frederic's insistence Crane began *Active Service* in November. When it went badly he turned aside to write **"The Monster"** in the evenings of a single week.

This powerful story, the only one of Crane's stories to deal with a whole civilian community rather than a few individuals, has its scene laid in Whilomville, New York, which was more or less Port Jervis, where Crane had lived as a child and where the young recruit of the *Red Badge* had enlisted. The monster is a Negro coachman who, rescuing his employer's child from a burning house, has had his own face burned away and has become harmlessly insane. Dr. Trescott, grateful and loyal, not only preserves Henry's life after the accident but also resolves to take care of him as long as he lives. But the children of the small town are terrified, the women upset, the men concerned.

Gossip makes the pathetic victim monstrous, enlarging the horror, till even Trescott's friends demand that he keep Henry elsewhere, and then abuse and desert the doctor when he will not. For Crane, in whom loyalty was almost the strongest personal emotion, the conflict was acutely dramatic. He could not—or did not—organize any such plot as Mark Twain's in *The Man That Corrupted Hadleyburg.* But Crane told his story with fierce sympathy for the victims and coldly multiplied the instances which show how much more cruel a community can be than perhaps any single member of it could. His fame had grown. One New York magazine refused the story, but another published it the next August.

In March 1898 he was writing "a new kind of play" with Joseph Conrad. Again a war intervened. Crane left for New York, to be rejected by the navy, and then to hurry as correspondent to Key West and Cuba. Though he was feverish and exhausted throughout the campaign and in general less effective than some of the other correspondents, he was officially mentioned for bravery at Guantanamo and now and then in his dispatches rose brilliantly above journalism. Having finished *Active Service* in Havana, he returned in October to New York, to collect some of his best work in *The Open Boat and Other Tales of Adventure.* Here in "Death and the Child" was the essence of what he had seen and felt of war in Greece. "Horses—One Dash," the story of his encounter with a Mexican bandit, though a briefer episode, still ranks close to "The Open Boat" as a transcript in fiction of a personal experience. "The Five White Mice," an invented story of a threatened deadly duel between some Mexicans and Americans in Mexico City, is Crane at his most intense in the passage describing the New York Kid's sensations as he faces the Mexican knife.

Good judges disagree as to which is the best of the Western stories. Willa Cather prefers "The Bride Comes to Yellow Sky," perfectly realistic, humane, humorous [see Further Reading list]. Jack Potter, town marshal, arriving by train with his bride in his frontier town, meets the drunken Scratchy Wilson on a rampage. Potter is unarmed, with his terrified wife beside him. Looking into Scratchy's venomous revolver, Potter does not, as some writer of talent might have made him, reflect on the awful brevity of human life and love, but sees what he may lose in images which only a writer of genius would have known how to put into Potter's downright consciousness. "He was stiffening and steadying, but yet somewhere at the back of his mind a vision of the Pullman floated: the sea-green figured velvet, the shining brass, silver, and glass, the wood that gleamed as darkly brilliant as the surface of a pool of oil—all the glory of the marriage, the environment of the new estate." Another writer might have made Scratchy, finally convinced that Potter is married and must therefore be spared, act in a burst of alcoholic chivalry. Not the more pungent Crane. His bad-man "was not a student of chivalry; it was merely that in the presence of this foreign condition he was a simple child of the earlier plains. He picked up his starboard revolver, and, placing both weapons in their holsters, he went away. His feet made funnel-shaped tracks in the heavy sand." There is more of Crane's sardonic doctrine in "The Blue Hotel," which H. L. Mencken prefers. A Swede comes to a Nebraska hotel resembling the actual one Crane had seen, expects to find life wild in the West, creates in a mild town

the turmoil he has been looking for, and is killed in a brawl. His death is not altogether the crazy accident it seems. Though it has no large meaning, it springs logically enough from the sleeping angers and resentments the Swede arouses in men who, left alone, would have been peaceful. Who is to blame? He, the men he first quarrelled with, the gambler who does the killing? "Every sin," one of the characters concludes, "is the result of a collaboration." Crane's doctrine though sardonic is also civilized. But "The Blue Hotel" is a little rambling as to structure and in art is inferior to "The Bride," which Crane himself thought was better than anybody had said in print.

The Open Boat volume did not include "The Blue Hotel," which appeared in 1899 with *The Monster and Other Stories,* the same year with the unsatisfying *Active Service* and the further poems of *War Is Kind.* Crane had gone in January to England, where he lived in Brede Place, a dilapidated manor in Sussex. The hospitable house swarmed with visitors and pets, and Crane had new friends: Joseph Conrad, H. G. Wells, Ford Madox Hueffer (later Ford), who all lived to write about the American's shining charm and lucid honesty. But he managed to read more than ever before, to continue the series of *Whilomville Stories* (1900), to compile the perfunctory *Great Battles of the World* (1901), to begin the satiric romance *The O'Ruddy* (finished by Robert Barr, 1903), to complete the Cuban sketches of *Wounds in the Rain: War Stories* (1900). Of the Spanish-American stories "The Price of the Harness" from *Wounds* and "An Episode of War" from the posthumous *Last Words* (1902) are of the same quality as Crane's best Civil War stories. The stories about children in Whilomville—notably "Lynx-Hunting," "Shame," and "The Carriage-Lamps"—stand up distinctively in the line that runs from the stories about Tom Sawyer and Huckleberry Finn to those about Penrod Schofield and William Sylvanus Baxter, less funny than Mark Twain's but more crisp and pointed than Booth Tarkington's. Crane could see comedy in Whilomville no less than the tragedy he had recounted in "The Monster." The Trescotts of that story reappear in happier adventures, and Henry Fleming, stern farmer of "Lynx-Hunting," is the young recruit of the *Red Badge* now grown old. To the final prolific, hectic period of Crane's life belongs also "An Illusion in Red and White," included in the London edition of *The Monster* (1901) and not unlike it in gruesome irony. There was small evidence of any loss of vigour in his work. But overdriven, pressed for money, interrupted, Crane was found in March 1900 to be far advanced in tuberculosis. He went in May to the Black Forest and died at Badenweiler in June, five months short of twenty-nine. (pp. vi-xvi)

It is as unfair to judge Keats solely by *Endymion* as Crane by the *Red Badge.* "The Open Boat" has more power for its length, "The Bride Comes to Yellow Sky" more humorous humanity, "The Monster" and "The Blue Hotel" more speculative implications, the *Whilomville* stories more comedy. It is of course an advantage for the *Red Badge* to be a longish story about a single hero, with whom readers have time to become acquainted. But the book is a novel which is a chain of connected sketches. Two hundred pages of short stories by Crane make up for their lack of unified force by their greater amount of variety. He was not primarily a novelist. His gifts were his intense perception and realization of what he had briefly seen or imagined, his bright freedom from dragging illusions, his insistence on writing about what really happened or must have happened, his mastery of lightning images. He was a story-teller without nonsense, a kind of poet among story-tellers. In a languid literary decade he used a living, perennial idiom. The decade of the 1920's, rediscovering him, recognized him as a surprising contemporary. **"The Monster"** exposed unimaginative small-town cruelty much as *Main Street* had recently done. **"The Bride Comes to Yellow Sky"** had Willa Cather's understanding of Western men. For that matter, the *Red Badge* resembled post-war novels of war rather than traditional romances. The short stories of fighting and rough adventure were not unlike Hemingway's. And the Bowery stories had some kinship with the later stories of poverty and misery under the depression. But the parallel should not be pressed too far. Crane is still a living writer not because he was prophetic but because he was excellent. Prophets come and go. It is excellence that is timeless. (pp. xvi-xvii)

> *Carl Van Doren, in an introduction to* Stephen Crane: Twenty Stories, *edited by Carl Van Doren, The World Publishing Company, 1945, pp. v-xvii.*

John W. Shroeder   (essay date 1950)

[*In the following excerpt, Shroeder argues that the theories of literary Naturalism often limited Crane's art, claiming that Crane's best work reached beyond the confines of Naturalistic principles.*]

It would be handy if I could say that whatever is wrong with Crane's art resulted from the want of challenge inherent in his naturalistic views. The proposition recommends itself by its neatness; presumably, an art based upon so limited a worldview cannot do very much. But the formulation will not stand. Even if it could be documented fully from Crane's works, it would still be suspect; things never work out this well for criticism. There are a number of bad or indifferent things in the Crane canon whose badness or indifference owes nothing to Naturalism. There is also at least one short story which is a triumph of Naturalistic thought and of art. But I think I can at least show that Naturalism, with distressing regularity, served to accentuate certain of Crane's artistic shortcomings, that Crane more often failed than succeeded when working within its limits, and that Crane's best work represents, if not a direct revolt from Naturalism, at least an effort to get beyond it.

Crane had extraordinary ability in certain of the areas in which ability counts. He had a rare skill in creating the charged master-symbol: the dominating image which opens whole dimensions of significance to fiction. Take the opening lines of **"The Blue Hotel"** as an example:

> The Palace Hotel at Fort Romper was painted a light blue, a shade that is on the legs of a kind of heron, causing the bird to declare its position against any background. The Palace Hotel, then, was always screaming and howling in a way that made the dazzling winter landscape of Nebraska seem only a grey swampish hush.

"The Blue Hotel," unhappily, contrives to go wrong despite this hopeful beginning. And the technique itself is apt to become ludicrous when handled badly. But when it

works, as it sometimes does, it gives us enveloping and integrating metaphors for some of the best of Crane.

Crane had, moreover, a well-developed sense for symbolic architecture. Let us take as our example here **"Death and the Child,"** the work that I had in mind when I spoke of Crane's one real Naturalistic triumph. The story opens before a battle:

> The peasants who were streaming down the mountain trail had, in their sharp terror, evidently lost their ability to count. The cattle and the huge round bundles seemed to suffice to the minds of the crowd if there were now two in each case where there had been three. This brown stream poured on. . . .

The metaphor which has been quietly developing in this description is now released:

> It was as if fear was a river, and this hoard had simply been caught in the torrent, man tumbling over beast, beast over man, as helpless in it as the logs that fall and shoulder grindingly through the gorges of a lumber country.

Crane next sets in opposition the forces embodied in the simile of the human river and those implicit in the mountain (which now takes on its full symbolic stature) of his first sentence:

> It was a freshet that might sear the face of the tall, quiet mountain; it might draw a livid line across the land, this downpour of fear with a thousand homes adrift in the current—men, women, babes, animals.

And the beginning of his second paragraph completes the array of the forces of the natural world:

> The blue bay, with its pointed ships, and the white town lay below them, distant, flat, serene. There was upon this vista a peace that a bird knows when, high in air, it surveys the world, a great, calm thing rolling noiselessly toward the end of the mystery.

The opposed forces are now transferred, the aimless confusion, fear, and hurry of the retreating peasants centering in Peza, the journalist, and the placid indifference of earth, sea, and sky centering in the babe—the Naturalist's "child of nature"—who plays unconcerned on the mountain while the war rages below him. At the end of the tale, Peza, who has retreated hysterically from the battle, finds himself in the presence of the child. This babe, his eyes "large and inscrutably wise and sad" as those of some animal, asks him, "Are you a man?"

> Peza gasped in the manner of a fish. Palsied, windless, and abject, he confronted the primitive courage, the sovereign child, the brother of the mountains, the sky, and the sea, and he knew that the definition of his misery could be written on a wee grassblade.

Perhaps I have been rather tedious in my quotations, but I know of no other way in which the perfection of Crane's technique, when at its best, can be displayed. Architecturally, this tale is a marvel. There is no waste effort; every description and every situation contributes to the total pattern. The final matching and resolution of the opposed forces leaves nothing unaccounted for. And I must add that the tale seems to me to be a marvel in more than in its architecture, since architecture itself is an element which not only contributes to but also reflects an indwelling and animating excellence. It is surprising that the artist who created **"Death and the Child"** should ever have made an artistic blunder.

But **"Death and the Child,"** unfortunately, is not typical. Crane's Naturalism, as I have said, usually conspired with certain of his creative deficiencies to overthrow him, and it should be worth our while to look into this business. Crane, to begin with, had an unholy genius for writing a story of no particular artistic validity merely in order to shovel into it a premise of no particular importance. **"The Little Regiment"** is mostly concerned with understating the remarkable discovery that brothers may conceal a real affection for one another beneath gruffness. **"A Grey Sleeve"** and **"Three Miraculous Soldiers"** announce circumspectly that love casts its eternal spell even in time of war. And two of Crane's novels, *Active Service* and *The Third Violet,* are apparently devoted to the proposition that women, though devious creatures, are the richest treasures to which the man of good heart can aspire.

Now certain of these works are pleasant enough, though pleasantness, to the best of my knowledge, has never been the criterion of literary merit. But when Crane determines to write around one of Naturalism's discoveries, he is apt to leave off being pleasant and to sink himself in what I can only call, with Scriblerus, "the bathos." It is impossible to illustrate what happens in these cases without examining a work in its entirety, a strategy precluded by demands of space. But we can get some notion of it from one of Crane's verses:

A man said to the universe:
"Sir, I exist!"
"However," replied the universe,
"The fact has not created in me
A sense of obligation."

Those critics who have dwelt with some satisfaction on this morsel seem to have forgotten that any village atheist can turn this sort of stuff out interminably. There is no particular trick to mouthing an ethical paradox. The verse exists solely for the paradox; it has no status whatever as poetry. And this error of writing to the service of empty revelations blights a surprising amount of Crane's work. The demands of Naturalistic irony magnify all his worst propensities. They give us such things as **"A Desertion,"** with its commonplace device of having a character talk, unwittingly, to a corpse (mankind's intentions mean nothing to the Universal Mechanic!). They give us **"A Mystery of Heroism,"** devoted, in its conclusion, to the accidental overturning (the Universe doesn't care!) of a pail of water that a soldier has ventured his life to draw. They give us, indeed, even *Maggie,* Crane's first novel, with its interesting mother who is persuaded to "fergive" the shortcomings of the daughter whom her own brutality and neglect (through a sequence of rigidly determined events) have sent out to walk the streets and finally to die. It will probably be urged that all this was fresh and new when Crane turned his hand to it. I doubt that it was fresh then, and it is certainly stale today. Great irony, irony with a purpose beyond itself, endures. This of Crane's does not. It is, I am afraid, irony at its lowest ebb.

Crane's peculiar habit of writing primarily for his Naturalistic moral seems even more reprehensible when we find it distorting works which begin with promise. **"The Blue Hotel"** is a ready example. It exists, mostly, for the convenience of a statement which every critic likes to quote when displaying Crane's Naturalism at large:

"We are all in it! This poor gambler isn't even a noun. He is a kind of an adverb. Every sin is the result of a collaboration. We, five of us, have collaborated in the murder of this Swede . . . that fool of an unfortunate gambler came merely as a culmination, . . ."

Doubtless this is most interesting and gratifying, but there is nothing in particular to justify it in the tale. What is interesting, indeed, is that the murdered Swede brought death on his head by what looks, in the story, like a remarkable effort of the will-to-destruction. Like the Hotel itself, the man screamed and howled until his fellows were forced to kill him. What is interesting, I suggest, is the way in which Crane has let his Naturalistic tag falsify the direction of his whole story.

This flaw, fatal to Crane's art, can be traced in too many places. It leads to a repetition which can easily become tedious. Such stories as **"The Five White Mice,"** **"Horses— One Dash,"** **"The End of the Battle,"** **"A Mystery of Heroism,"** and *Active Service* repeat tags and motifs until we begin to suspect that their author is actually not trying very hard. Crane's tales of the Mexican border seem little more than his tales of the war translated to a warmer climate. There is a place for repetition in literature, certainly. There are problems which must be met again and again in the artist's unending search for precision of definition. But Crane's repetitions in these stories—precisely because he has nothing in particular to define—are not of this sort. They seem, instead, to be the reiterations of a mind lulled into inertia by its reliance upon a system of thought inherently incapable of stirring it to action. For Naturalism, I suggest, too often seemed to Crane a philosophic peg upon which to hang his stories. And in proportion to the external strength which he fancied he saw in the peg, Crane permitted his creative power to go into abeyance. This is not to say that the stories which have fallen under my censure are without merit; Crane at his worst can still offer us an exactness of perception and an integrity toward his matter which are rare in art. But it is to say that they are not so important as to require much of the reader's time.

Crane, certainly, too often took his ease in the Naturalistic Zion; within the limits of Naturalism, he was moved but once to the creative effort of mastering, digesting, and evaluating his matter. Crane needed the stimulation of something more challenging, of one of those "problems that matter" that I left dangling on an earlier page.

Well, what does matter? What problems are of an intensity sufficient to call out a valid creative effort? I do not mean to be so foolish as to set down a list of eternals in art. But I can point to something that has mattered. *The Scarlet Letter, Moby-Dick, The Ambassadors, A Farewell to Arms,* and *The Waste Land*—and I trust that no one will object to my regarding these works as touchstones— are heterogeneous enough on their surfaces. But if we bother to peer beneath these surfaces, if, this is to say, we take the trouble to find out what is behind Hester's long penance, Ahab's God-insulting quest, Strether's growth into total awareness, Lieutenant Henry's separate peace, and the voice of the Thunder, we will find a common problem there. And we might define the problem, giving our definition not too much latitude, as that of salvation. (pp. 119-23)

As a definitive study of that salvation which Crane expressly makes his theme, *The Red Badge of Courage* is somewhat less than adequate. The novel is a promise rather than a fulfillment. In it, we discover Crane mapping a strategy under pressure and fighting an action with whatever weapons come to hand. But if it is only a promise, it is at least a very hopeful one. The vision of the haunted universe to which it attains holds, when taken together with the concern for salvation from this universe, the possibility of some future creative act of power and authority. And the intensity of the vision is itself good warrant that the artist will persist in the direction of such an act.

And Crane did. In two later and lengthy short stories—**"The Open Boat"** and **"The Monster,"** both written in 1897—he recapitulated the antagonisms basic to *The Red Badge*. The haunted vision is still there. It is possible to detect in **"The Monster"** (particularly in the powerful scene in which Henry Johnson rescues little Jimmie Trescott from the fire) precisely the same elements which went into the battle-imagery of *The Red Badge*. . . . But all the idiosyncrasies of the vision, all the false directions and incoherencies, have been purged. Compare, as an instance typical of Crane's advance, the unhappy invocation in *The Red Badge* to nature as "an existence of soft and eternal peace" to the famous delineation in **"The Open Boat"**:

> This tower was a giant, standing with its back to the plight of the ants. It represented in a degree, to the correspondent, the serenity of nature amid the struggles of the individual—nature in the wind, and nature in the vision of men. She did not seem cruel to him then, nor beneficent, nor treacherous, nor wise. But she was indifferent, flatly indifferent.

In one sense, this is yet another of those Naturalistic tags which I have condemned, in the bulk, as Crane's worst foes. But the difference between this achieved definition and the mere tag is crucial. In the first place, what might have been a tag has been transfigured by its successful animation of a precise image; it is, I repeat, an achieved insight. We feel that Crane had to work for it. And in the second place, Crane does not permit himself to rest in this statement. His loose tags are typically the ends to which his stories move—they provide a target which can too easily be hit. This, conversely, serves as a stimulus; it dictates further definition: an effort to get beyond or at least to find out what the real implications are. It is not accidental that **"Death and the Child"** is as centrally concerned with this antagonism of man and nature as are **"The Open Boat"** and **"The Monster."**

Logically, I suppose, a vision of nature's indifference should cancel out the equally powerful vision of Nature as somehow possessed by forces deadly to man. It seems somewhat curious that the same work which contains this clear and definite statement of indifference should also speak of the "wrath" of the ocean, which "growls" at least three times and whose waves rage "like a mountain cat." It is curious, too, that the prospect of drowning in this viciously animated sea should be styled "a cessation of hostilities." The answer, of course, is that Crane reacted to the indifference as strongly (and in much the same way) as did Melville to his more direct vision of nature as actively evil.

Crane felt the subtle threat implicit in the indifference so forcibly that he was moved to characterize it as positively malignant. The logical force of such a reaction is probably slight; the poetic force, on the other hand, is extreme. To nature's deadly indifference, Crane, in **"The Open Boat,"** again and conclusively opposes "the subtle brotherhood of men." The opposition is much the same in **"The Monster,"** which records two attempted salvations—each having those metaphysical overtones which by now expect—of man from nature: the first, Henry Johnson's rescue of Jimmie Trescott from the fire; the second, Dr. Trescott's rescue of Henry (burned and maimed by the flames) from death. And explicit in this second rescue is Crane's recognition that salvation's validity inheres in its being a consciously willed readiness to accept the responsibility and consequences of the mythic battle:

> "He will be your creation, you understand. He is purely your creation. Nature has very evidently given him up. He is dead. You are restoring him to life. You are making him, and he will be a monster, and with no mind."

Judge Hagenthorpe's speech presages an important shift in the strategy of the battle. The people of Whilomville abjure and oppose the doctor's refusal to submit in nature's resignation of Johnson to death. Trescott's fellows—in a renunciation of manhood perhaps tragic in view of the issues involved—react to his battle according to the dictates of thing. But Crane has not lost sight of these issues:

> "He will be what you like, judge," cried Trescott, in sudden polite fury. "He will be anything, but, by God! he saved my boy."

I imagine that my discussion has made **"The Open Boat"** and **"The Monster"** seem rather less interesting and more uncompromisingly didactic than the palates of most readers will tolerate. The fault, of course, is not Crane's but mine. My intentions (which have dictated a certain inattention to the artistic totalities of these works) are limited to an indication of how these two stories advance beyond the partial achievement of *The Red Badge* by their repair of whatever elements maimed the validity of the earlier novel. Essentially, the advance is from a diffuse and inchoate response to the central problem to an integrated and final literary mastery of it. In *The Red Badge* we seem to have the record of a running battle, and it is, to be sure, a battle of heroic dimensions. But in these two short stories (and I must add to them **"Death and the Child,"** which fights the same battle with a different emphasis) we have the artistic victory. Very few of Crane's works are without some effectiveness. The stories and novels that I have condemned would quite likely suffice to make a decent literary reputation. But Crane's claim to a place among the significant American writers, I think, must depend upon these three short stories. And in view of their achievement, I incline to believe that we must allow that claim. (pp. 126-29)

John W. Shroeder, "Stephen Crane Embattled," in The University of Kansas City Review, *Vol. XVII, No. 2, Winter, 1950, pp. 119-29.*

Robert Wooster Stallman   (essay date 1952)

[*An American critic, editor, and poet, Stallman is a leading scholar of Crane's life and work. His works* Stephen Crane: A Biography *(1968) and* Stephen Crane: A Critical Bibliography *(1972) are generally considered among the most authoritative texts of their kind (see Further Reading list). In the following excerpt, Stallman contrasts Crane's obsession with writing from experience and his proven ability to write effectively from imagination, paying particular attention to "The Open Boat."*]

When we approach the work of Crane we are instantly struck by the impact of his greatness, and we marvel not only at that quite inexplicable uniqueness of his technique and style but also that so much in so short a span as eight writing years could be produced by a mere boy who, dying at twenty-eight, left behind him more than enough perfections to place him solidly among the half-dozen major artists of American fiction in the 19th Century—not in the first rank with Hawthorne and Melville and Henry James but, counting work for work, in the second rank with Poe and Howells and Twain. Crane perfected as many works in fiction as Twain and Poe—at his best in a half-dozen stories and one novel—*The Narrative of A. Gordon Pym.* Luckless in everything else, Crane had the great luck—phenomenal among writers—to write two works of art having major importance in American letters and to write them before he was twenty-two. He first broke new ground with *Maggie: A Girl of the Streets,* the then sordid realism of that work initiating the literary trend of the next generation. *Maggie* is a tone painting rather than a realistic photograph of slum life, but it opened the door to the Norris-Dreiser-Farrell school of sociological realism. In *The Red Badge of Courage* and **"The Open Boat,"** that flawless construct of paradox and symbol, Crane established himself among the foremost technicians in American fiction. **"The Open Boat"** is a perfect fusion of the impressionism of *Maggie* and the symbolism of *The Red Badge of Courage.* The two main technical movements in modern American fiction—realism and symbolism—have their beginnings here in these early achievements of Stephen Crane. (pp. 244-45)

Crane was intense, volatile, spontaneous—what he wrote came unwatched from his pen. He wrote as he lived, and his life was shot through with ironies. If he won any "grace" from that "cold voyage" it was, I think, the artist's gift of ironic outlook, that grace of irony which is so central to his art. Irony is Crane's chief technical instrument. It is the key to our understanding of the man and of his works. He wrote with the intensity of a poet's emotion, the compressed emotion which bursts into symbol and paradox. All his best works are built upon paradox. They are formed upon ironic contrasts between ideals or romantic illusions *and* reality.

Actually, Crane wasted his genius. Under the mistaken notion that only those who have suffered shipwreck can become its interpreters, he expended himself in a misspent search for experience. Wilfully and needlessly he risked his life—among bandits in Mexico, under shellfire in Cuba and Greece as war correspondent, and off the Florida seacoast as a filibustering seaman in the disaster which befell him when he survived shipwreck after suffering thirty hours at sea in a ten-foot dinghy. It was natural that Crane

should want to see actual warfare after writing about it, and four years later as war correspondent in the Graeco-Turkish War he tested the psychological truth of his imagined picture. "My picture was all right!" he told Conrad. "I have found it as I imagined it." But at what a cost! Exposures endured in Cuba wrecked his health and impaired his art—nothing vital came from his war experience. And the pity of it all is that it could have been otherwise. He could have lived in one of his brothers' homes and done his writing there. He could have retreated from life to calculate it at a distance, as Hawthorne and James did. Instead, he deliberately chose to get as close to life as possible.

He wanted to get at the real thing and so he stood all night in a blizzard, in order to write **"Men in the Storm"**; to get at the real thing he spent a night in a Bowery flophouse in order to write **"An Experiment in Misery"**; to get at the real thing he traveled across the Western prairies, and out of it he got **"The Blue Hotel"** and **"The Bride Comes to Yellow Sky"**; out of Mexico he got **"Horses—One Dash!"** and other sketches; and out of Cuba and Greece impressions of war for *Wounds in the Rain,* stories like **"Death and the Child"** and the novel *Active Service.* But was there any need for Crane to experience a blizzard in order to write **"Men in the Storm"**? Wouldn't an imaginary rather than an actual blizzard have served just as well, since the germinal idea of the story is about a *symbolic* storm—the storm of social strife? Familiarizing himself with New York tenement life certainly wasn't necessary for the germinal idea of **"An Auction,"** in which he depicts the social shame of a poor couple whose household goods are auctioned off amidst the derisive mockery of a parrot and a gaping crowd. No personal experience of Bret Harte's country was needed to write parodies of Bret Harte's Californian tales—in **"Moonlight in the Snow," "Twelve O'Clock,"** and **"A Self Made Man."** Much of Crane's anecdotal material might just as well have originated in the experience of others, and in fact some of it did—for example, the incident used in **"The Lone Charge of Francis B. Perkins"** was taken from Ralph Paine.

Crane excels in the portrayal of mental turmoil, and for this psychological realism his creative imagination required no firsthand experience. His most directly autobiographical tales are **"The Open Boat"** and **"Horses—One Dash!"** **"The Open Boat"** is a direct transcript of personal experience, but it is personal experience transformed into an impersonal and symbolic representation of life: the plight of man tossed upon an indifferent sea. Crane transcribed it all from his experience, but he converted every detail into symbol, designed every image into a schemework of relationships, and manipulated the original facts and their sequence to form a patterned whole, a construct possessing a life of its own. He created his facts into patterns of contrast—the men in the dinghy *and* the people on the shore, the *white* and the *black* waves, the *sea* and the *land,* etc.—and he converted them into symbols—*viz.* the oar of the oiler, the windmill, etc. The only source that explains the calculated design and patterned significance of **"The Open Boat"** is the conceiving imagination of the artist.

His two greatest works represent two opposite methods of creation: art created from imagined experience and art created from actual experience. The single marvel he wrung from actual experience was **"The Open Boat,"** and the marvel of it is that he at once transcribed life and converted it into art. Yet a paradox is here established, for the masterpiece which he salvaged from his expense of greatness (as Gorham Munson was first to point out [see Further Reading list]) could have been conceived without any personal experience—as *The Red Badge of Courage* is there to testify. Crane's best works do not vindicate or support the creative principle by which they were generated.

There is thus an ironic contradiction between Crane's theory of creation and his art. His infrequent comments about art—oblique hints given out in an offhand air—amount to no more than the singlestick standard of sincerity and truth to the facts of experience. "My creed was identical with the one of Howells and Garland," he wrote in a letter of 1896. The creed of veritism which Hamlin Garland preached, the theory that art is founded upon personal experience and is copyistic of reality, Crane echoed when, not long before his death, he told a friend: "You can never do anything good aesthetically . . . unless it has at one time meant something important to you." His theory was that the greater the artist the closer his contact with reality. Yet his art was at its greatest when he wrote at some distance from the reality he had experienced, or when (as in **"The Upturned Face"** and **"An Episode of War"**) he wrote out of no personal experience at all.

In his quest for and immersion in experience Crane stands at the headstream of what has been defined as the dominant American theme and literary trend—exemplified in Ernest Hemingway, Sherwood Anderson, and Thomas Wolfe, who put the same premium upon personal experience. At his best Crane used not the experienced event but the event distilled for the thematic potentialities it suggested. The exception is **"The Open Boat,"** but here—as with Conrad in his "Heart of Darkness," which is taken straight from life—the personal experience served simply as the canvas for the recreated picture. For Crane and Conrad alike, contacts with reality provided hints for characters, details of locality, themes and germinal situations. But Crane seldom presents minute descriptions of people or scenes, and details of locality are not photographically recorded. The locality of **"The Blue Hotel"** has symbolic import and could have been sketched without firsthand experience of it. Crane could have written it without leaving New York City. The fight which he witnessed and tried to stop during his trip west (when in Lincoln, Nebraska) became the fight which he depicted in **"The Blue Hotel,"** but the germinal idea for the story might just as well have had a literary source instead of this personal one. **"The Blue Hotel,"** though it has been labeled a Hemingway story, is identical in germinal conception with Robert Louis Stevenson's formula: a certain scene and atmosphere suggest the correlative action and persons for that particular locality, and they are so used as to express and symbolize it. The atmosphere of the old blue hotel, the psychic quality of its screaming blue, impels and foreshadows the action which expresses it—the murder of the Swede.

It was realism that Crane aimed at—a photographic copy of real life. But Crane is, in essence, no realist. He believed, like Chekhov, that his task was to show persons and things as they really are, yet the persons of his fiction are not per-

sons but just Everyman—the synthetic figures of a Morality Play or a medieval tapestry, the typical representatives of a group (the young soldier from the farm, the Bowery bum, the cowboy). In **"A Self Made Man,"** for example, we get a character called Thomas G. Somebody. Crane was always symbolizing. Henry Fleming, being a more sensitive and imaginative person than the ordinary soldier, is not solely a type (as George Wyndham, in a preface to a collection of Crane's war stories, was first to point out). One might argue that all of Crane's characters have certain marked idiosyncrasies which set them apart from the type they represent, yet types they are as well as individuals. If there is any one point of common agreement among Crane's critics, it is the point that Crane in presenting a character (to quote Bushman's summing up) "was *always* at the same time dealing with generalities. . . . His characters are *representatives;* they are individuals *and* representatives of large groups." (pp. 245-48)

Every Crane short story worth mentioning is designed upon a single ironic incident, a crucial paradox, or an irony of opposites; all of them are built out of anecdotal material, and all are concerned with the same subject—the moral problem of conduct. Crane's method of construction is similar to the method that Chekhov employs. He constructs his stories by building up to a crucial moment of impasse and collapse. A Crane story consists of that moment when the characters confront the inescapable impasse of their situation, they are caught and boxed in by fate, and then—the moment of spiritual collapse—"nothing happens," and they are left with a sense of loss, insignificance, or defeat, futility or disillusionment. Crane and Chekhov were among the first to eliminate plot.

Crane's best short stories, after **"The Open Boat,"** are **"The Bride Comes to Yellow Sky"** and three war stories— **"A Mystery of Heroism," "An Episode of War,"** and **"The Upturned Face."** A slight thing but a perfection, **"The Upturned Face"** is built upon a paradox. The story is a parable: the ritual of burying a dead man is exposed as a ghastly outrage, more real than riflefire itself. Crane's grotesquerie here is integral to his theme. In **"The Blue Hotel"** it is out there on the page, and it is misspent. The story ends with the grotesque image of the corpse of the murdered Swede whose eyes stare "upon a dreadful legend that dwelt atop of the cash-machine: 'This registers the amount of your purchase.' " Here is the legitimate ending of the story. The tone here is at odds with the off-key tone of the appended section, and the theme here is at odds with the trumped-up theme announced in the irrelevant and non-ironic conclusion. **"The Blue Hotel"** happens to be Hemingway's favorite among Crane's stories, Willa Cather singles it out, and one or another of Crane's critics rate it as "one of the most vivid short stories ever written by an American." But it does not stand up under critical scrutiny. I don't think it needs to be demonstrated that **"The Monster,"** another famous anthology piece which has received undeserved acclaim, is not a unified structural whole. The opinion that **"An Experiment in Misery"** is "far more important than the more famous and accessible *Red Badge of Courage* or such stories of mere physical accident as **"The Open Boat'"** (as Ludwig Lewisohn would have it) can be dismissed without comment.

Crane constructs his stories to effect a single mood, or a series of moods with each unit in the series composed of a contrast. *Maggie,* a sentimental melodrama that borders upon travesty, concludes with the orgy of melodramatic emotion to which Maggie's mother gives vent over the death of the daughter whom she has brutalized and driven into the streets. The final turnabout consists of her last words—a parody of pious sentiment—"Oh, yes, I'll forgive her! I'll fergive her!" The grotesque buffoonery of this mock lamentation is comic enough, but there is grim tragedy in the underlying theme that all is sham, even between mother and daughter. All Crane stories end in irony. Some of them, like *Maggie* and *George's Mother,* end in a minor note—"not with a bang but a whimper." That is the characteristic ending of Chekhov's stories, as one of his critics has pointed out. Crane is a master of the contradictory effect. **"The Open Boat,"** like Chekhov's story "The Kiss," is constructed of alternating moods, each built-up mood of hope or illusion being canceled out by contradictory moods of futility, despair, or disillusionment. This method of the double mood ("qualitative progression," as Kenneth Burke defines it) was Flaubert's major technical discovery. It is the form of *Madame Bovary,* of Joyce's *Portrait of the Artist as a Young Man* and *The Dubliners* (notably "The Dead"), and of almost all of Chekhov's and Katherine Mansfield's short stories. It is the form of Melville's masterpiece "Benito Cereno" and of one of the best pieces Hawthorne wrote—that Kafka-like parable, "My Kinsman, Major Molineaux."

"The Open Boat" and *The Red Badge of Courage* are identical in form, in theme, and even in their configurated patterns of leitmotivs and imagery. The opening scene of *The Red Badge of Courage* establishes the same hope-despair pattern as the very last image of the book—"a golden ray of sun came through the hosts of leaden rain clouds." This sun-through-rain image, which epitomizes the double mood pattern that dominates every tableau in the whole sequence, is a symbol of Henry's moral triumph and it is an ironic commentary upon it. In **"The Open Boat"** the hope-despair mood of the men is established (and at the same time the point of view prepared for) in the opening sentence—"None of them knew the colour of the sky"—and the final scene repeats the same contrast mood. At the end when the men are tossed upon "the lonely and indifferent shore," the once barbarously abrupt waves now pace "to and fro in the moonlight," and as the sea changes so, we are made to feel, the men change in heart. They experience a tranquillity of mind now, a serenity that is signified by the seemingly quieted waves. But this peacefulness is deceptive, for actually the violence of the angry sea remains unabated. Their victory over nature has cost them one of their brotherhood—the oiler lies face downward in the shallows.

When Crane began writing fiction he began, like Conrad, as a symbolic artist. One of his very earliest stories, **"Men in the Storm,"** is an experiment in symbolism. Yet the greater number of his stories are nonsymbolic. When he does attempt symbolism all too often his potential symbols collapse. The pathetic episode of **"An Auction,"** for one example, intends to be symbolic but remains merely pathetic. In a good number of stories he wastes what he renders, namely realistic details that could readily have been converted to symbolic use. His symbolic technique is best studied in **"The Open Boat"** and *The Red Badge of Courage.* In **"The Open Boat,"** the very beginning of the story prepares for the final incident, the death of the oiler, by

a symbolic detail. The oiler is represented by the thin little oar he steers: "It was a thin little oar and it seemed often ready to snap." In both these works Crane charged every realistic detail with symbolic significance. (pp. 257-60)

Symbols are generated by parallelisms and repetitions. The chattering fear of a frightened squirrel who flees when Henry Fleming throws a pine cone at him (Chapter VII) parallels the plight or state of feeling of the hero when under shellfire. In **"The Open Boat"** an implied correlation is created between the confused mind of the men and the confused, irrational and "broken sea." Their mental state is obversely identified with the gruesome and ominous gulls who hover over them, sitting "comfortably in groups" and appearing utterly indifferent to the human plight. Again, the unconcern of the universe is symbolized in the wind-tower which stands before them as they head for the beach:

> This tower was a giant, standing with its back to the plight of the ants. It represented in a degree, to the correspondent, the serenity of nature amid the struggles of the individual—nature in the wind, and nature in the vision of the men. She did not seem cruel to him then, nor beneficient, nor treacherous, nor wise. But she was indifferent, flatly indifferent.

The death of the oiler symbolizes the treachery and indifference of nature, and it is through his death that this truth becomes revealed to them. At the end when they hear "the great sea's voice," they now understand what it says (what life means) because they have suffered. They have suffered the worst that the grim sea can exact from them—"they felt that they could *then* be interpreters." Thus the whole moral meaning of the story is focused in the death of the oiler. At the beginning (the very first image of the story), "None of them knew the colour of the sky"; but now they know it. The death of the oiler is foreshadowed and epitomized in the song recited by the correspondent during a moment of childhood reverie. He had known this verse when a child—"A soldier of the Legion lay dying in Algiers"—but then he had never regarded the death of this soldier as important or meaningful. He had never felt any sympathy for this soldier's plight because then he himself had not yet experienced it. "It was less to him than the breaking of a pencil's point." (This image of the pencil point correlates with the opening description of the delicate oar of the oiler, which seemed "often ready to snap.") The soldier's death foretells the oiler's death, the one being an analogy of the other. That Crane stands as an innovator in the technique of fiction is evidenced by his using this structural device of analogy, both in **"The Open Boat"** and in *The Red Badge of Courage.* It was first exploited by Flaubert, and later by James, Chekhov, and Joyce.

What is important to any artist is that he believe in his themes, not that he experience them. Crane passionately believed in the theme that no man can interpret life without first experiencing it, and he put his belief into actual practice. The result was **"The Open Boat."** *The Red Badge of Courage,* however, is the product of *imaginative* belief in the same theme. And that fact sums up the paradox of Crane's artistic career. **"An Episode of War"** contradicts Crane's personal theory. The theme that no man can interpret life without first experiencing it is here inverted. The lieutenant, because he is wounded, sees life with new insight because he is removed from the flux of

Crane on His "Little Creed of Art"

You know, when I left you [shortly after the completion of the Sullivan County sketches], I renounced the clever school in literature. It seemed to me that there must be something more in life than to sit and cudgel one's brains for clever and witty expedients. So I developed all alone a little creed of art which I thought was a good one. Later I discovered that my creed was identical with the one of Howells and Garland and in this way I became involved in the beautiful war between those who say that art is man's substitute for nature and we are the most successful in art when we approach the nearest to nature and truth, and those who say—well, I don't know what they say. Than that they can't say much but they fight villainously and keep Garland and I out of the big magazines. Howells, of course, is too powerful for them.

If I had kept to my clever Rudyard-Kipling style, the road might have been shorter but, ah, it wouldn't be the true road. The two years of fighting have been well-spent. And now I am almost at the end of it. This winter fixes me firmly. We have proved too formidable for them, confound them. They used to call me "that terrible, young radical," but now they are beginning to hem and haw and smile—those very old coons who used to adopt a condescending air toward me. There is an irony in the present situation that I enjoy, devil take them for a parcel of old, cringing, conventionalized hens.

In a letter to Lily Brandon on February 29, 1896, as quoted in Melvin Schoberlin's introduction to The Sullivan County Sketches of Stephen Crane *(1949).*

life and can observe it instead of merely experiencing it. The symbol of his insight is his wound, for it is his being wounded that changes him and enables him "to see many things which as a participant in the fight were unknown to him." Now that he has no part in the battle, which is to say no part in life itself, he knows more of life than others. Life, seen now through this new point of view, appears like something in "a historical painting," or fixed and statue-like. In structure the story is formed of alternations of moods, perspectives of motion and change shifting into picture-postcard impressions where everything is felt as fixed and static. Where we get the point of view of the wounded we get *at the same time* the point of view of the unwounded, and this device of the double vision, which was later employed so expertly by Joyce in "The Dead," Crane first introduced in **"The Open Boat."** Things viewed by the men at sea are viewed as though they were men on land. This double vision in the point of view manifests the two-part contrast of Crane's theme, sea and land symbolizing two ways of life. (pp. 261-62)

Like Flaubert and James and Conrad, Crane is a great

stylist. Theme and style in *The Red Badge* and in **"The Open Boat"** are organically conceived, the theme of change conjoined with the fluid style by which it is evoked. The deliberately disconnected and apparently disordered style is calculated to create confused impressions of change and motion. Fluidity characterizes the whole book. Crane interjects disjointed details, one nonsequitur melting into another. Scenes and objects are felt as blurred, they appear under a haze or vapor or cloud. Yet everything has relationship and is manipulated into contrapuntal patterns of color and cross-references of meaning.

Like Conrad, Crane puts language to poetic uses, which, to define it, is to use language reflexively and to use language symbolically. It is the works which employ this reflexive and symbolic use of language that constitute what is permanent of Crane.

It is the language of symbol and paradox: the wafer-like sun, in *The Red Badge;* or in **"The Open Boat"** the paradox of "cold, comfortable sea-water," an image which calls to mind the poetry of W. B. Yeats with its fusion of contradictory emotions. This single image evokes the sensation of the whole experience of the men in the dinghy, but it suggests furthermore another telltale significance, one that is applicable to Stephen Crane. What is readily recognizable in this paradox of "cold, comfortable sea-water" is that irony of opposites which constituted the personality of the man who wrote it. It is the subjective correlative of his own plight. The enigma of the man is symbolized in his enigmatic style. (p. 269)

> *Robert Wooster Stallman, "Stephen Crane: A Revaluation," in* Critiques and Essays on Modern Fiction, 1920-1951: Representing the Achievement of Modern American and British Critics, *edited by John W. Aldridge, The Ronald Press Company, 1952, pp. 244-69.*

James B. Colvert   (essay date 1958)

[*Colvert has written extensively on the life and literature of Stephen Crane. In the following excerpt from an article written early in his career, Colvert discusses the importance of language and style to meaning in Crane's short fiction, specifically "The Open Boat."*]

As a stylist, Stephen Crane puzzled some of his contemporaries. One critic, reviewing *The Red Badge of Courage* in 1900, identified him as one of the worst offenders of a new school of writers who, "in their effort to be vivid and striking, have allowed themselves to be carried away into extremes. The straining after effect and the extravagant use of onomatopoeticism here become so evident as to be uncouth". . . .

Critics of a later generation were not so much concerned with Crane's eccentricities of style. One reason, perhaps, is that readers in the twenties, accustomed to the experiments of the imagists and symbolists, no longer expected writing to adhere to the prose norm of the 1890's, a compromise between the nineteenth-century grand style and the plain style of the literary realists. A more important reason is that academic criticism by this time had already firmly attached to Crane's writing a literary label which encouraged the critic to ignore, largely, the question of style. He was a Naturalist. And since the Naturalist—particularly one of the school of Zola, to which Crane was assumed to belong—is theoretically indifferent to style, critics generally gave their attention to the ethical implications of his "mechanistic" world view, reading in his work a vision of man as a helpless and driven animal at the mercy of all-powerful forces about him. Beyond a few observations about his extraordinary color imagery and his predilection for ironic understatement, critics, especially the academic critics. seldom pursued the question of his language. (p. 34)

But Crane cannot rightly be read in this way. His method, unlike that of the realists, is metaphorical, imagistic, and symbolic. The burden of meaning in his fiction is carried in large part by image, metaphor, recurring motifs, contrasts in tone and mood, and other suggestive devices—in other words, by style. Consider, for example, the stylistic indirection of the writing in the first chapter of **"The Open Boat."** The poetically heightened opening sentence ("None of them knew the color of the sky") sets the dramatic tone of the passage, suggests the condition of mental stress of the men in the boat, and establishes the point of view to be developed—the point of view of the men totally absorbed in the experience of the rushing waves. The diction and regularized rhythm of the second sentence ("Their eyes glanced level and were fastened upon the waves that swept toward them") sustains the poetic heightening (chiefly in the phrase "glanced level"), fixes more firmly the point of view, and enforces the image of the men's fearful concentration on the threatening sea. The comparatively irregular third sentence is nearer to the rhythmic norm of prose ("These waves were of the hue of slate, save for the tops, which were of foaming white"), but toward the end it is again regularized ("and all of the men knew the colors of the sea") into a rhetorical and rhythmical balance with the first sentence ("None of them knew the color of the sky"). Coming in the middle of the paragraph, this gives the paragraph something of the balance and design of a stanza of poetry, a subtle commitment carried out in the deliberate onomatopoeia of the last sentence, which imitates the movement of the waves in the first half and suggests in the buzzing, sibilant sounds and broken rhythms of the last part the cruel threat of the imagined rocks:

> The horizon narrowed and widened
> and dipped and rose,
> and at all times its edge was jagged with waves
> that seemed thrust up in points like rocks.

Obviously the language here is not so highly organized rhythmically as the more or less tightly metered language of poetry, but if this analysis is acceptable it should suggest that Crane's style is more consciously poetic than the prose "norm" which Rahv seems to have in mind. Crane does in this sense put language to poetic uses, and it would seem that the techniques of poetry analysis, used with discretion and with regard for the more expansive and more explicitly dramatic structure of his fiction, are valid and necessary if we are to grasp the full meaning and significance of his writing. And to get at his meaning—to search out not only the structure of his art but also the nature of the world view which it expresses—is to remove from his best writing the stigma of a naive and ingenuous philosophical naturalism and find in it, as Edward Garnett did

years ago, something of the "perfect fusion of [the] forces of passion and irony [which] creates Crane's spiritual background and raises his work, at its finest, into the higher zone of man's tragic conflict with the universe" [see Further Reading list].

No reader could find this meaning in his work without taking style into account, for it is in style that this meaning exists in Crane's fiction. To read, for instance, the image of nature's wrath in **"The Open Boat"** into the author's world view is to fall into the error which leads Shroeder to conclude that contradictory visions of the sea as both hostile and indifferent are proof of Crane's confused "Naturalism" [see excerpt dated 1950]. But it is important to understand that these different visions of nature are aspects of Crane's perception of irreconcilable contradictions in reality. To the men, whose vision is concentrated with such fierce intensity upon the rolling sea, an intensity suggested in their exquisite perception of the violent contrast between the slate-colored waves and their crests of boiling white and suggested further in their vivid sense of the shifting, swelling motion of the sea—to these men, then, the hostile appearance of the waves *is,* at this moment, their absolute reality. "As each slaty wall of water approached, it shut all else from the view of the men in the boat, and it was not difficult to imagine that this particular wave was the final outburst of the ocean, the last effort of the grim water." But from the point of view of the narrator (and the reader), whose sense of the situation is not affected by an imprisoning wall of jagged waves, their reality might well be something else. "Viewed from a balcony," the narrator states later on, "the whole thing would, doubtless, have been weirdly picturesque. But the men in the boat had not time to see it. . . ."

This ironic contrast suggests a theme so central to Crane's consciousness that it can be taken as almost a definition of his world view, the vision of life governed by his profound sense of the consequences of our faulty perceptions of reality. The grand subject of his fiction is man's struggle to bring into some sort of meaningful order the confusions and contradictions of experience. His heroes, burdened with a perceptual machinery which renders them incapable of reconciling all the apparently disparate elements in their experience, stand uncertain and defenseless in a flux of imperfectly comprehended events. One of Crane's letters shows, I think, his sense of the meaning of this limitation of consciousness:

> I understand that a man is born into the world with his own pair of eyes, and he is not at all responsible for his quality of personal honesty. To keep close to this personal honesty is my supreme ambition.
>
> There is a sublime egotism in talking of honesty. I, however, do not say that I am honest. I merely say that I am as nearly honest as a weak mental machinery will allow. This aim in life struck me as being the only thing worth while. A man is sure to fail at it, but there is something in the failure.

Crane's heroes rarely have such a clear insight into their own limitations for seeing the world clearly and truly. More often they are compelled to maintain in their private worlds the images of themselves which their fallible consciousness demands. They must be the darlings of the gods, the central facts of creation, the aspiring masters of nature and themselves. Bound in darkness, they must be children of light—or what they think is light.

When we speak of Crane's ironical style we refer properly to the general relation between this attitude and the verbal forms which express it, not merely to the fact that his writing is normally couched in the language of ironic understatement. "Irony," Kierkegaard observes, "is an existential determination and nothing is more ridiculous than to suppose that it consists in the use of a certain phraseology, or when an author congratulates himself upon succeeding in expressing himself ironically. Whoever has irony has it all day long, not bound to any specific form, because it is the infinite within him" [*Kierkegaard's Concluding Unscientific Postscript* (1941)].

But our question is how irony in this sense is expressed in the structure and style of Crane's writing, and for a characteristic example we may return to the opening section of **"The Open Boat,"** where two apparently contradictory ideas about the reality of the sea are set up not only in direct, openly communicative statement, but also—and more significantly—in the images of space, color, and motion and in the rhythm, balance, and tone of the sentences. I have mentioned how the image of the waves as threatening, pointed rocks suggests to the men that nature is hostile and how the contrary idea is introduced in the narrator's statement that the scene, "viewed from a balcony," might be merely picturesque. But before the narrator intrudes to state it openly and discursively, the idea is evoked by stylistic indirection. The tone and direction of reference of the first sentence of the second paragraph ("Many a man ought to have a bathtub larger than the boat which here rode upon the sea") seems to express not so much an opinion of the narrator as a self-conscious protest from the sailors who, overwhelmed by the pathos of their situation, cry out against the injustice of their plight. Although there are ironic overtones in the conditional *ought* and in the implicit contrast of the domestic bathtub with the nearly swamped boat, still the main expressive force of the sentence is nonironical because the cry can be taken as a just and accurate expression of the genuine pathos of their situation. But the ethical reproach expressed in the sentence which immediately follows ("These waves were most wrongfully and barbarously abrupt and tall") must be taken ironically: to a detached observer ocean waves are neither right nor wrong, barbarous nor civilized. Clearly another attitude is admissible; the sea is perhaps weirdly picturesque or, as the correspondent comes finally to believe, merely indifferent.

But only admissible, not necessarily true; nature is only *perhaps* indifferent or picturesque. The reservations are important, indeed, the very essence of the ironic view; for the ironical man, though detached from the world of contradictions he perceives, does not pass final judgments upon them. "In fact," as Andrew Wright says [in "Irony and Fiction," *The Journal of Aesthetics and Art Criticism,* XII (September 1953)],

the ironist is deeply concerned with both aspects of the contradictions he perceives; and this concern leads to an ambivalence of attitude to one side and to the other—to both at once. Searching the orchards of human experience he finds the bittersweet apple of confusing appearance and ambiguous essence—and he becomes a man of the divided, the ironic, vision.

This has led some to feel that "the basic feature of every irony is a contrast between a reality and an appearance." But the matter is not so simple: the ironist is not sure which is and which merely seems.

The ambivalence of attitude of the true ironist bears greatly upon the structure and meaning of **"The Open Boat,"** for in his handling of point of view and imagery, Crane always implicitly allows for errors of perception—his own as well as the men's. Though nature appears at different times in different guises, sometimes cruel, wrathful, deadly to man; sometimes wildly beautiful, picturesque; and sometimes merely indifferent—still none of these aspects, the detached narrator knows, necessarily excludes the others. The language always allows for perceptual error. To the men the waves only "*seemed* thrust up in points like rocks." Seen from a balcony the sea would *doubtless* have been picturesque. It was *probably* splendid, it was *probably* glorious. It merely *occurs* to a man that nature does not regard him as important, and the "high cold star" is the word the correspondent *feels* that nature says to him. Sometimes, as we have seen, the narrator seems to be *in* the boat, seeing and feeling as intensely as the men, sharing sympathetically their conclusions about the meaning of their plight; at other times he seems to be observing their situation from afar, seeing it then critically, dispassionately, or even mockingly.

Consider how the tension between these conflicting points of view is basic to the ironic effect of the argument between the cook and the correspondent about the difference between a life-saving station and a house of refuge. The cook's assertion that they will be rescued by the life-saving crew is like a proposition in a formal debate, challenged after a brief question and answer by the correspondent's formal counter assertion. The futile impasse is moderated by the oiler's "Well, we're not there yet," and then the cook, unwilling to abandon his hopeful position, again asserts his conviction that they will finally be rescued by a crew from the shore. The passage ends with the skeptical oiler's repeated "We're not there yet." The formal design of this colloquy, with its balance and contrast of assertion and counter-assertion and the refrain-like interpolations of the oiler, gives to the men's speculations a tone of ironic presumption. The effect is powerfully reinforced when the narrator later states almost casually: "It is fair to say here that there was not a life-saving station within twenty miles in either direction; but the men did not know this fact, and in consequence they made dark and opprobrious remarks concerning the eyesight of the nation's life-savers."

Ironic tension is also sustained in the leitmotifs which refer to various contradictory aspects of nature. To the men, the sea gulls seem at one point to be allies of the hostile sea, for "the wrath of the sea was no more to them than it was to a covey of prairie chickens a thousand miles inland." Against the malice—if indeed it is malice—of the gull which attacks the captain's head, the men are almost helpless. The captain waves it "gently and carefully" away with the heavy painter just as the oiler gingerly and skillfully navigates the hostile sea with a "thin little oar . . . [which] seemed often ready to snap." When the gulls came close "and stared at the men with black beadlike eyes," they then seemed "uncanny and sinister" and "struck their minds at this time as being somehow gruesome and ominous." But only at this time, for later, when the birds are seen going in "slanting flight up the wind toward the gray desolate east," they seem less a symbol of an ineffable, perhaps demoniac malice, than a remote and beautiful design in nature.

The shark, the unnamable "thing" whose "enormous fin" cuts "like a shadow through the water" is to the correspondent both admirable and horrifying. Subjectively, it is, like the gulls, a symbol of nature's inscrutable malice; still, in his despair and exhaustion, the correspondent can also see the shark objectively. It does not affect him with "the same horror that it would if he had been a picnicker," and at the same time that he looks dully into the sea and swears in an undertone, he can reflect that "the speed and power of the thing was to be greatly admired." But later the image of this terrible "thing" seems to the narrator to suggest indifference rather than hostility. "The thing which had followed the boat and waited had evidently grown bored at the delay. There was no longer to be heard the slash of the cutwater, and there was no longer the flame of the long trail."

In the end the correspondent, to whom the "high cold star" and the wind-tower are the correlatives of nature's indifference, concludes that it is just this which is the significant reality of his experience:

> This tower was a giant, standing with its back to the plight of the ants. It represented in a degree, to the correspondent, the serenity of nature amid the struggles of the individual—nature in the wind, and nature in the vision of men. She did not seem cruel to him then, nor beneficent, nor treacherous, nor wise. But she was indifferent, flatly indifferent.

The passage is always read as an expression of not only the correspondent's conclusion, but of Crane's as well, as if at this point in the story the ironic contradictions are resolved in a final statement of the author's naturalistic world view. Daniel Hoffman, commenting on the meaning of the oiler's death, makes the point that the correspondent at the end of the story is still under Crane's ironic inspection, the evidence being according to Hoffman the fact that the correspondent sees not the oiler as the men's true sacrificial savior, but the "haloed and saintlike" vacationer who rushed into the surf to rescue the foundering men. The whole question of the theme of sacrificial death in Crane is, I think, debatable, but Hoffman's feeling that Crane's irony extends beyond the correspondent's final conviction about the relation of man to nature is crucially significant. "The truth of the correspondent's interpretation," Mr. Hoffman says in reference to this failure of consciousness, "lies not in his last impressions but in the manner in which he recreates the entire experience in the reader's imagination" [*The Poetry of Stephen Crane*].

The correspondent's passionate conviction that his experience has led him to the final truth, however deeply moving, is after all only a passionate conviction. The ironic overtones of other convictions, held at other times just as passionately, echo contradictions. It is suggestive that the story closes on an image of the sea as romantically and mysteriously beautiful:

> When it came night, the white waves paced to and fro in the moonlight, and the wind brought the sound of the great sea's voice to the men on shore, and they felt they could then be interpreters.

Who can say in what various ways the survivors interpret their experience or what one way could be understood to exclude the others? In the reverberating ironies of the last word, charged with the cumulative meanings evoked in the poetic indirections of Crane's style, the final meaning of the men's experience escapes at last into mystery. (pp. 38-45)

> *James B. Colvert, "Style and Meaning in Stephen Crane: 'The Open Boat'," in* Studies in English, *Vol. XXXVII, 1958, pp. 34-45.*

Thomas A. Gullason   (essay date 1960)

[*A notable Crane scholar, Gullason has edited, contributed to, or written such volumes as* The Complete Short Stories and Sketches of Stephen Crane *(1963) and* Stephen Crane's Career: Perspectives and Evaluations *(1972; see Further Reading list). In the excerpt below, Gullason presents Crane's story "The Monster" as a successful and unified work in which society serves as the symbolic monster of the tale and ostracism as a central theme.*]

"The Monster" is a "problem" story—a cause and effect story—one of the best of its kind in American fiction. The story is skillfully told; it is unified; it succeeds in achieving its intention. Crane was not interested in depicting Henry Johnson as the monster; the monster is society, and it becomes the anti-heroic central character only after Henry's tragedy. Crane, then, is primarily interested in effects. The story rightly presents this problem of effects after the cause for Henry's disfigurement and imbecility has been laid.

The twenty-four chapter divisions serve Crane's purpose well, for he presents each ironic chapter as a dramatic scene. At times, he focuses on the individual; then he widens his arc gradually, immersing the whole of the Whilomville community in the developing action. Crane plays between these two poles, and as he does so, he deepens his satire on individuals who represent the community's monstrosity, hypocrisy, stupidity, and savagery; simultaneously he deepens the atmospheric sense of ostracism, which slowly permeates the action and is climactically present at the story's end. The several minor climaxes (like the fire) are created before the major one to give more emotional force to the theme.

The opening chapter-scene sets in motion the atmosphere of impending ostracism, the symbolic action, which expands and gains in momentum in the following chapters. Little Jim Trescott, while riding his cart, accidentally creates a "monster" by destroying a peony. He tries to "stand it on its pins, resuscitated, but the spine of it was hurt, and it would only hang limply from his hand. Jim could do no reparation." Jim's father, Doctor Trescott, punishes his son by not allowing him to play any longer that day. Here, in little, is foreshadowed Henry Johnson's accident and the "problem" of the story.

Crane extends the symbol of the peony incident by linking Jim's destiny with Henry's, who takes care of the doctor's horses. Further, fuller treatment is given to Henry. The townspeople, who have the important function of a chorus, sometimes hostile, sometimes friendly, sometimes contradictory, are "impressed" by him. Though Henry is described as happy and confident, there is an omen of his future: ". . . he turned away from the scene of his victories into a narrow side street, where the electric light still hung high, but only to exhibit a row of tumble-down houses leaning together like paralytics."

The arc slowly widens into the group world. Here, as elsewhere, Crane depends on a structure of ironic contrasts to build up the atmosphere of potential disaster. The gaiety of a band concert is followed by the sinister note of a fire, which breaks out at Doctor Trescott's house. As Crane moves the action to the immediate scene of the fire before and during the arrival of the firemen, he portrays the anxiousness of the crowd, the reactions of the man who originally saw the fire, the rescuer, Henry Johnson, the converging of the various elements of Whilomville society, and a climax. Though Jim is rescued, the monster is created when one of Doctor Trescott's jars splinters and pours down into Henry's upturned face.

Now having clearly delineated the cause of Henry's disfigurement and imbecility, and having magnified the atmosphere of doom, Crane passes to the community's spirit, preparing the way for the major action of the story—the indictment of society as the monster (and the transference of the sense of ostracism from Henry to the Trescotts). For example, the young boys who are watching the fire are satirically portrayed. Crane also satirizes the adult world. There is the man with "information" who is completely misinformed. Another adult's role is to deliver the awful final judgment: "Oh, they'll die sure. Burned to flinders. No chance. Hull lot of 'em. Anybody can see."

The extended description of the group during the fire is the important introduction to the way in which it will react to this monster created by chance. Effects and their importance in the ensuing action have their proper motivation. At first, the effect on the town is wholesome. Judge Hagenthorpe welcomes the distressed Trescotts. The town newspaper is eulogistic and misinformed as it announces the death of Henry Johnson, but at least the editorial has a salutary effect. The boys of the community see Johnson as a "saint." And Miss Bella Farragut, to show her remorse over the supposed loss of her lover, exaggerates her relationship and announces "that she had been engaged to marry him."

There is an abrupt counter movement and a clear transference of the monster symbol from Henry to the Whilomville community, and the sense of ostracism from Henry to Doctor Trescott. The judge advances a monstrous suggestion, which he considers just: "No one wants to advance such ideas, but somehow I think that that poor fellow ought to die. . . . You [Doctor Trescott] are restoring him to life. You are making him, and he will be a monster, and with no mind." Trescott ignores the judge's advice and attempts to repay Johnson's bravery by having a fellow Negro, Alec Williams, take care of him. This solution has the same effect as it did on the judge. There is the short-lived welcome; then there follows a growing fear of having accepted the monster. Alec displays his monstrous hypocrisy by going to the judge and complaining that he can no longer keep Henry because his children cannot eat

and his wife cannot receive callers. In reality what he wants is more money.

Another movement from the individual to the group world follows—this time to Reifsnyder's barber shop, where the group repeats and extends the "problem" of the monster. The group's thinking is evident when several of Reifsnyder's customers argue over the questions posed earlier by the judge; and they take sides on the issue.

There is the return to the individual again and a more heightened sensitivity to Alec's new life with the monster. With higher pay, he is like a "balloon" and does not know that he is being ostracized by his neighbors. Deflation quickly sets in, however, for Alec returns home to find that Henry has disappeared; so he runs wildly, looking for Doctor Trescott. Meanwhile, his family dramatizes the full meaning of Henry's escape: they stand "quaking" until daylight.

This striking contrast of happiness and fear, seen earlier in Henry's visit to his girl friend and in the episode of the band concert, becomes increasingly meaningful to the Whilomville community when Theresa Page gives a party. One girl sees the wandering Henry from the window and is so badly frightened that she "was not coherent even to her mother." This arc of fear widens even more. Henry visits Bella and her mother, frightening them both away. A climax of fear is reached when the crowd responds to the roaming monster. They "chased him, firing rocks." Here, for the first time, Doctor Trescott personally feels the effects of his loyalty to Henry. The police chief tells him that Winter, the father of the frightened girl, wanted to have him arrested.

Following this, there is a choral "relief" when Crane turns to another monster, Martha Goodwin, an old maid whose occupation is to have "adamantine opinions" about everything. She is the most "savage critic" in town. She says of Trescott: "Serves him right if he was to lose all his patients." In this way she foreshadows the gradually widening breach between Trescott and the community.

Crane moves to the children's world to study further the effects of Trescott's humanitarianism. Little Jim and his friends play a cruel game with the pathetic Henry. They charge one another with cowardice, for no one is brave enough to walk up to Henry and touch him. After Jim succeeds in this ritual of courage he says to another: "You ain't afraid, hey? If you ain't afraid go do it, then." Doctor Trescott returns to witness this scene and becomes more grimly aware of another effect of his humaneness. His own child has turned into a monster.

Further shocking effects pile up. Trescott is angrily turned away by his former patient Winter, when he attempts to attend to his daughter. Reverberations of this incident follow and Martha Goodwin discusses them. She conveys the truth of the situation—that Winter's daughter, supposedly sick, attends school. Yet Martha displays her hypocrisy by contradicting her earlier hostility toward Trescott. As she condemns the whole town for being "silly," Martha argues with others over the Hannigans who are moving out of the neighborhood as a protest over Trescott's stand against the community. The conversation dissipates into a piddling argument as to exactly where the Hannigans are going to move. Ironically enough, the major issue— Trescott's "problem"—is completely forgotten.

The community's increasing hostility is represented by four men, who call on Trescott and try to convince him that Henry should be sent away "up the valley" or to a public institution. Trescott rejects the group's proposal. For this, he receives the final repercussions from the Whilomville world. The doctor returns home to find his wife crying. She usually receives callers on Wednesdays and only one guest arrived. Trescott tries to console her, and as he surveys the empty scene at the story's climactic end, he silently feels the last monstrous step taken by the community: "As he sat holding her head on his shoulder, Trescott found himself occasionally trying to count the cups. There were fifteen of them." Trescott's duty to a man who has saved his son has been paid in full—with ostracism.

This last chapter encloses the action superbly. Throughout, the rhythm of the story, the unity of it, is clearly pronounced and effectively modulated. It is similar to the rhythm of the sea, as described in **"The Open Boat"**: "The horizon narrowed and widened, and dipped and rose and at all times its edge was jagged with waves that seemed thrust up in points like rocks." After a full study of the horizon of Whilomville—looking at the "problem" narrowly, then widely, its effects salutary, then monstrous—Stephen Crane shows what is left at the end of the story: society's "edge," jagged like rocks. (pp. 663-68)

> Thomas A. Gullason, "The Symbolic Unity of 'The Monster'," in Modern Language Notes, Vol. LXXV, No. 8, December, 1960, pp. 663-68.

A. M. Tibbetts (essay date 1965)

[In the following essay, Tibbetts posits that "The Bride Comes to Yellow Sky" is often misinterpreted by critics as "serious allegory" instead of "nearly pure comedy."]

"The Bride Comes to Yellow Sky" has perhaps been misread more often than any other story of Crane's. Many critics misread it because they try to interpret it as serious allegory instead of appreciating it as comedy. R. W. Stallman believes, for example, that the marshal and the badman "represent two opposite worlds or points of view: the idealistic world of spiritual values whose force lies in its innocence, and the non-imaginative world of crass realities" (*Stephen Crane: An Omnibus*, New York, 1952) [see Further Reading list]. Robert Barnes states that the story is a "conflict of the East vs. the West" and that the marshal's new wife is "the symbol of Eastern civilization, duplicity, and evil" (Item 39, *The Explicator*, 16, April, 1958).

There are probably two reasons for such misreading of **"The Bride."** First, Crane's short-story technique, which was formed by an arresting mixture of modes and strategies, seems to have been created on purpose to mislead unwary readers. Like Mark Twain, Ambrose Bierce, Bret Harte, and others whose writing fell into the tradition of frontier humor and literary comedy, Crane worked hard the veins of burlesque, irony, and serio-comic exaggeration and understatement. In his belief that life was a long and bitter trick, Crane actually seems closest to Bierce. But none of the literary comedians had Crane's control of metaphor and image. The lines that one always remembers from a Crane story are those that fuse an ironic state-

ment of a bitter, terrible, or frightening condition with an equally strong poetic statement. Here, for instance, is a passage from **"The Open Boat,"** in which the sea's horizon is described as having an edge "jagged with waves that seemed thrust up in points like rocks":

> A singular disadvantage of the sea lies in the fact that after successfully surmounting one wave you discover that there is another behind it just as important and just as *nervously anxious to do something effective in the way of swamping boats*. . . . There was a *terrible grace* in the move of the waves, and they came in silence, save for the *snarling of the crests* (italics added).

Many writers of Crane's time could have produced the first of these two sentences, but few if any of them could have written the second.

A probable second reason why critics tend to misread **"The Bride"** is that they are accustomed to read Crane as a writer of portentous and symbolic tragedies. From the early *Maggie*, to *The Red Badge of Courage*, to the fine, late stories like **"The Monster," "The Blue Hotel,"** and **"The Open Boat,"** Crane worked in poetic sentences freighted with dark meaning. Superficially, **"The Bride"** has a fictional ring similar to the other great stories. But it must be read differently, for it is nearly pure comedy.

In fairness, I should say that a few critics have mentioned comic aspects of **"The Bride,"** but none has treated the story in detail as a comedy. G. W. Johnson has referred to "the comic aspects of the 'transaction' which occurs between two different conventions . . . " (*PMLA*, 78, 1963). Edwin Cady calls the story "a hilariously funny parody of neo-romantic lamentations over 'The Passing of the West' " (*Journal of English Literary History*, 28, 1961). R. B. West hesitates at calling it a comedy of manners, but adds that "if it is not, we have no traditional name for such a story" (*American Literature*, 34, 1962). Perhaps the best discussion of the story is in the few paragraphs that Eudora Welty devotes to it in her "The Reading and Writing of Short Stories," *Atlantic Monthly*, February, 1949. In a sharply accurate phrase, Miss Welty calls **"The Bride"** a "playful story, using two situations, like counters."

Structurally, **"The Bride"** is built like many of Crane's best stories. It is carefully divided into dramatic scenes, and it could easily be staged as a play. (In the late nineteen-forties, an excellent short movie was made from the story.) The first scene presents the town marshal of Yellow Sky, Jack Potter, and his bride as they sit in the train waiting for its arrival at the marshal's town, Yellow Sky. They are honest and simple persons, not young, but too inexperienced to play the part of newlyweds without great awkwardness.

The second scene is a partial flashback; it begins in time at the same moment as the first scene and its function is exposition: the men in the Weary Gentleman saloon tell a drummer from out of town about the ancient gunman Scratchy Wilson, who is a superb shot but harmless except when he is drinking. "When he's sober," explains the barkeeper, "he's all right—kind of simple—wouldn't hurt a fly—nicest fellow in town. But when he's drunk—whoo!" Scratchy intends to shoot up the town, and the barkeeper boards up his place to ride out the storm.

Crane shows us Scratchy for the first time in the third

scene. The old gunman, drunk and blazing away with two sixshooters at various targets, including the saloon, is looking for a fight but cannot find one. He remembers his old enemy, the marshal, and staggers away to the marshal's house, where he yells for Potter to come out. In the fourth and last scene, the paths of the two men meet as Potter and his bride round the corner heading for their new home and come upon Scratchy loading one of his pistols. The gunman waves his weapon angrily at them until Potter introduces his new wife. At the sight of the two together and at the knowledge of their marriage, Scratchy's rage is gone, and he walks sorrowfully away dragging his feet. The comedy is ended.

The language of the story is also that of Crane's best work. His metaphors and images are brilliant and precise. When they first see Scratchy, Potter and his wife are afraid: "Potter's mouth seemed to be merely a grave for his tongue. . . . As for the bride, her face had gone as yellow as old cloth. She was a slave to hideous rites, gazing at the apparitional snake." In Crane's description of the couple's reaction to the Pullman, he employs one of his sharpest images: "He pointed out to her the dazzling fittings of the coach; and in truth her eyes opened wider as she contemplated the sea-green figured velvet, the shining brass, silver, and glass, the wood that gleamed as darkly brilliant as the surface of a pool of oil."

However, Crane's customary dramatic, ironic, and poetic techniques in this story are generally either overridden by comic effects or shaped for the ends of comedy. The marshal and his bride are more than faintly ludicrous on the train. The fear of the men in the saloon is comic, as is the sudden deflation of the bragging drummer who, after ducking behind the bar, has "balm . . . laid upon his soul at sight of various zinc and copper fittings that bore a resemblance to armor plate." Scratchy is made out to be a holy terror, but his actions and appearance imply otherwise. He accurately and purposefully shoots in front of a dog instead of at it, and his major targets consist of pieces of paper and adobe walls. Dressed like a child's idea of a cowboy, in a maroon shirt and red-topped boots "of the kind beloved in winter by little sledding boys on the hillsides of New England," the old gunman is obviously a comic figure playing a childishly attractive game. As Eudora Welty remarks, "the more ferocious Scratchy is, the more we are charmed." Even when he faces Potter and his bride, Scratchy avoids shooting him; he merely talks about it, and although Potter is doubtful of his antagonists's harmlessness, the reader is convinced that the marshal is safe.

Throughout **"The Bride"** Crane uses comic devices with great sureness. There is tongue-in-cheek understatement in his catalogue of the men drinking in the saloon: "One was a drummer who talked a great deal and rapidly; three were Texans who did not care to talk at that time; and two were Mexican sheep-herders, who did not talk as a general practice in the Weary Gentleman saloon." Crane's favorite device is comic overstatement. The marshal's marriage is called an "extraordinary crime" that was "an important thing to his town. It could only be exceeded by the burning of the new hotel." Scratchy's drunken bellowing is called the "chanting [of] Apache scalp-music." In describing the actions of his characters, Crane uses echoes of and allusions to the epic to attain comic overstatement. The bar-

keeper becomes "the man of bottles." Jack Potter is not merely Scratchy's enemy; he is "his ancient antagonist." And when no one answers his challenges, Scratchy addresses the universe and calls "to the sky" like a hero out of Homer.

Occasionally Crane employs a sort of visual comedy that is close to slapstick. The marshal and his wife in the Pullman are little better than two hayseeds, the butt of joking throughout the car. They are terribly embarrassed and self-conscious. The Negro porter looks down on and bullies them, laughing at them as they leave the train. Potter's trying to tip the porter without drawing attention to himself is perfectly constructed rustic slapstick comedy: "Potter fumbled out a coin and gave it to the porter, as he had seen others do. It was a heavy and muscle-bound business, as that of a man shoeing his first horse."

All of these devices and scenes either anticipate or support the comedy of the confrontation of the "ancient antagonists" who have been involved in a burlesque of the Western feud. Holding a gun on the brave marshal, who is afraid to face the town when it finds out about his marriage, and who has just been caught skulking around back streets trying to get home without being seen, Scratchy works himself into a rage that disappears like a pricked bubble when the bride is mentioned. "No!" he says. And then in a splendid anticlimax of parodic gallantry, he asks: "Is this the lady?"

The feud that Scratchy has enjoyed so much is over. "I s'pose it's all off now," he says, and like a child who has lost something forever he walks away dragging his feet, making "funnel-shaped tracks in the heavy sand." But **"The Bride Comes to Yellow Sky"** is a comedy that implies a happy ending. Surely the marshal and his bride will live happily ever after; Scratchy Wilson, now that the object of his feuding attentions is no longer available, will undoubtedly reform and get religion; and even the dreadful *shivaree* that Potter was so frightened of will probably turn out to be no worse than an ice cream social at the Baptist Church. (pp. 314-16)

> *A. M. Tibbetts, "Stephen Crane's 'The Bride Comes to Yellow Sky',"* in English Journal, *Vol. 54, No. 4, April, 1965, pp. 314-16.*

Leedice Kissane (essay date 1966)

[*In the excerpt below, Kissane asserts that through metaphorical language Crane imparts more meaning in "The Open Boat" than he may have consciously intended.*]

When Crane wrote his newspaper account of the sinking of the *Commodore,* his own escape with three others in the lifeboat, and their rescue thirty hours later, those hours in the boat were pointedly omitted. Said he: "The history of life in an open boat for thirty hours would no doubt be instructive for the young, but none is to be told here and now." Clearly the author was saving this material for what he knew would be a great story—man against the forces of the universe. Though the narrative he later wrote, [**"The Open Boat"**], has the elements of adventure, its interest resides more profoundly in the consciousness of the narrator, in his coming to recognize the inequality of the struggle which is the condition of life, in his acceptance of it, and finally in his sensing of the solaces which make life under its inexorable condition endurable.

Laying bare the psyche of his protagonist was equally the author's purpose in *The Red Badge of Courage,* but the language employed in the two works is strikingly different. To describe the human conflict in which Henry Fleming is engaged, with its gunfire, smoke, wounds, loud cursing, fear, and death, Crane's metaphors are outlandish and violent. They convey the strangeness with which the chaos impinged on the sensibilities of the inexperienced young soldier. In **"The Open Boat"** the metaphors are of another sort. As Emerson wrote in *Nature,* some sixty years before Crane's setting adrift:

> A man conversing in earnest, if he watch his intellectual processes, will find that a material image more or less luminous arises in his mind, contemporaneous with every thought, which furnishes the vestment of the thought. Hence good writing and brilliant discourse are perpetual allegories. The image is spontaneous. It is the blending of experience with the present action of the mind. It is proper creation.

A situation which pits man against the implacable vastness of the sea demands linguistic vestments of a different nature from those used to suggest the confusion of battle.

Take for example such a metaphor as "Canton flannel gulls." Canton flannel was a fabric much used in the time of Crane's boyhood for sleepingwear, undergarments, even sheets. Its texture was fleecy soft, its color gray or white. To attribute the qualities of this material to sea gulls is startlingly evocative, yet touched with irony, for the gulls are actually hard and intrusive with their beady eyes and annoying persistence. Another figure often noted is this: "The waves rippled like carpets on the line in a gale." Carpets as Crane knew them were thin (no doubt woven of household rags) and were frequently hung on the clothesline where they were hand-beaten by means of a heavy wire beater. They had to be this very kind of thin rag-carpet in order to ripple in the fashion Crane, the impeccable observer, ascribes to them. Even the figure showing the riskiness of moving about in the boat has the aptness of real experience: "It was easier to steal eggs from under a hen than to change seats in the dinghy."

These are only a few of the material images that rose in the author's mind as he sought to express the thoughts and sensations of the correspondent during his hours in the boat. Almost without exception they are drawn from domestic routines he knew as a boy. "In **'The Open Boat'** things viewed by the men at sea are viewed as though they were men on land," says R. W. Stallman [in *Stephen Crane: An Omnibus* (1952); see Further Reading list]. Furthermore, could we not say, things at sea are described in terms of specific experiences the men have undergone on land, blended with present impressions or actions of the mind to achieve what Emerson calls "proper creation." For revealing simultaneously the external situation of the men in the boat and the internal workings of the correspondent's consciousness, these domestic figures are eminently well chosen, their consistency serving as a unifying force in the work.

But Crane's use of metaphorical language in **"The Open Boat"** performs a function beyond the aesthetic. It reinforces his theme by stressing the puniness of man in contrast to the vastness of the physical universe. Its effect throughout the tale is to reduce man in order to magnify the unevenness of his struggle against nature. Memories of carpets on the line, of the feel of fleecy flannel, of gathering eggs—all are those of childhood. The human being is belittled by these figures into puerility, a state in which he is even less well equipped for his uneven struggle.

He is rendered negligible as well by the lowliness of the metaphors—the ordinariness of the life reflected in them with its commonplace chores, activities of the kitchen (where Stephen as a boy must have spent much of his time), and the many indications of near-poverty and humble household arrangements. This suggestion of paltriness in man's stature and conditions is borne out by the prevalence of understatement or litotes: e.g., "Neither the oiler nor the correspondent was fond of rowing at this time." The trivial mundanity of the cook is revealed by his question: "What kind of pie do you like best?" Even the admirable captain is made to seem faintly ridiculous—"like a man looking over a board fence"—as he floats toward shore clinging to a fragment of the boat.

As if these glimpses of human littleness do not sufficiently reduce man, as a crowning indignity he is equated with lower forms of animal life: "The tower was a giant with its back to the plight of the ants." In the famous outcry "Why was I allowed to come so far and nibble the sacred cheese of life?" the speaker parallels himself by implication with an insignificant mouse.

This is Crane's method of showing the bigness of the forces that encompass man. He never expatiates on the expanse of water surrounding the men in the little boat, characterizing only the waves within the radius of their vision. As an example there is this statement, referring to night at sea: "The two lights were the furniture of the world." The emphasis here is not on the untenanted ocean, but on the two pinpoints of light which are its only visible objects. To designate these transitory and ephemeral glimmers, "furniture" seems an oddly specific term. But in its connotation of being exclusively man-made and used by man, and in its limited and humdrum quality, it points up that contrast between human existence and cosmic regime which is the author's chief concern.

If the conflicting forces engaged in this tale are man and nature, the psychic struggle clearly involves man's attitude toward the forces of nature. In tracing the steps the correspondent takes in reaching a fixed conclusion, the author's figures of speech prove most revealing.

At first the man in the boat looks upon nature as an enemy—maliciously cruel and vengeful. "The waves were most barbarously abrupt and tall" pictures faceless savagery endowed with a killer's ferocity. The mousetrap figure mentioned above demonstrates the most wanton cruelty of all, for just as the timid victim approaches the very stuff of life, the fatal trap is sprung. Though the correspondent cries out against such injustice, as he may have protested the slaughter of mice in his mother's kitchen, his cry is rhetorical and seems to expect no clemency.

As the hours in the dinghy pass and the man rows alone at night, his judgment of nature alters. Not gratuitously cruel, perhaps, but surely nature is irresponsibly, chancily menacing. The shark that flashes through the dark water near the boat is likened to a great, gleaming knife, another household object dreaded for its accidental as well as intentional deeds of blood. This creature appears soon after the correspondent's tirade against Fate—"that old ninny-woman"—as an old hen who knows not her intention. He may be thinking of the one of the three mythical sisters who holds her scissors poised to cut man's tenuous thread of life. The shark is an appropriate cutting agent, and the severing of man's life by its agency is as utterly a matter of chance. When the shark veers away as casually as it came, the hit-or-miss quality of Fate or chance is underscored.

At this point the correspondent arrives at the unwelcome truth that nature really does not care. "She is indifferent, flatly indifferent." She would not regard the disposal of him as maiming to the universe. He longs, in a fit of juvenile frustration, to fling bricks at the temple, but in the watery waste around him there are neither bricks nor temples. "A high cold star on a winter's night is the word he feels that she [nature] says to him."

There is no mistaking the inevitability of this edict. The figure of the star is not only cold and remote; it is not to be questioned, and it will not change. Its message is final. This figure closes a section of the tale, and the next one opens with the literary allusion to the soldier who lay dying in Algiers.

Like other figures of speech, literary allusion jets from deep in the subconscious. Unlike them, it is born not of an actual experience but of an intellectual impression—not a material image as Emerson described it, but a mental one. To the narrator the coming into his mind of this bit of verse was mysterious (for he had even forgotten it) but not irrelevant, for it "chimed the notes of his emotion"—the emotion induced by the word from the high, cold, indifferent star.

The narrator has already recognized as precious the comradeship of the men in the boat as they confront the ruthlessness of their common enemy. "The best experience of his life," he calls it. But as a solace for cold indifference and threatened annihilation, a more cosmic comfort is needed, and this is suggested by the thought of the soldier's plight.

> A soldier of the Legion lay dying in Algiers;
> There was lack of women's nursing; there was dearth of
>   women's tears;
> But a comrade stood beside him and he took that com-
>   rade's hand,
> And he said, "I never more shall see my own, my native
>   land."

The correspondent recalls that as a school boy he had been bored at the repetitive sing-song of his classmates as each in turn droned this passage from memory. He had cared little about that far-off lonely death. "Less than the breaking of a pencil point," he remembers. Yet now, pictorially vivid, the scene flashes on his inner eye—the low, square buildings, dry sands, the moribund soldier clutching his bleeding wound. And retroactively, as it were, his sympathy wells up. He is sorry.

Though Crane arrives at this rush of pity in a roundabout way, his purpose is clear enough. Only through his own experiencing of outrageous fortune and the imminence of death has the correspondent gained maturity enough to feel compassion for the universal human condition. To feel warm consideration for those close to one whose plight is identified with one's own is natural enough, but to know pity for suffering in general is a transcendent virtue. And it is comforting to know that such human pity exists, especially when one has just perceived the futility of an appeal to the forces that control the world.

Possibly the reference to the remembered poem has another and deeper meaning. Although it is evident that Crane's metaphors, like all metaphorical language, carry a greater weight of significance than at first seems obvious, more unusual are the indications that this significance may be partly or even wholly unintended by the author. Support for this view can be found in Mark Schorer's fine study of metaphorical language—"Fiction and the 'Matrix of Anology' " [*Kenyon Review,* XI (Autumn 1949)]. Emily Bronte, the critic points out, learned from her own metaphors, as her genius operated to uncover images that meant more than she consciously knew. "Her rhetoric altered the form of her intention," says Schorer. "It is her education; it shapes her insight."

The change in attitude toward the suffering Legionnaire may have more to reveal than the correspondent's growth in spiritual stature and the comforting implication that universal compassion exists as a sort of general solace for human misfortunes. The second line in the quotation provides a clue—"There was lack of women's nursing; there was dearth of women's tears."

Crane maintains a jeering attitude toward women throughout his tale (there is his reference to Fate as an old ninny-woman, an old hen who knows not her intention) and this at first would seem to be intensified by the bathos of the quoted line: "there was lack of women's nursing; there was dearth of women's tears," especially as rendered with the customary juvenile inflection. Yet the memory of the stanza *in its entirety* prompts the correspondent's spontaneous pity. The implication is plain: If man must venture into far lands and uncharted seas in his physical and psychic quests, he has need *in extremis* of the comfort of woman and the solace of her tears.

The very quality of the metaphors that Crane employs throughout this work suggests a submerged tenderness for home and mother that the author would have scorned to betray. The figures, as we have seen, are drawn from boyhood activities, mostly bounded by kitchen, backyard, and chicken coop. These are the provinces of the women of the household. Here they dispense the comfort and order which a young boy may resent, only to remember it later with longing.

There is ambivalence as well in the treatment of the middle-aged women with coffee-pots "and other remedies sacred to their minds" who follow in the wake of the male rescuer, a naked man who wears like a saint a halo around his head. These are ninny-women, no doubt—old hens—whose faith in their nostrums is scorned in the phrase "sacred to their minds." Yet the very word *sacred* portrays the author's unconsciously altered intention. *Sacred* parallels the saint-like accoutrements of the man rescuer. It is the very word used repeatedly in the key phrase "the *sacred* cheese of life." The remedies are sacred to a woman's mind because they assist her in her peculiar function—that of soothing, ministering to, and nurturing life. They are sacred to all for that reason. *Sacred* becomes, then, a sort of transferred epithet.

Finally the need of women, their love and tears, is implicit in the manner in which Crane tells of the oiler's tragic end. The land welcomes him, too, though he is dead; he is received with hospitality, only a different (cold) hospitality—that of the grave. Throughout the tale the land is the *desideratum;* glimpsing land and trees is equated with nibbling the sacred cheese of life. There is comfort in the hospitality of even a grave on land (where it can be visited and wept over). Hospitality has feminine overtones.

Though clearly attesting to Crane's deterministic beliefs, this tale of the men in the boat cannot be termed pessimistic. There are human influences that mitigate the admitted indifference of nature to insignificant man. One is the association with one's fellows that Crane joyously proclaims; one is the capacity for universal pity, which he feels can be learned through suffering; and one is the love of women which he yet seems to spurn. But the indication of this love is incontrovertibly present, buried in the language. I. A. Richards lists as one of the values of metaphor its ability to "smuggle in," in a semi-surreptitious way, whatever is needed for the wholeness of experience. It is largely through Crane's inadvertent choice of figures that his readers sense the wholeness of his meaning and along with protagonists, learn to be *interpreters.* (pp. 18-22)

> Leedice Kissane, "Interpretation through Language: A Study of the Metaphors in Stephen Crane's 'The Open Boat'," in Rendezvous, Vol. 1, No. 1, Spring, 1966, pp. 18-22.

Andrew Lytle   (essay date 1966)

[*Former editor of the literary quarterly* Sewanee Review, *Lytle is also a noted critic, novelist, and short story writer whose work is deeply informed by the values of Christianity and the Southern agrarian movement of the 1930s and 1940s. In the following excerpt from his collected essays,* The Hero with the Private Parts, *Lytle offers a close examination of action, image, and language in "The Open Boat" in order to determine the nature of the protagonists' view of the universe.*]

The sinking of the *Commodore* is the only instance I know which allows for a strict comparison between journalism (even in Eliot's sense) and fiction. After his rescue Crane wrote for the press, along with the Captain and others, his own story of the disaster. It is good; it is the best of journalism, but it is not fiction; nor was it meant to be. (p. 60)

Journalism in Crane's day was closer to fiction than it is now. The mechanical formulae of platitude as the norm would not come for another generation or so; so that at its best, as it is in "Stephen Crane's Own Story," the news story has at times the same authority as fiction. But the reader must wait for **"The Open Boat"** to know what it is to be at sea, to be within six inches of death minute by minute, at the height of a storm which lasts for thirty hours. Of course there is the obvious suspense: will the men get ashore? But this is merely the statement of a desired end; it is not the action itself. The shipwrecked, except at intervals, are not involved with rescue (this is their concern, of course); they are involved, to use Arthurian terms, with the dolorous quest, unconsciously, neverthe-

less truly; and this enforced quest becomes ignorance changed into knowledge and especially self-knowledge before a continuing precarious plight. This is the way in which the ordinary man becomes a hero or fails in manhood. With the frail support of a ten-foot dinghy four men, the injured captain, the cook, the oiler, and the one alien to the sea, the correspondent, confront the ocean (the elemental) at its most destructive phase. Without water there can be no life, but that which is benign and sustaining is merely one part of the dualism which holds in reserve, for its own mysterious reasons, the opposite or destructive power. Such is the course of learning these men are forced to undertake. They are at the mercy of one element, but they are affected by all four; to say four is to say the elements are pagan. The outcome of the action will show whether the cosmos to the shipwrecked is pagan and whether they so view it.

Four elements, four men in the boat who comprise the basic qualities of men acting as men. We begin with this. The captain is the legal and moral authority; he is the sovereign power. The cook is the one who attends to and satisfies appetite. The oiler has all of the craftsmanship and deep knowledge of the sea; he is the one who can make a thing work or go, and it is these qualities as expressions of his character which allow the captain, by ordering them, to bring the men to shore. It is also these qualities which make of him and not the captain the hero-victim. The correspondent is the outsider and so is better able to interpret what takes place. But particularly he is the man of words; and it is by means of words, artfully employed, that actions are most fully known. For these reasons the point of view must lie with him. We have a definite clue. He wonders why he is there, and to wonder is the beginning of knowledge. He enters the minds of all, but he is an actor, too, and finds himself most identified with the oiler. He is the twin and counterpart, but the articulate and imaginative part of the oiler, who only does.

Each of the men is, in a way, the protagonist, for each by his office (not personally) represents an intrinsic part of man. These parts must be seen not as allegory but as offices; that is, the man of appetite is a cook; sovereignty is specified by what it means to be a captain of a ship, not of infantry. But it is the correspondent who is the actual protagonist, for he is changed by the action. The others are there to be interpreted by him in the course of his learning. They are real but in a sense become his creatures. He is writing the story after the fact, to understand the experience and what it has done for him, which he cannot know unless he knows the others in their roles. Only fiction can do this, since facts are elusive and require a point of view and an imagination to fit them together. **"The Open Boat"** being fiction, Crane is not himself either but his own creature, along with the companions in sorrow.

The action opens not with the melodramatic incident of the crazed stevedore but with the now famous sentence, "None of them knew the color of the sky." Here is a simple sentence; yet it is mysterious. What it holds is the essence of the action: the kernel. It is the felt weight of this which induces the mystery and establishes in the first sentence the suspense and tone which will be maintained. This sense of the conflict can only be felt, because it takes the long middle and the shock at the end to fuse together the entire meaning at a specific moment. And this moment of course closes the action. A story whose opening lacks this feeling of weight, of a revelation about to be illumined, will be discursive and suggestive rather than intrinsic and absolute. The shipwrecked do not know the color of the sky, because to remove their eyes for an instant from the mountainous waves will swamp the boat. Nor can they remove their eyes: they are fixed by the threat and object of death. As in any crisis of violence man, by being immersed, can act only out of his instincts and reflexes. These men we are told know all the colors of the sea; that is, they have the particular knowledge of the ways of the sea. But being so caught up, they cannot use it. They are virtually in this beginning in a state of ignorance. Meaning develops as they suffer and learn.

The author's most urgent technical problem must have been the kind of comparisons to make. To use only pictures of the sea and its effects upon them would have produced monotony. No element in the natural world is finally isolated. Where there is the sea, there is the sky above which holds the breath of life and, as the winds blow it, the threat of death. Fire at sea is a harder matter, since it is the opposite of water and only in alchemy can conjoin with it. But there are the stars, the lights in the night, the streak of phosphorus. Once water is a spread of white flames. But the images most used are from the land. The sea and the land contain the conflict, the threat of annihilation and the hope of salvation. It is towards the land their desperate eyes most often turn. Can they free themselves of the waves and safely come to shore? In "Stephen Crane's Own Story," when trying to launch a life-boat, he compares their effort to that of moving a brick schoolhouse. Either instinctively or consciously here he got the substance of his structure. In their peril the land could only seem safe, kind, and longed-for, but this is only half its meaning. In their desperation they, at first, ignore what is hidden.

Because the eye is in the moving boat, the horizon narrows and widens, dips and rises, in fact refuses to make of the landfall a fixed and stable place. The motion of the sea dominates. All things, including the land, are liquid and threatening. Nowhere in the universe does there seem to be a firm place to stand. The waves are thrust up in points like rocks. To be tossed upon rocks is to be spitted; to be rolled in the breakers may be to drown. The threat of the waves is thus reenforced by something equally dangerous on the land. The entire paragraph gives us the shipwrecked in an almost hopeless condition, just after the ship goes down. The next paragraph says that a man ought to have a bath tub larger than the boat which here rides upon the sea. The tub, misplaced in the ocean, because of its misplacement makes visual the immensity of the ocean, the fragility of the dinghy, and the slight chance of survival. And what could be more opposite to what is happening to them than the safe luxury of a warm tub behind a locked door.

These seemingly contradictory effects follow throughout, but particularly in the first two parts. The boat is a bucking bronco. As the wave approaches, the little boat rises for it like a horse taking a fence outrageously high. It rides down the slaty wall of water, which seems the final outburst of the ocean. The waves have a terrible grace and they come in silence, "save for the snarling of the crests." Silence against the sound of the crests makes the reader

both see and hear in the wave the threat of the ocean. Not only has he here in the way no one can doubt brought together sound and silence, exact opposites; but he further enlarges the effect by yoking together things ordinarily never compared, and he does this by what they have in common, terror. The slaty wall is an actual terror in itself, but the terrible grace and the snarling implies the beast crouching or springing. The tiger of the news story takes on now its proper effect. And further the land is no longer the simple hope for refuge. The men are still caught up. They do not notice the changing of the hours; their faces are gray in the wan light of breaking day; they are still unable to be aware of anything more than the sea colors changing from slate to emerald green (the foam tumbles like snow). Against the elemental forces, to view the men at dawn, the author makes a violent shift of view. He puts it in a balcony, as if the spectator were comfortably watching a melodrama, something "weirdly picturesque." This is so removed from the actual predicament as to imply an indifference to their fate, to make it unreal. It is almost as if they were already dead. At least the unreality of a view from a balcony makes of the land, their hope of refuge, a place not to be believed in. Now, against the sea and those threats from the land similar both in kind and appearance to the sea, the author places a short dialogue between the cook and the correspondent. In spite of the fuller knowledge of what the land holds for these shipwrecked men, for the moment hidden in the enveloping comparisons, they can only see the shore as a good. The cook speaks hopefully of a house of refuge as being near. In his anxiety he confuses it with a life-saving station. The correspondent corrects him. They contradict each other; that is, they argue about a hypothetical situation. The oiler, the seaman, returns them to reality. "We're not there yet," he says.

These sea-land comparisons contain both the enveloping action, or the conditions forever constant upon the human and natural scene, and the action itself. In this short dialogue the action begins to withdraw from that which envelops it, begins to specify, although it does not yet make clear the fullness of what is amorphous. This withdrawal is never a severance. It merely gives shape to that which is hidden but everpresent. It is as old as the fall of man, since man falling into his predicament always falls into his original plight, a plight, though unique, common to all. The individual conflict is the only way to show their common predicament. The fear of death is an abstraction until it withdraws from the general into a particular effect. The sense of fear may be in a group, but each member will feel it according to his capacity. The artist manages to make this apparent by the use of his various tools, the most important of which is the sensibility. Its five parts make the word flesh.

Parts two and three continue and emphasize the ambiguity which relates land to sea, only now the action begins more and more to show it. The crest of the waves suggests a hill, not mountains of water, high and formidable but not impossible to mount. The danger seems less present than the snarling beast, although the situation remains precarious. Canton flannel (soft for babies and croup) gulls fly about them. They sit down upon the water, before the men, as at home as prairie chickens a thousand miles inland. They sit near patches of sea weed which undulate like carpets in a gale. All these domestic comparisons of comfort and safety converge through the gulls and then through one gull into the action itself. They make a particular effect. They stare at the men with black bead-like eyes. Their unblinking scrutiny seems uncanny and sinister. The occupants of the boat hoot at them. The one gull threatens by side-long jumps in the air, "chicken-fashion," to roost upon the captain's head. The captain would like to knock it in the head with a painter, but he waves it gently away and carefully. This enforced restraint brings to a point the six inches of gunwale and the turbulent waters, immediate and threatening.

The overwhelming, absolute threat of death which the mountains of water pose in the beginning remains, but in a state of suspension. It becomes the shape of their predicament. The senses begin to work and make the feelings of the four, their responses to particular objects, carry the increasing tensions of the conflict as it moves inevitably toward the climax. The cook bails, the captain directs, the correspondent and the oiler row, sometimes together, sometimes separately, and the care with which the rowers change places compares them to Dresden figurines. And then he who is relieved is no longer china. He drops into the cold water of the boat and is instantly asleep. Touch and sight show the menace of growing fatigue. Their waning strength is thus opposed to the tireless waves. In the beginning the oars seem too frail. Any moment the weight of water may snap them in two and thus doom the boat, but towards the end they are as heavy as lead. This different use of touch measures the time at sea and the mounting fatigue which diminishes their chances of escape. To say that men are tired does not show them so, but the changing weight of the oars does. Nor can statement make time pass either. But time is very important. It is another measure of the men's resistance. It is rendered in various ways, but sight, the sovereign sense, is sharpened upon a small still thing in the moving horizon. This is the lighthouse at Mosquito Inlet and nobody can see it at first but the captain, he whose attention is ever alert. Indistinctly this grows from a pin point, out of a long black shadow upon the sea, until it is an upright shadow upon the sky: substances of hope but insubstantial to sight, matter yet not matter. The horizon still moves; substance cannot be relied upon. However, sea weed imitating earth tells them they are making progress towards land.

We now approach the long middle. The fury of the sea has decreased, but only so far as to allow the shipwrecked to be consciously aware of the danger, to assess their chances. They have been cast away not in the pink of condition but overworked and hungry, and the captain has a broken arm. The men strain almost to the verge of collapse, but the captain by some stratagem, each time, prolongs the struggle. As he hangs over the water jar, he hears and sees and inwardly interprets the particularities, the quality of the threats; so that in each command quietly given, he speaks with his proper authority and adds to this the great moral force of knowledge they all now begin to acquire. Sometimes he has them hoist his overcoat on an oar for sail, at times he has the cook make of an oar a rudder, so that both the oiler and the correspondent can rest together. Even when the boat capsizes and they are in the surf, he speaks above its roar and instructs the cook and the correspondent.

But as the land slowly rises out of the sea and the light-house rears high, the captain himself voices their suppressed fear. Even he confuses the house of refuge (which doesn't exist) with the life-saving station (which is twenty miles away). Their irrational state of mind, where rescue is concerned, finds its expression in denying the facts. To accept the facts just then would bring them to despair, so great is their stress and so inadequate their means for survival. But there comes a respite. The land continues to rise beautifully out of the sea. Another sense now is used: sound. They hear the low thunder of the surf: the threat of death and the hope of salvation, just where the black line of the sea and the white of sand join, that border they must pass over and which now is fixed in their sight. The wind has changed, but their moment seems to be upon them. They grow cheerful, find cigars and matches. "Everybody took a drink of water."

But it is a false hope. The house the captain has seen as the house of refuge or life-saving station is just a house in a summer resort. They are forced to abandon the false illusion which unspoken fear established in their minds as fact. The surf though far away sounds thunderous and mighty. The captain is the first to confront the reality again, which is that if they are to be saved, they will have to do it themselves and presently, for "if we stay out here too long, we'll none of us have the strength left to swim after the boat swamps." They willingly face up to the enemy, and with understanding, not complete but sufficient for the moment. They exchange addresses, with constraint accepting the possibility of death. This is a kind of moral triumph before the obvious dangers at that place where land and water meet.

It is at this time that the correspondent, in interpreting for all, uses a rhetorical language which seems to violate the established tone. "If I am going to be drowned—if I am going to be drowned—if I am going to be drowned, why, in the name of the seven mad gods who rule the sea, was I allowed to come thus far and contemplate sand and trees? . . . my nose dragged away as I was about to nibble the sacred cheese of life? . . . If this old ninny-woman Fate cannot do better than this, she should be deprived of the management of men's fortunes. . . ." and it goes on. Actually there is no violation. This is one of the correspondent's voices. The false rhetoric is a part of the professional cynicism of journalism which views all appearance as false or suspect. It is not even a pretense to belief, for the gods here invoked are pagan gods the correspondent no more believes in than he believes in the Christian order of Heaven. He who was taught to be cynical of men does believe in and knows at the time that the fellowship with the other men in the boat would be the best experience of his life. This feeling of comradeship discovered for the correspondent his own humanity, but he is not yet fully saved, not so long as he uses the falsely pagan figures of speech. To be halfsaved on this quest is to ask for further trials. And this is exactly what the ocean and the doubtful shore have yet to give.

As they draw nigh to land, it is seen the billows will surely swamp the boat. The oiler announces the dinghy won't live three more minutes and asks the captain to let him take it to sea again. It takes supreme skill to execute this. The oiler rows them back into their predicament, towards the desolate orient and a squall marked by clouds "brick-red like smoke from a burning building." Moral fatigue as

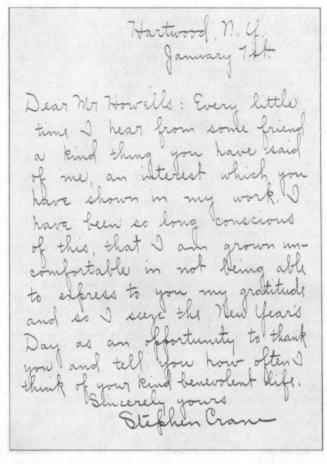

Hartwood, N. Y.
January 1st.

Dear Mr Howells: Every little time I hear from some friend a kind thing you have said of me, an interest which you have shown in my work. I have been so long conscious of this, that I am grown uncomfortable in not being able to express to you my gratitude and so I seize the New Year's Day as an opportunity to thank you and tell you how often I think of your kind benevolent life.
Sincerely yours
Stephen Crane

Letter by Crane to William Dean Howells, January 1, 1896.

up," when the oarsman falters. The long strain has made the cook indifferent to danger. He withdraws into a dream of food. He asks what kind of pie the oiler likes best. The man whose office it is to attend to the appetite of others now expresses his longing for shore in dreams of his own. This is the only time the oiler becomes agitated. To the correspondent the mention of food brings to mind no "cheese" of life but its very bread. They are made to suffer twice over, in their physical need and the land's comforts which the mention of food makes them so keenly aware of.

Throughout the night the oiler and the correspondent exchange places, each rowing after he is no longer able to row. And then in the deep reaches of the night the correspondent is left alone with the full responsibility of his office, for even the captain, he thinks, is asleep. We now approach the climax for all, and for the protagonist the long dark night at sea becomes the dark night of the soul. The correspondent is to be isolated, until he feels himself the one man afloat upon all the oceans, so that the "wind's voice is sadder than the end." There remains this night nothing to sustain him but himself. Before the complex mystery which surrounds him, he begins to change, finding his cynicism no help for what confronts him. The boat is so small that the men touch, their feet reaching under the sea even to the captain. They exist almost as one body, under the pressures of their predicament. But the correspondent does not share this, for he alone is conscious. Fire is the appropriate element to illuminate his predicament. There are two lights, one to the north and one to the south. "The two lights were the furniture of the world." This expresses his aloneness, but the shark trailing its prosphorus suggests death, although its light is harmless. Then there are the stars. All of these exempla of fire, because they are remote and cannot immediately affect him, either for good or ill, represent his confinement to himself. This is his trial, and he accepts it as he leans over the boat and swears softly into the sea.

During the rest of the night, the management of the boat requires the others to take their parts with him. He returns to them changed. Part six opens with "If I am going to be drowned . . . " but the rhetoric fails him. The complaint is very short. The indifference of Fate makes him say but "I love myself." At once he is presented with the vanity of this. His rebellion, the lack of a temple to pelt with brick, quickly declines into a pathos and knowledge of any man's supreme insignificance. "A high cold star on a winter's night is the word" he feels that she (nature) says to him. This is the point of change for him. The star is so remote it might be the core and shine of eternity, and nothing at this moment could so reduce him or make him suffer the humility without which no man is reborn. To make it concrete, out of his unconscious suddenly he is hearing a verse he had forgotten. As a child it had meant no more to him than a pencil point breaking. Like the ninny-woman Fate it belongs to a foreign world. Through his changing sense of himself, it now becomes present, no longer foreign but a local instance, as is his suffering, of the universal predicament of mankind, everywhere beset and tried by those forces of nature (for so far does he see) everywhere about, lying in wait to try and judge the spirit and resistance of man.

A soldier of the Legion lay dying in Algiers;

well as physical shows in the collapse of the rower into the cold sea-water sloshing to and fro in the bottom of the boat, being drenched without being awakened, within an inch of the waves, into which, if the boat should capsize, he would have "tumbled comfortably out upon the ocean as if he felt sure it was a great soft mattress." This is a small climax of the ambiguity in the land-sea images. The castaways' bitter retreat is made poignant by seeing a man on shore waving his coat. Other men arrive. But what a distance between those at sea and those on land. All the possibilities of rescue pass before those in the dinghy, but the men on land are as helpless to help as they are to receive it. When the four realize this, and also realize that they must spend a night upon the ocean, they revile those on shore and particularly the one waving his coat. The coat is a message of sympathy, but the night closing down makes the land seem hostile. After the land has vanished but not the low drear thunder of the surf, the correspondent berates the pagan gods about his possibility of drowning. But this time he speaks only about a third as much. This lessening of his use of such rhetoric is a clue to the meaning of its function.

They now literally enter the night sea journey. The oarsman can barely see the tall black waves. The rest lie heavily and listlessly in the boat. The captain droops over the water jar, but he still commands, saying, "Keep her head

There was lack of woman's nursing, there was dearth of
 woman's tears;
But a comrade stood beside him, and he took that comrade's hand,
And he said, "I never more shall see my own, my native
 land."

Out of the isolation of himself from all living creatures, before the point of eternity and in the presence of death (the
shark), the correspondent is able to transform sound into
sight (the rhythm of the verse into visual images), and out
of this combine all the senses into a belief in and apprehension of a real soldier dying in the sands of Algiers. These
sands become more real than the real sands before him by
a kind of reversal, as he is purged of false rhetoric. The
word becomes itself, and out of sorrow for himself has
grown a compassionate sympathy for all. This is the measure of the extremity of his change. But even yet he does
not understand it. The danger of the waves and the shut-in
night does not allow him time for contemplation. He
largely feels as much as exhausted muscle and attention
will allow. But when morning breaks and it is clear no help
is coming and the captain decides to run the surf, then nature to the correspondent (and he speaks for all) seemed
neither cruel, nor wise, nor beneficent, nor treacherous—
merely indifferent.

The sense of this represents the purgation of "fine" language and the illusion of false aid. There is nowhere a subterfuge for reality, the approaching crisis which in an instant will be death or salvation. The third great wave
swamps the boat and they tumble into the January water;
but the warning of that from which they must turn away
but, whatever the outcome, must face, comes to the correspondent as the waters from the second wave tumble into
the boat. His hands were on the thwarts. He quickly withdraws them as if he were afraid of wetting his fingers, he
who has been sleeping in water, been saturated by it, and
from the extremity of his fatigue would have rolled into
it as upon a soft mattress. I suppose, in fiction, the sense
of touch has never been so well used, nor can one find so
rare an example of the authority of rendition over that of
statement. The nerves, in prostration, reach that exquisite
feeling which brings to touch its euphoria and the falling
away from this exquisite feeling into the listlessness of no
response. Physically, then, the nerve ends, having reached
this condition, a condition where water is felt as fire (one
feels this in the quick withdrawal) represent the transcen-
dance of fatigue, the weapon of the sea against the shipwrecked, who will now enter the water with only the resistance their separate persons in the mystery of their spirits
may show. Also in this touch is the final concentration of
the unspoken fear of death, of hope and despair, also unspoken but revealed in full by this action, a repugnance for
their condition and for nature, the four elements, and the
final denial of any pathetic fallacy. Once in the water the
shore seems like scenery upon a stage. Although almost
in reach and touch, to turn at this moment the real shoreline into an artificial setting for entertainment is an irony
almost too finely drawn; it also sustains by the imagination
what touch has done for the flesh. By now we feel all the
false rhetoric has been strained away. The correspondent
says simply, in the wonder of an innocent, "I am going to
be drowned? Can it be possible? Can it be possible?" His
isolation from himself is his conquest over self. He is now
ready for the final act and understanding.

The captain in the water, holding on to the boat, still gives
directions above the mighty noise of the surf. The cook in
a life preserver is ordered to turn on his back and use the
oar. The oiler needs no direction. He swims rapidly towards land, ahead in the race, as if he had suffered no fatigue; but the correspondent is ordered to come to the
boat, when a wave lifts him and carries him completely
over it to waters in which he can stand, but only for an
instant. So fine a hair is drawn in his fate, which is settled
by a man on shore running, shedding his clothes until he
is naked as upon the first day, as the natural man free of
all inhibiting social conventions. He drags the cook
ashore; the captain still in his office of authority directs
him next to the correspondent whom he pulls by the hand.
Suddenly the man cries "What's that?" The correspondent says, "Go."

It is the oiler, in the shallows, face down. His head touches, between each wave, the sand. The two elements of
water and earth are now brought together in their complete meaning. The ambiguity of life-death is resolved in
the oiler's body. And in human terms, sustaining the elemental, the dead body of the oiler and the live naked body
of the man from the shore, whose charitable love saves
some of them, represent life and death which the shoreline
holds, the one aspect the forbidding and the other the
hopeful. If the irony, however, becomes final in the oiler's
body, the paradox remains to the end: one dies, the others
live. The one most knowledgable of the sea, who has
brought the others to safety, cannot save himself. Both life
and death are here, but only after a respite does the correspondent, speaking for the survivors and perhaps for the
dead, receive the full impact of learning. "When it came
night, the white waves paced to and fro in the moonlight,
and the wind brought the sound of the great sea's voice
to the men on shore, and they felt that they could then be
interpreters." From the ignorance of the first line, "None
of them knew the color of the sky," the ignorance of absolute action, they now have graduated into the knowledge
of the possibilities of all experience; that is, they can now
interpret, at last, what has happened to them and what,
therefore, can happen to all men. Like a destructive beast
nature is always lying in wait to undo mankind. The elements may be indifferent but the mysterious, fateful circumstance depending upon the supernatural can save or
destroy. Those who escape and those who fall define a
mystery. The oiler is there for proof. And from the wind
the sea carries to the men on shore this message. The basic
element of life, air without which we cannot live, is the
agency of the final mystery. Earth and water are forever
present, the physical grounds for action, but the air in its
physical and symbolic meaning carries the final authority
of knowledge, the conditions of man in life and in the presence of the supernatural. The shipwrecked understand
now the price of things as well as the mystery. They know
one does not earn his life once and for all, for the beast remains in ambush, whether at sea or on land or within the
human heart, pacing to and fro. Although the natural
man, the innocent man, (he does not know or care whether
he has clothes on or not) loves his neighbor as himself and
shines like a saint (angel), the ending does not necessarily
show them all turned Christians. They in this knowledge
which is experience may still be pagan. Their learning
could be in the limits of stoicism. This kind of withdrawal
of ignorance could be the answer to the mystery they have
suffered. But it seems more likely that the correspondent

who entered this adventure cynically now crowns his learning and change with a Christian image, even though he may have reached only the threshhold of faith, such as the early Christians knew. Perhaps it is this which makes them all feel, as the correspondent interprets for them, "that they could then be interpreters." (pp. 62-75)

> Andrew Lytle, " 'The Open Boat': A Pagan Tale," in his The Hero with the Private Parts, Louisiana State University Press, 1966, pp. 60-75.

Eric Solomon   (essay date 1966)

[*Solomon's* Stephen Crane: From Parody to Realism *is considered an important contribution to Crane studies. In his book Solomon asserts that Crane parodied conventional nineteenth-century literature to develop his own fiction. In the following excerpt from this study, Solomon discusses Crane's Western short stories as parodies of the Western, myth-making fiction popular during Crane's life.*]

The myth and the reality of the American West provided Stephen Crane with the setting for some of his most brutally violent and richly humorous stories. . . . Crane accepted many of the Western traditions and made them vibrant in his short fiction. Simultaneously he cast a cold eye on the myth of the Western hero. Crane laughed at this myth which had become degraded into hardened stereotypes by the 1890's. As Mark Twain in *Roughing It* was able both to parody romantic notions of gold seekers and desperados and at the same time to create in Scotty Briggs and Jack Slade vital portraits of those types—real, humorous, generous, vernacular—so Crane undercut the myth for the sake of the imbedded reality that he had observed, then reconstructed the myth, beyond parody, into tales that approximate Western tragedies. While Crane's funniest stories are clearly anti-Westerns, employing the mode largely to reject it, his most impressive tales accept the Western ideas of individualism, violence, strength, and honor. (pp. 229-30)

Stephen Crane's early Western story **"Horses—One Dash"** . . . is a revealing and not wholly successful amalgam of parody and thriller. The bare plot is that of a thriller: an Easterner named Richardson, accompanied by a comic Mexican servant, José, puts up for the night in a Mexican village where a group of sinister desperadoes later arrive. These outlaws are blood-thirsty and eager to butcher the supposedly sleeping Richardson for the sake of his expensive saddle and spurs. Our hero sneaks out at dawn and rides to safety after a wild chase across the plains. Certain parodic elements are obvious in this recital of the plot. The usual Western hero is not afraid, and he almost never runs. Crane seems a bit uneasy with his attempts at comic incongruity, however. He wants something heroic for the story and settles for Richardson's horse, a tough, capable pony. Although the choice is understandable, given Crane's love for horses, it confuses the comic tone with some sentimental clichés out of *Black Beauty*. While travestying the myth of the fearless hero, Crane supports the myth of the noble horse (a naturalistic gambit, to be sure), and he fails of his desired effect. (p. 240)

The story is an interesting failure, for we see Crane experimenting with methods of enclosing the Western reality he admired—in this case, a horse's loyal courage—within an envelop of ridicule of Western myth—here the idea of the lone hero in conflict with an outlaw gang. Crane is not sure where he wants to deflate and where he wants to identify, and the story suffers. He solves the problem in his next Western tale, where wry humor and bitter cruelty, identification with and disgust for the protagonist, join in a story that is a triumph in the Western form.

"A Man and—Some Others" . . . is heroic and anti-heroic, funny and terrible, absurd and inevitable. By comprehending the pardoxes inherent in the Western setting, where freedom mixes with isolation and courage is a part of savagery, Stephen Crane uses his distortion of the traditional view of the hero to create a work of fiction that moves beyond derision to a terrible beauty.

The tale opens with a marvelously evocative panorama of isolation. Dark mesquite spreads from horizon to horizon; the world seems an unpeopled desert, and only a blue mist in the far distance reminds a sheep herder of the existence of mountains, of another world. Here following a central theme of American literature, the theme of loneliness, Stephen Crane tells his story of the lonely hero, self-dependent on a range peopled only by hostile Mexicans who insist that he leave or be killed. (pp. 242-43)

By playing off his flawed Western protagonist against a figure who comes on the scene as a surrogate for the narrator—an innocent Easterner whose stirrups do not fit—Crane complicates the characterization. True, Bill is a killer who lives by a revolver that has taken the lives of several men. Crane overwrites his hymn to the gun, comparing it to an eagle's claw, a lion's tooth, a snake's poison, but the weapon is a friend to this utterly friendless man. . . . Bill [is revealed] to be an uneasy combination of strength, amorality, vulnerability, and shame. Crane's achievement is special, for in a short story primarily dedicated to rapid action he has created an enigmatic figure who breaks down a Western stereotype and engages the reader's sympathy. (pp. 245-46)

The story comes to a swift, expected, problematic, and nearly tragic end. The reader suddenly realizes that the stranger is of some importance himself, as more than a pendant. Crane implies that increased understanding emerges from the few hours that Bill and the stranger share in the violent landscape. Thus, though the story ends as it must with Bill's death, this end is also a beginning, the real start of the stranger's story; for he too, during the Mexicans' final charge, shoots and kills. In that moment when a panther is born in his heart, understanding and perhaps manhood are also born. Whatever is born, however, comes in the blaze of Bill's last passion. Crane only impressionistically hints at the facts of the ultimate gunfight. It is a "picture half drawn" . . . that resembles a dream, so violent is the action. Forever in the young man's memory will certain lines and forms stand out from the incoherence, the author insists. The stranger learns the lessons of the West, the real West: that it is easy to kill a man; that a man who can die with dignity is a "good" man (a term that defies further definition). (pp. 248-49)

Knowledge is the key element in many of Crane's subsequent Western writings. In 1898 he wrote a pair of stories featuring two youths, the San Francisco Kid and the New York Kid. These two are audacious, bantering, and tough, and Crane might have been planning a series; the progress of the New York Kid from city streets to Mexican towns and then to gun duels, bears a superficial resemblance to the early career of Billy the Kid. While the first story, **"The Wise Men,"** is negligible, **"The Five White Mice"** utilizes the Western setting to dramatize a young man's education into the ways of fear and bluff. Like the earlier tale, much of the narrative of **"The Five White Mice"** involves an elaboration of the Kid's gambling efforts. (p. 249)

His most famous Western comedy, **"The Bride Comes to Yellow Sky,"** written that same year, combines parodic humor and chastening realism in a similar but more consistently sustained manner.

"The Bride Comes to Yellow Sky" is the triumphant example of Stephen Crane's mixture of parody and realism in his fiction. The parody of the convention is a basic part of the story's continuity, and creates, rather than comments on, the dramatic movement. The first section gently scoffs at the tradition of romance in the Western story. The newlyweds, Marshal Jack Potter of Yellow Sky and a bride who is neither pretty nor young and who has been a cook before her marriage, contribute to a travesty of the familiar Western love plot, in which marriage comes at (or after) the end and in which the couple is usually young and handsome. . . . Much of the humor derives from the behavior of Potter and his bride, who are awkward and embarrassed in the great Pullman car—an Eastern, dignified sanctum replete with Victorian ornament and Negro porters. Indeed, the act of marriage itself strikes Potter as a betrayal of the Western, Yellow Sky ethos. He is condemned in his own eyes for betraying two traditions: he has tarnished the person of Marshal, a figure fearsome and independent, and he has tampered with the custom of partnership—he has not consulted his male friends.

"The Bride Comes to Yellow Sky" is a study of identities. Although insecure in his new role as married and responsible official, Jack Potter is conscious of his change from his former role as the lone marshal, ever ready for a fight. His opposite, Scratchy Wilson, cannot face his own two roles. For in reality Scratchy is the town bum, an aging cowboy who is an anachronism. (James Agee, in his movie version of the story, emphasized this aspect of Scratchy by making him a handyman who cleans out cesspools.) But when drunk, Scratchy reverts to his former role of tough gunfighter. In order to sustain this conception of himself, Scratchy must define it against his antagonist, Marshal Potter in his earlier guise as typical marshal of the Old West, untrammeled and quick on the draw. The serious element of this comic tale comes from Scratchy Wilson's recognition that, with Potter's shucking off his character as mythic marshal, Scratchy cannot retain his own particular dream role as mythic Western gunfighter. (pp. 251-53)

The second part of the story opens in a world of complete contrast to the Eastern Pullman: the setting is Western, the bar of the Weary Gentleman Saloon, twenty-one minutes before the train bearing the Potters is to arrive. The time shift enables Crane not only to sketch rapidly the plot situation but also to evoke the familiar Western background. Crane supplies an Easterner, a drummer, to serve

as an outside observer who must learn about the local mores and the customary epic drunks of Scratchy Wilson that disturb the dozing atmosphere. Scratchy's binges are formulaic, and the formula depends upon Marshal Potter to bring the ceremony of shouting and shooting to a halt by engaging in a ritual fight with Scratchy. The bar is locked, and its inmates, supported by the two Western staples (guns and whiskey) that have turned Scratchy loose, take cover. Scratchy's position in the Yellow Sky social order becomes manifest: he is "a wonder with a gun," "the last one of the old gang that used to hang out along the river here," and, when sober, the "nicest fellow in town." . . . That is, Scratchy is a living cliché of the Old West, a quick draw, a deadly shot, a rough with a heart of gold: in every way outdated. And the section closes on that most hackneyed of all Western dime-novel phrases, echo of a thousand descriptions of Indian or badman attacks, "Here he comes." . . . The travesty is that this attack is reduced to the singular absurdity of one old man. (pp. 253-54)

All worlds meet in the final episode when the relic of the Old West runs into the new bourgeois and his wife. The narrative brings together the modes of thriller (Scratchy's hair-trigger threats), comedy (the incongruous situation of a drunken old man confronting a blushing pair of newlyweds), and realism (the pathetic realization that age and time have triumphed). The staple of Western fiction, two strong men face to face, meets with mockery once more, just as in **"Horses—One Dash"** and **"The Five White Mice."** The tradition in this case cracks wide open because the marshal is unarmed. Marriage has removed him from the Western scene: "He was stiffening and steadying, but yet somewhere at the back of his mind a vision of the Pullman floated: the sea-green figured velvet, the shining brass, silver, and glass . . . all the glory of the marriage, the environment of the new estate." . . . Scratchy's world crumbles, the circle breaks: "There ain't a man in Texas ever seen you without no gun. Don't take me for no kid." . . . But Scratchy is a kid—in a kid's costume, playing a child's game, in the world of children's books and dime novels, in his case, sadly, in the realms of second childhood. (pp. 254-55)

The image is a particularly rich one. As in the funnel of an hourglass, the sands of Scratchy Wilson's time have run out; he leaves his footprints on these sands as his dreams end and his life closes in.

Still, the story is parody, Crane's kind of parody. All the *données* of the Western story are reversed; the empty forms are shattered. The marshal is an unarmed honeymooner; the gunman is a childish old man; the gunfight is aborted. The basic devices are comic—misunderstanding and ridicule. Yet parody need not preclude seriousness. We recall the reason given by young Ike McCaslin for killing the bear in William Faulkner's story: he does it before it will be too late, before the final day, when even the bear wouldn't want it to last any longer; for then the woods would be gone, destroyed by civilization's weapons, the sawmill and the railroad. Civilization's weapons have come to Yellow Sky, and they are stronger than Scratchy's guns. It is already too late for Scratchy Wilson. The gunfighter should have died the way he wanted, in the traditional manner—with his boots on, as the familiar phrase goes—according to the violent ritual of his calling. **"The Bride Comes to Yellow Sky"** is a beautifully balanced combination of humor and pathos, tightly, almost rigidly, organized; it is perhaps Stephen Crane's finest example of the creative uses of parody. (pp. 255-56)

Perhaps **"The Bride Comes to Yellow Sky"** is Stephen Crane's outstanding combination of parody and realism: **"The Blue Hotel,"** Crane's best-known, most anthologized and analyzed story, depends on parody less strongly but still capitalizes on the technique, and moves even closer to the stuff of tragedy.

The idea behind the story, one of the finest of all Western tales, is the search for identity and the desire of an outsider to define himself through conflict with a society. And this outsider, because of his internal contradictions, fails in Crane's world, a world once described as analogous to Hemingway's universe "of man damaged and alone in a hostile, violent world, of life as one long war which we seek out and challenge in fear and controlled panic." **"The Blue Hotel"** articulates such a conception as the battle-lustful Swede strides through the snowy winds of Fort Romper, a deserted village on an earth that one could scarcely imagine peopled. . . . (pp. 257-58)

The world that the Swede discovers in the West is dreadful and absurd, and the story chronicles the outsider's defeat, what Stephen Crane terms "a tragedy greater than the tragedy of action." . . . In simplest outline, **"The Blue Hotel"** tells of the initial victory and eventual defeat and death of an odd, disturbed stranger. The story treats, in a mixture of fantasy, realism, and parody, the fear that drives men to acts of violence. The narrative raises many questions as to the nature of fear and courage, the responsibility for a man's death, the inability of men to communicate. The questions appear throughout and not all find answers by the end of the tale, which is as problematical as most of Crane's best fiction. From the start of the long story, where no one will discuss fear or death with the Swede, to the conclusion where he has lost fear and gains death, a note of inevitability prevails. Stephen Crane once spoke of the kind of tragic event that was "not the tragedy of a street accident, but foreseen, inexorable, invincible tragedy." In this 1898 story another innocent in the long list of Crane naïfs that stretches back to Henry Fleming and Maggie must meet the test of experience. According to R. W. B. Lewis, the story of the fall of Adamic man usually appears in American writers' later works, in which they sum up their experiences of America and probe the tragedy inherent in the innocence of the new hero. In **"The Blue Hotel,"** the hero, the Swede, new to the Western world that he perceives in dime-novel commonplaces, falls victim to some of the very conventions that Stephen Crane reduces to parody throughout his Western fiction. (p. 258)

Stephen Crane's Western stories make a fitting climax to the essentially parodic approach that defines his fiction from start to finish. In his powerful and dramatic Western adventures, Crane laughs at the formulae of the Western story; without commitment he still manages to employ the traditional evocative qualities of the form while engaged in the process of criticizing the form itself.

With a style that is at once clear and ambiguous, language that is precise and evocative, settings that are immediate and impressionistic, dialogue that is lucid and vernacular, prose that is concentrated and rich, structure that is firm and flexible, Stephen Crane created an impressive body of fiction. With a philosophy of life that is bleak yet tough-minded, Crane viewed man in many situations of tense conflict—with nature, society, himself. Even in his most severe indictments of human and environmental limitations, however, Stephen Crane never lost sight of the ridiculous. Crane's major fiction most often commences in parody and concludes in creativity. He derided conventional slum sentimentality, mocked temperance fiction, glanced at certain excesses of sea tales, triumphantly made the conventions of war literature his own best medium, showed contempt for the stories of small-town America, and caricatured the narratives of the Old West. In his best work parody and realism become one. **"The Blue Hotel"** represents powerfully by the logic of the story's own action the typical development of Stephen Crane's imagination throughout his fiction. In the story he moves from an idea of stereotyped Western myth, to parody, to reality—the movement the Swede literally makes from his arrival with his head filled by mythic fears, to the absurd hotel, to the real saloon. So Crane generally views the traditional abstraction, cuts it to pieces through parody, then puts it together his way, redefining the actuality behind the abstraction. **"The Blue Hotel"** actually brings the parodic approach to its logical culmination, for the Swede is a living parody, a badly scared Don Quixote nurtured on dime-novel fiction, whose death, in the finest irony of all, is both a parody of art and the sole reality of his life. (pp. 281-82)

> *Eric Solomon, in his* Stephen Crane: From Parody to Realism, *Cambridge, Mass.: Harvard University Press, 1966, 301 p.*

Robert Narveson (essay date 1969)

[*In the following essay, Narveson suggests that the character of the Easterner in "The Blue Hotel" is, like the other characters in the story, a fool whose final words constitute a moral that is "a part of the story but not the moral of the story."*]

"The Blue Hotel" is a favorite with both professional critics and common readers; I suspect it would be generally accepted as Stephen Crane's best story if it were not for the puzzling ending, in which the Easterner offers a "moral" that baffles not only the poor cowboy to whom he states it, but also the reader. The problem is this: If the "Swede" brought his fate upon himself, as the whole story makes us believe, the Easterner is wrong when he claims that "five of us have collaborated in the murder of this Swede," or at the very least his count should include a sixth, the Swede himself. Even so amended, the Easterner's statement would strike most readers as an outrageous distortion of the depicted events. And as if this were not hard enough to take, the Easterner then goes on to make the silly pronouncement that "usually there are from a dozen to forty women really involved in every murder." All in all, it seems best to take seriously Crane's own protest that his stories "have no moral in tow," and to look for a view that makes the Easterner's moral a *part* of the story but not the *moral* of the story.

Readers of **"The Blue Hotel"** will recall how a terrified Swede from the East manages to irritate everyone in the hotel of a Nebraska town and then get himself into a fight with Johnny, the hotel-keeper's son; how he wins the fight and swaggers off through a snowstorm to a saloon, there to offend the town's professional gambler and be killed by him. The dead Swede, we remember, lies with his eyes fixed on the legend above the cash-machine: "This registers the amount of your purchase." The full horror we feel at this ironically appropriate legend may be stated roughly like this: "Granted, the Swede was *asking* for trouble and *deserved* trouble, but this is rather too much!" Nor do we doubt that such a reaction is what Crane intends; and therefore, since some sort of rejoinder to that grim cash-machine is surely in order, the story may appropriately go on for a page or two after this sudden denouement.

In the controversial final pages, the anticipated rejoinder does indeed appear. "Months later," the Easterner and a cowboy who was also present at the hotel are discussing the incident and its aftermath. When the cowboy takes up, in effect, the view of the cash-machine that the Swede brought his death upon himself, the Easterner counters with his totally different explanation. All the men connected with the incident, according to him, were guilty of complicity in the Swede's murder, Johnny by cheating at cards just as the Swede had charged, the three witnesses by not standing up for the Swede when he was in the right, and the gambler by reacting to provocation.

Unfortunately, if this is meant as a convincing corrective to the crude notion of poetic justice stated by the cash-machine, Crane has blundered the job, just as some critics charge. We readers, like the cowboy, feel injured and rebellious; unlike him, however, we need not cry out "blindly" against this "fog of mysterious theory." We have the advantage of guidance from the narrator, who supplies us with perspectives on the events not available to the simple cowboy or the subtle Easterner, or to anyone else within the story. One paragraph in particular stands out from the surrounding narrative as an uncharacteristic bit of explicit commentary. It occurs as the Swede makes his way through the blizzard from hotel to saloon:

> He might have been in a deserted village. We picture the world as thick with conquering and elate humanity, but *here*, with the bugles of the tempest pealing, it was hard to imagine a peopled earth. One viewed the existence of man *then* as a marvel, and conceded a glamor of wonder to these lice which were caused to cling to a whirling, fire-smitten, ice-locked, disease-stricken, space-lost bulb. The conceit of man was explained by this storm to be the very engine of life. One was a coxcomb not to die in it. However, the Swede found a saloon. [Italics added.]

The stark nihilism implied—perhaps—by this passage has often been noted. My italics call attention, however, to the words *here* and *then*, which strongly indicate an *ad hoc* intent. Man and nature may be viewed from this perspective while it is storming, but of course it is not always storming. Though it is our privilege to apply this storm-evoked view of things beyond the story if we please, Crane is not lending his authority to the attempt. By the same token, I should think, he is inviting us—without insisting—to apply this view to the story in which it occurs. Critics who have tried to do so have generally decided it cannot be done satisfactorily and have therefore concluded that the passage is an obtrusion on the story, and a flaw. I want to suggest a reading that reverses that judgment.

It is usually assumed that the "conceit" that is "the very engine of life" is a general notion held by people that their existence somehow matters in the scheme of things. I think this is true. But the people in the story act in a fashion that suggests an additional, more qualified, meaning of "conceit." The story is full of extravagant behavior. People do things from sensible or at least understandable motives, but go beyond the bounds suggested by taste, or decorum, or common sense, or whatever it is that provides a balance wheel to human behavior in any particular instance. The first example of this is Scully's choice of a paint color that makes his hotel "scream and howl" even against the dazzling winter landscape. But nearly every thing and every action in the story is similarly excessive in some way—"profligate," to use one of Crane's own terms: Scully's hospitality, the wind's violence, the stove's humming, Johnny's cardsharping, the cowboy's board-whacking, the guests' washing and drying, the gambler's respectability, the townsmen's acceptance of him—all this and much else besides. It is as if men have taken a cue from the extremes of climate and developed extreme notions of the behavior appropriate to their circumstances. That these notions arise from a peculiar form of "conceit" is suggested by Crane's use of the word "coxcomb" immediately afterward in the same passage. Most critics have read this word as meaning simply a fool, but a coxcomb is a special sort of foolish fellow, whose foolishness consists of a kind of vanity, a mistaken notion about the behavior appropriate to his sort of person. The manners of a coxcomb are caricatures of what is proper for the person he conceives himself to be. And so it is with the people in this story—with one apparent exception. Until the final scene, the quiet, rational Easterner has been a model of decorum, with only a lapse or two during the fight.

In that final scene, the Easterner, too, is shown to be one of those for whom "conceit" is the "very engine of life." *His* foolish vanity is pride in his superior awareness and understanding. When he finds the cowboy disagreeing with him about the Swede, he flies into a rage and attacks the cowboy "violently," calling him a fool and bewildering him with arguments for group complicity. Are we supposed to be convinced by the Easterner's line of reasoning? Throughout the story one thing causes another in believable fashion right through to the fatal stabbing, and we are thus ready to agree that if things had been different "the Swede might not have been killed." But that is a pretty flimsy ground upon which to build a case for moral responsibility. It is rational and commendable for the Easterner to feel guilt for refusing to "stand up and be a man" when he knew the Swede was right about Johnny. It is irrational and foolish for him to blame himself for the Swede's death, when he could not have known at the time and still cannot know whether acting differently would have changed the outcome. Just as with the verdict rendered by the cash-machine and echoed by the cowboy, we react to the argument of the Easterner by thinking, "There is something in what you say, but you go too far."

Earlier in the story the Easterner had been sensitive, controlled, and shrewd; now, however, we are forced to revise our estimate of him. His rage, his rhetoric, his sense of guilt—all are excessive. To wallow in the costfree luxury of collective guilt is both emotionally cheap and intellectually sloppy. The absurd business about the "dozen to forty women" is the final tip-off that Crane's mocking irony is again at work. We conclude from the Easterner's pronouncements not that he has discerned the "moral" of the whole affair but that his actions here are of a piece with so many others throughout the story.

"The conceit of man was explained by this storm to be the very engine of life." There is no more necessity to believe that this storm has offered the final and conclusive statement about life than there is to believe that the sunshine at the end of *The Red Badge of Courage* is nature's approval of Henry Fleming's rosy hopes. Like so many other statements in the story this one is to some degree undercut by its own excess. It does, however, apply to the events of this particular story well enough for us to be intrigued by it. It suggests why we should not take the Easterner any more seriously than the cash-machine. And finally, it explains why the title of the story, **"The Blue Hotel,"** is so totally apt. The color of the hotel stands as the first and most striking expression of a form of "conceit" characteristic of actions in the story from beginning to end. (pp. 187-91)

> Robert Narveson, "Notes on 'The Blue Hotel'," in Prairie Schooner, *Vol. XLIII, No. 2, Summer, 1969, pp. 187-91.*

James Nagel (essay date 1973)

[*In the following essay, Nagel examines structure and theme in Crane's story "An Experiment in Misery," revealing five thematically and imagistically independent sections that contribute to the tale's overall literary scheme.*]

Perhaps the most significant artistic achievement among all of Stephen Crane's fiction of the Bowery is **"An Experiment in Misery,"** a story originally published in the New York *Press* in 1894. It is not a long story, but it is carefully structured, breaking into five mutually contributory units (each with its own theme and imagery) which culminate in a powerful final paragraph the point of which is lost if the preceding sections have not been read closely. The story begins with an impressionistic passage typical of Crane's openings: "It was late at night, and a fine rain was swirling softly down, causing the pavements to glisten with hue of steel and blue and yellow in the rays of the innumerable lights." Into this setting comes the protagonist, a young man another character once calls "Willie," who is "going forth to eat as the wanderer may eat, and sleep as the homeless sleep." The *as* and *may* indicate that he is in reality neither a wanderer nor homeless, but engaged in some kind of experiment, some kind of scientific, detached investigation of a social condition. It is this detachment which erupts in guilt at the end, linking conclusion and introduction, and resolving the undefined emotion of the beginning.

In response to the insults of young boys, who mistake him for a hobo in his tattered clothes, he becomes dejected and searches for an "outcast of highest degree that they two might share miseries. . . ." He moves through City Hall Park to Chatham Square, where he finally finds the people he has been searching for, beaten men who stand like "chickens"—a dehumanizing image which recurs again in the conclusion. With these men he aligns himself and spends the evening watching an indifferent city: cable cars

of "formidable power" which give out a "loud fierce cry of the gong"; people leave "scar-like" tracks in the mud; and an elevated station which looms over all like a "crab." Thus part one ends; the youth has entered a world of depravity, identified with its inhabitants, and has felt the oppressive power around him which threatens him in his new and assumed impotence.

Part two takes place in a saloon described with particularly communicative imagery: "The swing doors, snapping to and fro like ravenous lips, made gratified smacks as the saloon gorged itself with plump men, eating with astounding and endless appetite, smiling in some indescribable manner as the men came from all directions like sacrifices to a heathenish superstition." The obvious imagistic implication is that the environment kills and devours human beings (a suggestion which explains the death-images in the flop-house in part three). The youth "allowed himself to be swallowed," indicating a volitional control on his part that most of the customers undoubtedly lack. After beer and soup, he sees a "man with oily but imposing whiskers, who was presiding like a priest behind an altar," an ironic simile given the man and the condition.

The most important event in part two is the introduction of a "reeling man" who, after his initial appearance, is continually known as the "assassin." "His head was a fuddle of bushy hair and whiskers, from which his eyes peered with a guilty slant. In a close scrutiny it was possible to distinguish the cruel lines of a mouth which looked as if its lips had just closed with satisfaction over some tender and piteous morsel. He appeared like an assassin steeped in crimes performed awkwardly." The function of the assassin is to act as a guide for Willie, as a physical guide to the flop-house and as a moral guide to an understanding of the degradation and pathos of the lives of the poor. Once that is realized, it can be seen that the guilt and cruelty and crimes in the assassin's face are reflections of the world around him and not of his inner character. His capacity for appreciation and joy is expressed when the youth offers to give him three cents to add to his money for a bed for the night: "The assassin's countenance became instantly radiant with joy. His whiskers quivered with the wealth of his alleged emotions. He seized the young man's hand in a transport of delight and friendliness." The youth draws back "coldly," indicating a restraint of emotion and suggesting again his scientific detachment. Thus the second section introduces the remaining major character and implies through its imagery something of the destructive and hostile force of environment.

Section three is the most important in the story and its full significance is accessible only through its imagery. The assassin leads Willie to a nearby flophouse and his first real look at the poor. As soon as he enters "from the dark and secret places of the building there suddenly came to his nostrils strange and unspeakable odours, that assailed him like malignant diseases with wings. They seemed to be from human bodies closely packed in dens; the exhalations from a hundred pairs of reeking lips; the fumes from a thousand bygone debauches; the expression of a thousand present miseries." The imagery of the odors as "malignant diseases" suggest a sociological pathology which will soon express itself in pervasive images of death; the reference to "dens" underscores the animalistic quality of life in the Bowery. The imagery throughout the section, expressed as Willie's view of his new environment, suggests that living under these conditions is in itself a kind of death: Willie's locker is like a "tombstone," and on the cots next to his he sees "the forms of men sprawled out, lying in death-like silence, or heaving and snoring with tremendous effort, like stabbed fish," an image which fuses animal and death references. The youth's bed feels like a "slab" and the man next to him sleeps "corpse-like": "The man did not move once through the night, but lay in this stillness as of death like a body stretched out expectant of the surgeon's knife." The man's rôle is thus passive and receptive to the destructive will of external forces the results of which can be seen in the figures of the rest of the men. "For the most part they were statuesque, carven, dead. With the curious lockers standing all about like tombstones, there was a strange effect of a graveyard where bodies were merely flung." The implication that such life is really living death is made inescapable through repetition. The remainder of the section concerns responses to the unavoidable inferences: the first response is expressed symbolically in the wail of a sleeping man; the second, Willie's, is reserved for the conclusion of the story.

A man, dreaming on a cot in the corner, unconsciously uttered "long wails that went almost like yells from a hound, echoing wailfully and weird through this chill place of tombstones where men lay like the dead." The animal image again reinforces the suggestion of dehumanization, and the cry itself becomes a symbolic protest of grief and despair, almost exactly like that of the girl in **"An Eloquence of Grief "** and of the dog in **"A Dark Brown Dog."** All of these cries transcend immediate depravity to become emblems of universal anguish. But the sound in itself is not as important to the story as the effect it has on Willie, to whom

> these were not merely the shrieks of a vision-pierced man: they were an utterance of the meaning of the room and its occupants. It was to him the protests of the wretch who feels the touch of the imperturbable granite wheels, and who then cries with an impersonal eloquence, with a strength not from him, giving voice to the wail of a whole section, a class, a people. This, weaving into the young man's brain, and mingling with his views of the vast and sombre shadows that, like mighty black fingers, curled around the naked bodies, made the young man so that he did not sleep, but lay carving the biographies for these men from his meagre experience.

The passage is the most important in the story, and, perhaps in all of the Bowery tales. It is, first of all, an overt expression of the social protest dimension of the story, expressed in a memorable and symbolic cry. And, second, it deals directly with the other major theme, that of Willie's psychological growth toward compassion and a mature grasp of the condition of life for these men. The boy's insomnia indicates a rapidly developing sensitivity and a strong emotional and intellectual shock.

The activity of the morning, as the men scratch their fleas and rustle about getting dressed, suggests something of the responsibility for such conditions. There seems to be nothing inherently depraved about the men themselves but simply about their place in an artificial social configuration: "A few were parading in unconcerned nakedness. Here and there were men of brawn, whose skins shone clear and ruddy. They took splendid poses, standing massively like chiefs. When they had dressed in their ungainly garments there was an extraordinary change. They then showed bumps and deficiencies of all kinds." This passage indicates the dichotomy between man as he is "naturally" and man as he is seen in the given social context. The depravity is clearly in the society and not in the individuals.

With the end of section three, Crane has made the major points of the story and the action moves swiftly to a conclusion. The major function of part four is to extend the implications of the flophouse in both temporal and spatial dimensions. Willie and the assassin go to a restaurant the following day and drink coffee out of bowls. "The bowls were webbed with brown seams, and the tin spoons wore an air of having emerged from the first pyramid. Upon them were black moss-like encrustations of age, and they were bent and scarred from the attacks of long-forgotten teeth." The passage is not only functional for description and mood, but also extends the thematic implications of the poverty back into time. Degradation is not a modern phenomenon: it goes back through the history of the users of these bowls and, metaphorically, to the ancient Egyptians. The spatial extension of theme comes from the previous reference to "pyramids" and from a long rambling speech from the assassin on the subject that things are tough all over. He reiterates his economic failures in New York, in the South, in Toledo, and in northern New York State; nowhere was he able to keep a job and attain social respectability. The section ends with grim irony and pathos, with the assassin commenting to Willie that they have been living like "Kings" and the boy's caution that another day and another struggle await them. "But the assassin refused to turn his gaze toward the future. He went with a limping step, into which he injected a suggestion of lamb-like gambols. His mouth was wreathed in a red grin."

Section five completes the cyclical structure of the physical action of the story by returning Willie to City Hall Park. His psychological aspect has changed in several ways, however. He now fits easily into the timeless tedium of the pattern of life of the decadent. His perspective has changed, and he now sees the good clothes of people on the street as emblems of the unattainable: "They expressed to the young man his infinite distance from all that he valued. Social position, comfort, the pleasures of living were unconquerable kingdoms. He felt a sudden awe." The gigantic buildings around him become expressions of a nation that cares only for the successful, and the sounds around him voice the hopelessness of the condition of the poor.

These realizations lead to a suggestive concluding paragraph: "He confessed himself an outcast, and his eyes from under the lowered rim of his hat began to glance guiltily, wearing the criminal expression that comes with certain convictions." There is ambivalence in his feelings: guilt for being at first an objective "experimenter" amid social conditions that demand the utmost compassion, and guilt by association with a class looked down upon with suspicion by the social norm. Thus, while the spatial movement is cyclical, the psychological action of the story moves from the boy's curiosity to despondency and finally to guilt. The effect, given the compassion of the reader, is to show Willie's psychological development and to "commit the reader himself to an act of identification and sympathy" [Maurice Bassan, "The Design of Stephen Crane's Bowery 'Experiment,' " *Stephen Crane: A Collection of Critical Essays,* edited by Maurice Bassan (1967); see Further Reading list].

Thus Crane has organized his fictive material to support the theme of social protest which is artistically expressed in images of pathology, depravity, and death, and brought dramatically to a conclusion through cyclical structure (suggestive of the continuity of poverty) and linear psychological development of the protagonist (showing his fully realized compassion and commensurate guilt). (pp. 169-74)

James Nagel, "Structure and Theme in Crane's 'An Experiment in Misery'," in Studies in Short Fiction, *Vol. X, No. 2, Spring, 1973, pp. 169-74.*

Charles E. Modlin and John R. Byers, Jr. (essay date 1973)

[*In the following excerpt, Modlin and Byers suggest that "The Monster" is a unified and sustained religious allegory that moves, "as in the gospel according to St. John, from the state of man's condition under Old Testament Law to the state of his condition under New Testament Grace," becoming "not only Crane's commentary on the state of Christendom but also his assessment of the lost condition of man."*]

"The Monster," one of Stephen Crane's most neglected major stories, has been troublesome to critics with its seemingly unsatisfactory plot development and its generally puzzling theme. Because, like many of Crane's works, "The Monster" contains an abundance of religious images and overtones, a few critics have attempted to attach an allegorical significance to the story. . . . A close textual examination of "The Monster" shows that Crane used a definite and complete religious pattern as the shaping principle of his art. The twenty-four sections of "The Monster" move, as in the Gospel according to St. John, from the state of man's condition under Old Testament Law to the state of his condition under New Testament Grace, but an impossible Grace in a totally naturalistic environment.

Section I sets the scene for Crane's religious statement. An idyllic frame of the father mowing his lawn with his small son playing at trains in the flower garden, the scene becomes extremely important in a religious context. Jimmie, in allowing his engine Number 36 to destroy a peony, has committed a sin in the garden. In confessing his sin to his father, Dr. Trescott, and in being told that he cannot play in the garden for the rest of the day, Jimmie stands as a representative of the pre- and post-Edenic Adam living under the Old Covenant of Law and cast out of his earthly bliss by a loving but legalistic God. Dr. Trescott, like God who "in the cool of the day" becomes aware of the sin of Adam and Eve, learns from his son of the broken flower while he tends his grass "in the coolness and peace of the evenings after supper." During the "judgment" of the doctor, Jimmie, like Adam and Eve, who hide themselves from God when he confronts them, does not look at his

father; and, then, like the primordial parents, he goes away, out of the garden.

In Section II, Jimmie, heavy with his burden of guilt ("he felt some kind of desire to efface himself"), leaps from the world of the Old Covenant to the world of the New Covenant in his short walk to the symbolic stable, where he finds Henry Johnson cleansing the doctor's buggy. Grinning "fraternally" at his small friend, Henry accepts him and provides "solace" by declaring himself a brother in sin. But Henry is "a light," and "eminence," and his "glory" is beyond Jimmie's understanding. On one point, however, the two are in agreement; they both see the doctor as nothing less than the moon, and to be in an "eclipse" is to be "disgraced." Further, whenever "Jimmie appeared in his shame [Henry] would bully him most virtuously, preaching with assurance the precepts of the doctor's creed, and pointing out to Jimmie all his abominations." Moreover, "the saintly Henry" sometimes allows Jimmie a part in the ritualistic cleansing of the buggy-wheel while he is "still gory from unspeakable deeds." Jimmie is aware of the "sublimity" of Henry as he drives Dr. Trescott about the country. And it is the "ceremony" of the washing of the wagon wheel and the sprinkling water that for Jimmie "slowly consumed the remembrance of a late disgrace." Henry delights in the "reverence" and "admiration" that the child has for him.

Section III focuses on the stable hand Henry Johnson, who begins to assume the full role of Christ in his last days. As the section opens, Henry has just eaten his supper, as a matter of fact his last supper before the fire which destroys not only his face but his mind. In preparation for his entrance into the city and thence to the courtship of Miss Bella Farragut, Henry is "like a priest arraying himself for some parade of the church." Only two items of his apparel are mentioned—his lavender trousers and his "straw hat with its bright silk band." Likewise, only two items are mentioned with which Christ is led to the cross—the purple robe and the platted crown of thorns. As Henry passes by Reifsnyder's barber shop, the lawyer Griscom's "you ought to see the coon that's coming" is reminiscent of Pilate's "Behold the man." Reifsnyder rushes to the window "marvelling" and utters the shortened epithet for Jesus, "Chee!"

The brief scene at the home of the Farraguts in Watermelon Alley furthers the plot with the "saffron" Miss Farragut suggestive of Judas Iscariot, the son of Simon (Bella's younger brother is named Sim), in that she, like Judas, is a study in appearance rather than reality. When Bella first sees Henry at a distance, she is in a plain dress, which she hastens to remove for a more elegant gown. Although "Henry saw it all," saw the whole pretense, in the awkwardness "he was simply perfect." Bella exclaims to her mother at the end of the evening, "Oh, ma, isn't he divine?"

Sections IV and V serve to bring the whole town of Whilomville together to witness the fire which causes Henry Johnson's act of sacrifice. Into the anticipatory crowd at the band concert there suddenly comes the sound of the fire whistle whose "giant voice from the night" stirs even the "cynical young men" into action. From the Methodist church comes an additional sound in the night—a "solemn and terrible voice, speaking from the clouds," like the "voice from heaven" of the Almighty in John 12:28, who proclaims the glorification of His name at the approaching death of Christ.

In Section VI the burning home of Dr. Trescott becomes the hell from which Jimmie must be saved. As the fire begins to creep from room to room the windows of the house appear to be stained with blood, and "fireimps" seem to be inside fathering all the colors of the fire. The flames become "bloody spectres at the apertures of a haunted house." To this inferno, then, comes the crowd, from which one man stands out in particular. He runs with an "almost fabulous speed" and wears lavender trousers and crumples a straw hat with a bright silk band in his hand. As Henry rushes into the house, flames have just burned a cord supporting the "Signing the Declaration." On an allegorical level the falling engraving may be equated with the Old Covenant, and it is Henry who is about to declare, through his sacrifice, the New Covenant.

In Section VII, Henry, on the upper level of the burning house, makes his way toward Jimmie's room to act out the role of saviour. Scooping up the child, here suggestive of mankind long since cast out of the garden of innocence, Henry tries to save Jimmie by the same path that he had come into the house—the front door. He sees, however, that the former way, i.e., life, is blocked. Through life he cannot save Jimmie. Thus, "He was submitting, submitting because of his fathers, bending his mind in a most perfect slavery to this conflagration." His yielding to this "perfect slavery" marks the end of Henry Johnson's earthly life; he must find a way other than through life to save the representative Jimmie.

It is then that Henry remembers the staircase to the laboratory, a descent which carries him and his burden into the symbolic hell of the doctor's experimental room. "All manner of odors assailed him during this flight. They seemed to be alive with envy, hatred, and malice," clearly reflective of the seven deadly sins in hell. Further, "The room was like a garden in the region where might be burning flowers," a satanic garden of evil. Amid the "deadly" smoke and the multicolored flames, Henry encounters a "delicate, trembling sapphire shape like a fairy lady," a sort of queen of hell. Henry shrieks and ducks out of her way but is unable to avoid her and his head bows "as if his neck had been struck." In falling on his back Henry allows Jimmie to roll away across the floor to safety. As Henry lies helpless at the base of a desk, a "ruby-red snakelike thing" from a splintered vial above him drops "with mystic impulse" upon his face. Thus, Henry Johnson, one-time stable hand, is no longer recognizable as a human being.

Dr. Trescott arrives home in Section VIII. Breaking down the door to the smoke-filled laboratory, he finds his son wrapped in a blanket and carries him to the safety of the lawn. Then in the terror of the moment, he becomes aware that Henry Johnson is still inside. He dashes toward the burning house again, only to realize that he is unable to rescue the sacrificed Henry.

Section IX opens with the thrill of the fire at its peak. Joining the other fire wagons is now significantly the Never-Die Company Number Three, like "a chariot dragged by a band of gods." Among all of the fire companies there is a good natured competition. Even the people of the crowd choose sides and declare which company is better, and

they "supported their creeds with no small violence," a suggestion of church rivalry. From the scene of the fire three cots are borne away by twelve firemen. In this "solemn parade" each man in the stretcher party "gained a reflected majesty." These twelve are clearly suggestive of the twelve disciples, and the crowd recognizes their importance, for, it "made subtle obeisance to this august dignity derived from three prospective graves."

In Section X Henry is presumed dead and thus fulfills the terms of the Christian allegory in perishing in his role as Jimmie's saviour. The town, glad to think well of him in death, "turned a reverent attention to the memory of this hostler." Bella Farragut establishes her own personal claim to Henry, announcing that they had been engaged. To the boys of the town Henry's name becomes "the title of a saint." Forgotten is the taunt with which they had formerly followed Henry:

> Nigger, nigger, never die,
> Black face and shiny eye.

The couplet takes on ironic meaning in Section XI, however, as Henry does gain an immortality of sorts. His face is burnt away and his entire body is enveloped mummy-like in bandages, save for an "unwinking eye." Its "scrutiny" and "magic" are a haunting reminder to Dr. Trescott of the moral dilemma posed by Henry's survival. The doctor's constant attendance upon Henry derives from a sense of obligation to him for his sacrifice: "He gave himself for—for Jimmie. What am I to do for him?" It is at this point that the earlier references to Trescott as a God-figure take on significance, for he in effect holds the power of resurrection. When he chooses to restore Henry to a spectral life, however, he bestows a dubious blessing, as Judge Hagenthorpe points out: "He is purely your creation. Nature has very evidently given him up. He is dead. You are restoring him to life. You are making him, and he will be a monster, and with no mind."

Section XII describes the conditions of Henry's dormancy prior to his re-entry into the world of the living. Shrouded again like a corpse, "wrapped to the heels in an old-fashioned ulster," he walks beside Dr. Trescott "slowly and carefully, as if he were learning," to the horse and buggy. He is now a "dark figure," a "dim form in the gloom," taken on a twilight journey to a destination "on a great black hill-side." The home of Alek Williams, Henry's caretaker, is, like the classical hell, guarded by fierce dogs and surrounded by a "dark sea of grass," which the carriage must negotiate to reach a sulfurous "beach of yellow light." Trescott leads the "silent shape" to the light and gives over his charge to Alek with the instructions to "put him to bed." In the "revelation of the light" Alek for the first time realizes the full extent of Henry's wounds and, giving "the yell of a man stabbed in the heart," addresses the grievously fallen Henry: "Ma Lode amassy! Who'd ever think? Ma Lode amassy!" He is "aghast" as he repeats the epithet "Ma Lode!" As the three "shadows" enter the "golden doorway," they are met by Alek's wife. She shrieks when she sees Henry, and her six children, like hellish imps, seek refuge in "a wailing heap" behind the stove, their proper symbolic element.

Henry's stay at the hellish abode of the Williamses, like Christ's harrowing of hell, turns out to be a vexing experience for his keeper. Ironically, however, it is Alek who, in finagling a raise from the judge, refers to Henry seven times in Section XIII as a devil. Section XV retains this distortion, as Alek sees himself, in achieving an extra dollar's pay, as a worldly hero, "the unconquerable Alexander Williams." Despite this lofty self-image, it is apparent that in the public eye he, as a keeper of the dead, has become a devil. On the way home he passes a fellow church deacon, Zeke Paterson, and in his high spirits fails to note that "Paterson had definitely shied into the dry ditch as they came to the point of ordinary contact." Nearing home, Alek, as the harrowed prince of hell, is reminded of his usurped kingdom and approaches "as if it were the fortress of an enemy." He is challenged by his own hounds of hell, who "discovering their lord, slunk away embarrassed," Alek's wife reacts to his arrival "as if he were a spectre." The attention shifts, however, to their charge within "the dreaded inner door," where they pay "the homage due to a corpse or a phantom." In the "intensely black and solemn night," Mary "adopted the attitude used always in church at funerals. At times she seemed to be upon the point of breaking out in prayer." As she stares "aghast," Alek opens the door to Henry's tomb-like room—"six feet one way and six feet the other way." Finding it like the tomb of Christ, empty except for a radiance of light, Alek howls three times, "He's gone!" and runs out into the night calling to a God-like Dr. Trescott: "It was as if Trescott was poised in the contemplative sky over the running negro, and could heed this reaching voice—'Docteh Trescott!'"

The barber shop patrons in Section XIV are a world apart from Henry Johnson, whom one man calls "the most terrible thing in the world." When Reifsnyder the barber tries to show some compassion for Henry, a customer facetiously responds: "You're kicking because if losing faces became popular, you'd have to go out of business." This "flint hearted" attitude foreshadows the reaction of the town to the escaped Henry.

In Sections XVI-XVIII Henry returns to town and, as in the accounts of Christ's resurrection, makes several dramatic appearances in the world of the living, all of which result only in rejection. The first takes place at a children's party where Sadie Winters sees him "looming spectrally" at the window. She later describes the creature she has seen as "simply a thing, a dreadful thing."

Henry's second visitation is to Watermelon Alley, where he re-creates his former romantic role with Bella Farragut. While Henry's demeanor is that of a perfect gentleman, each of the Farraguts rejects him: Sim falls off the porch railing when Henry arrives; Bella crawls away from him; Mrs. Farragut, presumably an invalid, runs off frantically and jumps over a high fence.

The third appearance occurs on the main street and results in his rejection by the town at large. He causes a riot and is pursued by a rock-throwing mob. To Trescott's concern over Henry's welfare the chief of police responds that "there isn't much of him to hurt any more, is there? Guess he's been hurt up the limit."

Section XIX introduces Martha Goodwin, who, as her last name ("Good-one") suggests, stands alone in her courage and belief. Like the biblical Martha, who reprimanded Christ himself for allowing Mary to sit at his feet while she (Martha) did the housework, Crane's Martha has such strong convictions that she "alone would defy the universe if she thought the universe merited this proceeding." When the town gossip, appropriately named Carrie Dungen, announces that Henry Johnson has escaped, Martha with her clear biblical connotations replies, "This, my prophecy, has come to pass." The "prophecy" is not explained or illuminated. The only explanation is that Martha in her own mind had already determined her belief that Henry would not die. Here, on an allegorical level, it is as if Martha Goodwin has accepted and proclaimed the fact of Henry Johnson's resurrection from the dead.

Henry's final indignity occurs in Section XX when even Jimmie, posing to his friends as "the owner and exhibitor of one of the world's marvels," betrays him. Jimmie becomes a hero in the eyes of the boys by daring to approach and touch the veiled monster. With this touch, he, like Doubting Thomas, demonstrates his failure to keep faith with his saviour. Supporting the betrayal theme of the section are the crowing sounds of the boys, suggestive of Peter's betrayal of Christ.

Henry's only response to his treatment—the last view of him in the story—is described in a passage which would seem to represent his Christ-like ascension to a completely spiritual plane, a symbolic renunciation of all human identity: "The monster on the box had turned its black crêpe countenance toward the sky, and was waving its arms in time to a religous chant: 'Look at him now,' cried a little boy. They turned, and were transfixed by the solemnity and mystery of the indefinable gestures. The wail of the melody was mournful and slow. They drew back. It seemed to spell-bind them with the power of a funeral." The mockery of Henry is ended with the arrival of Dr. Trescott. The boys, who are "used to being sent out of all manner of gardens upon the sudden appearance of a father or a mother," leave "much in the manner of frustrated and revealed assassins." The incident amounts to a second infraction of garden rules—occurring this time in the back garden behind the stable and involving a man instead of a peony—and new disgrace for Jimmie, who suffers "the loss of his position as a lad who controlled the privileges of his father's grounds. . . ."

Section XXI consists of a pair of reprimands. In the first, Dr. Trescott, the God figure, reprimands Jimmie, the representative of mankind, for having abused Henry Johnson, the Christ figure. In the second, however, it is Trescott who is reprimanded by Jake Winter for, in effect, having created the abomination which has terrified his daughter Sadie. In denying Trescott the opportunity of treating Sadie in her apparent affliction, Winter repudiates Trescott's divine faculties, the same medical skills that have resurrected Henry.

In Section XXII, Carrie Dungen again dashes in to announce to Martha and Kate the quarrel of Jake Winter and Dr. Trescott. While Kate and Carrie are clearly on the side of Jake Winter, Martha rises to her full stature and announces that she would not be terrified of Henry Johnson no matter what the town thinks. Carrie and Kate are willing to accept whatever the town says, but Martha flies in the face of the town and accepts only those things which her own mind tells her are so.

Four prominent citizens, including Judge Hagenthorpe and John Twelve, pay a visit to Dr. Trescott in Section

XXIII to argue against his ruin and for the disposal of Henry Johnson in some genteel way. The visitors understand or at least pretend that they understand Trescott's duty toward Henry, but they cannot forgive the doctor for destroying his own position. They, like the chief priests in John 12:10, who "consulted that they might put Lazarus also to death," as well as those who condemn Christ in John 19:7 ("We have a law, and by our law he ought to die, because he made himself the Son of God"), want the return of the old way rather than this new horror. But Dr. Trescott is adamant, Not even a public institution will do in this case. Henry Johnson has saved the representative Jimmie, and hence Dr. Trescott alone can be responsible for the now disfigured stable hand.

In the concluding Section XXIV, when Dr. Trescott comes home from his work on the day when his wife Grace receives callers, he finds her alone and troubled. Although she has set out fifteen cups and plates of teacakes, only one person has called, Mrs. John Twelve. The twelve here seem to represent the original disciples, and Crane would appear to be saying that not only the small town of Whilomville but also the world has rejected Grace, not Grace Trescott alone but the Grace of the New Covenant. Man is incapable of understanding or accepting a truly spiritual idea.

"The Monster," unified and consistent religious allegory, reflects Crane's view that man lives in a naturalistic world which has dispelled the myths of Old Testament Law and New Testament Grace. Man's life, Crane says, is grounded in the hard reality of materialism and certainly not in something as unreal or spiritual as the spectral Henry Johnson or Christ. Thus, **"The Monster"** becomes not only Crane's commentary on the state of Christendom but also his assessment of the lost condition of man. (pp. 110-13)

> *Charles E. Modlin and John R. Byers, Jr., "Stephen Crane's 'The Monster' as Christian Allegory," in* The Markham Review, *Vol. 3, No. 6, May, 1973, pp. 110-13.*

Alan Trachtenberg (essay date 1974)

[*In the following excerpt, Trachtenberg examines Crane's sketches of urban life at the turn of the twentieth century, focusing on the companion pieces "Experiment in Misery" and "Experiment in Luxury." Trachtenberg interprets a multi-fold experimentality in these works, stemming from Crane's use of point of view, literary techniques, and his adaptation and extension of journalistic traditions and style.*]

In the nineteenth century the big city appeared often in the guise of mystery. To be sure cities always have baffled the stranger with their labyrinths of streets and lanes, moving crowds, noisy markets, obscure carvings on gates: each a unique entity of family and clan and inner places closed to the outsider. Concealment in some measure is inherent in cities. But with new developments in the nineteenth century, particularly in large centers like Paris, London, and New York, mystery deepened beyond initial appearances and developed into a pervasive response. It was deeper too than the middle-class curiosity about the demimonde to which Eugene Sue catered, although the veiled

---

Crane on His Development As a Writer

As far as myself and my own meagre success are concerned, I began the battle of life with no talent, no equipment, but with an ardent admiration and desire. I did little work at school, but confined my abilities, such as they were, to the diamond. Not that I disliked books, but the cut-and-dried curriculum of the college did not appeal to me. Humanity was a much more interesting study. When I ought to have been at recitations I was studying faces on the streets, and when I ought to have been studying my next day's lessons I was watching the trains roll in and out of the Central Station. So, you see, I had, first of all, to recover from college. I had to build up, so to speak. And my chiefest desire was to write plainly and unmistakably, so that all men (and some women) might read and understand. That to my mind is good writing. There is a great deal of labor connected with literature. I think that is the hardest thing about it. There is nothing to respect in art save one's own opinion of it. . . .

Personally I am aware that my work does not amount to a string of dried beans—I always calmly admit it. But I also know that I do the best that is in me, without regard to cheers or damnation. When I was the mark for every humorist in the country I went ahead, and now, when I am the mark for only 50 per cent of the humorists of the country, I go ahead, for I understand that a man is born into the world with his own pair of eyes, and he is not at all responsible for his vision—he is merely responsible for his quality of personal honesty. To keep close to this personal honesty is my supreme ambition. There is a sublime egotism in talking of honesty. I, however, do not say that I am honest. I merely say that I am as nearly honest as a weak mental machinery will allow. This aim in life struck me as being the only thing worth while. A man is sure to fail at it, but there is something in the failure.

> *In a letter to John Northern Hilliard in January, 1896(?),* Stephen Crane: Letters *(1960).*

---

lives of outcasts and criminals contributed a large share to the sense of urban mystery. The pervasive image now shows the city as a perilous and problematic experience for its own citizens as well as strangers, its whole reality hidden within denser crowds, closed off much the way older vistas are now blocked by taller, inexplicable buildings. We find the image on all levels—in guide books and newspapers, in popular Gothicized "mysteries," in serious poetry and fiction: the city as a swarming mass of signals, dense, obscure, undecipherable. (p. 265)

The street in particular appeared as the locus of curtained, displaced experience. The idea of mystery came to be particularized as the notion of space fragmented, regularized, specialized. The consciousness of differentiated space use can be traced in guide books for "strangers" and street directories, themselves perfect expressions of the radical incompleteness of any street experience. Often dressed with literary devices and Gothic coloration drawn from the *mysteries,* these verbal maps convey the city as interlocking spaces occupied by functions increasingly unintelligible to each other, in short, as space mystified. (p. 267)

By the end of the century spatial barriers appeared threatening and intolerable, and in the rhetoric of reformers the idea of *mystery* itself was the veil which hid the sight of the lower orders and their quarters from the "public," the readers of newspapers and the payers of taxes for whom the slums were par excellence an "elsewhere" shrouded in awe and fear. What Stephen Crane called "the eternal mystery of social conditions" begged for solution. Such popular titles in the 1890s as "People We Pass," "The Nether Side of New York," "How the Other Half Lives," confirmed the by then conventional trope of a fragmented urban landscape; the *mystery* or problem is located entirely in the alarming incommunicability among what Robert Park early in the twentieth century described as the "moral regions," the patterns of segregation which make the city "a mosaic of little worlds which touch but do not interpenetrate."

In 1894 Crane published a number of city stories and sketches in the daily press in New York. He thought well enough of these experimental pieces to consider collecting them as "Midnight Sketches." Considering their origins as newspaper sketches, these mainly short, deft impressions of New York street life seem more like apprentice work than finished inventions. One of the reasons for their interest is, however, exactly the fact of their having been produced for the press as newspaper performances. If the stories show the young writer, still in his early twenties, experimenting with language to develop an appropriate style, the newspaper itself must be taken into account as a given of the experimental situation. Crane derived the form itself, the "sketch," from the newspaper, and at a deeper level the form provided a challenge, a barrier to be overcome.

The big city daily, especially as it developed in the 1890s, has its *raison d'etre* chiefly in the mystification of urban space, a mystification it claims to dispel as "news" yet simultaneously abets as "sensationalism." The newspaper addresses itself abstractly to a "public" which is the collective identity each isolated urban consciousness is invited to join, a neutral space held in common as the negation of hidden private space. The motive of the metropolitan press, Robert Park writes, is "to reproduce as far as possible, in the city, the conditions of life in the village." In villages "everyone knew everyone else, everyone called everyone by his first name." The tactic of searching out "human interest," of making the commonplace seem picturesque or dramatic, is an attempt to fill the distances inherent in mystified space with formulaic emotion fostering the illusion of distance transcended. In their daily recurrence newspapers express concretely the estrangement of an urban consciousness no longer capable of free intimacy with its own material life. In their form the wish for the

commonplace or the demystification of social distance co-exists with the wish not to dispel mystery, to retain as surrogate experience the aura of awe, allurement, fear which surrounds street experience.

Crane was not an ordinary reporter on assignment; he wrote as a "literary" observer, a personal reporter of city scenes. His sketches were not "news"; nor were they entirely fiction, though he was capable of "making up" an account of a fire which never occurred and placing it in the New York *Press* as a signed report. The sketches present themselves as personal reports from and on *experience,* frankly colored by a personal style. The convention of such stylized reporting already existed in New York journalism as an expression of the newspapers' need to transform random street experience into *someone's* experience. The convention provided Crane with an opportunity to cultivate an authentic style as a vehicle of personal vision. The danger was that pressure to distinguish his vision, to make his signature recognizable, would lead to stylization.

Choosing themes familiar to newspaper, magazine, and novel readers, Crane developed a distinctive manner, a kind of notation which rendered physical scenes in highlighted color and sound. "When Everyone is Panic-stricken," his fire report hoax, opens:

> We were walking on one of the shadowy side streets west of Sixth Avenue. The midnight silence and darkness was upon it save where at the point of intersection with the great avenue there was a broad span of yellow light. From there came the steady monotonous jingle of streetcar bells and the weary clatter of hooves on the cobbles. While the houses in this street turned black and mystically silent with the night the avenue continued its eternal movement and life, a great vein that never slept nor paused. The gorgeous orange-hued lamps of the saloon flared plainly and the figures of some loungers could be seen as they stood on the corner. Passing to and fro the tiny black figures of people made an ornamental border on this fabric of yellow light.

The effect is painterly, precise, impressionistic. Crane's eye for detail, his ability to take in a scene and convey its sense, its contours, in a few telling strokes, suggest important correspondence between his visual intentions and that of impressionist painters and photographers. The notation here, and typically in the city sketches, seizes a passing moment and formalizes it as a picture drawn from a precise physical perspective—from the shadowy side street toward the great avenue and its gorgeous yellow light. Within the formalization the scene contains motion, the potential for change, for the appearance of the sudden and the unexpected. The potency is held in the carefully constructed spatial relation between the black, silent houses in "this street" and the unsleeping, flaring life of the avenue. The relation has, moreover, the potential of an ironic contrast, one which does in fact emerge as the "grim midnight reflection upon existence" of the narrator and his companion (identified only as "the stranger"), "in the heavy shadows and in the great stillness" of the street, are disputed by a sudden "muffled cry of a woman" from one of the "dark impassive houses" and the "sound of the splinter and crash of broken glass, falling to the pavement." The pictorial patterns of the opening paragraph give way to the frenzy and excitement of a midnight fire. Like the shadowy street itself the stranger suddenly flares into life, clutches the narrator's arm, drags him to the blazing house, himself a mirror of its vehemence. Through his responses Crane registers the effective transformation of the scene from shadow to blaze, from grimness to frenzy: "The stranger's hand tightened convulsively on my arm, his enthusiasm was like the ardor of one who looks upon the pageantry of battles. 'Ah, look at 'em! look at 'em! ain't that great?' " The spatial relations and contrasts of the opening picture contain, in short, visual elements corresponding to the little drama which this fake news story performs.

A similar dramatization of visual detail and spatial relations to deepen and complicate conventional newspaper action appears in many of the sketches. Their interest lies in the fact that Crane used the occasion—the "personal" or "feature" reporter in search of copy—to develop techniques for rendering events on city streets as unique and complex experiences. Defining his literary problem from within such conventions posed certain difficulties; literalism, sensationalism, sentimentality were the ogres of the newspaper story Crane had to slay in his own work. From within the conventions Crane was able to discover a ground for genuine creation. That ground lay chiefly within the spatial structure of the common city story. Crane grasped the element of *mystery* within that structure and made it the basis of his point of view.

The most prominent and sensational of the spatial images in this period was that of the "other half," represented by the maze of streets and alleys and courtyards in lower Manhattan. In his famous exposures of living conditions in the slums, Jacob Riis, reporter for the New York *Sun,* excavated place names like Mulberry Bend, Bottle Alley, and Bandit's Roost. These names joined the "Bowery" as signals of forbidding and exotic territory. Illustrating his stories and books with photographs that explored to the "darkest corner," Riis established a pattern of spatial penetration which provided his readers with vicarious expeditions into mysterious quarters. His technique was that of a guided tour; his aim, to convert the reader from passive ignorance to active awareness and caring. In the sensations of his disclosures lurks some residue of the city *mystery.* . . . The strategy is to place the reader in a moral relation of outrage, indignation, or pity. But it remains a touristic device; the reader is not permitted to cross into the inner world of the slums—into its own point of view—and see the outer world from that perspective. The moral stance which defines the "other half " as "problem" assures distance.

The portrayal of "low life" in much of the popular writing of the period employed analogous devices to preserve distance—devices of picturesque perspective or sentimental plot which protected the reader from the danger of a true exchange of point of view with the "other half." The danger appears as such in an interesting passage in an essay on "New York Streets" by William Dean Howells. In his walks through the "wretched quarters," he writes, he permits himself to become "hardened, for the moment, to the deeply underlying fact of human discomfort" by indulging himself in the "picturesqueness" of the scene: "The sidewalks swarm with children and the air rings with clamor as they fly back and forth at play; on the thresholds the mothers sit nursing their babes and the old women gossip together," etc. He remarks then, shrewdly, that "in a pic-

ture it would be most pleasingly effective, for then you could be in it and yet have the distance on it which it needs." To be *in it,* however, is "to inhale the stenches of the neglected street and to catch that yet fouler and dreadfuler poverty-smell which breed from the open doorways. It is to see the children quarreling in their games and beating each other in the face and rolling each other in the gutter like the little savage outlaws they are." This reality, if you are a walker in the city, "makes you hasten your pace down to the river" and escape. The passage confesses at once to the denials of the picturesque view and the offensiveness of an unmediated view.

How then was "low life" to be viewed? For Howells, for Riis, and for many concerned writers, a moral posture supplied the necessary screen of protection from an exchange of subjectivities. But the possibility of such an exchange—indeed its necessity if the logic of the convention were to complete itself—is implicit in the spatial pattern. It is precisely this possibility that Crane recognized in his city sketches—a possibility which provides the formal structure of two of the most ambitious of the city stories, the companion pieces **"Experiment in Misery"** and **"Experiment in Luxury,"** and which illuminate his stylistic intentions throughout the sketches. (pp. 268-73)

Crane's recognition of the "mosaic of little worlds" and its demands upon representation is manifest in one of the best-known of the street sketches, **"The Men of the Storm."** The sketch is of a crowd of homeless men observed on the street during a blizzard as they wait with growing impatience and dangerous discontent for the "doors of charity" to open. Images of the homeless and jobless waiting for charity on the street were common in the writing and graphics of the period. Crane's piece differs from the standard treatment in several crucial ways. It is not a social study; it neither excites compassion for the men nor induces social guilt in the reader for their plight. It is a rendering of a scene, a depiction of a space, as objective as Alfred Stieglitz' street photographs with a hand-held camera in the same year. Crane's concern is with the phenomenon before him and his writing is almost surgical in its sureness of stroke. He writes to achieve an accurate statement of the feeling of the scene and his details are physical correlatives of the men's feelings of pitiless cold, biting wind, and snow that "cut like knives and needles." The men are driven by the storm "like sheep in a winter's gale." Viewed from without, they are also seen as possessing a collective subjectivity. For example, in their fierce condition they still can swear "not like dark assassins, but in a sort of American fashion grimly and desperately it is true but yet with a wondrous under-effect definable and mystic as if there were some kind of humor in this catastrophe, in this situation in a night of snow-laden winds."

A picture of a desperate scene—of men subjected to cold wind, snow, and hunger, alternately clinging to each other for warmth and fighting with each other for shelter—the sketch is also a highly pointed study in the problematics of point of view. Drawn from a detached floating perspective, the sketch contains several limited points of view, each located spatially and each characterized by a feeling linked to its space. The opening paragraphs present a picture of late afternoon busy streets as the blizzard begins to swirl upon pedestrians and drivers of vehicles and

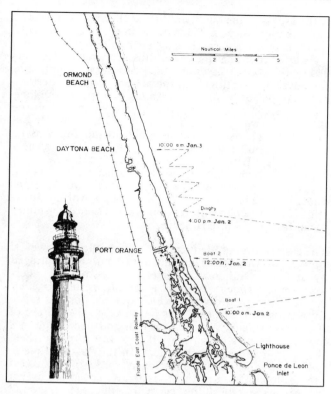

The course of the dinghy in which Crane was stranded with several other men, following the wreck of the steamship Commodore, January 1, 1897. Out of this experience, Crane wrote "The Open Boat."

horses. The mood is grim at first: people are huddled, drivers are furious, horses slip and strain; "overhead the trains rumbled and roared and the dark structure of the elevated railroad stretching over the avenue dripped little streams and drops of water upon the mud and snow beneath it." But the next paragraph introduces a more hopeful note. The perspective shifts momentarily to an interior, "to one who looked from a window"; the clatter of the streets, softened by snow, "becomes important music, a melody of life made necessary to the ear by the dreariness of the pitiless beat and sweep of the storm." The warmth of the interior in which such musings are likely pervades the paragraph; the shop windows, "aglow with light," are "infinitely cheerful," and now "the pace of the people and the vehicles" has a "meaning": "Scores of pedestrians and drivers wretched with cold faces, necks and feet, speeding for scores of unknown doors and entrances, scattering to an infinite variety of shelters, to places which the imagination made warm with the colors of home." The objective scene has been constructed to reveal a subjective mood—the storm is pitiless but the imagination warms itself with images of doors, entrances, home: "There was an absolute expression of hot dinners in the pace of the people." Crane then introduces a conjectural point of view inspired by the scene: "If one dared to speculate upon the destination of those who came trooping, he lost himself in a maze of social calculations. He might fling a handful of sand and attempt to follow the flight of each particular grain." But the entire troop has in common the thought of hot dinners: "It is a matter of tradition; it is from the tales of childhood.

It comes forth with every storm." Social calculation might be pleasant, diversionary, but trivial. All classes are reduced to those who speed home in the blizzard warmed with the thoughts of food, and those who do not. At this point Crane performs the sketch's most decisive modulation of perspective: "However, in a certain part of the dark West side street, there was a collection of men to whom these things were as if they were not." The stark negative halts all calculation.

The narrator has subtly worked upon the reader's point of view, freeing it from the hold of customary feeling so that it might receive freely a newly discovered "moral region," the territory of "half darkness" in which occurs another kind of existence. In the description which follows Crane twice again introduces a shift in perspective in order to confirm better the spatial independence of his own. At one point, across the street from the huddled men, the figure of a stout, well-dressed man appears "in the brilliantly lighted space" of the shop window. He observes the crowd, stroking his whiskers: "It seemed that the sight operated inversely, and enabled him to more clearly regard his own environment, delightful relatively." The man's complacency is echoed at the end of the sketch as the narrator notes a change in expression in the features of the men as they near the receiving door of charity: "As they thus stood upon the threshold of their hopes they looked suddenly content and complacent, the fire had passed from their eyes and the snarl had vanished from their lips. The very force of the crowd in the rear which had previously vexed them was regarded from another point of view, for it now made it inevitable that they should go through the little doors into the place that was cheery and warm with light."

By projecting in the contrasted points of view a dialectic of felt values, Crane forces the reader to free his own point of view from any limiting perspective. Crane thus transforms the conventional event of turning corners and crossing thresholds into a demanding event: a change of perspective which as its prerequisite recapitulates a number of limited perspectives. Crane's **"Men in the Storm"** differs, for example, from a characteristic "literary" treatment of the same theme such as Howells' "The Midnight Platoon" by its achievement of a point of view superior to, yet won through a negation of, perspectives limited by social, moral, or aesthetic standards. Howells' piece concerns a breadline as it is perceived from a carriage by a man who comes to recognize himself as comfortable and privileged. The figure in the story approaches the scene as a "connoisseur of such matters," enjoying the anticipation of "the pleasure of seeing"; he wants to "glut his sensibility in a leisurely study of the scene." The breadline is to him "this representative thing" and he perceives in the crowd of hungry men "a fantastic association of their double files and those of the galley-slaves whom Don Quixote released." . . . Aware that the men look back at him with equal curiosity, he suddenly recognizes his own "representativity." To them, he realizes, he stands for Society, the Better Classes, and the literary picturesque notions dissolve as he feels himself face to face with the social issue. Howells here confronts the social distance, portrays it as filled with middle-class rationalization, and ends with a "problem": what are "we" to do about these men and their suffering?

For Crane, the question is as if it were not. He writes from a curiously asocial perspective—or, at least, a perspective disengaged from that of the typical middle-class viewer; he approximates (though he does not yet achieve) the perspective of the men. That is, what Howells sees as a thoroughly social matter of how the classes view each other, Crane sees as a technical problem: how to represent the scene before him. He is not concerned with converting the reader to social sympathy (perhaps distrustful or weary of the condescension of such a stance), but with converting the sheer data into *experience.* He writes as a phenomenologist of the scene, intent on characterizing the consciousness of the place (which includes its separate points of view) by a rendering of felt detail. Each of Crane's images resonates with significance as a component of the episode's inner structure of feeling; the exactness of the correlation of detail to feeling leads, in fact, to the frequent mistake of describing Crane as a Symbolist. His *realism,* however, in the phenomenological sense, points to the significance, indeed the radicalism, of these sketches. For Crane transforms a street scene, a passing sensation for which a cognitive mold is already prepared in his reader's eye, into a unique experience.

If, following Walter Benjamin, we require that works be "situated in the living social context," then the immediate context is that established by the author with his reader; it is in that relationship that the possibility of each becoming "real" and particular for the other exists. In this case, the relationship is mediated by the sketch's appearance in a newspaper, and at a deeper level, by its formal expression of the newspaper motive: a "human interest" observation on a street. But typically the newspaper does not permit its own formal qualities so intense and exact a realization. Newspapers respond, as I have pointed out, to the increasing mystification, the deepening estrangement of urban space from interpenetration, from exchange of subjectivities. But their response is to deepen the crisis while seeming to allay it. In their typographical form, their typical verbal usage, they serve, Benjamin writes, "to isolate what happens from the realm in which it could affect the experience of the reader." By isolating information from experience, moreover, they deaden the capacity of memory; the lack of connection among the data of the newspaper page reduces all items to the status of "today's events." The newspaper, Benjamin writes, "is the showplace of the unrestrained degradation of the word." (pp. 274-78)

Yet, as Benjamin argues, within the logic of the newspaper lies a possible condition for the salvation of the word—in the new relationships it fosters between writer and world, between writer and reader. Crane accepted the condition of newspaper production and produced within it work which, with the complicity of his careful reader, converts the data of street life into memorable experience. He thus transvalues, or as Benjamin would put it, "alienates" the apparatus of production and forces his reader to become an accomplice, that is, to become himself an experimenter in mystified space. The best example among the sketches, an example which reveals Crane's motives almost diagrammatically, is the often misunderstood **"Experiment in Misery."** In this and in its companion piece, **"Experiment in Luxury,"** published a week apart in the New York *Press,* Crane presents a figure, a "youth," who enters opposite social realms—in the first a seedy lodging house, in the second the mansion of a millionnaire. The report in both cases is of the quality of life, of the awareness which inhabits each interior. The method in each "Experiment" is to convey the inner feeling by having the youth "try on" the way of life. The spaces are thus presumably demystified by the youth's assuming the point of view implicit in the physical structures and the actions of their interiors. For example, as he lounges with his rich friend, smoking pipes, the youth feels a sense of liberty unknown on the streets. "It was an amazing comfortable room. It expressed to the visitor that he could do supremely as he chose, for it said plainly that in it the author did supremely as he chose." Before long "he began to feel that he was a better man than many—entitled to a great pride." In each case the narrative point of view projects the youth's consciousness; he is made into a register of the world-as-it-is-felt of the particular setting. In this way Crane transmutes social fact into felt experience.

The stories are not identical in their strategies, however. Both begin with a frame in which the youth is encouraged by an older friend, in a conversation on a street, to undertake the experiment. As companion pieces they together confront the great division which was the popular mode through which "society" was perceived in the culture of the period: luxury and misery, rich and poor, high and low, privileged and underprivileged. Intentionally then, they comprise a social statement. In the "luxury" piece, unlike the other, Crane consciously works from a social proposition: his "experiment" is an attempt to discover if indeed the inner life of the very rich justifies the "epigram" "stuffed . . . down the throat" of the complaining poor by "theologians" that "riches did not bring happiness." The motive of the "misery" story is less overtly ideological: it is to learn of the "tramp" "how he feels." The narrative technique of the "luxury" story differs from the other in that the youth carries on his "experiment" along with a simultaneous inner dialogue based on observation and self-reflection. He learns that the rich do, after all, live pretty well, if insipidly. He could "not see that they had great license to be pale and haggard." The story assumes a point of view in order to shatter a social myth. Being rich makes a difference.

Discursive self-reflection plays no role in the companion sketch. In fact, to intensify attention on the experience itself, and to indicate that the social drama of displacing one's normal perspective already is internalized in the action, Crane discarded the opening and closing frames when he republished the story in a collection of 1898. In his revision he also added to the opening paragraphs a number of physical details which reinforce and particularize the sense of misery. Streetcars, which in the first version "rumbled softly, as if going on carpet stretched in the aisle made by the pillars of the elevated road," become a "silent procession . . . moving with formidable power, calm and irresistible, dangerous and gloomy, breaking silence only by the loud fierce cry of the gong." The elevated train station, now supported by "leg-like pillars," resembles "some monstrous kind of crab squatting over the street." These revisions and others suggest an intention more fully realized: the creation of physical equivalents to the inner experience of a "moral region" of misery.

The first version makes clear that the youth's "experiment" is a conscious disguise in order to search out "experience." "Two men stood regarding a tramp," it opens; the youth "wonders" how he "feels" and is advised by his older friend that such speculations are "idle" (a finely ironic word, as is "regarding") unless he is "in" the tramp's condition. The youth agrees to "try" it: "Perhaps I could discover his point of view or something near it." The frame opens with an awareness, then, of what the older man calls "distance," and establishes "experiment" as a method of overcoming it. So far the situation recalls the wish of Howells' witness of the breadline to penetrate distance, as it does the situation in many similar down-and-out pieces in the period. For example, in *Moody's Lodging House and Other Tenement Sketches* (1895), also a collection of newspaper sketches, Alvan Francis Sanborn writes: "the best way to get at the cheap lodging-house life is to live it,—to get inside the lodging house and stay inside. For this, unless one possesses a mien extraordinarily eloquent of roguery or misery, or both, a disguise is helpful." Crane's youth borrows a disguise from the "studio of an artist friend" (this suggestive detail is dropped in the revised version), and begins his experiment: as Crane puts it with a note of irony, the youth "went forth." The irony is directed at the hint of naïve chivalric adventuresomeness in the youth and prepares for the authentic conversion of his subjective life to follow.

In what follows the youth proceeds downtown in the rain; he is "plastered with yells of 'bum' and 'hobo' " by small boys, he is wet and cold, and "he felt that there no longer could be pleasure in life." In City Hall Park he feels the contrast between himself and the homeward bound "well-dressed Brooklyn people" and he proceeds further "down Park Row" where "in the sudden descent in the style of the dress of the crowd he felt relief, and as if he were at last in his own country" (this last significant detail was added in the revision). The youth begins to inhabit this other country, first by occupying himself with "the pageantry of the street," then "caught by the delectable sign," allowing himself to be "swallowed" by a "voracious" looking saloon door advertising "free hot soup." His descent deepens. The next step is to find someone with "a knowledge of cheap lodging houses," and he finds his man in a seedy character "in strange garments" with a strange guilty look about his eyes, a look which earns him the youth's epithet of "assassin." The youth confesses himself also a "stranger" and follows the lead of his companion to a "joint" of "dark and secret places" from which assail him "strange and unspeakable odors." The interior is "black, opaque" and during the night the youth lies sleepless as the dormitory takes on the grim appearance of a fiendish morgue. Near him lies a man asleep with partly open eyes, his arm hanging over the cot, his fingers "full length upon the wet cement floor of the room." The spirit of the place seems contained in this image. "To the youth it seemed that he and the corpse-like being were exchanging a prolonged stare and that the other threatened with his eyes." The "strange effect of the graveyard" is broken suddenly by "long wails" that "dwindle to final melancholy moans" expressing "a red and grim tragedy of the unfathomable possibilities of the man's dreams." The youth feels now that he has penetrated to the deepest recesses of the tramp's condition.

But at this point Crane performs an important act of distancing the narrative from the point of view of the youth. Fulfilling the earlier hints of his naïveté, Crane now has the youth interpret the shrieks of the "vision pierced man"

as "protest," as "an impersonal eloquence, with a strength not from him, giving voice to the wail of a whole section, a class, a people." An ideological romance settles in his mind, "weaving into the young man's brain and mingling with his views of these vast and sombre shadows," and he "lay carving biographies for these men from his meager experience." With morning and sunlight comes the "rout of the mystic shadows," however, and the youth sees that "daylight had made the room comparatively commonplace and uninteresting." The men joke and banter as they dress, and some reveal in their nakedness that they were "men of brawn" until they put on their "ungainly garments." The normalization of feeling in this morning scene is crucial. When the youth reaches the street he "experienced no sudden relief from unholy atmospheres. He had forgotten all about them, and had been breathing naturally and with no sensation of discomfort or distress." The respiratory detail confirms the point; he is now indeed in his own country, where he might feel after breakfast that "B'Gawd, we've been livin' like kings." In the expansive moment his companion "brought forth long tales" about himself which reveal him as a confirmed hobo, always cadging and running from work. Together they make their way to City Hall Park, the youth now one of "two wanderers" who "sat down in a little circle of benches sanctified by traditions of their class." In the normalcy of his behavior he shows that his experience of misery, since the night before, has become less meager.

The story closes as the youth on the bench becomes aware of a new substance in his perceptions. Well-dressed people on the street give him "no gaze" and he feels "the infinite distance" from "all that he valued. Social position, comfort, the pleasures of living, were unconquerable kingdoms." His new world and theirs were separate countries. The separateness is discovered as a difference in perspective, in how the world is seen, felt, and accepted. Now, the tall buildings in the background of the park are "of pitiless hues and sternly high." They stand "to him" as emblems "of a nation forcing its regal head into the clouds, throwing no downward glances." "The roar of the city" is now "to him" a "confusion of strange tongues." Estrangement has become his own experience, no longer a "thought" about the original object of his perception, the tramp. The youth, and through him the reader, has attained an experimental point of view expressed in an act of the eyes in the concluding sentences: "He confessed himself an outcast, and his eyes from under the lowered rim of his hat began to glance guiltily, wearing the criminal expression that comes with certain convictions." The conviction itself, of being excluded by the overarching buildings, accounts for the new perspective.

The two "experiments" conclude that the rich are banal but live well, and that the homeless poor are victims whose inner acquiescence is a form of cowardice. More important than such "meanings" are the strategies compressed in the word "experiment." In these strategies lie the specifically urban character of Crane's writings, a character which is his calculated invention out of the materials of the newspaper culture. Crane's "experiments" implicate Zola's but go beyond them. In the misery sketch "experiment" denotes the subject as well as the method; the sketch is "about" the youth's experiment, an anatomizing of the components of the naturalist's enterprise of investigating human life in its social habitat. But Crane is concerned with the investigator, with the exercise of the logic of investigation upon his subjectivity. The experiment transforms the youth, and it is through that transformation that the life of the city's strangers becomes manifest. The youth is transformed only provisionally, however; he is not converted, not reclassified as a tramp. His experiment is literally a trying-out, a donning of a costume in order to report on its fit and feel. In order to live provisionally as a stranger in another country he must have estranged himself even more deeply to begin with, that is, he must already have disengaged himself from all possible identities, from social identity as such. Crane recognized that the inner form of the newspaper culture was itself "experiment" and to fulfill its logic of disengagement was a prerequisite for recovering "experience" from the flux of the street. Crane's city sketches are "experimental" writing in the sense, finally, that they confront the transformation of literary relations (the writer's relation to his subject and to his reader) implicit in the big city's mystification of social and psychic space; they invent stylistic procedures for re-creating the word as experience.

Crane's direction was a descent to the street and to the constricted visions which lay there as broken images. Out of these he forged a unifying image of his own, a vision of a city peopled by nameless, desolate creatures, strangers to each other and to their own worlds. "The inhabitant of the great urban centers," writes Paul Valèry, "reverts to a state of savagery—that is, of isolation. The feeling of being dependent on others, which used to be kept alive by need, is gradually blunted in the smooth functioning of the social mechanism. Any improvement of this mechanism eliminates certain modes of behavior and emotions." Crane's vision is of a world already confirmed in its isolation, a world shocking in the absence of those "certain modes of behavior and emotion" which make subjective experience possible. The exchange of subjectivity performed by the youth rarely occurs among the characters of his city fiction; instead, violence always threatens as the promise of heightened sensation in defiance of the blunting mechanisms: a wail, a scream, a fire, a clutched arm. Crane's city people seem always ignitable, verging toward the discharge of feeling in riot. His own narrative point of view remains cool and aloof, however; his spatial penetrations end at the edge of sympathetic identification. Unlike Theodore Dreiser, he was little interested in character, little interested in exploring the versions of reality his style transcends. The expense of his expert technicianship was the larger novelistic vision Dreiser achieved. Dreiser also descended to the popular, to the banal, but the points of view of his characters were not provisional guises; he took them as self-sufficient acts of desire. Dreiser's city is a theme as well as a place: a magnet that attracts. Less than a place, Crane's city lies in the structured passages of his point of view; it is situated in his technique, in its processes of disengagement and recovery. His sketches are experiments in reading the "elsewhere" of the street. (pp. 279-85)

Alan Trachtenberg, "Experiments in Another Country: Stephen Crane's City Sketches," in The Southern Review, *Louisiana State University, Vol. X, No. 2, April, 1974, pp. 265-85.*

John Berryman (essay date 1976)

[*Berryman is probably one of the most important, and certainly one of the most widely read, of modern American poets. His own work developed from objective, classically controlled poetry into an esoteric, eclectic, and highly emotional type of literature. In his own words, he has called poetry "the means by which the writer can shape from an experience in itself usually vague, a mere feeling or phrase, something that is coherent, directed, intelligible." Berryman's* Stephen Crane *(1950; see Further Reading list) is a biography that amended some of the inaccuracies of the first Crane biography by Thomas Beer (see Further Reading list). In the following excerpt from a slightly revised version of an essay that originally appeared in 1960, Berryman provides a detailed examination of method and style in "The Open Boat," focusing on Crane's use of language particularly in the story's opening paragraph.*]

To his title **"The Open Boat,"** Stephen Crane appended this subtitle, "A Tale Intended to be after the Fact: Being the Experience of Four Men from the Sunk Steamer *Commodore*." The shipwreck, of which the men's experience in the boat is the aftermath, actually occurred early in 1897. When Crane got ashore safely with the captain and the cook, he wrote a long dispatch to his New York paper (he was a reporter) about the shipwreck, which they published.

His dispatch does not describe the experience in the boat. Now the story is said by him, in the subtitle, to be "after" (in accordance with) the *fact*, "*being* the *experience* of," and so on. Shall we expect then to hear the true story of the ordeal? (pp. 176-77)

The opening sentence reads: "None of them knew the color of the sky." Why are we told first a fact so flat and odd, a negative fact? Perhaps we are being told this *instead* of something else we expected to hear. You may say, "But the story begins with this sentence!" No, it began with its title, and subtitle, and it is in the light of both that we read the first sentence. An expectation *has* been disappointed, for when one hears of an open boat, and four men in it from a sunk steamer, perhaps the first thing one thinks of is the excellent view they unfortunately have of the sky and their deep interest in the weather it foreshadows. "Completely wrong," Crane is saying. "You know nothing about the matter." The men are watching the sea, with anxiety about the waves, presumably (we do not *know* yet—the sea may even be calm), and watching the horizon, with an equal anxiety to see it (we do not know yet how far out they are). The line, thus, is far more *businesslike* than anything one expected. It has the effect, shall we say, of bringing the reader's gaze—as if taking him by the back of the neck—*down* from the skyey expectations of the title and subtitle to what is *level* (this word then occurs immediately) and a matter of human efficiency. Crane's opening sentence is *anti*-heroic, that is to say, standing as it does like a blunt sentry, in the forefront of what looked to be an epic of the sea. Anti-heroic and ironic, in view of the "big" opening (high-keyed, exalted) that the reader presumably expected.

But it is a curious fact that this very prosaic though active sentence makes a line of formal verse. It is an iambic pentameter, what is called a heroic verse, with trochaic substitution in the opening foot. No doubt the line is not so intense or highly coloured as the first line of a poem on this subject might be, but the character of the rhythm, being formal, is antithetical to the sentence's anti-heroic muscular meaning and tone. This author desires to take possession of the reader, on several fronts simultaneously, at once. In this first sentence, the reader, made aware that the men are watching the sea, immediately understands the true scale of the experience to come. The quality of the thought of the sentence, at the outset, forces the reader to begin to think *with* the men. What looks like an impersonal declarative sentence is really in its effect personal, questioning, psychological. At the end of just a page or so, this process of obliging the reader to enter the boat (and share the men's experience) has gone so far that Crane can say "the faces of the men must have been gray" and we are inside—though *not* yet with the correspondent, only with all four.

Clearly, Crane's opening sentence, by *not* being about the sky but about—what? well, something else—introduces a complication. The longer second and third sentences are not only explanatory but *resolving,* and the resolution comes in almost the rhythm of the complication: "and all of the men knew the colors of the sea."

A wave has passed. Almost at once a second wave begins. "Many a man" is mock-heroic in tone (burlesquing heroic style) and the bathtub carries on the low-comedy sense. But the effect of the sentence is not comic. This dry, gay, senseless remark—as one critic has said—enables Crane to contrast, as in a flash of lightning, the most comfortable and sheltered situation conceivable (a bath in one's own bathtub) with on the other hand the sinister wilderness of wave and wind, where a man *owns* ("ought to have") nothing except, precariously, his life. But there is something more. A bathtub exists to fill with water—and with this sinister glimpse of the dinghy shipping water (we have not even been openly told yet that she is), the second complication is over. The wave is about to break, and in the famous sentence that follows, it does break: "These waves were most wrongfully and barbarously abrupt and tall. . . ." The sentence itself appears to swell and tower like a wave in the ear and mind, after the light, odd little sentence preceding: its long, mournful middle sounds ("most wrongfully and barbarously") are succeeded so rapidly by the extremely surprising, fast word "abrupt" and the even shorter, also sinister "tall," that it is a little as if a comber had loomed and broken over oneself. But the key word is "barbarously." The men are here in a world that has nothing to do with bathtubs. Civilization has been obliterated for them, and their ordeal is going to be primitive, barbarous. Notice, finally, that the tone has risen so very high in the part of the sentence we have been studying that Crane, in order to be able to get on with his narrative, drops his tone sharply in its second half, to make a technical remark; which has also the effect of saying that the barbarous is being confronted, at any rate, with skill.

So much for the opening paragraph, which is certainly one of the fastest, subtlest, toughest operations in American prose. Then each of the four men in the boat has a little paragraph to himself. The first thing to be observed about the four of them is negative: we spoke of "skill," and it immediately follows tht not one of the four men is a proper

sailor. Instead, we have men (in poor condition, as it will turn out) from the galley, the engine room, the passenger cabins, and the bridge—and the man from the bridge is injured. It follows that they will not be able to summon much except courage and endurance to save themselves. The author is clearly an author strongly given to irony.

Crane's treatment of the first man, the cook, is the reverse of heroic. There does not seem to be anything wrong with him and yet he is not doing anything; his costume is undignified, so is his speech, so is his fatness, so is the evident fear with which he regards the two inches of gunwale. This general impression is somewhat neutralized, however, by the last thing we hear, that he "invariably gazed eastward over the broken sea." This tone is more elevated than that of the rest of the paragraph, his intensity is communicated, and, after all, he does seem to be exercising a role: he is lookout.

The mock-heroic tone partly characteristic of the opening paragraph makes the semi-clownish cook the perfect character, of the four, to introduce first. What is our surprise, then, to hear far *less* about the oiler—almost nothing except that he is steering with a thin little oar and raises his body sometimes to avoid water. Is he going to prove even more insignificant in the story than the cook? Or is the author holding his fire, as with the cook there seems no reason to think he may be doing? All we can note at the moment is surprise.

Of the correspondent we hear, if possible, less still. He is rowing, watching, wondering "why he was there." But is this less? Surely with "wondering" we enter briefly the mind of the correspondent, as we never did the cook's mind, much less the oiler's. The notion of an explanation for the ordeal begins, with this verb, to reverberate in the story. It is suggested to us that at least one of our main points of view—notwithstanding the general tact of Crane's third-person narrative—is going to be that of the correspondent.

It is obvious, instantly, that one of the things Crane has been doing with the others is holding his fire in order to do a proper job on the captain. Injured, shipless, he is lying down (the others squat or sit), and the quality of his reflection and memory (of his foundering ship) is conveyed by Crane in language which has none of the irony that has characterized the opening page down to this point. The others are anxious, working. He is withdrawn. One realizes at once that his situation is not going fully to be that of the others: in a sense, his defeat has already taken place, fate can do nothing worse to him. He still gives orders—his "profound dejection and indifference" do not extend to an abandonment of his duty to the others; but he gives them in a voice "deep with mourning, and of a quality beyond oration or tears," and one does not receive an impression that the captain's fate is going to be the major concern of this story.

Whom, then, does it seem the story is going to be about?—at the end of this first page, that is; for a good reader is sensitive to as many as possible of an author's announcements and foreshadowings (*and omissions,* which is often the way announcements are made and suggestions conveyed).

The cook? Hardly. Of course, the author may have surprises in store for us; but a good author does not work in terms of surprises so much as of expectation, discussed later. It is unlikely that Crane will have misled us to that extent. The cook—just as we know him so far (and do we ever learn more?)—does not seem fitted to be either the hero or the victim of a tale one of whose keynotes is set by the august paragraph about the captain. We have to say hero *or* victim, naturally, because we do not know how the story will turn out. But it is unlikely to turn out either a simple tragedy or a simple escape story—considering the complexities of tone we have been examining on its first page.

The oiler? Conceivably; for we know nothing about him yet; the author may be making us wait, and it is a little striking that the first thing we learn, after the four characterizing paragraphs, is the oiler's name. Those paragraphs have already made it apparent that we are in the hands of an author who does not lightly reveal his characters' names: he is concerned, rather, with their roles, perhaps with their fates.

The correspondent? Conceivably; but, if so, in a very different way from the way the story will be about the oiler, if it proves to be. The correspondent, as one would expect, reflects and inquires.

Or all four? A study of the story's form will take us further, but how intense and elaborate is the initial impression made just by one paragraph and a little cast of characters.

The ordeal dramatized in the story has three parts, each growing out of, and superseding, the part preceding (this is true even of the first part, as will be clear in a moment), and each having a theme different from what one expected. The seven sections into which Crane has divided his story, that is, we may see as three waves. Each gathers, swells, breaks, and is followed by another, until the final word of the story brings the movements to a conclusion. But then this word itself shows that the three movements were one movement only. Far more than is the case even with most really good stories, **"The Open Boat"** reserves its true meaning to its actual final word.

What would the title, and the initial line of explanation ("A Tale," etc.), lead us to expect the story to be about? Hardship, certainly; fear; the relation between man and nature. But the first wave of the story (Sections I-III) is not about these things, essentially. It is about comradeship—the relation between man and man—and its basic tone is optimistic. At first no land is visible at all, then II ends with a "pin" appearing on the horizon, and the words "serenely" and "cheerful" are applied to the men. Section III strengthens this feeling at its close with the exquisite iteration "Slowly the land arose from the sea . . . Slowly and beautifully the land loomed out of the sea," and the men light cigars. The climax of this wave comes at the beginning of III, with "the subtle brotherhood of men that was here established on the seas." A man, that is to say, in his ordeal, is not alone; he may trust other men, and must, and does, and finds that they will help him. This is a *preliminary* conclusion, in the light of the rest of the story, but two things are to be noted about it at once. In the first place, it is, for this author, an unusually *hopeful* way of seeing man's situation. In Crane's earlier works, *Maggie* and *The Red Badge of Courage,* and in his later stories, such as **"The Blue Hotel,"** men are seen as either

Crane in 1897, after his ordeal in the dinghy.

completely alone or as *collaborating into disaster.* In the second place, this brotherhood is not arrived at easily or at once. As against the cliché that men in adversity stick together, Crane is careful to show these men quarrelling toward the end of Section I; so that the establishment of brotherhood comes as an achievement.

The second wave (Sections IV-VI) is concerned powerfully to question both this brotherhood and the nature of the ordeal itself. Its tone is very dark; all three of its sections end in gloom.

Already in part one, it was clear that the brotherhood was established against an enemy, the Sea, which is envisaged as animal: "There was a terrible grace in the move of the waves, and they came in silence, save for the *snarling* of the crests" and "There was a preparatory and long *growl* in the speech of them." The nature of this enemy is now to be explored. But the brotherhood itself—to deal with this first—is seen as both partial and incompletely operative. It does not include the men on the shore, who can only stand and wave, not help. So, are men able to help their fellow man in crisis, after all? Moreover, the brotherhood does not spare the correspondent his agony in the night—though we have to qualify this statement with a reminder that the captain *is* awake and with him, without his knowing it until later. Men must undergo their crises of rage and fear essentially alone.

To move now toward the nature of the enemy: man's fear is of death, but his rage is directed, rather, toward what is going to cause his death—that is to say, nature. But is nature man's enemy? To the extent that it is going to cause his death, one would think so. But in that it *cannot receive rage,* it is not after all an enemy: "he at first wishes to throw bricks at the temple, and he hates deeply the fact that there are no bricks and no temples." The final formulation of the truth about nature is reserved to the third part of the story: here it is enough to know that *nature is not an enemy,* so far as man's *expression of emotion* is concerned. Therefore, in one of Crane's subtlest passages (in Section VI), the rage and fear are transformed into *self-love* and *self-pity.* Nature does not hate man but does not love him either, and does not pity him; and so if he needs these emotions, he must supply them himself. There is irony, of course, even in this view, but it is a tenderer irony than most of Crane's, and the paragraphs about the soldier of the Legion dying in Algiers form one of his most beautiful achievements. (Technically, they get their effect by holding back and holding back in order to accumulate enormous pressure on the simple word "sorry" in the final sentence, making it ring in the mind.)

The dramatization of nature, in the correspondent's mind, as the shark, then, was false or misleading, and in the third part of the story we hear what nature *is:* she is "indifferent, flatly indifferent." Emotion directed toward her—anger or entreaty—is wasted. What is wanted is something very different; *understanding* of her. With this conception, however, we are approaching the word with which the story ends, and before entering on that final subject, it is necessary to understand the death of the oiler.

The oiler's death is the price paid by the men for the salvation of the other three. He dies as a sacrifice. Nature is indifferent, but the arrangements of nature—so to put it—exact tribute. From the narrative point of view, it has to be the oiler who dies because of the disqualifications of the other three. The cook is lacking in dignity, the correspondent is the perceiving mind, and the captain is already injured (a sacrifice must be in perfect condition). But somebody must die; man (the four men in the boat) does not escape scot-free from ordeal; and so the oiler perishes.

And now for the word "interpreters," toward which the entire story has been moving.

This unexpected and dramatic word lifts the story explicitly to a plane that has earlier only been implied. The experience, and *only* the experience, of nature's most dangerous and demanding ordeals, fits man to do what it is most his duty and power to do: to *explain*—explain what nature is, what man is, what matters. The whole story, then, has in some sense been a metaphor, and the ordeal of the boat only an instance of what can happen to man and what it means, what qualities the experience of nature requires. The best imaginable comment on Crane's word "interpreters" is the splendid passage with which William Faulkner closed his Nobel Prize address in 1950:

> I decline to accept the end of man. It is easy enough to say that man is immortal simply because he will endure: that when the last ding-dong of doom has clanged and faded from the last worthless rock hanging tideless in the last red and dying evening, that even then there will still be one more sound: that of his puny inexhaustible voice, still talking. I

refuse to accept this. I believe that man will not merely endure: he will prevail. He is immortal, not because he alone among creatures has an inexhaustible voice, but because he has a soul, a spirit capable of compassion and sacrifice and endurance. The poet's, the writer's, duty is to write about these things. It is his privilege to help man endure by lifting his heart, by reminding him of the courage and honour and hope and pride and compassion and pity and sacrifice which have been the glory of his past. The poet's voice need not merely be the record of man, it can be one of the props, the pillars to help him endure and prevail.

(pp. 177-84)

John Berryman, "Stephen Crane: 'The Open Boat'," in his The Freedom of the Poet, *Farrar, Straus and Giroux, Inc., 1976, pp. 168-84.*

Bill Christophersen (essay date 1982)

[*In the following excerpt, Christophersen applies several acknowledged definitions of Expressionist art to cite elements of Expressionism in Crane's short story "The Upturned Face."*]

Because his works presented a new vision and because his technique was both experimental and protean, Stephen Crane's fiction has puzzled critics since its inception. He has been pigeonholed as a Naturalist, congratulated as an Impressionist, and hailed as the father of Realism and Symbolism in modern American fiction. To some extent, all these labels pertain and lend insight. Yet there remain elements in Crane's fiction that defy even these wide-ranging categories. Crane's **"The Upturned Face"** is a short story in which certain of these elements are foreshortened to good advantage.

Few critics have dealt with **"The Upturned Face"** to any appreciable extent. This is surprising, since it is invariably included among Crane's five or six best pieces, alongside such relentlessly analyzed stories as **"The Blue Hotel"** and **"The Open Boat."** Such critical neglect may well reflect perplexity over a story that seems remote both in tone and technique from many of Crane's earlier works, works which were satisfactorily explained in terms of Naturalism or Impressionism. It is only because these established critical handholds have been so exhaustively exploited that one feels justified in introducing yet another stamp to the parcel of Crane's fiction. I believe **"The Upturned Face"** represents the epitome of an important, if unattended, strain in Crane's canon: a strain best characterized as Expressionist.

"The Upturned Face" is the story of two officers, Timothy Lean and "the adjutant," obliged to bury a fallen comrade during a battle. They are sitting ducks: the enemy has their precise range, and their position cannot be maintained another hour. The officers, assisted by two nondescript privates, dig a grave, "say a few words"—though neither can remember the proper service—and, after much vacillation, inter the corpse until all that remains visible is the "chalk-blue face." Meanwhile, one of the privates is hit. Lean grabs the shovel, sends both privates to the rear and continues the job himself amid the whine of bullets. When the adjutant, who has wavered indecisively from the outset, wavers yet again, suggesting "Perhaps we have been wrong. . . . It might have been better if we hadn't buried him just at this time," Lean explodes, damning the senior officer. Thoroughly shaken, Lean proceeds with the burial and the story ends, a "plop" of mud on the corpse's face sounding the final note. (pp. 147-48)

The *vision* Crane presents in **"The Upturned Face,"** although not altogether unique, differs from that of most of his other works. [John] Berryman characterizes it in terms of abstracted form and rarefied emotion: " . . . it [**"The Upturned Face"**] affects one as pure symbol, senseless and ghastly, like one of Goya's last etchings, and has the posthuman quality of certain late art by other masters" [John Berryman, *Stephen Crane* (1950); see Further Reading list]. Though one wishes he had named these "other masters," Berryman's allusion to Goya is significant. Carl Zigrosser cites Goya as an eminent precursor of the Expressionist painters of the twentieth century [*The Expressionists: A Survey of Their Graphic Art* (1957)].

The German critic Hermann Bahr, in his manifesto entitled "Expressionism" [in *Paths to the Present: Aspects of European Thought from Romanticism to Existentialism*, edited by Eugen Weber (1960)], defines the term and evokes the spiritual ambience which sired it:

> Never yet has any period been so shaken by horror, by such a fear of death. Never has the world been so silent, silent as the grave. Never has man been more insignificant. Never has he felt so nervous. . . . Distress cries aloud; man cries out for his soul; this whole pregnant time is one great cry of anguish. Art too joins in, into the great darkness she too calls for help, she cries to the spirit: this is Expressionism.

Bahr goes on to explain Expressionism as a reaction to Impressionism, which he derogates as a superficial and passive reflection of bourgeois culture. The Expressionist, Bahr notes by way of contrast, "tears open the mouth of humanity," proclaiming "the time of its silence, the time of its listening is over." Edvard Munch's painting *The Shriek* epitomizes this Expressionist archetype.

Expressionism, Bahr elaborates, is an assertion of the individual ego in a machine age which has all but annihilated ego and individual response. The particular suddenness with which Germany unified to become a highly industrialized capitalist society after the Franco-Prussian War probably accounts for the flowering of Expressionism in that country in particular. Expressionism, one may see, is modern man responding to the "death of God," and to what Ludwig Rubiner called "[Darwin's] evolution swindle." Bahr traces its antecedents to the magic signs and drawings of primitive savages, ritualistic or superstitious attempts to deal with a mystery of fear that cannot be rationalized.

The practical translation of this emotional matrix into Expressionist art is concisely described by Eugen Weber [in *Paths to the Present*]:

> Expressionists tried to go beyond the surface meaning of any particular situation to its deeper emotional meaning and it is the emotions—the hope, the dread, the love or the horror contained in a situation or an object (whether human or not)—that they tried to express rather than the visible surface realities. To do this they used distortion, exaggeration that ends in caricature, and a brutal, slashing color.
>
> (pp. 151-52)

Crane's **"The Upturned Face"** bears these earmarks of Expressionism. Its setting and conflict alone constitute an archetypal Expressionist scenario. Two men are poised over a corpse on a battlefield. "[A] windy sound of bullets" peppers the air. The dead man's face stares blankly from the ground. Such mise-en-scene approaches the poignancy of myth; it is, as Berryman suggests, "pure symbol, senseless and ghastly."

The adjutant stands alongside Lean, asking questions. In uttering the opening words "What will we do now?"— words which resonate far beyond their immediate fictional scope in significance—the superior officer, the presiding figure of authority, throws up his hands and abdicates. This abdication is as crucial to the story as that visual counterpoint, the "chalk-blue face." The adjutant, the one who might rightfully be expected to have the answers, has no answers: for Timothy Lean there is no one to "lean" on, no oracle, however tarnished, to consult for answers.

Instead, questions beset Lean: the senior officer's questions, Lean's questions, and that ultimate question mark, the upturned face, constituting at once an urgent personal appeal and an impersonal, inscrutable source of anxiety. Neither the adjutant nor Lean knows how to answer these various questions. Neither one remembers the burial service (so much for the slim security of protocol). Neither is familiar with even the practical aspects of interring a corpse, let alone the ritual.

Their uncertainties regarding the burial are complicated by their unwillingness to accept their friend's death—an unwillingness implicit in the way they defer covering him up. Similarly, the fear engendered by their exposed position is compounded by a metaphysical fear of the unknown (death in the abstract as well as the unseen enemy sharpshooters)—a fear which is concretized and concentrated in the dead man's chalk-blue visage. This fear of the unknown is dramatized by Crane's depiction of the contending armies. The Rostina sharpshooters, we are told, have the exact range of Lean's troops; "Lean's prostrate company of Spitzbergen infantry" is, on the other hand, "firing measured volleys." Victims of invisible marksmen, they go through the motions of returning the fire, but their retaliation is blind and perfunctory. This image of inadequacy and vulnerability is reiterated in the sudden anxiety of the privates whom Lean orders to dig the grave. "The men, thus caused to lower their glances to the turf, became hurried and frightened merely because they could not look to see whence the bullets came."

Lean's composure almost fails at the point where he recites what little he can remember of the burial service:

> "Perceive, we beseech, O, Father, the little flying bubble and—"
> Lean . . . stopped with a hopeless feeling and looked at the corpse.

Clearly the irony becomes unbearable. Where is this Father? How will the little flying bubble make it safely through the gunfire? The plight (like the image) is cruel; man is insignificant, vulnerable.

It is against this entire, unspeakable state of affairs that

Lean explodes when he curses the pathetic and indecisive adjutant. His insubordinate outburst, directed against the only figure of authority in evidence, is the Expressionist shriek par excellence—a cry of mutiny, conveying the affronted sensibility of man at that moment during which the modern world dawns on him in all its senselessness and horror.

From the moment of that utterance, Lean is, for all intents, alone. Even the catharsis of open defiance is limited: the spell of hysteria is not broken. The face remains, waiting to be dealt with. The "plop" of mud on the dead man's face yanks us back from subjective involvement to a distanced, cosmic perspective, unmasking man's meager worth in a universe bereft of all authority, justice, or humanity save that brought to it by the individual. It is perhaps Crane's bitterest irony.

What finally distinguishes **"The Upturned Face"** is Crane's personalized treatment of this abstract vision. While the vision itself can be recognized in other of Crane's works, nowhere else is it rendered so intensely. Lean and the adjutant exist as human characters, afraid to touch a corpse, in a way that many characters in Crane's earlier sketches never do. Moreover, such kindred visions as **"An Experiment in Misery"** and **"The Men in the Storm"** fail to achieve the emotional force that sets this work apart.

Crane's Expressionist vision also embodies many techniques later employed in Expressionist art and drama. Here we would do well to recall Crane's letter to Pinker in which he envisions the story as a thirty-minute stage piece. Some techniques **"The Upturned Face"** shares with Expressionist theater include the use of lurid visual effects ("the chalk-blue face"), an ambience of darkness, grotesqueness, and unreality, the use of disturbing aural effects (the "whiz" and "crack" of bullets, the "plop" of mud), and an almost theatrical emphasis on dialogue culminating in a climactic outburst—verbal outcry being a literal as well as a figurative motif in Expressionist statement.

With regard to dialogue, **"The Upturned Face"** features broken, fragmented speech, a stylistic device common to Expressionist theater:

> The adjutant began to babble. "Well, of course . . . a man we've messed with all these years . . . impossible . . . you can't, you know, leave your intimate friends rotting on the field. . . . Go on, for God's sake, and shovel, *you*." (The ellipses are Crane's.)

In addition, Lean's own telegraphic speech tends toward "the harsh, heartless and aggressive economy of . . . dialogue, which . . . was to become one of the most important styles prevailing in Expressionism" [Walter H. Sokel, *The Writer in Extremis: Expressionism in Twentieth-Century German Literature* (1959)].

Also of Expressionist stamp is the ambiguous rendering of setting and character in **"The Upturned Face."** We know nothing of the war being described—neither when, where, nor why it is being fought—and next to nothing of the characters involved, especially the dead man. When characters and situations are deindividualized to such an extent, the reader is invited (if not compelled) to consider

them in an abstract light. Such paring down of situation and character to the essence is central to Expressionism. Thus, Kokoschka's *Murderer the Women's Hope* calls for a cast of "Persons," consisting of a "man," a "woman," and a "chorus" of "men *and* women." Similarly, the setting is unspecified, denoted merely as "black ground" and "tower" against a "night sky."

Addressing a different medium, Ludwig Meidner writes of the pictorial necessity for a focal point in Expressionist painting. "The focal point is vital for the composition," he writes; "It is the most intense part of the picture and the climax of the design" [Ludwig Meidner, "An Introduction to Painting Big Cities," *Voices of German Expressionism,* edited by Victor H. Meisel (1970)]. Crane, whether consciously or not, employs such a focal point: the pastel face. This image acts like a visual magnet. Like Socrates' wounded foot in *Alkibiades Saved,* the face is a perpetual mute reminder of a grim reality underlying every action.

Moreover, the dead man's face constitutes a virtual mask. Yvan Goll, in an important document of Expressionist theater entitled "Two Superdramas," writes: "We have forgotten entirely that the primary symbol of the theatre is the mask." According to Goll, the mask is significant in two respects. The first of these is that "In the mask lies a law, and this is the law of drama. Non-reality becomes fact" [translated by Walter H. Sokel in his *Anthology of German Expressionist Drama* (1963)]. Goll is addressing the metaphoric function of Expressionist theater—the projection of abstract ideas into symbols that Sokel has discussed. His viewpoint is seconded by Paul Kornfeld's "Epilogue to the Actor": "Let him [the actor] not deny the theatre or try to feign reality. . . . Let him . . . pick out the essential attributes of reality and be nothing but a representative of thought, feeling, or fate!" [In Sokel's *Anthology of German Expressionist Drama*]. This concept approximates myth, as does Crane's story. **"The Upturned Face"** portrays an archetypal situation, man confronting his own insignificance in a hostile universe, rather than a Naturalistic slice of army life or a sample of "what war is really like." The face, in particular, is not so much a specific face, with three days' growth and a tooth missing, as it is a chalk-blue abstraction, a death mask.

The second significance of the mask, according to Goll, is its ability to shock:

> Art . . . to be in any way effective, must slay workaday man; it must frighten him as the mask frightens the child, as Euripides frightened the Athenians who staggered from the theatre. . . . Man . . . should learn to cry again.

In **"The Upturned Face,"** we are left with "two men . . . at the edge of hysteria, Lean stuttering, the adjutant crying out, pale, to go on" (Berryman). It is the sight of the grotesque face that sustains the tension and reduces the officers to the verge of collapse, curdling the reader's blood meanwhile. (pp. 152-57)

Crane shared with the Impressionists a concern with the inscrutability and mutability of reality as perceived by the senses—a concern which informs nearly all his mature work from **"The Open Boat"** to **"The Blue Hotel"** to *The Red Badge of Courage.* Yet if the dominant chord in his work is an Impressionist concern with reality, the subdominant strain may well be an Expressionist refusal to accept the bitter implications a reality thus coldly viewed holds for man.

Ultimately, this notion of Expressionism must be seen as part of a larger process: namely, a change in peoples' attitude with respect to the world and their place in it. [James B.] Colvert notes, for instance, in his discussion of *The Red Badge of Courage* ["Structure and Theme in Stephen Crane's Fiction," see *Modern Fiction Studies* entry in Further Reading list]:

> The novel treats four stages in Fleming's growth toward moral maturity. In the beginning he is unable to distinguish between his heroic dreams and hopes and the actual condition of war. Then follows a period of confusion and doubt. . . . Next he goes through a period of desperate but futile struggle. . . . In the end . . . he learns to see the world in its true light . . . to bring his subjectivity into harmony with the reality which his experience makes clear to him.

This ontogenesis is no more than a capsular version of every man's emotional entry into the modern world. Individual stories may reflect a part of this process, if not the whole. Various fictional postures (Naturalism, Impressionism, Expressionism) may reflect particular aspects of this process. Yet in the end the entire process must be viewed and synthesized if Crane's fiction is to be responsibly assessed. (pp. 160-61)

> *Bill Christophersen, "Stephen Crane's 'The Upturned Face' as Expressionist Fiction," in* Arizona Quarterly, *Vol. 38, No. 2, Summer, 1982, pp. 147-61.*

John R. Cooley (essay date 1982)

[*Cooley is an American author and essayist who has written about contemporary American literature, Harlem Renaissance writers, and the depiction of black characters in works by white writers. In the following excerpt from his* Savages and Naturals, *Cooley discusses Crane's depiction of the character Henry in "The Monster," finding that while he succeeds as a well-defined character in the early sections of the story, he loses definition in the later sections because of distancing by the author.*]

Crane's portrait of the black coachman Henry Johnson [in **"The Monster"**] is a far cry from the blatantly racist portraits of writers such as Thomas Dixon and Charles Carroll. Crane brings to this work the complexity of theme, finely honed irony, and depths of human compassion associated with the best of his writing. In **"The Monster"** he attempts to distinguish between the savagery of civilized whites in their reaction to a disfigured black man and the very unsavage, unmonsterlike reality of his life.

At the time of its publication William Dean Howells gave the novella high praise, although many other critics have disfavored it. In a perceptive contemporary discussion of the novella, Donald Gibson has termed it "in certain respects . . . the most ambitious piece Crane ever attempted." It is, as Gibson and many others have commented, Crane's most critical portrait of society. Not only does the story reveal the pettiness, the ingrained fears, and prejudices of white America, it provides a dilemma

through which to test the moral fiber of a man of principle. This man is Dr. Trescott, physician in the town of Whilomville, New York, and Stephen Crane's portrait of a "good man," a man even Christlike in character. The second hero of the novel is Henry Johnson, Dr. Trescott's black coachman, who saves the good doctor's son by carrying him through the burning inferno of the Trescott house. Charles Mayer expresses the heroic twinship of employer and employee in this way: Trescott's "moral act is the counterpoint of Henry's physical heroism." The thrust of most discussions of **"The Monster,"** however, has been to examine the interplay between Trescott and the Whilomville community and largely to overlook the hero and "villain" of the story, Henry Johnson. (pp. 38-9)

The issue here is how sensitively does this brilliant social realist portray the black servant who is the focal center of his novel? Is Crane able to establish and maintain a counter-distinction between public opinion of his character and the complex, anguished, private reality of this man? It is not enough to say that Crane attempted a difficult task in exploring race relations and moral values; the final test will be of Crane's own integrity to the character of Henry Johnson. One may turn to Ralph Ellison's *Invisible Man* or Richard Wright's *Native Son* for comparison. Ellison and Wright, it should be said, never lose sight of their protagonists while describing the reactions of white society to them.

In the opening pages of **"The Monster"** Crane attempts to provide a detailed and individual portrait of Henry Johnson. Henry and Dr. Trescott's son Jimmy are best of friends. Crane comments, "He grinned fraternally when he saw Jimmy coming. These two were pals. In regard to almost everything in life they seemed to have minds precisely alike." The insertion of "seems" saves the description from racist assumptions. The reader soon learns that Henry is more than a "pal"; he is able to console Jimmy when the boy is in trouble with his father, and even to mediate between the two. In the evenings, when Henry dresses up for town, Crane writes that he "was more like a priest arraying himself for some parade of the church." . . . Forced by society to an inferior position, he can at best imitate white society and pretend he is a gentleman. "There was no cakewalk hyperbole in it. He was simply a quiet, well-bred gentleman of position, wealth, and other achievements out for an evening's stroll." . . . Like "Nigger Jim" and Huck Finn, Henry and Jimmy are pals, but Henry is also seen here as an adult and an actor who shifts roles frequently to make the best of his situation as a black man in a town like Whilomville.

The power of Crane's irony becomes apparent now. Henry's reception by the townsfolk stands in contrast to the portrait of him Crane has just drawn. One white man hails him with, "Hello, Henry! Going to walk for a cake tonight?" Further down the block another comments, "Why, you've got the cake right in your pocket, Henry!" Crane's intention in these comments is not certain until later in the story when his satire of the white townsfolk becomes unmistakable. The whites here are obviously not responding to the Henry Johnson whom Crane has just described but to their ingrained minstrel image of a black man "dressed up" for their entertainment rather than his own. Henry seems accustomed to this treatment; it is the way of Whilomville.

Even though Henry is among the first to reach the burning Trescott house, flames are already "roaring like a winter wind among the pines." He rushes up the flaming staircase, but by the time he has gotten little Jim, the staircase is engulfed in flames. After a moment of hesitation and panic, he recalls the back stairway that leads down and out through Dr. Trescott's laboratory. Once down the stairs, he pushes open the door to confront a garden of burning flowers. . . .

> There was an explosion at one side, and suddenly before him there reared a delicate, trembling sapphire shape like a fairy lady. With a quiet smile she blocked his path and doomed him and Jimmy. Johnson shrieked, and then ducked in the manner of his race in fights. He aimed to pass under the left guard of the sapphire lady. But she was swifter than eagles, and her talons caught in him as he plunged past her. Bowing his head as if his neck had been struck, Johnson lurched forward, twisting this way and that way. He fell on his back. The still form in the blanket flung from his arms, rolled to the edge of the floor and beneath the window. . . .

(pp. 39-41)

The great horror of the scene comes from the realization that it represents a domestic jungle that Henry, like O'Neill's Emperor Jones, must cross in order to survive. The panther flame that leaps at him, the sapphire flame of the "fairy lady," the ruby-eyed, "scintillant and writhing serpent" . . . may be seen as various manifestations of racism and inhumanity harbored in the "good" people of Whilomville. The jeers and taunts hurled at "supremely good-natured" Henry earlier in the evening were prelude to this scene and are contained in it. The flaming jungle is neither Hell nor Africa, but a white physician's laboratory. The implied savagism refers not to the black man, Henry, but to the townsfolk in their reactions to Henry's disfigurement. Crane's intended effect here is quite the opposite of the jungle portraits presented by Vachel Lindsay and Eugene O'Neill. The "writhing serpent" represents the sin of racial injustice, or more generally, all acts that debase character and subvert honest relations.

At Trescott's insistence, Henry is brought forth, "a thing which he laid on the grass." From this point on, even Crane begins referring to Henry with increasing detachment. It is at first puzzling and disturbing that Henry is maimed in the laboratory of the man whom Crane admires most among the people of Whilomville. Crane chooses to test Trescott precisely because he sees admirable qualities in the man. Trescott is the only character in **"The Monster"** who might have wisdom, humanity, and strength of character sufficient to maintain integrity and understanding during the events that follow.

The "Morning Tribune," which had sent a boy up hourly to see if Henry had yet died, finally goes to press announcing his death. Now that it seems likely he will not live, people begin referring to him as "a saint." Crane implies through this sentiment not only that a society desires to kill its heroes so that it may properly praise them, but that to the white community there is something especially noble in the sacrificial death of a black man while saving a white child. It would be comforting for the whites to believe both that blacks were born to serve and that Henry and "his race" also recognized white superiority and were willing to sacrifice their lives to protect it.

In contrast to the town's hero worship, Crane gives a very different scene at Judge Hagenthorpe's house, where Henry had been taken after the fire. His head and body, frightfully burned, are covered in bandages; all that is visible is "an eye, which unwinkingly stared at the judge." Trescott sleeps and eats at the judge's house, keeping an almost continuous vigil, doing what he can to facilitate Henry's recovery. In his desire to do the medically "right" thing, to save a life, Trescott does not consider the possible mental and physical disfigurement that might attend Henry's survival.

The judge has considered these possibilities, and comments to Trescott: " 'He will hereafter be a monster, a perfect monster'." . . . Later he adds, as his mind begins to work on the subject, " 'He will be your creation, you understand. He is purely your creation. Nature has evidently given him up. He is dead. You are restoring him to life. You are making him, and he will be a monster and with no mind'." . . . Perhaps as the judge argues, Trescott errs in struggling to save Henry. It is clear from his reply he is working partially out of self-interest. " 'He will be what you like, Judge,' cried Trescott, in a sudden polite fury, 'He will be anything, but, by God! he saved my boy'." . . . Not once does he consider the kind of life Henry could have or where he will live and who will care for him. Could the judge's comment that Trescott's act is one of the "blunders of virtue" be Crane's criticism of the doctor, despite his admiration for the man? As Hagenthorpe said, the Henry Johnson once known is dead and what emerges from the ashes depends on one's perspective. To the judge he is a blunder of indiscriminate healing; to the doctor he is a savior; to the town he is a monster.

Crane's metaphor of facelessness is analogous to Ralph Ellison's metaphor of invisibility. The former Henry Johnson is no longer, and in his stead society places its desired substitutes. "He now had no face. His face had simply been burned away," and in its place whites and blacks substitute the masks they desire. Yet his physical facelessness also brings into focus that virtual facelessness he quietly tolerated in the white community before the fire. In the passing scenes, as this process occurs, Crane juxtaposes the innocence of Henry with the monstrous inhumanity of Whilomville.

Not only is the doctor's practice dwindling as a result of gossip about Henry, but insults and threats are hurled at the family. One of his neighbors moves away in protest. Next, Trescott is visited by a self-appointed committee of four of the town's "very active and influential citizens." They have come, they say, out of friendship and concern, lest he "ruin himself " over this "silly" matter. Their message is, in essence: even if there are a lot of fools in Whilomville stirring up this mess, it is senseless for you to "ruin yourself by opposing them. You can't teach them anything, you know." . . . The members of the committee pose a considerable threat to Trescott's position, for they appear as the voices of reason and good sense. Instead, they are the voices of rationalization. Before their scrutiny all issues of moral judgment dissolve into matters of practicality and profitability. (pp. 42-4)

In Crane's world survival is difficult; survival with integrity is almost impossible. The condition of warfare is all-pervasive in his fiction. In fact, it is Crane's richest symbol for man's condition. As in *The Red Badge of Courage* and

"The Open Boat," Crane is interested here in studying man under stress. In all three works, as Sy Kahn has observed, "forging and tempering an answerable courage and code is the repetitive situation." If Trescott is as strong as he seems, he and his family will manage with Henry under their care, despite the town.

What is most regrettable about **"The Monster,"** however, is Crane's shift in emphasis in the latter half, from Henry to Dr. Trescott. For all his care to avoid stereotyping Henry, Crane retreats further and further from him as the story progresses. By the end he is almost a forgotten character, totally absent from the last ten pages of the novella. From the time of the fire, neither Crane nor his readers get near Henry again. First an unblinking eye stares out from beneath bandages, then the reader hears reports of what he has done, what he looks like, as observed from windows, open doors, porches, from the corner of a barn. As a result, Henry is removed from the center of our vision, and almost from our concern. The finely honed irony of contrast between the Henry whom Crane described and the Henry seen by the white townsfolk is lost in the latter half of **"The Monster."** The reader does not know if his face is really as hideous as described, or what humanity remains beneath the "faceless" face. For the reader Henry Johnson has become an invisible man.

Why does Crane retreat from his focus on Henry and shift his attention to Trescott? Had he created a creature he could no longer work with? Had he created, in fact, a monster rather than the outward visage of a monster? Or is Crane, the supreme ironist, not only in control of his craft but intentionally testing the reader's identification and sympathy? Perhaps he intended **"The Monster"** to read us, to see whether his readers sided emotionally with Whilomville, even if intellectually with Dr. Trescott.

The Stallman biography of Crane documents the notion that " **'The Monster'** was an appeal for brotherhood between white and black" [see Further Reading list]. In a very limited sense the story achieves this end—the fidelity of Trescott to Henry *is* admirable—but at great expense in its development and handling of black character. Unfortunately, most commentary on **"The Monster"** has forgotten to look at Crane's other black portraits or to consider the novella's treatment of race. Stallman, at least, observed that "Crane's social irony is that the white man's face is also disfigured—by white society's cruelty to the Negro." (pp. 45-6)

The literal fire and disfigurement are to stand for the real, though often disguised, injuries suffered particularly by black Americans. Yet after the fire Crane does not restore Henry for the reader. He does not distinguish between the symbolic disfigurement of Henry represented by the actual injuries and the Henry who must reside beneath the "monster" if one is to continue identifying with him. This is where Crane fails. There is nothing left of Henry for the reader to identify with; he is figuratively dead. Consequently one must shift identification and sympathy to Dr. Trescott.

Briefly consider Henry during his visit to the black community after his injury. Crane describes him here and through the remainder of the tale as "the monster," "it," "the terror"; he has Henry raise a "deprecatory claw" while addressing the Farragut women. Although they see him as the monster they have been warned about, Crane presents Henry's speech in minstrel fashion. Henry Johnson makes a succession of low and sweeping bows, scraping his feet and mumbling. . . . Instead of suffering from shock, one sees that Henry has been reduced by Crane to the comic Sambo stereotype. Yet to the other blacks of "Watermelon Alley" he has been transformed into a monster. In their desperation to get away from Henry the black residents shriek and screech; one of them even breaks her leg attempting to scale a fence. Regrettably, Crane chose to use familiar stereotypes rather than attempt the much more difficult task of detailing Henry's mental and physical injury while maintaining his humanity and individuality.

Crane's description of Alek Williams, the black man who tended Henry for a time, is even more derisive. Alek is obviously Crane's attempt at a comic black portrait. He is described as obsessively superstitious, inexcusably lazy, and continually amusing. He asks for more money from Judge Hagenthorpe because his frightened children cannot eat. They imagine Henry to be the devil. Alek stands before the judge, "scratching his wool, and beating his knee with his hat." While arguing for a raise, he "began swinging his head from side to side in the strange racial mannerism." . . . The portrait, with its comic touches and its racial generalizations, is unnecessary for the story's development and is inexcusable.

The only other glimpse of the much-altered Henry Johnson occurs in chapter twenty, where Jimmy Trescott leads his companions to the edge of the Trescott barn so they can gape at Johnson. Crane writes that Jim slowly "sidled into closer relations with *it*," referring to Henry, but fails to show even a hint of the old friendship. On a dare, Jim runs up and touches Henry. "*The monster* was crooning a weird line of negro melody that was scarcely more than a thread of sound, and *it* paid no heed to the boy" (my italics . . .). This is the reader's last glimpse of Henry Johnson. It is as if in his mental derangement he were slipping back in time, becoming more thoroughly a primitive figure. He croons softly and submits to his condition. Crane made this same point while describing the fire. "He was submitting, submitting because of his fathers, bending his mind in a most perfect slavery to this conflagration." . . . During the fire Henry chose to act and resisted the flames while he could. But now Crane has rendered him incapable of either understanding his plight or of resisting it. Whatever is to be done for Henry must either be done by the Trescotts of Crane's world or it will be done by the fools of Whilomville. (pp. 46-8)

The regrettable, though inescapable conclusion is that Crane's "monster" got away from him. He could no longer work with Henry, except at considerable distance, because he had lost the critical distinction he started with—between the monster mask and the man beneath the mask. By the end of the novella there is only mask; somewhere along the way the man had ceased to be. Even though Crane fails to sustain the portrait of Henry, his novella remains a very significant failure. Crane is most skillful, after all, in exposing the potential savagism of Whilomville toward blacks and all scapegoats, and it appears that he intended a fully developed and sustained portrait of Henry. Yet one must judge what is, not what might have been. Crane's portrait of Henry Johnson reflects an artistic maladroitness in handling a character who demanded utmost care, and in a piece of fiction otherwise finely wrought. Further, it reflects a sadly limited racial consciousness, despite all good intentions, in one of America's most astute and compassionate social realists. (p. 49)

John R. Cooley, "The Savages," in his Savages and Naturals: Black Portraits by White Writers in Modern American Literature, University of Delaware Press, 1982, pp. 37-88.

Bettina L. Knapp (essay date 1987)

[Knapp is an American educator and critic who has written numerous critical studies, chiefly of French literature. In the following excerpt from a chapter of her book Stephen Crane, Knapp provides an overview of stories in Crane's The Open Boat, and Other Tales of Adventure.]

In his short stories, Crane adheres to Poe's dictum: the tale should form a "totality . . . there should be no word written, of which the tendency, direct or indirect, is not to the one pre-established design." Like a poem, each tale forms a complete unit, every portion contributing to its final impact and effect upon the reader. Each tale is a self-contained drama. Some have a sting to them; others have an epigrammatic quality that intensifies their momentum and shattering climax. Excitement is generated by controlled, barely sensed actions, which may be nothing more than a minor occurrence, such as a blizzard. Crane's tales aim at realism. They deal with the conflict between illusion and reality or the inner and outer worlds. Neither romantic nor charming, as are Washington Irving's The Sketch Books, Crane's stories show detachment, coldness, and a remote quality, lending a mythical touch to such tales as "The Bride Comes to Yellow Sky" or "The Open Boat." A feeling for nature and for natural man is molded directly into his colorful landscapes and precise descriptions of people and things. The earthiness of his terse, colloquial dialogue is alternately humorous, sardonic, and searing. The stories' musicality also lends them a poetic and incantatory quality.

Crane did not probe his characters' souls as Hawthorne did. Instead he silhouetted them in the light of specific situations or through character traits, giving brief insights here and there. Like Twain, he injected humor into his stories—not Huckleberry Finn's light-hearted banter, but rather satire wedded to bold similes. Unlike Twain, he never romanticized his protagonists nor alluded to nostalgic moments. Crane banished sentimentality and gushy romance, opting for realistic optical images, which under scrutiny reveal the truth of a situation. In this art form, Crane is on a par with masters such as Maupassant, Flaubert, Chekhov, Tolstoy, Gogol, Melville, Hawthorne, James, and Conrad. He knew how to use form, color, and drama to heighten the desired effects. Crane was a superb verbal photographer. His close-up and distant shots, possessed of some indefinable magical powers, remain indelibly fixed in the mind's eye.

"The Pace of Youth" (1895) is situated in the seaside resort of Asbury Park, New Jersey, where the twelve-year old Crane lived with his widowed mother. It focuses on a single image of intense appeal to a child: a glittering and exciting merry-go-round, which dominates not only the events but the characters as well. Stimson is the owner of the "Mammoth Merry-Go Round," with its "whirling circle of ornamental lions, giraffes, camels, ponies, goats, resplendent with varnish and metal that caught swift reflections from windows high above them." The fabulous carousel elicits excitement and ebullience from the children, who cling to the animals on which they ride. Amid all of this joy stalks Stimson, who has learned of his daughter Lizzie's elopement with Frank, his impresario. Despite his wife's pleading, he takes his revolver and runs "hatless" to hail a hack. Once inside, he orders the driver to gallop through the streets and catch up with the buggy that Lizzie and her lover had taken moments earlier. Excitement is intensified as the two vehicles race each other. But when Stimson realizes his hack is falling behind, his hopes of stopping his daughter are dashed. "His whole expedition was the tottering of an old man upon the trail of birds," Crane explains. Age has intervened; the generation gap has made inroads in his relationship with his daughter. He represents a dying past; she, the joyous future. Stimson gives up the race. It is no use. As he makes "a gesture of acquiescence, rage, despair" he suddenly becomes aware of the fact that he forgot his hat. This detail is of monumental importance since it makes him realize that he is no longer in the running.

"One Dash—Horses" (1896) was the first of a group of tales Crane wrote about his trip to the West and Mexico. For some years he had dreamt of seeing those open spaces and endless skies. He was fascinated by the myth of this land of promise and excitement with its very different codes, customs, and characters.

"One Dash—Horses" is based on a real incident in which Crane and his guide, riding into Mexican back country, spent the evening in a local adobe tavern. When Crane saw a drunken bandit, Ramon Colorado, eyeing him, obviously thinking Crane was a "rich" American, he reached for his revolver and stared unflinchingly at the bandit. Ramon Colorado, stunned by the courage of this foreigner, seems then to have changed his mind. The arrival on the scene of girls and musicians draws the bandit's attention away from Crane and his guide, permitting them to slip out of the tavern, mount their horses, and ride away. Soon, however, they notice they are being pursued by the bandit and his cohorts. The terror in their hearts encourages them to gallop on until they meet a troop of rural militia.

Crane does not emphasize the men in his tale; instead he focuses on and humanizes the horses. For example, when the narrator, fearing for his life, drives his steed to incredible speed he looks at the animal with deep confidence, as if it also knew the danger at stake: "The little animal, unurged and quite tranquil, moving his ears this way and that way with an air of interest in the scenery, was nevertheless bounding into the eye of the breaking day with the speed of a frightened antelope." Having reached safety, the narrator again stares at his little horse and becomes aware of his deep love for the animal.

The protagonist's terror is depicted as a race against time. The speed of hoofbeats as bits and pieces of landscape flash by, the rhythmic noise of the dashing horses, the sweat and breathlessness generated by the tremendous effort being expended symbolize the chaos of the unresolved situation. In the tavern scene, for example, fear is built up

Crane in his study at Ravensbrook Villa, Oxted, Surrey, 1897.

by foreboding reds and lambent hues: "the deep silence of the pale rays of the moon" as opposed to "the red spears of the fire," shedding their tones in a room "slowly flooded to its middle with a rectangle of silver light." Through economy of words Crane achieves a work of powerful impact. (pp. 145-48)

"The Five White Mice" (1896) is a wry story that . . . features two gun-slinging, venturesome, jocular youths, the San Francisco and New York Kids. . . . After rolling up more and more aces, the New York Kid finds himself and his two drunken companions, the San Francisco Kid and Benson, facing some Mexican desperados on a street, "as dark as a whale's throat at deep sea." The sober Kid is terrified; he remembers what easterners had said about western lawlessness, about the cruelty of cowboys and desperadoes. He sees himself dead and his family grieving for him. He waits, motionless, as he observes his enemies. He is terrified at the thought that he might not be able to draw his gun quickly enough. What if he drops it at the crucial moment or it gets entangled in his coat tails? "The sober Kid saw this [Mexican] face as if it were alone in space—a yellow mask smiling in eager cruelty, in satisfaction, and above all it was lit with sinister decision." The Kid suddenly decides to step forward. He grips his revolver. Crane increases the suspense by taking a moment out to caricature the entire incident, inviting the reader into the Kid's imaginary world. "He recalled that upon its black handle was stamped a hunting scene in which a sportsman in fine leggings and a peaked cap was taking aim at a stag less

than one eighth of an inch away." The contrast between the gravity of the Kid's present situation and the romantic visions carved on the holster of his revolver encourages wry laughter along with feelings of fright at the thought of the dangers at stake. "At the supreme moment the revolver came forth as if it were greased and it arose like a feather. This somnolent machine, after months of repose, was finally looking at the breasts of men." The reader learns, in a form of interior monologue, why the Kid was filled with rage as he took aim. The Mexicans "slunk back, their eyes burning wistfully," never giving him a chance to prove his courage. "The whole thing had been an absurd imposition." They all leave. "Nothing had happened". Nothing, yet everything is compressed into that one traumatic incident: fear, self-pity, courage, and will power.

"A Man and Some Others" (1897) also deals with the trauma of sustained terror and the serenity that follows the acceptance of one's mortality. A sheepherder, Bill, decides to fight the murderers stalking him. Feelings of anxiety and alienation build as Crane focuses his camera's eye on stark background images: "Dark mesquit spread from horizon to horizon. There was no house or horseman from which a mind could evolve a city or a crowd. The world was declared to be a desert and unpeopled." Crane now fills the reader in on Bill's past, giving the present situation a sense of perspective. Bill was once the owner of a rich mine in Wyoming, but lost the mine playing poker. He then became a cowboy, gambled again, and once again found himself destitute. He then worked as a bouncer, a killer, and, finally, a sheepherder in Texas. The story now pursues its course in the present. A Stranger approaches Bill, who warns him to leave because killing is in the offing. Minutes later, some Mexicans charge Bill. The Stranger screams. "As the guns roared, Bill uttered a loud grunt, and for a moment leaned panting on his elbow, while his arm shook like a twig. Then he upreared like a great and bloody spirit of vengeance, his face lighted with the blaze of his last passion." Bill is dead.

A sense of compassion, greater, perhaps, than in Crane's previous stories, prevails in **"A Man and Some Others."** Bill's past and his laconic statements to the Stranger let the reader understand the dignity of a man who once was a killer and the ease with which life may be ended. At the end of the tale, the Stranger looks at the "body contorted, with one arm stiff in the air" that lies in his path. "Slowly and warily he moved around it, and in a moment the bushes, nodding and whispering, their leaf-faces turned toward the scene behind him, swung and swung again into stillness and the peace of the wilderness."

"The Open Boat" (1898), one of America's finest short stories, describes the adventure that satisfied Crane perhaps most fully. He said once that he wanted to go "to some quarter of the world where mail is uncertain." He did just that when he accepted Bacheller's assignment in November, 1896 to cover the Cuban Revolution. Thick fog enshrouded the St. Johns River as the Commodore set sail from Jacksonville with Crane aboard. Although Captain Edward Murphy had taken the precaution of hiring a local pilot to help the vessel out of the harbor, it struck a sand bar. The following morning, the Commodore was towed free, but Murphy neglected to review the damage done the ship, which continued on into deeper waters. By the time the leak was discovered, there was no hope of saving the ship. Although the Captain tried to steer it back to the harbor, the pumps and engines gave out and it foundered. Passengers and crew were ordered into the lifeboats. Crane's conduct during this harrowing ordeal was superb: he soothed frightened men, helped bail out water, and acted like a born sailor. After the crew was in the lifeboats, Crane, the Captain, the cook and the oiler climbed into a ten-foot-long dinghy.

Although the boat managed to stay afloat on the high seas, Crane's harrowing experience was far from over. The mate's lifeboat capsized and the men on it drowned. Crane was deeply moved by the courage of the sailors who drowned: no shrieks, no groans, only silence.

The remaining lifeboats reached land the following day. The dinghy, however, could not get ashore because of the rough surf and so remained out at sea. No one on shore could see or hear the men in the dinghy. The captain fired his pistol but to no avail, and the men were forced to spend another night in the dinghy, rowing frantically to prevent being swallowed up by the rough seas. They then decided to row to Daytona Beach and try to make it through the breakers there. But the boat overturned, and they had to swim. A man on the beach saw what happened and ran for help. All but the oiler were saved. (pp. 149-52)

Its poetry and rhythmic schemes make **"The Open Boat"** the match of Melville's "White Jacket" and the best of Jack London and Joseph Conrad. This tale's unusually punctuated sentences of contrasting length simulate the heart beat of man under extreme stress, producing an incantatory quality. Crane's sensual images of man struggling against the sea remain vivid long after the reading of **"The Open Boat."** The salt spray and deafening roar of the waves pounding against the dinghy can almost be tasted and heard.

"Flanagan and His Short Filibustering Adventure" (1898) also focuses on the sea. Written under intense pressure, the story is entertaining, but not comparable to **"The Open Boat"** in either technique or subject matter.

"The Bride Comes to Yellow Sky" (1898), however, is another masterpiece of restraint, concision, and heart-stirring drama. The action takes place mostly in the mind of Sheriff Jack Potter, who goes off to San Antonio to bring back his bride to Yellow Sky. Disquietude and guilt seem to mark his every thought and gesture during the long train trip home with his new wife. The "heinous crime" that torments Sheriff Potter is that he has not informed his friends—the citizens of Yellow Sky—about his forthcoming marriage. The personality of the groom—in contrast with the usual image of the Western sheriff who with gun and badge imposes order on a lawless society—is revealed as he looks at his bride tenderly and shyly shows her "the dazzling fittings of the coach." Although trying to impress her, the sheriff remains modest and humble. He then slips into town via the back entrance in order to keep out of sight. The couple has almost reached their home when a drunken outlaw, Scratchy Wilson, approaches them and pulls out his gun. He intends to settle his affairs by fighting Potter. "I ain't got a gun on me, Scratchy," answers the Sheriff. Scratchy doesn't believe him. How could a sheriff be unarmed? "If you ain't got a gun, why ain't you got a gun? Been to Sunday-school?" When Potter tells him he has just been married, Scratchy Wilson is stunned—he "was like a creature allowed a glimpse of another world. He moved a pace backward, and his arm with the revolver dropped to his side."

Sheriff Potter broke the frontier code in two respects: by his marriage, and being gunless. His image tarnished, he is no longer a role model. Scratchy Wilson can not conceive of living in a town with a married sheriff. As for Potter's not carrying a gun: "There ain't a man in Texas ever seen you without no gun." Like the Sheriff, whose train trip was so filled with anxiety, Scratchy is also caught in a maze. This new situation spells trepidation. A single incident serves to point up the meaning of dread, not the dread encountered in **"The Open Boat,"** but the fear of change and apprehension that comes with the shattering of illusions and preconceived notions. With humor and irony, Crane demolishes the images of the brash, aggressive, loudmouth sheriff and the blood-thirsty outlaw and creates instead the two unforgettable characters of **"The Bride Comes to Yellow Sky."** (pp. 155-56)

"The Blue Hotel" (1898), which takes place at Fort Romper, Nebraska, is another of Crane's finest tales. It has many facets. Each character plays a role in keeping with his personality. Although the narrator apprehends only some of the truths implicit in the tale, the reader, through the metaphor of the blue hotel, is able to grasp the entire picture.

The Palace Hotel in Nebraska is painted blue, a fact of utmost importance: "a light blue, a shade that is on the legs of a kind of heron, causing the bird to declare its position against any background." This premonitory image, offered the reader at the very outset of the tale, implies metaphorically the fixity and intractability of the protagonist's view of people.

A Swede enters the Blue Hotel. Like the heron in the opening image, he is anchored to his unalterable preconceptions. He is certain that the people frequenting the Blue Hotel are lawless and cruel and that he may even be killed here. He masks his terror by adopting a swaggering gait and behaving in an arrogant manner. Like several other of Crane's characters, the Swede is an easterner prejudiced against the Wild West by dime novels and not by real life. Scully, the proprietor of the hotel, reveals himself to be just the opposite of the Swede's notion of the gun-happy Westerner; in fact, he looks "curiously like an old priest." He offers the Swede warmth, hospitality, and a drink in a show of friendliness, but to no avail. The Swede continues to act aggressively and defiantly. He even insults the proprietor and the habitués. "A guest under my roof has sacred privileges," Scully says. But the friendliness Scully offers the Swede is rejected. The Swede is convinced that the Blue Hotel, which looks more like a church with its icons and stained glass windows, spells violence and death.

Scully persists; he offers the Swede a fine meal and encourages him to join a group of friendly card players. The Swede then accuses the host's son, Johnny, of cheating, and a fight breaks out. Of course, Johnny is no match for the Swede. He is knocked to the ground almost immediately and the Swede would have continued hitting him had the others not intervened.

The Swede, convinced that he is in *real* danger, leaves the Blue Hotel in a blizzard to search for a safe place. "In front of it [another bar] an indomitable red light was burning, and the snow-flakes were made blood-color as they flew through the circumscribed territory of the lamp's shining." Another premonitory image: the red light presages blood and death. The Swede enters the "sanded expanse before him" and pours himself a whiskey. He then begins boasting of having "thumped the soul out of a man down here at Scully's hotel." Those present "encased themselves in reserve" and when the Swede invites the guests—a gambler, businessmen, a district attorney, and others—to drink with him, they refuse with "quiet dignity." Enraged by their rejection, the Swede virtually explodes. Putting his hand on the shoulder of the gambler, he invites him once again to drink with him and is once again refused. "What? You won't drink with me, you little dude! I'll make you!" the Swede roars, holding the gambler by the throat and dragging him from his chair.

> There was a great tumult, and then was seen a long blade in the hand of the gambler. It shot forward, and a human body, this citadel of virtue, wisdom, power, was pierced as easily as if it had been a melon. The Swede fell with a cry of supreme astonishment.

The story does not end with this. Crane must add his dash of irony. The gambler is given three years in prison for murder. As for Johnny of the Blue Hotel, he *had* cheated, the reader learns, but because "the game was only for fun." The guest who actually saw the sleight of hand had said nothing. Everyone, then, is guilty of the Swede's murder, Crane suggests—the criminal who did the stabbing as well as the collective who did nothing to prevent it.

Fear, masked by arrogance, and the impossibility of modifying role models are the themes of **"The Blue Hotel."** The fierce, graphic descriptions of the howling blizzard reproduce the nerve-shattering momentum built up within the hotel. The tale revolves around the Swede, who harangues and assaults the other guests, projecting his own inadequacies upon them. Because he wants to give the impression of being strong and virile, he has built up a paranoic system of defenses against presumed enemies. Scully, the spiritual leader of the hotel group, prevents an outbreak of violence as long as it is humanly possible. The Swede's heavy drinking, begun in the Blue Hotel, continues in the saloon. He feels manic elation over his victory in his fight with Johnny. The blinding snowstorm symbolizes the Swede's lack of vision, his inability to see into himself and, therefore, into others. He is unable to assimilate the kindness he was shown at the Blue Hotel; nor can he interpret the harsh atmosphere of the saloon. Like the heron of the opening image, he stands fixed in his ideas, oblivious to his surroundings, and it is his rigidity and blindness that cause his death.

Like **"The Open Boat," "The Blue Hotel"** deals with the theme of brotherhood as well as that of hostility. The Swede is given shelter from the storm, and is invited into a community of friendly people. But because they failed to understand the meaning behind the Swede's hostile behavior, the other characters are as blind and set in their ways as the Swede. As Crane suggested, **"The Blue Hotel"** is "a whirling, fire-smitten, ice-locked, disease-stricken space-lost bulb"—a microcosm of society and the world.

Fascinated by the dichotomies of eastern and western landscapes, of wild and churning seas, Crane, like Melville, Poe, and Conrad, uses his painter's eye to reveal strikingly vast spaces and war-torn areas. His verbal canvases, marked in blues, whites, reds, ochres, browns and blacks, portray scrubby ranges, low hills, blinding snows, and ferocious seas. He uses the detail to reveal the whole; he scrutinizes the isolated incident to explain the larger drama. He reveals a personality type in a swift and often elliptical manner, a situation in stonelike, language divested of all extraneous elements. (pp. 158-62)

> *Bettina L. Knapp, in her* Stephen Crane, *Ungar, 1987, 198 p.*

David S. Gross   (essay date 1988)

[*In the following excerpt, Gross focuses on Crane's Western stories and relates themes and elements of style in these tales to those elements in the literary works of Naturalism, Modernism, and Postmodernism.*]

In this essay I shall seek to relate both the themes, the meanings of Crane's stories and, especially, his narrative strategies, the forms of discourse he employs, to the dominant naturalism of his day, to the modernism which was just then emerging and even to the postmodernist positions of our day. These categories are of course not formal, strictly philosophical positions, but rather refer to literary and artistic styles, schools, movements which embody or show the influence of (stand in a parallel position to) various philosophical movements. These include the American pragmatism of Dewey or James, the logical positivism which followed (naturalism), existentialism after Kierkegaard, Heideger and Nietzsche (modernism) or the linguistic-based analytical philosophy of Pierce, the late Wittgenstein, Derrida and others which has become so influential (postmodernism).

What makes Crane remarkable, and sets him apart immediately from the watered down naturalism which dominated in both the academic and the popular culture of his day, is that while he situates his stories within such a discursive formation, and even gives passionate assent to some of its tenets, he subjects it all the while to devastating ironic scrutiny. Crane agrees with the aspect of what I have called naturalism which deals in the debunking of revealed truth—the "positive" or progressive aspect of what Adorno and Horkheimer call the *dialectic* of the Enlightenment [Max Horkheimer and Theodor W. Adorno, *Dialectic of Enlightenment* (1973)]. This issue centers on the critique of modes of thought and discourse which for centuries were deformed and dominated by religion, by what the progressives of the Enlightenment usually called "superstition." This defiant critical thought allowed for the broadening of what Bakhtin would call the conceptual horizons of the dominant belief systems of the day; this *critical*, active side of what would become naturalism thus constituted a key component in the enabling conditions, the ideological conditions of possibility of both the French Revolution and hopes for a revolutionary transformation toward social justice in the years since then.

But the other side of the dialectic of the enlightenment is the "instrumental view." Adorno, Horkheimer and other participants in the theoretical project of the Frankfort school like Marcuse and, more recently, Habermas have placed great stress on the inhuman, destructive side of so-called "Progress," the manipulative, cold-blooded and mechanistic side of a triumphant rationalism. This is Blake's Urizenic "single-vision," Shelley's "excess of the calculating faculty", a blindly confident bourgeois rationalism, which translates as "Chamber of Commerce" boosterism politically, the "scientific" view, so central to dominant thought and discourse that it might properly be said to constitute the cultural logic of high capitalism. This is the authoritative position, one which would brook no argument, what Bakhtin calls "the word of the father."

Both sides of the Enlightenment are strongly present in the thought and cultural practice of naturalism, a movement which, in fiction, achieved a brief period of greatness in the last quarter of the nineteenth century, especially in France and England, in the influential novels of Emile Zola and Thomas Hardy. In America the movement never produced "world class" major texts like Zola's and Hardy's, though certain novels of Upton Sinclair, Frank Norris and others have achieved near-canonical status, and both domestically and from across the Atlantic the movement exerted significant influence on American culture. Fiction in the naturalist mode in this country generally tended to rely heavily on mechanistic determinism and the melodramatic, sensationalist plot devices of commercial popular fiction. In fact, as Fredric Jameson has pointed out, the most significant legacy of the naturalist movement here was the creation of the epistomological givens, the conditions of narrative possibility of the popu-

lar novel. The naturalism which was "in the air" in Crane's time included thus the assumptions of popular fiction, the point of view of a good part of the non-fiction as well, both in serious essays in a place like the *Atlantic* or in philosophical journals and in journalistic reportage in the popular press. This movement in thought and cultural practice contained many contradictory elements, and embodied both the liberating and the repressive sides of its Enlightenment heritage.

Crane's position is this: he likes the hard-nosed pragmatism of the empirical, "common sense" version of naturalism, which assumes the absurdity of any faith-based moral order or belief in an a priori *meaning* in human life or in the universe. Crane wants to accept naturalism and agree with the view that will become central to the "scientific" view in the social sciences and logical positivism in philosophy, to the extent that it supports his atheistic debunking of any naively confident and positive view of human social existence and "progress." Thus the power of nature, exterior to human will and purpose. This belief is everywhere a significant element in Crane's stories, perhaps most centrally not in the Westerns but in **"The Open Boat."** Crane seeks always to emphasize the vanity of any grand view of human will and purpose where we might be seen as natural lords and rulers of the universe and the planet. The power of natural forces—the weather, the sea—are key elements in the non-human or even inhuman world we are shown to inhabit in Crane's stories.

But such natural forces are not the only elements of this world Crane shows us where causal forces seem to operate so independently of human volition or desire. The forces of chance are also important to Crane's debunking of a simplistic positivism which is so central to naturalism and to main-stream modern thought in general. Beyond that, though, Crane's ironic vision calls into question simplistic notions of progress or truth through his foregrounding and questioning of the conventions and cliches of culture (revealing them to be part of a powerful, inhuman order), and even the individualistic notions of the self which are so difficult to see and to critique, so central are they to the hegemonic cultural logic of capitalism.

Luck, chance, the aleatory, uncanny, the throw of the dice—hints and traces of everything that is powerful and exterior to the human—these are the elements in Crane's work that take it beyond naturalism and the hegemonic dominant view and link it to both modernism and postmodernism in ways that still seem unusual and new, which some readers still find disturbing. In the Introduction to the Signet Classic edition of **The Western Stories of Stephen Crane** the editor, Frank Bergon, says of this side of Crane:

> Crane's concern with the importance of luck in the outcome of individual showdowns differs from that of most Westerns, where victories are traditionally due to merit. Most distinctive of **"One Dash—Horses"** however is that at moments of the story's greatest intensity, the author breaks into the narrative in his own voice with a direct address to the reader or a comic aside or an unexpected wisecrack that destroys the immediacy of the drama.

Bergon continues his discussion by observing of one such interruption in the story: "There are few readers who have not been troubled by" it. I think readers with a taste for postmodernist narrative strategies will be likely to find such moments in Crane's stories not merely disturbing but fascinating and effective. This "weird" side of Crane is most noticeable in certain formal strategies, discursive devices—something about the narrative voice. It is most pronounced and strange-seeming in certain passages of exposition which go so far as to comment not only on the fictional nature of all narrative, foregrounding the formal artifice of "the Western," but even to the point of talking about key events in the story in terms of grammar, as in the famous passage near the end of **"The Blue Hotel"** where "the Easterner" and "the cowboy" are discussing the killing of the Swede and other events in the story. The Easterner observes: "We are all in it! This poor gambler isn't even a noun. He is a kind of an adverb. Every sin is the result of a collaboration."

Crane's metaphors make explicit his belief in the priority of discourse, that the way we form our words about something is almost totally dominant and determining in what we think to be true about it. Thus Crane joins modern thought after Nietzsche and Saussure in its insistence on the shaping power of culture—Levi-Strauss' notion of the self as an "effect of structure," culture thinking us. Crane makes that dialectical leap away from a dominant and hegemonic naturalism to an as yet explosive and subversive modernism again and again by foregrounding the discursive strategies in his stories and in all stories, by explicitly raising questions about the genre of "the Western" within his masterful employment of it.

As I observed before, this side of Crane usually shows itself in passages of exposition, and is conveyed by something strange in the narrative voice. Crane describes it himself within a passage of exposition describing the discourse of Scully the saloon keeper in **"The Blue Hotel."** "Scully's speech was always a combination of Irish brogue and idiom, Western twang and idiom, and scraps of curiously formal diction taken from the story-books and newspapers."

There is certainly no Irish brogue in the narrative voice I am talking about, but there certainly is "Western twang and idiom," as well as the idiom and perspective of the jaded, cynical big-city newspaperman from the East, and, especially, "strange scraps of curiously formal diction" taken from journalistic reportage and other non-fictional forms as well as the style of the popular Western of Bret Harte and others. Some good examples can be drawn from the magnificently extended chase scene in **"One Dash—Horses."** Crane had himself come West looking for "the West" in 1895, and had been chased by a band of Mexican desperados on that occasion. Here Richardson, his autobiographical American protagonist, and Jose, his Mexican servant, are in just that situation, racing across the desert at dawn, fleeing a pack of outlaws who have been terrorizing them all night in a tiny Mexican village. In the middle of the chase scene Crane begins a paragraph like this "Jose's moans and cries amounted to a university course in theology. They broke constantly from his quivering lips. His spurs were as motors." Here is the next paragraph in its entirety:

> Crimson serapes in the distance resembled drops of blood on the great cloth of plain. Richardson began to dream of all possible chances. Although quite a humane man, he did not once think of his servant.

> Jose being a Mexican, it was natural that he should be killed in Mexico; but for himself, a New Yorker—He remembered all the tales of such races for life, and he thought them badly written.

In both the comment on the university course in theology and the reference to "the tales of such races for life," Crane is calling our attention to the discursive formations, patterns of discourse and culture which dominate our thinking, even as he demonstrates their inadequacy, and even their absurdity.

In **"A Man and Some Others"** there is a chapter which contains a major piece of the action in the story which is entirely without dialogue, direct discourse, which begins and ends with the kind of self-conscious inflated rhetoric—at once ironic, even self-ironic and sincerely meant and uttered—which I have been presenting. In this story two Americans—one an "Easterner" of the sort of transparent stand-ins for himself which he used so often, and the main character, a former strikebusting brakeman, management thug and New York saloon keeper who has ended up as a sheep-herder in West Texas—are ambushed at night by a band of Mexicans who have been trying to drive the American off the range. Earlier in the story Crane had laconically observed, "Strange and still strange are the laws of fate." In this chapter he begins with a passage of description which includes the following:

> Finally, when the great moon climbed the heavens and cast its ghostly radiance upon the bushes, it made a new and more brilliant crimson of the camp-fire, where the flames capered merrily through its mesquite (sic) branches, filling the silence with the fire chorus, an ancient melody which surely bears a message of the inconsequence of individual tragedy—a message that is in the boom of the sea, the sliver of the wind through the grass-blades, the silken clash of hemlock boughs.

In a few swift paragraphs of very effective, highly economical narrative description, Crane describes the attack of the Mexicans. They gleefully shoot full of holes what they take to be the sheepherder's defenseless sleeping body, only to find out too late that they have been shooting into a dummy, when one of their number is laid low by a shot which rings out in the dark. They flee in the night, and Crane ends the chapter with explicit repetition:

> The silence returned to the wilderness. The tired flames faintly illumined the blanketed thing and the flung corpse of the marauder, and sang the fire chorus, the ancient melody which bears the message of the inconsequence of human tragedy.

This tone and the point of view it expresses links Crane clearly with Existentialism, as well as with all those varieties of modern thought in which the power of language, of discourse is emphasized. Always in Crane it is a matter of the shaping power of language, especially the language and belief system of the popular Western and the Horatio Alger self-help literature of the time. Crane derides the false simplicities and easy assurances of such forms of discourse even as he emphasizes their shaping power—the action and interaction, mutual influence and interpenetration of texts and textualities. This is not an idealist view which would assert that there is nothing but texts, no reality outside of thought and its formations, but rather a powerful awareness that all our notions of truth and of meaning are always textual.

What links Crane to modernism and postmodernism then is this concentration on language and culture, and on the cultural constitution of the subject. It is, in fact, this trait in Crane which is so startlingly postmodern, his central focus on "the problem of the subject." A central focus of contemporary theory has been the problematic nature of the subject—what we mean when we say "I." To problematize our notion of the self calls into question ideological notions of "identity," all the various forms of bourgeois individualism and the fetish of "the individual"; all that constitutes one of the principle components of that movement in thought and cultural practice to which the name "postmodernism" has been given. . . . Derrida and others have made the subject or the self a primary focus of their deconstructive project, following Nietzsche in subjecting to ruthless criticism and exposure the illusions of selfhood or identity as some mysterious given (of genetics or some other aspect of "fate") rather than as the specific product of certain material practices and experience such as institutions or cultural formations. Since Freud the delusions of the (bourgeois) ego have been exposed as such (whence his famous claim to have accomplished a third Copernican revolution, following the astronomer's disclosure that "man" was not the center of the universe, and Darwin's that "He" is but one species among many, to have shown "him" that he is not even master in his own house). More recently, Jacques Lacan's theories describing the self or ego as a product of insertion (inscription) into the symbolic order and his project of the "decentering of the subject" have been a major influence in postmodernist thought.

Crane seems clearly to have realized the importance of these matters, at just about the same time that Freud was beginning to develop them theoretically. His greatest story, **"The Blue Hotel"** is almost exclusively focused on the ways in which the Swede as subject is constantly foregrounded and called into question. He wants/expects the West he has arrived in—Nebraska in the winter in a blizzard—to be the West of the Western—and he's both right and wrong to expect that, insane to expect it, absolutely correct in his expectations. His "paranoia" as outsider is fully justified both in terms of the way they all turn on him and cheer openly for his adversary in his fist fight in the snow with Scully's son Johnnie, and in the way he is killed by the gambler at the end of the day. And in turning on him as they do the leading citizens in the tavern—like the hotel proprietor and representative entrepreneur Scully, the Cowboy, and the Easterner/reporter/Crane figure enact the dark, ugly side of the Western myth of the frontier. There the absence of civilization is felt in the blandishments of Scully as capitalist seller of his services, as in the cynical refusal to get involved of the saloon keeper and the Easterner—and in the individualist indifference and ability to ignore another's plight which characterizes them all.

The Swede is crazy because his attempt to enter the symbolic order of "the West" by means of discursive strategies governed by the generic conventions of the popular Western don't work; while he decodes properly, the residents resent him as outsider and refuse to grant that he's got the West right. Thus Crane is part of postmodernism not only

in his profound understanding of "the problem of the subject" as embodied in the Swede and who he thinks he is and has to be in "the West," but in his "nihilistic" deconstruction of the project of philosophy as a whole, his conviction as to the inadequacy of all theoretical attempts to configure reality in a way that does not lie.

There is something that mocks all reliable meaning in those strange, laconic, straightforward statements, addressing the reader directly in passages or brief moments of exposition which I have concentrated on here. Near the end of **"The Blue Hotel"** Crane has the Swede say to the patrons of the saloon, one of whose seemingly peaceable number will in a few minutes murder him with a knife for having laid a hand on his shoulder uninvited: "Yes, I like this weather. I like it. It suits me." Crane then observes, "It was apparently his design to impart a deep significance to these words." The cumulative effect of such interventions in the text is most strange, what Bergon calls "disturbing." They foreground the language, problematize the everyday cultural practices, formations of discourse which are normally taken for granted—like remarks about the weather. And somehow, at the same time in the precise context within which they occur (this is the uncanny, that something in the narrative voice) they contribute to a radical deconstruction of all abstract thought, including the theoretical project to which my essay attempts to contribute.

At the very end of **"The Blue Hotel,"** after the passage about characters in the story as noun and adverb cited before, Crane has "the cowboy" cry out his expression of empty bravado, confusion and refusal of responsibility "into this fog of mysterious theory." Mysterious or stupid or mystifying theory would seem to characterize Crane's view of the philosophies whereby humans seek to make sense of their lives, even as he recognizes that we cannot not think within such cultural formations. Like Nietzsche, and like modern deconstruction, Crane seems to feel that he has done all he can if he can deconstruct the myths and other patterns which give shape to desire and to fear, so that in that reflexive awareness may be the beginning of the difficult project of getting beyond those particular cultural formations, toward some other ones, which might not be based on such primitive and destructive versions of what it means to be human.

In a letter to a friend written immediately after his trip out West in 1895 Crane seeks to disassociate himself from the view of culture of the eastern United States, "a detestable superficial culture which I think is the real barbarism." (Crane's phrase is a remarkable anticipation of Walter Benjamin's famous remark, that "there is no document of civilization which is not at the same time a document of barbarism.") In that context he offers this striking definition: "Culture in its true sense, I take it, is the comprehension of the man at one's shoulder." All of Crane's work seems the fruit of that project of understanding, comprehension. And he took nothing for granted as he sought to understand human beings and the way they make sense of their world. For that reason he sought always to make us see and understand the role of language and of what is called culture in constituting us as the persons we take ourselves to be. (pp. 16-20)

David S. Gross, "The Western Stories of Ste-

phen Crane," in Journal of American Culture, *Vol. 11, No. 4, Winter, 1988, pp. 15-21.*

FURTHER READING

Adams, Richard P. "Naturalistic Fiction: 'The Open Boat'." *Tulane Studies in English* IV, (1954): 137-46.
Focuses on what Adams views as deliberate inconsistencies in Crane's view of nature in "The Open Boat" as simultaneously indifferent to and organically united with humanity. Adams considers this conflict fundamental to all Naturalistic literature.

Anderson, Sherwood. Introduction to *The Work of Stephen Crane: Midnight Sketches and Other Impressions,* edited by Wilson Follett, vol. XI, pp. xi-xv. New York: Russell and Russell, 1926.
Brief, appreciative, and impressionistic introduction to Crane as a writer.

Bassan, Maurice, ed. *Stephen Crane: A Collection of Critical Essays.* Englewood Cliffs, N.J.: Prentice-Hall, 1967, 184 p.
Collection of previously published criticism on Crane, including pieces on his short fiction by Bassan, William Bysshe Stein, and Daniel Weiss.

Beer, Thomas. *Stephen Crane: A Study in American Letters.* 1923. Reprint. New York: Octagon Books, 1972, 248 p.
First Crane biography. Beer's biographical work was enthusiastically accepted when it was first published, for it closed many of the curious biographical gaps in Crane's life. Though more recent biographers and critics point out factual errors in the book, it is still generally regarded as an important contribution to Crane studies.

Berryman, John. *Stephen Crane.* The American Men of Letters Series. n.c.: William Sloane Associates, 1950, 347 p.
Biography that amended some of the inaccuracies of the first Crane biography by Thomas Beer (see above in Further Reading list).

Brown, Bill. "Interlude: The Agony of Play in 'The Open Boat'." *Arizona Quarterly* 45, No. 3 (Autumn 1989): 23-46.
Examines the many possible meanings and applications of "play" as occasioned by the narrator's statement in "The Open Boat" that, "an overturned boat in the surf is not a plaything to a swimming man."

Cather, Willa. Introduction to *The Works of Stephen Crane: Wounds in the Rain,* edited by Wilson Follett, vol. IX, pp. ix-xiv. New York: Russell and Russell, 1926.
Finds Crane to be an Impressionist who is "the best of our writers in what is called 'description' because he is the least describing."

Collins, Michael J. "Realism and Romance in the Western Stories of Stephen Crane." In *Under the Sun: Myth and Realism in Western American Literature,* edited by Barbara Howard Meldrum, pp. 138-49. New York: The Whitston Publishing Co., 1985.
Analysis of "The Five White Mice," "The Bride Comes to Yellow Sky," and "The Blue Hotel." Collins posits

that in these works Crane applied elements of the Western romance form to realistic content, creating an "ironic myth" that illuminates reality.

Cox, James Trammell. "Stephen Crane As Symbolist Naturalist: An Analysis of 'The Blue Hotel'." *Modern Fiction Studies* III, No. 2 (Summer 1957): 147-58.
Detailed analysis of "The Blue Hotel" which determines that Crane's "fictional method is that of the symbolist rather than the naturalist." Cox regards the "stove" as the central symbol of this short story.

Ditsky, John. "The Music in 'The Open Boat'." *North Dakota Quarterly* 56, No. 1 (Winter 1988): 119-30.
Discusses elements of musicality in Crane's text, using principles of the relationship between literature and music as presented by Anthony Burgess in his book of essays *This Man and Music* (1974).

Ellison, Ralph. "Stephen Crane and the Mainstream of American Fiction." In his *Shadow and Act,* pp. 60-76. New York: Random House, 1964.
Examines *The Red Badge of Courage* and several Crane short stories as an expression of Crane's moral struggle and his depiction of social reality.

Follett, Wilson. Introduction to his *The Work of Stephen Crane: "The Monster" and "The Third Violet",* Vol. III, pp. ix-xxii. New York: Russell and Russell, 1925.
Through comparison of these two works, Follett arrives at the generalization about Crane's writing that "the story which is personal is weak, and the story which is impersonal is a thing of power."

Garnett, Edward. "Stephen Crane and His Work." In his *Friday Nights: Literary Criticisms and Appreciations,* pp. 201-17. New York: Alfred A. Knopf, 1922.
Appreciation of Crane's work, including commentary on his short fiction.

Gibson, Donald B. *The Fiction of Stephen Crane.* Carbondale and Edwardsville: Southern Illinois University Press, 1968, 169 p.
Thorough and balanced interpretive study of Crane's fiction.

Gullason, Thomas A., ed. *Stephen Crane's Career: Perspectives and Evaluations.* New York: New York University Press, 1972, 532 p.
Valuable and comprehensive collection of essays which includes reminiscences, early criticism of Crane's works, and a wide range of more recent interpretive studies. Also included in this book are four Sunday school stories by Crane's father, Reverend Jonathan Townley Crane.

Hafley, James. " 'The Monster' and the Art of Stephen Crane." *Accent* XIX, No. 3 (Summer 1959): 159-65.
Sees Crane's "The Monster" as an examination of moral values. In this regard Hafley finds the short story similar to "The Open Boat" and "The Blue Hotel."

Hagemann, E. R. "Crane's 'Real' War in His Short Stories." *American Quarterly* VIII, No. 4 (Winter 1956): 356-67.
According to Hagemann, his purpose in this essay is "to indicate specifically the facets of war as Crane understood them and presented them in his short stories," dividing his analysis into six parts: "(1) the individual soldier, (2) the lure of violence, (3) the effect of continual

warfare on the soldier, (4) heroism and duty, (5) death, (6) and the violation of the natural scene."

Katz, Joseph, ed. *Stephen Crane in Transition: Centenary Essays.* Dekalb, Ill.: Northern Illinois University Press, 1972, 247 p.

Collection of essays published here for the first time. Includes criticism on the short stories by E. R. Hagemann and Max Westerbrook.

Kent, Thomas L. "The Problem of Knowledge in 'The Open Boat' and 'The Blue Hotel'." *American Literary Realism: 1870-1910* XIV, No. 2 (Autumn 1981): 262-68.

Describes "how epistemological uncertainty is generated for both the reader outside the texts and the characters within the tales."

Linson, Corwin K. *My Stephen Crane.* Syracuse, N.Y.: Syracuse University Press, 1958, 115 p.

Lyrical, intimate portrait of Crane by an esteemed American painter and close friend, covering the years 1891 to 1895.

McFarland, Ronald E. "The Hospitality Code and Crane's 'The Blue Hotel'." *Studies in Short Fiction* 18, No. 4 (Fall 1981): 447-51.

Thorough study of the hospitality motif in Crane's short story "The Blue Hotel."

Metzger, Charles R. "Realistic Devices in Stephen Crane's 'The Open Boat'." *The Midwest Quarterly* IV, No. 1 (October 1962): 47-54.

Argues through an examination of realistic elements in "The Open Boat" that Crane's masterpiece is "a very realistic piece of writing."

Modern Fiction Studies, Stephen Crane Number V, No. 3 (Autumn 1959): 195-291.

Issue devoted to Crane studies by notable Crane critics such as Eric Solomon, Thomas Gullason, and R. W. Stallman. This special issue includes interpretive essays on *The Red Badge of Courage, Maggie: A Girl of the Streets,* and "The Blue Hotel," among others.

Morace, Robert A. "Games, Play, and Entertainments in Stephen Crane's 'The Monster'." *Studies in American Fiction* 9, No. 1 (Spring 1981): 65-81.

Contends that in "The Monster" adults and children participate in games on both conscious and unconscious levels and in both frivolous and serious matters, perpetuating misconceptions about other characters as well as their own self-delusions.

Munson, Gorham B. "Prose for Fiction: Stephen Crane." In his *Style and Form in American Prose,* pp. 159-70. Garden City, N.Y.: Doubleday, Doran and Co., 1929.

Utilizes Crane's stories "The Open Boat" and "The Reluctant Voyagers" as examples of appropriate and inappropriate tone in literature. Munson also discusses the art of reading in terms of differences between "verbal" and "experiential" reading.

Nagel, James. "The Narrative Method of 'The Open Boat'." *Revue des Langues Vivantes* 39, (1973-75): 409-17.

Explores Crane's narrative techniques in "The Open Boat," particularly in regard to shifts in point of view.

Proudfit, Charles L. "Parataxic Distortion and Group Pro-

cess in Stephen Crane's 'The Blue Hotel'." *University of Hartford* 15, No. 1 (1983): 47-53.

Illustrates how "The Blue Hotel" dramatizes what psychiatrist Harry Stack Sullivan has termed "the parataxic mode" in interpersonal relationships.

Roth, Russell. "A Tree in Winter: The Short Fiction of Stephen Crane." *New Mexico Quarterly* XXIII, No. 2 (Summer 1953): 188-96.

Asserts that in Crane, "puritanism and the spirit of place have merged: he has struck even deeper roots into his native soil than Twain."

Satterwhite, Joseph N. "Stephen Crane's 'The Blue Hotel': The Failure of Understanding." *Modern Fiction Studies* II, No. 4 (Winter 1956-57): 238-41.

Satterwhite proposes that "The Blue Hotel" develops the theme that "society, by its failure or refusal to understand individuals within it, can as effectively destroy a man as can the sea. The [protagonist of this story] is as much a victim of his environment as is Billy the oiler whom the surf destroys in 'The Open Boat'."

Schirmer, Gregory A. "Becoming Interpreters: The Importance of Tone in Crane's 'The Open Boat'." *American Literary Realism: 1870-1910* XV, No. 2 (Autumn 1982): 221-31.

Examines the narrator's changing voice throughout "The Open Boat" as a reflection of the tension and interplay between the view of man as helpless and insignificant in an indifferent universe, and that of men bound together in the face of that indifference.

Stallman, Robert Wooster, ed. *Stephen Crane: An Omnibus.* New York: Alfred A. Knopf, 1952, 703 p.

Anthology of Crane's works with critical introductions written by Stallman.

——. *Stephen Crane: A Biography.* New York: George Braziller, 1968, 664 p.

Comprehensive biography which updates the earlier Crane biographies of Thomas Beer and John Berryman. Stallman's book includes a helpful bibliography and checklist of Crane's work.

——. *Stephen Crane: A Critical Bibliography.* Ames, Iowa: The Iowa State University Press, 1972, 642 p.

Comprehensive annotated bibliography of works by and about Crane.

Starrett, Vincent. Introduction to *Men, Women and Boats,* by Stephen Crane, pp. 9-20. New York: The Modern Library, 1921.

Introduction to an influential early collection of Crane's short fiction that deeply effected a revival in Crane studies. Starrett provides a brief personal overview of Crane's literary life and career, proclaiming a preference for Crane's short stories over his novels and poems.

Van Doren, Carl. "Stephen Crane." *The American Mercury* I, No. 1 (January 1924): 11-14.

Perceptive assessment of Crane's literary contribution. Van Doren maintains that Crane's literary canon was the beginning of modern American literature.

Warner, Michael D. "Value, Agency, and Stephen Crane's 'The Monster'." *Nineteenth-Century Fiction* 40, No. 1 (June 1985): 76-93.

Warner analyzes what he regards as contradictions in

Crane's attitudes toward his characters in "The Monster."

Weatherford, Richard M. *Stephen Crane: The Critical Heritage.* The Critical Heritage Series, edited by B. C. Southam. London: Routledge & Kegan Paul, 1973, 343 p.

Collection of early critical reviews of Crane's works, including several of his short story collections.

Isak Dinesen

1885-1962

(Pseudonym of Baroness Karen Christentze von Blixen-Finecke; also wrote under the pseudonyms Tania Blixen, Osceola, and Pierre Adrézel) Danish short story writer, memoirist, novelist, and translator.

Considered among the most accomplished Danish authors of the twentieth century, Dinesen drew upon Gothic, Decadent, and Romantic literary conventions for her atmospheric short stories. According to critics, her tales transform reality into artifice, achieving what Lionel Trilling characterized as "an air that leads [the reader] to believe that they are involved with truth of a kind not available to minds that submit to strict veracity." To augment her often fantastic plots, Dinesen frequently distanced her tales temporally and geographically, using eighteenth- and nineteenth-century Europe, China, and Persia as settings. Her characters are similarly exotic, often appearing as grotesque yet heroic figures, defined by an aristocratic moral code. Frequently caught up in events beyond their immediate understanding, these men and women ultimately perceive themselves as participants in a tragicomedy authored by God. Eric O. Johannesson observed that in Dinesen's fiction, "all of life becomes a great story in which we human beings have our own little story to enact to the best of our ability and knowledge. The characters who have faith in the story are rewarded with a sign or an image, discover their identity, and accept their destiny. Some of them are tragic figures, others are comic; but whether they are villains, victims, or fools does not seem to matter in the long run, for ultimately they are all marionettes and thus in the hands of God and the storyteller."

Born to wealthy parents in Rungsted, Denmark, Dinesen was ten years old when her father committed suicide. According to Parmenia Miguel, her official biographer, Dinesen reflected that upon her father's death she "was pushed into the foremost row of life, bereft of the joy and irresponsibility of childhood." Tutored at home by a series of governesses, Dinesen demonstrated an early aptitude for languages, drama, and art. In 1903, she entered the Royal Academie of Fine Arts in Copenhagen to study painting, a pursuit that influenced the intricate descriptive style of her fiction. Dinesen left the Acadamie a few years later and began writing. In 1907 she published her first tales in the Danish periodical *Tilskueron* under the pseudonym Osceola, the name of her father's beloved German shepherd dog. Such early stories as "Grjotgard Älves n og Aud" (Grjotgard Älves n and Aud"), "Eneboerne" ("The Hermits"), and "Pl jeren" ("The Ploughman") intertwine romance with nature and the supernatural, while "Familien de Cats" ("Family de Cats") satirizes bourgeois pretensions. During this period, Dinesen fell in love with her second cousin, Hans von Blixen-Finecke, who, to her disappointment, did not return her feelings. As a result, Dinesen left Denmark to live in France and later Italy. Upon returning to Denmark in 1912, however, Dinesen unexpectedly announced her engagement to Hans's twin brother, Baron Bror von Blixen-Finecke. In 1913, with advice

and capital provided by Dinesen's family, Blixen journeyed to British East Africa and purchased a six-thousand-acre coffee farm outside Nairobi, Kenya. Dinesen joined her fiancé early the following year, and the couple were promptly married.

Dinesen adjusted well to life in Africa, often going on safari with her husband and socializing with British aristocrats, who later inspired many of her fictional characters. Dinesen also developed an abiding interest in and admiration for the native Africans employed on her farm, particularly her personal servant, Farah, who became her friend and confidant. Several months after her arrival, however, Dinesen contracted syphilis from her unfaithful husband. She returned briefly to Denmark for treatment, and though the primary symptoms were arrested, the disease continued to affect her throughout her life. In Africa, her husband's infidelity persisted, while the farm suffered numerous financial setbacks. Her family eventually dismissed Blixen and appointed Dinesen as the sole manager of what became known as the Karen Coffee Company. Although Dinesen refused to divorce her husband, writing in a letter to her brother that "there is far, far too much binding us together from all the years of difficulty we have shared here," Blixen himself ultimately initiated their divorce. In 1918 Dinesen met Denys Finch Hatton, a free-spirited British pilot and hunter who became her lover and the primary audience for her tales. In the years that followed, the financial condition of the Karen Coffee Company worsened. Dinesen later recalled in *Daguerreotypes, and Other Essays,* "During my last months in Africa, as it became clear to me that I could not keep the farm, I had started writing at night, to get my mind off the things which in the daytime it had gone over a hundred times, and on a new track." In 1931 Dinesen auctioned the farm and, later that year, learned that Finch Hatton had been killed when his plane crashed in Taganyika. Both these and many other of Dinesen's African experiences are recounted in her two lyrical memoirs, *Out of Africa* and *Shadows on the Grass.*

Dinesen continued to write after returning to Denmark, adopting as a pseudonym her maiden name and the Hebrew word Isak, meaning "one who laughs." As with later volumes, she composed the stories of her first collection, *Seven Gothic Tales,* in English, the language she spoke while in Africa, then translated them into Danish. While *Seven Gothic Tales* garnered considerable critical accolades in the United States and Great Britain, Danish reviewers dismissed the collection, citing its lack of social and psychological realism then favored by most Danish writers. In the decades following its publication, however, commentators from Dinesen's homeland have increasingly regarded *Seven Gothic Tales* as among the most original and important contributions to their contemporary literature.

Many critics compare *Seven Gothic Tales* to the *Arabian Nights* and the *Decamaron.* Like these and other works based in an oral tradition, *Seven Gothic Tales* emphasizes action and description rather than overt intellectual analysis. In "The Roads Round Pisa," for example, Dinesen intertwines tales of religious fanaticism, romantic intrigue, and murder as she chronicles the adventures of a duke in early nineteenth-century Italy. Critics also discern the influence of the oral tradition in Dinesen's assertion that only through story telling can humanity emulate divinity. Donald Hannah commented: "[The narrator] is turned into a surrogate for God, omniscient and all-powerful in the world he has created by his edict. And his word is not to be gainsaid. All tribulation is finally justified by the revelation of the design, and by the quality of [his] imagination displayed through this revelation." Such a revelation occurs in "The Deluge at Norderney" when a Cardinal directs his aristocratic companions to give up their places on a boat to peasants during a flood. Stranded in a hayloft as a result, the Cardinal suggests that they pass the time by telling their life stories. After each character divulges their innermost secrets, the cardinal reveals that he is in fact a murderous imposter. He then compares himself to Jesus Christ, another man, according to the masquerading cardinal, whose elaborately designed ruse saved the lives of others.

Along with *Out of Africa,* Dinesen's next collection of short stories, *Winter's Tales,* solidified her standing in the Danish literary community. While greatly similar to *Seven Gothic Tales,* this collection features a simpler narrative style and more easily recognizable settings as evidenced in such stories as "The Young Man with the Carnation" and "The Invincible Slave-Owners." Perhaps the best-known short story from *Winter's Tales* is "Sorrow-Acre," which is based upon a medieval folktale and set in eighteenth-century Denmark. In this story, a lord promises to spare the life of a serf convicted of stealing if the prisoner's mother mows an acre of grain in one day, a task normally performed by three men. Although the lord's enlightened nephew protests, the mother accepts and clears the acre by sunset only to die as she completes the task. Considered among Dinesen's most successful short stories, "Sorrow-Acre" shows, according to Robert Langbaum, "what such a manorial culture was like and how different its values were from ours—[suggests], one gathers from the story, that you cannot speak of the past as evil since our ideas of good and evil have changed." Following *Winter's Tales,* Dinesen composed two more collections of short stories, *Last Tales* and *Anecdotes of Destiny,* the latter of which contains, among other stories, the noted "Babette's Feast." Although both collections elicited critical praise, most commentators agree that *Seven Gothic Tales* and *Winter's Tales* constitute Dinesen's most significant contributions to the short story genre.

In her later years, Dinesen became an icon of Danish literature, accepting younger authors into her home in Rungsted, Denmark, and giving public lectures despite her fragile health. In 1962 she succumbed to emaciation, the result of her long struggle with syphilis. Evaluations of her work following her death have often centered upon her memoirs of Africa, yet most critics assert that her short story collections will remain her most respected literary achievements. While occasionally impugning the elitist tenor of her stories, commentators laud her artistry, imagination, and wit as enduring aspects of her fiction. Aage Henriksen wrote in her *Isak Dinesen/Karen Blixen* that "the qualities that have led to Karen Blixen's literary fame are the first ones to strike the readers of her stories. The exquisite and refined narrative manner and the mysterious and fantastic elements of their plots have given her readers a somewhat intimidating impression of her: Karen Blixen as the aristocrat and sybil in Danish literature, the great anachronism who manages to combine old culture with archaic unculture. But this portrait reveals only half the truth, and it suffers a bit from banality. There is much spirit in Karen Blixen's writings, but not so much witchcraft as people have tended to impute to them; she enchants without bewitching. And her aristocratic manner never outweighs her piety."

(For further information on Dinesen's life and career, see *Contemporary Literary Criticism,* Vols. 10, 29; *Contemporary Authors,* Vols. 25-28, rev. ed.; *Contemporary Authors New Revision Series,* Vol. 22; and *Contemporary Authors Permanent Series,* Vol. 2.)

PRINCIPAL WORKS

SHORT FICTION

Seven Gothic Tales 1934
Winter's Tales 1942
Last Tales 1957
Anecdotes of Destiny 1958
Osceola 1962

OTHER MAJOR WORKS

Sandhedens Haevn (drama) 1936
Out of Africa (memoir) 1937
Gengaeldelsens Veje (novel) 1944
 [*The Angelic Avengers,* 1946]
Skygger paa Graesset (memoir) 1960
 [*Shadows on the Grass,* 1961]
Daguerreotypes, and Other Essays (nonfiction) 1979

Mark Van Doren (essay date 1934)

[*The winner of the Pulitzer Prize for poetry in 1940, Van Doren was among the most prolific American authors of the twentieth century. He composed poetry, novels, short stories, plays, and criticism while editing numerous popular anthologies. He also wrote accomplished studies of Shakespeare, John Dryden, Nathaniel Hawthorne, and Henry David Thoreau and served as the literary editor and film critic for the* Nation *during the 1920s and 1930s. Van Doren's criticism is aimed at the general reader, rather than the scholar or specialist, and is noted for its lively perception and wide interest. Like his poetry and fiction, his criticism consistently examines the inner, idealistic life of the individual. In the following excerpt, Van Doren praises the short stories of* Seven Gothic Tales *as original, ornate portraits of a mythical world.*]

If, as Dorothy Canfield lets fall, the pseudonymous author of [***Seven Gothic Tales***] is a continental European "writing in English although that is not native to his pen," we have here a linguistic triumph for which there is probably no precedent. Barring a few slips from idiom which are so attractive as to seem premeditated, the English of the book is such as I for one have never seen written by a foreigner to the language, and none too often by those in the grammar born. And if, as rumor has it, the author is a Danish woman who never wrote a book before, we have a phenomenon so astonishing as to be incredible. Not that I disbelieve it, for of a person, man or woman, Dane or Albanian, who can write like this I am willing to believe any miracle.

The time of the tales is the nineteenth century, usually before 1850, and the place is Europe—Denmark, Italy, France, or Switzerland, though the prevailing skies are northern; the people have such names as Nat-og-Dag, De Coninck, Pellegrina, and Pozentiani. As for the stories themselves, they are mad after a peculiar fashion which gives the most modern possible meaning to the second word in the title. When Horace Walpole and his contemporaries called their stories "Gothic" they referred to the presence in them of oversized specters whose antics were reminders of some great, fantastic period long since past. This later author must refer, then, to the presence in her tales of such eccentric and overdeveloped personalities as seem already, now that we are in for an age of righteousness when the simplest men shall lead us, practically prehistoric. The individual, we hear, is out of date. Well, here he is as once he was—heightened, of course, in order to be visible at all, but heroic in his waywardness and splendid in his decay. Here are people whom fortune and genius have so specialized and refined that their cruelty, their kindness, their ugliness, their beauty, their fanaticism, their fairness, or whatever it is that has shaped them into these forms, is in itself art. They are a gallery of portraits out of that age which Matthew Arnold helped to define when he wrote an essay about "Doing As One Likes." These are Arnold's barbarian aristocrats, doing as they like in a world which quaintly suffers them to be as grotesque and fascinating as mankind can manage to be. The Europe of the book is perhaps that Europe which so many prophets say is dying on its feet. But what feet, and what fine words before the head and shoulders fall!

Isak Dinesen is a twentieth-century Zélide who manifests all the sensibilities and despairs of the time. One of her people, Mira the story-teller, regrets that he has grown silent as he has lost his fears. "When you know what things are really like you can make no poems about them. . . . I have become too familiar with life; it can no longer delude me into believing that one thing is much worse than another. The day and the dark, an enemy and a friend—I know them to be about the same." Yet something is left to Mira. "Every night, as soon as I sleep I dream. And in my dreams I still know fear." So Isak Dinesen can be supposed to have dreamed these tales; they sound like that, they are both luminous and plastic, both phosphorescent and marmoreal; and they would appear to be the final expedient of one who had no other way of proving that the world still is, or within a century was, no less exciting than it used to be. Episodes are piled upon episodes, or wrapped around the body of a tale like so many bands of silken leopard hide; personalities, announced at the start as perverse, grow to heroic stature as swift sentences develop an appropriately astonishing prose theme. Everywhere the prose is cool, certain, comprehending, disenchanted. Morten De Coninck, returning as a ghost to his father's mansion, declares: "We have been amateurs in saying no, little sisters. But God can say no. Good God, how he can say no. We think that he can go on no longer, not even he. But he goes on, and says no once more." Cardinal Hamilcar, or rather the man in bloody bandages whom we take to be the Cardinal, knows how to speak of a civilization which seems to him to have lost the glory of an ancient time when there were other and better gods: "No human being with a feeling for greatness can possibly believe that the God who created the stars, the sea, and the desert, the poet Homer and the giraffe, is the same God who is now making, and upholding, the King of Belgium, the Poetical School of Schwaben, and the moral ideas of our day."

The time has come, they say, when we must look with abhorrence upon a novelist who wastes any more talent upon characters who are laws unto themselves. May there be a moment, however, for these utterly graceful and outrageous people of Isak Dinesen. It is possible that we shall never see their like again.

Mark Van Doren, "They Do as They Like," in The Nation, *New York, Vol. CXXXVIII, No. 3589, April 18, 1934, p 449.*

Eric O. Johannesson (essay date 1961)

[*In the following excerpt from his* The World of Isak Dinesen, *Johannesson reviews the primary characteristics of Dinesen's short fiction.*]

"I have always thought that I would have cut a figure at

the time of the plague of Florence." This quotation from *Out of Africa* suggests the kind of role that Isak Dinesen has conceived for herself. Like Selma Lagerlöf, who liked to regard her audience as children listening to stories, Isak Dinesen has always imagined herself in the classic role of the storyteller, as a modern Scheherazade. Her tales are so imbued with the spirit of storytelling that one might venture to assert that the basic theme running through them all is, in fact, the storyteller's defense of the art of the story.

It was evidently the long droughts of Africa that made Dinesen into a storyteller. Because she felt the need of collecting her energy, she began, she says, "in the evening to write stories, fairy-tales and romances, that would take my mind a long way off, to other countries and times." These were stories that she had previously told to her friends, particularly to Denys Finch-Hatton, for Denys, says Dinesen, "had a trait of character which to me was very precious, he liked to hear a story told."

The storyteller needs an audience, and in this respect Dinesen was fortunate. In Africa she found eager listeners among the natives. While the art of listening to stories has been lost in Europe, Dinesen maintains, "the Natives of Africa, who cannot read, have still got it; if you begin to them: 'There was a man who walked out on the plain and there he met another man,' you have them all with you, their minds running upon the unknown track of the men on the plain." Together, her friends and the natives must have encouraged Dinesen's faith in the story, in "something you can tell. Like one can *tell Ali Baba and the Forty Thieves* but one could never *tell Anna Karenina.*"

The reference to the *Arabian Nights* is not without significance. The stories that make up this immortal collection are, as Dinesen suggests, dependent on the oral tradition of storytelling, they are tales to be told. Moreover, they are told with a specific purpose: they are told in order to change the morbid mind and cold heart of the King. In accomplishing this purpose, they also indirectly proclaim the power of the story.

It is, as Hans Brix has said, difficult to trace with certainty specific influences on Dinesen's tales because her heritage as storyteller is so vast and varied. She is, as she puts it, three thousand years old because she is telling the old tales over again. The stories of the Bible, the Norse sagas, the *Odyssey,* the classic collections of folk tales: they have all stimulated her imagination and influenced her manner of storytelling.

Still, if one were to single out the work that has meant the most to Isak Dinesen, it would undoubtedly be the *Arabian Nights*. Dinesen's tales are replete with allusions to this book, and she often employs the exotic Orient as the setting for her tales. Haroun al Raschid is often referred to: his habit of masquerading has appealed to the imagination of a writer who loves to cultivate this histrionic habit. The philosophy of Islam with its emphasis on acceptance seems to have influenced Dinesen profoundly. In Africa, on the farm, the people about her must have seemed like some of the figures in the *Arabian Nights,* and their attitudes to life, for which she expresses great understanding, like those of faithful Mohammedans.

The stories in the *Arabian Nights* are arabesques in the true sense of the word. They are intricate stories woven around interlaced tales. Many of Dinesen's tales resemble such arabesques, intricate embroideries with stories within the story. The Gothic tales, in particular, belong to this type. (pp. 8-10)

Dinesen's tales, like the stories in the *Arabian Nights,* proclaim the belief in the all but magic power of the story to provide man with a new vision and a renewed faith in life. Her figures are often Hamlet figures, melancholy young men or women who wait for fate to lend them a helping hand, who wait for the storyteller to provide them with a destiny by placing them in a story, or by telling them a story. The degree of probability or improbability of the tale is of little consequence, for in a world transformed by fantasy all is possible.

While the influence of the *Arabian Nights* on the art of Isak Dinesen seems the most profound and far-reaching, there are undoubtedly many other works of art that have left their marks on her mode of storytelling. The Book of Job, the *Decameron,* the comedies of Shakespeare, the tales of Voltaire and E. T. A. Hoffmann, of Alfred de Vigny and Barbey d'Aurevilly, the novels and tales of Walter Scott, Stendhal, Robert Louis Stevenson, Selma Lagerlöf, and Joseph Conrad: all of these, and many others, have probably influenced the art of Dinesen in one way or another. Her tales are a veritable gold mine for students of comparative literature.

Among the writers of the works listed above some are novelists, but most of them are, primarily, writers of tales. The names that are conspicuously absent are those of the creators of the modern psychological novel, the novel that cannot be *told*. In Dinesen's conception of fiction the story and the psychological novel are at opposite poles.

In several of the *Last Tales* Isak Dinesen has, contrary to her practice, made some very explicit and significant comments about her own art. Embedded in these tales is an eloquent defense of the story, of romance.

In one of these, **"The Cardinal's First Tale,"** a lady who has just been listening to Cardinal Salviati's story of his life remarks:

> Your Eminence, in answer to a question, has been telling me a story, in which my friend and teacher is the hero. I see the hero of the story very clearly, as if luminous even, and on a higher plane. But my teacher and adviser—and my friend—is farther away than before. He no more looks to me quite human, and alas, I am not sure that I am not afraid of him.

The Cardinal feels "that is all in the order of things," but adds:

> I see, today, a new art of narration, a novel literature and category of belles-lettres, dawning upon the world. It is indeed, already with us, and it has gained great favor amongst the readers of our time. And this new art and literature—for the sake of the individual characters in the story, and in order to keep close to them and not be afraid—will be ready to sacrifice the story itself.

The Cardinal then goes on to praise the novel as "a noble art, a great, earnest and ambitious human product." "But," he continues, "it is a human product. The divine art is the story. In the beginning was the story."

He further maintains that "a story has a hero to it," while "by the time when the new literature shall reign supreme you will have no more stories, you will have no more heroes." "The world," he says, "will have to do without them, sadly, until the hour when divine powers shall see fit, once more, to make a story for a hero to appear in." The disappearance of the story is followed by the disappearance of the heroine, the hero's prize and reward: "By the time when you have no more stories," says the Cardinal, "your young women will be the prize and reward of nobody and nothing. Indeed, I doubt whether by then you will have any young women at all." The hero will "see his lady disrobed of her story or her epos and, all naked, turned into an individual."

The story, the divine art, is different. "The story," says the Cardinal, "according to its essence and plan, moves and places these two young people, hero and heroine,— together with their confidants and competitors, friends, foes and fools—and goes on." The story provides for the hero and for the heroine but "does not slacken its speed to occupy itself with the mien or bearing of its characters, but goes on" toward its "promised end."

The latter remark occasions the lady to remonstrate against this approach to storytelling. "What you call the divine art," she tells the Cardinal, "to me seems a hard and cruel game, which maltreats and mocks its human beings." To which the Cardinal makes this reply:

> Hard and cruel it may seem, yet we, who hold our high office as keepers and watchmen to the story, may tell you, verily, that to its human characters there is salvation in nothing else in the universe. If you tell them—you compassionate and accommodating human readers—that they may bring their distress and anguish before any other authority, you will be cruelly deceiving and mocking them. For within our whole universe the story only has authority to answer that cry of heart of its characters, that one cry of heart of each of them: *"Who am I?"*

This eloquent dialogue in defense of the story presents an interesting argument. Most readers, like the lady, would probably disagree with the Cardinal's point of view, arguing that the modern psychological novel, which seeks to give the illusion of the very flow of the human consciousness, brings us closer to a definition of character. Still, an eminent critic such as Lionel Trilling seems to feel that the Cardinal's argument is quite valid. . . . [He] comments with regard to the dialogue in **"The Cardinal's First Tale"**: "The less concerned with story we have become, and the more concerned we are with characters and with understanding them, the less we have been able to perceive and conceive character." . . . (pp. 10-13)

In the story fate is character: the story moves the hero and the heroine and their attendants toward the "promised end," the moment when they discover the answer to their quest for identity. The storyteller is responsible for his characters, for he is the authority before whom they "may bring their distress and anguish." The storyteller must provide a destiny for his hero or his heroine, and he does this by putting them into a story. The greatest happiness from the hero's point of view is to become part of a story. Many of Dinesen's characters express their delight at having finally entered into a story.

In **"The Diver"** the "happy" man listening to the poet's story about Saufe, the theology student who once tried to make himself a pair of wings in order to be like the angels, turns out to be that same Saufe. Having heard the poet's story, he says:

> Once I had the welfare of the Softa Saufe, of whom you have just told me, much at heart. By this time I had almost forgotten him. But I am pleased to know that he has got into a story, for that is probably what he was made for, and in future I shall leave him therein confidently. Go on with your tale, Mira Jama, story-teller, and let me hear the end of it.

Whether the stories are true or not does not matter in the least, which is fortunate, since Dinesen's stories are, in the words of Trilling, "all lies. Their matter is magic and witchcraft, infants exchanged at birth, brothers and sisters who marry unknown to each other, beautiful giantesses, undying passions,—suchlike nonsense." The tales are told, as Trilling says, "with an air that leads us to believe that they are involved with truth of a kind not available to minds that submit to strict veracity." Dinesen's stories are often contrived and improbable, but in the skillful hands of the storyteller the characters are brought to their appointed end, to the moment of insight.

Some readers undoubtedly feel, like the compassionate lady in **"The Cardinal's First Tale,"** that Dinesen's approach to storytelling is "a hard and cruel game" because it reduces the characters, the human beings in the story, to marionettes, to puppets moved by "divine powers" and their representative, the storyteller, "the keeper and watchman to the story." In Dinesen's tales life itself becomes a marionette comedy, and the figures appear like such marionettes.

One of the remarkable features of Dinesen's style is the use of images, and one of the most common types suggests a mechanical or artificial behavior or being.

In **"The Deluge at Norderney"** the movements of the four central figures in the boat are compared to those of "four marionettes pulled by the same wire." Calypso von Platen-Hallermund finds her uncle asleep in his bed, only "a poor little doll stuffed with sawdust, a caricature of a skull."

In **"The Old Chevalier"** Baron von Brackel thinks of the husband of his former mistress as "the gigantic shadow, upon the white back-curtain, of an absurd little punchinello." Nathalie is compared to a doll, and the Baron thinks that "her bright painted cheeks looked even more like a doll's above her fair naked body."

In **"The Monkey"** Boris sees himself in his mind, "in his white uniform, as a marionette, pulled alternately by the deadly determined old lady and the deadly determined young lady." (pp. 14-16)

If Dinesen's human figures are described as if they were marionettes, they are also treated like marionettes. They become involved in patterns of events so fantastic that they are not able to grasp the significance of these events while they are taking place. However, in the end they are rewarded, they are rewarded with an insight into their problems. Thus it would not be correct to argue that they are reduced to being mere marionettes. Paradoxically enough, their marionette status lifts them to a higher plane. Dinesen's tales tend, in fact, to become epiphanies because they concentrate on the turning point in human experience, the moment when the truth is revealed and we see in a flash the pattern of meaning. Though they are often as fantastic and as improbable as the intrigues of opera librettos, these tales do bring this epiphany to the characters.

A few years ago W. H. Auden published some reflections on opera and drama which seem particularly relevant in this context. "The librettist," says Auden,

> need never bother his head, as the dramatist must, about probability. A credible situation in opera means a situation in which it is credible that someone should sing. A good libretto plot is a melodrama in both the strict and the conventional sense of the word; it offers as many opportunities as possible for the characters to be swept off their feet by placing them in situations which are too tragic or too fantastic for "words." [*Partisan Review,* January-February, 1952]

This statement seems very relevant here. In Dinesen's tales a credible situation is, I think, a situation in which it is credible that someone should tell a story. The plot seems often but a reason for getting some people together so that they can tell stories.

Auden continues with the remark that the golden age of opera, from Mozart to Verdi, "coincided with the golden age of liberal humanism, of unquestioning belief in freedom and progress." Since we no longer live in such an age some have hazarded the opinion that operas are impossible. Auden disagrees: "That would only follow," he says, "if we should cease to believe in free will and personality altogether. Every high C accurately struck demolishes the theory that we are the irresponsible puppets of fate or chance." This seems again a statement very applicable to Dinesen's tales. Dinesen's figures often appear as mere puppets because they serve the plot, but through the story they attain to new levels of awareness, to a mating with destiny, which indicates, precisely, that they are not irresponsible puppets of fate or chance. To the high C of the opera corresponds the moment of vision or insight in the tales.

With very few exceptions Dinesen's plots serve exactly this function: they are designed to provide a central figure, or several figures, with a new vision or insight. A glance at the various tales reveals that most of them have a specific relevance to the predicament of a central observer who is himself sometimes implicated in the action. The tale as a whole, or the part of it told to him, is designed to provide him with a new vision of life. This explains, incidentally, why so many of Dinesen's central characters are melancholy dreamers, observers of life, who wait for destiny to provide them with a sign. The melancholy hero as such does not necessarily interest Isak Dinesen: she needs a melancholy figure as a focus because he is by his very nature waiting to receive an insight of some kind. He is waiting for the storyteller to move him. A few examples will illustrate this.

In one of the *Winter's Tales,* "A Consolatory Tale," the central figure is the writer Charlie Despard. As the story begins he is sitting in a café in Paris. He is in a state of utter despair, and feels that it is a curse to be a writer. His friend Aeneas arrives. During the course of the evening, the latter tells Charlie a story, "a consolatory tale," which makes him see his position as a writer in a new light. He has been given a valuable insight into life, and he will go on writing.

"The Young Man with the Carnation" is also a story about Charlie Despard. He is in a state of despair over his writing ability, and the mistake he commits in sleeping in someone else's bedroom with someone else's mistress is like a sign from God that he should not despair. When he realizes his mistake and goes over the details of the nights before, "with the experienced eye of an author of fiction, they moved him as mightily as if they had been out of one of his own books. . . . 'Almighty God,' he said from the bottom of his heart, 'as the heavens are higher than the earth, so are thy short stories higher than our short stories'." There is an expression of rapture, laughter, and delight in his face. A light has fallen upon him, and "it seemed that he was to see himself, within it, as God saw him, and under this test he had to steady himself by the table." The mistake has brought him a new insight into his own life, and into his condition as an artist.

In **"The Roads Round Pisa"** a young Dane "of melancholy disposition," Augustus von Schimmelmann, is waiting for a sign. Brooding about the truth of his life, he wonders: "But what will happen to me now? I do not know what to do with myself or my life. Can I trust to fate to hold out a helping hand to me just for once?" And he thinks of the little smelling bottle he carries in his pocket, once given to a maiden aunt of his when she was traveling in Italy. At the end of the tale he is given an identical smelling bottle by the old Lady Carlotta, and he feels that there is in this coincidence, "in this decision of fate, something which was meant for him only—a value, a depth, a resort even, in life which belonged to him alone, and which he could not share with anybody else any more than he would be able to share his dreams." His role in the marionette comedy of life has been determined. His reward for being a good marionette is—a smelling bottle.

Even the other figures in the tale come to a realization of some sort. Lady Carlotta realizes that

> . . . life is a mosaic work of the Lord's, which he keeps filling in bit by bit. If I had seen this little bit of bright color as the centerpiece, I would have understood the pattern, and would not have shaken it all to pieces so many times, and given the good Lord so much trouble in putting it together again.

The old Prince Pozentiani realizes that "we fail because we are too small." "Too small I have been," he says, "too small for the ways of God."

In **"Sorrow Acre"** the events bring to Adam a new awareness of his own destiny and a deeper understanding of life. The events of the day bring to him "a deeper sense of pity with all that lived than he had ever known." Later, "his pity with all creation" comes to include the uncle, too. Then he suddenly sees "the ways of life . . . as a twined and tangled design, complicated and mazy," and realizes that "it was not given him or any mortal to command or control it. Life and death, happiness and woe, the past and the present, were interlaced within the pattern." He realizes that all that lives must suffer, and he becomes aware of the unity of all things, "the secret which connects the phenomena of existence." He feels that "this hour was consecrated to greater emotions, to a surrender to fate and to the will of life."

In **"Alkmene"** the young squire Vilhelm comes to realize that "the forces amongst which I had been moving were mightier and more formidable than I had guessed, and that my whole world might be about to sink under me." The parson, too, seems to have had "a sudden and splendid revelation" on his deathbed, having cried out "that now he understood the ways of the Lord."

Emilie Vandamm in **"The Dreaming Child"** is also given a deeper understanding of life through a child, the dreamer Jens. She comes to realize that the boy was her own child, her and Charlie Dreyer's son. After the death of Jens she understands everything: "there is a grace in the world, such as none of us know about. The world is not a hard or severe place, as people tell us. It is not even just. You are forgiven everything. The fine things of the world you cannot wrong or harm. They are much too strong for that." She feels "the generosity of the world."

To Jensine in **"The Pearl"** the added pearl brings a new insight, a realization that she will never conquer "these people, who know neither care nor fear. It is as in the Bible; I shall bruise their heel, but they shall bruise my head."

In **"The Old Chevalier"** Baron von Brackel tells his tale to his young friend in order to illustrate a theme, recurrent in the literature of the past, which they were discussing: "namely, whether one is ever likely to get any real benefit, any lasting moral satisfaction, out of forsaking an inclination for the sake of principle."

At the end of **"The Heroine"** Frederick Lamond is provided with "such a vision of life, and of the world" as none of the faces which the great masters paint had ever given him. (pp. 19-24)

[The] majority of the tales are designed to provide a central observer with a new insight into life. These insights are of various kinds. Some figures are brought to realize the unity and interdependence of all things. Others are brought to a realization of the greatness and scope of God's imagination, and an acceptance of the fact that we are only marionettes in God's great marionette comedy. Others learn that the condition of man must be accepted as it is, though it is fraught with injustice and suffering, for God is just, and God is great. Others attain a vision of life as a noble and elevated game in which the players must obey the rules, though it entails paying a high price.

Thus Dinesen moves her figures to their appointed end. They are treated like dolls, like marionettes, but they reach a new awareness, experience a moment of recognition.

One might argue, at this point, that it is in the nature of the short story as such to concentrate on a turning point in experience, and that there is nothing unique about Dinesen's method.

There is a difference, however. If we consider, for a moment, the tales of Joseph Conrad, the difference becomes quite apparent. In the tales of Conrad the action moves inexorably toward the moment of recognition, and the crisis occurs, as Morton Dauwen Zabel says, "when, by a stroke

Dinesen in 1913, just prior to leaving Denmark for British East Africa to marry Bror Blixen.

of accident, or by an act of decision or error rising from the secret necessities of temperament, a man finds himself abruptly committed to his destiny." The moment of recognition is "the stroke by which fate compels recognition—of one's self, of reality, of illusion, error, mistaken expectation, and defeat." [*Craft and Character in Modern Fiction*]. Character is fate.

In Dinesen's tales, on the other hand, very little of what happens to a man has to do with his character, with "the secret necessities of temperament." The moment of recognition is compelled by fate. When the hero recognizes that his imagination has not been sufficient to fathom the workings of destiny, he does not regard the events which have taken place as motivated by his own nature. Unlike Conrad's heroes, who indulge, as Zabel puts it, in "long recitatives, monologues, and self-inquisitions," Dinesen's figures lack insight into their own nature: they are waiting for destiny to mold it. Thus fate comes to determine their character, providing them not only with an answer to the question "Who am I?" but also with a recognition of the nature of reality.

In treating her figures as marionettes, and in letting them discover their identities, their characters, through their fates, Dinesen has clearly revealed her dependence on the oral tradition of storytelling and romance. Her tales are, as Trilling says, "always *told* rather than written." [*The Griffin*, January, 1958]. But the characteristic qualities of Dinesen's tales are by no means peculiar to her mode of expression: they are the characteristic qualities of the tale as a literary genre.

Oral storytelling requires a narrator. Such a narrator is often present in Dinesen's tales. Very often a tale contains stories within the story: the characters are telling each other stories. In some other cases the narrator is absent, but in such instances we are, I suppose, to look upon Isak Dinesen herself as the storyteller, masquerading for Karen Blixen.

The narrator's language is highly mannered, and yet very simple, direct, and concrete. Abstract reflections are rare because the storyteller *thinks* in stories. As Dinesen has pointed out, at the heart of the story is a tale, something that can be told, rather than an idea or mood.

The storyteller's world is a world with firm outlines and distinct texture on distance. The settings, the events, the human beings that compose this world, are seen in perspective, as if from a great height, complete and perfected.

The characters are types, never individuals, never "characterless" (as Strindberg called the complex figures of his psychological dramas). They are larger than life, and their behavior is artificial and stylized. The imagistic style of the oral tale never delves deeply into their minds: abstract qualities and states of mind are rendered by means of concrete images. The minds of men are things, as it were. The names of the figures and their gestures are exaggerated. They act as if they were on the stage, plucking quotations out of the air in order to define their roles, which are often re-enactments of classical or mythical roles. The events are never unique or isolated, but have already been fitted into an orderly pattern in which they stand out very clearly within a meaningful relationship: they have become ritual and myth.

The oral tradition of storytelling seems always to depend on a certain distance between the storyteller and his materials. The tapestry quality of a story by Dinesen is dependent on this perspective. As Staffan Björck has pointed out, this distance is Dinesen's "distinguishing mark as a writer, both means and end for the art of narrative she has chosen and the superiority of which she defends so unhesitatingly." It is, as Björck says, "only through the distance that the characters derive their definite outlines, the distance in descriptive technique, the distance in time and space, the distance in degree of reality to the unreal figures of the dream, the stage, and the marionette world." [*Dagens Nyheter,* November 4, 1957]. A brief survey of the tales in regard to setting and character will indicate the accuracy of this observation.

With very few exceptions Dinesen's tales are set in the past. They are, however, not set in an indefinite past, but within a clearly defined period of time, the nineteenth century. Most of the tales bear clear indications of dates, and the greatest number of them are confined to the period between 1830 and 1875.

As far as the physical setting is concerned, Dinesen shows a decided preference for exotic milieus. Only in the **Winter's Tales** does the Danish setting seem to be predominant. France and southern Europe are the usual settings of the **Seven Gothic Tales,** and Italy is the scene of most of the **Last Tales.** Norway is the setting of several tales, and it must be remembered that in the early half of the

nineteenth century Norway was still a wild and romantic country. Eight of the tales involve very exotic scenes: the West Indies, China, Persia, the Indian Ocean.

The reason for Dinesen's use of such exotic settings is probably quite simple. The motive is undoubtedly similar to that of other writers of romance: a desire to liberate the imagination from the fetters which too familiar an environment imposes upon it.

When the English writers of Gothic tales, a Mrs. Radcliffe, a Horace Walpole, a "Monk" Lewis, chose the scenes for their tales, they usually selected an exotic setting in the past. Thus *The Mysteries of Udolpho* and *The Castle of Otranto* were set in Italy, and Lewis' *The Monk* in Spain.

"This longing for the south," says Eino Railo in his study of the Gothic writers in England, *The Haunted Castle,* "for any alien and distant setting, is typical of romanticism, and reflects the effort of their imagination to break away from the fetters of homely experience." To these Gothic writers the exotic setting was "a territory and an atmosphere where, freed from the narrow confines of their surroundings, their visions, passions and the characters with whom they dealt, could develop to dimensions that in any other connection would have been both impossible and unendurable."

It comes as no surprise that Isak Dinesen, who must have used some of these writers of Gothic tales as models for her own romances, should employ a similar type of exotic setting in order to gain an equal degree of freedom to develop her fantastic plots.

The choice of the decades around 1830 and 1840 for many of the tales is probably not without significance. This is a time of social change: the values of *l'ancien régime* are in a state of rapid decline. It is the time of Louis Philippe, of the rise of the bourgeoisie to power, of Romanticism. For Dinesen with her definite aristocratic sympathies these decades must be of particular interest.

This is also a time which saw the publication of works by a great number of the writers with whom Isak Dinesen seems to have strong affinities. Some of the novels and tales of Hans Christian Andersen appeared during these decades, as did some of the most significant novels of Stendhal. Two French aristocrats, kindred spirits of Isak Dinesen, Barbey d'Aurevilly and Alfred de Vigny, published their best works during these years. Søren Kierkegaard, also a Gothic writer in many ways, published his novel *Either-Or* in 1843, and two other writers, Edgar Allan Poe and Eugène Sue, appeared on the scene, the former with a number of fantastic tales, the latter with *The Mysteries of Paris* in 1842-43 and *The Wandering Jew* in 1845, two Gothic masterpieces.

The reason for Dinesen's placing a number of the tales in the 1870's is somewhat more difficult to explain. These tales (**"Copenhagen Season," "Babette's Feast," "The Old Chevalier"**) are usually less Gothic, more modern in spirit, and warmer in tone, if not nostalgic. They are frequently set in Paris. These tales also seem to render the actual life of the time more intimately, more concretely. One of the reasons for this is probably, as Christian Elling suggests, that these were years which Dinesen knew intimately through accounts by her father. . . . (pp. 24-9)

While the 1870's seem to have been chosen by Dinesen in order to bring the figures in the tales somewhat closer to us, the intention in most of the tales is to remove the characters from us by placing them at a great distance in time and space. For this reason we find that the specific and detailed aspects of the setting are hardly ever rendered concretely or intimately, but in a fantastic, symbolic, or stylized manner.

The fantastic setting is, of course, most common in the purely Gothic tales. We need only think of Horace Walpole's Strawberry Hill as a model. Convents, medieval castles in ruins, high mountains, deep forests, and the sea are common Gothic settings. (pp. 29-30)

In **"The Monkey"** we are introduced to Hopballehus, a fantastic two-hundred-year-old castle owned by Athena's father. To the young Boris von Schreckenstein it is a building "so enormous that it fell in with nature, and might have been a little formation of the gray rock," and he says that "it had always appealed to his imagination":

> It was in itself a fantastic place, resting upon a large plateau, with miles of avenues around it, rows of statues and fountains, built in late baroque and now baroquely dilapidated and more than half a ruin. It seemed a sort of Olympus, more Olympic still for the doom which was hanging over it.

To Boris it is "a mysterious, a glorified, abode," and when he walks into it he has a feeling "like walking into a cathedral."

Deep in the forests of East Prussia is the convent Closter Seven, the setting of the main action in **"The Monkey."** The building does not seem fantastic: the strangeness of the convent is due to the fact that it is a kind of Noah's ark. It contains:

> . . . a whole world of pets of all sorts, and was well aware of the order of precedence therein. There were here parrots and cockatoos, small dogs, graceful cats from all parts of the world, a white Angora goat, like that of Esmeralda, and purple-eyed young fallow deer. There was even a tortoise which was supposed to be more than a hundred years old.

In **"The Caryatids"** the water mill is a fantastic setting in which Childerique is introduced to magic and witchcraft by the gypsy. She thinks of the gypsy as a viper and of the mill as a viper's nest where strange and unknown powers are at work. In this story the setting mirrors Childerique's mood. We move from the idyllic forest glade with the mellow, golden light, and the green cool shade in the opening scenes, when Childerique is happy and ignorant of the curse, to the somber landscapes in the latter part of the story, with thunder and rain in the forest, when she has become acquainted with the truth about herself and her husband.

It is generally true of Dinesen's tales, as Brix maintains, that natural phenomena appear only when "they are intimately connected with the description of people." Nature and the landscape mirror terror, happiness, and sadness, reflecting various moods. The moon, winds, thunder and lightning, the night add a theatrical note which is undoubtedly intentional. The settings of most of the tales are meant to be artificial, props, backdrops for the stage on which the characters move like so many puppets. (pp. 30-32)

In some of the tales the setting is, however, purely symbolic. This is the case in **"Sorrow Acre."** Here the landscape and the buildings form a geometric figure, a pyramid, which becomes a symbolic representation of the feudal organization of life. The irregular mosaic of meadows and cornfields tells of the life of the peasants, as does "the blurred outline of thatched roofs." A little higher up lies the red-tiled church "with the faint horizontal line of white cemetery-wall" around it. The church is described as a "plain, square embodiment of the nation's trust in the justice and mercy of heaven." "But where, amongst cupular woods and groves, the lordly, pyramidal silhouette of the cut lime avenues rose in the air, there a big country house lay." The lime trees parade around the manor and form a "green pyramid," speaking of "dignity, decorum, and taste." In this setting, plainly symbolic, a story of human suffering and human dignity is unfolded, illustrating the order on which this feudal world is based.

In **"The Pearl"** the bourgeois Jensine panics at the sight of the Norwegian mountains, having believed that nature was and should be horizontal in expansion as in the low, undulating Danish landscape. In Norway she is introduced to a new dimension of life, while her husband, who knows neither fear nor terror, is at home in the vertical realm: the mountains are his playground. In this story about courage and fear the mountains are a symbolic, moral landscape.

One of the basic features of Dinesen's art is her tendency to transform all of life into artifice. Very often she looks at the landscape with a painter's eye, and it is significant to note that the author once intended to become a painter. Christian Elling comments also on the fact that Dinesen seems to use paintings as models for her descriptions of nature [*Danske Digtere i det Tyvende Aahundrede*]. (pp. 32-3)

In some cases descriptions are rendered through the use of metaphors and similes: the landscape is compared to a work of art. In **"Sorrow Acre"** it is said that "the fields, the hills, and the woods were as still as a painted landscape." In **"The Poet"** a similar type of description is used: "The rich hues of night have withdrawn, oozed away like the waves from a shore, and all the colors of daytime lie dormant in the landscape like in the paints used for pottery, which are all alike gray clay until they come out in the furnace."

The world of Isak Dinesen contains a large gallery of characters. Sometimes one character appears in several tales, but that is an exception to the rule: Augustus von Schimmelmann appears both in **"The Roads Round Pisa"** and in **"The Poet,"** and the storyteller Mira Jama both in **"The Dreamers"** and in **"The Diver."**

Most of the characters are colorful and vivid figures with splendid names, original ideas, and exciting lives. Many are aristocrats, high-ranking people of noble birth—kings, princes, and cardinals. About half of them are artists or somehow involved with the arts. Many are students of theology, highly interested in religious speculations. With regard to their character traits, they fall into a few fairly well-defined categories, or types.

The first type is the standard hero or heroine of much Romantic literature: the melancholy young man or woman, so fashionable in the literature of the 1830's and 1840's. We need only think of Kierkegaard's Frater Taciturnus or Stendhal's Lucien Leuwen. This Hamlet figure, very common in Danish literature, appears in various guises in the tales. He is the observer of life, contemplating himself thoughtfully in the mirror, wondering about the truth and the meaning of existence, unable to commit himself to any course of action, waiting for fate to lend him a helping hand.

Thus Count Augustus von Schimmelmann sits in an *osteria* near Pisa waiting for fate to give him a sign. He is said to be "of melancholy disposition," and he contemplates himself thoughtfully in a little pocket mirror on several occasions. He thinks about truth. Some years later he reappears in **"The Poet,"** older, but still of the same "heavy and melancholy disposition": "He wanted to be happy but he had no talent for happiness." He is a dilettante, a fine connoisseur of art and pleasure.

Prince Giovanni in **"The Roads Round Pisa"** is possessed of a melancholy "about which the whole province grieves."

The two De Coninck sisters in **"The Supper at Elsinore,"** Fanny and Eliza, are "born melancholiacs" who talk of life "with the black bitterness of two Timons of Athens," and feel unreal in their relation to the world as if they were only two reflections in a mirror. "The fatal melancholy of the family" has also affected the young hero of "true romance," their brother Morten, the hero of Elsinore. (pp. 33-5)

A second rather common type in Dinesen's gallery is the stereotyped fearless hero or heroine of romance who embraces life and danger with courage and pride. These characters, whom Elling refers to as "the irresistible ones," are usually found among the aristocrats. They are very different from the members of the bourgeoisie, who are imbued with fear, afraid to commit themselves, and unwilling to pay the price of life.

Morten De Coninck is a melancholy figure like his two sisters, but he is also one of the irresistible ones, a heroic figure without knowledge of fear or guilt who has had the courage to say no to the secure and comfortable life in Elsinore which has stifled the spirits of Fanny and Eliza. His great love and passion are his ship and the sea.

Heloise in **"The Heroine"** not only bears a name that reminds someone of "all the sound of heroic French history," but she is like a lioness, and not the least afraid, in spite of the precarious situation in which she finds herself. Confronted with the danger of the moment "she became," says Frederick, "still more heraldic, like a lioness in a coat of arms." She is a master of the world "and will stand no nonsense from it. She is the descendant and the rightful heiress, of conquerors and commanders, even of tyrants, of this world."

In **"The Pearls"** Alexander is a dashing Romantic hero who prefers the vertical Norway to the placid and horizontal Denmark because he is, unlike his wife Jensine, devoid of fear. Unlike Jensine he does not worry about tomorrow. In the same story Henrik Ibsen appears in the guise of the artist as hero: he is not afraid to commit himself to a career as a dramatist, though it is a path full of uncertainties and difficulties.

A third major group of characters is composed of those whom we might call the possessed, the fanatics, characters whose lives are governed by an idea.

Miss Malin Nat-og-Dag is possessed by an idea. Being "a lady of the strictest virtue," she has for years believed herself "to be one of the great female sinners of her time." She is accompanied by Countess Calypso von Platen-Hallermund and together they give an appearance of "wildness." They are likened to two tigresses, "the cub quite wild, the old one only the more dangerous for having the appearance of being tamed." Neither of them is the least bit afraid in the situation in which they find themselves. Miss Malin is totally indifferent to fate, and Calypso is possessed by "that simple and arrogant optimism which takes for granted that nothing can go wrong." Both of them are proud and fanatic aristocrats.

Lady Flora Gordon in **"The Cardinal's Third Tale"** is also, like Miss Nat-og-Dag, "a fanatic virgin." She is also a proud aristocrat whose loathing of humanity is of such magnitude that it is compared to Jonathan Swift's. She is suspicious of all of creation and of the Creator. She is supremely arrogant, shrinks from any touch, and lives in proud and splendid isolation. (pp. 36-8)

There are, however, a few men among the possessed. Kasparson, royal bastard, valet, and actor, wants to play a great role once in his life, and is willing to go to any lengths in order to realize his ambition. Johannes Ewald in **"Converse at Night"** is possessed by the idea of "mythos." The hero of **"A Country Tale,"** Squire Eitel, is possessed by the idea of justice, and feels that he must atone for the injustice done to the peasants by his father. The young Saufe in **"The Diver"** is possessed by the idea of being able to fly like the birds because birds "must be, of all creatures, most like angels."

By placing the action of the tales in the past and in far away lands, Dinesen frees her imagination from the restrictions that too familiar an environment would impose upon it. And by creating a great distance between the storyteller and the characters of his story, she transforms the figures in the tales, she succeeds in transforming them into "luminous" heroes and heroines who appear larger than life and on a "higher plane."

One of the outstanding features of Dinesen's style is, as has already been noted, her use of metaphors and similes. Like Father Jacopo in **"The Cardinal's Third Tale"** she seems to feel "that it is wise and pious to call attention to likenesses." It is important to consider here not only what types of metaphors and similes are used but what in particular inspires the author to use them. Many of these figures of speech fall into one of three categories: those involving animals, those involving flowers, and those involving marionettes. All of them serve for the most part to exaggerate the proportions of the characters and to remove them from the ordinary human plane.

In connection with a discussion specifically of Dinesen's use of metaphors and similes involving animals, it is interesting to note her fondness for animal imagery in general. Bird images are the most common, with the swan recurring more frequently than any other particular bird.

Among the numerous wild animals the lioness, tigress, and lion cub are notably common. And there are many images of snakes and fish.

One might speculate on the reasons for Dinesen's great fondness for animal imagery. Her twenty years among the many exotic animals of Africa must have influenced her greatly in this respect. Incidentally, in Africa Dinesen was herself referred to as a "lioness" by the natives. Her reading of LaFontaine and Aesop, and of the Bible, must have had a great influence on her style. Finally, there is the possible influence of her father, who was a great lover of animals.

Some examples of Dinesen's use of animal metaphors and similes will indicate the functions which they serve.

Miss Nat-og-Dag is one of the most colorful figures in the tales. Along with Calypso she is imbued with the racial pride of a vanishing aristocracy, and has an appearance of wildness: "To the rescuing party it was as if they had taken into the boat two tigresses, one old and one young, the cub quite wild, the old one only the more dangerous for having the appearance of being tamed." Being a "fanatical virgin" she has always been on the lookout "like a fighting-bull for a red cloth, or a crusader for the sign of the half-moon, for any sign of the eye of lust, in order to annihilate the owner without pity." When at the age of twenty-seven she finally decided to choose one of her suitors, "she felt like a very tall bitch surrounded by small yapping lap dogs." Having come into a great fortune at the age of fifty, she has been liberated from most earthly cares. When that happened, "a weight fell away from her; she flew up to a higher perch and cackled a little."

Through the use of similar figures of speech involving animals Athena von Hopballehus becomes a grotesque figure. She is said to have "a pair of eyes for a young lioness or eagle," and she stands on one leg "like a big stork." During the seduction scene in which Boris thinks of himself as a bull in the Madrid arena, Athena draws herself up "as a snake does when it is ready to strike." She is compared to "a young she bear," relying on her great strength, and she has a "lioness's roar deep within her voice."

While these animal images serve to make the figures in the tales into grotesque, sometimes comic, larger-than-life characters, the similes and metaphors pertaining to flowers serve to remove the characters from the realm of individuality to the realm of symbol.

Flowers are invariably used in connection with women. The most common is the image of the rose.

When Baron von Brackel first meets Nathalie in **"The Old Chevalier,"** he wonders at her, "as one would wonder at finding a fresh bunch of roses in a gutter." Her undressing inspires him to speak of the woman of "those days," those days when woman was like a perfect work of art. He speaks of the waist shooting up "like the chalice of a flower, carrying the bust, high and rounded as a rose." In those days clothes were designed to disguise, not to reveal, the body: for this reason it was indeed "a revelation to us every time she stepped out of her disguise, with her waist still delicately marked by the stays, as with a girdle of rose petals." In those days there was no question as to which was more important, the idea of woman, or the individual woman. Women were brought up to become representa-

tives of the idea of woman: "slowly the center of gravity of her being would be shifted from individuality to symbol."

Isak Dinesen has often indicated that in her attitude concerning women she is a kindred spirit to Baron von Brackel. In a talk given in 1953 she expressed some of her now undoubtedly old-fashioned views about men and women and the differences between them. To Dinesen man is the being who acts: "A man's center of gravity, the quality of his being, consists of what he accomplishes and does in life." The woman, on the other hand, has her center of gravity in "what she is." A man *does* something, a woman *is* something (beautiful, charming) or *means* something by her very being (like the Virgin Mary or the Maid of Orleans). Men think in terms of the result of an action or activity, women find their fulfillment in the activity itself (embroidery). As artists men create works of art while women become, or are, works of art (actresses, singers, dancers). The power of woman is the power of the acorn, which is powerful by virtue of its fidelity toward its own nature.

With this distinction between men and women and its emphasis on the idea of woman rather than the individual, it is not surprising that the flower—the rose in particular—is employed in the tales as a symbol of the idea of woman. Like the acorn, the flower is what it is; and it is powerful insofar as it fulfills its own nature.

This correspondence between the idea of woman and the rose is developed in **"A Country Tale."** A young woman and a young man are walking in the wood. No word is spoken. The young woman lets her glance glide lovingly and happily over the forest scenery, while the young man ponders the vocation of man. To the young man it is as if he did not himself see the landscape before him, "but only through her knew that it existed, and what it meant." Then the similarity between the young woman's being and the rose is developed:

> She did not turn toward him; she rarely did so, and very rarely on her own offered a caress. Her form and color, the fall of her rich dark hair and the lines of her shoulders, her long hands and slim knees, in themselves were caresses; her entire being and nature was to enchant, and she craved for nothing else in life.

The young man thinks: "The vocation of a rose is to exhale scent; for that reason do we plant roses in our garden. But a rose on its own exhales a sweeter scent than we could ever demand of it. It craves for nothing else in life." The young man, however, returns to his thoughts. (pp. 39-43)

In **"Copenhagen Season"** Adelaide von Galen is called **"The Rose of Jutland,"**

> . . . as if all the land of the peninsula, from the dunes of the Skague to the pastures of Friesland, had gone to make up soil for this one fragrant, fragile flower. The rose swayed pliantly to the breezes, youthfully and naively alluring in color and scent, but it stood on an exceedingly high hill.

Here the rose metaphor seems to suggest the idea of woman as a prize, a value, only to be obtained through some kind of heroic action. It is significant that the image of the rose is most frequently used in those tales which center around one of Dinesen's central motifs, the motif of aristocratic pride and heroism.

There is a second device by which Dinesen removes her characters from the ordinary human plane and places them on a larger-than-human footing. That is the device of using literary and mythical references metaphorically, i.e., of comparing the characters to familiar figures from literature and mythology.

Thus Kasparson in **"The Deluge at Norderney"** is called "a curious Sancho Panza for the noble knight of the church." Miss Nat-og-Dag is compared to Sigrid the Haughty, ancient Queen of Norway, who once "summoned to her all her suitors amongst the minor kings of the country, and then put fire to the house and burned them all up, declaring that in this way she would teach the petty kings of Norway to come and woo her." Jonathan Maersk plays the role of the melancholy Timon of Athens. Calypso, when she went to cut off her breasts, "took a candlestick in one hand and a sharp hatchet in the other, like to Judith when she went to kill Holophernes." (pp. 43-4)

In Dinesen's world the names of the characters are often very significant. Some of them are, of course, rather ordinary names (Anders Kube, Jens Jespersen), but others are so exaggerated that they become grotesque or humorous. Unlike most contemporary writers, who give to their figures rather common, everyday names (or no names at all), Dinesen is fond of long picturesque names such as Calypso von Platen-Hallermund, Boris von Schreckenstein, Hamilcar von Sehestedt, Augustus von Schimmelmann, or Adelaide von Galen.

In some cases the names are significant in that they point toward some mythical or literary role being enacted by the character. In **"Sorrow Acre"** Adam is probably enacting such a mythical role.

At other times the derivation of the name is indicative of the role played by the figure. As Elling points out, the name Kasparson suggests a derivation from the name Caspar Hauser, the famous adventurer, and Kasperle, the marionette figure. Olalla resembles the character by the same name in a short story by Robert Louis Stevenson entitled "Olalla." Boris von Schreckenstein has a name not surprisingly composed of the German word for terror, and "-stein," probably from the famous Gothic figure Frankenstein.

The third method used by Dinesen to make her figures larger than life is the exaggeration of physical appearances, gestures, and physiological effects. It is safe to say, I think, that the figures in contemporary fiction are largely of average physical appearance. . . . With this lack of emphasis on physical appearance goes the avoidance of the theatrical effects of exaggerated gestures and physiological reactions. In Dinesen's world the contrary is true. Many of the figures in the tales are remembered because of their unusual physical qualities. The expressive gesture is very common, and physiological changes are used on the whole to indicate emotional changes. Dinesen's figures undergo great changes of appearance under the influence of passion. This is, of course, a very characteristic feature of the art of romance.

Dinesen's emphasis on physical traits that are out of the ordinary can be seen clearly in her description of the two

giantesses, Athena and Flora Gordon. Miss Nat-og-Dag has a very large nose, and it is often mentioned. In some cases such descriptions are used for a purely comic effect. Thus in **"Copenhagen Season"** the painter's face is said to look like the posterior of an infant.

Exaggerated gestures and physiological reactions are frequent particularly in the ***Seven Gothic Tales.*** In **"The Deluge at Norderney"** the four people just rescued sit in the boat "white as corpses." Jonathan turns pale at the sight of the collapsing granary. The Cardinal falls down "in a dead faint," and when he wakes up he "stares wildly at them." (pp. 45-7)

These physiological effects and exaggerated gestures are so common that the number of examples could be multiplied greatly. **"The Dreamers"** affords innumerable examples.

In ***Winter's Tales*** the element of exaggeration is toned down somewhat, but the note of theatricality is still very evident. In **"Sorrow Acre,"** for example, Dinesen uses exaggerated gestures in order to achieve a stylized and elevated effect.

The old uncle has a "grand, ceremonial manner" about him even when he solemnly proclaims that "it will be a hot day." He speaks with "his majestic nose a little in the air," and "gravely" or with "deep gravity." For his wife he is "a stately consort." Speaking to Adam about the divine art of comedy he appears as an "erect, ceremonious prophet." Perplexed by Adam's outbursts he turns around with an expression in his eyes of "stately surprise." . . . As the tragedy of Anne-Marie nears its appointed end he dresses up "in a brocaded suit that he had worn at Court." The movements of Anne-Marie as she cuts the corn appear more and more like the movements in a divine rite.

The actions and gestures of the old lord in **"Sorrow Acre"** illustrate how a strong emphasis on expressive gesture produces a theatrical effect. The theater is an important element in Dinesen's world. Her figures are actors and actresses in plots that are like theatrical extravaganzas. They are often imbued with a strong sense of the fact that they are, in effect, acting in a tragedy, or a comedy, or a ballet, or a ritual of some sort.

The old uncle in **"Sorrow Acre"** is acting a part in a kind of ritual, but also in a tragedy (Anne-Marie's) and in a comedy (his own). There are many instances in the tales of such theatrical and mythical performances.

Kasparson in **"The Deluge at Norderney"** is by profession an actor and plays his role as the Cardinal to the hilt. From the very first moment he behaves like an actor. When the people of the resort applaud his heroism he bows "his head a little, with an exquisite irony, in the manner of a hero upon the stage." The final scene between Kasparson and Miss Nat-og-Dag is grand theater. The hayloft becomes a *salon* under Miss Nat-og-Dag's tutelage, and the marriage ceremony is pure theater.

In **"The Monkey"** Boris is acting: "The deepest and truest thing" in his nature is "his great love for the stage and all its ways." To Boris the theater is real life. On the evening of the seduction he feels his friends would have been delighted with him for "he had never played better." With great care he applies his mask before the mirror and decides to wear black in order to accentuate the role of the unhappy lover. Looking at Athena, he is pleased "with his *jeune première* of the night. Now that they were upon the stage together he read her like a book."

In **"The Roads Round Pisa"** all of the figures are playing in a marionette comedy and are, as such, not really aware of the fact that they are actors in a play. The scene between Agnese and Prince Nino is, however, highly conscious theater. Speaking to each other of their strange adventure, they quote lines from Dante's *Divina Commedia*. (pp. 48-50)

In several of the *Winter's Tales* the figures are really playing appointed parts in a myth or ritual, but as with the marionette figures in **"The Roads Round Pisa"** they are not aware of their roles. For this reason their behavior cannot be termed consciously theatrical. Jens in **"The Dreaming Child,"** Alkmene, and the sailor boy play such roles.

In the *Last Tales* there are two examples of pure theater. In **"Copenhagen Season"** Ib and his sister play in a classical tragedy, and in **"Converse at Night"** Johannes Ewald and the King act in a kind of opera buffa or ballet, Johannes Ewald as Yorick and the King as Orosman.

In **"Tempests"** the conversation between Herr Soerensen and Malli Ross models itself after the lines of Shakespeare's play.

An additional feature might be mentioned. This is the habit of some of the figures in the tales to pluck quotations out of the air and use them very consciously. A good example is seen in the final speech of the fish in **"The Diver"**: "Man, in the end, is alarmed by the idea of time, and unbalanced by incessant wanderings between past and future. The inhabitants of the liquid world have brought past and future together in the maxim: *Après nous le déluge.*"

In a recent interview Isak Dinesen spoke of the comic spirit in her stories: "I do often intend a comic sense, I love a joke, I love the humorous. I often think that what we most need now is a great humorist." Asked what humorists she likes to read, she answered that "all the writers I admire usually have a vein of comic spirit. Writers of tales always do, at least." [*Paris Review,* Autumn, 1956].

The last remark is an interesting observation. The storyteller tends, as we have seen, to regard life from a distance, and so does the comic artist. As things seem to hurt less when they have been put into a story, so life takes on the quality of being a great human comedy when regarded from a distance. To tell tales is to be a humorist. If the story is a divine art, so is comedy.

The world of Dinesen is permeated with a comic vision of life. It is perhaps best defined as a kind of romantic irony, often found among some of the storytellers Dinesen admires: E. T. A. Hoffmann, for instance. In the final analysis, it is a profound humor.

Dinesen the romantic ironist is the Baroness Blixen hiding behind a number of pseudonyms. Like many modern writers Karen Blixen places herself at an ironic distance from her own stories. Osceola, Pierre Andrézel, Isak Dinesen: these are three pseudonyms, and the tales published under these names are, in addition, frequently told by narrators who do, or do not, participate in the action. This is, of course, a common technique among contemporary writers, who are fond of ambiguity and complexity. It is an element of Dinesen's art which must be kept in mind when we try to define the nature of the imagination that has projected the world of the tales. Isak Dinesen, like her famous countryman Søren Kierkegaard, alias Victor Eremita, is an artist of the mask and a master of irony.

A further aspect of Dinesen's romantic irony has to do with her attitude to art and the artist, to the story and the storyteller. We have already spoken of Dinesen's loyalty to the story, of her defense of the story. In the universe of story which she creates, God Himself is a great storyteller, but also a great charlatan, God and Devil in the same person. Thus the storyteller, God's representative here on earth, is also a bit of a charlatan. There is in Dinesen's tales an attitude toward the artist which is similar to Thomas Mann's: the artist is not quite respectable, he is a confidence man; it is by no means certain whether he is in the service of God or the Devil. The storyteller is seen in an ironic light. Even the story, no matter how divine, is a form of deception, an illusion, a dream, disguising the essential nothingness of life. As such it does, however, become a heroic defiance of nothingness, for it requires courage to meet the deception of life with a still greater form of deception.

The tales are, of course, filled with various comic effects, and life as a whole is often conceived as a human comedy authored by a comic divinity who "loves a joke." But Dinesen's comic vision goes deeper than that, and it is for this reason that I choose to call it humor.

Humor blends laughter and tears, joy and sorrow, pleasure and pain. There is in Dinesen's tales, says Jørgen Gustava Brandt, a feeling of "life as play, game, and as tragic seriousness." Comedy and tragedy are interwoven. Like Adam in **"Sorrow Acre"** Dinesen seems to feel that one must come to terms with contradiction, suffering, and pain before life can really begin. This is a conception of humor very close to that expressed by some of the German Romantics. In humor the German Romantics discovered, says William G. O'Donnell in a recent essay on Kierkegaard's humor, "a deep, enduring, warmhearted, Germanic feeling of kinship with all forms of life. It rests upon a sympathy for one's fellow-sufferers in a world out of joint. It springs from the heart and is almost another name for love." This kind of humor is very common in many of the tales: the insight into life which so many of Dinesen's heroes and heroines receive is very often precisely of this nature.

Humor, as understood by Isak Dinesen, is an affirmation and acceptance of life in all its forms, the opposite of rebellion. Writing from Germany during the last war, from a society dedicated to the belief in the omnipotence of the human will, Dinesen spoke of her own faith in the one attitude to life which was forbidden in Germany: "The strange kind of reliance on the grace of God, which one calls humor."

Humor is then a kind of yes-saying to life, an acceptance of whatever fate will bring, and the theme of acceptance is a profound one in Dinesen's tales. But, in saying yes to life, the figures in the tales are also acknowledging the authority of the story and the divine storyteller. Thus Dinesen weaves her tales in such a way that the two themes become one: acceptance of life is a defense of the story. It is no surprise, for this reason, that Dinesen is fond of telling the old tales all over again, that she is a writer of pastiche, for old stories become myths, patterns that God has found useful over and over again. (pp. 50-3)

> *Eric O. Johannesson, in his* The World of Isak Dinesen, *University of Washington Press, 1961, 168 p.*

Dinesen on the origins of *Seven Gothic Tales*

During my last months in Africa, as it became clear to me that I could not keep the farm, I had started writing at night, to get my mind off the things which in the daytime it had gone over a hundred times, and on to a new track. My squatters on the farm, by then, had got into the habit of coming up to my house and sitting around it for hours in silence, as if just waiting to see how things would develop. I felt their presence there more like a friendly gesture than a reproach, but all the same of sufficient weight to make it difficult for me to start any undertaking of my own. But they would go away, back to their own huts, at nightfall. And as I sat there, in the house, alone, or perhaps with Farah, the infallibly loyal, standing motionless in his long white Arab robe with his back to the wall, figures, voices and colors from far away or from nowhere began to swarm around my paraffin lamp. I wrote two of my *Seven Gothic Tales* there.

Now I was back again in my old home, with my mother, who received the prodigal daughter with all the warmth of her heart, but who never quite realized that I was more than fifteen years old and accustomed, for the past eighteen years, to a life of exceptional freedom. My home is a lovely place; I might have lived on there from day to day in a kind of sweet idyl; but I could not see any kind of future before me. And I had no money; my dowry, so to say, had gone with the farm. I owed it to the people on whom I was dependent to try to make some kind of existence for myself. Those Gothic Tales began to demand to be written. . . .

> *From "On Mottoes of My Life" in Daguerreotypes, and Other Essays, 1979.*

Howard Green   (essay date 1965)

[*In the following excerpt, Green examines Dinesen's concept of a "divine art" that brings the audience "face to face with the extraordinary, the unique, the inexplicable, the unpredictable."*]

With her taste for paradox, Isak Dinesen must have been amused at her own popularity. She saw her audience grow with every volume since the *Seven Gothic Tales* appeared

twenty-five years ago, until at the time of her death in 1962 she had become almost the object of a cult (nor by any means an esoteric one) despite the fact that her stories might never have been anything more than a treat for connoisseurs. Written by a Danish aristocrat under a name not her own and in a language not her own, they are old-fashioned in manner, remote in subject matter and uncongenial in theme. It is surely ironical that we, who have been brought up on Progress, on Scientific Thought, and on the Common Man, should be so fond of a writer for whom Progress is an illusion, Scientific Thought a joke, and the Common Man an unthinkable bore. (p. 517)

But mainly, of course, it is due to her unique narrative gifts, for her tales have a flavor unlike anything else in modern fiction. "I have always thought," she wrote in *Out of Africa,* "that I might have cut a figure at the time of the plague of Florence. Fashions have changed, and the art of listening to a narrative has been lost in Europe. The Natives of Africa, who cannot read, have still got it; if you begin to them: 'There was a man who walked out on the plain, and there he met another man,' you have them all with you, their minds running upon the unknown track of the men on the plain. But white people, even if they feel they ought to, cannot listen to a recital." It is just because fashions have changed, however, that she cuts a figure among us now, for nobody else satisfies that particular kind of elemental narrative pleasure as well as she does. Her tales are indeed recitals, not "private" recitals in the modern mode, where a casual manner and a chatty idiom suggest that the author is speaking to the individual reader alone, but "public" recitals, as if she had an audience assembled around her. And the stately and deliberate elegance of her style, with its somewhat archaic bouquet, suggests that we are all taking part in a ritual, a quasi-religious ceremony, ourselves being the congregation and she the priestess. The suggestion is not accidental.

She is really not so much a writer of short stories as a story-teller, in the old-fashioned sense of that term. Like every competent writer of fiction, she can hold our attention with a good narrative, but she does more than that. She also creates a singular and compelling world whose unfamiliar atmosphere and strange events excite that appetite for the unknown to which fiction makes its deepest and most primitive appeal. Nowadays there are very few writers who can do that, or perhaps very few who want to do it, for invention of this kind is out of style. Not, as we are so often told, because the literary imagination has withered—what could be more astonishingly imaginative than the work of a Proust or a Joyce or a Mann?—but because it has been turned in other directions by the historical changes which have encouraged realism in its various forms. Typically, the twentieth-century writer uses his imagination not so much to invent new worlds as to find subtle and complex ways of portraying the world we already know.

And so fiction is more sophisticated, both metaphysically and psychologically, than ever before, but to Isak Dinesen this is not necessarily an improvement. As Cardinal Salviati, the narrator in **"The Cardinal's First Tale"** remarks *à propos* of the nineteenth-century realistic novel, its practitioners have become so obsessed with the individual characters that they sacrifice the story itself. And when the lady to whom he is speaking objects that these characters are fascinating in their living, breathing closeness to the reader, he replies: "Mistake me not . . . the literature of which we are speaking—the literature of individuals, if we may call it so, is a noble art, a great, earnest and ambitious human product. But it is a human product. The divine art is the story. In the beginning was the story. At the end we shall be privileged to view, and review, it—and that is what is named the day of judgment." This is curious theology for a prelate, but Dinesen is most worth paying attention to precisely when she sounds most playful, and to revive the story as a "divine art" (however curious *that* may seem in a modern writer) was just what she had in mind.

The "human product," she felt, was too rational. For no matter how uncompromisingly irrational our fiction may appear—however romantic in attitude, abstruse in subject matter, or obscure in technique—it is always ultimately rational because it depicts experience in terms the human mind can somehow assent to. This is just as true of a James Joyce as of a Jane Austen, the difference being one of degree not of kind. But, as Dinesen sees it, although such art may gratify our need for bringing order out of chaos, the order it establishes is merely an illusion. In *Out of Africa* she recounts how a lawyer once tried to explain to her what the phrase "an act of God" signified in a legal contract: " 'No, no Madam,' he said, 'You have not quite caught the meaning of the term. What is completely unforeseeable, and not consonant with rule or reason, that is an act of God.' " Her stories depict the workings of this God, who is not in the least rational, but who is, on the contrary, a highly imaginative being, impatient with systems, fond of exercising his "terrifying fancifulness" (to quote the heroine of **"Echoes"**), and—as she is repeatedly at pains to point out—delighting in change. "The real difference between God and human beings," reflects Boris in **"The Monkey,"**

> was that God cannot stand continuance. No sooner has he created a season of a year, or a time of the day, than he wishes for something quite different, and sweeps it all away. . . . And human beings cleave to the existing state of things. . . . It is all wrong . . . to imagine paradise as a never-changing state of bliss. It will probably, on the contrary, turn out to be, in the true spirit of God, an incessant up and down, a whirlpool of change. Only you may yourself, by that time, have become one with God, and have taken to liking it.

The "divine art," then, as opposed to the "human product," should reflect the true spirit of God by bringing its audience face to face with the extraordinary, the unique, the inexplicable, the unpredictable. We would expect its form to be correspondingly unconventional—at least as outlandish as in *Tristram Shandy* or *Ulysses*—but Isak Dinesen's technique is imperturbably conservative. This inconsistency may be partly a caprice to exemplify her own philosophy, and the more we know her, the more likely this seems. However, divine art, like human art, no doubt entails certain compromises, and I suspect she saw that any divine prodigies of form would be self-defeating, for whoever wants to keep an audience confronted with the unexpected, and at the same time maintain an air of public story-telling, cannot very well afford complicated narrative techniques. And so we find none of those experiments with time or consciousness or language which abounded in fiction during her lifetime. Not that she is unaware of them. She simply finds they get in the way. They adulter-

ate the Story. "The story," as Cardinal Salviati observes, "does not slacken its speed to occupy itself with the mien or bearing of the characters, but goes on." "Speed" is hardly the first word her own stories bring to mind, but, for all their leisurely pace, the narrative momentum is sustained with consistent and notable skill. She establishes the mien and bearing of her characters carefully enough, but it is event rather than character which concerns her, unlike most of her contemporaries, who emphasize the inner world of thought and feeling precisely because they share her conviction (on whatever grounds of their own) that the outer world of events is largely inexplicable and unpredictable. Finding it harder and harder to determine what is "real" in that fast-changing outer world, they tend to deal increasingly with actions which by older standards seem inconsequential. The extent to which this inclination can carry a novelist is painfully exemplified by Samuel Beckett, whose characters sink deeper into catatonia with each succeeding novel.

So it is particularly hard at this moment in history to do what Isak Dinesen proposed for herself, namely, to write "eventful" fiction which will have the robust narrative appeal of an earlier age but which will also embody in its events the modern idea of universal mutability. Did she succeed?

Brilliantly, as far as the narrative aspect is concerned. But the philosophy she seems only to have finessed.

For she appears to have no real taste for what is or could be happening now. *Out of Africa* and *Shadows on the Grass* show how courageously and with what stoic and ironic acceptance she underwent the vicissitudes of her own life, but the ruling mood of these autobiographies is elegiac. They are laments for the past, not in the least celebrations of the changeful present. And almost all her stories are set in the past, usually in the eighteenth or early nineteenth centuries, and so although they are full of surprises and mysteries—a high-bred prioress turns into a monkey, an aristocratic lady of total and ruthless chastity catches syphilis without ever having touched a man, a hanged adventurer returns from the grave to dine with his two sisters—they are the surprises and mysteries of the world as it was, as it might have been, or quite often as it never conceivably could have been. We are naturally more inclined to tolerate improbabilities in the long ago or far away, and to trade on that inclination has always been the privilege of romance. But it is hardly open to a writer whose stories are supposed to depict God's universe as a whirlpool of real and present change.

And so she would appear to be a bit of a charlatan, concealing her inability to find authentic matter for the story as divine art behind a brilliant and ingenious treatment of spurious matter. So much, we might think, for her divinity.

But she is elusive when you try to seize her. Like the wild animals she describes so sympathetically in *Out of Africa*, she has a talent for evading you when you least expect it. If she is a divine artist, she will presumably stand in the same relationship to her stories and to her readers as God does to his cosmos and to his subjects, the essence of which is conveyed in the **"Tales of Two Old Gentlemen,"** where we find out why there are no genuine female atheists. It is because man—as opposed to woman—is always confusing himself by trying to interpret the relation between divinity and humanity in terms of his own normal experience: "He will lose breath—and heart—in search and investigation. The ladies, whose nature is nearer to that of the deity, take no such trouble, they see the relation between the cosmos and the Creator quite plainly as a love affair. And in a love affair search and investigation is an absurdity, and unseemly." It turns out that we have in fact lost breath and heart by coming to the conclusion that because she is something of a charlatan her art cannot really be divine, since—from her point of view—our conclusion is simply an unwitting tribute to her divinity: "To my mind," says her most eloquent spokesman, the self-styled Cardinal in **"The Deluge at Norderney,"** "there never was a great artist who was not a bit of a charlatan, nor a great king, nor a god. The quality of charlatanry is indispensable in a court, or a theater, or in paradise. Thunder and lightning, the new moon, a nightingale, a young girl—all those are bits of charlatanry, of a divine swank." In short, just when we think we have had her, we discover that it is she who has had us. Her stories, for all their air of being innocent period pieces, are booby traps for the reader who thinks himself clever enough to look beneath their decorative surface in the spirit of search and investigation . . . absurd and unseemly behavior for which she makes a fool of him. And the very joke is another sign of her divinity. "I love a joke," she observed to an interviewer for the *Paris Review,* "I love the humorous," and this is because, as we shall see in a moment, she holds the divine view of creation to be essentially comic. Her God is very unlike the solemn and Sunday being we are accustomed to. Not only is he a bit of a charlatan, he is also very much of a joker. "The Lord likes a jest," remarks Pellegrina Leoni in **"Echoes"**; and, as he comes to the end of his tale, Mira Jama, the story-teller in **"The Dreamers,"** says, "I have been trying for a long time to understand God. Now I have made friends with him. To love him truly you must love change, and you must love a joke, these being the true inclinations of his own heart."

So it may be that she has indeed recreated the story as divine art—that is, if her premises are to be taken seriously. But how seriously are they to be taken? She has such a pronounced taste for mockery that this is a very difficult question to answer, but we can at any rate be sure of one thing. However fanciful her esthetics and her theology may be, however much or however little she may really believe in them, they serve her to explore what, with deep and evident seriousness, she feels to be the central problem of human existence: how do we face destiny in a world we can only make sense of by supposing it, either literally or metaphorically, to be in the hands of a capricious and frolicsome God?

There is the way of the bourgeois, who fears the unpredictable, who aims to eliminate it and with his systems and methods and sciences to make life secure, orderly and comfortable. This is the modern Western way, which is forlorn, even stupid, in the face of God's "terrifying fancifulness." Dinesen came to sense its shortcomings by observing the native squatters on her farm, who were "in life itself within their own element, such as we can never be, like fishes in deep water which for the life of them cannot understand our fear of drowning." This admirable quality was born of their rapport with destiny: "The Kikuyu are adjusted for the unforeseen and accustomed to the unexpected. Here they differ from the white men, of whom the

majority strive to insure themselves against the unknown and the assaults of fate. The Negro is on friendly terms with destiny, having been in her hands all the time; she is to him, in a way, his home, the familiar darkness of the hut, deep mould for his roots. He faces any change in life with great calm."

Then there is the noble way, which embraces this sense of destiny, understands that life must accordingly be tragic and accepts it uncomplainingly as such. "The true aristocracy and the true proletariat of the world are both in understanding with tragedy. To them it is the fundamental principle of God, and the key—the minor key—to existence. They differ in this way from the bourgeoisie of all classes, who deny tragedy, who will not tolerate it, and to whom the word of tragedy means in itself unpleasantness."

And finally there is the divine view, which only a few mortals—the true elite—can reach and sustain: it goes beyond tragedy and sees the universe as comic, not "funny" indeed, but comic in an ironic sense which subsumes tragedy and makes it ultimately understandable. This is nowhere better expressed than in **"Sorrow Acre,"** a story set in eighteenth-century Denmark. The events are seen mainly through the eyes of a young man, whose name is (significantly) Adam and who is imbued with the new humanitarian ideas of the day. His uncle, a nobleman of the old regime who is identified (with equal significance) only as "the old Lord," has offered to withdraw charges of arson against the only son of an elderly widow, one of his tenants, if in one day she can mow a field of rye which is normally three days' mowing for a man. She accepts, performs the task on a burning and sultry day, and dies as she completes it. The situation, repugnant to Adam's democratic notions, provokes a discussion between the two, in the course of which Adam has occasion to observe that tragedy is a noble, even a divine phenomenon.

> "Aye," said his Uncle solemnly, "a noble phenomenon, the noblest on earth. But of the earth only, and never divine. Tragedy is the privilege of man, his highest privilege. The God of the Christian Church himself, when he wished to experience tragedy, had to assume human form. And even at that," he added thoughtfully, "the tragedy was not wholly valid, as it would have become had the hero of it been, in very truth, a man. The divinity of Christ conveyed to it a divine note, the moment of comedy. The real tragic part, by the nature of things there, fell to the executioners, not to the victim. Nay, my nephew, we should not adulterate the pure elements of the cosmos. Tragedy should remain the right of human beings, subject, in their conditions or in their own nature, to the dire law of necessity. To them it is salvation and beatification. But the Gods, whom we must believe to be unacquainted with, and incomprehensive of, necessity, can have no knowledge of the tragic. When they are brought face to face with it they will, according to my experience, have the good taste and decorum to keep still, and not interfere.

> "No," he said after a pause, "the true art of the Gods is the comic. The comic is a condescension of the divine to the world of man, it is the sublime vision, which can not be studied, but must ever be celestially granted. In the comic the Gods see their own being reflected as in a mirror, and while the tragic poet is bound by strict laws, they will allow

the comic artists a freedom as unlimited as their own . . .

"And here on earth, too," he went on, "we who stand in lieu of the Gods and have emancipated ourselves from the tyranny of necessity, should leave to our vassals their monopoly of tragedy, and for ourselves accept the comic with a grace. . . . Indeed," he finished his long speech, "the very same fatality which, in striking the burgher or peasant will become tragedy, with the aristocrat is exalted to the comic. By the grace and wit of our acceptance hereof our aristocracy is known."

There is a remarkable passage in *Out of Africa* describing how she came to this acceptance in her own life. It was towards the end of her stay in Africa. Two old friends had just died—the aged Kikuyu chief Kinanjui and the Englishman Denys Finch-Hatton, athlete, musician, lover of art, and sportsman—two men who stood for the "old Africa" she loved and admired so much. Her coffee farm, never very prosperous, had steadily been losing money, and the prospect of having to give it up had become correspondingly more menacing. She knew she had to make a decision, but she was confused and tormented. "If I looked in the right place, I reflected, the coherence of things might become clear to me. I must, I thought, get up and look for a sign." And so she walked out of the house and stood a few minutes watching the fowl run about, among them a big white cock. A little chameleon came out of the grass. "The Chameleon stopped up dead at the sight of the cock. He was frightened, but he was at the same time very brave, he planted his feet in the ground, opened his mouth as wide as he possibly could, and, to scare his enemy, in a flash he shot out his club-shaped tongue at the cock. The cock stood for a second as if taken aback, then swiftly and determinately he struck down his beak like a hammer and plucked out the Chameleon's tongue." In the next few days it dawned on her that she *had* been given her sign, that the gods she had invoked had indeed answered her: "The powers to which I had cried had stood on my dignity more than I had done myself, and what other answer could they then give? This was clearly not the hour for coddling, and they had chosen to connive at my invocation of it. Great powers had laughed to me, with an echo from the hills to follow the laughter, they had said among the trumpets, among the cocks and Chameleons, Ha, ha!"

She was in fact forced to give up the farm shortly afterwards and return to Europe, a move which meant the desolation of being exiled from what she considered to be her spiritual home. . . . For she deemed herself an aristocrat (remember that for her aristocracy was mainly a quality of instinct and temperament, not merely an accident of birth), and in a world otherwise submerged by the grey bourgeois tide, Africa seemed one of the few places where an aristocrat might still contrive to feel at home. Here she had stayed for seventeen years, and now she was being turned out. Yet she knew at heart that even if she had been able to stay, her situation would eventually have become hopeless. This was 1931, and she saw that the old Africa was being crushed beneath the pressures of the twentieth century. The brute fact was, that wherever she lived she would find herself out of tune with the age: as an aristocrat born into a democratic world, she had simply been born too late. This was the existential joke, as it were, which

God had played on her and for which he was now saying, "Ha, ha!" This was her fatality, and her code required that she make her aristocracy known by the grace and wit of her acceptance thereof, welcoming it in the spirit of comedy—"gaiety transfiguring all that dread," to use Yeats's phrase—looking God straight in the eye, and returning jest for jest.

How?

By outfacing destiny, by insistently remaining an aristocrat despite the impossible circumstances, not obtusely, but with a fine ironic self-consciousness, always alive to the bizarrerie of her situation. (pp. 517-25)

It was, she knew, only by being in some way a wit out of season that she could ever attain her own wild hope; it would have to be through the power of her mind, not of her person. In Africa, on her six-thousand acre farm, with its numerous dependents and native squatters to whom she was physician, magistrate and demi-god rolled into one, she had been a Lord of the Manor in an almost feudal sense—an aristocrat in the flesh, as it were. In Europe, where this was impossible, if she wanted to be an aristocrat at all, she would have to be an aristocrat of the imagination, making her domain the gift for story telling she had developed to while away the time when drought enforced long days of idleness on the farm. But a writer who elects to be a wit out of season is liable to become pretentious or quaint or simply tiresome. These were the risks she faced, and it was characteristic of her to elect a path which, in respect to those dangers, was as hazardous as any she could have chosen. In literary terms the jest would be as daring and arrogant as she could make it: she would write Gothic fiction.

So she called her first book *Seven Gothic Tales,* and the titles of the succeeding books—*Winter's Tales, Last Tales, Anecdotes of Destiny*—seem to be deliberately noncommittal as if to avoid suggesting any change of intention. For all her tales are essentially Gothic in mode or feeling. There is a generally aristocratic or exotic ambiance; there are handsome but fated heroes, beautiful but melancholy heroines; there are mysterious sins; there is an aura of illicit or perverted sex; there is often a flavor of horror, violence or death; there is an obsession with the grotesque, the unaccountable and the coincidental; and even where the narrative concerns itself with more common matters, there is the constant play of an intensely baroque sensibility.

Now to take such a musty and flyblown genre, to transform it into an elegant embodiment of her own philosophical convictions, and to make of it a popular success as well as a *succès d'estime*—that was literary daring of a high order. And there was arrogance to match it both in the substance of those convictions, so antagonistic to our own, and in the way she inveigled us into swallowing them under the guise of innocent entertainment. In fact, her jest was so successful that she contrived not only to avoid looking pathetic in our eyes, but even to make us feel as if we looked rather pathetic in hers. For we are left perpetually uncertain what to make of her departures from probability and frequently non-plussed by a tenuousness of motive (as, for example, in **"The Old Chevalier"** and **"The Roads Round Pisa"**) which is wiredrawn to the point of sheer obscurity. "Who, then," demands the narrator in one of the *Last Tales,* an ancient beldame who is a story-teller by profession, "Who, then, tells a finer story than any of us? Silence does. And where does one read a deeper tale than upon the most precious book? Upon the blank page." There are many such "blank pages" in Dinesen's fiction: they serve to keep alive the casual reader's sense of her divine inscrutability and they put the careful reader in his place by making him feel there is something he is simply too dense to understand. She could say with one of her heroes, the young writer Charlie Despard, "I have laid a wager with Satan about the soul of my reader, I have marred his path and turned terrors upon him, caused him to ride on the wind and dissolved his substance, and when he waited for light there was darkness."

But it is precisely here, where she is being most godlike in her cavalier treatment of the reader, that she does carry her jest a shade too far, and beneath the mask of divinity, cool and ironic in its detached timelessness, we glimpse an expression which is familiar, very human and unmistakably time-bound.

For nothing more readily betokens the specifically modern than an amalgam of irony and deliberate obscurity. Its presence in her work (for whatever reasons of her own and despite the air of eternity she so skilfully conjures up with her designedly unmodish techniques) makes us wonder if she isn't, after all, a good deal closer in thought and temperament to her contemporaries than both she and some of her more bemused admirers would lead us to suppose, and if her suggesting that we might regard her as a kind of latter-day Boccaccio, aloof from the currents of modern literature, isn't perhaps as extravagant as anything in her own fiction.

Almost every modern writer of any stature is tempted to be intentionally esoteric, or at least "difficult," because he knows that real understanding will come from the happy few and not from the public at large. Now the few may be happy in this situation, but the writer himself seldom is, since nobody really enjoys seeing his audience shrink; his malaise and resentment tend to aggravate the temptation and drive him from mere esotericism into a wilful obscurity which both expresses his contempt for the philistine and helps repair some of the damage alienation does to his ego. . . . For the same reasons, the writer is prone to radical doubts about the very function and value of the art he practises, which can haunt him and become obsessive in his work to the point of turning art into its own subject matter and the artist into his own hero—Proust is the purest example—and Dinesen's stories betray this obsession repeatedly, in either direct or symbolic terms.

The consequence of this situation is a characteristic double ambiguity. The artist is likely, first, to be ambiguous towards art itself, which at one moment he feels to be the most real of human activities and the most important, at another the most illusory and the most trivial; under one aspect metaphysical revelation, under another mere game. And, second, he is likely to be ambiguous about his own role: is he wise man or joker, priest or entertainer, prophet or charlatan—or is he all these at once? Together, these ambiguous feelings encourage a kind of irony which is typical of our age. The writer, not always consciously perhaps, tries to purge himself of his own uncertainties by transferring them to us, leaving us to some degree in doubt as to how seriously we are supposed to take what he is saying. . . . This ambiguousness may help convey the belief that in a fragmented age an honest writer cannot commit himself wholly to any certainties, but it also allows him to evade fully defining the significance of that belief by taking refuge in a self-created enigma.

Dinesen employs these ambiguities so assiduously that she puts us in the position of Mrs. Humphry Ward in Max Beerbohm's famous cartoon. The novelist is pictured as a little girl with her uncle Matthew Arnold. He is leaning debonairly against the mantlepiece, gazing down at her with a benevolent and jocular smile, as she demands plaintively, "Why, Uncle Matthew, Oh why will not you be always wholly serious?" (pp. 526-29)

We know [Dinesen] is in earnest about the problem of human destiny, but we do not know how much she is in earnest about the terms she uses to work the problem out, namely, those exotic views of God and the aristocracy which her stories inculcate so deftly and for which *Out of Africa* and *Shadows on the Grass* so tactfully elicit our sympathy. For in an age of total war and concentration camps, a philosophy whose ultimate wisdom was to look on human tragedy as a divine joke would not only be anachronistic but repulsive, and she was far too perspicacious to be unaware of that.

The fact is that Dinesen's ideas are rather like Dickens' characters: intensely real in the world their maker creates for them and almost equally unreal out of it, unreal not because they are irrelevant to life but because their relevance is mythical rather than naturalistic. Likewise, the elite envisioned by Dinesen is a highly symbolic and romantic creation (in some ways even sentimental, although the sentimentality is obscured by her wit and urbanity) and its relation to the world of everyday conduct is very oblique. Her aristophilia and her whimsical theology honor some virtues not currently in fashion and provoke us to call certain democratic complacencies into question, but the truth they embody is psychological rather than directly ethical. They remind us that in the free play of fantasy and invention there is a reality our rather grimly utilitarian view of the imagination makes us lose sight of. And that is where her essential achievement lies.

The strength of her appeal, as I have said, is in her narrative inventiveness, in her remarkable ability to arouse and gratify our curiosity and our sense of wonder; but the unique fascination of her work is in the subtle and elusive mockery of her attitudes and in her brilliant juggling of extravagant situations and ideas. Her "truth" lies not in these things themselves, but in the lambent and shimmering elegance of the pattern she creates with them.

And by an irony she would certainly have been the first to appreciate, Dinesen—the uncompromising advocate of the age-old—could now be considered the very *avant-garde* of the *avant-garde.* For nowadays so much is made of the absurd in art (most of it, alas! so dismally labored) and she is the true and incomparable virtuoso of absurdity. When the Cardinal in **"The Deluge at Norderney"** (an impostor, but a great artist in his impostures) reflects on God's courage in creating the universe, he exclaims: "What an overwhelming lesson to all artists! Be not afraid of absurdity; do not shrink from the fantastic. Within a dilemma, choose the most unheard-of, the most dangerous solution. Be brave, be brave!" Dinesen was indeed brave.

She had the courage of the Cardinal's convictions and, in an unpropitious age, created an absurd and fantastic world which would have been a credit to her own wayward God.

In one of her stories, she reminds us that "a name is a reality," and perhaps we had better not forget this as we read her. For she assuredly had her own reality in mind when she chose to write under the name of "Isak."

It means "laughter." (pp. 529-30)

Howard Green, "Isak Dinesen," in The Hudson Review, *Vol. XVII, No. 4, Winter, 1964-65, pp. 517-30.*

Robert Langbaum   (essay date 1965)

[*A professor of English at the University of Virginia, Langbaum composed the acclaimed critical studies* The Poetry of Experience *and* The Mysteries of Identity, *which examine the concepts of myth, tradition, and identity as envisioned by such authors as Robert Browning, William Wordsworth, and William Butler Yeats. In the following excerpt from his book-length study of Dinesen, which was reprinted in 1975 as* Isak Dinesen's Art: The Gayety of Vision, *Langbaum focuses upon Dinesen's short story "The Deluge at Norderney" and discusses what he perceives as tragicomic elements of her art.*]

The posthumous volume, **Osceola,** opens with an unfinished and hitherto unpublished story that Isak Dinesen wrote around 1905 when she was about twenty. Entitled **"Grjotgard Álvesøn og Aud" ("Grjotgard Álvesøn and Aud"),** it is based on Snorri Sturlason's Norse King sagas that, along with the other Icelandic sagas, Mrs Dinesen used to read to the children. An amazingly powerful piece of work, **"Grjotgard"** is romantic in its reconstruction of archaic modes of feeling and thinking, in the sense it conveys that the people of the story are different from us. The people of the story are at a point of transition between paganism and Christianity that is analogous to the point at which Isak Dinesen was to find her Africans.

The two stories published in 1907, **"The Hermits"** and **"The Ploughman",** deal with nature and the supernatural and seem to be companion pieces. Both deal with the old theme of the demon lover, but the thing that makes them romantic is the meaning they give to the supernatural theme. The lovers are demonic because their energies are associated with the energies of nature, so that our sympathy is with them. **"The Hermits"** is about the sea; the lover is a ghost who wins the heroine over to his element, the sea, and she dies. **"The Ploughman"** is about the earth; the lover's mother is a witch and his energies, amoral as the untamed earth's, are rendered evil by their clash with society. He recalls the highly moral heroine to her proper element, the earth, but she redeems him by harnessing his energies—she sets him to plough the earth.

The talent exhibited in these two early efforts is less that of a storyteller than of a lyric poet, a romantic nature poet. The author's interest does not seem to be in the story but rather in evoking a sense of nature; the story rises as a kind of emanation from the scene. Like other beginning writers of romantic sensibility, Isak Dinesen had to learn what to

do with the characters that materialize all too easily out of a mood or a landscape. Yet to the end she most often started with, as she put it, an atmosphere, a place, an "air", and she let the story grow from that.

Of the four elements, she liked to say, air was her element. Air was what she considered a work of art, whether a painting or a story, ought to have; the thing she remembered about a painting or a story was its air. **"Supper at Elsinore"** grew out of an attempt to render the air of that harbor town; **"The Invincible Slave-owners"** grew out of a visit to Baden Baden and an attempt to render its faded charm; and in writing **"Sorrow-acre",** she began by rendering the air of an old Danish manor at sunrise, then she put a figure into the landscape and went on. Her two rather crude stories of 1907 have, therefore, greater bearing on her future development than has the far more successful **"Family de Cats",** an incisive little satire of the bourgeoisie, which appeared two years later and which is in its quite different vein a finished piece of work.

Although **"The Family de Cats"** is Isak Dinesen's only straight satire, the satirical element is never absent from her later work as it is absent from the stories of 1907. One might say that she achieved a fusion of the styles of 1907 and 1909, and that the later stories are more or less successful just to the extent that both styles are present. On the one hand, the later stories show the sort of ironical awareness of their own extravagance which is absent from the stories of 1907; on the other hand, the irony of the later stories does not dispel their imaginative quality. In her best stories, Isak Dinesen achieves the peculiarly romantic kind of satire that feeds and is fed by imaginative activity.

Different as are the styles of 1907 and 1909, the moral ideas are the same. **"The Family de Cats"** continues the morality of nature of the first two stories, for it treats good and evil as problematical abstractions from an original moral unity identical with the oneness and vitality of nature. The point of the satire is that the two poles of what Blake calls "the cloven fiction" cannot exist without each other, and that it is relative and problematical which name, good or evil, can be applied to any person. All three stories look ahead to Isak Dinesen's rediscovery in Africa of the romantic morality of nature she brought there.

Her first attempt to bring together fantasy and satire, the styles of 1907 and 1909, is to be found in **"Revenge of Truth",** the marionette comedy which she wrote as a girl of sixteen or seventeen, then rewrote in 1915 when she was thirty, and finally revised and published under the name of Karen Blixen-Finecke in 1926. It is significant that she first combined the two styles by means of marionettes, for marionettes and the Book of Job are the references that recur most often in her work. They are both used to answer the same question—how to find the ideal in the real, the absolute in the relative. They would seem to offer opposite answers—the Lord's lyrical celebration of the life of nature as against lifeless dolls. Yet to understand Isak Dinesen is to understand the sense in which the two answers can be reconciled. For she likes the extremely natural and the extremely artificial; she is a nature writer and a writer about styles of art and civilization. Her references to Job tell about one aspect of her art—the intensification of the natural to yield the ideal. But her references to marionettes tell about the twin aspects of her art—the imaginative intensity with which she bodies forth the ideal and the satire which invokes the ideal to criticize the real. The marionettes also illustrate her use of characters as both naturalistic representatives of their own relative viewpoints and stylized agents of the plot, representatives of the absolute.

In using marionettes, Isak Dinesen for the first time calls attention to the art form itself as part of what she is saying. Marionettes offer a simplified diagram of the double vision that makes art art; for we play along with the pretense that they are not marionettes, that they have purposes of their own, while perfectly aware that someone is pulling the strings. The latter awareness is in the case of marionettes so exaggerated as to make every marionette play a comedy no matter how painful the material. Although Isak Dinesen was never again to use marionettes, the marionette comedy helps us understand some of her most characteristic qualities—the deliberate emphasis on artifice and the imposition on painful material of a comic awareness, the awareness that someone is pulling the strings, as an answer to the story's problems.

Comedy has always made a certain self-parodying use of the form to solve the problem of the play. Events reach an impasse, and the playwright with a smile and a flick of the wrist pulls a god down from the machine or turns up somebody's long-lost daughter. In self-consciously modern literature, the comic solution takes on a metaphysical significance as a way of dealing with the materials of modern disorder. The writer points up the chaos of life by reminding us that his solution is a mere trick of art—as in Brecht's *Threepenny Opera* where, after the hero has been saved from hanging by an unexpected pardon, the cast reminds us in a sardonic song, "Happy Ending", that in life it would not work this way.

But there is also in modern literature an even more complex use of the comic solution which goes a step farther and says that what looks like a trick of art is symbolic of some ultimate order in life, which uses the artifice to project a vision of order upon the naturalistic vision of disorder. This is the understanding of artifice behind the highly "esthetic" nineteenth- and twentieth-century literary talk about marionettes, dolls, masks and the stylized movements of the dance. Since this talk is directed against scientific naturalism, it is more belligerent—it conceives artifice as more artificial—than the traditional understanding which takes the formal aspects of art rather more for granted. The Aristotelian idea is that the order in art corresponds to the order in nature. The modern theorist says that the order in art symbolizes an order in nature which we cannot perceive, hence the more artificial the symbol, the more it sets our ordinary perceptions at nought, the better; but if we could understand nature completely, we would understand it as we understand a work of art—we would understand it, in Coleridge's phrase, as "the art of God". We need the whole of this concept to understand Isak Dinesen's references to both the Book of Job and marionettes, to understand the sense in which she is a nature writer and a writer about styles of art and civilization.

In two perceptive radio talks, published as *Karen Blixen og Marionetterne* (*Karen Blixen and the Marionettes*), the Danish critic, Aage Henriksen, says that Isak Dinesen uses the marionettes as symbols in the myth which is central to her work, the myth of the fall [*Isak Dinesen/Karen Blixen*]. The point is that the self-consciousness that came

with the fall made man imperfect, because it gave him the possibility of separating his own will from God's. Since the fall, perfection has consisted either in having no consciousness, like marionettes, or in having unlimited consciousness, like God. The mechanical doll, the most inhuman possible image, becomes therefore a symbol of divinity.

Henriksen applies the ideas of the most complete discussion we have of the esthetic significance of marionettes, the brilliant "Dialogue on the Marionette Theater", written at the turn of the nineteenth century by the German playwright Heinrich von Kleist, who also wrote tales that combine, like Isak Dinesen's imaginative intensity with satire. A famous dancer remarks in the dialogue that "the puppets could be very effective teachers of the dance". When the author asks how the puppeteer manages "the confusion of strings" necessary "to direct the small limbs in the intricate rhythms of the dance", the dancer replies that the limbs are not separately controlled. " 'Each puppet', he said, 'has a focal point in movement, a center of gravity, and when this center is moved, the limbs follow without any additional handling. After all, the limbs are pendula, echoing automatically the movement of the center.' "

The esthetic principle is that the artist does not consciously govern a multitude of details which it would be beyond anyone's capacity to govern. His conscious intention is simple, but if it is esthetically right, if it is at "the center of gravity", the ramifications will automatically follow. It is the automatism that transforms nature into art.

The dancer admits that the marionette's dance is not entirely mechanical; it is to some degree expressive of the puppeteer. Yet he goes on to speculate that " 'this last vestige of human spirit can be eliminated from the marionettes; and then their dance would be completely mechanized' "—it would be perfect. If an artisan would build him a marionette according to his directions, that marionette could " 'perform a dance which neither I nor any other capable dancer of this era could duplicate' ". The marionette would be perfect because the placement of its center of gravity would be, paradoxically, " 'more true to nature than in the common marionette' ". The completely mechanical artwork would meet, in other words, the natural ideal; for if the center of gravity were just where it ought to be, then all intentions would be subsumed, the right intention would be built in and there would be no need or possibility for conscious intention to intervene between nature and art. Since the puppeteer could no longer exercise choice, the completely mechanical marionette would never, like human dancers, slip into affectation. (pp. 46-51)

Art is the back door to Eden—art that delivers us from self-consciousness through ritual or, in Yeats's phrase, dying into a dance. " 'We see,' " says the dancer, " 'that in the natural world, as the power of reflection darkens and weakens, grace comes forward more radiant, more dominating.' " Art, however, gives knowledge too, so that it restores

> "a purity that has either no consciousness or consciousness without limit: either the jointed doll or the god."

"Therefore," I said, a little distracted, "we must eat

from the tree of knowledge again and fall back into a state of innocence."

"By all means," he replied, "that is the last chapter in the history of the world."

We have here the central myth of romantic literature; it is the secularized and psychologized version of the central myth of Christianity—the myth of the fall and redemption. Concerned less with sin than with the question whether sin was possible at all, whether values had any objective reality and the self any relation to the outside world, the romanticists interpreted the fall as a fall in perception—a fall into the analytic fragmentation of a world which was once perceived singly, a world in which subject and object, fact and value, and the values themselves, beauty, truth and goodness, had no separate names. All this is in English literature most explicitly set forth by Blake, who takes off from the theological paradox of the Fortunate Fall—the paradox that man, in regaining Eden through moral choice and an awareness of God's grace and love, will have gained a greater Eden than that unconscious state of innocence which he lost. In the romantic version, the paradox is interpreted to mean that art recaptures for consciousness the data of unconscious knowledge and thus regains for us our lost unity of perception through an expansion of consciousness. That is the meaning of Kleist's conclusion.

In Isak Dinesen's stories, we have already seen how an artist in life sets in motion events that take over of themselves, producing a pattern and meaning beyond the character's intention. The artist-character is like Kleist's puppeteer; the events are like the dead limbs of the marionettes; the point where the human turns into the divine artwork is the point of transcendence where art and nature meet. At the point of transcendence, Isak Dinesen's characters lose the naturalistic identities they have had in the story and become automatons of some higher artwork. Sometimes they are compared to marionettes; sometimes they take on the mythical identities required by some other form of art.

When he suggests in the end that the cure for consciousness is more consciousness, Kleist's dancer uses as an example a concave mirror where " 'the image vanishes into infinity and appears again close before us' ". This follows the author's story about a young man who "lost his innocence" because he became aware of his own beauty in a mirror. Isak Dinesen uses mirrors in her stories—in **"Roads"**, for example—with just the meaning Kleist assigns them. In Milton's *Paradise Lost,* Eve's first act after she has been created is to gaze longingly at her own reflection in water; and the suggestion is that the fall began at that moment. In Isak Dinesen, there are many scenes in which young women, like so many Eves, first discover their womanhood by falling in love with their own nakedness in a mirror.

The theme symbolized by the mirror—a theme I would call the mysteries of identity—emerges from the romantic interpretation of the fall. Since the romanticists interpreted the fall as a fall in perception, they saw the main problem left by it as a problem of epistemology or psychology. The problem was how to regain a connection with the outside world, how to find a basis for action or an action adequate to one's awareness of one's own potentiality. The

question was at what level of behavior—and in literature through what kind of plot—a person manifests his true self.

Isak Dinesen is an important writer because she has understood the tradition behind her and has taken the next step required by that tradition. Like the other, more massive writers of her generation—Rilke, Kafka, Mann, Joyce, Eliot, Yeats, too, though he is older—she takes off from a sense of individuality developed in the course of the nineteenth century to the point of morbidity, and leads that individuality where it wants to go. She leads it back to a universal principle and a connection with the external world. The universal principle is the unconscious life of man and nature, which, welling up in the human consciousness as myth, is the source of civilization, individual consciousness, and our concept of God's unlimited consciousness. It seems to have been the function of the literary generation born in and around the decade 1875-1885—the generation after that of Nietzsche, Frazer and Freud, the great explorers of myth and the unconscious—to effect a transition from the individual to the archetypal character: from the novel, with its separation of psychological and external data, to the myth which speaks with one voice of both.

Thomas Mann, in an essay of 1936 called "Freud and the Future", speaks of the transition in his own fiction from the psychological and naturalistic *Buddenbrooks* to the mythical *Joseph and His Brothers.* Speaking of the "point at which the psychological interest passes over into the mythical", Mann says: "It is plain to me that when as a novelist I took the step in my subject-matter from the bourgeois and individual to the mythical and typical my personal connection with the [psycho] analytic field passed into its acute stage." The connection lies in the answer, which is "the innermost core of psychoanalytic theory", to "the mystery of the unity of the ego and the world". The answer lies in the perception to which psychoanalysis leads us that "the apparently objective and accidental" is "a matter of the soul's own contriving", that "the giver of all given conditions resides in ourselves". When we remember, Mann explains, all Freud has revealed about "error, the retreat into illness, the psychology of accidents, the self-punishment compulsion", we realize that it is through our deepest desires that we make connection with external events.

The psychological interest passes over into the mythical at that psychological depth where we desire to repeat mythical patterns. Life at its intensest is repetition. Mann tells us that the ego of antiquity became conscious of itself by taking on the identity of a hero or a god. Caesar trod in the footsteps of Alexander, and Cleopatra made herself into the earthly embodiment of Ishtar, Hathor and Isis. (pp. 51-4)

These examples from Mann help us understand the style of so many characters and scenes in Isak Dinesen—the godlike qualities of Prince Potenziani in **"Roads"**, and the lovers quoting Dante at each other. They help us understand, as we shall see, the big moment in **"The Deluge at Norderney"** when Miss Nat-og-Dag says to Kasparson, " *'Fils de St Louis, montez au ciel!'* " Isak Dinesen's characters are, like Mann's antique figures, artists of their own personalities in that they know what powers they draw upon.

Mann also helps us understand the comic element in this view of life as repetition. For he describes the characters of his *Joseph* as puppets who know they are puppets reeling off, in the hoaxing of Esau the Red for example, "a plot abiding from past time and now again present in a jest". The effect is actually, as Mann makes clear, tragicomic; for Mann's characters feel the emotions they know they are representing. They are like and unlike puppets in a way which helps us understand the quality of *Seven Gothic Tales,* the way in which it is like and unlike **"Revenge of Truth"**. The word of Mann's which best describes the quality of *Seven Gothic Tales* is "blithe"; for the word implies in Mann's context the triumph over difficulties, the triumph of comedy over tragedy. It is this blitheness—"a blithe skepticism . . . a mistrust that unmasks all the schemes and subterfuges of our own souls"—that Mann sees as Freud's contribution to the art and humanism of the future. The mythical view, says Mann, although it came early in the life of the race, is in the life of the individual "a late and mature" view.

In describing the mythoi of tragedy and comedy, Northrop Frye tells us that we reconcile ourselves to tragedy, which is the myth of autumn or death, because it leads by implication to comedy, which is the myth of spring or rebirth. If Frye is right, then tragicomedy ought to be the vehicle of the complete or ultimate vision—which may be why Greek tragedy finished with the tragicomedies of Euripides, and why Shakespeare finished by writing those curious last plays that illustrate better than anything else in literature the ripeness or blitheness of which Mann speaks. (pp. 54-5)

Isak Dinesen, who published her first volume at forty-nine, must be understood as starting at the stage of vision appropriate to old writers. In taking the pseudonym Isak—which means laughter—she must have remembered Sarah, who laughed when she bore Isaac because she thought it a fine jest of the Lord's to give her, after a lifetime of barrenness, a child in her old age. "And Sarah said, God hath made me to laugh, so that all that hear will laugh with me" (Genesis 21:6). *Seven Gothic Tales* was both Isak Dinesen's late-born child and the vehicle of the laughter she wanted everyone to hear. Her laughter is the laughter of rebirth—of wonder at the power of the divine imagination that, having given her happiness in so unexpected a place as Africa, took it all away and then allowed her to recover what she had lost through imagination.

When we were talking once about the sense in which she used the word *tale,* Isak Dinesen said that she did not intend the word in the sense of the Danish *eventyr* (which Danes translate as *fairy tale* and associate with Hans Christian Andersen), but in the sense of Shakespeare's *Winter's Tale.* Her second volume of stories takes its title from Shakespeare's play, and the Danish title, *Vinter-Eventyr,* is a translation from the English. For the Danish titles of *Seven Gothic Tales* and *Last Tales,* she uses the word *fortællinger* which does not carry the connotation of fairy tale. If, following her hint, we assimilate her use of the word *tale* or *story* to Shakespeare's last plays, we may understand her to mean romance, but romance used to achieve tragicomedy—to subsume the opposition between the tragic and comic, that is discussed throughout her work, in the naive view of a child or primitive who sees a story as neither tragic or comic but as marvelous.

We have already seen how in **"Roads"** the events take over of themselves to turn the tragedy set in motion by Carlotta and Prince Potenziani into a divine marionette comedy. In the last story of *Seven Gothic Tales,* **"The Poet",** the man who tries to manipulate the other characters as though they were marionettes in a comedy of his own devising, finds that he has created instead a tragedy of which he is himself the tragic hero. (But even here he realizes, at the moment of his death, that in playing out his tragedy he has stepped into a divine artwork that is itself comic.) It is because the two stories make such a nice pair of opposites—showing, respectively, that comedy is the divine art and tragedy the human art—that in the author's arrangement, which is to be found in the British and Danish editions, they open and close the volume and, in their final effect, subsume tragedy and comedy in tragicomedy.

Only in the American edition [of *Seven Gothic Tales*] does **"Deluge at Norderney"** come first, presumably because the publisher felt it would draw readers into the volume. The American editors were not wrong to place **"Deluge"** first, for it is among Isak Dinesen's very best stories. I think it is her best because it is her wittiest. It combines the greatest number of her characteristic themes, and the most widely opposite effects. The wit fuses all these things into a story (pp. 55-6)

[Dinesen's narrative] style is built on the contrast of comic and tragic implications—the frivolousness of the romantic spirit and the ladies with their easels play against the hereditary role of the sea and the skeleton of the shipwreck. The contrast becomes even more violent when we learn

Baron Bror von-Blixen-Finecke, Dinesen's husband, in the drawing room of their East African house.

that "the peasants and fishermen of Norderney themselves learned to look upon the terrible and faithless gray monster westward of them as upon some kind *maître de plaisir*". It is a sign of the *embourgeoisement* of the peasants and fishermen as of the aristocracy that they have begun to flirt with "the dangerous powers of existence". The changed attitude toward the sea marks the end of the *ancien régime.*

When the sea shows itself in its full power, most of the guests depart. This happens in the late summer of 1835, when after a three days' storm the sea breaks through the dikes and floods the land. We hear of the stricken farmers, and of the already half-mythical figure of the 73-year-old Cardinal Hamilcar von Sehestedt, who is giving them miraculous support in their despair. Like the Cardinal of **Last Tales,** Cardinal von Sehestedt is Isak Dinesen's ideal figure in that he combines aristocratic lineage with spirituality. He also combines wit and imagination.

The old man was spending the summer in a fisherman's cottage, collecting into a book his writings on the Holy Ghost. For he held with the medieval divine, Joachim de Flora, that the testament of the Third Person of the Trinity remained to be written. He had with him "only a sort of valet or secretary, a man by the name of Kasparson .. a former actor and adventurer". In the collapse of the Cardinal's cottage at the start of the flood, Kasparson was killed and the Cardinal badly wounded so that he now wears during his rescue work "a long, blood-stained bandage wound about his head".

It is late afternoon when the last rescue boat of the day starts back with the remaining survivors from the bath. The miracle-working Cardinal is in charge There is a rich, crazy old maiden lady, Miss Malin Nat-og-Dag, "the last of the old illustrious race which carried arms two-parted in black and white, and whose name meant 'Night and Day' ". She has with her the sixteen-year-old Countess Calypso von Platen-Hallermund; the two ladies gave "that impression of wildness which, within a peaceful age and society, only the vanishing and decaying aristocracy can afford to maintain". On the way back, a peasant family signal them from the hayloft of a sinking farmhouse. Since the boat cannot hold more people, it is necessary for some of the passengers to change places with the family of the farmhouse. The Cardinal rises first, followed by Miss Malin, the Countess Calypso and a young man, Jonathan Mærsk. Since it is now dark, they will have to wait until dawn for a boat to return. The question is whether the boat will return before the farmhouse sinks.

The symbolism is perfect. These four choice souls are to spend the night in a sinking loft. There is nothing for them to *do;* they can only show what they *are.* There is a preliminary pause, like that marked by the tapping of the conductor's baton before the orchestra starts, then the story moves upward to a new level of imaginative intensity. The transition occurs in the following sentence: "As if they had been four marionettes, pulled by the same wire, the four people turned their faces to one another." The two couples, one old, one young, wait to begin the dance of wit.

At the Cardinal's suggestion, Miss Malin gets the dance going by playing the role of hostess, as though the hayloft were her salon and she had "death itself, like some lion of the season, some fine Italian tenor, out of the reach of rival

hostesses, waiting outside the door to appear and create the sensation of the night". We are told her story—that if she appears a bit off her head, it may be from choice. As a girl, she was a fanatical virgin who took too literally the Bible's words against lust. To Malin, a man's desire for her was "a deadly impertinence", like an "attempted rape". The man whom she finally picked out to marry, Prince Ernest Theodore of Anhalt, the most sought after young man of his time, could have found in Miss Malin "nothing striking but the price. That this thin, big-nosed, penniless girl, two years older than he, would demand not only his princely name and a full share in his brilliant future, but also his prostrate adoration, life-long fidelity, and subjection in life and death and could be had for nothing less,— this impressed the young Prince." He was so nervous about this first risk of refusal that he did not propose until the evening before his departure for war. He was killed at Jena. Miss Malin renounced all further thought of marriage, thus completing an old-fashioned story of monumental frustration. Her kind of sexual deficiency, which Isak Dinesen treats in several stories, comes from too high an idealism.

At fifty she came into a large fortune, but she was changed by "what changes all women at fifty: the transfer from the active service of life . . . to the mere passive state of a looker-on. . . . In her laughter of liberation there certainly was a little madness." The description of her madness is high comedy. "She believed herself to have been the grand courtesan of her time, if not the great whore of the Revelation. She took her fortune, her house, and her jewels as the wages of sin, collected in her long career of falls." If in young men she had taken the pursuit of adultery for the deed, she now took for the deed the acts of compliance she had not committed. By acknowledging her participation in that fall which she had already incurred through imagining it, she has, in Kleist's phrase, fallen back into the state of innocence that her fierce virginity had lost her. It is in this state of innocence regained, "this glow of milk madness and second youth", that we now find her.

The Cardinal introduces a new subject with one of those fantastic opening sentences that in Isak Dinesen sound like an orchestra striking up its first chords. " 'When, as a boy, I stayed for some time at Coblentz, at the court of the emigrant Duke of Chartres, I knew the great painter Abildgaard.' " The Danish painter, Abildgaard, used to tell the court ladies who came to have their portraits painted to wash off their powder and rouge, for if they would paint their faces themselves he could not paint them. The Cardinal reflects that this is what the Lord is continually telling us: " ' "Wash your faces. For if you will do the painting of them yourselves, laying on humility and renunciation, charity and chastity one inch thick, I can do nothing about them." ' " Such antinomian morality hardly suits a Cardinal, but it is part of the story's point and prepares us for a surprising revelation about the Cardinal; as does the reference to the Duke of Chartres who would have been, according to the chronology of the situation, Philippe-Egalité before he became in 1785 Duke of Orléans.

" 'Where in all the world did you get the idea that the Lord wants the truth from us?' " Miss Malin asks. " 'It is a strange, a most original idea of yours, My Lord. Why, he knows it already, and may even have found it a little bit dull. Truth is for tailors and shoemakers, My Lord. I, on the contrary, have always held that the Lord has a penchant for masquerades.' " She is talking about the difference between the quantitative truth, which is important only for people who have to take measurements, and the qualitative truth which gives life its value. The latter operates through concealment and even deception, through the symbolic mode of art. It is because the symbolic mode is enigmatic that its truth is not information but an evocation of life as having depths and extensions, connections with some infinite resource of power the consciousness of which gives us the courage to live life as though it were something grander than the utilitarian business of seeking pleasure and avoiding pain. The idea is at the heart of Isak Dinesen's defense of the old European order, which operated by symbols rather than facts.

They are " 'really of one mind' ", the Cardinal says gently. " 'This world of ours is like the children's game of bread and cheese; there is always something underneath—truth, deceit; truth, deceit!' " His point is that the mask reveals some deeper truth than the facts can, so the mask is after all true. " 'So speaketh the Arbiter of the masquerade: "By thy mask I shall know thee." ' " God is the Arbiter, and when at the day of judgment He lets fall His mask—it will be the supreme comic moment.

The Cardinal proposes that they let fall their masks. " 'Tell me who you are, and recount to me your stories without restraint.' " The Cardinal turns first to Jonathan Mærsk, whose story is comic, a little joke really, though it is about his fall into self-consciousness when he learned that he was the illegitimate son of a great nobleman, that he was in spite of himself a man of fashion. To escape this fact, he became a misanthrope; he was known in Copenhagen as Timon of Assens, after the seaport town on the island of Funen where he was born. But his very misanthropy became the fashion.

" 'What a story, Monsieur Timon,' " exclaims Miss Malin, " 'What a place this is! What people we are!' " They all share the qualities which make Jonathan so right. He has noble blood, the more he disdains his nobility the more he demonstrates it. He is a true wit; they are all true wits, which is why Miss Malin exults. She wants him for Calypso. He is the man to *see* Calypso; for if his problem is that he was seen only in his worldly or external aspect and therefore not in himself, Calypso's problem is that nobody could or would see her in her external aspect, her beauty, and nobody therefore could see her in herself.

Miss Malin's story about Calypso is in a comic vein far wilder, far more fantastic than Jonathan's story. She is more imaginative than Jonathan, and **"Deluge"** is designed to increase steadily in imaginative intensity. Miss Malin begins her story by naming the German romantic poet, Count August von Platen-Hallermund. " 'As he is not a man, but an angel,' " she says slyly, " 'we shall call him the Count Seraphina.' " He is Calypso's uncle; and she was raised, after her parents died, in his ivory tower, the castle of Angelshorn. Now the Count Seraphina, as the neuter name suggests, is not a man in two senses—he is not a human being and not a male. He " 'disliked and mistrusted everything female; it gave him goose flesh,' " Miss Malin continues. " 'His idea of paradise was, then, a long row of lovely young boys, in transparent robes of white, walking two by two, singing his poems to his music . . .

or otherwise discussing his philosophy, or absorbed in his books upon arithmetics.' " Count Seraphina dressed and educated Calypso as though she were a boy, until certain " 'signs' " made his " 'failure' " apparent. Then " 'he turned his eyes away from her forever' " and, we are told satirically, " 'annihilated her' ".

In figures like Counts Seraphina and Schimmelmann, and Jonathan Mærsk's father Baron Gersdorff, Isak Dinesen is satirizing estheticism and rationalism. Isak Dinesen associates esthetes, rationalists and moralists as opponents of instinct and experience—of reality. In considering Calypso annihilated, Count Seraphina is like the Schimmelmann of "In the Menagerie" (*Out of Africa*), who thinks that " 'the wild animals which run in a wild landscape, do not really exist' ", because no one sees them. Schimmelmann implicitly shares Count Seraphina's feeling that " 'the existence of the brute creation was an enigma and a tragedy' "; for both follow Descartes in assuming that things exist only inasmuch as they are thought about, so that the forms of life that are not self-aware must be machine-like. The Schimmelmann of **"Roads"** shows like Count Seraphina the desexualizing consequences of rationalism. Isak Dinesen is deliberately vague about whether Schimmelmann's and even Count Seraphina's homosexuality is active or only latent. That is because she is interested in their kind of homosexuality as a mental condition—as the inability of a mind to love anything beyond its own diagrammatic imprint upon the external world. To love women and wild animals, you have to believe in the concrete reality of objects other than the self. The esthete is not distinguished by his love of art but by his desire to organize all of life like a work of art; and he is, in his desire to see the imprint of human will and consciousness on everything, as rationalistic as the engineer.

To fit into this rationalistic environment, Calypso decides to do physically what so many women have for the same reason done psychologically—she decides to cut off her long hair and chop off her breasts. Hatchet in hand, she steals one night to a room where there is a long looking-glass and, as she sweeps down her clothes to the waist in front of the glass, we are given one of those scenes of Isak Dinesen in which a young girl discovers her nakedness in a mirror. It is the beginning of the fall—a sweet triumph among people who, like Miss Malin in her youth, have sinned in their attempt to avert the fall. Determined to preserve her womanhood, Calypso escaped from the castle to Miss Malin, her godmother.

Miss Malin has the Cardinal marry the young couple with a new rite appropriate to a marriage which can be consummated only in spirit and must be lived out in one night. When the ceremony is over, the Cardinal remarks on " 'the tremendous courage of the Creator of this world' ". For the Cardinal, had he made the world, " 'would not have dared to arrange these matters of love and marriage as they are' ". We fail, in other words, to understand reality because we are not imaginative enough; our plans and expectations are always too rational. The Cardinal makes the point explicit in one of those fine cries which, like Prince Potenziani's " 'Always we fail because we are too small' ", gives us a direct glimpse into the depth of tragic sincerity which we otherwise only sense in the special complexity of the wit. " 'What an overwhelming lesson to all artists! Be not afraid of absurdity; do not shrink from the fantastic. Within a dilemma, choose the most unheard-of, the most dangerous, solution. Be brave, be brave!' "

This is just what Isak Dinesen does to bring **"Deluge"** to its climax. The Cardinal proceeds to tell his story, " 'The Wine of the Tetrarch' ", which is the best of the three inset stories, as by its position it should be. It is not comic in the manner of the first two, for it takes off from the Gospels in subject and manner and has all the solemn resonance of a Biblical parable when it is read aloud in church.

> "As, then, upon the first Wednesday after Easter," the Cardinal began, "the Apostle Simon, called Peter, was walking down the streets of Jerusalem, so deeply absorbed in the thought of the resurrection that he did not know whether he was walking upon the pavement or was being carried along in the air, he noticed, in passing the Temple, that a man was standing by a pillar waiting for him. As their eyes met, the stranger stepped forward and addressed him. 'Wast thou not also,' he asked, 'with Jesus of Nazareth?'
>
> " 'Yes, yes, yes,' Peter replied quickly."

The great achievement of this story is its projection of inwardness. Each man seems to be wrapped in the aura of his own thoughts; the dialogue is heard as traveling a long distance from outside in. The effect is achieved through the stately diction and pace, through the use of stillness as a form of action and the management of pauses, through the steady deepening of implication that gives to every word and glance ultimate importance. The repeated play on *wine,* and *body* as it applies to wine, develops the ironic contrast between Peter and the other man, a robber whose concern with the events of Friday is that his friend was crucified with Jesus.

After inviting Peter for a drink at an inn, the robber asks whether his friend went to paradise on Friday as " ' "this Rabbi of yours promised" ' ". When Peter assures him that it is so, the man complains that the wine of Jerusalem has all turned bad since the earthquake. " ' "And good wine is my great pleasure. Now I do not know what to do." ' "

He tells how having heard of a shipment of priceless red Capri which the Emperor of Rome was sending to the tetrarch Herodes, he said to his friend, Phares, that he would give his heart to drink that red wine of the tetrarch's, and Phares said that to show his love for him he would kill the overseer of the transport and bury the wine until they could drink it together. Phares did all this, but was caught and condemned to be crucified. Disguised as a beggar, the speaker broke the law and got himself imprisoned with Phares in order to smuggle him a file and rope. The speaker was caught in the act of escaping, and Phares, who had already made good his escape, would not desert his friend, so the two were returned to prison and Phares was crucified on Friday. " ' "Since you are here, you got off somehow?" ' " Peter asks.

> " 'Yes; I got off,' said the man, and gave Peter a strange deep glance. 'I meant, then, to revenge Phares's death. But since he is in paradise I do not see that I need to worry. And now I do not know what to do. Shall I dig up this hogshead of the tetrarch's wine and drink it? . . . If that wine also has gone bad and gives me no pleasure, what am I to do then?' "

We can see the ironic parallel between the priceless red wine of the tetrarch and the blood of Christ; between Phares's self-sacrifice and Christ's; between Phares's plan to bury and resurrect the wine and drink it together, and the Communion ritual; between the robber's sense of the new dispensation and Peter's. Peter, however, is emotionally involved in the disparity and similarity. On the one hand, he only half attends to what seems a trivial complaint about wine; on the other hand, this robber unknowingly establishes a community of guilt between them. The man's question, " ' "Wast thou not also with Jesus of Nazareth?" ' " is the question Peter was asked when he denied Jesus three times, which is why Peter gives his affirmative answer three times quickly. (pp. 57-65)

What is for us an accumulating irony is for Peter an accumulating blasphemy which finally, when the man reveals what he is after, drives home to Peter his own far more serious blasphemy—for Peter knew what *he* was saying.

> " 'I have been informed that your Rabbi, on the night before he died, gave a party to his followers, and that at that time a special wine was served, which was very rare and had some highly precious body in it. Have you, now, any more of this wine, and will you consent to sell it to me? I will give you your price.'
>
> "Peter stared at the stranger. 'Oh, God, oh, God,' he cried, so highly affected that he upset his wine, which ran onto the floor, 'you do not know what you are saying. This wine which we drank on Thursday night, the Emperor of Rome cannot pay for one drop of it.' His heart was so terribly wrung that he rocked to and fro in his seat."

The upsetting of the wine brings back the Crucifixion.

Yet looking at the man, it came over Peter that he was " 'of all people in the world, . . . the one whom he could not help' ". We see why in the absolute opposition of their hopes. To Peter's " ' "Take up your cross . . . He will help you to carry it" ' ", the man declared he would need no help to carry a cross. If, before, we saw through the man's ironic uncomprehension a despair corresponding to Peter's, we now see by the same means a strength of character equal to Peter's. The man bares his chest and shoulders to show the crosses made by knife scars, and says disdainfully he would have lasted more than six hours on the cross. He rises to go, saying he must *meet* a transport of oil.

The man's future is made to seem harder than Peter's, and lonelier. When he reveals his name and we realize what it is that weighs upon his soul, he becomes in his opposite way as morally significant a figure, and we see that the ironic parallels of the story are the parallel paths to salvation of saint and hero—paths that never meet until infinity. " ' "What is your name?" ' " Peter asks.

> "He turned around and looked at Peter with hauteur and a slight scorn. He looked a magnificent figure. 'Did you not know my name?' he asked him. 'My name was cried all over the town. There was not one of the tame burghers of Jerusalem who did not shout it with all his might. "Barabbas," they cried, "Barabbas! Barabbas! Give us Barabbas." My name is Barabbas. I have been a great chief, and, as you said yourself, a brave man. My name

shall be remembered.' And with these words he walked away."

The repetition of the name is masterly and shows how in the mythical kind of story the revelation of a name is the revelation of a state of soul. Barabbas reminds us in his last sentence that he was indispensable to the famous drama he helped enact. Barabbas, Judas, Pilate, Caiaphas fascinate Isak Dinesen as the tragic figures in the divine comedy of the Passion. They were tragically sacrificed, their suffering is endless, in order to make possible Jesus's comic sacrifice, the happy outcome of which was never in doubt.

The story is punctuated by the longest pause in Isak Dinesen, a pause of a page and a quarter during which Jonathan rises, rejoins his wife, the two fall asleep, and Miss Malin continues to be transfigured before our eyes. Earlier we were told that "she looked like a corpse of twenty-four hours", now she "looked as if she were not going to sleep for all eternity", in the end she has "on her shoulders that death's-head by which druggists label their poison bottles". Finally, as if to answer the question of the point of the story, which has been standing between them, the Cardinal removes the blood-stained bandages from his head. " 'My name,' " he says, echoing Barabbas, " 'is Kasparson. I am the Cardinal's valet.' " He killed the Cardinal before the boat arrived to rescue them that morning. "The Wine of the Tetrarch" has been the vehicle of his self-revelation and self-defense.

Miss Malin's eye for nobility has been impugned, and she demands to know with whom she has passed the night. Kasparson reveals that he is what must be, for a Legitimist like Miss Malin, the most shocking thing possible—the bastard son of a moral bastard, of Philippe-Egalité, that Duke of Orléans who " 'voted for the death of the King of France' ". He is an actor by profession. As a child he danced in ballet, later he became a courtesan to the elderly noblemen of Berlin; he has been a barber in Spain, a printer of revolutionary papers in Paris, a dogseller in London, a slavetrader in Algiers, and the lover of a dowager principessa of Pisa. He has had a life the very opposite of the Cardinal's. Yet it is no less appealing to our imagination. We cannot, as a matter of fact, be sure that this new figure is not as much a fabrication as that of the Cardinal. The account of Kasparson's career sounds like a comic aria in an opera by Mozart or Rossini.

Beginning to regain confidence in her eye, Miss Malin joins in this new game. When Kasparson says that he has " 'stood in the great triangular shadow of the great pyramid' " in Egypt, she, not to be outshone in imagination, comes out with her wildest witticism. Obscene, grotesque, like nothing she has said before, it is a sign that she is joining hands with this new partner, that their dance of wit is becoming, as his unmasking and her transfiguration into a death's-head shows, a *danse macabre*. The mounting intensity of the comedy corresponds to the mounting intensity of the tragedy as morning approaches. " 'Ah,' " she says, " 'in Egypt, in the great triangular shadow of the great pyramid, while the ass was grazing, St Joseph said to the Virgin: "Oh, my sweet young dear, could you not just for a moment shut your eyes and make believe that I am the Holy Ghost?" ' " (pp. 65-7)

Without knowing it, Miss Malin has foreseen the substance of Kasparson's self-defense—that he wanted to show what he was capable of being, to manifest the Holy Ghost in himself. When Miss Malin asks why he wanted this role so much, Kasparson answers, " 'Not by the face shall the man be known, but by the mask' "—because the mask allows you to play out your unrealized potentialities.

Now we see why Kasparson was in a position to understand Louis-Philippe; he is his older brother and, as usurper of the Cardinal's role, he can understand the usurper of the throne of France. Like Barabbas, Kasparson is the criminal who usurped the right to live that should have been the saint's. Through the story of Barabbas, however, Kasparson is saying that the usurper is redeemed by the spirit of the good man whose place he has taken. We see by Barabbas's distaste for the old pleasures that the spirit of Jesus has possessed him, yet its effect is to make him more himself than ever. In the same way, Kasparson is possessed by the Cardinal's spirit at the climax of his career as actor and charlatan. Like Jesus with Barabbas, the Cardinal would in any case " 'have sacrificed his life for mine' ". And Kasparson has now the chance to die for these peasants and fishermen whom, as his mother's people, he loved like nothing else in the world. He would have served them had they called him master, and died for them had they worshipped him. Tonight, he concludes, " 'they have seen the face of God in my face' ". Like all Isak Dinesen's greatest characters, Kasparson wants nothing less than to play at being God.

The unmasking of the Cardinal negates the validity of everything he has been saying. Even the heroism is negated; for, as Miss Malin discreetly observes, if Kasparson is a murderer, then he is doomed whether the boat comes back to rescue them or not. With his whole performance negated morally, Kasparson proceeds to re-establish its validity in esthetic and existential terms. He is pleased to have created this night, and he has thoroughly enjoyed playing the role of the Cardinal.

> "For I have lived long enough, by now, to have learned, when the devil grins at me, to grin back. And what now if this—to grin back when the devil grins at you—be in reality the highest, the only true fun in all the world? And what if everything else, which people have named fun, be only a presentiment, a foreshadowing, of it?"

What if "we shall enjoy ourselves hereafter," speculates Keats in his *Letters,* "by having what we called happiness on Earth repeated in a finer tone". The romanticist wants not renunciation or conversion but the intensification of life as it is. To grin back at the devil is the very opposite of changing your ways; it is to intensify your own character to the point where, as Keats says of the intensity of art, "all disagreeables evaporate, from their being in close relationship with Beauty and Truth". The Minds that follow their own bent, says Keats, "would leave each other in contrary directions . . . and at last greet each other at the Journeys end". Art carries character to its journey's end, revealing in such opposite personalities as Kasparson and the Cardinal the same Holy Ghost.

Miss Malin, who has also created this night, and who has lived her virginity with such passion as to become one in erotic imagination with her opposite, the whore—Miss Malin breaks out with an utterance like song.

"And I too, I too," said Miss Malin in a voice which, although it was subdued, was rich and shrill, and which seemed to rise in the flight of a lark. As if she wanted to accompany in person the soaring course of it, she rose straight up, with the lightness and dignity of a lady who has had, by now, enough of a pleasant entertainment, and is taking her leave. "I have grinned back at him too. It is an art worth learning."

Her body follows the trajectory of her soaring emotion, just as Prince Potenziani's bullet follows the line of the song he is about to send forth when he dies of love. Kasparson having risen with her, she looks at him with radiant eyes and they consummate their "marriage" with a duet as well as a *pas de deux*.

> "Kasparson, you great actor," she said, "Bastard of Égalité, kiss me."
>
> "Ah, no, Madame," said Kasparson, "I am ill; there is poison in my mouth."
>
> Miss Malin laughed. "A fig for that tonight," she said. She looked, indeed, past any sort of poison. She had on her shoulders that death's-head by which druggists label their poison bottles, an unengaging object for any man to kiss. But looking straight at the man before her, she said slowly and with much grace: *Fils de St Louis, montez au ciel!*

This is the climax of absurdity and beauty—that the skinny old maid offers her lips as a stairway to heaven, and that she addresses to Kasparson the words reputed to have been addressed to Louis XVI by the priest who officiated at his execution. The beauty is in the imaginative penetration to the potentiality which the absurdity symbolizes by its very extravagance, its equivalent amount of energy. It is because they have made an artwork of the night, made of it an occasion for intense and stylized gestures, that we can see through the old maid to the *donna angelicata* of the high old Western tradition of ideal love, and through the bastard to the true son of St Louis, the exemplary ancestor of the royal line of France. He kisses her, and she concludes the dance with one of the most finely executed flourishes in all Isak Dinesen. "With a majestic and graceful movement she lifted up the hem of her skirt and placed it in his hand. The silk, which had been trailing over the floor, was dripping wet. He understood that this was the reason why she had got up from her seat." Brought back with such wit and style, the tragic note blends with the comedy and poetry to make the story's concluding chord.

The water, which had risen to the level of the hayloft, threatens the young couple asleep on the floor, and it is to stop Kasparson from waking them that Miss Malin suggests, through a swift recapitulation of her life, the sense in which they are all to be saved.

> She took one of the actor's hands in hers. "Wait a moment," she said softly, so as not to waken the sleepers. "I want to tell you. I, too, was once a young girl. I walked in the woods and looked at the birds, and I thought: How dreadful that people shut up birds in cages. I thought: If I could so live and so serve the world that after me there should never again be any birds in cages, they should all be free—"

She stops, because she sees between the boards the symbol of their liberation—the dawn which brings them not the

rescue boat but death. The image of bird flight, which in her climax of understanding she had only demonstrated by her voice and motion, she now uses to epitomize her life as leading to that climax. For she has freed them all from the conditions which would have made the hayloft a prison. By turning the hayloft into a stage of the free play of the imagination, she has given them the freest hours of their lives—hours which have prepared them to make death their ultimate triumph over conditions. After such words and gestures, rescue would come as an anti-climax; it would turn the night into a burlesque, as the old lord of **"Sorrow-acre"** would have turned Anne-Marie's ordeal into burlesque had he stopped it. The end of life is not safety but self-realization.

It is because they are, in meeting death blithely, going to be everything they want to be, that they are saved. Additional years of life could take them no farther toward self-realization. There are, however, two kinds of blitheness. The sleeping young couple will meet death perfectly, because they are innocent of the water, the "dark figure, like that of a long thick snake" on the floor of the loft. The sleepless old couple will meet death perfectly, because they have outstared it, they have grinned back at the snake in the Garden, they know everything. That is what Miss Malin means when she says in effect: Do not wake them, I too was young and knew freedom as potentiality, do not confront their freedom with conditions for they will not have time to regain it as we have. Innocence and Innocence Regained! The two couples together symbolize the whole progress of the imagination in the romantic version of the myth of the fall. (pp. 68-72)

> *Robert Langbaum, in his* The Gayety of Vision: A Study of Isak Dinesen's Art, *1964. Reprint by Random House, 1965, 305 p.*

Donald Hannah   (essay date 1971)

[*In the following excerpt from his* "Isak Dinesen" *and* Karen Blixen: The Mask and the Reality, *Hannah considers the primary role of imagination in Dinesen's tales.*]

Looking back on Karen Blixen's life from her earliest days at Rungstedlund, throughout the years in Kenya, and then until her death in the same house where she was born, it is possible to discern a kind of pattern in which the different parts of her life fall into place as components of a whole. With its marked symmetry of outline it would seem to have been shaped by circumstances with such an aesthetic eye for the over-all design that her life came to resemble a work of art. So at least Karen Blixen herself saw it. In an interview in *Berlingske Aftenavis,* 24th June, 1950, she regretted the fact that, in her later years, her eyesight had deteriorated. This had been a sad experience, it was true, but it was also one that had had its compensations, for it had meant that somehow things had become more beautiful. She compared this to the way that connoisseurs of art do not stand close to a painting, but take a few steps back so as to appreciate the full effect. 'Perhaps it is just that which the years do with us—or for us! Without any initiative on our part, they lead us back a couple of paces from life and adjust our eyes to get the total impression of what the artist meant.'

These remarks about life offer a precise analogy to what takes place in her stories. There too, by means of the distance maintained between reader and story, we are led back a few paces to get the total impression of what the artist meant by the arrangement of the component parts. Moreover, if Karen Blixen looks at life in the same way as she would view art, this contains a further implication for her work. In her case, unlike so many other writers, it is not only autobiographical experience which, even if very indirectly, provides material for the content of her stories; in addition, the fact that she saw life as a paradigm of art also principally determines their aesthetic form. And the reader, kept at a distance by her narrative form, thus gains the same perspective of her art as she gained of her own life.

In **"The Cardinal's First Tale"**, after he has narrated his story, the lady in black, who is given no further description than that, tells him that she finds he has now become remote and even rather inhuman. He admits the truth of the charge, but adds:

> 'You will see the characters of the true story clearly, as if luminous and on a higher plane, and at the same time they may look not quite human, and you may well be a little afraid of them. That is all in the order of things. But I see . . . today, a new art of narration, a novel literature and category of belles-lettres, dawning upon the world . . . And this new art and literature—for the sake of the individual characters in the story, and in order to keep close to them and not to be afraid—will be ready to sacrifice the story itself.

> 'The individuals of the new books and novels—one by one—are so close to the reader that he will feel a bodily warmth flowing from them, and he will take them to his bosom and make them, in all situations of life, his companions, friends, and advisers. And while this interchange of sympathy goes on, the story itself loses ground and weight and in the end evaporates. . . . The divine art is the story.'

What the Cardinal is really doing here, of course, is defending his author's conception of the importance of the story itself. The reader's attention (like the writer's) is focused upon the whole; it is not directed to the individual parts—such as the characters. ' "I write about characters who together *are* the tale," ' Isak Dinesen said in *Harper's Magazine* [February, 1965]. ' "I begin, you see, with the flavour of the tale. Then I find the characters, and they take over. They make the design; I simply permit them their liberty . . . I write about characters within a design, how they act upon one another." '

This seems an excellent account of what happens in her stories—except that it is extremely doubtful how far her characters are ever really permitted their liberty or allowed to 'take over'. On the contrary, they are kept in very taut leading strings by the author; they neither exist in their own right, nor indeed are they meant to. Isak Dinesen's imagination in the tales does not function primarily in terms of characterisation—one or two major traits are enough and the salient features are established. The characters are assigned to a few clearly defined categories, and the same types are found again and again.

There is also another side to these figures. In most of her stories what the characters say is at least as important as

what they do, and this is reflected in the emphasis which is placed upon the dialogue. Some of them are composed almost entirely of this—**"Converse at Night in Copenhagen"** is precisely what the title indicates; in others, like **"A Consolatory Tale"**, or **"The Cardinal's First Tale"**, the story is really told in order to illustrate or develop points in a conversation. In others like **"The Supper at Elsinore"** or **"The Deluge at Norderney"**, the crucial events have actually taken place before the tale starts, and the action consists in bringing the characters together into a place where they can talk. ' "Recount to me your stories,' the Cardinal says in **"The Deluge"** ', and this is what they do, in the conversation which lasts throughout the night until day-break. And even in those tales, like **"Copenhagen Season"**, where the stress falls more on the narration of events, Isak Dinesen places at least one eloquent figure to expound the main themes in the story, as a kind of fixed point around which the whole action revolves.

All of her chief characters then are good talkers—and good listeners. They develop their views at length, expatiate on their subjects, launch into flights of fantasy, illuminate their theme with flashes of wit, while the others listen until their turn comes, or put in a comment, *sotto voce*, which sets off another train of ideas. Sometimes there is a clash of opinion; more often it is a measured exchange of views, even a kind of ordered debate, like the series of ceremonious exchanges which take place between the old lord and his nephew, Adam, in **"Sorrow-Acre"**. But the debate is one really held within the mind of their creator rather than one giving the impression of originating from within the characters themselves. It is *her* eloquence which flows directly through them, while they remain immovably fixed in the category to which they have been assigned. What they lose in psychological depth, they gain in rhetorical eloquence; their inner life is externalised, and the movement of their thoughts is expressed through their speech and dialogue. The essence of the relationship between them, in short, consists of a series of verbal exchanges between various interlocutors much more than it is a relationship involving an interaction between fully individualised persons.

The contrast her fictional characters make with the people described in *Out of Africa* has already been noted; but it is possible at this stage to discern an additional reason for this. In the same interview in *Harper's Magazine* she explained why she wrote of characters within a design and of their inter-relationship: 'relations with others is important to me, you see, friendship is precious to me.' It is the reflection of the relationship of the living woman to flesh and blood people which helps impart such humanity and warmth to *Out of Africa*. In that book there *is*—to use the words of the Cardinal to the lady in black—an 'interchange of sympathy', one which is deliberately eschewed in the stories. Why is this excluded? And why is the nature of the relationships in her tales so different from that depicted in *Out of Africa*?

In the tales the focus is shifted from the individual persons to the story as a whole. This adjustment of focus is one defined with such clarity that on one occasion she even represented it in visual terms. The Danish critic, Aage Henriksen, in an essay on Isak Dinesen, says that she would keep her stories by her for years before publishing them, and would lend copies of them to her friends on the strict understanding that they replied to them. Once, a friend of hers, greatly daring, made his reply by writing a sequel; in return, he was given what amounted to a graphic demonstration of the act of the short story:

> 'What is this supposed to be?' Karen asked. 'It's supposed to be a counter-story,' her friend replied, who had in truth not really considered what it was supposed to be. 'A counter-story, is something which doesn't exist,' she said. 'Nor is there anything called that.' . . . 'I'll show you just what a story looks like,' and she drew a pentagram. 'There! There's nothing to add to this, and nothing to take away. In the same way a story is finished when it is completed.' [*Det quddornmelige Barn og andre Essays on Karen Blixen*].

It is the figure of the pentagram upon which Isak Dinesen concentrates, and the characters are visualised as being within this. The form of the story, therefore, does not so much develop organically as an interplay between plot and character, but is rather one which is imposed around the characters as a kind of elaborate frame which sets off their actions. A ballet-like achievement of pattern, executed with a stylised grace and a refined decorum is the effect Isak Dinesen often seeks to convey. As a result many of her tales are meant to be enjoyed aesthetically for the clarity and shapeliness of their structure and for the intellectual challenge they offer to unravel their meaning. The individual story is woven together into an intricate arabesque of plot-design; to work out the full consequences of the plot, to interlock all the parts together into an elaborately completed whole is, in fact, the process which engages Isak Dinesen's imagination to its fullest extent. And it is possible to illustrate this process by reference to her manuscripts.

'I begin with the flavour of the tale,' she said. Amongst her manuscripts there are about sixty suggestions and working-notes (all of them quite brief) for the novel, *Albondocani* which she was working on during the last years, but never completed. These notes show more precisely what this flavour consisted of, and give a considerable insight into certain aspects of the working of her imagination.

A few of them consist of a concept or an idea around which a story could possibly be constructed; others sketch out a situation or outline a plot. . . . (pp. 73-8)

Having got the initial idea or sketch of a situation, the next stage was the one which took Isak Dinesen most time. Keeping the drafts by her for years so that she had several different stories on the stocks at the same time, she would recast them again and again. The painstaking care with which she elaborated her plots is amply demonstrated by her manuscripts. She would take a particular incident in a story, amplify it in one draft, then becoming dissatisfied, would abandon it. Then she would start another version of the same incident, this time condense it, and try to fit it into another place in the story, until this too would be given up. Beginning all over again, she would rewrite the whole tale, re-arranging the sequence of the action, cutting here, transposing there, omitting some parts altogether, adding a detail here, altering a character's actions there. It is practically impossible to trace the chronological order in which the different drafts were written, and this is a direct consequence of the way in which she worked, weaving back and forth, constantly rearranging her material and shuffling the different parts around until they were finally composed into the order which satisfied her exacting demands. More evidence of the care to which even the smallest details were subjected is given in a reply which she made to some criticisms of **"The Roads round Pisa"** by the Danish scholar Hans Brix. Through a very detailed analysis of this tale Brix had tried to show certain inconsistencies in the plot. Isak Dinesen, however, turned the tables by refuting these objections in an even more minutely detailed analysis, showing the way in which it was constructed so that everything was interlinked to form an indivisible whole.

These manuscripts take us into her workroom and show us something of her method and the processes which the stories underwent during their composition, but it is also possible to discern the fundamental idea controlling these processes in her published work. In *Out of Africa* she describes a game she had been taught as a child; as an illustration of her method and intention it could hardly be improved upon:

> When I was a child I was shown a picture,—a kind of moving picture inasmuch as it was created before your eyes and while the artist was telling the story of it. This story was told, every time, in the same words.
>
> In a little round house with a round window and a little triangular garden in front there lived a man.

This house and garden are drawn on a sheet of paper. One night the man hears a terrible noise, rushes out, runs first one way then the other, and each time he does this, his movements are drawn on the paper. He stumbles over a big stone, falls into ditches, finds the water rushing out of a dam, and then has much trouble in plugging it. Finally he returns, utterly weary, to the house, and goes to bed. The next morning he looks out of the window and sees what it has all added up to—the picture of a stork. She adds this comment:

> I am glad that I have been told this story and I will remember it in the hour of need. The man in the story was cruelly deceived, and had obstacles put in his way. He must have thought: 'What ups and downs! What a run of bad luck!' He must have wondered what was the idea of all his trials, he could not know that it was a stork. But through them all he kept his purpose in view, nothing made him turn round and go home, he finished his course, he kept his faith. That man had his reward. In the morning he saw the stork. He must have laughed out loud then.
>
> The tight place, the dark pit in which I am now lying, of what bird is it the talon? *When the design of my life is completed, shall I, shall other people see a stork?*

The characters in Isak Dinesen's stories can also be deceived and have obstacles put in their way, but when the design of their life has been completed, the meaning is made plain—at the end of the story. Standing back and seeing the whole in retrospect, like the man looking back on the events of the previous night, the idea becomes clear—both to them and to the reader.

Isak Dinesen's major intention of showing the completed design, to which nothing can be added and from which nothing can be subtracted, gives one of the principle reasons for the fact that her tales are set in the past. As we have noted, the past is the dimension in which she felt her imagination could range most freely, and when asked on one occasion if all her tales were set in the nineteenth century, she indicated another of the reasons for this in her reply: 'I may begin in the eighteenth century and come right up to the First World War; my calendar is flexible. Those times have been sorted out; they are clearly visible.' And she goes on with words that directly recall her statement of what she believed took place in life as a result of the passing of time: 'The present is always unsettled, no one has time to contemplate it in tranquillity. No painter wants the subject right under his nose; one wants to stand back and study . . . with half-closed eyes.' [*Harper's Magazine,* February, 1965]

The fact that the setting in the past causes a distillation of the major issues and liberates the imagination is nowhere in Isak Dinesen's work better illustrated than in **"Sorrow-Acre"**, one of the finest of all her tales. It is based on a folk-tale from the south of Jutland; the details vary, but the most important version for our purpose is given in F. Ohrt's *Udvalgte Sønderjydske Folkesagn* (*Selected Folk-Tales from South Jutland*), published in 1919. This version runs as follows:

> During a flood with high tidal waves, a good deal of flotsam drifted ashore near Ballum. Amongst it, a young man from the town recognised some pieces belonging to his family, and started salvaging them. Whilst he was doing this, one of the robbers from Skærbæk came and wanted some of it. They started fighting, and the young lad unfortunately killed his opponent. At that time, however, these beach-robbers were so powerful that they had him condemned to death at the court-house. His mother, deeply distressed by this, went to the Count at his castle of Skakkenborg, told him of her grief, and implored him to show mercy towards her son. The Count promised her to do so on the condition that she must mow a field of barley between sunrise and sunset. This field was so large that four men would have much labour to cut it in one day. If she could do it, her son would be set free. The mother accepted the task, and did finish it. When she had cut the last handful with her sickle, she said,
>
>> Now the sun will set
>> Now God's mercy I will get.
>
> But at the very moment when she raised herself from her bent position, her back broke and she fell dead. The mother was buried in the churchyard at Ballum. On her grave, a stone has been laid, on which she is drawn with a sheaf and sickle in her arm. The field where she cut the corn is still shown. To this day it is known as Sorrow-Acre.

The date of the events giving rise to the folk-tale can be determined quite accurately since the flood took place in 1634. (pp. 79-82)

In **"Sorrow-Acre"**, a young man on the estate of a Danish nobleman has been accused of setting fire to one of the barns. Anne-Marie, his widowed mother, intercedes for him, and, like the mother in the folk-tale, is told that if she can cut a field of corn between sunrise and sunset her son will be set free. But if she fails, the case against her son will go through, and she will never see him again. To this

agreement the lord pledges his word and Anne-Marie accepts the conditions. We learn of this in retrospect, since the story begins with the thoughts and reminiscences of the lord's young nephew, Adam, newly returned from a long stay in England. It is through his eyes that we see much of the action, and the conflict of principles forming the core of the story emerges from the conversations which take place between the two men when Adam entreats the lord to retract his word, and thereby rescind the agreement with Anne-Marie. The lord steadfastly refuses to do this, and the rest of the story follows the folk-tale with the mother dying just as she has completed her task. The son is freed, and the field afterwards is named Sorrow-Acre.

From this some of the changes made will be apparent; two, in particular, are very significant. A completely new character, Adam, is introduced, and moreover his importance in the story is even stressed by the method of narration. The other major change is that the date at which the events take place has been altered. It is still kept in the past, but the times have been moved forward by well over a hundred years. This date is just as firmly given as in the folk-tale, though more indirectly. During the course of the story, Adam lends his uncle a book which has recently been published; it is described as a tragedy dealing with the gods of Nordic mythology, by Johannes Ewald (the same poet who had lived for a time at Rungstedlund), and it is clear the work is *Balders Død* (*The Death of Balder*), first published in 1775. The introduction of a new main character and a shift time from 1634 to about 1775—why are these changes made?

These two alterations are connected and together point to one of the major themes. The story is now set in the period when the long-established, semi-feudal, landed society of the eighteenth century (reminiscent of that in Kenya) is beginning to face the challenge of new ideas. And in this challenge, the ethos of the age in decline is more sharply defined and is made, in Isak Dinesen's own phrase about the winnowing effect of the past, 'clearly visible'. Moreover, the fact that it is *Balders Død* which gives rise to the discussions between Adam and his uncle is clearly intended not only to give the period in which **"Sorrow-Acre"** is set, but also to throw the clash between the opposing attitudes into even sharper relief. Ewald's drama centres on Balder, who in this work is a Nordic demi-god driven to his death by the force of his irresistible passion for Nanna, a mortal woman; although a demi-god, he is powerless to control his emotions. For the old lord the main significance of the book is that it marks the emergence of a new era, which 'has made to itself a God in its own image, an emotional God', and is thus in complete opposition to the ideal of responsibility and omnipotence upon which he bases his conduct, and which is represented for him by the ancient gods of classical mythology. In other words, the setting of the folk-tale has been transferred so that Isak Dinesen's short story now stands at the cross-roads of one of the great movements in European social and cultural history; and the figure of Adam is introduced to be the voice of the new age. . . . A ready sympathy is aroused by the views expressed . . . by Adam. But perhaps the sympathy is felt a little too readily and the identification with one character made too swiftly. For part of the greatness of **"Sorrow-Acre"** lies in the fact that the reader is gradually forced away from this incipient identification with one character, is made to stand at a distance, and thus gain a clearer insight and imaginative understanding of the old lord's role, and everything which this represents. In particular we are made to realise the full implications of what is merely a 'caprice' or 'whim' for Adam. The conflicting issues in **"Sorrow-Acre"** are not simply formulated in abstract terms in the discussions; they take on a life of their own which is rendered by the complete story. They are really threads woven into the finished pattern, and which must be related to the whole; indeed the reader is compelled to do this by the narrative method.

The artistry, by which the reader is made to look at the old lord's role with an imaginative perception and a gradually quickened understanding, needs to be stressed. The method of narration is actually used by Isak Dinesen to weight the scales against the lord, since we see him mainly through the eyes of a highly critical Adam. It is a criticism presented with scrupulous honesty and to which full weight is given. And although Anne-Marie dies at the supreme moment of her love and glory, having kept faith and finally conquered over all her tribulation like the man in the story of the stork, nevertheless, her sacrifice, exacted by the conditions imposed by the lord, is not minimised in any way. On the contrary, it has been counted, and counted against him, in the finely rendered description of her death at the end. But the old lord is neither individualised, nor given any very human quality; he appears in the story as remote and as inhuman as the Cardinal seemed to the lady in black. Like her, he is not even given a name, but remains from first to last simply 'the old lord'. He is in fact, the product of a completely disciplined imagination, imperturbably keeping its distance, holding its powers rigorously within bounds, dispassionately subduing to the total demands of the story any innate sympathy for a particular character, or any trace of nostalgia for a lost order of society.

Although the short story has a much more limited compass than the novel, it still remains clear that Isak Dinesen's imagination, when engaged in representing a past age, does not belong to that type—like Thackeray's, for instance, in *Henry Esmond*—which musters a wealth of historical detail into a composite picture, and reconstructs the life of a period in that way. Instead she fastens on the more general features of a past era and etches these in, sharply, but economically. The figure of the old lord is an example of this, for his lack of individualisation in the story is partly a reflection of his social position in that age. Thus he becomes a typical representative of the *ancien régime,* of its way of life and ideals. (pp. 83-6)

The reader's imaginative understanding of the old lord's character also extends to the part he plays. His character in the story is his part in life; the two cannot be separated, for they are made into one by the way in which he is presented. By her way of depicting him, Isak Dinesen succeeds, against all modern predilections, and against all odds, in investing his duties with a certain nobility and grandeur and in compelling our respect. He is seen as the embodiment of the duties of the great land-owners of the past both to their land and to the people living on it, as an incarnation of the principle of *noblesse oblige.* This, in turn, shows the part which the fine evocation of the Danish landscape at the beginning contributes to the whole. Here Isak Dinesen really does 'stand back and study a landscape with half-closed eyes'; but the details, painted in so deftly, are not there merely to provide local colour. Like the splendour of the descriptions in *Out of Africa,* which affords a fitting background to the heroic nature of life there, these details in **"Sorrow-Acre"** are also made to contribute to the total effect. The description is of a landscape—but of a landscape with figures; rendered in terms of the people who inhabit it, it ceases to be merely this, and becomes a land where life falls into an ordered pattern of existence, drawn by generations of people, traced by stability, marked by tradition and order, and maintained throughout the centuries by these same qualities (pp. 86-7)

In this rendering of a way of life, country-house and peasant hut, peasant and lord, are inter-dependent parts. **"Sorrow-Acre"** itself is but one field, a single piece in the mosaic of the Danish countryside. Much more is at stake for the lord than Anne-Marie's individual fate and destiny—or even his own. Representation of the unity of this life becomes the design of the story—design in every sense—which is reaffirmed at the close, when, in the evening-light, the people left in the field after Anne-Marie's death bind up the corn she has cut: 'the old lord stayed with them for a long time, stepping along a little, and again standing still. As it grew darker he could walk up quite close to them or move amongst them, without being recognised.'

The old order has been re-affirmed and the unity of this life endures—but for how long? As in Kenya, after Berkeley Cole's death, history itself and historical change break into this stable world, set in the past and enclosed within the framework of the story: Adam has his destiny to fulfil. His relationship to the lord's young wife is not elaborated, but the suggestion of their growing intimacy also forms part of the story. There is no heir to the land, and it has been foretold Adam that a son of his will inherit the estate. The setting in the past, which causes the conflict between the two ways of life, also indicates the way the issues will be decided. And it is one which heightens the old lord's stature into that of an indomitable figure defending a dying order.

One final point remains to be made about the lord, for concealed behind him can be discerned much of Isak Dinesen's own attitude. For him 'tragedy is the privilege of man, his highest privilege', whereas 'the true art of the Gods is the comic'. He develops this belief by saying that on earth, the aristocrats 'who stand in lieu of the Gods . . . should leave to our vassals their monopoly of tragedy, and for ourselves accept the comic with grace', and he acts accordingly by leaving to Anne-Marie her monopoly of tragedy. But if she is made into a tragic figure by the lord's actions, he is made into something very different by the author. By implying that the old lord will be made a cuckold by his young wife and Adam, Isak Dinesen has thus identified him with one of the most traditional figures of comedy. And in this lies the paradox. For by doing this, she has implicitly endorsed the validity of his attitude and beliefs, solely by means of the story itself and the turn it is given, not by any overt expression of sympathy with his ideals. The lord says that 'the very same fatality which, in striking the burgher or peasant will become tragedy, with the aristocrat is exalted to the comic. By the grace and wit of our acceptance hereof our aristocracy is known'. If these beliefs govern his behaviour in **"Sorrow-Acre"**, they also define with equal force that of Karen

Blixen herself as revealed in *Out of Africa*. The story's historical setting is eighteenth-century Denmark, but personal remembrance of grace and wit also constitutes a part of the imagination which created "Sorrow-Acre".

Some further qualities of Isak Dinesen's imagination, deriving from the fact that the stories are set in the past, can be explored by a comparison of the tale, "Copenhagen Season", with an unpublished one, "Carnival". "Carnival" is set in the mid-nineteen-twenties, and thus is exceptional in that it falls quite outside the period in which she usually places her tales. In it a supper-party is held in a large house on the outskirts of Copenhagen after a masked ball in the town. The guests come to the house in the fancy-dress they have worn at the ball; they are all depicted as bright young things of the period, and give, what is to us now, a rather faded air of determined frivolity. There is one character who is an exception to this: an elderly painter called Rosendahl, who is described thus:

> Since it seemed strange that such a very brilliant person should have a little full-moon face, with no features, hair or expression to speak of, indeed most of all like the posterior of a baby, the pupils of his painting school, who loved him, had developed a theory that there had been a shifting about in his anatomy, and that he had an eminently radiant and expressive face at the other place.

This is transferred almost verbatim to "Copenhagen Season", where it is used to describe the artist, Professor Sivertsen. But this is not the only similarity between the two stories.

In the conversation during supper, Rosendahl states that, in his belief, the present age is inferior to previous times because it has banished tragedy from life; the way in which this has been done, however, is never made very clear, for he does not see this in social terms, but instead illustrates this absence of tragedy aesthetically, in terms of painting. Black, he says, is necessary for a painting since it gives a contrast to all the other colours; if the painter is denied its use, all the other hues pale into insignificance. Similarly tragedy is an essential part of life, and it is really one of man's rights to be allowed to preserve a sense of the darker side of life. Talking of the slum-clearance recently undertaken in Copenhagen, he says: 'We had much trouble in making some of the old inhabitants move away,—good, decent people, who clung to the right of man, to preserve a little bit of darkness of their own.'

The remainder of the story can be quickly summarised. All the people present are well-off, and they decide to draw lots to see which one of them shall live on their pooled income for a year, during which time the others are to be penniless. A man enters at this point, dressed all in black as Zamor, Madame du Barry's Negro page. At the sight of him the painter thinks: 'These people see in him only a Carnival joke. But there is more here. Perhaps a good deal of suffering, despair, a surprise to the whole party.' A surprise it is. Holding up the party with a gun, he demands their money, saying that he is a desperate man and not to be trifled with since he has already killed one person, the woman who owned the antique shop where he worked. They treat this fairly calmly, and instead persuade him to take part in their lottery. One of the characters wins, and announces that she will take Zamor with her for the year 'to be my conscience. Shall I not be al-

lowed to have a conscience, Rosie? Something black in my life, a little *mouche* on my soul?'

The plot has been rather baldly summarised because one can thus see the significance of the striking contrast this story, taking place in the twentieth century, makes with the rest of Isak Dinesen's work, set a hundred to a hundred and fifty years ago. The highly melodramatic nature of the plot is very apparent, and this is even heightened by the incongruity this makes with such features of twentieth-century life as slum-clearance and with the modernity of the characters—most of them have sports-cars, one of them has his own aeroplane. In "Carnival" the representation of an historical period has really dwindled to a passing reference to an antique shop. Nevertheless, although the plot is melodramatic, it is no more so than most of Isak Dinesen's other tales; there is little to choose between the plot of this story and, say, that of "The Deluge at Norderney", where a valet murders his master, the Cardinal, in order to impersonate him; or that of "The Supper at Elsinore" in which the ghost of a pirate returns to Elsinore to visit his two sisters. In these stories, however, the melodrama, instead of being incongruously at odds with the contemporary scene, becomes simply one more aspect marking the story off from our own day and age. It is not only the author's imagination that is liberated by setting the stories in the past, so too is the reader's.

If the way in which the modern age has banished tragedy from life is never made clear in "Carnival", in "Copenhagen Season" this becomes a major theme. (pp. 87-91)

The story is set in Denmark in the eighteen-seventies and its remoteness from the present is stressed. It is a period for Isak Dinesen hall-marked by a code of honour, and it is just as obvious from this story, as it was from "Sorrow-Acre", that an age which held honour so dearly is one which Isak Dinesen's imagination found much more congenial than modern times. Ib Angel, based as we have seen upon her father, has fought a duel of honour, even though duels have been prohibited. The age is also one nearing its end and standing on the threshold of the present. But before it finally passes away, it gives Ib, the epitome of the period, the opportunity to perform a tragic action by steadfastly maintaining its code.

Ib Angel is in love with Adelaide, who belongs to one of the noblest families in the Danish aristocracy. (p. 91)

The social position of Adelaide's family plays an essential part in the tale. Ib Angel does not belong to the aristocracy, and the barrier this establishes entirely precludes any question of marriage between them. In what is to be their last meeting, which takes place in secret, it is made clear that if he personifies the honour of his age, Adelaide is also representative of it in another way. Without realising the implication of her suggestion, she tells him that she is willing to go on meeting him illicitly:

> For a second her total and absolute ignorance of the coarser facts of life, which was the *fine fleur* of her education and upbringing—as of the education and upbringing of all noble young girls of her age—and had been obtained with such a tenacity of purpose and such continuous watchfulness as later ages cannot imagine or believe, awakened in him the reverence which was the highest product of the education of all noble young men . . . He knew well

enough what, according to the code of orthodox morality he ought to say to her . . . But orthodox morality had become a thing of the vanished past . . . Here at last were Ib and Adelaide, alone in the universe . . . And then, just then, at the moment when he had quashed all outside laws, the law of his own being spoke out and passed sentence on him.

Ib sacrifices his love to his code of honour and thus fulfils the conditions which Professor Sivertsen had stated as being necessary for tragedy.

In **"Carnival"**, the past with its idea of tragedy offers a contrast to the present, but it is one only stated, and remains a shadow without substance. The situation is exactly reversed in **"Copenhagen Season"**, there, a past era is concretely described, takes on form and substance, and by means of this the present time is weighed in the balance and found wanting. Like Professor Sivertsen, who condemns the times to come because, lacking honour, they lack also the conditions necessary to create a tragedy, Isak Dinesen's moral condemnation of the present and approbation of a past ethos are also expressed in aesthetic terms and implicitly testified to by the very existence of the story itself.

So far we have been considering the way in which Isak Dinesen's imagination functions particularly in its concern with the past, but there is also a way in which it is engaged with the present, namely, in the person of the reader of her tales. 'It is not a bad thing in a tale that you understand only half of it,' Lincoln Forsner says in **"The Dreamers"**, before embarking upon his story; it is a remark that represents another facet of Isak Dinesen's attitude to the reader, and the story of **"The Young Man with the Carnation"** helps define this more closely.

The main character, Charlie Despard, is a writer who believes that his creative imagination has now atrophied so that he will never be able to write another book. He feels that he has been turned from 'a human being into printed matter', and that of his own free will, but without, until then, counting the cost, he has exchanged all the things that constitute life for 'the words that describe them'. Arriving late at night in Antwerp to rejoin his wife, he goes up to her hotel room and gets into bed without waking her. Shortly after, he hears someone try the door, opens it, and finds a young man with a carnation in his buttonhole standing outside. The man apologises when he sees Charlie, and leaves. But Charlie is unable to sleep and begins to speculate about the young man, for, in his thoughts, he has come to represent everything in life he himself has renounced in order to become an artist. . . . He gets up and goes down to the harbour where he spends the rest of the night in an inn talking to some sailors; during the time he is there, he feels his imagination again stirring to life and tells them a story.

In the morning Charlie returns to the hotel, meets his wife, then discovers that the room he had entered the previous evening was in fact not hers. His imagination now even more aroused by the mystery in which he has inadvertently been involved, he decides that he will write a story about it:

> As Charlie now looked back on the happenings of the night, with the experienced eye of an author of

fiction, they moved him as mightily as if they had been out of a book of his own. He drew in his breath deeply. 'Almighty God,' he said from the bottom of his heart, 'as the heavens are higher than the earth, so are Thy short stories higher than our short stories.' He went through all the details slowly, and surely, as a mathematician sets up and solves an equation.

A rather obtrusive colloquy follows between God and Charlie, in which God maintains that to be isolated from life is an irrevocable edict imposed on the artist; through this dialogue Charlie Despard becomes reconciled to his lot and sees life as providing the raw material for the artist's creative imagination and human existence being of importance because it affords a subject for aesthetic activity. The tale ends with his thoughts returning to the young man and the story he is now certain he will write about him.

His solution to the equation posed by the young man is that he has witnessed a romantic assignation between two lovers, and it is this assignation he will write his story about; but it is by no means certain that this interpretation is the only construction which can be placed on the events since other possibilities easily suggest themselves to the reader. And the fact that the options are left open is something deliberately intended by Isak Dinesen. **"The Young Man with the Carnation"** is really a kind of palimpsest; one interpretative design has been drawn and made complete, but beneath this pattern, other outlines can be discerned. The tale not only describes the way in which the artist's creative faculties are aroused; the reader's imagination is also awakened by following the events and attempting to square them with his own interpretation.

At the same time the story has certain radical flaws. The description of Charlie Despard going through the details of the plot like a mathematician setting up, and then solving, an equation, reveals a disturbingly high degree of contrived ingenuity, and the plot itself is more like the preliminary sketches for a story one finds among Isak Dinesen's manuscripts than a tale that has gradually been enriched over a long period of time by her usual vein of fantasy. And the similarity with these working-sketches is really no coincidence, since the story is actually meant to illustrate the role allotted the reader within her scheme of artistry as a whole. Further evidence of this—and one which exposes even more clearly the weaknesses of this story—is provided by **"The Caryatides"**.

Although it appears in *Last Tales*, **"The Caryatides"** was actually written many years previously; like **"Carnival"** it was originally intended as part of *Seven Gothic Tales*, but was subsequently dropped from that collection. First published in Danish in 1938 as an unfinished tale by the Swedish literary periodical, *Bonniers Litterära Magasin*, it was still incomplete when included some twenty years later in *Last Tales*. . . .

There really seems no doubt that the story is deliberately left unfinished. The length of time between writing and first publishing it (at least four years, since *Seven Gothic Tales* came out in 1934), and then all the years that elapsed before it was finally included in *Last Tales*, point very strongly to this. But the most convincing reason lies in the fact that without a shadow of a doubt it *is* best that it finishes where it does and the riddle remains unsolved.

The main house of the "farm in Africa, at the foot of the Ngong Hills." Dinesen stands before the entrance.

It is better that the reader's imagination should be stimulated to try and unravel the Gordian knot than that the sphinx-like author should go on to cut it; nor is it surprising that she did not dare go on—and run the risk of an anti-climax.

The problem in **"The Caryatides"** is a much more integral part of the plot than in **"The Young Man"**, and there is a highly imaginative aura cast around all the events by a gypsy, who has the reputation of being a witch, and plays a key-role in the action. Moreover, whereas Charlie Despard was an artist with no roots anywhere, here the characters are firmly placed in a particular context, and again it is one which defines the role they play in the story—particularly that of the women, as Caryatides, who uphold a semi-feudal world by the position they occupy in it. Philippe is married to a woman, who, he discovers after their marriage, is really his sister. If the true nature of their relationship is revealed, it will bring the world of their estate, together with the lives of all those dependent upon them, down in ruins. The story breaks off before Philippe's wife discovers the truth, but she may—or may not—be about to do so.

"The Caryatides" is really a virtuoso exercise in pure ambivalence; the reader is mischievously teased into participation in the game—and most of his enjoyment of the story must stem from this fact being recognised. The

sphinx is really wearing a smile. 'It is not a bad thing in a tale that you understand only half of it'; it is more, it is an essential condition of Isak Dinesen's art.

In his essay, "Notes on the Novel" [in *The Dehumanization of Art and Other Writings on Art and Culture*] Ortega y Gasset writes that, if we examine the way in which the novel has developed from its beginnings to the present day, we can observe that, from being narrative and indirect, the novel has become direct and descriptive, or, what he calls, 'presentative'. It is a generalisation that would require some considerable qualification when applied to the novel's development as a whole, but its interest lies in the way Ortega defines 'presentative':

> . . . . when we are fascinated by a novel is is not because of its subject, not because we are curious to know what happened to Mr So-and-so. The subject of any novel can be told in a few words and in this form holds no interest. A summary narration is not to our taste; we want the novelist to linger and to grant us good long looks at his personages, their being, and their environment till we have had our fill and feel that they are close friends whom we know thoroughly in all the wealth of their lives. That is what makes of the novel an essentially slow-moving genre as either Goethe or Novalis observed. I will go even further and say that today the novel is, and must be, a sluggish form—the very opposite therefore of a story.

As a description of what Isak Dinesen does *not* do this could hardly be improved upon. She neither lingers in this way, nor gives us good long looks at her personages, nor do we ever become close friends. On the other hand, 'summary narration' could hardly be bettered as a description of her technique: her method is that which Ortega criticises sharply when employed by the novelist:

> We want to see the life of the figures in a novel, not to be told it. Any reference, allusion, narration only emphasizes the absence of what it alludes to. . . . When I read in a novel 'John was peevish' it is as though the writer invited me to visualize, on the strength of his definition, John's peevishness in my own imagination. That is to say, he expects me to be the novelist.

This is precisely an account of what happens with Isak Dinesen. We, too, as we have noted, are always kept aware of what is absent in her tales: given a summary, we are expected to amplify it until the full meaning is grasped. In fact the principle of omission operates just as stringently in her stories as it did in *Out of Africa,* and becomes a basic part of her artistic design; for it is a design in which the reader's imagination is compelled to participate in the very act of creation.

Her tales frequently seem baffling whilst reading them—and they are made deliberately so by the author. Time and again motives for the characters' actions are concealed, links in the plot are obscured, the significance of incidents is veiled at the time they happen, and their meaning is only elucidated later. This does not constitute wilful mystification for its own sake. The characters do trace out a meaningful design, but they are not fully aware of its import until the end—nor is the reader. If they are left in the dark, he too is given very little light. In retrospect, however, everything is clarified, but like the characters, the reader has to work at this. Assigned a part to play, he is made to play it by her conception of the artist's function: Isak Dinesen calls the tune and it demands an attentive listener. And all this is done in accordance with a definite creed that an atmosphere of mystery and a state of half-knowledge is the indispensable condition for calling the imagination into play—in life as well as in art.

The fundamental question this raises then is why does Isak Dinesen place such a high value on the role of the imagination? What, in the last analysis, is her conception of the artist's function and of his relationship to the reader? A description of this relationship is given in **"A Consolatory Tale"**, the other story in **Winter's Tales** in which Charlie Despard appears. Quoting the injunction to love thy God, he changes it somewhat. ' "Thou shalt," ' he says, ' "love they art with all thy heart, and with all thy soul, and with all thy mind. And thou shalt love thy public as thyself. . . All human relationships have in them something monstrous and cruel. But the relationship of the artist to the public is amongst the most monstrous." ' And after a while he continues:

> 'But do not imagine . . . that I have no compassion on the public, or am not aware of my guilt towards them . . . I have had to read the book of Job, to get strength to bear my responsibility at all.'

> 'Do you see yourself in the place of Job, Charlie?' asked Æneas.

> 'No,' said Charlie solemnly and proudly, 'in the place of the Lord.'

> 'I have behaved to my reader,' he went on slowly, 'as the Lord behaved to Job.'

In his essay, 'Religion, Poetry and the "Dilemma" of the Modern Writer' [*Literary Essays*], David Daiches points out that the central problem raised by the book of Job is that of theodicy, of the justice of the ways of God to men, and that this has long been a central theme in literature. 'The answer,' says Daiches, 'is generally given in terms of attitude rather than of logic. Job's problem disappears in a note of wonder—wonder at the grandeur and immensity of creation.' This is the course adopted by a writer like Milton, for example, who answers the questions posed by religion mainly in literary or aesthetic terms. Isak Dinesen also offers an answer in terms of an attitude and of an aesthetic concept, even if it is a more self-consciously elaborated and explicative aesthetic. She herself gave the reason for the frequent references to the book of Job found in her work in one sentence. Describing the Africans in *Out of Africa,* she writes that when they speak of the personality of God, they do so 'like the last chapters of the book of Job; it is the same quality, the infinite power of imagination, with which they are impressed'. It is this quality which also impresses her, and lies at the heart of her conception of the artist's function and of the part played by the imaginative faculties.

The artist and God are akin in the power of the imagination they both possess, even if that of God is greater. God and the imagination are really synonymous terms for Isak Dinesen. When God speaks out of the whirlwind to Job, He pleads, says Charlie 'the defence of the artist and of the artist only'. In fact He simply proclaims the omnipotence of His own imagination, and does not even attempt to justify the treatment meted out to Job in any moral or logical terms. And in the same way that God, in His behaviour to Job, asserts a majesty that may not be questioned, so too is the artist vindicated in his treatment of his characters and of the reader. Art thus becomes ultimately a religion, and the artist himself is turned into a surrogate for God, omniscient and all-powerful in the world he has created by his edict. And his word is not to be gainsaid. All tribulation is finally justified by the revelation of the design, and by the quality of the artist's imagination displayed through this revelation. The parallel this suggests with her own life is obvious. Moreover, if it is the fact that she saw life as a paradigm of art which ultimately determines the aesthetic form of her tales, this also has a concomitant effect. For the truth is that Isak Dinesen believes that life can be understood—and only fully understood—by the analogy it offers with art. We are, all of us, artists, creating the story of our lives in the very process of living, and striving to grasp its full significance through our imaginative faculties.

The artist in his work is like God in creation—indeed, according to one of the aphorisms she wrote among the notes for *Albondocani,* he becomes God: 'It is blasphemous to introduce God into novels and writing (the writer *is* God).' This belief opens a further perspective. We have noted previously that she uses the omniscient author technique in such a way that the reader never forgets her presence as the story-teller; that she continually interposes the *persona* of the narrator between us and the narration of events; and that our awareness of these qualities is sharpened by her distinctive idiom. But in the light of this belief we can see that these aspects of her narrative technique are all parts of a much more comprehensive scheme of ideas. The fullness of creation witnesses to the presence and the glory of a supreme power—whether it be God or the artist. If God is the Supreme Author, the author himself is God made everywhere manifest in his creative work. Isak Dinesen's narrative technique is not one chosen only because it best suited her genius; it constitutes an indivisible part of what she has to say. It is, in reality, a means of expressing her fundamental belief about the artist's supreme power, and of keeping the reader aware of this: through the form itself of the tales her creed is expressed and its validity demonstrated.

The situation of the artist tallies with that of God at further points. In **"The Cardinal's First Tale"**, the Lord catechises the artist-priest before his ordination:

> 'You are aware,' he said, 'that I am almighty. And you have before you the world which I have created. Now give me your opinion on it. Do you take it that I have meant to create a peaceful world?' 'No, my Lord,' the candidate replied. 'Or that I have,' the Lord asked, 'meant to create a pretty and neat world?' 'No, indeed,' answered the youth. 'Or a world easy to live in?' asked the Lord. 'O, good Lord, no!' said the candidate. 'Or do you,' the Lord asked for the last time, 'hold and believe that I have resolved to create a sublime world, with all things necessary to the purpose in it, and none left out?' 'I do,' said the young man. 'Then,' said the Master, 'then, My servant and mouthpiece, take the oath!'

In the same way Isak Dinesen does not create a neat and pretty world, not a peaceful one, nor one easy to live in. And this needs stressing, since, although the world of her fiction does offer a release from actuality, it is neither an escape into an idealised state of existence nor a flight into an easier sphere of life. Nevertheless, she does in a very definite sense create a sublime world of the imagination, remote from ordinary life, with all things necessary for understanding it, and with nothing left out.

As God fashioned man to work out the divine purpose, so too the artist fashions his characters to work out a story. In order to do this God has need of man ('it is even doubtful,' says Charlie Despard, 'whether the Lord is not more dependent upon Job than Job upon the Lord'); in the same way the artist has need of his characters. And just as God moves in a mysterious way his wonders to perform, so also does the artist—indeed to create a sense of mystery is one of his major functions.

The final analogy with God is the most far-reaching of all, and it is one which shows that in this aspect Isak Dinesen's work must be seen as contributing its part to what is possibly one of the chief endeavours of art in our time—the attempt to find an aesthetic equivalent for a Christian tradition regarded as moribund. At the beginning of **"The Young Man with the Carnation"** Charlie Despard's situation in life is like that of Job's. 'The love of God and the certainty that in return God loved him beyond other human beings, had upheld him in times of poverty and adversity . . . But now he felt that God had turned away from him. . . . He had become estranged from God, and how was he now to live?' At the end, God speaks to him

in the same terms as he spoke to Job and reveals the fullest extent of his imaginative design; Charlie is reconciled to his lot and understands God's purpose—but only because his own imagination has been re-awakened. Similarly, Isak Dinesen believes that the questioning of God's purpose by Job is caused by a lack of understanding resulting from a failure of the imagination to comprehend God's ways with mankind. When God at last reveals the whole scope of his plan of creation, Job can then say with humility: 'Who is he that hideth counsel without knowledge? therefore have I uttered that I understood not; things too wonderful for me, which I knew not.'

It is the same answer we are made to give; we become as Job. For Isak Dinesen, only by the exercise of the imagination, in life, as well as in art, can we comprehend the design, understand the purpose of our existence—and be reconciled to our lot. This is the full extent of the function and the importance of imagination for her. (pp. 92-102)

> *Donald Hannah, "The Function of Imagination," in his* "Isak Dinesen" and Karen Blixen: The Mask and the Reality, *Putnam & Company, 1971, pp. 73-102.*

Marcia Landy   (essay date 1978)

[*In the following excerpt, Landy contends that Dinesen recreated in her short fiction the oral tradition of storytelling through her use of myth, dreams, and the presence of death.*]

Isak Dinesen was a storyteller. She worked in a genre which has become increasingly rare in the modern world, one which has been identified more with men than with women. She knew well the difference between the modern novelist and the storyteller, much as Marxist critics Georg Lukacs and Walter Benjamin know and describe that difference. Her preference for the tale is based on her self-conscious recognition of the differences between the oral and the written tradition in fiction and her desire and ability to recreate in writing the earlier conditions of telling a story. The conflicts, language, settings, and modes of characterization reveal Dinesen's bias against modernism and against bourgeois society. No Marxist, Dinesen uses class issues, particularly the historical vantage point of aristocracy, to expose bourgeois sentiment and behavior as a mask for personal security, exploitation, and privilege.

To understand Dinesen's narrative art, one must understand her conception of the tale or "anecdote" and of the role of the storyteller. She rejects psychological analysis in her works, most particularly analysis of the Freudian variety. In her presentation of character, she strives for the typical. Her stories have much in common with the folk tale. She sets her tales in earlier times, preferring past to contemporary history. The present exists by implication, and by contrast. Furthermore, the presence of death in many of her tales gives them a sense of urgency and authority so necessary to the storyteller, as Walter Benjamin tells us.

In his classic essay, "The Storyteller," Benjamin emphasizes the authoritative role of the storyteller. That authority derives from a knowledge of the role death plays in determining life choices: "death is the sanction of everything that the storyteller can tell. He has borrowed his authority from death. In other words, it is a natural history to which his stories refer back." The knowledge of death, of loss, of change, and of endings gives historical perspective. Death is a great teacher, and the storyteller is a sage who "has counsel—not for a few situations, as the proverb does, but for many, like the sage." (pp. 389-90)

Though Isak Dinesen, like Franz Kafka, uses myth, dreams and parable, she is not interested in complex but futile constructions of reality, nor does she view life solely from the perspective of failure. The crucial, but difficult, element to describe in her work is the peculiar combination of simplicity and complexity. The simplicity derives from the basic life and death situations in which she places her characters, from the representative nature of her portraits and plots, and from the narrator's active concern to shape a moral context for an eagerly listening audience. The complexity derives from the writer's toughness, her refusal to sentimentalize or to evade conflict, and especially from the knowledge that storytelling recreates and affirms the human process of constructing reality. For Dinesen, the emphasis on dialogue between author and audience and among the characters is a paradigm for community.

Of the craft of storytelling, which she explores throughout her work, she finds:

> Fashions have changed, and the art of listening to a narrative has been lost in Europe. The Natives of Africa, who cannot read, have still got it; if you begin to them: "There was a man who walked out on the plain, and there he met another man," you have them all with you. . . . But white people . . . they have been accustomed to take in their impressions by the eye. [*Out of Africa*]

Allowing for her limited cross-cultural knowledge of "Natives of Africa" and "white people," what Dinesen acknowledges here is the reciprocal context for storytelling. The integral relationship between storyteller and auditor is a paradigm for unalienated relationships. The ear, hearing, represents a more active and shared experience than the eye which represents a more abstract and differentiating experience and thus is more isolating. . . . The oral tradition which stands behind the tale nourishes and maintains the validity and importance of social discourse. Dinesen sees herself as a modern Scheherazade; the narrative techniques of the *Arabian Nights* and of the *Decameron* are influential in her tales. Her reflexiveness about the art of storytelling is as integral to her tales as is the content which explores reciprocity.

A brief look at the influences which have moulded Dinesen's narrative concerns reveals the choices she made in her role of storyteller. Her indebtedness to the Scandinavian oral tradition has been noted by her critics. Along with the *Arabian Nights* and the *Decameron,* Shakespeare's influence ranks high. Her *Winter's Tales* are structured around dominant Shakespearian motifs—the relationship between art and nature, loss and recovery, and the pastoral elegiac vision as a vehicle for exploring these motifs. One finds allusions to the German romantics in her work in the exploration of the Gothic, the nostalgic, the appeal of the South, and in her interest in the creative individual. She also draws on the history and literature of eighteenth and nineteenth-century France in order to give her tales a setting which shows a society in transition.

Many of her tales are drawn from Danish society in the nineteenth century, and her locations are often pastoral.

The setting of her stories and the situations she describes give an aura of historical legitimacy. She sets her characters during times of war (**"The Heroine"**), of revolution (**"The Dreamers"** and **"Babette's Feast"**), and of impending natural disasters (**"The Deluge at Norderney"**). As in *Out of Africa,* they record a passing world and they juxtapose older values against emerging contemporary values. The tales are anecdotes of human actions in the face of deluges, tempests, struggles with the soil, with the seasons, and with avoidable and unavoidable human conflicts. The pastoral is the storyteller's haven. It is a propaedeutic genre, enabling the narrator to explore affinities between human beings and nature, the inevitable estrangement between the two, the consequences for the estrangement through loss and death, and the potential for confronting and transcending limitations. Because of its established conventions, its emphasis on correspondences, and its concern with elemental situations, it enhances the authority of the narrator and the representativeness of character and situation.

Through memory and reconstruction, the tale provides the reconciliation to death and loss. The act of discourse, like culture, compensates for discontinuity in nature. In Dinesen's tales, characters typify the old and new. They are captured in moments of crisis and choice. They are memorable—both author and personages—not for their personal suffering, their internal conflicts, but for their heroism or cowardice and because they are not self-indulgent. A classic example in the tales of Dinesen's predilection for the anecdotal and typical is **"The Heroine"** (*Winter's Tales*). This tale is strikingly reminiscent of the work of another storyteller: Guy de Maupassant's "Boule de Suif." Héloise, the heroine, is asked by one of the German officers during the Franco-Prussian war to appear nude before him, and by so doing to save the lives of the other people stranded with her in a German town and trying to make their way back to France. She refuses to make the decision. She calls on the other members of the group to decide. They decide not to let her do this in their behalf, even if this means their death. Years later, we learn when she and the narrator meet again, that she is an actress and appearing in the nude is not at all an unusual thing for her to do. Her heroism, therefore, consists in allowing others to act heroically, since the act would have cost her very little. She thus subordinates her own personal desires in the interests of others. The actions are simple. Furthermore, Dinesen avoids any psychological exploration of the heroine's behavior. She prefers to see Héloise's actions as arising from the exigencies of the war situation. Héloise typifies the potential people have for heroism when confronted by a life and death situation.

"The Heroine," like many of the other tales, is a parable. The description of the events as an anecdote gives them their parabolic character. It is the moment of crisis that stands out and other kinds of analysis are irrelevant. The reader has no difficulty accepting Héloise's actions, her explanations of these actions, and the author's choice of this anecdote. This tale is an excellent example of the way Dinesen subordinates personality to events. It demonstrates too, in Benjamin's terms, how death plays an important role for the storyteller, reinforcing the aura of authority and wisdom.

Behind Dinesen's heroes and heroines is the heroic stance of the storyteller herself. Unswervingly, she pursues meaning, totality, and a vision of life which identifies basic opposing tendencies and which seeks to mediate these oppositions. The mythical, the familiar, and the typical is all-important to her. Her treatment of character in the tales, like her comment on the life of white settlers and the Africans in *Out of Africa,* are principally concerned with collective truths and with community. She explores the relationship of individuals to each other. She rejects partial truths. Storyteller, characters, and readers are invited to explore their deepest needs and desires, contradictory though they may seem to socially legitimated forms of behavior, in order to arrive at more fundamental insights about behavior.

Dinesen, the storyteller, is not diverted by complexity. She is able to identify conflict, to isolate the parties to the conflict, and to utilize these oppositions to convey basic moral truths. She is undaunted by psychological interpretation and ambiguity. Her tales thrive on the identification of conflict and opposition.

If characters are pitted against each other, the tales characters tell about themselves are also juxtaposed. Heroic and conventional views of experience are contrasted, class opposes class, aristocrat and peasant, aristocrat and bourgeois, and bourgeois against peasant and native. In **"Sorrow-Acre"** (*Winter's Tales*) the lord of the manor is starkly pitted against the peasant woman, Anne-Marie. He refuses to revoke a harsh sentence he has passed on Anne-Marie's son who has transgressed against him. He demands rigid satisfaction, and Anne-Marie provides that satisfaction by substituting herself, through plowing the lord's acre all alone, for her son. She plows the large field, with the lord looking on, and she succeeds in finishing the work. She thus frees her son from the death sentence, but she herself dies from the effort. She fulfills her tragic role by sacrificing her life for her son's.

The tale is unrelenting. There is no mitigation of her suffering so that Dinesen may advance the idea that heroic action is more important "than the mere avoidance of pain." No liberal humanitarian ideas intervene with the harsh fulfillment of her tragic role. Dinesen refuses to blur the conflict. She introduces Adam, a young man opposed at first to the actions of the lord, in order to juxtapose a modern perspective. There is no compromising the opposition between lord and peasant. She forces the reader thus to confront differences in class, role, and status and the consequences of these differences. She seems to be asking the reader to explore the sentiment inherent in liberal bourgeois attitudes much as she does in other tales and in *Out of Africa.* In this way, she focusses on the situation which produces oppositions rather than on the nature of individual suffering. The conflict between dominant and subordinate is clear.

While Dinesen's tales are often set in the past, she does not seem to be employing an earlier historical period as an anodyne to contemporary confusion and anomy; she uses the clearer outlines of past social relations to confront the reality of pain, suffering, and death and the need to confront them heroically. In place of sentiment, she offers clarity

and the necessity of action. For example, **"The Invincible Slave-owners"** explores the complex relations between master and servant, domination and subordination. The two sisters, Mizzi and Lotti, actually reverse roles of master and servant. The young man, Axel Leth, who is in love with Mizzi, acts for a while as a servant of the two women, and from this experience he gains insight into the relations between master and slave:

> Axel realized and understood, the umbrella in his hand—with reverence, since he was now in livery—that the slaveowner's dependency upon the slave is as strong as death and cruel as the grave. The slave holds his master's life in his hand, as he holds his umbrella. (*Winter's Tales*)

Axel's freedom consists in this understanding of mutual dependence. One must be able, like him, to experience and then step aside from the master-slave relationship in order to perceive alternatives. Though he experiences pain and loss as a result of this knowledge, the pain of freedom is preferable to the loss of freedom. Dinesen takes advantage of the role-reversals in the story to reacquaint the reader with basic and familiar truths about relationships.

In **"The Deluge at Norderney"** (*Seven Gothic Tales*), Dinesen explores with great reflexiveness the relationship between natural disaster, death, and storytelling. The tale is told under the most elemental of circumstances. Some survivors are stranded in a hayloft as the flood waters rise. They have not escaped the flood as others have done. As a matter of fact, they have allowed others to go in their place. As the flood increases, they spend their time, like the Florentine exiles from the plague in Boccaccio, telling each other stories. The narrator focusses her efforts on the context for the stories and on the tellers of the tales. She stresses particularly the relationship between death and storytelling. The Archbishop says in the full knowledge of imminent danger:

> Has not the Lord arranged for us here a day of judgment in miniature. It will soon be midnight. Let it be the hour of the falling mask. If it be not your mask, or mine, which is to fall, let it be the mask of fate and life. Death we may soon have to face, without any mask. In the meantime we have nothing to do but remember what life be really like. Come, Madame, and my young brother and sister! As we shall not be able to sleep, and are still comfortably seated here, tell me who you are, and recount to me your stories without restraint.

And so the characters proceed to construct stories about themselves which tell who they are, until dawn and the flood waters begin to penetrate the loft. The final lines of the story are not about death but about the ending of tales: "A ce moment de sa narration . . . Scheherazade vit paraître le matin, et, discrète, se tut."

In developing this conjunction between death and storytelling, Dinesen often uses masks, disguises, and dramatic roles in order to underscore the relationship of nature and artifice. As in the pastoral, masks or disguises signal changed social relations, changed attitudes, and particularly the humanly constructed nature of social roles and of creativity in contrast to natural phenomena.

Dinesen is not a writer to elevate personal honesty. Only in confronting death are human beings without masks and roles. She is much too aware of the subtle interplay between external events and individuals to accept the idea that individuals confront events without being constrained by roles, by self-illusions, and by others' role-playing. The interplay between individuals and their society is dialectic. Economic necessity, social class and structure, sex differences, natural obstacles determine the character, and character in turn can exercise a certain limited influence on events. Dinesen's emphasis on masks and disguises underscores the boundaries and the constraints under which human beings live. The mask, like the story, stresses the nature and necessity of form and of artifice, and the reality of social forms as opposed to romantic notions of authenticity.

Freedom and necessity are as much related as are men and women in Dinesen's work. The characters in **"The Deluge at Norderney"** cannot alter the reality of the flood, but they do determine the way in which they confront disaster; the way they tell their tales is symbolic of the way humans live in the face of death.

Masks, role-playing, and disguises serve still another function in Dinesen's storytelling art. They help deflect the reader from motive onto action. This is another way in which she diverts her reader from becoming involved in the individuating aspects of personality. Since events in Dinesen evolve from people talking to each other, interacting with each other, and since social life too evolves out of the conflicts engendered by the demands of social roles, Dinesen's concern is to plumb the various strategies individuals use to fulfill or circumvent certain roles. In this respect, her tales are dramatic.

Dinesen's mode of storytelling is a reflection of the content itself, which portrays individuals as fulfilled through events and through history. She has a wide array of devices other than the mask to convey the themes of the tales and the attitudes of the characters without resorting to probing psychological analysis and extreme individualization. Eric O. Johannesson has enumerated many of these techniques, specifically focussing on the role of theatre, puppets and marionettes, and on masks. Of the mask, in particular, he notes:

> The tales woven around the motif of the mask . . . express the same basic theme, a central one in Dinesen's view of life: the need for a life of adventure, freedom, and imagination felt by those who for one reason or another are trapped, are unable to experience life fully. [*The World of Isak Dinesen*]

Johannesson identifies the importance in Dinesen's storytelling of redeeming contemporary life's banality. Benjamin stresses this dimension of the storyteller as separating him from the novelist and reporter. This emphasis on role-playing and on earlier historical situations is a reproach to contemporary bourgeois reality with its pompous concern for security, for sincerity, and for sentiment.

Donald Hannah, too, views Dinesen's use of masks and her emphasis on the importance of acting as her main weapon against realism and particularly psychological realism:

> It is this concept of the person's other self as an actor, staging a performance which determines Isak Dinesen's method of characterization. It follows the same lines traced out by the stories: these

are not realistic, and neither is the characterization a psychologically-oriented realistic one. And this is so, despite the fact that many of her characters are really split personalities—but not split in a psychological sense. If her characters do have a kind of introspective quality, the analysis they conduct is of their acting procedures much more than it is an exploration of their processes of thought. [*Isak Dinesen and Karen Blixen*]

Many of Dinesen's characters play many roles; they are often performers in a professional, social, or aesthetic sense. They are protean. In **"The Dreamers,"** for example, Pellegrina Leoni is in different contexts revolutionary, courtesan, and artist. Héloise is a professional actress. Leoni, in both tales where she appears, is an opera singer. Babette is an ordinary cook; she is also a great artist and a magician of sorts. Malli in **"Tempests"** is an actress, and when confronted by the choice of marriage and security or acting, she chooses the rich and protean challenges of art rather than the constraints of domesticity. Dinesen fills her tales with changelings. Some of her characters are accused of being witches; a few are actually witches. These characters share the common need and desire to resist simplistic views of the self and of social reality. Metamorphosis and ambiguity prevail in order to enhance the multiple possibilities open to human beings in their quest for meaningful action. Characters are most appealing in Dinesen when, in both tragic or comic terms, they are exploring and testing reality and their potential for experiencing life. Life can only be fully appreciated when it has been lived without regard for security or the need to escape decisions.

A look at Dinesen's life reveals the same disregard for conventional roles, the same rejection of secure self-definitions as her characters. She too was an adventurer. Going off to Africa was not a common pattern for a young woman of her social status. Her divorce from Baron Bror von Blixen-Finecke and her attempt to manage the coffee plantation alone reveal too an independence of spirit. Her struggles to succeed financially and her succumbing to failure, her ability to turn to literature as a means of self-expression and support also testify to her own flexibility and adventurousness. And her ability to be creative in spite of many years of illness and excruciating physical pain certainly reveals her resistance to self-indulgence and despair. In an important sense, she metamorphoses the many losses in her life—the loss of the plantation, the death of Denys Finch-Hatton, and the loss of her health—into art, into her tales. The transformation of the uninteresting aspects of pain and loss into the imaginative properties offered by play, dream, and art is what interested her.

Robert Langbaum probes the "mysteries of identity" in Dinesen thus:

> We understand that the volume [*Seven Gothic Tales*] has all along been asking the following questions: How do we navigate between experience and tradition, between fact and myth; and where, among the different aspects we show to people, and among the metamorphoses we pass through in the different stages of our life, is our identity? [*The Gayety of Vision*]

Dinesen had her own disguises. She passed from being Karen Blixen to being Isak Dinesen, to being, at one point, Pierre Andrézel. She was Danish, but she wrote in English. She was wife, manager of a coffee plantation, and later writer. She was the public person who gave dramatic readings of her tales and at the same time the private person who lived at Rungstedlund, dressed not in the chic clothes which she wore in public but in slacks and a bulky sweater. (pp. 390-98)

The artifice of the tales allows Dinesen to explore a wide range of roles and of behavior. Characters realize themselves through events and through the artifice of language, of verbal reconstruction. In formulistic fashion, so many of the tales and the tales within them, are triggered by questions such as "Who are you?" asked in one case by the lady in black in **"The Cardinal's First Tale"** (*Last Tales*). And typical of the responses in other stories, the Cardinal says, "Allow me, then, in order to save my modesty to answer you in the classical manner," that is, by telling a tale, which is what he does. Count Augustus in **"The Roads Round Pisa"** looks into the mirror and asks this same question, as does Calypso von Platen-Hallermund in **"The Deluge at Norderney."** The "classical manner" to which the Cardinal refers is not a casual use of language; it refers back to the epic and oral tradition where the individual role was inseparable from genealogy, social role, and narration.

The individual's sense of community and of humaneness is validated through others. The narrator in **"The Roads Round Pisa"** comments on the necessity and pitfalls of people's dependency on each other:

> So your own self, your personality, and existence are reflected within the mind of each of the people whom you meet and live with, into a likeness, a caricature of yourself, which still lives on and pretends to be, in some way, the truth about you. Even a flattering portrait is a caricature and a lie. (*Seven Gothic Tales*)

Dinesen recognizes the importance of reflection, while at the same time understanding that the reflection is not the total truth. Here is the essence of her presentation of character and situation. The wisdom and humor in Dinesen derive from the simultaneous recognition of the human need for communication and yet the need to be cautious in interpreting the quest for knowledge.

As in fairy tales, the quest motif is repeated in tale after tale. Characters take to the road, journey on the sea, or contemplate a journey like Charlie Despard in **"The Young Man with the Carnation."** The journey motif is also part of the "classical manner" in the tale. The plots in the tales are not unique. Identity is not unique. Dinesen does not value originality but, like the oft-repeated dream, familiarity. "I know your tale," says Mira in **"The Dreamers"** (*Seven Gothic Tales*), "I have heard it before. Now I believe that I made it myself." Details, settings, the names of characters change, but the essentials of the plot remain simple and similar and familiar: the plot of revenge, betrayal, loss, love requited and unrequited, the wager, the sacrifice, and renunciation. What unifies all of these plots and her characters is the conflict between the desire to experience life and the retreat into security. For example, Laura in **"The Young Man with the Carnation,"** like Jensine in **"The Pearls,"** seeks the safety of domesticity and the denial of contingency. . . . (pp. 398-99)

[Laura] hemmed herself in by her refusal to go beyond the sentimental notion of her "love" for her husband, and by so doing she denies her husband and denies experience. Charlie Despard, her husband, by contrast is eager to escape the restraining and cloying aspects of predictable bourgeois behavior. He rejects contemporary material definitions of success preferring to experience adventure. Adventurers in Dinesen, however, are not restricted to one sex. Agnes della Gherardesci in **"The Roads Round Pisa"** is another of Dinesen's adventurous spirits. She "got into her head the notion that she looked like Milord Byron . . . and she used to dress and ride as a man, and to write poetry" (*Seven Gothic Tales*).

Dinesen frequently shows how roles and attitudes are interchangeable. In her exploration of the relations between men and women she plays with the conventional male dominant and female subordinate opposition. She not only sees the mutual dependency of the sexes, but she shows how the nature of that dependency may vary from one relationship to the next. The challenging element for her is the complex amalgamation of the qualities that constitute the self. Designations of male and female transcend biological distinctions and belong to both sexes alike. Relationships between men and women are characterized by the quest for totality or its denial. Her vision and role as storyteller is to probe and uncover that totality. The union of male and female, the kinship of all created things, are characteristic of the storyteller's world. . . . To deny these relationships is to deny creation and life itself.

For example, in **"The Deluge at Norderney,"** Dinesen shows in this story of Calypso how the denial of others is equivalent to the denial of life. Only through the mirroring of self through others, through art, and through language is it possible to restore the integrity of the self. Count Seraphina in his rejection of Calypso's womanhood denies a part of himself. He almost succeeds in convincing her of her invisibility. Until she can create herself in her own human and female image, she is incomplete: "she knew that she did not exist, for nobody ever looked at her" (*Seven Gothic Tales*). But as she wanders around the palace in her isolation, she discovers a large painting portraying centaurs and satyrs "following, adoring, and embracing young girls of her own age and of her own figure and face." She looks in a mirror, and she experiences identification with the nymphs:

> She looked at them for a very long time. In the end she returned to her mirror and stood there contemplating herself within it. She had the sense of art of her uncle himself, and she knew by instinct what harmonized together. Now a hitherto unexperienced feeling of a great harmony came upon her.

This is a good example of the quest for harmony or totality so characteristic of Dinesen's storytelling. Many other of her characters look, like Calypso, for wholeness, but frequently are frustrated from experiencing the harmony she finds. They find themselves in the position of the characters described by the comic myth Aristophanes recounts in Plato's *Symposium,* unable by circumstance or disposition to find their missing counterparts. Or, in a more tragic vein, a character like Alkmene in the story of that name, lives out a life of religious penance and renunciation, unable to accept the terms of her life and unable to transcend self-denial through others who could help her experience plenitude. In a tale like "Alkmene," the unity of experience is not located in the character, but in the knowledge of the narrator who, by showing the unrealized alternatives, points the reader to the potential of unity.

One of Dinesen's most anthologized tales in *Winter's Tales* is "The Sailor Boy's Tale," a tale that orchestrates many of Dinesen's dominant concerns. It is a tale too that is most reminiscent of a work which exercised a great influence on Dinesen's writing, Coleridge's "Rime of the Ancient Mariner." Her friend, Denys Finch-Hatton, introduced her to it, and one can see echoes of it in other Dinesen tales. There are many reasons why the Coleridge poem should have appealed to Dinesen. It is a poem which stresses the role of the narrator, particularly the hypnotic effect he has over his auditors, and which stresses the cathartic effect on the storyteller and auditor. Dinesen's tale explores the idea of the violation of nature and its consequences, and the unity "Of all things both great and small." The exploration of isolation and community pervades Dinesen's tale much as it does the "Rime." The Coleridgean concern for reconciliation among human beings, and between human beings and nature is also Dinesen's. Finally, Coleridge's poem with its use of archetypal situations and characters, its emphasis on the supernatural, has its counterpart in Dinesen's tale. Dinesen's tale is a particularly good example of the characteristics of the storyteller as described by Benjamin: one finds the magical properties of the fairy tale, the kinship with nature, the familiar as opposed to the unique, the presence of the maternal image, the concern with death, a simplicity of narration, and the presence of words of counsel.

"The Sailor Boy's Tale" should, according to Dinesen, have opened *Winter's Tales,* for it contains many of the thematic elements of the other tales in the volume. The action takes place aboard ship and on land. The first significant action on the sea journey is between the young sailor boy and a falcon which has been trapped on the ship's mast. But, unlike the Mariner who kills the Albatross, the sailor boy frees his bird. He acknowledges his kinship with the falcon: "He thought: 'That bird is like me' " (*Winter's Tales*). In freeing her, however, the boy is injured by her. In exchange, he angrily hits her on the head. They are reunited and reconciled when he finds her later, metamorphosed into a wise old Lapp woman who saves him from some Russian sailors seeking revenge for the death of a comrade killed by the sailor boy on his way to meet his sweetheart. The woman reveals her former identity to him: "That day you climbed up by the shrouds of the topgallant-mast to help her [the falcon] out, in a stiff wind, and with a high sea. That falcon was me." Moreover, she tells him that she is saving him because he is "a boy . . . who will kill a man rather than be late to meet your sweetheart. We hold together, the females of this earth."

Dinesen makes the explicit equation between the female bird, the young girl, and the old Lapp woman. The unity between human beings and nature and males and females is essential to the tale. The old Lapp woman is symbolic of a matriarchal power belonging to women, a power which men often violate as they violate other creatures in nature. This community to which the sailor boy now belongs is contrasted to the group of men aboard the ship who mock his actions in saving the bird and also to the Russian sailors who would obstruct him in his quest for the young girl. Thus Dinesen stresses the dependence of

the community on nature and the importance of being true to one's desires in spite of threatening obstacles. The ritualistic elements in the tale—the falcon, the exchange of objects, the metamorphoses, the roles of the boy, the girl, and the old woman—like the ritualistic elements in the "Rime of the Ancient Mariner"—move the reader beyond the idiosyncratic aspects of character and situation to basic and typical aspects of human life. The wisdom of the storyteller can be seen in her ability to give the events their representative and universal nature. She also reveals that actions are neither arbitrary or incomprehensible. As narrator, Dinesen derives her authority from making the basic identifications and connections which gives these parables their power. This is not a mystical knowledge. Dinesen's authority is evident in the way she presents her words of counsel. She induces general truths from events and the observations feel right. The reader does not experience her statements as moralizing or as simplistic proverbs.

In describing the tale of Kitosch, the unfortunate servant in *Out of Africa,* Dinesen gives another good example of the narrative authority which permits her to provide moral comment. She says in "Kitosch's story":

> By this strong sense in him of what is right and decorous, the figure of Kitosch, with his firm will to die, although now removed from us by many years, stands out with a beauty of its own. In it is embodied the fugitiveness of the wild things who are, in the hour of need, conscious of need, conscious of refuge somewhere in existence: who go when they like: of whom we can never get hold. (*Out of Africa*)

In this passage, one can find too a similar motif as in Dinesen's later tales, the reverence for the wild things like the falcon in **"The Sailor Boy's Tale,"** and one can read her open admiration for those free spirits who will not allow themselves to be dominated and brutalized by others or who will not dominate and brutalize others. (pp. 400-03)

Even more significantly, she uses [Kitosch's death] . . . to describe the heroic, decorous, and dignified way the African transcends the brutality of the white settler. Kitosch dies like an aristocrat. One finds throughout her work this emphasis on an aristocracy deriving not from the privilege of class but from self-respect and fearlessness in the face of adversity. Another word Dinesen substitutes for aristocracy is pride, and of pride she says:

> People who have no pride are not aware of any idea of God in the making of them, and sometimes they make you doubt that there has ever been much of an idea, or else it has been lost, and who shall find it again? They have got to accept as successes what others warrant to be so, and to take their happiness, and even their own selves, at the quotation of the day. They tremble with reason, before their fate. (*Out of Africa*)

Not interested in worldly definitions of success, Dinesen sees as more important the feeling of dignity and the necessity of action to negate despair. A passage like the above is not merely an appendage to her work but an integral part of the narration. Because of her capacity to make events simple, powerful, and typical, she has earned the right to her counsel.

Furthermore, her reflexiveness about the necessary authority of the storyteller is evident in many of the tales through her description of the narrator's role. In **"The Cardinal's Third Tale,"** she has the Cardinal say:

> "And I too," with these words Cardinal Salviati broke the silence that followed upon the Spanish Ambassador's story. "I, too, can tell a tale which may somehow illuminate our theme."
>
> As ever he spoke slowly and quietly, and as ever the sweetness and authority of his voice captured the circle round him. (**Last Tales**)

This is a typical passage from Dinesen. Her tales are filled with writers and storytellers. Some tales have one narrator. In others, there are several as in a chain story. Both men and women tell tales: the Virgin Prioress in **"The Monkey,"** Aeneas in **"A Consolatory Tale,"** the three narrators in **"The Dreamers,"** the men and Miss Nat-Og-Dag in **"The Deluge at Norderney,"** and in **"The Blank Page"** the "old coffee-brown, black-veiled woman who made her living by telling stories" (**Last Tales**). Many of the inset tales were recited by Dinesen in her public appearances on radio and in live performances before an audience. She did not read the stories; she told them. Whether in her public appearances or in her tales where she holds you hynotically like the Ancient Mariner, there is the sense in which involvement in the tales approximates a public and collective event quite different from the conventional privacy associated with the act of reading.

By focussing the reader on the role of narration and on the shared experiences in storytelling, she connects the experience of the reader and the writer, the author and the public. Her most dramatic exploration of this relationship is in **"A Consolatory Tale."** Through the comments of Charlie Despard, "the scribe," the relationship of the writer and the public is analogized to marriage: "All human relationships have in them something monstrous and cruel. But the relation of the artist to the public is amongst the most monstrous. Yes, it is as terrible as marriage" (**Winter's Tales**). He also compares the relationship to that of Job and the Lord in the Book of Job:

> "I have behaved to my reader," he went on slowly, "as the Lord behaves to Job. I know, none so well as I, how the Lord needs Job as a public, and cannot do without him. Yes, it is even doubtful whether the Lord be not more dependent upon Job than Job upon the Lord. I have laid a wager with Satan about the soul of my reader. I have marred his path and turned terrors upon him, caused him to ride on the wind and dissolved his substance and when he waited for light there was darkness."

In the prologue to this tale and in the "consolatory" tale which follows, we see orchestrated the relationship between the teller and the audience, the element of the sacred in that relationship, the importance of conflict and of illumination, and the parabolic quality of the narration. Dinesen's choice of the tale with its anti-modernist, anti-bourgeois biasses is corroborated, in several significant ways, in George Lukacs' discussions of the modernist novel. Briefly, her affinities with Lukacs are to be found in her emphasis on narration rather than description, action rather than contemplation, the concrete rather than the abstract. She too recognizes the problematic and alienated social origins of the modernist novel with its individualistic and subjective orientation. But Dinesen's critique of bourgeois society and her treatment of collectivity are

not based on any dynamic idea of class struggle, nor do her narratives reflect any concrete actuality of that struggle. In this respect, her role as storyteller is more exemplary of Walter Benjamin's description of the storyteller [in his essay "The Nature of the Work of Art in the Age of Mechanical Reproduction," *Illuminations*]. Her tales betray a "sensibility to the archaic," a striving toward unity, a recognition of the value of repetition, ritual, and familiarity as opposed to the exhaustible nature of modern publishing, especially of journalism, and, above all, of the recognition of the importance of death for determining moral values. Benjamin had more sympathy than Lukacs with modernism and with the ability of the technological media to demystify culture and to liberate the masses from capitalism. While aware of the tendency of the media to render politics aesthetic and non-political, he also saw their mass potential. Dinesen's storyteller abandons Benjamin at this threshold of modern technology. The farthest she can go in her narration is to keep alive the art of storytelling and thus to reassert through discourse the dignity of human beings and the importance of community. (pp. 403-06)

> Marcia Landy, "Anecdote as Destiny: Isak Dinesen & the Storyteller," in The Massachusetts Review, *Vol. XIX, No. 2, Summer, 1978, pp. 389-406.*

Robin Lydenberg   (essay date 1978)

[*In the following excerpt, Lydenberg maintains that in her tales Dinesen offered an unconventional portrait of the role of female adolescence in which "the idealism, imagination, and androgynous energy of youth become crystallized as permanent and absolute values."*]

In her strange and archaic Gothic tales the Danish storyteller Isak Dinesen, who did not begin her literary career until she was over forty, sketches a unique portrait of female adolescence. Dinesen deviates from the conventional psychological and sociological approaches which treat adolescence as part of a larger chronological sequence, as a transitional gap between childhood and maturity. Instead, she views the female adolescent in **Seven Gothic Tales** through a rarified aesthetic prism in which the idealism, imagination, and androgynous energy of youth become crystallized as permanent and absolute values.

The conventional view of adolescence as we find it expressed in such classic texts as Helene Deutsch's *The Psychology of Women* and Simone de Beauvoir's *The Second Sex* is determined by a chronological perspective and social commitment which set maturity and adaptation as the indisputable goals of individual development. Adolescence is perceived as a transitional limbo, a suspension, an "emotional vacuum between a world that is disappearing and another that has not yet come into being" (Deutsch). Because of the social and biological nature of her female destiny, the adolescent girl may well contemplate the uncertain future with more ambivalence than her male counterpart. The childhood she is about to leave behind has been active and freely androgynous; the maturity she must achieve calls for passivity and feminine submission. While this transitional stage is marked by passive expectation, it is also a time of deep internal struggle in which the young girl suffers most acutely the contradiction between "her status as a real human being and her vocation as a female" (de Beauvoir). (pp. 521-22)

Dinesen does recognize the transitional function of adolescence within the individual's development, and she portrays her adolescent heroines in the process of their unsettling confrontation with the external adult world. At the same time, however, she thoroughly regrets the inevitable loss of the freedom and potential of adolescence, and her deep ambivalence towards the social and spiritual restrictions of maturity forms the basis of a strong empathy with her adolescent heroines. Dinesen inhabits with these young girls an atemporal fictional universe in which the child's past is never irretrievable nor the adult's future inevitable, where with the power of dreams one may well hope to vanquish or transform a banal and restricted reality. Declaring her allegiance ultimately to the creative potential of the imagination rather than to the exigencies of any social reality, Dinesen glorifies the adolescent as the courageous upholder of an aesthetic vision of the world "as it should be."

Within the highly poetic world which Dinesen constructs in her fiction, the transitional quality of adolescence is seen as a convergence rather than a vacuum, an intersection rich in potential, its confusion offering a wondrous multiplicity. In language very similar to that used to characterize the uncertainty of adolescence, the poet and critic Louise Bogan describes the elusive and transitional quality of *Seven Gothic Tales,* suspended "at the end of one thing as much as at the beginning of another: caught back in the nostalgia for the past and filled with premonitory anguish" [*Selected Criticism*]. What Bogan perceives in the chiaroscuro uncertainty of Dinesen's tales is a reflection of poetic creativity, of the "incompletely lighted and fantastic nineteenth century soul" which found expression in, among other literary forms, the gothic novel.

In choosing to write gothic tales, Dinesen adopted a genre of extremes and ambiguities, an expanded fictional universe in which boundaries were erased, in which past and present, dream and reality, man and god, could be confused or interchanged. Hovering in the uncharted areas between the strictly delineated territories of the realistic novel and the purely supernatural narrative, the gothic novel depends for its generic identity on uncertainty. In the often iconoclastic transgression of natural law and social convention which it describes and in the imaginative potential which grows out of its generic uncertainty, the gothic novel has much in common with the transitional chaos and rebellious spirit of adolescence. Dinesen thus discovered in gothic fiction a sympathetic literary atmosphere in which her adolescent heroines might flourish.

Gothicism itself, both in its fictional and architectural forms, has often been characterized as adolescent in style. (pp. 523-24)

While many critics remark on the adolescent quality of the gothic style, few have recognized that the nature of the adolescent experience itself provides a major thematic focus of gothic fiction. With a startling consistency the gothic novel presents heroines (Emily in *The Mysteries of Udolpho,* Antonia in *The Monk*) fresh from the convent, their virtue suddenly exposed to a world of dangers and deceptions. . . . Unlike the *Bildungsroman* which also examines the precarious passage from childhood to adult

life, the gothic novel associates the conflicts of adolescence primarily with the process of sexual maturation. Ellen Moers has written recently that the gothic novel provided a fictional "device to send maidens on distant and exciting journeys without offending the proprieties" [*Literary Women*]. I would add that these journeys derive their intensity to a large degree from the uncertain circumstances and identity of the gothic heroine as she passes not only through external dangers but through the internally chaotic changes leading from childhood to a mature sexual identity.

The traditional gothic heroine displays either a feminine passivity and helplessness inherited from the heroine of the eighteenth-century sentimental novel or a childish willfulness so fiercely epitomized in Catherine Earnshaw of *Wuthering Heights.* Dinesen deviates from both of these types, creating in her gothic heroine the noble and androgynous figure of a disciplined soldier. The young girls in *Seven Gothic Tales* partake of the heroism which Dinesen perceives as the essence of adolescent sensibility. In describing the heroic idealism and regal aloofness of the Somali natives among whom she lived in Kenya, Dinesen evokes as the very symbol of these qualities the European adolescent: "In such young Europeans too, the code of honour, the deadly devotion to the grand phrase and the grand gesture is the passion urging them on to heroic deeds and heroic self-sacrifice, and also at times sinking them into a dark melancholy and resentment unintelligible to grown up people" [*Shadows on the Grass*]. The devotion to honor and grand pomp as well as the passionate and self-destructive isolation of adolescence are dramatized and dignified in Dinesen's gothic heroines. (pp. 524-25)

[One] brave warrior is Athena Hopballehus of **"The Monkey,"** at once as mythic and ungainly as her name, who radiates a "feeling of invincibility, like a young captain advancing into fire with a high courage, overbearingly." Such military metaphors occur frequently in Dinesen's descriptions of her heroines and lend a more epic stature to the "intensified self-confidence" typical of adolescence. What is most striking in the "sturdy sailor boy" or the powerful giantness of Dinesen's tales is the distinctly androgynous quality from which they draw their energy and strength. This androgyny is personally anachronistic, stemming from the bisexual identity of childhood, but it is also anachronistic in a broader historical sense. The warrior virgins of **Seven Gothic Tales** carry with them the feudal nobility and uncompromising honor of an age of myth or early romance wherein the female was permitted to take part in heroic adventure.

Personal, historical, and even a primitive mythic nostalgia are united in the heroine of **"The Monkey."** Rejecting her cousin Boris' marriage proposal, Athena clings to the freer and more heroic atmosphere of a childhood in which she has been treated as both daughter and son, glorified in her father's imagination "wearing the old coats of armor of Hopballehus." When she fights to protect the independence of this androgynous freedom against Boris' sexual assault, Athena uses none of the "feminine inspiration to scratch or bite" but attacks with the frank fierceness of a she-bear, with the mercilessness of a carnivorous beast. Paradoxically, as long as Dinesen describes her as a "creature"—a giant stork, a lioness, an eagle—her heroine maintains an intense humanity. For it is particularly in her affinity with the world of animals and plants, removed from the conventions which define and restrict her behavior as a woman in society, that the young girl may still feel herself a free human being.

Caught himself between a lingering nostalgia for his own pastoral and androgynous adolescence and the social destiny which demands that he become a husband, a father, an "expert on food and morals," Boris divines and respects Athena's resistance: "This is the tragic maiden's prayer: From being a success at court, a happy, congratulated bride, a mother of a promising family, good Lord, deliver me. As a tragic actor of a high standard himself, he applauded her." Boris admires in Athena what Dinesen admires in the Somali natives—the purity of her uncompromising style, the persistence in her of the autonomous spirit of adolescence.

From a pragmatic social perspective the adolescent's heroic and uncompromising imagination appears as a passive and compensatory faculty, secondary and inferior to the accomplishment of action and interaction in the world. In the female adolescent in particular an excessive fantasy life is seen as prolonging the immature narcissistic stage of her development and isolating her for a longer period than her male peer from productive involvement in the world. In the ambiguous universe created by the conventional un-

certainties of the gothic genre and its unique transformations in Dinesen's modern tales, there is no such clear distinction between fantasy and reality. Nor does Dinesen as a storyteller perceive the world of the imagination as an isolated or antisocial enclosure, as the province of a feminine passivity.

In Dinesen's fiction imagination *is* activity, and the dream creates its own communicable reality. **Seven Gothic Tales** projects a romantic fictional universe in which action is not the healthy realization of desire or idea but its destruction, a finite limit imposed on the vaster universe of the possible. In contrast to the conventionally feminine portrait of the adolescent girl as passive and restricted within her narcissistic fantasies, Dinesen's young heroines embody in their actions and dreams the "palpable energy" and "imagination of possibility" which form the core of androgyny. Athena, for example, does not dissipate her imagination in girlish daydreams of imaginary lovers immobilized in admiration of her beauty, but recalls the excitement and violence of a bear hunt she witnessed as a child and longs to enter battle with the King of Ava and his army of tigers. She reads the history of the French Revolution, declares herself a Republican, and would "cut off the heads of all the tyrants of Europe."

We may always trace in Dinesen's stories the hand of the mystic as well as that of the historian; and if her adolescent

Denys Finch Hatton, a close companion of Dinesen's in Africa.

heroines deviate from a conventional norm it is because she portrays them in a world as rich in wondrous surprise as it is in physical and social restrictions. Far from isolating her from the world, Athena's imagination reveals to her the magic reality offers. For in Dinesen's aesthetic world view reality is merely the universe as imagined by God—a divine fantasy which differs from the fantasies of men and women only in its superior audacity. Dinesen's adolescent heroine need not compromise her private dream-life by surrendering to a more limited reality because she is most often surprised and seduced into the world through its unimaginable sensuality and complexity.

Protected and isolated until the final scene of **"The Monkey"** by the "magnet, the maelstrom quality of drawing everything . . . into her own being and making it one with herself," Athena finally becomes aware of Boris as "a being outside herself." Their witnessing of the horrifying and hilarious metamorphosis in which the old Prioress and her spritely monkey change bodies shocks the young girl out of her proud but barren isolation. From the cool and abstract aloofness with which she earlier declares "If I have a child . . . my father will teach him astronomy," Athena is awakened to the erotic idea of man's animal nature, an idea for which she has been prepared by her active and androgynous imagination. Like Dinesen's other adolescent heroines, Athena need not compromise her fantasies by surrendering to a more limited reality because the strange reality of Dinesen's tales will always be able to surprise and seduce her with its complexities.

Despite the affirmation of life and sensuality which pervades *Seven Gothic Tales,* there are no happy adjustments to maturity for its young heroines. The adult world introduces the young girl to pain and tragedy even as it robs her of noble independence and androgynous autonomy, and Dinesen shares her heroines' ambivalence towards this restricted universe. Dinesen perceives the overcoming of the self-enclosed isolation of adolescence as insufficient recompense for the abdication of its freedom and irresponsibility, and for many of her heroines the rite of passage from childhood to maturity proves violent, cruel, and often fatal. With authorial omniscience or the wisdom of experience, Dinesen remains far more concerned than her fictional characters with what is lost in the process of maturation than with what is gained.

A magical weightlessness and an imminent possibility of flight emblemize for Dinesen this tenuous adolescent freedom she prizes so highly. Shifts in an individual's consciousness are often measured in *Seven Gothic Tales* in relation to the law of gravity. The young girl Fransine of **"The Poet,"** for example, has glided untouched through her marriage to a very old man, her early widowhood, and her subsequent engagement to another mature suitor with a calm indifference. She exists in an angelic isolation from the world, represented in her perfection of the technical dance maneuver, the *ballon,* which gives her a "lightness that is not only the negation of weight, but which actually seems to carry upwards and make for flight . . . as if the matter itself had here become lighter than air." The Councillor sees in this lightness an emblem of purity, and perceiving that a young dancer can leave the earth with such ease, he begins to doubt the very fall of man. We find a similar bird-like quality in the calm bearing of Athena,

"Still, safe in her great strength . . . standing, as was her habit, on one leg, like a big stork." Just as Fransine recalled for the Councillor a paradisiacal innocence, Boris is reminded of the freedom of his own childhood by Athena's dark image of potential flight, as "her big cloak, blowing about her, threw strange shadows upon the gravel, like a pair of large wings."

When the adolescent heroine leaves behind the androgynous autonomy of childhood and becomes integrated into society as a woman, she sacrifices this weightless freedom. After the shock of the physical intimacy of her struggle with Boris, Athena has "given up her habit of standing on one leg, as if it now required both her legs to keep her upright and in balance." Fransine, shaken from her narcissistic indifference by her desire for Anders, is weighted down by longing and despair, "like the lead in the little wooden figures which children play with, like the weight tied to dead seamen's feet, which keeps them standing up, swaying at the bottom of the sea." Dinesen's ambivalence towards the inevitable passage from childhood to maturity is revealed most clearly in her depiction of this transition as a gradual weighting down of the young girl's being, as an accumulation of bonds which imprison her on the earth. As the young woman descends from her lofty and dream-like isolation, drawn by a sensual and painful desire for possession of the external physical world, she finds herself unexpectedly overcome by the law of gravity.

The self-sufficient autonomy which allowed the female adolescent to be narcissistically content in her private world—for as Boris explains to the Prioress, the *horror vacui* does not function above thirty-two feet—gives way to an erotic need of others. This desire may focus on a real or imagined lover or on some cherubic infant, the ultimate weapon and disguise of the god of love, who awakens simultaneously erotic desire and maternal instinct. Dinesen presents woman's childbearing function as the primary force which anchors her to the earth and to the flesh. This instinct is present even in earliest childhood when the little girl's "delicate roots in the dark mould of the past," in her own birth, and in her mother's flesh, are nurtured by what Dinesen warns is the dangerous occupation of playing with dolls.

Far more repressive than the woman's natural biological destiny, however, is the symbolic destiny imposed on her by the social patterns of a masculine culture. Maintaining her metaphor of the flight, Dinesen describes the transition from adolescence to maturity as the shifting of the young girl's "center of gravity . . . from individuality to symbol." While she honors the heroic stature of the individual clothed in "epos," in the grandeur of a goddess' symbolic robes, Dinesen shrewdly represents the motivation behind man's deification of woman in the frank confession of the old Bishop in **"Supper at Elsinore"**: "We, all of us, willingly grant her the title of angel, and the white wings, and lift her up on our highest pedestal, on the one inevitable condition that she must not dream of, must even have been brought up in absolute ignorance of, the possibility of flight." Cemented on her pedestal or confined within a sonnet, woman can only dream, as all of Dinesen's heroines do, of glorious freedom and flight.

Even the young bride Childerique in **"The Caryatids"** who seems to have "taken to her element" and fulfills her sexual role in a sublime harmony with nature—does not escape the weight of the pedestal to which her feet have been fixed by an adoring husband. She achieves at best a circumscribed flight, a domesticated sublimity. Her husband accepts with ease her periodic disappearances into a distant dream world because he knows she is weighted within, her vitality "balanced down" to assure her return to earth. He sees her spiritual excursions only as exotic shopping trips from which she returns with "fresh flowers to adorn her home."

Immortalized in marble or stone, this domestic goddess is represented by Dinesen as a reluctant architectural support of the great houses, guardian of the lands, upholder of the earthly and bourgeois structures of family and society. It seems to Childerique a cold and banal destiny, without the freedom either of gypsies or queens. The young wife longs to throw the weight from her shoulders, to try the magic as well as the poison of the world of adventure outside her domestic confines. Childerique is only one of many Dinesen heroines who scorn the passivity of Eve, longing to overcome the restrictions of sexual polarity in equal competition with men. Such, Dinesen explains, was the nature of the "noble striving" of competition between Adam and Lilith, a competition which ended in woman's triumphant return to her heavenly home.

Out of his fear of the freedom and androgynous independence of her adolescence and out of an equal distrust and awe of the alien mysteriousness of her mature fertile body, man constructs around woman a ritual aura of ceremony and formality in the hopes of restricting and controlling her power. With an astute understanding and enjoyment of divine irony, Dinesen demonstrates how this domestic goddess may turn on her makers and fulfill her role with a vengeance. The symbol of childhood freedom and innocence which her adolescence once offered to man is metamorphosed into the formidable symbol of domestic authority and censure; from the creature of angelic lightness which was the female adolescent grows the woman who is a "law of gravity, like property."

This weighty creature appears in her most fierce incarnation as the fictional Madame Knudsen [in *Out of Africa*], invented by Dinesen to explain an old Danish sailor's aversion to the land and its society: "She was the woman who ruins the pleasure of man, and therein is always right. She was the wife of the curtain-lectures, and the housewife of the big cleaning days, she stopped all enterprises, she washed the faces of boys and snatched away the man's glass of gin from the table before him, she was law and order embodied." Dinesen sees womanhood at its best as an ironic play, an expression of divine humor in the manner of Fransine's danse, "done, lightly, as in jest." If she takes her vocation too seriously, Dinesen warns, this earth goddess may become the enemy of all who yearn for freedom—men and women alike.

This transformation, however, is not inevitable or irreversible. Dinesen perceives adolescence as a particular attitude towards the world and towards the self, not strictly delineated within a psychological or physiological period of individual development. Dinesen expresses the timelessness of adolescent sensibility most clearly in the surprising affinity she establishes between her adolescent heroines and the spirited old crones who often dominate her stories. Because they have returned to or maintained the heroic idealism, the imaginative creativity, and the androgynous en-

ergy of adolescence out of knowledge rather than innocence, these old women reflect (more consciously than the young heroines who are caught up in its tumultuous transitional changes) the *absolute* nature of adolescence.

Let us consider the extreme example of the de Coninck sisters in **"Supper at Elsinore"** who have sustained for a lifetime the same uncompromising rejection of a banal domestic destiny which marks Athena's youthful idealism. These two "flying Dutchwomen" have treasured their secrets and romantic dreams like a precious trousseau, and although in their old age they must beat their arms to keep warm, Fanny for one still carries in her breast the soul of a "great, mad, wing-clipped bird," the fierce androgynous yearning for flight. Although they are cold and barren, there is a grandeur in the bleached out old skulls of these spinsters who have denied their womanly flesh to become "spiritual courtesans" devoted to their impossible dreams.

The strength Dinesen attributes to her warrior virgins is reclaimed by the mature woman who has ceased to be a sexual entity. When Boris thinks he has cleverly manipulated his old aunt to his own purposes, he is surprised to discover the power which lies hidden in the "narrow, wooden chests of old women": "all at once he got such a terrible impression of strength and cunning that it was as if he had touched an electric eel. Women, he thought, when they are old enough to have done with the business of being women, and can let loose their strength, must be the most powerful creatures in the whole world." Although similar to the reckless freedom of the adolescent who has not yet taken on the burden of what Spacks calls "taking care," the burden Dinesen represents in her image of the **"Caryatids"** upholding the great houses, the strength of old women is perhaps even more intense for having been so long repressed.

Far from regretting the confines or transgressions of their past lives, Dinesen's old women tend to launch into a new imaginative life after menopause, filling in the gaps of their experience not pathologically but with irony and wit. Miss Malin in **"Deluge at Norderney,"** for example, counters the strict virginity which ruled her life with recollections of an imaginary past in which she reigned as one of Europe's most infamous courtesans. Dinesen explains obliquely that what changed Miss Malin was "what changes all women at fifty: the transfer from the active service of life . . . to the more passive state of looker-on." Miss Malin's menopausal retirement is thus described as a liberation from the law of gravity, as the resumption of the free imaginative flight of adolescence: "A weight fell away from her; she flew up to a higher perch and cackled a little. . . . [The] old woman who had seen to her safety could dive down into any abyss of corruption with the grace of a crested grebe." The perspective of this venerable aristocrat who, like the old Somali women, has seen "all of life and through it" parallels in its satiety the innocence of the adolescent who has seen nothing: both are free of the earth, free of its morality, free of the law of gravity.

Dinesen's gothic crones complete their lives by generating a lively harmony of temporal and sexual polarities: the rejuvinated spirit in the old body, the untouched spinster who becomes a "spiritual courtesan," the masculine courage of heart within the old woman's narrow bosom. To Dinesen the old woman is complete because she combines the strength of both sexes, because she has been elevated above all polarities—not to the point where they disappear but to the point where they converge once again as they did in the undifferentiated potential of early adolescence.

Perhaps the strongest testimonial to the survival of the spirit of adolescence is Isak Dinesen's own continued identification with its freedom and potentiality. When she abandoned the bourgeois Victorian and piously Unitarian atmosphere of her matriarchal home in Denmark to embark on an uncertain future in the hills of Kenya, Dinesen felt that she was finally experiencing a liberation known only in her adolescent dreams. The same metaphor which emblemizes the heroic grandeur of adolescence is used by Dinesen to describe her elation on beginning her life in Africa at the age of twenty: "Here at last one was in a position not to give a damn for all conventions, here was a new kind of freedom which until then one had only found in dreams. It was like beginning to fly where one seemed to have left the law of gravity behind. One might get a little dizzy, it was a little dangerous as well, it took courage. . . . But it was glorious, intoxicating." Not only did the native culture Dinesen encountered in Kenya reflect her own predilection and respect for the adventurous idealism of adolescence, but the African landscape itself seemed to reproduce in her spirit the soaring freedom of the adolescent's indulgence in a dreamlike profusion of possibilities.

In the second volume of her African reminiscences, *Shadows on the Grass,* Dinesen juxtaposes two photographs of herself. One shows a young woman, jaunty and boyish in her kakhi shorts against the background of the hills of Africa and the other reveals the sharply alert face, withered almost to a skull, of the sophisticated Danish writer. The spirit in the two photographs is the same: that of a woman of limitless energy, daring imagination, and a peculiarly seductive androgyny. Forced at the age of forty to leave her farm in Kenya and her active life of adventure, Dinesen turned to storytelling as a means of support. She brought to this new undertaking the same reckless imaginative intoxication and energy she experienced in Africa, concentrating those qualities in her unique celebration of the female adolescent in her gothic tales. (pp. 525-32)

> *Robin Lydenberg, "Against the Law of Gravity: Female Adolescence in Isak Dinesen's 'Seven Gothic Tales'," in* Modern Fiction Studies, *Vol. 24, No. 4, Winter, 1978, pp. 521-32.*

David H. Richter   (essay date 1985)

[*A professor of English at Queen's College of the City University of New York, Richter is the author of* Fable's End: Completeness and Closure in Rhetorical Fiction *and* Ten Short Novels. *In the following excerpt, Richter provides an explication of Dinesen's short story "The Sorrow-Acre," centering upon the tragic relationship between Adam and his young aunt.*]

Perhaps none of Isak Dinesen's novellas has been more admired, and certainly none has been more widely anthologized, than **"Sorrow-Acre,"** originally published with her **Winter's Tales** in 1942. This lyrically tragic tale, set in Denmark in the 1770s, invokes many of the persistent themes that haunt Dinesen's work: the contrast between the cruel beauty of the *ancien regime* and the more prosaic humanitarian ethos of modern democracy that will inevitably displace it; the inextricable connections between men and the land they live on; the arcane routes by which men seek and find their destiny; the perverse and terrible costs which love exacts. These themes have been sensitively and eloquently elucidated in the published criticism on Dinesen [Robert Langbaum's *The Gayety of Vision,* Eric O. Johannesson's *The World of Isak Dinesen,* and Donald Hannah's *'Isak Dinesen' and Karen Blixen* (see excerpts above)]. . . . What these critics, and others, seem to me to have misunderstood about Dinesen's **"Sorrow-Acre"** is not her themes but her plot. Or her plots, rather. For it is my basic thesis that **"Sorrow-Acre"** is informed by two interlocking plots, one overt and obvious, which no reader can conceivably miss, the other merely hinted at through foreshadowing allusions which previous commentators have misread or read but in part. The brief essay that follows will concern itself with the covert plot of **"Sorrow-Acre,"** its relation to the more visible plot, and why Dinesen may have adopted the apparently risky strategy she chose of structuring a story around a plot so enciphered that it might easily remain a mystery.

The open or visible plot of **"Sorrow-Acre"**—which to my mind is the subordinate one of the two—has its source in a Jutland folk-tale collected by Ohrt and retold by Paul la Cour in 1931. . . . The story, as it appears in **"Sorrow-Acre,"** concerns a widow, Anne-Marie, whose only son Goske has been accused of setting fire to a barn belonging to the "old lord" on whose landed estate they work. Anne-Marie pleads with the old lord to save her son, and the old lord offers her a bargain: if she will mow in one day a rye-field that would be work for three men, he will let her son go; if she fails, the boy will be sent away to be judged and she will never see him again. On the day after the ordeal, Anne-Marie begins mowing the field, quickly at first, then much more slowly as her strength ebbs and as the heat of the day takes its toll. In the presence of a crowd of peasants gathered to commiserate with and encourage her, and in the presence of the son for whom she made the bargain, Anne-Marie finishes the field just at sunset, only to collapse, dead from exhaustion.

While this story occasionally occupies the foreground of Dinesen's narrative, particularly at the denouement, for the most part it forms the backdrop against which a very different figure is traced. This takes the shape of a debate between the old lord and his young nephew, Adam, whom most commentators correctly take to be the focal character of the story. On the day set for the mowing, Adam has just returned to his ancestral estate from England, where he has absorbed the liberal and humanitarian values current there in intellectual circles, and which we today would associate with Jefferson or Rousseau. As he walks to the mansion at the centre of his uncle's feudal estate, Adam experiences a recrudescence of intense love for the soil of his forefathers, which he senses wishes to claim him, body and soul; these feelings are qualified, however, by his awareness of how alien his values have become to the hierarchical structures of autocracy physically emplanted in the topography of the manor. As Adam stands listening, in the morning, to the old lord's exposition of the bargain he has made with Anne-Marie, he says nothing to challenge his uncle's decree, but as the day wears on the drama being played out in the rye-field weighs ever heavier upon his conscience, and he is driven to remonstrate with his uncle: " 'In the name of God . . . , force not this woman to continue.' " The old man answers Adam calmly and reasonably from within his aristocratic and feudal values: that Anne-Marie chose to accept the ordeal as freely as he chose to offer it; that his word, once given, is to him as sacred as that Word out of which the world was created; that his decree, if cruel as those of the Greek gods, at least allows the woman the beauty of a tragic destiny to which gods themselves cannot aspire. . . . Adam is finally driven to declare that, rather than stay in a land where such brutality must be, he will leave Denmark and go, not to England, where the feudal structures are incompletely eradicated, but to America, in whose fields and forests his more modern ideas reign supreme.

But this is not where Dinesen leaves the matter. In a long passage of interior monologue written with an intensity that marks it as the emotional climax of the story, Adam reverses his decision and decides to stay on his uncle's estate. The passage begins with the old lord's bitter benediction upon Adam's choice to go to America: " 'Take service, there, . . . with the power which will give you an easier bargain than this: That with your own life you may buy the life of your son.' " This refers, most obviously, to the bargain the old man had concluded with Anne-Marie, but it also alludes to the uncle's private sorrow—the death of his only son, who was to inherit the manor. Though the old man has married himself the bride intended for his dead son, and may, Adam thinks, have children by her, Adam sees as he had not before the old man's suffering, and his ever-present dread of "the obliteration of his being" through the failure of his direct line. And as Adam contemplates his uncle with pity and forgiveness, he recognizes that beneath his liberal values was a stronger, universal vision which determines him not to leave but to stay. To make this vision comprehensible it must be quoted at some length:

> He saw the ways of life, he thought, as a twined and tangled design, complicated and mazy; it was not given him or any mortal to command or control it. Life and death, happiness and woe, the past and the present, were interlaced within the pattern. Yet to the initiated it might be read as easily as our ciphers—which to the savage must seem confused and incomprehensible—will be read by the schoolboy. And out of the contrasting elements concord arose. All that lived must suffer; the old man, whom he had judged hardly, had suffered, as he had watched his son die, and had dreaded the obliteration of his being. He himself would come to know ache, tears and remorse, and, even through these, the fullness of life. So might now, to the woman in the rye-field, her ordeal be a triumphant procession. For to die for the one you loved was an effort too sweet for words.

> As now he thought of it, he knew that all his life he had sought the unity of things. . . . Where other young people, in their pleasures or their amours, had searched for contrast and variety, he himself had yearned only to comprehend in full the oneness of the world. If things had come differently to him, if his young cousin had not died, and the events that followed his death had not brought him to Denmark, his search for understanding and harmony might have taken him to America. . . . Now they have been disclosed to him today, in the place

where he had played as a child. As the song is one with the voice that sings it, as the road is one with the goal, as lovers are made one in their embrace, so is man one with his destiny, and he shall love it as himself.

As Adam decides to stay, he feels the hour 'consecrated . . . to a surrender to fate and to the will of life," and as he speaks of his altered plans to his uncle a roll of Jovian thunder signals the fateful choice. But Adam is not afraid: he thinks, in his present *amor fati,* that "he had given himself over to the mightier powers of the world. Now what must come must come."

But just what is it that "must come"? What is the fate that Adam has accepted with such gravity? This is what I have called the covert plot of **"Sorrow-Acre,"** for it is not so much told to us as it is enciphered by Dinesen in the loose ends and stray details surrounding the visible story. One common view is that expressed by Robert Langbaum: "It is the destiny of Anne-Marie and the old lord to die, and it is the destiny of Adam to inherit the lord's estate and marry his young wife." Another view is that of Johannesson, who speculates that Adam will cuckold his uncle; the latter, we are told, "is a comic figure because . . . he will have a son produced for him by his wife and Adam." Now while there is evidence to support elements of both these views, neither is very congruent with the tone Dinesen uses to describe Adam's acceptance of his fate, or Adam's reflection, a little later on, that "Anne-Marie and he were both in the hands of destiny, and destiny would, by different ways, bring each to the designated end." The sombre tone of Adam's vision, and his foresight of a link with Anne-Marie's tragic destiny, suggest a very different fate for Adam than the inheritance of a valuable estate or a sexual romp with his uncle's beautiful young bride. Contemplating either destiny would require little in the way of *amor fati.* I believe, however, that when Dinesen's hints are read as a whole, the story in which one infers Adam will play the role of protagonist would be more like that of Tristan and Isolde than like Chaucer's "Merchant's Tale." There will indeed be a love-affair between Adam and his youthful aunt, a love-affair that will culminate in the birth of a child; but Adam's fate will be to die, at the hands of his uncle or his minions, sacrificing himself to save the woman and their son.

The common ground of all three interpretations is the future connection between Adam and his uncle's seventeen-year-old bride, and indeed this is the element of Dinesen's covert plot that is most difficult to miss. Our inferences are primarily cued by the lengthy digression Dinesen makes from the visible story to portray this girl, who plays no explicit part either in Anne-Marie's tragedy or in Adam's fateful decision. Dinesen's language is somewhat coy here, but the portrait clearly enough indicates her sexual frustration. . . . [Mild] hints that the old lord may be impotent are validated by the bride's dreadful "consciousness of an absence" in her life, her longings for "the being who should have been there" in her embrace, "and who had not come." This absence is quite clearly sexual, for it is when examining her nude and lovely body in the looking-glass that she most intensely fees "a *horror vaccui* like a physical pain." That Adam will be the one to fill this vacuum, to complete her inchoate longings, is first hinted at when the bride tears herself from her unpleasant meditation by thinking instead about "her new nephew arrived from England," with whom she plans to "ride out on the land." The activities of Adam and his aunt on the day the narrative is set are chaste enough, of course, but their thoughts about each other, their ride together, and their collaboration in a musical duet as the curtain is drawn upon them symbolize even as they presage the love-affair we can foresee.

That this will be an illicit affair, rather than a more staid romance that will wait upon the death of Adam's uncle, is largely implicit in the sexual urgency of the bride's physical frustration, taken together with the absence of any suggestion that the old lord is soon to die. But there are other hints as well. The young bride's middle name, for one thing, is Magdelena, traditionally identified with the fallen woman of the seventh chapter of the Gospel according to Luke. For another, there is the prophecy made to Adam back in England: "When at Ranelagh an old gypsy woman looked at his hand and told him that a son of his was to sit in the seat of his fathers." If we take the prophecy seriously, and in the literal way such foreshadowing is generally to be taken in tragedies and folk-tales, it suggests that, while a son of his will possess the manor, Adam himself will *not* be its inheritor. Thus one must reject the Langbaum interpretation, and accept the Johannesson, as far as it goes. But Johannesson's notion that the covert plot of **"Sorrow-Acre"** is a cuckold comedy is unsatisfactory for quite a number of reasons.

The first and perhaps most unanswerable reason is that already mentioned: that the tone of **"Sorrow-Acre"** is tragic, not merely in the section devoted to the destiny of Anne-Marie but in that devoted to Adam and his fateful decision to remain on his uncle's manor. Here Adam foresees that "he himself would come to know ache, tears and remorse," which is far from suggesting that his love-affair will be a bedroom farce devoid of serious consequences. Second, Johannesson's formulation is structurally off kilter, for his view takes the old lord to be the protagonist of this comedy, whereas it is clear from the narrative point of view that it must be Adam that is the protagonist of the novella's covert plot. Finally, there are a great many subtle hints within the text that death, rather than birth or love, is the focus of Adam's fate.

First off, there is Adam's name, recalling the Biblical Adam, our once innocent forefather who was betrayed by woman into death. Second, there is Adam's sense, on his first approach to the manor house, that he has been invited there by the dead ("Dead people came towards him and smiled upon him. . . . "). Next, there is the tragedy by Johannes Ewald which Adam brings with him and leaves with his uncle. It is not named in the text, but the conversation it kindles suggests that it must be the 1775 verse drama of *Baldurs Død,* which centers upon a young god who dies, driven by his passion for a mortal woman. Fourth, there is the sinister aspect to the young bride's sexual fantasies, which imply that loving her would be a most dangerous thing. . . . Fifth, there is the recurrent pair of lines from Gluck's *Alceste,* repeated three times within the novella: "Mourir pour ce qu'on aime, C'est un trop doux effort." These lines about dying for the one you love are not only translated within Adam's interior monologue, they are alluded to as the curtain is discreetly drawn upon him and his aunt, for it is Alceste's aria which the two are playing and singing together. They apply, obvi-

ously, to Anne-Marie, who sacrifices herself for her son, but in his interior monologue Adam apparently applies them to his own case. Finally, there is Adam's sense, already alluded to, that his fate and that of Anne-Marie are somehow linked, that they are "both in the hands of destiny" which will bring each of them to "the designated end"; in the context this makes even more ominous Dinesen's guarded statement, "Later on he remembered what he had thought that evening."

Arching over all these details, and marshalling them into perspective, is the reader's desire to make the fullest possible sense of Dinesen's story, to take this "twined and tangled design" and find in it a "pattern," to unify this work of literature and participate in its harmonies in the same way that Adam wants to decipher the hidden unity and harmony of life. It is this aesthetic sense that has dictated Adam's decision to stay, just as it is the old lord's aesthetic sense that has made him stage-manage the tragedy of which Anne-Marie is the protagonist. And I suspect that Dinesen trusted the aesthetic sense of her readers to complete, to stage-manage in their own minds, the tragedy linked to the visible one of which Adam is the protagonist. And, if we have been following her implications correctly, a single denouement, the completion of Anne-Marie's sacrifice and death, will serve as the katharsis for both. Anne-Marie, as a peasant-woman, is the heroine of a tragic folk-tale; Adam, as befits his higher birth and station, will be the hero, not of a folk-tale or a fabliau, but of a variant of the tragic myth of Tristan.

It is in fact a misapplication of Dinesen's aesthetics that led Johannesson and Hannah to posit a cuckold-comedy as the covert plot of **"Sorrow-Acre."** Their argument is based upon the old lord's view that, just as the omnipotent Greek gods could not be tragic, so too the aristocrats of Denmark "who stand in lieu of the gods" should "leave to our vassals their monopoly of tragedy." But it is only the old lord himself who, in his omnipotence and amorality, like the greek gods, is beyond the reach of the tragic. His nephew is no Zeus; he is more like the Norse gods of Asgaard who, the old lord tells us, "had, at all times, by their sides those darker powers which they named the Jotuns, and who worked the suffering, the disasters, the ruin of our world"; and like the Norse gods, like the Baldur of Ewald's drama, Adam in his limitations possesses the capacity for tragedy. The old lord quite explicitly identifies Adam with Baldur: the new age, which Adam represents "has made to itself a god in its own image, an emotional god. And now you are already writing a tragedy on your god." To put it another way, the old lord, from his Olympian perspective, may indeed view himself as a comic figure, a deceived Vulcan whose Venus has strayed. But from Adam's perspective—and given the point of view it is his angle that we share—his destiny to love the young bride, to father her son, and to die sacrificing himself for them is indeed a tragic fate, which his uncle characterizes as the highest human privilege:

I have tried to show how the demands of tone, of parallel structure, of point of view, and of details and verbal allusions all collaborate to convey the covert tragic plot of **"Sorrow-Acre."** But if we can agree that Dinesen has succeeded in organizing her story in such a way, then we must also paradoxically admit that she has failed. She has failed, at least, to convey her covert story to five sensitive readers whose studies I have cited, and therefore, one suspects, to most of those who have perused her novella. To the initiated, Adam says in his interior monologue, the pattern of life, that complicated and mazy design, "might be read as easily as our ciphers—which to the savage must seem confused and incomprehensible—will be read by the schoolboy." And yet Dinesen has so enciphered the primary plot of her story that few of her readers are likely to make it out. For those who succeed, the pleasures of tacit collusion with the author are intense and refined indeed; for those who fail—and here is Dinesen's insurance policy—most will have not sense of what they have missed.

The fact is that Isak Dinesen was an elitist in more ways than one. The reception of **Seven Gothic Tales** had suffered in Denmark, critic Tom Kristensen remarked, from the common readers' reaction to "their too aristocratic tone, verging on snobbery," Though Kristensen felt that the **Winter's Tales** had more "humanity" than the earlier book, it is clear that her defense of the *ancien regime,* her contempt for democratic vistas, are by no means absent from the later collection, which includes **"Sorrow-Acre."** And as an elitist, Dinesen was very unlikely to have been averse to reserving some of her work's secret pleasures for a select group of kindred souls capable of following her indirections and allusions. Like Joyce's *Finnegans Wake,* whose meaning is encrypted in thousands of puns in dozens of living and dead languages, like Nabokov's "The Vane Sisters," whose hidden denouement is encoded in the initial letters of the last paragraph's words, and like Dinesen's own **"The Roads Round Pisa,"** whose ending requires the reader to decipher an obscure symbolic passage in Dante, **"Sorrow-Acre"** is a story that is also part puzzle, a reflection of its author's intellectual snobbery and a challenge, moral as well as intellectual, to the reader's own. (pp. 82-8)

> *David H. Richter, "Covert Plot in Isak Dinesen's 'Sorrow-Acre',"* in *The Journal of Narrative Technique, Vol. 15, No. 1, Winter, 1985, pp. 82-90.*

John Updike (essay date 1986)

[*Considered a perceptive observer of the human condition and an accomplished stylist, Updike is among America's most distinguished men of letters. Best known for such novels as* Rabbit Run *(1960),* Rabbit is Rich *(1981), and* Rabbit At Rest *(1990), Updike portrays Protestant, middle-class Americans who search for meaning in their lives while facing the painful awareness of their morality and basic powerlessness. A contributor of literary reviews to various periodicals, he has written the "Books" column in the* New Yorker *magazine since 1955. In the following excerpt, adapted from his introduction to the sixtieth-anniversary edition of* Seven Gothic Tales, *Updike briefly reviews Dinesen's life and explores her attitudes toward courage, sex, and religion, as evidenced in* Seven Gothic Tales.]

When the Book-of-the-Month Club offered **Seven Gothic Tales,** by Isak Dinesen, as its selection for April of 1934, its newsletter said simply, "No clue is available as to the pseudonymic author." But even then, with some detective work by the newspapermen of Denmark, this utterly obscure author was emerging into the spotlight as one of the most picturesque and flamboyant literary personalities of the century, a woman who had "style" as well as a remarkably grave and luminous prose style, and whose works as they followed her veiled debut seemed successive enlargements of her dramatic persona. She relished what she called "the sweetness of fame" and the company of the great and glamorous; she received in her native Denmark and while traveling elsewhere the attention due a celebrity. . . .

Karen Christentze Dinesen was born in April of 1885, in a manor house near the coast, 15 miles north of Copenhagen. Her father, Wilhelm Dinesen, the younger son of a Jutland landowner (who had once traveled through Italy with Hans Christian Andersen), was a soldier, adventurer and writer, whose epistolary memoir, *Letters From the Hunt,* ranks as a minor classic of Danish literature. Karen's mother, Ingeborg, came from a family of wealthy traders and merchants. She married Wilhelm in 1881 and within five years was the mother of three daughters, of whom Karen, nicknamed Tanne, was the second. Two more children, both sons, followed in the next decade. Tanne was her father's favorite and confidante; all the greater the blow, then, to the little girl when Wilhelm, whose careers in both politics and literature had taken discouraging turns, and who had a history of restlessness and "soul-sickness," committed suicide, by hanging, shortly before Tanne's 10th birthday.

Karen grew up, in the strongly feminine company of her mother and sisters and servants and aunts, as the family fantastic, who from the age of 10 or 11 concocted plays that were performed within the domestic circle, the children and their friends taking the parts of Columbine and Harlequin, Blancheflor and Knight Orlando. In adolescence she became obsessed with the figure of her dead father and the notion that his ideals and romantic spirit had descended into her. When, in her early 20's, she published a few tales in Danish magazines, it was under the pen name Osceola. Osceola was the name of Wilhelm's dog, with whom the father and daughter used to take their walks. In 1934 Isak Dinesen explained to a Danish interviewer that she had taken a pen name "on the same grounds my father hid behind the pseudonym Boganis . . . so he could express himself freely, give his imagination a free rein. . . . In many things I resemble my father." And when, in early 1914, at the near-spinsterish age of 28, she married, it was to a Swedish aristocrat, her cousin Bror Blixen, who like her father was restless, impractical and cavalier. Though he was to be an unfaithful husband, he gave her two wedding gifts beautifully faithful to her sense of herself: he made her a baroness, and he took her to Africa. . . . In British East Africa, English became her daily language; and in the person of her handsome, Etonian, Oxonian lover, Denys Finch-Hatton, she for the first time encountered a fully involving intellectual partner, a brilliant and playful stimulant to her own intelligence and her storyteller's gift. She liked to think of herself as Scheherazade, and in Denys she met her Sultan. Also, in the Kenyan highlands she encountered two societies, the African and the white settlers', colorfully imbued with the aristocratic notions of honor, fatalism and daring that had always attracted her. Many of the 19th-century exotics of **Seven Gothic Tales,** in fact, are based on originals met in the semifeudal world, simultaneously raffish and posh, rough and luxurious, around Nairobi.

Her situation, when at the age of 46 she was at last compelled to return to Denmark, might be described as ignominious. Her marriage long ended, her farm bankrupt and sold to a real estate developer, her lover recently dead in the crash of his airplane, her body tormented by the complications of tabes dorsalis (syphilis of the spine), she was received into her mother's household as a prodigal daughter, a middle-aged adolescent. Setting up shop in her father's old office, she picked up notebooks and ideas she had been toying with for 10 years while in Africa.

The manuscript of *Seven Gothic Tales* was ready by the spring of 1933, but, rich and strange and free as it was, had difficulty getting into print. Several English publishers rejected it; Thomas Dinesen, however, had befriended an American writer, Dorothy Canfield, who was on the Book-of-the-Month Club's first board of judges, and sent his sister's manuscript to her in Vermont. Miss Canfield was impressed, and urged the book in turn upon her neighbor, Robert Haas, a publisher whose firm later merged with Random House. He published the book in January of 1934, and the Book-of-the-Month Club offered it to its members, Miss Canfield writing in the newsletter the report that memorably begins, "The person who has set his teeth into a kind of fruit new to him, is usually as eager as he is unable to tell you how it tastes." The new fruit met critical acclaim and, unexpectedly, commercial success as well. (p. 3)

[In 1959, she spoke to an] interviewer about *Seven Gothic Tales* with what he reported as embarrassment. It was "too elaborate," she said, and had "too much of the author in it." [In 1985] Pauline Kael, film critic of *The New Yorker,* took the occasion of the Meryl Streep movie [*Out of Africa*] to tell us, with her customary verve and firmness, that Isak Dinesen's "baroque stories are lacquered words and phrases and no insides. Some seem meant to be morality tales, but you never get the moral. . . . *Seven Gothic Tales* are a form of distraction; they read as if she had devised them in the fevered atmosphere of all-night debauches." This verdict echoes the prim censoriousness of the young Danish reviewer Frederick Schyberg, who wrote when the book was new, "There are no normal human beings in *Seven Gothic Tales.* The erotic life which unfolds in the tales is of the most highly peculiar kind . . . There is nothing, the reviewer finds . . . behind [the author's] veil, once it is lifted."

Well, as Dorothy Canfield advised half a century ago, "Take a taste, yourself." Enter a deliciously described world of sharply painted, dramatically costumed heroes and heroines, posing, with many a spectacular gesture and eloquent aria, in magnificent landscapes maintained by invisible hands as a kind of huge stage set. This operatic Europe, like opera itself, would call us into largeness. One character is "hurt and disappointed because the world wasn't a much greater place than it is," and another says of himself at a moment of crisis, "Too small I have been, too small for the ways of God." Though Isak Dinesen's leisurely and ornate anecdotes, which she furnishes with just enough historical touches to make the stage firm, have something in them of the visionary and the artificial, they are not escapist. From the sweeping flood of the first story to the casual and savage murder of the last, they face pain

and loss with the brisk familiarity of one who has amply known both, and force us to face them, too. Far from hollow and devoid of a moral, the tales insistently strive to inculcate a moral stance; in this her fiction especially suggests that of Hemingway, who thought well enough of her to interrupt his Nobel Prize acceptance speech with a regret that she had not received it. Both authors urge upon us a certain style of courage, courage whose stoic acceptances are plumed with what the old Cardinal, in the first Gothic Tale, calls "divine swank." Dinesen even called this quality *"chic,"* ascribing it to the costumed Masai warriors who, "daring, and wildly fantastical as they seem, are unswervingly true to their own nature, and to an immanent ideal." She also admired, in Africa, the Moslems, whose "moral code consists of hygiene and ideas of honor—for instance they put discretion among their first commandments."

This admiration of the warrior's code surprises us in a woman. She was a feminist, but of an oddly unblaming kind, who includes within her ideal of the energizing sexual transaction what is heedless and even hostile in the male half of the sexual dichotomy. The three men she most loved—her father, her husband, her lover—all conspicuously failed to shelter her, and she took their desertions as a call to her own largeness. This call, which reverberates throughout her tales in all their abrupt and sternly mysterious turnings, was, it would appear, more easily heard and understood in the land of Emerson and Whitman than in tightly inhabited England and Denmark. America played the role of Africa or an older Europe: a place of dangerous freedom, of natural largeness and of *chic,* discreet natives. The discretion in Dinesen's writing, the serene and artful self-concealment even in her memoirs, is an aspect of the personal gallantry which, in the social realm, masked her frightful bouts of pain and debility with the glamorous, heavily made-up, in the end sibylline persona who ought to be entertaining.

The teller of tales would ennoble our emotions and our encounters with divine fatality. Isak Dinesen wrote that we must take "pride in the idea God had, when he made us." She was a theist of a kind (and was much twitted about this by her brother Thomas, a sensible Danish atheist). For there to be "divine swank," after all, there must be a divinity. She placed these Gothic Tales in the Romantic era when God, no longer housed in churches and institutions, was thought to be outdoors, in the mountains and sunsets. But even this evaporated divinity seems in the tale-teller's 20th century too benign to be credible, too unironical a guarantor of our inner sense of honor. In **"The Dreamers,"** the storyteller Mira Jama asserts of God, "To love him truly you must love change, and you must love a joke, these being the true inclinations of his own heart." Such a deity feels pre-Christian—a vitality at the dark heart of things. One of the many magical atmospheric sentences in **"The Poet"** runs, "The stillness and silence of the night was filled with a deep life, as if within a moment the universe would give up its secret." The brand of stoicism which these tales invite us to share is not dispassionately Roman or of the pleasure-denying Protestant variety; it has Viking intoxication and battle-frenzy in it. Intoxication figures frequently in Isak Dinesen's work, and mercilessness was part of the storyteller's art as she construed it: the story must pursue its end without undue compassion for its characters. Combat lies closer than compassion to the secret of *Seven Gothic Tales,* and its exhilaration is their contagious mood. (pp. 3, 37)

John Updike, " 'Seven Gothic Tales': The Divine Swank of Isak Dinesen," in The New York Times Book Review, *February 23, 1986, pp. 3, 37.*

FURTHER READING

Aiken, Susan Hardy. *Isak Dinesen and the Engendering of Narrative.* Chicago: University of Chicago Press, 1990, 350 p.

Explores gender, sexuality, and representation in Dinesen's fiction.

Gossman, Ann. "Sacramental Imagery in Two Stories by Isak Dinesen." *Wisconsin Studies in Contemporary Literature* 4, No. 1 (Winter 1963): 319-26.

Examines Dinesen's symbolic use of the sacrament of communion in "Babette's Feast" and "Echoes."

Handler Burstein, Janet. "Two Locked Caskets: Selfhood and 'Otherness' in the Work of Isak Dinesen." *Texas Studies in Literature and Language* XX, No. 4 (Winter 1978): 615-32.

Examines Dinesen's attitudes toward women in her writings.

Henriksen, Aage. *Isak Dinesen/Karen Blixen: The Work and the Life.* New York: St. Martin's Press, 1988, 197 p.

Personal and critical reflections upon Dinesen and her short stories.

Høyrup, Helene. "The Arabesque of Existence: Existential Focus and Aesthetic Form in Isak Dinesen's 'The Roads Round Pisa'." *Scandinavica: An International Journal of Scandinavian Studies* 24, No. 2 (November 1985): 197-210.

Argues that "The Roads Round Pisa" "epitomizes the existential focus of Isak Dinesen inasmuch as it is the result of an urgent need to interpret existence from the viewpoint of the individual."

Thurman, Judith. *Isak Dinesen: The Life of a Storyteller.* New York: St. Martin's Press, 1982, 495 p.

Exhaustive biography of Dinesen.

Weed, Merry. "*Märchen* and Legend Techniques of Narration in Two 'Tales' by Isak Dinesen." *Journal of the Folklore Institute* XV, No. 1 (January-April 1978): 23-44.

Explores the influence of European fairy tales upon Dinesen's narrative style.

Whissen, Thomas R. *Isak Dinesen's Aesthetics.* Port Washington, NY: Kennikat Press, 1973, 130 p.

Argues that Dinesen offered art as a substitute for God.

———. "The Magic Circle: The Role of the Prostitute in Isak Dinesen's Gothic Tales." In *The Image of the Prostitute in Modern Literature,* edited by Pierre L. Horn and Mary Beth Pringle, pp. 43-51. New York: Frederick Ungar Publishing, 1984.

Contends that the character of the prostitute in Dinesen's fiction symbolizes "woman at ease with her own mystery and strangely empowered by it."

John Gardner

1933-1982

(Full name: John Champlin Gardner, Jr.) American short story writer, novelist, poet, critic, author of children's books, essayist, dramatist, and editor.

Gardner's career, although relatively short, was diverse and distinguished. He worked in nearly every genre, including children's fiction, opera libretti, and scholarly criticism, and his writings reflect the rich legacy of Western culture. While primarily recognized as a novelist, Gardner wrote two volumes of short stories that are similar to his longer fiction in both theme and content. Freely parodying the techniques and themes of such stylistically diverse writers as Homer, Edgar Allan Poe, and Herman Melville, Gardner incorporated philosophical ideas from the past in order to show their relevance to the present, often focusing on the redemptive power of love and art, and the relationship between good and evil. William Kennedy commented: "Gardner is the Lon Chaney of contemporary fiction, a writer without a personal psychography in his work. He seems sprung not from life but literature, history and ideas, a man making books with other books as a starting point, but a writer of enormous range and inventiveness. His prose is regal. What he is is a splendid showoff."

Gardner was born in Batavia, New York, and spent his childhood on the family farm. After receiving his Ph.D. from the University of Iowa, he taught medieval literature and creative writing at numerous colleges and universities, most notably Southern Illinois University for eleven years. Gardner continued to teach throughout his literary career, and both Western New York State University and Southern Illinois were influential in his writing. Many of Gardner's stories and novels are set in these locations, while others have such historical backdrops as ancient Greece or medieval Scandinavia. Gardner's first novels, *The Resurrection* and *The Wreckage of Agathon,* earned a modest amount of critical attention, but the publication of *Grendel,* a retelling of the eighth-century epic poem *Beowulf* from the monster's point of view, established Gardner's reputation as an important new writer. This work was followed by such critical and popular successes as *The Sunlight Dialogues, Nickel Mountain,* and *October Light,* which won the National Book Critics Circle Award for fiction in 1976. Gardner's popularity diminished somewhat in the late 1970s, following the publication of his controversial book of critical theory, *On Moral Fiction.* In this work, Gardner stated that an artist is responsible for creating works that affirm life and present inspirational visions, and he harshly criticized nearly all of his contemporaries for being more concerned with "technique" than "truth." Gardner's unflattering remarks can perhaps be blamed for the largely negative reviews of his last novel, *Mickelsson's Ghosts.* Several months after the book's publication, Gardner was killed in a motorcycle accident, only days before his intended wedding.

Gardner's characteristic emulation of such writers as Poe, Melville, Franz Kafka, and Samuel Taylor Coleridge prompted steady critical commentary throughout his ca-

reer. Although some considered this practice to be a smoke screen concealing a lack of profundity, several critics maintained that it epitomized the belief Gardner expounded in *On Moral Fiction.* As a moral writer, Gardner's most significant theme concerned the ability of faith to vanquish the destructive forces of nihilism, and he believed that fiction, above all else, could accomplish this act. He "stole" from other writers, Blanche H. Gelfant noted, "because as creators of fiction they possess what he most esteems—the imagination, the will, the power to shape a personal style, that is, to shape a personal vision. To have shaped one's vision in art is to have asserted one's being; and that *does* matter, as the act of life." While Gardner's pervasive literary consciousness resulted in both consternation and praise from critics, he was roundly applauded for his strong, self-conscious narratives and his adroit handling of myriad fictional modes, including fantasy, satire, myth, and allegory.

Gardner's first collection of short fiction, *The King's Indian: Stories and Tales,* revolves around the motif of illusory life and the hazards of blind compliance and passivity. "The Warden" pays homage to Franz Kafka's *The Trial* and "In the Penal Colony" through its use of irony, ambiguity, and eerie atmosphere. Herr Vortrab, an assistant to a prison warden, continues to carry out executions and pardons relayed by the warden although he has not seen the man in some time. He becomes more confused after he sees the warden shoot himself in the head in a cemetery, and then get up and walk away. Though shaken, Herr Vortrab resumes his actions, deferring to mute authority and questioning nothing. The title novella of the collection, *The King's Indian,* is a tragicomic work that elicited varying critical reactions. A tall tale with nuances of, among many other works, Melville's *Moby-Dick* and Coleridge's *The Rime of the Ancient Mariner, The King's Indian* chronicles the story of Jonathan Upchurch, who is himself relating his life to a listener named John Gardner. Upchurch says that as a youth, pirates cunningly got him drunk and persuaded him to buy their battered boat, the *Jolly Independent,* with money he had saved to buy a farm. After taking it out on the ocean, the boat swamps and Upchurch is rescued by the *Jerusalem,* a whaling ship carrying a crew of dead men and slaves who, although supposedly deceased, subject him to lunacy, villainy, deception, and illusion. Several reviewers professed Gardner's blend of philosophy, fantasy, and parody to be overwhelming and pretentious, but the majority were impressed with his creative study of human nature versus free will. The most critically acclaimed stories in the *King's Indian* collection are overt, contemporary tales of the conflict between faith and disbelief. "John Napper Sailing through the Universe," which concerns a painter who struggles against nihilism and despair, and "Pastoral Care," the account of a Presbyterian minister whose passionate sermons inadvertently provoke a radical student to blow up his church, are two such works.

The Art of Living, and Other Stories follows the philosophy of art Gardner delineated in *On Moral Fiction.* Characteristically, the ten tales contain a wide variety of settings and characters, and include both realistic and fantastic approaches; however, nearly all the stories treat a single theme: the value of art as a life-affirming moral force. While some critics asserted that this collection contained the same self-indulgent tone as many of Gardner's novels and essays, most praised the volume's capricious qualities. Anne Tyler observed: "These are miracles of stories— fully realized, far-reaching, greater than the sum of their parts. It's a wonder a single volume can contain them all." "Nimram" centers upon the relationship between a famous symphony conductor, Benjamin Nimram, and a terminally ill sixteen-year-old girl. A chance meeting on a flight to Chicago changes both their lives—the girl's plight helps Nimram realize the banality of the anxiety that has come with his fame, and she receives strength through the power of his music after attending a symphony which he conducts. "Redemption" concerns an adolescent farmboy who must cope with immense guilt after he accidentally kills his younger brother with a tractor. This highly personal tale is based on a tragic event from Gardner's childhood. At the age of twelve, Gardner killed his seven-year-old brother Gilbert in a similar accident, and the story evokes the anguish and fear that Gardner claimed haunted him for decades after the accident. The boy in "Redemption" is able to survive the tragedy when he takes up the French horn and is introduced to the life-affirming joy of music. Another personal story, the critically acclaimed work "Come on Back," recalls a Welsh boy's childhood in rural New York State. After the death of a beloved uncle, the youth is ushered into an appreciation for Welsh ceremony and ritual when his family helps him discover the beauty of the cultural songs his uncle so dearly loved. This story has been praised for its rich detail and imagery.

Those critics and writers adamantly opposed to the ideas Gardner presented in *On Moral Fiction* have tended to dispute Gardner's contention that art can radically change people's lives and have questioned the value of his work. Nevertheless, Gardner remains widely respected for artistically presenting principles in which he so strongly believed. Additionally, numerous critics have argued that the metaphysical elements and ubiquitous literary aestheticism of Gardner's short stories reveal not only an astute creative mind, but also a respect for the intelligence of his audience. In a review of *The King's Indian,* Kelly Cherry commented: "What Gardner does so successfully, and what too many writers in America today fail to do, is to examine and dramatize philosophical motives. He shows us the relation between idea and character or event, and he gives us back the intelligence that American literature, in its eagerness to conform to that Procrustean bed that certain critics made for it, lopped off. He gives us the whole person."

(For further information on Gardner's life and career, see *Contemporary Literary Criticism,* Vols. 2, 3, 5, 7, 8, 10, 18, 28, 34; *Contemporary Authors,* Vols. 65-68, 107 [obituary]; *Dictionary of Literary Biography,* Vol. 2; *Dictionary of Literary Biography Yearbook: 1982;* and *Something about the Author,* Vols. 31, 40.)

PRINCIPAL WORKS

SHORT FICTION

The King's Indian: Stories and Tales   1974
The Art of Living, and Other Stories   1981

OTHER MAJOR WORKS

The Complete Works of the Gawain-Poet (criticism) 1965
The Resurrection (novel) 1966; revised edition, 1974
The Wreckage of Agathon (novel) 1970
The Alliterative Morte Arthure (criticism) 1971
Grendel (novel) 1971
The Sunlight Dialogues (novel) 1972
Jason and Medeia (epic poem) 1973
Nickel Mountain (novel) 1973
The Construction of the Wakefield Cycle (criticism) 1974
The Construction of Christian Poetry in Old English (criticism) 1975
Dragon, Dragon, and Other Tales (children's book) 1975
Gudgekin the Thistle Girl, and Other Tales (children's book) 1976
October Light (novel) 1976
A Child's Bestiary (children's book) 1977
In the Suicide Mountains (children's book) 1977
The King of the Hummingbirds, and Other Tales (children's book) 1977
The Life and Times of Chaucer (biography) 1977
The Poetry of Chaucer (criticism) 1977
On Moral Fiction (criticism) 1978
Poems (poetry) 1978

Vlemk the Box-Painter   (novella) 1979
Freddy's Book   (novel) 1980
The Temptation Game   (radio drama) 1980
Death and the Maiden   (drama) 1981
Mickelsson's Ghosts   (novel) 1982

Kelly Cherry (essay date 1974)

[*In the following excerpt, Cherry praises Gardner's ability to incorporate philosophical motives into the short stories collected in* The King's Indian.]

You learn to walk along the edges of your brain inconspic-
uously, the way you approach life in a new neighborhood.
One day you have the terrific, unexpected good fortune to
make a friend who is already at home in your head.

Clearly, friends must be cherished. It's true John Gardner's popularity is immense, but that would be a poor reason not to extol his new work as greatly as it deserves.

And does it deserve to be extolled! What Gardner does so
successfully, and what too many writers in America today
fail to do, is to examine and dramatize philosophical motives. He shows us the relation between idea and character
or event, and he gives us back the intelligence that American literature, in its eagerness to conform to that Procrustean bed that certain critics made for it, lopped off. He
gives us the whole person.

In each of the first five stories in Gardner's . . . [*The
King's Indian*], the whole person is a professional man—
minister, doctor, monk, prison official, poet—confronting
the chaos that greets us even in our own back yards when
we explore to the limit those ideas we otherwise blithely
act on. The confrontation may be, often is, comic—but
there's a feverishness to the fun, at least in these opening
stories. When the laughter dies down, we're left with a
minister reluctantly attending the very "wildman" who
damns him, or with a doctor healing cloned children, a
monk clinging to the knight of faith for dear life.

"The Warden" is an especially wonderful story. In it, Herr
Vortrab, the warden's so-called amanuensis and general
factotum, is intellectually seduced into compassion. Recognizing the intimate connection between the Cartesian
cogito, "I think, therefore I am," and the assumption that
God exists, Gardner draws a vaguely malevolent, unfathomable warden who may have altogether absconded with
past and future time, leaving us empty-handed, with nothing to go on but an *as if* philosophy.

From one point of view, this is Descartes' "Deceiver"; but,
says Descartes in the *Second Meditation,* "Without doubt
I exist also if he deceives me." A world sustained by deception isn't Paradise; it's Kafkaesque, gloomy, erratic; the
mood is dark and quarrelsome. Riddled with references to
European history, this story derives its power from the
way it plucks at every man's sense of helplessness.
Vortrab's only salvation is to hold mind and body in perfect tension, like balanced scales, sacrificing neither. The
trouble is, without an assurance of benign order, we—
everyman, Vortrab—have no criterion for distinguishing
between illusion and reality. Which is which? Meanings

merge; a burial detail becomes a jury, or disciples; phe-
nomenology is precisely the most untrustworthy interpretation of things.

In a dazzling twist of perspective, three stories about a
royal court whose mad queen feels herself frequently to be
a toad make similar points so playfully and plainly that a
child would have to love them, as an adult has to applaud.
These pieces are absolutely nutty. The foiled villain Vrokror stamps his foot and calls his fellow characters "mani-
acs"—and so they are, a feudal company of fools as hilarious and appealing folklore. They all, including Vrokror,
like one another so well that we've got to like them too.

In the title story [*The King's Indian*], a long and convoluted quest for freedom, Gardner flicks back and forth between the comic and the tragic, Gothic parody and high
seriousness, with the virtuosity of a lizard's tongue or of
the rather satanic hypnotist, Dr. Luther Flint, who is
given to appearing, chameleonlike, in various guises
throughout.

While an angel acts as host, a mariner recounts for his
guest the tale of a young man with the fine name of Jonathan Upchurch, and how he was taken aboard the *Jerusalem.* Here, the *Jerusalem* is a whaling vessel, or, again, a
slaver; it is everywhere a microcosm of the world. America, alas, used to be understandably known as the new Jerusalem.

Jonathan's voyage involves him with sailing mates and
harpooners who soliloquize in the manner of Melville,
psychic disturbances and oddities out of Poe, big white
birds hatched by Coleridge, or, as Melville preferred,
"God's great, unflattering laureate, Nature." But the primary problem is free will and its relation to time, which
Gardner turns over and over again, in a dizzying display
of literary showmanship.

Near the end of Upchurch's tale, its author steps onto the
stage, insisting on his own reality as a celebrant "of all literature and life." The reader will discover like remarks
elsewhere. . . . This coyness, though no crime, is mildly
irksome, because an outfront consideration of the writer's
standing among his own characters could have led to interesting effects.

The other charge that may be made against some of the
stories is that they don't always move speedily—but the
same complaint has been voiced about Conrad, and that's
okay company to be in. Ultimately, Gardner's con is the
King's Indian, a sophisticated defense that transforms a
reluctant attack into "the fighting game *par excellence.*"
It's played out in an ending so splendidly vulgar, wacky,
and acute that the reader experiences a surprising lift of
the spirit, a rush, such as Meno's slave must have felt, surrendering to the Socratic method.

*Kelly Cherry, "Gardner's Characters Give Fic-
tion Back Its Intelligence," in* Chicago Tribune, *December 1, 1974, p. 3.*

William Kennedy (essay date 1974)

[*Kennedy is an American novelist who has written such
works as* Ironweed *(1983) and* Quinn's Book *(1988). In
the following review of* The King's Indian, *Kennedy fo-*

cuses on the idea of "illusory life" as the collection's main theme.]

A serious case can be made for how little John Gardner resembles himself. Now he's an epic poet, now an epic novelist, now a medieval monster, now a simulated Poe or Melville. He is the latter two, and more, in . . . [*The King's Indian*, a] new collection of his short fiction, the title story a remarkable novella, full of marvels.

Gardner is the Lon Chaney of contemporary fiction, a writer without a personal psychography in his work. He seems sprung not from life but literature, history and ideas, a man making books with other books as a starting point, but a writer of enormous range and inventiveness. His prose is regal.

What he is is a splendid show-off. Look Ma, I'm Kafka. He is Kafka in "The Warden," a story of illusory life, which is the dominant theme of most of these stories and tales. Herr Vortrab is an assistant to the warden of a prison where men are kept in chains in dungeons, never charged with a crime, some for presumably religious heresies. Vortrab relays the warden's directions to underlings, but lately he hasn't seen the warden. He believes he hears him pacing in his office, but the warden will not respond to knocks or messages. Neither will the higher echelons of the system of justice. Gardner is not merely parodying *The Trial* and "In the Penal Colony" in this, but using their moods, their ambiguities, their bizarre ironies out of homage both to the stories and their inventor. With the theme of mute authority dictating men's destinies, Gardner does not improve on Kafka, but Kafka starts from him. Herr Vortrab finally does see the warden, in a cemetery, holding a pistol, his forehead blown open. But when the warden walks off, Herr Vortrab, uncertain of what he has seen, resumes his life as before, pretending the warden exists, not quite sure he doesn't, issuing pardons and death sentences in his name. Mute authority reigns. Illusion runs the world.

In "The Temptation of St. Ivo" the illusion overtakes an overzealous medieval monk, Brother Ivo, a genius at decorating sacred manuscripts with "zoomorphic capitals"—letters layered with designs of dragons, the phoenix, bears, birds, "coiled, unwitting in the larger design of an A or an O." Then one day Brother Nicholas invades Brother Ivo's life, accuses him of being homosexual. Is it an invitation? He hounds Ivo, tells him he has found a phoenix and intends to murder it. Ivo confesses the hounding, but his confessor says he's overworked, under a strain and should pray for perception. Does Brother Nicholas really exist? Is he really old Nick? We assume as much but the reality of his presence drives Ivo into the night forest to a rendezvous, not with the phoenix or with the devilish Nicholas, but with—ah, the shining fantasy of a repressed cloister queen—a knight errant in full armor, on horseback, clutching a sword. Ivo accepts an invitation to mount the horse, hugs the knight, smells his sweat, and they ride off together in the moonlit mist, Ivo enroute to sainthood?

In "The Ravages of Spring" Gardner turns to Poe for framework and tone, writing elegant literary spookery. Consider this from this most modern writer:

> The door through which they led me . . . opened on a circular wooden stairway with a rail worn smooth by many climbings in the night, a pitch-

dark room as airless as dreams of the grave. At what was perhaps the third turning, I saw light above, frail and unearthly—the lumination of the storm. It grew brighter, more ominous. I could feel the giddying sway of the tower. But at last we arrived, despite all that—came out into the world of Hunter's ungodly laboratory.

The story is one of a mysterious house, tornado terror, a mad doctor, witchery and clones, all in support of Gardner's conclusion that "no work of evil men or devils is finally impressive compared with the vastness of the universe or the hopeful imagination," a bit of self-congratulation here, since Gardner is the most hopeful imagination at hand. He is never the tragedian. Evil folks do dastardly deeds all right, but they usually get theirs, and the goodbodies are still around at the finale.

The prime goodbody in this collection is John Napper, a painter from the story "John Napper Sailing Through The Universe." Gardner appears in this as another man named John, a poet writing an epic poem about Jason (a devilishly clever disguise: Gardner has also written an epic poem about Jason). But Gardner proves to be little more than a presence in the story, a pair of eyes to see John Napper descending into life's blackest, most despairing regions through his art, yet never ceasing to see the best side of all that life has to offer. "Marvelous" is Napper's vision of most things. Though this is a slight story which seems more like homage to a friend than competition for the other elaborate work in this collection, it suggests itself as one key to Gardner's psyche: he is not like Napper but he wishes he were. (p. 19)

Elsewhere he is also a fabulist, a teller of fairytales in three stories of Louisa, the freckle-faced, red-headed frog queen, and her husband, King Gregor ("bold King Gregor" was the name the king applied to himself, but it never caught on). These tales are amusing, fanciful, forgettable.

But unforgettable is *The King's Indian,* the novella that ends the collection. The major frame for this bravura piece is *Moby Dick,* as told not only by Melville but also Poe again, Conrad, Stevenson, Wilde, Pirandello, Hawthorne and Ingmar Bergman, among others, the amalgam suffused with the surrealist muse.

The narrator is a grizzled ancient mariner named Jonathan Upchurch, who is in heaven, recounting his story (while a sleepy angel serves drinks) to a listener who turns out to be John Gardner by name. The frame is an antique device, which Gardner uses for presumably the same reasons he uses so many obsolescent and obscure words—"some mysterious egritude of mind," "sensual, quisquos old Ovid," "in the fuliginous silence we both preferred"—to make this take a homemade museum of both language and literature.

The narrator and Gardner are finally an intrusion in the tale, not because of the device but because of Gardner's explanation just before the story's last gasp. He says that "with the help of Poe and Melville and many another man" he wrote this book, filled with doubts. But he adds that the book "is not a toy but a queer, cranky monument, a collage: a celebration of all literature and life; and environmental sculpture, a funeral crypt."

(Did he want to bury Melville? Perhaps. Be done with such an impossible hero once and for all.)

But these final lines are merely Gardner's uncertainty about what he had sculpted. He is a worrier, trying to avoid the judgment of others in advance. Will they really say he stole from Melville? How could they not? But will they know the theft had a purpose: flattering that grand spook with abject homage? How could he imagine they wouldn't know and approve?

The tale is so outlandish, so full of magic and the occult, so brimming with fraudulent visions and deceptive symbols and conversations with the Holy Ghost and hoaxes and illusions and the most outrageous coincidences, that it instantly explains to potentially miffed Melvilleans that Gardner is not propagating borrowed wisdom but only humble story. His tale of Jonathan Upchurch—a youth mesmerized by the magician Flint and his strange daughter Miranda, then robbed by pirates, fingered by nature, rescued by that doomed whaling ship, the *Jerusalem* (carrying a crew of dead men and slaves and commanded by Captain Dirge) and then damnedly destined to ride out the voyage's lunacy and villainy and murder and deception and illusion on the grandest possible scale—all this is done with such verve and fraudulence and with such an outlandish concatenation of improbabilities (ventriloquists, a spontaneously combustive man, ghost ships, angel birds) that no one could possible accuse Gardner of venal literary piracy, only of joyful trickery.

Even the wisdom he does propagate between segments of his narrative is itself suspect, transplanted to that mystical whaler from Gardner's own overflowing rhetoric bank in order to give us yet another illusion—that this story means something. Melvillean rhetoric must mean something mustn't it?

No.

Only the plot of this tale matters, standing as it does for that profoundest of human truths: that life is one goddamn thing after another. All other interpretations of this work are illusory. And if you believe that we can get on with the story. (pp. 19-20)

> *William Kennedy, in a review of "The King's Indian," in* The New Republic, *Vol. 171, No. 23, December 7, 1974, pp. 19-20.*

Alan Friedman (essay date 1974)

[*An American critic, Friedman has written several scholarly works, including* The Turn of the Novel *(1966). In the following review of* The King's Indian, *Friedman maintains that Gardner's short fiction lacks the fantastic and magical elements of his novels.*]

It's been several years since I first stumbled over a book by John Gardner. I dusted myself off, examined my bruises, and have been engaged ever since in a running debate. I run as I read, trying to escape, muttering literary objections, and Gardner pursues, snuffling and wild-eyed, hurling book after book. From time to time I glance back over my shoulder and observe that he's still got his fangs locked on something apparently foul and indigestible. It may very well be human, I reflect uneasily, but quite possibly it is only the stem of his pipe.

That first book was *Grendel.* (Gardner's two earlier books

had missed me.) *Grendel,* the revelations of a monster is an eerie *tour de force* that manages to transmogrify the Old English epic of Beowulf into a modern English nightmare. Part of its astonishing force lies in the conception. It is the first story. My 5-year-old son plunked himself down at my typewriter one day and painstakingly typed out his first story. It was very short: "A monster came into my house."

Gardner gives us the soul of the monster, brooding on the philosophical torments of its position. He gives us the house—civilization itself—the great hall of Hrothgar. He takes us down into the subterranean world from which the monster arises, and brings us back, again and again, to the slaughter. The monster dies but he remains on the mind's retina, an afterglow, gleaming with subearthly radiance.

Nevertheless, while reading, I had doubts aplenty. The work seemed somehow unreliable, always interesting, even gorgeous, but not human. Not a novel. A myth in a pressure-cooker. A fiction in a Fryeing pan. The author, I too hastily assumed, must be a most extraordinary Beowulf scholar, and *Grendel* his pipedream.

I was unprepared for *The Sunlight Dialogues,* aimed at me and striking. Here, for all its hocus-pocus, was a human chronicle, one demanding a genealogy and List of Characters (eighty-one!) and displaying a wealth of interlocking plots and scenes. A grand work. Yet top-heavy. That book-long debate between Clumly, the Man of Law, and his daemonic agonist, the Sunlight Man: was it not too carefully posed, staged and unconvincing? (p. 1)

Nickel Mountain, his next work, had a gentler impact. By the meandering path of *A Pastoral,* as he subtitled the book, Gardner had mounted to the broad highroad of fiction. He had, in fact, come that well-traveled way before. His first novel, *Resurrection,* which I recently picked up with caution, was conventional enough, though immensely agitated by the Consolation of Philosophy and the preparations for dying. Now in *Nickel Mountain* he moved with an unexpected quietness, a high density of simple feeling, a longwave serenity of mood. The melancholy reflections of pastoral upstate New Yorkers were suddenly persuasive. Gardner the Trickster had effectively retired behind and within the work, placidly paring his claws.

Frankly, I felt safe, no longer threatened by monsters and daemons.

Now at last a volume of his shorter fiction has come to hand. ***The King's Indian*** is a collection which gives us, as a prism might, the spectrum of Gardner's vision from the infra-red of his Gothic horrors to the purple poses of his romantic realism. . . . In Gardner's prose, darkening landscapes churn and fearful houses come clattering to ruins as in Poe. Inaccessible authority and bizarre injustice creak on as in Kafka. A queen can turn into a toad and a peasant lass into a princess as in Lewis Carroll and Grimm reality. And on the high seas of this raging art, a mutinous Bounty of a Wandering Dutchman can meet a wizard of Oz.

But hold on tight. "Life . . . is preposterous." So begins **"The Ravages of Spring,"** the second tale in this collection. How preposterous that the narrator should tell us this at all, though his banality is self-confessed. Yet how right that word is for Gardner's world. Not absurd, but preposterous. It's absurd to be tossed in a single story "from one sphere of reality to another," but it is downright preposterous to be nudged at the same time from one sphere of fiction to another. Into this pastiche of Poe rushes Kafka's "Country Doctor" whose runaway horse, like its original, thrusts its head into the house to hurry matters along.

The narrator of these tales is apt to be an *homme moyen raisonnable.* A man who will ponder things exhaustingly with "one ear cocked toward the infinite." A minister, a doctor, a monk, or a warden. A man preternaturally aware of his role in tradition, including his literary tradition. Against nihilism, against panic, these ponderers cling to "the ancient regulations" as Gardner clings to his traditional forms, while all around him and them "conditions grow monstrous." Kafka's K. may have been unjustly accused; Gardner's prisoner, rotting in his cell, was never accused.

For all the author's seriousness, however, a playfulness, often dreadfully Romantic—an uppercase Agony—flits in and out of his text. "I have fled like a tortured ghost from one green courtyard to another . . . " There is something less than desperate in his "centuries of despair," something delicious in the cyclones and twisters that blow "great black tons of clouds" through these pages. A few of the pieces, like **"John Napper Sailing Through the Universe,"** have a self-indulgent congratulatory tone that repels—or excludes—me. The "Tales of Queen Louisa," obsessively madcap and fraught with calculated *frisson,* depend on a very special brand of humor that is not to my taste: "The forces of evil do exist! Ha ha!" Possibly, some of the tales may be journeyman's work, the sorcerer's apprentice on his way to becoming a master. In others, the mastery dazzles and the magic is black.

The last offering in this collection is a short novel, **The King's Indian,** which lends its title to the volume as a whole. It is John Gardner's most rambunctious work to date, as long as *Grendel* and rivaling it in ingenuity, if not obsession. In a tavern we overhear an ancient mariner. From there we set off on a mysterious whaling voyage. At first the ghostly accents in the cellarage of the narrative and the hold of the ship are Coleridge's and Melville's (not only *Moby Dick,* but *Benito Cereno, Billy Budd, The Confidence Man* and so on). Then ominous waves begin to rock the boat—Stevenson, Conrad, Twain, Shakespeare, Homer—the vast literature of the sea, of necromancy, of hoaxes. Gardner's voyage makes its way through a tempest of literary refractions that almost capsizes, but never quite sinks, the most outrageous sea yarn this side of Jules Verne and the Sargasso Sea.

> I could tell you a tale, if ye'd understand from the outset it has no purpose to it, no shape or form or discipline but the tucket and boom of its highflown language and whatever dim flickers that noise stirs up in yer cerebrium, sir—the boom and the bottle we chase it with—fierce rum of everlasting sleep, ha ha!—for I won't be called a liar, no sir! not when I speak of such matters as devils and angels and the making of man, which is my subject, sir.

Fair enough. Stunning enough. But when the guest hesitates, the ancient mariner goes so far as to instruct him in poesy. " 'Tell on, old loon!' yer supposed to say."

"That face! . . . that face! Where <u>have</u> I seen that face?"

Gardner's first professional publication: a cartoon in the July, 1948 issue of Seventeen *magazine.*

And what are *we* supposed to say? New writers are expected to stand on the shoulders of earlier ones. Some of them, however, prefer to place a couple of bodies of earlier work on their lap, manipulate the dummies, and speak with their predecessors' voices. They become literary ventriloquists: Mann, for instance, in "The Holy Sinner" and Joyce through enormous sections of *Ulysses.* This preference may be unusual, but it is neither unique nor perverse.

Oddly, Gardner feels the need to justify it. "Shall I strip myself naked and cry out, shameless . . . it was like THIS in our time? Better the cover of my dungeon fiction . . . " More ingenuously still, he assures us that his tale, which he enters in *propria persona,* is not "a cynical trick," not "one more bad joke of exhausted art," but "a celebration of all literature and life." I do not myself care for such nervous self-congratulation. But apologetics aside, there's no doubt that Gardner plays his game with gravity and dignity.

There will be readers who enjoy the game: it's fun to have one mirror on the road and another in the library. These readers will find Gardner's formal masks an irony, enriching the archetypal stories he tells, which might otherwise be too simple, uncapturable. And there will be irritated readers who will see mere artifice; flashing lights and sharp practice; at best a distraction that keeps blurring a genuine literary experience. In my own judgment, Gardner is in many places too cunning for his own good. He is a virtuoso, roguish, fluent, self-indulgent. But elsewhere the undeniable power of his imagination transcends the question of his method altogether. Collages or not, bamboozling or not, his ventriloqual fictions do suddenly grow nerves and breathe with an awesome, independent life. Often when he throws his voice, I respond like the crew aboard the whaler who are mesmerized by the villain. An unwilling suspension of disbelief grips me—I must believe—until the villain snaps his fingers to remind me that he is John Gardner.

Which brings me at last to the first piece in this new volume. **"Pastoral Care"** is not a tale, not a pastiche, not a trick, but a straightforward contemporary story, enormously appealing, about the encounter between an up-to-the-minute Presbyterian minister and the perfect monster for our time, the idealistic student. This work will stand comparison with the standard great stories of contemporary fiction. What more could one ask? Well, might one not ask with respect whether it is too much like those other great stories? I don't mean a reasonable facsimile. I mean an unreasonably flawless item in a highly developed genre. Yet in that sense predictable. For what of its impact? As the blows fall, their shocks are easily recognized: their direction, their significance, their very form. In the midst of the usual epiphany I found myself longing for the complex litanies and amazing grace of his voices and mirrors. I felt comfortable with the story. There was no menace. And I kept on wishing he would bare those literary fangs of his, a bit forced perhaps, but grinding away at reality. (pp. 1-2)

Alan Friedman, "A John Gardner Spectrum From Gothic Horrors to Romantic Realism," in The New York Times Book Review, *December 15, 1974, pp. 1-2.*

Thomas R. Edwards   (essay date 1975)

[*In the review excerpted below, Edwards asserts that absurdity is a recurring motif in* The King's Indian *and, referring to Gardner's gift for language and atmosphere and his impersonations of the writings of Edgar Allan Poe, Franz Kafka, and Herman Melville, describes the collection as a book best suited for teachers of literature.*]

Novels by and/or about teachers of literature can be a tiresome subgenre which, since it's hard to imagine anyone else being interested, seems usually intended *for* teachers of literature. The assumptions that the scholastic life somehow represents life itself or that it qualifies one to practice literature aren't ones that dentists or bus drivers or shoe salesmen seem to make about their own professions, a modesty that ought to be encouraged. Still, it is a pleasure to find pieces from the academy with life in them.

The stories in *The King's Indian* allow John Gardner to put on a variety of narrative masks, from that of teller of hip fairy tales about anxiety, madness, and marital strain to jaunty impersonations of Poe, Kafka, Melville, and John Gardner. And of course the beauty of masks is that they can come off whenever an effect is required. For example, **"John Napper Sailing Through the Universe,"** a tale of *la vie bohème* centered on an artist with the same name as the illustrator of Gardner's *Sunlight Dialogues,* is told by a narrator named—like a good many other people in the book—John, a college teacher who like Professor John Gardner lives on a farm in southern Illinois and is writing an epic poem about Jason and Medea. Or consider the moment toward the end of the novella *The King's*

Indian, when the pretense that a Yankee-style Ancient Mariner is recounting his strange adventures turns out to be yet another hoax in a story of hoaxings compounded:

> This house we're in is a strange one, reader—house or old trunk or circus tent—and it's one I hope you find congenial, sufficiently gewgawed and cluttered but not unduly snug. Take my word, in any case, that I haven't built it as a cynical trick, one more bad joke of exhausted art. The sculptor-turned-painter that I mentioned before is an actual artist, with a name I could name, and what I said of him is true. And you are real, reader, and so am I, John Gardner the man that, with the help of Poe and Melville and many another man, wrote this book. And this book, this book is no child's top either—though I write, more than usual, filled with doubts. Not a toy but a queer, cranky monument, a collage: a celebration of all literature and life; an environmental sculpture, a funeral crypt.

That does seem quite a lot for a book to be.

Here, I suppose, Gardner is thinking less of Poe and Melville than of someone like the John Barth of *Chimera* and "The Literature of Exhaustion." In any case, I wish Gardner weren't so eager to join the game of self-conscious fiction. Insisting on the arbitrariness of illusions puts all the cards in the novelist's hand, and I feel a little surly about Gardner's assumption that I, the reader, am safely "real" (how can he be so sure?) while letting me see that "John Gardner the man that . . . wrote this book" is just another disguise of a trickster who, like any teacher, has reserved the real power for himself.

It's not inevitably a bad thing for a novelist to teach in a college and know a lot about literature and modern thought. One of the best stories here, **"Pastoral Care,"** takes place in a college town in southern Illinois beset by revolutionary student unrest. To be sure, the troubled protagonist is a clergyman, not a teacher, but the professions have their resemblances. Elsewhere the voices are those of a literate country doctor, a medieval monk, a prison administrator, a smart parent amusing his kids with more than they're likely to grasp; and in all these clerkish voices one hears an academic man trying out hypothetical other selves in situations in which a literary education can exercise itself to greater effect than it usually does on campus.

Gardner's Grendel and Sunlight Man were deracinated professors, too, speculative minds placed in situations whose hostility or indifference provided a splendid tragicomic stage for eloquent failure. And *Nickel Mountain,* his most restrained and best novel, has fine moments in which "ordinary" people are granted the emotional equivalent of intellectual subtlety, moments that work because self-consciousness and self-irony are not attached to them.

Nothing in *The King's Indian* matches these successes. The recurrent motif is craziness, not the depressing madness of the real world but in the more amusing sense of "crazy" that in bookish conversation (like "marvelous," "incredible," and "unbelievable") simply means exciting and imaginative. A country doctor who has read a great deal of Poe takes refuge from a tornado in an old farmhouse inhabited by a mad geneticist, long thought dead, who has perfected a technique for duplicating living creatures; the geneticist turns out to be a clone himself, and after he's destroyed by the tornado the doctor finds, and true to his science and his humanity preserves, several repulsive child-clones of the original Hunter. In another story, a pious monk is beset by the anarchic whispers of freedom and crime of Brother Nicholas, a philosophical relative of the dragon in *Grendel* ("Your rules are absurd. The order of the world is an accident. We could change it in an instant, simply by opening our throats and speaking"). In another, a bewildered functionary tries to keep a Kafkaesque prison running as the mysterious Warden grows silent and invisible. And so on.

Much of this is made tolerable by Gardner's great gifts for language and moral atmosphere. But only in the title story, *The King's Indian* (referring, appropriately, to a chess gambit), is there anything like the amplitude of form and conception needed to keep Gardner's eloquence from swamping the fable. Young Jonathan Upchurch (who, in one of Herbert L. Fink's handsome illustrations, looks rather like the author) plans to leave Boston for (yes) southern Illinois; but at a tavern he falls in with pirates (whose captain is called Pious John, evidently another form of "Jonathan Upchurch") and drunkenly buys from them an unsound small boat, the *Jolly Independent,* with the money he'd saved for a farm. Enraged and humiliated, he sails recklessly into the Atlantic and is rescued from his not so jolly independence by the whaler *Jerusalem,* bound for the South Pacific with (oddly) slaves below deck. Jonathan, a resourceful youth of the kind that pervades American fiction, becomes a member of the crew and tutor to the ravaged Captain Dirge's intriguing daughter Augusta, with whom he promptly falls in love.

I won't attempt to summarize the elaborate reality games that follow, except to say that, a time-loop being suspected, the *Jerusalem* may be the ghostly double of the *Jerusalem* that may have gone down with all hands off the Vanishing Isles some years before; the Captain may be—no, wait, *is*—the mesmerist Flint who performed in Boston with his daughter Miranda in Jonathan's childhood, but it takes a while to locate the real Flint among his clockwork surrogates, especially since he's a master ventriloquist and hypnotist, and there are distracting mutinies, murders, and rapes going on all around. But we get an upbeat ending, in which Upchurch and Augusta-Miranda set sail for the seacoast of southern Illinois while Old Glory flutters overhead:

> "—Homewards, my sea-whores," I shouted from the masthead. "—Homewards, you orphans, you bandy-legged, potbellied, pig-brained, belly-dancing killers of the innocent whale! Eyes forward [Upchurch himself is wall-eyed], you niggers, you Chinese Irish Mandalay-Jews, you Anglo-Saxons with jackals' eyes! We may be the slime of the earth but we've got our affinities! On to Illinois the Changeable!"

Academic vaudeville can be good fun, and Gardner in these stories does play with classic American uneasiness, the mixture of fascination and mistrust toward portentous appearances, the yearning to strike through the mask even as you fear that there will, after all, be nothing much behind it. But *The King's Indian* is irksome in its reaching for the outrageous, the crazy, the (I'm afraid it must be said) cute, and I can only hope that it has done this immensely gifted writer some good to get these things out of his system. (p. 34)

Thomas R. Edwards, "Academic Vaudeville," in The New York Review of Books, *Vol. XXII, No. 2, February 20, 1975, pp. 34-6.*

Ronald de Feo   (essay date 1975)

[*In the following excerpt, de Feo negatively reviews* The King's Indian, *charging Gardner with employing exaggerated, pretentious philosophy.*]

Though I admire John Gardner's talent, ambition, and inventiveness, I've never been able to warm up to his work. The author has what might be called a sweet tooth for philosophy. He is often so determined to inject philosophical dialogues, concepts, and references into his work that he will introduce them even if they break the mood of the tale he is telling, interrupt the action, appear totally absurd, pretentious, and contrived in context. For example, in *Grendel,* Gardner's clever, though at times stifling takeoff on the Beowulf story, the title character visits a dragon who speaks in the following manner: "Importance is primarily monistic in its reference to the universe. Limited to a finite individual occasion, importance ceases to be important." The reader is, of course, willing to accept the fantasy of the book and go along with the talking monster business, but must he contend with a dragon who sounds as if he's conducting a seminar in philosophy? Such a passage not only destroys the mood of the fiction (for we can only believe that the philosophic author is spouting these very carefully chosen words), but it also gives the piece a bloated quality.

Almost all of Gardner's books have suffered from this peculiar brand of inflation and heavy-handedness. Although the reader appreciated the meticulous rendering of small-town life in *The Sunlight Dialogues,* he couldn't accept the contrived philosophical tug of war between Sheriff Clumly and the Sunlight Man (whose at-the-drop-of-a-hat monologues were too artfully structured to be believed). . . . [*Nickel Mountain*] was almost a welcomed change of pace. In this somber rural tale focusing on an inarticulate outsider, the irritating philosophical passages were noticeably, mercifully absent. The novel really didn't work—it was too cold and studied and the characters never truly sprang to life—but at least it did promise a less pretentious Gardner to come.

Unfortunately, *The King's Indian,* Gardner's latest book, is filled with the same type of self-indulgence that marred so many of his earlier efforts. And to make matters worse, there is in this collection of tales a good amount of still fashionable, though by now tedious, literary game-playing—in-jokes on narrative technique and the art of fiction, allusions to other writers and their work, the use of contemporary jargon in historical pieces. In several of the stories, Gardner makes a conscious effort to emulate various writers of the past. We detect traces of Poe and Kafka in **"The Ravages of Spring."** The narrator, a country doctor, regards life as preposterous, and well he should since he himself seems trapped in a preposterous tale—a little too calculatedly ridiculous and eerie for its own good. **"The Warden,"** one of the slightly more successful stories, concerns a warden's assistant who hasn't seen his mysterious boss for some time. The tale has a nice Kafkaesque quality, but Gardner's "philosophical" intrusions break its spell. The assistant, who, not surprisingly, goes home to read Descartes, chats with a philosophic prisoner ("There are two bodies, the rudimental and the complete . . . ") and a parent who is apparently taken with Swedenborg and Spinoza. The three stories dealing with mad Queen Louisa are supposed to be sparkling and witty, but come across as silly sketches tossed off by a professor between classes. However, if you can accept a description of battling knights one moment and a queen saying "Let's go skinny-dipping" the next, you should find the pieces hilarious. Of the two stories with a contemporary setting, **"Pastoral Care"** is the more accomplished and substantial. In fact, this refreshingly quiet piece, focusing on a Presbyterian minister's encounter with a student, shows that Gardner can do without his bag of tricks—the story is direct and effective.

Sadly, that bag of tricks is fully employed in the title story (a novella, actually) and the results are maddening. *The King's Indian* is a huge crazy comic invention in which a host of authors are evoked and parodied—Melville, Hawthorne, Poe, Coleridge, Charles Brockden Brown, to name only a few. Jonathan Upchurch's narrative, describing his voyage on a whaling ship populated by an insane cast of characters, is totally outrageous, containing enough twists and turns of plot, hoaxes, conspiracies, coincidences, to support dozens of tales. Gardner obviously had fun writing it, and I wish I could report that I had fun reading it. But one gets the idea soon enough, and the tale, for all its mad energy, rapidly becomes a bore. It goes on and on, for no particularly good reason, and finally, exhausted at last, it self-destructs. Even in this piece of overdrawn whimsy Gardner the philosopher cannot rest. That the philosophizing contrasts too sharply with all of the nonsense obviously makes little difference to the author.

The King's Indian surprises me on two counts. One, that a writer of Gardner's sophistication could settle for such philosophical and literary doodling. And two, that so many critics could be charmed by the performance. This kind of encouragement Gardner surely does not need. (pp. 234-35)

> Ronald de Feo, "A Sweet Tooth for Philosophy," in National Review, New York, Vol. XXVII, February 28, 1975, pp. 234-35.

George Levine   (essay date 1975)

[*In the review of* The King's Indian *excerpted below, Levine contends that the collection is characterized by strong, self-conscious narratives and an ecumenical literary consciousness.*]

John Gardner tells stories. A hundred years ago he might have been a great popular novelist, serious in the way popular novelists then could be. As it is, his story-telling is mixed with a good deal of philosophizing, solemn and playful, and with a lot of modern post-narrative self-consciousness. In a very few years he has tried an astonishing number of fictional modes, each time working from a strong narrative tradition, each time questioning it, each time returning. (p. 291)

No doubt Gardner has Dickensian ambitions, but where Dickens was a genuinely popular writer, Gardner is a professor. No doubt also, on the evidence of the novels, he is a remarkably learned and good one; but as a writer he not

only earns the rewards, he pays the price of professing. Dickens could unselfconsciously make myths out of the materials of a popular culture in which he participated. Gardner makes, or rather unmakes, myths out of the materials of a very high culture playing about the pop; almost every word he writes seems to bear upon it the scar of the past of Western literary culture. He is cursed, or blessed, by a characteristic modern literary consciousness.

What writer we might care about these days isn't? Barth, Borges, Nabokov, Pynchon, Coover. But with Gardner it is a little different. Though literary virtuosity is almost a condition of serious writing these days, though literary games are both part of the sport and part of what really counts, Gardner plays the game most of the time with a straight-forwardness that makes me feel—happily and uneasily at once—that the real name of his game is narrative. Even as he includes (in all of the stories I have read) elements to undercut the traditions of narrative he uses, each story depends for its strength and energy on the suspect narrative itself. So he gives us a gallery of nihilistic philosophers, of magicians and sleight-of-hand people. And always, somewhere behind the continuous sequence of actions, there is a bomb of meaninglessness waiting to explode the mythic significances just as we are getting comfy with them.

Still, enduring behind nihilism, meaninglessness, violent disruptions, there is Gardner saying yes, winking a bit shyly, and wall-eyed at the embarrassment of saying it under the burden of all that knowledge. And I think the effort to say yes is the clue to the strange way his apparently very modern perceptions of narrative-as-lie, of inanity, of inconsecutiveness seem to be edging backwards, not to parody and rejection, but to affirmation and acceptance of the narrative-epic-novelistic tradition. The way to come out smiling (or almost) is, after you've shown that you understand all the limits, all the falsifications and mistaken assumptions, to end by writing your own crazy narrative, to assimilate without mockery the elements of such traditional fiction that can survive the curse of professorship and disenchantment. (pp. 291-92)

Having tried just about everything else in the way of story telling, Gardner gives us, in *The King's Indian,* a volume of short stories and a novella. All of them are more or less overtly autobiographical, or are made to seem that way; and without really telling us much about him (except what I guess his friends would pick up) they nevertheless ring true. They are full of professorial fun, cloaked in science fiction or gothic horror or fairy tale. And yet each of them has a central figure who seems very Gardnerish. The first hero is a man of words, a preacher in a Southern Illinois Church (near, coincidentally, where Gardner teaches). He has evoked the distrust of his parishioners because he insists on social responsibility, and he inadvertently attracts a revolutionary youth to blow up his church. And what is the power of language? The second hero is a Southern Illinois doctor, caught in a cyclone during which he finds a mad and wicked genius who clones himself into wicked young duplicates. The third is a medieval monk in a Browningesque complication of envy and haunting who has given up his art of illuminating manuscripts to work in the fields. And so on. In one story Gardner figures as an actor himself, the narrator describing a wild artist who has come through a period of darkness to see "the best in everything."

In their brevity and in their more or less obvious and deliberate evocation of Poe, Kafka, Browning, medieval romance, and science fiction, these stories are all fairly effective. But the book gets much better as Gardner's manifestations become more and more wildly fanciful, less and less disguised in the clothing of the real. The second set of three stories is pure fantasy, playing with the narrative traditions of the fairy tale, transmogrifications and heroic rescues, reminding us of the arbitrariness of sequence and characterization, and, of course, of *Alice in Wonderland.* The insane and beautiful Queen Louisa invents a family and a world, happy (except for occasional lapses into a toad) in the midst of playful violence and horror which purports to be sane and obeys quite arbitrary rules.

But the novella, *The King's Indian,* may be the best thing Gardner has done so far. It is so dazzlingly literary, so promiscuously allusive and parodic, that it would seem impossible to take the narrative seriously. But Gardner's ultimate virtuosity is that while making fun of some of the central narratives of the last two hundred years, he has to bring us up short at the end of every section in order to disengage us from the mere story, to force us to face the fact that there are other larger issues. It is the work of an effective Sunlight Man, of a real trickster whose tricks are his real subject.

Of course, the ostensible narrator of the story, Jonathan Upchurch, a nineteenth century American mariner out of Nantucket (oh!), is really John Gardner, though he isn't really. We know too much to associate a narrator with the real author—or to dissociate him. Anyway, there's a fine and quietly funny illustration (at last, in *The King's Indian,* Gardner has got himself a first-rate illustrator, as all nineteenth century novelists should), a drawing of a wall-eyed young man, surely Jonathan Upchurch, dressed like a young ancient mariner, surely John Gardner, as any dust jacket picture will confirm. He stoppeth two of three. And sure enough, near the end, John Gardner, happily loose and seriously unserious, having played almost as many tricks as one hundred fifty pages will sustain, enters to talk: "And you are real, reader, and so am I, John Gardner the man that, with the help of Poe and Melville and many another man, wrote this book. And this book, this book is no child's top either—though I write, more than usual, filled with doubts. Not a toy but a queer cranky monument, a collage: a celebration of all literature and life; an environmental sculpture, a crypt."

I honor the words, though they teeter on embarassment: a queer and cranky monument—to Poe and Melville, to Coleridge and Conrad, to Dickens, to Whitman and Mark Twain, to Mary Shelley and Wilde's *Dorian Gray,* to the traditions of narrative and the possibilities of belief. This strange retelling of the ancient mariner's story is the record of a hoax, and of hoaxes within hoaxes, of enormous and gratuitous lies; and it is a celebration of hoaxing. The question remains—and it will, I think, be the test of Gardner's art as he develops and faces the doubts with which he says he is now writing—whether, while a celebration of literature, it is a celebration of life as well.

The story is full of the staple elements of Gardner's fictions: the magician, the materialist cynic, the redemptive

power of love. Particularly, it is a desperately funny and simply desperate struggle to make narrative work beyond all embarassment; and it is built on the faith that narrative is the way to say yes to life. No matter how far Upchurch pushes, he can't quite get to the center of the hoax. Each villain fades into another, while the price of the game goes up in the cost of lives. Yet Upchurch ends with the holy ghost sitting on his shoulder in the form of a sea-boobie. As the ship tacks alee (what a marvelous set of pages parodying technical sea talk we get here from the boy who dreamed of living in Southern Illinois) he cries to the bird, "You better hang on there, bird," to which the Holy Ghost replies, "Hang on yourself, thou fucking lunatic."

The ultimate redemption here, as in most of Gardner's work, may not be of souls, but of narrative. The raped and disfigured Miranda (woops! Shakespeare) "blesses him unawares" by loving him; but neither Upchurch nor Gardner concludes by throwing his story into the sea and living without magic. Neither can survive without stories, without lies, without hoaxes.

With all this extraordinary inventiveness, Gardner is faced with the problems of many of the best writers of our time: how to work in a medium for which their imaginations thirst—in a kind of dead sea—but which everything they know makes them distrust. In allowing himself to play these wild games out in the open, to temper his half-embarassed solemnities with arch professorial and obscene jokes, Gardner may be getting close to honoring his own best instincts as a writer. Still healthily afraid of making sense of appearances, myths of his stories, it's certain Gardner wants to do it. Even if the Holy Ghost is obscene, he is some kind of spirit. As the hero of the Browningesque story earlier in the book suggests, "It's nerve-wracking business, knight-errantry." Still, Gardner is doing his knight-errant's trick almost everywhere in this volume. Now if he can only continue being open about the games he plays . . . (pp. 295-97)

George Levine, "The Name of the Game," in Partisan Review, *Vol. XLII, No. 2, 1975, pp. 291-97.*

Roger Garfitt   (essay date 1975)

[*In this largely negative review of* The King's Indian, *Garfitt cites "Pastoral Care" as the only story of merit in the collection, asserting that it is the least fabulous.*]

The King's Indian offers a striking illustration of the difference between fiction and fabulation. In the opening story, **"Pastoral Care"**, a Presbyterian minister tries to shepherd the remnant of his flock through bewildering changes. The buildings they had raised out of tithes and covenants stand empty. Their Foreign Missions are rejected as colonialist agencies. What is the use, he reflects, of telling them "that that was the point of Christianity. All systems fail: psychologies, sociologies, philosophies, rituals. To believe in any firm system whatever, even Foreign Missions, is to be left—like Adam biting into the apple—with a taste of blowing ashes." Hopelessly he preaches "the Church-in-crisis", and creates only a crisis in elderly minds. When a student revolutionary attends his radical sermons, it seems that at last he has an audience—and then the bombings begin.

In the title-piece [*The King's Indian*], a tale that occupies a third of the book, the same themes, the eclipse of faith, the collapse of order, are given a fabulist treatment. With a whimsical echo of *The Ancient Mariner,* "the guest" is told by "an old loon" the tale of Captain Dirge and the whaler *Jerusalem* sailing out of Boston, or rather, out of Melville. We are inside a two-fold artifact, a duplicity more than matched by subsequent events, for Captain Dirge is none other than Dr Flint the illusionist, and the ship is in pursuit of her own shadow, last seen foundering off the Vanishing Isles. A rum tale, with more than a pinch of Pynchon in it: the hero, Jonathan Upchurch, mesmerized by Flint in childhood and bewitched by Flint's daughter Miranda, is drawn after them as helplessly as Slothrop, in *Gravity's Rainbow,* is drawn by a Pavlovian reflex to the V2 rockets. The universe is random and determinist: it proceeds from a whim, from a terrible emptiness.

The fabulists are restoring to the novel the theological dimension of epic, but the pantheon is deserted and epic turns inevitably to farce. The *Jerusalem* is crewed by bunkum professors and flim-flam men, "all the while solemnly declaiming the opinions of Leibniz or Marx or Winckelmann", as if our systems have themselves come down to bunkum and flim-flam. "Shall I strip myself naked", asks John Gardner in one of the intervals in the narrative, "and cry out, shameless, to stone-deaf graveyards and children uncreated, Brothers, Sisters, it was like THIS in our time? Better the cover of my dungeon fiction"—better, for one thing, because it resolves the problem of combining serious inquiry with a narrative interest.

Flint the illusionist is himself, it seems, the victim of a trick. Mr Gardner raises the tale's elaborate edifice in order to collapse it, for history's collapse is where Jonathan finds Miranda:

> mere girl, mere woman, humanity's showpiece, transformed by nineteen centuries of pampering to a stage creation, tinselled puppet painted, taught speech by troubadours—championed by knights who knew her lovely and probably unfaithful—philosophized by painters and jewellers and poets—and now the theatre had collapsed on her, ground her to the staddle, revealed what she was . . . her whole soul silently bawling as mine was, bellowing for no more illusions, no more grand gestures, just humdrum love such as children and plants feel.

There is a parallel again with *Gravity's Rainbow,* where the Schwarz-kommando finally discover their mystic pattern in the dereliction around them. The fable ends, in other words, where fiction has to begin. When it comes to the real material of human experience, *The King's Indian* has shot its bolt and concludes in a puff of whimsy with a new Jerusalem:

> Rankless, ruleless, they were learning to be a community of sorts on the mutilated ship. No more geniuses, no more great kings. Only wild pale-faces, contemplative Apaches.

Here Mr Gardner's fabling falls dangerously short of his fiction. Jonathan is joined to Miranda in "humdrum love", as if that somehow solved everything. It merely exchanges one daydream for another. Like Thomas Pynchon, Mr Gardner gives all his attention to the structure, and leaves the characters as ciphers. In **"Pastoral**

Care", working within the much smaller compass of a short story, he shows what "humdrum love" really involves. There is more heroism in Dr Grewy, the church elder struggling to remake his faith, than in the entire voyage from Nantucket to the Vanishing Isles. Even the "contemplative Apaches", translated from fable to fiction, have substance in **"Pastoral Care"**: here they are ragged hippies, adrift and stoned. One of them, a pregnant girl, walks off a moving train. The story ends with the minister, himself by now adrift, offering what comfort he can: " 'Trust me', I say. . . . I force myself to continue. I have no choice."

A darker ending than the fable's, but finally more heartening, because it is free of flim-flam. There is a self-indulgence inherent in fabulism that turns it to grand guignol. The other tales in the book are amusing exercises with even less allegorical charge than *The King's Indian.* **"Pastoral Care"** stands as a lonely exemplar of fiction in the front of this volume, a signpost to a road not taken.

> *Roger Garfitt, "Fiction and Fabulation," in* The Times Literary Supplement, *No. 3848, December 12, 1975, p. 1477.*

Keith Neilson (essay date 1977)

[*In the essay excerpted below, Neilson lauds the diverse stylistic modes in* The King's Indian *and examines the literary roots of several stories.*]

With *The King's Indian,* a fascinating assortment of short stories, John Gardner consolidates his position as America's literary Proteus. He can apparently do anything he wants to with language and assume whatever artistic identity may suit his fancy. In his longer fictions he has written a straightforward realistic novel (*The Resurrection*), an ironical medieval epic (*Grendel*), a modern epic laced with quasi-Platonic dialogues (*The Sunlight Dialogues*), a reinterpreted classical myth (*Jason and Medeia*), and a contemporary "pastoral" (*Nickel Mountain*). In *The King's Indian* he further expands his range to include contemporary social realism, gothic science fiction, Absurdist parable, medieval fairy tale, and fantastic high seas adventure. The literary echoes include Poe, Melville, Coleridge, Browning, Kafka, and Cabell, to mention only the most obvious.

But how, the scholarly critics puzzle, can a writer so unabashedly "literary" and so blatantly philosophical be so commercially popular? The answer is simple and obvious: unlike many of his contemporaries, but in common with those masters he mimics, Gardner is a superb storyteller. And no better example of his skill as a "yarnspinner" can be cited than the title work in this collection, *The King's Indian.* In this story he exploits the "tall tale," the high seas yarn, the gothic romance, the classical quest, the suspense mystery, the literary hoax, and the science fiction parable. The result is almost—but not quite—a modern masterpiece in nineteenth century garb.

The narrator of the tale, Jonathan Upchurch, spins a grotesque fantasy that veers back and forth between the barely possible and the hallucinatory. He speaks with the ornate, high-blown rhetoric of nineteenth century melodrama, but has a hard edge and sense of irony that is distinctly modern. The bizarre setting (either an ancient pub or an ante-room in Heaven) and the tall tale approach give the preposterous events and their ambiguous implications the same type of credibility generated by Poe's *The Narrative of Arthur Gordon Pym* and Coleridge's *The Rime of the Ancient Mariner*. Jonathan finds himself on a whaler which may also be a slave ship of the sort found in Melville's *Benito Cereno*. His captain, a man appropriately named "Dirge," is a madman (reminiscent of Ahab in *Moby Dick*) on a peculiar quest to find the site where, he is convinced, his ship has *already* (in another time dimension) gone down. The Captain has a daughter, Augusta, who becomes Jonathan's tutee, and the daughter has a huge black hound of the gothic romance variety. Hovering mysteriously at the periphery is Jeremiah, a blind prophetic old man who reminds one of Tiresias in Greek Tragedy.

A mutiny? A love affair? A philosophical quest? Surely this is enough plot for even a Melville at his most ambitious. But, as Jeremiah says, "there are no divisions, no dualities, only monstrous mirrors." At the point where the action of the story seems to have been resolved, Gardner starts spinning his mirrors. The mutiny and ensuing slaughter occur—but who is rebelling against whom? Is Dirge, the defeated Captain, also (as a sailor named Wilkins states) the victim of a cruel hoax perpetrated by his employers? Or are those employers themselves victims of Dirge's trickery? Is Dirge even Dirge? Or is he a Spiritualist and bunkum artist named Luther Flint? Is Augusta actually Flint's daughter Miranda and his partner in crime? . . . Once he starts things spinning, Gardner does not stop until we are exhausted. His narrative manipulations in this story must rank as one of the most impressive *tours de force* in contemporary letters.

But in the end there are too many mirrors, too many reflections. We are fooled by Gardner's plot twists and thematic flip-flops so many times, especially in the last thirty pages or so, that we dizzily back off. He is simply too adroit and ingenious. It is like the magician who audaciously insists on doing his sleight of hand over and over before us until we finally catch on. And, as we begin sighting the skillfully palmed cards and the silks up the sleeve, we cease to wonder at the tricks themselves and appreciate only the transparent dexterity of the magician; simple admiration replaces awe.

Though considerably less ambitious, **"The Warden,"** a short story in the manner of Franz Kafka, is probably a more effective example of Gardner's "derivative" writing. So complete is Gardner's immersion in the mode and themes of this great predecessor that **"The Warden"** could probably be inserted in an edition of Kafka's collected stories without anyone spotting the forgery. An underling named Vortrab finds himself running a prison by default. The Warden is presumably still there, pacing behind a closed door, but he does not communicate and so the decisions are left to his assistant. Vortrab "carries out orders" (his own) that he knows are ridiculous in the name of an authority which probably does not exist. In the pattern typical of Kafka's "heroes," he acts counter to the logic of his situation because if he did otherwise he could not act at all.

His other "derivative" stories are not so successful, however, and probably illustrate dangers inherent in such a self-consciously literary approach. The "Mad Queen Louisa" stories, medieval satires reminiscent of James Branch

Cabell's "Poictesme Romances," can be dismissed as moderately amusing finger exercises, but **"The Ravages of Spring"** and **"The Temptation of St. Ivo"** are more seriously flawed.

In **"The Ravages of Spring,"** the author sends Kafka's "country doctor" on an unwilling errand to Poe's "house of Usher." The "Roderick" figure he finds there (John Hunter) turns out to be a mad scientist, and the whole affair degenerates into B-movie science fiction. In **"The Temptation of St. Ivo,"** Gardner amplifies the conflict in Browning's "Soliloquy in a Spanish Cloister," gives it homosexual overtones and hints of demonism, and resolves it with a gratuitous flight into crude fantasy. Both stories seem contrived and strained, bereft of emotional commitment or intellectual control.

Even in the best of his derivative stories, Gardner seems aware of the pitfalls of such a method. Toward the end of *The King's Indian*, he intrudes himself into the story and addresses the reader. . . . But why would an author feel the need to tell us directly that his writing is serious? Does he feel that his virtuosity undercuts his intentions or that his real voice is being lost among the literary echoes? It is, perhaps, not surprising that the only stories in which Gardner's own feelings and ideas are clearly expressed are the two nonderivative, realistic, contemporary stories, **"Pastoral Care"** and **"John Napper Sailing Through the Universe."**

"Pastoral Care" is about the Reverend Pick, a liberal Protestant minister, whose sense of self and meaning are threatened by an "idealist" who acts out the full implications of the clergyman's ideas: he blows up churches. Pushed to the extreme, the Reverend Pick abandons his intellectualizations and becomes his role: "I am no one, for the moment; a disembodied voice; God's minister. . . . 'Trust me,' I say. . . . I force myself to continue. I have no choice."

"John Napper Sailing through the Universe" is the story of another modern man, a painter-sculptor, who is forced to the edge by a vision of contemporary meaninglessness. By sheer will power Napper forces himself to affirmation. This forced optimism seems to be Gardner's basic posture, and it is one that is consistent with his previous efforts. All of the stylistic gyrations, the philosophical gamesmanship, and the literary mimicry evident in *The King's Indian* finally boil down to a passion for meaning and order in the face of contemporary nihilism and chaos—hardly a unique theme in modern writing, but one that touches raw nerves.

Gardner's most ambitious and exciting fictions are impressive, but lack authenticity; his most authentic works are without the scope and power of his full virtuosity. What remains now is for the two to be synthesized. For all of his spectacular skill, talent, versatility, and energy, John Gardner has not, as yet, quite achieved full mastery over the most important elements of all, his own vision and voice. (pp. 4036-38)

Keith Neilson, in a review of "The King's Indian: Stories and Tales," in Survey of Contemporary Literature, *Vol. 6, edited by Frank N. Magill, revised edition, Salem Press, 1977, pp. 4036-38.*

Gardner on What Makes a Good Story

A story is the most valuable thing in the world. Nothing is as precious as a good story, a perfectly told story. It fascinates in a way nothing else in the world, not even music, can fascinate us. Fiction must be a totally honest, serious thing, even if it's kidding around and playing jokes. The relationship between a writer and a reader ought to be a model love relationship. It ought not to be a rape, which is what happens when the writer's tricking the reader, pushing the reader on, making the reader angry. It ought not to be a cruel and cunning seduction; something very clever at the beginning that will seduce the reader into reading the story. It's a love relationship, in which you give the reader the best story you can think of.

In an interview with Ed Christian, Prairie Schooner, *Vol. 54, No. 4 (Winter 1980-81).*

Anne Tyler   (essay date 1981)

[*An American novelist and short story writer, Tyler has written numerous works, including* The Accidental Tourist *(1985), which won the National Book Critics Circle Award, and the Pulitzer Prize-winning novel* Breathing Lessons *(1988). In the following excerpt, Tyler reviews* The Art of Living, and Other Stories, *praising the entire collection, particularly Gardner's ability to stop a story's action and allow his characters to "suddenly speak out, seizing a single moment of stillness to state their concerns."*]

[*The Art of Living*], John Gardner's new collection of short stories—his first in seven years—is a small, solid, chunky volume, of a satisfying weight. In fact it seems unusually heavy for its size, but that may be a subjective impression. This is a collection so bounteously packed with plots and people and ideas, you imagine it must have a higher density than other books.

Of the ten stories, two are fairytales—a form that Gardner has used with stunning effectiveness over the years, retaining all its conventions but embroidering upon it, deepening it, adding wry twists of reality and extra layers of meaning. Another story is a fantasy of the Edgar Allan Poe variety. There is a quiet, richly textured piece that reads like a reminiscence, and a story inspired by the world-weary stranger in Thomas Mann's "Disillusionment," and even a kind of sustained joke—a Minnie Pearl-style comedy of revenge. The tone varies constantly; a realistic narrative is followed by something spun from thin air. As a result, the book avoids the pitfalls of most single-author collections. It's never repetitious or predictable, even when read at one sitting.

In **"Stillness,"** a woman returning to downtown St. Louis envisions her own younger self standing on a street corner. She wonders what this girl would have imagined if she could see the present-day St. Louis—if the bustling, thriving street of the 1940s had suddenly fallen silent, the crowds vanished, the buildings "gone solemn, like prison or mausoleum walls," and "nothing else stirring but two pigeons overhead and a newspaper blowing along the pavement." It's a wonderfully vivid moment that stops us in our tracks, and the impact is doubled at the story's end.

In another slip in time, the famous and successful hero of **"Nimram,"** while traveling first class on a jet, finds himself back on a train of his boyhood. Every detail is clear—the discolored plush of the seats, the passenger with the hacking cough, the conductor writing and muttering. Here, the purpose of the moment is to make us comprehend the value of all the years that the hero has lived since. His seatmate—a dying 16-year-old girl—will never have those years; but it's only after Nimram's vision that the reader feels the tragedy.

"The Music Lover," a story both sad and hilarious, describes a man who compulsively attends concerts after his piano teacher wife dies. Although a musical ignoramus, he may be the only listener to react appropriately to a contemporary piece in which a cello is sawed in half: "He wrung his fingers, groaned, covered his eyes, and on one occasion cried out loudly, 'Oh my God! My God!' . . . He caught the pale hand of the lady beside him . . . and whispered, violently shaking, 'Insane!' " . . .

But the masterpiece is **"Vlemk the Box-Painter,"** in which an artist paints a picture so real that it speaks. Here John Gardner is in his element. He invents an entire culture; he gives the fairytale plot an added dimension by rounding out each character; and he injects a good measure of humor. (The talking portrait, for instance, is a marvelously spiky little individual; and there's a would-be axe murderer whose potential goes unfulfilled only because he's a perfectionist and can't find the "aesthetically perfect set of murder victims.") Finally, he raises any number of questions about the validity of beauty and the purpose of art, and other matters not normally tackled in a story about enchanted princesses.

What links such diverse stories, in fact, is exactly such questions. Over and over, characters involved in absorbing and active plots will suddenly speak out, seizing a single moment of stillness to state their concerns. A cook in the title story [**"The Art of Living"**] says, "The thing a person's gotta have—a human being—is some kind of center to his life, some one thing he's good at that other people need from him, like, for instance, shoemaking. I mean something ordinary but at the same time holy, if you know what I mean." The dying young girl quotes her Uncle Charley: "He says the most interesting thing about Noah's Ark is that all the animals on it were scared and stupid." An ex-poet reflects that "to fools, nothing *can* be said; to the wise, nothing *need* be said . . . Who learns anything—I say anything—from poetry?"

These are miracles of stories—fully realized, far-reaching, greater than the sum of their parts. It's a wonder a single volume can contain them all.

Anne Tyler, "Little Miracles," in The Detroit News, *May 10, 1981, p. 2J.*

Julian Moynahan   (essay date 1981)

[*Moynahan is an autobiographer and professor of En-*

glish literature. In the following review of The Art of Living, *he discusses Gardner's dominant theme of the relationship between life and art in conjunction with the artistic theories Gardner advanced in his essay* On Moral Fiction.]

Most of the 10 stories in John Gardner's new collection [*The Art of Living*] develop the common theme of art and its vexed relation to life. This was also the subject of Mr. Gardner's book-length essay, *On Moral Fiction,* published in 1978. There he made substantial use of Tolstoy's argument for a strictly moral art. . . . Certainly it is possible that Mr. Gardner runs a comparable risk in following up his moralizing essay on fiction with stories closely related to it in theme. But before addressing that problem let's recall what *On Moral Fiction* had to say.

In it he argues that all good art, including prose fiction, should be moral. By this he means it should be life-enhancing, protecting human existence from the dark forces of chaos (the "trolls") pressing in from all sides and coming up from below, seeking whom they may devour. In making this argument he is quite hard on many of his fellow writers, issuing such dismissive decrees as "bad art is always basically creepy; that is its first and most obvious identifying sign. Warhol. Philip Roth," and savaging Thomas Pynchon for his "winking, mugging despair." E. L. Doctorow and Norman Mailer are issued flunking grades and Samuel Beckett barely passes, while John Fowles, for reasons not entirely clear, makes the very sparse Honor Roll. These magisterial judgments are consistent with Gardner's idea that "true art treats ideals, affirming and clarifying the Good, the True and the Beautiful," that "real art creates myths a society can live instead of die by."

While there is something of the Welsh preacher, full of righteousness, in John Gardner, perhaps even something of the upstate New York prophet in a direct line from Joseph Smith, many pages of *On Moral Fiction* make lively reading, and it's a positive pleasure to see various fashionable gloom spreaders and doomsday peddlers get it in the neck. Yet one wishes that Mr. Gardner gave more evidence of having deeply meditated on modern history, and that he would avoid such juvenile terms as "creepy" in assessing mature art and artists. . . . On the other hand, Mr. Gardner's title story, **"The Art of Living"**—about a small-town chef slaughtering and ragouting a small black dog stolen from a pet store—is very creepy. . . . (pp. 7, 27)

The worst thing about this story is not its central event, or the idea that event may illustrate, but its technical ineptness. The narrator, supposedly a member of an adolescent motorcycle gang during the early years of the Vietnam War, looks back on that period from a time considerably later but never establishes any significant relation between "then" and "now." His and his companions' speech patterns of the earlier period lack flavor and verisimilitude, and the various Italian-American males connected with the restaurant where the canine feast is prepared are hard to tell apart. Also, the story lacks a consistent economy of treatment, so that we are told too much about this or that person or incident, too little about others. The thing reads like a try at a novel that didn't work out, not like a crafted short story.

Rather better is the story **"Nimram."** The title character is a prominent conductor of late-Romantic symphonic music, much preoccupied with his own success, who finds himself next to a 16-year-old girl on a flight from the West Coast to Chicago. It turns out she is dying of an incurable disease, and this shows Nimram his vulgarity in worrying about being recognized in public or being interviewed by *People* magazine. In a brief epilogue, the child is brought to Orchestra Hall, where Nimram is conducting a hugely augmented Chicago Symphony in Mahler's Fifth Symphony: " . . . she had never in her life heard a sound so broad, as if all of humanity, living and dead, had come together for one grand onslaught."

Here no doubt is an instance of art's life-affirming quality, but is it truly what a young girl with an incurable disease, who has had some recent experience playing in the string section of her school orchestra, would hear in the music? I don't think so. This tiresome "humanizing" of music tends to be a vice not of the young, but of fiction writers and second-string critics meeting deadlines.

There is clumsy writing, as when it's said of the conductor that

> When he'd put behind him, at least for public appearances, that famous "Beethoven frown"—once a private joke between his wife and himself but now a thing as public as the mileage of his Rolls, since his wife had mentioned both, in an unguarded moment, to an interviewer—he'd discovered that smiling like a birthday child as he strode, tails flying, toward the light-drenched podium came as naturally to him as breathing, or at any rate as naturally as the second-nature breathing of an oboist.

This lurching style of excessive (bearish) parenthetical remarks may be a try at rendering in prose the overloaded, "stretched" musical idiom of Mahler or Bruckner. That would not explain or justify, however, comparable excesses in the prose of the next story, **"Redemption,"** where one sentence, beginning "Because she had, at thirty-four . . . ," lurches on for 94 words before reaching its main clause. **"Redemption"** is about learning, through musical study and the example of an ancient Russian teacher of the French horn who had survived the Bolshevik terror, how to live with the anguish and sorrow of having contributed inadvertently to a brother's accidental death.

The best story in **The Art of Living** is **"Come on Back."** It is a heritage piece about rural and Welsh roots which produces pleasing variations on the theme of art through an informed, affectionate look at the Welsh passion for choral singing. By far the worst and longest story is **"Vlemk the Box-Painter,"** a tedious pseudo-medieval allegory about the painting of a "speaking likeness" of a princess on a rosewood box. There is nothing to be said in its favor, except that Mr. Gardner, in conceiving it, going on with it and publishing it, shows the courage of his moral convictions. (pp. 27-8)

Julian Moynahan, "Moral Fictions," in The New York Times Book Review, *May 17, 1981, pp. 7, 27-8.*

Charles Champlin   (essay date 1981)

[*Champlin is the arts editor for the* Los Angeles Times. *In the review of* The Art of Living *excerpted below, he asserts that the stories are sometimes marred by authorial aloofness, but praises Gardner's ability to translate personal recollections into art.*]

The death of the short story has been prematurely reported, as the [*Los Angeles Times*] book editor was saying a few weeks ago. It has simply changed its principal residence from periodicals to hardcovers.

The latest collection to appear is John Gardner's ***The Art of Living and Other Stories.*** This is the American, and indeed the upstate New York John Gardner, not the English chap who lately committed an ersatz James Bond.

The U.S. Gardner is an author of multiple interests, a scholar specializing in medieval literature, a poet, essayist, novelist and biographer who has also written three books of fairy tales for children.

His *The Life and Times of Chaucer* is a remarkable piece of literary detective work (and elegant writing), reconstructing the poet-politician and his tumultuous world from a comparative handful of facts and clues.

Some of his novels—*The Sunlight Dialogues, Nickel Mountain, October Light*—reflect Gardner's upstate upbringing and his life as an author-scholar revisiting and reinspecting his own past. This I find the most impressive of his fiction—minutely accurate, crankily funny and quite moving. The sense of passage and loss, but also of self-discovery, is at once familiar and original. I may of course be prejudiced; I know and recognize the territory.

But at heart Gardner is I think above all a fabulist. He is even more at home in the past of the sagas than in Batavia, eager to be a teller of tales, fables, epics. (He has done an epic poem called *Jason and Medeia*.)

He is thus a man of several voices, and various of them are to be heard in ***The Art of Living.*** The first story, **"Nimram,"** a contemporary piece about a chance meeting of a symphony conductor and a dying teenaged girl, seated together on an airliner, has a strikingly timeless aspect. The revelations for both from their encounter might not have been much different had they met on a schooner or a stagecoach.

Another of the stories, **"The Music Lover,"** acknowledges its debt to Thomas Mann, and is set in a previous but undated Middle Europe. **"Vlemk the Box-Painter"** is an extended fairy tale of sorts, complete with princesses, castles and courtiers, a tale extended to novella length although not the better for it. . . .

"Trumpeter," the name of a dog from whose viewpoint the tale is told, is another castle-set fable, wrought with irony.

The title story, **"The Art of Living,"** and a few others arise in the upstate experience. These too are somehow touched with fable, dealing with characters and events that may be larger than life or longer than time, or both. An eccentric chef in a small-town beanery once a week does something magical like Peking duck. He decides on an Asian delicacy with dog its chief ingredient and the local motorcycle guys uneasily do his foraging for him. All quite strange, and

with overtones as a gesture of solidarity with suffering Vietnamese.

"Come on Back" is a story in the form of a recollection of growing up Welsh in America. **"Redemption"** watches the growing up and healing of a boy who has killed his brother in a tractor accident.

What diminishes the collective power of the Gardner stories is that they seem at last to be exercises in style and voice, set pieces that make the reader continually aware of the author manipulating, mixing, coloring the material, and somehow standing apart from it.

The stories are not without passions or a feeling of real experience recalled and translated into art. But the emotions seem freeze-dried by intellect or possibly embalmed by the processes of literature, joy and anguish described rather than evoked.

The power of other collections of stories, as by Elizabeth Spenser most recently—or John Cheever, John O'Hara, Irwin Shaw—is in the persisting tone of voice and angle of attack, which makes each story seem part of a larger whole, an embracing vision.

The novel is obviously a congenial form for Gardner and in fact some of these long stories seem to be trying to be novels; in their length they compromise briefer ends by violating the unity of time and event and that gives the short story its unique strength and impact.

> Charles Champlin, "Breathing Life into the Short Story," in Los Angeles Times, *May 19, 1981, p. 6.*

Peter Collier   (essay date 1981)

[*Collier is an American novelist and biographer. In the following review of* The Art of Living, *he lauds Gardner's strong narratives and the collection's undercurrent of myth and fable. Collier also maintains that several of the most successful stories in this volume concern death and guilt.*]

The Art of Living has everything we have come to expect in John Gardner's fiction—the ability to cast a narrative spell, extravagances of the imagination, a pronounced tendency to shove events in the direction of myth and fable. This collection of stories shows once again that Gardner is one of our brainiest writers—a scholar of effects as well as texts. . . . The common theme uniting the stories in this book is the concern with art—the art of the writer, to be sure, but also the art of characters who must get along with life lived in the shadow of dread.

Of the two or three really first-rate pieces in this collection, **"Nimram"** is possibly the one that shows Gardner with all the balls in the air, confidently juggling his effects and creating his magic. It is about Benjamin Nimram, a renowned conductor who finds himself on an airplane with a teen-age girl who is frightened to death on her first flight even though she is terminally ill. The God of his own creation in the music he makes, Nimram is also lordly in his attitude toward the fears that besiege most people. "He'd heard friends speak from time to time, about their fear of dying and the feeling was not one he scorned or despised; but the fact remained, he was not the kind of man who had it." But in the course of the flight, as he tries to make sense of his pity and compassion for the girl, he experiences new doubts about his hold over the materials of his life. He is particularly shaken by an offhand comment the girl makes about the animals on Noah's Ark—survivors like himself—being scared and stupid. This vision of the Ark blindly heading toward Ararat, powered by fear and nescience, stays with Nimram as he leaves the plane. But Gardner concludes the story with a marvelous final scene in which the conductor is at the podium, the dying girl watching from the balcony as he begins to coax from the orchestra a sound like "the breathless dead of the whole world's history, awaiting the impossible." Art is our thin chance, our only hope against death and dismay.

"Redemption," a story that attracted considerable attention when it was first published in the *Atlantic,* is about Jack Hawthorne, a boy who kills his brother with a tractor. Fearing that he is a "spiritual defective" and irremediably evil, Jack is unable to step out of the abyss. His only solace is his French horn. One day he goes to his teacher, a gnarled Russian emigre, and watches him try out a new instrument.

> He began to play now not single notes, but, to Jack's astonishment, chords—two notes at a time, then three. He began to play runs. As if charged with life independent of the man, the horn sound fluttered and flew crazily, like an enormous hawk hunting frantically for escape. It flew to the bottom of the lower register, the foundation concept F, and crashed below it, and on down and down, as if the horn in Yegudkin's hands had no bottom, then suddenly changed its mind and flew upward in a split-second run to the horn's top E . . . then lightly dropped back into its own home range, and, abruptly, in the middle of a note, stopped. The room still rang, shimmered like a vision.

It is this perfect soundful silence, this vision of perfection, a Yeatsian ideal of art triumphant over the vagaries of fate, that brings Jack back to life.

"The Stillness" is a wonderful story about a seriously ill woman driving with her husband through St. Louis, where she grew up, and reconstructing the past in a way that allows her to face her future. In the title story, "The Art of Living," a chef deals with the death of a son killed in Viet Nam by preparing an exotic dish of Imperial Dog. This is Gardner's metaphor for the work of the writer himself—taking an unpalatable and chancy ingredient like black dog and, through a sheerness of artistry, making a dish that is not only tasty but somehow *right* as well.

So, when Gardner is good, he's very good. He's never bad, let alone horrid, but he is sometimes tendentious and self-indulgent, windy in his advocacy; in John Updike's words, "a forced flower." In some of the stories in *The Art of Living,* there seems to be an insufficient bond between the human and the abstract, the fiction and the moral.

"The Problem of Art," for instance, is a sort of English 1A lecture. "Vlemk the Box-Painter," which is twice as long as some of the stories mentioned above but half as good, is a tedious tale about a painter capable of painting portraits of such realism that they seem alive. It is a situation that gives Gardner too great a latitude for a discussion of art and reality of life that not only imitates art but is nothing without it.

But we overlook the fact that some of the characters in these stories, like the portrait on the queen's box, tend to matter to us. It may be that this collection, like others of Gardner's work (with the exception of *Grendel*), is not always as finely controlled as it might be. Yet it is work that takes itself seriously, work that always gives good weight. At one point the chef in "The Art of Living" says:

> If he's an artist, what a man does, or a woman, is make things—objects which nobody asked him to make or even wanted him to make, in fact maybe they wanted him *not* to. But he makes them, and once people have them in their hands or standing there in front of them, people for some reason feel they would like to take them home with them. . . . That's what it is all about. Making life startling and interesting again. . . .

At his best, that's what John Gardner does in this collection: make life interesting.

Peter Collier, "John Gardner's Wizardry Brings His Art to Life," in Book World—Chicago Tribune, *May 24, 1981, p. 1.*

Bruce Allen   (essay date 1981)

[*In the excerpt below, Allen asserts that the most effective stories in* The Art of Living, *most notably "Come on Back," are those that are the least abstract.*]

If the author of such basically dissimilar books as *Grendel, October Light,* and that curmudgeonly manifesto *On Moral Fiction* is noted for any particular qualities, they are probably his distinctively energetic and impudent variety and vitality. Some of the variety, at least, surfaces in the 10 stories comprising . . . [*The Art of Living,* a] new collection, Gardner's first since *The King's Indian* (1974).

For example, there's the least typical story here, "The Joy of the Just," which portrays a moralist turned avenger, an elderly woman bent on destroying her (perfectly innocent) "offenders." The conception is promising, but the development is repetitious and dull—finally, it's a pointless story, enlivened only by some combative Bible-quoting.

Whenever Morality *per se* doesn't rear its head, Art does. "Trumpeter," for another example, announces itself as a picturing of "the only kingdom in the world where art reigned supreme"—but it relaxes into anthropomorphical whimsy. . . .

Several other stories ("Nimram," "Redemption," "Stillness") deal with the evocative or restorative powers of art (specifically, music). "The Music Lover"—an acknowledged steal from Thomas Mann—contrasts the ravaged emotions of an elderly "concert devotee" against the pomposities of a satanic composer, whose music becomes in performance an avant-garde exercise in atonality and discord. Here again we feel the "moral fiction" argument stirring: an advocate of "decency" in art opposes "one of those fashionable nay-sayers."

The contours of fable are traceable elsewhere. "Vlemk the Box-Painter" is an interminable allegory about a painter whose creations assume their own life—thus complicating and compromising his. The idea that artistic creations enter, despite themselves and their creators, into "reality" also suffuses "The Library Horror."

The idea that Art is more than a match for Life also (almost) animates ["The Art of Living"], the title story (note the reversible nature of that title?), the silly tale of a . . . restaurant cook who thinks he's an artist and a gang of smalltown layabouts who yearn to be feared as "motorcycle hoods." Gardner uses the standard medieval forms of knightly quest and formal debate, setting up a dialectic between the claims of social organization and individual freedom. But the elements never cohere: arbitrary whimsy and atrocious dialogue keep us at a distance from the world of the story.

I read on, rubbing my eyes, wondering if there would be any relief from this fun-and-games obsession with those enormous cloudy abstractions Art-and-Morality, Art-and-Life; this tepid schoolmarmish medievalism.

Well, there is relief, in the splendid story **"Come on Back."** This is a loving portrait of a Welsh farming community in upstate New York, and an intimation of adulthood for the young narrator enthralled by his elders' penchant for singing and "magic." It isn't really a story (though the dying of a beloved uncle provides a narrative thread); rather, a refreshing immersion in period and local detail. Though Gardner is often a slapdash writer, he has here achieved some beautiful observations ("fish poked thoughtfully in and out among the shadows of underwater weeds") and images (Welsh choruses sing "in numerous parts, each as clearly defined as cold, individual currents in a wide, bright river"; a blacksmith shop was "a dark, lively place full of coal smell, iron smell, and horse smell. All day long it rang like a musical instrument . . . ").

The art that created **"Come on Back"** doesn't need any fabulistic trimmings or justifications. I hope that the artist who created it will pass beyond defending and examining Art, and keep on producing it.

> Bruce Allen, "From Gardner, Short Stories Dimmed by Abstractions," in The Christian Science Monitor, June 24, 1981, p. 17.

Michael Kreyling (essay date 1982)

[In the laudatory review of The Art of Living excerpted below, Kreyling discusses Gardner's theory of life and art—which involves reconciling oneself morally with society—and examines several stories with this theme.]

If we did not know that John Gardner had written a polemical book called On Moral Fiction, we would still hear the resonant voice of an author concerned with the moral issues faced both by his characters and by himself as maker of art in **The Art of Living and Other Stories.** The art of living is the art of living morally, and that art is won by those persons who have reconciled the natural demands of the assertive self with the social obligation to allow other selves an equal freedom. Gardner's sense of morality, in his criticism and fiction, aims at the calming of this tension. To the self, life appears exclusively personal, yet each one of us knows, Gardner would argue, that life is shared with others. When and if the second arm of the duality is severed, a person runs the risk of the immoral life. Authors are immoral when they sever ties with characters they have created or with readers whom they have approached and engaged. Gardner supplies examples of both in On Moral Fiction. The characters in the ten sto-

ries in **The Art of Living** are captured in moments when this choice is put to them. They must—whether they are conscious of the choice or not—act morally by accepting the paradoxical fate of subject-to-self and object-to-other, or act immorally by abolishing the human paradox by an act of solipsism.

"Nimram," the first story in the collection, clearly sets the moral issue. Nimram is a renowned symphony conductor, perhaps the most flamboyantly egotistical role an artist can play. On a night flight from Los Angeles to Chicago we find him cuddled up with himself in the first class section. His expressions reflected in the jet's window, his reveries of his houses, his Rolls, his reputation, his wife who is deeply devoted to his private and public selves are the topics of his thoughts. The stewardess guides a young woman to the seat next to Nimram. The girl is frightened of flying, and the storm into which they are to take off does not ease her anxiety. Instead of becoming grist for Nimram's thoughts, the girl lets him know that she is dying of an incurable disease. And, to Nimram's further chagrin, she does not recognize his name.

The story comes from the ripples of this encounter, for Nimram reviews his life in the light of the dying girl. Her mortality covertly undermines his assumption of immortality: he assures her with the confidence of God that the jet will not crash. Safely in Chicago, Nimram and the girl separate, but she sees him later from the audience as he, revelling in his mastery of orchestra and audience, conducts like an angelic creature far above the rest of us. The story pits the two characters in a moral arena, but Gardner's verdict is tantalizingly withheld. We are not told outright whether Nimram is immoral in his hubris, or whether the girl is at fault for a timid retreat from her shortened life.

"Redemption," the following story, makes use of the vivid local color of Gardner's western New York State. Jack Hawthorne, as a young boy, saw the tractor he was driving accidentally fall into reverse and crush his younger brother. Jack seems to waver on the lip of a deeply egotistical guilt, for he becomes reclusive and hard-hearted. He nearly slips into the abyss of solipsism when he hesitates to say grace while his younger sister watches. But he performs the rite, and gives her the sign that he is still in the community of lives that nourishes them all. Redemption does not come from these rites, however, but from Jack's discovery of music and a teacher who steps into the role vacated by his weak father. **"Redemption,"** then, is also about the forces tugging the human being two ways—into total self-immersion or into interaction with other people in a spiritually and artistically nourishing community. Jack is rescued for a moral life by his choice of art over private guilt.

"The Joy of the Just" is a story that uses the grotesque in character, tone, and incident in a way that is reminiscent of Flannery O'Connor. Something about the handsome young preacher and his self-centered wife rankles Aunt Ella Reikert. She orchestrates a series of "accidents" the purpose of which appear to be to bring the preacher back within the realm of human fallibility. His wife had run Aunt Ella's truck off the road, and the preacher had conspired to keep his wife's name in the clear. But vengeance is only the simple name for what Aunt Ella desires. In the end she successfully ruins the preacher and his wife, surreptitiously getting them drunk just before the Sunday evening service—at which the preacher sets fire to his own church. One can imagine how O'Connor would have handled the same materials; Gardner's way is to be more explicit about the moral issues, to spell out the sin of the preacher and the justification of Aunt Ella. (pp. 77-8)

"Come on Back" is perhaps the most successful of the stories, but not for its originality. In form it has been written a thousand times: a young man, a member of a small but tightly-knit familial and cultural community, confronts the mysteries of life and death and is eventually ushered into full membership in the group with a ritual that serves as the climax of the story. Gardner invests this story with a genuine feeling and a deeply ingrained knowledge of people and place. His characters simultaneously stand out from and take their places in the fabric of the Welsh community which is the center of the story. The boy's relationship to this community, and his sure initiation into moral living as a function of life shared with others—those long dead, now living, and not yet born—succeeds with a confident touch in the telling and in the feeling.

"The Art of Living," the final story, succeeds less well, for there is too much overt preaching. Instead of gaining life from their human connections, the characters of "The Art of Living" seem too thickly attached to the author's thematic structure. They say things that are thematically appropriate but not dramatically fitting. The central incident, the killing, cooking, and eating of a dog, is thematically managed but artistically clashes with the temper the story seems to strive for.

John Gardner is not a cloistered writer—that is, he places demands on his skills of invention and narrative; he'll try the equivalent of cooking dog. He is . . . the artist as worker, persisting in his work through all phases from art to whatever is less. The moral decision is to keep talking, writing, to avoid the temptation to lapse into a self-centered silence. What Gardner offers in these stories is frankly offered: life as he has known it, seen it, felt it; communicated in good faith to an audience in whom he believes. (pp. 78-9)

> *Michael Kreyling, in a review of "The Art of Living, and Other Stories," in* Studies in Short Fiction, *Vol. 19, No. 1, Winter, 1982, pp. 77-9.*

Gregory L. Morris   (essay date 1984)

[*The following excerpt is taken from two chapters of Morris's book-length study on the fiction of John Gardner,* A World of Order and Light: The Fiction of John Gardner. *In the first half of the excerpt, Morris covers the collection* The King's Indian, *which he contends examines both the theory and ethical nature of art. The second half of the excerpt examines* The Art of Living, *which, according to Morris, focuses on "one of Gardner's larger philosophical obsessions: the relation of the artist to his art and to his life."*]

Short story collections are often random affairs, chance bits of writing thrown together with no plan or reason other than to paste up something large enough to sell. Such is not the case, however, with *The King's Indian: Stories and Tales* (1974). It is a complex construction—blueprinted, developed, designed—meant by Gardner to stand for many things. The several stories (nearly all published earlier) are composed and grouped along definite lines of thought; they stand capably enough alone, but when brought together, even the most striking tours de force blend submissively into a large and more impressive whole. Each of the three sections study and drive home a point, yet all are welded skillfully into a coherent collection that, when finished, strikes the reader with the consolidated force of a novel.

One of the aims of *The King's Indian* is to highlight the strange and largely unrecognized landscape of southern Illinois. The collection was written and published during Gardner's tenure at Southern Illinois University, and the book forms, in a way, a group of one that might join the Batavia and the Catskill groupings. (Actually, one might also include the short story "The Joy of the Just," in *The Art of Living,* which is also set in southern Illinois.) Gardner, even in the largely fantastical stories of the book's middle section, used the area around Carbondale as a setting and an evocation: "If I was going to write a book about Southern Illinois, which in fact I did in *The King's Indian,* that's another, completely different feeling. There it's as if human beings had never landed; the human beings—the natives, anyway—seem more like gnomes." Remember that the book's title is qualified: *Stories and Tales.* Gardner is pursuing a genre—the ghost story—with all of its magic and shadow and inexplicability; and to conjure up the necessary emotion he must also conjure up the necessary setting.

As a sort of footnote to *The King's Indian,* Gardner wrote a short piece for *Vogue* magazine entitled "Southern Illinois." The article is interesting in its restatement of the mystery and otherworldliness that Gardner was striving for in *The King's Indian.* At one point Gardner remarks of southern Illinois: "It's the only place I know that—in Merlin's old-fashioned, rather stern sense—is still magical." It is this sense of part fable, part truth, part arabesque that Gardner chases in his collection. Moreover, there are things characteristic of this region of the country that Gardner employs in several of his stories (whether or not they are admittedly set in southern Illinois), characteristics that he expounds upon in this article. When Gardner writes the following, one automatically thinks back to **"The Ravages of Spring"**:

> You get a good early spring, hopefully one without a late, killing frost that will knock out the peach and apple crops; the hickories, oaks, and maples leaf out . . . a hundred varieties of flowering bushes; and you get your small basin of loam plowed up. Then, out of nowhere, one afternoon, comes a yellow-green sky and a dark mass of clouds moving in from the southwest, maybe a shaft of black that will prove a tornado—sometimes two or three of them are visible at once—and the whole world goes silent. The birds, the horses, even the crickets stop to listen.
>
> On rare occasions, when the storm is in no hurry, the first thing you hear is the creeks breaking. Flash floods strike faster than a stranger would believe. . . . You hear the rain coming then and, if a tornado's behind it, the approach of a sound like a hundred old-fashioned railroad engines. It's time to go down cellar, though it may not be much help if the twister decides to hit head on.

Later on, Gardner recalls: "The region's had its violent

people, too—riverboat murderers, in the days when the Ohio and the Mississippi were big business; union men and scabs who killed for the dubious pleasure of digging coal; moonshiners and bootleggers, racists, comic but deadly small-time racketeers." This is the southern Illinois of the nineteenth century, the southern Illinois that Jonathan Upchurch lights out for in *The King's Indian.* Finally, writing of the southern Illinois of today, Gardner says: "Though they listen to the radio and watch TV, they still, some of them, say magic spells, sing ancient songs about iron men (knights), and examine strangers with a wary eye." From this southern Illinois spring the gap-toothed madwoman of **"The Ravages of Spring,"** the knights and witches of **"The Temptation of St. Ivo"** and "Tales of Queen Louisa," and the murmuring congregation of **"Pastoral Care."** It is the ghostly breeding ground of Gardner's crazed cast of characters, a land where the outlandish seems everyday and where people learn the marvel of surprise.

The King's Indian serves another and more important purpose: it is Gardner's testament to art. At its very center the book is an examination of artistic theory and practice. Gardner has explained that

> The whole book is a study in aesthetics—aesthetics I think in the only sense that really counts, as it expresses people through a theory of beauty. Aesthetics can never be completely abstract, it has to be derived from the physical expression of a theory in people's feelings and lives, so that to study it you make up characters and you show what happens if they shape their world by this aesthetic standard or by that one—this idea of the sublime or that one—and hopefully what you come to is true art, which everybody can share in. It puts all artistic approaches in perspective. The true story teller, like Jonathan Upchurch, in *The King's Indian,* is a model for all artists—intuition in the service of King Reason—therefore the eternal artist, God on earth. So basically it's a book about aesthetics, a subhead under metaphysics. It *is* my book about aesthetics.

The King's Indian is, in fact, a tangible monument (and memorial) erected by Gardner with the aid of artists—visual and literary, solicited and drafted, dead and living—allied to a specific aesthetic tradition. (pp. 116-18)

[While] it is clear that a portion of the collection is concerned with the function of art and its ethical nature, it should be noted that *The King's Indian* is also a discussion of Gardner's favorite pair of metaphysical opposites: anarchy and order. The book is constructed in such a way that Gardner first examines the social, moral, and philosophical implications of the contrasting impulses toward order and anarchy, and their relation to the artistic effort. This is done in the five stories contained in book 1, "The Midnight Reader." Gardner follows this with a study of the artistic imagination itself—what it is made of, how it functions, and how it orders and disorders the world. This is the focus of book 2, "Tales of Queen Louisa." In book 3, "The King's Indian: A Tale," Gardner self-consciously combines both themes, telling a story (or tale) that reveals the creative process at work and that shows the obstacles and choices with which the serious artist is faced. Character, narrator, and author all become involved in the same problem, that of matching imagination to reality.

In **"Pastoral Care,"** the opening story in "The Midnight Reader," the narrator (all five stories in book 1 are narrated in the first person) is a Carbondale minister enjoying the cool freedom of the neo-orthodoxy. The Reverend Pick delights in his objectivity and his self-conscious intelligence; he literally "picks" apart the antiquated institution that has overgrown into *"The Church."* "The institutional church is not the church at all, I say to them, but a foul encrustation, a birthday party for a man who's left town and forgotten to leave us a forwarding address." He is skeptical of his own role as spiritual shepherd, unsure of where he is leading his charges, encouraged only by the shared folly of pastor and herd: "If I weren't ridiculous—balanced (*vanitas*) on my pulpit stool—I might easily grow scornful, indifferent to these people. And if my pitiful flock were not confused and unhappy, they would joyfully go out into the world and leave my church empty. We need each other. I give them a vision they only half understand, a vision vaguely exciting, though alarming." Pick is so critical of himself and so aware of the silliness of the pumped-up human ego, that he is unable to really *feel* the uncertainty of his congregation. The relationship between preacher and parish is a symbiotic one in which both parties feed off of the other's despair and mockery.

From his pulpit, Pick attacks the futility of system-building and its inbred perniciousness. . . . All systems, in their claims to inclusiveness and surety, are defective. It is intellectual arrogance to believe that man can solve all of his own problems merely by erecting a scaffold and a skeleton of old and weary ideas. What nags at Pick is his failure to calm the soul (his and others'); doubt is necessary, but there must first be some belief strong enough to withstand the doubting.

When Pick interviews the young stranger—"Beyond all doubt a maniac, or else stoned. Or Christ come down to check on me"—he finds himself pressed to self-examination. The young man is a bomber, a lunatic, an acclaimed anarchist; yet, like the Manichean universe, he is innocent and blessed as well: "Still gazing at me, benign, inhuman, he backs away through the outer office. At the far door he gives me a peace sign and suddenly—amazingly—smiles. He has a beautiful smile. His eyes are like Brahma's. He vanishes." The stranger is Christ-like, Pick sees, in his ability to sanctify and also to destroy. He persuades Pick that anarchy, when politically and (it seems) morally justified, is correct. Tradition should not be deified, but should be challenged, and should perhaps be destroyed. Pick is led by the man's argument to a sermon on the parable of the fig tree, a parable which Pick reads as an anarchist tract on a dead institution: "The prophet's tree of Judah started well. . . . Only with time did it lose vitality and purpose. That happens, you know, with human institutions. . . . Any institution, life-style, program, can be vital at its inception but become, in time, an obstacle, a sickness." To the usual reading of the statement, "Render unto Caesar what is Caesar's," Pick adds: "The saying admits of a more radical interpretation: If Caesar usurps the rule of God, decrees that immorality is moral, then resist him; blow up the Pentagon." What Pick does not realize is that he advocates the very thing he condemns: the seizing of godhood by the ungodly, the Promethean theft.

It is too late for Pick to recant, however, or to at least mol-

Gardner, in an illustration by Herbert L. Fink, as the character Jonathan Upchurch in the title novella of The King's Indian.

lify the harshness of his words. The intruder has heard and has acted upon Pick's advice. The police station goes up in flames, torn apart by a bomber's imprecise morality, and the connection is made: *"Bomber linked to local minister."* Pick flees his church, escapes into the wilderness. . . . [He] simultaneously acknowledges his responsibility and admits his guilt, but it is not enough. Almost in the same breath comes the news of the destruction of his own church, a fact that sends him whirling toward despair and nihilism: "It does *not* matter. The truth explodes out of the night and the sound of wheels. The world is dying—pollution, old, unimportant wars, the grandiose talk of politicians, the whisper of lovers in cheap motels. The sentence of death is merely language, a pause between silences." Pick loses his faith and adopts the unreliable anarchy and pessimism of a different generation.

It requires another accident, every bit as enormous and tragic as the bombings, to shake Pick from his resignation, and when the hot and iron-heavy train blasts the young hippie girl halfway to infinity, he is recalled to proper reason. He dons once more the mask of consoler and sustainer of souls, loses his self-consciousness and confesses his helplessness: "I am no one, for the moment; a disembodied voice; God's minister. The wildman stumbles, drops to one knee, groaning, gushing tears. Cautiously, I touch his shoulder. 'Trust me,' I say. (The fall is endless. All systems fail.) I force myself to continue. I have no choice." It is the "miraculous resurrection" that Gardner has spoken of. Pick is retrieved, brought back from the deathfulness

of lost belief and egotism, by a chance but compelling act of faith. Pick learns the usefulness of what one might call "applied faith." It is the sort of faith that is left after an eternity of puzzling and pain and reversal; it is a faith that, though perhaps temporary and imperfect, succeeds in easing the pain (personal and universal) provoked by a world that at times appears too evil for belief. It is a Gardneresque retreat to orthodoxy, to emotional metaphysics, and to the virtues beyond the institution. (pp. 119-22)

The world in **"The Temptation of St. Ivo"** is . . . the world of medieval monks and temptors. Brother Ivo is an artist, an illustrator of Biblical texts—an excellent one, the best—but he is humble and well aware of his human, Fred Clumly-like condition: "I am old. Fifty. My weight's in my miserable belly. My arms and legs are like a sickly old woman's, as white as potato sprouts under the cassock, and as flabby, as jiggly, as buttocks." Ivo's universe is ordered about the monastery and God's irreducible law that turns the world into a pattern, as intricate but as related as one of his drawings:

> The scheme of providence demands of us all that each man humbly perform his part, sing his own line in the terrestrial humn, as the planets are singing, unheard, above us, and with charity forgive those to left and right when they falter. That may sound pompous, simpleminded, but it's true, or anyway I hope it's true. A man can go mad, discarding all tradition, reasoning out for himself the precise details of celestial and terrestrial law. I've been there. Live by rule, as all Nature does, illuminating the divine limits exactly as ink fills invisible lines. . . . We are merely instruments, and he who denies his condition will suffer. The world is a river, and he who resists the pressure of Time and Space will be overwhelmed by it.

Ivo's is the mind of the medieval cleric: ordered, devout, without questions. But it is not the mind of an artist, for it lacks imagination and the willingness to "resist the pressures of Time and Space."

This is why he hates Brother Nicholas: "Long-nosed, eagle-eyed, his flowing hair more black than a raven's . . . whispering, brazenly defying the rule." Nicholas is the third of Gardner's anarchists, a "devil" who teases Ivo toward violence and violation: "He willfully, pointlessly strikes out at me. He scorns all rule, defies all order for mere anarchy's sake." Nicholas challenges Ivo's graybearded concept of order and obedience; he dares Ivo to exercise his will and discover what lies beyond the monastery walls, filling his ears with black whispers: *"Brother Ivo, your rules are absurd! The order of the world is an accident. We can change it in an instant, simply by opening our throats and speaking."* Nicholas emphasizes the freedom of will and the grand possibilities of choice. He reduces it, in fact, to a matter of personal responsibility for Ivo by forcing him to a decision: *"Brother Ivo, I've decided to murder the Phoenix. I've discovered where it lives. . . . You don't believe in the Phoenix, Brother Ivo? I give you my word, you're the only man who can save the beast. . . . Do not be too hasty in judging my project, Brother Ivo. Many notable authors have spoken of the Phoenix, and holy men among them. . . . Despite all that, you deny the bird's existence. Very well! But it exists, nonetheless, and I have found it, and I mean to murder it. Prevent me if you can!"* Brother Nicholas is out to destroy the Phoenix—its mythology and symbolism. The Phoenix is the emblem of God's order and design, and the emblem of Ivo's delicate workmanship, all interwoven, as Ivo realizes: "I remember when he looked at the Phoenix with which he makes fun of me now. A design as perfect—I give thanks to God—as anything I've done." It is also the symbol of the resurrected Christ, the promise and the hope: "And in the feathers of the bird, ingeniously, almost invisibly woven, the characters RESURREXIT." It drives Ivo to prayer and to an overblown consciousness of his sin, and bolsters his belief in the laxity of his "order." (pp. 124-25)

The matter is complicated by Nicholas's own claims on art; like Ivo he illuminates . . . the Biblical texts, and Ivo begins to wonder whether it is his own duty to save his brother-artist: "A man cannot be a master artist if he lies to himself, settles for illusions. . . . What if I, a fellow artist, was his soul's last human hope? What selfishness, then—what spiritual cowardice—that I refused him what he asked, a companionable voice!" Ivo must choose, as Nicholas once must have chosen: Do I keep silent, maintain my vows, obey the doctrine; or do I purposely speak out, break all pledges, and perhaps save a soul while contravening all tradition? Just how far should one extend the limits of human freedom? . . . Ivo is . . . [a] human being coming to terms with the notion of existential freedom. If the skies are deserted, what difference does it make whether one opts for compliance or rebellion?

This is the question Ivo poses to his confessor. Ivo cries, "Rules are my only hope against his nihilism," and the confessor answers: "True, if it's nihilism. On the other hand, as you've suggested, if all his acts are a devious plea for help—if his terror in an abandoned universe is as great as your own this moment—then surely you'd be right to break the rule. It would be the act of a saint, a soul whose purity is beyond the rules that protect and keep the rest of us." The fact that it is Brother Nicholas behind the confessional curtain does not change the essence of the challenge or the promise. It is *action* which will drive Ivo to sainthood . . . ; it is evil, in all of its tortuous ambiguity, that tugs ordinary man to something blessed. Remember, it is *St.* Ivo—and he wins his sainthood by seeking to save the Phoenix, by *breaking,* not following, holy law.

So he ventures into the forest (as we already know, the Gardneresque haunt of sinners and anarchists), anxious and crushed with despair: "I abandon hope. I have lost Brother Nicholas, though I'm by no means confident that he has lost me. . . . I am afraid, sick unto death with fear. I have no faith that the universe is good, as I have thought. Yet I am here. I have no choice." It is the exact situation that the Reverend Pick finds himself in, and that which all men and women tested by a possibly empty universe find themselves confronting. Nor is he alone in the forest. As tradition would have it, there is a knight, Gardner's archetypal symbol of virtue and hope (crazy-headed or not), pursuing the "nerve-wracking business of knight-errantry." Together they try to outface the darkness and the silence, faith and nobility allied against an indefinable evil:

> "There's something in there," he whispers, and closes his visor. We peer into the darkness. It seems to me that I see Brother Nicholas standing motionless in the blackness of the forest eaves. He stares straight at us, smiling his mysterious, scornful smile.
>
> *Nothing means anything,* the figure whispers.
>
> Faster than lightning, the dagger has flown from the gauntleted hand. We do not hear it strike, consumed by moss, dead trees, the darkness at the heart of things. *Nothing means anything,* the forest whispers. The knight is trembling. The face still seems to smile at us. But it is not a face, we know now—some trick of light—and the voice is not the Devil's voice but some heavy old animal in its lair, unable to sleep because of age.
>
> "Mistake," my defender whispers.

Perhaps there is something in there, perhaps not. What matters is our willingness to break free of an aged and rickety system, and at least peer into the forest, even if it means breaking a few of the old rules. Gardner is not counseling anarchy here, but a sort of virtuous antinomianism which has as its base an authentic and tested ethic. By going to the forest, Ivo both exercises his will and liberates his imagination; he joins belief (his own religious tradition) with vision (the knightly perseverance) and emerges with an aesthetic and a canonization.

This idea of the forsaken universe is taken up once more in **"The Warden,"** a Kafkaesque, Borgesian tale set somewhere in the vastness of a nowhere land. The universe becomes a prison, and "the Warden has given up every attempt to operate the prison by the ancient regulations. Conditions grow monstrous, yet no one can bring them to the Warden's attention." Vortrab, the chief guard, can no longer draw any sort of response from behind the Warden's door; he can only knock and listen to the pacing that stretches on into the night. It is an absurd place where guards game and laze about and prisoners are held for no crime or reason. In the bowels of the prison lies an old, blind, sticklike man, a professor (or so he's called by Heller, the man who knows him best) who speaks oracularly upon mind and matter:

> There are gradations of matter of which man knows nothing, the grosser impelling the finer, the finer pervading the grosser. . . . The ultimate, unparticled matter not only permeates all things but impels all things, and thus *is* all things within itself. This matter is God. . . . There are two bodies, the rudimental and the complete, corresponding with the two conditions of the worm and the butterfly. What we call "death" is the painful metamorphosis. Our present incarnation is progressive, preparatory, temporary. Our future is perfected, ultimate, immortal. The ultimate life is the full design. . . . Only in the rudimental life is there any experience of pain, for pain is the product of impediments afforded by number, complexity, and substantiality. That is not to say that the rudimental life is bad, however painful in a given case. All things, after all, are good or bad only by comparison. To be happy at any one point we must have suffered at the same. Never to suffer would be never to have been blessed. But in the inorganic life, pain cannot be; thus the necessity for the organic.

There is no immateriality, says the Professor, only successively finer degrees of matter. All—in life and in death—is body, flesh, and bones. Cells do not die and give way to spirit, but are refined into a purer form. Moreover, pain is a necessary part of material existence; it defines our lives and gives reason to our happiness. The idea is nearly Sufic in its progression through finer (more spiritual?) levels of matter, and the Professor seems to be in a transition stage, somewhere beyond pain and suffering, entering the complete and "inorganic" body.

Such thoughts naturally breed uneasiness and stir sleeping ghosts. Vortrab attempts to deny the Professor's metaphysics, but the ideas (and the haunting, strangely southern Illinois landscape) tug at his reluctant imagination and pull him toward vision: "I had a feeling of standing outside myself, as if time and space had stopped and in one more second would be extinguished. As quickly as the queer impression came it passed, faded back into shadow like a fish. And for some reason impossible to name, I was left with a feeling of indescribable, senseless horror, a terrible emptiness, as if I'd penetrated something, broken past the walls of my consciousness and discovered . . . what?" In the instant that Vortrab releases his hold on consciousness and on material, worldly demands, he jumps outside of the bounds of time and space. (pp. 125-28)

Vortrab is not a man given to such fancies, suppressing imagination instead of encouraging it. Those who let their thoughts run free, those who are characters of imagination, Vortrab brands as crazy and wrong-headed. It is a trait he cannot understand in his own father, "a foolish old man, but one with all his sensibilities refined by landscape painting" (a hint at the story to follow, a fore-image of John Napper?). The old man insists (perversely, Vortrab contends) upon confusing the Professor with the long-dead Josef Mallin, imaginatively resurrecting the anarchist, "a nihilist, destroyer of churches, murderer of medical doctors" (note the echoes of earlier Gardner anarchists in book 1) from an ugly and bloody past:

> The period of Mallin's imprisonment . . . was a terrible strain on all of us. He was a brilliant devil, black-haired and handsome and deadly as a snake, so cunning at bribing or persuading the guards that at last the Warden himself took charge of holding him. It was shortly after his death that the Warden began that interminable pacing in his chamber. Mallin's execution, I might add, was unpleasant. His crimes were the worst of the three main kinds of which the laws speak, so that, after the decapitation, his head was thrown to the sawdust in the village square, to be eaten by dogs, as the law requires.

The father understands the effect of the dead upon the living. He sees, through lunatic eyes, the psychic connection between Mallin and the Warden: "The minute the axe comes down on Joe Mallin, the Warden's life will go fsst!" He knows why the Warden paces behind his door, unresponsive, obsessed. He knows of the existence of ghosts, of the life that runs on beyond reason. As Gardner has maintained, the father is an artist and a creator who has experienced the madness which is art. . . . The father haunts his own son just as Mallin haunts the Warden. He echoes the Professor's very words, conjures up the emotions that strike at Vortrab, and pierces his consciousness with the violence of a fist through glass.

What is more, the old man is the only person who understands what motivated Mallin and his wanton, anarchical viciousness: "The unpleasant facts of life, [Mallin] claims,

charge the human soul with longing. They drive a man to make up a world that's better than ours. But that better world is mere illusion, says Mallin; and illusion, being false, a mere cowardly lie, is as foul as actuality. So he goes at the universe with dynamite sticks.—It's a natural mistake." The anarchist is merely the artist who finds illusion contemptible. The artist creates a better world, content with his counterfeit; the anarchist finds all worlds—real and painted—absurd and abhorrent, and so destroys. Josef Mallin is the bomber in **"Pastoral Care,"** the mad geneticist of **"The Ravages of Spring,"** and the long-down-the-line descendant of Brother Nicholas in **"The Temptation of St. Ivo."** He is Gardner's fictional anarchist-clone. One can either choose, says Gardner, to play the artist and create, improve, and believe in the value of this life; or one can choose to deny the worth of this world and set at its foundations with hand, bomb, pen, or brush, bent upon bringing it all to the ground.

Even Heller can sense the oddity and ultimate preposterousness of it all. When Vortrab finally lets on that he has not seen the Warden in months, Heller laughs and asks, "Why, then . . . what makes you think he's there?" He admits to his abandonment and to the fact that no one is in charge. There is no one to order the burial of the Professor, who has finally passed from the organic to the inorganic life, yet Heller takes charge, telling Vortrab: "My people . . . have a long history of dealing with absurd situations. Leave everything to me." Heller knows something of the folly of a world divided between mind and matter, spirit and flesh. He has heard the Professor's talk for too long not to have invested some of his faith in the crepuscular; at the Professor's funeral, when all the ghosts convene (eleven dark-cloaked Jews, the Warden with a forehead shot away, and somewhere, I am sure, the spirit of Josef Mallin), Heller tries to persuade the empirically minded Vortrab of the possibility of a ghost race, dead spirits returning angry to a world that insisted upon the reality of "sticks and stones." Vortrab holds fast to his stubborn realism—or he holds at least until he sees the vision of the Warden, a dead man haunted to the point of suicide. Such things change a person: "I no longer bother to deny that I am frightened, hopelessly baffled, but neither do I pretend to believe that sooner or later he will answer my knock. I need rest, a change of air, time to sort out my thoughts."

So there they sit, Vortrab and Heller, guarding a prison that grows more absurd with each day. When a peddler tries to pawn off a book (a ghostly pirate of Sartre's *Being and Nothingness*) attacking humanity's puny attempt to deal with the world's duality, Vortrab runs him off with his walking stick and muses:

> [Heller] thinks I'm mad, of course. Each new regulation I bring "from the Warden," each new pardon or death sentence, increases his despair. I understand his feelings. I do what I can for him. "If Order has value, you and I are the only hope!" I whisper. He nods, mechanically, stroking his beard.
>
> I worry about him. Late at night, when he should be asleep, I hear Heller pacing, occasionally pausing, deep in thought.

The pacing goes on. What Mallin was to the Warden, so the Professor seems to become to Heller. Only Vortrab, the unimaginative one, fails to see what is happening, fails to see the futility of the illusion (it is an unartistic illusion). It is as if Heller knows that he is doomed; he knows nothing will change, that Vortrab and all the other "stubborn realists" will continue to insist upon a confused and inflexible kind of order that fits upon this world like an old uniform on a man grown well-bellied. It is the kind of order that kills art and makes it a ghost and a memory.

Not until we reach **"John Napper Sailing through the Universe"** does Gardner offer us a complete picture of how the artistic imagination makes its way through a disordered and deadly universe. Napper, as a painter, has made the journey from negation to affirmation, has made it with a genuine sense of suffering and cost. It is evident in his work. The "old" John Napper, as Gardner discovers, is blanketed in shadow and bleak denial:

> From out of the closet and under the bed we dragged some old John Napper paintings. They were a shock: dark, furious, intellectual, full of scorn and something suicidal. Mostly black with struggles of light, losing. He'd been through all the movements, through all the tricks, and he thoroughly understood what he was doing—a third-generation master painter. Understood everything, it seemed to me, but why he kept fighting instead of slitting his wrists. No sense of the clownish in the universal sorrow. No sense of dressing up, putting on gray spats, for the funeral.

This is the pretransitional Napper, the Napper (like the Professor) still going through the necessary suffering and living the rudimental life. He has yet to begin to "sail."

The transitional work of Napper reveals a change of attitude and aesthetic: he has gone Romantic. Of one such midway work, Gardner writes: "It had Turner things in it—illusions of movement, sultriness, light seen through cloud, the faintest suggestion of a ship, trouble. The universe was churning." The world has suddenly become less morose and more hopeful. The key is in the agonizingly slow breakthrough of light; it is the symbol of faith working its way out of the black morass of nihilism and hands-in-the-air acquiescence. The world broods one moment, smiles the next; the trick is to catch the brief reflection between the changes.

Not until Napper grows completely lunatic, "full of joy, mad Irish," does he move on to that world of pure imagination where happiness is a blend of pain and release from pain. It is there on his canvases where, as Gardner sees,

> at the center of all that joyful movement that shadows away toward not quite joyful—the face hangs perfectly motionless, holy. . . . He'd gone to the pit, in those Paris paintings, fighting for his life, squeezing the blood from his turnip of a world to hunt out the secret life in it, and there was none there. He'd hounded light—not just visual light—straining every muscle of body and mind to get down to what was real, what was absolute; beauty not as someone else had seen it but beauty he could honestly find himself, and what he'd gotten was a picture of the coal pocket.

That vision of light must come after one works his way through the darkness. It is an earned vision, says Gardner, one that signals a metamorphosis (as the Professor called it). An untested faith is naïve and shallow and washes out

in the first storm. Neither must one stop at an unchallenged despair; as Napper has learned, art consists of a struggling—intellectual, emotional, physical—with the darkest elements of existence. In the end, also like Napper, you may not actually come upon the light, but you will find something there that is worthwhile. It drives you to madness, an excess of imagination and feeling that leads you to "see the best in everything." The artist creates the world *ex nihilo* (not, as Hunter says in **"The Ravages of Spring,"** *"Nihilo ex nihilo"*); it is an imposing responsibility, one that can take a man to drink or to anarchy, or even to a redefined belief in the light at the "world's dark center." What Gardner deplores is the denial of imagination in the pursuit of order; if anyone is crazy, it's the person who labors to maintain a system that is colorless and broken down and beyond its time.

This is part of the lesson of book 2, "Tales of Queen Louisa." The stories in this section (and the story **"Trumpeter,"** published elsewhere) are fantasies, fairy tales that are more akin to Gardner's children's stories than to his other adult fiction. Furthermore, Gardner does not mean for us to take them *too* seriously; we should first enjoy them, and *then* think about them. We should approach them with all the capacity for belief and wonder of a child, but also with the adult consciousness of their "made-upness." If we are going to accept the world as it is, says Gardner, we must accept as well its mystery and improbability and fancy. We must use, in other words, the imagination that many of us abandoned when we grew solemnly out of childhood.

In the first story, **"Queen Louisa,"** we are introduced to the mad queen—mad beyond reasonable doubt, a person who shifts between woman, lizard, and toad with all the facility of an unfettered imagination. She dismisses the shadowy worries that afflict her by providing them with nothing to stick to; she is the symbol of a consciousness that is basically artistic and full of bright vision and light. She is a woman who works by intuition—"These hunches of hers were infallible"—and by a graced lunacy.

When the kingdom (momentarily without its king) is threatened, Queen Louisa rides out to meet the destroyer-witch who haunts an abandoned mystery. What she finds is that

> the garden's stone walls were encased in ice, as was every tree and shrub and leftover flower stalk. But in the center of the garden there was a glorious rosebush in triumphant bloom, such bloom as would hardly be natural on even the warmest summer day. And beside the bush there was a horrible ugly old witchlike person who was trying to cut down the rosebush with an axe. With every swipe she took, the trunk of the bush grew wider and stronger, and the roses bloomed more brightly. At the feet of the ugly, witchlike person, an old red hound lay whimpering and whining.

The rose bush is an emblem of virtue and regenerative good; random attempts at evil inadvertently breed beauty, and are powerless against a healthy imagination. The witch is an anarchist and an existentialist. . . . When the knights rush in to slaughter the witch and her wolves, Louisa halts everything with a loud "Stop!"—and all *is* stopped, though not explained, because she is the queen and that is all that matters. What she does not tell them is that the whole scene was a creation and an artifice:

"She'd admit, in all fairness, that perhaps the rosebush *was* cut down, since she was insane and could never know anything for sure, and perhaps the whole story was taking place in a hotel in Philadelphia."

Louisa (and Gardner) are playing fairy tale tricks (the sort of tricks Gardner devises in *In the Suicide Mountains,* his adultish children's tale), tricks that turn a dog into a king and a pack of wolves into a band of monks and a witch into a lady-of-waiting. The story comes close to self-conscious, self-parodying fiction, with Gardner perhaps even drawing himself in at the very end: "The boy beside the coachman said: 'Isn't this a marvelous tale to be in?' The coachman, who was silver-haired and wise, gave his nephew a wink. 'You barely made it, laddie!' " Queen Louisa has the artist's mentality which rests upon a benign madness—the sort of madness evident earlier in John Napper—She can forgive malevolence and rebellious youth because her mind makes significant leaps of reason. She need not make all of the connections, touch all of the logical points of progression: the gaps she fills in with imagination.

She is a vivid contrast to her husband, King Gregor—or *Bold* King Gregor "as he liked to call himself and as he'd tentatively suggested from time to time that he might not unfittingly be called, but it had never caught on"—who is reasonable and rational and overburdened with the responsibilities of state. He is pestered and pricked with madness and folly (thus the title, **"King Gregor and the Fool"**), and it is affecting his work—which is unfortunate, since

> he dearly loved his work, and he was good at it. That was why he spent too much time at it, as the Fool kept pointing out, and tended to neglect his family. No doubt it was true that it was because of his neglect that Mad Queen Louisa spent more and more of her time these days as an enormous toad, though in her natural shape she was the most beautiful queen in the world. And presumably it was why his daughter—if it was true that, as Queen Louisa insisted, he had a daughter—had run away from home and only recently returned, having gotten herself into trouble and having no one to turn to.

Gregor is an orderly man surrounded by chaos. He finds life "baffling," a conglomeration of idiot ways, and his one wish is "to introduce, in his own small way, some trifling note of sense" into a kingdom that is rapidly splitting into silliness and skinny-dipping.

The poor man cannot even fight a proper war. The field is a mess, ranks are broken like disparate parts of a jigsaw puzzle, and bodies are hewn apart with no sense of medieval, chivalric propriety. To make matters worse (or perhaps for a moment better), Queen Louisa decides to visit her husband and see exactly what it is a king does during his day. In anticipation of the Queen's appearance, Gregor and his foe, Just King John, hastily reorder the field, realigning scattered troops and dragging corpses and horse-flesh into the cover of the woods. When Louisa approaches, the signals are given and the armies quicken. . . . Louisa knows evil and stupidity when she sees it, and in her beautiful insanity she can stop it with a word (remember the rosebush and the witch). Even her ally, the Fool,

senses the ludicrousness of the kingly business of killing, and circulates a couplet that fairly giggles:

> You think I'm small because I'm lazy;
> But big brave knights get killed. That's crazy!?

It sends King Gregor over the edge, demanding the Fool's head. When the Fool claims biblical origin for the poem, Gregor calls in King John (sleepy-eyed and in nightcap) to rule upon the issue (John is known to be a biblical scholar). And Just King John for once lives up to his name, siding with the lunatic element in pronouncing: "Yes! . . . The passage is distinctly Biblical. Loosely." John's decision restores a bit of order and peace to the kingdom and sanctions Louisa's sweet, solving madness. Gregor is a decent and high-minded man, but he is caught up in the transition of systems and institutions, and he causes disasters. Louisa tries to turn the world humane by affirming life and art—and you *have* to be a little crazy to do that.

Only a crazy woman would pluck a peasant stranger-woman and call her her daughter, which in the story **"Muriel"** we discover did happen. Muriel is a sane girl who, by an act of chance insanity, sees her life and circumstances changed in an instant. Gone are the poverty and humility and the wan existence—but "the best thing about suddenly having been turned into a princess was that Muriel escaped all those tiresome and ultimately dangerous ideas that her friends imagined it was necessary to maintain." These are the ideas that turn pennilessness into a religion and interpret power as a purely repressive, political fact. As Muriel insightfully tells her peasant friends, describing Queen Louisa: "She's a very fine person, in whichever shape. She organizes great charity balls and calls off wars and heaven knows what. She's majestic, really. I believe she's a kind of saint." Such ideas become dangerous when they are organized and lead toward anarchy, which is something with which Muriel (*née* Tanya) is familiar.

She has been to the forest, and as anyone who reads Gardner knows, "no one ever came to the great, dark forest but rapists and anarchists and outlaws." She has met—been abducted by, in fact—the grim, murderous Vrokror, anarchist-pirate. Yet he has a certain sympathetic appeal that Muriel finds winning: "No man on earth was ever more beautiful and tragic, though certainly he was possessed by the Devil." He is "angry and malevolent" but he has "suffered more anguish than have most men of eighty." He is a man turned sadly wrong by misfortune and the accidents of life, and even the possibility of Muriel's love cannot save him at the moment: "Tanya . . . within our lifetime I will destroy all governments, all ideas of station. Peasantry I will make an obscure, archaic word. . . . I have penetrated the grotesque stupidity of things as they are."

What is most pernicious about Vrokror's way of thinking is its ability to trap the old peasant friends of Muriel, turning their heads toward revolution and destruction. The confrontation between king and rebel is inevitable; mayhem prevails, the peasants lie battered and bleeding, and Vrokror escapes (for a purpose, we find later). Only Queen Louisa can put it all back together again, as once more by a vast act of imagination she brings everyone back into the fold, turning peasants into royalty, shepherds and milkmaidens into princes and princesses. No one dies, though all suffer, and Louisa is not about to let anyone off without a lesson. . . . Vrokror is left hissing on a mountainside, the useless anarchist in a magical kingdom. As Louisa says, "All error begins . . . with soreheads." If you're going to be an anarchist, recommend Louisa and John Gardner, you had best be a "joyful anarchist," one who sees the possibilities that exist for a positive disorder. It is always better to build than to tear down—it makes people happier.

Gardner concluded this section with a story entitled **"Trumpeter,"** which was published separately in *Esquire* in December 1976, and later included in *The Art of Living and Other Stories.* Trumpeter is Queen Louisa's dog, a silent observer and reasoner of the ways of the Queen and her kingdom. Trumpeter knows that the original princess has died, that Muriel-Tanya is a substitute offered by Louisa's fine distraction, yet he also understands the sort of blurred reason behind the Queen's actions, understands "that in making them her children, as perhaps they were indeed, since the life of a dog is but a heartbeat, so to speak, in the long span of man, the queen had brought happiness to a kingdom that had suffered, before that, grave troubles—peasants against royalty, 'madness against madness,' as the minstrel said: an obscure saying; but Trumpeter, in his heart, understood it." This "madness against madness" is at the heart of the "Tales of Queen Louisa"—the idea of proper and improper forms of madness; the one makes you an anarchist, the other makes you an artist. (Note how in this wonderful kingdom, even the dog can intuit, can feel "in his heart," the rightness of things.)

All that is left to perfect the kingdom is the marrying of Muriel, and Louisa (after opening up the treasury to pirates and thieves, thus eliminating greed and want and cutpursery) delivers her masterstroke: she pairs the princess with "Vrokror the Terrible" (he, too, must have a title it seems), displaced and exiled anarchist, a man reduced to living "all alone on the top of a mountain, eating tundra plants." Louisa yanks Vrokror out of his isolation, matches him with the beauteous princess Muriel, and turns the kingdom into a stylized bit of lawlessness, a crystal vase: "The palace was full of light—beyond the windows, thick darkness. Nothing was wrong; nothing could go wrong. It was a balanced kingdom, the only kingdom in the world where art reigned supreme." Louisa is the consummate artist. She is physical light and vision; her lunacy is sublime and inspired, and touched with an humane intuition that urges her toward sainthood (Muriel's earlier judgment is exactly on the mark). She draws together opposites, synthesizes, and comes up with the ideal measure of compromise and hope. She is the Gardner aesthetic personified: the transforming, transmogrifying, light-bearing artist. (pp. 128-37)

With *The Art of Living* (1981), Gardner brought together nearly all of his previously uncollected short stories and satisfied an old desire to consolidate all of the random fiction he had floating about in various journals and magazines (only the title story had been unpublished). Curiously, while none of the stories in this collection is as intensely personal as the patently autobiographical **"John Napper Sailing through the Universe"** in *The King's Indian,* at least three of the stories—**"Redemption,"** **"Stillness,"** and **"Come on Back"**—draw unmistakably upon Gardner's own history for their substance. In a way, *The Art of Living*

ing is a working through of problematical parts of Gardner's past, a sort of therapy in prose by which Gardner comes to at least a temporary truce with private emotional bogies.

More important, though, *The Art of Living* demonstrates with amazing consistency one of Gardner's larger philosophical obsessions: the relation of the artist to his art and to his life. All but three of the stories in this volume deal directly with art in one of its forms or another, and two of those remaining stories (**"Come on Back"** and **"The Art of Living"**), while not concerned with bona fide artists, do examine the roles of what might be called "unsuspected artists," or people who work artistically in unusual or even quite mundane ways. That, in fact, is the lesson of *The Art of Living:* there is the artistry of creation (the art of the composer, the painter, the writer) and there is the artistry of life (the art of the individual who lives life as it should be lived, artistically). For Gardner, life should and must be transformed into art, or into *an* art. In some way, the artist should be better equipped to live the artistic and (Gardner would say) moral life, but even he must sometimes be made to see the transformative possibilities of his art and to accept the responsibilities that are inherent in the nature of the artist. Contrarily, the "unsuspected artist" often lives the artistic life, masters the "art of living" unconsciously, and only in epiphanous moments of brilliant clarity and emotional crisis is made aware of the blinding power of art in life. Art, Gardner believes, is infectious and undeniably effective; it has the ability to chastise death, to negate loss, and—as all of Gardner's fiction tells us—to illuminate the darker and more painful mysteries of our existence.

In the first story in the collection, **"Nimram,"** Gardner examines one of his favorite "games of opposites": the matter of good and bad luck. Benjamin Nimram is a toweringly successful symphonic conductor, a man blessed with comfortable public and private lives. He is one of those creatures who occasionally seems to loom over the rest of mankind, a man larger than his name or reputation. He rages and loves like a god, yet he is consciously aware, behind his "Beethoven frown," that he is "a fortunate accident, a man supremely lucky." . . . Gardner, like Taggert Hodge in *The Sunlight Dialogues,* believes in the separation of the lucky and the unlucky, believes that we are born with certain portions of good and bad fortune, and that those who ascend are those who are randomly, unforeseeably blessed. It is totally illogical, and impossible to rationally explain.

Nimram himself does not understand it, as he discovers on his flight to Chicago. Nimram shares a first-class seating with a teen-aged girl named Anne, a girl whose physical features could, in another life, have made her Nimram's daughter. Anne is dying; she is one of the negatively elect. Death is an immediate, inescapable fact for her, yet she fears it, as she fears her plane ride, her first, only when she thinks about it, when she puts the fact into words and declares it. Anne is the symbol of life's most unbearable paradox: death is neither just nor reasonable, but accidental. Time, which Nimram had "consumed too fast to notice he was losing it . . . was time the girl would never get." Gardner throws two of the "chosen" together, juxtaposes good and bad fortune to bring home to Nimram the tragedy that sits beside him. Nimram's sense of responsibility and his singular sense of fear for others throw him into a general metaphysical confusion of doubt and wonder, and make him uncertain of his own thought and feeling:

> It wasn't pity he felt, or even anger at the general injustice of things; it was bewilderment, a kind of shock that stilled the wits. If he were religious—he was, of course, but not in the common sense—he might have been furious at God's mishandling of the universe, or at very least puzzled by the disparity between real and ideal. But none of that was what he felt. God had nothing to do with it, and the whole question of real and ideal was academic. Nimram felt only, looking at the girl—her skin off-color, her head unsupported yet untroubled by the awkwardness, tolerant as a corpse—Nimram felt only a profound embarrassment and helplessness: helplessly fortunate and therefore unfit, unworthy, his whole life light and unprofitable as a puff-ball, needless as ascending smoke. He hardly knew her, yet he felt now—knowing it was a lie but knowing also that if the girl were really his daughter it would be true—that if Nature allowed it, Mother of tizzies and silences, he would change lives with the girl beside him in an instant.

How do you behave if you are one of the elect, one of the walking gods on earth? How do you deal with the injustice that sprouts in the gap between good luck and bad? Nimram's heart opens up, almost upon human reflex, with love for the doomed girl, but that is intellectually not enough. Nimram, the fortunate, temporary hero-god must act to redeem that injustice through his art.

Which is what Nimram does the following night in a performance by the Chicago Symphony of Mahler's Fifth, a performance which Anne attends. The moment is compactly epic, epiphanous. The god descends; Nimram springs upon the stage "like a panther," light angling off his hair like lightning flashes, and draws the orchestra into him, commands them with his presence, makes player and conductor one. Anne feels the magic of it all. . . . Art, in all of its brilliant lucidity, redeems for an instant the tragic darkness of life. Nimram becomes god-pilot-conductor, turning death's scythe into a life-giving arc of sound; man does not descend, but ascends into that realm of spirit and light where time and space fade, where the souls of past and present conjoin, where death is defeated. The act of the artist elevates man, transforms matter into spirit in a sort of aesthetic holiness. It is an act that is repeated throughout Gardner's collection, and one which ultimately closes the book, in a gathering of living and dead, in a direct echo of this first story.

This theme of art as redemptive force comes through most clearly and most intensely in the second story, **"Redemption,"** which is Gardner's personal attempt to redefine a particularly painful part of his memory. The story is based on the tragic death of Gardner's younger brother Gilbert in a farming accident in the home-fields of Batavia, New York. Gardner talked of this memory in an interview in *The Paris Review,* and explained how the story served as a deliberate exorcism: "Before I wrote the story about the kid who runs over his younger brother . . . always, regularly, every day I used to have four or five flashes of that accident. I'd be driving down the highway and I couldn't see what was coming because I'd have a memory flash. I haven't had it once since I wrote the story. You really do

ground your nightmares, you *name* them." Guilt, it should be clear by now, is an integral part of Gardner's universe, and in **"Redemption"** Gardner attempted a reconciliation with his own private nightmares and misplaced responsibilities.

Death is typically most brutal in its effect on the living, and the tragedy of David Hawthorne's death is felt most clearly by his family. Dale Hawthorne, the father, is profoundly affected, is in fact "nearly destroyed by it":

> Sometimes Jack would find him lying on the cow-barn floor, crying, unable to stand up. Dale Hawthorne . . . was a sensitive, intelligent man, by nature a dreamer. . . . He loved all his children and would not consciously have been able to hate his son even if Jack had indeed been, as he thought himself, his brother's murderer. But he could not help sometimes seeming to blame his son, though consciously he blamed only his own unwisdom and—so far as his belief held firm—God. Dale Hawthorne's mind swung violently at this time, reversing itself almost hour by hour, from desperate faith to the most savage, black-hearted atheism. Every sickly calf, every sow that ate her litter, was a new, sure proof that the religion he'd followed all his life was a lie. Yet skeletons were orderly, as were, he thought, the stars. He was unable to decide, one moment full of rage at God's injustice, the next moment wracked by doubt of His existence.

This disparity, as Nimram calls it, between the real and the ideal hits at Hawthorne as it hits at every person blasted by tragedy and the world's illogic. His mind turns, at times, to suicide and a sort of metaphysical escape, but he ultimately settles on literal physical escape, becoming a fugitive from his family and home. He abandons responsibility, leaves his son, daughter, and wife to mourn their loss among themselves, to survive as *he* hopes to survive.

His wife, Betty, survives in her changedness. She weeps alone at night, and embraces her children "whenever new waves of guilt swept in." She is the emotional center who through her strength of character and sense of love keeps "her family from wreck." Phoebe, the daughter, survives through an abiding child's belief in a God whose wisdom outruns his logic and justice; she sticks unthinkingly, as a girl her age would do, to her faith, tested for the first time by the world's unpredictability.

Jack Hawthorne, too, survives, through a long ordeal of doubt and guilt and sorrow. He doubts his own ability to love and to feel for anyone or anything: "He'd never loved his brother, he raged out loud, never loved anyone as well as he should have. He was incapable of love, he told himself. . . . He was inherently bad, a spiritual defective. He was evil." Jack plummets to the depths of philosophical despair, damning himself for the accident of his brother's death. Like his father, Jack eventually comes to doubt the necessity of his existence, bemired as he is in the certainty of his own damnation: "The foulness of his nature became clearer and clearer in his mind until, like his father, he began to toy—dully but in morbid earnest now—with the idea of suicide." The facticity of death, as Gardner has illustrated before, is the ultimate moral test. It drives us down, sinks us, and challenges us to submit or to respond. If we submit, we become nihilists; if we respond heroically, we rise to love and to believe once again.

Dale Hawthorne responds by returning to his family, who surround him in a tableau of forgiveness: the prodigal father come home. He is a man much changed by his experience; the luster has left his eyes and his body seems empty of its old energy. There is a new sobriety about him that tells you he has faced down tragedy and survived—not necessarily prevailed, but survived. Jack does not immediately perceive the agony his father has suffered, and so rages at him with a censorious sort of hatred. He isolates himself from the family, refuses the consoling, healing influence of those who love him, and turns to his music and to his French horn for solace and some sort of intuitive philosophical comfort.

At the end of the story, Jack visits his horn teacher in Rochester, Arcady Yegudkin, "the General." Yegudkin is an old man, an artist and a sufferer and, with his misshapen wife, a survivor. He is pathetically human—"In his pockets, in scorn of the opinions of fools, he carried condoms, dirty pictures, and grimy, wadded-up dollar bills"—but when he plays the horn, he becomes a god, a transformer of matter into spirit. . . . On the outer limits of art exists a transmogrified world, a world "suspended in space" and time, a world that Jack Hawthorne longs to know and to explore. For now, however, he can only cry . . . at the beauty and the elusiveness of his vision, and fall once more into the arms of the world around him: his family, his art, his ability to love. There is much to suffer

JOHN GARDNER

1933–1982

"MASTERY HOLDS FAST."

"Through the study of technique—not canoeing or jogging or slinging hash—one learns the best, most efficient ways of making characters come alive, learns to know the difference between emotion and sentimentality, learns to discern, in the planning stages, the difference between the better dramatic action and the worse. It is this kind of knowledge that leads to mastery. . . . Mastery is not something that strikes in an instant, like a thunderbolt, but a gathering power that moves through time, like weather."

—John Gardner
The Art of Fiction

John Gardner worked to make the creative writing program at SUNY-Binghamton "the best in the world." The University shares his vision and reaffirms its own commitment to his ideal.

Before his death, John Gardner initiated a fund-raising campaign to help insure the continued excellence of the creative writing program at SUNY-Binghamton. Contributions to the John Gardner Creative Writing Endowment can be sent to: The SUNY-Binghamton Foundation, Vestal Parkway East, Binghamton, N.Y. 13901.

After Gardner's untimely death, his colleagues at the State University of New York at Binghamton ran this full-page ad in the New York Times Book Review *as a tribute.*

and to enjoy before he can transform the world as Yegudkin can, to take someone soaring and dipping as this artist has taken him. There is always the promise, though, that one's art can and will redeem, will erase the guilt and assuage the pain, will return one's faith and peace-in-sleep. That is the magic of art.

Gardner goes after the quality of this magic in **"Stillness,"** another autobiographical story. It is one of two Carbondale stories in the book, and seems clearly modeled on Gardner's past: Joan and Martin ("Buddy") Orrick are surely John ("Bud" as his parents call him) Gardner and his first wife Joan, and Orrick with his crewcut, leather jacket, and "unpublishable novels" is the Gardner in the jacket photo of the rare hardback edition of *The Resurrection.*

In this story, however, the remembrances belong to Joan Orrick, who while on a lecture trip with her husband, recalls her days as an accompanist in a dance school in St. Louis. Like Jack Hawthorne in the previous story, Joan Orrick has artistic dreams of grandeur: she wants to go to Paris, to play piano, to find the magic. She plays for Pete and Jacqui Duggers—Duggers School of Dance—and she remembers the artistry, the "magic" of Pete Duggers when he moved:

> The speed and lightness with which Pete Duggers danced were amazing to behold, but what was truly miraculous, so that it made you catch your breath, was the way he could stop, completely relaxed, leaning his elbow on empty air and grinning as if he'd been standing there for hours, all that movement and sound you'd been hearing pure phantom and illusion. That was unfailingly the climax when he danced: a slow build, with elegant shuffles and turns, then more speed, and more, and more and still more until it seemed that the room spun drunkenly, crazily, all leading—direct as the path of an arrow—to nothing or everything, a sudden stillness like an escape from reality, a sudden floating, whether terrible or wonderful she could never tell: an abrupt hush as when a large crowd looks up, all at the same moment, and sees an eagle in the sky, almost motionless, or then again, perhaps, the frightening silence one read about in novels when a buzz-bomb shut off over London. He stood perfectly still, the piano was still, his young students gaped, and then abruptly reality came back as the piano tinkled lightly and he listlessly danced and, as he did so, leaned toward his students and winked. "You see? Stillness! That's the magic!"

That stillness is the stillness that occurs as the artistic aftermath; it is the stillness in the crowd at Hudiksvall as they stare at the statue of St. George and the Dragon, in *Freddy's Book,* the stillness in the cork-lined room in Rochester as Yegudkin puts down his horn. For an instant, time and space are truly suspended; art performs miracles, magic. This is Gardner's vision.

For Joan Orrick, Paris never comes—at least not in her first forty years. Married half her life, bogged down in the mundaneness of life with a man who sleeps "exactly as he'd always slept, winter and summer," plagued by headaches and sleeplessness—she is a long way from the stillness of that studio in the heart of St. Louis. The future looms tiresomely certain and transparent, full of as much disappointment as the past. Hope seems to lie in the recapturing of that stillness and in the re-creation of that magic—not necessarily in the same fashion (it could just as easily have been in the lunatic antics of her great-uncle blasting at tornados with his shotgun), but with the same intent. To have the world transformed, just briefly, to see art working at its best, to play in Paris and to turn Paris into an otherworld: that is the miracle the artist seeks.

The working—and counter-working—of this miracle is the subject of the story **"The Music Lover,"** which is a rewriting of Thomas Mann's "Disillusionment" (as Gardner says, "The most gallish thing I've ever done"). The "music lover" in this instance is Professor Alfred Klingman, a dusty, eccentric old man whose obsequiousness insinuates pain and pathetic sorrow. However, as Gardner writers, "Every man who survives in this world has at least one area in which he escapes his perhaps otherwise miserable condition, and for Professor Klingman, this area was music." Music, as it was for the girl in **"Nimram"** and for Jack Hawthorne in **"Redemption,"** is an escape and a salvation for Klingman. At concerts, Klingman scurries in, his eyes like lunatic eyes, his white hair flying, "looking terrified and slightly insane." Though amazingly ignorant of the technicalities of the music he hears—the number, the key—Klingman enjoys a profound intuitive knowledge of the work that surpasses the sheer intellectual efficiency of the schooled listener. Indeed, his sensitivity borders on the embarrassing, for

> no one could be more responsive to the anguished wellings and sweet palpitations of the music itself. When Mahler was played, or even the coolest, most objective of Bruckner, tears would run streaming down Professor Klingman's nose, and sometimes he would sob audibly, so that everyone around him was made uncomfortable. . . .

Klingman allows himself to be transported by the music, to ascend and to swoop as the music directs or takes him. Klingman *feels* the music and the artistry.

One night, however, Klingman attends a concert featuring "three contemporary pieces" of music. The evening is a disaster. The music is dissonant and harsh and obscene: Klingman "wrung his fingers, groaned, covered his eyes, and on one occasion cried out loudly, 'Oh my God! My God!' " Klingman's actions are intuitive, emotional reactions to the inherent perniciousness of the music, a perniciousness intended by the composer, Klingman later learns, when the music's composer draws Klingman into a cafe to drink and to talk with him about the piece.

The composer is a young man, full of anger and disillusionment. Like many of Gardner's anarchists, he is dressed in black, with eyes "unnaturally bright and alert" and with "strikingly long white fingers." The composer tells Klingman of his youth, of his life as a clergyman's son in a home dominated by "a punctilious cleanliness and a pathetic, bookish optimism" that is reminiscent of Bishop Brask in *Freddy's Book.* . . . Life, for the composer, was little more than words, language, constructs of an alphabet and a rhetoric. When actually confronted with the stuff of life, then, the composer found existence paltry, dull, and unpromising: again, the disparity between the real and the ideal. Life *is* often unequal to the words that describe it; that is the danger of ignoring life for the descriptions of life. Disillusioned, the composer turned to creating works of antiart, music that joked at life and the art that tried to capture or glorify it. The composer is one

of Gardner's artist-cynics, writing, composing, or painting bad, exhausted art. That is why Klingman reacts so violently to the discordance of the music, for he senses the inherent malevolence and destructiveness of the thing. The music curses life instead of showing its manifold nature of good and evil. The composer has "transformed" music into bad rhetoric, has stripped the music of its magic, has replaced the "stillness" with the painful cries of a man betrayed by art. (pp. 184-93)

"Vlemk the Box-Painter" is a fable or parable for artists. Strictly speaking, **"Vlemk"** is a novella, one that Gardner published separately in 1979, but in spirit it is a fairytale lesson. In some ways, it is a fabulistic parallel to Gardner's earlier story, **"John Napper Sailing through the Universe,"** for the fictional career of Vlemk follows a line similar to the true-to-life career of the artist John Napper. Vlemk descends and ascends, goes from darkness to light much in the manner of Napper, who had to pass through his own "dark" period before achieving the clarity and light of his present style.

Vlemk, as the title states, is a box-painter, an artist, and a very good one at that. In fact, he is the best:

> Though he was not old and stooped, though old enough by several years to grow a moustache and a beard that reached halfway down his chest, he was a master artist, as box-painters go. He could paint a tiny picture of a grandfather's clock that was so accurate in its details that people sometimes thought, listening very closely, that they could make out the noise of its ticking. He painted flowers so precisely like real ones that one would swear that they were moving just perceptibly in the breeze, and swear that, pressing one's nose to the picture, one could detect a faint suggestion of rose smell, or lilac, or foxglove.

Yet Vlemk, like so many of Gardner's characters, has another side, a monstrous side that sends him reeling into staggering drunkenness and makes friends of villains and thieves and knaves. He is trapped by his monstrousness, just as he is trapped by the metaphors of his art: " 'What a box I'm in!' he would cry, looking up from the gutter the next morning. It had long been his habit to think in terms of boxes, since boxes were his joy and occupation."

One morning, while Vlemk lies passed out in the street-filth, he is noticed by the Princess. Ashamed of his condition and smitten by the woman's astounding beauty, Vlemk resolves to call upon the Princess at her castle home. The Princess is taken by Vlemk's openness and grants him his wish to visit her again, but on one condition: that he paint a picture of the Princess's face so realistic and accurate that it actually speaks.

So begins Vlemk's decline. As he works on the painting, he is besieged by "morbid, unsettling ideas." . . . Vlemk begins to doubt the condition of beauty in life. He even begins to doubt the purpose of his art and his ability as an artist to reproduce that beauty. He becomes wary of his craft, fearful "that the paint was controlling him, creating not an image of the Princess but something new, a creature never before seen under the sun." Vlemk wants desperately to cling to his belief in the reality of beauty, but he feels a need tugging him to redefine that reality. His painting turns into something of itself, attains a life—altogether different from what he had planned—of its own. The face reveals things better left unshown, "faint but unmistakable hints of cruelty, vanity, and stinginess." And as these traits emerge, so does Vlemk's repressed doubt: "He began to perceive clearly the fact that he'd known all along but had never quite confronted: that Beauty is an artist's vain dream; it has, except in works of art, no vitality, no body."

Paradoxically, though, his painting does spring to life, asserts its vitality, its "virtual existence," as Langer would call it. The face on the box becomes Vlemk's personal "library horror." All the while Vlemk is at work finishing the portrait, he is conscious of one thing: "Having come to understand the Princess, both the best and the worst in her, poor Vlemk had fallen hopelessly, shamelessly in love." Yet that is not the worst of Vlemk's dilemma, for the picture is indeed so lifelike that it begins to speak, and its first words are a fitful, doomful curse upon the unlucky box-painter: "You shall never speak a word until I say so!" Vlemk, then, is doubly cursed. He is held by the Princess's demand to create a painting so true to nature that it shall speak, a curse of horrible intensity for the artist; then he is cursed to dumbness when he is close to lifting the initial curse with his painting.

Part of Vlemk's problem is that he receives such bad advice. He talks with a world-weary old monk (shades of Bishop Brask) who tells him that beauty is evanescent, "momentary in the mind," and that "by the highest standards I am able to imagine, I have never known a beautiful woman . . . or even a good woman, or even a relatively good mother." Vlemk's trio of mismatched friends do him no better. One is a poet who no longer writes poetry because no one is capable of learning anything from it: "My audience . . . has, collectively, the brains of one pig. . . . Perhaps I underestimate pigs." He now filches people's jewelry and kidnaps people's children. One is a violinist who no longer makes music because his audience is his enemy and his music noise. He now steals and pilfers the pockets of the wealthy: "There's no real money in it, but the response of the crowd is tremendous." The third is an axe-murderer—though he has yet to claim his first victim. He is the least agreeable of all: "He had a mouth made unpleasant by small, open sores, and eyes that seemed never to fix on anything but to stare with fuming discontent in whatever direction his small, shiny head was turned." The axe-murderer is a nihilist, a believer in "the power of evil." . . . All three men . . . are dreamers, ineffectual, cynical, dried-up artists who have rejected their art for weak lies and poor opinions. Nihilism, Gardner seems to say, is little more than intellectual sour grapes.

Vlemk, unfortunately, is ripe for such unwisdom. His art first turns sterile, dry, and Vlemk gives up his skill. Then it turns vicious and vile as he explores the darkest sides of the Princess, probes the ugliness and evil that he has been told is the sum of our existence. He paints "Reality boxes" that portray the varieties of man's potential monstrousness, and he achieves a new sort of mastery: "He was painting, after all, as no other box-painter in the world could paint, making discoveries as rare as any scientist's. He was coming to such a grasp of life's darkest principles—and at the same time discovering, as he chased his intuitions, such a wealth of technical tricks and devices—that not a dozen fat books could contain what he had learned in one day." Vlemk spends his days turning out

boxes each "more sinister than the last, more shamelessly debauched, more outrageously unfair in the opinion of the picture that could talk, which she now did rarely, too angry and too deeply hurt to give Vlemk the time of day." Art turns into a mean obsession that pleases no one, not even the axe-murderer, not even Vlemk. There is no joy (it is only delusion), no miracle, no magic in Vlemk's art. The light has given way to the darkness. Vlemk's vision is all bleakness and scorn.

The Princess, meanwhile, has begun a personal moral lapse of her own. She sees in the picture of herself (which Vlemk has left her as a gift) the same disturbing traits that had bothered Vlemk, and she is so molested by these "hints of cruelty, vanity, and stinginess" that she considers tossing the painting into the fire. The painting's conscious perversity drives the Princess to distraction and to a sort of enlightenment, pointing up that persistent disparity between what is and what seems to be, between what the Princess "felt to be her best self and knew to be her worst." Still she rejects the several portraits in Vlemk's studio as falsities, coming to see them as veritable curses upon her, or as symbols of the curse that Vlemk himself has placed upon her. What that curse is, the Princess hardly knows, but even her father the king feels it and implores her to "go to the box-painter. Beg him to remove the curse. Otherwise we're doomed."

The curse, as it turns out, is the fact of the love that both Vlemk and the Queen (as she becomes upon her father's death) feel, but fail to openly acknowledge. The Queen visits Vlemk, and sees in him a changed man and a changed artist. And she falls beneath the spell of that change. . . . The Queen apes Vlemk's descent (or mock-descent) into cynicism, joining in disguise the cutthroat world of the tavern. She misreads the curse, defining it as a fear instead of a joy. Rule turns into misrule; the kingdom reverts to chaos and lunacy, but not a beneficent, blessed lunacy. Not until the Queen learns to deal with the portrait— "She's your own very self, a picture so real it can speak. Surely you can find a way to live with your own very self!"—can she return the country and herself to order and sanity.

Vlemk considers helping her by repainting the picture on the talking box, but each time he resolves to try, he fails because "the terrible truth was that he loved with all his heart that saucy, incorrigible little picture on the box— and no doubt also the Queen, since the two were identical." Fraught with his impotence, Vlemk returns one evening to the tavern and to his three old friends, who have suddenly turned successful. The ex-poet writes verses for a cardboard-box company ("Got troubles? Out-fox 'em! Box 'em!"). The ex-violinist writes music for advertising jingles for the cardboard-box company, pickpocketing symphony themes instead of overcoats. And the axe-murderer: "I chop up wooden boxes to make the phosphor sticks people buy in those little cardboard boxes. They're getting to be all the rage, these phosphor sticks. They're easier than a flint. Also, sometimes children burn down hotels with them. Ha ha!" The three failures have turned into successful, if compromised, frauds. Reality has shifted once again. And it drives Vlemk home to repaint the Queen's face—but without its flaws and insinuations of malice. In the magic of the moment and the repainting, Vlemk reverses the curse, turns the painting mute, leaving both artist and art dumbstruck when they go to see the Queen.

The Queen is near death, a symptom of the painting's effect upon her soul and of her misinterpretation of Vlemk's character. She is intent upon dying and seeks atonement for her sins; she wants to be retrieved, if only for a last moment, from the despair that has tugged her down. Reality, however, is not always as it seems to be. When the box is thrown into the fire, it cries out to Vlemk for salvation; the curse—well, there was no curse upon the box, for it could talk all the time. It merely wished to spite Vlemk, just as the Queen had wished to spite him, for the portrait is indeed the Queen's "own very self." The Prince, the Queen's suitor, reveals himself a married man and leaves, but not before revealing a part of Vlemk's puzzle to him: "Surely . . . my dear Vlemk, you painted what you *thought* was a picture of perfection, but it came out exactly as it had been before you started!" The Queen, like the rest of us, is a hapless mixture of good and evil, perfection and fault. That is what Vlemk had painted, what the portrait had harped upon, and what the Queen had denied. Eventually, the box itself proposes the odd but obvious solution: a marriage of box-painter and Queen ("It's *odd* of course. . . . No doubt we'll have our critics."). Love finally emerges through all of the hatred and doubt, and people "muddle through." The kingdom—like other of Gardner's kingdoms—turns to a rule by art. Strange things happen in such a kingdom—opposites attract, artists marry queens, seasons change unpredictably and instantly. The castle doors open upon a winterscape where there previously was autumn. Art has worked its magic: "In every direction except straight above, the world was white and lovely, as if the light came from inside the snow. Straight above—or so it seemed to Vlemk, standing with one hand on his beard, the other in his pocket—the sky was painfully bright, blinding, as if someone had lifted the cover off the world, so that soon, as usual, everything in it would be transformed." Reality and matter and the world are transmogrified by the lunacies of love and art. Darkness gives way to light, blinding light, the sort of light that blinds the Devil in *Freddy's Book* and illuminates the hero's eyes, the sort of light that turns the Vermont landscape mystical in *October Light,* the sort of light that pierces the blackness of John Napper's painting and bursts upon Queen Louisa's kingdom. It is the same redemptive and transformative light that shines through all of Gardner's fiction.

With **"Vlemk the Box-Painter"** Gardner caps his study of the "acknowledged artist," of the artist-by-profession, and in his final two stories he takes a realistic look at the "unsuspected artist" whose art is in his living. **"Come on Back"** details, in a closely autobiographical way, the workings of art to redeem (as it did in **"Redemption"**) mankind from sorrow and loss. The story is set in Remsen, New York, a town very near Gardner's own Batavia. Remsen is infected with the magic of its Welsh settlers; it is almost a fairyland where myth is nearly as real as fact and where the young narrator's imagination is filled with legends of a people who really seem to believe in angels. It is a world of light, where music is a form of communion and exhilaration and art, so that the singing festival—the Cymanfa Ganu—becomes a sort of holy expression and catharsis.

One of the paradoxes of light is that it cannot exist without the parallel existence of darkness. In Remsen, the darkness runs beneath the surface, is hinted at, in the character of the narrator's Uncle Charley. Charley's world is the world of the song, of the Cymanfa Ganu. The boy's grandmother tells him: "Singing's got its place. But a body can get to thinking, when he's singing with a choir, that that's how the whole blessed world should be, and then when he comes down out of the clouds it's a terrible disappointment." When the darkness strikes, as it so often does, in the form of an accident to Charley, the man's world begins to crumble. His body weakens and fails, his flesh goes thin, and his will fades to a whimper. Accidents bring guilt, even to those who are not responsible, even to the young boy who stands aside and tries to make sense of all the confusion going on about him. The boy sees his uncle drifting into uselessness and impotence, a man wasted by sudden despair, cynical even of his own Welsh myths.

Eventually, the boy attends his first Cymanfa Ganu ("Means 'Come on Back' . . . 'Come on Back to Wales' "), and despite—or perhaps because of—his youth he feels the magic of the celebration. . . . It is all a part of that mysterious, magical, miraculous uplift and ascension that is art. For a moment the soul is suspended, removed from the material world, and transported; several souls become one, a unity.

Sometimes, though, even the magic is not enough. Charley drifts off, disappears, finally reappears to the family a suicide, a victim of his despair. Sorrow splinters and deadens the family; the union is temporarily broken; the voices lapse: "Slowly the whole conversation died out like embers in a fireplace, and as the stillness deepened, settling in like winter or an old magic spell, it began to seem that the silence was unbreakable, our final say." This is the stillness that *precedes* art, part of the same magic at work in **"Stillness"** and **"Vlemk."** The silence lasts until the first timid voice breaks through, inviting others to join it in a personal, familiar Cymanfa Ganu, a welcoming back to Wales of Uncle Charley, a resolution of the combined guilt and sorrow of those left behind in Remsen. Art has redeemed the souls of both the dead and the mourning, defeating time and space in the instant of a song.

In the final and title story, **"The Art of Living,"** Gardner repeats this celebratory motif, demonstrating how there is indeed an art to living, how we are all sorts of unsuspecting artists, how we all participate in the miracle that is art. Arnold Deller is a cook, a man of seemingly ordinary talents who takes an extraordinary approach to his work. Food, to Deller, is an "art," and Deller himself a self-described "artist." He is also a sufferer. He has lost his son in Vietnam, a loss that has transformed him into a human-monster reminiscent of Henry Soames in *Nickel Mountain.* Finnegan, the recollecting narrator, describes Deller: "Cooks are notoriously cranky people, but Arnold was an exception. Why he should have been so even-tempered seems a mystery, now that I think about it—especially given his fondness for rant and given the fact that, as we all found out, he was as full of pent-up violence as anybody else at that time. Nevertheless, even-tempered he was. Sometimes when certain kinds of subjects came up, his eyes would fill with tears; but he never swore, or hardly ever, never hit anybody, never quit his job in a huff." Deller possesses that "lidded wrath" that consistently threatens to turn man into a beast, that outruns the modes of expression and converts itself into violence and overwhelming emotion. It is that bit of Grendel in all of us.

Deller is also a philosopher and a humanist. He has (to quote another Gardner fiction) "first-class opinions." The world is in chaos, Deller tells Finnegan's gang, and the temptation is just to back off, to turn irresponsible: "But it's no good, leads straight into craziness. The thing a person's gotta have—a human being—is some kind of center to his life, some one thing he's good at that other people need from him, like, for instance, shoemaking. I mean something ordinary but at the same time holy, if you know what I mean. Very special. Something *ritual*—like, better yet, cooking!" Man must have an art and a purpose. Man's potential for artisthood, in fact, is one of the things that distinguishes him from other forms of life: "People can get the idea life's just instinct, no trick to it. But we're not animals, that's our great virtue and our terrible dilemma. . . . We've got to think things out, understand our human nature, figure out how to become what we are." And part of that understanding is learning how to love, which is in truth learning how to live: "Love by policy, not just instinct. That's the Art of Living. Not just instinct; something you do on purpose. Art!"

Deller begins talking the lunacy that is art. The narrator feels the craziness of things in the rushing of his blood, like a drunkenness, to his head. He feels the dead son rising in Deller's memory as it always does when the cook unleashes his emotion: "My boy Rinehart had a certain dish over there in Asia, a certain dish you might think no American would touch, given our prejudices. But it was made so perfectly, it was so downright outstanding, sooner or later you just had to give in to it. . . . It wasn't just food, it was an *occasion*. It was one of the oldest dishes known in Asia. Sit down to that dinner . . . you could imagine you were eating with the earliest wisemen in the world." The dish is cooked dog. The *occasion* is art, a ritual, a celebration. It is the artist's responsibility to create that occasion, that ritual, that celebration. . . . The artist's function is to redeem, through his art, the lost and sorrowed and guilty. We have seen it in **"Nimram,"** in **"Redemption,"** in **"Vlemk,"** in **"Come on Back"**—and we see it here.

Despite their doubts ("It was all pure bullshit"), the gang finds a dog for Deller, assists in the celebration of the ritual. For Finnegan, the narrator, the action springs from love and from an intuitive sense of the necessity of the thing. He knows that Deller is "crazy-serious," but he also knows that Deller believes in the morality of the covenant of the artist and in his sanctioned lunacy. . . . The artist possesses an inherent conviction of the rightness of his art and is obliged to an aesthetic and holy fidelity to it. The failed artist "sells out," turns cynical and spiteful. The faithful artist maintains his madness.

So the celebration finally comes off. The repugnance, the horror, the violence—all are overcome in the transcendence of the moment. What begins in doubt ends in affirmation as the magic of art once again works its transforming wonder:

> There was no sign of the thousands and thousands of dead Asians, or of Rinehart either, but it felt like they were there—maybe even more there if there's

no such thing in the world as ghosts, no life after death, no one there at the candlelit table but the few of us able to throw shadows on the wall. Say that being alive was the dinner candles, and say they burned forever over this everlasting meal of Imperial Dog. Then we were the diners there now, this instant, sent as distinguished representatives of all who couldn't make it this evening, the dead and the unborn. Everybody was feeling it, the importance of what we were doing—though it wasn't *what* we were doing that was important. . . . We were all, even Arnold, a little shocked, but in the darkness beyond where the candles reached, Rinehart nodded, and a thousand thousand Asians bowed from the waist.

The essence of the celebration, of the art, is what matters. The overpowering emotion of the ritual is what manifests itself as art. The method might vary—a Mahler symphony, a Welsh hymn, a dinner of Imperial Dog—but the end is the same. The souls come together from the corners and the depths of the world. Art brings life to death and light to darkness. For one lost moment in time, there are no roots, no ties, no connections to the material world. For that one moment all is strangely holy. For that one moment one captures the art of living. (pp. 196-205)

Gregory L. Morris, in his A World of Order and Light: The Fiction of John Gardner, *The University of Georgia Press, 1984, 259 p.*

FURTHER READING

Allen, Bruce. "Settling for Ithaca: The Fictions of John Gardner." *The Sewanee Review* LXXXV, No. 3 (Summer 1977): 520-31.

> Discusses several Gardner works, including the collection *The King's Indian,* and asserts that Gardner's principal concern in his fiction is the tension between social order and individual freedom.

Christian, Ed. "An Interview with John Gardner." *Prairie Schooner* 54, No. 4 (Winter 1980-81): 70-93.

> Critically acclaimed interview in which Gardner offers insight into his writing methods, his sources of literary inspiration, and the genesis of his fiction.

Fitzpatrick, W. P. "John Gardner and the Defense of Fiction." *Bulletin of the West Virginia Association of College English Teachers* 4, No. I (1977): 19-28.

> Maintains that the stories in *The King's Indian* are postmodern fiction, and that the collection mainly examines the constant transformations of human perception.

Henderson, Jeff, ed. *Thor's Hammer: Essays on John Gardner.* Conway, Ark.: University of Central Arkansas Press, 1985, 197 p.

> Collection of fifteen essays chiefly covering Gardner's novels and *On Moral Fiction,* but also examining his short stories.

Howell, John M. *John Gardner: A Bibliographical Profile.*

Carbondale, Ill.: Southern Illinois University Press, 1980, 158 p.

Detailed compilation of various publications by and about Gardner, including essays, letters, and speeches. Contains an afterword by Gardner.

Morace, Robert A. *John Gardner: An Annotated Secondary Bibliography.* New York and London: Garland Publishing, 1984, 364 p.

Comprehensive bibliography that includes interviews, speeches, critical essays and books, and chronological reviews of Gardner's fiction.

Morace, Robert A., and VanSpanckeren, Kathryn, eds. *John Gardner: Critical Perspectives.* Carbondale, Ill.: Southern Illinois University Press, 1982, 171 p.

Contains twelve essays which discuss such diverse themes as the structure of Gardner's fiction, his characterizations, and the analogy of *On Moral Fiction* to his short stories.

Vernon, John. "John Gardner's Loss Was Our Loss." *Binghamton Press* (19 September 1982): E1-2.

Posthumous tribute by a friend and colleague of Gardner. Classifies Gardner's major works as realistic novels and extended fables, and praises the compassion and power of his writing in both fields.

Margaret Laurence

1926-1987

(Born Jean Margaret Wemyss) Canadian novelist, short story writer, memoirist, essayist, editor, and translator.

A prominent figure in contemporary Canadian literature, Laurence earned international acclaim for realistic fiction that focuses on the individual's quest for self-realization. Her most respected and popular works feature protagonists from fictitious Manawaka, Manitoba, a small Scots-Irish community on the Canadian prairies that Laurence derived from her native town of Neepawa. The Manawaka series, comprised of four novels and the short story collection *A Bird in the House*, examines the interwoven relations of four generations of the town's families, concentrating on five women protagonists who seek literal and metaphorical escape from the stifling values of their forebears. Admired for the evocative power of her characterizations and settings in these and earlier works, as well as for her passionate valorization of quotidian Canadian life, Laurence was revered by her compatriots, many of whom agree with David Stouck's assessment that "the first writer to create a feeling of tradition among Canadian novelists [was] Margaret Laurence." Although Laurence is best known as a novelist, her two short story collections, *The Tomorrow-Tamer* and *A Bird in the House*, served to bolster her reputation, with some critics regarding the latter collection a central achievement in her fiction. Like her longer works, Laurence's stories typically employ simple prose, well-defined characters, and strong, clear narrative lines to delineate such themes as freedom, exile, order, disorder, and change in an unsentimental, elegiac tone.

Critics observe that the events of Laurence's life often informed her fiction. Born in Neepawa, Manitoba, Laurence was four years old when her mother died of a kidney infection. Her death compelled Laurence's maternal aunt to leave her Calgary teaching position and return to Neepawa to care for her young niece. When Laurence was five, her aunt married Laurence's father, Robert Wemyss, who died of pneumonia four years later. Laurence was then raised by her aunt in the home of her maternal grandfather, a stern, dominating man upon whom Laurence modeled the strict grandfather of the stories collected in *A Bird in the House*. In 1944, after earning a scholarship, Laurence left Neepawa for Winnipeg's United College, where she wrote short stories, became involved with social reform issues, and met Jack Laurence, a civil-engineering student whom she married in 1947. In 1949 the couple traveled to England and then to Africa, where Laurence's husband directed a dam-building project for the British Protectorate of Somaliland (now Somalia), and she explored the oral narratives of the Somalis. This endeavor inspired Laurence's translation *A Tree for Poverty: Somali Poetry and Prose*, the first collection of Somali works to appear in English. In 1952 the couple moved to Gold Coast (now Ghana). Jack continued with engineering work, and Margaret cared for their two small children and pursued her interests in African culture. As a result, Gold Coast became the setting for two early volumes of Lau-

rence's fiction—her first novel, *This Side Jordan*, and her first short story collection, *The Tomorrow-Tamer*—both of which focus on the implications of personal and political independence through depictions of African communities torn between cultural inheritance and Western modernization. Laurence's African experiences also inspired her travel memoir *The Prophet's Camel Bell*. Based on diary entries from her sojourn in Somaliland, this work discusses how Laurence's study of African colonialism helped shape her literary objectives, stimulating interests in racial equality, women's emancipation, and the promotion of national literatures of emergent nations, including Canada.

In 1957 the Laurences returned to Canada, settling for five years in Vancouver, British Columbia. There the author completed her African fiction and began her first book in the Manawaka cycle, *The Stone Angel*. Laurence finished this novel after separating from her husband and moving with her children to England in 1962, where she lived for more than a decade, though making frequent visits to Canada. While writing *The Stone Angel* and her next two Manawaka novels, *A Jest of God* and *The Fire-Dwellers*, Laurence published a number of short stories, which she later collected in her volume *A Bird in the House*. These stories continue the Manawaka cycle and are generally recognized as Laurence's most autobiographical works. In 1974, after accepting a position as writer in residence at Trent University in Canada, Laurence settled permanently in Lakefield, Ontario. That same year she published her final novel, *The Diviners*. The culmination of both her Manawaka cycle and her literary career, *The Diviners* is often regarded as Laurence's most ambitious work and constitutes what the author called her "spiritual autobiography." In addition, the social issues that permeated Laurence's previous fiction—women's individuation, equality among Canada's racial groups, and the literary validation of Canadian experience—are frequently said to find their resolution in this novel. In the years following *The Diviners*, Laurence published *Heart of a Stranger*, a collection of her critical and autobiographical essays, and several children's books. Her memoir, *Dance on the Earth*, was published after her death in 1987.

According to Granville Hicks, the stories in Laurence's first short story collection, *The Tomorrow-Tamer*, "evoke the humor, the drama, the pathos, and the tragedy that result when two kinds of civilization are brought together." Set in Gold Coast during the 1950s, when it and other African nations were moving from colonialism to independence, these stories focus on the experiences of native Africans and British colonialists caught in a changing social, political, and economic atmosphere. Laurence exhibited sympathy toward the African people in these stories, while also displaying understanding and compassion toward the colonialists. In one story from this collection, "The Drummer of All the World," Laurence explored the evolution of the relationship between the narrator, the son of an English missionary, and his childhood friend Kwabena, son of an African nurse, as the political changes around them cause conflict between them. Another often-discussed story from this collection, "Godman's Master," relates the parabolic tale of Godman Pira, a dwarf with oracular powers who is released from bondage by the kindness of a stranger named Moses Adu. Freed to do as he pleases, Godman chooses to serve his redeemer despite Moses's pleas for Godman to enjoy his newfound freedom: " 'There is more to freedom,' [Moses] said, 'than not living in a box.' " Godman is finally released against his will when Moses gets married. A year later when Godman and Moses meet in the street, Godman recounts without bitterness the suffering he endured after Moses let him go and before he established a livelihood as a practicing oracle, concluding, "I have known the worst and the worst and the worst, and yet I live. I fear and fear, and yet I live." Henry Kreisel described "Godman's Master" as "a marvelously condensed account of the evolution of a frightened and exploited little dwarf into a self-reliant human being. . . . [It is] a microcosm of the human condition in general and of the African experience in particular."

A Bird in the House, Laurence's second book of short fiction and the fourth work in her Manawaka series, is a chronologically ordered collection of stories linked by character, setting, and theme that depicts episodes from ten years in the life of narrator Vanessa MacLeod, a ten-year-old girl living with her parents and grandmother MacLeod in her grandmother's house in Manawaka during the economically depressed 1930s. These stories capture such events as the death of Vanessa's grandmother, the birth of her baby brother, the death of her father, and

her family's ensuing move to the home of her austere and puritanical grandfather Connor, whom Vanessa despised for his harshness. The collection ends with grandfather Connor's death and a brief epilogue in which Vanessa returns twenty years later to her grandfather's monumental brick house and finally comes to terms with the house, her ancestors, and her culture. Clara Thomas observed that "for Margaret Laurence, the writing of these stories was a journey back in time and memory, to exorcise the intimidating ghost of her grandfather, and to sublimate her youthful bitterness towards him in the processes of art until all bitterness was burned away and the old man became part of her and Canada's past—grandfather Connor standing for all the proud, tough, puritanical pioneers who were Canada's 'upright men.' "

Laurence's status as a leading chronicler of Canadian life has endured in the years since her death. Her African fiction has been praised for its perceptive and evocative portraits and studied for its insights into her literary development. Her Manawaka cycle is widely considered among the most poignant and important depictions of life in Canada during the twentieth century. Focusing on such issues as freedom, exile, order, disorder, and change, Laurence endowed her fiction with a wide thematic scope to encompass her overarching conviction that human endeavor persist against a disordered and transitional universe. Although *The Tomorrow-Tamer* has been relegated by several critics to the level of apprentice work, *A Bird in the House* is considered by many to approach the accomplishment of her novels. In his study of Laurence's short stories, Frank Birbalsingh echoed the opinions of other critics when he concluded that *A Bird in the House* is among Laurence's greatest literary achievements, as it "treats her main themes with a formal excellence unattained by the rest of her fiction."

(For further information on Laurence's life and career, see *Contemporary Literary Criticism*, Vols. 3, 6, 13, 50, 62; *Contemporary Authors*, Vols. 5-8, rev. ed., 121 [obit]; *Something about the Author*, Vol. 50; and *Dictionary of Literary Biography*, Vol. 53.)

PRINCIPAL WORKS

SHORT FICTION

The Tomorrow-Tamer 1963
A Bird in the House 1970

OTHER MAJOR WORKS

This Side Jordan (novel) 1960
The Prophet's Camel Bell (travel memoir) 1963; also published as *New Wind in a Dry Land*, 1964
The Stone Angel (novel) 1964
A Jest of God (novel) 1966; also published as *Now I Lay Me Down*, 1968; and *Rachel, Rachel*, 1968
Long Drums and Cannons: Nigerian Dramatists and Novelists, 1952-1966 (criticism) 1968
The Fire-Dwellers (novel) 1969
Jason's Quest (children's book) 1970
The Diviners (novel) 1974
Heart of a Stranger (critical and autobiographical essays) 1976
The Olden Days Coat (children's book) 1979

Six Darn Cows   (children's book)   1979
The Christmas Birthday Story   (children's book)   1980
Dance on the Earth   (memoir)   1989

Granville Hicks   (essay date 1964)

[*Hicks was an American literary critic whose famous study* The Great Tradition: An Interpretation of American Literature since the Civil War (*1933*) *established him as the foremost advocate of Marxist critical thought in Depression-era America. During this period, Hicks believed it was the task of literature to confront sociopolitical issues. After 1939 Hicks denounced communist doctrine and adopted a less stringently ideological posture in his literary criticism. In the following excerpt, Hicks praises Laurence's powers of insight and evocation in the stories collected in* The Tomorrow-Tamer.]

The Tomorrow-Tamer [is] a collection of ten stories about present-day Africa. The country in which they are laid, which is in process of transformation from colonialism to independence, is, I suppose, Somaliland. These are not stories to point a political moral or to denounce prejudice. What they do is to evoke the humor, the drama, the pathos, and the tragedy that result when two kinds of civilization are brought together.

Mrs. Laurence sees many facets of the situation. In the first story, for example, **"The Drummer of All the World,"** she introduces a missionary's son who is drawn to the old, traditional ways. Returning to Africa after ten years in England, he finds that the new ways have triumphed: "The old Africa was dying, and I felt suddenly rootless, a stranger in the only land I could call home." Then, on the other hand, there is **"The Pure Diamond Man,"** which pokes fun at an Englishman who is full of romantic ideas about primitive Africa. Another humorous story, **"The Perfume Sea,"** shows what strange forms adaptation can take: an Armenian hairdresser, abandoned by the white ladies who were once his support, succeeds when he advertises, "African Ladies a Speciality."

In **"The Merchant of Heaven"** Mrs. Laurence portrays the dismay of a missionary when he learns what Africa is like—a theme that has often been treated before but which she treats with fresh subtlety. The title story describes an African born in the most primitive sort of society who succeeds in making what seems to be a successful adjustment to technology, only to be destroyed by the conflict of old and new. The story suggests that, though the new is bound to triumph, the old will survive for a long time.

Unusual varieties of conflict are explored. An African girl who has been educated in England is enrolled in a missionary school in the land of her parents, where she is utterly miserable. **"Godman's Master"** is a grotesque account of an eccentric sort of adjustment. **"The Voices of Adamo"** is a tragedy of misunderstanding. **"A Gourdful of Glory"** is both robust comedy and a sardonic comment on the inevitability of disillusionment.

Mrs. Laurence has a style that permits her to make the most of her knowledge of Africa. Here, for example, is part of a description, too long to quote in full, of a small town "growing sluggish under the sedative sun of late morning":

> Pariah dogs on the road snarled over the corpse of a cat; then panting, tongues dribbling, defeated by sun, they crawled back to a shaded corner, where their scabrous hides were fondled by an old man in a hashish dream. Footsteps on the cracked and scorching pavement lagged. Even the brisk shoes of white men slackened and slowed. The market women walked tiredly, their head-trays heavy, their bare feet pressing the warm dust into ripples and dunes. Babies slung on their mothers' backs allowed their heads to loll forward and whimpered at the sweat that made sticky their faces. A donkey brayed disconsolately. Voices droned low. Laughter like melted honey poured slowly.

But more important than the author's ability to give the reader a sense of the country is her insight into its people, black and white. Although she clearly has great sympathy for the natives, she does not plead their cause. She simply makes us see them as they are, in all their bewildered complexity. Each story is built upon an insight, and each is so constructed and written that the insight comes to the reader as a kind of revelation. This is indeed a writer to be welcomed. (pp. 25-6)

Granville Hicks, "Neighbor to the North Makes News," in Saturday Review, *Vol. XLVII, No. 24, June 13, 1964, pp. 25-6.*

Hilda Kirkwood   (essay date 1964)

[*In the following excerpt from a favorable review of* The Tomorrow-Tamer, *Kirkwood compares Laurence with and finds her superior to Canadian writer Ethel Wilson and cites Laurence's principal theme in these stories as "the impact of technical civilization on tribal life, and more specifically on individuals."*]

Margaret Laurence is undoubtedly the Canadian writer of the moment in the field of the short story. With the exception of one or two of Hugh Hood's stories, nothing as fine as her **"Perfume Sea"** and **"A Gourdful of Glory"** [in **The Tomorrow-Tamer**] has come our way since Ethel Wilson wrote *Equations of Love*. Although separated by many years in age and outlook these two writers have some characteristics in common. Dr. Pacey once said that Ethel Wilson had "the innocent eye." Mrs. Laurence has above all the compassionate eye, and they share an infallible ear for revealing conversation in which the voice of the speaker is in his own words. There is also the difference that "innocence" implies in the sense of cool objectivity, the childlike view which is uncommitted. Mrs. Laurence *is* committed, nay involved with her Africans and without the slightest hint of condescension. It is too late for *that* attitude.

Her underlying theme, which runs so movingly through her travelogue, *The Prophet's Camel Bell*, that is, the impact of technical civilization on tribal life, and more specifically on individuals is expressed creatively in her short stories and it is of interest to see the use of her factual material as it is transformed.

"The Perfume Sea" does not stand the test of time quite as well as the incomparable **"Gourdful of Glory"**. The first concerns the adaptation of two white mis-fits to a community changing from white to black control. While the characters of the hairdressers Doree and Archipelago are unforgettable, the tricky ending detracts a little from the pleasure of re-reading.

The character of Mammii Ama in **"A Gourdful of Glory,"** her place in the market world, her naive conception of what freedom means and her natural magnificence are embodied in fifteen short pages of flawless and near perfect story telling. Nothing could have been added or subtracted from this story and Mrs. Laurence has never exceeded it, although this collection is well up to her high standard.

"Godman's Master," one of the most ambitious, is the reverse side of a story called **"The Rain Child."** They are both marvellously perceptive explorations of the cruelty of transition. In the first a Europeonized African comes back to Ghana. His name is Moses and he is indeed a leader into the new world. The scene in the house of the village oracle conjures up the malevolence and the power of African black magic and the charlatanism of the exploiters of credulity. Moses overcomes this evil of his own people and is able through his strength to free another who is a victim of it. It is a subtle and complicated story about the relationship of two black men to one another, to their past and to the bewildering present, and about the limits of slavery and freedom. **"The Rain Child"**, on the other hand, gives us a little African girl born and raised in London and brought back at puberty to a board school for native Ghanian girls. She is unable to make the transition and is destroyed by it as her mother had been by her move in the opposite direction.

In **"The Merchant of Heaven"**, also a masterful story, the ignorance and arrogance of a well-meaning missionary are sadly exposed. He is defeated by Africans fundamentally wiser than he.

Mrs. Laurence's style is simple and powerful. She has a warm and lusty sense of humour which helps to make her sympathetic with the Africans she knows so much better than outsiders who have taken a condescending view of their culture. Her psychological insight, coupled with a poet's eye and a skill which is entirely unpretentious combine in an art which enables us to view what she has seen and understood of the dark countries through her Compassionate Eye.

Hilda Kirkwood, "The Compassionate Eye," in The Canadian Forum, Vol. XLIV, No. 522, July, 1964, p. 94.

Edward Weeks (essay date 1970)

[*Weeks served as editor of the Atlantic Monthly Press from 1928 to 1938, as editor of the* Atlantic Monthly *magazine from 1938 to 1966, and has continued to serve as senior editor and consultant to the Atlantic Monthly Press since 1966 He has written and edited numerous books, including several collections of his own memoirs. In the following excerpt, Weeks provides a favorable review of* A Bird in the House, *commenting on the universal appeal of Laurence's subject matter and themes.*]

[In] **A Bird in the House,** the reader is projected into the midst of a likeable American family who are going about

the business of life with the little grudges and groans, the laughter and the heartache which taken together keep us sane. The fact that the action occurs in a small town in Manitoba during the Depression makes not the slightest difference, for what happens to these people could happen in any American household at a time when there was too much work and too little money.

The special thing about **A Bird in the House** is that the narrative comes to us through the mind and senses of the only daughter, Vanessa MacLeod, who is ten when the story begins and twenty when it ends. There is nothing cute about Vanessa; she is old for her years, intuitive in what she pieces together about her elders, and very partisan in her sympathies.

Her father is a doctor, the hard pressed general practitioner who when he is paid, if he is paid, is more likely to receive a side of bacon or a leathery chicken than a good hard dollar or two. Vanessa is passionately on his side; she knows he is having a hard time and is being unfairly maligned by her grandmother, and she is right. Vanessa rebels against the dominance of age; she watches her Grandfather Connor, a big strong-willed man, who demands that life be ordered to suit him: she watches him intimidate her mother, she watches him drive away the suitors for her unmarried Aunt Edna; and her rage at times is such that she would gladly kick him.

Her mother she adores, and by eavesdropping and by inference she knows more about her mother than she can reasonably explain. She objects to being endowed with a younger brother, and when Baby Roderick is born, Vanessa is torn between jealousy and pity for the depleted woman she loves. Vanessa has an impudent affection for her Uncle Dan, who drinks more than is good for him, and when he reels in unexpectedly for a bit of their sanctimonious Sunday night supper, and begins to quarrel with Grandfather, she is all ears. It takes great skill to keep this story within the expanding horizon of this young girl and yet make it so revealing of the adult world.

Margaret Laurence, the author of this book, is a Canadian, and good writers in Canada have been few and far between, perhaps because the Dominion has been so long linked to the Victorian tradition. But there is nothing parochial about Mrs. Laurence; she has lived with her civil engineer husband in Ghana and Somaliland, and one of the best of her early books, **The Tomorrow-Tamer,** is evidence of her attachment to West Africa. Her country is the country of the heart. Now in **A Bird in the House** she comes home to the continent and the people she knows best.

Edward Weeks, in a review of "A Bird in the House," in The Atlantic Monthly, Vol. 225, No. 3, March, 1970, p. 144.

Honor Tracy (essay date 1970)

[*Tracy is an English travel writer, novelist, short story writer, and translator whose nonfiction work has received high critical praise. In the following excerpt from an unfavorable review of* A Bird in the House, *Tracy faults Laurence for unimaginative and uninspired treatment of her subject matter—childhood—and characterizes these stories as material to mark time until Lau-*

rence returns to the success of her earlier novels and travel essays.]

Some authors, such as Colette, write of their childhood because it was the vivid and delectable period in their lives. Others, like Dickens, do so to free themselves from its memory. Still others, like Thomas Mann, hope to find in this way a clue to a puzzle. But these are specialists, and few. There is a whole corpus of humdrum childhood chronicles which owes its being to the writer's lack of other material. Either he is too young to have acquired any or he has used up—if only for the time being—what there was: whatever the cause, the results are apt to be pretty small beer.

The eight stories, or rather pieces, which make up *A Bird in the House* are no exception. There is the protagonist Vanessa, filling copybooks with romantic tales from the age of 8; there are her grandfather Connor, Irish Protestant and holy terror; her placid yielding grandmother Connor; her harum-scarum but lovable stage-Irish great uncle Dan; her sweet mother Beth; her dedicated doctor father Ewen; her tough, smoking, drinking aunt Edna, whose admirers are scared off by grandfather Connor when not by herself; and her Grandmother McLeod, who boasts of ancient lineage, superior breeding and six different kinds of cake for tea, but is in fact the daughter of an Ontario vet. The time is the great slump of the thirties, the scene a small Canadian town named Manawaka.

Nothing very much happens. Grandfather Connor has a flaming row with Dan one Sunday after luncheon, whereupon grandmother Connor, taking Dan's part, unexpectedly proves a match for the old bully. There is the birth, bleakly supervised by grandmother McLeod, of Vanessa's brother. Her father dies in an epidemic: Vanessa and Beth have to move in with the Connors. Vanessa is allowed to keep a halfbred Husky pup which, ill-treated by a delinquent boy, grows savage and is destroyed behind her back. Edna marries a middle-aged Baptist with an ulcer, who laughs a lot at his own jokes. The war comes, and Vanessa falls in love with an airman who turns out to be married. Grandfather Connor has a stroke and dies; his daughters can hardly believe it, while Vanessa feels nothing like as liberated as she would have expected.

We have been here many times before, which would not matter if there were some urgency in the writing to compensate us. But Mrs. Laurence appears to be wearied by it herself, to the extent of not even editing the tales before incorporating them in a book. Twice, in nearly identical terms, she tells of Ewen's dying after only a week's illness, of Vanessa's withdrawal after his death, of Dan's stage-Irishry, of grandfather Connor's being "still handsome," of his burning a mixture of poplar and birch for economy, of his detestation of card-playing, smoking and drinking; and she was surely a-snooze at her proofs when she passed "the Almighty's contention that wine was a mocker and strong drink was raging."

As often happens when material is thin, there are frequent bursts of jeweled prose—"dirt must not be tracked in upon the blue Chinese carpet with its birds in eternal motionless flight and its waterlily buds caught forever just before the point of opening"—as well as make-weight description that might well be parody—"She turned away and bent her dark head over the big woodstove that said 'McClary's

Range' in shining script across the warming oven at the top." And we can only presume that the rhetorical flourish at the end of almost every piece is intended to pull the thing together and give it a semblance of point.

This is a carping way to go on, but as a novelist and travel writer . . . Mrs. Laurence stands high. Were this collection to be judged by women's magazine standards, she would doubtless receive an A-plus: as it is, let us merely say that she has been marking time, treading water or getting her breath back, and eagerly await her return to form.

> *Honor Tracy, in a review of "A Bird in the House," in* The New York Times Book Review, *April 19, 1970, p. 40.*

George Woodcock   (essay date 1970)

[*Woodcock is a Canadian educator, editor, and critic best known for his biographies of George Orwell and Thomas Merton. He also founded one of Canada's most important literary journals,* Canadian Literature, *and has written extensively on the literature of Canada. In the following excerpt from a review of both* The Tomorrow-Tamer *and* A Bird in the House, *Woodcock notes a marked progression from the former collection to the latter, stating that in* A Bird in the House *Laurence presents "a world far tighter, far more self-consistent, far more directly apprehended and expressed than that of* The Tomorrow-Tamer."*]

As a short story writer, attracting attention in little magazines like *Prism* and university journals like *Queen's Quarterly,* Margaret Laurence first made Canadian readers aware that a new voice of major importance had emerged among them.

Those early stories were exotic in the most literal sense; they emerged from the experiences of years the author spent as an engineer's wife in an Africa growing towards independence. The West African stories—which complement Margaret Laurence's descriptive books on life in Somaliland—were collected in 1964 into a volume entitled *The Tomorrow-Tamer* (title of one of the individual stories), and this has now been republished . . . at the same time as Mrs. Laurence's new book of stories, *A Bird in the House,* makes its appearance.

Whether this simultaneous presentation of the two collections was merely coincidental, or a result of the publisher's planning, it reminds one forcibly of the multiple claims Margaret Laurence has established to being accepted as one of our finest prose writers. For she is much more than an excellent novelist. *The Prophet's Camel Bell,* a narrative of her life in Somaliland, is a combination of autobiography and travel writing of a quality neither genre often attains in Canada. Her *Long Drums and Cannons* is a workmanlike presentation of a vital phase in African literary history. And the volumes under review, taken together, clearly establish her as one of the three best short story writers at work in Canada today.

There are similarities between the two books, but there is also a remarkable progression. Each, of course, has its own kind of unity, its own special mark. In *The Tomorrow-tamer* the physical look and feel of Africa are recorded with a precise and brilliant brushwork; perhaps the impasto is at times rather heavily applied, but the impressions of a tropical environment press so weightily on the stranger who enters it that they often do appear exaggerated to those who have not experienced them. Temporally the stories are united by the fact that all are devoted to the period of Margaret Laurence's own life in Africa, and in theme they are united because each in its way records a displacement; all the characters and their predicaments are involved in a larger and essentially political pattern—the complex of changes that affects individual lives and fates when a country gains its own identity through independence.

The main flaw in *The Tomorrow-tamer* is the obviously didactic intent, for in almost every story there is a moral which the author has not sufficiently absorbed into the fabric of the action. For example, **"A Gourdful of Glory"**, the tale of an African market woman's triumph on the day when freedom comes to her country, has much of the blunt pointmaking that has marred officially approved Russian fiction over the past two decades. Yet the awkwardness with which the theme is handled in that particular instance is exceptional. The best stories follow the pattern of alienation implied in **"The Drummer of All the World"**, which concerns a missionary's son, brought up among Africans and accustomed to think Africa his home, to whom independence and the hostilities it unleashes even among children who shared the same nurse's breast bring a disillusioning realization. "The old Africa was dying," he muses, "and I felt suddenly rootless, a stranger in the only land I could call home."

Here is a truer ring than in **"The Perfume Sea"**, where two European hairdressers who have deliberately cut their roots with the past find a comfortable place in the new Africa. **"The Perfume Sea"** is so evocatively written that the surface charm of the story at first woos one into accepting its pleasing fantasy, but one is unconvinced by the denouement, which projects a dream brilliantly but hollowly fulfilled. It is the stories which accept that for strangers African dreams will go unfulfilled, which apply this knowledge even—in the case of **"The Rain Child"**—to Africans returning from Europe, that are the most urgently felt pieces in *The Tomorrow-tamer.* In comparison, the stories about Africans struggling with the changing world that engulfs them have a remoteness of feeling, almost as if one were reading a translation, and, indeed, in a way they are translations, for, however sensitively Margaret Laurence may have absorbed and understood the traditions of Ghanaian peoples, we are always aware that she is expressing them in an alien idiom.

Thus, though I regard a third of the stories in *The Tomorrow-tamer* as remarkably successful, and admire the atmospheric quality of all of them, I find the book as a whole incompletely satisfying. I would find it hard to justify a similar judgment of *A Bird in the House.* For here one enters a world far tighter, far more self-consistent, far more directly apprehended and expressed than that of *The Tomorrow-tamer.*

A Bird in the House is a group of stories about a girl growing from childhood into adolescence in a fictional Manitoba town. The stories are populated for the most part by the same cast of characters: Vanessa MacLeod, her parents, grandparents, aunts and uncles, with other small-town characters appearing on the periphery of this tightly-

knit world of two connected but rival families, the professional MacLeods and the pioneering Orange-tinged Connors. Story flows into story, to such an extent that when they are collected a perceptible development from one to the other becomes evident, and it is hard to know whether to define *A Bird in the House* as a collection of tales or as a loosely knit and unconventional novel.

The autobiographical content of *A Bird in the House,* the solid basis of personal experience, is even more evident than in *The Tomorrow-tamer.* Much in the earlier book was obviously invented, but, though there are clearly many wholly imaginary incidents in *A Bird in the House,* one feels that as a whole it is an illuminated series of variations on Margaret Laurence's own experience of a depression-age childhood in a Manitoba small town very similar to Manawaka, where the action of *A Bird in the House* is enacted.

By predicament as well as by place the people of *A Bird in the House* are united, and here—as in *The Tomorrow-tamer*—the sense of alienation is crucial, though now it is not the transformation of a society so much as the failure of a society that sets the tone. Society in general having failed, the natural social units become important again, and families are willy-nilly reunited, Aunt Edna coming home from jobless Winnipeg, Dr. MacLeod moving in with his widowed mother because his patients can no longer pay him in cash; the depression in fact renews the pioneer intensity of relationships within small and threatened groups, and that intensity Margaret Laurence mordantly evokes.

A Bird in the House shows the same power of creating a convincing background as *The Tomorrow-tamer,* but here, because it is not an exotic setting that is being portrayed, the brushwork is even more exact, while the colours are modulated in sombre tones rather than in clashing vividnesses. But it is not merely the setting that is so superbly appropriate and sufficient in *A Bird in the House.* Perhaps the most notable achievement is the skill with which Margaret Laurence has shown the lives and emotions of older people through a child's eye, until in the end the child moves into the age when those emotions become identical with hers, and the perceiver becomes the perceived. (pp. 82-4)

George Woodcock, "Jungle and Prairie," in Canadian Literature, *No. 45, Summer, 1970, pp. 82-4.*

Henry Kreisel (essay date 1970)

[*Kreisel is an Austrian-born Canadian educator, writer, and critic whose short stories have appeared in many Canadian magazines and several anthologies of Canadian and American short fiction. In the following essay, Kreisel characterizes Laurence as a short story writer in the classic tradition: her works display strong, clear narrative lines; well-defined characters; and clean, simple prose.*]

Some ten years ago I wrote an article on Margaret Laurence, at a time when she was not yet widely recognized [see Further Reading list]. It began as a review of her first novel, *This Side Jordan,* but since I had been reading some of her African stories in *Tamarack Review* and *Prism,* I expanded my review to deal with these stories, especially with **"Godman's Master,"** which seemed to me a marvellously condensed account of the evolution of a frightened and exploited little dwarf into a self-reliant human being who can say in the end, 'I have known the worst and the worst and the worst, and yet I live. I fear and fear, and yet I live.' It seemed to me then a microcosm of the human condition in general and of the African experience in particular.

Re-reading the story now, I still find it immensely moving. It is still my favourite among the African stories that Mrs Laurence collected in **The Tomorrow-Tamer and Other Stories,** first published in 1963 and now re-published in the New Canadian Library series.

Reading the ten stories collected there along with the eight stories brought together in **A Bird in the House** gives one a very clear view of precisely what kind of a short-story writer Margaret Laurence is. She stands very clearly in the tradition of the classic story tellers. Her stories are strongly plotted and the narrative line is always very clear. She goes about her business in a brisk, straight-forward manner. She really *tells* a story, and the reader certainly always knows where he is. There is a very clear beginning, a middle, and an end. Her stories usually move to a decisive climactic moment. The prose is clean and simple and beautifully shaped; the characters are precisely observed and sharply portrayed.

All these are characteristic virtues of Mrs Laurence's work, and they make that work among the most distinguished now produced in Canada. At the same time one must note that she is not very adventurous in exploring the possibilities of the short-story form. The structure of her stories rarely varies. I am not saying that this is a fault, I simply note it as a fact. In a way, I wouldn't wish it otherwise, for clearly her approach serves her in general very well indeed. Occasionally (in **"The Perfume Sea,"** for example, or in **"The Merchant of Heaven"**), the resolution is a trifle pat, slick even, but for the most part she avoids the temptation of too neat a resolution in order to bring a story to a close.

When I first read the African stories, they had a certain topical as well as artistic interest for me. Africa was very much in the news, as one after another the countries of the continent gained its independence. The bright new dawn was coming, the phoenix was rising, and in a way Margaret Laurence was supplying an emotional background to events. Not that she was ever a topical writer, and that is why her stories have retained their freshness. Her Africa is nevertheless the Africa of the transition from colonial status to at least formal independence. She is concerned with showing the impact of the white man on the native Africans in so far as this impact is made manifest in the acts of missionaries, soldiers, and minor administrators, and in the ambiguous relationships that are the result of a clash of cultures.

The point of view in the stories, both implicit and explicit, is that of the liberal tradition as this is embodied in a long line of English writers, for example, in E. M. Forster's *A Passage to India*. This point of view is implicit in the dramatic situations she chooses, and it is made explicit in a passage like this from **"The Drummer of All the World"**:

We were conquerors in Africa, we Europeans.

Some despised her, that bedraggled queen we had unthroned, and some loved her for her still-raging magnificence, her old wisdom. But all of us sought to force our will upon her. My father thought he was bringing Salvation to Africa. I no longer know what salvation is. I only know that one man cannot find it for another man, and one land cannot bring it to another.

Mrs Laurence's characters are caught in the process of change. Most of them have an extremely strong sense of their roots, but they find themselves suddenly inhabiting a familiar landscape in which the landmarks have mysteriously shifted, so that though everything seems the same, nothing is the same. The characters know who they are, but not exactly where they are (for example, in **"The Tomorrow-Tamer," "The Voices of Adamo,"** and **"Godman's Master"**). And what is true of the Africans is also true of the whites. Their Africa, too, is changing; they, too, live in a familiar country that has suddenly become a strange place.

Political Africa is in the background of the stories. It enters the narratives for the most part obliquely, as for example in **"A Gourdful of Glory,"** where Mamii Ama discovers that you still have to pay bus-fare even after Freedom.

In **A Bird in the House,** Margaret Laurence returns to her own roots, deep, deep in Manitoba. We are far, far from Africa, and yet perhaps not so very far. For here, too, we see a landscape that is at once familiar and yet extraordinarily strange, a landscape of the memory. We are given here the Manitoba of the 1930's, a bleak, pinched, puritanical environment rendered for us by a young girl, Vanessa MacLeod. Yet the voice is curiously mature. It is really an older Vanessa recalling what the young Vanessa experienced. The people who have imposed themselves most strongly on her imagination are the grandparents, especially Grandfather Connor, and her Aunt Edna, a woman full of life and vigour, thwarted, but never completely crushed by the times and the environment in which she must live. The Connors are among the finest character portrayals Mrs Laurence has given us.

Both the African and Canadian stories are marked by a strong, elegiac tone. In both, the old and the very young predominate. Both celebrate (that is the word I want, though it may seem strange to use it in this context) worlds that are in the process of passing or have already passed. Margaret Laurence is anything but sentimental about the world she renders. There is no suggestion that the old world—either in Africa or in the Canadian West—was in any way superior to the new. There is no nostalgia. There is only the honest rendering of a landscape, both physical and emotional, that made a powerful impact on the writer's imagination and in the act of recalling and shaping becomes a timeless place. And that is a kind of celebration. (pp. 91-4)

> *Henry Kreisel, "A Familiar Landscape," in The Tamarack Review, No. 55, 1970, pp. 91-2, 94.*

Clara Thomas   (essay date 1972)

[*Thomas is a Canadian educator, critic, and biographer whose extensive works on Canadian writers and litera-*

ture include Margaret Laurence (*1969*) *and* The Manawaka World of Margaret Laurence (*1975*). *In the following excerpt, Thomas surveys the stories in the collections* The Tomorrow-Tamer *and* A Bird in the House, *focusing on the authorial "voice" Laurence assumes in these tales.*]

Margaret Laurence lived in Africa from 1950 to 1957, for the first two years in Somaliland and then in Ghana. **The Tomorrow-Tamer** stories are all set in Ghana just before it became an independent nation; they demonstrate from many angles the effects of the processes of independence on individual Ghanaians and on the bewildered Europeans who were caught up in the agonising splendour of the hopes of an emergent nation. More than that, in every line they give evidence of the enormous impact of Africa and her African experiences on the creative talents of Margaret Laurence. Very seldom has "culture shock" had such a positive outcome—in the ranks of Canadian writers one has to go back to Susanna Moodie to find a complement, an Englishwoman whose experiences of early Canada jolted her into the creative energy that her *Roughing It in the Bush* displays. There, however, the analogy ends, for Susanna's powers, though strong, were all fragmented and finally unrealised; in contrast, there is a stunning success of technique in Margaret Laurence's stories, an unerring instinct to suit the form to the substance and the voice to the character. Furthermore, and more important, Africa was in every way a positive, releasing experience for Margaret Laurence—every story gives evidence of her intense sympathy for the Ghanaian people and the African culture that was so new to her.

The Tomorrow-Tamer stories are all built from the point of view of the ironist—not the ironist who assumes superiority and so condescends to her subjects, but the ironist who sees at once the immense vitality and the enormous contradictions of joy and pain, of hopes and achievements amongst the people of an emergent nation. Margaret Laurence indicates her own assessment of her three African-set works, *This Side Jordan, The Prophet's Camel Bell* and **The Tomorrow-Tamer,** when she says [in "Ten Years' Sentences," *Canadian Literature*, No. 41 (Summer 1969)]:

> They were written out of the milieu of a rapidly-ending colonialism and the emerging independence of African countries. They are not entirely hopeful books, nor do they, I think, ignore some of the inevitable casualties of social change, both African and European, but they do reflect the predominantly optimistic outlook of many Africans and many Western liberals in the late 1950s and early 1960s.

Perhaps the first and most essential challenge to any writer is to find the right "voice" for his material; in every one of **The Tomorrow-Tamer** stories, the main character is, in some large sense, an outsider. Some of the stories have a first person narrator and some a third, but in each case, Mrs. Laurence, an outsider herself, can readily identify with the particular person who tells the story or about whom the story is told. So, in **"The Drummer of All the World,"** Matthew, whose missionary father thought he was bringing salvation to Africa, is the speaker and he tells the story of his past out of the sadness and rejection of his present:

> Since then very little has happened to me. I do my job adequately but not brilliantly. My post is to be given to an African soon . . . I shall be leaving soon. . . . the squalor, the exultation, the pain. I shall be leaving it all. But—O Kwabena, do you think I will ever forget?

In **"The Merchant of Heaven,"** Mr. Ketteridge, who has been long enough in Africa to know and to accept that he will always, essentially, be an alien, tells the story of Brother Lemon who comes to Africa an "apostle . . . replete with faith as a fresh-gauged mosquito is with blood." Brother Lemon fails in his "work" of saving souls and leaves, bewildered and disappointed, but still invincibly armoured with zeal and blind complacency. But Ketteridge bought The Black Christ painted by his African friend, Danso, and,

> Sometimes, when I am able to see through black and white, until they merge and cease to be separate or apart, I look at those damaged creatures clustering so despairingly hopeful around the Son of Man, and it seems to me that Brother Lemon, after all, is one of them.

"The Rain-Child" is narrated by Violet Nedden, who knows that she is not only an outsider in Africa but that she is also, irrevocably, an exile from England, her homeland. She can understand and sometimes help others, like young Ruth and the orphan child Ayesha, who are fated to be forever homeless:

> Sitting in my garden and looking at the sun on the prickly pear and the poinsettia, I think of that island of grey rain where I must go as a stranger, when the time comes, while others must remain as strangers here.

Similarly, the point and sympathy of each one of the stories which is narrated in the third person rests on an outsider. In **"The Voices of Adamo,"** Adamo has lost his tribe, his home and therefore his true identity; he believes that he has found a new home in the British regimental band, but his pathetic transference of love and loyalty only ends in tragedy. In **"Godman's Master,"** Godman Pira had not been part of the world of men as long as he had been used as a slave-oracle by a fetish priest. He finally finds his manhood and his life's meaning in freely doing what before he had been forced to do by his master. . . . It is not such an easy thing, to find where the laughter is hidden, like gold in the rock. One has to be skilled for this work. The *pirafo* used to be fine jesters, and now, perhaps again . . .

> And Godman Pira waved to Moses and hopped up to take his place with the other performers on the broad and grimy stage.

This ending fans out beyond Godman Pira to enclose in its irony all of us, "performers on the broad and grimy stage," the world of men.

In **"The Perfume Sea,"** the delicately fantastic, funny and moving pair, Mr. Archipelago and Dorree are drawn together in their loneliness and their sensitivity one to the other. They survive in the new Africa because they adapt to its requirements and so for them, finally, the brine-laden wind from the sea, which Mr. Archipelago calls *"eau d'exile,"* was not only "bitter and salt, but to them it was warm, too."

Only the final story, **"A Gourdful of Glory,"** is told from the inside, by Mamii Ama, who stands for everything positive and hopeful in the newly independent Ghana. Then, when Free-Dom actually comes, Mamii Ama becomes the outsider herself—she was humiliated by the worldy wisdom of the white woman, who knew that the buses would not automatically give her free rides, and that there could be no sudden transformation to a land of flowing milk and honey for everyone. But Mamii Ama regains her faith—and so the book ends:

> Inspired, Mamii Ama lifted the gourd high above her head, and it seemed to her that she held not a brittle brown calabash, but the world. She held the world in her strong and comforting hands. 'Free-Dom he come', she cried, half in exultation, and half in longing. 'Free-Dom be heah now, dis minute!'

Margaret Laurence has a gift for the expressing of tone and mood through a turn of phrase in conversation or through the judicious phrasings of a double-edged word. She has also a highly developed instinct for a key dramatic scene which will be the climax of the story's movement and will bring about its swift denouement. And she has a vivid power of description—of scenes and people given full dimensional quality by their details of sight, sound and smell, and of characters like Mr. Archipelago, who by their very vivid strangeness take on life in our imaginations. Most importantly, all of these stories are infused and buoyed up by Mrs. Laurence's immense excitement about the land of Ghana and its people. Her enthusiasm is lit by understanding and a great sympathy, but nevertheless, her stories have qualities of disengagement and detachment which keep them on a middle range of irony, muting their satire on the one end of the scale and their tragedy on the other. In Africa, Margaret Laurence was very aware of herself as irrevocably alien, like the characters her stories illuminate. . . . (pp. 25-8)

The stories that make up *A Bird in the House* are, in one sense, told very much from the inside, for these are autobiographical stories and the facts of Margaret Laurence's childhood are the facts of Vanessa Macleod's. With this important difference—Mrs. Laurence has inevitably used every writer's requirement and prerogative—the selection of *some* facts, *some* details and *some* occasions and the heightening and highlighting of these in the interests of her art. The writer who sets out to write a memoir or an autobiography is inevitably selective also: but the writer who undertakes to use autobiographical detail in the compressed, demanding genre of the short story is particularly bound to be so. Consequently, we have the skeleton of a life-story and yet by no means *simply* a life-story: the highs and lows of Vanessa Macleod's developing take on some of the broader implications of the painful yet glorious process of every child's growing up and out into a wider world.

In another sense, as in the African stories, Margaret Laurence is illuminating the experiences of an outsider; for Vanessa, as every child must be, is a stranger to the world she observes around her. And throughout the stories she is seeking and finding, often painfully, keys both for understanding and for entering the adult world. Vanessa, her father Ewen, a doctor, and her mother, Beth, live with her grandmother Macleod in the Canadian prairie town of Manawaka in the 1930s. She visits grandfather and grand-mother Connor in the Brick House, grandmother Connor dies, a baby brother is born and her father dies. Then Vanessa, her mother and small brother go to live with the Connor grandparents, her aunt Edna is married, a young cousin goes mad, grandfather Connor dies—and finally Vanessa arrives at the very edge of adulthood and of Manawaka, poised and impatient for flight into the larger world.

There is a great deal of death and a great deal of sadness in the background facts of these stories. There is also the milieu of the depression and drought years of the '30s which stunted opportunity and sometimes bred bitterness in two generations of Canadians. And there are the twin hazards of grandmother Macleod's pseudo-helplessness and disappointed gentility and grandfather Connor's baffled resentment that everyone cannot be as tough and successful as he has been in his pioneer generation. But through all the battling, Vanessa grows up, always vulnerable, but increasing in understanding and sympathy, and with a toughness of will that finally links her to her grandfather.

Grandfather Connor is, in fact, the hero of *A Bird in the House:* he had been a pioneer in Western Canada; he had cowed his children and infuriated his granddaughter; but in his own inarticulate way, he had loved his wife and had been as pitifully bewildered by the circumstances which defeated him as he had been justifiably proud of his achievements. Though Vanessa detested him, she grew to pity and finally to understand and respect him. For Margaret Laurence, the writing of these stories was a journey back in time and memory, to exorcise the intimidating ghost of her grandfather, and to sublimate her youthful bitterness towards him in the processes of art until all bitterness was burned away and the old man became part of her and Canada's past—grandfather Connor standing for all the proud, tough, puritanical pioneers who were Canada's "upright men". . . . (pp. 28-9)

The adult world seen through the eyes of a child, the maturing of the child, innocence to experience—this is so populated a branch of literature as to constitute a genre in itself. To attempt to stake out a new claim in the field is certainly a challenge to a writer but at the same time a very great hazard. Here again the problem of "voice" is paramount: how was Margaret Laurence to present Vanessa's world as the child understood it unless she let Vanessa speak the story? How was she to project the understanding of Vanessa's older self on the child's world, to fuse the two understandings, to juxtapose them or to blend them in harmony? Her solution could be compared to a technique of double exposures: her narrator became Vanessa, the woman, who both takes on the voice and the attributes of the child she was and, at the same time, remains her present self, far older and wiser in compassion. Often the two Vanessas blend perfectly, with acceptance but not indulgence of the older self for the younger; sometimes they quite obviously separate in their tones and the dimensions of their knowledge, but still successfully. . . . Sometimes the technique is not successful and the child, Vanessa, seems too contrived, with a cuteness as embarrassing as a bad pun: "My grandmother was a Mitigated Baptist. I knew this because I heard my father say, 'at least she's not an unmitigated Baptist. . . .' " But failures are rare because Margaret Laurence's taste and restraint in the handling of her material are remarkably sure and successful.

What finally becomes somewhat oppressive in the collected stories, however (and this would not have been so as they were singly written and published), are the restrictions of their circumference and the sameness of their final effects. Vanessa's world is a small circle and it is constantly impinged upon or threatened by death, the depression, and the fears and effects of two world wars. It is a world of harsh edges, muted colours or no colours, in contrast to the irrepressible brilliance of Margaret Laurence's African world. Its surfaces are all rough and it is dominated by grandfather and the Brick House, symbols of the roughness of all the elements that buffeted Vanessa into maturity. . . . (p. 30)

Moreover, though the episodes are convincingly unique to Vanessa (the sensitive but tough-minded child we see growing through these stories) and though the vivid phrases are true (both to Margaret Laurence's talent and the place, time and idioms of her people), there is a fated sameness about Vanessa's path. Each story ends with some recognition that is a step towards maturity; sometimes we finish with a limited child's point of view, as in **"To Set Our House in Order":**

> I could not really comprehend these things, but I sensed their strangeness, their disarray. I felt that whatever God might love in this world, it was certainly not order.

And sometimes the adult Vanessa's perceptions finally beam through to lighten the gloom of grandfather Connor in her background:

> Many years later, when Manawaka was far away from me, in miles and in time, I saw one day in a museum the Bear Mask of the Haida Indians. It was a weird mask. The features were ugly and yet powerful. The mouth was turned down in an expression of solemn rage. The eyes were empty caverns, revealing nothing. Yet as I looked, they seemed to draw my own eyes towards them, until I imagined I could see somewhere within that darkness a look which I knew, a lurking bewilderment. I remembered then that in the days before it became a museum piece, the mask had concealed a man.

There is, however, an overriding justification for the collection of these stories; they do give us more in their sum than in their several separate entities. In collection they make a unique contribution to our literature in a particular Canadian time and place, under the deadening blows of the depression and drought of the '30s. The voice of Aunt Edna with its carry-over of "I'll tell the cock-eyed world" slang of the '20s is the voice of a Canadian generation whose chances were killed, or at the least constrained, for a decade. Grandfather Connor's attitudes estranged him from his children and his grandchild, but his concept of a rigid, authoritarian, patriarchal society was as valid to his generation's vision as it was alien to theirs. And there is, throughout the course of these stories, a cumulative building to the character of grandfather; he moves away from Vanessa's childish conception of him as an overbearing, domineering old man to take on a mythic proportion. And finally, in **"Jericho's Brick Battlements,"** the last story. Margaret Laurence intends—and

achieves—a real catharsis of pity for the man and admiration for his type. . . .

> He looked exactly the same as he had in life. The same handsome eagle-like features. His eyes were closed. It was only when I noticed the closed eyes that I knew that the blue ice of his stare would never blaze again. I was not sorry that he was dead. I was only surprised. Perhaps I had really imagined that he was immortal, Perhaps he even was immortal, in ways which it would take me half a lifetime to comprehend. . . .

> "You know something, Beth? Aunt Edna went on, "I can't believe he's dead. It just doesn't seem possible."

> "I know what you mean," my mother said. "Edna—were we always unfair to him?"

> My aunt swallowed a mouthful of rye and ginger ale.

> "Yes, were were," she said. "And he was to us, as well."

Aunt Edna's ironic voice implicates us all. Here finally, as in **"Godman's Master,"** Margaret Laurence has fanned out beyond Vanessa's story to enclose us in recognition of the inevitability of estrangement and the possibility of understanding between generations and among all men. (pp. 31-2)

> *Clara Thomas, "The Short Stories of Margaret Laurence," in* World Literature Written in English, *Vol. 11, No. 1, April, 1972, pp. 25-33.*

Patricia Morley   (essay date 1976)

[*Morley is a Canadian educator and critic who has written numerous studies of Canadian writers, including Margaret Laurence (1981). In the following excerpt, Morley identifies the "search for spiritual freedom" as a recurring theme in Laurence's short fiction, which the author explores through "patterns of imagery, characterization, and narrative structure."*]

The vision which underlies Margaret Laurence's fiction is remarkably unified. Whether one considers her long fiction or her short, her African oeuvre or her work with a Canadian setting, Laurence's theme of themes remains the search for spiritual freedom, and the difficulties inherent in that search. This paper is concerned with this recurring theme in Laurence's short stories as seen through patterns of imagery, characterization, and narrative structure.

There is nothing sentimental about this vision. Man is rarely free, and no one knows this better than Laurence. The other side of the coin is bondage, entrapment, alienation. Some of the bonds are forged by her characters for themselves; some are imposed from without, through various ironies of circumstances beyond their control. Alienation and exile are seen as forms of bondage or psychic slavery. In story after story, Laurence depicts an often agonizing struggle to break these bonds, to overcome alienation, to achieve an integration both personal and social which is imaged as a freedom to love and to accept love, to share, to meet, to touch. Such a state, Laurence implies, is our spiritual home, the human goal, the grail. In stories where the mode is primarily ironic and tragic, the focus is upon the forces which block movement towards this goal. In stories where the structure is comic, the characters are successfully engaged, difficulties notwithstanding, in the long trek home.

"The Rain Child" (1962) is an early version of the theme. In, many ways, this African story prefigures Hagar's experience in *The Stone Angel,* even to the phrase "Pride has so often been my demon. . . ." Every character in the story save Kwaale, the beautiful young African girl, is and remains an exile. And even Kwaale is excluded, by her youth and limited experience, from the full sharing which her own culture expects and demands. The implacable Kwaale has no pity for Ruth, the African girl who is culturally white but imprisoned in a black skin; Kwaale has not yet experienced alienation and suffering. She has never been a stranger in the land of Egypt, Violet Nedden thinks, using the archetypal story from the Old Testament which underlies Hagar's name and experience. Both teacher and headmistress are exiles, and Violet's love for the country only deepens her sense of exclusion from it. Other exiles include Ayesha, the child prostitute, and Yindo, the Dagomba boy from the northern desert who expects no mercy from strangers in a foreign land. " 'No got bruddah dis place,' " Yindo stammers fearfully, when he is discovered with Ruth. The teachers, Ruth, her equally displaced parents, Ayesha, and Yindo are all strangers in a hard land, outcasts, rain children. One type of rain is tears. In Laurence's poignant image for the human condition, the English climate and the tropical (the cause of Violet's deformity), the contrasting and excluding cultures, and the resulting human suffering, are brilliantly coalesced.

The title image of **"The Half-Husky,"** like the rain child and the stone angel, suggests the paradoxes of human nature and experience. The creature who is half dog half wolf, half domesticated half wild, half loving half vicious, is also Everyman, set in a world which typically evokes both responses. In **"The Rain Child,"** Ruth begins to learn hatred by being hated: "I noticed then how much thinner she had grown and how her expression had altered. She no longer looked like a child. Her eyes were as implacable as Kwaale's." Similarly, Nanuk learns to hate through Harvey's sadistic tormenting. After the pepper incident, Vanessa notices how wolfish Nanuck looks, with his lips drawn back in a devil's grin. Harvey's stone transforms the dog into a demented fury, and its young owner Vanessa into someone who wants to injure Harvey "in any way available."

The stolen telescope forces Vanessa to face the conditions which have spawned Harvey. The ugliness of the human relationships involved are reflected in the physical squalor, the rust, the weeds, the disorder. His aunt's hatred and contempt for her nephew is absolute, and evokes the same feelings in Harvey. Vanessa is like Ruth, reacting to the story of Ayesha's slavery with naive horror, "the look of someone who recognizes for the first time the existence of cruelty" (**"The Rain Child"**). Cruelty results in bondage. Nanuk and Harvey are "safe to go free." Harvey's aunt, along with the rest of mankind, appears to be on the loose thanks to some cosmic laxity or neglect. The sins of the fathers are indeed visited upon the children unto the third and fourth generation. It is a bitter story, reflecting the dark side of Laurence's vision.

"Godman's Master" is my favourite from the African collection, possibly because the dwarf 's experience is an analogue for the housewife's, as well as for mankind's. Whether read as a statement on Women's Liberation or simply as a universal parable, the story is both witty and profound. Perhaps Laurence intuits that the seriousness of the theme demands humour. The introductory description of the storm, for example, whimsically compares the egrets, wrapped in their cloak wings, to flocks of sorcerers. The little man squeaks, or scuttles, now a cockroach, now a mouse. And the names! Moses Adu is the dwarf 's first deliverer, the one who leads the little man out of slavery yet who cannot bestow freedom. *Moses:* the lawgiver, the Pharaoh-confronter, who led his people towards but not into the Promised Land; *Adu:* adieu, or à Dieu; *Godman,* called "halfman," the little barely human creature or "man-forsaken little god" who aspires to be a free man and who grows into that stature. God-in-man? God's man? In the full context of the story, the name seems to carry these suggestions. Moses' wife is called Mercy. Freedom, in Laurence's fiction, is seen to be a gift which is both a mercy bestowed and also a birthright to be won through infinite desire and struggle, like Jacob wrestling with the Angel, an archetypal narrative which Laurence takes from Genesis and uses repeatedly in her fiction. The witty title suggests both the African who refuses to continue in the role of master, and God, or perhaps human destiny, which includes freedom.

Once free of the village priest, Godman would prefer simply to exchange an unkind master for a kind one. Freedom can be frightening. To work for money, to support himself and be responsible for himself, appears an impossible task. He is quite willing to keep house. If he learned man's work half as well as woman's, Moses tells him, he would be a great success. As Moses begins to understand Godman's dependence, even worship, he is horrified: " 'There is more to freedom,' he said, 'than not living in a box.' . . . He and Godman were bound together with a cord more delicate, more difficult to see, than any spun by the children of Ananse. Yet it was a cord which could strangle."

So the unwilling Godman has the opportunity for freedom forced upon him. And he survives. In Moses' next view of him, a year later, Godman's smallness is his glory: "There sat Godman, flamboyant as a canna lily in scarlet turban and green robe." Man the truant, *pace* Pratt. Godman's story is as flamboyant as his costume. " 'I have known the worst and the worst and the worst,' " he concludes, " 'and yet I live. I fear and fear, and yet I live.' " As must we all, Moses adds. The story closes with the tiny descendant of court jesters taking his place with the other performers "on the broad and grimy stage": the human comedy, African-style.

The stories which make up *A Bird in the House* are linked by character, setting, theme. The primary link is formed by the narrative voice, that of the child-cum-woman Vanessa McLeod. These links are so effective that the collection might be called a novel, and more than one critic has made this claim. Laurence grants that the net effect is similar to that of a novel, but describes the flow-lines as being vertical rather than horizontal, as they are in a typical long fiction. The threads of Vanessa's life are presented separately, not simultaneously. But the narrative voice, with its control over fictive time, is handled in the same way in these stories as it is in Laurence's novels.

Vanessa is a budding writer, curious and observant, who describes herself as "a professional listener." This is obviously a good device for a first-person narrator. Comically, Vanessa sometimes conceals herself by sitting quietly in plain view, and sometimes puts her ear to one of her listening posts, round holes in the bedroom floors which had once been used for stovepipes.

The motif of entrapment is more frequent here than that of achieved freedom. But Vanessa moves through these stories of pain and disappointment, of laughter and love and hatred, on her own path of slow growth, towards the partial freedom of her early adulthood. She will go to university, a freedom denied to her mother. Yet in some indefinable way, Vanessa does not feel nearly as free as she had expected to feel. The book ends with Grandfather Connor's death and, in a short epilogue, Vanessa's revisiting (twenty years later) the Brick House that had been both her grandfather's home and his monument.

The Brick House, a central metaphor in the collection, is identified with her grandfather, with his inherited Scots-Puritan culture, and, ultimately, with Vanessa herself. She has feared and fought the old man; yet he proclaims himself in her veins. Similarly, Laurence came in maturity to recognize the strengths, the desirable qualities, of a culture she had once despised for its harshness. Fortress or prison? The Brick House is introduced in the first story with military metaphors: it is "sparsely windowed as some crusader's embattled fortress in a heathen wilderness"; its trees are "sternly protective," its guillotine lawn mower beheads the wildflowers and "helmeted snapdragons stood in precision".

The last two views of the Brick House, however, evoke different moods and attitudes. We see, first, its stable-garage, home of the MacLaughlin-Buick: "I remembered myself remembering driving in it with him, in the ancient days when he seemed as large and admirable as God", and second, its neglected state of disrepair. *How are the mighty fallen in the midst of battle.* The trumpets are sounded and Jericho's Brick battlements are fallen down. Once again, the story's title provides the central image and the theme. But Vanessa has come to terms with the Brick House, with her ancestors and her culture, and passed beyond.

A Bird in the House, taken as a whole, is the story of Vanessa's growth. It is her spiritual odyssey, as *The Stone Angel* is Hagar's. Like the novel, its themes are bondage, flight, and freedom. Vanessa is ten in the first story, eleven in the second and third. In the fourth, where her father dies, she is between the ages of twelve and seventeen; in the fifth, between eleven and eighteen; in the sixth, between six and thirteen. She is fifteen in the seventh, and between twelve and twenty in the last. There is a development in the type of suffering, the quality of pain endured, which parallels Vanessa's chronological growth. The first three stories deal with love and loss through death, on a relatively simple level. The fourth connects the death of her father with Vanessa's loss of religious faith. The next three introduce the older adolescent to social evils too complex to be cured by any individual; to psychic depression and breakdown; and to sadism. Finally, the last story

treats of two flights to freedom (Vanessa's, and Aunt Edna's) using apocalyptic images of a heavenly chariot and victorious warfare. Near the beginning of the last story, a depressed Vanessa fears that her fictional heroine Marie is trapped for life. Then the twelve-year-old girl clambers into Grandfather's old car and recalls driving with him in early childhood: "*A-hoo-gah! A-hoo-gah! I was gazing with love and glory at my giant grandfather as he drove his valiant chariot through all the streets of this world*". Aunt Edna escapes by marrying a local man. Her suitor works for the C.N.R.: again, the travel archetype. Grandfather's basement rocking chair is a comic chariot which airs his rage. And Vanessa's last action is to drive away from Manawaka. Free?

"The Sound of the Singing" contrasts freedom with bondage through the medium of three personalities. Grandfather Connor's "upright" nature is matched by his brother's "downright" one. Dan is considered by the townsfolk to be downright lazy, downright worthless, a downright fool. Bound by his moral concepts, Grandfather feels like a caged man at the enforced idleness of Sunday, and holds his family in a kind of bondage. Yet he supports his family, and his brother too. Neither man is truly free. Grandfather lacks Dan's *joie de vivre,* a quality to which Vanessa is drawn and which she symbolically pursues at the story's end. Road, journey, quest. Balanced between unpleasant rectitude and irresponsible, childlike gaiety stands Grandmother Connor: "Acceptance was at the heart of her. I don't think in her own eyes she ever lived in a state of bondage. To the rest of the family, thrashing furiously and uselessly in various snarled dilemmas, she must often have appeared to live in a state of perpetual grace, but I am certain she didn't think of it that way, either." The quotation is from **"The Mask of the Bear."** But in the first story, it is Grandmother Connor who rebukes a self-righteous lack of charity in her husband and welcomes Dan back into their house.

The second story contrasts two kinds of spiritual order, one obvious and rigid (which Vanessa rejects), and one subtle, immaterial, free. The latter is large enough to accommodate such radically different personalities as Grandmother MacLeod, her husband, and her son. The description of Vanessa's paternal grandmother, "unaware that her hair was bound grotesquely like white-feathered wings in the snare of her coarse night-time helmet," evokes multiple suggestions of entrapment and freedom. Grandmother's blue Chinese carpet features birds in eternal motionless flight, and water-lily buds "caught forever just before the point of opening."

God loves Order, she tells Vanessa. By *order,* Grandmother means balanced accounts, a well-stocked cellar, and all emotions under lock and key. Fear and expressed weakness are disorders which do not belong in Grandmother's universe. She yearns for social prestige, whereas her husband yearned towards classical Greek drama, and his son, Vanessa's father, for travel to exotic lands. These unfulfilled yearnings are caught up in Vanessa's musings at the story's end, as she thinks of the leather-bound volumes of Greek, the elaborate tea-table, and the pictures of leopards and green seas." She knows that her father has lied to his mother about the way in which his brother died, although, in Grandmother's phrase, "the MacLeods do not tell lies." Even the older Vanessa (for the narrative voice speaks from two points in time, simultaneously) understands only that the world before her is not subject to order of the type advocated by Grandmother MacLeod.

Laurence's reader, however, has been given an anagogic image of a spiritual order large enough to embrace this pain and confusion. In the anagogic perspective, everything in the universe is potentially identifiable with everything else; an anagogic metaphor is an image which suggests that it may be identified with the entire cosmos. Laurence's anagoge is the circular rose-window of the MacLeod house. It contains "glass of many colours which permitted an outlooking eye to see the world as a place of absolute sapphire or emerald, or if one wished to look with a jaundiced eye, a hateful yellow." The image picks up such traditional symbols as the circle, and the rose. Even a common phrase such as "seeing the world through rose-coloured glasses" contributes to its ecumenical suggestions. The glasses through which Grandmother views the world are "a hateful yellow," but this colour is transformed later in the story by connecting it with poplar leaves and the sun. Vanessa intuits that the individuals in her family are too different for any simplified system to contain. But sun imagery dominates the closing paragraphs. And the window's rainbow colours are the individual components of light. Even a ladybird, seemingly "unaware that she possessed wings and could have flown up," contributes to the unobtrusive but intricate pattern of images that supports Laurence's theme.

The central four stories focus on pain, fear, entrapment, despite numerous touches of humour. The Haida mask conceals a lurking bewilderment, like Grandfather Connor's pain, untouchable in the cellar retreat. The mask is described as ugly, powerful, with an expression of sullen rage. It is only after her grandmother's death that Vanessa recognizes the mask of anger as a covering for her grandfather's repressed yearnings. The bear has claws, too, sufficient for frightening away Edna's suitor and teaching Vanessa that love and loss belong to Manawaka and not simply to ancient Egypt. The juxta-position of the two key incidents, the routing of Edna's Jimmy and the death of Grandmother Connor, enrich the symbols of mask and bear and ground them solidly in human experience.

When Vanessa's father dies, the bird trapped between the two layers of her window is not simply an omen of death but an image of trapped humanity, apparently capable only of meaningless movements. The empurpled religious visions of Noreen are as unacceptable to Vanessa as the rigid Puritan code of Grandmother MacLeod. Vanessa, reacting to her father's death by striking Noreen, is also the bird, blindly battling to get out.

The loss of her father precipitates a loss of faith which is a kind of psychic death. Where is he now? *Rest beyond the river. I knew now what that meant. It meant Nothing. It meant only silence, forever.* In a later story, Vanessa thinks of the view of God she has held since her father's death: "Distant, indestructible, totally indifferent." **"A Bird in the House"** ends with Vanessa's discovery, years later, of an old photo of a girl. There is a French inscription. She remembers what her father has said about the war, and his old unfulfilled desire to travel. Perhaps the French girl had meant some brief and unexpected freedom. But her father is now dead, and the understanding which Vanessa would like to share with him is imprisoned within her. Once again, Laurence returns us to her title image, the bird. The bird, remember, did go free before the father's death. But nothing relieves the severity of the story's ending.

"The Loons" identifies a halfbreed Indian girl and, by extension, her entire people, with the lonely phantom lake birds: "Plaintive, and yet with a quality of chilling mockery, those voices belonged to a world separated by aeons from our neat world of summer cottages and the lighted lamps of home." Two cultures, light years apart. Vanessa's neighbours live in brick houses. The Tonnerres occupy a huddle of lean-tos, ramshackle huts built of materials salvaged from the town dump. At thirteen, Piquette has no interest in the woods around the MacLeod cottage, thereby dashing Vanessa's romantic image of the Indian. Piquette attempts to protect herself from the pain of living by withdrawal. At seventeen, Piquette is engaged to an English boy and her eyes betray "a terrifying hope." Neither before nor after the shack fire which ends Piquette's life can Vanessa forget that look: wild, mocking, yearning, untameable. Incompatible with brick houses. This is Vanessa's first recognition of adult social guilt. Speaking of the story, Laurence traces the alienation of the Métis back to the nineteenth century and identifies the loons with that ancestral past.

Withdrawal is also the protective mechanism used by Vanessa's older cousin Chris in **"Horses of the Night."** This portrait of an intelligent and imaginative youth crushed by a combination of outer and inner factors strikes me as the bleakest story Laurence has written. Chris craves order and beauty, and is given a family where dirt and disorder prevail. He craves work—the opportunity to create, to contribute to social needs—and is denied a job until the Depression is broken by World War Two. He craves gentleness, and finds violence. After his breakdown, Vanessa remembers "the brave and useless strokes of fantasy against a depression that was both the world's and his own." The title image is beautifully suggestive: of the dread, destruction-laden Horses of the Apocalypse: of the dark and terrifying depths of the mind, fears which are also imaged by the prehistoric monsters who once inhabited the lake near Chris's home and, finally, of his fantasy horses, Duchess and Firefly, "swifting through all the meadows of summer."

The psychic breakdown of Brother Lemon, in the African collection, might be compared with the story of Chris. But the symbols of hope in **"The Merchant of Heaven"** are more prominent, and the prevailing tone ironic rather than tragic. The American evangelist comes to Africa to acquire souls. Just souls. Bodies—whether racked with tropical disease, crippled, hungry, or blind—are not Brother Lemon's concern. The metaphors here are blackly comic. Brother Lemon is "replete with faith as a fresh-gorged mosquito is with blood." Like his own water-purifier, the evangelist is a soul-purifier, "sucking in the septic souls and spewing them back one hundred per cent pure." The Jacob archetype, one of Laurence's recurring metaphors, takes a demonic form: "Jacob-like, he came to wrestle for the Angel's blessing, and instead was bent double with cramps in bowels from eating unwashed salad greens." How could his struggle be successful, in this form, as Laurence's ironies make clear?

Brother Lemon's name contains multiple puns, a kind of

word-play which engages the author's wit even when she is most serious. *Lemon* is archaic for *lover*: the abstractions of the evangelist's love are even more Manichean than the concept of *cortezia* in Provencal poetry; Danso calls the evangelist his "dear citric sibling"; and, in contemporary slang, a *lemon* is a *failure*.

The final metaphor, and the story's focus, is Danso's picture of the Nazarene, depicted as an African: strong, capable of laughter, and surrounded by diseased beggars. Earlier, we have been given a glimpse of Brother Lemon's deprived childhood in an unpainted American farmhouse. His mental and emotional deprivations match the Africans' physical ones. The epiphany provided by the painting moves beyond its technical limitations: "Sometimes, when I am able to see through black and white, until they merge and cease to be separate or apart, I look at those damaged creatures clustering so despairingly hopeful around the Son of Man, and it seems to me that Brother Lemon, after all, is one of them." And with this, the title expands from the simple level of irony into an apocalyptic reference, with God as the heavenly seeker of souls.

"The Drummer of All the World" deals with freedom and captivity on many levels, personal, national, cultural. Both squalor and beauty are caught in the anagogic metaphor of "the Drummer of all the world, drumming on himself, the Drum of drums." The English narrator loses this vision and is excluded from the country he loves, while the Africans remain excluded from opportunity and a decent standard of living. Freedom here is demonic, the freedom to discard illusion.

The mood in **"The Perfume Sea"** is quite different. Exile is treated comically, although the pain caused by isolation is not minimized. The story breathes a spirit of reconciliation, expressed in a pattern of baroque and amusing metaphors. The tall gaunt Doree and the plump little hairdresser, Archipelago, are grotesques who nevertheless express the universal pathos and loneliness of human existence. Pigeon and crane, they walk on the African beach "with hands entwined like children who walk through the dark." Each is the other's sanctuary. Their economic and personal freedom has been achieved, as Archipelago puns, "By an act of Mercy," combined with their own courage and love.

In **"The Tomorrow-Tamer,"** Laurence contrasts the types of freedom afforded by two different cultures. Faith, humility, acceptance, and service lie at the heart of the freedom which is to be found within the religious culture of the village of Owurasu. This is curiously close to Grandmother Connor's type of freedom. The service of God, or of the gods, is perfect freedom. The ironically-named Emmanuel, the African bridge-builder, typifies the rootless freedom of a secular, technological culture. Emmanuel's life is "to make money, and spend it." His non-community is the society of those like himself who move from job to job. The lack of understanding between the two cultures is portrayed with humour and pathos. The village elders send Kofi to work on the bridge as a test.

The young man is eventually seduced by a vision of money and power. Laurence sets the gods of the two cultures in ironic juxtaposition. Kofi's silver shillings resemble moons, and the bridge is painted silver, "moon-bright in the kingly sun." Kofi's fall from grace in a moment of ex-

ulting self-deification suggests the Icarus myth, and the concept of *hubris* from classical Greek tragedy. Kofi's act is also a betrayal of the values of his own people. His proud ambition is ironically fulfilled when his people weave both his death and the new bridge into their myth.

At the end of the African collection, the mammy trader calls freedom a sun thing, a sweet thing, a piece of free gold. The glory-filled gourd is the common life of these people. Busfare must still be paid, after Independence, yet Mammii Ama confronts the Englishwoman as an equal. A child-like exuberance is common to both characters and symbols here. The story is not one of Laurence's best, but by placing it at the end of the collection she draws attention to its theme. (pp. 19-25)

The Laurentian theme of exile has received considerable critical attention. George Woodcock, for example, speaks of the "sense of alienation" as crucial in *A Bird in the House.* Clara Thomas sees in Laurence's fiction both "the inevitability of estrangement and the possibility of understanding between generations and among all men and women." But the comic spirit of reconciliation in this body of fiction, and the recurring archetype of the spiritual quest, have not, I think, been sufficiently emphasized.

In an interview with Clara Thomas and Irving Layton published in 1972, Laurence notes a similarity between many of her themes and those of Layton. She describes her work as follows: "When I first began writing, the theme to me then seemed to be human freedom and in a profound sense it still is human freedom. But this is linked with survival, which, as you say, has to be linked with some kind of growth and I would express this in terms of an inner freedom." An author is not always his or her own best critic. But Laurence's self-verdict is, I believe, peculiarly apt. Her fiction is designed to be lived with. It wears well. And with successive rereadings, the underlying concerns become clear. These are survival, growth, inner freedom. The long trek home. (pp. 25-6)

> *Patricia Morley, "The Long Trek Home: Margaret Laurence's Stories," in* Journal of Canadian Studies/Revue d'etudes canadiennes, *Vol. XI, No. 4, November, 1976, pp. 19-26.*

Arnold E. Davidson   (essay date 1981)

[*Davidson is a Canadian educator, editor, and critic. In the following excerpt, he examines the subject matter and narrative technique of* A Bird in the House, *focusing on the title story as an example of Laurence's concern throughout her fiction with the relationship between past and present.*]

Canada's Yoknapatawpha County is surely Manawaka, Manitoba. Indeed, Margaret Laurence has produced a number of works almost Faulknerian in their focus on the intertwining lives of different characters who all grew up in one fictional setting. From this small Western town, her protagonists may travel as far as Vancouver to the west or England to the east, yet they never really leave Manawaka behind. In other words, one of Laurence's main themes is the continuing presentness of the past. In five books so far—four novels, *The Stone Angel* (1964), *A Jest of God* (1966), *The Fire-Dwellers* (1969), and *The Diviners* (1974), and one volume of interconnected short stories, *A Bird in the House* (1970)—she shows how different adult characters struggle to come to terms with unsettling memories of—or other perturbing mementoes from—their Manawakan past. She also shows how the river of memory runs both ways, how the past is reshaped from the perspective of the present and the present is built on the ruins of the past.

Perhaps Laurence's basic theme is best exemplified in her most recent work, *The Diviners,* a book that has consolidated her reputation as one of Canada's foremost novelists. But this author can also effectively accommodate her material to the narrower confines of the short story, so much so that her art, I would argue, is most evident in her short stories. . . . I therefore purpose to examine the book of stories in some detail and to do so primarily through an assessment of the title story, which effectively illustrates both the subject matter and the narrative technique that informs the entire volume. As Robert Gibbs has observed in his introduction to *A Bird in the House,* Laurence employs a "structural principle whereby the shape of the whole recapitulates that of the parts." And conversely, the shape of one part anticipates that of the whole.

The story that provides the title for the entire volume [**"A Bird in the House"**] comes near the middle of the book and that tale also takes its title from a mid-point episode. So an analysis—of both the story and the book—might well begin with a summary account of what "a bird in the house," on the most immediate levels, signifies. The bird was a sparrow that had managed to get itself "caught between the two layers of glass" of a storm window. Vanessa MacLeod, the child-protagonist and retrospective adult-narrator of each story, "could not bear the panic of the trapped bird." She rushed to free it. But by opening the inner window she merely released the captive creature into a larger cage, whereupon "it began flying blindly around the room, hitting the lampshade, [and] brushing against the walls." "Petrified" and "revolted," Vanessa was afraid that she would soon see the bird "lying broken on the floor" and angry that Noreen, the servant girl, might make some typical religious comment such as "God sees the little sparrow fall." The actual comment, however, was more perturbing than the anticipated one: " 'A bird in the house means a death in the house,' Noreen remarked." Even more upsetting, the prophecy soon proves correct. Later in the winter the protagonist's doctor father dies from the same flu that he had cured in others, including his daughter.

The death foreshadowed by the trapped sparrow is of pivotal importance in the whole work. The Depression had earlier forced Dr. MacLeod to move himself and his family into his widowed mother's home. No one, including Vanessa's Grandmother MacLeod, found that living arrangement comfortable. But with the demise of the father, "everything changed." At the end of **"A Bird in the House"** the MacLeod house is sold. Grandmother MacLeod is taken in by a daughter in Winnipeg. The mother, with her two children, goes to live with her father. Vanessa, who found her Grandmother MacLeod difficult and forbidding—"I'm sorry," she early realized, was the password in Grandmother's house—soon discovers that her autocratic Grandfather Connor is even less appealing. The young girl exchanges one house where she does not really belong for another one that is still more constraining.

Thus Laurence has the central event in the story image the central situation in the book, a situation that is itself magnified by what happens in the story. No wonder Vanessa, in her Grandmother's house, was so disturbed by the sparrow's plight. But the child protagonist could only sense what the adult narrator can show—that the bird's predicament symbolized her own.

This same episode is significant for still another reason. An earlier indicated, Vanessa angrily anticipated what Noreen's reaction to the bird would be and was then upset when the servant girl voiced a comment other than the expected one. But Noreen's superstitious statement, Vanessa immediately realized, was not her real response either. It was Noreen who picked up the fallen sparrow, "cradled it with great gentleness between her cupped hands," carried it downstairs, and set it free: " 'Poor little scrap,' she said, and I felt struck to the heart, knowing she had been concerned all along about the sparrow, while I, perfidiously, in the chaos of the moment, had been concerned only about myself." The child here obviously and at once recognizes that she has not judged justly. Clara Thomas has persuasively argued that the whole book turns on the recognition and revision of more substantial misjudgments and thereby shows Vanessa coming to terms with the previously unperceived realities of her past. In a second sense, then, the title of the volume is appropriate. A bird in the house, the event that provides a summary symbol for the whole book, also provides a central synecdoche.

Synecdoche and symbol, it should here be observed, are also connected in a different fashion. Both derive—the former directly, the latter indirectly—from the complex narrative perspective through which these stories are structured. Thomas rightly observes that "the adult world seen through the eyes of a child, the maturing of the child, innocence to experience—this is so populated a branch of literature as to constitute a genre in itself." This common form entails, however, a definite technical difficulty. To voice her own experience, Vanessa must be allowed to "speak the story." But the narrator also has to indicate how her experience should be interpreted, and interpretation requires a mental and emotional sophistication, a level of awareness, that is precisely what youthful protagonist-narrators generally lack. One common solution to that basic problem is to have the undiscerning narrator conveniently provide symbolically significant details that can be appreciated only by the perceptive reader, a technique masterfully utilized by such major authors as James Joyce in *Dubliners* or Ernest Hemingway in the early Nick Adams stories. But Laurence, as Thomas points out, employs a different "solution," which can "be compared to a technique of double exposures: the narrator became Vanessa, the woman, who takes on the voice and attributes of the child she was and, at the same time, remains her present self, far older and wiser in compassion and understanding." The river of experience runs both ways too. As the past and the present are each partly relived in the other, imperfect early visions must necessarily be substantially revised. Thus the central synecdoche, Vanessa misjudging Noreen, is itself another version of the central symbol, the trapped bird. The child was a captive in a house not her own but she was also a captive of her own childhood, of her innocence and inexperience.

Vanessa senses this second captivity too, as her regular listening to conversations that she does not understand at-tests. The first story, in fact, begins with a description of "the old Connor place," which will presently be one of Vanessa's prisons, and then progresses to an account of what transpired during one particular Sunday visit. Vanessa, already "a professional listener" who had discovered that the "best concealment was to sit quietly in plain view," practiced her art to her considerable confusion throughout what was, the reader—and the mature Vanessa—can both later realize, a standard Connor family crisis.

The parameters of Vanessa's childhood experiences delimit the substance of the stories; the difference between her voice as a young girl and her voice as an older woman determine their tone; but their meanings substantially derive from the juxtapositions and parallels established as past and present partly interpenetrate. And again we can examine the central scene in the title story, for it also illustrates that third and final point. The sparrow's situation obviously mirrors the daughter's, but, equally important, it reflects something of the father's—something more than his impending death. Indeed, with respect to the father, the meaning of the significant bird—like memory and experience—flows both ways. What is partly an ominous portent also serves as a retrospective symbol, a representation of the obvious imperfections of Dr. MacLeod's past life. Like his daughter, he too reluctantly inhabits a house not his own.

"A Bird in the House" begins by suggesting that the father is subject to various undefined psychological constraints and captivities. These suggestions are tenuous. Vanessa can only half understand what her father can only half articulate, so the reader must function in the interstices between the father's and the daughter's tangled limitations. Nevertheless, the necessary clues are provided, starting with the first sentence in the story: "The parade would be almost over by now, and I had not gone." Vanessa was "pained" because she was "betraying" her father, but it would have been even more of a betrayal to try to take seriously a small procession led by the town's half-uniformed Civic Band augmented by the regular Salvation Army Band, the Remembrance Day pretense that Manawaka was the home of heroes. The middle-aged men, marching out of step as the two bands played out of rhythm, were not the young soldiers that they might once have been. For Vanessa, they were "imposters," and, as she later attempts to explain, "They look silly. . . . Marching like that." But the daughter soon finds that, in a different sense, her father had not been quite the soldier that he later pretended to be. To atone for the criticism implicit in her faltering explanation as to why she avoided the parade, she tries to show that she can understand his war experiences, and particularly the most disturbing one, the death of his brother. She asks a penetrating question and thereby discovers that, contrary to the official story of an "antiseptic" expiration in a hospital, her father, as a young man, had helplessly watched his still younger brother die, grotesquely, in the trenches. The daughter's reaction was "horrified awe," tears. The roles she had anticipated were immediately reversed: "Now I needed him to console me for this unwanted glimpse of the pain he had once known."

Laurence shows that the daughter then achieved, as would be expected, only a glimpse. The full significance of other details—overheard conversations, the many pictures the grandmother had of her dead son compared to the one photo of the living son—never registered, and Vanessa did not perceive how much her father was motivated by unassuaged guilt, and how his former pain was endlessly protracted. Yet the reader should see that Ewan MacLeod held himself responsible for his brother's death and for his mother's continuing unsolacable sorrow. Furthermore, to make some reparation to his mother by becoming, as much as possible, the son she would prefer to have, he must be unfair to his wife. That double burden was intolerable, yet, as the author demonstrates in one crucial scene, it could not at all be lightened. An exchange between the parents begins with the father's comment, "I never thought things would turn out like this, did you?" For the listening Vanessa, that simple question elicits a confusing response: " 'Please—' my mother said in a low strained voice, 'please, Ewan, let's not start all this again. I can't take it.' " The "conversation" soon ends:

> "I'm sorry," my mother repeated, blowing her nose.
>
> "We're both sorry," my father said. "Not that that changes anything."

Neither could speak the unspeakable. In a sense that the daughter did not then understand, "I'm sorry" was indeed the motto of the MacLeod house.

Only later, with the final episode in the story, could Vanessa begin to comprehend more fully what her father's plight must have been: "During the Second World War, when I was seventeen and in love with an airman who did not love me, and desperately anxious to get away from Manawaka and from my grandfather's house, I happened one day to be going through the old mahogany desk that had belonged to my father." What she discovered was a secret drawer containing the picture of a young lady and a letter written in French. Because of her own too clearly perceived situation, she could partly comprehend the significance of the "absurdly old-fashioned" face in the photograph and the undecipherable missive: "I looked . . . at the girl, and hoped she had meant some momentary and unexpected freedom, I remembered what he had said to me, after I hadn't gone to the Remembrance Day parade." A parallel falls more clearly into place. What he had said, consoling his daughter, was that she should not cry because "it wasn't all as bad as that part [the death of his brother]. There were a few other things." And equally unclearly, explaining the first confusing explanation: "Those of us who came back mostly came back here, or else went no further away from town than Winnipeg. So when we were overseas—that was the only time most of us were ever a long way from home." How telling that "other things" might have been the main solace of his life, that his greatest freedom was probably achieved while serving in the Great War. The last line in the story is thus most appropriate: "I grieved for my father as though he had just died now."

What she, at seventeen, can see is that, alive, he had been dying all along. What she does not yet see is that his death was perhaps a paradoxical attempt at life and the only later escape that he could allow himself. Certainly the timing of that death is suggestive. After the birth of a son—who is given the name of the father's dead brother at the request of the child's grandmother and despite the mother's objections—it is as if Dr. MacLeod, partly settling one account by increasing another, has done the best he can do and decides that it is time to depart. But later, in **"Jericho's Brick Battlements,"** the last story in the book, the retrospective narrator who visits her father's tomb and notes that he "had died when he was the same age as I am now" can perceive the common element in his death and her life, for that recognition is worked into her account of his demise and particularly into the episode that gives both that story and the book its title.

Because the stories all embody essentially the same pattern, it is not necessary to consider them individually and in detail. Each is similar to the title story in that a crucial experience in Vanessa's earlier life is recounted from a perspective that indicates both the young girl's immediate reaction to that event and her later more comprehensive retrospective assessment of its significance. And since adult revision allows for artistic vision, the older narrator regularly emphasizes those elements in her earlier experience that can best provide symbolic approximations of her remembered plight. Consequently, in the separate stories, different birds, both real and metaphoric, differently inhabit different houses. These symbols can, of course, extend far beyond Vanessa. In the first story, ironically titled **"The Sound of Singing,"** the grandmother's canary has accepted its captivity—and seldom sings. Similarly, the grandmother finds little occasion for outpourings of happiness in her marriage to Grandfather Connor. But unlike the mostly silent canary, the loons, in a story of the same name, sound their wild song. Even more important, they will not remain in the world of men at all. Neither does Piquette Tonnerre, the tubercular halfbreed girl, who spent one summer with Dr. MacLeod and his family. **"The Loons"** concludes by describing how disastrously Piquette's "terrifying hope" for happiness in marriage ended, a tragedy more fully examined in *The Diviners*. Yet even from the brief account provided by her mother, the eighteen-year-old Vanessa can understand that, as children on the lake, "Piquette might have been the only one, after all, who had heard the crying of the loons."

Other possible paradigms more obviously image the protagonist's situation. Vanessa, in one story, **"The Mask of the Bear,"** sees her grandfather callously subvert his daughter's romance. Later he will similarly try to tyrannize over her. Or, in **"Horses of the Night,"** one of the most moving tales in the book, Vanessa tells of a cousin whose problems, she recognizes, are much greater than hers. He plans to escape the narrow limitations of his life by going to war but then evades the different dehumanization of that war through the still more desperate one of insanity. Even Grandfather Connor, the protagonist's chief antagonist, is trapped in his own concept of himself as a self-made man. Raging in the cage of his retirement, he only confirms the trap. In fact, most of the characters reflect the book's central metaphor and are thus symbolically interconnected. Simply put, the stories chart how they are all caught up in parallel captivities and engaged in divergent flights.

The most significant of these flights is, naturally, Vanessa's. And it is in the overall portrayal of her protagonist that Laurence best demonstrates the breadth of her artistic vision. To start with, Vanessa's first captivity is her con-

strained childhood, which encourages imaginative escapes and sets her on the road to her vocation as a writer. Then, as an apprentice writer, she encounters even more clearly what she has already experienced as a confused child. The most basic "cage" in the book is the immediate limitations of self. The youthful protagonist is trapped by what she is, by her inexperience as well as by her limited experiences, particuraly those experiences with which she has not yet fully come to terms. That last phrase suggests the other essential captivity assessed. As earlier observed, one of Laurence's most persistent themes is the problem of "time and the personal and ancestral past." Characters are all, to a degree, prisoners of their past. But that condition can be a final self-defeat, as with Grandfather Connor, a "pioneer" still surviving beyond his time, or, as with Vanessa, the beginning of a personal liberation. The child endures Manawaka; the adolescent about to leave for university can look with some magnanimity on some of what she has experience; the older adult narrator can more fully review Manawaka. Through these somewhat different characters, Vanessa makes—and retrospectively maps—her course to self-determination. In effect, she frees herself psychologically by remembering a place she earlier left physically and by then restructuring or re-creating those memories into meaningful stories.

The young Vanessa reacts passionately to her life's story; the somewhat older Vanessa re-examines sympathetically; the author, a mature Vanessa, writes analytically, with an objectivity impossible to the "trapped" child. But the adult narrator too is trapped in a new cage, in the subtler cage of memory that makes youth look grander in retrospect as age limits possibilities and admits to compromise where once was only promise. The child, rebelling against one cage, is, in some ways, freer than the mature writer who, ultimately, has turned life into fiction, categorized emotions, confined what was fluid for her earlier self into narratives as balanced and structured as autobiographies tend to be.

But Vanessa—the naive child, the rebellious adolescent, the mature writer—is not, despite the autobiographical details in these stories, Margaret Laurence. Beyond the narrator who delimits her life's story, is the fictionalist who frees it. If in one sense the author is the exhibitor of cages, the proponent of the human condition, with all its limitation, then she is also the master of escapes. For Laurence, the last escape is art, the achievement of an extra dimension. The young Vanessa is an aspiring writer who composes imitation conventional romances. As an adult, she is a promising writer who explores the partly fictitious realities of her past and does so by conjoining her present voice with her former ones. Yet the author, a better artist, can underscore and emphasize the tones of those voices and the details they report to show how Vanessa regularly speaks both more and less than she knows. Laurence's larger perspective gives us, then, a number of interconnected short stories—different portraits of a future artist as various young women—that well reward the reader's careful attention. And just as the title story exemplifies the art that informs the whole volume, so too can *A Bird in the House* illustrate the subtle techniques that shape the other Manawakan novels. (pp. 92-100)

Arnold E. Davidson, "Cages and Escapes in Margaret Laurence's 'A Bird in the House'," in The University of Windsor Review, *Vol. XVI, No. 1, Fall-Winter, 1981, pp. 92-101.*

Laurence on autobiography in her fiction

[*A Bird in the House* comprises] a number of short stories set in Manawaka and based upon my childhood and my childhood family, the only semi-autobiographical fiction I have ever written. I did not realize until I finished the final story in the series how much all these stories are dominated by the figure of my maternal grandfather, who came of Irish Protestant stock. Perhaps it was through writing these stories that I finally came to see my grandfather not only as the repressive authoritarian figure from my childhood, but also as a boy who had to leave school in Ontario when he was about twelve, after his father's death, and who as a young man went to Manitoba by stern-wheeler and walked the miles from Winnipeg to Portage la Prairie, where he settled for some years before moving to Neepawa. He was a very hard man in many ways, but he had had a very hard life. I don't think I knew any of this, really knew it, until I had finished these stories. I don't think I ever knew, either, until that moment how much I owed to him. One sentence, near the end of the final story, may show what I mean. "I had feared and fought the old man, yet he proclaimed himself in my veins."

> *In her essay "A Place to Stand On," from her book* Heart of a Stranger *(1976), as quoted by George Woodcock in his* The World of Canadian Writing *(1980).*

Frank Birbalsingh   (essay date 1982)

[*In the following excerpt, Birbalsingh appraises Laurence's stories in* The Tomorrow-Tamer *and* A Bird in the House, *focusing on themes of order, disorder, and the nature of freedom, while characterizing the former collection as "apprentice work" and the latter as "the centerpiece of the author's art."*]

[Laurence's] African books are rightly regarded as apprentice work, training ground on which the author exercises untried imaginative resources and narrative skills which are later to be deployed, in more developed form, on her principal subject—Canada, particularly Western Canada in the 1930s and 40s. While there is no dispute about the African books' representing the initial stages of Laurence's development as a writer, it is not entirely correct to suppose that these books, or her African experience as a whole, have influenced her thinking significantly: this early work contributes mainly to a development of technique.

The other point at issue concerns the relationship between Laurence's short stories and her novels. Again, there is no dispute with the prevailing judgment that the author's fin-

est work is the collective achievement of the novels rather than the short stories. But this judgment is misleading insofar as it neglects the formal excellence of stories in the second collection, *A Bird in the House.* These stories are not only more convincingly dramatic than those in *The Tomorrow-Tamer* individually, they come as close to artistic perfection as Laurence has ever attained. Naturally, they lack the scope and total, if flawed, excellence of the longer novels—*The Stone Angel, The Fire Dwellers* and *The Diviners;* but they present, in almost perfect miniature form, the elements that appeal most in the author's writing—the pathos and elegiac tone which evolve from her portrayal of persistent human struggle against a permanently disordered universe.

The stories in *The Tomorrow-Tamer* first appeared in various periodicals during the 1950s. The unavoidable outsider's point of view in these pieces is frankly recognized by the author. . . .

Although ultimately Laurence's candor is the product of her own complex personality, this personality itself is unmistakably stamped by her upbringing in Western Canada during the 1930s and 40s. Perhaps this is why we so readily associate her candor, open-mindedness and willingness to do right with the rather hopeful North American innocence of Henry James's transatlantic heroines. Isabel Archer's approach to Africa would be completely different from Madame Merle's—as different as Laurence's fictional view of Africa is from the views of Europeans like Conrad in *Heart of Darkness* and Joyce Cary in his four African novels. (p. 30)

Laurence's African stories tread between Conrad's wary pessimism and Cary's suspect optimism: they present candid descriptions of African situations and problems accompanied by an apparently instinctive suspension of judgment. As Conrad engages in painful confrontation with Africa and Cary suspiciously celebrates it, Laurence seems eager to justify her experiences in Africa.

In a typical story, **"The Drummer of All the World,"** the narrator, son of an English missionary, grows up with Kwabena, the son of his African nurse. The story accurately describes the ethnocentric paternalism yet technological "progressiveness" of the narrator's culture, the fundamental integrity of Kwabena's traditional culture, the ensuing conflict, the psychological implications of this conflict and the apparent impasse they produce in the postcolonial world. There is sympathy for everyone and everything; there are no absolute villains. The mood is one of tolerance, understanding and a super-compassionate willingness to justify, or to find reasons for justifying, every human activity, good as well as bad. Laurence does not actually justify British colonialism, for she leaves no doubt about its disastrous effects; but she discerns value or benefit in the activities of some British people in Africa.

"The Merchant of Heaven" describes the coarse ethics of Brother Amory Lemon, "proselytizer for a mission known as the Angel of Philadelphia." Brother Lemon's commercial zeal, racist insensitivity and plain ignorance are all illustrated. His attitude toward African culture is similar to that of the narrator's father in **"The Drummer of All the World"**; it is liberalpaternalistic, based on a social-Darwinist model originating in the second half of the nineteenth century. This view, the sustaining creed of many stalwart Empire-builders, places Africans at a low social and cultural level from which they are expected gradually to rise on an ascending scale of linear, evolutionary development. In this view colonialism is intended to provide benevolent contact with "higher" European cultures which will promote the process of social and cultural uplift in Africa—hence the related concepts of "the white man's burden" and "the civilizing mission."

In **"The Drummer of All the World"** the narrator's father says of Africans, "Remember, they're like children, these people"; and Brother Lemon calls the Akan religion "idolatry, paganism." But although their faults are exposed, these characters are not vilified. They are seen to possess redeeming aspects of behavior. Kwabena expresses grateful if grudging respect for his friend's father: "That was the thing about your father. He did not like us—that is true. He did not understand us. And we did not like or understand him. Nearly everything he did was wrong. But at least he did not want us to stand still." While he recognizes their limitations, Kwabena nevertheless attributes some value to the liberal-paternalistic activities of former Empire-builders. So too in her more contemporary saga of misguided evangelism, Laurence reserves some respect, even affection, for Brother Lemon. Her narrator, a supposedly neutral English observer called Will Kettridge, is "amused" and "rather touched" when he first meets Brother Lemon with his cine-camera and projector, his antimalarial drug and water-purifier. Kettridge comments, "I was almost sorry that this was not the Africa of Livingstone and Burton." And in the end, after Brother Lemon leaves Ghana in disillusionment, Kettridge observes a portrait of Christ by the African painter Danso.

> I bought Danso's picture. Sometimes, when I am unable to see through black and white, until they merge and cease to be separate or apart, I look at those damaged creatures clustering so despairingly hopeful around the Son of Man, and it seems to me that Brother Lemon after all, is one of them.

The "damaged creatures" are "a group of beggars sore fouled, their mouths twisted in perpetual leers of pain," and the narrator's identification of Brother Lemon with them relieves the offensiveness of his commercialized evangelism by showing that he is a suffering sinner. His "offense" is the result of a sinful, fallible nature which we all possess. We and the author are therefore not in a position to judge Brother Lemon.

The missionaries in both stories are shown as people whose human fallibility leads them into vices such as cultural imperialism, racism, insensitivity and rudeness; but their underlying motive of helping to elevate members of a less developed culture is acknowledged as virtuous. Laurence suggests that any human being, placed in the circumstances of her characters, is likely to act more or less like them. In other words, the missionaries, because of human fallibility, are victims of circumstances. So are we all. All vices or offenses, indeed all human actions, are either justifiable or pardonable.

In the story **"The Tomorrow-Tamer"** an African character is examined in a light similar to that shed on the two missionaries. Villagers are reluctant to accept the construction of a bridge in their area because it conflicts with their traditional beliefs. The god of the river over which the bridge is to be built has first to be appeased. This hap-

pens when the seventeen-year-old protagonist Kofi throws himself into the river and drowns. Like the missionaries in the previous stories, Kofi is placed in confused, disordered circumstances produced by colonialism. He struggles as best he can, and since he loses his life in the process, he is certainly a victim of his circumstances. But his (destructive) death is also constructive, and because of this ambivalence in his achievement he cannot be rightly condemned. This process of fallible humanity placed in limiting (disordered) circumstances and producing action of ambivalent value is one that we observe throughout the author's fiction.

Laurence's presentation of Kofi underlines her view of an imperfect or disordered world which reduces all human beings to the same victimized condition. Since we are all victims, we have no right to victimize others. In her book *Heart of a Stranger* she mentions a biblical quotation which "has always meant a great deal" to her: "Also, thou shalt not oppress a stranger: for ye know the heart of a stranger, seeing ye were strangers in the land of Egypt." The quotation entails a belief in the sameness of human experience and hints that that experience is nearly always one of alienation, suffering or victimization. Of the characters looked at so far, the two missionaries and Kofi are all victims—Kofi most of all. The missionaries appear as mildly pathetic and evoke a little sympathy. We feel more sympathy for Kofi because he suffers most. Laurence's fiction is most successful when the pathos is greatest and the elegiac tone at its most intense; and these effects are achieved when her fiction conveys as pervassive a sense of suffering, loss or transience as possible. In *The Tomorrow-Tamer* these effects are best achieved in **"Godman's Master."**

The hero of this story is Godman Pira, a dwarf who is kept locked up in a box by Faru, an ex-convict. Moses Adu rescues Godman and gives him a job cooking and keeping house for him. Godman likes the job and does not want to leave when Moses asks him to. He regards Moses as his priest and is happy to serve him forever.

> "You saved me," he [Godman] said. "You cannot deny that you saved me. I would have died if I had stayed there much longer. You lifted the lid of the box and let me out. It was no other man. You were the one. Who else, then, should protect me? Who else should I serve? Who else's name should I forever bless? You freed me. I am yours."
>
> Moses put his head down onto his hands.
>
> "There is more to freedom," he said, "than not living in a box."
>
> Godman fixed ancient eyes upon Moses.
>
> "You would not think so if you had ever lived in a box."

Ill-equipped by size and shape for normal life, Godman is ready to embrace slavery even, so long as it assures him of survival.

Eventually Moses gets married and Godman is forced to leave. One year later Moses meets Godman, who has set up a new business practicing his old skill as an oracle. Far from bearing him a grudge, Godman is delighted to see Moses: "Lucky for me I am alive at all," he tells Moses, "after the way you treated me. Oh, I don't hold it against you now, but you must admit it was cruel"; and without any bitterness or self-pity, he recounts his sufferings after Moses threw him out. Moses is simply confounded by Godman's defiance, ingenuity and ceaselessly surging, confident cheerfulness. He congratulates him on his success; but the little man merely shrugs; "I have known the worst and the worst and the worst," he says, "and yet I live. I fear and fear, and yet I live." These sentiments are quintessential Laurence: they are uttered in one way or another by every major character she has created. They issue readily, for instance, from the lips of Hagar Shipley, the superbly resilient and spirited, ninety-year-old heroine of *The Stone Angel*. In Laurence's fiction colonialism, physical deformity, old age are only some of the consequences of an imperfect world order—that is to say, of cosmic disorder. Her chief characters are depicted as victims of this disorder, yet they struggle on, human frailty and fallibility notwithstanding. Out of this struggle and the loss and suffering that it entails comes pathos, genuine feeling for our mortality and for the transience of human life.

This comparison between Godman Pira and Hagar Shipley raises the question of African influences in the author's work. Either her vision of a disordered world originates in Africa or, as is more plausible, is conceived out of her cumulative experience, principally during her formative years in Canada, though it may have been further stimulated by her later travels in Africa and elsewhere. The unity of the vision, applied to all her fiction, reinforces the latter view. This view is not only more plausible but is supported by essentially Calvinist attitudes which imply a stern if not cruel God who is responsible both for a disordered creation apparently incapable of change and for human beings whose sense of fallibility (guilt) and capacity for enduring misfortune through hard work are their foremost qualities.

Calvinist influences are not unusual in someone of Scottish Presbyterian background. In an interview Laurence admits to coming "from a people who feel guilty at the drop of a hat, who reproach themselves for the slightest thing, and for whom virtue comes out of work . . . and that's something very Calvinistic." But her fiction does not reflect the cramping sense of spiritual impotence and guilt that more orthodox Calvinism inspires, for example, in the novels of her compatriot Hugh MacLennan. All that is claimed here is that Laurence's fiction shows strong traces of Calvinist influences in its philosophical outlines. Her close reading of the Pentateuch on her way out to Africa reinforces the biblical sources of her thinking. The weight of evidence strongly suggests that, in broad outline at least, the author's thinking had taken fairly solid shape before she reached Africa.

Laurence herself regards the general theme in her African writing as "the nature of freedom." She states that by the time she wrote *The Stone Angel* this theme had changed to one of "survival." This acknowledgment of change is unnecessary when Godman and Hagar may be seen as engaged in the identical struggle for freedom and survival within a disordered world. Perhaps the author is acknowledging the righteousness of the movement for freedom from colonial rule which dominated West Africa during the time she was there. At any rate, as Moses Adu says, freedom does not merely imply liberation from physical slavery or political subjection: it is also spiritual, permit-

ting access to all the human resources one can muster in one's struggle for survival. (pp. 31-3)

Convincing and committed as her African characters may be, Laurence's characters in her Canadian books are considerably more so. There really is no comparison between the compelling conviction and solidly grounded authenticity of her Canadian books and the well-meaning, sympathetic interest she takes in Africa. Nor is this difference unexpected or unrecognized. . . . The certainty is felt in every utterance of Hagar Shipley and in every line of *The Stone Angel*. While the African stories are convincing enough in the sense that the characters lack neither sincerity nor consistency, they lack the comprehensive certainty of the Canadian books. Godman Pira and Hagar Shipley are shaped in the same philosophical mold to illustrate identical attitudes; but where thoughts are concerned, for absolute authenticity of idiom, feeling and gesture, the African does not come within a mile of the Canadian. Hagar's whole prairie, puritan, provincial way of life is recorded, thought for thought and feeling for feeling, with an insider's authoritative control over the most finely documented details. And nowhere is this insider's control of Canadian subjects more evident than in *A Bird in the House.*

A Bird in the House consists of eight stories dealing with the childhood experiences of the narrator Vanessa MacLeod, a name that may be taken as a pseudonym of the author. Order, or the lack of it, is a preoccupation in most stories—for example, in **"To Set Our House in Order,"** which describes the birth of the narrator's brother. This birth is seen by Vanessa, from her child's point of view, as a mysterious accident, like the death of her baby sister, her uncle's partial loss of eyesight or her paternal grandfather's ability to read Greek. To Vanessa these events do not fit into a discernible pattern. Yet her grandmother keeps reminding her of a favorite thought of her own father—Vanessa's great-grandfather: "God loves order." This thought utterly baffles the child, because it seems to contradict the disorder she observes in the mysterious accidental happenings around her. Hence her conclusion: "I could not really comprehend these things [her observations], but I sensed their strangeness, their disarray. I felt whatever God might love in this world, it was certainly not order." This is not the conclusion of a mere child, however: it accurately describes the veritable universe of Laurence's fiction, one in which people's lives are governed by random chance and mystery and in which their experiences seem disparate, incoherent, lacking order. In the Canadian stories this disorder is presented as cosmic, inherent in the nature of things. In the African stories it is a direct consequence of colonialism, which itself is a symptom of cosmic disorder.

By the time she narrates **"Horses of the Night,"** Vanessa's father has died and her world is further disrupted: "After my father died, the whole order of life was torn. Nothing was known or predictable any longer." One day Vanessa's cousin Chris takes her to a lake on the prairie, where she is overcome by her response to pristine innocence and prehistoric wilderness: "It was like a view of God which I had held since my father's death. Distant, indestructible, totally indifferent." Parallels with the remote neutrality and unbending sternness of the orthodox Calvinist deity do not have to be searched out; they reappear in a long conversation that Chris has with Vanessa when he is twenty-one and she still a teen-ager.

> "People usually say there must be a God," Chris went on, "because otherwise how did the universe get here? But that's ridiculous. If the stars and planets go on to infinity, they could have existed forever, for no reason at all. Maybe they weren't ever created. Look—what's the alternative? To believe in a God who is brutal. What else could He be? You've only got to look anywhere around you. It would be an insult to Him to believe in a God like that. Most people don't like talking about this kind of thing—it embarrasses them, you know? . . . If there's a war, like it looks there will be, would people claim that was planned? What kind of a God would pull a trick like that?

This passage confirms the cosmic nature of disorder and intriguingly suggests it might be the result of a divine joke.

God as trickster or jester is not an unfamiliar concept in Laurence's fiction. Her novel *A Jest of God* conveys precisely the idea of the heroine's experiences' being jokes played on her by God. This heroine, Rachel Cameron, wins great sympathy as a hapless pawn in the hands of a capricious and brutal deity. This is also the case with Chris in **"Horses of the Night."** He joins the army but is discharged because of a mental breakdown. He struggles as best he can against disorder imposed on him by a malign God to satisfy His own perverse sense of humor. But when this disorder forces Chris to kill his fellow men, he falls back to his last line of defiance: "They could force his body to march and even to kill, but what they didn't know was that he'd fooled them. He didn't live inside it any more." As a record of victimization in a disordered world, the account of Rachel's or Chris's misfortunes produces genuine pathos. As a rule, pathos is greatest in those stories where the struggles of the characters are persistent and determined—for example, in **"Godman's Master"** and *The Stone Angel*. This is why *A Jest of God* and **"Horses of the Night"** evoke less pathos: the struggles of Rachel and Chris are poignant enough, but her suffering and his presumed loss of sanity are not produced out of as intense a dramatic conflict as in **"Godman's Master"** and *The Stone Angel*.

Apart from Vanessa, the most important character in *A Bird in the House* is Grandfather Connor, whose authoritarian hold on the family is indiscriminate, intolerant and inflexible. Grandfather Connor's response to a disordered universe is an austere, severely puritanical code of behavior that attempts to preserve some semblance of order in his family, although it limits the freedom of individual members. **"Mask of the Bear"** illustrates his cruelty to his brother Dan and to his daughter Edna; his cruel actions make it appear that he lacks feeling; but feelings do surface when Grandmother Connor dies. As his granddaughter discovers, the old man's severity is merely a mask for more human emotions concealed inside him. For he too is a fallible human being who finds that it helps to wear a mask of severity and unbending firmness all his life in order to sustain him in his struggle against disorder. In the end Grandfather Connor's daughters—the narrator's mother and aunt—acknowledge that the family are as unfair to the old man as he is to them.

In the world of Laurence's fiction disorder evokes in her

main characters tough, spirited, unbending resistance, mixed with weaker, more human emotions. The ambivalence and uncertainty produced out of this mixture registers as fallible human behavior. Fallibility is as inescapable as Calvinist guilt; for we are all tarred with the same brush. After he is dead, Vanessa recognizes an echo of her grandfather in her own voice. And in the final story, when she returns to Manawaka some twenty years after the earlier events, she reacts to the occupants of Brick House with an impulsive, willful severity that is reminiscent of him. She confesses: "I had feared and fought the old man yet he proclaimed himself in my veins." The word *proclaimed* is significant in placing a positive value on Grandfather Connor's personality: his firm severity is both a strength and a weakness, since it sustains him in his fight against cosmic disorder while it alienates him from his family.

Laurence clearly implies that the essence of fallible humanity which Vanessa had inherited from her grandfather will pass on through her to her descendants, as it was passed on to her grandfather through his forebears. Moreover, while her grandfather's outbursts of cantankerous impetuosity result from his own struggle with cosmic disorder, his outbursts serve to perpetuate disorder by creating injustice for other members of the family. This further implies that disorder is a permanent feature of normal life and an ineradicable consequence of our mortality. If this is not exactly the dark Calvinist view of original sin, of our very humanity's—the very fact of birth—being sinful, it readily fits an author who describes herself as coming from "a Scots-Irish background of stern values and hard work and puritanism, and who grew up during the drought and depression of the thirties and then the war."

Laurence's vision suggests that it is precisely by virtue of its capacity for endurance and suffering that our humanity proves to be our saving grace. The humanity of her characters is defined by their capacity to suffer hardship and endure loss. Her chief characters are all victims. Those like Godman Pira, Hagar Shipley and Grandfather Connor, who actively oppose their victimization, win greatest sympathy from the reader. Those like Chris and a majority of the African characters, who are more passive victims, have less artistic appeal. Laurence's best characters are active victims, and one of the best—certainly the best in *A Bird in the House*—is Piquette Tonnerre. Like Godman Pira, Hagar Shipley and Grandfather Conner, Piquette is the victim of a diseased world order (disorder): her mistake is to be born, to grow up, to be human; and her most striking assertion of this humanity is her capacity to endure loss, without feebleness or self-pity. Piquette clings to life as desperately as does any other Laurence character. She does not stop to consider or debate the issues of her victimized condition: she is bent only on survival. . . . This tenaciously enduring will to live is what we observe in the best of Laurence's characters: it is both a virtue and a vice; it brings out the best and the worst in them; it is, in short, both the blessing and the curse of their humanity. (pp. 33-5)

Part of the aim of this essay has been to argue against both the emphasis and the praise given to Laurence's African stories. Not that these stories lack merit; but they occupy no more than third place in importance and quality in a Laurence canon which consists firstly of the three long novels and secondly of *A Bird in the House,* the center-piece of the author's art—not because it is her best book, but because it treats her main themes with a formal excellence unattained by the rest of her fiction.

As far as themes are concerned, . . . Laurence's preoccupation with victimization gives her much artistic scope in a country which feels it has more than its share of victims in an age when the techniques of victimization are more sophisticated and more widespread than ever before. It is notable that members of the Tonnerre family appear in more than one of the author's books, because the Métis (of French-Indian ancestry) are victims of English-speaking Canadians, who are victims of the British and Americans, who are victims of cosmic disorder. With her profoundly Calvinistic feeling for suffering, loss and transience, Margaret Laurence brilliantly illuminates the whole condition of the Tonnerres of this world. In so doing she illuminates the human condition, for we are all tarred with the Tonnerre brush. (p. 36)

> Frank Birbalsingh, "Margaret Laurence's Short Stories," in World Literature Today, Vol. 56, No. 1, Winter, 1982, pp. 30-6.

Giovanna Capone   (essay date 1985)

[*In the following excerpt, Capone presents the theme of order as Laurence's principal concern in* A Bird in the House.]

In Margaret Laurence's *A Bird in the House* the distance between the real and the imaginary is the ordering theme of the cycle of stories, built as they are on the spaces between experience and its imaginative reconstruction. In these stories time constantly stretches both ways, and the future is mirrored in the past while dwelling in it. This special sense of 'memory' is underlined in the words spoken in silence by the narrator near the end of the last story: 'The memory of a memory returned to me now. I remembered myself remembering. . . .'

As the stories follow one another the confrontation of the narrator's reconstructions with her childhood vision of the world gradually becomes more explicit. The importance of childhood and adolescence from the creative viewpoint is indicated in Laurence's essay, "A Place to Stand On," when she cites Graham Greene: 'The creative writer perceives his world once and for all in childhood and adolescence, and his whole career is an effort to illustrate his private world in terms of the great public world we all share.'

In *Heart of a Stranger* Laurence writes of her own life in Neepawa:

> When I was eighteen I couldn't wait to get out of that town, away from the prairies. I did not know then that I would carry the land and town all my life within my skull, that they would form the mainspring and source of the writing I was to do, wherever and however far away I might live.
> This was my territory in the time of my youth, and in a sense my life since then has been an attempt to look at it, to come to terms with it. Stultifying to my mind it certainly could be, and sometimes was, but not to the imagination. It was many things, but it was never dull.

Margaret Laurence's leaving of Neepawa has its parallel in Vanessa MacLeod's leaving of Manawaka in *A Bird in the House.* The leaving is like an emergence from the womb, a long and exhausting birth. Not unlike Rachel in *A Jest of God,* Vanessa too seems laboriously to emerge 'from the tomb-like atmosphere of her extended childhood,' and here too the protagonist-author refers to her emergence as 'partial defeat' and 'partial victory.' She attempts to break 'the handcuffs of her own past,' but her insight makes her understand that there will never be such a thing as total liberation from her ancestors. And it will therefore be a problem of freedom which is at stake: political freedom for a country and a people, personal freedom for an individual, the victory always being only partial anyway.

Freedom and birth represent substantially the same theme. Every birth in Laurence's writing is difficult, starting with Vanessa's brother's in the story **"To Set Our House in Order,"** down to the dubious one in *A Jest of God:* everything 'struggles into life,' as the entrance into life is hard. And it is all the fault of order—the house to be kept in good order at all costs—that Vanessa's mother risks losing her baby and her own life. Life and birth are closely related to order, and order means, above all, beginning and knowing where to begin from. Knowing where to begin from is one of the recurring themes of the Canadian intellectual: does one begin from Canada, from England or one's European mother-country, from one's own region, from somewhere else? Where should one locate one's own birth?

The place of order then is *par excellence* the house. In *Bird* there are various houses, all ancestral, not only the more orderly ones belonging to the MacLeods and the Connors, but also the less orderly ones of the Tonnerres and of Uncle Wilf at Shallow Creek. Each house represents an epic of its own, with its own story and dramas; each world, inside each house, remains separate from the others in both time and space, 'a world separated by aeons.' This is especially true of the Tonnerres' and Uncle Wilf's houses, which represent remote worlds, forever rejected and hopeless, worlds still to be got in touch with, but whose separateness and disorder have led what once were youthful hopes of life to death and destruction. That is why not far from Uncle Wilf's house the menacing 'footprints in the rocks' can be seen, evidence of the past permanently imprinted in the bedrock on which the country is based, traces of that remote past which it is imperative to get in touch with.

The established order within Vanessa's maternal and paternal grandparents' houses is rigidly hierarchical and patriarchal, governed as it is by the severe figures of the grandparents, the young parents being frail, almost inexistent, figures, crushed by life and too soon dead, weaker than the patriarchs, and their true victims. Of Margaret's frail real mother, who died when she was still a child, and her father's remarriage to her aunt, there remains no trace in *Bird.* Once the heroic chapter of the pioneer grandparents is over, the parents succumb before external forces—the Depression that holds the country in these years—and internal ones inherent in everyday life. In the houses of order the task of keeping things in their place is by tradition assigned to women. Aunt Edna and the mother are relegated to doing nothing but set the house in order. As for the grandparents, Grandmother MacLeod and Grandfather Connor, order is something they simply expect, each one in his or her own image. All this reflects the conflict between two generations: here the parents' generation is sacrificed to guarantee a screen against external reality that changes precipitously, forced by the economic climate, and the immutable and 'ordered' reality of family background. Whatever hardships they may have suffered, the pioneer grandparents' sacrifice was a more celebrated epic and acknowledged as heroic, not like the middle generation's obscure attempt to set things in order. Order is equally to be found in the immutability of traditions, in the cliché-ridden immobility of the Scottish clans to which each belongs, in family mottos to be followed, almost impersonated. For Grandmother MacLeod each person must correspond to the everlasting fixity of her own heraldic motto: *'Be then a wall of brass. Learn to suffer. Consider the end. Go carefully.'* Though reassuring to her grandmother, none of these slogans reassures Vanessa.

Order is negated freedom, and freedom is often seen as being denied to creatures of nature, whether men or animals. There is a bird in Margaret Wemiss Laurence's family coat of arms, and it is perhaps no mere chance that images of birds run throughout her work. In **"To Set Our House in Order"** Grandmother MacLeod's hair looks like white-feathered wings. A sparrow that has fled into the attic troubles Vanessa's sleep. As Vanessa tidies up while her mother is in hospital risking her life, this is the way she depicts herself: 'I stood there holding the feather duster like a dead bird in my hands.' The MacLeod house has never seemed like home to the child, with its too formal appearance, its turret decorated with ferns, its verandah embellished with a profusion of wrought-iron scrolls and well-composed curls, and its circular rose-window.

Here all is alien territory, forbidden to the games and the inevitable disorder of the child, who is invited by Grandmother to use the back stairs and to stay upstairs so as not to make a mess, and induced by her own craving for freedom to seek secluded corners, quaint nooks, hidden places in the house. In this double microcosm the disposition of the inhabitants of the house is precise: grandmothers live in the living-rooms, mothers—that is Mother and Aunt Edna—in the kitchens, Grandfather and the child concealed, Father outside.

Grandmother MacLeod lives in the myth of the aristocracy, and with each step recollects her late husband, a successful doctor who was well-off in the community and who remains a silent implied reproach to her son Ewen. Ewen counts just a few scrawny birds in payment for his work, and so little money that he cannot afford to hire a maid to keep the house in order. 'My accounts were always in good order, and so was my house,' Grandmother MacLeod insists, as she adopts her own father's warning, 'God loves Order,' with which she afflicts Vanessa: 'You remember that, Vanessa. God loves Order—he wants each one of us to set our house in order.' The warning extends far beyond housecleaning, but cleaning the house stands for keeping life's moral order, caring for one's soul. This warning about order suggests the equation of order and death. For Vanessa, precociously conscious that her mother is risking her life to give her a brother, the equation is ominous.

In the houses, however, order is always elusive. No one

there is in the place where he or she would like to be, everyone would have preferred to be someone else and to live somewhere else. Grandmother MacLeod wished she could have been an aristocrat, Father a traveller and a sailor, Roderick a doctor, Grandfather MacLeod a Greek scholar; Aunt Edna would have liked to marry young and work in town, Mother to take a degree and continue her education and Cousin Chris to go to the university and to pursue life. Each one is out of place and each finds it difficult to perceive the uneasiness of the other. Vanessa's father refers to Grandfather MacLeod, remarking that he must always have been a lonely man, and that he himself in his own youth had not been able to understand his father. 'Sometimes a thing only hits you a long time afterwards' is Vanessa's father's comment regarding his relationship with his father, and this of course applies as well to Vanessa's personal experience; only years later will she be able to see this world of her childhood with different eyes. As for Grandmother MacLeod, the father's comment is that 'the house is still the same, so she thinks other things should be, too. It hurts her when she finds they aren't.' The conclusion that Vanessa reaches, after having experienced so many emotions and sensed so many contrasts during the span of a few days, is not so much to understand rationally as to feel deeply and permanently from then on the disarray, and to sense the sinister associations of the word 'order': 'I could not really comprehend these things, but I sensed their strangeness, their disarray. I felt that whatever God might love in this world, it was certainly not order.'

This is perhaps a good point at which to remark on Vanessa's choice of language. Here all is founded on the vocabulary of intuition. The child depicts herself as a 'professional listener,' she has the vocation of the observer; as in Laurence's novels to come, it is almost an artist's credo which Vanessa voices regarding her childhood: 'I had long ago discovered it was folly to conceal oneself. The best concealment was to sit quietly in plain view.' The refined use of the vocabulary of intuition reflecting the child's sensitivity and sensibility rather than plain rational understanding is worth noting. Vanessa is a juvenile storyteller by vocation; and side by side with the life she is living, she lives the story she is currently making up, so that at times a word from reality evokes a literary atmosphere, a sentence, or a paragraph from a would-be story. More often than not these are stories with a tragic ending, like the ones about the old man dying of pneumonia while assisted by a beautiful Métis lady, or the baby that drowns while being baptized by total immersion in the Wachakwa River. One of the stories she is writing is about pioneer life, entitled *The Pillars of a Nation,* but when she is told that Grandfather Connor in his day had been a pioneer, she feels disappointed and abandons it.

Using the language of intuition, she portrays her apprenticeship. The sadness of her mother and Aunt Edna is 'such a new thing, not to my actual sight, but to my attention,' that a sudden and almost physical pain gives her the sense of having lost something: 'some comfort had been taken from me.' Progressively she learns perceptiveness. The acquisitive, accumulative process of these lessons constitutes the profound motivation beneath these stories, loose like all the apprenticeships of life, fragmentary like all the dictates of experience, and, like the natural and vital disorder of things, hard to set in order. But the artist has an order of his own. The pace of his imagination is the pace of the mind moving through memory in a quest for meaning, not for an explicit abstract order, but rather for the shape, sense, and sentiment—the vital pulsation—of the past. Laurence chooses to narrate what memories endure in her, what is part of her. In the end order coincides with the individual, and the measure of order is the artist herself, in her internal imaginative reality.

Time is Vanessa, a developing creature; time is with her, in her advancement towards her own life. Time is movement, everything changes incessantly; and through the theory of things glimpses of meaning, truth, and divinity will be perceived. As for the rest, all is fragmentary, like the structure and so-called 'order' imposed by men, captured by the fragmentary order of memory. Only imagination is able to grasp order and time without their coming to signify death.

The time of the beginning of a story exemplifies the time of the story; the short is thus akin to poetry. More than showing her reader that symbols do exist, Laurence shows that things are in themselves symbolic, and that they are especially so when connected with the theme of freedom. Almost everything in her writing points toward some sort of negated liberty recurs in the theme of birds and other animals seen as being trapped, menaced or extinct: Grandmother Connor's canary Birdie, the caged wild bear that represents Grandfather Connor, the half-husky that stands for the Métis such as the Tonnerres, the loons, representing the original Indian inhabitants of the country eradicated by so-called civilization, the dinosaurs to which Grandfather Connor and Grandmother MacLeod are equated, and finally the bird in the house, emblem of the father. Though born to be free, to travel and see the world, the father's only freedom may have been confined to the season of the war. The world he saw then was only a Europe of trenches and destruction and death: his death symbol will be the bird in the house, trapped like him, generous and beaten, and destined to die young.

The caged bear is Grandfather Connor. When offended he withdraws from the living-room and retreats to his cavern in the basement, where he sits cross and mute in his rocking chair, squeaking out a reproachful warning for the whole house, which almost trembles from it, so oppressive is his irritated, intolerant presence down there: 'From his cave . . . the angry crunching of the wooden rockers against the cement floor would reverberate through the house, a kind of sub-verbal Esperanto, a disapproval which even the most obtuse person could not fail to comprehend.' Vanessa associates the Bear-Grandfather with the never-seen Great Bear Lake, perceived only on the maps like an imagined vastness of black water that lies in an unknown place beyond the known prairies and the fenced fields, a place where nature is indomitable and impregnable. Grandfather may be an intermediary to the world that is aeons away, where still 'there was no feeling about the place.' This sets the 'savage' Grandfather Connor in contrast to the extremely 'civilized' Grandmother MacLeod, so that a fight between the two would be nothing less than 'like a brontosaurus running headlong into a tyrannosaurus.'

In this period Vanessa is writing her hundredth story, *The Silver Sphinx*. A passionate story of love and death, it is inspired by the Bible, which is her only reading experience

and only source for such feelings; her love scenes are spoken in the hieratic language of the Song of Solomon. The story is an exotic pastiche set in ancient Egypt, and its auburn-haired heroine, when left by her lover, can feed only on avocados. The love and death scenes have the sombre splendor of Ecclesiastes. However, though 'Both death and love seemed regrettably far from Manawaka and the snow, and my grandfather stamping his feet in the front porch of the Brick House,' it is in the Brick House that Vanessa for the first time encounters experiences of love and death.

Her first perception of what real love is reaches her during a visit of Aunt Edna's boyfriend and occurs as a story of conflicting sentiments and renunciation linked to the difficulty of finding a job during the Depression. Grandfather is unkind and rough towards the guest, hurting Edna. The couple withdraws to another room while Vanessa, the eternal eavesdropper, approaches her listening post. The conversation between the lovers is bitter and painful, and in the end pitiless reality overwhelms affection. That night Vanessa overhears Aunt Edna crying in her loneliness, whispering the name of the man she will no longer be able to love. All of a sudden Vanessa is struck by the absurdity of what she thought was love in her barbaric queen, and she sees that like every human image, that of human love and suffering is made up of contrasts: 'I could not reconcile this image with the known face, nor could I disconnect it,' she thinks. 'I thought of my aunt, her sturdy laughter, the way she tore into the housework, her hands and feet which she always disparagingly joked about, believing them to be clumsy. I thought of the story in the scribbler at home. I wanted to get home quickly, so I could destroy it.' The image of passion, the reality of love, true pain, Aunt Edna's sacrifice to solitude—this superior order—will linger from now on in the narrator.

Another life experience that Vanessa apprehends here is death—Grandmother Connor's death. Left in the care of Grandmother MacLeod in the house-museum, she has not been able to visit the Connor's house-monument so frequently: 'Without my mother, our house seemed like a museum, full of dead and meaningless objects, vases and gilt-framed pictures and looming furniture, all of which had to be dusted and catered to, for reasons which everyone had forgotten.' At the death of her beloved Grandmother Connor, Vanessa is again caught eavesdropping; but the season of spying is almost at an end: 'I could no longer eavesdrop with a clear conscience, but I justified it now by the fact that I had voluntarily removed myself from the kitchen,' the adults' place. It is here that she realizes how complex the reality of pain can be, and how unexpected, unexplored, and unfathomable feelings of guilt and merit link the quick and the dead in inscrutable ways.

That *Bird* is an extraordinary celebration of clichés finds its confirmation in the title story, the story of the death of Vanessa's father. The country-girl, hired at last by the MacLeod household to 'make order,' announces a death when she sees a sparrow trapped indoors: 'A bird in the house is a death in the house.' The scene is full of horror, but what dominates the story is above all grief and the comprehension of grief. Vanessa justifies herself to her grandmother for not having gone to the Remembrance Day parade by formally telling her she is sorry. Then, after thinking over again what the parade means to her grandmother—the remembrance of her son Roderick's death—Vanessa repeats: 'I'm sorry'; but it is only when she is fully aware of why she is saying it that she really feels she means what she says, attaining the comprehension of grief. In an analogous episode occurring during the Second World War, when she is seventeen and herself in love with an officer, Vanessa casually discovers the photograph of a girl, whom her father may have briefly loved during his service in Europe; only then will she really feel the acute pain for the whole of her father's life, which was so ungenerous towards him. She finds herself hoping that the brief moment he lived with that girl had meant freedom to him. And only then can she really feel her father's death. The whole book is her way of saying a protracted 'I'm sorry' and of revisiting the clichés and digging out their meanings, both mysterious and charged with confirmation.

After the death of her father the house-monument, the mythical 'Sunday place,' becomes the 'everyday place.' Grandmother Connor is no longer there. Grandfather Connor has been debunked: 'The rocking chair trick was used fairly often, and when my mother and Michael and I were doing the dishes we would hear the reproachful *screee-scraaw* coming from Grandfather's cavern,' his prison-refuge. And there is now a Michael in Vanessa's life, a presence of short duration, rapidly eliminated from the scene by Grandfather, as in Aunt's time. (Edna has meanwhile succeeded in marrying a bolder boyfriend who in the eyes of the grandfather has the merit of having prevented the house from catching fire, daring to invade his territory and desecrate his cave by laying hands on the furnace located there). Michael leaves, but Grandfather has been clear-sighted: the young man, it turns out, was married after all. Vanessa must of course suffer because of this, but she will cure her own sorrow, although about this as about everything that happens to her during these years, she will later have to observe: 'and yet, twenty years later it was still with me to some extent, part of the accumulation of happenings which can never entirely be thrown away.' Like Edna before her, she now becomes frantic to get away from Manawaka and the Brick House—'Jericho's Brick Battlements,' as she will humorously call this place, as remote and embattled as an outpost.

She leaves to go to town and study at the university, and will come back only for Grandfather's death two years later; during the funeral oration for him she hears the story of a pioneer by the name of Connor as if it were an entirely new person, a 'stranger,' a persona, a fictional character:

> He had come from Ontario to Manitoba by the Red River steamer, and he had walked from Winnipeg to Manawaka, earning his way by shoeing horses. After some years as a blacksmith, he had enough money to go into hardware business. Then he had built his house. It had been the first brick house in Manawaka. Suddenly the minister's recounting of these familiar facts struck me as though I had never heard any of it before.

After twenty more years Vanessa will again come back, but she will not go to visit her grandfather's tomb: 'There was no need. It was not his monument.' She will go instead to his true monument, the Brick House, symbol of the man's immortality, which Vanessa feels proclaiming itself in her veins, while the immortality of the mother—the deep reason perhaps why the mother in this collection out-

lives the father, whereas Laurence's own real mother dies when she is still a girl—will be found in the imperishable 'clichés of affection.' (pp. 161-69)

*Giovanna Capone, " 'A Bird in the House':
Margaret Laurence on Order and the Artist,"
in* Gaining Ground: European Critics on Canadian Literature, Vol. VI, *edited by Robert Kroetsch and Reingard M. Nischik, NeWest Press, 1985, pp. 161-70.*

Helen M. Buss   (essay date 1985)

[*In the following excerpt from her monograph* Mother and Daughter Relationships in the Manawaka Works of Margaret Laurence, *Buss focuses on relationships between Vanessa and several female, mother-surrogate characters in* A Bird in the House.]

The lives of Laurence's female artist-figures, like the lives of her other heroines, are placed firmly in the context of the mother-daughter relationship. In *A Bird in the House* we discover the experience of this relationship to be the primary motivating factor in the shaping of the female-artist. In *The Diviners* we find how a creative relationship of mother and daughter is integrated with the artistic process itself. Thus we move from a psychological view of the nature of this bond to a religious view; we move toward Laurence's most positive statement of the mother-daughter relationship as it becomes the source of inspiration for the artist-figure.

In the closing story of *A Bird in the House,* "Jericho's Brick Battlements," Vanessa's mother Beth tells her that she has sold the MacLeod silver and Limoges and asked for help from the family to get Vanessa to college. The daughter protests:

> "What have you done?" I cried. "Canvassed the entire family?"
>
> "More or less," my mother said calmly, as though the tigress beneath her exterior was nothing to be surprised about. "Father is also selling some bonds which he's been hanging onto all these years."
>
> "Him! How did you do that? But I'm not taking a nickel of his money."
>
> My mother put a hand on my shoulder.
>
> "When I was your age," she said, "I got the highest marks in the province in my last year high school. I guess I never told you that. I wanted to go to college. Your grandfather didn't believe in education for women then."

In this moment of truth between mother and daughter we not only begin to see the "tigress" that Beth has hidden for a lifetime from the view of her daughter and others, but also, as readers, we are forced to reassess much of their relationship and much of the book's content in the light of this new knowledge of Beth's lost opportunities and the different future she hopes for her daughter.

On the surface, *A Bird in the House* would seem to be largely about the dominance in the lives of others of the Manawaka patriarch, Timothy Connor. Beth would appear to be, to her daughter's eyes, one of the chief defenders of Timothy's authority. In the opening story, **"The Sound of Singing,"** she hurries Vanessa along to dinner at "the Brick House" with, "you know how your grandfather hates people to be late." When Vanessa chants, "Step on a crack, break your grandfather's back," Beth responds, "that's not very nice Vanessa . . . I always thought it was your mother's back." Vanessa is "hurt that she could imagine the substitution to have been accidental, for I had genuinely thought it would please her." She quickly learns that she cannot openly enlist her mother as ally against her grandfather. Indeed, her rebellious spirit must develop underground through her eavesdropping on her mother's real opinions, as voiced to Beth's sister Edna.

Signe Hammer, who has described the "underground" nature of the mother-daughter relationship, also emphasizes that the daughter often receives a "double message" from the mother, one in which the daughter is encouraged to obey the patriarchal definition of her womanhood and another message which pushes the girl toward defining her identity in more achievement-oriented ways. Vanessa, quite literally, receives a "double message"; her mother insists on her obedient submissiveness to Timothy and his ideas and yet engages, with Edna, in the expression of quite opposite viewpoints. In these stories much of what Vanessa learns about her mother's real views is a truly espionage effort since she hears them by listening through stove pipes or air vents or by making herself invisible. "The best concealment was to sit quietly in plain view" she explains, as she yearns to hear her mother's and Edna's whispered rebellions.

Aunt Edna, a mother-surrogate in many ways, represents for Vanessa a more obviously rebellious and self-directed female figure than her mother. When Beth reprimands Vanessa for criticizing her grandfather, Edna defends Vanessa and corrects Beth. The two women, in their physical appearance, seem to be the two sides of femininity that she needs to reconcile. Beth is described as "slight and fine-boned, with long-fingered hands like those on my Chinese princess doll, and feet that Aunt Edna enviously called 'aristocratic' which meant narrow. . . . Aunt Edna on the other hand, was handsome and strong but did not like being so."

The attempt to heal the results of the "double message"—that the female is either fine and beautiful (but weak) or tough and strong (but unacceptable), combined with maternal disapproval of the expression of her viewpoint—leads Vanessa to turn to writing. She first imagines a story of a man "sick to death in the freezing cabin with only the beautiful halfbreed lady (no woman) to look after him." The "beautiful halfbreed lady (no woman)" is a combination of beauty and strength; the slightly exotic and unacceptable connotations of "halfbreed" reflect the beginning of an awareness of an archetypal female character that appears later in Vanessa's stories as "some barbaric queen, beautiful and terrible, and I could imagine her, wearing a long robe of leopard skin and one or two heavy gold bracelets, pacing an alabaster courtyard and keening her unrequited love."

The emergence of such a figure in the young female writer is in response to both personal and cultural needs. Psychologically, Vanessa must invent a version of womanhood that is not as powerless as her two maternal figures, her mother and her aunt. On a cultural level, the split our society makes between the feminine as beautiful and the feminine as strong must be healed by the irruption of this figure in the imagination of the creative girl, in order to create the archetypal wholeness that the feminine worldview seeks. In *The Great Mother,* Neumann defines the collective and individual manifestation as "the primordial image or archetype of the Great Mother . . . [it is] not . . . any concrete image existing in space and time, but . . . an inward image at work in the human psyche. The symbolic expression of this psychic phenomenon is to be found in the figures of the Great Goddess represented in the myths and artistic creations of mankind." Outside her writing, Vanessa finds no such manifestations; she searches her family circle in vain for the qualities of womanhood that rise unbidden in her fictional creations. Much space in the first four stories is devoted to an analysis of the "womanhood" of five characters: Beth, Edna, Agnes Connor, Grandmother MacLeod and Noreen. While Beth and Edna represent two potentially positive but imprisoned versions of womanhood, the two grandmother figures can be seen as the two traditional modes by which women adapt and hide their true selves to meet the demands of the patriarchy.

Grandmother Connor, more admired by Vanessa, adapts by channeling her strength into a kind of sublime and tolerant detachment. She attempts to ignore what she cannot change and works in the lives of others in only the most indirect ways. Yet all those around her credit her with an enormous depth of feeling and colossal strength, and hold a saintly image of her. As Vanessa puts it, "it was a family saying that she couldn't tell a lie if her life depended on it." Through her, Vanessa sees the Old Testament religion softened and humanized: "to her everything in the Bible was as gentle as she herself. The words were spiritual only, strokes of lightness and dark and the wounds poured cochineal." Less positively, Agnes Connor is obedient to the point of exhaustion to her oppressive and possessive husband, Timothy. When she finally does ask something for herself, that Timothy be tolerant of her brother Dan, she is really asking the favor for the benefit of a man. Her defenses of her daughters against Timothy are largely strategies to avoid confrontation. Since her daughters are convinced that she will be terribly hurt if they make a fuss, the paternal dictatorship is reinforced. There is no proof that Agnes ever objected to Timothy's refusal of an education for their daughter. Thus the saintliness of Agnes consists of silence and detached serenity.

Vanessa receives an insight into the other side of sainthood when, eavesdropping as usual, she hears a conversation between her mother and her Uncle Terence following Agnes' funeral. Terence has just revealed that their father was once unfaithful to their mother:

> "How could he?" my mother said in a low voice.
>
> "Oh Terence. How could he have done that? To Mother, of all people."
>
> "You know something, Beth?" Uncle Terence said. "I think he honestly believed that about her being some kind of angel. She'd never have thought of herself like that, so I don't suppose it ever would have occurred to her that he did. But I have a notion that he felt all along she was far and away too good for him. Can you feature going to bed with an angel, honey? It doesn't bear thinking about."

"Terence, you're drunk," my mother said sharply, "As usual."

"Maybe so,' he admitted. Then he burst out, "I only felt, Beth, that somebody might have said to Vanessa just now, 'Look baby, she was terrific and we thought the world of her, but let's not say angel, eh?' All this angel business gets us into really deep water, you know that?"

Vanessa not only begins to learn more tolerance of her grandfather whose ways are often her own, but she also realizes that the struggle to achieve the saintly model of womanhood, represented by her Grandmother Connor and to some degree her own mother, is often achieved only by way of cutting off real human contact and love.

On the other hand, the grandmother who is recognized as both physically weak and not admirable, Grandmother MacLeod, turns out to have a perverse strength that Vanessa must grudgingly admit. In **"To Set Our House in Order"** we receive several descriptions of Vanessa's paternal grandmother which show her to be, in the young writer's mind, a kind of negative version of the queenly character she writes about: "at the top of the stairs . . . Grandmother MacLeod . . . standing there in her quilted black satin dressing gown, her slight figure, held straight and poised"; her voice is "distinct and ringing like the tap of a sterling teaspoon on a crystal goblet"; she is "steel-spined despite her apparent fragility." Stoically, she scolds her son for "encouraging the child to give way" to emotion when Vanessa's mother is in a long and difficult labor. Grandmother MacLeod is obsessed with her possessions and cannot be stopped from buying fine linen even in the depths of the Depression. To Vanessa, she is the hypochondriac occupant of the walnut spool bed which "had obviously been designed for queens or giants . . . my tiny grandmother used to lie within it all day when she had migraine, contriving somehow to look like a giant queen." Her words of guidance for Vanessa are "God loves order," but through watching the tragedy of the lost life around this woman, Vanessa learns "that whatever God might love in this world, it was certainly not order." Grandmother MacLeod has opted for the materialistic concept of womanhood as defined by patriarchal values. She has spent her life being refined, reserved, physically manicured and correct, by surrounding herself with the physical paraphernalia of being "a lady."

With sainthood and ladyhood rejected as unworthy models, a bizarre yet curiously powerful kind of female figure enters Vanessa's life. Noreen, the hired girl from the country, embodies a version of womanhood outside Vanessa's middle-class experience. With her physical earthiness and religious excesses Noreen, like Rachel's Calla, is a shocking contrast to the other two women in the MacLeod house. Beth spends some time trying to improve Noreen by getting her to shave under her arms; Grandmother MacLeod refuses even to speak to the girl; Vanessa herself, however, is fascinated:

I began to think of her as a sorceress, someone not quite of this earth. There was nothing unearthly about her broad shoulders and hips and her forest of dark red hair, but even these features took on a slightly sinister significance to me. I no longer saw her through the eyes or the expressed opinions of my mother and father, as a girl who had quit school at grade eight and whose life on the farm had been endlessly drab. I knew the truth—Noreen's life had not been drab at all, for she dwelt in a world of violent splendours, a world filled with angels whose wings of delicate light bore real feathers, and saints shining like the dawn, and prophets who spoke in ancient tongues, and the ecstatic souls of the saved, as well as denizens of the lower regions—mean-eyed imps and crooked cloven-hoofed monsters and beasts with the bodies of swine and the human heads of murderers, and lovely depraved jezebels torn by dogs through all eternity. The middle layer of Creation, our earth, was equally full of grotesque presences, for Noreen believed strongly in the visitation of ghosts and the communication with spirits. She could prove this with her Ouija board.

Noreen is the first female figure of any spiritual dimension that Vanessa has encountered.

Because it is Noreen who has made the dire prediction, "A bird in the house means a death in the house," when Vanessa's father dies, she becomes the focus of Vanessa's spiritual and physical anguish: "I hit Noreen as hard as I could. When she swung around, appalled, I hit out at her once more, my arms and legs flailing. Her hands snatched at my wrists, and she held me, but still I continued to struggle, fighting blindly, my eyes tightly closed, as though she were a prison around me and I was battling to get out." When Noreen tries to assure Vanessa that her father is in heaven, the girl responds coldly with, "He is not in Heaven, because there is no Heaven." At this moment, just when Vanessa has lost her faith in the traditional patriarchal religion of her father's world, Noreen has taken on the darkest side of the maternal world that is emerging in Vanessa's consciousness: she seems to be the terrible mother who devours the hero in death. Actually, however, Noreen represents an aspect of the feminine that is essential but which Vanessa has not integrated into her psyche.

In the youthful Vanessa's writing career, her creative efforts have ceased. She stopped writing her pioneer stories, "The Pillars of the Nation," because she found out that her disliked Grandfather Connor was one of those brave pioneers she so worships. After turning to love stories she realizes that love in a fallen world is too complicated when she hears Edna crying for her lost love. Her cliched world of expiring pioneers, half-breed ladies and barbaric queens has been much shaken by the powerlessness of the women around her, the death of her father and the terrifying implications of womanly strength and power represented by Noreen. "Everything changed after my father's death," Vanessa says. Not just economic and social arrangements, but her whole world-view is changing. She has lost the one positive male character that tied her to patriarchal values. She has not gained the insight to establish her own values in their place. Her mother has needed her daughter to be adult and maternal during the crisis and Vanessa remembers that "I stayed close beside my mother, and this was only partly for my own consoling, I also had the feeling that she needed my protection." In the past Beth has sought this care from her sister Edna. Now she turns to her own daughter. The daughter is strong but much of her own bitterness and confusion remain unexpressed except in her brief fight with Noreen.

For Vanessa, the writer, the expression must come later

in life through her writing. Significantly, although the childhood scribblings end at this time, the stories of the adult Vanessa, the stories we are reading, reflect a marked change in narrative technique. In "Crossing Jordan: Time and Memory in the Fiction of Margaret Laurence," Sherrill Grace notes that "with *A Bird in the House* (1970) and *The Diviners* (1974), Laurence herself discovered the philosophical and technical means to present her vision of past, present and future embodied in characters young enough to re-create the past in the present process of living." The technical device involved here is the wide-ranging breakdown of historical time which begins with the fifth story of the *Bird* collection, **"The Loons."** As Grace says, "each of the first four stories has a comparatively simple temporal structure" whereas "the last four stories . . . are convoluted, moving back and forth over long stretches of the past, stitching the past, as it were, into the 'spiritual fabric' of the present." I would suggest that, as in the case of *The Stone Angel,* the primary reason for the technical change is to dramatize the breakdown of the old patriarchal world that at her mother's urging Vanessa lived in and believed in. The traditional order has collapsed, and accordingly the masculine logic of cause and effect, linear time and tightly organized plots also come to an end. Vanessa begins now to employ the logic of "Eros" and to search for more subtle connections between events. Similarly, instead of merely reflecting the problem, she begins a detailed exploration of the lives of the victims of the patriarchal world.

Thus in **"The Loons"** the underside of the pioneer conquest of the West is shown in the form of the tubercular Piquette Tonnerre. The youthful Vanessa has turned away from Piquette at thirteen in favor of cliched versions of Indians, and turned away again from the young woman Piquette in embarrassed discomfort. The middle-aged narrator attempts to deal with the world that created a Piquette, dead with her babies in a tragic house fire. **"Horses of the Night"** diagrams what happens to a sensitive young man as he attempts to block out his emotions in order to become the success that the materialistic and belligerent world demands and wherein manhood is equated with material success and the ability to kill. In **"The Half-Husky"** Vanessa sees the negative mirror-image of the world which made her grandfather's boast of self-made success possible.

In each story the youthful Vanessa is vaguely aware of her own implication in the world that caused these victims' fates but cannot consciously accept that the same world she grew up in is also an evil and fallen world. At the end of **"The Loons,"** the adult narrator comes to a realization of her own limitations when she says, "it seemed to me now that in some unconscious and totally unrecognized way, Piquette might have been the only one, after all, who had heard the crying of the loons." Similarly, with reference to Chris's tragic life, at the ending of **"Horses of the Night"** she notes how her youthful self found it difficult to speak the half-realized truth out loud: "I could not go on, could not say that the letter seemed only the final heart breaking extension of that way he'd always had of distancing himself from the absolute unbearability of battle." At the end of **"The Half-Husky"** she admits her own unfairness in not being able to speak to Harvey Shinwell's violent aunt. She had first seen the dog as victim of Harvey's sadism, then Harvey as victim of his aunt's violence. In

turn, she had vaguely understood that the aunt was pandering to something in her grandfather's attitude.

She does not, however, finally confront the unfairness of the world she has lived in until the moment of truth with her mother. Then it is that for Vanessa "Jericho's Brick Battlements" tumble down.

I mentioned at the beginning of this discussion that this moment alters the mother and daughter relationship for Vanessa and Beth and forces our reassessment of the events of the stories. Two important realizations emerge. Beth has been able to do for her daughter what she was never able to do for herself: stand up to her own father. In addition, Vanessa's search for victims had led her to the mother. The implications for Vanessa are contained in those two statements referred to earlier: that she is not "Free" and that her mother's death remained "unhealed" the longest. The reader senses that for the middle-aged Vanessa the telling of the stories has been a way of healing and freeing herself.

Much of what she is integrating into her psyche through the writing remains unconscious. On a conscious level Vanessa realizes that although "I feared and fought the old man, yet he proclaimed himself in my veins." Thus, on the one hand, the book is about Vanessa's coming to terms with her grandfather as a patriarchal figure and the feminine vision remains unspoken for Vanessa herself. At the same time, however, this feminine vision is available to the reader through Laurence's subtle use of bird symbolism.

Throughout the collection the female characters are associated with trapped birds. Grandmother Connor keeps a canary in a cage. Vanessa tells us that "when I asked my grandmother if the bird minded being there, she shook her head and said no, it had been there always and wouldn't know what to do with itself outside." Grandmother MacLeod has a "Chinese carpet with its birds in eternal motionless flight." Piquette is associated with the vanishing loons. Vanessa hears trapped sparrows in the attic. Grandfather Connor says that Edna has "no more sense than a sparrow." The feather duster that Vanessa uses to dust her Grandmother's precious possessions is "like a dead bird."

The most obvious use of the symbol, of course, is to be found in the title story of the collection, where a bird is caught between two layers of window glass and Vanessa releases it into the further captivity of her room. Terrified, she sees that "The sparrow had exhausted itself. It lay on the floor, spent and trembling. I could not bring myself to touch it. Noreen bent and picked it up. She cradled it with great gentleness between her cupped hands. Then we took it downstairs, and when I opened the back door, Noreen set the bird free." This story, like the others, is on the surface largely concerned with Vanessa's relationship to the paternal world. In this case we are being told the story of her father's death. Thus the statement by Noreen that "a bird in the house means a death in the house" seems a prediction of the father's death. On another level, however, it is Vanessa's paternal world that is dying. Thus Noreen's prediction must be seen in a larger context, that of the growth of unconscious matriarchal feelings and values.

Joseph L. Henderson in "Ancient Myths and Modern Man" describes symbols as "the means by which contents of the unconscious can enter the conscious mind, and they also are an active expression of those contents," and he goes on to observe that "the bird is the most fitting symbol of transcendence." In the Vanessa stories the bird has become the symbol of female entrapment, not just in a sociological sense but in a psycho-spiritual one. It is important to notice, for example, that it is Noreen, the only maternal figure of any religious dimension, that releases the bird. Robert Gibbs in his introduction to the collection has said that this title story is the "localizing of her [Vanessa's] own release, her own uncaging." But Laurence means us to see the uncaging as something more than a simple gaining of personal freedom. The attention she has given to the symbolic significance of Noreen and her influence in Vanessa's life suggests that the "release" is the feeling of previously caged feminine feelings and values. These have been present in the youthful Vanessa's writing in the figure of the barbaric queen. The more conscious dimension of these feelings and values takes the form of a changed consciousness of the older Vanessa narrator who is now able to write the victim stories and who is able finally to see the "tigress" in her own mother.

Thus, in the Vanessa stories, Laurence makes an important statement about the motivation of the female artist. Vanessa writes to free herself, to tell the story of the maternal world existing unrealized and often unnoticed inside the patriarchal structure. In telling these stories Vanessa defines her own womanhood by describing its shaping influences. Appropriately, these ideas are expressed not so much on the conscious planes of plot but on the level of image and symbol.

Esther Harding has said of Modern woman's dilemma that "if woman is out of touch with the feminine principle . . . she cannot take the lead in what is after all the feminine realm—that of human relationship," and she feels that if women "are to get in touch with their lost feminine side it must be by the hard road of conscious adaptation." I would suggest that this is the very process Laurence is depicting in her two kunstlerromans. In *A Bird in the House,* the process is somewhat implicit: the mother-daughter relationship exists as a subtle underplay and is presented largely through imagery and the narrator's growing artistic preoccupation with female figures. In *The Diviners,* however, the mother-daughter relationship is used as the very principle of structural and thematic organization. (pp. 54-64)

> *Helen M. Buss, in her* Mother and Daughter Relationships in the Manawaka Works of Margaret Laurence, *University of Victoria, 1985, 88 p.*

W. J. Keith   (essay date 1987)

[*Keith is an English educator, editor, and critic who has published several works on Canadian writers. In the following excerpt, he offers a consideration of Laurence's "Uncertain Flowering," an obscure early story that was the first of her works set in Africa. Keith regards this tale as an important link between Laurence's non-fictional treatment of her time in Somaliland, Africa,* The Prophet's Camel Bell, *and her African fiction collected in* The Tomorrow-Tamer.]

In 1953 Laurence published a short story entitled **"Uncertain Flowering"** in the fourth number of *Story: The Magazine of the Short Story in Book Form,* edited by Whit and Hallie Burnett. As the contributors' page remarks, "this is her first story published in the United States." It is not, however, included in the standard Laurence bibliographies and checklists, nor, so far as I know, has any commentator discussed it. Perhaps the story was forgotten because it appeared during a time of resettlement and changed addresses after the Laurences moved from Somaliland to the Gold Coast; one of its chief claims to interest, indeed, lies in the fact that it is set in Somaliland and thus provides an interesting link between the non-fiction material later written up in *The Prophet's Camel Bell* and the African stories that grew out of her Gold Coast (Ghana) experiences.

Because **"Uncertain Flowering"** seems to be unknown and is not readily available, a summary of the plot may be helpful. The chief character is a sixteen-year-old English girl named Karen Aynsley, and we first encounter her on a plane bound for the Somaliland Protectorate, where she is to spend her school holidays with her parents, Philip and Jo Aynsley. She is weeping, but we do not understand why until later. A cockney sergeant in an adjoining seat tries to strike up a conversation, but she is curt in her replies. "You *are* a funny kid," he comments, and she bridles at this remark. We soon realize that she is at the painful stage of growth between girlhood and womanhood.

On arrival at Bor Mado in Somaliland, she is met by her parents, who still treat her as a child, her father referring to her kindly but inappropriately as "bairn." Not only do their references to child friends and childhood pursuits grate on her, but it becomes clear that the relationship between her parents is on the point of break-up. Karen has long been aware of the situation, and this explains her initial tears. She is roused only by mention of her pony and the prospect of a gymkhana. A few days later, Karen rides off with an old Somali servant named Yusuf to an old haunt of hers which, in Yusuf's words, is "fit only for those who dream dreams." After an exchange in which she is surprised to find that she is speaking once again in Somali without realizing it, she tells him that it was a place where she used to come "to pray." She finds, however, that she can no longer do so.

The climax of the story occurs at a dance following the gymkhana. Karen is standing "unobtrusively beside one of the doors . . . just far enough around the corner to be out of sight of the dancers," overhears her father engaged in an affair with a family friend, and comes to suspect that an army captain is her mother's (latest) lover. A young and somewhat drunk lieutenant, Howard Tavershaw, is detailed to escort Karen home early. She soon extracts from him confirmation of her parents' affairs and confides that she herself "had an affair in England." This provokes Tavershaw into making love to her; as Laurence rather coyly puts it, he "pulled her closer to him and let all his young longing for a woman take her as its object." The final revelation comes when he discovers that she was a virgin. Asked why she implied the contrary, she admits: "I don't know." Her last words—to herself—are: "You think I should be glad. . . . You really think I should be glad. . . . "

"Uncertain Flowering" is a workmanlike, often quite accomplished, but ultimately somewhat formulaic story. The sense of place is evoked economically and effectively, and Laurence's ear for dialogue is remarkably skilful. She has an enviable capacity to convey meanings and implications that are not directly expressed in conversation. Karen's situation, poised between child and adult, is sensitively portrayed without ever suggesting condescension. The weakness of the story lies in its contrived quality. Revelation follows revelation too relentlessly; we are too conscious of authorial control over the material. Thus the sergeant's "you *are* a funny kid" is balanced by Tavershaw's "you *are* a queer kid" and "you *are* a peculiar kid." Similarly, the sergeant's offering her a cigarette to show that he no longer considers her a child is echoed when Karen herself insists on a gin and lime rather than "squash or lime" from Tavershaw. One feels, however, that these formal effects are imposed upon the narrative from outside; in short, the story seems to arise less from a sense of personal urgency on Laurence's part as from a dogged determination to produce a "well-made" fiction.

Its fascination resides in the glimpses it affords of attitudes and preoccupations that are to recur elsewhere in Laurence's writing. This is her first attempt at fiction created out of her African experience, and it is an index of her caution that she writes not about the Somalis themselves but about the British administrative class. Clearly, she has not yet thought her way through to the kind of vision that is to distinguish the stories that constitute *The Tomorrow-Tamer.* The scene between Karen and Yusuf is perhaps the most tender in the whole story, and it is significant that he understands her better than the whites. While they can only see her as a child, Yusuf remarks shrewdly: "You are no child. . . . But you are not a woman, either." Her automatic switch into Somali is poignant evidence of an emotional bond, but the scene is close to a dead-end so far as the plot is concerned. References to "the proud impoverished Somalis with enigmatical eyes" and "the quavering sadness of the songs the Somalis chanted around their fires"—first hint, perhaps, of Laurence's interest in the material that became *A Tree for Poverty*—read a little too much like "local colour" exoticism. At the same time, they indicate the direction in which Laurence's interests will move.

In addition, there are some intriguing and more specific connections with Laurence's later writings. Yusuf the servant, who had served with the Camel Corps in "the later Mullah Campaigns," may well have been based on the "old warrior" who is central to the twelfth chapter of *The Prophet's Camel Bell.* The general subject of young people coming to Africa—and coming to terms with Africa—is explored later in **"The Drummer of All the World"** and **"The Rain Child"** (both in *The Tomorrow-Tamer*). Here it is a simple return from school on Karen's part, but in **"The Drummer of All the World"** a black/white childhood friendship is involved, while in **"The Rain Child"** the girl is an African born and educated in England who is encountering Africa for the first time. The increase in subtlety is noticeable. Again, Karen's dislike of being called "kid" or "child" or "bairn" looks forward to later reactions by Rachel Cameron in *A Jest of God* and by Morag in *The Diviners,* while the rather contrived overhearing scene anticipates similar (and, in my view, similarly overcontrived) scenes in *The Stone Angel, A Bird in the House,* and *The Diviners.* More dramatically, the realization after the love-making that the girl was a virgin is repeated, with greater violence but at the same time with greater poignancy, in the scene between Johnnie Kestoe and the young black prostitute (who is also "very young, not more than sixteen") in the twelfth chapter of *This Side Jordan.* Above all, the pervasive sense of sexuality as a sub-text within the story, the strong impression we receive of Karen as a growing physical being, underlines the extent to which this is a recurring and developing preoccupation in Laurence's major work.

One significant difference, of course, between **"Uncertain Flowering"** and the other African stories is that here Laurence focuses almost exclusively on the group that she later categorizes, in the fourteenth chapter of *The Prophet's Camel Bell,* as "the imperialists." This is doubtless another reason why the story has been overlooked. Once she realized that she had a rich and suitable subject in stories about Africans approaching political and personal independence, this story would have seemed conventional and even trivial. The political undercurrent is always secondary here. The British are characterized with some asperity but not totally without sympathy. Seen in virtual isolation from the Somalis, they are ridiculous in their weaknesses but are also presented as victims in a situation which, as individuals, they did not create, and which they cannot control. Karen herself transcends the categories; she is offered not politically as an imperialist but individually as a child-woman. By the same token, however, the story's connection with Africa may thus be seen as merely incidental. The "well-made" quality of the construction cannot wholly disguise the split between theme and setting. This is, then, apprentice work, but for serious students of Canadian literature it represents an important first step in the development of Margaret Laurence as a writer of fiction. (pp. 202-05)

W. J. Keith " 'Uncertain Flowering': An Overlooked Short Story by Margaret Laurence," in Canadian Literature, No. 112, Spring, 1987, pp. 202-05.

FURTHER READING

Darling, Michael. " 'Undecipherable Signs': Margaret Laurence's 'To Set Our House in Order'." *Essays on Canadian Writing,* No. 29 (Summer 1984): 192-203.

Identifies the opposition of order and disorder as the central theme in "To Set Our House in Order." Referring to the narrator/protagonist of the story, Vanessa MacLeod, Darling states that "in giving order to her own life by retelling the events of her childhood, Vanessa learns that seemingly obvious differences conceal deeper affinities, and that an apparently rigid order may be only a flimsy structure hiding a chaotic turmoil."

Harrison, James. "The Rhythms of Ritual in Margaret Laurence's *The Tomorrow-Tamer.*" *World Literature Written in English* 27, No. 2 (Autumn 1987): 245-52.

Examines how Laurence utilizes character, plot, and "certain syntactic and rhetorical mannerisms" to illuminate in *The Tomorrow-Tamer* difficulties in West Africa's quest for independence from Britain.

Journal of Canadian Studies 13, No. 3 (Fall 1978).
  Special issue devoted to Laurence that includes four of Laurence's previously uncollected short stories, as well as other pieces by and about the author.

Kreisel, Henry. "The African Stories of Margaret Laurence." *The Canadian Forum* (April 1961): 8-10.
  Thematic analysis of Laurence's African stories and her novel *This Side Jordan,* focusing on themes of freedom and dignity.

Lecker, Robert, and David, Jack, eds. "Margaret Laurence: An Annotated Bibliography." In their *The Annotated Bibliography of Canada's Major Authors: Volume One,* pp. 47-101. Downsview, Ontario: ECW Press, 1979.
  Extensive, annotated bibliography of works by and about Laurence.

Middlebro', Tom. "Imitatio Inanitatis: Literary Madness and the Canadian Short Story." *Canadian Literature,* No. 107 (Winter 1985): 189-93.
  Examines Laurence's treatment of the theme of insanity in "Horses of the Night."

Morley, Patricia. *Margaret Laurence.* Twayne's World Author Series: A Survey of the World's Literature, edited by Robert Lecker. Boston: Twayne Publishers, 1981, 171 p.
  Critical biography.

Nancekivell, Sharon. "Margaret Laurence: Bibliography." *World Literature Written in English* 22, No. 2 (Autumn 1983): 263-85.
  Unannotated bibliography updating Lecker and David's 1979 work (see above in Further Reading list).

Thompson, Kent. Review of *A Bird in the House,* by Margaret Laurence. *The Fiddlehead,* No. 84 (March-April 1970): 108-11.
  Focuses on Laurence's use of narrative voice and point of view in *A Bird in the House.*

Woodcock, George. "The Human Elements: Margaret Laurence's Fiction." In his *The World of Canadian Writing: Critiques & Recollections,* pp. 40-56. Vancouver: Douglas & McIntyre, 1980.
  General appraisal of Laurence's fiction, including her short story collections *The Tomorrow-Tamer* and *A Bird in the House.*

Prosper Mérimée

1803-1870

(Also wrote under the pseudonym Clara Gazul.) French short story writer, dramatist, poet, critic, novelist, historian, and translator.

Mérimée is generally considered one of France's greatest short story writers. Critics contend that his insightful depictions of human nature exhibit both an emotional restraint reminiscent of Stendhal and an economy of language and psychological detail similar to that of Gustave Flaubert. Though best known for his short stories and novellas, Mérimée excelled in many genres. His historical novel *Chronique du règne de Charles IX* (*1572: A Chronicle of the Times of Charles the Ninth*) attests to his interest in history and his narrative skill; his plays, which are clever imitations of Spanish dramas, are considered by many to be more successful than their models; his letters, the most renowned of which are collected in *Lettres à une inconnue* (*Letters to an Unknown*), are noted for sensitively illuminating facets of Mérimée's enigmatic personality. In addition, Mérimée achieved recognition as a statesman and French translator of Russian literature. Yet, such celebrated works of short fiction as "Mateo Falcone," "La Vénus d'Ille," and *Carmen,* the story that inspired Georges Bizet's opera, perhaps most strikingly portray Mérimée's concise, detached prose style and exemplify his greatest achievements.

Born in Paris, Mérimée was raised among the artists, critics, and writers who attended his parents' literary salon. At the Lycée Napoléon, Mérimée demonstrated proficiency in languages and literature, and upon graduation pursued law at the University of Paris. Instead of studying, however, he frequented the Parisian salons, where he met French author Stendhal, who became a close friend and supporter of Mérimée's literary efforts. In 1824 Mérimée began writing articles on the Spanish theater for *Le Globe,* a Paris journal, and collaborated with Stendhal on a play that was never produced. The next year *Le théâtre de Clara Gazul* (*The Plays of Clara Gazul*) appeared, a volume of dramas written by Mérimée but presented as the works of a Spanish actress. Similarly, in 1827, Mérimée published *La guzla,* a collection of ballads that were purportedly transcribed from Serbian by Hyacinthe Maglanovitch. Though intended by Mérimée as parodies, these works were well received by an unsuspecting public, few of whom doubted their authenticity.

Between the years 1829 and 1830 Mérimée published short stories in the *Revue de Paris* and *Revue française.* These stories form the core of his early efforts in the short fiction genre and were later collected in book form as *Mosaïque.* In 1831 Mérimée gained employment as a civil servant and by 1834 was appointed Inspector General of Historical Monuments, a position that satisfied his interests in antiquities and travel. As Inspector General and later as a senator under Napoléon III and Empress Eugénia, Mérimée journeyed throughout France, southern Europe, and the Near East, gathering material for both his fictional and historical writings. During the mid-1860s Méri-

mée's health declined, and he began spending winters in Cannes, where he wrote his final short stories.

Mérimée's first attempt at the short story form, "Mateo Falcone," established him as a master of the genre. Called by Walter Pater "perhaps the cruellest story in the world," this tale combines detached narration, concise description, and poignant, though limited characterization to delineate how a Corsican father's devotion to family honor drives him to kill his only beloved son for betraying the family's name. Masterful in his control of the story's passionate events, Mérimée also employs techniques of local color writing to render an accurate and convincing portrait of nineteenth-century Corsican life, though at the time Mérimée had never visited the island. Another of Mérimée's early stories that utilizes local color is "Tamango," an ironic yet realistic depiction of the West African slave trade. In this tale Mérimée satirizes both civilized humanity and the myth of the Noble Savage through the actions of the central character, African chief Tamango, who naively trades his people to a Frenchman named Ladoux (Gentle). After realizing his mistake, Tamango pursues Ladoux's ship, christened L'ésperance (Hope), managing to board and organize a mutiny. Unfortunately, the freed slaves starve when no one is able to navigate the ship back to shore. Critics note that "Mateo Falcone" and "Tamango," though powerful narratives, present relatively simple character types, whereas another short story, "Le vase étrusque," is built upon a more complex character that many commentators liken to Mérimée himself. Mérimée's enigmatic personality has long been a subject of discussion among critics, most concurring that the acerbic wit and detached nature that he revealed in his salon personality was, as in the cold, impersonal tone of his writings, a mask for deeply felt emotions. Thus when Mérimée writes protagonist Auguste Saint-Clair in "Le vase étrusque," "He was able to conceal from others the emotions of his too tender heart; but, in locking them up within himself, he made them a hundred times more cruel for him," Mérimée's words are generally interpreted as autobiographical. Through the sensitive, sympathetic portrayal of Saint-Clair, a man driven by jealousy toward his tragic death, critics observe that Mérimée successfully delineated the complex nature and motives of a character type unique in his writings.

"La Vénus d'Ille" ("The Venus d'Ille"), inspired by the myth of Venus, mixes Mérimée's characteristic verisimilitude with the supernatural, marking a new phase in his short fiction. The narrator of this tale, a Parisian intellectual interested in archeology, lends credibility to an otherwise fantastic story of an ancient statue of Venus that becomes animated after having been unearthed in a Pyrenean village. The statue bears an inscription that the narrator translates as "beware if she loves you," although few villagers heed this warning. Later, a young man carelessly places his fiancée's wedding ring on the statue's finger, but when he attempts to remove the ring, the statue closes its fingers on it. In the end, the statue fatally crushes the bridegroom in an embrace on his wedding night. Frank Paul Bowman posited that " 'Vénus d'Ille' presents the myth of love in its pure state," suggesting that the story concerns both the seductive and destructive natures of love, a theme Mérimée established through such details as the ominous inscription and the fear as well as desire that the statue's presence elicits.

Also during this time, Mérimée composed his highly acclaimed novella *Carmen*. Some critics have commented that the eponymous character of this popular work provides a human counterpart to the statue in "The Venus d'Ille." Arthur Symons noted that "in this story all the qualities of Mérimée come into agreement; the student of human passion, the traveller, the observer, the learned man, meet in harmony . . . ," creating a work of local color that has become "the symbol of Spain." Mérimée's fascination and appreciation of Mediterranean culture is engagingly apparent in the vibrant Spanish setting of this frame novella in which an archeologist encounters Don José, a soldier turned bandit, who relates the tragic story of his passion for the free-spirited gypsy Carmen. Mérimée's prose style is strikingly exhibited in this narrative, which incorporates the archeologist's ironic perspective with Don José's sincere confession of Carmen's murder. Atypical in this work is Don José's colorful and metaphorical speech, so unlike the impersonal tone of Mérimée's more sophisticated narrators. First published in 1845, *Carmen* appeared in a revised edition in 1847 in which Mérimée added a final chapter of discourse on the customs and language of gypsies that has roused controversy among critics who have variously characterized this addi-

tional chapter as illustrative of Mérimée's scorn for fiction, representative of the separation between the story and the reader, and supportive of the story's emphasis on local color. More recently P. W. M. Cogman asserted that "the final chapter represents the triumph of the academic self and the definitive extinction of juvenile curiosities," noting also that the revised edition highlights Mérimée's thematic concern with the opposition of constraint and freedom.

After 1847 Mérimée stopped writing fiction for nearly two decades and concentrated on historical works. Beginning in 1866, however, Mérimée wrote three new stories and resurrected an older story, "Il viccolo di Madama Lucrezia," which were posthumously collected as *Dernières nouvelles* (*Last Stories*). "Lokis," a story inspired by myth, is generally considered Mérimée's best work in this last volume. "Lokis" concerns a Lithuanian woman who is purportedly raped by a bear and later gives birth to a son, Szémioth, who exhibits bearish tendencies. Eventually, Szémioth kills his bride on their wedding night, and she is found with teeth marks on her neck. Similar to "The Venus d'Ille," the subject matter of "Lokis" involves the destructive capacities of unleashed passion; only in this later tale, Mérimée seems also to focus on a primitive animal force that is a component of even the most civilized human beings. Despite the fantastic plot, as in "The Venus d'Ille," Mérimée controls the structure of the narrative with detailed description and employs a reliable narrator to make the supernatural believable. Nevertheless, A. W. Raitt commented that "it is difficult to overlook the physical impossibility on which ['Lokis'] depends."

Although interest in Mérimée's work has declined in the years since his death, *Carmen* has remained popular in the twentieth century through the ballets, films, and new stagings of Bizet's opera that it has inspired. In the past, commentators as diverse as Henry James and George Brandes praised Mérimée's short stories and historical works, and more recent critics laud Mérimée's narrative skills and objective prose style. Many critics also concur that Mérimée's last works attest to his unfailing narrative skill, as well as evidence a reneowed creative power in his later years. While scholars rarely fault Mérimée's work, some have asserted that his abilities are essentially technical and that his work lacks emotion. However, most critics agree that Mérimée's enduring appeal lies in the objectivity and lucid precision of his prose. V. S. Pritchett perhaps best captured the essence of Mérimée's style when he termed it "crystalline, exact, apparent."

(For further information on Mérimée's life and career, see *Nineteenth-Century Literature Criticism*, Vol. 6.)

PRINCIPAL WORKS

SHORT FICTION

La double méprise (novella) 1833
    [*A Slight Misunderstanding*, 1959]
Mosaïque 1833
"La Vénus d'Ille" 1837; later appeared in *Colomba*
Colomba (novella and short stories) 1841
    [*Colomba*, 1843]
Carmen (novella) 1845; revised edition, 1847
    [*Carmen*, 1878]

Nouvelles 1852
Dernières nouvelles 1873
The Writings of Prosper Mérimée. 8 vols. (poetry, drama, novellas, short stories, novel, and letters) 1905
Oeuvres complètes. 12 vols. (poetry, drama, novellas, short stories, novel, and letters) 1927-33
The Venus d'Ille, and Other Stories 1966

OTHER MAJOR WORKS

Le théâtre de Clara Gazul [as Clara Gazul] (drama) 1825
  [*The Plays of Clara Gazul,* 1825]
La gazula (poetry) 1827
La Jacquerie (drama) 1828
Chronique du règne de Charles IX (novel) 1829
  [*1572: A Chronicle of the Times of Charles the Ninth,* 1830]
La carosse de Sainte-Sacrement [as Clara Gazul] (drama) 1830
L'occasion [as Clara Gazul] (drama) 1830
Histoire de Don Pèdre Ier, roi de Castille (history) 1848
  [*History of Peter the Cruel,* 1849]
Lettres à une inconnue. 2 vols. (letters) 1874
  [*Prosper Mérimée's Letters to an Incognita,* 1874; also published as *Letters to an Unknown,* 1897]
Correspondance générale. 17 vols. (letters) 1941-64

Henry James (essay date 1874)

[*James was an American-born English novelist, short story writer, critic, essayist, and dramatist of the late nineteenth and early twentieth centuries. As a novelist James is renowned for his psychological acuity and complex sense of artistic form, while as a literary critic he is admired for his lucid and insightful commentary. James respected the self-consciously formalistic manner of contemporary French writers, particularly Gustave Flaubert, which stood in contrast to the loose, less formulated standards of English novelists. On the other hand, he favored the moral concerns of English writing over the often amoral and cynical vision that characterized much of French literature in the second half of the nineteenth century. In the excerpt below, which originally appeared in the* Nation, *James reviews* Dernières nouvelles, *admiring Mérimée's conciseness, yet concluding that stories in this posthumous volume will add "little to the reputation of one of the 'first French writers'."*]

Edmond About somewhere speaks of Madame Sand and Prosper Mérimée, "the two greatest French writers." Without exactly agreeing with M. About, the reader interested in literary matters in France may have a high enough opinion of the author of **Colomba** and the **Double Méprise** to be thankful for this posthumous volume of tales. Unfortunately, the stories before us will add little weight to the opinion; though, indeed, they remind us agreeably of the author's limited but singularly perfect talent. Mérimée had long ago given the measure of his power as a storyteller, and it was hardly to be hoped that this little collection of literary remnants would place it in a new light. . . .

[We] confess that Mérimée's chiselled and polished little fictions, and indeed, the whole manner and system of the author, have always had a great fascination for us. He is, perhaps, the most striking modern example of zealous artistic conciseness—of the literary artist who works in detail, by the line, by the word. There have been poets who scanned their rhythm as narrowly as Mérimée, but we doubt whether there has ever been a prose writer. His effort was to compress as large an amount of dramatic substance as possible into a very narrow compass, and the result is that, though his stories are few and short, one may read them again and again, and perceive with each reading a greater force of meaning. Some of the earlier ones are most masterly in this pregnant brevity; the story seems to say its last word, as the reader lays it down, with a kind of magical after-resonance. We have often thought a selection might be made from these tales, and presented to young narrators as a sort of manual of their trade—a guide for the avoidance of prolixity. Mérimée's subjects are always of the romantic and picturesque order, dealing in action, not in sentiment. They almost always hinge on a violent adventure or chain of adventures, and are strongly seasoned with bloodshed and general naughtiness. There are a great many sword-thrusts and pistol-shots, and a good deal of purely carnal love-making. At the beginning of his career the author had a great relish for Spanish local color, and several of his early works are richly charged with it. The *Théâtre de Clara Gazul,* written, we believe, before he was twenty-three, is a series of short tragic dramas on the picturesque cruelties and immoralities of Old Spain. One of his masterpieces, **Carmen,** published later, is the history of a wonderful *gitanilla*—a princess among the heroines who have dared much for love. With his brutal subjects and his cynical style, Mérimée is doubtless thoroughly disagreeable to such readers as are not fascinated by his artistic skill. To tell a terrible little story without flinching—without expressing a grain of reprobation for the clever rascal who escapes under cover of the scuffle in which his innocent rival has his brains blown out, or a grain of compassion for the poor guilty lady whose husband or father, brought upon the scene by the crack of pistols, condemns her to a convent cell for life; not to be sentimental, not to be moral, not to be rhetorical, but to have simply a sort of gentlemanly, epicurean relish for the bitterness of the general human lot, and to distil it into little polished silver cups—this was Mérimée's conscious effort, and this was his rare success.

Some of his best stories are those in which a fantastic or supernatural element is thrown into startling relief against a background of hard, smooth realism. An admirable success in this line is the "Venus d'Ille"—a version of the old legend of a love-pledge between a mortal and an effigy of the goddess. . . . Mérimée, making his heroine an antique brozen statue, disinterred in the garden of a little château in Gascony, and her victim the son of the old provincial antiquarian who discovered her, almost makes us believe in its actuality. This was the first known to us of Mérimée's tales, and we shall never forget our impression of its admirable art. The first and much the best of the stories in the present volume, "Lokis," deals with a subject as picturesquely unnatural. A Polish lady is seized by a bear, and dragged for five minutes toward his hiding-place. She is rescued in time to save her life, but her reason has succumbed to her terror, and she remains for ever a monomaniac. A few months after her disaster she gives birth to a son. Mérimée tells us the son's story. We recommend it to readers not averse to a good stiff horror. Our author's last years were very silent, though **"Lokis,"** indeed, was published shortly before his death. He broke his silence in a flimsier cause in producing the mildly scandalous tale of the **"Chambre Bleue."** Among the papers found at the Tuileries after the flight of the Empress, as the story goes, was the MS., tied with blue ribbons, of this little performance *à la* Crébillon Fils. Worthy, perhaps, of the circle for which it was composed, it adds little to the reputation of one of the "first French writers." But we strongly suspect that Mérimée's best things will be valued for many years to come. Among writers elaborately perfect in a somewhat narrow line he will hold a high place; he will always be admired by the votaries of "manner." Twenty years hence, doubtless, clever young men, reading him for the first time, will, in the flash of enthusiasm, be lending his volumes to appreciative female friends, and having them promptly returned, with the observation that they are "coarse." Whereupon, we suppose, the clever young men will fall to reading them over, and reflecting that it is quite right, after all, that men should have their distinctive pleasures, and that a good story by Mérimée is not the least of these. We should add that our author gave some attention to Russian literature, and that the best thing in the present volume, after **"Lokis,"** the extremely energetic little tale called **"Le Coup de Pistolet,"** is a translation from Pushkin. (pp. 169-72)

> *Henry James, "Mérimée's Last Tales," in his* Literary Reviews and Essays On American, English, and French Literature, *edited by Albert Mordell, Vista House Publisher, 1957, pp. 169-72.*

Walter Pater   (essay date 1890)

[*Pater was an English essayist, novelist, and critic who is regarded as one of the most famous proponents of aestheticism in English literature. Distinguished as the first major English writer to formulate an explicitly aesthetic philosophy of life, he advocated the "love of art for art's sake" as life's greatest offering, a belief that he exemplified in his influential* Studies in the History of the Renaissance (1873) *and elucidated in his two-volume novel* Marius the Epicurean (1885 and 1892). *In the following excerpt from an essay that is considered a seminal study of Mérimée's work in the English language, Pater emphasizes the impersonality of the author's art.*]

So disparate are [Mérimée's] writings that at first sight you might fancy them only the random efforts of a man of pleasure or affairs, who, turning to this or that for the relief of a vacant hour, discovers to his surprise a workable literary gift, of whose scope, however, he is not precisely aware. His sixteen volumes nevertheless range themselves in three compact groups. There are his letters—those *Lettres à une Inconnue,* and his letters to the librarian Panizzi, revealing him in somewhat close contact with political intrigue. But in this age of novelists, it is as a writer of novels, of fiction in the form of highly descriptive drama, that he will count for most; *Colomba,* for instance, by its intellectual depth of motive, its firmly conceived structure, by the faultlessness of its execution, vindicating the function of the novel as no tawdry light literature, but in very deed a fine art. The *Chronique du Règne de Charles IX,* an unusually successful specimen of historical romance, links his imaginative work to the third group of Mérimée's writings, his historical essays. (p. 854)

[The *Chronicle of Charles the Ninth* is cheerful] because, after all, the gloomy passions it presents are but the accidents of a particular age, and not like the mental conditions in which Mérimée was most apt to look for the spectacle of human power, allied to madness or disease in the individual. For him, at least, it was the office of fiction to carry one into a different if not a better world than that actually around us; and if the *Chronicle of Charles the Ninth* provided an escape from the tame circumstances of contemporary life into an impassioned past, *Colomba* is a measure of the resources for mental alteration which may be found even in the modern age. There was a corner of the French empire, in the manners of which assassination still had a large part. "The beauty of Corsica," says Mérimée—

> is grave and sad. The aspect of the capital does but augment the impression caused by the solitude that surrounds it. There is no movement in the streets. You hear there none of the laughter, the singing, the loud talking, common in the towns of Italy. Sometimes, under the shadow of a tree on the promenade, a dozen armed peasants will be playing cards, or looking on at the game. The Corsican is naturally silent. Those who walk the pavement are all strangers: the islanders stand at their doors: every one seems to be on the watch, like a falcon on its nest. All around the gulf there is but an expanse of tanglework; beyond it, bleached mountains. Not a habitation! Only, here and there, on the heights about the town, certain white constructions detach themselves from the background of green. They are funeral chapels or family tombs.

Crude in colour, sombre, taciturn, Corsica, as Mérimée here describes it, is like the national passion of the Corsican—that morbid personal pride, usurping the place even of grief for the dead, which centuries of traditional violence had concentrated into an all-absorbing passion for bloodshed, for bloody revenges, in collusion with the natural wildness, and the wild social condition of the island still unaffected even by the finer ethics of the duel. The supremacy of that passion is well indicated by the cry put into the mouth of a young man in the presence of the corpse of his father deceased in the course of nature—a young man meant to be common-place. "Ah! Would thou hadst died *malamorte*—by violence! We might have avenged thee!" In Colomba, Mérimée's best known creation, it is united to a singularly wholesome type of personal beauty, a natural grace of manner which is irresistible, a cunning intellect patiently diverting every circumstance to its design; and presents itself as a kind of genius, allied to fatal disease of mind. The interest of Mérimée's book is that it allows us to watch the action of this malignant power on Colomba's brother, Orso della Rebbia, as it discovers, rouses, concentrates, to the leaping-point, in the somewhat weakly diffused nature of the youth, the dormant elements of a dark humour akin to her own. Two years after his father's murder, presumably at the instigation of his ancestral enemies, the young lieutenant is returning home in the company of two humorously conventional English people, himself now half Parisianised, with an immense natural cheerfulness, and willing to believe an account of the crime which relieves those hated Barricini of all complicity in its guilt. But from the first, Columba, with "voice soft and musical," is at his side, gathering every accident and echo and circumstance, the very lightest circumstance, into the chain of necessity which draws him to the action every one at home expects of him as the head of his race. He is not unaware. Her very silence on the matter speaks so plainly. "You are forming me!" he admits. "Well! 'Hot shot, or cold steel!'—you see I have not forgotten my Corsican." More and more, as he goes on his way with her, he finds himself accessible to the damning thoughts he has so long combated. In horror, he tries to disperse them by the memory, of his comrades in the regiment, the drawing-rooms of Paris, the English lady who has promised to be his bride, and will shortly visit him in the humble *manoir* of his ancestors. From his first step among them the villagers of Pietranera, divided already into two rival camps, are watching him in suspense—Pietranera, perched among those deep forests where the stifled sense of violent death is everywhere. Columba places in his hands the little chest which contains the father's shirt covered with great spots of blood. "Behold the lead that struck him!" and she laid on the shirt two rusted bullets. "Orso! you will avenge him!" She embraces him with a kind of madness, kisses wildly the bullets and the shirt, leaves him with the terrible relics already exerting their mystic power upon him. It is as if in the nineteenth century a girl, amid Christian habits, had gone back to that primitive old pagan version of the story of the Grail, which identifies it not with the Most Precious Blood, but only with the blood of a murdered relation crying for vengeance. Awake at last in his old chamber at Pietranera, the house of the Barricini at the other end of the square, with its rival tower and rudely carved escutcheons, stares him in the face. His ancestral enemy is there, an aged man now, but with two well-grown sons, like two stupid dumb animals, whose innocent blood will soon be on his so oddly lighted conscience. At times, his better hope seemed to lie in picking a quarrel and killing at least in fair fight, one of these two stupid dumb animals; with rude ill-suppressed laughter one day, as they overhear Columba's violent utterances at a funeral feast, for she is a renowned *improvisatrice*. "Your father is an old man," he finds himself saying, "I could crush with my hands. 'Tis for you I am destined, for you and your brother!" And if it is by course of nature that the old man dies not long after the murder of these sons, (self-provoked after all) dies a fugitive at Pisa, as it happens, by an odd accident, in the presence of Colomba, no violent death by Orso's own hand could have been more to her mind. In that last hard page of Mérimée's story, mere dramatic propriety itself for a moment seems to plead for the forgiveness, which, from Joseph and his brethen to the present day, as we know, has been as winning in story as in actual life. Such dramatic propriety, however, was by no means in Mérimée's way. "What I must have is the hand that fired the shot," she had sung, "the eye that guided it; aye! and the *mind* moreover—the mind, which had conceived the deed!" And now, it is in idiotic terror, a fugitive from Orso's vengeance, that the last of the Barricini is dying.

Exaggerated art! you think. But it was precisely such exaggerated art, intense, unrelieved, an art of fierce colours, that is needed by those who are seeking in art . . . a kind of artificial stimulus. And if his style is still impeccably correct, coldblooded, impersonal, as impersonal as that of

Mérimée at age five in a portrait by his mother, who was a well-known children's portrait artist of the early nineteenth century.

Scott himself, it does but conduce the better to his one exclusive aim. It is like the polish of the stiletto Colomba carried under her mantle, or the beauty of the fire-arms, that beauty coming of nice adaptation to purpose, which she understood so well—a task characteristic also of Mérimée himself, a sort of fanatic joy in the perfect pistol-shot, at its height in the singular story he has translated from the Russian of Pouchkine. Those raw colours he preferred; Spanish, Oriental, African, perhaps, irritant certainly to cisalpine eyes, he undoubtedly attained the colouring you associate with sun-stroke, only possible under a sun in which dead things rot quickly.

Pity and terror, we know, go to the making of the essential tragic sense. In Mérimée, certainly, we have all its terror, but without the pity. Saint-Clair, [In **"Le Vase Etrusque"**], the consent of his mistress barely attained at last, rushes madly on self-destruction, that he may die with the taste of his great love fresh on his lips. All the grotesque accidents of violent death he records with visual exactness, and no pains to relieve them; the ironic indifference, for instance, with which, on the scaffold or the battle-field, a man will seem to grin foolishly at the ugly rents through which his life has passed. Seldom or never has the mere pen of a writer taken us so close to the cannon's mouth as in the **"Taking of the Redoubt,"** while **"Matteo Falcone"**—twenty-five short pages—is perhaps the cruellest story in the world.

Colomba, that strange, fanatic being, who has a code of action, of self-respect, a conscience, all to herself, who with all her virginal charm only does not make you hate her, is, in truth, the type of a sort of humanity Mérimée found it pleasant to dream of—a humanity as alien as the animals, with whose moral affinities to man his imaginative work is often directly concerned. Were they so alien, after all? Were there not survivals of the old wild creatures in the gentlest, the politest of us? Stories that told of sudden freaks of gentle, polite natures, straight back, *not* into Paradise, were always welcome to men's fancies; and that could only be because they found a psychologic truth in them. With much success, with a credibility insured by his literary tact, Mérimée tried his own hand at such stories: unfrocked the bear in the amorous young Lithuanian noble, the wolf in the revolting peasant of the Middle Age. There were survivals surely in himself, in that stealthy presentment of his favourite themes, in his own art. You seem to find your hand on a serpent, in reading him. (pp. 857-60)

Mérimée, a literary artist, was not a man who used two words where one would do better, and shines especially in those brief compositions which, like a minute intaglio, reveal at a glance his wonderful faculty of design and proportion in the treatment of his work, in which there is not a touch but counts. That is an art of which there are few examples in English, our somewhat diffuse, or slipshod, literary language hardly lending itself to the concentration of thought and expression, which are of the essence of such writing. It is otherwise in French, and if you wish to know what art of that kind can come to read Mérimée's little romances; best of all, perhaps, **"La Vénus d'Ille"** and **"Arsène Guillot."** The former is a modern version of the beautiful old story of the Ring given to Venus, given to her, in this case, by a somewhat sordid creature of the nineteenth century, whom she looks on with more than disdain. The strange outline of the Canigou, one of the most imposing outlying heights of the Pyrenees, down the mysterious slopes of which the traveller has made his way towards nightfall into the great plain of Toulouse, forms an impressive background, congruous with the many relics of irrepressible old paganism there, but in entire contrast to the *bourgeois* comfort of the place where his journey is to end, the abode of an aged antiquary, loud and bright just now with the celebration of a vulgar worldly marriage. In the midst of this well-being, prosaic in spite of the neighbourhood, in spite of the pretty old wedding customs, morsels of that local colour in which Mérimée delights, the old pagan powers are supposed to reveal themselves once more, (malignantly, of course) in the person of a magnificent bronze statue of Venus recently unearthed in the antiquary's garden. On her finger, by ill-luck, the coarse young bridegroom on the morning of his marriage places for a moment the bridal ring only too effectually (the bronze hand closes, like a wilful living one, upon it), and dies, you are to understand, in her angry metallic embraces on his marriage night. From the first, indeed, she had seemed bent on crushing out men's degenerate bodies and souls, though the supernatural horror of the tale is adroitly made credible by a certain vagueness in the events, which covers a quite natural account of the bridegroom's mysterious death.

The intellectual charm of literary work so thoroughly designed as Mérimée's depends in part on the sense as you read hastily perhaps, perhaps in need of patience, that you are dealing with a composition, the full secret of which is only to be attained in the last paragraph, that with the last word in mind you will retrace your steps, more than once, it may be, noting then the minuter structure, also the natural or wrought flowers by the way. Nowhere is such method better illustrated than by another of Mérimée's quintessential pieces, **"Arsène Guillot,"** and here for once with a conclusion ethically acceptable also. Mérimée loved surprises in human nature, but it is not often that he surprises us by tenderness or generosity of character as another master of French fiction, M. Octave Feuillet, is apt to do, and the simple pathos of **"Arsène Guillot"** gives it a unique place in Mérimée's writings. It may be said, indeed, that only an essentially pitiful nature could have told the exquisitely cruel story of Matteo Falcone precisely as Mérimée has told it; and those who knew him testify abundantly to his own capacity for generous friendship. He was no more wanting than others in those natural sympathies (sending tears to the eyes at the sight of suffering age or childhood) which happily are no extraordinary component in men's natures. It was, perhaps, no fitting return for a friendship of over thirty years to publish posthumously those *Lettres à une Inconnue,* which reveal that reserved, sensitive, self-centered nature, a little pusillanimously in the power, at the disposition of another. (pp. 861-63)

The intimacy, the effusion, the so freely exposed personality of those letters does but emphasise the fact that *impersonality* was, in literary art, Mérimée's central aim. Personality *versus* impersonality in art:—how much or how little of one's self one may put into one's work: whether anything at all of it: whether one *can* put there anything else:—is clearly a far-reaching and complex question. Serviceable as the basis of a precautionary maxim towards the conduct of our work, self-effacement, or impersonality, in literary or artistic creation, is, perhaps, after all, as little possible as a strict realism. "It has always been my rule to put nothing of myself into my works," says another great master of French prose, Gustave Flaubert, but luckily, as we may think, often failed in thus effacing himself, as he too was aware. "It has always been my rule to put nothing of myself into my works" (to be *disinterested* in his literary creations, so to speak) "yet I have put much of myself into them": and where he failed Mérimée succeeded. There they stand—Carmen, Colomba, the "False" Demetrius—as detached from him as from each other, with no more filial likeness to their maker than if they were the work of another person. And to his method of conception, Mérimée's much-praised literary style, his method of expression, is strictly conformable—impersonal in its beauty, the perfection of nobody's style—thus vindicating anew by its very impersonality that much-worn, but not untrue saying, that the style is the man:—a man, impassible, unfamiliar, impeccable, veiling a deep sense of what is forcible, nay, terrible, in things under the sort of personal pride that makes a man a nice observer of all that is most conventional. Essentially unlike other people, he is always fastidiously in the fashion—an expert in all the little, half-contemptuous elegances of which it is capable. Mérimée's superb self-effacement, his impersonality, is itself but an effective personal trait, and, transferred to art, becomes a markedly peculiar quality of literary beauty. For, in truth, this creature of disillusion who had no care for half-lights, and, like his creations, had no atmosphere about him, gifted as he was with pure *mind,* with the quality which secures flawless literary structure, had, on the other hand, nothing of what we call *soul* in literature:—hence, also, that singular harshness in his ideal, as if, in theological language, he were incapable of grace. He has none of those subjectivities, colourings, peculiarities of mental refraction, which necessitate *varieties* of style—could we spare such?—and render the perfections of it no merely negative qualities. There are masters of French prose whose art has begun where the art of Mérimée leaves off. (p. 864)

Walter Pater, "Prosper Mérimée," in The Fortnightly Review, *Vol. 54, No. CCLXXXII, November 1, 1890, pp. 852-64.*

Paul Bourget   (essay date 1920)

[*Bourget was a French critic, novelist, and short story writer whose revolutionary critical study* Essais de psychologie contemporaine *(1883) is regarded as a prototype of modern psychological criticism. In this work, Bourget applied techniques of psychological analysis to literary criticism, interpreting works of literature according to an author's attitudes toward the moral and philosophical issues of his or her age. In the following excerpt, Bourget maintains that Mérimée's personality, which was controlled on the surface despite strong underlying emotions, was best suited for expression in the short story form.*]

The real truth of a literary artist reveals itself in the motives which make him choose a certain medium, a certain style to express himself. It may be objected that a desire for success will influence an artist, but that fact, in itself, is a guide to his character; we can distinguish, for example, between a Chateaubriand, highly talented but spoiled by his sense of the audience and a Stendhal, in love with truth, and quite incapable of adapting himself to public taste. Besides, even in his searching for success, the artist seeks a medium where his particular gifts will have full expression. (p. 346)

We have no trustworthy guides to [Mérimée's] personality except his works, and although he was one of those writers who systematically hide themselves behind their creations, we could reconstruct from his writings the essential qualities of his character. This year is the fiftieth anniversary of his death and many of us will read again some of his vigorous stories, *Colomba, Carmen,* "le Vase Etrusque," "Tamango," "la Venus d'Ille," "Matteo Falcone," "l'Enlèvement de la Redoute." If Mérimée was never extravagantly popular with the public, at least he never suffered that ebb and flow of popular opinion which carried too high and then too low—before their true level was ascertained. . . . [Hippolyte] Taine, about 1875, in the preface to the *Lettres à l'Inconnue,* remarked already the stability of Mérimée's reputation.

The reason lies, I think, in the complete accord of the writer with his work; it is not only his intellectual expression, but the expression of his character, of his most intimate and secret personality. This fundamental identity of the artist and his creation gives the impression of a perfect, an absolute coördination and employment of all the faculties of the artist. His compositions remain a living organism to which you can add nothing and from which you may take nothing away.

Such a success is not a matter of chance. It implies natu-

rally an artist of superior personality, and also—I come back to my original thesis—the choice of a medium thoroughly adapted to that personality. Mérimée of the stories—his true glory is as a story-teller—fulfills both conditions. If we study the man as he is authentically described, and if we recall the laws of the specialized art of the story, we will clearly perceive why the author of **"Matteo Falcone"** chose that medium, why he excelled in it, his originality as a writer of stories, and his limitations.

It has been a commonplace to say that Mérimée was dominated from his youth by the fear of being deceived. His motto 'Remember to Distrust' has been frequently quoted, not always with the correct implication. . . . This motto is the device of a highly strung man who was frightened, when still very young, by the violence of his own emotions. It is himself he distrusts and not others. We find this admission in the clearly autobiographical pages he devotes to Saint Clair, his moral twin, in the **"Vase Etrusque."** He shows him to us reserved, taciturn, 'hiding from others the emotions of his too sensitive soul.' And he adds: 'In stifling his emotions he made them a hundred times more cruel. The world knew him as a hard and thoughtless man, but in his solitude his uneasy imagination created torments for him, more frightful than he could possibly have confessed to anyone.' As Mérimée was a writer who valued his words accurately and delicately, the painful intensity of such words as *cruel emotions, torments, frightful* shows the nature of his confession. 'At the age when one receives enduring impressions his sensitiveness was ridiculed by his comrades. He was proud and studied how to hide all expressions of what he felt to be a shameful weakness.' Saint Clair assumes a mask of coldness. His distrust is a defensive measure. Knowing that he can be too easily wounded, he tries to protect himself from word and look. Mérimée has described himself, a sensitive, emotional man, self-repressed.

To distrust your own sensitiveness always means to distrust to a greater or less degree Life in general. Mérimée grew up among impressions which accentuated his natural tendency to pessimism. Born in 1803, ten years after the Terror had covered France with blood, he was brought up among survivors of those dreadful days. His parents had known intimately some of the victims and talked about them with their friends. Tragedies of private life which, for us, are confused in the immense collective tragedy, stayed in their memories as individual sorrows which they had witnessed. War was everywhere, culminating when Mérimée was thirteen years old, in disaster and invasion. Contemporary memoirs tell us what kind of stories were told by veterans of the Grande Armée between campaigns, the stubborn battles in Prussia, Spain, and its ambushes and savagery, Russia and the terrible retreat. A chronicle of heroism and death, more exalted but no less bloody than that of the Revolution. In the *Partie de Trictrac,* in the opening chapters of *Colomba,* and especially in **"l'Enlèvement de la Redoute"** we find the proof that the boy to whom these tales were told received a profound and lasting impression. We see in Mérimée's moral constitution two strongly marked traits—admiration of energy and an acute sense of the latent ferocity of the human animal. To these characteristics and to his repressed emotionalism we must add another quality—a radical atheism such as the survivors of the Encyclopedic philosophy of the eighteenth century professed and taught.

These remarks seem quite foreign to the purely professional question—why did Mérimée definitely specialize in the story as against other forms of literature and excel in it—but they will perhaps help us to answer it. Let us begin by admitting that he had the natural, innate gift of story-telling, the *Lust zum fabulieren* as Goethe said. But we have noted in Mérimée the habit of repressing his emotions, and we can suppose that such a habit induced the practice of control of all his expansive faculties. Evidently he was no lover of expansion either in a story-teller or in other artists. As a poet he would have chosen the concise rigor of the sonnet, as a dramatist, the one-act play, as a story-teller he found in the short story an adequate expression of his customary attitude of repression. He derived the same satisfaction from condensing his narration that a Walter Scott or a Dumas found in expanding their own. I do not mean that he boiled down a novel plot. The story is not, in any sense, a short novel. If you will take a masterpiece in each medium, **"Matteo Falcone,"** for example, and *la Cousine Bette,* and try in imagination to lengthen one and shorten the other, you will realize how such a process denatures the original. The matter of each is too different; in the story it is an episode, in the novel a series of episodes. The episode which the story describes must be detached, isolated, while the novel, whose effect lies in the continuity, the culmination of episodes, must unite them together. It works by development, the story by concentration. Single episodes in a novel may be very slight, almost insignificant, as in *Madame Bovary* and *l'Education Sentimentale,* but the episode treated in a story must be intensely significant. The novel permits and can command a diversity of tone and color. The genial and vulgar figure of Creval in *la Cousine Bette* is contrasted with the bitter cruelty of the poor mother. The story demands a unity of tone, a few touches perhaps, but ones which work for a single effect. (pp. 346-48)

Colomba, that tragedy of Corsican vendetta could very well have been treated as a novel. It would have sufficed to give the episode of the assassination of Colonel Della Rebbia a value equal to that of his son's return, and to insert between the two episodes, the analyses of the sentiments of the son and of his sister. Mérimée seduously avoided this treatment and subordinated everything to the episode of the son's return. That is the way to treat the material in a story. *Carmen,* the most typical of his productions, is one hundred pages long; *la Double Meprise* is shorter, **"Tamango"** forty pages, **"Matteo Falcone"** less than thirty, and **"l'Enlevement de la Redoute"** only eleven. But these quick stories are so striking, so dramatic, so rich in observation, that they make a stronger impression on the reader than whole volumes.

All of these stories are tragic. *Colomba* is the history of a murder revenged by two others. The hero of *Carmen,* Jose Navarro, is a bandit who stabs his mistress. Matteo Falcone shoots his own son; Tamango, an African chief, brings about a revolt of the slaves on board a slave ship: the crew is massacred, and then the victors die of starvation on board the ship they cannot navigate. *La Double Meprise* and **"le Vase Etrusque"** are laid in Paris but the plot is no less tragic. . . . (pp. 348-49)

Mérimée's obvious contempt for civilized persons and his weakness for rougher human types, nearer to primitive animalism, is explained by his wish to portray strongly char-acterized individuals. He sought them in countries which orthodox sociology regards as backward, where the race has not been disciplined and policied into a dead level of uniformity, such as Andalusia, Navarre, Greece, and Asia Minor. If his scene is laid in a more civilized setting, he hardly ever fails to introduce a reference to those half wild, barbaric countries, which he loves, such as the words of Théodore Néville on his return from Egypt in the luncheon scene of the **"Vase Etrusque,"** or the adventure of Darsy at Lanaca in the **Double Meprise.** The influence of Lord Byron, whose prestige affected so many young Frenchmen of the period is reflected in this romantic liking for the outlaw of Spain in the Orient. But in Mérimée's case, the impulse is more than a mere external suggestion. While the picturesque quality of a Carmen or a Don Jose Navarro attracted him as a literary artist who chooses Goya models for his etchings, he found, as a philosopher, a new vigor in contact with these simple and brutal energies. Of all conceptions of the universe, the materialistic is the most frozen and lifeless. . . . Mérimée suffered from the spiritual *malaise* induced by the nihilism of his philosophy. He felt his spiritual vitality growing weaker, but did not understand the reason for this condition. He attributed it to the diminishing force of modern civilization, like Stendhal, who suggested that the mediocrity of his days was due to the fact that the streets were safe and life too well ordered and too thoroughly policed. Like Stendhal, he reinforced his own colorless days by imagining the life of half-barbaric people, poor in culture but rich in sensation and in will. Almost he preferred them criminal. Both Stendhal and Mérimée thought that they were protesting against the hypocrisies and conventions of their day. If their psychological lucidity had not been disturbed by the prejudices of their philosophic theory, they would have realized that they were actually seeking the sacred thrill of mystery, of the unknown, which their theories denied. They sought the unknown, in the dark gulf of human passion at its paroxysm.

We can understand, knowing this quality of his mind, why Mérimée, whom we know to have been ironic to the point of cynicism, gives in his stories an impression of gravity, almost of severity. . . . He formulates no creed and presents no reasons. As a story-teller he states a detached episode of life. A story cannot show the genesis of action or its results. Its end is to present the action, as vividly, as strongly as possible. You may think what you like about it, the storyteller gives you the statement of facts; if they seem to you to present a problem of life or of philosophy, answer it if you can. For Mérimée the fundamental problem, which includes all the others, was definitely answered. Human existence has no human significance. He lived by this desperate theory and he overcame the paralysis of its negation by his labor as an artist, by his passionate and critical work as a writer.

His thoroughness of self-criticism gave him a perfection of technique, thanks to which his stories, most of them written before 1840, have held the admiration of writers with the stability which astonished Taine. Mérimée justified the old saying 'Excel, and you will live.' In studying the construction of these stories one can appreciate the quality of self-criticism which controlled their composition. One realizes how keenly their author had analyzed the art of the story, whose secret complications are only known, perhaps, to those who have tried this medium.

The first difficulty is credibility, to make your story real. . . . [The storyteller] cannot insinuate the reality of his story; he must impose it, a performance all the more difficult, if his story is exceptional—out of the ordinary. See with what skill Mérimée handles the difficulty in *Carmen,* a story laid in a setting entirely foreign to familiar experience. He must make this highly melodramatic adventure natural, almost an every day affair. To tell his story he employs the first person, the *I,* which takes you into his confidence, which familiarizes the story. . . .
(pp. 349-50)

The reader admits as a perfectly natural thing, the visit to Spain, of an archæologist anxious to verify the text of the *Bellum Hispanense* on the location of the battlefield of Munda. In imagination he follows him to Cordova, where he engages a guide and horses, and sets out. We see him stopping to water his horses and unsaddle in a gorge of the Sierras. The stage is set; we can believe in it, and the apparition of Jose Navarro in this solitary spot, a circle surrounded with rocky peaks, is not astonishing, as the narrator does not make the mistake of presenting him as an extraordinary person. He is a horseman who dismounts, like the archæologist, attracted by the water, and the shade of a clump of live oaks. He only describes him as 'a strong, young man of middle height, with proud and rather sombre eyes.' A more detailed or striking description and you would have felt the writer striving for his effect. An easy, incidental description is in this instance the cunningest ruse of the artist who will achieve his effect in due season. An exchange of cigars, a dialogue, an evening passed together in an inn, and, by one detail after another, the unknown traveler discloses himself as a bandit. The rest follows indisputably. Twenty-one pages and twenty-four lines have sufficed for this act of witchcraft.

Each of Mérimée's stories can be analyzed in this way. He is a master in endowing his dramas with verisimilitude. And he has also to a supreme degree what—for lack of a better term—I may call the gift of Presence. Many excellent novels have not this particular quality. They tell a true story, the events described actually took place, but not *before our eyes.* To use a vulgar but expressive metaphor—the actors are not in the same room. In Mérimée's, as in Balzac's works, they are always visible. The sense of their presence is the more remarkable as it is not brought about by description or dialogue. Mérimée did not believe in description—he gives the reason somewhere *à propos* of a failure to reproduce the Venus de Milo: 'a few millimetres of difference in the nose and this beautiful face is utterly changed. But you cannot, in black and white, express this difference between the original and a bad copy.' He reduced dialogue to essential words. The explosive scene—if I may use that term—where characters explain themselves at length was repugnant to his taste of concentration. Count the replies between Carmen and her lover when he was going to kill her. There are only eleven, of which six have less than twenty words, and the longest only seven lines. He imposes the sense of being present by a careful choice of very small details, very simple but illuminating. Read the beginning of *Carmen* and see how it shows us Jose Navarro by a series of gestures. First, Jose is waked from his sleep—one hand on his gun, the other on the halter of his horse; second, he released the horse, and his gun, at first horizontal, points toward the ground; third, he sits down without laying aside his gun and accepts a cigar. His

origin is betrayed by the way he pronounces his S; he is from the north, and his situation by the pleasure with which he inhales the smoke of his cigar. 'How long it is since I have smoked!' . . . Mérimée worked by the use of exact detail, without comment. To imagine these details, to set them in the proper perspective, one must have a mental vision of photographic precision, unencumbered with useless detail, a mind of confident certainty which seizes only the significant in faces, attitudes, and words.

These short stories, so real, so vivid, are written in a classic style, which contrasts with the language of the prose writers who followed the tradition of Chateaubriand and Hugo. . . . Mérimée would not have been logical in his own discipline if he had not restrained himself to the somewhat dry but clear, solid style of our national tradition. . . . Mérimée's style is so personal, so adapted to his character, that we cannot conceive that he could have written otherwise, just as we cannot conceive that he, being the sort of person he was, could have worked in a different kind of medium. If his work has faults, they are his faults. He lacked enthusiasm, *abandon,* the religious values, and these faults are reflected in his work. But how many other qualities he had and shows in his writings— the first of all—Truth! Matthew Arnold said of Wordsworth that all his verses were not necessary. . . . Of Mérimée's stories we have the right to say that they are all necessary, so thoroughly in his case are the author and the man a unit. (pp. 350-52)

Paul Bourget, "Prosper Mérimée, Writer of Stories," in The Living Age, *Vol. CCCVII, No. 3983, November 6, 1920, pp. 346-52.*

Albert J. George   (essay date 1956)

[*In the excerpt below, George explores some of the technical and experimental aspects of Mérimée's short narratives that the critic asserts helped to advance the short fiction genre.*]

The strange unity of Mérimée's work can perhaps best be grasped from a knowledge of the man's personality. . . . Ugly and timid, he protected himself with a razor wit and a cynicism strengthened by a glacial bearing. This complete egoist never became anyone's disciple or dupe; he stood aloof to watch life roll by with disdainful tolerance. Mérimée viewed the world with jaundiced eyes. For him it was an unpleasant antheap, agitated by the superstitiously religious, "cette canaille de dévots." He preferred the aristocracy of a man on horseback like Napolean III to democracy, for he had no faith in the intelligence of the common man or any taste for his manners.

It is not surprising, therefore, that such an attitude colored his work, or that he approached the art of storytelling with a keen appreciation for irony, the sense of which had been strongly reinforced by a careful reading of Sterne. A sharp awareness of the ridiculous tempered his choice of subjects, his exploitation of character, and his comments on the meaning of his stories. Hence, all types of irony can be found intermingled in his work: *verbal irony,* most often by understatement, as in *Colomba,* when he describes French bureaucracy of the English upper classes; *irony of manner,* a pretense of naïveté or open-eyed wonder, as in the Abbé Aubain; *dramatic irony,* that created by the twist of events, as in "Tamango" or the "Partie de trictrac"; and *cosmic* or *romantic irony,* the satire of frustration, of men's highest aspirations. This last constitutes one of Mérimée's most common techniques, evident in his better works, the **Double Méprise** or the "Vase étrusque," both bitter comments on the destiny of man.

That Mérimée was not a professional writer makes it difficult to secure any very helpful information from him. Certainly he was not given to theorizing on the nature of his avocation. Writing was a side line for M. l'inspecteur général des monuments. He commented rarely on his art and these few instances are interlaced through a voluminous correspondence. Thus, the only way to uncover his aesthetics is to inquire how he put together his narratives and then poke amidst these findings for his notions of the brief tale and what, if any, contributions he made to its development.

The subject matter gives no help. The locales of the nineteen stories range from France, to Spain, to Corsica, Africa, Denmark, and Russia. Mérimée deals with the fantastic in the "Vénus d'Ille," religion in "Fédérigo," slavery in "Tamango," and honor in **Colomba.** Such catholicity of taste reveals only a man close to romanticism who apparently exhibited little originality of background and theme. His plots are full of animated statues, ghosts, slave kings, consumptive mistresses, gypsy girls and illicit lovers. He seems, in fact, to have drawn heavily on the literary clichés of his time.

Similarly, most of the techniques he favored were also commonplace. The plots are shaped as sequential narration articulated by causality, though without any implication of determinism; they are told by a pseudo-author who occasionally interjects a caustic observation. These are presented as framework constructions, stories within stories ("Sorcières espagnoles," "Il Viccolo di Madama Lucrezia"), with a goodly seasoning of foreshadowing to titillate the reader ("Ames du Purgatoire"). Mérimée relies heavily on such exotic elements as distant lands, primitivism, dreams, visions and folklore. And each story contains a carefully calculated dose of local color which particularizes and sets historically such clichés as the Noble Savage, the Priest, the Luckless Lover, the Honest Harlot, or the Jeune France.

Yet, closer observation shows that Mérimée offers more than just a resumé of the commonplaces of romanticism. Certainly he used all the themes in vogue, but, having learned his trade from Diderot and Sterne, he proffers them to the reader slightly out of focus, to create a universe in which only *his* will seems operative and beyond caprice. . . . The usual stock romantic plots were given strange twists. Mérimée delighted in ambiguous endings, leaving the reader to wonder whether the statue of Venus really crushed the boy or whether Charles XI actually did have a vision. Certainly the pure in heart will never understand "Lokis." The Abbé Aubain resembles Jocelyn, but a clever and scheming one. Tamango may be a noble savage but his stupidity lands him in the kind of slavery which only an abolitionist British government could imagine. (pp. 29-31)

This kind of focus makes his work more interesting, perhaps, yet he deserves higher praise as a technician and a contributor to the development of short prose fiction. For all his mockery this satirist took his art seriously, and a close scrutiny of the variety of stories at which he tried his hand reveals a passion for experimentation which would enrich the medium he used. The short narrative he had chosen deliberately. He was not interested primarily in the development of incidents multiplied around a boy-girl entanglement—which would have led him to the romance; nor was he attracted by the possibility of creating fully-rounded characters by the slow erosion of cause-effect on a personality—which would have led him to the novel. Both these forms required settings spatially and temporally elongated. Rather he preferred to draw on the dramatic possibilities of life's ironies at given moments, to work with the explosive tensions which such compression made possible. This choice in essence limited him to the domain of the briefer narrative: the exploitation of a severely limited number of incidents, focussed to produce rapidly the maximum of effect; the development of character in a single situation. Both of these would further be restricted by considerations of time and space; the psychological time of the characters as well as the reader's sense of time, the space of the fable as well as the geography of the plot.

With a full appreciation of these boundaries, Mérimée experimented with the various problems involved in manipulating characters in limited time and space as he sought the frontiers of his medium. He would consequently write nineteen stories, no two of the same kind, and use a multiplicity of techniques to produce such divergent types of narrative as "Mateo Falcone," the **Double Méprise,** "L'Enlèvement de la redoute" and **Colomba.**

Within these very short works his concern for psychological time caused Mérimée to treat incident variously, depending on the way in which he hoped to exploit it. Thus, the "Enlèvement de la redoute" occurs over a period of perhaps an hour, during which time Mérimée hoped to give a picture of people at a highly interesting moment. Since it is not a complete story and has, substantially, no plot action, the "Enlèvement" closely resembles the sketch as practised by Irving. On the other hand, in "Mateo Falcone" and the "Vénus d'Ille" everything is directed, in Poe-like fashion, toward the production of a single effect, concentrated, and stripped to barest essentials. All action is exteriorized, and passes in rapid tempo through a single crisis to explode in the climax, then decline in a brief dénouement.

The longer forms, too, include the same range of experimentation. . . . ["Ames du Purgatoire"] commonly called a *nouvelle* in contradistinction to the shorter *conte,* necessitated giving the reader a longer sense of elapsed time because the subject would naturally take longer to mature, without the staccato explosiveness of the *conte.* Since compression would in this instance ruin the attainment of the effects desired, in the **Double Méprise** it led Mérimée to slow his tale with the repitition of a long and unimportant anecdote. Similarly, in the "Vase étrusque" he marred the smoothness of his main plot by indulging in an ironic digression on the habits of the Jeune-France during a bachelor dinner. He was not now concerned with effect or exposition, but with revelation, with the portrayal of character, the psychological delineation of personality.

Thus a part-time writer made a major contribution to the history of the forms he practised. As a good romanticist he experimented, and this experimentation provided later men with an idea of how much could be expected from the medium of the short prose fiction. His productions were interesting, certainly; but, more important, they were historically meaningful and artistically distinguished. (pp. 31-3)

Albert J. George, "Prosper Mérimée and the Short Prose Narrative," in Symposium, Vol. X, No. 1, Spring, 1956, pp. 25-33.

[The] recipe for a good fantastic tale is well-known: begin with firmly delineated portraits of strange but possible characters, and give their features the most minutely observed reality. The transition from what is strange to what is marvellous is imperceptible, and the reader will find himself surrounded by the fantastic before he realises that the real world has been left far behind.

Mérimée as quoted by A. W. Raitt in his Prosper Mérimée, 1970.

Frank Paul Bowman   (essay date 1960)

[*Bowman is an American educator and critic whose studies in French literature include* Prosper Mérimée: Heroism, Pessimism, and Irony *(1962). In the following excerpt, Bowman examines Mérimée's use of mythology and narrative devices in his short story "La Vénus d'Ille," positing that these elements enhance the universality of the tale's theme.*]

Among Mérimée's stories, the **"Vénus d'Ille"** merits particular attention. With it he opened his "major phase," turned his back on the romantic experiments of his youth, and began the series of works similar in form, style, and length by which he is best known. He himself considered it his masterpiece, a significant judgment in an author usually very derogatory about his own works. Valery Larbaud, who shared this appreciation, justified it by noting that Mérimée here managed to give the maximum of verisimilitude to the maximum of supernatural. This is an achievement in which Mérimée could, and probably did, take pride, but his preference may also have been for the plot itself, which he was to repeat twenty years later in **"Il Viccolo di Madama Lucrezia."** This is the only instance of his repeating a plot, though he often repeats details—and of these the **"Vénus"** possesses an exceptional number: superstitions concerning Friday, dissertations on the excellence of contraband chocolate, complaints about the riotousness of wedding feasts, the ironic transition in conversation from horses to women, and so forth. More importantly, here the device of the narrator, so frequent in his writing, is found in its most developed form. Finally, the action of the **"Vénus"** illustrates with exceptional clarity that conjunction of love and death, so central a part of the "romantic agony," which in various forms is widespread in Mérimée's writing.

In the **"Vénus,"** Mérimée turned for his inspiration to a myth. Like many an agnostic, he was very much interested in religion, superstition, and mythology. The early *Guzla* is already full of pastiche folk-lore, and he utilized such material in many of his later works, often for "local color," occasionally as a plot source. (p. 475)

The nature and origins of myths were frequent subjects of discussion in the early nineteenth century, especially because of the renascence of philological studies. Mérimée was familiar not only with the traditional Enlightenment attitude on the subject, but also with the thought of Niebuhr, Creuser, and Max Müller. In all probability he also knew the theories of Herder and Vico, if not at first hand then through Ballanche, Quinet, Fauriel, or Cousin. His own attitude combines open-minded receptivity with frequent attacks on the excessive use of theories he himself elsewhere employs. His synthesizing intelligence posits that myths are composed of various elements and thus open to a variety of interpretations. For example, he was quite struck by the recurrence of the same legend in different places and cultures, recurrence he encountered both in his reading and in his travels; however, in accordance with the procedures of the Enlightenment, he uses this phenomenon to suggest a discrediting similarity between Greek mythology and Christian dogma. In one instance he treats Euhemerism ironically, and in another states that myths undoubtedly contain a considerable portion of historic reality; in the **"Ames du purgatoire"** he offers an Euhemerist interpretation of the Jupiter myth and of that of Don Juan. (p. 476)

More significantly, Mérimée rejects Grote's notions that myths primarily serve an esthetic purpose. He felt myths express the faith of the Ancients, in the form of a particular language or system of metaphors common to various cultures. He could have derived this idea from either Vico or Max Müller. The historical or philosophical importance he gives to myth is justified by the conviction that mythology has preserved for us very old ideas on the impenetrable secrets of this world, ideas which are hardly any more extravagant and in their form infinitely more poetic than the explanations of later philosophers. Like us, the Greeks expressed notions normally inaccessible to man in a flux of images in order to make them comprehensible. Myths then constitute a form of fabulation similar to that of later literature and whose product remains available to future generations. At the same time, myths offer an opportunity to express ideas inaccessible to man, or at least to put in concrete form an abstraction which otherwise couldn't effectively be expressed. Mérimée rejects the notions that the Greeks invented myths solely for the purpose of telling stories, and one can be suspicious of any such interpretation of Mérimée's writings. Rather, he himself probably used fiction and particularly myth to express ideas otherwise difficult to communicate. Such was I think the case with the **"Vénus d'Ille."**

For the story does make use of a myth; Mérimée didn't haphazardly attach the name of the goddess of love to his statue. The host is constantly making a show of his knowledge and thereby identifying the statue with the whole Venus-Aphrodite tradition; he even attributes to her a role as a titular deity. The statue overlooks a garden, a traditional position for Venus the goddess of fertility. But Mérimée is at pains to insist that this ancient copper statue, long buried in the earth, is black. This is Aphrodite androphonos, the man-slayer. She is a jealous goddess who punishes those who betray her; she is intimately associated with death. Although there is no record in antiquity of the particular legend on which the story is based, it only represents the combination of the traditional figure of destructive Venus with equally venerable stories about the consequences of the exchange of rings. (pp. 476-77)

According to Stendhal, Mérimée felt that the best way to create the fantastic was to dress the hero "en gilet de flanelle," and, once he had found the structure of his tale, this is what he did. In the **"Vénus"** the action has a purely literary provenance, whereas the particular setting Mérimée gave it (including the narrator) is derived from direct observation. It is striking that Mérimée, accustomed to manufacturing exotic works or historical novels in accordance with romantic fashion, should have turned "realist" and brazenly moved this fantastic tale into the good bourgeois age of Louis-Philippe, hardly notorious for its ghosts. The story, in detail if not in structure, is one of his most autobiographical. The statue is a combination of the Venus at Vienne and the one at Quinipili, both of which he describes in his travel reports. The village archeologist Peyrehorade is Puigarri, whose name, slightly changed, becomes that of the bride. Puigarri was guilty of false (especially Phoenician) place-name etymologies such as Peyrehorade proffers, though the false etymology of *Néra* is closer to one Mérimée himself had made. The M. de P. who sends the narrator to see Peyrehorade is Mérimée's friend Jaubert de Passa. The nonfantastic details of the story are taken directly from the observations of Mérimée as Inspector of Historical Monuments. What better source than direct observation? But there is notoriously little, if any, such observation in *La Guzla, Clara Gazul,* **"Mateo Falcone," "Djoûmane,"** or **"Lokis,"** even if Mérimée pretended there was. This use of direct observation serves the esthetic purpose of making the flannel vest more realistic; but, by its topical nature, it also serves to project the author Mérimée into his story, involve him vicariously in the mythic situation. He transposed the legend, told in medieval times about antiquity, into the age of Louis-Philippe because that was the age in which he lived, and he wanted to put himself into the tale. This is made clear by his use of the narrator.

The narrator of the **"Vénus"** serves the traditional purpose of procuring a greater "suspension of disbelief"; he is a man like ourselves, whose relation to the events is similar to that of the reader. He witnesses everything and guarantees the veracity of what happens. He is cleverly depicted as hesitant, unwilling to believe, and finally overwhelmed by the force of the evidence; and the reader's reactions go along with his. He effectively expresses within the story the attitude the author desires to create. Such a narrator appears, in varying degrees of importance, in nine of Mérimée's tales, always serving among other things to give our awareness of the fictional nature of fiction a structure within the tale. But, as Theophil Spoerri has rightly remarked, one of Mérimée's great achievements was to integrate the framework of a story into the story itself and by the device of the narrator accentuate this framework in order to lead us as close as possible to the abyss without ever allowing a sense of real danger to arise, giving us firm ground on which to stand while we peer down. Compared to the other narrators, the one in the **"Vénus"** is the most developed; he represents an extreme point in Mérimée's art. He sees things, meets people, witnesses the statue's vengeance, first toward the young rock-throwing urchin and then toward the hero. He is an honored guest of the Peyrehorade family, and is even admitted to the marriage festivities, which are quite intimate because the Puygarrig family is in mourning. From an expository point of view, all he doesn't see directly is told to him, he is our only source for the tale; in contrast to **Carmen** no other person even speaks for very long. The ideas and reactions of others are only presented through dialogue with him. He thus occupies a much more important place in the tale than does the narrator in any of the other stories; the integration of framework and action is here at its most complete.

In addition, just as the realistic detail of this story is so autobiographical, likewise the narrator is much closer to being Mérimée, than is, for example, the narrator of **Carmen.** If the latter stems from the Inspector of Historical Monuments, the former is this inspector, even including his professional deformation. (pp. 478-79)

However, in acquiring this realism, the Parisian narrator has lost, to a great extent, those traits which create a condescending attitude on the reader's part toward the narrator of **Carmen.** There Mérimée makes sure the narrator doesn't interfere too much with our emotional reaction to the plight of Carmen and Don José. In the **"Vénus,"** he is more intelligent, indeed endowed with a rather subtle capacity to face the demands of daily life. This is especially demonstrated in the intelligent and sympathetic, never annoying way in which he treats the problem of the sophisticated Parisian confronted with the rather excessive good will and hospitality, not to mention amateur erudition, of the provincial. He maintains his cosmopolitan identity, while at the same time appreciating the virtues of his hosts. Whereas the narrator of **Carmen** seems to want to submerge the heroes of his tale in the categories of Gypsy or Basque, the narrator here perceives the individual rather than the category. The erudition of the narrator in **Carmen** is satirized; here he is almost omniscience itself.

Strikingly, Mérimée even proceeds to endow his narrator with a certain responsibility in the disaster. There are some, the innocent and unsophisticated, such as the mother, the villagers, the bride, who from the beginning have recognized the menacing danger of the statue; these are the people who give credit to myth and superstition. The intellectuals, the *procureur du roi,* the victim's father, and especially the narrator, refuse to pay any attention to these fears; those who can't act recognize the danger, and those who are intelligent and could act refuse to see it or do anything. The person best placed to understand and act is the narrator; he correctly interprets the inscription on the statue to mean "Beware if she loves you," sees that *turbul* stands for *turbulenta;* he is sensitive enough to recognize the tiger-like, diabolic, menacing face of the statue. What is more, excepting the victim, he alone knows that the ring has remained on the statue's finger; he is informed that the finger has tightened on the ring but, in order to avoid getting wet in the rain, prefers to assume that his menaced informant is drunk. . . . Finally he hears Venus mount the stairs, but even then will not admit that this might be the statue. Of all the characters in the story, he is best placed to understand what is going on and to impede the course of the disaster; more than a mere witness to these events, he is in a negative sense responsible for them.

In this way, Mérimée's self-projection into the tale acquires a new dimension; by the use of autobiographical realism and by the device of the narrator he at the same time tries to increase the credibility of the story, and to suggest his own personal involvement in it and the problems it presents, to offer a vicarious presentation of himself, in which that self does not come off very well.

The full implications of this are evident if one recalls the subject matter of the story. This is, again, black Aphrodite, the goddess of love who causes death. The story opens with the evocation of death and destruction—the Puygarrig family is in mourning, and the statue's first act is to break someone's arm. The theme of a fatal, wounding Venus is reiterated page after page (at times with humorous intent) by the mother, the villagers, M. de Peyrehorade, the narrator. And the dénouement fully justifies this theme, the synthesis of love and death, which is a major element in Mérimée's abyss. Love, like the Vénus of Ille, is invincible, inevitable, and disastrous. (This conviction was I suspect particularly strong in Mérimée when he was writing this story, for sometime before October 1832 he suffered a disappointment in love of which he was still writing in his correspondence in July 1833 and which probably inspired the *Double méprise* and, less directly, the "Vénus d'Ille;" we unfortunately know practically nothing about this affair.) The incredible beauty and fascination of the statue is frankly attributed to . . . the presence of disdain, irony, and cruelty; she is the fatal woman *à l'état pur*. More often in Mérimée the female is the victim of the male, but in five stories we meet the fatal woman. . . . In many of his tales, love has as its outcome the death of the beloved. In "Lokis," the groom eats his bride on their wedding night; in *Inès Mendo,* Mendoza's infidelity to his saintly bride pushes her to death. Arsène Guillot dies of a broken heart, complicated by the injuries received upon throwing herself out the window. In *Le Ciel et l'enfer,* Dona Urracca almost has her lover killed out of jealousy. The more violently people love, the more deadly that love can be. The eternal triangle is resolved by the death of one or two lovers at the hands of the remaining parties. This is true not only of *Carmen* (she is, as Luppé remarks, a Vénus of Ille in the flesh), but also of *La Famille de Carvajal,* where the daughter kills her father in order to put an end to his incestuous pursuits, and of many of the ballads and plays. In the "Vase étrusque," Saint-Clair's jealousy involved him in a mortal duel, and then Mathilde pines away. This death exists only as a possibility in "Il Viccolo," but the fascination of the story comes from the use made of the idea of the woman who kills in loving. In the "Chambre bleue," death takes place in the next room and turns out to be only a matter of spilt red wine. "Djoûmane" presents in dream form a voluptuous obsession which ends in human sacrifice. This includes a great majority of Mérimée's love stories. In others, the theme is introduced subtly or metaphorically. Even in *Colomba,* Miss Lydia's feelings for Orso are heightened by his entrance into the violent world of the vendetta.

Then, for Mérimée, the "Vénus d'Ille" presents the myth of love in its pure state. Venus, terrible and vengeful goddess, accepts only one tribute, that of human life. The mere repetition of this plot in "Il Viccolo" indicates the extent to which this theme constantly remained before him. However, in "Djoûmane" the theme is presented as a nightmare from which hero and reader awaken; in the *Carvajal* ironically as an example of "romantisme noir," an obedience to literary fashion which need not be taken seriously; in *Carmen* as stemming from the violent love and jealousy of primitives, not civilized people; in "Lokis" as a sort of biological abnormality. "La Chambre bleue" represents the extreme transposition, or bowdlerizing of the theme.

The "Vénus d'Ille" is unique in that there is no such sugar-coating to the pill. Here, on the contrary, the death is effected by the mythic deity who personifies love and thus this death is generalized; Venus becomes identifiable with fate. The use of myth gives the love-death synthesis a general applicability which Mérimée suggests nowhere else. The myth did not serve a purely esthetic purpose, it offered the opportunity to express in concrete form an idea it was otherwise necessary to hide or disguise. Here, what is usually abnormal and exotic takes place among us, among people we know (through moving the legend into the nineteenth century and using autobiographical local color). Even worse, through the responsibility of the narrator, our double within the tale, we are intimately involved in the viciousness of Venus. On the occasion when he uses a myth for the structure of his story, Mérimée has us behold the abyss more purely and more clearly than anywhere else. If elsewhere the implication is that this is an exotic or historical problem, or a misunderstanding, here the reader's representative within the story, the narrator, who is also patently linked to the author, is caught in the very heart of the theme. (pp. 479-82)

Frank Paul Bowman, "Narrator and Myth in Mérimée's 'Venus d'Ille'," in The French Review, *Vol. XXXIII, 1960, pp. 475-82.*

A. W. Raitt   (essay date 1970)

[*Raitt is an English editor and critic whose critical study* Prosper Mérimée *is considered the definitive biography of the author in the English language. In the following excerpt from his book, Raitt surveys technical and thematic characteristics in Mérimée's short stories, discerning three major phases in their development.*]

Certainly the brief tale proved much more suitable for Mérimée's special requirements than either the novel, the prose poem or the drama. He was never able to master the problem of imposing unity on diversity in a longer work of imagination, and the more ambitious his intentions were, the more he was liable to end up with a series of juxtaposed but disparate elements. As Pierre Trahard has pointed out, in his early years Mérimée practised a 'divergent aesthetic', which led to fragmentation and disunity; in 1829 he realised the virtues of a 'convergent aesthetic', and by restricting his canvas to small dimensions, was able to impose on it a coherence and a density which had hitherto escaped him [in Trahard's *La Jeunesse de Prosper Mérimee*]. Thereafter almost all his imaginative writings were brief narratives. He had discovered the form best attuned to his own temperament and was thereafter little inclined to go outside it.

There are many reasons why Mérimée felt so much at home with the short story. Compared with the novel, it gives little scope to a writer whose view of the world is broad and complex. On the other hand, by its very compactness, it offers excellent opportunities to anyone who is more concerned with effects than with causes, since a point can be made effectively without the necessity for those preparations and explanations which the novel normally requires. Thus that inveterate scepticism which made Mérimée suspicious of all generalisation tended to unfit him for novel-writing, while pushing him towards a reliance on individual facts that corresponded exactly to the bounds of the short-story form. Indeed, Mérimée's reluctance to visualize happenings on a large scale is one of the defects of a work like the *Chronique*. Moreover, his predilection for sudden, violent action, unencumbered by lengthy dialogue or diagnosis, sorted well with a genre which, by definition, demands concision. The pressure of strong emotions, which sometimes makes his longer works appear schematic in their succession of unexpected events, produces an intensity of feeling in the short tales that is perfectly expressed by a single dramatic act. Even Mérimée's style lends itself admirably to short-story writing: the urgent, clipped tones, the blunt statements of fact, the direct assault on the reader's sensibility are the ideal instrument for the tale as Mérimée conceived it. As early as 1831, Sainte-Beuve provided this penetrating summary of the qualities which drew Mérimée to the short story:

> the broad view of things does not suit him, his mind is too positive to believe in it; he believes in clearly defined, circumstantial facts, each carried to the logical conclusion of its special form of passion and of its expression in physical reality; the rest strikes him as so much smoke and cloud.

The result is that when Mérimée first tried his hand at a short story early in 1829, he achieved mastery at one stroke. How far this success was brought about by deliberate calculation and how far it was an instinctive divining of a new technique it is hard to tell. Mérimée only rarely indulged in theorising about literature, and that for the most part in the later years of his life, when he drew on his own experience to appreciate the skills and problems of other authors. What is certain is that his handling of the short story owes little to any of his immediate predecessors in France. One has only to look at the works of Charles Nodier, the acknowledged master of the short story in the 1820s (and whom Mérimée was to succeed in the Academy in 1844), to see how vast is the gulf which separates the tales of *Mosaïque* from the great majority of earlier French stories. Where Nodier narrates slowly, amiably, digressively and verbosely, Mérimée strips his tales down to their bare essentials, makes every word and every detail count, and drives the action forward with relentless energy. In this way, he ensures that the short story acquires an identity and a character of its own—to quote one historian of the form,

> unhampered by tradition or the urge to write novels, he became the first French writer to treat brief fiction as more than a dehydrated novel or a miniature long romance.

(pp. 122-24)

Oddly enough, those tales which most strongly indicate this development are those written first, in 1829—"**Mateo Falcone**," "**La Vision de Charles XI**," "**L'Enlèvement de**

la redoute" ("**The Storming of the Redoubt**"), "**Tamango**" and "**Federigo**"; the two which date from 1830—"**La Partie de tric-trac**" ("**The Game of Backgammon**") and "**Le Vase étrusque**"—deal with more complicated psychological states and consequently require a more circumstantial mode of narration. The earlier group deals largely with the uncomplicated natures of brutal primitives—a Corsican peasant, a West African negro chief, soldiers in the thick of a murderous battle—whereas the second investigates the subtler reactions of a more civilised milieu (though violence is no less present here). It is the preoccupation with the spontaneous urges of people whose natural reactions are not stifled by convention that enables Mérimée to treat his subjects with such exemplary succinctness. The more delicate and profound the psychological dissection is to be, the more time the author needs for the operation, and the general direction of Mérimée's art after 1830 is consistently towards greater finesse and precision in the analysis of motive and feeling. (pp. 124-25)

In nearly all these tales, he concentrates on a single situation of crisis and omits all description, comment or character-drawing which is not directly relevant to it. In "**Mateo Falcone**," the action obeys the unities as strictly as any classical tragedy: the peasant's son betrays the bandit he has hidden, the father returns, discovers the boy's treachery and shoots him. In "**L'Enlèvement de la redoute**" all the glory and savagery of 1812 is condensed into a rapid account of one short but bloody combat. In "**La Vision de Charles XI**," the king's sinister prophetic vision is related as abruptly as it happened. In "**Tamango**," though the action covers a longer period, there is an equal sense of precipitancy in the story of the negro slave-trader who is shanghaied by an unscrupulous French captain, succeeds in rousing the slaves to massacre the crew, only to see them all perish when they find they cannot sail the ship. "**Federigo**" has a more complicated anecdote about a scamp who ingeniously tricks both God and the Devil, but Mérimée did not take it very seriously—he hesitated before including it in the collection and then excised it from subsequent editions. Even the two tales written in 1830 do not allow their slightly looser form to detract from their confinement within the strict bounds of economy and unity. Roger's remorse for having caused a man's death by cheating in "**La Partie de tric-trac**," Saint-Clair's unreasoning jealousy and its fatal consequences in "**Le Vase étrusque**" may be more complex emotions than Mateo's cruel sense of honour or Tamango's animal cunning, but they are depicted with the same deft attention to detail and the same swiftness of movement.

Perhaps the most telling feature of Mérimée's art in the laconic concision of these tales is his brilliant use of the significant detail to enlist belief, to concentrate interest and to provide a concrete image for the mind to fasten on. From his earliest critical writings to his late literary studies, Mérimée regularly stressed the importance of singling out the one detail which would give the whole work, whether in fiction, in painting or in architecture, a centre and a term of reference. (pp. 125-26)

This principle is much in evidence in the *Mosaïque* stories. The cupidity of young Falcone when the sergeant bribes him to reveal the whereabouts of the bandit he has hidden is given a palpable physical presence by the shining watch which is dangled in front of his face as a reward:

meanwhile the watch was swinging to and fro, and sometimes bumped against the end of his nose. At last, little by little, his right hand rose towards the watch: the tips of his fingers touched it; and all its weight was resting in his hand, though the sergeant-major still held on to the other end of the chain. . . . The dial was sky-blue . . . the case newly polished . . . in the sunlight it seemed to be on fire . . . The temptation was too strong.

(p. 127)

But Mérimée is also a master of the apparently inconsequential touch or unnecessary piece of information which carries conviction precisely because it is there for no visible reason. The endings of his tales illustrate this. **"Mateo Falcone"** concludes, not with the death of the boy, but with the father saying: 'Send a message to tell my son-in-law Tiodoro Bianchi to come and live with us,' thereby indicating that the tragic death of the child is only an incident in a continuing sequence of existence, that the waves of time will soon wash away the name written in sand. . . . The most brutal intrusion of an indifferent reality comes at the end of **"La Partie de tric-trac."** The story is being told by the captain of a ship lying becalmed somewhere at sea. Just at the moment when he is about to describe Roger's death, he is interrupted by the sighting of a whale, breaks off his tale and thinks only of the new diversion which has presented itself. Mérimée concludes laconically: 'I was never able to find out how the unfortunate Roger died.' The reader is at once impressed by the air of honesty and naturalness which emanates from this admission, and disturbed by the coolly ironic detachment of an author who can bring a moving story to such an incongruously abrupt close. Credibility and impersonality are equally served by this highly sophisticated technique of assumed casualness.

The style, too, by its precision and its sobriety, creates an impression of truthful frankness. Mérimée has often been reproached with having a colourless style. To the extent that he cultivates no rhetorical effects, that his sentences are simple and direct, that his images are neither frequent nor original, that the tone is generally conversational, there is something in this criticism. But the very absence of poetic flourishes, emotional tirades or elaborate convolutions makes his language the ideal vehicle for short stories which aim both to convince and to shock. 'My antipathy for stylistic brilliance is so strong that I kill it off where-ever I find it', he declared in 1831, and the fact that he writes with such anonymous detachment gives his tales the dry crispness of the reports of a trained observer, concerned only to present a factual statement of events. But Mérimée did not seek the same kind of impersonality as Flaubert. He makes no attempt to disguise the presence of a story-teller or to avoid the introduction of phrases expressing personal opinions: several of the tales in *Mosaïque*—"Mateo Falcone," "L'Enlèvement de la redoute" and "La Partie de tric-trac"—are told in the first person, and the others contain frequent authorial interjections. However, this serves to create a distancing effect—the narrator of **"Mateo Falcone,"** for example, has such a shadowy existence that the author's personal involvement is decreased rather than enhanced by his presence, and the officer and the ship's captain in the other two stories simply make it clear to us that Mérimée is repeating hearsay for which he accepts no responsibility. The creation of a false identity behind which he can shelter unseen is a de-

vice which he will use to even greater effect in **"La Vénus d'Ille"** and *Carmen.* Similarly, when in **"Le Vase étrusque"** Mérimée uses autobiographical material which for him carries an unusually high charge of personal emotion, he deliberately affects a tone of almost supercilious amusement to describe his hero, Saint-Clair.

These effects of aloofness and impassiveness damp down any pathos latent in the subject-matter of the tales—to see just how much Mérimée has left unspoken, one needs only to glance at Balzac's "Un Drame au bord de la mer" ("A Drama by the Seaside"), in which the theme of a father killing his son to redeem the family honour is treated with heavy stress on the horror of the deed and the remorse it would later inspire. Yet the events of all these brief anecdotes burn with a white heat of passion. Mateo's fierce pride compels him to destroy what he loves most dearly; Roger's shame at having caused a man's death by cheating at backgammon is so overwhelming that he courts and finds death in action; Saint-Clair is consumed by silly, pointless jealousy until he too is killed by it. The savage instincts of Tamango, the horror-stricken shudder of Charles XI, the unreasoning actions of soldiers in the heat of battle, all reveal the same view of humanity as constantly shaken by feelings and appetites which it cannot control and which defy rational analysis.

As G. Hainsworth has pointed out, the contrast in **"Tamango"** between those reputed to be savages and those reputed to be civilised is instructive. Mérimée (who as a good liberal, a friend of Fanny Wright and a frequenter of the Stapfer salon was accustomed to hearing slave-trading indignantly condemned as a degrading and inhuman practice) begins his story with a series of sarcastic digs at the hypocrisy of dealers in black ivory: the ironically named Captain Ledoux generously allows a space of five feet by two for each negro during the six-week voyage, ' "for the truth is", as Ledoux told the shipowner to justify this liberal measure, "negroes are, after all, human beings just as much as white men" '. But as the story develops it becomes clear that it is anything but abolitionist propaganda. A kindly interpreter turns loose a few slaves, 'who ran off in all directions, completely at a loss to know how to get back to their homeland two hundred leagues from the coast', and those who try to seize their new liberty are, like Tamango himself, selfish, brutal, and above all stupid. 'The sum of the tale, clearly, sets in parallel savagery and civilisation, to the greater glory of neither.' Human nature is shown as never far from the basic animality of passion, and Mérimeé takes sardonic pleasure in demonstrating that the elegant and sophisticated Saint-Clair is just as much the plaything of his unstable emotions as an uneducated primitive like Tamango.

It is this combination of highly controlled narrative craft and uncontrollable feeling which gives Mérimée's tales their unique flavour. Keeping the tightest possible rein on his own reactions, relating events with the imperturbable technical mastery of a born *raconteur,* never allowing the tone to rise above that of urbane conversation, Mérimée brings us to the very edge of the abysses which open up within our very being, allows us a terrifying glimpse into their depths, and then, with an off-hand shrug, returns us to the apparent security of ordinary existence. (pp. 127-31)

Which of the tales is most effective is ultimately a matter of personal choice. Certainly none makes a more powerful impact than **"Mateo Falcone."** The story itself is not new; a good half-dozen versions were already in print. Nor can Mérimée be given much credit for the details of local colour, since he had culled them all from various guidebooks and historical works about Corsica (after he had himself visited the island in 1839, he corrected some of the more glaring inaccuracies and removed the subtitle of *Mœurs de la Corse* (*Corsican Manners*) which in the meantime had become sadly dated). But if Mérimée's imagination invents little it excels at the selection and rearrangement of given materials and the vivid immediacy of **"Mateo Falcone"** is utterly convincing. Hastening through a series of linked crises—the arrival of the hunted bandit, the vain search by the troops, the bribe and its acceptance, the return of Mateo, the shooting of the boy—it maintains an almost unbearable tension. Few lines in French literature deliver a more stunning blow with simple means than the famous sentence relating the boy's death: 'Mateo fired and Fortunato fell stone dead.' The total absence of moral comment or inner psychological analysis concentrates attention exclusively on the action itself, but that is so carefully prepared and so full of emotive force that further explanations could only seem superfluous. The exact adjustment of outward deed or gesture to inward states of mind is always one of the great strengths of Mérimée's art. Here the contrast between the awfulness of the killing and the author's rigid refusal to capitalise on it conveys a sense of icy sobriety which fully justifies Walter Pater's description of **"Mateo Falcone"** as 'perhaps the cruellest story in the world' [see excerpt dated 1890].

"La Vision de Charles XI," Mérimée's first attempt at the ghost-story, seems somewhat less effective, perhaps because he himself surpassed it so brilliantly in later works, perhaps because the Gothic horrors of the vision barely escape meretriciousness. Its most interesting feature is the care taken to persuade us of its authenticity. Mérimée's claim that it is based on attested documents is not without justification (though in fact the papers in the Swedish archives to which he refers were apocryphal), and he adopts the calm, impartial style of a historian whose sole aim is to set out established facts. Moreover, the non-hallucinatory nature of the vision seems to be guaranteed by the bloodstain which remains on the king's slipper after the gory phantoms have faded—but that is a detail of Mérimée's own fabrication. In this story Mérimée deploys his gifts of minutely convincing narration to instil in us the same sense of uncomprehending unease as overcomes the supposed participants in the vision. Perhaps for the first time, a French writer has sought to use the supernatural, not as fantasy, as entertainment, as allegory or as a scarcely credible embroidery on reality, but as something which can inexplicably but incontrovertibly intrude into the fabric of ordinary life. If at the end of the tale we are uncertain whether or not to believe him, his purpose has been achieved. His own attitude to the occult is compounded of approximately equal parts of credulity and scepticism, and if he can insinuate the same doubts into the minds of his readers, he has effectively demonstrated to them how frail and unsteady is the position humanity holds in the universe.

"L'Enlèvement de la Redoute" has, from its publication, ranked with **"Mateo Falcone"** as a masterpiece of the short story. It has the same background of real or assumed authenticity as the two earlier tales, the same streamlined economy of execution, the same urgency of style, the same insistence on violence as an essential part of human life. Yet many readers would sense in it, as André Gide did in **"La Partie de tric-trac,"** 'an intolerable impression of useless perfection and well done homework'. No doubt it is an astonishing feat to have condensed into half a dozen pages the whole atmosphere of Napoleon's Russian campaign, but one wonders whether it was worth performing: inevitably, the epic sweep is missing, and no great human interest compensates for its lack. Technically, the tale is impeccable, but once that has been said, there is little to add.

"Tamango" is a more complex and a more disturbing work. Again Mérimée has documented himself thoroughly, and skilfully used his knowledge to authenticate the strange events which constitute his story. But here his ulterior motive, never clearly indicated though always implicit in the progress of the action, is, as we have seen, to set the savage beside the civilised man and to give an equally bitter picture of both. The irony which runs through the story serves not only this misanthropic end, but a variety of subsidiary purposes: to expose the horrors of the slave-trade, to ridicule the myth of the 'good savage', to give a grim reminder of the futility of unplanned humanitarianism, and generally to deride human folly, human greed and human ferocity. Little that Mérimée wrote has quite the same note of unrelieved pessimism as **"Tamango"**; its dark colours are enhanced by an acid humour in the style, which culminates in the ultimate incongruity of Tamango's career:

> The colonel of the 75th noticed him and took him on to play the cymbals in the regimental band. He learned a little English; but he never talked much. On the other hand, he drank rum and tafia to excess. He died in hospital of an inflammation of the chest.

"Federigo" has never enjoyed the popularity of its fellows, and Mérimée himself was unsure whether to include it in the collection. Yet this slight anecdote of a reprobate who by his cheerful trickery outwits both God and the Devil has an unpretentious charm of its own. How much this is due to Mérimée's own ingenuity is unsure, since the source of the story has never been clearly identified—but there is no reason to doubt his word that it derives from an old Neapolitan legend. The tone is light and unassuming, as befits a folk-tale which neither author nor reader takes very seriously; at most, one might see in it a vague prefiguration of the theme of **"Les Ames du Purgatoire"** (**"The Souls in Purgatory"**), Mérimée's version of the Don Juan story, which it resembles in that both treat the theme of the rogue who seeks to escape retribution for his misdeeds. But it would be going too far to diagnose it as a twinge from the conscience of an author who was well aware of his own transgressions of the conventional moral code; it remains no more than an amusing recital of a blithely and harmlessly irreverent folktale.

"Le Vase étrusque," on the other hand, bids fair to be considered as one of his greatest achievements. Based as it is on Mérimée's tempestuous affair with Émilie Lacoste, it contains in Saint-Clair a discreet but extremely revealing self-portrait which renders it doubly precious to his admirers. This current of genuine personal emotion, though half-hidden by the froth of surface frivolity, gives it a tragic colouring and a power to move which Mérimée is inclined to forfeit elsewhere by a too rigid refusal to admit any sympathy with his characters. The vacillations of the morbidly sensitive hero are portrayed with a remarkably delicate touch, and though Mérimée still prefers to reveal emotion through gesture and action rather than through abstract categorisation, the greater complexity of Saint-Clair's reactions induces him to treat the subject more spaciously than he had done with the relatively simple natures of Mateo or Tamango. Indeed, the long conversation at the stag-party during which Saint-Clair's jealousy is first aroused, though an outstanding example of natural and lifelike dialogue, moves sinuously through areas of no great relevance to the central topic. Mérimée, incorrigibly attracted by local colour, even manages to bring it into this Parisian tale (with a wry smile) by means of Neville's account of his travels in Egypt. But all this accentuates the essential intimacy of the tale. As in the two plays which were added in 1829 to the *Théâtre de Clara Gazul,* Mérimée has become fascinated by the tragic inconsistencies of human feelings, and these he traces with profound skill and insight. The agony of suspicion in a proudly solitary mind leads to a fatal petulance which is as pointless as jealousy of a dead man had been in the first place. The tragedy of **"Le Vase étrusque"** is all the more moving for being so unnecessary. It is perhaps Mérimée's harshest lesson on the fragility of human happiness. (pp. 131-35)

The tales of **Mosaïque** constitute one of the most remarkable collections of short stories ever assembled. Models of a genre which was still far from maturity, they retain today all of their whiplash force, and not even Maupassant has surpassed the best of them. Their qualities make them read as though they were still fresh from the press; even what might seem shortcomings are converted by Mérimée into positive elements in their success. (p. 136)

Between 1830 and 1846, Mérimée wrote eight tales, which include his finest achievements; thereafter, he was to forsake fiction for twenty years until, in an access of what he professed to regard as senile euphoria, he was tempted again. Though there is a gap of three years between **"La Partie de tric-trac,"** the last of the stories collected in **Mosaïque,** and **La Double Méprise,** which appeared in 1833, there is no dramatic change in his methods as a narrator, but rather a gradual development of trends already apparent in the earlier works. These middle-period tales are less abrupt and schematic; they display a much richer and subtler understanding of psychology; they use his mastery of technique to produce effects more complex and more profound. (p. 172)

The tales can roughly be divided into two groups, corresponding to Mérimée's two principal preoccupations in writing during these years. Into the first group, one may put those stories which deal with modern life in its falsity, its hypocrisy, its uncertainty—**La Double Méprise** (1833), **"Arsène Guillot"** (1844) and **"L'Abbé Aubain"** (1846), to which can be added **"Les Ames du Purgatoire"** (1834), since, although it is set in seventeenth-century Spain, its theme is closely connected with Mérimée's reactions to the life he was leading in the Parisian society of the 1830s. The second group comprises **"La Vénus d'Ille"** (1837), **Colomba** (1840), **Carmen** (originally composed in 1845) and **"Il Viccolo di Madama Lucrezia"** (which, though only published posthumously, dates from 1846); these sto-

ries are primarily concerned with the darker, more mysterious forces of life, whose eruption can destroy the superficial façade of civilisation as most of us know it. There is of course nothing rigid in this classification, for just as **La Double Méprise** uses a refined and elegant setting to demonstrate the destructive power of emotion, so **"La Vénus d'Ille"** adds to its main preoccupation with phenomena outside rational control an attack on the misplaced values of a society which seeks to deny the existence of such phenomena. But it may at least serve to clarify the complex of themes which underlies all these tales and which Mérimée's brusque, blunt manner makes it easy to overlook.

La Double Méprise was written in the summer of 1833, at the time when Mérimée was still leading a life of dissipation as a self-confessed scamp and very shortly after his tragic-comic affair with George Sand. These circumstances have an unmistakable bearing on the sad, simple tale of Mme Julie de Chaverny who, married to an unbearable brute but still virtuously faithful, finds herself seduced in the space of nine hours by the cynical Darcy and then dies of remorse. It would be absurd to pretend that Julie as a person owes much to George Sand, far too idiosyncratic a model to be used with impunity; but Julie's situation with a coarse, thoughtless, philistine, philandering husband is undoubtedly akin to George Sand's deteriorating relationship with the deplorable Casimir Dudevant, with whom she was thoroughly disillusioned by the time she met Mérimée. Likewise, Darcy, elegant but not rich,

A study of Mérimée as a young man.

caustic, mildly misanthropic, highly experienced with women, full of a half-mocking predilection for exoticism, can hardly fail to recall Mérimée himself as a slightly jaundiced observer might have seen him at that time—and that Mérimée was eminently capable of turning an acutely critical gaze on his own person is made very plain by his letters. Moreover, the double misunderstanding of which the title speaks, the mutual failure of Julie and Darcy to understand each other's motives, is exactly what had characterised the George Sand-Mérimée débâcle, the one vainly hoping to find in it the great love of a broken life, the other seeing it as an adventure to be undertaken with deliberately cold detachment.

But the story is anything but a banal autobiographical transcription. Two things above all interested him. The first and more prominent of the two is that of demonstrating how a woman who has always prized her fidelity to her marriage vows can, in a matter of hours, ruin her whole life by committing adultery with someone whom she scarcely even knows, let alone loves. In one sense, this is a further variation on the theme already exploited in **"Le Vase étrusque"** and **"La Partie de tric-trac,"** where an emotion totally foreign to a character's normal habits of behaviour suddenly seizes control of him and causes his existence to collapse in ruins, and as one might expect, Mérimée pitilessly emphasises how unaccountably swift Julie's fall has been: 'It was at four o'clock that she had seen Darcy for the first time.—Yes, *seen* him,—she could not say seen him *again*. . . . She had forgotten his features, his voice; for her he was a stranger. . . . Nine hours later she had become his mistress!' Once again, Mérimée has shown us the instability of feeling, the weakness of humanity, the impotence of principle or of conscious thought when an irrational desire flutters into the mind. (pp. 172-74)

This theme, however, mingles with another which is perhaps even more poignant: the inability of two people to communicate with one another, the infinite possibilities of misunderstanding even in the tenderest relationship. After Darcy has seduced Julie in his carriage on the way back to Paris, she is overcome by a flood of conflicting emotions which eventually merge into a desperate resolve to sacrifice all for love and elope with him to some distant land; at that very moment, the unmoved Darcy 'was very calmly putting his gladé-kid gloves on again', and Julie suddenly realises that, for him, she is no more than another conquest who will keep him pleasantly occupied during the winter. Her dying words, a few days later, are, significantly: 'Write to him that he doesn't know me . . . that I don't know him . . . ' Neither partner had been capable of seeing how the other was feeling: Julie had deluded herself into believing that Darcy was profoundly in love with her, whereas Darcy had supposed that she was simply ready for a passing affair. The misunderstanding kills Julie, and leaves Darcy as ironically unperturbed as ever. In the original text published in 1833, that was as far as the story went; tragedy arose from the misunderstanding, but it was exclusively Julie's tragedy, since her impressionability had made her the victim of a Don Juan who remained unaffected by her misfortune. But when Mérimée revised the story for a new edition in 1842, he altered the emphasis so as to give a less harsh view of Darcy's attitude and to suggest that he might have lost almost as much as Julie by their failure to see into each other's minds. A sentence

which had at first stated abruptly: 'Darcy was not in love' now read more dubitatively: 'Darcy had been wrong about the nature of his feelings: it must be admitted that he was not in love.' Darcy's reproaches of hard-heartedness, which finally decided Julie to succumb, were in 1833 uttered with 'his diabolical smile'; in 1842, he speaks 'in a voice so gentle that its tone was all the more moving'. Above all, the end of the story is given a new twist, so that instead of finishing with Darcy's ironical smile, it goes on to the profound melancholy of: 'These two people, for all the misunderstanding between them, were perhaps made for one another.'

That these changes are intended to add a new dimension to the tale is clear; that they succeed in doing so is less certain. The reader's general impression of Darcy remains what it was in 1833: a cynical seducer who may once have been capable of genuine feeling but who has become hardened by debauch. The lighter touches now added to the portrait seem to superimpose another image on it more than they modify the original physiognomy. Perhaps Mérimée wishes to alter the perspective because his own attitude to Darcy is no longer the same. In 1833, a Don Juan himself, he has presented a deliberately harsh, unsympathetic view of such a character—a man whose thoughtless search for pleasure can cause a woman's death. In 1842, less bitter, less inclined to self-reproach but still as pessimistic, he hints that Don Juan can frustrate his own chances of happiness just as much as those of the women he treats as his playthings. If the two themes had been equally prominent in the first conception of the tale, it might have been a more unified work; as it is, the suggestions of unrealised possibilities and missed opportunities do not marry perfectly with the idea of the mutability of human emotion.

The story thus remains primarily the account of Julie's succumbing in a few hours to the blandishments of a man who is in effect a stranger. In order to make this credible, Mérimée plans his narrative with quite extraordinary skill. He is not out for the facile enjoyment of satirising Julie's fallibility; he wants to make us understand it, believe in it, and feel for it, and to this end, he devotes meticulous care to the detailed motivation of her actions. Chaverny's unpardonable rudeness at the Opera, the assiduous but ineffectual courtship by young Châteaufort (who, by making her glimpse the possibility of adultery, unwittingly prepares the way for his rival), the memories of a past love and what might have been if it had led to marriage, the romantic adventures which the dashing Darcy had undergone in Cyprus, the alarm of the coach accident, Darcy's practised wooing of her in the long and fascinatingly organised conversation in his carriage—all these things are necessary preliminaries to Julie's fall. Nowhere else in Mérimée is there such delicacy and subtlety in the fine shades of psychological analysis. Moreover the analysis is carried out with more gentleness than acerbity, and for all the detachment of the style, *La Double Méprise* is, with **"Arsène Guillot,"** the best answer to those who would see in Mérimée only coldness and cruelty. In later years, he affected to disdain it: 'it's one of my wild oats, sown for money, which was given to someone of no great worth'. (Céline Cayot is meant.) But posterity has been kinder, and it was with good reason that, a few years ago, a committee of distinguished French writers and critics voted it one of the twelve best novels of the nineteenth century. (pp. 174-76)

La Double Méprise, fairly obviously, and **"Les Ames du Purgatoire,"** more deviously, relate to Mérimée's feelings about the life he and others of his generation were leading in the early 1830s. **"Arsène Guillot,"** though not written until 1844, does so with even less attempt at disguise. In 1832, at the time of his escapade with Pauline, Mérimée had noted: 'Thanks to her, I've made a lot of observations about the heart of Opera chorus-girls, and those girls known as *demi-castors.* I firmly intend to write a fine dissertation on them when I have time.' That the dissertation, when it came, would defend these humble sinners against the strictures of the well-bred ladies of high society was also predictable, Mérimée having frequently inveighed against those who condemned them from the security of wealth and status: to Jenny Dacquin in 1832, after recounting the misfortunes of one such girl, he had exclaimed bitterly:

> Be so good as tell me whether that young girl isn't infinitely more meritorious for leading the life she leads than someone like yourself, who has the extraordinary good fortune to have an impeccable background and such a refined nature that for me it is almost the epitome of a whole civilisation.

In the event, he is manifestly thinking of Céline Cayot when he comes to write his tale. Even the names are similar, and when Arsène Guillot complains that her lover cannot write her name correctly—'Yes, I'm called Arsène Guillot, G, U, I, two L's and he spells it with a Y!'—it is a direct reflection of Mérimée's own inability to remember the correct spelling of Céline's surname. The friendly affection he always felt for her is magnified here into a feeling of compassion for the heroine which almost verges on sentimentality. Nor can one doubt that his demonstration of the fundamental genuineness of the penniless Arsène is principally aimed at Valentine Delessert for whom he had abandoned Céline. Throughout the tale, he addresses himself with exaggerated respect to a supposed female listener who belongs to a higher social class than Arsène, and this can be none other than Mme Delessert, for whom, as he said himself, all that he ever wrote was destined. The engaging reprobate Max de Salligny, Arsène's ex-lover who is eventually stolen from her by the aristocratic Mme de Piennes, owes much to Mérimée himself: both are addicted to foreign travel, accustomed to high life as well as low life, elegant, humorous, modest, and zealous in their attentions to ladies.

But if the story has analogies with aspects of Mérimée's own life and opinions in the 1830s, its immediate cause is his fury with the neo-Catholic piety of the 1840s, which roused him to a peak of disgusted indignation about Easter 1843. Convinced that the devoutness of fashionable society was nothing but a hypocritical sham, Mérimée plainly intends **"Arsène Guillot"** to draw an exemplary contrast between the honest and unselfish simplicity of Arsène, who has to have a lover to support herself and her ailing mother, and who tries to kill herself when she is abandoned, and the ostentatious and conventional religiosity of Mme de Piennes, who in the end finds herself going off with the lover of the girl she had tried to convert. (pp. 178-79)

Ultimately more important than this polemical intent is the care and humanity Mérimée has shown in depicting the contrasting characters of Arsène and Mme de Piennes.

The portrait of Arsène is not a complex one—by definition, that would have been impossible—but it is deliberately and intensely compassionate, so that the whole tale is bathed in an emotive atmosphere unique in Mérimée's work. Certainly the light, ironic style and the swift narration hold feeling in check; but its presence is no less clearly felt for being veiled. At the end, it even comes to the surface in an uncommonly obvious form, when Arsène on her deathbed suddenly and unconvincingly cries: 'I have loved!' As one of Mérimée's critics has observed, if she were to say anything at all in those circumstances, it would have been: 'I have loved Max!' The greater psychological interest derives from Mme de Piennes, whose waverings between Christian charity and her inclination for Max are most adroitly analysed. Despite Mérimée's constant preoccupation with the notion of dupery and hypocrisy, he has not been content to portray Mme de Piennes as a two-faced deceiver. Instead, he has sought to understand how something which begins (however conventionally) as a charitable impulse gradually yields to the pressure of an emotion so unexpected that the person experiencing it cannot at first recognise it for what it is. (pp. 180-81)

When to these qualities of emotion and penetration is added a remarkable narrative dexterity, it is clear that **"Arsène Guillot"** deserves a high place in Mérimée's work. The last paragraphs are perhaps one of the most extraordinary foreshortenings of perspective in nineteenth-century fiction. Arsène has died, with Max and Mme de Piennes at her side. Mérimée turns to his imaginary female interlocutor to beg her not to jump to rash conclusions.

> Above all, never doubt the truth of my story. You do have doubts? Go to Père Lachaise cemetery; twenty paces to the left of General Foy's grave, you will find a very simple limestone tomb, always surrounded with fresh flowers. On the stone, you can read my heroine's name engraved in large letters: ARSÈNE GUILLOT, and, if you lean over the grave, you will see, unless the rain has already washed it off, a line delicately written in pencil: Poor Arsène! She is praying for us.

With all this to recommend it, one can only echo André Gide's praise: 'I never knew there was anything like that in Mérimée. Why is it not better known? [. . .] Yes, it is better than anything I thought Mérimée was capable of writing. Truly excellent.'

Two years later, Mérimée returned to an analogous theme with **"L'Abbé Aubain,"** in which, using the epistolary form, he tells how an ambitious young priest tricks a pious lady into obtaining his preferment for a better parish by pretending to be falling in love with her. It is a slight and anodyne work, which Mérimée claims is based on fact. . . . But whether or not the idea came to him from real life, it patently did not inspire him to anything more than the perfunctory relating of an amusing anecdote. Though there is a genially ironic twist to the end, the worldly priest and the lady deliciously thrilled by the prospective scandal of a clerical love affair are no more than inoffensively lightweight caricatures. If **"L'Abbé Aubain"** appeared anonymously, it is perhaps less because Mérimée feared another uproar than because he was aware that no other story of his was quite so unsatisfyingly insubstantial.

These then are the stories in which Mérimée's chief concern is the human situation in civilised society. On the other side stands the group of stories in which he investigates the sombre and irrational fatality of passion. The first of these tales, **"La Vénus d'Ille,"** published in 1837, was Mérimée's own favourite among his works—twenty years later, he declared: 'In my opinion, it's my masterpiece.' The outward form of this story of a statue of Venus which murders a bridegroom on his wedding-night because he has imprudently put his ring on its finger comes from Mérimée's activities as Inspector-General of Historic Monuments; indeed the first-person narrator is a mildly satirical self-portrait in which all the stress is on his erudition, his pedantry and his detachment from mundane considerations. (pp. 181-82)

In reality, **"La Vénus d'Ille"** is something far more interesting than an ingenious and technically impeccable ghost-story (though it is perhaps one of the most successful ever written). Mérimée's aim is neither merely to entertain us by making our flesh creep, nor yet to convince us—as Balzac and Nodier seek to do in their fantastic tales—of the existence of supernatural agencies, in which he firmly declined to believe. What he sets out to do is to revivify myth because, in his view, that is the only form in which certain truths can be made accessible to the human mind [see excerpt dated 1960]. Shortly after writing **"La Vénus d'Ille,"** he became passionately interested in the study of ancient mythology, and this is how he summarises one of the most significant conclusions which he reached:

> the general tendency of ancient mythologies is to leave first causes in what is perhaps a deliberate obscurity, while concentrating on some of their effects. Incapable of elucidating mysteries above human understanding, these myths distract our thought as far as possible from the crux of the difficulty.

"La Vénus d'Ille," with its obvious allusions to Greek and Roman mythology, proceeds in exactly that way.

It is after all no accident that the statue involved is that of Venus, the goddess of love, and, more particularly, according to the inscription on her arm, *Venus turbulenta*, love in its strongest, most violent, most disruptive form. The dual nature of the statue, both attractive and frightening, symbolises the dual aspect of passion as Mérimée saw it, at once irresistibly fascinating and horribly dangerous. He stresses these two characteristics whenever he describes the statue's features. 'Disdain, irony and cruelty could be read on that face which was nevertheless incredibly beautiful.' 'That expression of infernal irony', 'her expression of ironic spite', 'mischief almost shading into spitefulness'—these are some of the terms he uses to characterise the ambivalence of its charm. At the end, the unfortunate Alphonse de Peyrehorade dies because, in the thoughtless gesture of putting his ring on the statue's finger, he has unwittingly committed himself to this sinister power, and the symbolic overtones are evident in Mérimée's comment on the statue as it stands impassively in the garden on the morning after the crime: 'I felt as though I were looking at some infernal divinity gloating over the misfortune which had descended on the household.' At the centre of the tale is a conception of passion as a force at least as destructive as it is seductive—a conception never before propounded by Mérimée so forcefully as here.

But it is noteworthy, too, that the cruel goddess who represents this force comes from underground and from a far distant period of time. The milieu into which she is brought with such disastrous consequences is that of the provincial middle classes of early nineteenth-century France, and they are quite incapable of appreciating the real significance of the divinity of passion. M. de Peyrehorade regards the statue simply as an archaeological find, a valuable piece of sculpture, and jovially trots out all the well-worn quotations about being 'wounded by Venus' without ever pausing to think of their true meaning. As for his son Alphonse, Mérimée deliberately makes him into a rather wooden young man, interested in his bride only because she has a large dowry and otherwise mainly concerned with his own prowess at *pelota*. Love and marriage for him are no more than convenient domestic arrangements; in his scale of values, amorous feeling comes a very poor second to the Hippolytus-like pursuit of sport. Both father and son live by a superficial and conventional set of values, which prevents them from seeing the more alarming forces to which humanity will always be subject. Just as the statue of Venus has by the passage of time become hidden by the accumulation of earth above it, so the primitive urges of the basic emotions have become overlaid by the trivial pretences of modern civilisation. When the statue is brought to light, it repels as much as it fascinates, and calamity ensues; so we are powerless victims once passion has broken down the shams and protections with which we seek to nullify its existence.

One of the reasons why **"La Vénus d'Ille"** makes such a powerful impact on the reader is that these symbolic intentions are only dimly hinted at in the narration, which moves forward with the implacable urgency characteristic of Mérimée. One is above all conscious of an overpowering sense of material reality, so convincingly conveyed that there is no option but to believe in the intrusion of the supernatural when it occurs—and with it all the vaguely adumbrated mythical implications. . . . Stendhal felt that . . . the whole story is tainted with aridity, but Mérimée was prepared to risk boring some readers in order to establish the impeccable academic qualifications of his narrator, a man so immersed in archaeology that he could never be suspected of romancing.

Into this realistically painted setting, there gradually spreads a sinister and uncanny mood, as strange, disturbing, but credible details mount up: the workman's broken leg, the broodingly ambiguous expression of the statue, the enigmatic inscriptions on it, the stone which rebounds from it to hit the thrower, the marriage on the ill-omened day of Venus, Peyrehorade's hollow jocularity about the power of Venus, finally Alphonse's account of how he had been unable to pull his ring off the statue's finger. As for the killing itself, that is only narrated at second-hand, and we may have doubts about the sanity of the distracted bride. Indeed, the possibility of a natural explanation is not wholly excluded, since suspicion momentarily falls on a *pelota* player who had earlier been insulted by Alphonse. But in the end, while this intentional vagueness makes the tale more effective than a direct affirmation would be, we are likely to conclude that the statue is responsible, since Mérimée's ingenious arrangement of the circumstances makes that seem by far the most plausible explanation. The inevitability of the progression means that there is no head-on clash between incredulity and the incredible. Mérimée is indeed so far from abjuring his usual scepticism that, when a small boy naïvely asked him whether the statue had really killed Alphonse, he replied evasively: 'Goodness, child, I've no idea'—to which the boy, with sound common sense, objected: 'What, sir! You tell stories, and you don't even know them!'

The theme of the conflict between passion and civilised values which gives **"La Vénus d'Ille"** its richness and its resonance is taken up again in *Colomba* (1840), the product of Mérimée's stay in Corsica in 1839. (pp. 183-87)

The story has a readily apparent and symmetrical structure. Orso della Rebbia, after years of service as an officer in the French army, returns to his native Corsica to find himself torn between two women. On the one hand is his sister Colomba, who fanatically exhorts him to avenge his father's murder by pursuing a vendetta against the Barricini family whom she suspects of the crime; on the other hand is Lydia Nevil, the respectable young Englishwoman with whom he has fallen in love and who would immediately disown him if he were to do anything so barbaric. Of the two, Colomba is infinitely the more impressive creation, with, significantly, something of the same ambivalent power of attraction as the statue of Venus. When she thinks she has persuaded Orso to kill the Barricinis, her eyes sparkle with 'a malign joy', and as she sets out with him, Miss Lydia anxiously notices her 'sardonic smile': 'it was as if she could see his evil genius dragging him away to destruction'. Orso himself is all too conscious of the sinister side of his sister's lust for vengeance, and when she begs him to kill the Barricinis, 'he felt as though he were listening to some fatal, inevitable oracle demanding blood from him—innocent blood'. He even sees in her something diabolical, echoing so many other Mérimée characters in whom women inspire the terror of the devil: 'my sweet Colomba, I fear you are the devil himself'. But the demure and correct Lydia acts as a counterpoise, and Orso finds himself unable to choose between the primitive violence which Colomba urges on him and the unadventurous conformity with civilised standards which Lydia would have him observe.

By far the greater part of the story (Mérimée's longest, apart from the *Chronique*) is concerned with Orso's hesitation between the forms of behaviour represented by the two women. Born a Corsican, he might by nature be inclined to follow the fierce practice of the vendetta; but years of contact with the life of metropolitan France have given him another and more sophisticated set of standards which he is powerless to ignore. Even Lydia is aware of the uncomfortable duality of his situation, and, comparing him with the hero of Byron's *Corsair,* she says: 'He was something between a Conrad and a dandy. . . . I've turned him into a complete dandy, and a dandy with a Corsican tailor!' Orso's long indecisiveness, which is the real theme of the story, reflects Mérimée's inability to opt finally between the crude but genuine primitivism for which Colomba and Corsica stand, and the polite, superficial uniformity of that European civilisation exemplified by the prim and proper Lydia. *Colomba* is essentially the story of a dilemma, and in the end the dilemma remains unsolved. For Mérimée so arranges matters that the choice is eventually taken out of Orso's hands. Before he has made a decision, he is caught in an ambush in which the Barricinis fire on him, and when, despite a broken arm,

he kills them both with his return shots, he is simply saving his own life. As far as the real theme of the story is concerned, this is no more than an evasion of the issue. By a piece of dubious sleight-of-hand, Mérimée avoids having to conclude on the moral problem which has formed the whole basis of his tale.

Critics have often commented on the way in which *Colomba* fails to fulfil the expectations it arouses in us, without perhaps seeing quite what lies behind the sense of disappointment it leaves. Pierre Jourda for instance notes: 'he promised us a vendetta and tells us about an act of self-defence'. Guy Michaut goes even further and suggests that Mérimée has, out of habit, hoaxed both the public and himself: 'the powerful, poetic drama has turned into a picturesque anecdote'. The aesthetic effect of *Colomba* is notably weakened by this trick and its quality as a human document lessened. Mérimée has lacked the courage to face the tragic implications of the situation he has devised and wriggles out of it in what can only be described as a dishonest way. Orso never has to make up his mind and so can marry Lydia while keeping his sister's affection. The happy ending is contrived and as a result unsatisfying. But this is because Mérimée himself remains so uncertain over the basic issue underlying the whole story: primitivism or civilisation, passion or politeness—he refuses either to choose between them or to admit the impossibility of keeping both.

There are other reasons, too, why *Colomba* remains a relatively low-keyed work. One is that it is too visibly planned to show off representative antitheses, as was also the case with the *Chronique.* Every element in it is there for a fairly obvious reason of balance or symbolism. But where this method was reasonably effective in a work as diffuse and complex as the *Chronique,* the more tightly knit plot of *Colomba* reveals all too clearly the author manipulating his puppets for effect. It consequently never quite comes to life as an organic whole in the way that **"La Vénus d'Ille"** and *Carmen* do. Another flaw is Mérimée's slightly shamefaced but nevertheless very manifest predilection for local colour. Whole episodes, scenes and characters are included because they are so typically and picturesquely Corsican. . . . (pp. 188-91)

If *Colomba* ultimately fails because Mérimée is unwilling to come to terms with the consequences of his own thoughts and feelings, *Carmen* succeeds magnificently because there, more than anywhere else, he takes his conception of passion to its logical—and intensely tragic—conclusion. (p. 191)

The 1845 text of *Carmen* is simple in its outlines (it was only in 1847 that a major revision brought in an entirely new section at the end). It begins with a leisurely account, in the first person, of the acquaintanceship the narrator strikes up with the bandit Don José whom he meets during his archaeological researches in Spain, and of his subsequent encounter with Carmen herself. This leads into the main body of the tale, which is Don José's account, given to the narrator while awaiting execution for Carmen's murder, of how he had first set eyes on her, how he had deserted from the army and taken to banditry for love of her, how he twice killed men out of jealousy, and how he had finally murdered Carmen herself when he had realised that she could never be his alone. The function of the preamble, with its detached and pedantic narrator occupied only with ancient history, is similar to that of **"La Vénus d'Ille"**: to establish an atmosphere of normality in which the extraordinary figure of Don José will gradually but naturally take a grip on our imagination. Don José's narration will thus be authenticated by the credentials of Mérimée himself, who at the same time absolves himself from responsibility for Don José's criminal aberrations. There is a good deal of irony in this part, most of it directed inwards against himself, even to the extent of hinting in advance that it is all very trivial compared with the serious business of locating Munda:

> until my dissertation at last solves the problem which is keeping all the learned men of Europe on tenterhooks, I am going to tell you a little story: it in no way prejudges the interesting question of the site of Munda.

But once the narrator hands over to Don José, the irony vanishes. Mérimée has, as usual, protected himself by implying an ironic view of the whole proceedings; the irony is, however, confined to the preface and so enhances rather than detracts from the desperate sincerity of Don José's confession.

That confession itself, so rough-hewn, so terrifying, so monolithic that Charles du Bos has called it 'a literary menhir', is the real centre of the tale. Undoubtedly, its bleak tragic power comes from the masterly description of Don José's jealous passion and from the taunting figure of Carmen herself. It is the only place in his works where Mérimée dares to give a full-scale depiction, from the inside, of the ravages of passion, and as one might expect, Carmen, the object of this irresistible and all-consuming force, has much in common with the statue of Venus. As a gypsy, she too stands outside the confines of normal contemporary society and cannot be peacefully integrated into it. Almost her last words are: 'Carmen will always be free.' She too has associations with the supernatural, since she is a fortune-teller. Her hold over Don José is as absolute and as disastrous as that of Venus over Alphonse de Peyrehorade. Her beauty is as fierce and cruel as that of the statue:

> It was a strange and wild beauty, a face which at first called forth astonishment but which it was impossible to forget. Above all, her eyes had an expression both voluptuous and savage which I have never seen since in any other human gaze.

About her, as about the statue, there is something infernal, stated with such terse, casual simplicity that it almost passes unnoticed—' "You are the devil," I said to her. "Yes," she replied.' And like Colomba, she represents the lure of a dangerously free and lawless existence, which may liberate one from the shackles of society but also hurl one headlong to destruction. Clearly, the concept of passion she embodies is the same as that in **"La Vénus d'Ille"** and in *Colomba,* but because here it appears in a more humanly comprehensible form than in the one and is not subjected to the same devious evasiveness as in the other, it is more effective than in either.

A large part of this effectiveness comes from the fact that Don José speaks to us directly in his own words. There are no deflating comments, no anticlimactic asides, no flippant badinage. Don José believes passionately in the love he has experienced and recounts events with all the urgen-

cy and impact one might expect from a man under sentence of death. The habitual straightforwardness and energy of Mérimée's style are heightened here by the vivid speech of the soldier and bandit, in which colourful metaphors abound. . . . But despite the forceful images, Don José's normal speech is remarkably precise, exact statement of the barest, most immediate kind. Perhaps the most outstanding example of this, haunting in its simple affirmation of the cause of the tragedy, is what he reports Carmen as saying to him just before the murder: 'I don't love you any more, but you still love me, and that's why you want to kill me.'

Another result of allowing Don José to narrate is to make us go through all his hardships and torments with him. We too submit to the seductiveness of Carmen because we see her through his eyes—it is the same technique as Prévost uses to compel the readers of *Manon Lescaut* to acquiesce in Des Grieux's guilty passion for Manon. Indeed, the analogies between the works have not escaped the critics, and Sainte-Beuve described *Carmen* as 'a spicier *Manon Lescaut,* served in the Spanish style'. But *Carmen* is superior to the earlier novel by its more incisive writing, its more concentrated plot and its more evocative descriptions. In each case, the outcome is inevitably tragic, for neither Manon nor Carmen can accept the constraints which their lovers would impose on them; they fascinate, because they are unpredictable, and conformity would rob them of the very quality which makes them so attractive. 'Carmen will always be free'; sensual, animal, unspoilt, untamed, she cannot bow to the laws José insists on, so from the moment when José first falls in love with her (characteristically just after she has tried to commit murder), their fate is sealed. The sense of fatality and the constant presence of danger characterise his passion for her, and it makes its full impact on us because we live through it with him.

The Spanish atmosphere moreover sets it off to perfection. Whereas *Colomba* was written as a deliberate showpiece for Corsican local colour, the Spanish setting is made into a part of the very fabric of *Carmen.* The basic theme is universal in its dramatic simplicity, but Spanish in its full though unobtrusive localisation. The choice of detail here is particularly cunning; one may single out that gesture which so pleased Charles du Bos with its authenticity, when Carmen has failed to persuade Don José to kill and rob the narrator: 'then the gypsy cast a glance of profound scorn at him, and sitting down cross-legged in a corner of the room, she selected an orange, peeled it and began to eat it.' All these things are done with such rapid and economical dexterity that one scarcely realises all their implications and overtones. (pp. 192-95)

One could almost wish that that were the end of the story of Mérimée's middle-period tales. But in 1846 he not only wrote **"L'Abbé Aubain,"** one of his slightest works, he also produced **"Il Viccolo di Madama Lucrezia,"** which displays a high degree of narrative skill but is otherwise almost entirely empty. This tale of what appears to be a ghostly incident in Rome begins like another evocation of the dangers of passion, but in the end it mystifies us to no good purpose, since Mérimée supplies a natural explanation for all its mysterious events. It is a bare-faced hoax on the reader, written apparently for no other reason than the unworthy pleasure of hoodwinking us. The ambiguity always present in Mérimée's attitude to imaginative literature seems now to have sapped his will to create seriously. Since all fiction involves deception, why not remove everything from it except deception? A few months later, he confirmed this view by adding an extra section to *Carmen,* which consists exclusively of a brief essay on the language of the gypsies, in which he had been taking a highly professional interest. The last words of the story after this 1847 revision are these:

> That is quite enough to give the readers of *Carmen* a flattering idea of my studies of the Romany tongue. I shall end appropriately with a proverb: *En retudi panda nasti abela macha.* If you keep your mouth shut, the flies won't get in.

Few readers can have felt this as anything other than a deliberate and provocative anticlimax. (pp. 196-97)

The canker of doubt about the value of imaginative creations which had scarred Mérimée's works from the earliest times has now grown to such proportions that it completely inhibits their life. The hints of aloofness, of disbelief, of irony detectable in the incongruous endings of the *Clara Gazul* plays, in the atmosphere of imposture surrounding *La Guzla,* in the off-hand conclusion of the *Chronique* or in various asides in the short stories, now coalesce in what comes close to a repudiation of any work of the imagination. Scepticism was always an essential ingredient in Mérimée's art; finally it destroys it. After 1847, Mérimée takes his own advice and fends off the flies of doubt by keeping his lips tightly closed. Having indicated by his wilfully perverse revision of *Carmen* that he scorns his own literature, he abandons it completely for twenty years, turning instead to history, which had been attracting him increasingly and which struck him as proof against the sort of corrosion which had eaten away his never very strong confidence in the validity of fiction. (p. 197)

In the last four years of his life, Mérimée produced three stories: **"La Chambre bleue"** (**"The Blue Room"**) in September 1866, **"Lokis"** in the latter part of 1868, and **"Djoûmane"** early in 1870. . . . None of these late tales was intended for publication, and it was only at the insistence of Buloz that **"Lokis"** appeared in the *Revue des Deux Mondes* on 15 September 1869. **"La Chambre bleue"** and **"Djoûmane"** were published only after Mérimée's death. This hesitancy does not mean that Mérimée was in doubt about their quality—he took great pains over **"Lokis"** and had a surprisingly high opinion of the mediocre **"Chambre bleue."** But he was mildly bemused by his sudden recrudescence of interest in story-telling, apprehensive about the effect on public opinion of scabrous subjects treated by a senator, and generally disinclined to advertise works conceived as entertainments for his friends. In fact, these last stories, despite the twenty-year gap, retain the narrative skill of the earlier tales but their themes break new ground.

The first of them, **"La Chambre bleue,"** is the least impressive. With a series of knowing sniggers, Mérimée tells the banal story of a couple who go to a country hotel for an illicit weekend, find their bliss interrupted by sinister nocturnal noises in the next-door room occupied by an English lord, see with horror what appears to be blood seeping underneath the door—only to discover the following morning that the bibulous lord had upset his bottle of

port. It is a strangely pointless story, creating tension only to dissipate it with the announcement that it was all a misunderstanding. What Mérimée told his friends about the genesis of **"La Chambre bleue"** helps to explain the impression of gratuitousness which it leaves. According to the account he gave later to Jenny Dacquin, while he had been staying with the Empress at Biarritz in the summer of 1866, the guests had amused themselves by discussing how to behave in difficult situations, such as that of Rodrigue torn between his father and Chimène in Corneille's *Le Cid.* 'That night, having drunk too much strong tea, I wrote about fifteen pages on a situation of that kind.' For Turgenev's benefit, he went into more detail.

> I had intended my subject to be very tragic, and I had written the preliminaries to it in a facetious style so as to surprise the reader even more. As the thing was dragging on and boring me, I rounded it off with a joke, which is bad.

He also boasted of its immorality. The manuscript which he subsequently presented to Eugénie, is signed: 'Composed and written by Pr. MERIMÉE, jester to Her Majesty the Empress'.

But if Mérimée wanted to involve the reader in the moral dilemma of two lovers afraid to report an apparent murder lest their relationship be made public, he has sadly miscalculated. The problematic aspect of their situation is only touched on. What seems to have interested him most is the evocation of the emotions of the guilty couple as they arrive at the hotel, as they find their solitude disturbed by an officers' dinner, as they gradually come to suspect that some dreadful crime is being committed in the adjoining room. All this is done skilfully, with a light touch, but even more than **"Il Viccolo di Madama Lucrezia,"** it builds up its effects for no other purpose than the meretricious pleasure of a deliberately bathetic anticlimax. It is no more than an irritatingly childish hoax; perhaps it is significant that the two stories which stand on either side of the twenty-year period during which Mérimée devoted himself to history should demean fiction to the lowest level of deception. If Mérimée had given the tale the tragic ending he originally planned, maybe the lovers' dilemma would have been more dramatic and more gripping. Maybe too the latent association of eroticism with scenes of bloodshed and death which marks the other late stories would have been more forcibly expressed and would have given it something of that sinister, enigmatic and slightly repellent fascination which characterises **"Lokis"** and **"Djoûmane."** But one can only marvel at the self-delusion which led Mérimée to remark with satisfaction to Jenny Dacquin: 'it is not, I think, the worst thing I've produced, even if it was written in a great hurry'.

"Lokis" is very different. Relatively long, carefully planned, scrupulously documented, it is a work to which Mérimée from the outset attached some importance. Like **"La Chambre bleue,"** it was written for the Empress, and, if we are to believe the author, was meant to outdo in sensationalism the extravagant fantastic novels which in 1868 formed the staple diet of the Court at Fontainebleau. But it turned out more seriously: 'the trouble is that I immediately started to find it attractive, and instead of drawing a caricature, I tried to do a portrait'. First roughed out in August 1868, it was not finished until the following summer, and when Buloz pressed Mérimée to allow the *Revue* *des Deux Mondes* to print it, his resistance soon wilted. The story of the Lithuanian count whose mother was violated by a bear, and who had consequently always had bearish traits in his nature, which culminate in the murder of his bride on their wedding-night, is not original. Like the legend on which **"La Vénus d'Ille"** is based, it is an ancient story, retold, revivified and localised by Mérimée, which had often crossed his mind. The subject was clearly mapped out in 1867 when he had written to the young and pretty Lise Przezdziecka:

> you talk to me about hunting with such enthusiasm that I imagine you would rather like to find yourself face to face with a wolf, or even a bear. The first of these dreadful animals is all right, but I absolutely forbid you to have anything to do with bears; they are much too ill-bred to show respect to huntresses.
>
> (pp. 328-30)

The theme of the story is bizarre and disturbing. In his first draft, Mérimée had made it clear that Countess Szémioth was raped by the bear when it dragged her off into a thicket. But when he read **"Lokis"** to Jenny Dacquin, she objected to this scandalous postulate, and in deference to her wishes, he made the incident more vague, so that, as he remarked to Mme Delessert, 'timorous people who would refuse to believe in cross-breeding between *plantigrades* will be at liberty to assume that the hero's eccentricities derive from a pregnant woman's fright or fancy'. This decent obscurity does not alter the zoological prodigy on which the story rests: Michel Szémioth *is* the son of the bear. Various small touches hint at this relationship in the early part of the tale—his propensity for tree-climbing, the terror he inspires in domestic animals, the mysterious remarks of the witch-like old woman he meets in the forest, his crushing embrace of the girl he eventually marries, his sudden accesses of savage violence, his mother's madness. But the climax is reached when, after the wedding-night, the corpse of his bride Ioulka is found with teeth-marks in her throat. For Mérimée, there was in this gruesome theme something more than the arbitrary evocation of horror. To Turgenev, he made an uncharacteristic admission: 'if I were any good at writing verse, I would have made a poem out of it; I find something poetic in this mixture of humanity and bestiality'. In the story itself, this aspect of the action is made explicit when, in a conversation with the narrator and a doctor, the count asks for an explanation of 'the *duality* or the *duplicity* of our nature'. How does it come about, he wonders, that our passions can make us commit acts which our reason abhors? The implied answer is that, in all of us, there is a latent animal nature which is normally held in check by reason and morality, but which is liable to escape if reason momentarily loses its vigilance. (pp. 331-32)

So the idea of Szémioth having been fathered by a bear is ultimately used as a means of heightening dramatically the theme that there is a beast in all of us. Clearly, this is related to the treatment of the destructive force of passion to be found so often in Mérimée's work. In particular, "Lokis" resembles **"La Vénus d'Ille."** In both stories a pedantic narrator arrives in an out-of-the-way spot, witnesses a variety of more or less disquieting incidents, is present at a wedding, and the morning after discovers that one of the spouses has been the victim of a brutal and mysterious slaughter. This pattern emphasises the extent to which both works are concerned with the dangers of unleashed

erotic passion. But whereas **"La Vénus d'Ille"** treats this theme on the level of mythology, **"Lokis"** transfers it to that of pathology. The murder in the first story is the work of a statue symbolising Venus; in the second, it springs from the instinctive lusts of a young man. Whatever the implausible explanation for these lusts proffered by Mérimée, they are something which well up inside a human being, and which, it is suggested, any of us may feel. Sex, the most primitive of urges, releases the bestiality underlying even the most civilised of natures (Szémioth is presented as an affable, cultured and distinguished man in ordinary circumstances), and the woman, like Mlle de Puygarrig in **"La Vénus d'Ille,"** has a white-skinned, childlike innocence that marks her out as a predestined victim. The sexual implications are underlined both by the account of Szémioth's mother's experience with the bear, and by the overtly phallic imagery of the encounter with the old woman and her snake.

Nowhere has Mérimée penetrated further into the dark recesses of the human mind than in **"Lokis."** One is forced to envisage unpleasant possibilities about one's own constitution, which are all the more disquieting for being only half-spoken. If in the end **"Lokis"** remains distinctly inferior to **"La Vénus d'Ille,"** that is partly because it comes too close to repeating the effects of the earlier story, and partly because it is difficult to overlook the physical impossibility on which it depends. We are required to believe, not in the supernatural, but in a misstatement of the laws of physiology. Perhaps there are some obsessional undertones in this choice of a subject involving a sexual prodigy—Ioulka resembles Lise Przezdziecka, with whom Mérimée was conducting a platonic flirtation, and there must have been something frustrating in such a situation for a man of his once voracious sexual appetites. He has not succeeded in giving **"Lokis"** the same are of general human truth as **"La Vénus d'Ille."** The impression it gives is ultimately one of eccentricity, of abnormality; in the literal sense, it is a monstrous tale.

"Djoûmane" was the last story Mérimée wrote, begun in January 1870 and finished in March of the same year. It is supposedly related by a French officer fighting against the Arabs in Algeria. Exhausted by a long ride, he and his troops are obliged to set out again without sleep, but they first witness a performance by a snake-charmer, in which a little girl is bitten but recovers as if by miracle. The officer is then involved in a skirmish at a ford, becomes separated from his men, sees an extraordinary scene in which a magician apparently drowns a girl in a well with some sort of serpent swimming in its waters, wanders through passages cut in a rocky hillside, is welcomed into a luxurious chamber by a raven-haired beauty . . . and then awakes to realise that he had been dreaming while riding out in accordance with his orders. At first sight, one might be tempted to consider the final revelation as yet another instance of Mérimée's taste for anticlimactic deceptions, in the manner of **"La Chambre bleue."** But it does not cancel out the strangely fascinating quality of the dream sequences, so that one is forced to seek some profounder meaning in it.

Raoul Roche has provided a Freudian reading of the tale, regarding it as a reproduction of one of Mérimée's own dreams, and seeing in it the disguised expression of a passing desire for a young Jewish girl, figured by a recurrent

Portrait of Jenny Dacquin, the "unknown" with whom Mérimée corresponded for nearly four decades. Through this correspondence, Mérimée revealed passionate and tender emotions that he concealed in his public life and writings.

association of a snake with the girl's death and intensified by the oppression caused by his asthma. This reading is marred by the critic's failure to realise at what point in the story the dream begins; it is only when the officer, after the snake-charming incident, rides out with his troop towards the ford that his fatigue causes him to fall asleep on horseback. The dream thus opens with the arrival at the ford and the fight with the Arab leader: the rest is presented as part of the officer's waking experience. But that does not altogether disqualify M. Roche's theory, since Mérimée's sexual obsessions might just as much be translated by the images of what he states to be reality as by those which he specifically attributes to a dream—the more so as the two parts of the tale are thematically very closely related. In support of his opinion, one might add that not only is the '-mane' of **"Djoûmane"** the phonetic equivalent of the termination '-mann' common in Jewish surnames, but that the first syllable 'Djoû' is almost a transcription of the English word 'Jew'. Moreover, Mérimée must often have fallen asleep while looking at his father's picture *Innocence feeding a serpent,* which hung in his bedroom. The inconsequential flow of images, the almost surrealistic illogicality of the action, the obvious sexuality of certain scenes, Mérimée's own casual remark to Jenny Dacquin

that in **"Djoûmane"** 'there is a lot about love', which is not an immediately noticeable feature, all legitimise a psychoanalytic approach to the story.

Not that one need follow M. Roche in diagnosing its origins in a guilty fancy for a little Jewish girl. In the latter years of his life, Mérimée sought the company of attractive young women with whom he bantered about love—Olga de Lagrené, Lise Przezdziecka, the Duchesse de Castiglione-Colonna. Superficially, these amorous friendships were innocent; beneath the surface, they undoubtedly offered the ageing Mérimée a somewhat shame-faced compensation for his vanished sexual powers. The idea of real sexual contact with one of these girls would have been unthinkable, given his age, his ill-health and his loss of potency. But it must always have been there as a culpable temptation, and this seems to be one of the reasons for the hints that the girl in **"Djoûmane"** is Jewish. Like many Frenchmen of his class and generation, Mérimée had been vaguely and as it were automatically anti-semitic—in 1849, for instance, he had recommended a bookseller to Sobolevski with the words: 'he's a Jew, but he has a good stock', and in 1854, he joked that Jews repelled him 'as much for their conduct under the government of Pontius Pilate as for their love of money'. Yet he appreciated the charms of Jewish prostitutes, and in 1830 had happily announced to Sutton Sharpe that the cargoes of newly arrived whores included some 'splendid Jewesses with fine large black eyes, and delicate feet'. In this way, Mérimée associated illicit sexual pleasure with a taboo on Jewishness, and no doubt this comes out in the Semitic references in **"Djoûmane,"** rather than any specific attraction to a young Jewess.

The preoccupations of **"Djoûmane"** are highly personal, which is possibly why Mérimée kept it for himself and a few intimate friends. It has much less relevance to the human situation in general than **"Lokis,"** and in any case contains much less narrative substance. The gratuitousness of the sequence of events militates against dramatic tension, and there is not much inducement for the reader to delve below its surface. It is only if one takes the trouble to decode the perhaps inadvertent symbolism with which it is strewn that it appears as a work of any cogency or inner necessity. Even then, its interest scarcely extends beyond that of being a curious and slightly sinister document on the subterranean workings of Mérimée's emotions.

Though this isolated outcrop of stories at the end of Mérimée's life includes no masterpieces, it does represent an interesting new departure in his art. The style and the narrative techniques are still those he had used twenty years earlier. But they serve different purposes. More clearly than he had ever done before, Mérimée tries to penetrate the mysteries of the subconscious. That the result is wholly satisfactory in literary terms may be doubted, even though these stories are nowadays more highly rated by critics than they used to be. They are too strange, too disconnected, too individual to be accessible even to a sympathetic public. Nevertheless, without them, something would be missing in our image of Mérimée: a direct glimpse into the steamy, tangled undergrowth of his mind. He was taken aback by this sudden return of an imaginative inspiration he believed to be long dead, and attempted to dismiss it as a manifestation of senility.

> When you are young, you can call on women of
> easy virtue in broad daylight; a venerable old man

like myself, if he still thought about such women, would only visit them in secret. I'm reaching the stage of second childhood, and I may be weak enough to go on writing stories, but I have sense enough to show them only to my friends.

He only agreed to the publication of **"Lokis"** when readings of it at Court had convinced him that most people would misunderstand it, and chance alone assured the survival of the other tales. This sense of shame betokens a fear that he is exposing himself without defence. That he did so is both their strength and weakness. They initiate us into the most secret parts of his personality, and the protective structures so prominent in his earlier fiction have largely collapsed. But the constraint and reticence, always essential to his art, have also been damaged, and the result, if more revealing, is also less telling. (pp. 332-37)

> *A. W. Raitt, in his* Prosper Mérimée, *Eyre & Spottiswoode, 1970, 453 p.*

Kathryn J. Crecelius   (essay date 1982)

[*In the following excerpt, Crecelius compares Mérimée's short piece "Federigo" to various extant versions of a folktale commonly known as "The Smith Outwits the Devil," illustrating how Mérimée's innovations in character, plot sequence, and setting "transformed a folktale into a short story."*]

While it is true that **"Federigo"** does belong to the tradition of which the story of "Bonhomme Misère" is a part, Mérimée did more than gather and translate popular legends. He was being too modest when he denied himself credit for a charming tale, and the critics too gullible in believing the disclaimer of a notorious *mystificateur*.

"Bonhomme Misère" is a variant of a folktale type identified by Aarne and Thompson as number 330, known generally as "The Smith Outwits the Devil," and occasionally as "The Gambler and the Devil," particularly in Germanic countries. A close relative is "The Devil in a Knapsack (Bottle, Cask)." This tale is attested all over Europe and seems to have origins in classical Antiquity; it is related to the Sisyphus myth. Each variant of the tale has innumerable versions, depending on the region of origin, local customs and appropriate local color. Mérimée's version combines "le merveilleux chrétien" with references to Pluto, Cerberus and the Underworld. Although he insists that his tale is Neapolitan in origin, the reason he chose this city is unknown as is the manner in which he came in contact with the original. . . . The researcher is limited to those versions of the tale that have been collected and analyzed by folklorists, but the existence of other, lost versions that might have been Mérimée's starting-point cannot be excluded. There is, however, sufficient internal evidence to show that whatever his source, Mérimée transformed a folktale into a short story.

The basic elements of tale 330 are quite simple. A smith (or farmer, carpenter, etc.) receives three wishes as a reward for having lodged Jesus, accompanied by his twelve disciples, or in some cases just Peter or Peter and Paul. He asks for a pear tree (or fig tree, apple tree, etc.) that holds fast anyone daring to take a fruit; a seat or bench, sometimes near the hearth, from which no one can get up without the smith's permission; and a deck of cards with which

he will always win. By means of the first two gifts, the smith extorts longer life from Death, who has come to call him; in some versions, no one else dies while Death is stuck to the tree or the bench. When the smith's time is up, he is refused entry to heaven, for he has not earned a place there, and he neglected to ask Jesus for salvation as one of his gifts. Upon his arrival in hell, the smith plays cards with the devil, and for each game won obtains a soul. After winning varying numbers of souls (his own, twelve, two hundred, a whole regiment), he returns to heaven where he and his companions are admitted.

This schematic plot description of the traditional tale reveals two noticeable differences between **"Federigo"** and the standard version. First, Federigo is neither a smith nor an artisan of any sort. . . . Like the Spielhansl of the German tale, he loves to gamble (certain variants of the tale present protagonists who are gamblers at the beginning), and he is extremely fond of wine and women. Second, Mérimée briefly sketches Federigo's past, for unlike the standard tale, **"Federigo"** does not begin with Jesus' visit. After ruining twelve young men who later became outlaws and died without confession in a fight with the *condottieri*, he too, was ruined and lost all his fortune except for a small property near Cava, to which he has retired. Three years after these events, Jesus and his twelve apostles seek lodging in his home. Federigo receives them graciously and as well as his reduced circumstances permit. For his hospitality, he is given three wishes. Despite Peter's urging, he does not ask for salvation, but rather requests that his deck of cards always win, that whoever climbs his orange tree might not descend without his permission, and that whoever sits on the stool next to the fire might not rise without his leave. This is all granted.

There is a third and crucial difference between the standard form of the tale and **"Federigo."** Aarne and Thompson divide the story into four parts [in "The Types of Folklore," *Folklore Fellows Communications*, 184 (1961):121-23]. The first, Contract with the Devil, is found neither in **"Federigo"** nor in most of its closest relatives, although it originally was an important element, since it provided the reason for the smith's desire to play cards with the Devil to free himself from his contract. The second sequence, Receipt of Magic Objects, pertains to Jesus' visit. The third part is the Deception of Death, who must grant longer life to the hero, and the fourth is Expulsion from Hell and Heaven, during which phase the cards are used. The folktales gathered all over Europe by folklorists scrupulously observe this order. Mérimée, however, has changed the order of the plot elements and has moved the fourth step, involving the playing of cards and winning of souls, so that it follows the receipt of magic objects. This, along with the preamble concerning Federigo's past, provides greater plot motivation than in any of the folk versions and makes **"Federigo,"** like Mérimée's other stories, a tightly-constructed narrative, with no superfluous details or action. By rearranging the elements so that they follow one another in a logical fashion, Mérimée has transformed a folktale into a short story, where each action is motivated by what precedes it. (pp. 57-9)

Federigo's descent into hell is extremely interesting, for Mérimée's description of this event does not correspond to that found in any of the folk versions, and is likely the result of his excellent knowledge of the classics. Hell is the

Netherworld of Pluto and is located in Sicily, which is in accord with classical mythology. The references to Pluto and Cerberus elicit immediate recognition from the reader, and make the story less abstract and more *vraisemblable.* Instead of bringing the traditional honeycakes to distract Cerberus, guardian of Pluto's realm, Federigo is accompanied by his favorite hound, who succeeds so well at amusing Cerberus that several months later she gives birth to a litter of monsters. Federigo wins all twelve souls from Pluto, who tires of losing and tricks him into leaving. He returns home to live out his life on his old estate, with the souls in a sack. . . . (pp. 60-1)

From this point on, "Federigo" follows the standard pattern. Death visits him twice, and due to the sticking power of the tree and the stool is twice compelled to add one hundred, then forty years to Federigo's life, which he proceeds to enjoy fully. (p. 61)

When the last forty years have passed, Death comes for Federigo, who must accompany her this time, since he has run out of ways to trick her. He is ready to go, along with his sack, since he has lived a full life. Pluto refuses him in hell. . . . The fact that he has already been in hell makes him known to Pluto and makes Pluto's refusal understandable. Purgatory will not accept him, for he is in a state of mortal sin. Saint Peter is outraged that he would dare enter heaven, since he did not ask for salvation at the time he was given three wishes, but Federigo reminds him that this welcome is very unlike the one he received when he arrived with Jesus and the other disciples so long before. Jesus is willing to let him in, but without the souls that accompany him, as they are damned. . . . Federigo has thus managed to have a longer life than usual, enjoy all of life's pleasures, do a good deed and even save his soul.

Clearly, Mérimée has done more than translate a popular folktale. His primary contribution to the tradition of "The Smith and the Devil" lies in his extensive refashioning of the original material. Like any good nineteenth-century storyteller, he has endowed his protagonist with a personality and a past, both of which motivate his behavior. Federigo is not a type, but a character whose actions derive from a certain psychology. The generosity that led him to welcome Jesus and his disciples impells him to atone for the injustice he did the men he ruined, while the brashness with which he wins their souls from Pluto is a trait he demonstrates throughout the tale, but especially at the end. Mérimée has not neglected the local color for which he is justly famous and has placed his character in a geographical and social context. Since the tale is short, as is its model, Mérimée uses key words that express succinctly the atmosphere he is trying to create while minimizing description and narration. Thus, *malandrins* and *condottieri* place the tale in the middle ages, the time most propitious to the unfolding of these events, *Cava* describes its geographical location, *Pluton* stands for the Netherworld. These key words also provide a certain narrative consistency and serve in a somewhat tautological fashion to confirm the information concerning the tale's provenance given in the narrator's initial note. The narration is terse and ironic, as is generally the case in Mérimée's stories. The tale is tightly structured, and no detail is extraneous. The heightened structural coherence obtained by changing the order of the basic plot sequence is reinforced

by the balance created by the recurrence of the number twelve—twelve gamblers ruined, twelve disciples and twelve souls won.

No one knows why Mérimée did not consider this tale very highly and included it in only the first edition of *Mosaïque.* He was often a hard judge of his own work. Yet he could hardly have dismissed "Federigo" for its lack of originality, since he borrowed from many sources for all his works, adapting them to his specific literary needs. Perhaps the explanation for his elimination of "Federigo" from later editions is that he felt that the light, fairy-tale, optimistic tone of "Federigo" was ill-suited to a collection of stories dealing with death, tragedy and the darker side of human passion. "Federigo" is one of the very few stories by Mérimée with an unequivocally happy ending. This ending contrasts sharply with those of the other stories of *Mosaïque,* such as "Mateo Falcone," "Tamango" and "Le Vase étrusque," where all suffer, both the good and the bad. This is very unlike the moral of "Federigo," which shows that generosity and perseverance are rewarded.

In addition, he may also have been unhappy with the positive depiction of religion and the naïve view of miracles and salvation expressed by the tale. Mérimée was decidedly anticlerical all his life. His works reflect his conviction that most piety is either a sham or a form of self-deception ("Arsène Guillot"), and most representatives of the church hypocrites ("L'Abbé Aubain"). His stories and novels denounce ignorance and credulity in all spheres of life, but most especially in connection with religion. Although the religious elements in "Federigo" are necessary and intrinsic parts of the tale, Mérimée may well have thought in later years that his story was inconsistent with his own views on religion and so withheld it from newer editions of his works.

Mérimée took his inspiration from a common folktale, of which there are one hundred French versions alone. Not only has his story been unquestioningly accepted by critics as a simple translation of an Italian tale, but "Federigo" has had the ironic fortune of being included by folklorists in lists of Italian variants of type 330. Close comparison with European folktales of the same type reveals that "Federigo" differs from the known versions in ways that are literarily and structurally significant. "Federigo" deserves to be considered a short story and assigned its rightful place in Mérimée's *oeuvre.* (pp. 61-3)

Kathryn J. Crecelius, "Mérimée's 'Federigo': From Folktale to Short Story," in Studies in Short Fiction, *Vol. 19, No. 1, Winter, 1982, pp. 57-63.*

Kathryn J. Crecelius (essay date 1986)

[*In the following excerpt, Crecelius discusses Mérimée's novella* Colomba *as a hybrid text that combines elements of the vendetta tale with those of the detective story and offers a metafictional interpretation of the work.*]

Colomba can be viewed most profitably as a work whose very subject is the process of interpretation: it represents the successful attempt to forge a unified conception of two events, a murder and its revenge, in light of and despite the multiple interpretations to which each of those events is subject.

When *Colomba* was written in 1840, the classic detective story as we know it today had not yet been developed by its acknowledged father, Edgar Allan Poe. Poe had many precursors, however, some of whom Mérimée knew and read, particularly Balzac and Bulwer-Lytton; he had in fact himself already employed detective-like methods in **"La Vénus d'Ille."** It is clear from *Colomba* that he sensed the techniques which are central to the genre, especially the false clues and the delayed revelation of the name of the murderer. He also realized that the question of point of view is intrinsic to detective fiction, where all clues must be construed in the proper fashion to lead to the truth. Since the status of truth and its attendant value, justice, is the real subject of *Colomba,* Mérimée turned to this relatively new genre and added it to a much older one to create a hybrid text that, much like its hero, benefits from the association of two traditions.

Colomba combines two literary forms in complementary ways. It announces the detective story, but adheres to the older genre of the vengeance tale as well. Indeed, punishment is rarely a part of the detective story, which is concerned only with the uncovering of guilt. Nonetheless, *Colomba* is very much a detective narrative that follows a course from confusion to clarity, ending with the synthesis of three contrasting viewpoints and agreement as to the identity of the murderer of Ghilfuccio della Rebbia. The punishment section describes an opposite movement, going from convergence to divergence, so that the epistemological situation at the end of *Colomba* mirrors that of the beginning, with the crucial exception that the reader has had access to all of the information contained in the story.

On a superficial level, the plot of *Colomba* is one of the oldest and simplest in literary history: a young man returns home and avenges his father's death. To be more accurate, one would have to add that he acts largely at the instigation of his sister. This brief description, however, does not take into account all of the events in *Colomba,* for although the story ends as anticipated with the son's revenge, the end does not come in the way it was expected. In fact, nothing in *Colomba* is predictable. Each chapter reveals new twists to an increasingly complicated plot which is resolved in a satisfactory way not by premeditated violence, but by a bold act of interpretation.

At the outset, the story appears to involve a conflict between the necessity for revenge demanded by primitive custom and the Europeanized hero's unwillingness to revert to his cultural heritage. Indeed, this is the way that *Colomba* has traditionally been read. A. W. Raitt's criticism that "Mérimée has lacked the courage to face the tragic implications of the situation he has devised and wriggles out of it in what can only be described as a dishonest way . . . " is based on the assumption that this situation involves an either/or choice that the hero must make. For this reason, the dénouement appears inconsistent with this dilemma and is described by Raitt as a "trick" [see excerpt dated 1970]. Trahard also views the story as the opposition of two value systems, with the twist that in the end the protagonists have switched positions. . . . (pp. 225-26)

This view of the story, where Orso and Colomba stand for two diametrically opposed traditions, ignores the existence of a third character whose presence is crucial to the outcome of the plot. The polar opposition in the work is not between Colomba and Orso, but rather between Colomba and Miss Lydia Nevil, with Colomba the embodiment of primitive custom and Lydia the epitome of European civilization. Orso, the Corsican metamorphosed into a French army lieutenant, is a hybrid product of the two different systems the women represent. There are in fact three choices open to Orso, each represented by one of the main characters.

At the beginning of the story, Orso, Colomba and Miss Lydia have very different views of the events which occurred in Pietranera two years previously and of the action that these events demand. Each constructs a potential plot out of the information he or she possesses concerning the death of Colonel della Rebbia, and each strives to see that plot fulfilled, to impose it upon the other characters. The extraordinary achievement of *Colomba* is that all succeed, for these three contradictory plot possibilities are consolidated into one comprehensive narrative. No one plot is valorized over another. Each attains its own ending at the proper time, while the whole narrative ends in a manner consistent both with the individual, conflicting plots and with its own higher level of organization. Unlike Mérimée's **"Mateo Falcone"** (1829), where Fortunato's crime is his failure to participate in the interdependence of two orders, *Colomba* turns the older story inside out to depict a successful compromise in which all parties are ultimately satisfied and in which the tragic potential of the situation is turned into one of Mérimée's rare happy endings.

From Colomba's viewpoint, the plot is clear. Orso must avenge his father's death in the Corsican manner. Colomba has no doubt as to the identity of her father's murderer(s), and merely awaits their punishment. To this end, she attempts to restore Orso to Corsican values, thoughts and even costume, so that he may fulfill her plan of retribution. Colomba gives life to the story, for without her insistence, there would be no settling of scores. Both dove (as her name implies and as she calls herself in her *ballata*) and tigress, she is an imposing figure to those around her; like Carmen, she is thought to be "le diable en personne."

Colomba begins to achieve a mythic dimension that is quickly dispelled for the reader by the unexpected resolution of her quest for vengeance: despite her perseverance and almost religious belief in the justness of her cause, Colomba does not succeed in the plan which Orso quickly realizes she has made for him. . . . She does not arrive at her anticipated goal precisely because she does not completely control her brother, nor even the events of her own making. This is shown clearly when Colomba mutilates the ear of Orso's horse and then attributes to the Barricinis this base act. . . . The significance of this insult is less profound for Orso than for his supporters, and Colomba's goad backfires. Instead of remaining in town and punishing the affront, Orso continues on his way to intercept the Nevils. Had Colomba's plan succeeded, the ending of the story might have been quite different. This incident demonstrates that Colomba is not some sort of omnipotent demon, but a woman of strong conviction who can and does miscalculate the extent of her influence.

Miss Lydia Nevil perceives the problem much as does Colomba, but from the opposite perspective. She is anxious to see Orso's civilized side prevail in his quest for justice, not his Corsican nature. Lydia is the perfect complement to Colomba. Lydia's education and sophistication have almost obscured her natural sentiments, whereas Colomba's ignorance allows for an instinctive appreciation of poetry, as her reaction to Orso's reading from Dante reveals; indeed, she is herself a poet according to an oral tradition of improvisation. Both women demonstrate an indomitable strength, as well as a softer side. While Lydia is at first seen to be flighty, she becomes stronger and more dependable as the situation warrants. Conversely, once her dream of vengeance has been satisfied, Colomba is transformed into a young woman of style, very proper and elegant. Lydia ultimately becomes responsible for clearing Orso's name and for concluding the story happily. Her ideal plot is fulfilled when she helps establish that Orso did not betray his European training, and her romantic dreams are realized when she and Orso are married. Her Corsican trip is a success in both a moral and a material sense.

Orso is initially somewhat detached from the problem of his father's death and the passions it raises. He has returned to Corsica solely to settle his affairs and see Colomba married so that he may return to Europe to live. He views Colomba's suspicions as unreasonable and unfounded, and is satisfied by the official explanation as to the identity of his father's murderer. It is only slowly, and after what he deems to be acceptable proof of the Barricinis' guilt, that Orso is drawn into the web of Colomba's plans. Even then, he does not automatically resume the vendetta as his village expects of him. Defined by the text, the vendetta is a self-perpetuating system which blindly continues, so that often its causes have been forgotten with the passage of time and its victims are hardly implicated in the dispute. It is this mindless propagation that Orso cannot accept. As the product of a rationalist, military education, he looks only to legal proof and testimony to determine guilt and exact justice. In the plot that he elaborates, he seeks to reconcile the two forces that hold equal claim to him, to avenge his father, but by civilized means.

In seeking to weave these three conflicting plots together, *Colomba* becomes a detective story in which the initial question posed by the text—Will the murderer be punished and if so how?—is slowly displaced by a more pressing one, namely—Who is the murderer? Indeed, it is difficult to prosecute a murderer until his identity has been firmly established. Yet at the beginning of the story, there are at least two suspects, one of whom is dead; while Colomba alone believes that the Barricinis are guilty, the official explanation points to Agostini. To vindicate her, and so that justice may be done, Colomba's charges must be proven, which they are via a series of investigations of allegations and counter-allegations concerning the circumstances of della Rebbia's death that occupy a full two-thirds of the narrative. The description of the events leading up to the murder forms that part of the detective story that Todorov describes as "absente mais réelle." Absent, because the events occurred before the time of the narration, but nonetheless very real because of their importance in designating the murderer, this mode of plot is usually the main concern of the detective who pieces evidence together in order to find the guilty party. In *Colomba,* however, there is no single detective; rather, the characters and the reader are all actively engaged in assembling bits of the

puzzle supplied by informants, first, to identify the murderer and, then, to see him punished.

Both Colomba's and Orso's plots require the positive identification of their father's murderer. The circumstances of his death are revealed to both the characters and the reader in a variety of ways that show the multiple perspectives to which the murder is subject. The first to evoke this unhappy event is the sailor on the boat that brings Orso and the Nevils to Corsica; his account is brief, and makes clear that he believes Orso is returning home to fulfill the vendetta. This communication is responsible for attracting Lydia's notice, for until then the young soldier had struck her as unworthy of her attention. The narrator is the next source of information; he follows the hallowed tradition of beginning *in medias res,* filling in the past while his characters sleep. . . . He divulges all the facts necessary to the reader, beginning with the origin of the feud between the della Rebbias and the Barricinis, describing its avatars during the lives of Giudice Barricini and Ghilfuccio della Rebbia, and ending with the murder of the latter and the inquest, led by Giudice Barricini as town mayor. Orso himself speaks to Lydia about his father's death, as well as Colomba's suspicions concerning the Barricinis which he does not share. Finally, the prefect presents his explanation of the origin of the false letter attributed to the outlaw Agostini which was the immediate cause of della Rebbia's death. This precipitates Colomba's search through her father's papers and her refutation of the prefect's thesis, which eventually persuades Orso that her allegations were correct.

It is possible to discern in *Colomba* an epistolary subtext, where characters are linked by what they write rather than what they say. In fact, most of the details concerning della Rebbia's murder are revealed through letters. (pp. 226-29)

Colomba's vindication provides a powerful scene, composed of two warring families, a harried prefect who is trying to prevent further bloodshed, two outlaws as witnesses and their trained dog. Colomba is sublime as she presents proof that Tomaso Bianchi had no reason to write the letter attributed to Agostini, thereby destroying all theories that placed blame for her father's death with anyone other than the Barricinis.

The detective story is now complete. The murderer has been found and Orso's plot conforms more closely to Colomba's. However, one important item remains: that the guilty be punished. Accordingly, the text returns to its original question: Will the Barricinis be punished and how? It is at this juncture in the narrative that the neatly assembled pieces of the puzzle do not follow the expected order. At this point, both the characters and the reader have the same amount of information; all are convinced of the Barricinis' guilt. This common knowledge will soon be lost, however, as the narrative enters the punishment phase. Indeed, by the novella's end, there are as many different versions of the ensuing action as there had been of the murder in the beginning. After tying the individual plots so closely together, the final dénouement produces further loose ends.

Orso's opinions are changed completely by Colomba's proofs. The prefect also seems convinced. There is a brief skirmish, after which Orso writes to invite the Barricinis to a duel. They refuse, and indicate in their letter that this provocation will be made known to the authorities; later, Orso's letter becomes damaging evidence against him. In the midst of all this activity, Lydia writes to announce her arrival and her happiness that altercations have ceased; evidently she received Orso's first letter relating his belief in Tomaso's guilt, but not the second in which he announced that the whole village was in a state of siege. Lydia's letter is really the immediate cause of the dénouement, for Orso sets out to meet her and her father, to warn them of the state of affairs in Pietranera and to ascertain if they wish to continue their trip despite the danger. On the way, he is ambushed by Vincentello and Orlanduccio Barricini, and kills them both.

Colomba ends as anticipated from the beginning: Orso avenges his father's death by killing his enemies. Yet he does so in a most unexpected manner, neither in a European-style duel, as he had envisaged, nor by cold-blooded murder, as demanded by tradition, since neither of these solutions would have satisfied Lydia's plot. Instead, he is forced to kill his enemies in self-defense. This scene is narrated for the benefit of the reader, who has no doubt as to the circumstances of the killing; it is clear that Orso fired only when fired upon. There are no eye-witnesses, although the shots are heard by two parties, the outlaws, who discover the bodies, and the Nevils, who are passing through the area and who hear shots which they recognize as coming from the rifle Col. Nevil gave Orso. However, neither they nor their guide paid much attention to the order in which the shots were fired. Moreover, the word of the outlaws is unacceptable to the authorities on account of their extra-legal status. . . . When the evidence seems to go against Orso for lack of reliable witnesses, and also because of his letter of challenge to the Barricinis, Lydia assures the prefect that she and her father can confirm the outlaws' assertion that Orso fired only when fired upon.

The status of this statement is ambiguous, because it is simultaneously a lie and the truth. It is a lie because Lydia does not know who fired first. Her heart tells her that Orso could not have provoked the violence, and her love, plus her desire to protect him, forces her to exculpate him. Yet from the reader's point of view, her statement is thoroughly in accord with the actions as recounted, and so is not a falsehood. This lie, then, is the source of the happy ending, for the Nevils' testimony is considered to be unimpeachable; an autopsy further confirms that Orso was alone at the moment of the attack. Thus, by a well-meaning fiction, Lydia has saved the situation and restored the order that should have been. Each of the three individual plots has been brought to its own end. . . . (pp. 230-31)

As the ambush scene shows, interpretation and viewpoint are not only central to the plot of *Colomba,* but to its narration as well. Mérimée uses the technique of limited point of view, where only one person's understanding of a situation is given, in a variety of ways in *Colomba* so that several different perspectives are expressed. As in the case of the detective novel, Mérimée is again experimenting with a technique that others later perfected. Henry James became famous for presenting via third-person narration a character's view of events, particularly in *What Maisie Knew* (1897), where the child cannot comprehend the importance of what she sees. (pp. 231-32)

Miss Lydia is the pivotal figure in the story, and her plot is closely tied to the initial tone of the narration. From the beginning, the narrator's view of her is definitely uncomplimentary. She is shown to be spoiled, rude and a bit silly. She is ridiculed as belonging to that class of tourists who view everything with scorn and find nothing on their trip to please them. In fact, Lydia travels not to entertain or educate herself, but rather to impress her friends with the unknown wonders she alone has seen. Her sole reason for assenting to the trip to Corsica is precisely so that she might be the first Englishwoman to go there. . . .

Although educated, Lydia seems to possess the same romantic imagination shown by other of Mérimée's heroines. At first, Orso does not interest her. . . . However, once she learns Orso's story, from an "être prosaïque" is instantly transformed into a fascinating person. . . . She immediately reinterprets his physiognomy and his character in the light of her new information. This interest, aided by Lydia's own desire for excitement, leads to her further involvement in Orso's destiny and her attempt to prevent his embroilment in a potentially dangerous situation. (p. 232)

Once interested in Orso, she treats him seriously and tries to help him deal with the difficult situation which confronts him. As the story becomes more complicated, Lydia's character grows in importance and stature. The narrator loses his mocking tone and closes the distance which initially separates him, as well as the reader, from the story.

This change in the narrator's tone parallels Lydia's change in viewpoint: he mocks her as she mocks the world, but once she begins to enter the story in earnest, he treats her with more respect and his story not as a mere *divertissement* but as a significant puzzle. This shift in attitude can be explained by the desire on the part of the narrator to present only the character's viewpoint, to limit the information he reveals to what she knows and thinks. Mérimée does not pursue this limited viewpoint in a systematic way: neither Colomba nor Orso is shown in the same manner. In *Colomba,* Mérimée uses this subjective vision of a character to emphasize the problem of interpretation which is central to the story: where the narrator sees a frivolous *enfant gâtée,* the prefect discerns a bright young woman.

While the narrator shows Lydia's perspective in a special way, he also controls the way his own narrative is presented, through self-conscious narrative techniques. This becomes especially evident in the sixth chapter, where he lightheartedly explains why he began the story in the middle. . . . The awkwardness of the flashback technique is here underlined by the narrator's ironic stance rather than minimized. He deliberately calls attention to the artifice of his narrative, indicating that its arrangement is dependent solely upon his volition, and not any external requirement; further, he suggests that the narrative act itself always eludes the kind of seamless construction and closure desired by the reader, being ruled instead by arbitrariness.

Equally jarring is the narration of the beginning of the penultimate chapter. Most of the loose ends of the story have been tied up and Orso's vengeance is complete. Suddenly, there is a change in focus to an "objective" view written in journalistic style; this style is even specifically referred to in the first paragraph. . . . This is the style in which traditional stories begin, with characters presented from afar before being named and situated within the action, before acts of interpretation actually begin. (pp. 232-33)

This distancing underscores the multiplicity of possible viewpoints, including that of the press, and the impossibility of ever arriving at a consensus. The time of narration of *Colomba* is not clear; it is certainly some time after the fact, as indicated by numerous hints in the text. . . . Further, the perspective as well as the investigation which time allows is revealed in the information that when the outlaws spoke to the perfect along with the feuding families, the door had been double-locked by the servant . . . . This kind of distance further reinforces the conviction that little is certain and that all is subject to interpretation, to further study and more information.

It is significant that the last word of this story, as in Mérimée's **"Le Vase étrusque"** and *La Double Méprise,* is left to an outsider, to society in the form of a farmer. In this scene, the final mysteries are solved, and still one more is presented. Colomba confronts Giudice Barricini, old and broken by the death of his sons. He reveals the lie on which much of the story is based, for not only was he responsible for the false letter signed Agostini, but he also tore out the page upon which della Rebbia had written his assassin's name and replaced it with one naming Agostini. It is not surprising, however, to discover that even Colomba's truth was imperfect, for she demanded the death of both sons, when only Vincentello was guilty. In order for her to obtain vengeance, she had to go farther than was necessary. (pp. 233-34)

Colomba strikes terror into the old man; he sees her as some sort of demon, with mysterious powers that enabled her to read the sheet of paper he had burned. This view is shared by the farmer who cares for him. . . . Certainly Colomba's effect on the old man is bewitching, and she is presented throughout the story as having an almost supernatural strength of character. Yet her strength comes from her convictions, and her weakness is also shown, particularly in her failure to dominate Orso. Rather than confirm Colomba as a witch with supernatural powers (at worst she can be called single-minded and uncharitable to her enemies), the farmer's parting remark serves merely to emphasize further the vast differences in the scope of individual viewpoints. She knows nothing of Colomba's past, she can only speculate based on what she has seen and her own prejudices. In this respect, she joins the reader, as well as the narrator and the characters, who all create their own private version of the events of which they have knowledge.

In this story, events exceed the ability to perceive them. The more closely *Colomba* is read, the more it appears to present both a typology of literary generation and a mirror of the critical act. *Colomba* is a fiction which, on the one hand, is based on a concatenation of fictions, lies and obfuscations, deliberate and inadvertent, and which, on the other, details the analysis of fiction to discover the truth.

The status of truth is the central question in *Colomba.* While certain facts can be proven indisputably false, few earn the right to be deemed "true." Truth depends on information and viewpoint, and we have seen both in the plot and in the narration that these two elements are subject to change. What is one person's truth is another's falsehood, or uncertainty. The fictions which comprise *Colomba* are themselves of ambiguous status; the narrative path leading to the accusation of the Barricinis is strewn with lies that are proposed, examined and rejected until a final version of the murder is attained. Most of the lies in the story are exposed, but not all: Lydia's true-lie is not subject to examination, nor is Colomba's lie regarding the mutilation of Orso's horse.

These two latter statements remain within the reader-narrator relationship, beyond the reach of the other characters. The second is especially interesting, for it demonstrates further that certain mysteries are never explained and some misunderstandings never clarified; it represents a narrative path to another dénouement which was not taken and which remains unexploited. Had Orso reacted as expected to Colomba's lie, he would not have ridden into the ambush. These unexplored lies are also important because they contradict the promise inherent in detective stories, and in fiction in general, that, at the end, truth will be discovered and told. Here, truth is discovered, but revealed only to the reader; characters never have access to certain information.

Indeed, like many of Henry James' stories, *Colomba* is constructed around a central lacuna, a blank which is known only to the narrator, the reader, and one of the characters, but not to those whose actions depend on it. James, of course, exploited this structure systematically and extensively, eventually making the lacuna absolute by excluding both reader and narrator from key knowledge in *The Turn of the Screw.* In *Colomba,* this blank is not a void, but rather a generator of meaning, for it constitutes the juncture where truth and justice meet. Paradoxically, the truth disappears in the ambush scene, but when the dust settles, justice emerges.

In a very real way, narrative form and technique in *Colomba* acquire a moral dimension. The text posits a relationship between justice and narrative, for all the different plot possibilities are forged into a single plot which not only reaches a consonant ending, but which provides for a happy ending by allowing Orso's acquittal. Were the truth to be revealed, namely that Lydia did not know who fired first, the testimony of the outlaws would probably not have been enough to save Orso from prison. The narrative's quest for an appropriate end parallels the plot's demand for justice for Orso, and for his father. This is not surprising, for both the narrative and the judicial system in *Colomba* have been shown to depend upon the investigation of fictions to reach their goals. The moral and epistemological implications of this relationship are extremely telling, for justice is seen to be more important and more desirable than truth; by the same token, it is possible to argue that successful fictions are held to be superior to the elusive "facts."

Lydia's assertion forms the true crux of the story, both in terms of the plot and in a philosophical sense, for it combines all the various elements elaborated by the text. It involves truth and fiction, and their accompanying questions of interpretation, for Lydia, like a detective, assesses the facts that are presented and devises a vision of them which suits her desires and her knowledge of the situation. Her testimony is indeed the ultimate fiction, for her statement is true even if she does not know it. She has achieved the proper combination of truth and imagination which characterizes literature itself.

Lydia not only forms an interpretation, however, she imposes it upon the world. It will be remembered that Fortunato tried the same tactic, but failed, for his fictions did not take into account the requirements of the society around him. Lydia is not like some of Mérimée's characters, Saint-Clair and Julie among them, who make no attempt to have their ideas and fantasies coincide with those of their contemporaries. Rather, Lydia is an active being who tries to control her own destiny and in so doing forges her own plot and designs her own happy end. Although it is generally true, as Frank Bowman asserts, that Mérimée found literature "a meaningless substitute for action," [see Further Reading list] in *Colomba*, at least, literature is seen to be a form of action which is both successful and just. (pp. 234-36)

> *Kathryn J. Crecelius, "Narrative as Moral Action in Mérimée's 'Colomba',"* in *Nineteenth-Century French Studies, Vol. XIV, Nos. 3 & 4, Spring-Summer, 1986, pp. 225-37.*

P. W. M. Cogman   (essay date 1988)

[*In the excerpt below, Cogman studies the multiple points of view evidenced in the frame narrative of* Carmen, *assigning emphasis to Mérimée's revised final chapter, which Cogman asserts "highlights a key thematic opposition . . . between constraint and freedom."*]

When it was first published in the *Revue des Deux Mondes* of 1st October 1845, Mérimée's *Carmen* did not contain the concluding chapter on gypsy customs and language, which was only added in the 1847 publication in volume and in all subsequent editions. This chapter has always posed problems for commentators. Some have just treated it as an excrescence: for Trahard it is a 'dissertation pédante' that weakens the thrust of the story; for A. W. Raitt, it is a 'wilfully perverse' addition [see excerpt dated 1970]; for M. J. Tilby, 'little more than a learned appendix'. For these critics, the central interest of the story is the study of Don José's passion for Carmen. In the course of time interest has tended to slide back from Carmen herself, no longer the 'personnalité si nette' that Dupouy evokes, but seen increasingly as 'unknowable', just as her gypsy world is 'incomprehensible to both Don José and the narrator', and has shifted to Don José's love for her, whether seen literally or read allegorically, as it is by Tilby for whom it mirrors the relationship between the Romantic fiction-maker (Carmen, an analogue of the creative writer and of the text) and his reader, 'as gullible as José and . . . well disposed towards the seductive myth of Carmen the *femme fatale.'*

Most of those who have attempted to justify the final chapter have done so in terms of external tactics by the author with respect to a real or potential public, by attributing it for instance to a desire to display his philological knowledge or to fill up a thin volume (Parturier), to attenuate the publication by an Academician and a *fonctionnaire ministériel* of spicy tales of smugglers and gypsy girls, or out of *dandysme,* to affect detachment from an exciting

Portrait of Mérimée in 1868.

narrative (Dupouy). Similarly for Raitt, it indicates Mérimée's scorn for literature, the attitude of the author to his story. But to the extent that Mérimée might be seeking to guide the reader's response to the story, the pedantry of the chapter functions as a part of the story; the fullest of such 'internal' justifications is given by F. P. Bowman, who sees the 'obtrusive erudition' of the first and last chapters as a deliberate choice, and ultimately designed to provoke our dissociation from the Narrator (as I shall term the *savant* who relates his two encounters with Don José) and our identification with Don José, and an aesthetic effect of distancing between the story and the reader [see Further Reading list]. The main other internal explanation has been to shift the interest from Carmen and Don José and hold that the story is essentially a study of local colour and gypsy life. This would seem to be even more problematic. If we are to learn about gypsy life, why the elaborate narrative framework that Mérimée has set up? Why the fact that if *Carmen* has survived in multiple versions in different media: opera, ballet (Roland Petit, notably), film both of the story and of Bizet's opera, with local colour (Francesco Rosi) or updated (Preminger's *Carmen Jones,* Godard's *Prénom Carmen*), or even combining the two as in Carlos Saura's flamenco version, it is above all a character (Carmen herself) or the relationship between her and Don José (the Narrator almost invariably falls by the wayside) that survive? What I shall seek to demonstrate is the possibility of integrating the final chapter with the story in a way that both relates to the central issues of the story without evacuating traditional human interest, and makes it functional in terms of the elaborate narrative technique that Mérimée has adopted. . . . (pp. 1-2)

In Barbara Herrnstein Smith's dictum, 'a story is always . . . someone telling someone else that something has happened': relating also in the sense that it sets up a pattern of relationships. The most obvious of these is that between narrator and audience or narratee. But there is also the relationship between narrator and story. In the case of Mérimée, this has generally been explored by critics who have focussed their attention on the reliability or otherwise of Mérimée's narrators, notably that of **"La Vénus d'Ille"**: is he a reliable witness who can guarantee the veracity of events [see excerpt dated 1960], or someone whose limited perspective and restricted understanding allows a supernatural explanation to arise? The same problem arises in *Carmen:* how do we view Don José's account of Carmen? Is she demonic, as he presents her, and as Dupouy is inclined to agree; or is this just an illusion, or even an illusion which is parallel to *our* wishful thinking? To do so however is to treat Don José as storyteller as a unitary figure, when in a homodiegetic narrative (to use Gérard Genette's term) such as those of both the Narrator and Don José, in which the narrator plays a part in his own story, a key relationship is that between the narrator who is narrating and the narrator as protagonist of his own narrative. . . . [For] my purposes, it will be sufficient to distinguish older and younger selves in that the older selves only narrate (Don José in his cell, the Narrator in 1845), the younger selves are the actors in their respective tales. This is essentially a question of point of view, or focalization: are we restricted to what the younger self sees at the time, or do we see from the angle of the older narrator?—and it is a dimension that is often crucial in Mérimée. An extreme instance is **"Il Viccolo di Madama Lucrezia,"** in which the whole interest of the story depends on the narrator presenting the events just as they were experienced by his younger self. His older self intervenes occasionally to judge critically the character of his younger self. . . . He gives no hint however of facts or discoveries to come. This preserves ambiguity (are the events supernatural?) and suspense, which spring from the narrator imagining that he is at the centre of the mysterious events going on (the woman who threw him a flower, the shot from the empty house), whereas in fact they are directed at Don Ottavio (who, though he does not realize it, is his half-brother). But the ambiguity is sustained only by a trick: the older narrator suppresses to the end of the story a key fact, namely his resemblance to Don Ottavio. We are forced to attribute the fact that he did not notice it when he first met him to his egoism, vanity and self-centered unawareness. . . . (pp. 2-3)

This suggests that the question of defining focalization is in practice not totally clear-cut, but is above all a question of emphasis. Of the two theoretical focalizations available in a homodiegetic narrative, Mérimée takes advantage both of the point of view of the hero (to sustain suspense) and of the narrator (to generate amusement at the expense of his younger self). It is in any case *prima facie* unlikely that an older man would portray things solely as experienced by his younger self, with no sign of later discoveries

about the world or about himself, or that he would be content to surrender the narrative advantages of the perspective of the hero by viewing things totally with hindsight. Insofar as one can distinguish between a focalization on the hero and on the narrator, it must be based on a difference between the two (generated by their chronological separation). This difference may consist simply on the level of information (unawareness/knowledge of physical resemblance) or, on a deeper level of self-awareness, it can be produced by age and experience (juvenile vanity/mature detachment). In *Carmen* Mérimée exploits both possible focalizations (hero or narrator) and the two main types of difference on which they can be based (knowledge of facts or evolution of character).

In the case of Don José's tale, the focalization is not restricted to his younger self. As the older Don José tells his tale to the Narrator in prison, having turned to a life of crime, under sentence of death for 'plusieurs meurtres', having killed Carmen (though neither the Narrator who sees him in gaol nor the reader knows this yet), he views the successive incidents of his past life in the light of these later developments. His constant interventions from this vantage point, aware of what his actions are going to lead to, contribute to the sense of fatality that he seeks to instil in his audience. (pp. 3-4)

The creation of a sense of fatality by constant interventions also corresponds to the older Don José's tactics of self-exculpation: it is only after the event that one can seek to apportion (or shift) blame. Not only does he blame Carmen when he kills her . . . , he presents her (as she herself did) as 'le diable', while also blaming Carmen's character on her upbringing. . . . What these inconsistent explanations have in common is that they shift any blame from the young Don José. The older Don José who seeks to do this repeatedly invokes the Narrator's agreement, as narratee, in an appeal for sympathetic understanding of his position. . . . (p. 5)

As he relates his past to the Narrator, the older Don José not only retrospectively invests it with inevitability, exculpates himself, and appeals for understanding, but also crucially distorts his career and the image he seeks to give of his own character. In the rapid account he gives of his life before meeting Carmen, we can detect (though he glosses over it) a young Don José resistent to discipline and study . . . ; someone whose violence and lack of self-control in a quarrel has led to a fight, perhaps to death and flight from the law and the consequences of his actions. . . . One could note Don José's characteristic shifting of the blame, firstly to national characteristics, then to the victim as instigator of the quarrel. It is not clear that it actually led to a death. Don José's flight *could* be explained for other reasons (e.g. fear of revenge attacks), but if so, why should he not say so? If we assume this to be the case, are we not making the assumptions that Don José wants the Narrator (as narratee) to make—to give him the benefit of the doubt? The very lack of explicitness in the account is already a sign of evasiveness, a pointer to a recourse to violence Don José seeks to underplay, a murder he wishes to forget. The rapid, perfunctory nature of the narrative is significant in that he wants to locate the start of his life of dishonour and crime with his meeting with Carmen. . . . Don José's account of his flight [from the army] immediately afterwards is coloured by his lack of awareness of what is happening. . . . He jumps over the transition from being a fugitive from justice and the army to involvement at Carmen's suggestion in a smugglers' band. . . . (pp. 5-6)

The standard view of Don José is of a man, weak perhaps, but virtuous, destroyed by love [according to Bowman]: 'Don José tries to remain true to his duty as a soldier and firmly resists Carmen, but he weakens and his passion plunges him into a world of crime'. Raitt speaks of the 'desperate sincerity' of his confession. . . . Most readers, however sceptical they may be of the way in which his love for Carmen leads him to blame it on her supposed magical powers, tend to overlook the fact that when he meets Carmen, he has *already* been in a brawl, and perhaps killed a man—as of course he does in his accusation when he is about to kill her. . . . (p. 7)

Against this *escamotage* and attenuation could be set those things which Don José's account highlights. Recurrent amongst these is the importance he attaches to his (noble) birth. . . . He is equally proud of his Basque origins and of his language. . . . Having achieved (after his initial murder) a position in the army, he dwells on his desire, unlike the card-playing and sleeping Spanish soldiers, to occupy himself usefully making a chain, and expects promotion. After his demotion, he remains ambitious. . . . He rejects the chance offered by Carmen to escape from prison. . . . He expresses shame at his degradation, at being on guard duty as a 'simple soldat', shame at 'la belle vie que j'ai menée' as a bandit. If he rejects Carmen's proposal to get Garcia killed in ambushing the Englishman, it is again because of his national 'honour' . . . Here he is at pains to stress continuity and identity between his past and present selves which he can only do by seeing both from the point of view of the present, striving thereby to impose on the Narrator a false, or at best misleading, image of persistent allegiance to a certain ideal through the vicissitudes of his past life.

The Narrator adopts the other available narrative point of view by restricting his narrative in general to an internal focalization on his younger self. When he first meets Don José, we see the Narrator's growing suspicions about him, implied in the details he notes: the man's ignorance of the region, his knowledge about horses; but the narrative does not go beyond the synthesis that the young Narrator could draw at the time. Likewise he cannot tell *why* his guide Antonio distrusts the stranger they have met. This is essential to effects of surprise, both when he first meets Don José, and later in Cordoba. . . . (pp. 7-8)

This distinction between the points of view adopted by Don José and the Narrator in their narratives hinges on the difference in information between their older and younger selves: the Don José who relates his life knows all that will happen to him; the Narrator relating his Spanish adventures presents them as seen by someone not knowing what will happen next. But the distinction can also be made if there is a change in character or self-awareness between the two selves at issue. It is significant in this respect that a considerable time has elapsed between the Narrator's experiences in Spain and the moment of narration. He met Don José in 1830 (the date is given at the start of his narrative); the one specific indication he gives of the time of writing, 'il y a de cela quinze ans,' makes it the time of first publication (i.e. 1845), and the idea of a specific

time of writing or production of the narrative, posterior by some time to the events narrated, is reinforced by the reference 'forward' to the supposed future monograph on the site of the battle of Munda.

The Narrator, in 1830, is naïve. We see through the account (seen from the point of view of his gullible young self) of the watch incident, and realize what Carmen is up to, as she asks the time to find out if he has a watch worth stealing before deciding whether to accept his invitation to the *nevería;* and enquires if it is really gold; no surprise for us when it is missing. The young Narrator has demonstrated an incautious ostentation in showing it off in the library, and has something of the foreigner's vanity that characterizes the narrator of **"Il Viccolo di Madama Lucrezia"**: quite apart from his academic convictions about the site of Munda (and the error of those who disagree with him), he *knows* ('je connaissais . . . ') the Spanish character, as he knows Spanish pronunciation, and so feels safe with Don José even if he is a bandit, to the extent of thinking him 'doux et apprivoisé'. We might reflect that the Narrator is lucky in coming across an untypical bandit: a Garcia would not have been that scrupulous. . . . But this knowledge and the confidence it instils have limits. Worried when he learns of his guide's plan to betray Don José, he takes precautions (moving his gun) before waking him, and his knowledge of pronunciation doesn't help him to pin down Carmen: it is she who has to tell him that she is a gypsy. (p. 8)

The young Narrator abroad also has a fascination with exotic sex. What after all is he doing down by the Guadalquivir at nightfall when the women bathe? He is eager to enjoy 'un spectacle . . . ' with the other men there and fondly imagines 'Diane et ses nymphes au bain'. If he knows that the bellringer is now 'incorruptible', Mérimée would seem to be slyly hinting that the Narrator has found out from experience. He is all *too* willing to let himself be picked up by Carmen, when she comes and sits by him, lets her mantilla slide to reveal her head—she plays the same trick in front of Don José, and when he takes her off to gaol—and initiates the conversation, using smoking as a pretext. Even at the time, the Narrator seems somewhat ashamed of what he has laid himself open to: when he says that he doesn't take steps to recover his watch by recourse to the law. . . .

The older Narrator is readier to admit another curiosity of his younger self, namely magic, though his desire to declare himself free of such superstitions even then ('guéri') ['cured'] points to an interest which clearly extends beyond the merely academic. . . . (p. 9)

A third aspect of the young Narrator's interest in marginal and forbidden areas lies in his fascination with bandits and illegality. . . . The Narrator's attraction to bandits may happen to echo Mérimée's, but what is more important is the role of this attraction in the economy of the story. In all three areas (sex, magic, bandits) a gap can be sensed between what he felt then and the ironic attitude of the older self who stresses the difference. . . . Insofar as we sense this gap, we can see that the restriction to the point of view of the Narrator's younger self is largely true only of information, to justify effects of surprise, but less so in terms of moral perspective and self-awareness. A key feature of the tone of the Narrator's account of his experiences of 1830 is the delicate balance maintained between the two selves: we share both the younger Narrator's anxiety, unable to follow the conversation in Romany between Don José and Carmen, and uncertain what is to happen next to him, and the older Narrator's somewhat condescending calm, as he underlines his young self's incomprehension . . . with a growing literary deliberation and with a wry, detached humour at the expense of the naïve youngster who has got himself into this predicament. . . . (pp. 9-10)

The final chapter does not have this double perspective. The footnotes to Don José's narrative have served as a constant reminder that we are not hearing his account at first hand, but the record of it by a Narrator who now knows Romany. The concluding chapter is unambiguously by the older Narrator. The extent to which we identify him with Mérimée (who did make a trip to the Vosges in 1845, like the Narrator) is again less significant than the gap between his older and younger selves. The final chapter represents the triumph of the academic self and the definitive extinction of juvenile curiosities. It is methodical: he works through the distribution of the gypsies, their jobs (men, then women), their physique, their morality and attitudes to themselves and to others, to death and religion, to magic (a long passage), their origins, their language, of which (unlike the younger Narrator) he now has an extensive knowledge. The gypsies have become just an object of study. The approach is generally impersonal. . . . If the element of personal experience comes in . . . , he is a witness, an anthropologist who is merely recording, and who is not involved as he was with Carmen and Don José. He makes no difference between direct experience and what other people have told him. . . . As regards sex, he now shows . . . not so much . . . fascination as the sardonic attitude to morality of an experienced man . . . , and the conversation he quotes as a commentary on Borrow's anecdote which purports to demonstrate their virtue displays a clear cynicism: offers of money to tempt gypsy girls have to be pitched at the right level. He certainly has no longer a gullible fascination with magic: the anecdote of the woman duped about her lost lover and his sardonic comment . . . make it clear that gypsy 'spells' dupe only the naïve *payllo* and serve as a source of profit. Overall we are now offered a generally deromanticized view of gypsy life: smuggling 'et autres pratiques illicites' figure after more conventional activities, such as horsetrader, vet, tinker. (pp. 10-11)

This distinction of two selves in the Narrator, active/narrating, Romantic/academic, does not just give a role in the economy of the story to the final chapter. As we have seen, this chapter in any case does no more than develop more explicitly, and with an element of caricature, something that is present in the story from the start, and was consequently already present in the original (1845) version. The distinction is also important in that it highlights a key thematic opposition (if not *the* key thematic opposition) around which the story is constructed: that between constraint and freedom. This opposition existed already in the younger Narrator, seduced from his academic quest for Munda first by his curiosity in a bandit, then by a gypsy girl. It takes two forms in Don José. One is external: jealous Don José (constraint) is in conflict with Carmen's desire for freedom. The other, internal, lies

in the conflict between the proud and ambitious Don José and instability and violence. After the initial brawl (or murder) he seeks social reintegration, a return to order, by enlisting as a soldier, When Carmen repeatedly and in various ways seduces him from the path of duty, we know that that duty is the more important to him because of his previous lapses. Finally, Carmen herself is by no means a spirit of pure 'freedom'. . . . But she frequently invokes gypsy law or code in argument, as if she were bound by it. Admittedly, with her it is difficult to tell when a statement is just a tactical move (or a lie): for instance, she won't emigrate, she says, because it would involve breaking a promise to her Gibraltar friends. Nevertheless there is a consistency in her attitude to gypsy law which leads ultimately to it being, in a sense, the cause of her death and a factor in terms of which she has to define her freedom. . . . Before Garcia's death, she asserts that Don José has no rights over her because he is not her *rom;* after his killing, she concedes Don José's new rights under their law . . . , while at the same time asserting her independence, which can now exercise itself only in death.

Thus for all the characters there exists, in various forms, an opposition between various forms of constraint: duty to friends, debts of honour, family pride, academic integrity on the one hand, and on the other, impulses of passion, violence, personal curiosities, individualistic self-assertion. What interests Mérimée is not so much the value of one or the other, so much as the *tensions* set up between the two. There is a moral issue, one that the Narrator toys with when he allows Don José to escape the law. . . . But the moral issue is not honestly posed by the Narrator here (he may seek to excuse his betrayal of his duty as a citizen in the light of another 'duty', hospitality; in fact it was out of his own capricious fascination with the bandit), and it is in any case eluded at this point by the opportune arrival of the soldiers. . . . We may well feel frustrated in **Colomba,** where we are led to *expect* the resolution of the moral issue (should Orso stay true to the primitive vendetta code of Corsica or to that of 'civilized' society?) one way or the other before it is eluded by the ambush which enables Orso to kill in self-defence, an act which satisfies the Corsican code of vengeance without sacrificing what he owes to his European education. In **Carmen** it is more a question of the reader being alerted to an issue that gives rise to central thematic tensions, tensions which also inform the narrative structure and give it *interest.* Garcia's view of Carmen would be of minimal interest because it would contain minimal tension . . . ; there is more in the view of Carmen by a soldier who represents law and order; even more when that soldier is a fugitive from the law trying to achieve social reintegration; even more in a restrained academic's view of Don José's view, especially when that academic is also a Peeping Tom seeking thrills in magic and in consorting with bandits. In Carmen's and Don José's case, the irreconcilable demands of constraint and freedom lead to their deaths; in the case of the Narrator, the triumph of the law is embodied in the final chapter in the death of his younger self. (pp. 11-12)

P. W. M. Cogman, "The Narrators of Mérimée's 'Carmen'," in Nottingham French Studies, *Vol. 27, No. 2, November, 1988, pp. 1-12.*

FURTHER READING

Bowman, Frank Paul. *Prosper Mérimée: Heroism, Pessimism, and Irony.* Berkeley: University of California Press, 1962, 205 p.

    Detailed analysis of Mérimée's writings, focusing on what Bowman views as the pessimistic nature of the works and Mérimée's conception of heroic qualities within a fatalistic world.

Brandes, George. "The Romantic School in France." In his *Main Currents in Nineteenth-Century Literature,* Vol. V, pp. 239-46, 260-80. New York: Macmillan Co., 1904.

    Discusses a "passion for strength" that Brandes discerns in both Mérimée's personality and literary works.

Hamilton, James F. "Pagan Ritual and Human Sacrifice in Mérimée's 'Mateo Falcone'." *The French Review* 55, No. 1 (October 1981): 52-9.

    Examines Mérimée's blending of pagan myth and elements of the Romantic aesthetic in his story "Mateo Falcone."

Lapp, John C. "The Dénouement of Mérimée's 'La chambre bleue'." *Modern Language Notes* LXVI, No. 2 (February 1951): 93-7.

    Places the seemingly gratuitous ending of Mérimée's tale "La chambre bleue" within a satiric context to demonstrate the carefully planned structure of the story.

Lethbridge, Robert, and Tilby, Michael. "Reading Mérimée's 'La double méprise'." *The Modern Language Review* 73, No. 4 (October 1978): 767-85.

    In-depth metafictional study of Mérimée's novella *La double méprise* in which Lethbridge and Tilby posit that "Mérimée's story is not concerned merely to *illustrate* the hardly original dichotomy of fiction and reality but to *involve* the reader in the problematics of telling and reading and the associated activity of interpreting."

Pritchett, V. S. "Books in General." *The New Statesman and Nation* XXVII, No. 675 (29 January 1944): 79.

    Positive reconsideration of Mérimée's short fiction.

Saintsbury, George. Introduction to *The Writings of Prosper Mérimée,* by Prosper Mérimée, pp. ix-lxv. New York: Croscup and Holby Co., 1905.

    Surveys Mérimée's literary canon, assigning specific merit to his short narratives.

Sivert, Eileen Boyd. "Fear and Confrontation in Prosper Mérimée's Narrative Fiction." *Nineteenth-Century French Studies* VI, Nos. 3-4 (Spring-Summer 1978): 213-30.

    Thematic study of fear in Mérimée's short fiction.

Smith, Maxwell A. *Prosper Mérimée.* New York: Twayne Publishers, 1972, 199 p.

    Critical biography.

Symons, Arthur. "Prosper Mérimée." In his *Studies in Prose and Verse,* pp. 26-41, New York: E. P. Dutton and Co., 1904.

    Significant biographical account, highlighting aspects of Mérimée's temperment, artistic ideals, and scholarly endeavors.

Wells, B. W. "The Fiction of Prosper Mérimée." *The Sewanee Review* VI, No. 2 (April 1898): 167-79.

    Overview of Mérimée's short stories and novellas.

Ivan Turgenev

1818-1883

(Full name: Ivan Sergeyevich Turgenev; also transliterated as Sergeyevitch, Sergheïevitch, Serguéivitch, Serguèvitch, Serguiéiévitch, and Sergyéevitch; also Toorgenef, Tourghenief, Tourguénief, Turgeneff, Turgenieff, and Turgéniew) Russian novelist, short fiction writer, dramatist, poet, and essayist.

The first Russian author to achieve widespread international fame, Turgenev was designated his country's premier novelist by nineteenth-century Westerners and is today linked with Fedor Mikhailovich Dostoevsky and Leo Tolstoy as one of the triumvirate of great Russian fiction writers of the nineteenth century. Although his novels have in some ways obscured the popular and critical reputation of his short stories and novellas, he initially established his critical reputation for his sketches collected in *Zapiski okhotnika* (*A Sportsman's Sketches*), and many of his best known works are written in the short story form. These include "Dnevnik lishnego cheloveka" ("The Diary of a Superfluous Man"), "Mumu," and "Stepnoi Korol' Lir" ("A King Lear of the Steppes"), as well as the novellas *Asya, Pervaya lyubov'* (*First Love*), and *Veshnie vody* (*The Torrents of Spring*). Turgenev's novels generally utilize third-person narration and reflect a deep concern with the politics of his homeland, depicting Russia's tumultuous political environment from the 1840s to the 1870s; his short fiction, usually written in the first person, often focuses on the everyday lives of peasants and the love affairs of aristocrats. Turgenev's fiction in both genres is noted for its psychological truth, descriptive beauty, and haunting pathos.

Turgenev was born in the city of Orel into a family of wealthy gentry. His father, by all accounts a charming but ineffectual cavalry officer, paid little attention to his son and became involved in numerous extramarital affairs after marrying Turgenev's mother, Varvara Petrovna, for financial gain. Turgenev's childhood on the family estate of Spasskoye was largely dominated by Petrovna, whose treatment of her favorite son Ivan alternated between excessive affection and mental and physical cruelty; she ruled Spasskoye and its 5000 serfs with the same arbitrary power. Biographer's have cited Petrovna's influence to explain the development of Turgenev's personality—particularly his horror of violence and hatred of injustice—and his fiction is often populated by strong-willed females and well-meaning but ineffectual male protagonists. During his early childhood, French was the primary language spoken in Turgenev's household, and critics often propose that Turgenev learned Russian vernacular from the Spasskoye serfs. When he was nine years old, the family left the country estate for Moscow, where he attended various boarding schools before entering Moscow University in 1833. There he earned the nickname "the American" due to his interest in the United States and his democratic inclinations. In 1834, Turgenev transferred to the University of St. Petersburg. Upon graduation, he decided to study abroad, and in 1838 he enrolled at the University

of Berlin in Germany. During the next several years he studied Latin, Greek, and philosophy but never finished his degree. Although he returned to Russia in 1841, he spent the remainder of his life between his homeland and western Europe.

Although Turgenev had begun writing poetry as a student in St. Petersburg, publishing his first verses in 1838, biographers generally cite the narrative poem *Parasha,* published in 1843, as the beginning of his literary career. The volume attracted little attention from his contemporaries, however, and more important to his subsequent life and literary development were the friendships he made in the mid-1840s. During this period Turgenev met Pauline Viardot, a successful opera singer from a Spanish family of gypsies who was married to a director of the Italian Opera in Paris. Although Turgenev's letters indicate a grand passion for Viardot, the singer was not attracted to Turgenev and their relationship is believed to have been platonic; Turgenev periodically lived with Viardot and her family and their relationship endured for the rest of his life. Turgenev also became a close friend of Vissarion Grigoryevich Belinsky, an extremely influential literary critic who believed that literature must both mirror life and promote social reform. A political liberal and ardent advocate of Westernization who sought to bring Russia's culture and political system closer to that of Europe, Belinsky was closely associated with *Sovremennik* (the *Contemporary*), a radical periodical edited by Nikolay Alekseevich Nekrasov in which Turgenev published his first popular short story, "Khor and Kalinych." The story contrasts two Russian peasants, one a sly, practical, and crudely adept man capable of attaining a modest position despite his social status, the other a poetic dreamer who reaps only a meagre harvest because the landowner of the property he works demands that he assist him in hunting every day.

Although Turgenev continued to write poetry and also attempted several works of drama, the success of "Khor and Kalinych" convinced him to write a series of related pieces between the years 1847 and 1852, all first published in the *Contemporary* and later collected and published in book form as *Zapiski okhotnika* (*A Sportsman's Sketches*). In these sketches, which range from brief slices of life to fully realized stories, Turgenev drew on his experiences at Spasskoye and expressed his love for the land and people of rural Russia by adopting the persona of an aristocratic hunter in the country. Common to the volume is the theme of the injustice of Russian serfdom. Because of this omnipresent concern, *A Sportsman's Sketches* is frequently compared with Harriet Beecher Stowe's anti-slavery novel *Uncle Tom's Cabin,* published in 1852. Unlike the American novel, however, Turgenev's work is understated, his moral message implied rather than overt. At their first publication, Turgenev's stories proved enormously popular with almost everyone but government officials. When Turgenev later wrote an admiring obituary of Nikolay Gogol and was refused publication by St. Petersburg censors in 1852, he instead published the piece in Moscow. He was arrested and jailed for a month, then placed under house arrest at Spasskoye for nearly two years. Although ostensibly arrested for excessive approval of a suspect author, Turgenev was more likely detained as the author of the controversial *A Sportsman's Sketches.* When the serfs were finally freed in 1861, many credited the volume with having helped to effect their emancipation.

During his month in prison, Turgenev wrote "Mumu," a famous and frequently explicated work praised for its sensitive indictment of serfdom. The story focuses on Gerassim, a gigantic, deaf-mute serf who loses the girl he loves when the mistress of his estate arranges the girl's marriage to another man. Gerassim finds a substitute love object in Mumu, a small dog he rescues from a river, but is forced to drown Mumu after it is cornered in the mistress's house and bares its teeth to her. The cruelty and oppression of serfdom is evident in the mistress's inhumane treatment of both Gerassim and Mumu as animals, while Gerassim's size and strength establish him as a heroic symbol of the proletariat, submissive yet nursing a growing resentment that prophesies the coming emancipation of the serfs. Turgenev's first novel, *Rudin* (*Dmitri Roudine*), features several character types that recur in his subsequent works, including a protagonist reminiscent of the hero of Turgenev's earlier story "Dnevnik lishnego cheloveka" ("The Diary of a Superfluous Man"), a famous literary portrait of a Byronic "Russian Hamlet" whose effectiveness is nullified by his tendency toward self-analysis. Turgenev's next work, the novella *Asya,* addresses the infeasibility of

mutual love and may have some basis in his friendship with Mikhail Bakunin at the University of Berlin, with whom he lived closely for a year before courting his friend's sister. In *Asya,* a gentlemen narrator known as N. N. becomes close friends with a young man named Gagin, whose half-sister, Asya, the illegitimate daughter of Gagin's father and a serf girl, tries to interject herself between the two in a desperate plea for attention. Torn between his close friendship with Gagin and his growing attraction to Asya, N. N. comes to understand Asya's loneliness and frustration but becomes another of Turgenev's "superfluous men," capable of thought and reflection but unable to express his love even as Asya exits his life.

Following the outbreak of the Franco-Prussian War in 1870, Turgenev traveled to England with the Viardots, later moving to Paris, France, before settling on his summer estate on the Seine at Bougival. In ensuing years he befriended such literary personages as Emile Zola, Guy de Maupassant, and Gustave Flaubert, while completing some of his most celebrated works of short fiction. *Pervaya lyubov'* (*First Love*), a novella that some critics believe derived from his unrequited love affair with Viardot, details the love of a sixteen-year-old boy for Zinaida, a devious but alluring lover of power and personal freedom who keeps her weak-willed suitors in suspense by toying with their affections. However, Zinaida herself becomes a prisoner of her passion for the boy's father. Edward Garnett commented: "Here we tremble on the magic borderline between prose and poetry, and the fragrance of blossoming love instincts is felt pervading all the fluctuating impulses of grief, tenderness, pity and regret which combine in the tragic close. The profoundly haunting apostrophe to youth is indeed a pure lyric."

Turgenev's interest in the dramatic potential of the plays of William Shakespeare is evident in his acclaimed story "Stepnoi Korol' Lir" ("A King Lear of the Steppes"), in which Martin Kharlov, a man of large physical stature like Turgenev himself, divides his estate between his daughters after experiencing a dream foretelling his impending death. Loosely following Shakespeare's plot, Kharlov is evicted as a result of the manipulations of his greedy son-in-law three weeks later, and the story ends as Kharlov climbs to the top of his former manor and, in grief and anger, falls to his death while trying to dismantle the roof. A. V. Knowles commented that " 'A King Lear of the Steppes,' with no obvious social message, is a chronicle of family discord and human weakness. Powerfully written and accurately detailed, it leaves the reader lamenting for the human condition, for which Turgenev offers no palliative." During the last fifteen years of his life, Turgenev returned to the short story as his predominant form. His later stories often focus on the effect of fate or the supernatural upon helpless individuals, and he often concurred in his correspondence with the opinions of various critics that these later works were trivial and lacking in social importance. One exception, however, is the novella *Veshnie vody* (*The Torrents of Spring*), in which a young gentleman, Dmitri Sanin, meets and falls in love with Gemma, a beautiful young girl from a modest family, while returning from a foreign tour to Russia via Germany. However, Sanin soon forgets his vows and succumbs to "the torrents of spring" after falling in love with Madame Polosoff, a married heiress who is alternately frank and charming, cruel and malicious. She soon discards

Sanin, who is left to contemplate his own thoughtlessness after learning that Gemma has married another man in the United States. According to Henry James, this novella "has a narrative charm that sweetens its bitter waters. . . . [*Spring Torrents* illustrates] the element of folly which mingles, in a certain measure, in all youthful spontaneity, and makes us grow to wisdom by the infliction of suffering."

Throughout the twentieth century, Turgenev's literary reputation has remained generally stable. Modern commentators agree that Turgenev's fiction is distinguished by solid literary craftsmanship, vivid descriptions, and convincing characterizations. Commentators also note that his characters, who are identifiable as both unique human beings and representatives of universal human qualities, are drawn with a psychological penetration made more effective by the suggestive use of word and action, rather than the overt exposition of the narrator. Critics often contend that Turgenev was particularly adept at portraying women in love and at creating an unsentimentalized atmosphere of pathos in his unhappy love stories. Scholars suggest that Turgenev's fiction reveals his own sense of the futility of life, but add that he tempered his essentially pessimistic outlook with an appreciation of life's beauty. As Turgenev himself remarked, "Everything human is dear to me."

(For further information on Turgenev's life and career, see *Nineteenth Century Literary Criticism*, Vol. 21.)

PRINCIPAL WORKS

*SHORT FICTION

"Dnevnik lishnego cheloveka"   1850
    ["The Diary of a Superfluous Man" published in *Mumu and the Diary of a Superfluous Man*, 1884]
"Mumu"   1852
    ["Mumu" published in *Mumu and the Diary of a Superfluous Man*, 1884]
Zapiski okhotnika   1852
    [*Russian Life in the Interior; or, The Experiences of a Sportsman*, 1855; also published as *Tales from the Note-Book of a Sportsman*, 1895 and as *A Sportsman's Sketches* in *The Novels of Ivan Turgenev*,   1895]
Asya   1858
    [*Annouchka*, 1884; also published as *Asya* in *The Novels of Iván Turgénieff*, 1904]
Pervaya lyubov'   1860
    [*First Love* published in *First Love, and Punin and Barburin*, 1884]
"Stepnoi Korol' Lir"   1870
    [*A Lear of the Steppe*, 1874; also published as "A King Lear of the Steppes" in *The Novels and Stories of Iván Turgénieff*, 1903]
Veshnie vody   1872
    [*Spring Floods*, 1874; also published as *The Torrents of Spring* in *The Novels of Ivan Turgenev*, 1897]
Polnoe sobranie sochinenii. 10 vols. (novels, novellas, short stories, dramas, poetry, criticism, and letters) 1891

The Novels of Ivan Turgenev. 15 vols.   (novels, novellas, short stories, and poetry)   1894-99
The Novels and Stories of Iván Turgénieff. 16 vols.   (novels, novellas, and short stories)   1903-04
**Three Short Novels*   1948
A Nest of Gentlefolk, and Other Stories   (novel and short stories) 1959
Selected Tales   1960
Polnoe sobranie sochinenii i pisem. 28 vols.   (novels, novellas, short stories, dramas, poetry, criticism, and letters)   1960-68

OTHER MAJOR WORKS

Parasha   (poetry)   1843
Rudin   (novel)   1856; enlarged, 1860
    [*Dmitri Roudine*, 1873; also published as *Rudin* in *The Novels of Ivan Turgenev*, 1894]
Dvoryanskoe gnezdo   (novel)   1859
    [*Liza*, 1869; also published as *A House of Gentlefolk* in *The Novels of Ivan Turgenev*, 1894 and as *A Nobleman's Nest* in *The Novels and Stories of Iván Turgénieff*, 1903]
"Gamlet i Don Kikhot"   (essay)   1860; published in the periodical *Sovremennik*
    ["Hamlet and Don Quixote" published in periodical *Poet Lore*, 1892]
Nakanune   (novel)   1860
    [*On the Eve*, 1871]
Ottsy i deti   (novel)   1862
    [*Fathers and Sons*,   1867; also published as *Fathers and Children* in *The Novels of Ivan Turgenev*, 1899]
Dym   (novel)   1867
    [*Smoke*, 1868]
†*Mesyats v derevne*   (drama)   1872
    [*A Month in the Country* published in *The Plays of Ivan S. Turgenev*, 1924]
Nov'   (novel)   1877
    [*Virgin Soil*, 1877]
Stikhotvoreniya v proze   (poetry)   1882
    [*Poems in Prose*, 1883; also published as *Senilia*,   1890]
The Plays of Ivan S. Turgenev   (dramas)   1924
Literary Reminiscences and Autobiographical Fragments   (sketches and essays)   1958
Turgenev's Letters   (letters)   1983

*Most of Turgenev's works were originally published in periodicals.

**This work includes the short story "The Diary of a Superfluous Man" and the novellas *First Love* and *Asya*.

†This work was written in 1850.

V. G. Belinsky   (essay date 1848)

[Belinsky is considered the most influential Russian literary critic of the nineteenth century. He initiated a new trend in critical thought by combining literary appreciation with an exposition of progressive philosophical and political theory. He made his most notable contributions to literature during his later career as chief critic for the progressive review Otechestvennye Zapiski (Notes for the Fatherland), *and later, for* Sovremennik (The Con-*

temporary). *In these publications, he embraced a form of humanitarian socialism and became the predominant spokesman in the Russian intelligentsia's campaign against serfdom, autocracy, and orthodox religion. In the following excerpt from an essay written in 1848, Belinsky surveys Turgenev's short fiction and concludes that while Turgenev lacks creative imagination, he excels in the observation and faithful rendition of actual life.*]

Mr. Turgenev began his literary career by writing lyrical poetry; among his shorter verses are three or four noteworthy plays, as for instance "The Old Landowner," "A Ballad," "Fedya," and "A Man Like Many Others." However, he came off well with these plays because they either do not contain anything lyrical or their principal feature is not lyricism but hints at Russian life. (p. 66)

He also tried his hand at the narrative; his **"Andrei Kolossov"** contains many splendid sketches of characters and Russian life, but as a story, this work as a whole was so queer, inconsequential, and clumsy that very few people noticed the good points it really contained. It was then obvious that Mr. Turgenev was seeking a path of his own and had not yet found it, for this is not a thing that anybody can always easily or quickly find. Finally Mr. Turgenev wrote a story in verse, **"The Landowner,"** not a poem, but a physiological sketch of the life of the landowning class, a joke if you will, but a joke that somehow turned out to be much superior than any of the author's poems. Its racy epigrammatical verse, its gay irony, the faithfulness of its pictures, and at the same time an integrity sustained throughout the work—all tend to prove that Mr. Turgenev has discovered the real genre of his talent, has found his own element, and that there are no reasons why he should give up verses entirely. At the same time there appeared his story in prose, **"Three Portraits,"** which reveals that Mr. Turgenev had found his real road in prose as well. Finally his story **"Khor and Kalinich"** appeared in the first issue of the *Contemporary* of last year. The success of this short story, which had been published in the "Miscellany" column, was unexpected for the author, and induced him to continue his hunter's sketches [collected in *A Sportsman's Sketches*]. Here his talent was fully displayed.

Evidently he does not possess a talent for pure creative genius; he cannot create characters and place them in such mutual relationships in which they form themselves of their own accord into novels or stories. He can depict scenes of reality that he has observed or studied; he can, if you wish, create, but only out of material that is ready at hand, provided by actual life. This is not simply copying from real life; the latter does not provide the author with ideas but, as it were, suggests them to him, puts him in their way. He reworks the ready-made substance according to his ideal and gives us a scene, more alive, more eloquent and full of meaning than the actual incident that prompted him to write the scene; this sort of thing requires a certain measure of poetical talent. True, his entire ability sometimes consists only in faithfully describing a familiar person or an event of which he was a witness, since in actual life there are sometimes phenomena which, when faithfully put on paper, have all the features of artistic fiction. This, too, requires talent, and talents of this kind have their degrees. In both cases Mr. Turgenev possesses a highly remarkable talent. The chief characteristic feature of his talent lies in the fact that he would hardly be able faithfully to portray a character whose likeness he had not met in actual life. He must always keep his feet on the soil of reality. For that kind of art he has been endowed by nature with ample means: the gift of observation, the ability swiftly and faithfully to grasp and appreciate any phenomenon, instinctively to divine its causes and effects, and thus through surmise and reflection to complement the store of information that he needs, when mere inquiries explain little.

It is no wonder that the short piece **"Khor and Kalinich"** met with such success. In it the author approached the people from an angle from which no one had ever approached them before. Khor, with his practical sense and practical nature, his crude but strong and clear mind, his profound contempt for womenfolk and his deep-rooted aversion to cleanliness and neatness, is a type of Russian peasant who has been able to create for himself a position of significance under extremely adverse circumstances. Kalinich, however, is a fresher and fuller type of the Russian peasant; he is a poetical nature in common folk. With what sympathy and kindliness the author describes his heroes, and how he succeeds in making the readers love them with all their hearts! In all, seven sportsman's stories were published last year in the *Contemporary*. In them the author acquaints his readers with various aspects of provincial life, with people of diverse rank and condition. Not all his stories are of equal merit; some are better, others are worse, but there is not one that is not in some way interesting, entertaining, and instructive. So far, **"Khor and Kalinich"** remains the finest of all these sportsman's tales; next comes **"The Steward"** and then **"The Freeholder Ovsyanikov"** and **"The Counting-House."** One can only wish that Mr. Turgenev will write at least entire volumes of such stories.

Although Turgenev's story **"Pyotr Petrovich Karataev,"** which appeared in the second issue of the *Contemporary* for last year, does not belong to his hunting tales, this work is just as masterly a physiological sketch of the purely Russian character, and with a Moscow flavor at that. In this story, the author's talent is as fully expressed as in the finest of his hunting tales.

We cannot but mention Mr. Turgenev's extraordinary skill in describing scenes of Russian nature. He loves nature not as a dilettante but as an artist, and therefore he never tries to present it only in its poetical aspects, but takes it exactly as it appears to him. His pictures are always true, and you never fail to recognize our Russian landscapes in them. (pp. 67-9)

> *V. G. Belinsky, "A Survey of Russian Literature in 1847: Part Two," in Belinsky, Chernyshevsky, and Dobrolyubov: Selected Criticism, edited by Ralph E. Matlaw, E. P. Dutton & Co., Inc., 1962, pp. 33-82.*

Gustave Flaubert (letter date 1863)

[*The most influential French novelist of the nineteenth century, Flaubert is remembered primarily for the stylistic precision and dispassionate rendering of psychological detail in his classic work* Madame Bovary. *Although his strict objectivity is often associated with the realist and naturalist movements, he rejected this classification, and his talent is considered by many critics to defy such categorization. Flaubert struggled throughout his career to overcome a natural romantic tendency toward lyricism, fantastic imaginings, and love of an exotic past. A meticulous craftsman, he sought to create a prose style "as rhythmical as verse and as precise as the language of science." In the following letter to Turgenev, Flaubert expresses admiration for his friend's writing.]*

Dear Mr Turgenev,

How grateful I am for the gift you sent me! I have just read your two volumes [containing *Sportsman's Sketches, Rudin,* **"Diary of a Superfluous Man,"** and **"Three Encounters"**], and really must tell you that I am delighted with them.

I have considered you a master for a long time. But the more I study you, the more your skill leaves me gaping. I admire the vehement yet restrained quality of your writing, the fellow feeling that extends to the lowest of human creatures and brings landscapes to life. One perceives and one dreams.

Just as when I read *Don Quixote* I feel like going on horseback along a white and dusty road, like eating olives and raw onions in the shade of a cliff face, your **Scenes from Russian Life** make me want to be shaken alone in a telega through snow-covered fields, to the sound of wolves howling. Your work has a bittersweet flavour, a sadness that is delightful and penetrates to the very depths of my soul.

What an artist! What a mixture of emotion, irony, observation and colour! And how it is all blended together! How you achieve your effects! What mastery!

You manage to encompass general points while writing about the specific. How many things that I have felt and experienced myself have I found in your work! In **"Three Encounters"** amongst others, and especially in **Jacob Pasynkov,** in the **"Diary of a Superfluous Man,"** etc., everywhere.

But what has not received enough praise in your work is the heart, that is, a sustained emotion, an indefinable deep and secret sensibility. (pp. 38-9)

> *Gustave Flaubert, in a letter to Ivan Turgenev on March 16, 1863, in* Flaubert and Turgenev, a Friendship in Letters: The Complete Correspondence, *edited and translated by Barbara Beaumont, The Athlone Press, 1985, pp. 38-9.*

Henry James   (essay date 1883)

[James was an American-born English novelist, short story writer, critic, and essayist of the late nineteenth and early twentieth centuries. He is regarded as one of the greatest novelists of the English language and is also admired as a lucid and insightful critic. His commentary is informed by a receptivity to European culture, particularly English and French literature of the late nineteenth century. In the following excerpt from a review originally published in slightly different form in The North American Review, *April, 1874, James praises Turgenev's sensitivity, detailed observations, and*

sympathetic characterizations before briefly surveying the author's short fiction.]

[M. Turgénieff] belongs to the limited class of very careful writers. It is to be admitted at the outset that he is a zealous genius, rather than an abundant one. His line is narrow observation. He has not the faculty of rapid, passionate, almost reckless improvisation—that of Walter Scott, of Dickens, of George Sand. This is an immense charm in a story-teller; on the whole, to our sense, the greatest. Turgénieff lacks it; he charms us in other ways. To describe him in the fewest terms, he is a story-teller who has taken notes. This must have been a life-long habit. His tales are a magazine of small facts, of anecdotes, of descriptive traits, taken, as the phrase is, *sur le vif.* If we are not mistaken, he notes down an idiosyncrasy of character, a fragment of talk, an attitude, a feature, a gesture, and keeps it, if need be, for twenty years, till just the moment for using it comes, just the spot for placing it. . . . He has a passion for distinctness, for bringing his characterization to a point, for giving you an example of his meaning. He often, indeed, strikes us as loving details for their own sake, as a bibliomaniac loves the books he never reads. His figures are all portraits; they have each something special, something peculiar, something that none of their neighbours have, and that rescues them from the limbo of the gracefully general. We remember, in one of his stories, a gentleman who makes a momentary appearance as host at a dinner-party, and after being described as having such and such a face, clothes, and manners, has our impression of his personality completed by the statement that the soup at his table was filled with little paste figures, representing hearts, triangles, and trumpets. In the author's conception, there is a secret affinity between the character of this worthy man and the contortions of his vermicelli. This habit of specializing people by vivid oddities was the gulf over which Dickens danced the tight-rope with such agility. But Dickens, as we say, was an improvisatore; the practice, for him, was a lawless revel of the imagination. Turgénieff, on the other hand, always proceeds by book. What could be more minutely appreciative, and at the same time less like Dickens, than the following portrait?

> People in St. Petersburg still remember the Princess R———. She appeared there from time to time at the period of which we speak. Her husband was a well-bred man, but rather stupid, and she had no children. The Princess used to start suddenly on long journeys, and then return suddenly to Russia. Her conduct in all things was very strange. She was called light, and a coquette. She used to give herself up with ardour to all the pleasures of society: dance till she dropped with exhaustion, joke and laugh with the young men she received before dinner in her darkening drawing-room, and pass her nights praying and weeping, without finding a moment's rest. She often remained till morning in her room stretching her arms in anguish; or else she remained bowed, pale and cold, over the leaves of a hymn-book. Day came, and she was transformed again into an elegant creature, paid visits, laughed, chattered, rushed to meet everything that could give her the smallest diversion. She was admirably shaped. Her hair, the colour of gold, and as heavy as gold, formed a tress that fell below her knees. And yet she was not spoken of as a beauty: she had nothing fine in her face except her eyes. This even, perhaps, is saying too much, for her eyes were grey and rath-

er small; but their deep keen gaze, careless to audacity, and dreamy to desolation, was equally enigmatical and charming. Something extraordinary was reflected in them, even when the most futile speeches were passing from her lips. Her toilets were always too striking.

These lines seem to carry a kind of historical weight. It is the Princess R—— and no one else. We feel as if the author could show us documents and relics; as if he had her portrait, a dozen letters, some of her old trinkets. Or take the following few lines from the admirable tale called **"The Wayside Inn"**.

> He belonged to the burgher class, and his name was Nahum Ivanoff. He had a thick short body, broad shoulders, a big round head, long waving hair already grizzled, though he was not yet forty. His face was full and fresh-coloured; his forehead low and white. His little eyes, of a clear blue, had a strange look, at once oblique and impudent. He kept his head always bent, his neck being too short; he walked fast, and never let his hands swing, keeping them always closed. When he smiled, and he smiled often, but without laughing and as if by stealth, his red lips parted disagreeably, showing a row of very white, very close teeth. He spoke quickly, with a snarling tone.

When fiction is written in this fashion, we believe as we read. The same vividly definite element is found in the author's treatment of landscape. . . . There is an even greater reality, because it is touched with the fantastic, without being perverted by it, in this brief sketch of the Pontine Marshes, from the beautiful little story of **"Visions"**.

> The cloud before my eyes divided itself. I became aware of a limitless plain beneath me. Already, from the warm soft air which fanned my cheeks, I had observed that I was no longer in Russia. This plain, moreover, was not like our Russian plains. It was an immense dusky level, overgrown, apparently, with no grass, and perfectly desolate. Here and there, over the whole expanse, glittered pools of standing water, like little fragments of looking-glass. In the distance, the silent, motionless sea was vaguely visible. In the intervals of the broad beautiful clouds glittered great stars. A murmur, thousand-voiced, unceasing, and yet not loud, resounded from every spot; and strangely rang this penetrating, drowsy murmur, this nightly voice of the desert. . . . "The Pontine Marshes," said Ellis. "Do you hear the frogs? Do you recognise the sulphur?"

This is a cold manner, many readers will say, and certainly it has a cold side; but when the character is one over which the author's imagination really kindles, it is an admirable vehicle for touching effects. Few stories leave on the mind a more richly poetic impression than *Hélène* [*On the Eve*]; all the tenderness of our credulity goes forth to the heroine. Yet this exquisite image of idealized devotion swims before the author's vision in no misty moonlight of romance; she is as solidly fair as a Greek statue; his dominant desire has been to understand her, and he retails small facts about her appearance and habits with the impartiality of a judicial, or even a medical, summing-up. The same may be said of his treatment of all his heroines, and said in evidence of the refinement of his art; for if there are no heroines we see more distinctly, there are none we love more ardently. It would be difficult to point, in the

blooming fields of fiction, to a group of young girls more radiant with maidenly charm than M. Turgénieff's Hélène, his Lisa, his Katia, his Tatiana and his Gemma. For the truth is that, taken as a whole, he regains on another side what he loses by his apparent want of joyous invention. If his manner is that of a searching realist, his temper is that of an earnestly attentive observer, and the result of this temper is to make him take a view of the great spectacle of human life more general, more impartial, more unreservedly intelligent, than that of any novelist we know. Even in this direction he proceeds with his characteristic precision of method; one thinks of him as having divided his subject-matter into categories, and as moving from one to the other—with none of the magniloquent pretensions of Balzac, indeed, to be the great showman of the human comedy—but with a deeply intellectual impulse toward universal appreciation. He seems to us to care for more things in life, to be solicited on more sides, than any novelist save George Eliot. Walter Scott cares for adventure and bravery and honour and ballad-figures and the humour of Scotch peasants; Dickens cares, in a very large and various way, for the incongruous, comic and pathetic; George Sand cares for love and mineralogy. But these writers care also, greatly, and indeed almost supremely, for their fable, for its twists and turns and surprises, for the work they have in hand of amusing the reader. . . . M. Turgénieff lacks, as regards form, as we have said, this immense charm of absorbed inventiveness; but in the way of substance there is literally almost nothing he does not care for. Every class of society, every type of character, every degree of fortune, every phase of manners, passes through his hands; his imagination claims its property equally, in town and country, among rich and poor, among wise people and idiots, *dilettanti* and peasants, the tragic and the joyous, the probable and the grotesque. He has an eye for all our passions, and a deeply sympathetic sense of the wonderful complexity of our souls. He relates in **"Mumu"** the history of a deaf-and-dumb serf and a lap-dog, and he portrays in **"A Strange Story"** an extraordinary case of religious fanaticism. He has a passion for shifting his point of view, but his object is constantly the same—that of finding an incident, a person, a situation, *morally* interesting. This is his great merit, and the underlying harmony of his apparently excessive attention to detail. He believes the intrinsic value of "subject" in art; he holds that there are trivial subjects and serious ones, that the latter are much the best, and that their superiority resides in their giving us absolutely a greater amount of information about the human mind. Deep into the mind he is always attempting to look, though he often applies his eye to very dusky apertures. There is perhaps no better evidence of his minutely psychological attitude than the considerable part played in his tales by simpletons and weak-minded persons. . . . Almost always, in the background of his groups of well-to-do persons there lurks some grotesque, underwitted poor relation, who seems to hover about as a vague momento, in his scheme, of the instability both of fortune and of human cleverness. Such, for instance, is Uvar Ivanovitsch, who figures as a kind of inarticulate chorus in the tragedy of *Hélène*. He sits about, looking very wise and opening and closing his fingers, and in his person, in this attitude, the drama capriciously takes leave of us. Perhaps the most moving of all the author's tales—moving, not in the sense that it makes us shed easy tears, but as reminding us vividly of the solidarity, as we may say, of all human weakness—has for its hero a person made imbecile by suffering. The admirable little story of **"The Brigadier"** can only be spoilt by an attempt to retail it; we warmly recommend it to the reader, in the French version. Never did Romance stoop over a lowlier case of moral decomposition, but never did she gather more of the perfume of human truth. To a person able to read but one of M. Turgénieff's tales, we should perhaps offer this one as a supreme example of his peculiar power; for here the artist, as well as the analyst, is at his best. All rigid critical formulas are more or less unjust, and it is not a complete description of our author—it would be a complete description of no real master of fiction—to say that he is simply a searching observer. M. Turgénieff's imagination is always lending a hand and doing work on its own account. Some of this work is exquisite; nothing could have more of the simple magic of picturesqueness than such tales as **"The Dog," "The Jew," "Visions," "The Adventure of Lieutenant Jergounoff," "Three Meetings,"** a dozen episodes in the *Memoirs of a Sportsman.* Imagination guides his hand and modulates his touch, and makes the artist worthy of the observer. In a word, he is universally sensitive. In susceptibility to the sensuous impressions of life—to colours and odours and forms, and the myriad ineffable refinements and enticements of beauty—he equals, and even surpasses, the most accomplished representatives of the French school of story-telling; and yet he has, on the other hand, an apprehension of man's religious impulses, of the *ascetic* passion, the capacity of becoming dead to colours and odours and beauty, never dreamed of in the philosophy of Balzac and Flaubert, Octave Feuillet and Gustave Droz. He gives us Lisa in *A Nest of Noblemen,* and Madame Polosoff in *Spring-Torrents.* This marks his range. Let us add, in conclusion, that his merit of form is of the first order. He is remarkable for concision; few of his novels occupy the whole of a moderate volume, and some of his best performances are tales of thirty pages.

M. Turgénieff's themes are all Russian; here and there the scene of a tale is laid in another country, but the actors are genuine Muscovites. It is the Russian type of human nature that he depicts; this perplexes, fascinates, inspires him. His works savour strongly of his native soil, like those of all great novelists, and give one who has read them all a strange sense of having had a prolonged experience of Russia. We seem to have travelled there in dreams, to have dwelt there in another state of being. M. Turgénieff gives us a peculiar sense of being out of harmony with his native land—of his having what one may call a poet's quarrel with it. He loves the old, and he is unable to see where the new is drifting. American readers will peculiarly appreciate this state of mind; if they had a native novelist of a large pattern, it would probably be, in a degree, his own. Our author *feels* the Russian character intensely, and cherishes, in fancy, all its old manifestations—the unemancipated peasants, the ignorant, absolute, half-barbarous proprietors, the quaint provincial society, the local types and customs of every kind. But Russian society, like our own, is in process of formation, the Russian character is in solution, in a sea of change, and the modified, modernized Russian, with his old limitations and his new pretensions, is not, to an imagination fond of caressing the old, fixed contours, an especially grateful phenomenon. A satirist at all points, as we shall have occasion to say, M. Turgénieff is particularly unsparing of the

new intellectual fashions prevailing among his countrymen. (pp. 212-20)

It was not, however, in satire, but in thoroughly genial, poetical portraiture, that our author first made his mark. *The Memoirs of a Sportsman* were published in 1852, and were regarded, says one of the two French translators of the work, as much the same sort of contribution to the question of Russian serfdom as Mrs. Stowe's famous novel to that of American slavery. This, perhaps, is forcing a point, for M. Turgénieff's group of tales strikes us much less as a passionate *pièce de circonstance* than as a disinterested work of art. But circumstances helped it, of course, and it made a great impression—an impression that testifies to no small culture on the part of Russian readers. For never, surely, was a work with a polemic bearing more consistently low in tone, as painters say. The author treats us to such a scanty dose of flagrant horrors that the moral of the book is obvious only to attentive readers. No single episode pleads conclusively against the "peculiar institution" of Russia; the lesson is in the cumulative testimony of a multitude of fine touches—in an after-sense of sadness that sets wise readers thinking. It would be difficult to name a work that contains better instruction for those heated spirits who are fond of taking sides on the question of "art for art." It offers a capital example of moral meaning giving a sense to form and form giving relief to moral meaning. Indeed, all the author's characteristic merits are to be found in the *Memoirs* with a certain amateurish looseness of texture which will charm many persons who find his later works too frugal, as it were, in shape. Of all his productions, this is indeed the most purely delightful. We especially recommend [**"Foma, the Wolf"**], the little history of Foma, the forest-keeper, who, one rainy night, when the narrator has taken refuge in his hut, hears a peasant stealing faggots in the dark, dripping woods; rushes forth and falls upon him, drags the poor wretch home, flings him into a corner, and sits on in the smoky hovel (with the author, whom we perceive there, noting, feeling, measuring it all), while the rain batters the roof and the drenched starveling howls and whines and imprecates. Anything more dismally real in a narrower compass we have never read—anything more pathetic, with less of the machinery of pathos. In this case, as at every turn with M. Turgénieff, "It is life itself," we murmur as we read, "and not this or that or the other story-teller's more or less clever 'arrangement' of life." M. Turgénieff deserves this praise in its largest application; for "life" in his pages is very far from meaning a dreary liability to sordid accidents, as it seems to mean with those writers of the grimly pathetic school who cultivate sympathy to the detriment of comprehension. He does equal justice—joyous justice—to all brighter accidents—to everything in experience that helps to keep it within the pale of legend. Two of the Sportsman's reminiscences are inexpressibly charming— [**"Byezhin Prairie"**], in which he spends a warm summernight lying on the grass listening to the small boys who are sent out to watch the horses at pasture, as they sit chattering to each other of hobgoblins and fairies; and [**"The Singers,"** a] truly beautiful description of a singing-match in a village ale-house, between two ragged serfs. The latter is simply a perfect poem. Very different, but in its way as characteristic, is the story of **"A Russian Hamlet"**—a poor gentleman whom the Sportsman, staying overnight at a fine house where he has been dining, finds assigned to him as room-mate, and who, lying in bed and staring at him grotesquely over the sheets, relates his lugubrious history. This sketch, more than its companions, strikes the deep moral note that was to reverberate through the author's novels. (pp. 221-23)

[The novella *Spring-Torrents*] strikes us at first as a reproduction of old material, the subject being identical with that of *Smoke* and very similar to that of the short masterpiece called **"A Correspondence."** The subject is one of the saddest in the world, and we shall have to reproach M. Turgénieff with delighting in sadness. But *Spring-Torrents* has a narrative charm that sweetens its bitter waters, and we may add that, from the writer's point of view, the theme does differ by several shades from that of the tales we have mentioned. These treat of the fatal weakness of will that M. Turgénieff apparently considers the peculiar vice of the new generation in Russia; *Spring-Torrents* illustrates, more generally, the element of folly which mingles, in a certain measure, in all youthful spontaneity, and makes us grow to wisdom by the infliction of suffering. The youthful folly of Dmitri Sanin has been great; the memory of it haunts him for years and lays on him at last such an icy grip that his heart will break unless he can repair it. (pp. 236-37)

On his way back to Russia from a foreign tour he meets, at Frankfort, a young girl [Gemma] of modest origin but extraordinary beauty—the daughter of an Italian confectioner. Accident brings them together, he falls in love with her, holds himself ardently ready to marry her, obtains her mother's consent, and has only, to make the marriage possible, to raise money on his Russian property, which is of moderate value. While he is revolving schemes he encounters an old school-fellow, an odd personage, now married to an heiress who, as fortune has it, possesses an estate in the neighborhood of Sanin's own. It occurs to the latter that Madame Polosoff may be induced to buy his land, and, as she understands "business" and manages her own affairs, he repairs to Wiesbaden, with leave obtained from his betrothed, to make his proposal. The reader of course foresees the sequel—the reader, especially, who is versed in Turgénieff. Madame Polosoff understands business and much else besides. She is young, lovely, unscrupulous, dangerous, fatal. Sanin succumbs to the spell, forgets honour, duty, tenderness, prudence, everything, and after three days of bewildered resistance finds himself packed into the lady's travelling-carriage with her other belongings and rolling toward Paris. But we foresee that he comes speedily to his senses; the spring-torrent is spent. The years that follow are as arid as brooding penitence can make them. Penitence, after that night of bitter memories, takes an active shape. He makes a pilgrimage to Frankfort and seeks out some trace of the poor girl he had deserted. With much trouble he obtains tidings, and learns that she is married in America, that she is happy, and that she serenely forgives him. He returns to St. Petersburg, spends there a short, restless interval, and suddenly disappears. People say he has gone to America. The spring-torrents exhale themselves in autumn mists. Sanin, in the Frankfort episode, is not only very young, but very Russian; how young, how Russian, this charming description tells.

> He was, to begin with, a really very good-looking fellow. He had a tall, slender figure, agreeable, rather vague features, kindly blue eyes, a fair complexion suffused with a fresh red, and, above all that genial, joyous, confiding, upright expression, which at the first glance, perhaps, seems to give an air of limitation, but by which, in former times, you recognised the son of a tranquil aristocratic family—a son of the "fathers," a good country gentleman, born and grown up, stoutly, in those fruitful provinces of ours which border on the steppe; then a somewhat shuffling gait, a slightly lisping way of speaking, a childlike laugh as soon as any one looked at him,. . . . health, in short, freshness and a softness,—a softness!. . . . there you have all Sanin. Along with this he was by no means dull, and had learnt a good many things. He had remained fresh in spite of his journey abroad; those tumultuous impulses that imposed themselves upon the best part of the young men of that day were little known to him.

If we place beside this vivid portrait the sketch, hardly less expressive, of Madame Polosoff, we find in the mere apposition the germ of a novel.

> Not that she was a perfect beauty; the traces of her plebeian origin were perceptible enough. Her forehead was low, her nose rather thick and inclining to an upward inflection; she could boast neither of a fine skin nor of pretty hands and feet. But what did all this signify? Not before the 'sanctity of beauty'—to use Puschkin's words—would he who met her have stood lingering, but before the charm of the powerful half-Russian, half-Bohemian, blooming, womanly body—and he would not have lingered without a purpose.

Madame Polosoff, though her exploits are related in a short sixty-five pages, is unfolded in the large dramatic manner. We seem to be in her presence, to listen to her provoking, bewildering talk, to feel the danger of her audacious, conscious frankness. Her quite peculiar cruelty and depravity make a large demand on our credulity; she is perhaps a trifle too extravagantly vicious. But she is strangely, vividly natural, and our imagination goes with her in the same charmed mood as with M. Turgénieff's other evil-doers. Not without an effort, too, do we accept the possibility of Sanin's immediate infidelity to the object of the pure still passion with which his heart even yet overflows. But these are wonderful mysteries; its immediacy, perhaps, best accounts for it; spring-torrents, the author would seem to intimate, *must* flow, and ravage their blooming channels. To give a picture of the immeasurable blindness of youth, of its eagerness of desire, its freshness of impression, its mingled rawness and ripeness, the swarming, shifting possibilities of its springtime, and to interfuse his picture with something of the softening poetizing harmony of retrospect—this has been but half the author's purpose. He has designed beside to paint the natural conflict between soul and sense, and to make the struggle less complex than the one he has described in *Smoke,* and less brutal, as it were, than the fatal victory of sense in **"A Correspondence."** "When will it all come to an end?" Sanin asks, as he stares helpless at Maria Nikolaievna, feeling himself ignobly paralysed. "Weak men," says the author, "never themselves make an end—they always wait for the end." Sanin's history is weighted with the moral that salvation lies in being able, at a given moment, to turn on one's will like a screw. If M. Turgénieff pays his tribute to the magic of sense he leaves us also eloquently reminded that soul in the long run claims her own. He has given us no sweeter image of uncorrupting passion than this figure of Gemma, the frank young Italian nature blooming in northern air from its own mere wealth of joyousness. Yet, charming as Gemma is, she is but a half-sister to Lisa and Tatiana. Neither Lisa or Tatiana, we suspect, would have read popular comedy with her enchanting mimicry; but, on the other hand, they would have been withheld by a delicate, indefinable conscientiousness from caricaturing the dismissed lover of the day before for the entertainment of the accepted lover of the present. But Gemma is a charming piece of colouring, and all this only proves how many different ways there are of being the loveliest girl in the world. The accessories of her portrait are as happily rendered; the whole picture of the little Italian household, with its narrow backshop life, in the German town, has a mellow enclosed light in which the reader gratefully lingers. It touches the figure of the usual half-fantastic housefriend, the poor old ex-barytone Pantaleone Cippatola, into the most vivacious relief.

We always desire more information about the writers who greatly interest us than we find in their works and many American readers have probably a friendly curiosity as to the private personality of M. Turgénieff. We are reduced, however, to regretting our own meagre knowledge. We gather from his writings that our author is much of a cosmopolitan, a dweller in many cities and a frequenter of many societies, and, along with this, an indefinable sense of his being of a so-called "aristocratic" temperament; so that if a man's genius were visible to the eye, like his fleshly integument, that of M. Turgénieff would be observed to have, say, very shapely hands and feet, and a nose expressive of the patrician graces. A friend of ours, indeed, who has rather an irresponsible fancy, assures us that the author of *Smoke* (which he deems his masterpiece) is, personally, simply his own Pavel Kirsanoff. Twenty to one our friend is quite wrong; but we may nevertheless say that, to readers disposed now and then to risk a conjecture, much of the charm of M. Turgénieff's manner resides in this impalpable union of an aristocratic temperament with a democratic intellect. To his inquisitive intellect we owe the various, abundant, human substance of his tales, and to his fastidious temperament their exquisite form. But we must not meddle too freely with causes when results themselves are so suggestive. The great question as to a poet or a novelist is, How does he feel about life? what, in the last analysis, is his philosophy? When vigorous writers have reached maturity we are at liberty to look in their works for some expression of a total view of the world they have been so actively observing. This is the most interesting thing their works offer us. Details are interesting in proportion as they contribute to make it clear.

The foremost impression of M. Turgénieff's reader is that he is morbidly serious, that he takes life terribly hard. We move in an atmosphere of unrelieved sadness. We go from one tale to the other in the hope of finding something cheerful, but we only wander into fresh agglomerations of gloom. We try the shorter stories with a hope of chancing upon something pitched in the traditional key of "light reading," but they strike us alike as so many ingenious condensations of melancholy. **"A Village Lear"** is worse than **"The Antchar"**; **"The Forsaken"** is hardly an improvement on **"A Correspondence"**; **"The Journal of a Superfluous Man"** does little to lay the haunting ghost of **"Three Portraits."** The author has written several short dramas. Appealing to them to beguile us of our dusky vapours, we find the concentrated tragedy of **"The Bread**

of Charity," and, by way of an after-piece, the lugubrious humour of **"The Division."** Sad beginnings, worse endings, good people ineffably wretched, happy ones hugely ridiculous; disappointment, despair, madness, suicide, degrading passions, and blighted hopes—these seem, on first acquaintance, the chief ingredients of M. Turgénieff's version of the human drama; and to deepen our sense of its bitterness we discover the author in the background winding up his dismal demonstration with a chuckle. We set him down forthwith as a cold-blooded pessimist, caring for nothing in life but its misery and for nothing in misery but its pictorial effects—its capacity for furnishing cynical epigrams. What is each of the short tales we have mentioned, we ask, but a ruthless epigram, in the dramatic form, upon human happiness? Evlampia Charloff, in **"A Village Lear,"** drives her father to madness and death by her stony depravity, and then joins a set of religious fanatics, among whom she plays a great part as the "Holy Mother of God." In **"The Bread of Charity,"** a young heiress brings home to her estates her newly-wedded husband, and introduces him to her old neighbours. They dine with him, and one of them, an officious coxcomb, conceives the brilliant idea of entertaining him by an exhibition of a poor old gentleman who has long been hanging about the place as a pensioner of the late parents of the young wife, and is remarkable for a dumb canine attachment to herself. The heartless guest plies the modest old man with wine, winds him up and makes him play the fool. But suddenly Kusofkin, through the fumes of his potations, perceives that he is being laughed at, and breaks out into a passionate assurance that, baited and buffeted as he is, he is nothing less than the father of the mistress of the house. She overhears his cry, and though he, horrified at his indiscretion, attempts to retract it, she wins from him a confession of the fact that he had been her mother's lover. The husband, however, makes him swallow his words, and do public penance. He turns him out of the house with a small pension, and the curtain falls on the compliment offered this fine fellow by the meddlesome neighbour on his generosity: "You are a true Russian gentleman!" The most perfectly epigrammatic of our author's stories, however, is perhaps that polished little piece of misery, **"A Correspondence."** A young man, idle, discontented, and longing for better things, writes, for a pastime, to a young girl whom he has formerly slightly known and greatly esteemed, who has entertained an unsuspected and unrequited passion for him, and who lives obscurely in the country, among very common people. A correspondence comes of it, in the course of which they exchange confidences and unburden their hearts. The young girl is most pitiable, most amiable, in her sadness, and her friend begins to suspect that she, at last, may give a meaning to his aimless life. She, on her side, is compassionately interested, and we see curiosity and hope throbbing timidly beneath the austere resignation to which she had schooled herself, and the expression of which, mingled with our sense of her blooming beauty of character, makes of Maria Alexandrovna the most nobly fascinating, perhaps, of our author's heroines. Alexis Petrovitsch writes at last that he must see her, that he will come to her, that she is to expect him at such a date, and we imagine tenderly, in the unhastening current of her days, the gentle eddy of her expectation. Her next letter, after an interval expresses surprise at his non-appearance; her next, several months later, is a last attempt to obtain news of him. The correspondence closes with his confession, written as he lies dying at Dresden. Just as he was starting to join her, he had encountered another woman, a dancing-girl at the opera, with whom he had fallen madly in love. She was low, stupid, heartless; she had nothing to recommend her to anything but his senses. It was ignoble, but so it was. His passion has led him such a life that his health is gone. He has brought on disease of the lungs, by waiting for the young lady at the opera-door in the winter nights. Now his hours are numbered, and this is the end of all! And on this lugubrious note the story closes. We read with intent curiosity, for the tale is a masterpiece of narration; but we wonder, in some vexation, what it all means. Is it a piece of irony for irony's sake, or is it a disinterested picture of the struggle between base passion and pure passion? Why, in that case, should it seem a matter of course for the author that base passion should carry the day? . . . If we pursue our researches, in the hope of finding some method in this promiscuous misery, examples continue to seem more numerous than principles. The author continues everywhere to imply that there is something essentially ridiculous in human nature, something indefeasibly vain in human effort. We are amazed, as we go, at the portentous number of his patent fools; no novelist has drawn a tenth as many. The large majority of his people are the people we laugh at, and a large fraction of the remainder the people we half disgustedly pity. There is little room left, therefore, for the people we esteem, and yet room enough perhaps, considering that our very benevolence is tempered with scepticism. What with the vicious fools and the well-meaning fools, the prosperous charlatans and the grotesque nonentities, the dead failures and the sadder failures that regret and protest and rebel, the demoralized lovers and the jilted maidens, the dusky pall of fatality, in a word, suspended over all human things, it may be inferred that we are not invited to a particularly exhilarating spectacle. . . . We lay down the book, and we repeat that, with all the charity in the world, it is impossible to pronounce M. Turgénieff anything better than a pessimist.

The judgment is just, but it needs qualifications, and it finds them in a larger look at the author's position. M. Turgénieff strikes us, as we have said, as a man disappointed, for good reasons or for poor ones, in the land that is dear to him. Harsh critics will say for poor ones, reflecting that a fastidious imagination has not been unconcerned in his discontentment. To the old Muscovite virtues, and especially the old Muscovite *naïveté,* his imagination filially clings, but he finds these things, especially in the fact that his country turns to the outer world, melting more and more every day into the dimness of tradition. The Russians are clever, and clever people are ambitious. Those with whom M. Turgénieff has seen himself surrounded are consumed with the desire to pass for intellectual cosmopolites, to know, or seem to know, everything that can be known, to be astoundingly modern and progressive and European. . . . An imaginative preference for dusky subjects is a perfectly legitimate element of the artistic temperament; our own Hawthorne is a signal case of its being innocently exercised; innocently, because with that delightfully unconscious genius it remained imaginative, sportive, inconclusive, to the end. When external circumstances, however, contribute to confirm it, and reality lays her groaning stores of misery at its feet, it will take a rarely elastic genius altogether to elude the charge of being morbid. M. Turgénieff's pessimism seems to us of two

sorts—a spontaneous melancholy and a wanton melancholy. Sometimes in a sad story it is the problem, the question, the idea, that strikes him; sometimes it is simply the picture. Under the former influence he has produced his masterpieces; we admit that they are intensely sad, but we consent to be moved, as we consent to sit silent in a death-chamber. In the other case he has done but his second best; we strike a bargain over our tears, and insist that when it comes to being simply entertained, wooing and wedding are better than death and burial. **"The Antchar," "The Forsaken," "A Superfluous Man," "A Village Lear," "Toc . . . toc . . . toc,"** all seem to us to be gloomier by several shades than they need have been; for we hold to the good old belief that the presumption, in life, is in favour of the brighter side, and we deem it, in art, an indispensable condition of our interest in a depressed observer that he should have at least tried his best to be cheerful. The truth, we take it, lies for the pathetic in poetry and romance very much where it lies for the "immoral." Morbid pathos is reflective pathos; ingenious pathos, pathos not freshly born of the occasion; noxious immorality is superficial immorality, immorality without natural roots in the subject. We value most the "realists" who have an ideal of delicacy and the elegiasts who have an ideal of joy.

"Pictorial gloom, possibly," a thick and thin admirer of M. Turgénieff's may say to us, "at least you will admit that it *is* pictorial." This we heartily concede, and, recalled to a sense of our author's brilliant diversity and ingenuity, we bring our restrictions to a close. To the broadly generous side of his imagination it is impossible to pay exaggerated homage, or, indeed, for that matter, to its simple intensity and fecundity. No romancer has created a greater number of the figures that breathe and move and speak, in their habits as they might have lived; none, on the whole, seems to us to have had such a masterly touch in portraiture, none has mingled so much ideal beauty with so much unsparing reality. His sadness has its element of error, but it has also its larger element of wisdom. Life *is,* in fact, a battle. On this point optimists and pessimists agree. Evil is insolent and strong; beauty enchanting but rare; goodness very apt to be weak; folly very apt to be defiant; wickedness to carry the day; imbeciles to be in great places, people of sense in small, and mankind generally, unhappy. But the world as it stands is no illusion, no phantasm, no evil dream of a night; we wake up to it again for ever and ever; we can neither forget it nor deny it nor dispense with it. We can welcome experience as it comes, and give it what it demands, in exchange for something which it is idle to pause to call much or little so long as it contributes to swell the volume of consciousness. In this there is mingled pain and delight, but over the mysterious mixture there hovers a visible rule, that bids us learn to will and seek to understand. So much as this we seem to decipher between the lines of M. Turgénieff's minutely written chronicle. He himself has sought to understand as zealously as his most eminent competitors. He gives, at least, no meagre account of life, and he has done liberal justice to its infinite variety. This is his great merit; his great defect, roughly stated, is a tendency to the abuse of irony. He remains, nevertheless, to our sense, a very welcome mediator between the world and our curiosity. If we had space, we should like to set forth that he is by no means our ideal story-teller—this honourable genius possessing, attributively, a rarer skill than the finest required for producing an artful *réchauffé* of the actual. But even for better romancers we must wait for a better world. Whether the world in its higher state of perfection will occasionally offer colour to scandal, we hesitate to pronounce; but we are prone to conceive of the ultimate novelist as a personage altogether purged of sarcasm. The imaginative force now expended in this direction he will devote to describing cities of gold and heavens of sapphire. But, for the present, we gratefully accept M. Turgénieff, and reflect that his manner suits the most frequent mood of the greater number of readers. If he were a dogmatic optimist we suspect that, as things go, we should long ago have ceased to miss him from our library. The personal optimism of most of us no romancer can confirm or dissipate and our personal troubles, generally, place fictions of all kinds in an impertinent light. To our usual working mood the world is apt to seem M. Turgénieff's hard world, and when, at moments, the strain and the pressure deepen, the ironical element figures not a little in our form of address to those short-sighted friends who have whispered that it is an easy one. (pp. 238-52)

Henry James, "Ivan Turgenieff," in his French Poets and Novelists, *Bernhard Tauchnitz, 1883, pp. 211-52.*

Edward Garnett   (essay date 1917)

[*Garnett was a prominent editor for several London publishing houses who discovered or greatly influenced the work of many important English writers, including Joseph Conrad, John Galsworthy, and D. H. Lawrence. He also published several volumes of criticism. In the following excerpt, Garnett offers a chronological survey and appraisal of Turgenev's short stories.*]

In addition to his six great novels Turgenev published, between 1846 and his death in 1883, about forty tales which reflect as intimately social atmospheres of the 'thirties, 'forties and 'fifties as do Tchehov's stories atmospheres of the 'eighties and 'nineties. Several of these tales, as *The Torrents of Spring,* are of considerable length, but their comparatively simple structure places them definitely in the class of the *conte.* While their form is generally free and straightforward, the narrative, put often in the mouth of a character who by his comments and asides exchanges at will his active rôle for that of a spectator, is capable of the most subtle modulations. An examination of the chronological order of the tales shows how very delicately Turgenev's art is poised between realism and romanticism. In his finest examples, such as **"The Brigadier"** and **"A Lear of the Steppes,"** the two elements fuse perfectly, like the meeting of wave and wind in sea foam. "Nature placed Turgenev between poetry and prose," says Henry James [see excerpt dated 1883]; and if one hazards a definition we should prefer to term Turgenev *a poetic realist.* (pp. 163-64)

[In 1846] appeared **"The Jew,"** a close study, based on a family anecdote, of Semitic double-dealing and family feeling: also **"Three Portraits,"** a more or less faithful ancestral chronicle. This latter tale, though the hero is of the proud, bad, "Satanic" order of the romantic school, is firmly objective, as is also **"Pyetushkov,"** whose lively, instinctive realism is so bold and intimate as to contradict the compliment that the French have paid themselves—

that Turgenev ever had need to dress his art by the aid of French mirrors.

Although **"Pyetushkov"** shows us, by a certain open *naïveté* of style, that a youthful hand is at work, it is the hand of a young master carrying out Gogol's satiric realism with finer point, to find a perfect equilibrium free from bias or caricature. The essential strength of the realistic method is developed in **"Pyetushkov"** to its just limits, and note it is the Russian realism carrying the warmth of life into the written page, which warmth the French so often lose in clarifying their impressions and crystallizing them in art. Observe how the reader is transported bodily into Pyetushkov's stuffy room, how the Major fairly boils out of the two pages he lives in, and how Onisim and Vassilissa and the aunt walk and chatter around the stupid Pyetushkov, and laugh at him behind his back in a manner that exhales the vulgar warmth of these people's lower-class world. One sees that the latter holds few secrets for Turgenev. . . . [In 1844] had appeared **"Andrei Kolosov,"** a sincere diagnosis of youth's sentimental expectations, raptures and remorse, in presence of the other sex, in this case a girl who is eager for a suitor. The sketch is characteristically Russian in its analytic honesty, but Turgenev's charm is here lessened by his overliteral exactitude. And passing to **"The Diary of a Superfluous Man,"** we must remark that this famous study of a type of a petty provincial Hamlet reveals a streak of suffused sentimentalism in Turgenev's nature, one which comes to the surface the more subjective is the handling of his theme, and the less his great technical skill in *modelling* his subject is called for. The last-named story belongs to a group with which we must place *Faust, Yakov Pasinkov,* **"A Correspondence,"** and even the tender and charming *Acia,* all of which stories, though rich in emotional shades and in beautiful descriptions, are lacking in fine chiselling. The melancholy yearning of the heroes and heroines through failure or misunderstanding, though no doubt true to life, seems to-day too imbued with emotional hues of the Byronic romanticism of the period, and in this small group of stories Turgenev's art is seen definitely dated, even old-fashioned.

In **"The Country Inn,"** we are back on the firm ground of an objective study of village types, with clear, precise outlines, a detailed drawing from nature, strong yet subtle; as is also **"Mumu,"** one based on a household episode that passed before Turgenev's youthful eyes, in which the deaf-mute Gerassim, a house serf, is defrauded first of the girl he loves, and then of his little dog, Mumu, whom he is forced to drown, stifling his pent-up affection, at the caprice of his tyrannical old mistress. The story is a classic example of Turgenev's tender insight and beauty of feeling. As delicate, but more varied in execution is **"The Backwater,"** with its fresh, charming picture of youth's *insouciance* and readiness to take a wrong turning, a story which in its atmospheric freshness and emotional colouring may be compared with Tchehov's studies of youth in *The Seagull,* a play in which the neurotic spiritual descendants of Marie and Nadejda, Veretieff and Steltchinsky, appear and pass into the shadows. This note of the fleetingness of youth and happiness reappears in **"A Tour of the Forest,"** where Turgenev's acute sense of man's ephemeral life in face of the eternity of nature finds full expression. The description, here, of the vast, gloomy, murmuring pine forest, with its cold, dim solitudes, is finely contrasted with the passing outlook of the peasants, Yegor, Kondrat, and the wild Efrem.

The rich colour and perfume of Turgenev's delineation of romantic passion are disclosed when we turn to *First Love,* which details the fervent adoration of Woldemar, a boy of sixteen, for the fascinating Zinaida, an exquisite creation, who, by her mutability and caressing, mocking caprice keeps her bevy of eager suitors in suspense till at length she yields herself in her passion to Woldemar's father. . . . Here we tremble on the magic borderline between prose and poetry, and the fragrance of blossoming love instincts is felt pervading all the fluctuating impulses of grief, tenderness, pity and regret which combine in the tragic close. The profoundly haunting apostrophe to youth is indeed a pure lyric. Passing to **"Phantoms,"** . . . the truth of Turgenev's confession that spiritually and sensuously he was saturated with the love of woman and ever inspired by it, is confirmed. In his description of Alice, the winged phantom-woman, who gradually casts her spell over the sick hero, luring him to fly with her night after night over the vast expanse of earth, Turgenev has in a mysterious manner, all his own, concentrated the very essence of woman's possessive love. Alice's hungry yearning for self-completion, her pleading arts, her sad submissiveness, her rapture in her hesitating lover's embrace, are artistically a sublimation of all the impressions and instincts by which woman fascinates, and fulfils her purpose of creation. The projection of this shadowy woman's love-hunger on the mighty screen of the night earth, and the merging of her power in men's restless energies, felt and divined through the sweeping tides of nature's incalculable forces, is an inspiration which, in its lesser fashion, invites comparison with Shakespeare's creative vision of nature and the supernatural.

In his treatment of the supernatural Turgenev, however, sometimes missed his mark. **"The Dog"** is of a coarser and indeed of an ordinary texture. With the latter story may be classed **"The Dream,"** curiously Byronic in imagery and atmosphere, and artistically not convincing. Far more sincere, psychologically, is **"Clara Militch,"** a penetrating study of a passionate temperament, a story based on a tragedy of Parisian life. In our opinion **"The Song of Triumphant Love,"** though exquisite in its jewelled mediaeval details, has been overrated by the French, and Turgenev's genius is here seen contorted and cramped by the *genre.*

To return to the tales of the 'sixties. **"Lieutenant Yergunov's Story,"** though its strange atmosphere is cunningly painted, is not of the highest quality, comparing unfavourably with **"The Brigadier,"** the story of the ruined nobleman, Vassily Guskov, with its tender, sub-ironical studies of odd characters, Narkiz *and* Cucumber. **"The Brigadier"** has a peculiarly fascinating poignancy, and must be prized as one of the rarest of Turgenev's high achievements, even as the connoisseur prizes the original beauty of a fine Meryon etching. The tale is a microcosm of Turgenev's own nature; his love of Nature, his sympathy with all humble, ragged, eccentric, despised human creatures, his unfaltering, keen gaze into character, his perfect eye for relative values in life, all mingle in **"The Brigadier"** to create for us a sense of the vicissitudes of life, of how a generation of human seed springs and flourishes awhile on earth and soon withers away under the menacing gaze of the advancing years.

A complete contrast to **"The Brigadier"** is the sombre and savagely tragic piece of realism, **"An Unhappy Girl."** As a study of a coarse and rapacious nature the portrait of Mr. Ratsch, the Germanized Czech, is a revelation of the depths of human swinishness. Coarse malignancy is here "the power of darkness" which closes, as with a vice, round the figure of the proud, helpless, exquisite girl, Susanna. There is, alas, no exaggeration in this unrelenting, painful story. The scene of Susanna's playing of the Beethoven sonata (chapter xiii.) demonstrates how there can be no truce between a vile animal nature and pure and beautiful instincts, and a faint suggestion symbolic of the national "dark forces" at work in Russian history deepens the impression. The worldly power of greed, lust and envy, ravaging, whether in war or peace, which seize on the defenceless and innocent, as their prey, here triumphs over Susanna, the victim of Mr. Ratsch's violence. The last chapter, the banquet scene, satirizes "the dark forest" of the heart when greed and baseness find their allies in the inertness, sloth or indifference of the ordinary man.

"A Strange Story" has special psychological interest for the English mind in that it gives clues to some fundamental distinctions between the Russian and the Western soul. Sophie's words, "You spoke of the will—that's what must be broken," seems strange to English thought. To be lowly, to be suffering, despised, to *be* unworthy, this desire implies that the Slav character is apt to be lacking in *will,* that it finds it easier to resign itself than to make the effort to be triumphant or powerful. The Russian people's attitude, historically, may, indeed, be compared to a bowl which catches and sustains what life brings it; and the Western people's to a bowl inverted to ward off what fate drops from the impassive skies. The mental attitude of the Russian peasant indeed implies that in blood he is nearer akin to the Asiatics than the Russian ethnologists wish to allow. Certainly in the inner life, intellectually, morally and emotionally, the Russian is a half-way house between the Western and Eastern races, just as geographically he spreads over the two continents.

Brilliant also is **"Knock-Knock-Knock,"** a psychological study, of "a man fated," a Byronic type of hero, dear to the heart of the writers of the romantic period. Sub-Lieutenant Teglev, the melancholy, self-centered hero, whose prepossession of a tragic end nothing can shake, so that he ends by throwing himself into the arms of death, this portrait is most cunningly fortified by the wonderfully life-like atmosphere of the river fog in which the suicide is consummated. Turgenev's range of mood is disclosed in **"Punin and Baburin,"** a leisurely reminiscence of his mother's household; but the delicious blending of irony and kindness in the treatment of both Punin and Baburin atones for the lengthy conclusion. . . . In considering **"A Lear of the Steppes,"** *The Torrents of Spring* and **"A Living Relic,"** we shall sum up here our brief survey of Turgenev's achievement in the field of the *conte.*

In *The Torrents of Spring* the charm, the grace, the power of Turgenev's vision are seen bathing his subject, revealing all its delicate lineaments in a light as fresh and tender as that of a day of April sunlight in Italy. *Torrents* of Spring, not Spring Floods, be it remarked, is the true significance of the Russian, telling of a moment of the year when all the forces of Nature are leaping forth impetuously, the mounting sap, the hill streams, the mating birds, the blood

in the veins of youth. The opening perhaps is a little over-
leisurely, this description of the Italian confectioner's family, and its fortunes in Frankfort, but how delightful is the
contrast in racial spirit between the pedantic German
shop-manager, Herr Klüber and Pantaleone, and the lovely Gemma. But the long opening prelude serves as a foil
to heighten the significant story of the seduction of the
youthful Sanin by Maria Nikolaevna, that clear-eyed
"huntress of men"; one of the most triumphant feminine
portraits in the whole range of fiction. The spectator feels
that this woman in her ruthless charm is the incarnation
of a cruel principle in Nature, while we watch her preparing to strike her talons into her fascinated, struggling prey.
Her spirit's essence, in all its hard, merciless joy of conquest, is disclosed by Turgenev in his rapid, yet exhaustive
glances at her disdainful treatment of her many lovers,
and of her cynical log of a husband. The extraordinarily
clear light in the narrative, that of spring mountain air,
waxes stronger towards the climax, and the artistic effort
of the whole is that of some exquisite Greek cameo, with
figures of centaurs and fleeing nymphs and youthful shepherds; though the postscript indeed is an excrescence
which detracts from the main impression of pure, classic
outlines.

Not less perfect as art though far slighter in scope is the
exquisite **"A Living Relic,"** one of the last of *A Sportsman's Sketches.* Along with the narrator we pass, in a
step, from the clear sunlight and freshness of early morning, "when the larks' songs seemed steeped in dew," into
the "little wattled shanty with its burden of a woman's suffering," poor Lukerya's, who lies, summer after summer,
resigned to her living death. . . . (pp. 164-75)

Lukerya tells her story. How one night she could not
sleep, and, thinking of her lover, rose to listen to a nightingale in the garden; how half-dreaming she fell from the top
stairs—and now she lives on, a little shrivelled mummy.
Something is broken inside her body, and the doctors all
shake their heads over her case. Her lover, Polyakov, has
married another girl, a good sweet woman. "He couldn't
stay a bachelor all his life, and they have children."

And Lukerya? All is not blackness in her wasted life. She
is grateful for people's kindness to her. . . . She can hear
everything, see everything that comes near her shed—the
nesting swallows, the bees, the doves cooing on the roof.
Lying alone in the long hours she can smell every scent
from the garden, the flowering buckwheat, the lime tree.
The priest, the peasant girls, sometimes a pilgrim woman,
come and talk to her, and a little girl, a pretty, fair little
thing, waits on her. She has her religion, her strange
dreams, and sometimes, in her poor, struggling little voice
that wavers like a thread of smoke, she tries to sing, as of
old. But she is waiting for merciful death—which now is
nigh her.

Infinitely tender in the depth of understanding is this gem
of art, and **"A Living Relic's"** perfection is determined by
Turgenev's scrutiny of the warp and woof of life, in which
the impassive forces of Nature, indifferent alike to human
pain or human happiness, pursue their implacable way,
weaving unwittingly the mesh of joy, anguish, resignation,
in the breast of all sentient creation. It is in the *spiritual
perspective* of the picture, in the vision that sees the whole
in the part, and the part in the whole, that Turgenev so
far surpasses all his European rivals.

To those critics, Russian and English, who naïvely slur
over the aesthetic qualities of a masterpiece, such as **"A
Lear of the Steppes,"** or fail to recognize all that aesthetic
perfection implies, we address these concluding remarks.
"A Lear of the Steppes" is great in art, because it is a living organic whole, springing from the deep roots of life itself; and the innumerable works of art that are fabricated
and pasted together from an ingenious plan—works that
do not grow from the inevitability of things—appear at
once insignificant or false in comparison.

In examining the art, the artist will note Turgenev's method of introducing his story. Harlov, the Lear of the story,
is brought forward with such force on the threshold that
all eyes resting on his figure cannot but follow his after-
movements. And absolute conviction gained, all the artist's artful after-devices and subtle presentations and side-
lights on the story are not apparent under the straightforward ease and the seeming carelessness with which the
narrator describes his boyish memories. Then the inmates
of Harlov's household, his two daughters, and a crowd of
minor characters, are brought before us as persons in the
tragedy, and we see that all these people are living each
from the innate laws of his being, apparently independently of the author's scheme. This conviction, that the author
has no prearranged plan, convinces us that in the story we
are living a piece of life: here we are verily plunging into
life itself.

And the story goes on flowing easily and naturally till the
people of the neighbourhood, the peasants, the woods and
fields around, are known by us as intimately as is any
neighbourhood in life. Suddenly a break—the tragedy is
upon us. Suddenly the terrific forces that underlie human
life, even the meanest of human lives, burst on us astonished and breathless, precisely as a tragedy comes up to
the surface and bursts on us in real life: everybody runs
about dazed, annoyed, futile; we watch other people sustaining their own individuality inadequately in the face of
the monstrous new events which go their fatal way logically, events which leave the people huddled and useless and
gasping. And destruction having burst out of life, life
slowly returns to its old grooves—with a difference to us,
the difference in the relation of people one to another that
a death or a tragedy always leaves to the survivors. Marvellous in its truth is Turgenev's analysis of the situation
after Harlov's death, marvellous is the simple description
of the neighbourhood's attitude to the Harlov family, and
marvellous is the lifting of the scene on the after-life of
Harlov's daughters. In the pages . . . on these women,
Turgenev flashes into the reader's mind an extraordinary
sense of the inevitability of these women's natures, of their
innate growth fashioning their after-lives as logically as a
beech puts out beech-leaves and an oak oak-leaves.
Through Turgenev's single glimpse at their fortunes one
knows the whole intervening fifteen years; he has carried
us into a new world; yet it is the old world; one needs to
know no more. It is life arbitrary but inevitable, life so
clarified by art that it is absolutely interpreted; but life
with all the sense of mystery that nature breathes around
it in its ceaseless growth.

This sense of inevitability and of the mystery of life which
Turgenev gives us in **"A Lear of the Steppes"** is the highest demand we can make from art. If we contrast with it
two examples of Turgenev's more "romantic" manner,

Acia, though it gives us a sense of mystery, is not inevitable: the end is *faked* to suit the artist's purpose, and thus, as in other ways, it is far inferior to **"Lear,"** *Faust* has consummate charm in its strange atmosphere of the supernatural mingling with things earthly, but it is not, as is **"A Lear of the Steppes,"** life seen from the surface to the revealed depths; it is a revelation of the strange forces in life, presented beautifully; but it is rather an idea, a problem to be worked out by certain characters, than a piece of life inevitable and growing. When an artist creates in us the sense of inevitability, then his work is at its highest, and is obeying Nature's law of growth, unfolding from out itself as inevitably as a tree or a flower or a human being unfolds from out itself. Turgenev at his highest never quits Nature, yet he always uses the surface, and what is apparent, to disclose her most secret principles, her deepest potentialities, her inmost laws of being, and whatever he presents he presents clearly and simply. This combination of powers marks only the few supreme artists. Even great masters often fail in perfect *naturalness:* Tolstoy's *The Death of Ivan Ilytch,* for instance, one of the most powerful stories ever written, has too little of what is typical of the whole of life, too much that is strained towards the general purpose of the story, to be perfectly *natural.* Turgenev's special feat in fiction is that his characters reveal themselves by the most ordinary details of their everyday life; and while these details are always giving us the whole life of the people, and their inner life as well, the novel's significance is being built up simply out of these details, built up by the same process, in fact, as Nature creates for us a single strong impression out of a multitude of little details.

Again, Turgenev's power as a poet comes in, whenever he draws a commonplace figure, to make it bring with it a sense of the mystery of its existence. In **"Lear"** the steward Kvitsinsky plays a subsidiary part; he has apparently no significance in the story, and very little is told about him. But who does not perceive that Turgenev looks at and presents the figure of this man in a manner totally different from the way any clever novelist of the second rank would look at and use him? Kvitsinsky, in Turgenev's hands, is an individual with all the individual's mystery in his glance, his coming and going, his way of taking things; but he is a part of the household's breath, of its very existence; he breathes the atmosphere naturally and creates an atmosphere of his own.

It is, then, in his marvellous sense of the growth of life that Turgenev is superior to most of his rivals. Not only did he observe life minutely and comprehensively, but he reproduced it as a constantly growing phenomenon, growing naturally, not accidentally or arbitrarily. For example, in *A House of Gentlefolk,* take Lavretsky's and Liza's changes of mood when they are falling in love with one another; it is Nature herself in them changing very delicately and insensibly; we feel that the whole picture is alive, not an effect cut out from life, and cut off from it at the same time, like a bunch of cut flowers, an effect which many clever novelists often give us. And in **"Lear"** we feel that the life in Harlov's village is still going on, growing yonder, still growing with all its mysterious sameness and changes, when, in Turgenev's last words, "The storyteller ceased, and we talked a little longer, and then parted, each to his home." (pp. 176-83)

Edward Garnett, in his Turgenev: A Study, *W. Collins Sons & Co., Ltd., 1917, 206 p.*

Vladimir Fisher   (essay date 1920)

[In the following excerpt taken from a book-length study originally published in Russian in 1920, Fisher offers an objective survey of Turgenev's short fiction and insists, contrary to popular critical opinion, that fate plays as great a role as the destructive love impulse in the downfall of Turgenev's protagonists.]

Turgenev's novels have overshadowed his stories. And in general, the latter were somehow unlucky. The critics, in the person of Belinsky, met the first story [**"Andrey Kolosov"**] rather coldly. The success of *Notes of a Hunter* at the end of the 1840s and the beginning of the 1850s prevented the public and the critics from appreciating the great merits of the stories. The reflected light of the fame of *Notes of a Hunter* fell on two of the stories—**"Mumu"** and **"The Inn."** But after that began the era of the novels, which happened to coincide with the blossoming of the Turgenev story. But the vivid social significance of the novels crowded the stories out of the foreground. True, our socially minded critics noted some stories, but more was said apropos of them than about them . . . ; some stories provoked bewilderment (**"Phantoms,"** **"Enough,"** **"The Dog"**); others enjoyed success among the public as entertaining reading (**"The Song of Triumphant Love"**); they were always published enthusiastically in journals, they were translated, but they were little studied.

In the scholarly literature that has arisen recently, the stories have been addressed in order to treat questions of one sort or another that occur in connection with the study of the writer's worldview . . . or of his "manner." . . .

But the Turgenev story has its special interest if only because it is the product of the writer's pure inspiration, which does not lay claim here to the solution of any social questions, for which solution, in the opinion of certain people, Turgenev had no gift.

The autobiographical significance of Turgenev's stories, however, has been established, although hardly studied thoroughly. The writer's declaration that his entire biography is in his works relates primarily and especially to his stories. He himself pointed especially to the story *First Love.* But that does not mean that the Turgenev story is of purely subjective origin. On the contrary, its interest is more objective, and the subjective image in the story stands not in the foreground, but, for the most part, at a double or triple remove: the person in whom we recognize the author is often the witness in a story, the observer, the narrator, but not the hero. The author draws not so much on experiences from his own life as on observations.

If one looks at Turgenev's stories from the biographical point of view, one will have to single out, in the first place, those that treat family legends and the author's family recollections; the first such story in time is **"Three Portraits,"** which treats the author's ancestors on his maternal side; the figure of his mother is encountered, as is well known, in the stories **"Mumu,"** **"A King Lear of the Steppe,"** and **"Punin and Baburin"**; that of his father, in the story *First Love.*

Other stories shed light on the author's school years: the narrator or hero is a university student or preparing to be one, and, moreover, at Moscow University; the author's brief stay at the latter left an incomparably greater mark on his artistic memory than did his stay at Saint Petersburg University, about which so much is said in "Memoirs of Literature and Life." But a Moscow coloration prevails in a great number of Turgenev's stories, beginning with **"Andrey Kolosov"** and ending with **"Klara Milich,"** and also forms an organic part of the majority of his novels.

The stories in a third category cover the "years of wandering": the narrator or hero travels abroad, as Turgenev himself travelled after finishing his education; these are **"Three Meetings,"** *Asya,* and ***Spring Freshets,*** the autobiographical nature of which has been established.

The other stories are probably also autobiographical to a certain degree, although that is more difficult to establish, so varied is their coloration.

Establishing the autobiographical element in Turgenev's stories is extraordinarily important for elucidating the process of their creation, but not for elucidating their essence: Turgenev's stories do not give a sequential history of the author's inner life, as do Tolstoy's works. Personal recollections, meetings, and observations only gave Turgenev the material out of which there arose something, but in its essence something different from poetic autobiography. (pp. 43-5)

The autobiographical origin of the majority of Turgenev's stories affects their form noticeably: the majority of them (twenty-five out of thirty-four) are narrated in the first person, while in the novels, whose plots are for the most part invented, that form of narration is not encountered. At the same time, the first person in the story is not the main person, and often is quite peripheral. But the author needs him for the form, and he, the author, expends considerable energy to create him, and in such a way that the reader does not confuse him with the author. . . .

Thus, Turgenev, while needing the fiction of narrators, is anxious in every way to leave him in the shade, not to introduce him into the plot if at all possible, and not to restrict himself with his manner. In fact only in a few stories is the narrator the main person, for instance, *Asya;* in the majority of instances he plays a secondary role, as in the story *Yakov Pasynkov,* or he plays no role at all other than that of a viewer, observer, witness, for instance, **"The Brigadier."**

And nonetheless in the corpus of Turgenev's stories autobiographical or subjective traits appear every now and then; now we see a young master, the son of a female estate owner, then a young university student, now a traveller, then a hunter, now simply an elderly tall gentleman with graying hair. From time to time the narrator is a mouthpiece for the author's worldview or the author's artistic credo.

But there are quite objective narrator characters too: such is the Kaluga estate owner Porfiry Kapitonych (**"The Dog"**), the priest (**"Father Alexey's Story"**), and the old man (**"The Watch"**). There are absolutely undistinguished, fictional narrators, for instance, Mr. X (**"A Strange Story"**).

Turgenev's lack of desire to imitate a narrator's manner does not come, of course, from an inability to create experiments such as Karl Ivanovich's story in Tolstoy. A superb authority on mores, Turgenev has a masterful command of other people's speech and knows how to convey its slightest nuances, including pronunciation.

But poetic autobiography is present in Turgenev's stories only as an element and does not comprise their essence. Cultural realia, which saturate many of Turgenev's stories, are an element and a material, too, but cultural realia do not comprise their essence either. . . . One additional surface aspect of Turgenev's stories that ought to be recognized as such is the socio-historical element. In telling about Sanin and Gemma's love (***Spring Freshets***), the writer notes the awkwardness that Sanin feels when the prospect of selling his peasants presents itself to him. It is clear that this has very slight relation to the story's plot. But it is remarkable that Turgenev always dates his narratives precisely and indicates the place of action precisely. In general, that is the accepted practice in historical novels; it is also understandable that Turgenev indicates the years in his novels, which depict a specific moment in the history of educated Russian society. But what need have we to know that the action of the story **"Klara Milich"** transpires precisely in 1878?

In Turgenev the reader almost always learns in what year, or at least in what decade the action transpires. We learn that the action of **"The Desperado"** takes place in 1829, that of *First Love* in 1833, that of **"A Misfortunate Girl"** in 1835, that Sanin meets Gemma in 1840, and that he is 22 then, that **"A Correspondence"** relates to the years 1840-42, the action of *Faust* to 1850. The separate parts of the story **"Punin and Baburin"** are headed with figures: "1836," "1837," "1849," and "1861." Moreover, the time is marked by historical and historico-literary information. The story **"The Jew"** coincides with the forays abroad after the War of 1812; **"The Watch,"** with Alexander I's ascension to the throne; Baburin's exile, with the arrests that raged in 1849. The action of *First Love* occurs right "at the height of romanticism"; that of **"A Misfortunate Girl,"** at the time when Pushkin's Onegin is fresh in everyone's memory; **"Knock—Knock—Knock"** relates to the time of Marlinsky's great renown; Gemma reads Malss, a Frankfurt writer of the 1840s; the reader always knows what the heroes of a story read and what their literary tastes are: that characterizes them and the time. But, of course, only in part. So be it that Sanin was born in 1818, loves Gemma in 1840, reads Malss with her and contemplates selling his peasants. But if he had been born in 1848 and in 1870 loved a Gemma who was born later, the essence of their love would remain the same: the only difference would be that they would read someone other than Malss, and Sanin would have had to sell his estate instead of live people. Why does Turgenev need this chronology and illusion?

It is an almost unprecedented phenomenon. . . . This "historicity" of Turgenev's stories is only a surface aspect, an element, material, like autobiography and cultural realia. It is not an artistic necessity, but it is, for Turgenev, a psychological one.

In order to understand this, one must turn to those stories that happen to lack this chronology. These are primarily those stories that are the almost unmediated expression of the author's worldview—**"Phantoms," "Enough,"** and **"A Dream."** Here Turgenev's creativity is bared; here those "surface aspects" that were mentioned earlier do not turn up.

First, there is nothing autobiographical here: the author conveys his own attitude and worldview, true, but a general one that is not linked to any particular moment in his personal life.

Second, there are no conditions of place here, that is, cultural realia. In this regard, an especially interesting example is the story **"A Dream,"** where there is not even a single name, but human relations are shown in their essence.

Third, there are no conditions of time here: no dates, no historical or historico-literary information.

And in order to understand the Turgenev story at all, one has to disengage oneself from the autobiographical element, from cultural realia, from the historical background, because none of these things is of the essence; it is essential to contemplate human relations presented by Turgenev in the purity in which they are shown in the story **"A Dream."**

Thus, a Turgenev story's main interest is psychological and philosophical, although only in a few cases are the philosophy and psychology not made up in the colors of place and time.

In the story **"Phantoms"** precisely the absolute freedom from the fetters of time and space is observed. Ellis carries the hero off to distant places and distant eras. The result is horror, melancholy, despair. . . .

Of course the essence of Sanin and Gemma's relations [in *Spring Freshets*] would remain the same in another era as well, but Turgenev wants to see them alive; and for that he needs specifically Frankfurt, specifically 1840, Gemma's Italian gestures, and the reading of Malss, specifically Malss, not of Sudermann.

Nature as an elemental force, as a substance, is horrible. And life in its essence is petty, boring, flat, and terrifying in that there is nothing terrifying in it. But

> Look around—and the everyday world
> Is multicolored and marvellous

And so, fettering a person to a place, fixing him in the framework of chronological dates, and observing him in that little corner, after forgetting about the infinity that surrounds him—that is Turgenev's artistic mission.

"Stay!" he exclaims in the *Poems in Prose,* "remain forever in my memory as I now see you!" Another feature of Turgenev's worldview that influences the concepts of his stories in a specific way is a distinctive fatalism. While seeing only a phenomenon in the individual human, Turgenev sees a substance in human life, in the life of the masses. The aggregate life of people is such a complex combination of individual wills, such an interweaving of intersecting aspirations, that it is ruled by chance, which is not envisioned by any individual consciousness and for which no individual principle can establish norms. An individual thrown into the mass is powerless, like a straw in the wind, like a raindrop in a current: the drops create the current, but each individual drop is completely in the power of the current. Turgenev's most powerful poem, "The Crowd,"

expresses this sad capitulation of the individual to the mass.

An individual in an elemental mass of other individuals is given up to chance. The story **"Three Meetings"** is built on the play of chance. But in portraying life in general, Turgenev often ponders *"the mysterious play of fate* that we blind ones call blind chance" (*Faust*). "Neither can one alter one's *fate,* nor does anyone know himself, and besides, it's also impossible to foresee the future. In reality, nothing else happens in life except the *unexpected,* and we spend our whole lives doing nothing but accommodating ourselves to events" (**"A Correspondence"**).

Chance rules in life. Chance sends Vyazovnin to Paris, where he so stupidly runs up against a sword; chance brings Alexey Petrovich (**"A Correspondence"**) to the ballet, where he falls in love with a ballerina; chance brings N. N. together with Asya, Sanin with Gemma; chance turns Ridel's joke into the fatal reason for Teglev's suicide (**"Knock—Knock—Knock"**); chance governs the watch that invades the lives of the boys (**"The Watch"**); but fate often peeps out from behind chance. . . .

Therefore the life of an individual is not defined by his character. By virtue of his position an individual is inevitably passive; the active principle is the reality surrounding him. The perceived opinion about a weakness of will as the main trait of Turgenev's heroes has begun to waver recently. It is not weakness of will that makes many of Turgenev's heroes impotent in life and "superfluous," but something else, located outside themselves—fate.

In the story **"The Watch,"** the narrator's father, a minor business agent, after quarreling with his friend Latkin, curses him.

> Fate itself seemed intent upon discharging my father's last wish. Soon after the rupture . . . Latkin's wife, who, true, had been ill a long while, died; his second daughter, a three-year-old child, went deaf and dumb from terror in a single day: a beehive had gotten stuck around her head; Latkin himself had an apoplectic stroke and fell into extreme poverty.

No matter how Lavretsky's break with his wife may be motivated psychologically, one should not forget his Aunt Glafira's curse: "You won't make a nest for yourself anywhere!" In the story **"The Inn"** there is also the fickle finger of fate: Naum, who gets the inn through deceit, keeps being lucky; but

> after being a successful manager for some fifteen years, he arranged to sell his inn at a profit to another petty bourgeois. He would never have parted with his fortune if the following apparently insignificant circumstance had not occurred: for two mornings in a row his dog, sitting in front of the windows, howled long and plaintively; he went out onto the street for the second time, took a good look at the howling dog, shook his head, set off for town, and on that very day agreed on a price with the petit bourgeois who had long wanted to buy the inn. A week later he left for somewhere far away— outside the province; the new owner moved in, and what do you think? That same evening the inn burned down, not a single closet survived, and Naum's successor was left a beggar.

Fate sends Porfiry Kapitonych, a Kaluga estate owner

with a bald spot and a belly, a dog who perishes after playing a definite role in his life (**"The Dog"**). The same fate sends Lukeria (**"Living Relics"**) a disease and turns her from a "giggler, singer, dancer" into a saint.

Lukeria believes that that is God; but it is an unjust god who at the same time has a beehive get stuck to an innocent child's head; it is a god who gives Naum success in unfair business practices but punishes the innocent petty bourgeois who buys the inn from him; it is a god who manifests incomprehensible sympathy for Porfiry Kapitonych; it is a god who listens attentively to the curses of evil people, not the prayers of the good. His whims resemble those of the crotchety old woman who causes the mute Gerasim suffering (**"Mumu"**).

In Turgenev there are no people who forge their own happiness: all are blamelessly guilty, lucky without reason. All are doomed. That is precisely what a Turgenev story tells about. Generally speaking, it tells about how an outside force irrupts into a person's life, takes him into its universe, throws him here and there according to its arbitrary rule, and, finally, casts the shipwrecked person up unto his bank as a pathetic piece of debris. Moreover, fate does not reckon with a given person's predisposition toward one thing or another, but imposes a role upon him that is often beyond his strength. You would think him a Gogolian hero, but an adventure in the spirit of Pechorin happens to him.

So, Lieutenant Yergunov [in **"Lieutenant Yergunov's Story"**], a blood brother of Gogol's Zhevakin, has an adventure reminiscent of Lermontov's story "Taman."

Aratov, a relative of Podkolyosin, experiences a mysterious poem of love with a mystical ending (**"Klara Milich"**). (pp. 45-50)

Turgenev portrays the contact of tawdry people with the romance of life, of shallow and weak people with the mystery of love, and of sober people with the mysteries of nature.

In accordance with this, three moments are distinguishable in a Turgenev story:

> (1) The norm. The depiction of an individual in the ordinary conditions of life in which another writer would in fact leave that person, for instance, Goncharov.
>
> (2) The catastrophe. The violation of the norm thanks to the incursion of unforeseen circumstances that do not arise from the given situation.
>
> (3) The finale. The end of the catastrophe and its psychological consequences.

The moments are laid out in just such a sequence in, for instance, the story *Asya,* where N. N.'s trip is the norm; the catastrophe, his love for Asya; and the finale, N. N.'s lonely old age.

But these moments may follow in reverse sequence: the finale, that is, the depiction of the consequence of the catastrophe, may be at the beginning; then follows the story of the norm and of the catastrophe that came after it. The story **"A Correspondence,"** for instance, is composed in that way, where the hero's death is told at the beginning, and then the norm unfolds from his correspondence—his

relations with Marya Alexandrovna; and the catastrophe—his affair with the French singer.

The repetition of similar moments sometimes occurs in one and the same story: a finale turns into a norm which, in turn, is violated by a second recurrent catastrophe, which leads to a new finale.

That is how the story **"A Dream"** is constructed. The first norm here is the narrator's parents' happy, easygoing trip, about which his mother tells him later (chapter 9); the catastrophe is the appearance of the stranger, who becomes the narrator's father; the finale is the ruined life described at the beginning of the story, in the first chapter. That finale has turned into a norm. The new appearance of the stranger and his death comprise the second catastrophe in the story, which brings with it a new finale that comprises the contents of the last fragment of the story (beginning with the words "My mother and I never spoke of him"). (pp. 50-1)

The moment in a Turgenev story that I have called the norm consists of a realistic depiction of the hero's circumstances of life. These norms can be reduced to several types. The main ones are the following:

> (1) The narrator of the hero of the story is a student or preparing to be one; he lives in Moscow more or less independently, more or less sociably.
>
> (2) The narrator or hero of the story travels abroad, without definite aims.
>
> (3) The narrator or the hero of the story arrives in his village on business or as a consequence of the absence of business.

The transition from the norm to the catastrophe is accomplished by Turgenev with the help of a plot that provides the story's surface interest. The appearance of a female character usually serves to put the plot in motion. The moment of the appearance by the woman—usually the one who enters the room—is a very important turning point in the story. If the norm is portrayed for the most part realistically, then the plot intrigue is distinguished by its romantic character. The female character who appears in Turgenev is almost always full of enigmatic, mysterious, enticing beauty. Moreover, she stands in contradiction to the surrounding milieu. . . . The question of how that creature could turn up in this milieu arises; interest is aroused, the story's tempo increases. This tension is already felt in the conveying of the impression made by the heroine's appearance: it stuns, amazes, strikes, and rivets the narrator to the spot. The center of attention from that moment on is the female character, and the narrator's role is unimportant: he may be the hero of the story, like Sanin, or the hero of *Asya,* or he may remain an accomplice, a go-between, a witness, as in the stories **"A Misfortunate Girl," "Punin and Baburin."**

And so, the realistic exposition in a Turgenev story represents a sort of thesis; the romantic plot intrigue, which thanks to the realistic grounding, accounts for the whole effect of the story, an antithesis.

The further transition to the catastrophe forms the synthesis. The female character does not remain a romantic daydream: having surprised the reader, she gradually stands out in bolder and bolder relief, becoming persuasive and lifelike. The realistic writer comes into his own. Upon the hero or narrator's close acquaintance with the heroine, the realistic and almost always wretched, sometimes difficult conditions of her life come to light. At home Zinaida (*First Love*) has decay, slovenly poverty, and a vulgar mother with an inclination to malicious litigation. Asya is the illegitimate daughter of an estate owner and has grown up in extremely abnormal conditions. . . . Finally, the enchanting Gemma (*Spring Freshets*), a representative of the petit bourgeoisie, the fiancée of the solid merchant Klyber, called upon to use her beauty to save her impoverished family's situation, and later—the wife of an American businessman. When her mother discusses quite practically the benefits of her marriage to Sanin, in the presence of the latter, Gemma feels extremely awkward.

However, a female character does not always initiate the intrigue in a Turgenev story; sometimes an animal (twice a dog, once a horse), sometimes things (**"The Watch"**) are the instrument of fate that brings on the catastrophe. But no matter what, the plot intrigue is always romantically unexpected; as is well known, Turgenev took special pains with it, finding that the absence of "invention" was the weak side of Russian writers. As Gutyar notes quite justly, the outline of a Turgenev work "is suggested only in part by the fate of those people who served as the prototypes of the story's protagonists." As applied to a Turgenev story, the term "catastrophe" does not have quite the same meaning as in a tragedy.

There is little of the tragedic in Turgenev, or the tragic in his works consists of the absence of tragedy where it ought to be, of the fact that the most terrible thing in life is that there is nothing terrible. But the term "catastrophe" is applicable here because what happens to Turgenev's protagonists bears the imprint of fate: both good fortune, which they are incapable of apprehending adequately, and misfortune, which turns out to be beyond their powers. The mother's story in **"A Dream"** is characteristic in this regard.

She is alone in a hotel room—her husband has gone to the club; she goes to bed. "And suddenly she felt so awful that she even turned cold all over and began to shiver. She thought she heard a light knocking behind the wall—the way a dog scratches—and she began watching that wall. An icon camp burned in the corner; the room was hung all around with damask. Suddenly something moved over there, rose a bit, opened up. And all black, long, that horrible man with the evil eyes came right out of the wall! She wanted to cry out and could not. She froze in fear. He came up to her quickly, like a beast of prey, threw something over her head, something stifling, heavy, white."

And so, that is how fate functions. Its emissaries penetrate walls covered with damask in which unclean doors are revealed. The turning point in the story is quite unreal. But Turgenev's devices are bared in general in **"A Dream,"** and if one ponders the essence of life's phenomena, the stranger's emergence from the wall is not the least bit any stranger than the appearance first of Gemma in Sanin's life, and then of Marya Nikolaevna; it is just that in the latter instance a realistic motivation is given such as is lacking in the first.

It has already been noted more than once that for Turgenev the supreme confirmation of the individual is love, and

Portrait of Pauline Viardot, a close friend of Turgenev.

that at the same time love is a pernicious, destructive, and dangerous force. Fate lures Turgenev's heroes into a whirlwind of passion, and whether they want that or not, it leaves them no choice: if they meet it head on, ruin and devastation threaten them; if they lack courage, they will be punished—by the misery of later regrets, like the hero of *Asya*, by the horror of emptiness and the fear of death, like Sanin, or a rejected love will make its claims on them from beyond the grave, as happens to the hero of **"Klara Milich."**

However, there are people on whom fate does not bestow its attention. There is a certain level of life, a fullness of sensations, to which not everyone is capable of rising. Only a person who rises to that point will experience life in full measure, but he will also drink the bitter cup of suffering; only with the level of passion do life and beauty begin. The idyll that Turgenev paints in the story **"Old Portraits,"** an idyll of old-world land owners, does not move him; Malanya Pavlovna's impenetrable stupidity, which her loving husband is also aware of, does not increase the delight of the idyll; and the fact with which the story ends destroys the idyll. In the story **"Two Friends"** that tranquil life is established in the finale: good Verochka, with her phlegmatic right, remains deaf to the language of passion, marries a husband once "without rapture," then marries a second time, to a person more comprehensible to her. "Pyotr Vasilievich, his wife, and all their domestics spend the time very monotonously—peacefully and quietly; they enjoy their happiness, *because on earth there is no other happiness.*" A specter of life, however, arises above theirs, and that is the memory of Vyazovnin; but he, himself incapable of rising to the level of passion, has flashed by in their life like a shadow, and they remain on the bottom. No catastrophe has occurred.

A catastrophe is possible only for those people who have the attributes necessary for reaching life in its fullness, even though they may have no desire to do so: passion nevertheless will pull them into the whirlpool. In the story *Faust,* Vera, thanks to her mother's efforts, has been seemingly insured against the element of passion since childhood. Its most powerful conductor, art, was removed. Vera leaves for the canopy of a marriage "without rapture," like Verochka; but a person from another world, with a copy of Goethe's *Faust* in his hands, turns up and "ploughed up raging voices" in the young woman. . . .

Real life prudently creates one marriage; fate, the romance of life, erects above it its own mighty superstructure, which crushes that marriage.

But the topic here has been individuals unwillingly carried away by passion, who shun it out of "fear" or good sense. There are those who play with fire, who set out into the ocean of passion without worrying about an anchor. Such is Zinaida (*First Love*). But the highest degree is to accept the cup of life without faint-hearted fear, but to limit oneself to the lofty commands of duty. Such is Yakov Pasynkov, who has made denial his principle. Those who have not stood at the necessary height also come to this conclusion. "Life is hard work. Denial, constant denial—that is its secret meaning, its unriddling: not the fulfilling of favorite ideas and dreams, no matter how elevated they might be, but the fulfilling of duty—that is what a person should worry about; without putting chains on himself, the iron chains of duty, he cannot reach the end of his days without falling." Only if a person is anchored to duty will he not be swept away by a catastrophe. (pp. 51-5)

The catastrophic nature of events in Turgenev's stories is often overshadowed by descriptions of storms; they are rather frequent (**"A Quiet Spot," *Faust, Spring Freshets,* "A Dream"**). And where there is no storm or tempest, it is overshadowed with the help of similes and metaphors. . . .

The storm of life, the storm of passion does its work and leaves debris. The debris of life's storm includes Chulkaturin, the heroine of **"Three Meetings,"** Alexey Petrovich of **"A Correspondence,"** the hero of *Faust,* Zinaida of *First Love,* the Brigadier, King Lear of the Steppe, and Sanin. Others perish, like the baron in the story **"A Dream,"** or Vera (*Faust*), or the hero of the story **"Klara Milich."** Others remain debris; moreover, something from the past remains in their hands, a romantic recollection. . . . (p. 55)

Vladimir Fisher, "Story and Novel in Turgenev's Work," translated by David A. Lowe, in Critical Essays on Ivan Turgenev, *edited by David A. Lowe, G. K. Hall & Co., 1989, pp. 43-62.*

Charles Morgan   (lecture date 1947)

[*Morgan was an English novelist and critic. The essay excerpted below was originally delivered as a memorial lecture on June 11, 1947, in honor of Lieutenant Gifford Edmonds, a soldier killed in battle during World War II. Here, Morgan uses Turgenev's novella* First Love *to refute critical charges that Turgenev's works present a sentimental or romanticized view of reality, contending that the story offers an honest and truthful rendition of life.*]

It is remarkable that, throughout the Western world, there is to-day a renewed interest in Turgenev, for, in more ways than one, Turgenev is a "test case." Our judgment of him must govern many other of our judgments in literature and in life. To recognize him as a great master is to profess our adherence to certain values which, taken together, almost define civilization itself; to shrug our shoulders at him, to think of him as a romantic aesthete whose work is no longer relevant to us, is, in effect, to renounce Western civilization as an inheritance from Greece and from Christianity, and to adopt an altogether different view of the nature of man and of his place in the scheme of things. (p. 102)

Turgenev was of an aristocratic, not of a vulgar or, even, a popular mind. He was of a romantic, aesthetic and highly individualistic temperament. He was not a successful pamphleteer, or even, at heart, an ardent reformer. He was much more interested in the strange variability of the human, and particularly the feminine, intelligence and passion than he was in any collective plan for our improvement.

I am sure that there are some who will, therefore, frown upon him, and think that I am playing my cards very badly when I recommend him to a modern audience in these terms. They are entitled to frown; their brows, high or low, are their own to do with what they will; but they must not expect us yet, in this country, to fall into the totalitarian habit of praising artists for the wrong reasons. Therefore I repeat that though, by the standards of his time, Turgenev was presumably pink, I do not put that forward as a sop to Russophils. Indeed, I regard it as irrelevant. It is of much more interest to observe uncompromisingly that he was indeed aristocratic, romantic, aesthetic, highly individualistic, and that, in spite of this or because of it, his works, after a long period of neglect, are, in England, in France and in America, being everywhere retranslated, republished and newly discussed.

That is why I said at the outset that Turgenev was a "test case," and why I believe that his treatment of love—that is to say, of human nature, as he saw it, in its loveliest, its most tragic, its most fateful, and always its most revealing imaginative essence—is the key to the whole matter: the evidence upon which his case (and, by implication, the test case of civilization itself) is to be decided.

Let me, in order to be plain, state the issue in crude simplicity. If, when you see a woman, whether she be peasant or lady, what you are interested in is her uniqueness and the mystery of creation implied in that uniqueness; if the impulse of your mind is not to obliterate her uniqueness in a group or a category, but to emphasize it by entering into her being and re-imagining it from the inside outwards; if she is, for you, in her virtues and sins, her wisdom and follies, a private and a holy thing, and holy because private; if in her age you can read her childhood, in her gaiety her seriousness, in her sin her innocence, in her failure her aspiration, and even in her stupidities her dreams; if, in her flesh, her spirit appears; if, therefore, her love is, for you, an image, held for however brief an instant in however dark a mirror, of her immortality, and not simply a part of her animalism; if love is an emblem of wonder, of breed, of distinctiveness, and not a dull mechanism of repetitive fecundity; if to that extent and in that way you are in charity with your neighbour, then you are a romantic, you are a Turgenevian. But if, when you see a woman, whether she be peasant or lady, she is for you primarily a numbered inmate of the economic concentration camp and her love a compulsion to replenish it with slaves, then you are not a Turgenevian. This is the issue, and this is why an examination of Turgenev's treatment of love is, I think, of more than academic interest. It was for him, as it was for Keats, a key to life. We have to decide whether the key is truly made, whether it turns in the lock, and whether, when the door opens—if it does open—a real world or, as Turgenev's detractors say, a falsely romantic world, is revealed. It may also be of interest to look over the locksmith's shoulder and observe his craftsmanship.

This examination might be made in three ways. We might conduct an encyclopaedic study of his complete works—"had we but world enough and time." I should attempt to seduce you by exhaustive quotation, "and you should, if you please, refuse till the conversion of the Jews." A second expedient would be to attempt the encyclopaedic method, with one eye on the clock, to rush in panic from volume to volume, to illustrate arguments with instances of which only very devoted Turgenevians carry the context in their heads, and to sink down in the end, as so many lecturers do, panting and exhausted, in an entanglement of half-considered trifles. A third method, which I hope you will allow me to adopt, is to choose one masterpiece and concentrate upon it; to thank heaven that it is short and its anecdote simple—for nothing is more tedious than the retelling of an elaborate plot; to call in other witnesses as a matter of convenience now and then; but to invite you to consider Turgenev's method chiefly in the light of this one story.

It may be justly objected that, in other stories, altogether different characters are concerned in altogether different circumstances, and it is true that, if I were a German professor and you were a German audience, we should not venture to build our house upon so simple a plan or, as the Germans would say, upon so narrow a foundation. But as we are unregenerate English; and as, I think, the foundation, though small, is pretty deep; and as, after all, this is Wednesday afternoon and the sun is shining, let us take our chance. Let us examine the story called *First Love*. There are three good reasons for clinging to it: that it is enchanting; that it is the only story in the world of which I am prepared to say that it is flawless; and that it is the only story of Turgenev's of which I can hope, as a result of much industry, to pronounce the Russian names without being sent to the bottom of the class.

The story is told by Vladimir Petrovitch, remembering his youth, and this is how it begins:

> I was sixteen then. It happened in the summer of 1833.

I lived in Moscow with my parents. They had taken a country house for the summer near the Kalouga gate, facing the Neskutchny gardens. I was preparing for the university, but did not work much and was in no hurry.

No one interfered with my freedom . . .

You will see at once what I meant when I said that the story was flawless. When we remember how many stories, in order to be impressive or mysterious, in order, perhaps, to avert a charge of being old-fashioned, begin with elaborately confused dialogue between persons unknown, in a place unknown, at a time unknown, and leave us to fog it all out half-way through the second chapter, what a relief it is to observe the simplicity of the great masters attack:

> On an evening in the latter part of May a middle-aged man was walking homeward from Shaston to the village of Marlott . . .

—that is Hardy.

> Happy families are all alike; every unhappy family is unhappy in its own way. Everything was in confusion in the Oblonskys' house. The wife had discovered that the husband was carrying on an intrigue with a French girl . . .

—that is Tolstoy, not a supreme formalist as Turgenev was, but just as careful to be plain at the outset, to engage the reader's attention, to inform him quite simply of what is afoot.

Turgenev sometimes allows himself a little prelude in which to introduce a narrator, but his opening of his main story has always the same firmness and lucidity.

> It was in the summer of 1840. Sanin was in his twenty-second year, and he was in Frankfurt on his way home from Italy to Russia . . .

—that is the beginning of *The Torrents of Spring*. But, it may be asked, is there only one way to begin a story? No: there are a thousand ways. . . . To choose it rightly is the hardest of all our tasks. To begin too soon or to begin too late is the greatest of all our confusions. But once that choice is rightly made—(and Turgenev's choice was always accurate; he is never to be seen floundering in too much retrospect or starving for lack of it)—then, I believe, that there is a rule: namely, to establish, with the greatest possible economy of means, the place, the persons and the time; to arouse the reader's attention; and to announce the theme.

Turgenev's theme, in the story we are considering, is a double one: youth itself, the feel of being young and alive; and love. He loses no time in saying so; he never, never commits the sin of confusing a reader, of leaving him to wonder what the story is about and what he, Turgenev, is driving at. Vladimir Petrovitch has a horse to ride:

> I used to saddle it myself and set off alone for long rides, break into a rapid gallop and fancy myself a knight in a tournament.

That indicates at once the youthfulness of the young man and the fate that awaits him, for a knight in a tournament presupposes a lady whose favour he wears. Already, because Turgenev chose that brilliantly accurate phrase, we see the gleam of her eyes—but not yet the lady; she is anonymous; she is felt to exist, but her universality is as yet not limited—is not "crystallized," as Stendhal would have said—in a personality and a name. This is deliberate. In holding his heroine back, Turgenev is doing much more than prepare an entrance for her; he is making it clear that what he is writing about is love itself, and femininity itself, and not only a particular animal passion. So, in his next paragraph, he continues:

> I remember that at that time the image of woman, the vision of love, scarcely ever arose in definite shape in my brain; but in all I thought, in all I felt, lay hidden a half-conscious, shamefaced presentiment of something new, unutterably sweet, feminine. . . . This presentiment, this expectation, permeated my whole being; I breathed in it, it coursed through my veins with every drop of blood . . . it was destined to be soon fulfilled.

It was destined to be very soon fulfilled. Turn one page, and you are plunged into the enchantment. Near to the house in which Vladimir Petrovitch and his parents were living that summer was a dilapidated lodge. This had been rented by an impoverished Princess Zasyekin, herself *une femme très vulgaire* but the widow of an aristocrat. The gardens were separated by a fence, and Vladimir Petrovitch was in the habit of wandering about his garden every evening on the look-out for rooks. Now observe Turgenev's magic—how, in a few lines, he communicates, not a photograph of the girl, scarcely even a sketch of her character and appearance, and yet what I can only call the *flash* of her, and how that flash fires the trail in Vladimir Petrovitch, and how the flame leaps and runs within him.

> Suddenly I heard a voice; I looked across the fence, and was thunder-struck. . . . I was confronted with a curious spectacle.
>
> A few paces from me on the grass between the green raspberry bushes stood a tall slender girl in a striped pink dress, with a white kerchief on her head; four young men were close round her, and she was slapping them by turns on the forehead with those small grey flowers, the name of which I don't know, though they are well known to children; the flowers form little bags, and burst open with a pop when you strike them against anything hard. The young men presented their foreheads so eagerly, and in the gestures of the girl (I saw her in profile), there was something so fascinating, imperious, caressing, mocking, and charming, that I almost cried out with admiration and delight, and would, I thought, have given everything in the world on the spot only to have had those exquisite figures strike me on the forehead. My gun slipped on to the grass, I forgot everything, I devoured with my eyes the graceful shape and neck and lovely arms and the slightly disordered fair hair under the white kerchief, and the half-closed clever eye, and the eyelashes and the soft cheek beneath them. . . .
>
> "Young man, hey, young man," said a voice suddenly near me: "Is it quite permissible to stare so at unknown young ladies?"
>
> I started, I was struck dumb. . . . Near me, the other side of the fence, stood a man with close-cropped black hair, looking ironically at me. At the same instant the girl too turned towards me. . . . I caught sight of big grey eyes in a bright mobile

face, and the whole face suddenly quivered and laughed, there was a flash of white teeth, a droll lifting of the eye-brows. . . . I crimsoned, picked up my gun from the ground, and pursued by a musical but not ill-natured laugh, fled to my own room, flung myself on the bed, and hid my face in my hands. My heart was fairly leaping; I was greatly ashamed and overjoyed; I felt an excitement I had never known before.

> After a rest, I brushed my hair, washed, and went downstairs to tea. The image of the young girl floated before me, my heart was no longer leaping, but was full of a sort of sweet oppression.

"Full of a sort of sweet oppression." Remember Keats's phrase, describing the impact upon him of such a girl: "I feel escaped from a new and threatening sorrow. . . . There is an awful warmth about my heart like a load of immortality." (pp. 105-10)

Let me now glance here and there at Turgenev's development of his heroine, who is Zinaïda Alexandrovna, the old princess's daughter. As the tale is told by Vladimir in the first person, we see her always from the outside, and yet what we chiefly see is not her outside, but a glow from within her. Next morning Vladimir Petrovitch is sent with a message to the dilapidated lodge. He is presented to Zinaïda and she carries him off to wind wool. She is twenty-one, he sixteen; she laughs at him a little for being so young and he pretends to be older than he is.

> She was sitting with her back to a window covered with a white blind. . . . "And here I am sitting before her," I thought; "I have made acquaintance with her . . . what happiness, my God!" I could hardly keep from jumping up from my chair in ecstasy, but I only swung my legs a little, like a small child who has been given sweetmeats.

Then a young hussar comes and gives Zinaïda a kitten.

> "For the kitten—your little hand," said the hussar, with a simper and a shrug of his strongly-built frame, which was tightly buttoned up in a new uniform.
>
> "Both," replied Zinaïda, and she held out her hands to him. While he was kissing them, she looked at me over his shoulder. I stood stockstill . . .

It is a small but perfect instance of what I mean when I say—and I am afraid I have said it often—that an artist's duty is not to teach, to persuade, not even to describe, but to impregnate the imagination of a reader; to draw back a curtain and to say: "Look out, there is Zinaïda; see her with your own eyes! . . . Look out, there is a world to be created; create it yourself!" "While he was kissing them, she looked at me over his shoulder." How? With what expression? With what glance? Provocatively? Derisively? Affectionately? Gaily? Sadly? We are not told. Any adverb would have spoiled that effect—would have "exteriorized" us, would have made us observers of the outside of Zinaïda instead of drawing us into her, and compelling us, if we would see at all, to look out of her eyes, and to see, over the hussar's shoulder but from within her soul, Vladimir Petrovitch standing "stockstill." And any adverb would, correspondingly, have narrowed our sense of that glance's effect on Vladimir Petrovitch. Turgenev knows how to leave well alone. (pp. 110-11)

Soon afterwards the old Princess and her daughter dine at the Voldemars', and we receive Turgenev's first clear indication, very subtly conveyed, that what he is writing is not only a sketch of idealistic first-love, but a profound tragi-comedy of passion and the slavery of passion. Vladimir Petrovitch's mother, after the manner of mothers on such occasions, does not approve of her visitors, certainly not of Zinaïda.

> "A conceited minx," she said next day. "And fancy, what she has to be conceited about, avec sa mine de grisette!"

> "It's clear you have never seen any grisettes," my father observed to her.

> "Thank God, I haven't!"

> "Thank God, to be sure . . . only how can you form an opinion of them, then?"

What is to happen is that Zinaïda, to whom all men are slaves and who cannot resist the pride of tormenting them, is herself to become the slave of Vladimir's father; and this fragment of dialogue is Turgenev's premonitory hint. The cruelty of passion, hitherto a weapon in Zinaïda's hands, is to turn its point back upon her. She whom we first saw slapping her adorers with small grey flowers that burst open with a pop on their foreheads; she who uses the game of forfeits to humiliate them and to emphasize their blind obedience to her; she who made a kind of playful ritual of stabbing one of them with a pin, foretelling that he would only laugh when she did so, and triumphing in his laughter; this brilliant, gay and, at heart, tender creature, is to submit so abjectly and with such obsessed pleasure to the elder Voldemar that the final scene of the story is that in which the boy, an unseen observer, sees his father strike Zinaïda with his riding-switch. She is at an open window; Vladimir's father, outside the house, is leaning in to her across the sill.

> I began to watch; I strained my ears to listen. It seemed as though my father were insisting on something. Zinaïda would not consent. I seem to see her face now—mournful, serious, lovely, and with an inexpressible impress of devotion, grief, love, and a sort of despair—I can find no other word for it. She uttered monosyllables, not raising her eyes, simply smiling—submissively, but without yielding. By that smile alone, I should have known my Zinaïda of old days. My father shrugged his shoulders, and straightened his hat on his head, which was always a sign of impatience with him. . . . Then I caught the words: 'Vous devez vous séparer de cette . . .' Zinaïda sat up, and stretched out her arm. . . . Suddenly, before my very eyes, the impossible happened. My father suddenly lifted the whip, with which he had been switching the dust off his coat, and I heard a sharp blow on that arm, bare to the elbow. I could scarcely restrain myself from crying out; while Zinaïda shuddered, looked without a word at my father, and slowly raising her arm to her lips, kissed the streak of red upon it. My father flung away the whip, and running quickly up the steps, dashed into the house. . . . Zinaïda turned round, and with out-stretched arms and downcast head, she too moved away from the window.

That, apart from Zinaïda's death, is to be the end of the story.

Now, having looked ahead so far, having seen a little, but as yet by no means all, of what Turgenev is driving at, let us see what his method is and what his attitude of mind is towards love, and how that method and that attitude are peculiar to him and make him the artist he is.

His attitude of mind is, first of all, compassionate, and his method gentle. Never was there a man less given to violence of thought or of style. He did not, as the fierce materialists do, divide human beings or human motives or forms of human behaviour into abrupt categories to be labelled for perpetual praise or perpetual damnation. There are psychologists who, hearing the tale that I have just outlined—the tale of the face-slapping, the forfeits, the pin and the whip—would say that Turgenev's story was of the masochism and the sadism of passion, and, if they were story-tellers, they would tell it in those ugly terms. The idea of setting it in a context of a boy's first-love would seem to them utterly false. They would brutalize it in the cause, as they supposed, of naturalistic and materialistic truth, and would despise Turgenev for what they would regard as his avoidances. The question we have to ask is whether they are right or whether his truth is in fact more profound and more genuinely realistic than theirs.

If we are to be fully aware, not only of Turgenev's romantic spell, but of his veracity, it is important to notice two things: that he never allows us to lose sympathy with Zinaïda, and yet that he is completely unsparing of her. Enchantment and criticism go hand-in-hand, as they do in life.

After the game of forfeits the boy goes home and to his own room. Zinaïda's face floats before him in the darkness. Then the scientific observer in Turgenev smilingly intervenes:

> At last I got up, walked on tiptoe to my bed, and without undressing, laid my head carefully on the pillow, as though I were afraid by an abrupt movement to disturb what filled my soul.

But then his father calls at the lodge, and everything begins to change for reasons that the boy does not yet understand. But he understands the cruelty inherent in love.

> Zinaïda . . . amused herself with my passion, made a fool of me, petted and tormented me.

(pp. 112-14)

This unsparing criticism of Zinaïda is followed by the boy's discovery that she herself is beginning to suffer as her victims suffer. It is one of Turgenev's most compassionate scenes:

> One day I was walking in the garden beside the familiar fence, and I caught sight of Zinaïda; leaning on both arms, she was sitting on the grass, not stirring a muscle. I was about to make off cautiously, but she suddenly raised her head and beckoned me imperiously. My heart failed me; I did not understand her at first. She repeated her signal. I promptly jumped over the fence and ran joyfully up to her, but she brought me to a halt with a look, and motioned me to the path two paces from her. In confusion, not knowing what to do, I fell on my knees at the edge of the path. She was so pale, such bitter suffering, such intense weariness, was expressed in every feature of her face, that it sent a pang to my

heart, and I muttered unconsciously, "What is the matter?"

Zinaïda stretched out her hand, picked a blade of grass, bit it and flung it away from her.

"You love me very much?" she asked at last. "Yes."

I made no answer—indeed, what need was there to answer?

"Yes," she repeated, looking at me as before. "That's so. The same eyes,"—she went on; sank into thought, and hid her face in her hands. "Everything's grown so loathsome to me," she whispered, "I would have gone to the other end of the world first—I can't bear it, I can't get over it. . . . And what is there before me! . . . Ah, I am wretched. . . . My God, how wretched I am!"

"What for?"

(p. 114)

In episode after episode Turgenev now develops his theme: that in love (and, therefore, in life itself) as we are, in spite of ourselves, both tyrants and victims, we are little entitled to set ourselves up as judges, and shall certainly be wrong if we try to make creation conform to the rigid pattern of a materialistic orthodoxy. In human nature, motive cannot be divided into compartments, for conflicting motives co-exist in the human heart, and are to be seen *through* one another. This is not, in the popular sense, an optimistic theme. It prescribes no anodyne against suffering, nor does it presuppose that by organization we can guarantee happiness to ourselves. But it does presuppose that we live, not in herds under a roof with guards at the door, but in the airs of heaven, and that it is wiser and more just, when lovely woman stoops to folly, to listen to the aeolian music arising from the strings of her individuality and to recognize the beauty of this music, than to destroy all music by the violence of our own screaming. What Turgenev is always seeking is harmony—a harmony which can arise only from recognition, by a sensitive ear, of life's differing notes: a harmony which we hear sometimes, then lose again; a harmony which, if only we ourselves can make ourselves be still and listen, is audible in experience, but which is drowned or converted into chaotic discord if, like the materialists, we shout or whine.

In this spirit he invites us to consider Zinaïda and Vladimir Petrovitch, and even the boy's father. Vladimir Petrovitch is so happily love's fool that when Zinaïda mockingly bids him jump off a fourteen foot wall, he jumps unhesitatingly and collapses at her feet. As he recovers consciousness he hears her say: "How could you do it? How could you obey? You know I love you. . . . ," and "her fresh lips began covering my face with kisses . . . they touched my lips." Is that rapture foolishness in him, or the assurance that she loves him hypocrisy in her? You may answer, "She loved the father; therefore she was lying to the son"; but she was not lying; she was speaking out of Turgenev's charitable wisdom, out of his acceptance of the infinite complexities of the human heart. Others are satirical; others are ironical; but no one else, I think, has Turgenev's gift of loving irony. Other men condemn first and perhaps forgive afterwards, but the gods and Turgenev observe and forgive *at the same time*. That, perhaps, is why the modern world is beginning to turn to him again.

That, perhaps, is why his play, *A Month in the Country*, which is almost a companion piece to **First Love**, was regarded throughout the 'twenties and 'thirties as too thinly romantic for commercial production, and why, when at last it was produced during the war at the St. James's Theatre, it drew all England. In this play there is again a story of first love. More important, the elder woman, Natalya, though different from Zinaïda in age and circumstance, is, like Zinaïda, such a woman as Turgenev loved to paint—a woman to whom love comes as a delicious madness, which, though she cannot resist it, she is able, with a detached part of herself, to criticize. Turgenev understood, and was able to express, the truth that passion is a solvent of the barriers set up by conscience and habit between the good and the evil in men. Those who are led by it to folly and misery are to be pitied, not condemned—perhaps not even to be pitied, for is not imaginative life, though it lead to suffering, better than imaginative stagnation, and is not love an imaginative flux? Because he held this view of love—a view which allies it with poetry rather than with morals or biology—he has been accused of being a sentimentalist. But that was not Tolstoy's view of him or Flaubert's. It is a recent view, based upon the abject Marxian philosophy that only matter is real and that all of us, except our flesh, is delusion. Turgenev was, in fact, a realist, and a realist the more profound because his realism, informed by poetic vision, took account of the intangible. His people may appear at first to be creatures of unaccountable mood; but, as we live with them, we begin to understand that all their moods, their contradictions, their changes of mind, spring from his grasp of one over-riding truth: that men, and women even more certainly than men, are capable, not only of motives successive and conflicting, but of wanting and not wanting a thing *at the same instant*. It is this that gives to his love-stories a kind of scintillating elasticity. No one—except a character here and there that is too closely identified with political theory, and these characters are his weakness, not his strength—no one, apart from these, is rooted in opinion. His people are even a little dazzled, as we all are when we are awake, by the kaleidoscope of vision; they dance with truth.

Let us then take one last glance at Zinaïda and Vladimir Petrovitch before we part from them. She has become his father's mistress and at last the boy knows it. He has seen them out riding together; he has pursued them into the garden, a jealous Othello with a knife, and at sight of his father has dropped the knife. He is in rapture and despair; so, even more terribly, is she. His family is moving back to Moscow. The summer holiday is over. Vladimir Petrovitch goes to the lodge to say goodbye: . . .

> "I have come to say good-bye to you, princess," I answered, "probably for ever. You have heard, perhaps, we are going away."
>
> Zinaïda looked intently at me.
>
> "Yes, I have heard. Thanks for coming. I was beginning to think I should not see you again. Don't remember evil against me. I have sometimes tormented you, but all the same I am not what you imagine me."
>
> She turned away, and leaned against the window.

"Really, I am not like that. I know you have a bad opinion of me."

"I?"

"Yes, you . . . you."

"I?" I repeated mournfully, and my heart throbbed as of old under the influence of her overpowering, indescribable fascination. "I? Believe me, Zinaïda Alexandrovna, whatever you did, however you tormented me, I should love and adore you to the end of my days."

She turned with a rapid motion to me, and flinging wide her arms, embraced my head, and gave me a warm and passionate kiss. God knows whom that long farewell kiss was seeking, but I eagerly tasted its sweetness. I knew that it would never be repeated. "Good-bye, good-bye," I kept saying . . .

She tore herself away, and went out. And I went away. I cannot describe the emotion with which I went away. I should not wish it ever to come again; but I should think myself unfortunate had I never experienced such an emotion.

He never spoke to her again, though he saw her once more on the occasion when his father struck her with a whip. Four years later, hearing that she was in town, he tried to see her again, but went too late. She was already dead.

That is all. What emerges above all else is an impression of beauty and truth. Nothing has been distorted, nothing falsified. The life depicted has been full of suffering, even of waste and folly, and yet it has not been either ugly or in vain. For Turgenev, the material things we touch and measure—even Zinaïda in her grave, "those dear features, those eyes, those curls, in the narrow box, in the damp underground darkness"—though they may be objectively real, are not the only reality; they are certainly emblems as well as objects, and perhaps emblems only.

Emblems of what? Turgenev is not a dogmatist. He gives no precise answer to that question, but makes us aware that there is an answer. To know that there is an answer is to accept life in the Turgenevian sense, to observe suffering and rapture with an equal eye; not, as a man, to be restive; not, as an artist, to scream. This, I think, is what Tolstoy meant when he said that he valued Turgenev "just because he is not restive." Dostoevski, he added, was restive, and so his "wisdom and heart ran to waste. . . . Turgenev," Tolstoy declared, "will outlive Dostoevski, and not for his artistic qualities but because he is not restive."

This story of **First Love** is evidence in support of Tolstoy's verdict. No story is emotionally more highly charged, and yet none is less "restive" or enables us to understand more clearly why a man so different from Tolstoy as Henry James should have spoken of Turgenev as "the least unsafe man of genius" he had met. I owe that reference to Sir Edmund Spriggs, and I think it is valuable to notice that so distinguished a man of science, in his Harveian Oration delivered before the Royal College of Physicians in 1944, chose Turgenev as an instance of the application to art of the Harveian method.

By the Harveian method (he said) is meant the use of observation and experiment guided by knowledge and thought. Opposed to it is thinking, or ac-

cepting what others have said, without the control of looking and trying.

This goes to the root of my contention: that Turgenev, accused by his opponents of being a romantic avoider of the truth, is better equipped than they are, both by his method and by his temperament, to reveal human nature and to inspire those guesses—no less scientific because they are guesses—without which the seeming contradictions of human nature cannot be reconciled. But Turgenev is not a sentimentalist. Hear how he ends his love story:

> I remember, a few days after I heard of Zinaïda's death, I was present, through a peculiar, irresistible impulse, at the death of a poor old woman who lived in the same house as we. Covered with rags, lying on hard boards, with a sack under her head, she died hardly and painfully. Her whole life had been passed in the bitter struggle with daily want; she had known no joy, had not tasted the honey of happiness. One would have thought, surely she would rejoice at death, at her deliverance, her rest. But yet, as long as her decrepit body held out, as long as her breast still heaved in agony under the icy hand weighing upon it, until her last forces left her, the old woman crossed herself, and kept whispering, 'Lord, forgive my sins'; and only with the last spark of consciousness, vanished from her eyes the look of fear, of horror of the end. And I remember that then, by the death-bed of that poor old woman, I felt aghast for Zinaïda, and longed to pray for her, for my father—and for myself.

There let us leave it. We have been in the presence of a great artist and a gentle man of whom there is need in this restive, bitter and opinionated world. Unless civilization is utterly destroyed by those whose materialism has brought it to the very edge of madness, Turgenev will become, I think, more and more a contemporary, because a universal and spiritual force. But it is not for his opinions that he will live. No novelist, not even Tolstoy, lives for his opinions. He will live, as Tolstoy does in *Anna Karenina*, because he knows how to evoke the scent and touch of a woman, and how to love her, and how, like the gods themselves, to forgive her her sins.

He knows how to enable us to re-imagine and to receive into ourselves the uniqueness of each human experience, the solitary miracle of each man's and each woman's being alive; because, for example, he knows, not only how to describe a woman or how to analyse her character, but how to evoke her scent, her touch, her presence, her being she, as in her own heart she is herself and none other; and so, for all her faults, how to love her, and how, in that love, to abstain from judgment of her, and how, not presuming himself to forgive any creature, to pray for her in the same prayer that he prays for himself. (pp. 115-19)

Charles Morgan, "Turgenev's Treatment of a Love-Story," in Essays by Divers Hands, *n.s. Vol. XXV, 1950, pp. 102-19.*

Marc Slonim   (essay date 1950)

[*Slonim was a Russian-born American critic who wrote extensively on Russian literature. In the following excerpt, Slonim seeks to illuminate Turgenev's philosophy of life and its effect on his writings.*]

Turgenev called himself a Realist, and defined his artistic aim as the truthful and dispassionate portrayal of life. He often pointed out his own objectivity: being a Westernizer did not prevent him from presenting the Westernizer Panshin (in *A Nest of Gentlefolk*) unfavorably and making him come off second-best in the argument with the Slavophile Lavretsky; being an anti-Nihilist did not deter him from bringing out all the good points and even virtues of Bazarov; being an atheist did not affect his sympathetic comprehension of Liza's religious feelings.

Belinsky praised Turgenev's precise observation, his capacity for grasping the essence and the peculiarities of each character, and his superb artistry in revealing the causes and effects of human actions and in describing nature [see excerpt dated 1848]. Although he is justly considered one of the world's greatest storytellers, the story itself never attracted Turgenev: the plots of his novels and tales are so simple as to appear slight, and always hinge on the reversal of a love affair. The main thing for him is to show men and women, their relations and their emotions and ideas, without ever attempting a thorough psychological analysis—he always leaves such an analysis to the reader. The latter, however, it put on the right path by hints, allusions, and the mood created by landscapes and the rhythm of the language. The actual work of psychological penetration is done behind the scenes of the novel, by the highly intelligent author who allows only the ultimate results of his exploration to appear in his writings.

This method is responsible for the kind of psychological impressionism or imagism we always find in Turgenev's novels and stories. Turgenev has stated that he wrote not because certain incidents or adventures had occurred to him, but because he had in mind the representation of a certain person, whom he tried to conceive with factual and psychological completeness (he even wrote, for his own use, preliminary biographies of all his main characters). (p. 263)

This concreteness assumes the form of absolute compactness and economy of words. Turgenev's art is very different from Goncharov's factual thoroughness, Dostoevsky's metaphysical depth, or Tolstoy's universality. Turgenev limited himself in the scope and range of his writings, as well as in his ways of expression. His novels are short; the action unfolds without digressions or parallel plots and usually takes place in a brief span of time; the protagonists are reduced to a minimum: the author does not indulge in any analysis of their feelings or their behavior, always employing the method of indirect allusions and understatements.

When he wants to clarify a detail, however—to demonstrate Insarov's strength, for instance, or Bazarov's skeptical attitude toward accepted authorities—he does not beat around the bush but comes straight to the point. The dialogue—adroitly individualized and functional in psychological portrayal—also serves for the exposition of ideas. His protagonists not only talk, but also discuss facts and abstract concepts. Rudin and Lezhnev deliver long speeches on various subjects; Lavretsky and his friend Mikhalevich discuss the men and trends of the 'forties; Bazarov and Paul Kirsanov have arguments over love, science, and esthetics; Potughin and Litvinov exchange lengthy opinions on Europe and Russia's destinies. In gen-

eral, Turgenev's heroes are defined more by what they say than by what they do.

It can be said of all his novels that they had the definite purpose of representing the aristocracy and the intelligentsia in their intellectual and social metamorphosis and that they form a gallery of Russian types as they actually existed between 1840 and 1870. His short stories, more concerned with the love episodes in the life of aristocrats, mostly Superfluous Men, are a sort of poetic accompaniment to the novels, although esthetically they are the best part of his literary bequest. But, if most of Turgenev's writings were social novels, what was their message? And, if there was none, what constituted their central theme, and what did they convey, and continue to convey, to their readers?

Turgenev did not see in life only material for his imagination. He looked for topics and people that corresponded to his personal inclinations. All the works of this objective realist were highly subjective and unraveled many inner conflicts that had tormented him since his early youth. He possessed a great gift for understanding contradictions, for picturing with an equal persuasiveness an idle aristocrat, a Nihilist, a dreamer, or a practical man. Was it objectivity or ambivalence? It certainly could not be explained, as some critics have attempted to do, only by his insight and tolerance.

There was another reason for Turgenev's noncommittal attitude. A rational atheist, he did not believe in God and showed little enthusiasm for humanity. He kept to the middle of the road in politics, went along with the gradual reformers, was on friendly terms with radicals, but never committed himself to any definite group. In art he defended the objective representation of reality, praised harmony and balance as the main principles of an aimless estheticism, and took pride in the fact (contested by the critics) that his novels, both long and short, neither proved anything nor attempted to do so. He certainly appreciated freedom, human dignity, education, culture, and progress, but he never displayed any ardor in proclaiming those values.

As a matter of fact, there was very little positive affirmation in his work. The friends of his youth, such as Belinsky, Bakunin, and Herzen, had been enthusiastic about philosophy, anarchism, or Socialism; his contemporaries, such as Gogol, Dostoevsky, Tolstoy, struggled for religion, God, or morality—but Turgenev did not identify himself with any doctrine or intense belief. Here, again, he kept to the middle of the road, like an intelligent onlooker who enjoys the show but will never take part in it as an actor. He lacked religiosity, which some people believe to be a Russian national trait, and was hardly interested in the quest of all-embracing, all-absorbing concepts or systems of ideas. (pp. 264-65)

Whoever will read several of Turgenev's novels and tales in succession will not fail to notice that they all have unhappy endings. Rudin, Insarov, Bazarov, Nezhdanov, Chertopkhanov, Pasynkov—all meet sudden and, for the most part, violent deaths. Liza dies for the world's sake; Lavretsky continues to vegetate in a sort of deadly atonement. All the love stories also end with failure or death (**Spring Freshets, First Love, Asya**, "Clara Milich", "Phantom", **Faust,** and so on). In general, in Turgenev's tales something always happens on the threshold of fulfilment: accidents or catastrophes meet his men and women at the very door of happiness.

This is not accidental. Turgenev, like his hero Litvinov in *Smoke,* felt the vanity of human illusions and the absurdity of life. The idea of eternity terrified him; he speaks of it time and again, like a man who has a long and involved account to settle with it. His *Senilia*—the most complete and frank expression of his true self—repeatedly deals with the fear of death. **"A Conversation," "The Dog," "The Hag," "The End of The World,"** and a number of other poems in prose revolve around the one topic—the inevitability of annihilation. The mysterious female vampire Ellis in **"Phantoms"** (written in 1863) reflects his own qualms: 'Why do I shudder in such anguish at the mere thought of annihilation?' For merciless and aloof Nature the existence of man is no more important than that of a flea (**"Nature"**). From the summits of the Alps, for the Jungfrau and the Finsteraarhorn, centuries pass like seconds, and to them the humans in the valley look like ants who will disappear one day, leaving immaculate the white eternity of their snow (**"An Alpimalyan Dialogue"**). A blind woman of gigantic proportions pushes on a bony, stalwart female who holds the hand of a small, bright-eyed girl, the child struggles in vain, but is driven along—and these three figures are Fate, Force, and Freedom. Men are imprisoned within a circle of fatality—and there is nothing beyond its bounds except 'the clangorous barking from the thousand throats of death,' 'darkness, eternal darkness,' the interminable void of destruction. This fundamental pessimism overshadows not only the tales of Turgenev's old age but his earlier works, such as **"Andrei Kolossov,"** *Faust,* **"A Backwater," "Journey to Polessie,"**—all written in his thirties.

In one of his letters to Pauline Viardot he writes: 'I cannot stand the empty skies, but I adore life, its reality, its whims, its accidents, its rites, its swiftly passing beauty.' It was not an easy love. He fled from the 'empty skies' into the palpable reality of human affairs, he sought oblivion in the activity of others, in love and illusions. Eternity is madness, death is a nightmare, and Turgenev forgets them only when he meets some spontaneous manifestation of life, in beauty, action, or thought.

The charm of a momentary pleasure moves him to tears, for he always realizes how short and transitory it is bound to be. A green branch on a spring day fills him with tremulous delight: it is the very image of beauty, of the sweet joy of being. In his lecture, "Hamlet and Don Quixote," he gave preference to the Knight of La Mancha, since the Spaniard's illusions overcame his fear of death; his love of action liberated him from the burden of reflection, which dissects and kills the spontaneity of existence.

As a friend and disciple of philosophers, Turgenev, of course, was much closer to the Prince of Denmark than to the ecstatic Spanish hidalgo. In picturing the superfluous men he was in part making self-portraits, particularly when he showed how the self-analysis and self-criticism of his heroes destroyed their ability for action. But he admired the Don Quixotes, and he also loved men like Bazarov, Solomin, and Insarov, who were the very antithesis of himself.

Another curious aspect is his interest in political and social struggles. He was always excited by men's most spectacular activity—that of social transformation—because he was a patriot and sincerely loved his country and also because in this activity he found another affirmation of life, another evidence of 'whims and accidents,' which helped him to forget 'the toothless Ancient.' He was not energetic or particularly active by nature, but the others' expenditure of energy gave him a sense of security and heartened him, in the way the love of other people inspired him with joy and admiration, not unmixed with melancholy. Beauty was another, though momentary, victory over annihilation; contemplation of it brought a rapture enhanced by the consciousness of its evanescence. His tears of ecstasy were mingled with tears of regret.

Well aware of his inner conflict, he dreamt of harmony and the simple, natural life. In *Faust,* and in the **"Journey to Polessie,"** he came to the conclusion that 'the quiet and slow animation, the unhurried restraint of sensations and impulses, the equilibrium of health in every individual being, are the prerequisites of happiness.' The only lasting happiness lies in the serenity of a somewhat monotonous existence based upon instinct and resignation. The same law applies to art: a good work of art must possess the same equilibrium, the same poise, even when dealing with anxiety or madness. He praised highly 'the tranquility in passion' of the great tragic actress Rachel, citing her as an example of the highest esthetic achievement.

Here again his duality was patent. Although he was denied the romantic vision of happiness, all his heroes aspire to its bliss. This aspiration is an irresistible human need, a manifestation of the life instinct—and it is doomed to failure and annihilation. With incomparable poetry he describes this wistful expectation of soul and flesh, this flowering of desire and love, this hope of triumphing over the ruthless domination of time. The best pages of Turgenev are devoted to this promise of happiness that reaches its height in the awakening of love and in the springtime of nature. In **"Three Encounters"** the image of the tense, almost painful, silence of a magnificent summer night filled with scents and susurrations and cravings, with the languor and yearnings of mind and body, with a strange sensation of happiness—a promise and a recollection—is one of the most lyrical passages in the European prose of the nineteenth century; and as a parallel to these pages, there are the chapters describing Liza's love for Lavretzky in *A Nest of Gentlefolk.*

Turgenev never pictured the fulfilment of love, the satisfaction of the senses and of the heart. For him the apex had been reached before—in the highest and most intense moment of a dream that can never come true. (pp. 266-68)

Certain severe critics contend that Turgenev's search for beauty often turned into prettiness, while his art became arty. It is true that his softness and gentleness have at times a cloying aftertaste. He makes life and nature appear rather tame, he avoids mentioning the seamy side of reality or plunging too deeply beneath its surface, for fear of encountering the monsters of depravity, hatred, or abnormality. He takes great care not to pain or shock his readers, and his prose is decorous and seemly, suave and well-bred. His voice is never raised or altered; there are no surprises in his narrative, no breaks in his sentences. Whatever one may feel about this kind of literature, its craftsmanship is undeniable: Turgenev was an extraordinary artist.

This refined and intelligent writer whose irony—and there is far more irony in his works than is usually acknowledged—underscored his sadness, this accomplished stylist who believed that 'such a great, mighty, and free language' as Russian must have been given to a great people, this esthete who wrote social novels, this partrician who described the peasants, this democrat who sang requiems over the nobility, this realist who was so elegiac, this poet who was so precise, is one of the most beloved writers in Russia.

Widely read and enjoyed today, he will probably continue to be one of the most popular writers for many years to come—as long as his languor, his melancholic grief, combined with the exaltation in love and beauty, and his conception of art as an orderly arrangement of emotional values, still stir the poetic and esthetic senses of Russian readers. . . . (pp. 270-71)

> Marc Slonim, "Turgenev," in his The Epic of Russian Literature: From Its Origins through Tolstoy, *Oxford University Press, 1950, pp. 250-71.*

Edmund Wilson   (essay date 1958)

[*Wilson is generally regarded as among the foremost twentieth-century men of letters in the United States. A prolific and intelligent reviewer, creative writer, and social and literary critic, he exercised his greatest literary influence as the author of* Axel's Castle, *a seminal study of literary symbolism, and as the author of widely read reviews and essays in which he introduced prominent works of modern literature to the reading public. Wilson's criticism displays a fundamental concern for the historical and psychological implications of literary works. Alert to literature's significance as "an attempt to give meaning to our experience" and as a vehicle for the betterment of humanity, he also believed that "the real elements . . . of any work of fiction are the elements of an author's personality: his imagination embodies . . . the fundamental conflicts of his nature." Related to this idea is Wilson's theory, expressed in his study* The Wound and the Bow, *that artistic ability is compensation for a psychological wound. In the following excerpt, Wilson examines themes of evil and morbidity in Turgenev's shorter works, often relating these tales to circumstances in the author's life.*]

The work of Turgenev has, of course, no scope that is comparable to Tolstoy's or Dostoevsky's, but the ten volumes collected by him for his edition of 1883 (he omitted his early poems) represent a literary achievement of the concentratedly "artistic" kind that has few equals in nineteenth-century fiction. There are moments, to be sure, in Turgenev novels—*On the Eve* and *Virgin Soil*—when they become a little thin or unreal, but none can be called a failure, and one cannot find a single weak piece, unless one becomes impatient with **"Enough,"** in the whole four volumes of stories. No fiction writer can be read through with a steadier admiration. Greater novelists are more uneven: they betray our belief with extravagances; they bore or they fall into bathos; they combine poetic vision with rubbish. But Turgenev hardly even skirts these failings, and he is never mediocre; his texture is as distinguished as his temperament.

This texture barely survives in translation. Turgenev is a master of language; he is interested in words in a way that the other great nineteenth-century Russian novelists—with the exception of Gogol—are not. His writing is dense and substantial, yet it never marks time, always moves. . . . But this language will not reach the foreigner. How to render the tight little work of art that Turgenev has made of **"The Dog,"** narrated by an exhussar, with his colloquialisms, his pungent sayings, his terseness and his droll turns? And the problems of translating Turgenev are to some extent the problems of translating poetry. There is a passage in **The Torrents of Spring**—a tour de force of onomatopoeia—that imitates in a single sentence the whispering of leaves, the buzzing of bees and the droning of a solitary dove. This is probably a conscious attempt to rival the well-known passage in Virgil's First Eclogue and Tennyson's imitation of it:

> The moan of doves in immemorial elms,
> And murmuring of innumerable bees.

But it would take another master to reproduce Turgenev's effects, just as it took a Tennyson to reproduce those of Virgil, and a Turgenev to compete with these.

Since I am going to go on . . . to call attention to the principal themes that run all through Turgenev's work and to relate them to his personal experience, I must emphasize here the solidity and the range of Turgenev's writings. It is only in the later stories which deal with the supernatural that these underlying themes emerge as obsessions or hallucinations. They are otherwise usually embodied in narratives, objectively presented, in which the backgrounds are always varied and in which even the individuals who belong to a constantly recurring type are always studied in a special context and differentiated from one another. Turgenev is not one of the great inventors, as his two colleagues and Dickens are, but in his tighter, more deliberate art he is perhaps the most satisfactory of the company to which he belongs, for he never oppresses, as Flaubert does, by his monotony and his flattening of human feeling, or fatigues, as Henry James sometimes does when his wheels of abstraction are grinding, or makes us nervous, as Conrad may do, through his effortfulness and occasional awkwardness in working in a language not native to him with materials that are sometimes alien. The material of Turgenev is all his own, and his handling of it is masterly. The detail is always amusing, always characteristic; every word, every reference, every touch of description has naturalness as well as point; the minor characters, the landscapes, the milieux are all given a full succulent flavor. The genre pictures—the funeral supper at the end of **"An Unhappy Girl,"** the transference of the property in **"A Lear of the Steppes"**—are wonderfully organized and set in motion, though such exhilaration of movement as Tolstoy is able to generate in such episodes as the hunt in *War and Peace* and the races in *Anna Karenina* is quite beyond Turgenev's powers, as is the cumulative fun and excitement of the town celebration in Dostoevsky's *The Devils*. But neither can fill in a surface, can fit language to subject like Turgenev. The weather is never the same; the descriptions of the countryside are quite concrete, and full, like Tennyson's, of exact observation of how cloud and sunlight and snow and rain, trees, flowers, insects, birds and wild animals, dogs, horses and cats behave, yet they are also stained by the mood of the person who is made to perceive them. There are moments, though not very many, when the affinity between natural phenomena and the emotion of the character exposed to them is allowed to become a little melodramatic in the old-fashioned romantic way—the volcanic sunset in *Faust* when the heroine is herself on the verge of eruption—but in general Turgenev is protected from the dangers of the "romantic fallacy" by his realistic habit of mind.

Let me here, also, call attention to a story that seems to me a masterpiece and that sounds a different note from those I shall discuss later: **"The History of Lieutenant Ergunov,"** of 1867. This Lieutenant is a heavy and clumsy and extremely naïve young man who is highly susceptible to women and who regards himself as something of a dandy. Stationed in a provincial town, he becomes involved with a household that purports to consist of an elderly woman living with two nieces. They are of mongrel and dubious origins; one of them, who calls herself Colibri, is semi-Oriental, exotic. The Lieutenant never discovers that the two girls are prostitutes and that their bully is lurking in the background. His suspicions are not even aroused when he has dropped off to sleep on a couch one day and been awakened by the efforts of one of the girls—he is carrying government money—to detach from his belt his wallet. He becomes so fascinated by Colibri that it is no trouble at all for her to drug him. They rob him, bash in his head and, assuming he is safely dead, throw his body down a ravine. It is only his exceptional vigor that enables him in time to recover from this. The thieves have, of course, made their getaway, but he presently receives a long letter from the girl who tried to steal his wallet, in which she tells him that though she has "a bad morality" and is "flighty," she is not really "a villainess." She is terribly sorry about the whole thing; the others had induced her to lend herself to luring him to the house and then sent her away for the day. "The old villainess *was not* my aunt." She begs him to answer, but he never does. Ergunov all the rest of his life tells the story at least once a month.

It is typical of Turgenev's art that the anecdote in itself, as I have sketched it, cannot convey Turgenev's point. Nothing could be more different than a story, say, by Maupassant. There are no tricks of the professional raconteur, no sudden surprise at the end. We follow a steady narrative, built up with convincing detail. It closes calmly enough with Ergunov's shaking his head and sighing "That's what it is to be young," and displaying his terrible scar, which reaches from ear to ear. And it is only when we have finished the story that we grasp the whole implication of the triumph of good faith and respect for the innocent over the brutal violation of human relations. Ergunov is the side of Turgenev himself that never could believe at first that the people who exploited him were not honest. It is a question in **"Lieutenant Ergunov"** not of one of the author's obsessive themes but of a feeling that, for all his demons, all his ogresses and their helpless victims, continues to assert itself almost to the end of his work—Gemma's letter of forgiveness to Sanin, in the later *Torrents of Spring,* reversing the roles of the sexes in **"Ergunov,"** embodies the same moral—and a feeling that he shares with the creator of Myshkin as well as with the creator of Pierre. This instinct sets the standards for Turgenev's mind, and it is the basis of his peculiar nobility. It

is the essence of the life-giving drop that he has rescued from the cave of the reptiles.

But this story is almost unique. The positive force of honesty, even the survival of innocence—though they sometimes occur in the novels: Solomin in *Virgin Soil,* Tatyana and her aunt in *Smoke*—are excessively rare in these tales. There are examples of religious dedication—**"A Living Relic"** in *A Sportsman's Sketches,* **"A Strange Story," "A Desperate Character"**—but, especially in the last two of these, you feel that they are simply cases, included with the other cases, of the unhealthiness of Russian life. In general, the ogresses and devils continue to have the best of it, and the timid and snobbish young men continue to disappoint the proud women. . . . [In] 1857, ten years before **"Lieutenant Ergunov"**—this has happened to the heroine of *Asya* and to Gemma of *The Torrents of Spring,* and is to happen to the heroine of **"An Unhappy Girl"** (two of these the illegitimate daughters of gentlemen and one the daughter of an Italian confectioner). It is only in *First Love* that the girl under a social shadow is allowed to have a passionate love affair, and I am sure that it is partly to this, the exceptional element of sex interest, that the story owes its especial popularity—along with, for the same reason, *The Torrents of Spring*—among Turgenev's shorter fictions. Yet note that it is not the young boy but his father who enjoys Zinaida's love, and that Turgenev explained that the story was based on an experience of his own youth. The figure of Turgenev's father plays no such role in his work as that of Varvara Petrovna, but the aloof and dashing father of the narrator of *First Love,* who fascinates Zinaida and slashes her arm with his riding crop, evidently has something to do with the diabolic brother of **"The Song of Triumphant Love,"** who mesmerizes and rapes his sister-in-law. If the heroes in Turgenev are inhibited from going to bed with the women and do so only, still with inhibitions, when—as in *Smoke* or *The Torrents of Spring*—they, the men, are themselves seduced, the man who prevails over women is likely to treat them with violence and to become an embodiment of the Evil Force.

In the meantime, [Turgenev's mother] Varvara Petrovna is reappearing in **"Her Ladyship's Private Office"** . . . , and in **"Punin and Baburin,"** and the Lutovinova grandmother who killed the little serf boy turns up as a variation of the Varvara Petrovna character in Agrippina Ivanovna of **"The Brigadier."** The masculine Force of Evil, after lying in abeyance since **"The Wayside Inn"** of 1852, reappears five years later in **"A Tour in the Forest,"** and it is here for the first time invested—at least in the minds of the peasants of the story—with supernatural implications. This piece was added by Turgenev to a new edition of *A Sportsman's Sketches* published in 1860, but afterwards presented by the author—in his collected edition of 1865—in its chronological place. For it does not belong with the *Sketches*—it is more philosophical and more complex; it shows the development of Turgenev's art. I agree with Dmitri Mirsky in his admiration for **"A Tour in the Forest"**—with its wonderful descriptions of pine forests, its feeling for the non-human life of trees that both embraces and isolates human beings, that oppresses at the same time it calms. And in the forest the demon is found—Efrem, a bad peasant who fears nobody, who stops at nothing and whom his neighbors can do nothing about. (pp. 48-54)

In reading **"A Tour in the Forest,"** it occurs to one that this indigenous demon, against whom the people of the forest feel themselves utterly helpless, against whom they can have no redress, represents a constant factor in Russian life, an ever-recurring phenomenon of history: the bad master whom one cannot resist, Ivan the Terrible, Peter the Great, Stalin. The masculine Force of Evil reappears in **"An Unhappy Girl"** as Susanna's horrible stepfather, and in **"A Lear of the Steppes"** you have one male and two female villians, all more or less unaccounted for. In **"Lear,"** the two daughters of old Kharlov, who destroy him, no doubt dominate the son-in-law, but there is nothing to explain why both of them should have risen to such positions of power save the example of Varvara Petrovna, on whose character they present variations. Maria Nikolaevna in *The Torrents of Spring*—another strong and cunning peasant—is a still further variation. And thereafter, as Turgenev nears sixty, both the female and the male evil powers not only cease to wear the aspect of noxious products of the social system or even of elements of animal nature; they become supernatural beings, who prey upon and take possession, who swoop in on us from outside our known world. This development on Turgenev's part synchronizes—despite the fact that during the seventies he wrote, in *Virgin Soil,* his most ambitious social novel—with a haunting and growing sense of the nullity of human life and the futility of his own endeavors. . . . In the late *Poems in Prose,* this despondency has reached its nadir. You have, for example, the devastating dialogue between the Jungfrau and the Finsteraarhorn, which, waking or drowsing in the course of their millennia, see the human race, far below them, come to life, stir about for a little, and eventually die out like vermin. And at the same time the Force of Evil seems to rush in to fill this vacuum. These *Senilia,* as he calls them, are full of nightmares—the nightmare of the giant insect that fatally stings the young man, the nightmare of the end of the world, in which people in a country house are surrounded and swallowed up by a raging and icy sea.

These nightmares have begun in **"Phantoms"** of 1863, and this is followed, thirteen years later, by **"The Dream."** The element of the supernatural first appears in **"The Dog"** of 1866. This very curious story associates itself with **"Knock! . . . Knock! . . . Knock! . . . ,"** which follows it in 1870. Both deal with mysterious destinies, one fortunate, the other unfortunate—a suggestion of which is also to be found in *The Torrents of Spring* of 1871. In **"The Dog,"** the Force of Evil wears the aspect of the gigantic mad dog which persistently attacks the hero and from which he is only saved by his heaven-sent protector: a setter which has come to him first as an invisible but audible presence. The canine guardian angel is again, like the Lieutenant's innocence, a form of the life-giving drop. But this angel in the subsequent stories grows weaker and at last gives way before the Demon of Evil: the diabolic baron of **"The Dream";** the priest's son, possessed by the Devil, of **"Father Alexey's Story";** the sinister Renaissance sorcerer of **"The Song of Triumphant Love."** I do not agree with Mirsky that the realistic setting of these stories prevents them from being successful. They *are* certainly less compelling than the diabolic tales of Gogol, from which they may partly derive, for the reason that the world of Gogol, being always distorted and turbid, is more favorable for this kind of horror, but they are nonetheless creepy enough and can hold their own with any such fan-

tasies. The fault that one would find with them is rather that they are not merely horrible but hopeless. The forces that battle with the goblins are too feeble; they do not have a chance of success. Compare Gogol's vampire story *Viy* with Turgenev's **"Clara Milich,"** which fundamentally it somewhat resembles. It is not only that the rude village church in which the young student of Gogol keeps his terrible vigil with the girl in the coffin is closer to peasant folklore than the "small wooden house" in Moscow where Turgenev's student lives with his aunt and has his rendezvous with the dead Clara; Gogol's hero arouses more sympathy, puts up a better fight than Turgenev's, who is actually, like Sanin in *The Torrents,* more attracted than frightened by the vampire.

This story—of 1882, the last that Turgenev published—is, in any case, the culmination of the whole morbid side of his work. (pp. 55-8)

> *Edmund, Wilson, "Turgenev and the Life-Giving Drop," in* Literary Reminiscences and Autobiographical Fragments *by Ivan Turgenev, translated by David Magarshack, Farrar, Straus and Cudahy, 1958, pp. 3-64.*

Judith Oloskey Mills   (essay date 1971)

[*In the following essay, originally published in the* Slavic and East European Journal *in 1971, Mills compares Turgenev's* First Love *with his first published story, "Andrey Kolosov." Through analysis of image and symbol, Mills demonstrates how Turgenev's novella augments the theme of passionate love with a study of the psychological causes of arrested adolescence.*]

First Love has long been acclaimed as one of Turgenev's major artistic achievements. Despite the agreed-upon excellence of the work, however, the attention which it has received in the critical literature, Russian and Western, has been cursory. Typical of the statements acknowledging its quality is Freeborn's remark that in the years 1860-62 Turgenev brought the forms of the novel and the short story to perfection and that *First Love* is the most brilliant and enchanting of his stories. Other critical references to the story, similarly brief, usually concern the scantiness of plot or the story's biographical origins, especially in the depiction of the mother and the father. J. A. T. Lloyd observes, "of plot there is scarcely any," and notes that Turgenev's recall of youthful impressions is especially intense. Magarshack makes the same observations about the factual material in his biography of the author. André Mazon treats the story in terms of its factual correspondence to Turgenev's life, noting the departures made in the interests of realism.

The most extensive study of *First Love* in Russia is Ovsyaniko-Kulikovsky's thorough analysis of the heroine, Zinaida. A powerful force within the story, she fits, within broad limits, into the category of Turgenev's strong women. As such, she is often the focus of critical attention. Ovsyaniko-Kulikovsky considers her a personality formed on contradiction, loving power and freedom but herself becoming a slave to passion. Nina Brodiansky calls her the most enchanting of Turgenev's heroines. Both critics are concerned with a character analysis of Zinaida, attempting to define her personality and comparing her with other of Turgenev's women.

The one effort known to me to treat *First Love* as a whole has been made by Charles Morgan [see excerpt dated 1947]. He sees the chief virtue of this work in the achievement of the harmony which Turgenev constantly sought in his work. This harmony, in Morgan's opinion, resulted from Turgenev's innate sense of balance and of the civilized, which formed his point of view as a writer. It permitted him to see love and passion objectively, without condemnation and without employing the ugly naturalistic terms of sadism and masochism. Morgan's apology for Turgenev's objectivity, aimed at making him acceptable to the reader and critic more accustomed to contemporary naturalistic descriptions, should not be permitted to obscure other aspects of Turgenev's harmony. With equal justification we may posit of this work a structural harmony, resulting from Turgenev's skillful use of symbols and images. This concept of harmony is not negated by the role played in the story by passion. And although Turgenev does not use vivid naturalistic descriptions, neither does he hide the sado-masochistic elements in the love he treats. The torments of love in Turgenev's works have often been cited. Indeed, Irving Howe goes so far as to call him "a man, and, in some sense, a writer of disarranged sexuality."

Morgan identifies the two dominant themes of *First Love* as youth and love. Zinaida, the pivot of passionate exchanges, is young and experiencing her first passionate involvement. There is, however, another "first love," and Zinaida's pivotal position should not obscure the role of the youthful narrator, Volodya. This second young victim of first love has not received adequate consideration.

The narrator of *First Love* is another "superfluous man" of nineteenth-century Russian literature, a direct descendant of the narrators of **"Andrey Kolosov," "The Diary of a Superfluous Man,"** and *Asya.* Although the notion of the superfluous man had for Turgenev primarily political and social implications, the term is intentionally applied here to a psychological phenomenon. For it is the contention of this paper that in *First Love* Turgenev has supplemented the theme of passion with a study of the psychological causes of the superfluous man. The story presents at least a rudimentary analysis of the adolescent personality which is arrested in its development and remains permanently ineffectual. The causes of a psychological problem are delved into in a way which is not characteristic of Turgenev. That Turgenev intended this second theme to be an important and integral part of the story is, as I shall attempt to show, evident from his use of image and symbol.

The concept of the superfluous man with origins in an undeveloped adolescent psyche was not a theme totally new to Turgenev. It occurs also in his first story, **"Andrey Kolosov,"** although in a rather primitive form when compared to the later work. The two stories are similar in overall structure. They share the "framework" technique and the first-person narration of past events, which forces a certain objectivity about the experiences narrated. Both stories juxtapose an adolescent with a more mature man. The juxtaposition provides contrast, but it also serves to stifle the younger man's development.

In **"Andrey Kolosov"** Turgenev describes the unsuccessful attempts of the young narrator to emulate his ideal, Kolosov. Kolosov is the hero of the story, and the strength of his personality precipitates whatever action occurs. The attraction for him of the student group in which he moves rests on his ability to act decisively and spontaneously without introspection and without regret, a rare ability in that reflective age. He is a new "natural man" who responds immediately to his emotions without dissection or self-laceration. He has attained that knowledge of life to which the young romantics aspire but which constantly eludes them. His friend Shchitov is a less well developed variation on the same theme. The contrasting types are described in terms of maturity versus immaturity and also as "sensible" and its opposite. The opposition is reinforced throughout the story by Turgenev's choice of vocabulary. Kolosov and Shchitov, who are so much admired, are characterized as "sensible" and "to the point." Kolosov's presence among the students results in a "sensible conversation." Shchitov is able to calm the agitated group by a "sensible word."

The narrator is quite different. He is a product of the romantic thirties, representative of the contemplative generation. He is one of those young men who dream but the content of whose dream is illusory: "I wanted something, strove for something, and dreamed of something; I confess that even then I did not know very well what precisely I was dreaming of." As a substitute for activity, he becomes infatuated with Kolosov and tries to imitate him, seeking a pattern for proper activity. He would like to emulate Kolosov's "sensibility." He rejects an abstract discussion of what constitutes an "unusual man" in favor of a story on grounds that a story would be "more the point." However, in telling the story he continually slips into extensive description, reverting to his contemplative nature. His audience on two occasions demands that he get down "to business."

Although the narrator is chronologically young (eighteen) at the time of the events of the story, he is made to seem even more immature. He is called the "small man." Throughout the story he is connected with child imagery, with the implications of purity and innocence which stand in sharp contrast to Kolosov and Shchitov. He is one of the students whose "half-childish melancholy" is dissolved by Kolosov's sensible conversation. When the narrator first becomes infatuated with Kolosov, he venerates him "childishly." When the narrator postpones his talk with the girl's father, he says that the word "tomorrow" was invented for indecisive people and for children, and that he, like a child, was consoling himself with this magic word. The narrator thus defines himself not as an indecisive adult but as a child. The contemplative thirties pass, but the young man is arrested in his immature state: ten years later when he relates the story he has not changed. His permanent superfluous state results not from indecision but rather from arrested development.

The love story, which involves Kolosov and the narrator with the same girl, Varya, is less important for itself than for the light it sheds on those two personalities. Kolosov loves Varya but leaves her when he becomes bored. The narrator thinks he loves her and declares his love, but he takes flight at the thought of marriage. Varya transfers her love from Kolosov to the narrator with minimal effort. Insignificant to the action, she is merely the necessary female component of the triangle. She is certainly not the prototype for Zinaida.

Whereas in **"Andrey Kolosov"** Turgenev merely recorded the thwarted development of the superfluous man, in *First Love* he shows the process which actually stifles maturation. In the first story the theme was reinforced by the repetition of pertinent concepts. In the later story the same concepts are embellished by a system of symbols and images which give the theme a more definite structural pattern.

The contrasting male pair is the narrator Volodya and his father Pyotr Vasilich. Each is in love with Zinaida. The love theme is better developed in this story for it touches the three characters in depth and, with the exception of Zinaida's mother, extends to all the other characters in the story. Volodya would like to pattern himself after his father, but he is not so totally imitative as the narrator of **"Andrey Kolosov."** He aspires to Zinaida's love and is quite willing to act on his own. His spontaneous action, however, is curtailed by the other two principles. Volodya is trapped by his own lack of strength and by those who will in no way help him. The world in which adults live and act is always just beyond his reach.

The love to which Volodya aspires is for the exceptionally strong; it is never free of sado-masochistic elements. It means pain for all involved, yet it is for this reason all the more attractive. When Zinaida is first seen by the narrator, she is striking her admirers on the forehead with a small globular flower. This is symbolic of the pain awaiting those who become involved with her. (pp. 79-83)

Zinaida is imperious and totally in control. Not one of her suitors can make an impression on her, but each is used to her own advantage. Zinaida does not find her equal until she meets Volodya's father, who although he seems to be the least well developed main character in the story is the motivating force to the action and the definitive influence on both Volodya and Zinaida. With Pyotr Vasilich Zinaida learns that self-sacrifice can be as pleasurable as tormenting others, and with a recklessness that is rare even among Turgenev's heroines, she sacrifices herself for a moment of satisfaction. Ultimately he controls her, and the physical sign of this psychic power is the final whiplash on her hand. There is no place in the domain of Zinaida and Pyotr Vasilich for any of the others, least of all for Volodya. Volodya suffers pain, but his pain never reaches the intensity of that experienced by Zinaida and his father. Nor will he fully experience love.

Her daydream is another indication of Zinaida's unique position. In it Zinaida is a princess whose guests love her but receive no response from her. She is the feminine egotist whose world revolves around her. None but her equal should dare approach her. Volodya would try, but as he crosses the boundary, his destruction begins. Zinaida refuses to accept him and in the process forces him to remain a child. The image of the child pervades the story and has the same function as it did in **"Andrey Kolosov."** In their first conversation Zinaida defines the difference between them. "What a strange habit children have—she corrected herself—young people have not to speak openly about their feelings." Volodya is anxious to show her that she is not dealing with a boy, but when he falls unconscious from

the wall, she calls him "my dear boy." He does not respond to her kisses as an adult, realizing that he is still a "child." When she sends him off to play with her younger brother, she delivers another blow: "The arrival of this boy turned me into a boy as well." (pp. 83-4)

The impossibility of Volodya's even achieving equal status in love is evident in the changes which are made in the conventional symbol for the onset of love, the storm. Looking at it, Volodya can see lightning, but it is so far in the distance that the thunder is inaudible. The lightning itself is not especially vigorous. It flickers and trembles "like the wing of a dying bird." The storm's distance symbolizes the first timid intimations of love. Volodya will not experience its full force just as he does not feel the full force of the storm. The end is already in sight; the bird is dying. The use of a natural phenomenon to symbolize the development of love is a standard device in Turgenev. The storm here reinforces the impotence already present in the child motif.

Turgenev uses a set of symbols which well suits the psychological make-up of the characters and at the same time is part of the external action of the story. Zinaida imagines herself a princess. Volodya, when he is first introduced into the story, presents himself as a horseman and imagines himself a knight in a tournament. Before the action of the story begins, he thinks of himself as a figure equal to Zinaida. This image is intensified in the scene where he takes his rifle and goes out hunting. (Ironically his game is crows.) On first sight of Zinaida in the garden with her suitors he drops the rifle. This lack of presence is a portent of the relationship which will develop. It also puts him in sharp contrast to his father, who immediately prior to this action has been described as a man totally "self-assured and self-possessed."

Volodya's hopes are dashed the first time he sees her follow the figure of his father with her eyes. He wanted to go over to her, but his father's image had interposed and he could see that she no longer noticed him. To this point Volodya's only competition has been the circle of admirers to which he had been readily admitted. Zinaida is willing to grant him as much attention as she grants any of the others. But none of them will be able to compete with Pyotr Vasilich.

Volodya's father is not unkind to him but distant and unemotional ("My father treated me with indifferent affection"). Like Zinaida, he is inclined to treat Volodya as a child and to dominate him in a way which is inoffensive, yet harmful to him. The well-maintained distance between father and son is broken only to serve the father's purpose. He takes Volodya by the hand (like a child) into the garden to question him about the previous evening at Zinaida's. The scene is parallel to the one in which Zinaida demands truthfulness from him because he is still a "child." Except for an occasional distracted caress Pyotr Vasilich lets Volodya go his own way. Volodya resents this and seeks a relationship, sought also by the narrator of **"Andrey Kolosov,"** which would give him a pattern upon which to fashion his own maturity and masculinity. His father could if he wished with one word awaken the boy's confidence and trust ("with a single word, a single motion, arouse my unlimited confidence in myself"). But these words of encouragement are infrequent.

Zinaida strikes a heavy blow to his self-image when she designates him not a knight but a page: "From this day on I appoint you as my page." This epithet creates a bond between the child motif, which enters directly into the verbal exchange between Volodya and Zinaida, and the horseman-knight motif. It enters also into the plot and serves to generate another confrontation between father and son. Since Volodya has been designated page, Malevsky can urge him on to the garden rendezvous. Thus Volodya is put into the ludicrous position of holding the train of the princess as she goes to meet her lover. (pp. 84-5)

The father believes in the power of the dominant will. This will puts him in control of every situation and enables him to tame the wildest of horses—and Zinaida as well. It is the strength of will which Volodya would like to develop but is powerless to do so. The rivalry between father and son is played out in terms of horsemanship. Volodya likes to ride with his father but is only rarely permitted to do so. (Compare the infrequent and encouraging conversations.) Horsemanship becomes identified with masculine successes, and Volodya is deliberately excluded by both Zinaida and Pyotr Vasilich. As Volodya becomes more and more attached to Zinaida, in a way suggested by the captured-beetle image cited above, he ceases riding horseback ("I even stop walking around the environs and riding horseback"). Zinaida is thus an emasculating force. This impotence is further dramatized by the riding episode. Zinaida asks Belovzorov to procure a horse for her. Underestimating her riding ability, Belovzorov is afraid that the horse which he offers will be too spirited. But she is every bit as commanding as Pyotr Vasilich. The next day when Volodya sees Zinaida riding with his father, she is quite able to keep up with him, but Belovzorov and the other suitors, including Volodya, are left far behind.

A final incident summarizes this theme. It occurs after the family has returned to Moscow and Zinaida has supposedly been forgotten. Volodya is riding with his father and for the first part of the ride, with a considerable exertion on the part of his little horse, is able to pace the father's more powerful animal. However, after Volodya sees his father deliver the whiplash to Zinaida, he is no longer able to ride with him as an equal. On the return trip he is left behind, like Belovzorov earlier. The pattern of his personality as developed throughout the story is here reinforced. Volodya has learned that his father has continued a liaison which he has not even been able to begin. He will never be the equal of his father either in horsemanship or in overall capabilities. This is the last deadly blow to his maturation.

Although the plight of Volodya may be considered a secondary theme of *First Love,* Turgenev, as we have seen, has thoroughly integrated it into a complex system of symbols and themes, and this structural unity gives *First Love* the harmony for which it is justly esteemed. (pp. 85-6)

Judith Oloskey Mills, "Theme and Symbol in 'First Love'," in Critical Essays on Ivan Turgenev, *edited by David A. Lowe, G. K. Hall & Co., 1989, pp. 79-86.*

Victor Ripp   (essay date 1980)

[*In the following excerpt, Ripp examines Turgenev's stories collected in* A Sportsman's Sketches, *exploring such concerns as the Russian acceptance of serfdom despite its oppressive consequences for both peasant and landowner, the general theme of exile or homelessness, and the individual's attempt to impose order on the outer world.*]

In *Notes of a Hunter* Turgenev refrains from condemning men like the Westernizers, with their merely abstract ideal of social justice, but neither does he excuse them. On the one hand, he depicts an existing order of such strength that the individual's efforts to promote change are severely limited. On the other hand, the permanence of evil in the world of *Notes of a Hunter* is as much the result of the individual's failure to imagine change as the result of brute oppression. Turgenev shows characters who are bewitched by the values of the status quo.

His most telling evidence of the failure of the political imagination is the status of serfdom. Peasants as well as noblemen regard the institution as if it were some marvelous perpetual motion machine that should run down because of its design, but doesn't. The awe they feel at the spectacle seemingly keeps them from summoning any true resistance, however accurately they gauge the cruelty and injustice of the effects. **"Raspberry Spring"** is probably the sketch that offers the most sustained analysis of how serfdom induces moral passivity. While out hunting, the narrator decides to escape the mid-day heat by retreating to the tree-lined banks of a cool spring. There he encounters three peasants. They represent three different responses to the pressures of Russian reality. One peasant, Vlas, has come to Raspberry Spring on his way home after walking to Moscow (some three hundred miles) to apply for relief from an exorbitant *obrok* obligation. He has got no relief, no sympathy. And though the consequence of this is probably starvation, Vlas shows no surprise that his master has taken not the slightest interest in his plight, that in fact he had Vlas chased from his presence immediately. Masters are supposed to behave in such a way.

This is Turgenev's first of three insights into the psychological mechanism sustaining serfdom: even to those it most oppresses, it appears reasonable. Serfdom was clothed in the trappings of legality. It was not slavery, which depended on force and terror, but was rather part of a rationalized system that supposedly apportioned benefits to all. If the disadvantages to the serf were obvious— he could not own property, he was obliged to perform labor on his master's land or pay him a tax, he could be bought, sold, mortgaged, or given away—the law mentioned benefits also. A landowner was required to provide his serfs with a strip of land they could cultivate for themselves, he was obliged to arbitrate disputes, to open his grain reserves in time of famine, to refrain from "excessive" punishment. Such benefits appear ludicrously paltry, but it made considerable difference to the peasant, as exemplified by Vlas, that technically at least he was not dependent on his master's whim; he was part of a logical, though unfair, scheme.

The second peasant, Stepushka, at first seems to be in a better position than Vlas. By some remarkable oversight he has been allowed to fall outside the system of serfdom altogether. He has slipped through the bureaucratic grid, so that it is even doubtful, as the narrator notes with amazement, "if he was actually listed in the government census of serfs." But in the event, Stepushka's situation is not enviable. "Every human being," the narrator remarks, "has some sort of status in the social situation, has some sort of connection; every domestic is issued, if he gets no wages, at least a so-called 'flour allotment.' Stepushka received no subsistence aid whatsoever, he was not related to anybody; nobody was aware of his existence." In the summers he sleeps in a cubbyhole in the back of the hen-house, in the winters in the entry to the bathhouse; and his days are wholly taken up with scavenging for food.

This is Turgenev's second major insight into the workings of serfdom: it was not only legal, it was encompassing. There was virtually no life in Russia except within the prevailing system. In removing himself from accountability to the government, Stepushka removes himself as well from the only means in Russia by which men acquire social status and a measure of security. In fact, in escaping direct oppression, Stepushka comes close to losing all traces of humanity. The encompassing nature of serfdom suggests why, when peasants did manage to mount a rebellion, it was often carried out in the name of the tsar. The sanctity of the system was not challenged, only specific abuses of it. In general, though serfdom came into existence in Russia gradually and haphazardly, once in place it functioned efficiently in a crucial respect: men had great difficulty imagining an alternative way to live.

The last peasant, nicknamed Fog, is a liberated serf of almost seventy, and his response to serfdom is perhaps the most striking of the three. Fog had in the past served as a sort of major domo to a rich count, organizing a vast manorial estate so as to provide the maximum of pleasure and luxury for his master. He entered upon his duties so wholeheartedly that even now, years after, Fog still rhapsodically recounts the manner of life the count enjoyed, he still itemizes, with something approaching love, the various appurtenances of his master's pleasure: the numerous hunting dogs kept on silk leashes, the servants decked out in red caftans with gold braid, the marvelous snuffboxes, canes, wigs, and colognes. To sum up his memories of his master, Fog remarks, "When he set out to give a banquet—O Lord, Sovereign of my life—the fireworks would begin and so would the pleasure jaunts." That parenthetical expression is terribly revealing; for in such an expression of spontaneous enjoyment and undistanced enthusiasm, Fog reveals how fully his pleasures depend on pleasing the count.

This is Turgenev's third insight regarding serfdom: serfdom does not oppress all peasants equally. In certain cases, such as that of Khor' [in **"Khor and Kalinych"**], who is able to acquire his own business, there are rewards for extraordinary effort. In other cases, such as Fog's, the rewards are given almost randomly. In general, however, serfdom allows peasants to believe they have a chance to work out their own destiny, instead of having to accept the common dreary fate. (It helped that the details of how much serfs could legally hope to achieve was obscure. Even Turgenev, famed as an expert on peasant affairs, was unsure of all the laws. Only after studying the issue carefully does he write to Annenkov, "An enserfed individual does *not have* the right to acquire property except in the

name of his master.") The incremental differences in injustice seem to lighten the degradation all peasants suffered. Fog, for example, is so exhilarated by his proximity to wealth that he forgets completely his actual status—and forgets also that he should think of satisfying his own desires as well as his master's.

The climax of the sketch comes when Vlas recounts how his master drove him away when he applied for help. The peasants are confronted with the incontrovertible cruelty of slavery; and the stifling heat, which previously helped to explain their lackadaisical behavior, now seems to suggest that such an atmosphere of purposelessness cannot long continue. But Fog responds with only token sympathy, then returns to his fishing; Stepushka at first seems ready to remonstrate, but after a few disconnected words sinks into confusion and silence—a sequence of gestures befitting a man who is apparently free but actually powerless; and even Vlas himself proves curiously incapable of comprehending what he is saying, telling his story "with a mocking smile, as though it were someone else he was talking about." Thus the climax, instead of altering the situation the rest of the sketch has built up, only recapitulates it in a more intensive fashion. The evidence of great evil suggests there should be change; but there is none, because the evil is of a nature that prevents men from thinking of alternatives. The values of the status quo appear as pervasive as the heat, as correct as the sun.

Throughout **Notes of a Hunter,** Turgenev describes a complete lack of comprehension of one's own interests, a comprehension that is the prerequisite of politics. When a character manages to rise above the common level of degradation, it is not by ignoring and still less by combatting the prevailing order, but rather by accepting it most fully: men scramble to secure a more elevated place in the hierarchy of power, content to be oppressed if they can oppress others. In **"The Tryst"** a valet transforms a farewell meeting with his peasant girl lover into a vicious encounter, rebuffing her expressions of love in the haughty manner that he believes his superior position entitles him to. In affected and dandified tones, like a master speaking to an underling, he tells her, "Anyway, you've got no education—so you must obey when you're told to do something." In **"Ermolai and the Miller's Wife,"** Ermolai routinely exploits Arina's misfortune for his own sexual pleasure, pointedly oblivious to the social process that has degraded them both, if in different degrees. In **"The Steward,"** the title character curries favor with his master, a real tyrant who is restrained only by his wish to appear a progressive: the steward carries out the master's cruel impulses for him, unconscionably maltreating the peasants under his control. (pp. 61-5)

Turgenev's description of serfdom invites the reader to view **Notes of a Hunter** as a plea for the underdog. We are presented with a picture of terrible suffering; quite naturally, our sympathies go out to the victims. Although that response *is* part of the experience of reading **Notes of a Hunter,** it should not be the whole of it. The work is far from the spirit of Stowe's *Uncle Tom's Cabin.* Turgenev does more than elicit compassion for the peasantry. Indeed, the character who is most present, appearing on every page, is a nobleman. That, of course, is the narrator, and his predicament is finally the most compelling aspect of Turgenev's design. On the face of it, the narrator's life

Writers associated with the magazine Contemporary. *Seated from left to right are Iván Goncharóv, Turgenev, Aleksándr Druzhínin, and Aleksándr Ostróvsky; Leo Tolstoy and Dimítry Grigoróvich are standing.*

seems without problems, especially in comparison to the peasants'. He is materially well off, free to move around the countryside, capable, because of his education, of enjoying refined pleasures. These, however, are secondary characteristics. What defines the narrator, what makes him memorable, is his remarkable reticence about himself. It is a highly ambiguous quality. If it often appears as a becoming modesty, a means for the narrator to confer all value on his material, it must also, in a world where individual assertion is so difficult to attain, suggest powerlessness.

Since reticence is the form that the narrator's problem assumes, he can never fully express his unhappiness. There are only tremors of unease. One such tremor occurs at the end of the sketch **"The Tryst."** After the supercilious valet and his serf-girl lover Akulina have departed, the narrator emerges from his hiding place to retrieve the bouquet that Akulina has offered as a gift and which had been carelessly discarded. The sketch closes with these words: "I came home; but for a long time the image of poor Akulina would not leave my mind, and her cornflowers, withered long since, are treasured by me." In one perspective, the narrator's rapt attention to the cornflowers points beyond them to the pathetic circumstances of peasant life. But if

the focus is shifted slightly from background to foreground, it is the narrator himself who dominates the scene. His attention to the peasants, his sympathy and concern, turn out to be elements in the personality he is desperately constructing for himself. Nothing *seems* to block the narrator from asserting himself except his own disposition; on the other hand, the status quo in mid-nineteenth-century Russia often managed to shape the constraints on the individual into the form of a personal choice.

In fact the narrator enjoys only one moment of great and unrestrained feeling in the course of the book, one moment when his whole being comes into play. It is a moment of exuberant pleasure; but significantly it is also the single moment in *Notes of a Hunter* when we can best begin to identify the cause of his pervasive discontent. It occurs in the sketch **"Kas'ian of the Beautiful Lands,"** when the narrator stops to rest in a forest clearing:

> I lay down flat on my back and begin admiring the peaceful play of the tangled leaves against the far-off radiant sky. An amazingly pleasant occupation, this lying on your back in a forest and gazing upward. It seems to you that you are looking into a bottomless sea which is spreading wide beneath

you, that the trees are rising not out of the earth but
just as if they were the roots of enormous plants,
and going down, are plunging straight into those
glassily limpid waters. . . . You do not move—
you gaze; and there is no expressing in words how
joyous and gentle and delectable is the mood that
enters your heart. You gaze: and that profound
pure azure brings to your lips a smile as innocent
as [the azure] itself, as innocent as the cloud against
the sky . . . and all the time your gaze is receding
farther and farther into the tranquil shining abyss,
and is drawing you after it, and it is impossible to
tear yourself away from that height, from that
depth.

The narrator experiences the world in terms of a visuality
so powerful that it "draws" the rest of the man behind it.
The normal agencies of consciousness relax; only in the
absence of any mediating or interpretive reflex can the visual sense exert its effect fully. At this most intense moment, contemplation becomes equivalent to identification.
The seductive attraction of the "abyss" absorbs the narrator in a way that eradicates the line between the external
world and himself, a feeling that Turgenev captures in a
turn of phrase that unreservedly equates the qualities of
the narrator's smile with the qualities adhering in the sky.
The physical activity of lying down is thus a prelude for
a more radical change in attitude, an abdication of self-
control so total that the self virtually dissipates. At the end
of the passage "depth" and "height" are one, because it
is no longer clear if the narrator is outside the natural
world looking in, or inside looking out.

Though the emotion accompanying the activity appears to
be pleasure, it must be a most ambiguous pleasure for
someone who put as much stock in the ego as Turgenev.
If the result in this case is satisfying, the experience suggests grave risk: once the individual loses his sense of himself as an independent agent, capable of maintaining the
borders of his personality, what will happen should the enticing world prove evil instead of good, as it appears to be
in "Kas'ian of the Beautiful Lands"? Identification with
the world, allowing it fully to penetrate one's being, would
be a truly terrible event. In fact, the moment in the forest
clearing is less an ideal than a warning. It reveals Turgenev's persistent belief that man must confront the world;
but it also shows his fear that without a confident and
ready understanding of one's own prerogatives that confrontation can prove disastrous.

Though "Kas'ian of the Beautiful Lands" is the most
graphic evidence, Turgenev also implies the narrator's potential weakness in the face of the world's power in many
other passages of *Notes of a Hunter.* He places one piece
of information so directly on the surface of the narrative
that it almost escapes attention, but it is crucial. Virtually
every sketch begins with the narrator departing from his
estate and many end with his mentioning his eagerness to
return there. But beyond the fact that the estate is located
in Orel province, no information about it is given. We do
not learn the shape or color of the house, nor the dimensions of the grounds surrounding it, nor the variety of the
furniture within. Where there might have been a symbol
of stability and tradition, there is a vacuum. Though the
narrator could locate his residence on a map, in effect he
is homeless.

The concept of home always played a major role in Turge-

nev's thoughts. Partly, home implied domesticity. As an
expatriate and bachelor, he often wished for a place to settle, and his letters are filled with references to his desire
to build a "nest." But "home" also had political meaning.
Upon hearing in Rome that emancipation was nearing,
Turgenev wrote, "Now every man should be at home in
his nest." He meant his estate in Orel, in order to oversee
the new arrangements with the peasants; he also meant
Russia generally, and the chance to participate in the momentous social transformation. The emancipation promised not only liberation of the serfs but an end to the political dispossession of men like Turgenev.

The absence of a true home in *Notes of a Hunter* is presented as a palpable psychological lack. Because he has no
home to which to withdraw, the narrator must live out his
life in a sphere dominated by Russia's public values. Aside
from one or two small havens of personal pleasure, the
landscape of *Notes of a Hunter* contains only one element:
the system promoted by the central government. One sees
only the homogeneity of the status quo, a stretch of terrain
whose distinguishing features never change, whose moral
and political problems never get solved, because there is
no place where moral or political challenge could originate.

The one structure that would seem most likely to break
up this depressing desolation is explicitly denied an existence: Turgenev is scathing in rejecting the nobility as a
consequential political force. The sketches in the book
that deal with the nobility depict it as a collection of fatu-
ous and vague men—the presiding attitudes are neatly indicated in the description of the party at the opening of
"Prince Hamlet of Shchrigrov Province," a remarkable
gathering in that the only energy of the evening comes alternately from men posturing and men fearing that they
will be caught out posturing. Nothing more substantial engages them. But the most dismaying fact about the nobility, Turgenev shows, is that its shortcomings are less a matter of personal insufficiency than of the prevailing political
organization, hence less amenable to change. As the title
character of "Ovsianko the Freeholder" remarks, complaining of the present condition of the nobility, "Those
with smaller estates have all spent time working for the
government or else can't stay put in one place. As for the
bigger sort, there's no recognizing them." Ovsianko believes that the nobility was once a significant political
force, which has now degenerated. His belief in the golden
age of the nobility is mostly wishful thinking, but his remarks accurately describe the factors that retarded the nobility's contemporary influence: enticement into government service, no continuity of landholding, the economic
heterogeneity of the estate. Ironically, Ovsianko himself
symbolizes the dilapidated condition of the nobility: a
"freeholder" was a category halfway between the nobility
and the peasantry, with some of the obligations and privileges of each estate—the freeholder status had to remind
the Russian noblemen that the estate they belonged to was
open and fluctuating, and finally regulated not by themselves but by the government. It follows that the nobleman-narrator feels himself homeless and lacks and confident vision that might come from commanding at least a
small part of the world.

As depicted by Turgenev, the nineteenth-century nobility
derives as little psychological satisfaction from Russian

life as the peasantry. Material advantages do not guarantee a purposeful existence; political dispossession saps the spirit of individuals in drawing rooms as fully as it does the spirit of individuals in thatched huts. The surprising convergence of rich and poor is perhaps the most ominous element in Turgenev's design. The peasantry and the nobility are searching for happiness on the same narrow ground, and the moves of one jostle and unnerve the other. Throughout *Notes of a Hunter,* Turgenev makes the reader consider this question: can two groups exist in harmony when they are equally dispossessed politically but one has great social power over the other? The question, indeed, informs the way each word gets on the page. The nobleman-narrator always has great potential power over the peasants, who are only the material that fill his narrative. The narrator is sympathetic to peasant life, but his role must tempt him to exploit the thoughts and acts of others for his own ends. Can a nobleman in the mid-nineteenth-century Russia, however well intentioned, forbear using any means at his disposal to bolster his self-esteem?

"Bezhin Meadow" explores the ambiguity of the narrator's position. In this sketch the peasants make their greatest effort to resist the oppression of Russian life and to express their human potential. With the peasants engaged in a task that so clearly touches his most vital concerns, can the narrator stand coolly by? Would he not also try to assert his personality if he knew a way? Indeed, the sketch opens not by focusing on the peasants but by describing the narrator, at much greater length than is usual in the cycle. He appears in the precarious state of mind that was first described in **"Kas'ian of the Beautiful Lands"**: the external world has insinuated itself so fully that the outlines of his individuality seem about to give way—and this time the external world appears not beautiful but sinister. True, as the sketch begins, the narrator is lost, and that partly accounts for the unease he feels; but Turgenev by his style emphasizes a disorientation that is psychological as well as physical, and that turns unease into existential anxiety. The narrator is in a world where structure has disappeared, where all angles and purchase that might have been used to establish a sense of stability are lacking. The sky "drains" of color, the air "congeals," the night "sprawls out," darkness "pours down." The atmosphere oppresses and envelops, and the narrator's discriminating power flags. When in the course of his erratic wanderings he almost falls into an unseen ravine, it is symbolic not only of the nearness of physical extinction but of the deadly absorbing power of a world not properly kept at a distance.

Yet by the end of the sketch the narrator has managed to attain a remarkable mastery over his surroundings. The change is partly the result of impenetrable night passing into bright day, but again it would be wrong to give too much weight to mere circumstance. The narrator has somehow acquired a capacity to order and shape the world. (pp. 66-72)

The substance of the sketch is designed to explain the narrator's changed attitude, from his initial confusion to his final robust confidence. The process of change, however, is very subtle; for most of the sketch the narrator hardly pays any attention to himself. Instead, he gives himself over to considering the behavior of five peasant boys he encounters in Bezhin Meadow, where they are guarding a

herd of horses. To pass the time before they sleep, the boys take turns relating wonderous stories, and each reveals an imagination in full play. Occasionally, the story-teller constructs such miraculous horrors that he is as terrified as his listeners. Despite the atmosphere of foreboding, when a strange sound is heard one of the boys plunges into the dark thickets to see if a wolf is threatening the herd. The narrator is filled with admiration and respect. Indeed, all the boys appear remarkably self-assertive: the stories they have told, myths about water nymphs and hobgoblins, seem to have given them a measure of control over the world. The peasant boys have managed to transcend their environment, which is the rarest of events in *Notes of a Hunter.*

Turgenev makes clear that the boys' achievement requires very special conditions. The peasant boys exist apart from the more insidious influences of Russian reality. Chronologically, they are, as boys, free from some of the pressures adults must face; geographically, as the narrator's disorientating experience at the beginning of the sketch emphasizes, it is hard to find the way to Bezhin Meadow from the workaday world. The light from the bonfire around which the boys sit marks off a piece of ground that is a realm of its own. "When one sits where it is light," the narrator remarks, "it is hard to make out what is going on in the dark, and therefore everything even near at hand seemed to have black curtains drawn over it." In this circumscribed area, in this "ring of light," as the narrator twice calls it, the boys manage to act out their best creative impulses. Here they can assert their individuality. But, Turgenev shows, it is difficult to sustain the magical power of that "ring of light." In the last lines of the sketch, which constitute a postscript to the main action, we are told that one of the boys was killed in an accident shortly after the narrator's encounter with him. The evil and chaos of the world at large sooner or later make themselves felt.

The boys' attempts to impose order on the world must have a special interest for the narrator. Their attitude of bafflement and fear precisely parallels his own at the beginning of the sketch. Turgenev sets up that elegant symmetry of concerns to expose a welter of moral confusion. The narrator, instead of working through his own uncertainty, has simply positioned himself at a point of maximum self-interest, a spectator to others' work and risk-taking that proves happily relevant to his own life. Watching the peasant boys' effort to comprehend the world is inspiring, as watching manual labor can be inspiring. The very inadequacy of the boys' effort is bracing—if the boys manage as well as they do with such meager tools, the narrator with his greater capacities should have nothing to fear. By the end of the sketch, though he has done nothing and exerted little mental effort, he feels infinitely more in control than he did at the beginning. "Bezhin Meadow" presents a neat division of labor, the difficulties that the narrator experiences are resolved for him by the example of the peasant boys. But as with any division of labor, there is a threat of moral dissipation. The narrator is continually on the verge of exploiting the peasant boys, not for material gain but in order to bolster his sense of his own identity.

That may seem an extreme conclusion to draw from the commonplaces of literary method: the narrator's presence at the scene of the peasant boys' adventure is, after all, the best certification of the truth of his story. But it is Turgenev's great talent to let the reader see that seemingly dispassionate methodological choices may have moral implications. The action at Bezhin Meadow reveals the dubious nature of the narrator's position throughout *Notes of a Hunter:* a use of others in the hope of finding vicarious satisfaction, and a repression of the knowledge of one's own weakness through the contemplation of those who are weaker still. (pp. 72-4)

Turgenev's treatment of the narrator in *Notes of a Hunter* reflects the more typical reaction of a Russian progressive in the middle of the nineteenth century: a genuine altruism that creeps ineluctably toward self-servingness. The narrator-nobleman exploits his peasant characters not from malice but simply because they are near at hand. Indeed, at that moment in Russian history, it was virtually impossible for a writer who belonged to the nobility to have portrayed the peasantry with unambiguous sympathy. *Notes of a Hunter* thus emphasizes a general rule of literature that is often denied or glossed over: a writer's choice of a subject is never innocent. In a letter to Annenkov in May, 1853, Turgenev wrote: "The peasants have completely overwhelmed us in literature. That in itself would be nothing; but I am beginning to suspect that we, no matter how much we may fuss with them, still don't understand anything about them. . . . It is time to send the muzhiks into retirement." The military image in the first sentence indicates Turgenev's realization that the peasantry is equivalent to a foreign force. A literary work dealing with the peasantry therefore can easily become distorted. Even if the theme is fully incorporated into the narrative, the result would be like a country that defeats an occupying army by absorbing it into the native population. Tactically effective, the effort entails a tremendous sacrifice of moral integrity.

No peasant character plays a major role in the novels that Turgenev began to publish in 1856. In fact, there are few references to the peasantry in these works. Increasingly, he came to realize that if an author were to comprehend the fullness of Russian reality, he had to begin by exploring the terrain he himself occupied. The muzhiks had to be sent into retirement not because they had become a trivial subject—they would never be that in Russian history—but because a prior step was necessary before the topic could be confronted in a thoroughly honest and thoroughly effective manner.

Though *Notes of a Hunter* can be read in isolation from Turgenev's other works, and with great pleasure, it is as a stage in his career that it appears most powerful and sympathetic. It has the aspect of a question that urgently requires an answer. Most of the sketches show Turgenev's great willingness to engage the world around him, but the unfortunate result is that he is drawn into complicity with prevailing evil: Was there any way for a writer to describe mid-nineteenth century Russia while successfully projecting his own values, his own voice?

Turgenev's intention of surpassing the style of *Notes of a Hunter* was announced most emphatically in a letter from October, 1852 to Annenkov, who had for some time been urging him to take a new literary tack. He wrote:

All that you say I feel as clearly as you—it is irre-

futable—and I sign my name under every word. It is necessary to go along a different path—and to say good-bye to the old manner. . . . But here is the question: am I capable of something big, serene? Can I achieve clear, simple lines? . . . This I do not know and cannot know until I try—but believe me, you will hear something new from me or you will hear nothing.

The letter, though full of personal doubt and complaint, suggests the beginnings of an aesthetic. Turgenev's uncertainty about achieving "clear, simple lines" was partly the result of his belief that he lacked a novelist's skills. In fact, he never learned to construct intricate plots or to delineate complex mental states. The technical problems, however, signaled more profound problems of sensibility. The "old manner" exerted a tenacious attraction. He had become very proficient at it—so proficient that it had begun to appear less a chosen manner than his natural means of expression. At the same time, however, he had to admit that *Notes of a Hunter* was not a success; he had spoken in his natural voice, but he felt he had not been heard. The ambiguous attraction of the novel was precisely that it was an alien genre. Writing "something big, serene" meant a leap into unknown territory; it would require giving a wrench to habit and intuition. Turgenev could hope that the strain of writing in a new form would impart distinctiveness to his authorial voice, as muscles under strain acquire tone.

The clearest sign of his move away from naturalness in the elimination of the first person type of narration. This was more than a formal adjustment; it involved his views of personality. In *Notes of a Hunter* Turgenev tried for an unapologetic presentation of his pleasures, sympathies, and concerns, but he refused to cast these aspects of himself in an insistently political or social light. As a result, the narration is often silent at points where we expect comment. The narrator's social pedigree and political allegiances are usually only hinted at. When they are mentioned, they are treated as unproblematical facts, demanding no attention. The narrator never meets anyone who asks him about his daily occupation, his opinion of the government, his view of serfdom, and he does not think of questioning himself. Thus, for all his directness, the narrator occasionally slips from view. (pp. 74-7)

[Turgenev] was a nobleman in a period when the nobility's sense of purpose was questionable; a serf-owner in a period of emancipation; a man of amiable and conciliatory temperament in a period of ideological passion—indeed, almost all his political traits were of a sort to inspire unease. But in accepting politics as an important constituent of his personality, he also began to find relief; for it meant that in questioning who he was, he was simultaneously questioning the political order of his day. Russia turned out to be not the eternal fact it presented itself as, but rather a contingent and alterable human construction. (p. 78)

Victor Ripp, in his Turgenev's Russia: From "Notes of a Hunter" to "Fathers and Sons," *Cornell University Press, 1980, 218 p.*

Joseph L. Conrad   (essay date 1986)

[*In the following excerpt, Conrad analyzes Turgenev's novella* Asya. *In opposition to critics who view the young narrator's friend, Gagin, as a peripheral figure, Conrad suggests that he functions as a complex catalyst for the ambiguous sexual feelings of the narrator, who may be divided between his mutual attraction for both Gagin and for Gagin's half-sister, Asya.*]

Ivan Sergeevič Turgenev's short tale, *Asja,* is a remarkable reflection of its author's philosophy of life and the quixotic nature of happiness. Here we find the vague desires of innocent youth contrasted with the wisdom of the mature, and the central theme of the ultimate impossibility of mutual love and happiness found in many of Turgenev's literary works.

Asja is usually said to concern an incipient love between the narrator, N. N., and the story's namesake. Asja's love is treated sensitively and sympathetically; the narrator's retrospective view presents his own role rather negatively. At first glance the third major character, Asja's half-brother Gagin, seems to be peripheral to the love story; however, careful scrutiny reveals that he plays a far greater role than that identified by critics. Gagin is the least developed of the three, and midway in the story his role is diminished. Yet, for the first half he is regularly in view, and at the end he is instrumental in spiriting Asja away, thus apparently depriving N. N. of his chance for happiness. Such factors are important ones, and because of them Gagin cannot be dismissed as a secondary figure. Turgenev's presentation of the changing relationships between N. N., Gagin, and Asja is delicately ambiguous; the ambivalence evident in N. N. is central to the events.

Asja is indeed a tale of lost opportunity, of impossible love, but when we examine the nature of the theme of "impossible love," it becomes apparent that the situation is more complex than it seems. There are subtle indications of an immediate attraction between the narrator and Gagin, an attraction which causes jealousy between them with regard to Asja, and which is very likely the source of her bewildered confusion about N. N.'s intentions.

To demonstrate that there is not one but two incipient love relationships in *Asja,* attention must be focussed on several actions by the protagonists which previously have been overlooked, or perceived as unmotivated or puzzling. For example, at the beginning the narrator has been wounded emotionally by an unfortunate affair with a coquettish widow; wandering in the small German spa of S. (Sinzig), he hears the music and raucous activity from a fraternity party in the town of L. (Linz) across the Rhein, and he decides to visit it. This decision may merely seem to be evidence of the narrator's already proclaimed interest in observing people; yet, when considered in light of other details which will come out in the course of this analysis, it is significant that he admits that he enjoys looking at the (male) students' faces, their embraces, the "innocent coquetry of youth," their "passionate glances," their "joyous effervescence of life," and their "good-natured abandon" (*razdol'je*); all this has a touching, warming effect on him (*èto . . . menja trogalo i podžigalo*).

But just as he is considering joining that lively bachelor party he hears Russian spoken. Asja and Gagin are introduced into the story with a device often used by Turgenev, i.e., the sound of the voice: " 'Asja, have you had enough?' a man's voice suddenly said behind me in Russian. 'Let's stay a little longer,' replied another voice, a woman's, in

the same language." N. N. reacts: "My glance fell on a handsome young man in a cap and loose jacket; he had his hand through the arm of a young girl of medium height in a straw hat which concealed the upper part of her face." Worthy of note here are not only Turgenev's ever-present interest in fashion, but the suggestive facts that N. N.'s attention quickly focusses on the man and not the woman, and that half of Asja's face is hidden from view. (This detail parallels her role in the first half of the story, where she is seen flitting in and out of various locales, but is only a minor irritation to N. N. and Gagin.)

The narrator then describes his new acquaintances. Again his attention is drawn first to Gagin, whose description constitutes some twenty lines and concludes:

> I liked Gagin at once. There are in the world such happy faces: everyone likes to look at them, just as though they warmed or stroked you [*točno oni grejut vas ili gljadat*]. Gagin had such a face—kind, charming with large soft eyes and soft, curly hair. He spoke in such a way that, even if you did not see his face, you felt by the mere sound of his voice that he was smiling.

With its sensations of warming and caressing, the pleasant sound of Gagin's voice and the general softness of his appearance, N. N.'s description is very subjective and unusually sensual. Gagin's effect on him is not unlike that of a lovely young woman on a man of the narrator's age at the time of the event (about twenty-five); the reader senses that N. N. is smitten by the sight of his new acquaintance.

The impression created by Asja is equally subjective, but the description contains none of the tactile sensations associated with Gagin:

> The girl whom he called his sister seemed to me at first glance to be extremely pretty. There was something special, something that belonged only to her, in the cast of her darkish, round face with its small, fine nose, almost childlike cheeks, and bright black eyes. She was gracefully built, but somehow did not seem to be fully developed yet. She did not in the least resemble her brother.

(pp. 215-16)

That over the course of this first evening he has developed a close relationship to Gagin can be heard in their leave-taking (chapter 2): "It's time I went!" (*Pora!*), the narrator exclaims, and Gagin's response is the same: "Pora." Asja makes an attempt to be noticed: she chases after them, she cries out to the narrator that his boat has broken the reflection of the moon, the moonlight pillar in the waters of the Rhein, and she calls out: "Good-bye!" (*Proščajte!*), which is seconded by Gagin's intimate "Till tomorrow" (*Do zavtra*). It is possible that the friendly farewells (*"Pora,"* and *"Do zavtra,"* which are rather unexpected among cultured people of the gentry who have only just met) are used here because these Russians are fellow countrymen in a foreign land; however, this informality may also suggest an unexpected intimacy. (p. 217)

When Gagin serenades N. N. (!) the next morning (chapter 3), N. N. hastens to meet him. We are offered a physical description which is more like that of a girl: "With his wavy, shiny hair, open neck, and rosy cheeks, he [Gagin] was as fresh as the morning himself." Asja is not present. Entering a cozy garden (*sadik*) the two men sit down together and discuss their past and future. When N. N. speaks of his unhappy love for the widow, there is no strong response on the part of Gagin: after sighing once or twice in polite sympathy, Gagin invites him to see his sketches, and N. N. "immediately accepts."

It is with considerable ambiguity that Turgenev uses the next chapter (4) to demonstrate N. N.'s fluctuating attitudes toward Asja. His presentation of N. N.'s often contradictory reactions makes it difficult to determine exactly which direction the characters will take. When Gagin and N. N. find Asja climbing the ruins of a medieval castle, N. N. feels compelled to reproach her for her carelessness. If we have seen that he has found immediate rapport with Gagin, his reactions to Asja seem to vacillate between admiration and hostility. For after his paternal admonition concerning her welfare (*Ja gromko upreknul ee v neostorožnosti*), he appreciatively notes her "graceful figure, clearly and beautifully outlined against the clear sky." Yet he comments that he watched her "with an unfriendly feeling." He explains that her smile was strange, half-impudent, half-gay; he is perplexed by the unnaturalness which she projects. Although he continues to be attracted by her dark eyes, charming movements, and light-footed agility, he is vexed by her perpetual mobility and laughter. Observing her closely, he sees that she seems to be consciously striving to attract his admiration. He then notices that, suddenly ashamed at her own actions, she lowers her "long lashes and sits down modestly, as if she were guilty." Asja has indeed drawn his attention, for now he examines her face closely, and calls it the "most changeable face" (*samoe izmenčivoe lico*) that he has seen. Does this observation perhaps reflect, or project, his own subconscious inconstancy?

In a few short paragraphs Turgenev has shown N. N.'s positive and negative responses to Asja's unpredictable moods, and has established his heroine as a charming, yet puzzling, character who intrigues the reader; he leaves open the possibility of a romance between N. N. and Asja. But the bond between N. N. and Gagin has grown much stronger. Later the same day (chapter 4) Gagin rather familiarly (given their short acquaintance) and naughtily ("with a sly grimace" [*s lukavoj užimkoj*]) toasts the lady of N. N.'s heart. . . . Upon hearing the toast, Asja asks: "Does he really have, do you really have such a lady?" As if surprised by that possibility, she pauses for a moment, and her facial expression takes on a "challenging, almost mocking laugh." This shift may be intended to intrigue N. N. still further. And when she withdraws, she comments: "I thought you two would be more comfortable together" (*vam budet lušče vdoem*), thereby creating a void to stimulate N. N.'s curiosity. Conversely, it is also possible that she feels excluded from their company. Upon returning, she gives Gagin a geranium with the request that he imagine her to be the lady of his heart. But learning that N. N. is about to leave, she suggests that he instead give it to N. N. Gagin does so as if it were a sacred ceremony: "Gagin held out the geranium sprig to me in silence. I silently put it in my pocket." The solemnity of this scene may prompt the reader to ask: Is Gagin to be the "lady" of N. N.'s heart?

Asja's capricious behavior seems calculated to arouse N. N.'s interest, but at this stage he is already fundamentally attracted to Gagin. He confides in the reader: "The more

I got to know him, the more strongly did I get attached to him," and then offers an encomium on Gagin's "typical Russian nature [*duša*], truthful, honest, simple, but, unfortunately, a little flabby, without tenacity and inward fire." Addressing Gagin familiarly in the second person singular, albeit silently in thought, he observes: "You'll never work hard, you're incapable of pulling yourself together." Finally, he states that "it was impossible not to be fond of him; one's heart was simply drawn to him. We spent four hours together, sometimes sitting on the sofa, sometimes walking slowly up and down in front of the house, and in those four hours we finally became close friends." (pp. 217-19)

Something has happened to N. N. over the course of this day; returning to his hotel room "in a totally different mood" from that of the evening before, he confesses: "I felt almost angry with myself and could not calm myself for a long time. An unfathomable irritation was tearing me apart." Despite his stated belief that this irritating emotional turmoil is the result of his thoughts about Asja, the real cause of his confusion may be the involuntary attraction which he feels for Gagin. In any case it is noteworthy that he displays a lack of interest in women. The once-cherished note from his recent lover now has no meaning for him: "And the widow's note lay very quietly on the floor, shining white in the moonbeams." Asja has had a largely negative effect on his emotional well-being.

Far from being charmed by this enigmatic creature, he has the mildly condescending impression that she is a "totally Russian girl, indeed a common girl, almost a housemaid," and she reminds him of "homegrown Katjas and Mašas." His attitude toward her is now quite negative: he does not choose to spend time with her, for he has noticed her "sallow, faded little face" (*želtovatoe, ugassee ličiko*). Rather he invites himself to go with Gagin in search of suitable landscapes to paint. Once out in nature N. N. lies on the grass and tries to read, but unsuccessfully. Nor can Gagin paint. Yet when they concentrate on each other, their conversation begins to flow. Their discussion turns into a veritable whirlwind of ideas, which stimulates Gagin to lie down next to N. N. Then their conversation becomes even more animated: "Our youthful speeches flowed freely, sometimes passionate, sometimes wistful, sometimes ecstatic, but almost always vague." The reader may wonder why these words, so full of passion and ecstasy, are unclear; the reason for the narrator's confusion and apparently, Gagin's as well, may be the intimacy developing between them.

Gagin and N. N.'s impassioned discussion about life and nature is a major moment in the development of their mutual attraction. There has also been a striking change in Asja: when the men return from their day in nature, N. N. notices that she is quite subdued and displays none of the coquetry or affectation which irritated him so upon their previous meetings. Gagin nonchalantly observes that she has "decided to abstain and do penitence" (*post i pokajanie na sebja naložila*). While she may merely be trying another pose to catch N. N.'s eye, her serious behavior seems unmotivated, and the reader may ask, From what does she intend to abstain? From life, from happiness with N. N.? And why should she do penitence? These questions beg an answer, for she has committed no action as yet—

nor does she later in the story—which would be cause for such self-abnegation.

Gagin's observation arouses a number of other, equally contradictory questions: Why would a girl deliberately make herself unappealing? Is she only acting, in order to pique his curiosity? Or has she noticed the easy rapport between her brother and N. N., a union of spirits which apparently excludes her? Is she then confirming her lack of success, her inability to attract N. N.? Or is she trying desperately to get his attention? He does indeed notice her, but it is at this point that he remarks: "What a chameleon that girl is!", a comment which is not necessarily one of affectionate approval.

After some two weeks N. N. notes that Asja avoids him, and that she is "secretly distressed [*ogorčennyj*] or embarrassed [*smuščennyj*]." Turgenev does not tell us why, but leaves us to wonder: Has she seen that her brother and N. N. are unusually attracted to each other, and is she "distressed" and "embarrassed" by the awkward nature of her position? When N. N. criticizes her choice of reading matter (a French novel, probably a romance), she ashamedly puts the book down and runs outside to the garden. Rejection, not only of her physical self but of her intellect and heart, is more than Asja can endure.

Despite frequent cautions against doing so found in early nineteenth-century Russian literature and despite numerous negative comments about French literature found in Turgenev's letters from 1857, reading a French novel is a relatively harmless occupation for a young girl. But N. N. reads Goethe's *Hermann und Dorothea,* a "domestic epic," aloud to Gagin, not to Asja. This may only be an indication that these young men are confirmed "Romantics." But it is also possible that N. N. is suggesting something more intimate to his new friend. Asja, in a show of jealousy, keeps trying to draw N. N.'s attention, first by running in and out, and then by sitting next to him to listen to the tale. And the next day she surprises him once again: she has become "as domestic and sedate as Dorothea." But her naive attempt to woo N. N. is still unsuccessful. When (in one of Turgenev's stock devices) N. N. overhears her swear to Gagin that she loves only him, her brother, he is shocked. He reports that this chance discovery "suddenly confirmed [my] suppositions." Here the reader first assumes N. N. is referring to his earlier suspicion that they were not in fact brother and sister, but N. N. may have suspicions of a different sort, i.e., that Gagin and Asja are involved in an incestuous relationship, that Gagin is therefore heterosexual and that a close relationship between himself and Gagin is endangered. Support for this interpretation may be found in N. N.'s bitter exclamation: "Good Lord, they certainly know how to pretend! But why should they? Why try to fool me? I never expected it of *him* (emphasis added). And what a sentimental scene!" N. N. resents the fact that he has been betrayed, not by Asja, but by Gagin. (pp. 219-21)

Emotional turmoil is shown in all three principals (at the beginning of chapter 8) when Gagin receives N. N. with affectionate reproaches. Asja, who is thoroughly embarrassed by this scene, bursts out in apparently causeless laughter. Gagin is likewise embarrassed ([*on*] *smutilsja*), and N. N. becomes angry at her for upsetting them both: "I confess I was very vexed with Asja. I did not feel particularly at ease anyway, and now again that unnatural

laughter and those strange grimaces." In a vain attempt to gain N. N.'s attention, Asja keeps entering the room and running out again, and the conversation between Gagin and N. N. does not take hold. N. N. takes his leave coldly by lightly pressing Asja's hand and giving her a slight bow, whereupon Gagin, perhaps to assert his claim to N. N., volunteers (*vyzyvalsja*) to see him home.

On the way, they sit on a bench at a statue of a grieving Madonna to commune with nature; there they have a "remarkable" conversation. Gagin tells him Asja's history. N. N. agrees to listen, but "not without a certain bewilderment," and in retrospect he admits his jealousy: "I did not expect him to start talking *about her*" (emphasis added). Still, Gagin's story about Asja appeases N. N. After finishing, Gagin smiles "his quiet smile," and suggests they go home together. N. N.'s response: "I pressed his hand warmly."

Gagin confesses that Asja has noticed a change ("she . . . took it into her head to tell me that I was colder to her than I used to be"), and in a gesture perhaps intended to deflate any interest on the part of N. N. for his half-sister, tells him that she "[wants] a hero, a man who is out of the ordinary, or a picturesque shepherd on a mountain pass." Of course, N. N. is neither; on the contrary, he is simply an ordinary, if somewhat confused, young gentleman. Dropping the discussion of Asja, N. N. agrees that they should go to Gagin's. The latter responds with a good-natured but ironic smile (*on dobrodušno usmexnulsja*). Gagin's smile is puzzling unless seen in the context of a secret intimacy between them, which is then confirmed by N. N.'s confession: "I was feeling a kind of sweetness, namely sweetness in my heart, as though someone had secretly poured some honey into it."

In keeping with Turgenev's ambiguous presentation, N. N.'s reaction to learning Asja's secret may be read in at least two ways: Either he is relieved to know that Asja is not Gagin's lover, and that despite Gagin's remark about a hero or a shepherd, he foresees no hindrance to the further development of his relationship with her (the traditional interpretation), or he sees that the path is open to increased intimacy with Gagin. In either case, N. N.'s sense of relief, and the sweet conviction that all is well, mark a crossroad in the development of the love plot(s).

From this point on there is an unspoken struggle in both Gagin and N. N. to define their relationship and that of N. N. to Asja. This turn of events also marks the inception of N. N.'s love for Asja, and in chapter 9, he remarks that he began to understand her soul; he saw that

> a secret oppression weighed on her constantly; her inexperienced and misguided pride was struggling anxiously and in confusion; but she strove with all her being for truth. I understood why this strange girl attracted me; it was not only by her half-wild charm, which pervaded her slender body, that she attracted me; it was her soul that appealed so strongly to me.

The riddle posed here is: Just what is that "secret oppression"? Has N. N. only now begun to recognize that she has fallen in love with him and is attempting to interest him, or does he sense that she has guessed his feelings for her half-brother, and that her "inexperienced and misguided pride" is "anxious" and "confused" by the fact that he is not yet attracted to her? Is she striving to understand the relationship between the two men? This passage indicates N. N.'s new receptiveness toward her and shows his sympathy with her predicament; now he begins to look more kindly upon her.

Asja senses this change, for when N. N. asks her why she left them earlier, she answers: "I went away . . . because . . . I won't go away now. . . ." Though confused by N. N.'s previous ambivalence toward her, she seems to be relieved that he is, after all, interested in her and not in her half-brother. Yet when she innocently asks him about her brother's toast to the "lady of his heart," he responds with a half-truth: "Your brother was joking. I never cared for any woman, at least, I don't care for any now." It is of course possible that with this comment N. N. may be admitting that he has no interest in the opposite sex. His subsequent behavior seems to confirm this interpretation: when Asja asks what he finds pleasing in women, he exclaims, "What a strange question!" The result of this exchange is that Asja is somewhat embarrassed (*slegka smutilas'*) by his quick retort. But perhaps she has misunderstood: he may also be suggesting that he is open to a relationship with her. Turgenev allows the situation to remain ambiguous.

At the end of the chapter, when they are indeed coming closer in spirit, and Asja has hinted at her desire to go somewhere, to do something good (compare Natalja in *Rudin* [1856], and Elena in *On the Eve* [1860]), N. N. dances with her, and suffers from a confusion of sensual perceptions, punctuated by the "sweet sounds" of a Josef Lanner waltz, and Asja's "soft, feminine" nature. The mature N. N. belatedly confesses: "For a long time afterwards I remembered the touch of her tender body; for a long time I heard her quickened, close breathing; for a long time her dark, immobile, almost closed eyes in a pale but animated face, sharply outlined by fluttering curls, haunted me." All these new sensations caused the young N. N. to examine the conflicting emotions within himself.

Turgenev uses nature in a masterful way to reflect the younger N. N.'s inner turmoil. Chapter 10 is brief, less than a page; but it progresses very neatly from objective evaluation of events, to subjective perceptions of the Rhein and the stars reflected in the water's surface, then back to reflective consideration of the evening's events, and finally to the mature N. N.'s objective evaluation of what he really wanted at that time. After speaking of a "mysterious restlessness," he concludes: "A thirst for happiness has been kindled in me, . . . happiness to the point of satiety—that was what I wanted, what I longed for." His experience while crossing the Rhein focussed his attention on new desires; he began turning toward Asja and away from Gagin.

This transition is shown in the subsequent chapter. N. N., drawn to Asja, is not at all eager to disturb Gagin, who, in a mood quite different from his earlier, sweet disposition, is now in a fury: "He was standing all dishevelled and covered with paint before a stretched canvas and, brandishing his brush over it, he nodded almost fiercely to me, then took a few steps back, screwed up his eyes, and pounced on his picture again." His furious activity may reflect his jealousy over the attention N. N. is now paying to Asja, and he cannot accept his changed position. As N. N. and Asja converse, growing closer and closer emotion-

ally, and ultimately touch hands ("her hot little hand squeezed mine tightly"), Gagin checks this development by exclaiming: "Isn't this background a little too dark?" (*N.! ne temen ètot fon?*). The wording of the original is perhaps more symbolic than a direct translation suggests: *temnyj* has the basic meaning of "dark," but also has connotations of "suspicious," "fishy," and "(evil) lurking." Perhaps Gagin is suddenly feeling threatened by the closeness he has witnessed developing between his half-sister and N. N. If that is the case, the background has indeed darkened for him. His relationship with N. N. could be changed fundamentally as a result of this new interest in Asja. Thus, he quickly interrupts a major development which could jeopardize his position with N. N. In response to this challenging question, N. N. moves close to Gagin; Asja, in at least temporary submission to Gagin's will, withdraws to her room.

Gagin attempts to separate them again in chapter 12, when N. N. notices that something has changed in Asja which he cannot understand. She is pale; fixing her eyes on him, she accuses him of having a low opinion of her. He is about to reassure her that she is wrong, when Gagin asks loudly: "Why do you look so crestfallen, the two of you?" Twice rejecting her brother's offer to play another waltz, Asja exclaims: "Not for anything!" This abrupt rebuff of her brother's seemingly generous suggestion indicates her resentment at the interruptions, and may mark the beginning of her claim to N. N. In any case, it causes (the somewhat imperceptive) N. N. to ask himself if she could possibly be in love.

The same question both closes chapter 12 and opens 13, as N. N. also admits that "her image, the image of the girl with the affected laugh, had *wormed itself* [*vtesnilsja;* emphasis added] into my heart and that I wouldn't be able to rid myself of it soon." This would not be a curious reaction if N. N. were strictly heterosexual; but in the context of his already established relationship with Gagin, it highlights the inner struggle he experiences when confronted with the necessity of making a choice between hetero- and homosexual love.

Chapter 14 brings Gagin's explanation of Asja's confusion: "My sister Asja is in love with you." Since N. N. has already begun to wonder if Asja loves him, his reaction is quite unexpected: "I gave a violent start and half raised myself in my chair." The reason for this sudden response can only be deduced by conjecture: Is there a sudden fear that a woman's love may be the undoing of the relationship between the two young men? Gagin seems to be aware of the possibility, and calling N. N. a "very nice fellow," admits that he cannot understand "why she has so fallen in love" with him. He continues by saying that "she will ruin herself, certainly." And finally, Gagin, as if losing confidence in N. N.'s orientation, stammers "You are not going to marry her, are you?" Dumbfounded by these comments, N. N. responds: "How do you want me to answer such a question? Judge for yourself, can I now?" On the one hand, Gagin is momentarily reassured that his relationship with N. N. is not threatened; on the other, he is relieved that the danger of Asja's ruination, i.e., her love for a man who could not reciprocate, is passed. Revealing his ambivalent feelings toward them both, N. N. is at once elated and disturbed by her love, and then decides that "it's out of the question" that he should marry a "girl of seventeen with her character."

The mature N. N. explains his thoughts while on his way to the fateful meeting with Asja (chapter 16). Reflecting on the events of the past few days, he asked himself: "I had been thirsting for happiness, hadn't I? . . . It had become possible, and I was *hesitating,* I was *pushing it away,* I *had to* [*dolžen byl*] push it away. *Its suddenness disconcerted me. Asja herself,* with her fiery temperament, her past, her upbringing—*that fascinating but strange creature,* I confess, *frightened me.* My *feelings struggled within me* for a long time" (emphasis added). This passage is very revealing when read in light of N. N.'s attempt to make the choice whether or not to love conventionally, or to go against convention by showing his feelings for Gagin. His vacillation, his rejection of heterosexual love, his fear and the threatening presentiment Asja arouses in him, all force him to make a decision: "I can't marry her," he says; but, ever ambivalent, he adds, somewhat resignedly (and curiously, in view of what follows): "She'll never find out that I too have fallen in love with her."

At the beginning of their "secret meeting," when Asja hopes for N. N.'s declaration of love, he instead explains that he was obligated to tell her brother everything, to which she responds in disbelief: "Obligated?" This is a question perhaps shared by the reader, but one left unanswered. In the next few minutes, N. N. gradually falls under her spell ("Her eyes drew me after them, I forgot everything, I drew her to me"). but when she whispers "I am yours," the thought of Gagin, who disapproves of this meeting, causes him suddenly to stand back and shift the blame to Asja by reproaching her for confessing her love to her brother. At the same time he is aware that something is terribly wrong, and he thinks to himself: " 'What am I saying?' . . . and the idea that I was an immoral deceiver, that Gagin knew of our meeting, that everything had been misinterpreted [*iskaženo*], exposed [*obnaruženo*] kept ringing in my head."

These are telling statements: for if he is deceiving Asja by continuing the role of a potential lover, he is also deceiving Gagin. And what has been "misinterpreted"? What has been "exposed"? He continues: "You had no confidence in me, you doubted me," an accusation which could confirm her earlier suspicion of a relationship between her brother and N. N. While it is undoubtedly true that Asja is the one who is most hurt by this encounter, it is also the case that the young N. N.'s ambivalence is underlined by his own later recognition that "I could not understand how this meeting could possibly have come to such a quick, such a stupid end, how it could end when I had not said even a hundredth part of what I wanted to say, what I had to say, *when I had no idea myself how our meeting might end*" (emphasis added). And he reproaches himself angrily for letting such an ending come about. Revealing his confusion, he asks: "Was I really capable of parting from her? Could I bear to be without her? 'Madman! Madman!' I kept repeating bitterly."

This development has engendered a break in the relations between the two men. The next day (chapter 18) Gagin and N. N. are already uneasy with each other, and the following evening N. N. does not understand when Gagin refuses to discuss Asja with him and says only *Proščjte* ("good-bye" but also "farewell"). N. N. then utters "Till

tomorrow . . . tomorrow all will be decided." Here it is quite clear that the younger N. N. did not comprehend the finality of Gagin's word. The older, wiser N. N. does indeed recognize its meaning, for he says: "[I thought:] Tomorrow I will be happy! [But] happiness has no tomorrow, nor does it have a yesterday. It doesn't remember the past, it doesn't think about the future. It has only the present, and that is not a day, but a moment." Morning (chapter 19) brings a letter from Gagin, a note which hints at the real nature of the relationship between them. In his letter Gagin excuses himself by saying that he found no other way out of a situation which might become difficult and dangerous (*zatrudnitel'nyj i opasnyj*), and he writes: "There are prejudices I respect; I realize that it is impossible for you to marry Asja." . . .

Gagin has seen that their relationship is impossible for a number of reasons: society's disapproval, the emotional turmoil it has created in his half-sister, and his lack of confidence in N. N.'s constancy. The ingenious nature of Turgenev's ambiguity here is that, in the first place, these statements may refer to N. N.'s supposed "prejudice," i.e., Gagin's assumption that he would be unwilling to marry someone of the lower class (Asja, the illegitimate daughter of Gagin's father and a serf-girl), for doing so could conceivably lead to a difficult and dangerous situation for the couple. Thus, Gagin would be forced to remove her, thereby resolving N. N.'s predicament. Alternatively, Gagin may be implying society's disapproval of a homosexual relationship, which would lead to difficult and dangerous lives for the two men. In either case, he has "found no other way out," for he knows that it is "impossible" for N. N. to marry Asja.

By contrast with Gagin's response to the situation, this experience helps N. N. overcome his ambivalence; he asks: "What prejudices? . . . What right had he to steal her away from me?" And soon thereafter, when he reads Asja's note reproaching him for not having said outright that he loved her, he admits to his earlier confusion:

> I did not tell her I loved her. And indeed I could not have said it at the time. When I met her in that fateful room I still had no clear realization (*soznanie*) of my love; it had not awakened even when I was sitting with her brother in that senseless, oppressive silence. It flared up in me with irresistible force only a few moments later when, frightened by the possibility of misfortune (*ispugannyj vozmožnost'ju neščast'ja*), I began looking for and calling her, but then it was already too late. Asja would not have gone away if there had been a hint of coquetry in her and if her position had not been a false one.

N. N.'s mature assessment confirms the thesis of the present analysis. As a young man he was uncertain about his sexuality, did not know which way to turn, and was in terror of possible exposure of a relationship with Gagin; at the same time he recognized that Asja's situation vis-à-vis himself was false; it was impossible, given what she had witnessed prior to, and experienced during, their fateful meeting. But what of N. N. "now," twenty years later? Is his problem still unresolved? As if to confirm his sexual ambivalence, N. N. admits that

> fate ordered everything for the best by not uniting me with Asja; I comforted myself with the thought that I should probably not have been happy with

such a wife. . . . Condemned to the solitude of an old bachelor, I live out the lonely years. . . . And I myself, what has become of me? What has been left of those blissful and anxious days, those winged hopes and aspirations?

Close examination of Turgenev's romantic tale has demonstrated that *Asja* is not solely concerned with the inception of love between an impressionable young man and an enigmatic young woman, and that there are numerous statements, actions, and reactions within the text which are not readily obvious in terms of such a narrow scheme. These apparently inexplicable details are based in the relationship between N. N. and Gagin, and, together with the remainder of the work, form a love triangle with no clear resolution in terms of the narrator's own development. N. N. has moved from a reaction of being deeply hurt by his "wicked beauty," which made him seek a close, intimate, and comforting friendship with another male, Gagin, to a growing attraction for Asja, which is then cut off by Gagin, and finally to a state in which he is still unsure of his sexual orientation. For her part, Asja immediately recognized that his interest in Gagin was greater than in herself (note her formal "good-bye" and refusal to give her hand to N. N. in chapter 2); she was by stages perplexed, confused, and disturbed by her daily confrontation with this situation. Nevertheless, as a typical Turgenev heroine of this period of his writing (cf. Natal'ja, Zinaida of *First Love* [1859], and Elena), she gradually came to love her "hero" and, with however much timidity and hesitation, dared to force him to a decision. That action resulted in her own emotional devastation when she found (chapter 16) not only that he could not make a choice, but that his intimate bond to Gagin was stronger than she had imagined. But it was just this episode which forced N. N. to examine his own motivations and the essence of his sexualtiy. Clearly, Turgenev's novella is more complicated than has been assumed in the past.

For all of these reasons, *Asja* is a story of ambivalent love, one presented with sensitive ambiguity. Turgenev's skilled narration of the interlocking relationship among the three principals lends the tale considerable charm. Further examination of his novels and stories, and the curious history of his lifelong relationship with Pauline and Louis Viardot, may perhaps suggest similar instances of ambivalent love in Turgenev's life and works. (pp. 221-27)

> *Joseph L. Conrad, "Turgenev's 'Asja': Ambiguous Ambivalence," in* Slavic and East-European Journal, *Vol. 30, No. 2, Summer, 1986, pp. 215-29.*

Edgar L. Frost   (essay date 1987)

[In the following excerpt, Frost explores themes of lovelessness and isolation in "Mumu" while suggesting that the story functions as an indictment of Russian serfdom.]

There is only one instance in his story **"Mumu"** where Turgenev directly and uncompromisingly tells the reader that love exists, and those involved are Mumu and Gerasim. Mumu, we are told, "loved Gerasim alone," while for his part "Gerasim . . . loved her to distraction" (trans. mine—E. F.). In no other scene is the reader shown unquestionable, directly attested mutual love, and it is this

simple fact which Turgenev plays upon to structure the entire story and to characterize those who act it out. He does so, for the most part, by focusing on the absence of love rather than its presence. Such an approach is not surprising, since love in Turgenev's œuvre is usually illusory or short-lived. The only two characters that love each other and show their love are the dog and her master, and, while the depths of this relationship are shown, the lone instance of such love is outweighed by all the manifestations of its absence elsewhere.

The major example of one who does not love and is not loved is, of course, the *barynja,* and the primary victim of this negative force on the love scene is Gerasim. But it should be noted that there are several other instances of the absence of love in what is indeed a very sad tale. The unfortunate Tat'jana is loved by Gerasim, but does not return his feelings, at least not until it is too late; her main reaction to him is fear, and her main tactic in dealing with him is to try to stay away from him. The eternally rationalizing Kapiton, generally stupefied by drink, can hardly be said to be in love with Tat'jana; he is not opposed to the idea of matrimony, but when he learns that it is the excruciatingly shy laundress who has been chosen for him, he thinks painfully and exclusively of the threat Gerasim represents to him. Family life is also noteworthy by its absence, and the fact that the major characters have no families underscores the degree to which love is missing in their lives. (p. 171)

The first part of the story develops the ill-fated affair between Gerasim and Tat'jana; when it is finished, the stage is ready for his next love. In like manner, when the second object of his affection no longer exists, the action is again ready for a shift, and Gerasim leaves almost immediately, though he is first seen briefly by another of the serfs. The story develops by moving from one love episode to another, or, more precisely, from zero on the love scale, to fairly high, to the top of the scale, and then back down to zero. The episode with Tatjana is a step up and a preparation for the greater love the hero finds with Mumu. The love element, in its presence, its absence, and its degrees, dominates the narrative. For it to loom so large in the plot it must be a symbol for something very important in the lives of Gerasim and others—something, perhaps, more than just love itself. I would suggest that this something was the human dignity of which the serfs were deprived.

There is general agreement that Turgenev was outraged by the treatment of serfs, in general throughout Russia and in particular on his mother's estate. A sensitive person who felt guilty about the lot of the serfs, Turgenev is remembered as one who wrote feelingly about their great suffering and their qualities as human beings. . . . Turgenev felt very strongly that the serfs were human beings and should be treated as such. Thus, whether love stands for freedom, happiness, or something else, one can surmise that in the story it represents much that is denied Gerasim. He is a serf, and therefore his life is made incomplete. In the final section, Gerasim is home again, but he remains alone, loveless. He has no family, and the reader is told that he has no dog and sees no women. He is in familiar surroundings, but the story remains pathetic precisely because he has been cut off from the two beings that gave his life a deeper meaning through love, whether real or imagined.

Some might think it improper to speak of the relationship between Tat'jana and Gerasim as "finished," as I have above, since it never really begins, except on his part. Such an objection might be valid in one sense, but not another. While the love is a one-way affair, from Gerasim to Tat'jana, it is clearly an attempt on his part to deepen his life, and as such it is a foreshadowing of the real joy he finds in the joining of his life with Mumu's. Indeed, there is much evidence to link Tat'jana and Mumu. Both fill a void in the life of the hero, thus illustrating his otherwise empty fate at the hands of his mistress. One can scarcely help noticing the link between Tat'jana and Mumu, because of the way Turgenev structures the tale. As Tat'jana is about to leave for the remote country, to accompany her worthless husband, Gerasim comes out of his room and presents her with a red kerchief, an obvious sign of his affection for her. She responds by crying and by kissing him three times, and although the kisses are described as being "in the Christian manner," they nevertheless convey feeling for him. A few moments later, she is gone, but no sooner has the cart bearing her lurched out of his view than Gerasim turns off along the river and notices the as-yet-unnamed Mumu wriggling helplessly in the mud there, trying to extract herself.

It is, of course, quite a coincidence for Gerasim to stumble onto a new and greater love almost before the one he has lost is out of sight. The suddenness of the transition from Tat'jana to Mumu is such that it draws attention to the obvious and invites comparisons of the two objects of Gerasim's love. The precipitousness of the break also makes one mindful of the structure of the story, conveying the notion that something new and important is about to happen and thus setting up the ascendancy of the Mumu-Gerasim relationship.

The similarities between Tat'jana and Mumu make the work a Freudian delight—beginning with the fact that Mumu is a female and shares Gerasim's bed: "[She] immediately leapt onto the bed with a satisfied air." What is important, however, is not sex, but love and all that it stands for in the tale. And in that connection the links between Tat'jana and Mumu are instructive. Both are orphans of vague or unknown ancestry. Tat'jana has a worthless uncle, banished to the country and thus prefiguring her fate with her equally worthless husband. This and the existence of some other uncles are all we are told of her lineage. The author, in fact, pointedly tells us that "she essentially had no relatives." No mention is made of whence Mumu has come, and one can only surmise that she is unwanted progeny that someone has cruelly disposed of. Both characters have known hardship. The dog has been left to die in the river, and the woman has been oppressed since her early years. Furthermore, the two resemble each other physically. Tat'jana is described as "small, thin, fair-haired, with moles on her left cheek," while Gerasim spies near the river bank a "small pup, white with black spots." The unwanted whelp is also pictured as trembling with "all its . . . thin body." (pp. 172-73)

Tat'jana is a cowering type who trembles at the mention of her mistress's name and never talks to anyone if she can avoid it. Her only interest is in finishing her work on time. Turgenev's direct words about her are, "She was of an extremely mild, or, it would be better to say, timorous disposition," and, he adds, she "was deathly afraid of others."

There is a clear connection between the frightened woman and the intimidated dog that refuses to be enticed by the *barynja* and her servants.

Just as Tat'jana "trembled at the mere mention of the *barynja*'s name," so Mumu "began to shiver and flattened herself against the wall" upon being brought before the old woman. The words "Disposition . . . extremely mild, . . . timorous," cited before with reference to Tat'jana, are echoed when one reads "became very frightened and was ready to hurl herself toward the door" in the description of the dog's behavior before her mistress. The actions of Gerasim's two love objects are strikingly similar. Both are terrified of the old woman, and it is further significant that Tat'jana's fear exists, "although the latter hardly knew her by sight." The dread *barynja*, of course, is not acquainted with Mumu either, a fact not particularly noteworthy in itself but important as an added parallel between Tat'jana and Mumu.

The accumulation of such evidence would seem to make it difficult to deny that Turgenev had reason for equating the two—as, indeed, he had. And the reason was that he wanted to call attention to their desperate loneliness, isolation, and need of love, as well as their relationships with Gerasim. In a work so devoid of love, theirs is an eloquent connection, both with each other and with the hero. It is a deft touch in the Tat'jana-Mumu relationship that the connection . . . combines the ideas of love and a fawning, cringing attitude, two of the essential ingredients of the tale. And though the work is one of love and its absence, it is also one of the frightful cruelties perpetrated upon human beings and symbolized by the equal tyranny over a dumb beast and her dumb master. Within this scheme, too, Tat'jana serves as a link between Mumu and Gerasim, for she is of the dog's nature and the man's kind.

An avenue by which Turgenev airs the theme of nonlove is, certainly, the corollary of isolation. He begins by focusing on the solitary figure of the dictatorial old *barynja* and concludes by sketching the hero in his lonely hut, without family, with no romantic interest, and with no dog. In between, the author shows us the abandoned mongrel and the timid, then banished and isolated, Tat'jana. The work, as will be demonstrated, is partially organized around the theme of isolation. (pp. 174-75)

[The *barynja* and Gerasim] are alone in different ways, to be sure, but ironically enough they share equally the fate of being isolated from their fellow beings. Being thus isolated, they cannot love and be loved, a common bond of loneliness between the two.

For her part, the old woman has been cast off by others because of her age and her disposition, foul and surly. A widow, she is all alone though surrounded by servants and handmaidens. Her children have gone off to live their own lives and left her to the artificial company surrounding but not loving her. Unloved, she chooses to meddle in love and arrange a match between Kapiton and Tat'jana, where there is no love of one for the other. The *barynja*, to gain attention and company, feigns illness and fainting spells, but she never manages to break out of the enchanted circle of her loneliness and is forced to live out her last days in bitter solitude.

Gerasim is just as alone, but for very different reasons. First, he is alone because the cruel old woman has brought him to Moscow, where he plainly does not fit. Inured to the arduous toil of the country, where physical prowess and stamina are valuable, Gerasim scoffs at the tasks of the city. The countryside, where his staggering strength served him especially well and where he did the work of four men, is no preparation for the city environment, where he chafes at his relative inactivity. Clearing the yard of roosters and the walks of drunks is not worthy work for one with the air of a *bogatyr'* about him. While the work he performs in the country is also not of an exalted nature, still one has the feeling that Gerasim fits there. His size and strength are of a singular nature and cause him to stand apart from others, emphasizing his isolation, his loneliness, and, ultimately, his separation from love. This is the case even among his fellow serfs, and both they and Gerasim seem to realize it. His fellow workers keep their distance, and Gerasim "didn't like people to come to see him." The repelling, rather than attracting, qualities of Gerasim become evident when one reads, "Not everyone was willing to jeer . . . at Gerasim: he didn't like jokes." Tat'jana, however mousy and shrinking she may be, is still one of the crowd and can be teased, but Gerasim is not and cannot. The last paragraph in the tale begins, "I živet do six por Gerasim bobylem v svoej odinokoj izbe" ("And Gerasim still lives all alone in his lonely hut"). The words *bobylem* and *odinokoj* in combination serve to underscore the degree of loneliness in Gerasim's existence and to remind us that, however content he may be in the country rather than in Moscow, he has had to leave both of his loves behind. Embittered, he also cuts himself off from any future love. For Turgenev, isolation is terrible because it is a state in which one can neither give nor receive love, as we see through Gerasim's plight and through that of the *barynja*.

The difference, to an extent, between the *barynja* and Gerasim lies in his being deaf and dumb. His proportions and strength serve to make him heroic, and we are told that if it were not for his ailments, any lass in the village would be happy to link her life with his. But his physical handicaps isolate him completely, for they lend to his towering, imposing physique a frightening aspect that causes others to shun and fear him. Much is, in fact, made of what a wide berth others give him, and not just the timid-souled Tat'jana. "Everyone in the neighborhood began to respect him a great deal; even in the daytime passersby, not swindlers by any means but simply strangers, at the sight of the menacing yard-keeper waved him off and shouted at him as if he could hear their cries." And again, at the end of the narrative, "and a dog—what does he need a dog for? You couldn't drag a thief into his yard with a rope!" The stress here is on the threatening side of the hero, which contributes mightily to his isolation. But the reader is given a mixed portrayal of Gerasim, who is both terrible and wonderful. He is an unrefined manifestation of nature, and we are remiss if we fail to notice either aspect: the terrible, for he has that in him, or the marvelous, for he has that as well.

The terrible side of Gerasim is apparent enough—he cracks heads together, flings wrongdoers about as if they were so much chaff, and thrusts a threatening fist at any who dare to tease Tat'jana. The strength which can dislodge a horse and cart stuck in the mud also petrifies the loutish Kapiton with fear, causing him to refer to Gerasim as "tot-to, lešij, kikimora-to" ("that one, the wood-goblin,

the she-devil"). The choice of words, albeit from the unreliable Kapiton, is not without interest, for it functions to focus on the dark side of the hero. . . . Gerasim, as we are made to see very plainly, has a strongly developed negative side. The same can be said of the *barynja*, with the vital difference that there is nothing positive about her. She is terrible and only terrible, while Gerasim's positive attributes outweigh his faults.

Ironically, though, it is what he does to the one he loves most of all that best illustrates the terrible side of Gerasim—he drowns Mumu. There is a sense of fulfillment in the act, for he rescues the dog from a watery grave at one point, only to plunge her into one at another. Russia's serfs were often doomed to unhappiness, and this sequence of events serves to bring home the hopelessness of the existence of Gerasim. "Why bother to save the dog in the first place, if you're going to have to end her life later?" runs the implied question. It is, of course, a terribly poignant device to have the hero destroy the creature he loves. But why have him drown her? Perhaps precisely because it is a painful death, and not a quick one. Turgenev thus manages to elicit more sympathy from his readers—Gerasim has said he will kill the dog, and he does. He could do it another way, but no other way would fit quite so well in this particular tale. It demonstrates the blind, mute fury of a downtrodden people, the unthinking savagery of which they were capable. Yet, at the same time, it demonstrates their sometimes unbending honesty and straightforwardness. The act simultaneously attracts and repels.

In the story there is another dog, an old watchdog named Volčok, which is never taken off its chain. It lies about the yard day and night, firmly fastened to its place. But the most interesting thing about it is that it does not try to leave. Volčok, in Turgenev's words, "didn't demand freedom at all." This freedom—freedom to live and love—is also a central concern of the narrative. What better symbol of the situation of the serfs? Here we have an old dog, beaten down by age and experience, which has accepted its fate to the point of not even trying to change it. It barks quite halfheartedly, merely going through the motions. Obviously, Volčok will never lose his chains.

Mumu stands in the starkest of contrasts to this acceptance of one's fate. Until discovered by the old woman, she runs freely about the property and the city with her master. She enters his room, hops onto the furniture, and is familiar to the owners of the restaurant where Gerasim takes her for her last meal. She is, furthermore, a fighter, a creature with spirit. Even though weak, she is struggling for her life when Gerasim first chances upon her in the mud. Cornered by the *barynja* and her servants, she backs up against a wall and bares her teeth at the old woman. Stolen from her owner, she breaks free and returns to him. Moreover, in contrast to Volčok, she has a purpose in life, which is brought out in her barking. A good watchdog, she makes it known if there really is an intruder or something suspicious about. One may contrast this with the way Volčok lies curled up in his house, aimlessly emitting, from time to time, a hoarse, almost *silent* sound, "as if sensing all its futility himself." Mutatis mutandis, the Russian people lie silently and submissively in their hovels, living out their days, making no effort to attain freedom. Like Volčok, they bark hoarsely, almost silently, only now and then, and to no real purpose.

Gerasim, linked closely with the freedom-loving Mumu, is restless, and he finally gains some individual freedom by leaving Moscow for his native region. But, being a serf, he also shares some of Volčok's heritage. He, like Volčok, has almost no voice and is capable of making only one sound, an indistinct one at that. The Russian people had no voice in their own affairs, and Gerasim's dumbness—he cannot declare his love—symbolizes their total dependence on their owners.

Turgenev, it should be observed, used the world of sounds—alien to Gerasim—very effectively in his tale. He went far beyond employing it in its absence to represent the mere bondage of the serfs. Primarily, he used it as a link with love, once in connection with Tat'jana and on another occasion in reference to Mumu. In the first instance, Turgenev depicts Gerasim sitting on the side of his bed, "singing" mournfully. The scene is reported by the coachman Antipka, who peeps through a crack into Gerasim's room. What he sees is the dumb giant seated, head down and hand on cheek, swaying and shaking his head, now and then softly emitting his lowing sound. His eyes are closed, and no sound comes out except the mooing. The motion of his head is compared to that of coachmen or boathaulers, "when they drag out their mournful songs," and the effect of what Antipka sees is so strong that he stops looking through the crack, obviously unable to do so any longer. . . . The reason for this plaintive portrayal is Gerasim's loss of Tat'jana to Kapiton.

The second instance of sound-related depiction having to do with Gerasim also involves a loss, that of Mumu. There is a heart-rending scene in which she has been stolen from her owner, and he runs pitifully about the yard, asking all present whether they have seen her. A pathetic height is reached when Gerasim "turned away and again murmured [*promyčal*]: 'Mumu!'—Mumu didn't answer.'" The symbolism of the name "Mumu" itself is, of course, quite rich, and it is manifested tellingly here. The name, chosen by Gerasim, is an animal sound, specifically a bovine sound. Thus, it not only reinforces the animal imagery connected with the hero, but also reminds us in particular of his being compared with a young bull taken away by a train. Beyond this, however, it has another function, namely that of calling to mind again for the reader the fact of Gerasim's inarticulateness—literally his inability to speak and figuratively his inability to speak out in protest. We are told of Gerasim's "speech" (*myčan'e*), which Ožegov defines first as the lowing or mooing of cattle (or the bellowing of a bull) and second as speaking indistinctly or inarticulately. This overlapping of meanings thus makes "Mumu" the perfect name for the title character, and the scene in question especially pathos-filled. In sum, the two scenes of Gerasim's using sounds—one in which he "sings," and another in which he calls his dog—are directly love-related, each having to do with the loss of a loved one.

Mumu, the supreme symbol of unselfish, loyal love in the story, values Gerasim highly, and she is the force which changes his life. A willing sacrifice offered up by her master's hands, she becomes the symbol for the coming emancipation of the serfs in Russia. Simply put, she replaces Volčok in Gerasim's (i.e., the people's) life. Not indefinitely would the *mužiki* lie passively chained to the land owned by their masters. Gerasim remains a symbol of po-

tential energy waiting to be unleashed, rather than one of a force roaming unchecked over the land, but he is a powerful symbol whose explosiveness is hinted at in his terrible strength and in the fear and respect he inspires in others.

Gerasim has something of the paradoxical about him. He represents the Russian peasantry as a whole, and yet he is, after all, a very singular individual who stands out from the crowd in ways already enumerated. There is much that is heroic about Gerasim, and heroes by their nature stand above the masses. It is, however, a point well taken that figures like Sten'ka Razin and Robin Hood are beloved by the people and that they are, in the final analysis, of the people. C. M. Bowra, commenting on the nature of the hero, sheds light on the reason common folk feel at one with those greater than they are. "Even when the hero has supernatural powers and is all the more formidable because of them, they do little more than supplement his essentially human gifts." The hero, Bowra continues, "awakes admiration primarily because he has in rich abundance qualities which other men have to a much less extent." Gerasim is heroic because of his strength and because of his actions. But others can relate to him because of his human qualities, which Turgenev insisted on. In short, Gerasim becomes a folk hero very closely identified with the *narod*. He is already such a figure in the introduction to the tale, and his stature as such has grown and is reemphasized by its end. (pp. 175-79)

[Gerasim's portrayal also] stresses his humble station in life and his oneness with his fellow Russian peasants. With regard to the other servants in the household of the *barynja,* the narrator informs us that Gerasim "considered them his own," a necessary point if Gerasim is to serve as a symbol of his fellows. Not overly friendly with them, he nevertheless knows that his place is among them, and he gets along with them well unless they threaten Tat'jana or Mumu or misbehave in the territory where he has been assigned to keep order. (pp. 180-81)

[There] are numerous elements which link Gerasim with the peasant masses from which he has sprung. . . . Ironically, his opposite, the *barynja,* is also linked with this old world, but in a significantly different way: "The old *barynja* . . . followed the old customs in everything and kept numerous servants." This passage relating to the old woman also concerns the peasantry: it pointedly goes on to list the many different categories of such people she owns. One of the major points of the work is the inhumaneness of serf owners like the *barynja,* and the quote cited is used as an introduction to the person of Kapiton Klimov, already mentioned as the drunken husband of Tat'jana. The author goes to some lengths to demonstrate the worth of individuals such as Gerasim, then turns immediately around to document the extent to which they count for naught in the eyes of those like the *barynja:* she has dozens of them around and thinks of them primarily in terms of the type and amount of work they do, not of their value as human beings. Much of the balance of the narrative is achieved by the author's focusing on the similar, yet dissimilar, isolation of the *barynja* and Gerasim. The effect is heightened by the device mentioned here: by again demonstrating a sameness . . . and then pointedly showing the gap that exists between serf and owner. Gerasim yearns for Tat'jana, for the linking of his life with hers.

But the old woman, who has already removed the hero from his native element, now goes a step further, creating a match between Tat'jana and Kapiton. Her cruel capriciousness shatters Gerasim's dream, terrifies Kapiton, and saddles Tat'jana with a less than useless mate.

Still other details, such as the work he performs, identify Gerasim as a member of his class in society. Now hefting a whole load of firewood, now effortlessly handling a cumbersome barrel of water, Gerasim toils so energetically and efficiently that one involuntarily marvels at him, at the very nature of his prodigiosity. At the same time, one must agree with Ivan Aksakov that Gerasim as symbol of the people mirrors not only its "terrifying strength," but also its "inscrutable humility," of which we are reminded by Mumu's death. Disturbed enough to leave Moscow, Gerasim is still submissive enough to kill the thing he loves and to remain a serf, bound to the soil and working for its owner.

Isolation, the imagery of folklore, and the silence of the hero—who has no voice in either a literal or a figurative sense—have all been shown to play a role in the development of the story. In the end, however, the story comes back to the nullification of love, and it is in leading up to the turning point of Mumu's death that the author makes this plain. He does so by introducing a character named Ljubov' Ljubimovna, the senior "companion" of the old woman. The person in charge of carrying out the *barynja*'s orders and kept forever off balance by her whims is Gavrila Andreevič, the chief domestic servant of the household. It is this Gavrila who informs Kapiton of his impending marriage to Tat'jana. He also is put in charge of getting rid of Mumu after she has offended the mistress. The unhappy Gavrila ponders the situation and tries to anticipate how he should act in accordance with the capriciousness of the *barynja*. As he prepares for the final assault upon the barricaded Gerasim and Mumu, Gavrila turns to this "companion" with the transparent name. He speaks to her because she has been sent to him directly from the old woman. And who is this Ljubov' Ljubimovna? She, it turns out, is Gavrila's partner in crime, guilty of nothing very serious, perhaps, but certainly not manifesting any great love for her mistress by joining Gavrila in stealing tea, sugar, and the like from the household larder. And so, just before the climactic incident, Ljubov' Ljubimovna's name is mentioned several times, stressing the emptiness of the *barynja*'s life—there is no love in it, neither on the part of this appropriately misnamed servant nor on that of anyone else near the mistress. Servants can be employed, but the life they must shore up is artificial, involving no genuine love. The very opposite, to be sure, of the situation involving Mumu and her master.

These last two, the dog and the dumb peasant, are brought ever closer together in a demonstration of real love, before it is shattered by the cruelty of the aged tyrant. As Gavrila and his helpers cluster about Gerasim's door endeavoring to get him to open it, Mumu barks: "Here again sounded a hollow barking." In the phrase "hollow barking" ("glux-oj laj") one can scarcely keep from noticing the associations with deafness or indistinctness of sound inherent in the first word, the result of which is to unite man and dog more closely and poignantly. The man's "voice" and that of the dog are linked by the combination of words used by the author.

As the final severing of the relationship draws ever nearer, another connection suggests itself. After Gerasim has been deceived with regard to Tat'jana's drinking, we read of Tat'jana and Kapiton that "that same evening they . . . set out for the *barynja*'s with geese under their arms, and a week later they got married." If we compare this with the wording of a passage a few pages later, we find a strange echo pertaining to Mumu and Gerasim: stopping on the way to the boat, Gerasim "carried off two bricks . . . under his arm." . . . [The bricks] suggest a "wedding" between Gerasim and Mumu, foreshadowed by the actual but meaningless one between Kapiton and Tat'jana. It is another "couple," but what is borne under the arm this time is not geese, but bricks. Yet the parallel is tempting, for we see two twosomes formalizing their relationships. Neither pair constitutes a normal "couple"; yet each is setting out, clearly embarking on the process of linking themselves more closely. . . . [This is] confirmed by what follows. Gerasim has put on his festive *kaftan* as befits a groom, and Mumu's coat "shone spendidly," as one would expect of a bride's garment. At an earlier stage, Gerasim has been seen partaking of *šči*, and now he offers Mumu the same fare, "salting" what he gives her with one of his own tears, which falls into the bowl she is eating politely from. Finally, just before he straightens up and drops Mumu into the water, Gerasim remains motionless, as if in prayer, "having crossed his mighty hands on her back." It is appropriate for him to form a cross on her with his hands, for he is playing a dual role, betrothed and priest, the former as indicated above and the latter because it is he who conducts the sacrifice of which she becomes the victim.

When Gerasim opens his hands and Mumu disappears beneath the surface of the water, the "ceremony" ends. Indeed, the whole scene and the preparations for it are carried out ritualistically, as is appropriate for both a wedding and a funeral, which are equally represented. Great love is manifested throughout by both parties: Gerasim displays extreme solemnity and sadness, and Mumu shows complete trust in him, even as he holds her above the waves. The depiction of the love between the two is, of course, what makes the scene so terrible when it has ended, because they are then irreparably separated. The level of love has been brought back to zero, where it was at the outset of the story.

In the beginning, when Gerasim has been brought to the unfamiliar urban environment, we read of his initial unhappiness in the words "he didn't at first like his new life." The straightforward meaning of "ne poljubilos' emu" has to do with his not liking his life in the new milieu, but it is not difficult a few pages later to find an echo of the wording with a very different emphasis. "He grew fond of her" ("Poljubilas' ona emu") occurs in the author's description of how Gerasim falls in love with Tat'jana by stages. This phrase causes us to recall the one that came before it. When we compare the two, it is easy to see that the first refers to the absence of love in the hero's existence. The use of the similar but opposing phrases heightens the tragic nature of the narrative by emphasizing the contrast of his prior life and his new one. . . .

Gerasim, let it be said, had found no love in his earlier life, a point the introductory material on him makes amply clear. He lived in those days "apart from his brethren,"

The Turgenev estate at Spasskoye.

though, as already mentioned, he might have had his pick of the village lasses but for his dual physical afflictions. The key is not merely that he is loveless at beginning and end, but rather that there is a difference because of what has happened in between. There is a finality about his love-lessness in the end that is not there at the outset, and this is a very large and vital difference. What is significant is that his chances for love are taken away by his owner. But for the heartless old woman, he might have found a Tat'jana or a Mumu in the countryside—and his hut might not have been so empty. He might have shared it with a woman or a dog, perhaps both. But, as the author tells us in conclusion, "he has completely quit associating with women, doesn't even glance at them, and doesn't keep a single dog at his place."

The stress in the last paragraph of the story is on the ap-parent sameness of circumstances surrounding the hero. Three times Turgenev uses the phrase "as before"—first, in reference to Gerasim's strength, which is as great as ever; second, to let us know that Gerasim still does the work of four men, just as he used to; third, to indicate that his staid and sedate nature has remained the same as be-fore. It seems clear that the reason for the emphasis on all this sameness is to set up a distinct contrast between it and the one aspect that is not the same: the protagonist's op-portunity to love and be loved. Without this opportunity, Gerasim remains less than a man, which is exactly Turge-nev's point. Much more than a lachrymose dog story, **"Mumu"** was at the time of its publication—and remains today—an eloquent statement on the deprivations suf-fered by the Russian peasants, and its major device was the careful removal of love from Gerasim's sadly limited little world. (pp. 181-84)

> *Edgar L. Frost, "Turgenev's 'Mumu' and the Absence of Love," in* Slavic and East-European Journal, *Vol. 31, No. 2, Summer, 1987, pp. 171-86.*

A. V. Knowles   (essay date 1988)

[*In the following excerpt, Knowles assesses the short fic-tion of Turgenev's later career.*]

During the last decade or so of his life Turgenev continued to publish stories, but at irregular intervals. Despite his at-tempt to deal with contemporary Russia in *Virgin Soil*, after his unhappy experiences with *Fathers and Sons* and especially with *Smoke* he largely turned his back on cur-rent social and political questions. He is still at his very best in some of what he published then—***The Torrents of***

Spring and a few of the short stories—but in general the later works are of lower quality and less interest. Their mood is one of nostalgic regret, and Turgenev's pessimism about the human condition intensified. As the narrator of **"Punin and Baburin"** remarks: "I am old and ill and think mostly of death, which draws nearer with every day. . . . Only occasionally do I recall bygone years, happenings, faces; but then my thoughts do not dwell on the prime of my life or on my young manhood. They carry me back to my early childhood." Yet the former Turgenev is still apparent as earlier themes and preoccupations reappear, though now with a slightly different emphasis. Furthermore, although he had always asserted that he had no interest in the supernatural, some of his best later stories contain a strong element of the fantastic or the mysterious. (p. 104)

The stories **"Brigadir"** (**"The Brigadier"**), **"Istoriya leytenanta Ergunova"** (**"The Story of Lieutenant Ergunov"**), **"Neschastnaya"** (**"An Unhappy Girl"**), **"Strannaya istoriya"** (**"A Strange Story"**), **"Stepnoy korol' Lir"** (**"A King Lear of the Steppes"**), **"Stuk . . . stuk . . . stuk"** (**"Knock . . . Knock . . . Knock"**), **"Punin and Baburin,"** and **"Chasy"** (**"The Watch"**), all published between 1868 and 1876, reflect Turgenev's nostalgic mood. They are all set in the past, and many of them contain autobiographical elements.

"The Brigadier" (1868) is based on a letter Turgenev found amongst his mother's papers at Spasskoe. An elderly army officer who had made his career during the Napoleonic Wars is living in poverty in the country. He writes to the niece of a rich woman landowner asking for help and shelter. In his younger days he had been deeply in love with the landowner and had given her years of selfless devotion. It is a slight tale, but the letter itself, written in Turgenev's best style, is very moving. The story also avoids any sentimentality, as Turgenev always sought to do.

Although published in the same year, **"The Story of Lieutenant Ergunov"** is of more interest. It was written while Turgenev was finishing *Smoke,* and although it took him some time to complete, when composing it he showed his usual facility: he even boasted that he wrote the last twenty pages "in one day." When he finished it, in Baden-Baden, he told Pauline Viardot that it had turned out longer than he had originally planned, and it is clear that he took considerable care with the characterization of its two leading personages. He took the manuscript with him on one of his periodic visits to Russia and read it to friends who, while generally approving it, suggested some changes, for example, that he broaden the character of the "heroine" and tone down what some might consider the "immoral" nature of certain passages.

The story takes place at the end of the 1820s in the port of Nikolaev, a relatively new town founded in 1789, which, incidentally, Turgenev had never visited. It describes an incident in the life of the young Lieutenant Ergunov, one he was always ready to recall to anyone prepared to listen. Twenty-five at the time, Ergunov was placed in charge of the building of the shipyards in Nikolaev. Though inexperienced and something of a dandy, he was a prudent and trustworthy young man. He never played cards or drank, and shunned the company of others: he found his only pleasure in taking solitary evening

strolls around the town, admiring the flowers and sighing after young ladies he saw. He had a weakness for the fair sex, but he had never permitted himself any "foolishness." That he should succumb to temptation is not at all surprising.

One evening, while out walking in the town, he meets a distraught young woman who tells him that a cook has stolen all her possessions and that the police take no interest in her case. She is supposedly Emiliya Karlovna, nineteen, very good-looking and flirtatious. She takes him to her dismal home where he is introduced to Madam Fritsche, an unprepossessing Jewess who is apparently Emiliya's aunt. Later a man surreptitiously delivers a parcel that Ergunov thinks might have traces of blood on it. Emiliya, very defensive, claims that no men come to the house. The mystery deepens when Ergunov thinks he sees the man again as he leaves. He takes to visiting the house frequently, but the two (or is it more?) residents tell him nothing about themselves, and he never enters any other rooms but the one in which they receive him. On one occasion he falls asleep and suspects that Emiliya has tampered with his money belt; on another Emiliya invites him to the house, although she later denies it, and he meets someone said to be Emiliya's younger sister, the seductive Kolibri (in Russian: a hummingbird) who flirts with him, sings and dances, tempts the impressionable young man but permits him no more than a fleeting kiss. She is as mysterious about her life and the house as the others. While Ergunov is powerfully drawn to her, there is here no element comparable to those in certain other Turgenev stories, where the hero finds himself in the throes of an uncontrollable passion which leads to disaster. On another day Ergunov drinks a glass of drugged tea and gradually falls asleep, to dream, peacefully and serenely, of going with Kolibri to Turkey, and then to awaken in a hospital. The transition from reality to dream, the description of the dream itself, and the return to consciousness is extremely well done, and Turgenev was especially proud of these passages.

In the end the mystery is to a large extent cleared up. Ergunov had been drugged, robbed, beaten over the head, and left for dead by the man he had seen on his first visit to the house. It transpires that the four residents of the house are all on the run from the police, that their true names are not those given to Ergunov, that the man is a violent thief, and that the two girls are used by him and Madam Fritsche as bait for unsuspecting people, and that Emiliya and Kolibri are probably prostitutes as well.

The story was poorly received in Russia. "A very ordinary tale," the critics remarked: "Turgenev has regressed. The same marvelous style—but that's all"; "We expect more from Turgenev than empty, stale, old anecdotes." Even the praise was at best ironic: as the critic for one newspaper wrote, "only such a fine and subtle writer as Turgenev could have made such an elegant, artistic tale out of such empty subject matter." Although the story contains much that is typical of Turgenev, and even typical of him at his best, it is difficult to gainsay the contemporary critics. Turgenev always had difficulties with sheer invention. His best and most enduring works are based to a greater or lesser extent on his own experience or that of others about which he knew.

Turgenev was extremely sensitive when questioned about

his attitude toward the Jews, and always claimed he bore them no ill will. They appear infrequently in his stories, but the stereotyped characters in the early **"The Jew"** and the profession of the two Jewesses in **"Lieutenant Ergunov"** lent support to those who suspected he was tinged with anti-Semitism. **"An Unhappy Girl"** (1869), though, provides ample evidence to the contrary. It was written in Spasskoe, while Turgenev was on one of his regular visits to Russia and when, he admitted, he was overwhelmed by love for his native country and by memories of his youth. As in his first published story, **"Andrey Kolosov,"** he returns to his student days in Moscow when he first heard a similar story. The heroine, Susanna, is the illegitimate daughter of a landowner who never acknowledges her. He marries off her mother, a Jewess, who soon dies, leaving Susanna at the mercy of a sadistic stepfather. A love affair develops between Susanna and the son of her real father's brother. Simply because Susanna is a Jewess, the two older men attempt to hinder the young couple at every step. Susanna dies very suddenly, but the cause of her death is unclear: she might have died of natural causes, committed suicide, or been poisoned by her stepfather, who will inherit her income. Turgenev exhibits his usual skill at drawing convincing characters and recapturing the atmosphere of the past. Susanna's Jewishness is very finely detailed, and the manuscripts show that Turgenev went to much trouble to get it right. Susanna emerges as an extremely sympathetic character, in marked contrast to the few other Jews in his fiction, who are at best rather inferior people. Susanna's unhappy life and untimely death are the result primarily of her Jewish descent, a fact which engenders outrage in the reader's mind.

Throughout his career Turgenev had been interested in Russia's religious dissenters, the Old Believers, as we see from characters such as Kasyan in *A Sportsman's Sketches* or Akim in **"The Inn."** He was not at all concerned with their theological convictions, but rather with the social or moral problems they posed. In 1868 he drew up a plan for a long historical novel to be based on the seventeenth-century Old Believer priest Nikita of Suzdal, known to his detractors as Pustosvyat (His Holynothingness). Nothing came of this idea, but in 1870 Turgenev did publish a slight tale, **"A Strange Story,"** in which the daughter of a rich landowner, inspired by deep humility and Christian ethics, abandons a life of ease to devote herself to one of the uneducated "holy men" who wandered about the country living on charity. Although it does highlight the difficulties of the dissenters and present a picture of certain traits Turgenev admired in Russian women, it is ultimately no more than a frightful picture of particular aspects of Russian life.

The lesser known story **"Knock . . . Knock . . . Knock"** (1871) deserves attention for a number of reasons. It reflects Turgenev's views on the romanticism of the late 1820s and the 1830s and on what might be called the original "superfluous man," characters such as the heroes of Alexander Marlinsky's long-forgotten novels, Pushkin's Onegin, and Lermontov's Pechorin. "All sorts of elements were mingled in that type," says the narrator.

> Byronism, romanticism, memories of the French revolution, of the Decembrists—and the worship of Napoleon; faith in destiny, in one's star, in strength of will; posing and fine phrases—and a miserable sense of the emptiness of life; uneasy pangs of petty vanity—and genuine strength and bravery; generous impulses, and defective education, ignorance; aristocratic airs, and delight in trivial foppery. . . .

Turgenev's embodiment of such a "fatalist" is Lieutenant Teglev, whose story is told by his friend Ridel. In the 1830s Ridel used to visit his brother in Krasnoe Selo, near St. Petersburg, where he was stationed as a cavalry officer. There he meets Teglev, a man who believes passionately in "fate." Despite all appearances to the contrary, he firmly believes that he is destined to play a significant part in life. His conviction of his own greatness drives him to adopt the role of a "fatalist," which he supports by undertaking various "heroic" adventures. On the eve of Teglev's name-day Ridel spends the night in his house. Teglev tells him of certain occurrences, forebodings, and apparitions that he interprets as ill omens. As he prepares to sleep Ridel knocks on the hollow wall of his room for no apparent reason. Teglev interprets the knocking as a message from his former girlfriend Masha, whom he has deserted. Teglev goes out into the night looking for Masha's "ghost," hears a voice whispering his name, and is convinced that Masha has killed herself. The following day he receives confirmation of his worst fears and decides that he must follow her example. In the evening he gives Ridel a letter for his commanding officer and vanishes into the thick mist of the summer's night to commit suicide. Ridel tries to prevent this foolish act, but fails. Ridel later discovers that Masha has indeed died, but from cholera, and that the voice calling Teglev's name had been that of another woman looking for her lover, who happened to have the same first name as Teglev. The story ends on a melancholy note: "Yes, someone has observed truly of those who commit suicide: until they carry out their plan, no one believes them; and when they do, no one regrets them."

Throughout his adult life Turgenev had been concerned with what he saw as irrational elements in human life. As a child he had been aware of his parents' belief in ill omens. He often said that he had experienced telepathy, prophetic dreams, and forebodings in his own life. While spending the summer with the Viardots in France in 1849, he fell prey continually to strange sensations. None of these experiences boded, he believed, anything but ill. Such phenomena recur throughout his shorter stories, and they lend an air of inevitability to many events he describes.

A premonition that Teglev's life will end badly lies at the core of **"Knock . . . Knock . . . Knock."** The episode of the knocking occurs on Teglev's name-day, a fact to which he attaches the utmost importance. This feeling is reinforced by the fact that he has also that day given alms to an old woman who had promised "to pray for his soul." As Teglev begins to expect some fateful happening, even Ridel, who at first laughs at the "boring fatalist," is infected by his mood and feels something akin to compassion for Teglev. He discounts his faith in the destiny that rules his life as an affected pose, but still senses that some tragic fate did await him. And that turns out to be the case. Teglev might have died from "fatalism," or from his own foolishness; he might even have shared the death wish apparent in Pechorin's final days, but in spite of everything his forebodings of his own death prove accurate. However rational an explanation Turgenev might have provided for Teglev's visions, and however much the reader may wonder whether Teglev was predisposed to suicide or whether he was indeed under the sway of evil forces, the outcome still appears inevitable.

While the story did not attract much favorable criticism, Turgenev could not entirely agree with, say, Annenkov, who thought it altogether one of his lesser pieces. As Turgenev wrote to a correspondent in January 1877, "I consider the story successful—even if it does leave something to be desired and is a little weak. It is one of the most serious things I've ever written. It is a study of suicide, in particular of a contemporary, Russian kind—proud, meaningless, superstitious—and empty and ridiculous."

Turgenev's tendency during his later years to look at Russia's history emerges particularly in **"The Watch"** (1876) and **"Punin and Baburin"** (1874). The leading characters in both stories are two friends who recall Bazarov and Arkady in *Fathers and Sons* in the sense that one is distinctly dominant over the other. **"The Watch,"** a sort of picaresque parable, is set at the turn of the nineteenth century, during the reigns of Paul and Alexander I. The narrator receives a watch from his godfather, a corrupt government official. At first he is delighted with it, until a cousin—whose father has been exiled to Siberia for his radical activities and republican opinions—tells him the watch is no good, and that anyway he should not accept gifts from such a man as his godfather. The rest of the story details the boy's attempts to get rid of the watch, by hiding it, burying it, or giving it away. But it is all to no avail, because either pressure from his family and friend, or his own pride of possession compels him to retrieve it. In addition to demonstrating Turgenev's skill at recalling the past and his ability to enter into the mind of a young boy, the story might also be interpreted on a metaphorical level. The watch might represent Russia's existing social system, or else the corruption of the "old" Russia. The watch is finally disposed of by the republican-minded cousin, who throws it into a river but nearly drowns in the process. The allegorical meanings are clear.

Whether this view of **"The Watch"** is sustainable or not, the radical theme of **"Punin and Baburin"** is clearly central to it. The story is related by Petya, the young grandson of a tyrannical woman landowner, in four historical periods: 1830, 1837, 1849, and 1861. The first narration recalls Turgenev's own boyhood at Spasskoe. Baburin, appointed a clerk on an estate, brings his friend Punin with him. Punin is a gentle man who loves reciting poetry and stories that enchant the young narrator, whereas the strong-willed Baburin holds "republican" views: he opposes the arbitrary power landowners exercise over their serfs, and is himself before long dismissed.

The second section is set seven years later, when Petya is a second-year university student. A friend of Petya's, Tarkhov, is in love with Musa, an eighteen-year-old seamstress. It soon transpires that Musa is an orphan, and also illegitimate like Baburin, who has taken her under his wing in the same philanthropic spirit that moved him to support Punin. He is prepared to marry Musa but at the time she prefers Tarkhov and Baburin accepts her choice.

Twelve years later at Punin's funeral Petya again meets Baburin, now aged considerably and married to Musa. She is calmer and more determined, having lost what Petya calls her "vanity," or in other words her egoism and

her belief that love is the most important thing in life. When Baburin is arrested and exiled, Musa accompanies him. Although Turgenev does not say so, evidently Baburin was marginally involved in the Petrashevsky Circle, a radical organization active in Russia in 1847-48. Petya, while sympathetic to Baburin's republican ideals, voices Turgenev's own views in criticizing the efficacy of his methods: revolution, he argues, is impossible in Russia.

The story reaches its conclusion in 1861, as Baburin welcomes the emancipation of the peasants and dies soon afterward. It is symbolic of Turgenev's own disappointment with the results of the emancipation that Baburin, who, like Turgenev, had lived through the dark days of the reign of Nicholas I and into the brighter future initially apparently offered by Alexander II, should die at the very moment when all he had been striving for was theoretically achieved. His dreams of a free Russia, however, die with him.

Most of these stories, it must be admitted, are inferior to Turgenev's previous works. This does not hold, however, for **"A King Lear of the Steppes"** (1870), written as well and as convincingly as anything he ever published. Turgenev always admired Shakespeare, and once even tried to convert Tolstoy to his opinion. While based loosely on events that had actually occurred on an estate near Spasskoe, the story is nonetheless loosely and intentionally modeled on Shakespeare's tragedy.

"A King Lear of the Steppes" is started by a group of old university students who meet and then hear one of their number relate a story. The narrator, Dmitry Semenovich, recalls the time when, at fifteen, he was living on his mother's estate. The tale's leading personage, introduced in Turgenev's preferred manner by a physical description, is Martin Kharlov, a neighbor of the narrator's mother and a man of gigantic physical stature. He is a hard-working peasant farmer, stern, demanding, and fearsome, but also honest and proud. He lives in what he calls a "mansion," in reality a rather ramshackle manor house, much of which he built with his own hands. When he was forty the narrator's mother arranged to marry him off to a sickly seventeen-year-old orphan who bore him two daughters but died shortly afterward; the little girls were raised in the narrator's home.

Having established Kharlov's character and those of a few minor characters, Turgenev then describes Kharlov's elder daughter, Anna, a cruel woman, her mild-mannered, complaining, and grasping husband, Sletkin, and the younger, unmarried, haughty, and free-spirited daughter Evlampia. Both the daughters are physically very attractive. Thus in a few short chapters the leading characters and the setting for the story are all finely and vividly outlined.

One night Kharlov has a dream that he interprets as a forewarning of his imminent death, and so sets about drawing up a will to divide his estate immediately between his two daughters. Kharlov is confident of his power within his own family and insists his daughters will stand by him even after he gives them their inheritance. But his generosity proves to be foolishness.

From here on Turgenev expands the story. After the legal formalities of drawing up the will have been completed, there is a meal. When it is over, Souvenir, Kharlov's malicious brother-in-law, tells Kharlov that he has been silly in dividing up his property before his death. A sense of inevitability now pervades the story, compounded by Kharlov's continuing preoccupation with death.

After an interruption in the action, the imminent change in Kharlov's life indeed takes place. Sletkin, with Evlampia as his mistress now, has gained complete control of the estate and Kharlov, although still living in the house, is a mere shadow of his former self. Three weeks later Kharlov is dramatically evicted by Sletkin and his daughters, just as Souvenir had predicted, to be given refuge by the narrator's mother. Taunted by Souvenir, Kharlov suddenly climbs onto the roof of his former "mansion" and starts to dismantle it, beam by beam: "They shall not even have a roof over their heads either," he shouts in a frenzy. A vivid passage ends as Kharlov falls to his death, crushed by the roof's central beam.

Fifteen years later the narrator returns to the scene of the tragedy. Sletkin is dead, unmourned. Anna is the same as ever, still attractive but hard, selfish but an extremely efficient manager of the estate. The narrator wonders whether she deserves what he sees as her happiness, saying: "Everything in the world, good or bad, comes to man not through his deserts, but in consequence of some as yet unknown but logical laws which I shall not take upon myself to indicate, though I sometimes fancy I have a dim perception of them."

Rarely one to leave his stories at loose ends, in the final chapter Turgenev describes a fleeting meeting between the narrator and Evlampia, who has become the leader of a dissident religious sect, perhaps out of remorse, though we cannot be certain. True to himself, Turgenev refuses to moralize. "The storyteller fell silent, and we talked a little longer, and then parted, each to his home."

"A King Lear of the Steppes," with no obvious social message, is a chronicle of family discord and human weakness. Powerfully written and accurately detailed, it leaves the reader lamenting for the human condition, for which Turgenev offers no palliative.

Turgenev's writings of the 1870s were not extensive until he began *Virgin Soil*. Perhaps his only work of lasting significance and real literary merit was **The Torrents of Spring,** begun in the middle of 1870, completed at the end of the following year, and published in 1872.

The background for the plot was an encounter in Frankfurt in 1841 between Turgenev and an extremely beautiful young girl who rushed out of a tearoom to ask him to help her brother who had just fainted. Unlike his future heroine Gemma, the girl was not Italian but Jewish, and Turgenev himself, unlike Sanin, sensibly left town the same night, before he got further involved.

The themes of this remarkable novella are characteristic ones: the humiliation that love for an unworthy woman can bring with it, the unhappiness caused by the involvement of a weaker man with a stronger woman, the malevolent influence of sexual passion.

As the story opens, the fifty-year-old Dmitry Sanin is returning home from a party while ruminating on the vanity of the world and the uselessness of life. At home he casts his mind back thirty years to 1840 when, on his way from Italy to Russia, he stopped off in Frankfurt. As he passes a pastry shop a beautiful girl, Gemma, rushes out and asks him to help her brother, Emilio, whom, she thinks, is on the point of death. When Sanin revives him from what is apparently only a fainting fit, he is welcomed into Gemma's household as Emilio's savior. The impressionable Sanin cancels his plans to return to Russia and before long has fallen hopelessly in love with Gemma, who, however, is engaged to a repulsive German shopkeeper named Klüber. Eventually Sanin and Gemma realize they love each other, Gemma breaks off her engagement to Klüber, and she and Sanin agree to marry.

Turgenev then develops the story's main theme. Just as he is about to return to Russia to sell his estates, Sanin meets an old acquaintance, Polozov, who is married to a wealthy woman of peasant stock and notable physical attractions. Polozov convinces Sanin that his wife will buy his lands, but Polozova decides to seduce Sanin in order to wreck his projected marriage. Turgenev describes Sanin's seduction in some detail, an unusual thing for him. The description of sexual infatuation in this work is the most explicit in the whole of Turgenev's writings, and even he thought he was rather "immoral" in it. As the story ends a degraded Sanin is in the grip of an uncontrollable passion for Polozova. Sanin writes Gemma a despicable and cowardly letter, after which Polozova coldly keeps him for a while in the circle of her numerous admirers before discarding him.

As Leonard Schapiro has pointed out, there is one dominant theme in this fascinating tale: its interpretation of sex as an unconscious force capable of simply overwhelming reason. This theme had emerged earlier in, for example, **"A Correspondence,"** where the hero abandons an honest and self-sacrificing young girl for the physical attractions of a ballerina, but it is more to the fore here as the moving force of the story's action. Turgenev well knew Schopenhauer's notion that sex was a world energy operating outside man's conscious existence, and that love, however ethereal it might seem, is rooted in the sexual impulse alone. If Turgenev believed this, then his view had shifted, for in many of his earlier stories and novels a largely nonerotic love could have very serious and irrational consequences. But he would return to this subject some ten years later, as we shall see.

After the publication of *Virgin Soil* much of Turgenev's literary output contains an element of the supernatural, or at least the mysterious. This was by no means a new departure for him, but in the earlier stories the supernatural was but an element, whereas in the later ones it is central to the action. An interesting factor about most of these stories—usually told by a far-from-omniscient narrator—is that the strange events can be given a rational explanation even if Turgenev does not directly suggest one.

Turgenev's two stories of 1877 provide good examples of this change in emphasis: **"Son" ("The Dream")** and **"Rasskaz ottsa Alekseya" ("The Story of Father Alexis").** Both based on actual, or reported, events, they have a realistically convincing setting, which, some critics argue, diminishes their potential horror. But unlike E. T. A. Hoffmann or Gogol, Turgenev could never invent convincing stories of pure imagination. The young narrator of **"The Dream"** cannot fathom the strange events he describes, but the older reader can suggest plausible explanations for the mysterious combination of dream, coincidence, illness, fear, death—and the apparent disappearance of a corpse. Yet any explanation remains only a possibility. The supernatural element in **"Father Alexis"** is less mysterious but rather more frightening. The son of a priest begins his education in a seminary but then decides to go to university, abandoning the religious life. On his first visit home his parents find him a different person: he thinks he is possessed by the devil. During Holy Communion he sees a vision of the devil telling him to spit out the bread, which he does. Convinced that he is condemned to eternal damnation, he loses his sanity and soon dies. Turgenev could have written the story in a sensational manner, but instead relates it calmly, simply, and compassionately.

Arguably the best of these stories—and also more interesting in that they elaborate on some of the themes that had appeared in previous works—are **"Pesn' torzhestvuyushchey lyubvi"** (**"Song of Triumphant Love"**), published in 1881, and **"Klara Milich"** (1882). Dedicated to the memory of his friend Flaubert, and in style recalling the latter's *Legends,* **"Song of Triumphant Love"** is set in sixteenth-century Ferrara. Two friends, Mucius and Fabius, both handsome, rich, cultured, and artistically talented, fall in love with the beautiful Valeria, who must choose between them. Aided and abetted by her mother, Valeria chooses Fabius, where upon Mucius leaves, promising not to return until his love is a thing of the past. Valeria and Fabius marry and enjoy five years of complete happiness, spoilt only by their inability to have children. Then Mucius returns and settles nearby, with a very mysterious Malay servant. He also brings exotic oriental objects, including an Indian violin on which he plays an exultant melody describing the triumphant feelings caused by satisfied love. The effect of the music on Valeria is striking. Visions of Mucius haunt her by day, he appears in her dreams at night, and various nocturnal meetings apparently occur between them. Fabius stabs Mucius and believes he has killed him, but, revived by the Malay servant, he leaves the house never to return. One day, as Valeria is sitting at the organ, suddenly, as if of their own accord, the notes of the song of triumphant love burst forth. At this moment, for the first time, she feels the stirrings of new life within her womb. And there the story intriguingly ends.

Turgenev was a past master at describing the disturbing but nonetheless uplifting effects of human love, but never before, not even in *The Torrents of Spring,* had he written so vividly about an inability to cope with the impulses of a sexual passion, when the erotic appears as a profanation of sacred love.

This idea is further developed in **"Klara Milich,"** now subtitled "After Death." It is based on an actual occurrence, when an actress had committed suicide for unknown reasons by taking poison during a performance. An acquaintance of Turgenev's either saw her act and fell in love with her or else, according to some reports, conceived a passion for her only after her death; in any case his love led to serious mental illness. When he heard the story Turgenev thought it would make "a semifantastic tale in the manner of Edgar Allan Poe."

As in real life, Turgenev's heroine commits suicide by taking poison on stage. Aratov, his unfortunate hero, lives shut off from the world with an old aunt. A friend persuades him to go to a concert where an actress and singer

named Klara Milich will appear. At that performance Klara transfixes him with her hypnotic gaze, and soon afterward he receives an unsigned letter, which he guesses is from Klara, suggesting they meet. When they do Klara cannot put her emotions into words, and he does not know how to help her. A little later he reads in a newspaper of her suicide, caused, the report suggests, by an unhappy love affair. Aratov visits a provincial town to see her family, and learns from Klara's diary of her love for him.

From this moment on Aratov becomes obsessed with Klara, who haunts him in dreams and hallucinations. His health begins to suffer. He hears her voice during the nights; she appears before him, seductively, in his bedroom. On another occasion they kiss, and he senses her moist lips and the burning nearness of her body. "Not even Romeo and Juliet," he muses, "ever exchanged a kiss like that. But next time I shall be stronger . . . I shall possess her." The next time she appears to him, he throws himself upon her with the words "You have conquered me . . . Take me. . . . " His aunt discovers him on his knees with his head resting on the armchair where "Klara" had been sitting. A few days later he dies happily, deliriously declaring that he is Romeo who has just taken poison.

Turgenev's view that love is an illness, or even a poison, that destroys people's equilibrium and prevents them from thinking and behaving normally runs consistently through his fiction. So too does the notion that love leads in one form or another to death. That love should still have the same effect from beyond the grave is something new. And yet so finely is **"Klara Milich"** constructed and related, so convincingly are the characters, especially Aratov, drawn, that the reader believes in at least the possibility of a passion that can survive death. (pp. 105-17)

The two short stories **"Starye portrety"** (**"Old Portraits"**) and **"Otchayanny"** (**"A Desperate Character"**) were published under the general title *Otryvki iz vospominaniy—svoikh i chuzhikh* (*Fragments from Reminiscences—My Own and Others'*). While he was working on the former Turgenev apparently intended to write a new series of stories recalling *A Sportsman's Sketches,* which, it will be remembered, had grown out of the initial success of **"Khor and Kalinych."** He wrote to Annenkov on 22 November 1880: "It would be a miracle if **'Old Portraits'** were also to prove as fruitful." Unfortunately the miracle did not occur. **"Old Portraits"** appeared in 1881 in the liberal newspaper *Poryadok* (*Order*), edited by Turgenev's publisher of that time, Mikhail Stasyulevich, and **"A Desperate Character"** in the *Messenger of Europe* at the beginning of the following year. Neither of them ranks among Turgenev's best stories but both have their virtues and were relatively successful with the Russian critics upon publication and even more so abroad when translated into French and English.

In both stories Turgenev is in a nostalgic mood and unconcerned with contemporary problems. He also reverts to a style in which he had earlier proved himself a master, that of portraiture. Both are first-person narratives, although **"A Desperate Character"** is removed a stage when Turgenev has one member of a group relate the tale. Although both stories are clearly related to Turgenev's own experiences, in his preface to the first edition he declared "that I chose the first-person narrative form for my own convenience and so I ask the reader not to take the 'I' of the narrator exactly for the 'I' of the author. This is implied by the title of the fragments: 'Reminiscences—my own and *others.*' " The ones by the "others," however, were never written.

"Old Portraits" takes place "many years ago," in the 1830s, during the reign of Nicholas I, well before serfdom was abolished. It relates the story of Aleksey Sergeich Telegin, based on one of Turgenev's uncles, and his wife Malanya. They live a quiet, almost elegiac life in a typical manor house of the steppes, spacious but unostentatious. The only notable thing it contains is an immense collection of paintings. The house is ringed with office buildings, peasant huts, and a modest orchard, and the whole estate is set amid ten miles of empty steppe: "No lofty object met the eye; not a tree, not even a belfry," the narrator writes. Telegin is as apparently old-fashioned and at peace with the world as are the surroundings in which he lives. A conservative who believes that things have grown steadily worse since the death of Catherine the Great at the end of the previous century (he was born in 1760), Telegin is a religious man, and also well-read, at least in Russian literature published before 1800. Telegin's wife, Malanya, a former beauty, "the Moscow Venus," is devout and kind-hearted, but a rather empty-headed chatterbox.

Both Telegin and his wife die within a few months of each other in 1848, a year that sees the end of the idyllic pastoral Turgenev has been painting. But he concludes the story with a description of a happening that contrasts sharply with the charming picture of life on a typical country estate, and points up the darker side of serfdom to an extent far beyond anything found in *A Sportsman's Sketches.* When the narrator makes his final visit to the Telegin estate, one of Telegin's serfs comes to him in utter despair. It transpires that one of Telegin's neighbors, a man known for his brutality toward his serfs, has discovered that the man really belongs to him, and demands his immediate return. The kind-hearted Telegin offers him rather more money for the serf than is strictly necessary in such circumstances, but the neighbor refuses any monetary settlement. The serf, dreading his fate, threatens to kill his new owner rather than submit. Indeed, a bit later he does just that, and is sentenced to the mines for life. Turgenev's portrayal of the arbitrary nature of serfdom as an institution had never been clearer, not even in **"Mumu."** And yet, just as before, he leaves the story to speak for itself, with no explicit comment.

Annenkov told Turgenev, when the latter submitted **"Old Portraits"** to him for advice, that the serf should commit suicide as a form of protest against such inhumane treatment. But Turgenev rejected such a conclusion, for he believed peasants did not normally behave in that way. He understood that in adverse circumstances the Russian peasant normally accepted with fortitude whatever life offered him.

"A Desperate Character" portrays a disillusioned and rootless member of the Russian minor nobility. The outcome is a faithful picture of one of Turgenev's first cousins, Mikhail Alekseevich Turgenev, whom Turgenev had earlier described in a letter to Annenkov of 12 October 1860 as follows: "That crazy good-for-nothing who was nicknamed Shamil in the province had at one time a very decent estate, and then became a monk, a gypsy, and an army officer, and would now appear to have dedicated himself to the profession of drunkard and cadger. I have written to my uncle and asked him to support this dissolute buffoon at Spasskoe."

As the story opens, a group of eight people are discussing contemporary events. One remarks that he cannot understand men these days: there has never been anything like such desperate fellows before. The narrator of the story disagrees and relates the tale of his nephew, or rather cousin, Misha Poltev. Born in 1828 and brought up by his kindly yet strict, old-fashioned, limited, and religious parents, Misha was, until their deaths when he was eighteen, an obedient and even rather effeminate, young boy. Then a remarkable change occurs.

The next time the narrator sees Misha he discovers that he has sold the family estates for a trifling sum, dresses somewhat unusually, and spends his money on drink, horses, and riotous living among a band of gypsies. A few months later he turns up looking like an itinerant pilgrim and proclaiming that as he has now spent every penny he is going off to become a monk and seek atonement. He begins to write letters begging for forgiveness and asking for help, usually financial. A month or two later the narrator hears that Misha has become a junior officer in the Caucasus, but he turns out to be less than useless as an officer.

Misha later attributes his unpredictable behavior to wretchedness. "If one comes to oneself, begins to feel, to think of the poverty and injustice in Russia," he says, "Well, it's all over . . . one is so wretched—one wants to put a bullet through one's head. . . . One's forced to start drinking." Misha was also a passionate gambler, and upon being discharged from the army, he takes to a life of debauchery and joins a gang of drunken itinerant beggars. The narrator offers him a home if he will give up his heavy drinking, and Misha, in a fit of self-pity, accepts. His reformation does not last long. He grows wild and morose, and cannot stand the ordered way of life of the narrator's country estate, and so departs to resume his former ways. Later on he marries and tries to settle down, but is overcome by feelings of guilt and inadequacy, and soon dies. "He embodied," concludes the narrator, "a thirst for self-destruction, wretchedness, dissatisfaction. . . ."

Is Poltev little more than the last in a long line of memorable "superfluous men"? Or was Turgenev trying to make some comment about the people of the late 1870s, as many thought? In a letter of January 1882 Turgenev explained that he had tried to portray a type of person he knew from his own youth but who exhibited remarkable similarities with some contemporary young people. He was consequently criticized for maligning contemporary youth just as he had been some twenty years in connection with *Fathers and Sons.* This naturally upset him, yet he still believed that the youth of the time *were* the same type as his desperate character. Social conditions had changed, but there was still, he said, "the same recklessness, the same restlessness, the same lack of will, and the same vagueness and indeterminateness in what they are demanding." Turgenev offers no explanation for the strange personality of Poltev, but he recognizes the frightful waste that his life amounts to. (pp. 118-21)

A. V. Knowles, in his Ivan Turgenev, *Twayne Publishers, 1988, 144 p.*

FURTHER READING

Andrew, Joe. "The Lady Vanishes: A Feminist Reading of Turgenev's *Asya*." *Irish Slavonic Studies* 8 (1987): 87-96.
 Examines Turgenev's portrayal of the character of Asya in relation to the general perception of women in nineteenth-century Russia.

Brodiansky, Nina. "Turgenev's Short Stories: A Revaluation." *Slavonic and East European Review* XXXII, No. 78 (December 1953): 70-91.
 Offers interpretations of Turgenev's short fiction.

Eekman, Thomas. "Turgenev and the Shorter Prose Forms." In *Text and Context: Essays to Honor Nils Åke Nilsson,* edited by Peter Alberg Jensen, et. al., pp. 42-52. Stockholm: Almqvist & Wiksell International, 1987.
 Uses the short story collection *Sportsman's Sketches* to examine Turgenev's narrative technique.

Fitzlyon, April. *The Price of Genius: A Life of Pauline Viardot.* New York: Appleton-Century, 1964, 520 p.
 Contains frequent references to Turgenev's life and writings as they pertain to his relationship with Pauline Viardot.

Gettmann, Royal A. *Turgenev in England and America.* Urbana, Ill.: University of Illinois Press, 1941, 196 p.
 Useful reference guide to Turgenev's critical reception in England and America from 1855 to 1937.

Hart, Pierre R. "The Passionate Page: 'First Love' and 'The Little Hero'." In *New Perspectives on Nineteenth-Century Russian Prose,* edited by George J. Gutsche and Lauren G. Leighton, pp. 111-20. Columbus, Ohio: Slavica Publishers, 1982.
 Explores Turgenev's technique of characterization by comparing his novella *First Love* to Fedor Dostoevski's "The Little Hero."

James, Henry. "Ivan Turgénieff." *The Atlantic Monthly* LIII, No. CCCXV (January 1884): 42-55.
 James's fond personal reminiscences of his friend Turgenev.

Kagan-Kans, Eva. "Ivan Turgenev and Henry James: 'First Love' and 'Daisy Miller'." In *American Contributions to the Ninth International Congress of Slavists, Vol. II: Literature, Poetics, History,* edited by Paul Debreczeny, pp. 251-65. Columbus, Ohio: Slavica Publishers, 1981.
 Contrasts Turgenev's pessimistic world view with James's more optimistic vision as realized in their two novellas.

Landor, Mikhail. "*A Hunter's Sketches* as Read Today." *Soviet Literature,* No. 12 (1983): 160-67.
 A re-evaluation of *A Hunter's Sketches* and its influence upon modern authors.

Lord, Robert. "Prose." In his *Russian Literature: An Intro-duction,* pp. 86-182. New York: Taplinger Publishing Co., 1980.
 Contains general remarks on Turgenev's novels and short stories.

Lowe, David A., ed. *Critical Essays on Ivan Turgenev.* Boston: G. K. Hall, 1989, 175 p.
 A collection of previously published essays on Turgenev by such critics as Lev Pumpyansky, Richard Freeborn, and Vladimir Fisher (see excerpt dated 1920 in entry above).

Magarshack, David. *Turgenev: A Life.* London: Faber and Faber, 1954, 328 p.
 Discusses Turgenev's works in the context of his life.

Martin, Mildred A. "The Last Shall Be First: A Study of Three Russian Short Stories." *Bucknell Review* VI, No. 1 (March 1956): 13-23.
 Compares the Christian themes of Turgenev's "Biryuk" to those of Nikolai Gogol's "The Cloak" and Fedor Dostoevski's "The Thief."

Moser, Charles A. *Ivan Turgenev.* New York: Columbia University Press, 1972, 48 p.
 Biographical and critical monograph.

Schapiro, Leonard. *Turgenev: His Life and Times.* New York: Random House, 1978, 382 p.
 Biography.

Schefski, Harold K. "Novelle Structure in Turgenev's *Spring Torrents*." *Studies in Short Fiction* 22, No. 4 (Fall 1985): 431-35.
 Shows that *The Torrents of Spring* adheres to the structural devices of the German novella, particularly in its emphasis on the unfolding of a single plot.

Silbajoris, Rimvydas. "Images and Structures in Turgenev's *Sportsman's Notebook*." *Slavonic and East European Journal* 28, Vol. 2 (Summer 1984): pp. 180-91.
 Asserts that Turgenev created "a complex, highly evocative blend of unflinching observation upon 'things as they are' and a deep feeling of what things could become if transfigured by the power of the poetic principle."

Waliszewski, K. "Lermontov, Gogol, and Tourgueniev." In his *A History of Russian Literature,* pp. 227-98, 1927. Reprint. Port Washington, N. Y.: Kennikat Press, 1969.
 Overview of Turgenev's life and career.

Yachnin, Rissa, and Stam, David H. *Turgenev in English: A Checklist of Works by and about Him.* New York: New York Public Library, 1962, 55 p.
 List of English translations of Turgenev's works—both those published separately and those appearing in anthologies and periodicals—and a bibliography of secondary sources.

Zhitova, Mme. V. *The Turgenev Family.* Translated by A. S. Mills. New York: Roy Publishers, n.d., 179 p.
 Contemporary reminiscences of Turgenev and his immediate family by an intimate of the Turgenevs.

Virginia Woolf

1882-1941

(Born Adeline Virginia Stephen. Full name: Adeline Virginia Woolf. Also wrote under the pseudonym Radclyffe Hall.) English novelist, critic, essayist, short story writer, diarist, autobiographer, and biographer.

Acknowledged as a major figure of modern literature, Woolf is highly regarded both for her innovative fiction techniques and insightful contributions to literary criticism. Like her contemporary James Joyce, with whom she is often compared, Woolf revolted against the traditional narrative methods of her time and experimented with stream-of-consciousness prose and interior monologue, achieving particular acclaim with her novels *Mrs. Dalloway, To the Lighthouse,* and *The Waves.* However, Woolf first introduced many of these formal experiments in short stories that often present what Woolf termed "moments of being"—instances of intense sensibility during which disparate thoughts and events culminate in a flash of insight. In her short stories, which include "The Mark on the Wall," "Monday or Tuesday," "Kew Gardens," and "A Society," Woolf explored such themes as the elusive nature of storytelling and character study, the nature of truth and reality, and the role of women in society. Like her novels, these highly individualized, stylistic works are noted for their subjective explorations and detailed poetic narratives that capture ordinary experience while depicting the workings and perceptions of the human mind. Written in an elliptical and impressionistic style, Woolf's brief, apparently plotless stories are considered to have significantly influenced the development of modern short fiction.

Virginia Woolf was born into a talented and distinguished literary family in London, England, in 1882. The third of four children of Sir Leslie Stephen, a prominent literary scholar, and his second wife, Julia, a close friend to the family of William Thackeray, Virginia enjoyed a childhood atmosphere steeped in art and intellect. Sir Leslie, who is perhaps best remembered for compiling the prodigious *Dictionary of National Biography,* maintained friendships with figures of the Victorian intellectual aristocracy, often hosting visits from such eminent writers as Thomas Hardy, George Meredith, and Henry James. Although Virginia and her sister Vanessa, later a well-respected avant-garde painter, received no formal education, the lively and learned conversations that flowed through the Stephen's home and the uninhibited access to their father's extensive library provided a rich source for their private learning. In 1895 the Stephen's comfortable existence was disrupted by the sudden, tragic death of their beloved mother, Julia. Virginia's subsequent mental breakdown was the first of several that troubled her throughout her life.

The death of Sir Leslie in 1904 propelled Virginia into another state of depression, and early in 1905 she moved with Vanessa and their two brothers, Thoby and Adrian, to the Bloomsbury district of London. There they met weekly with several of Thoby's Cambridge associates to discuss the arts and together formed what is now known as the Bloomsbury group. Within this circle of friends that included, among others, John Maynard Keynes, Clive Bell, Vita Sackville-West, and Lytton Strachey, Virginia was exposed to a variety of modern theories on art and literature that deeply affected the development of her own ideas. Also during this time Virginia published her first literary essays and reviews, a practice she continued throughout her life. In 1912, following the death of Thoby from typhoid and the marriage of Vanessa to Clive Bell, Virginia married Leonard Woolf, a writer and socialist political figure, also among the Bloomsbury circle, whose stabilizing influence on Virginia is considered to have nurtured her literary career. Nevertheless, in 1913, after the publication of her first novel, *The Voyage Out,* Virginia collapsed from mental exhaustion, and the ensuing breakdown, her most severe, lasted several years.

In 1917, following Virginia's recovery the preceding year, she and Leonard founded the Hogarth Press—a business venture that was intended partly as a release from the anxiety Virginia experienced when writing, and which subsequently kept her from having to send her work to an outside publisher. The Woolfs launched Hogarth with a small printing of *Two Stories,* a book composed of Virginia's

"The Mark on the Wall" and Leonard's "Three Jews." Following the publication of Virginia's second novel, *Night and Day,* Hogarth issued *Monday or Tuesday,* fiction of a marked difference from her first two traditional novels and her only collection of short fiction to appear during her lifetime. By 1924 Hogarth had grown into a successful and respected business, publishing all of Virginia's writings as well as the early works of such writers as Katherine Mansfield, T. S. Eliot, and Sigmund Freud. During the period 1922 to 1941, Virginia immersed herself in writing fiction, completing the critically acclaimed novels *Mrs. Dalloway, To the Lighthouse,* and *The Waves,* which form the foundation of her literary reputation. In addition, her nonfiction works from this time, particularly *A Room of One's Own* and *Three Guineas,* established her as an important contributor to modern critical and feminist writing. Yet, despite these successes, Woolf feared the onslaught of another breakdown from which she perceived recovery impossible, and in 1941, she took her own life by drowning. The posthumous publication of many of Virginia Woolf's essays, short stories, journals, diaries, and letters attest to an abiding interest in her career.

In her short fiction Woolf typically focused on minute physical detail and experimented with stream-of-consciousness techniques, interior monologue, and symbolism to capture the subjective workings of human thought. Woolf wrote in her essay "Modern Fiction" that "everything is the proper stuff of fiction"; according to Woolf, each instance, each impression in life, no matter how unconnected it may seem, has its place. For example, in "Monday or Tuesday," perhaps her most speculative and experimental short piece, the narrator uses the flight of a heron to present an impressionistic delineation of city life in an attempt to discern the nature of truth amid the observable details of reality. Joanne Trautmann Banks stated that this story posits the notion that "[realizations] about the mind, the way it knows, and its involvement with the world outside, await us any Monday or Tuesday." "Kew Gardens," another story depicting the importance of everyday events, typifies Woolf's lyrical portrayal of varied narrative perspectives through the interior monologue of an omniscient narrator. In this seemingly plotless story, Woolf creates the atmosphere of an afternoon at London's Kew Gardens by fusing the shifting points of view of several people with those of a snail, insects, flowers, and even such inanimate objects as buses and airplanes. Woolf's sensuous imagery and elliptical style compress events and various subjective perspectives in this piece to evoke a unification among characters, achieving, as John Oakland has commented, a "collective theme-voice" that strikes order in the story's fragmented structure and parallels its theme of interconnected relations within life's apparent randomness. In "The Mark on the Wall" Woolf employs interior monologue to impart the musings of a narrator who, in speculating about a small detail on a wall, ponders a variety of topics, including personal reminiscence, history, and nature. Every rumination returns to the mark only to stray anew into reverie, as each of the narrator's seemingly meandering thoughts builds upon one another to create an intricate discourse on the nature of reality and truth.

Themes in Woolf's short fiction are intrinsically fused with narrative form. Similar to Joyce's short stories, in which epiphany is frequently an essential element,

Woolf's short fiction often depends on "moments of being" to delineate theme. Whereas Joyce's notion of epiphany focuses on the power of a single event to reveal truth, Woolf's "moments of being" encompass various incursions into time and place. Woolf wrote in her diary, "[What] I want now to do is to saturate every atom. I mean to eliminate all waste, deadness, superfluity: to give the moment whole; whatever it includes." Woolf's preoccupation with saturating individual moments with significance is perhaps most evident in "Moments of Being: 'Slater's Pins Have No Points.'" Here the protagonist, Fanny Wilmot, searches for a lost pin while she simultaneously attempts to gain insight into the personality of her elderly piano teacher, Julia Craye. In the brief time she searches for the pin, Fanny juxtaposes thoughts about Julia's past with the present and speculates whether this independent, unmarried woman is happy. The narrative returns after each rumination about Julia's life to Fanny's search for the pin until, finally, at the instant when Fanny finds the pin, she experiences the revelation that Julia is indeed happy.

Woolf's fascination with the elusive nature of storytelling, as well as the inherent difficulty of knowing character, provided subject matter for several of her short stories. In "An Unwritten Novel" Woolf explored this theme through the capricious mind of the narrator as she rides a train with a stranger, observing details of the unknown woman's appearance and behavior to construct a story surrounding her life. Noting the woman's mention of a sister-in-law, her pursed lips, nervous fidgeting, and obsession with rubbing a spot on the window, the narrator surmises that the woman, whom she names Minnie Marsh, is an unhappy spinster harboring guilt over an unnamed crime en route to a miserable visit with relatives. When, near the end of the tale, "Minnie Marsh" is happily greeted by her son at the train station, the narrator is momentarily stunned by the falsity of her conclusions, but soon renews her musings on the nebulous possibilities of the relationship between mother and son. In this and in several other stories, Woolf overturned conventional Edwardian precepts that relied on observable details to discern veracity and illustrated the unknowable nature of truth and character.

In both her fiction and nonfiction Woolf was devoted to raising the social consciousness of readers. Her disarming and often humorous feminist works are informed with pointed criticism of sexism, as well as praise for neglected women writers. "A Society," Woolf's short story that preceded her major feminist essays *A Room of One's Own* and *Three Guineas,* is considered one of her more traditional tales in terms of style, even though its subject matter sharply attacks Edwardian social and political customs. This story highlights ten years in the lives of a group of women who meet regularly to question conventions of art, literature, scholarship, law, and military achievement in a male-dominated society. One of the group's vows is to forgo having children until they have resolved their questions. However, when one woman, Castilia, becomes pregnant, a new resolution is adopted to allow only the unchaste into their society, and Castilia is appointed president. The story's ironic stance, humor, and extensive use of allusion to the Bible and mythology serve, for several critics, to elevate it above the level of polemic. Susan Dick noted that "A Society" is of great interest for "the extent to which Woolf reflects . . . with striking immediacy the historical and cultural context in which it was written."

Most critics acknowledge that Woolf's short stories frequently served as experimental studies wherein ideas for her works of longer fiction were originated and developed. (Her impressionistic exploration of subject matter, tone, narrative technique, and theme often found more expansive treatment and, certainly, more critical attention in her novels.) Yet, many commentators have contended that Woolf's experiments with poetic style, psychological focus, and subjective point of view expanded the limits of time and perception within the framework of the short story, influencing and contributing significantly to the development of modern short fiction. Jean Guiguet wrote: "[Just] as certain novelists have used the short story to emphasize and epitomize their vision of the world, Virginia Woolf sought to render in a few pages the essence of her universe. . . . From this very nature of her reality, Virginia Woolf was able to extract a principle of composition which may be considered a rule of the genre as she conceived it and through which, moreover, she carries on a tradition."

(For further information on Woolf's life and career, see *Twentieth-Century Literary Criticism*, Vols. 1, 5, 20; *Contemporary Authors*, Vol. 104; and *Dictionary of Literary Biography*, Vol. 36. See also the "Bloomsbury Group" entry in *Twentieth-Century Literary Criticism*, Vol. 34.)

PRINCIPAL WORKS

SHORT FICTION

Two Stories [with Leonard Woolf] 1917; also published as *The Mark on the Wall,* 1919
Kew Gardens 1919
Monday or Tuesday 1921
A Haunted House, and Other Short Stories 1943
Mrs. Dalloway's Party: A Short Story Sequence 1973
The Complete Shorter Fiction of Virginia Woolf 1985

OTHER MAJOR WORKS

The Voyage Out (novel) 1915
Night and Day (novel) 1919
Jacob's Room (novel) 1922
Mr. Bennett and Mrs. Brown (criticism) 1924
The Common Reader (criticism) 1925
Mrs. Dalloway (novel) 1925
To the Lighthouse (novel) 1927
Orlando: A Biography (novel) 1928
A Room of One's Own (essays) 1929
The Waves (novel) 1931
The Common Reader: Second Series (criticism) 1932
Flush: A Biography (biography) 1933
The Years (novel) 1937
Three Guineas (essays) 1938
Roger Fry: A Biography (biography) 1940
Between the Acts (novel) 1941
The Death of the Moth, and Other Essays (essays) 1942
The Moment, and Other Essays (essays) 1947
The Captain's Death Bed, and Other Essays (essays) 1950
A Writer's Diary (journal) 1953
Hours in a Library (essay) 1957

Granite and Rainbow (essays) 1958
Collected Essays. 4 vols. (essays) 1966-67
The Letters of Virginia Woolf. 6 vols. (letters) 1975-80
The Diary of Virginia Woolf. 5 vols. (diaries) 1977-84
Moments of Being (autobiographical essays) 1976

Desmond MacCarthy (essay date 1921)

[*MacCarthy was one of the foremost English literature and drama critics of the twentieth century. He served for many years on the staff of the* New Statesman *and edited the periodical* Life and Letters. *A member of the Bloomsbury group, MacCarthy was guided by their tenet that "one's prime objects in life were love, the creation and enjoyment of aesthetic experience, and the pursuit of knowledge." According to critics, MacCarthy brought to his work a wide range of reading, serious and sensitive judgment, interest in the works of new writers, and high critical standards. In the following excerpt from a review of* Monday or Tuesday, *MacCarthy, writing under the pseudonym Affable Hawk, stresses the impressionistic style of Woolf's stories.*]

In naming her new book **Monday or Tuesday,** Mrs. Woolf seems to suggest that this is the stuff, unlikely as it might appear, of which the mental life of any ordinary day is made. You may remember how in *The Voyage Out* the author was not satisfied with telling us what, at a given moment, her principal characters were doing, but took us from bedroom to bedroom of the large hotel in which they were staying, and described rapidly but with extreme precision how the occupants were simultaneously engaged. The effect of this was to impress us with the oddity and irrelevance of the setting which life provides for the adventures of the individual soul. We are used to a love story or a tragedy being set against the background of the irrelevant activities and indifference of nature, but a background made up of other human beings, each like a little clock keeping its own time and striking independently, had a curious effect. Anatole France sometimes uses this device lightly in the service of irony. In one of the best pieces in **Monday or Tuesday** it is used to produce a disconcerting poetic effect. The scene is an oval flower bed in Kew Gardens on a sunny afternoon. The author follows the thoughts not only of the different people who pass by, but of the snail that crawls tentatively along under the plants. First a man and his wife pass: he is thinking of a courtship, which years ago came to nothing, in Kew Gardens; she answers with her memories of a kiss, a kiss given her as a child by an old grey-haired woman. Then we become aware of the snail.

> In the oval flower bed the snail, whose shell had been stained red, blue and yellow for the space of two minutes or so, now appeared to be moving slightly in its shell, and next began to labour over the crumbs of loose earth which broke away and rolled down as it passed over them. It appeared to have a definite goal in front of it, differing in this respect from the singular high-stepping angular green insect who attempted to cross in front of it,

and waited for a second with its antennæ trembling as if in deliberation, and then stepped off as rapidly and strangely in the opposite direction. Brown cliffs with deep green lakes in the hollows, flat blade-like trees that waved from root to tip, round boulders of grey stone, vast crumpled surfaces of a thin crackling texture—all these objects lay across the snail's progress between one stalk and another to his goal. Before he had decided whether to circumvent the arched tent of a dead leaf or to breast it there came past the bed the feet of other human beings.

Now a madman and his keeper pass, and though the elderly man is mad, he hardly lives more completely isolated in the bubble of his own imaginings than others. His bubble is a bubble of more arbitrary fancies, but it is hardly less unreal. He is followed by two elderly women talking of sugar and household worries, and they by two lovers who are attempting to blend their bubbles. Once more under the unifying blaze of the afternoon sky we watch the tentative purposeful movements of the snail.

It is these iridescent, quickly-pricked, quickly-blown-again bubbles, made of private thoughts and dreams, which the author is an adept at describing. In neo-Buddhistic books we sometimes come across pictures of little human figures, like the nuclei in the many coloured albumen of their eggs, and we are told that these are people's auras. Auras, in the sense of temporary and shifting integuments of dreams and thoughts we all carry about with us while pursuing practical aims, are her subject-matter. **"The Mark on the Wall"** and **"The String Quartet"** are prose lyrical effusions which trace every streak and change in them. The first is a wonderful description of wool-gathering beside a fire; the second of such fancies as are woven like a cocoon round the mind while listening to music. . . .

In the piece called **"An Unwritten Novel"** she guesses at the inner life of a woman opposite her in a railway carriage—only to find she was entirely wrong. The contrast between the diversity and arbitrariness of the inner life and the uniformity and conventionality of the life without fills her alternately with laughter and amazement—and sometimes with contempt; for of the two the inner life seems to her incomparably the more vivid and real. But the inner life of dreams and straying thoughts has not authority to impeach the other, and when, as in **"A Society,"** she writes from contempt, her work is not her best.

> *Affable Hawk [pseudonym of Desmond Mac-Carthy], in a review of "Monday or Tuesday," in* New Statesman, *Vol. XVII, No. 417, April 9, 1921, p. 18.*

Winifred Holtby   (essay date 1932)

[*Holtby was an English novelist, essayist, and critic. She is best remembered for* South Riding *(1936), a highly acclaimed novel of her native Yorkshire county. In the following excerpt, Holtby discusses the experimental, poetic quality of Woolf's short stories collected in* Monday or Tuesday, *noting the author's use of free association, a technique that Holtby claims liberated Woolf's fiction from conventional prose standards.*]

May 18, 1924, was the date on which, when reading "Mr.

Bennett and Mrs. Brown" to the "Heretics" Society at Cambridge, Mrs. Woolf uttered her challenge to the Edwardian tradition. She had gone to the Edwardians, she said, asking them how to set about the novelist's proper business of creating character. How was she to create a woman, Mrs. Brown?

"And they said, 'Begin by saying that her father kept a shop in Harrogate. Ascertain the rent. Ascertain the wages of shop assistants in the year 1878. Discover what her mother died of. Describe cancer. Describe calico. Describe . . . ' But I cried 'Stop! Stop!' And I regret to say that I threw that ugly, that clumsy, that incongruous tool out of the window, for I knew that if I began describing the cancer and the calico, my Mrs. Brown, that vision to which I cling, though I know no way of imparting it to you, would have been dulled and tarnished and vanished for ever." (p. 98)

[Mrs. Woolf] had, in *The Voyage Out,* described a ship, described a villa, described the domestic arrangements of Helen's brother and of Mrs. Chailey. In *Night and Day* she had described the Hilberys' house, described Ralph's bedroom, described Richard Allardyce and the aunts and the correspondence about Cyril. And she was not satisfied. So she had forthwith flung the tools she had hitherto used out of the window, and had started again with an entirely new technique. In 1919 she published, as well as *Night and Day,* two little essays, **"Kew Gardens"** and **"The Mark on the Wall,"** entirely unlike anything that she had produced before. Two years later they reappeared in volume form, . . . together with several other sketches . . . , bearing the title *Monday or Tuesday.*

The fascination of that little book lies largely in the knowledge of what went before and what was to follow after.

In it Mrs. Woolf was experimenting, stretching her prose to the fullest limits of intelligibility, and sometimes beyond, seeing how far it was possible to discard description, discard narrative, discard the link-sentences which bind ideas together, seeing how far it was possible to write her prose from within, like poetry, giving it a life of its own. She was devising her new technique; she was testing possibilities and discovering her own powers. And what is particularly interesting about *Monday or Tuesday* is that it contains, as in an artist's sketch-book, brief designs and lightly traced outlines of each of the experimental styles, and even of the manners of thought, which Mrs. Woolf was to develop in that sequence of novels which leads from *Jacob's Room* to *The Waves.* (pp. 99-100)

[By] 1919 she had begun to question the necessity of all the heavy impedimenta of plot, narrative and description hindering the novelist. Why, she seems to have asked herself, should he be weighed down by all the external trappings of life? (They had, indeed, weighed her down in *Night and Day.*) It is all so long, so cumbrous, so unnecessary; why should we pander to the stupidity of readers, who might perhaps be induced to take these matters for granted? Poets, after all, do it. Poets present sensations, emotions and processes of thought, with only lightly indicated backgrounds. They reveal, rather than explain. They suggest. They illumine. They flash a torch through the darkness on to a child's green bucket, an aster trembling violently in the wind, or blades of grass bent by the rain, and leave us to imagine the wild storm-swept garden, and the children safely tucked in bed for the night. Poets have immense advantages over novelists.

In one essay, *Notes on an Elizabethan Play,* now published in *The Common Reader,* Mrs. Woolf draws her comparison between Ford's and Tolstoi's tragedies, between the poetical drama and the prose novel.

> Then, at once, the prime differences emerge; the long leisurely accumulated novel; the little contracted play; the emotion all split up, dissipated, and then woven together, slowly and gradually massed into a whole, in the novel; the emotion concentrated, generalised, heightened in the play. What moments of intensity, what phrases of astonishing beauty the play shot at us!
>
> (pp. 100-01)

> With all her reality, Anna Karenina could never say
> "You have oft for these two lips
> Neglected cassia!"

> Some of the most profound of human emotions are therefore beyond her reach. The extremes of passion are not for the novelist; the perfect marriage of sense and sound are not for him; he must turn his swiftness to sluggardry; keep his eyes on the ground, not on the sky; suggest by description, not reveal by illumination. . . . How, then, can we compare this lumbering and lagging art with poetry?

Mrs. Woolf, the critic, did compare it, and found that *Anna Karenina* came off after all not so badly in the comparison, and that *War and Peace* remained a great book. But Mrs. Woolf the artist would not let well alone. Why, indeed, should novelists resign themselves to their disadvantages? Why should they leave so much to the poets?

She did not want to write verse. She wanted to write prose. In 1920 she published in *The Athenæum* a review of an anthology of English prose in which she states her prejudice. "But no, I dare not breathe a word against English poetry. All I will venture is a sigh of wonder and amazement that when there is prose before us with its capacities and possibilities, its power to say new things, make new shapes, suggest new passions, young people should still be dancing to a barrel-organ and choosing words because they rhyme." It is plain that her mind was busy with the teasing subject. Twelve years later, in her "Letter to a Young Poet," she declares that her practice of writing prose has bred in her "a foolish jealousy" of poets. She wished to eat her cake and have it, to write prose while enjoying the freedoms of the poet.

In *Monday or Tuesday* we see her experimenting to see how it would work. The first sketch included in the volume, **"A Haunted House,"** is pure poetry. It presents pictures; it reveals a mood; it unites sense and sound; it eliminates all the external facts demanded by conventional prose; it suggests instead of describing, and it is written with a cadence which only just escapes being pure *vers libre.*

In a way, that is nothing new. Novelists have often slipped into something near the rhythm of poetry in moments of excitement. Dickens had done it—disastrously; Mrs. Woolf had, in an essay, defended Meredith for doing it. But neither the death of Little Nell, nor the meeting be-

Woolf, seated in the background, with her parents at their summer home in St. Ives.

tween Richard Feverel and Lucy, has quite the silvery, ethereal, de-la-Mareish music of **"A Haunted House."** (pp. 102-03)

But music and cadence are not the only gifts of poetry that Mrs. Woolf would borrow. There is the use of elimination, omitting descriptive and narrative facts, and relying on the reader's imagination to supply them. Why not set picture beside picture, phrase by phrase, as in a poem, and let their juxtaposition, unexplained, form its own meaning? Music does that; poetry does that. Why not prose? It was, on the whole, a more audacious innovation than the experiment with cadence. In each of these sketches she does it to some extent, but the most complete form of it is in **"The String Quartette."**

There is the colloquial opening: "Well, here we are, and if you cast your eye over the room you will see that tubes and trams and omnibuses, private carriages not a few, even, I venture to believe, landaus with bays in them, have been busy at it, weaving threads from one end of London to the other. . . . "

Then someone is saying that Regent Street is up, and the Treaty signed, and a word about the weather, and the memory darts back to the domestic tragedy of having forgotten to write about a leak in the larder; then forward to a relative now met after seven years. It becomes clear that Mrs. Woolf is at a concert, sitting with a hundred or so members of an audience, passive on gilt chairs, waiting for the music to begin. But we have to deduce for ourselves which are the thoughts in her mind, which the half-buried memories, which the words of her neighbours, and which the images suggested by the early Mozart quartette. (pp. 104-05)

It is the picture of a concert; it is a poem about music, about one individual's response to music; with a light sketching of figures, as though by Monet in his early work, their outlines dim, their attitudes' significant. There is no doubt that it is effective, though odd and teasing as a poem by Edith Sitwell. Difficult, delicate, requiring a touch so light and firm that only a brave artist would attempt it; a daring method, exposed to the complementary dangers of violence and weakness; but holding out entrancing possibilities.

Reading through the sketches, we come upon another trait. Here is a passage from **"The Mark on the Wall"**:

> I like to think of the tree itself: first the close dry sensation of being wood; then the grinding of the storm; then the slow delicious ooze of sap. . . . The song of birds must sound very loud and strange in June; and how cold the feet of insects must feel upon it, as they make laborious progresses up the creases of the bark, or sun themselves upon the thin green awning of the leaves, and look straight in front of them with diamond-cut red eyes. . . .

"How cold the feet of insects must feel. . . . " There is a comparable passage in **"Kew Gardens"** describing the light falling down through a flower-bed on to the smooth grey back of a pebble, the shell of a snail, or a raindrop. Such minute yet intense perception, such sympathetic intimacy with non-human objects, feeling the cold feet of insects, or the light expanding in a raindrop, such close identification of the emotion of the beholder with the thing perceived, belong to poetry rather than prose, or to the more delicate forms of decorative art. They require an observation as minutely accurate as it is imaginative, and a sense of the unity of all manifestations of life which dwells in the metaphors of the poets. To think oneself into the sensations of a tree or a stone is a poet's or painter's privilege. For a prose-writer it has its obvious dangers. Balance is hard enough to achieve at any time. . . . If we are to involve ourselves also in the sensations of trees and snails, where will it end? Jane Austen kept her observation quietly to the comedy of individual, decorous, middle class men and women. Tolstoi moved among wars and empires; Dostoievsky ranged through Heaven and Hell and all the disorders of the human spirit. And here is Mrs. Woolf applying an exquisite and microscopic observation to the cold feet of insects. (pp. 105-07)

The use of cadence, of elimination, of a microscopic observation, might have been enough for a less experimental writer. But there was another practice which Mrs. Woolf did not originate, but at which she was anxious to try her hand. (p. 107)

To lie still and let sensations, suggestions, thoughts stream through the mind, to attempt no arbitrary control, but to analyse and record the contents of the flowing river, as analysts record the nature of Thames water, that is an activity likely to attract writers of the generation that intellectually discovered the subconscious and invented the technique of free association.

"Kew Gardens" and **"The Mark on the Wall"** are both exercises in free association, with this difference. In **"The Mark on the Wall"** Mrs. Woolf shows herself sitting in winter time before the fire, smoking a cigarette after tea, and letting her eye rest on the burning coals, the chrysanthemums in the round glass bowl, and on the mark on the wall. As she watches it, she thinks of a crimson flag flapping from a castle town, of ants bearing a blade of straw,

the people who lived in the house before she did, the mystery of life, odd things one loses, immortality (at which she thinks herself as small as Hans Andersen's Thumberlina, so that the cup of a flower, as it turns over, deluges her with purple and red light), the dust which buried Troy, Shakespeare, thoughts that are pleasant because flattering to ourselves, flowers, the looking-glasses through which we look at life, followed by a very important speculation on the novelists of the future, followed by an indictment of generalisations, and boring masculine standards, of Sunday walks and Whitaker's Table of Precedency, followed by a thought that the mark may be a tumulus, which leads on to antiquaries and learned men in general, and an ideal world without specialists or superstitions; then a reflection on nature's game of prompting us to action as a remedy for painful thoughts, then on other remedies—thoughts of the impersonal world, a chest of drawers, wood, the trees from which wood comes, the fate of trees . . . suddenly there is interruption. Somebody stands over her, saying:

> 'I'm going out to buy a newspaper.'
>
> 'Yes?'
>
> 'Though it's no good buying newspapers. . . . Nothing ever happens. Curse this war! God damn this war! . . . All the same, I don't see why we should have a snail on our wall.'
>
> Ah, the mark on the wall! It was a snail!

Now though that seems, when summarised, to be an incoherent jumble of irrelevant reflections, in the essay itself each idea leads naturally from the other. . . . It is no less coherent than the "Argument" printed above a long eighteenth-century poem. And unpromising though the material may seem, the combined result has beauty. It derives unity from Mrs. Woolf's own consciousness. Her mind holds it together. There she lies, all the time, in her chair beside the fire, till interrupted by that sharp, dramatic violence. The external moment rushes with fierce impact upon the flowing thought. She is in the present world. It is war-time. Somebody wants to buy a paper. The dream-quality of her reflections are related to the horror of a world of action in which suffering, decisions, personalities, are immediately revealed.

The technical difference between **"The Mark on the Wall"** and **"Kew Gardens"** is that in the first, consciousness is centred in her own mind; in the second it is diffused among different centres. The garden itself is now the channel for thought. It is no longer a question of thoughts passing through her mind, but of light, insects, people, sounds, passing through the garden. The dimensions of the objects seen do not remain at the steady human size to which novelists have accustomed us; they suddenly diminish to the consciousness of a snail, who sees cliffs and lakes and round boulders of grey stone between the passage from one stalk to another; then suddenly they swing to the vast bird's-eye view from an aeroplane flying above the trees. (pp. 109-11)

To let the perspective shift from high to low, from huge to microscopic, to let figures of people, insects, aeroplanes, flowers pass across the vision and melt away—these are devices common enough to another form of art. They are the tricks of the cinema. Mrs. Woolf had discovered the cinema. There is no reason why it should monopolise powers of expansion and contraction. In **"Kew Gardens"** the external figures appear and disappear with such brilliant clarity that we could almost photograph them from the words. It becomes plain at once that here is a technique of writing which a novelist could use, given a keen visual imagination and a strong sense of design.

But external forms are not everything. Could the same free technique be applied to the fragments of thought, sounds heard, pictures seen, passing through the mind? When one sits in front of a fire, the thoughts are not always so fully formed as in **"The Mark on the Wall."** Dare one photograph by a mental camera the far more elusive procession of fancy, conversation, memory, reflection, of which one is conscious while, say, pouring out tea on a foggy afternoon?

Mrs. Woolf's attempt to do this, she calls **"Monday or Tuesday."** It is very brief, and is, perhaps, the most obscure of all her sketches. Possibly she chose it to give the title to her collection because it is the highwater mark of experiment. Further than this she dared not go. Beyond this point of individualism art ceases to be communicative; it becomes pure expression—an activity which may gratify the artist, but which has no more social significance than an exercise performed by a dancer in her private bathroom.

> Lazy and indifferent, shaking space easily from his wings, knowing his way, the heron passes over the church beneath the sky. White and distant, absorbed in itself, endlessly the sky covers and uncovers, moves and remains. A lake? Blot the shores of it out! A mountain? Oh, perfect—the sun gold on its slopes. Down that falls. Ferns then, or white feathers, for ever and ever.
>
> Desiring truth, awaiting it, laboriously distilling a few words, for ever desiring—(a cry starts to the left, another to the right. Wheels strike divergently. Omnibuses conglomerate in conflict)—for ever desiring—(the clock asseverates with twelve distinct strokes that it is mid-day; light sheds gold scales; children swarm)—for ever desiring truth. Red is the dome; coins hang on the trees; smoke trails from the chimney; bark, shout, cry 'Iron for sale'— and truth?
>
> Radiating to a point men's feet and women's feet, black or gold encrusted—(this foggy weather— Sugar? No, thank you—The commonwealth of the future)—the firelight darting and making the room red, save for the black figures and their bright eyes, while outside a van discharges, Miss Thingummy drinks tea at her desk, and plate-glass preserves fur coats—

It begins, apparently, with a mental picture. The mind sees a bird—a heron. The bird symbol is a favourite one. Mrs. Dalloway is like a blue jay; happiness is identified in *Orlando* with a kingfisher or heron's feather, ecstasy with a wild goose; in **"An Unwritten Novel"** the artist becomes "the hawk over the down." In *Jacob's Room* the metaphor reappears. The heron flies over an imagined landscape.

But while the visual imagination forms pictures, the will is at work, desiring that which Mrs. Woolf's will always desires—truth, the means to capture truth, to distil it in a few words. Then, breaking in upon will and imagination

come the sounds from the street, with their impact upon the alert and waiting senses. Imagination, will, fancy, registration by the senses of external experience, combine together in "Red is the dome; coins hang on the trees; smoke trails from the chimneys; bark, shout, cry 'Iron for sale'— and truth?" But we must have action as well. One cannot sit by a fireside registering sensations. Someone comes in for coffee after lunch—or possibly tea. The room by this time is dark enough to show the firelight, and outside in the town Miss Thingummy—all-the-Secretaries-in-the-world—drinks tea at her desk. One must permit conversation, on the foggy weather, on the Commonwealth of the Future, and make polite inquiries about sugar.

This is more than cinematograph technique. It is like an orchestra. Senses, thoughts, emotions, will, memory, fancies, the impact of the outside world, action and conversation each play a different instrument. Mrs. Woolf is now a conductor. She raises her arms, beckoning now to fancy, now to power, now to a noise of traffic from the street, now a polite inquiry about sugar. It is immensely complicated, immensely suggestive. The whole orchestra gets going at once, responsive to her beat. She must keep control. She must make some sort of harmony, of melody, some intelligible rhythm, some sequence that the listener can follow, or the music will dissolve into a confused cacophony of sound.

The question is, Can she do it? And the answer seems to be that it can be done, but only with extreme care, and only after most careful preparation of the audience. In *Jacob's Room* she uses the cinematograph method. In *Mrs. Dalloway* and *To the Lighthouse* she conducts the orchestra.

So she had got free. The old clumsy tools were out of the window. She had learned to use new and far more delicate and complex instruments. Writing had ceased to be a discipline and had become an adventure. It was true that her experience of life was still limited. She could not rattle round St. Petersburg, rape peasant girls, fight in the Crimea, manage estates, and lay up an enormous store of memories of action. Tolstoi's advantages were as far remote from her as ever. But she had something. If her knowledge of life was narrow, it was profound. There was no fear, no sorrow, no ecstasy, and no limitation that she could not penetrate. And now she had an entirely new technique. She could compensate herself for all the things she did not know by arranging in a thousand new patterns the things she did.

And suddenly, it seemed, something happened to her spirits. She learned gaiety. The little sketch called **"A Society"** is on an entirely new note. There had been comedy in *The Voyage Out* and humour in *Night and Day,* but in neither novel had there been gaiety. Now, in this strange little squib, gaiety dances; it is evanescent with hyperbole; it is debonair with nonsense. (pp. 111-15)

She did not use it for long; her sense of life is tragic rather than comic. But having discovered it, she never lost it again. Perhaps laughter is the first gift of freedom. In any case, after the publication of ***Monday or Tuesday,*** any discerning reader must have understood that Mrs. Woolf was free. (p. 115)

Winifred Holtby, in her Virginia Woolf, *1932.*

Reprint by Folcroft Press, Inc., 1969, pp. 98-115.

Marjorie Brace (essay date 1946)

[*In the following excerpt, Brace discusses Woolf's terror of the "unknowableness of people and the impossibilities of communion" that characterized the writing of her generation, attributing Woolf's resultant devotion to inanimate objects and nature in her short fiction to a new moral sensibility.*]

In an essay titled "The Traveller's-Eye View" Aldous Huxley refers to some writers who "exploit the spectator's emotion": "The most uninteresting human being, seen at a little distance by a spectator with a lively fancy takes on a mysterious charm, becomes odd and exciting. One can work up a thrilling emotion about distant and unknown people—an emotion impossible to recapture after acquaintance, but which yields place to understanding." Certain authors, however, gain their effect precisely by never trying to understand. . . . Katherine Mansfield, on the other hand,

> invents suitable lives for the fabulous creatures glimpsed at cafés—and how thrilling those fancied lives always are! . . . Her characters are seen with extraordinary brilliance and precision, as one sees a party of people in a lighted drawing-room at night, through a window, haloed with significance . . . The glimpse of the inhabitants sipping their tea is enormously exciting, but one knows nothing, when one has passed, of what they are really like.
>
> (pp. 489-90)

The serious writers of the twenties were very conscious of living in an age of transition, bereft of any desirable order of values; very aware of living breathlessly in motion, in time, without roots. Psychologically speaking, they had no home for quiet living. Alone and unsupported on an unfathomable journey, their personal lives were as if confined to hotel rooms. They were spectators in every sense, observing not only other people, but themselves, with that traveller's eye which perceives nothing but gesture. Emotions—and, above all, relations with others—were seen through lighted windows as dramatic postures, and so became false. To "understand" the human character became more and more impossible, not through ignorance or superficiality or love for mystery, but because on that disintegrating journey in which no fixed standard of judgment could endure, it was absolutely what was *unknowable*.

To Virginia Woolf the unknowableness of people and the impossibilities of communion were never, as to some of her contemporaries, comic or ironic or of intellectual interest, but terrifying. The devices others used for evading genuine characterization, the "scientific" analyses, the violent caricatures, the self-conscious satirical melancholy posturing, all these were repulsive to her serious and lyrical nature. That responsiveness to the truly alive which, in her literary essays, emerged in such tender appreciations of personalities from a warmer past, left her shivering but determined before the cold looming problems of her own time. Like one of the insects she loved to describe, we see her progressing erratically through her novels, feeling, as with painfully sensitive antennae along a chilly

wall, for some new approach to the mystery. With each novel, the characters become more shadowy and we have in their stead, almost alarmingly real—as large as life and twice as natural—seasons, boats, oceans, leaves, furniture; the very streams of consciousness, when not a highly lyrical poetry, sound like overheard conversations or the confessions a stranger might impart on a train. And in *A Haunted House,* her collected short stories,—some of them left unrevised at her death, some, even in final form, mere sketches—there is a kind of unity the novels, for all their elaboration, never achieved: the traveller's view has perhaps never been expressed with such purity, in all its super-vividness of seeing and hearing, its rocket-like bursts of excitement, its flat returns to the hotel room of the self.

Here is a reiterated motif of human departure from the haunted "houses" of the past:

> They wanted to leave this house because they wanted to change their style of furniture, so he said . . . very interesting people because one will never see them again, never know what happened next . . . we were torn asunder, as one is torn from the old lady about to pour out tea and the young man about to hit the tennis ball in the back garden of the suburban villa as one rushes past in the train. . . . Why, if one wants to compare life to anything it is being blown through the Tube at fifty miles an hour, with one's hair flying back like the tail of a race-horse.

Reality is something glimpsed as one tears past, something arrested, timeless; is a flower-stalk or the old lady about to pour tea.

But the old lady lives only in a picture. She is not "understood," she has no capacity for action other than to complete a gesture, and she fades like a landscape from our sight, her living and dying of obviously less significance to a traveller than the decay of her house or garden. This world in which old ladies may be equivalent in value to the weather or snails on a rock, while unquestionably it has uncovered new areas of awareness, has also brought fresh terror to individual experience, beside which the spectator's joy is seen dwindling to a nervous, transient release. In such a story as **"An Unwritten Novel"** the narrator, observing a tragic face on a train, invents a withered spinster's life story to suit it, only to have the fancy exploded when the "character" is met at the station by a son. And what is the reaction? "Well, my world's done for! What do I stand on? What do I know? Who am I? Life's bare as a bone." But almost at once (still aboard the train and not back in the hotel room) the last look "flooded her anew. Mysterious figures! Who are you? Where tonight will you sleep? . . . unknown figures, you I adore; if I open my arms it's you I embrace—adorable world!"

The note of hysteria is unmistakable: the traveller's intoxicating sense of illegitimate freedom is darkened by inevitable returns to a somehow equally spurious "reality," subjective as well as objective, where, alone and looking at himself, he is compelled to dissolve his *own* capacity for action by self-mockery: "I wish I could hit upon a pleasant track of thought, indirectly reflecting credit on myself. . . . Dressing up the figure of myself in my own mind, stealthily, not openly adoring it, for if I did that I should catch myself out . . ."

Virginia Woolf is least interesting when, defending, as it were, this powerless condition, she presents as the only possible foil the stock culprit of so many novels of the period: the ignoble person who has not the grace to realize his own self-imprisonment. Such are the humanitarians in **"The Man Who Loved His Kind"** who, anxious to prove their own way of loving humanity to be the only right one, end up by hating everybody. Similarly, there is the girl in **"The New Dress"** whose costume, designed to be exotic, appears only laughably eccentric to her once she arrives at a party where she is doomed to be either snubbed or bored because—we grasp the point only too quickly—her own unreflecting egotism turns all dresses and parties drab. We have met this girl too often before. We have been informed by too many writers that we *are* that girl, that, always taking ourselves to parties, we miss the thrills of observation through a lighted window.

We do not question the Baudelarian horrors of existence so poisoned by subjectivity that even the ocean speaks "un langage connu." What we do question is the finality of the either-or implication. Is it not just this artificial pendulum-swing between human falseness and an inhuman world of "mysterious figures" that adulterates such writing with a morally dubious quality? Is it not just as untenable and even smug, to be forever appreciative of our "honesty" and thrilled with the unknown?

Virginia Woolf's work never resolved this issue, but when it was confronted, as in her story **"Solid Objects,"** she created some of the most remarkable symbolic expressions of our time. Here is John, standing for Parliament—that is all we are told about him—who one day at the beach finds a lump of green glass so mysteriously significant that he begins hunting everywhere for similar objects for his mantel. "They were useful," Virginia Woolf tells us slyly, "for a man upon the brink of a brilliant career has any number of papers to keep in order—addresses to constituents, declarations of policy, appeals for subscriptions. . . . " Soon he finds a fragment of china so extraordinary that he misses a meeting trying to fish it from an obscure recess. "Set opposite the lump of glass it looked a creature from another world—freakish and fantastic as a harlequin. The contrast between the china so vivid and alert, and the glass so mute and contemplative, fascinated him." He begins to haunt wastelands, rubbish heaps, demolished houses, neglects everything in the search, and the day he is not elected finds him elate, for he has discovered "a most remarkable piece of iron, massy and globular, but so cold and heavy, so black and metallic, that it was evidently alien to the earth and had its origin in one of the dead stars or was itself the cinder of a moon. And yet it stood upon the same ledge with the lump of glass and the star-shaped china."

In this apparent negation of all human values, we find a partial and—in its very inadequacy—a desperate, almost noble attempt to re-invoke them on some unapproached plane. The documents, leading articles, cabinet ministers—that reality which made Virginia Woolf exclaim, "The military sound of the word is enough!"—these things had become so profoundly inimical to the interests of the other, inner reality (in turn horrified by its own isolation) that the two realities cancelled each other out. There was nothing but to establish entirely new relations as, waking from a nightmare, "one turns on the light and lies worshipping the chest of drawers, worshipping solidi-

ty, worshipping the impersonal world which is a proof of some existence other than ours. That is what one must be sure of."

An excess of moral sensibility and humaneness caused Virginia Woolf to move into an inhuman and morally irresponsible world, making her write of insects, trees, old boards and broken china as if they were inhabited in an ancient sense by gods and spirits. She was trying to shift perspective, to start all over again, by creating in the unconscious some life-giving pagan emotion which, roving through the detritus of civilization, might also move into relation with a chemical, mineral, biological, fourth-dimensional universe, and so toward a new morality.

The virtue of the spectator's view is that, tearing down houses and disrupting dead relationships, it helps this fresh start. Its defect is that no matter how great the artist's moral anxiety and sensibility, it makes quite hopeless those human relations the difficulty of which sent him on his travels at the beginning. That is why, in almost all the novelists of the transitional group, definite or memorable characters are sacrificed to the qualities of things that should be distinct from literature, such as psychology, or music or painting. But the truth of a psychological analysis, the significance in a musical theme or a picture is complete and not, as great literature is, implicit with potential action. More successfully than any prose writer of her time, Virginia Woolf was, with words, a musician and a painter. What she was not can be seen in comparison with the few who, working with her material and intention, were not dazzled by a new conception of time, but lived densely within it; who placed human beings in new relations with each other as well as with the physical world. (pp. 490-94)

But it is she who seems closer to us now, and prophetic. The martial sound of reality and the clashes of malformed egos have invaded the landscape as well as the midnight room with cold ferocity. We are reminded as we read her that journeys now have grimmer purposes, that the traveller no longer stops at those marvelous way-stations, those heavenly côtes d'Azur she explored so exquisitely. The general motivation of current fiction recalls those base persons whose lack of self-knowledge she repudiated with fastidious disgust. If we cavil at her writing like a painter, how are we to endure those novelists whose work, under such an analogy, could only be compared with some curious Landseer school, populated with people like vicious or noble dogs? who do not even comprehend the questions left unanswered by a previous literary generation? To be surrounded with what is dying, and to know it, is better than to mistake death for life. (pp. 494-95)

Despite our completed knowledge of the life bare as a bone at the journey's end, the rushing air is so alive, so cold and salty with the sea, so warm with flowering vines; and there is also the amazing piece of iron, solid and concentrated, to hold like a talisman in our hands. (p. 495)

Marjorie Brace, "Worshipping Solid Objects: The Pagan World of Virginia Woolf," in Accent Anthology: Selections from Accent, A Quarterly of New Literature, 1940-1945, *edited by Kerker Quinn and Charles Shattuck, Harcourt, Brace and Company, 1946, pp. 489-95.*

Woolf on the Art of Fiction

Look within and life, it seems, is very far from being "like this". Examine for a moment an ordinary mind on an ordinary day. The mind receives a myriad impressions—trivial, fantastic, evanescent, or engraved with the sharpness of steel. From all sides they come, an incessant shower of innumerable atoms; and as they fall, as they shape themselves into the life of Monday or Tuesday, the accent falls differently from of old; the moment of importance came not here but there; so that if a writer were a free man and not a slave, if he could write what he chose, not what he must, if he could base his work upon his own feeling and not upon convention, there would be no plot, no comedy, no tragedy, no love interest or catastrophe in the accepted style, and perhaps not a single button sewn on as the Bond Street tailors would have it. Life is not a series of gig lamps symmetrically arranged; but a luminous halo, a semi-transparent envelope surrounding us from the beginning of consciousness to the end.

Let us record the atoms as they fall upon the mind in the order in which they fall, let us trace the pattern, however disconnected and incoherent in appearance, which each sight or incident scores upon the consciousness. Let us not take it for granted that life exists more fully in what is commonly thought big than in what is commonly thought small.

"The proper stuff of fiction" does not exist; everything is the proper stuff of fiction, every feeling, every thought; every quality of brain and spirit is drawn upon; no perception comes amiss. And if we can imagine the art of fiction come alive and standing in our midst, she would undoubtedly bid us break her and bully her, as well as honour and love her, for so her youth is renewed and her sovereignty assured.

Excerpted from Woolf's essay "Modern Fiction" in her The Common Reader *(1925).*

Jean Guiguet   (essay date 1962)

[*In the following excerpt, which is a translation of Guiguet's book-length critical study of Woolf and her works that was originally published in 1962, Guiguet surveys and comments on the experimental nature of Woolf's short fiction in which she presents "moments of being."*]

With the exception of **"A Society"** and **"Blue and Green"** (originally published in March 1921, in the only collection to appear in her lifetime, *Monday or Tuesday*), Virginia Woolf's sketches and stories, eighteen in number, were collected by Leonard Woolf in a small volume, *A Haunted House and other short stories,* published in 1944. In his preface, Leonard Woolf indicates how Virginia Woolf wrote these pieces, thus suggesting the place they should be allotted in her work:

> All through her life, Virginia Woolf used at intervals to write short stories. It was her custom, whenever an idea for one occurred to her, to sketch it out in a very rough form and then to put it away in a drawer. Later, if an editor asked her for a short story, and she felt in the mood to write one (which was not frequent), she would take a sketch out of her drawer and rewrite it, sometimes a great many times. Or if she felt, as she often did, while writing a novel that she required to rest her mind by working at something else for a time, she would either write a critical essay or work upon one of her sketches for short stories.

Without questioning the fact that these brief compositions were sometimes considered by Virginia Woolf merely as interludes, and that the chance requirements of her profession induced her to write some particular story at one moment rather than another, if we looked no further than this statement of Leonard Woolf's we should be liable to neglect one important aspect of several of these writings: their experimental character. This is stressed in the Diary, and furthermore chronology provides an argument in favour of this hypothesis, which a study of the texts will confirm. In fact, the publication of the stories falls into three brief periods: 1917-1921, 1927-1929 and 1938-1940. Although these dates only enable one to give a rough estimate of the time of writing, they correspond too closely to the periods of exploration in Virginia Woolf's career for the coincidence to be a fortuitous one.

The first group in particular, which includes at least four stories prior to the composition of *Jacob's Room* and three that are contemporary with it, represents unquestionably an exploratory path which was to lead to that novel. With the other two groups, although the relations between the sketches and the novels of the same period are less clear, and as we shall see are confused by other links with earlier works, one of them coincides with the point when, feeling her way towards *The Waves*, Virginia Woolf lingered over *Orlando,* and the other with the point when, at the end of that long labour *The Years,* she was turning in the direction of *Between the Acts.* (pp. 329-330)

On the strength of these observations, I might have divided my study of the sketches between these three periods. However, I felt this would mean unduly stressing a single aspect of them which, though not unimportant, was secondary or at any rate supplementary; it would also mean neglecting their autonomous character. If, indeed, they may have served as exercises, they are something more than that. And I have chosen therefore to classify them according to other criteria, more appreciative of their individual character and thus more apt to encourage a just assessment of their merits. (p. 331)

I shall associate with ["**Kew Gardens**"] four other impressionist studies, **"Blue and Green"**, **"A Haunted House"**, **"Monday or Tuesday"** and **"The String Quartet"**. These five sketches are characterized by their lack of any dramatic framework and by their attempt to present, in a contiguity which creates continuity, the disparate elements of consciousness, made homogeneous by uniformity of tone and the absence of any precise reference to place or time. We have here moments snipped out of existence, without any "before" or "after"; the close of day between two flights of a heron through the sky (**"Monday or Tuesday"**), the space of time between the moment of taking one's seat in a concert hall and the moment of parting at the door (**"The String Quartet"**). The consciousness through which there flit sensations, perceptions, fragments of thought, images from the past and from elsewhere, fancies, words heard or spoken, has no face and no body. It does not exist in itself; it exists in what passes through it, making and unmaking it constantly, leaving the reader with the contradictory reality of this possession and this transience. One is tempted to speak of pure atmosphere. **"A Haunted House"**, with its opening phrase: "Whatever hour you woke there was a door shutting" might incline one to do so. But the ambiguity by which the inhabitants of the haunted house become one with the ghosts that haunt it is evidence of a different intention. The atmosphere, strictly speaking, is only one element in these stories. What they are trying to convey is, at the same time, the way in which it pervades the being who is immersed in it, and the way in which it emanates from him. For basically, the real subject is one moment of his existence, and it is in this respect that these sketches are on the way that leads to *Jacob's Room, Mrs Dalloway* and *The Waves*. And indeed their failure, or at least their uncertain character, can be explained when we set them beside the comparable moments that make up the later novels, for which they prepared the way. It is the accumulation and interconnectedness of such moments that brings to life Jacob or Clarissa, Susan or Bernard. If we isolate one moment, its resonances remain dead; cut off from its whole it becomes pale and lifeless; all that remains is a wonderful shimmering background where the human being is lost. Only **"Kew Gardens"**, perhaps on account of its greater complexity and the solidity of its structure, is fully successful; the others delight the eye and ear without satisfying the mind. The most extreme example, **"Blue and Green"**, goes outside the realm of reality to lose itself in the world of dream, where images are connected only by a slender thread. This arbitrary universe was not the one Virginia Woolf sought to explore, and that is doubtless why she proposed leaving it out of the later editions which she envisaged.

Of the same type as **"An Unwritten Novel"** are three other stories: **"Moments of Being," "The Lady in the Looking Glass"** and **"The Shooting Party"**. Despite differences of treatment and style, the general plan is the same. All four show the writer in quest of "Mrs Brown", according to the methods [she] set forth in the 1923 article ["Mr Bennett and Mrs Brown"]. In fact, Minnie Marsh in **"An Unwritten Novel"** is elder sister to Mrs Brown, and Virginia Woolf undoubtedly bore in mind the sketch—written in 1919-1920, when elaborating the typical figure on whom she based her theory.

"The Shooting Party", although the last in date of the series, is outwardly the closest to its prototype. As in **"An Unwritten Novel"**, the anonymous observer-narrator, sitting opposite an unknown woman in a railway carriage, reconstitutes from a few signs a whole section of the stranger's life, complete with settings and companions. At the end of the journey, the construction breaks down before a touch of reality: the son waiting on the platform relegates into the world of fancy Minnie Marsh, the maiden aunt with her unhappy love affairs and her miserly relations. In the same way, under the glare of the station lights Milly Masters, the poor tailor's daughter who has been seduced by the squire, turns into a very ordinary woman visiting London on some trivial errand. But whereas in **"An Unwritten Novel"** the makebelieve story keeps referring back to the real character for confirmation and impetus, in **"The Shooting Party"** it flows on uninterruptedly and thus gains an autonomy which seems a guarantee of authenticity, so that at the *dénouement* this para-reality withstands the corrosive power of facts. The author does not feel compelled to justify it, as she had done in the last paragraph of **"An Unwritten Novel"**. Even if all that really existed was "M. M.", the woman with the suitcase and the brace of pheasants, while the Squire, the manor and the shooting party were mere phantasms, these convince us and remain in our minds when the slender reality from which they were born has vanished into the past and oblivion.

In **"Moments of Being"** the observer, Fanny Wilmott, constructs out of fragments—gestures, appearances, words—the life and personality of her piano teacher, Julia Craye: her family circumstances, her manifestations of avidity, independence and frustration, all contribute to confirm the hypothesis of a narrow, disappointed life. Then suddenly Julia Craye takes Fanny in her arms and kisses her mouth. This revelation, without completely destroying the image Fanny had formed, reorganizes it around a different centre. The stress which had been laid on loneliness and pathos now falls on independence and will-power: what had seemed semi-failure becomes semi-victory.

Unlike **"An Unwritten Novel"** and **"The Shooting Party"**, **"Moments of Being"** contains a certain dramatic element closely linked to the general theme of the exploration of a personality. Although Fanny chooses unhappy solitude, the possibility of voluntary solitude is never absent, and a sort of tension arises which is only resolved in the final paragraph. Moreover, the conflict between the real and the imagined is not what is most essential in this story: the title indicates that it is more specifically concerned with the revelation which replaces this conflict and solves it by integrating the contradictory elements. The moment of being is at the meeting of the two worlds where, during the space of a privileged moment, we catch a glimpse of truth. This moment, defined here by the commonplace sentence "Slater's pins have no points", recalls Joyce's "Epiphanies", whose characteristic is the liberation of the revelatory power latent in an insignificant word or gesture.

"The Lady in the Looking Glass" might have been called **"An Unwritten Novel"**. In fact, in the effervescent mood that was to produce *Orlando*, Virginia Woolf notes in her Diary:

> But I can think of more books than I shall ever be able to write. How many little stories come into my head! For instance: Ethel Sands not looking at her letters. What this implies. One might write a book of short significant separate scenes. She did not open her letters.

The story ends on practically the same sentence. If the

mere fact that these letters were bills explains the indifference of Isabella Tyson, alias Ethel Sands, the revelation implied by this gesture is made dramatic by the slow preparation at cross purposes, the misunderstanding which is the theme of the story. **"The Lady in the Looking Glass"**, however, combines the psychological enquiry of **"An Unwritten Novel"** and the rich impressionism of **"Kew Gardens"**. This alliance is perhaps not unconnected with the exploration which Virginia Woolf was then undertaking for *The Waves*. That reality is distinct from our image of it is suggested, from the beginning, by the distinction between the real scene and its reflection in the looking glass. And paradoxically, as one might have expected from Virginia Woolf, the reflected image, with its precision and fixity contrasted with the confusion and movement with which real space is filled by the light and shadows, the air, the flowers, captures the essence of reality and reveals it. Isabella has disappeared into the garden; the observer's conception of her is suggested by her delightful home, her luxuriant garden. Her wealth implies happiness and success; her silence, mystery and passion, and the bundle of letters the postman has just flung on to the marble table bears witness to this. But when Isabella reappears in the mirror, the light that surrounds her figure reveals a very different truth: loneliness, indifference, emptiness, age—and the letters are only bills. (pp. 331-35)

With **"The New Dress"** we come to the stories which form part of what one might call the *Mrs Dalloway* saga, which comprises also **"The Man who loved his Kind"**, **"Together and Apart"** and **"The Summing Up"**. In this group, **"The New Dress"** stands apart. From its date, 1927, as well as from several pieces of internal evidence, it seems to be a reject left over from the novel. We see the famous party through the eyes of Mabel, a humble acquaintance of the Dalloways. Like the other guests in the novel, she is greeted in the cloakroom by Mrs Barnet, who sizes up each visitor's class and dress. The perspicacity of the old servant, already mentioned in the novel, lies at the root of Mabel's misfortunes; Mrs Barnet's attitude makes her aware of the unsuitability of her dress, and this feeling isolates her during the whole party, making her conscious, amidst all these rich people, of her own poverty, then of the failure of her life, and revealing to her, moreover, the vanity and sterility of such social contacts. After having endured the hypocrisy, indifference and selfishness of others and her own humiliation, she makes her retreat with a polite lie: "I have enjoyed myself enormously." This lie synthesizes all the lies, all the treacheries not merely of these few hours but of the whole of existence. We see from this that its setting is not the only factor that connects **"The New Dress"** with *Mrs Dalloway*. The satirical implications of the story are akin to those of the novel; at an even deeper level, through her pessimism, Mabel recalls Septimus, while like him she is connected with Clarissa by "a divine moment" of sea and sand and sun. Apart from the recurrence of this theme we may note also, as though referring to Peter Walsh and his life-story, Mabel's youthful daydream: she had pictured herself living in India, married to a hero, whereas Hubert, her husband, has a dreary subordinate job in the Law Courts. Finally, perhaps she was intended to form a parallel to Ellie Henderson, or else to take her place at the party. Like Ellie, in fact, Mabel is an outsider, reluctantly invited at the last minute, and is too poor to spend money on her dress. The distance that divides her from this world allows it to be seen, through her,

from a different angle to that of the other characters. Nevertheless, Mabel's viewpoint is as unlike Ellie's as is their way of dressing: Ellie is natural and sweet-tempered, whereas Mabel is timid and embittered. Perhaps Virginia Woolf was rightly reluctant to alter the atmosphere of the closing pages of her novel by this corrosive ingredient, and therefore relegated this character into the drawer where she kept her rough sketches.

In spite of all the links that can be found between the short story and the novel, **"The New Dress"** is none the less a perfectly self-contained narrative, with its own progress and peripeteia. Mabel, having gone through the hell of her shame and loneliness, reaches the safe shore of happy memories, which reconcile her to herself and her life; she acquires new strength and resolution; but is it through having looked in the mirror, having once again encountered the same Mabel that the others see? She can merely mumble a conventional falsehood, and goes back to her own truth.

The three other stories which take their setting from Mrs Dalloway's party, written considerably later, it seems, even if the idea of them occurred to Virginia Woolf while she was writing her novel, reflect the latter only indirectly. The atmosphere of a social gathering is conducive to the development of the theme which, like the setting, is common to all three. They are variants on the difficulty of communicating with other people. In **"The Man who Loved his Kind"** Prickett Ellis and Miss O'Keefe, both philanthropists in different ways, try in vain to tell each other of their common love for humanity, while exasperated by the sight of the frivolity and indifference around them. All that they are able to express, or to feel, is hatred! The same impossibility of mutual understanding divides the two characters of **"Together and Apart".** Just as Prickett Ellis and Miss O'Keefe failed to meet on the common ground of philanthropy, so Mr Serle and Miss Anning fail to make contact in their common recollections of Canterbury which, for a brief second, had given them a sense of closeness; but it was for a second only. They go back each to his solitude and separate, indifferent to each another. Whereas in **"The New Dress"** and **"The Man who Loved his Kind"** Virginia Woolf had given free rein to her sense of caricature and had got her effects by exaggeration, here she works in half-tones, suggesting the submerged world which she knows so well, where she can here and there use her characters for a meditation on her favourite themes. The same atmosphere recurs in **"The Summing Up"**, where a man and a woman are talking in Mrs Dalloway's garden. The woman, indeed, listens more than she speaks; she listens and thinks about something else, spell-bound by the perfection of the place and the moment. From this advanced point in our civilization she looks back, vaguely, to the primitive times when marshes lay where London stands, for the two extremes are the very substance of the soul, although the riddle of nature and man remains insoluble. This Sasha Latham is akin to Mrs Swithin in *Between the Acts* in her sense of cosmic continuity as well as in her calm, wondering acceptance of things human.

"Lappin and Lapinova" and **"The Legacy"** are abridged dramas of married life. They show, the first in a vein of heroic-comic fantasy, the second with a tension which is sustained from beginning to end with the help of dramatic irony, the deterioration of relations between a married couple, gradually slipping into what, in her note on the married relationship written in 1926, she called "the automatic customary unconscious days on either side". Since Virginia Woolf wrote a first version of **"Lappin and Lapinova"** in 1917 or 1918, returned to the theme and even wrote another story of the same subject towards the end of her life, we may assume that her opinions on this point never altered. Moreover, from the hesitancies of Rachel and Terence in *The Voyage Out* to the more concrete hostility between Isa and Giles in *Between the Acts,* every one of her novels touches on this problem. It is a common enough problem, no doubt, but with Virginia Woolf it acquires freshness through its implications. It is just a special case of the difficulty all human beings have in understanding and knowing one another, an example of the ignorance and loneliness from which we try in vain to escape. (pp. 336-39)

In **"The Legacy"** Gilbert Clandon, after the death of his wife Angela, gives their secretary Sissy Miller a brooch that Angela has left her, and reads through the diary she had left on purpose for him. He discovers from this how Angela had passed gradually from love, admiration and enthusiasm into lukewarmness, indifference and bored loneliness; how she had flung herself into social work, and met a certain B. M. with whom she seemed to have fallen in love. She had refused to go away with him; he committed suicide, and the last sentence in the diary reveals that she herself had died not as the result of an accident, but having deliberately chosen to give up a life that had lost its meaning and to join the man she loved—the brother of Sissy Miller—in death. (pp. 339-40)

"The Legacy" is Virginia Woolf's most dramatic story, in the sense that the riddle towards whose solution it moves with a sure art of suggestions and partial revelations, is connected with action rather than with a personality. The chain of events leading up to the *dénouement* provides a solid basis for the accompanying characterization, and confers on the whole more firmness and clarity of outline than is generally found in these stories.

The other four, while they bear the imprint of their author in detail of execution and in the suggestion of certain themes, seem to be, each in its way, incursions into less familiar fields. **"Solid Objects"** (1920) is a philosophical tale where, after an opening reminiscent of *Jacob's Room,* Virginia Woolf portrays a man who, having found a piece of glass brought in by the waves, fascinated by this "solid object"—truth, concealed and misunderstood—abandons a promising political career in order to devote himself to an eccentric search for other specimens of this reality. **"The Duchess and the Jeweller"** is a satirical portrait in the same vein as *The Years.* **"The Searchlight"**, which is not easy to label, is at the same time perhaps the least successful of all the stories and the most profoundly typical of Virginia Woolf. In the flash of a searchlight, a woman glimpses a fragment of the past—not even of her own past but of her grandmother's youth. The meaning of this fragmentary and fleeting revelation only appears in the closing lines: "The light . . . only falls here and there." The symbol of the telescope thanks to which the narrator's grandfather discovered the woman who was to become his wife links the story, after a fashion, with the searchlights that are raking the sky. But the whole thing remains vague; the

moment of vision loses its special flavour in the long drawn out narrative that is needed to clarify or communicate it. As for **"A Society"**, Virginia Woolf was surely right in wishing to exclude it from later editions. This social fable tells of the imaginary enquiry undertaken by a group of women into the basis of civilization, in order to decide whether it is worth while perpetuating the race. The general design is uncertain, the irony often clumsy. None the less this failed venture into militant literature, which Virginia Woolf had the good taste to cast aside, marks an interesting stage in her development. It contains the germs of *A Room of One's Own* and *Three Guineas;* it shows that her feminist attitude remained constant as regards education, marriage, literature and the liberal professions, as did her opinions about men of law, academics, soldiers and politicians. But it was to take another ten years, the experience of writing *Orlando* and perhaps too, the self-confidence that came from success to sharpen her verve. When the ideas of **"A Society"** had been developed and satisfactorily set forth in her pamphlets, this somewhat feeble story could be put aside as a rough draft. (pp. 340-42)

It is difficult to formulate any general judgment on such dissimilar pieces. If **"The Legacy"** and **"The Duchess and the Jeweller"** correspond, more or less, to the traditional conception of a short story, the rest can only be described as sketches or studies. In this field, as in that of the novel, Virginia Woolf refused to be bound by ready made formulae. Granted her hostility to any sort of "story", to the organization of events within a rigid framework of time and

Undated photograph of Woolf as a child.

space, it might be said that short story writing was a challenge to her. Yet just as certain novelists have used the short story to emphasize and epitomize their vision of the world, Virginia Woolf sought to render in a few pages the essence of her universe. "Moments of Being" might serve as sub-title for each of these fragments. They attempt, indeed, to convey the unique quality of an instant when the world of our senses and the inner world, the present and the past, the here and the elsewhere, like the different elements in a solution, suddenly combine to form that solid body, reality—which, a moment later, once glimpsed, is again dissolved into its elements. From this very nature of her reality, Virginia Woolf was able to extract a principle of composition which may be considered a rule of the genre as she conceived it and through which, moreover, she carries on a tradition.

She always starts from something mysterious or, at least, perplexing and disturbing, to which the closing lines provide an answer, most frequently an unexpected one. Only the group I have described as impressionist sketches cannot be thus characterized. The fact that these were all written between 1919 and 1921, in a period of experiment and exploration, after which Virginia Woolf wrote no more atmospheric sketches of this sort, inclines one to believe that she was aware of the limitations of the genre. If **"Kew Gardens"** remains a masterpiece, it is none the less true that it could not be safely imitated or reproduced. If many pages of *The Waves* show that Virginia Woolf put to good account its teaching and its potentialities, after the three attempted variants of 1921 she returned to the trail blazed by **"The Mark on the Wall"** and **"An Unwritten Novel"**. Supplementing her longer journeys through the world of appearances and through the years, these stories each represent a brief excursion from which, in her unremitting quest for reality, Virginia Woolf brought back some slight quarry—slight indeed but revealing of the depths in which it was discovered. (pp. 342-43)

> *Jean Guiguet, in his* Virginia Woolf and Her Works, *translated by Jean Stewart, The Hogarth Press, 1965, pp. 329-43.*

R. T. Chapman   (essay date 1972)

[*In the following excerpt, Chapman examines Woolf's use of perception in "The Lady in the Looking-Glass" as a means of organizing experience and compares her methods to tenets of Gestalt psychology.*]

A woman visits an old friend and is shown into her drawing-room to wait. Thinking how shallowly she knows her friend Isabella Tyson, the visitor attempts to create in her mind's eye a picture of what she is really like. This six-page short story [**"The Lady in the Looking-Glass"**] traces the imaginative processes which build up this picture until Isabella Tyson is "caught." Nothing is known of the thinker in the story; she is completely anonymous, and although everything is seen through her eyes and filtered through her consciousness, the interest is centered upon the object of her thoughts, Isabella Tyson. This is an unusual use of the interior monologue, for normally thought processes are revealed in order to give a deeper understanding of the thinker. Mrs. Ramsay, for instance, unlike her husband, never has a coherent or logical thought-pattern, and their mode of thinking is as important as the

content of their thoughts in defining their characters. In **"The Lady in the Looking-Glass"** we are interested in the processes of perception for their own sake and not for the sake of "character." A similar interest in the movement of the mind is seen in Virginia Woolf's first "experimental" work, **"The Mark on the Wall"** (1917), which now reads like the application of word-association and the Rorschach blot test to literature. **"The Lady in the Looking-Glass,"** first published twelve years after the early story, shows a much more sophisticated use of psychological concepts and highlights many of Virginia Woolf's enduring psychological preoccupations.

Reading *A Writer's Diary,* one is continually aware of Virginia Woolf's acute consciousness of the mind as a thinking instrument and, in her own case, as a very delicate instrument: "I must rinse and freshen my mind and make it work soberly on something. . . . I am taking a fortnight off fiction. My mind became knotted." Because of mental illness, work on *Night and Day* (1919) was limited to one hour per day, and the continued fear of "neurasthenic" breakdown must have contributed to Virginia Woolf's preoccupation with things psychological. As Leonard Woolf writes in *Beginning Again* (London: Hogarth Press, 1965): "Normally she was sane, but four times in her life she passed over the line which divides the sane from the insane . . . [but] . . . it seemed that deep down in her mind she was never sane." In *Mrs. Dalloway* (1925), she laid bare the insane mind of Septimus Smith, and in later novels she plumbed the depths of the "normal" mind. These excursions into the conscious and subconscious lives of her characters are so frequent and natural that in Virginia Woolf's writing the life of the mind is as "real" as physical existence. In *A Writer's Diary* she tells how she met her sister in Tottenham Court Road: "Both of us sunk fathoms deep in that wash of reflection in which we both swim about . . . I was thinking of a thousand things as I carried my teapot, gramophone records and stockings under my arm." Virginia Woolf's analysis and description of this "wash of reflection," both in her diary and in her fiction, reveal a remarkable ability for introspection and suggest an interest in, if not a detailed knowledge of, the writing of contemporary psychoanalysts, many of whom were published by the Woolf's own Hogarth Press.

"The Lady in the Looking-Glass" explores how the mind translates external facts into subjective knowledge and the relative validity of these types of truth. The problem is an epistemological one, and Virginia Woolf treated it discursively in her famous essay "Mr. Bennett and Mrs. Brown" (1924). Here she chastises Bennett and traditional Edwardian novelists for laying "an enormous stress upon the fabric of things. They have given us a house in the hope that we may be able to deduce the human beings who live there." In Bennett's novels the reader knows about Mrs. Brown: Virginia Woolf wants to *know* Mrs. Brown, and in *Mrs. Dalloway* and *To the Lighthouse* (1927) we see the "new novel" breaking free of the ties of conventional realism. She searches below naturalistic behavioral observation for that new reality defined in *A Room of One's Own* as lying beyond the mundane; it is "what remains over when the skin of the day has been cast into the hedge." **"The Lady in the Looking-Glass"** embodies the process of attaining this more profound reality and ends with such an epiphanous insight into the heart of things.

Clarissa Dalloway is said to have the gift of "knowing people almost by instinct. . . . If you put her in a room with someone, up went her back like a cat's; or she purred." So, too, the visitor to Isabella's drawing-room is extraordinarily perceptive to atmosphere:

> The house was empty and one felt, since one was the only person in the drawing-room, like one of those naturalists who, covered with grass and leaves, lie watching the shyest animals—badgers, otters, kingfishers, moving about freely, themselves unseen. The room that afternoon was full of such shy creatures, lights and shadows, curtains blowing, petals falling—things that never happen, so it seems, if someone is looking . . . and the room had its passions and rages and envies and sorrows coming over it and clouding it, like a human being. Nothing stayed the same for two seconds together.

This type of observation is different in kind from the photographic details of the realist; Virginia Woolf invests inanimate objects with an existence of their own, divorced from the neutralizing and humanizing effect of their being a part of human existence. The "otherness" of objects, the mystery inherent in their very existence ("Nothing stayed the same for two seconds together"), is a theme of Sartre's *La Nausée* (1938) and, more recently, of the *nouveaux romans* of Robbe-Grillet. But in these later novels it is the alien nature of the "otherness" which is stressed; in this short story the mystery, the newness of the experience, is attractive. Says Bernard in *The Waves:* "I fill my mind with whatever happens to be the contents of a room or a railway carriage as one fills a fountain pen in an ink pot." This total sensory awareness of the most minute nuances of atmosphere and feeling is characteristic of Virginia Woolf's writing, and it is those very qualities of mind which are usually implicit in the best descriptive writing that are self-consciously examined in **"The Lady in the Looking-Glass."**

When such qualities of observation are applied to people, it is generally said that one knows them well. Yet the "imaginative" grasp of Isabella is revealed as being unsatisfactory. Even the most perceptive acts of empathy are, in the final analysis, the weaving of beautiful myths around figments of one's own fancy, unless such intuitive grasping after knowledge is based upon observable reality:

> [Isabella] has gone presumably into the lower garden to pick flowers; or as it seemed more natural to suppose, to pick something light and fantastic and leafy and trailing, travellers' joy, or one of those elegant sprays of convolvulus that twine around ugly walls and burst here and there into white and violet blossoms. She suggested the fantastic and tremulous convolvulus rather than the upright aster, the starched zinnia, or her own burning roses alight like lamps on the straight posts of their rose trees. The comparison showed how very little, after all these years, one knew about her; for it is impossible that any woman of flesh and blood of fifty-five or sixty should be really a wreath or a tendril. Such comparisons are worse than idle and superficial—they are cruel even, for they come like the convolvulus itself trembling between one's eyes and the truth. There must be truth; there must be a wall. Yet it was strange that after knowing her all these years one could not say what the truth about Isabella was; one still made up phrases like this about convolvulus and travellers' joy.

The poetic phrases are here a cloak to truth; the free imagination is limited in its powers when divorced from fact, and the visions of the creative mind crumble if faced with flesh and blood reality. The two "ways of knowing" here contrasted are, in Virginia Woolf's terms, the Masculine and the Feminine—the ways of Mr. Ambrose and his wife; Mr. Ramsay and his wife; Bart Oliver and Mrs. Swithin. Virginia Woolf's portraits of the masculine intellect usually compare unfavorably with her feminine intuitives: the one is analytical, cold, rational, unfeeling; the other unifying, loving, and all-embracing. But in this story Virginia Woolf goes beyond a mere polarization of these two principles to suggest the limitations inherent in the feminine way of knowledge—beauty is not necessarily truth.

The mind moves from drifting fanciful images of the "tremulous convolvulus" to consider the hard facts about Isabella; perhaps these will lead towards the truth:

> As for facts, it was a fact that she was a spinster; that she was rich; that she had bought this house and collected with her own hands—often in the most obscure corners of the world and at great risks from poisonous stings and Oriental diseases—the rugs, the chairs, the cabinets which now lived their nocturnal life before one's eyes.

But the reflecting mind cannot stay with facts; it runs on (in the manner Virginia Woolf characterized as typically "feminine"), to associate, conjecture, surmise, and fill in for itself the missing pieces. It is as though the feminine mind cannot bear too much reality; concrete, external facts only having validity as stimuli to reverie—oriental *objects d'art* evoke thoughts of past exotic travels, and newly arrived letters throw forward the mind to imagine future happiness. The physical limitations of time and space are obliterated by this capacity of the imagination. All things are possible within the mind, and Virginia Woolf continually glories in this ability to transcend the limitations of life. Again Bernard, the spokesman for the writer in *The Waves,* best describes this freedom of the imagination: "I throw my mind out in the air as a man throws seeds in great fan flights, falling through the purple sunset, falling on the pressed and shining ploughland which is bare." Facts are bare, they need to be clothed. The "things [Isabella] talks about at dinner" represent merely the social persona, no more the truth than Bennett's "fabric of things." There is a deeper layer of truth than this: "It was her profounder state of being that one wanted to catch and turn to words, the state that is to the mind what breathing is to the body, what one calls happiness or unhappiness."

The movement of the mind gives form to this story; it is a thought-adventure, an ever progressing act of empathy, consciously aiming at a moment of insight. The mind is never at rest, it is forever pressing forward, mentally feeling in dark corners, attempting to discover a revealing detail: "If she concealed so much and knew so much one must prise her open with the first tool that came to hand—the imagination. One must fix one's mind on her at that very moment. One must fasten her down there." Again the mind is "thrown out in the air," Isabella is seen in the mind's eye cutting a spray of travellers' joy—perhaps she will be thinking about death: "[but] she was one of those reticent people whose minds held their thoughts enmeshed in clouds of silence." The quest for this higher reality seems to be floundering; is it ever possible to "know" any-one in this way? The story appears to be moving towards the solipsistic conclusion that each man is an island; facts are abstractions and lifeless, yet all imaginative attempts to "be" Isabella are purely subjective and reveal more about the thinker than the object of thought. Life is too fluid to "fasten her down"; the essence of existence is its continual metamorphosis into something other: "Nothing stayed the same for two seconds together." Is it only possible, then, to record impressionistically the flux and withdraw into silence? In *To the Lighthouse* Virginia Woolf postulates "a still space that lies about the heart of things"; it is this stasis which the visual arts portray, and it is this stasis which is presented in **"The Lady in the Looking-Glass"** as the culmination of a complex train of thought.

From the beginning of the story a distinction has been made between perception of life and the image of life in the looking-glass. . . . The mirror transforms life into something other; it is removed from the flux and caught within the frame, static, metamorphosed into glass. This mirror-image is a metaphor for a process of perceiving reality which is, most often, associated with aesthetics. The mirror here performs the function of formalizing the flux of experience into significant pattern, of imposing order upon the ceaselessly changing. This problem of form is central to much of Virginia Woolf's writing; Mrs. Dalloway and Mrs. Ramsay create meaningful patterns in their social lives, whereas Lily Briscoe, Bernard, and Miss La Trobe create their patterns in the media of paint, words, and drama. In their different ways all are bringing stasis to the flux, selecting and embodying what is important from the "incessant shower of innumerable atoms" that make up life and thus creating art. But the embodiment of the vision is a secondary process; what this story describes is the primary process basic to all aesthetic creation: the perception of significant form in life.

The act of perception involves a continual organization of sense data, and this process is acutely described in this story. Deep in thoughts of Isabella, the thinker is startlingly awakened to the present:

Suddenly these reflections were ended violently and yet without a sound. A large black form loomed into the looking-glass; blotted out everything, strewed the table with a packet of marble tablets veined with pink and grey, and was gone. But the picture was entirely altered. For the moment it was unrecognisable and irrational and entirely out of focus. One could not relate these tablets to any human purpose. And then by degrees some logical process set to work on them and began ordering and arranging them and bringing them into the fold of common experience. One realised at last that they were merely letters. The man had brought the post.

The mind, according to this account, continually translates crude experience into assimilated knowledge; the "large black form" and "marble tablets" are swiftly "drawn in and arranged and composed and made part of the picture" and recognized as a man bringing letters. This analysis closely resembles the account of perception given by *Gestalt* psychologists; Herbert Read summarizes these ideas in *The Philosophy of Modern Art*, quoting from Koffka, one of the founders of the *Gestalt* school:

Visual perception itself only makes sense, only becomes coherent, by virtue of an organizing faculty within the nervous system. We should not be able to cope with the multiplicity of impressions which the eye receives were we not, at the same time, capable of organizing these impressions into a coherent pattern. In the words of a *Gestalt* psychologist: 'Perception tends towards balance and symmetry; or differently expressed: balance and symmetry are perceptual characteristics of the visual world which will be realized whenever the external conditions allow it.

In these terms, art is the articulation, in a medium of communication, of a "good Gestalt." The mirror acts as a metaphor descriptive of this patterning quality of the mind, and the final perception of the story is, in fact, a "good *Gestalt.*"

Isabella Tyson approaches the house, and her friend can see her reflected in the looking-glass. All the former modes of perception are synthesized in this final view of Isabella; a new reality stands revealed:

She came so gradually that she did not seem to derange the pattern in the glass, but only to bring in some new element which gently moved and altered the other objects as if asking them courteously to make room for her . . . the looking-glass began to pour over her a light that seemed to fix her; that seemed like some acid to bite off the unessential and superficial and to leave only the truth. It was an enthralling spectacle. Everything dropped from her—clouds, dress, basket, diamond—all that one had called the creeper and the convolvulus. Here was the hard wall beneath. Here was the woman herself. She stood naked in that pitiless light. And there was nothing. Isabella was perfectly empty. She had no thoughts. She had no friends. She cared for nobody. As for her letters they were all bills. Looking, as she stood there, old and angular, veined and lined, with her high nose and wrinkled neck, she did not even trouble to open them.

The facts of Isabella's appearance are fused with an imaginative grasp of what she feels—previously Isabella had eluded being "placed," but now she takes her place within the frame, she completes the picture, and all the elements fall into a significant pattern. This *Gestalt*—the structuring, simplifying, and unifying of the multiplicity of experience into an epitomizing image—illustrates the active, creative faculty of the mind, suggesting that every good *Gestalt* is an unconscious act of creation. What appears to be a mystical, "epiphanous" flash of insight (imaged in Isabella's appearance in the mirror) is, in fact, an aesthetically pleasing structuring of sense data. The intellect and imagination combine, and the grasp they have of reality "feels" true. This truth is to perception what the "holiness of the heart's affection" is to the emotions and was, for Virginia Woolf, the highest form of knowledge. (pp. 331-37)

R. T. Chapman, " 'The Lady in the Looking-Glass': Modes of Perception in a Short Story by Virginia Woolf," in Modern Fiction Studies, *Vol. 18, No. 3, Autumn, 1972, pp. 331-37.*

Stella McNichol   (essay date 1973)

[*In the following excerpt from an introduction to* Mrs.

Dalloway's Party: A Short Story Sequence, *McNichol discusses what she considers Woolf's preoccupation, following the completion of her novel* Mrs. Dalloway, *with writing short stories that explore the dynamics of social gatherings as a microcosm of society at large.*]

The seven stories in [**Mrs Dalloway's Party**] belong to the period between *Jacob's Room* (1922) and *To the Lighthouse* (1927). The novel of that period is *Mrs Dalloway* (1925). The stories, as it were, surround that novel. It is not necessary to read the novel *Mrs Dalloway* in order to appreciate the book of short stories I have named **Mrs Dalloway's Party.** On the other hand, the book of short stories does enlarge one's understanding and appreciation of Virginia Woolf's work as a whole. It explains why, for example, the Mr and Mrs Dalloway who appear in *The Voyage Out* (1915) are still being written about in 1925. Virginia Woolf is not repeating herself; she is moving deeper into the Dalloway world, the society world, in order to fathom its power and question its values. The party created by Mrs Dalloway belongs to a particularly significant stage of Virginia Woolf's development as a novelist and a critic; it is significant biographically too.

Virginia Woolf loved society and its functions:

> The idea of a party always excited her, and in practice she was very sensitive to the actual mental and physical excitement of the party itself, the rise of temperature of mind and body, the ferment and fountain of noise.
>
> Leonard Woolf, *Downhill All the Way*

It was out of the excitement, the fluctuations of mood and temper, and the heightened atmosphere of the party that Virginia Woolf created the microcosm of society which she gives to us in her Mrs Dalloway stories.

But because of her severe bouts of illness in 1921 and 1922, the Woolfs had left London for the quiet of Richmond, though when Virginia was fit, they travelled to London to enjoy a limited social life. As her health improved in 1923 she began to feel imprisoned or cut off in Richmond and longed to return to the city, its noise and vitality. In early 1924 the Woolfs returned to London. The imposed restriction on her attendance at parties in the three years 1921 to 1923, and the return to a fuller enjoyment of society and its functions in 1924, seem to me to be reflected in her preoccupation with that world in the novel and short stories written roughly within those years.

It was on 27th April, 1925, when *Mrs Dalloway* was about to come out that Virginia Woolf made the following significant entry in her Diary:

> But my present reflection is that people have any number of states of consciousness: and I should like to investigate the *party consciousness*, the frock consciousness etc. The fashion world of the Becks . . . is certainly one; where people secrete an envelope which connects them and protects them from others, like myself, who am outside the envelope, foreign bodies. These states are very difficult (obviously I grope for words) but I'm always coming back to it. The party consciousness. . . .

It seems that Virginia Woolf actually did make an investigation into the 'party consciousness' in her group of Mrs Dalloway short stories. It is the psychology of the party,

the subtleties of the human being's reactions and anxieties under the conditions and limits imposed on him by the social occasion that are closely scrutinised by Virginia Woolf in *Mrs Dalloway's Party*. The artificiality of the occasion brings the reality to the fore or gives access to it. So, for example, Mabel Waring in **"The New Dress"** reflects:

> For the party makes things either much more real, or much less real, she thought. . . . She saw the truth. This was true, this drawing-room, this self, and the other false.

But for Mrs Vallance in **"Ancestors"**, on the other hand, the world of Mrs Dalloway's drawing-room is but a 'noisy bright chattering crowd' with which she contrasts the more worthwhile world of her childhood spent in the country, in Scotland. The two pieces, **"Introduction"** and **"The Man Who Loved His Kind"**, both explore the solitary reflections of the individual alone in the midst of a group of men and women who are united only in that they are physically placed together in the drawing-room or home of Mrs Dalloway. The actual title **"Together and Apart"** suggests what happens to two individuals at the party: Miss Anning and Mr Serle, introduced to each other by Mrs Dalloway, come together, or relate to each other, but only within the bounds of the party. They experience the 'old ecstasy of life' but their brief experience does not endure beyond the party or the story. There is, in other words, a brief 'coming together' which is resolved into a return to separateness or falling 'apart'. **"A Summing Up"**, the last story or chapter of **Mrs Dalloway's Party,** provides a key passage for an understanding of the short stories and of Virginia Woolf's 'party consciousness'. A tribute is paid to Clarissa Dalloway's creative ability. It is a bow to the hostess who is responsible for the occasion and the world she has created:

> This, she thought, is the greatest of marvels; the supreme achievement of the human race . . . and she thought of the dry, thick, well-built house, stored with valuables, humming with people coming close to each other, going away from each other, exchanging their views, stimulating each other. And Clarissa Dalloway had made it open in the wastes of the night. . . .

Yet the point of view of the story and of the actual summing up is complex like the party itself, for in a moment of disenchantment and detachment the person who made the bow to Mrs Dalloway asks herself if the party is after all nothing more than 'people in evening dress'.

Of the stories in the present volume **"Mrs Dalloway in Bond Street"** is the one most closely connected with the genesis of the novel *Mrs Dalloway*. It was intended originally to be Chapter One of that novel. Although the story is obviously heavily echoed in the novel, it was rejected from the novel by Virginia Woolf who herself published it independently as a short story in 1923. **"The New Dress"** was written in 1924 when Virginia Woolf was revising *Mrs Dalloway* for publication. In a pencil note to the manuscript opening of the story Virginia Woolf states:

> The New Dress
> At Mrs D's party
> She got it on this theory
> the theory of clothes
> but very little money
> this brings in the relation with

Cover of Kew Gardens *that was designed by Woolf's sister, Vanessa Bell.*

sex; her estimate of herself.

"Mrs Dalloway in Bond Street" and **"The New Dress"** are both connected with the genesis of the novel *Mrs Dalloway;* the other five stories written consecutively and probably not later than May 1925 form a kind of epilogue to it. Though the party goes on after the novel is finished Mrs Dalloway's is no longer its central consciousness. The focus now shifts from guest to guest revealing their reflections and insights. It is the other side of Mrs Dalloway's party. The seven stories or chapters, therefore, besides being all centred on Mrs Dalloway were also all written more or less at the same time as the novel.

The Mrs Dalloway stories, then, do form a related group in that they relate to each other thematically: the social theme and subject of the party and the actual or implied presence of Mrs Dalloway give a unity to them. There is, too, a simple narrative and chronological unity to the 'stories'. At the narrative level the first two stories in the present collection anticipate the party: Mrs Dalloway is in Bond Street on the morning of the day on which she is to give her party. The Man Who Loved His Kind meets Mr Dalloway in Dean's Yard and is invited to drop in on the party. The remaining five 'chapters' are set at the party and the final chapter does in fact provide A Summing Up.

The new book which I have called *Mrs Dalloway's Party* does have a definite, though very simple, compositional

form. The form it takes, or which I have given to it, was that intended originally for the novel *Mrs Dalloway.* That novel was first thought of as being possibly *At Home* or *The Party.* The Berg manuscript which contains Virginia Woolf's compositional notes for *Mrs Dalloway* has in it the following entry:

> Oct. 6th 1922. Thoughts upon beginning a book to
> be called, perhaps, At Home: or The Party:

> This is to be a short book consisting of six or seven
> chapters, each complete separately.
> Yet there must be some sort of fusion!
> And all must converge upon the party at the end.

This plan was abandoned by Virginia Woolf and the novel itself was altered radically in the course of its composition. But the plan fits perfectly the present volume of short stories. *Mrs Dalloway's Party* is a short book consisting of seven 'chapters', each complete separately and having, as I have tried to show, some sort of fusion, and all converging on or centring in the party.

Virginia Woolf's interest in the short story is something that can be traced back further than the sudden intense probing of the party and its world in 1925. By 1919 Virginia Woolf had proved herself to be a successful short story writer, particularly with the publication of *The Mark on the Wall,* and *Kew Gardens.* Or again, in experimenting with the form of the novel at the beginning of 1920 she finds her structural norm in the short story:

> Whether I'm sufficiently mistress of things—that's
> the doubt; but conceive (?) **"Mark on the Wall"**,
> **"K. G."** [**"Kew Gardens"**] and **"Unwritten Novel"**
> taking hands and dancing in unity. What the unity
> shall be I have yet to discover; the theme is a blank
> to me; but I see immense possibilities in the form
> I hit upon more or less by chance two weeks
> ago. . . .

With the completion of *Mrs Dalloway* at the end of 1924 Virginia Woolf with almost a sense of release, turns again, only with greater concentration, to the short story proper:

> —and then I shall be free. Free at least to write out
> one or two more stories which have accumulated.
> I am less and less sure that they are stories, or what
> they are. Only I do feel fairly sure that I am grazing
> as near as I can to my own ideas, and getting a tol-
> erable shape for them.

On 19th April 1925, Virginia Woolf states that she wants to 'dig deep down' into her short stories. Then suddenly on the following day one learns that something has obviously happened, for she adds in her diary that she has now six stories 'welling up' in her. Then again, on May 14th, Virginia Woolf writes that before beginning work on her new novel (*To the Lighthouse*) she must 'write a few little stories first'. The 'few little stories' are contained in the present volume. Within roughly the first six months of 1925, therefore, two of Virginia Woolf's major literary preoccupations were the exploring of what she refers to as the 'party consciousness' and the writing of short 'stories', or small fictional fragments, of whose exact nature she was herself unsure. The two preoccupations interlock in that the 'stories' together explore a collected or varied party consciousness. (pp. 10-17)

Stella McNichol, in an introduction to Mrs Dalloway's Party: A Short Story Sequence, *by Virginia Woolf, edited by Stella McNichol, The Hogarth Press, 1973, pp. 9-17.*

Jeanne Delbaere-Garant (essay date 1974-75)

[*In the following excerpt from a detailed analysis of "The Mark on the Wall," Delbaere-Garant assesses Woolf's apparently vague narration, claiming Woolf's form belies both the intricate organization of the piece and its delineation of her mature themes.*]

Commenting on **"The Mark on the Wall"** and **"Kew Gardens"** in *Two Cheers for Democracy*, E. M. Forster saw them as "lovely little things" which seemed "to lead nowhere"; they were, he said, "all tiny dots and coloured blobs, they were an inspired breathlessness, they were a beautiful droning or gasping which trusted to luck. They were perfect as far as they went, but that was not far, and none of us guessed that out of the pollen of those flowers, would come the trees of the future." A close reading of **"The Mark on the Wall"** shows that Forster was probably deceived by the "semi-transparent envelope" of the story and that if he had only looked long enough he would have seen the tiny dots and coloured blobs fall into place in a clear network of interconnected meanings and the narrator's apparently loose thoughts organise themselves into a pattern as rigorous as that of Virginia Woolf's best novels.

The surface effect of **"The Mark on the Wall"** is, one must admit, one of misty glassiness. It offers the eye an undifferentiated whiteness not unlike that of the wall on which the mysterious black spot is the only landmark. A saving plank for the reader as it is for the day-dreaming narrator, the mark breaks the reverie at regular intervals preventing it from losing itself in too much fluidity while also saving the sketch from complete formlessness. It is really the first organizing element of the text. But if it starts the train of thoughts it is in turn coloured by the very associations it has set in motion: first a hole made by a small nail, it becomes eventually a rose leaf left over from the summer, a tumulus projecting from the wall and a big nail driven into the wall two hundred years before and coming out again. The succession of these associations suggests a cyclical conception of history as a vast process of waste and repair, of pulling downwards and striving upwards, of burying and digging out.

The narrator wants to sink quietly into herself, "to slip easily from one thing to another, without any sense of hostility or obstacle," to go "deeper and deeper, away from the surface, with its hard separate facts." But the sinking into herself is also a descent into time. It leads her first to the former tenants of the house she now inhabits. Although she caricatures their tastes and conventional behaviour she also resents the brevity of her acquaintance with them. She finds it hard to admit that "one will never see them again". The mark on the wall, she thinks, was probably made by the small nail with which these people attached to the wall what must have been the miniature—carefully chosen to match the style of their furniture—of a lady with "powder-dusted cheeks and lips like red carnations."

Sinking deeper into herself the narrator now proceeds to examine other losses: her own past and a few objects remembered from her childhood like the bird cages, the iron-hoops, the steel skates, the Queen Anne coal-scuttles, the bagatelle board, the hand organ. These things have vanished now and lie with all that is dead "at the root of turnips." The solid Victorian age has gone too with its mahogany sideboards, its Landseer prints, its gods and devils. Deeper still are the disparate remains of all past civilisations which antiquarians dig out and put in museums: the foot of a Chinese murderess, a handful of Elizabethan nails, a great many Tudor clay pipes, a piece of Roman pottery, the wineglass that Nelson drank out of. The miniature buried yesterday comes out of the earth again, magnified into the detritus of all times. Likewise the separation from the former tenants—a miniature death—has expanded into the death of the retired-colonel-turned-antiquarian. The mark itself reflects both the magnifying and the burying/excavating process: it is no longer a small hole made by the nail which held up a miniature but a gigantic old nail revealing its head above the coat of paint and "taking its first view of modern life in the sight of a white-walled fire-lit room."

The death of the colonel-antiquarian marks the end of the human world in the narrator's descent into time. Her reverie has taken her to the time when there were only herbs and stars, water and flowers, an organic world of silence and beauty "without professors and specialists or housekeepers with the profile of policemen, a world which one could slice with one's thought as a fish slices the water with his fin, grazing the stems of the water-lilies hanging suspended over nests of white seaeggs . . . " At the end of the whole gnawing process of life are these white sea eggs which reconcile past and future in their round shape and, as a symbol of life, intimate that everything is going to start anew. Through a metaphor which enables her to effect the transition from earth to water the narrator reminds us that she has now reached the bottom ("down there") of her stream of consciousness which merges with the general flux of life.

Parallel with the track of thoughts that has just been described we can trace another track running from the very beginning and following the same movement. It is no longer concerned with concrete objects but with ideas, rules and facts. When the narrator had to part so suddenly from the man who lived in the house before her the latter was just saying that "art should have ideas behind it." Later in her reverie she imagines a shower of "ideas" falling down through Shakespeare's mind but she immediately dismisses the picture as "historical fiction," as an accumulation of facts and data which provide no real insight into the life they are supposed to illuminate. The word "fiction" remains floating in her mind and makes her think of what novelists are doing with reality, what they should do and what they are likely to do in the future: explore the rich depths of the individual soul and not only that "shell of a person" which can be seen by anyone.

All this theorizing is an obstacle to a smooth descent into herself. She dislikes such "generalizations" with the military sound of their first three syllables and all the memories they bring back to her mind: "leading articles, cabinet ministers—a whole class of things indeed which, as a child, one thought the thing itself, the standard thing, the real thing from which one could not depart save at the risk of nameless damnation." Just as she had dismissed "historical fiction" she now reacts against the Victorian imposition of a fixed way of seeing and knowing upon the spontaneous impulses of the individual, against the Sunday world of absolute truths in which she was brought up: "Sunday in London, Sunday afternoon walks, Sunday luncheons, and also ways of speaking of the dead, clothes, and habits—like the habit of sitting all together in one room until a certain hour, although nobody likes it. There was a rule for everything." Even tablecloths did not escape social conformity. Whitaker's Almanack and his Table of Precedency, expressions of "the masculine point of view which governs our lives, which sets the standard," become symbols of fixity and separateness counterpointing the white sea eggs with which, at the bottom of the stream, they are brought into dialectical opposition.

We recognize here many of the things Virginia Woolf satirized in her mature work: the superficiality of biographers in *Orlando,* the materialism of her contemporary fellow novelists in "Modern Fiction," the Victorian social system in *The Years* and, in general, all that is fixed, constraining and antagonistic to the freedom of the individual soul. This second aspect of reality is closely woven with the first, undergoes a parallel development and like the first also ends where it began. The retired colonel sends us back to the man who thought that art should have ideas behind it. Like him, he is a man with "ideas." They give him a pleasant feeling of self-importance when his wife is making plum jam or cleaning the study. He feels "agreeably philosophic" in accumulating evidence on the South Downs barrows. He, too, is abruptly interrupted when he is on the point of explaining something: he is about to communicate the results of his researches on the tumuli at the quarterly meeting of the local society when a stroke lays him low.

The two strands of meaning which, for clarity's sake, we have been obliged to consider separately are, in fact, the two opposite, inseparable and complementary faces of the Janus-like human reality: they represent two modes of knowing, two different approaches to reality: the "feminine" with its more passive, intuitive and all-embracing apprehension of things on the one hand, the "masculine" with its analytical bend and its tendency to leave its mark and impose its order upon life, on the other. They branch forth in the story, closely entangled with each other, in a growth which is organic rather than logical as is suggested by the plant imagery which also runs through the sketch and which, by placing the tensions between masculine and feminine inclinations on a different level, is a discreet but illuminating comment on their interrelatedness.

We pay little attention to the "three chrysanthemums" in the first paragraph, to the "lips like red carnations" of the lady on the miniature in the second or to the asphodel meadows in the third. Our eyes run listlessly over the opals and emeralds lying "at the root of turnips." But when the narrator takes us in imagination under the earth, together with things lost and dead "groping at the root of the grass" we recognize a familiar echo, remember the emeralds and begin to distinguish the first trait of another internal design. After depicting the slow and gnawing process of life which is responsible for all the losses mentioned

above, the narrator sees herself in the earth and feels there the "slow pulling down of thick green stalks so that the cup of the flower, as it turns over, deluges one with purple and red light." We do not know whether, at this stage, she remembers George Herbert's sweet rose whose "root is ever in its grave" but she certainly makes a similar association for immediately after this passage she no longer sees the mark as a hole made by a nail but as a "small rose leaf, left over from the summer."

On the surface the rose may appear as a mere automatic association with the "rose-shaped blots" of the preceding paragraph just as the dust may simply show that the narrator has not cleaned the mantelpiece very carefully. But deeper under the surface the link between rose and root, flower and dust becomes tighter. The dust on the mantelpiece expands into the more universally significant dust of Troy whereas the small rose leaf left over from the summer turns into the fragments of pots left over from a dead civilisation and "utterly refusing annihilation." This association of flower and dust, of life force and destroying process is further exemplified in the next paragraph when the narrator imagines herself talking about "a flower growing on a dust heap on the site of an old house in Kingsway," a flower whose seed must have been sown in the reign of Charles I. (pp. 457-61)

When we now look back to the "lips like red carnations" of the lady on the miniature and see that the simile is immediately preceded by the mention of "powder-*dusted* cheeks" (my italics) we realize that even at this early stage, the association flower/dust, vague and inarticulate though it was, was already present in the narrator's subconscious. Her description of our gradual perception of the world around us when we are born again after life could serve as a metaphor for the way in which we are gradually made aware in the next (both as readers and as human beings) of the close connection between life and death, pulling downwards and striving upwards. . . . (p. 461)

The narrator has now reached the still point where all tensions are resolved. But this moment of perfect balance and the impression of peace and security conveyed by the white sea eggs are only evanescent: the word "rooted" which immediately follows functions as an alarm signal and reminds us of the equation root/grave, tomb/womb which has been running throughout the story. We also remember that the whole train of associations which ends up here had been originally concerned with losses. As a matter of fact the narrator is now in danger of suffering the most important of losses: that of her own identity. On the point of being completely absorbed into nature she awakes, terrified at the threatened loss of identity. Like the rose she refuses annihilation and unconsciously conjures up Whitaker's Almanack as a rescuing power. But if this enables her to reaffirm her feminine identity as opposed to the masculine it is not yet enough to save her from dissolution. Only the world of matter offers sufficient contrast to the fluidity of her own subjectivity. She must "jump up" and see for herself what the mark on the wall really is. She sees it now as a "plank in the sea", something real and palpable which will bring her back to her own separate and finite self and prevent her from dissolving in the general flux. . . . (p. 461)

In its turn the comparison with a saving plank conjures up associations (plank-wood-tree) which provide her with an adequate symbol to unify and bring together not only the polarities of life but all the separate strands of the story: fusing into one single image the narrator's mental arborescence with the growth/destruction process at large the tree offers a significant objective correlative for the transcendental notion of the oneness of man and nature. (p. 462)

"It is full of peaceful thoughts, happy thoughts, this tree," the narrator comments. But just as she is on the point of taking each of these thoughts separately, of reaching some meaningful conclusion that would give coherence to her reverie, an unexpected "vast upheaval of matter" makes all the elements which had been so beautifully connected become "separate facts" again and tumble down like a house of cards. She is finally back to the surface, looking in vain for the mysterious thread which held Downs, tree, rose leaf, Whitaker's Almanack together in one single unified pattern. Like the Trissie of **"Kew Gardens"** she is left with the fragments of a vision and as in the other story it is a man who breaks the spell. For though he remains unidentified it is clear that the person who starts talking at the end belongs to the "masculine" world of Whitaker: he resorts to action ("I'm going to buy a newspaper"), needs facts ("Nothing ever happens"), does not shrink from mentioning the war and calls the mark by its name ("I don't see why we should have a snail on our wall").

After the long winding course of the narrator's reflection, this clear definition falls down with the force of a decree. It is like the blackness of the mark on the white surface of the wall, like the fixity of a rule on the flux of life. Here is "the masculine point of view which governs our lives, which sets the standard," the intelligence which, as Bergson says, "solidifies all that it touches." By defining the mark the man limits its infinite possibilities of spiralling expansion and puts a final stop to the dynamic relation between the narrator and the object. But paradoxically, though he breaks the reverie he also gives it shape by bringing it back to the time-bound and space-bound world of necessity, by enclosing it in the hard "shell" of objective reality. As Bergson puts it elsewhere: "the act through which life proceeds towards the creation of a new form and the act through which this form takes shape are two different, often antagonistic, movements."

The shape which then emerges is not unlike the mirror image of the snail in the narrator's mind: an inverted cone with lines reaching down towards the bottom of consciousness where opposites are temporarily reconciled and up again towards a recovery of identity, separateness and definition. The general design also reproduces the spiralling line of the shell: the small nail is replaced by a gigantic one, the miniature by all the possessions of a museum, the rose leaf grows into a tree, the separation from the former tenant becomes the death of the Colonel and the interruption of the narrator's automatic fancy becomes the breaking off of the whole reverie at the end. Things are repeated and magnified until something occurs which arrests the movement and fixes the form. If the external form of the story offers some analogy with the pattern of the shell its content curiously resembles the dark living centre inside: the emphasis on the mystery of life, on the burying and digging out reminds us of the contraction and expansion of the mollusc and suggests the inexhaustible energy of the vital impulse continually striving to escape from its bonds yet kept imprisoned in matter like the snail in its shell.

I hope that my analysis sufficiently demonstrates what a *tour de force* Virginia Woolf has accomplished here and how far we are from what Forster took for mere "inspired breathlessness." The snail not only reconciles the antinomies of the story by combining the fixed world of Whitaker with the free world of the narrator's consciousness, it also symbolizes Virginia Woolf's successful attempt at striking a balance between the "hard shell" of form and the fluidity of content. I am not even sure that my microscopic reading has detected all there was to detect, for each word is important, each new image closely related to the whole. Nothing is further removed from automatic fancy than this kind of prose which looks so much like it but is submitted, beneath the smooth surface, to an extremely strict organisation.

The vagueness of the surface is largely due to the fact that the reverie takes place in the pure time of consciousness in which all things merge and escape definition. The reader who takes such apparently precise indications as "the middle of January" or "a summer's evening" at their face value is bound to fall into the traps purposely laid by the author. If we examine all the implications of these time data we must necessarily come to the conclusion that they lead nowhere. (pp. 462-64)

"The idea has come to me that what I want now to do is to saturate every atom. I mean to eliminate all waste, deadness, superfluity: to give the moment whole; whatever it includes. Say that the moment is a combination of thought; sensation; the voice of the sea. Waste, deadness, come from the inclusion of things that don't belong to the moment; this appalling narrative business of the realist: getting on from lunch to dinner: it is false, unreal, merely conventional. Why admit anything to literature that is not poetry—by which I mean saturated?"

Woolf, from her A Writer's Diary *(1953).*

"The Mark on the Wall" contains in germ all the preoccupations of Virginia Woolf's mature fiction: the search for an androgynous synthesis of masculine and feminine inclinations, the individual's longing for fusion but fear of annihilation, the antagonistic though necessary interrelatedness of things and ideas, the need for the artist to stick to "marks" outside to keep firm control of form and structure. The miniature spiral on a still blank wall was to expand in increasingly wider circles until the writer's suicide—a distant echo and amplification of the smaller interruptions in the story—put a final stop to her life-long reverie. The mark itself became bigger as it left the wall for the sky or the ocean: the skywriting plane in *Mrs. Dalloway* or the lighthouse in the novel called after it are nothing but extensions of the original mark on the wall, this "lovely little thing" which—with all due deference to E. M. Forster—did lead somewhere. (pp. 464-65)

Jeanne Delbaere-Garant, " 'The Mark on the Wall': Virginia Woolf's World in a Snailshell," in Revue des langues vivantes, *Vol. 40, No. 5, 1974-75, pp. 457-65.*

Avrom Fleishman   (essay date 1980)

[*Fleishman is an American educator and critic who has written* Virginia Woolf: A Critical Reading *(1975). In the following excerpt, he provides an analysis of Woolf's short stories, which he categorizes as either linear tales that "start at one place or time or motif or verbal cluster and move through a number of others, arriving at a place, time, motif, or verbal cluster distinct from those with which they begin," or circular stories, whose "forms are those which begin and end with the same or similar elements."*]

The standard format for a critical study of Virginia Woolf is a series of chapters on the nine longer fictions, one after the other. The body of her short stories tends to be neglected, except as quarry for the longer works. In contributing to a revaluation of Woolf's achievement, I take up these stories to discover what is distinctive in their form and, by implication, their innovations within the development of the modern short story. (p. 44)

From the inception of critical discussion of the short story, the theory of its form has not moved much beyond Poe's notion of the unity of effect to be realized in a genre of limited means. While problems of subject (plot or no plot?), theme (point or no point?), and narrative (telescoping . . . exposition . . . development) still persist, the question of form has never approached resolution. The usual byway down which this trail leads is epiphany; since the most prominent of modern stories come accompanied by the theory of epiphany, it was inevitable that Joyce's term has been used in lieu of a concept of form. A recent study of epiphany recognizes the laxity of such usage; despite Joyce's emphasis on the suddenness of the epiphanic moment, "it has been fashionable to speak of one or another of his entire works as 'an' epiphany . . . If an epiphany is 'sudden,' as it is, then works as long as the average short story—and certainly any novel—simply cannot 'be' epiphanies, for they cannot be 'experienced' or apprehended immediately." The story, short or long, is not a single event but a form extended in time and, conceptually, in space as well.

If short stories are not unitary events but extended forms, they involve sequences of phenomena, verbal or representational. Morris Beja's definitions of epiphany are useful in defining story form, for he goes on to discriminate another frequent element of short fiction, the leitmotif. In the epiphany, Beja writes,

[T]here has to be some such revelation—and it is here that we must beware a common misconception that confuses Joyce's epiphany with the leitmotif, the obsessive image which keeps coming back into the consciousness of a character or into the work as a whole but which at no single time involves any special, sudden illumination.

This apt distinction between a series of repetitions and a salient event unfortunately avoids stating a possible relationship between the two: the epiphany may appear at the end of a sequence, either as a term that stands outside the "obsessive" chain and suddenly emerges to cap it, or as the final and crowning instance of the repetition itself—that is, either a new motif, like the coin of success and betrayal in Joyce's "Two Gallants," or a definitive statement of an established one, as in the protagonist's return to isolation in his "A Painful Case."

In this way, one can better appreciate the repetitiveness that appears so widely in modern literature—witness Pound, Eliot, Faulkner, Proust—but nowhere more strikingly than in the short story. What Frank O'Connor somewhat facetiously calls Hemingway's "elegant repetition" (on the model of "elegant variation") may be only a mannered extension of the repetitive patterns that mark the stories of Joyce, Mansfield, and Woolf. (pp. 49-50)

Virginia Woolf's short stories can be broadly divided into those that are formally linear and those that are formally circular. Another word on terminology here: the adjectives "linear" and "circular" are obviously metaphoric and, just as obviously, spatial. The use of these terms implies no exclusive disposition toward "spatial form" in Woolf: one might just as easily use the terms "progressive" and "returning," though these would emphasize the ongoing temporal flow of the narrative. *Linear* or *progressive* forms are those that start at one place or time or motif or verbal cluster and move through a number of others, arriving at a place, time, motif, or verbal cluster distinct from those with which they begin; while *circular* or *returning* forms are those which begin and end with the same or similar elements.

The earliest writing in *A Haunted House,* the main collection of Woolf's stories, is **"The Mark on the Wall."** This piece, without action, characterization, or setting, vividly raises questions about the demarcations of Woolfian prose: is it a story, an essay, or a prose poem? As the present analysis does not depend on these generic distinctions, I include **"The Mark on the Wall"** at least provisionally among the stories. The piece takes the form of a train of speculations on the character of a poorly perceived stimulus, an amorphous mark; this is a sequence of efforts in one direction, toward identifying something which is disclosed at the end of the sequence. This linear process begins at a particular time, "the middle of January in the present year," and moves through various later times at which hypotheses are framed: that the mark "was made by a nail," was not "made by a nail after all," "is not a hole at all," and "may have been caused by some round black substance"; that it is more prominent than a spot, "seems actually to project from the wall," and is perhaps the "head of a gigantic old nail," or alternatively "a rose-leaf, a crack in the wood." Having moved beyond seeing the mark as an indentation, then as a flat surface color, to seeing it as a projection, and after running through a number of more or less probable projecting objects, the conclusion is reached: "Ah, the mark on the wall! It was a snail." Those who know and love this piece will agree that my account of its form leaves out the rich and humorous meanderings of the prose, in which the narrative "I" moves from uncertainties and desires ("I wish I could hit upon a pleasant track of thought") to a declaration of indeterminacy ("No, no, nothing is proved, nothing is known"), and on to a final set of thoughts which the speaker describes as "worshipping the impersonal world." It would require further analysis to determine the form created by the interweaving of these subsidiary tracks, but it should already be clear that **"The Mark on the Wall"** is not "free association" but a controlled linear form.

Another way of looking at the form of **"The Mark on the Wall"** is to see it as the *progressive definition* of a term, by interpretation of an ambiguous sign, the mark. Other Woolf pieces having this linear form are **"Solid Objects"** and **"The New Dress."** **"Solid Objects"** begins with a similar, undefined visual stimulus: "The only thing that moved upon the vast semicircle of the beach was one small black spot." The story does not go on to examine the spot but instead supplies a series of references for the pronoun "it," by which that small black spot is designated. The second sentence reads: "As it came nearer to the ribs and spine of the stranded pilchard boat, it became apparent from a certain tenuity in its blackness that this spot possessed four legs; and moment by moment it became more unmistakable that it was composed of the persons of two young men." The initial reference of "it" is thus to human beings, or at least to their bodies: "nothing was so solid, so living, so hard, red, hirsute and virile as these two bodies for miles and miles of sea and sandhill." After setting out the tale of one protagonist's infatuation with a piece of glass found on the beach, and his progressive obsession for collecting other *disjecta membra,* a climax is reached upon his discovery of a "remarkable piece of iron" to which he (or the teller of the tale) attaches cosmic significance. Seen as a meteorite, "alien to the earth," this object now becomes the main reference for the pronoun, "it": "It weighed his pocket down; it weighed the mantelpiece down; it radiated cold." A final turn in the fate of this pronoun is given at the denouement, when the second protagonist tries to fathom his friend's obsession, which has caused the loss of his parliamentary career and his withdrawal from society: " 'What was the truth of it, John?' asked Charles suddenly, turning and facing him. 'What made you give it up like that all in a second?' 'I've not given it up,' John replied." For the man-of-the-world Charles, "it" is simply worldly success, but John clearly has another ideal in mind—though it remains unclear where that value lies. The pronoun thus begins with the "solid" bodily life of two friends, moves on to the metaphysical implications clustered around the solitary being of ordinary objects, and finally comes to rest in a suggestive juxtaposition of worldly and more profound values. Form here is a significant elaboration of the story's initial verbal donnée.

Another story formed as a series of identifications of the pronoun "it" is **"The New Dress"**—this time with associations closer to the jazz-age sobriquet for sex appeal. The story begins with the frumpy heroine's arrival at Mrs. Dalloway's party and her uneasiness about her new dress: "it

was not right . . . No! It was not *right.*" The dress is, however, only the first of the protagonist's shortcomings to be designated by "it" in the course of the story: "Everybody knew why she did it—it was from shame, from humiliation." When Mabel tries to play the game of social intercourse, the pronoun reaches a watershed: "Ah, it was tragic, this greed, this clamour of human beings . . . it was tragic, could one have felt it and not merely pretended to feel it." "It," then, is not simply Mabel's dress or her inadequacy, but the entire emotional life in which she fails to participate. And yet, she remembers "divine moments" in her life when she has said to herself " 'This is it. This has happened. This is it!' " At this point of elaboration, a climax is reached: Mabel envisages a future in which "she would become a new person. She would be absolutely transformed . . . and it would be always, day after day, as if she were lying in the sun . . . It would be it!" Articulating this ultimate self-identity, the action concludes as Mabel makes her departure. The form of the story emerges as a progressive widening of the key term from direct reference to the new dress, to a broad indication of possible lifestyles, and on to an even more suggestive association with some integral state when, at the peak, "It would be it."

These prose pieces represent a simple form of linear organization in which a given, often insignificant term becomes a repetitive pattern, and is then subjected to a series of modulations and enhancements—mainly by shifting the context so that the key term enters into new relations and opens up varied possibilities. When the key term is so simple a thing as a mark on a wall or a neutral word like "it," the form of the story is, as it were, a making of something out of nothing—or, as a similar process is described elsewhere in Woolf, a "building it up."

A related group of stories takes a form similar to this gradual expansion or emergent creation, but in such a group there is no single term which moves through a sequence. Instead, a *series* of items is set out, the final item emerging as the key one. The most famous instance of such an organization is the well-known **"Kew Gardens,"** in which eight beings or kinds of being are observed as they saunter through the botanical gardens. First comes the general class: "men and women." There follow a married couple remembering the past; a snail (who appears three times in all); a mystical and somewhat disturbed old man and his younger companion; "two elderly women of the lower middle class," looking for their tea; a young couple, also thinking of tea amid the glow of their romance; a group of aerial beings, including a thrush, butterflies, and an airplane; and finally, the voices. After lulling us with what seems a random and casual series of passers-by, the story reaches a new level of intensity at its final paragraph:

> It seemed as if all gross and heavy bodies had sunk down in the heat motionless and lay huddled upon the ground, but their voices went wavering from them as if they were flames lolling from the thick waxen bodies of candles. Voices. Yes, voices. Wordless voices, breaking the silence suddenly with such depth of contentment, such passion of desire, or, in the voices of children, such freshness of surprise; breaking the silence? But there was no

silence; all the time the motor omnibuses were turning their wheels and changing their gear; like a vast
nest of Chinese boxes all of wrought steel turning
ceaselessly one within another the city murmured;
on the top of which the voices cried aloud and the
petals of myriads of flowers flashed their colours
into the air.

This crescendo of the repeated word "voices" emerges as
the final and triumphant term in the series of elements
presented by the story. The voices are, indeed, a chorus
of all the beings who have trooped through Kew Gardens,
those named and all the others that might have been listed—come at last to expression and united in a common
life. It is difficult to distinguish form and content in this
beautiful piece; even the simplest description of the form
verges on an interpretation of the content, and I must content myself on this occasion with singling out the linear
progression by which **"Kew Gardens"** reaches its heights
at the close.

Three other stories follow the **"Kew Gardens"** form of serial presentation, with a significant final term. **"An Unwritten Novel"** in some respects resembles **"The Mark on
the Wall"** as a succession of speculations on the identity
of an unknown being, in this case an elderly lady sitting
in a railway carriage, but it also builds up to a peak by adding one item after another in an imaginative construction
of a human identity. This peak is the discovery that the
little old lady is not a spinster on her way to visit her
brother and sister-in-law, where she will be victimized and
unwelcome, but that she is instead the mother of a son
who comes graciously to meet her at the station. The
movement from novelistic imaginings to the hard kernel
of reality is paralleled by the movement of the train which
carries the observer and the observed. . . . We might consider this an example of *parallel* linear form, in which the
spatial sequence and the perceptual sequence move along
together to a joint arrival.

"Together and Apart" is a simpler exercise, merely following the course of a conversation in which two middle-aged
and typically self-absorbed people try and fail to communicate. The conversation takes the form of a set of variations on the verbal motif "Canterbury," interlaced with
other repetitive verbal patterns (like Miss Anning's self-
rallying phrase, "On, Stanley, on"). . . . This is Virginia
Woolf at her satirical best, but the form is perhaps too simple: the party guests come together, go through their travesty of conversation, and reach a peak of absurdity in the
final line: "whatever they may do, they can't spoil Canterbury."

The last story I would classify among the linear forms is
"The Man Who Loved His Kind." As in **"Together and
Apart,"** a party conversation leads here to mutual hostility
and separation, but the formal sequence is somewhat different. The movement of action and language is entirely
unremarkable up to the final page; then, in the last four
paragraphs, the phrase from which the story draws its title
is employed four times. . . . There are other linear movements at work, among them repeated references to the humanitarian anecdotes the interlocutors thrust upon one
another, but the story achieves a clear direction only in the
last phase, where the repetition of the key term signals a
height of satirical dismissal.

It will be observed that three of the seven stories described

as linear are of the **Mrs. Dalloway's Party** group, which
has recently been established as a unit by publication in
a separate volume [see McNichol excerpt dated 1973]. The
group contains none of the best of Woolf's stories, and
some of them are decidedly sketchy, as is suggested by
their having remained in manuscript; but their appearance
as a group gives rise to reflections on the compositional
order of Woolf's stories. Of the twenty-three pieces published in collected volumes, five were composed in 1925,
making this the year of most intensive short-story writing
in Woolf's career. For the hypothesis that this intense activity also marked a turning point in her mode of composition, the following facts can be considered: all of the seven
linear pieces date from 1925 or before, while all but three
of the thirteen stories to be described as circular are of the
period 1925 and after. (Two others among the latter group
are difficult to date, but Leonard Woolf's Foreword to *A
Haunted House* suggests treating them among the later
stories.) There is no evidence of a concerned change, but
only of a gradual shift in Woolf's characteristic form from
the linear to the circular model.

The simplest kind of circular form is the return at the close
of a story to the prominent use of a significant *word* which
has been introduced at or near the outset. Three stories
conform to this model. **"The Duchess and the Jeweller"**
sums up its opening account of a posh West End jeweller's
career with an extended metaphor: "Imagine a giant hog
in a pasture rich with truffles; after unearthing this truffle
and that, still it smells a bigger, a blacker truffle under the
ground further off. So Oliver [Bacon] snuffed always in the
rich earth of Mayfair another truffle, a blacker, a bigger
further off." After the jeweller is duped by the duchess and
by his own social-climbing, he looks at the fake pearls he
has bought: "This, then, was the truffle he had routed out
of the earth! Rotten at the centre—rotten at the core!" The
note of irony does nothing to enhance the comic extravagance of the initial use of the metaphor, but it brings off
the conclusion roundly.

Similarly, **"Lappin and Lapinova"** opens and closes with
a definition of the imposing term "marriage." "They were
married," it begins. "The wedding march pealed out."
After a poignant account of the couple's imaginative personification of each other as rabbits, and after the stern re-
buke to imagination delivered by their upper-middle-class
milieu, the dream and the relationship come to an abrupt
end: "So that was the end of that marriage." We have
learned nothing significant about the nature of modern
marriage, but the form of the story has been neatly rounded off.

The third of these word-closed stories is **"The Legacy"**; as
in many another tale, the title acts as the controlling focus
throughout, but it is mentioned only at the beginning and
end. (pp. 53-9)

A more elaborate use of this simple circular form is
evinced in four stories, each of which opens and closes
with approximately the same *sentence*. The most obvious
instances of this type are the sentences "People should not
leave looking-glasses hanging in their rooms" in the story
"The Lady in the Looking-Glass," and "Slater's pins have
no points" in **"Moments of Being."** Such stories do not
gain their force merely from the repetition of an ironic understatement or a disconcerting irrelevancy. In the former
case, the looking-glass is a continuing focus throughout.

The action consists mainly of the changes in a room in the course of a day, as recorded by a passive but knowing field of vision, a mirror. Revelation comes when the lady of the house is brought under the mirror's relentless scrutinizing power, and is seen as starkly as the objects of her house. (p. 60)

In **"Moments of Being,"** the reappearance of the opening sentence in the final paragraph is considerably more complicated than in the story of the mirror. For one thing, the sentence is repeated in two other forms: once as the epigraph of the story (with capitals and quotes, as in a motto) and again in the course of the text, with an altered verb form: "Slater's pins having no points . . ." This pattern interweaves with a number of others in a way so complicated as to make this one of the most interesting of Woolf's stories. One of the patterns is the time scheme, which begins with present action, introduces a past report on an even earlier state of affairs (Miss Kingston's information about Julia Craye's early life), fills out the portrait of Julia with brief images of her at other times of life—meanwhile adding other notes on the protagonist's recent encounters with Julia—and finally returns to the present for a momentary vision of the subject which takes in the whole past: "All seemed transparent, for a moment, to the gaze of Fanny Wilmot, as if looking through Miss Craye, she saw the very fountain of her being spurting its pure silver drops. She saw back and back into the past behind her . . . She saw Julia—."

This temporal pattern cannot be assimilated to the circle traced by the repeated references to Slater's pins, unless we face up to a subject that seems to have been avoided in discussions of this story. For there is one other significant action at the close: the elderly piano teacher kisses her young pupil on the lips, at the precise moment of her vision of Julia's being. It seems crass to labor the point, but this intuition of homosexuality is part of the total vision of Julia which Fanny achieves. Throughout the narrative, numerous statements have underscored Julia's independence, especially of marriage, and indeed her separation from other people, with the exception of her brother: "there was in Miss Kingston's voice an indescribable tone which hinted at something odd; something queer in Julius Craye; it was the very same thing that was odd perhaps in Julia too." The next sentence associates this insight with the pin: "One could have sworn, thought Fanny Wilmot, as she looked for the pin, that at parties . . . [Miss Kingston] had picked up some piece of gossip . . . which had given her 'a feeling' about Julius Craye."

Later, when Fanny speculates on Julia's repeated rejection of offers of marriage, a perception of her sexual preferences is again accompanied by the search for the pin: "The setting of that scene [of rejecting a suitor] could be varied as one chose, Fanny Wilmot reflected. (Where had that pin fallen?)." Finally, the moment of vision is triggered by Fanny's finding the pin and her simultaneous discovery of Julia's self-sufficient happiness: "Fanny Wilmot saw the pin; she picked it up. She looked at Miss Craye. Was Miss Craye so lonely? No, Miss Craye was steadily, blissfully, if only for that moment, a happy woman." What seems clear from this repeated association of the search for the pin and the revelations of Julia's sexual disposition is that an arbitrarily chosen object has achieved symbolic status by the time it is repeated at the close. (Or is a pointed and

elongated object, capable of linking and of pricking, once kept in hand but presently lost, chosen entirely arbitrarily?)

What is much less clear is the continued activity of the pin. At the opening, the pin has fallen from Fanny's dress, where it held a rose. When Fanny finds the pin and sees Julia in ecstasy, Julia is holding a carnation upright in her lap. Immediately after Julia kisses Fanny, the following sentences occur: " 'Slater's pins have no points,' Miss Craye said, laughing queerly and relaxing her arms, as Fanny Wilmot pinned the flower to her breast with trembling fingers." Which flower and whose breast? We are not told. Only the emphatic repetition of the motto stands out clearly in this disturbing, but highly formal, finale.

Another story in which an initial sentence figures in the conclusion may be mentioned in passing: **"Ancestors,"** one of the newly published Dalloway stories, opens with a reference to an overheard remark: "Mrs. Vallance, as she replied to Jack Renshaw who had made that rather silly remark of his about not liking to watch cricket matches, wished that she could make him understand . . ." After prolonged reflections on all she has lost in life through the absence of her parents, the protagonist returns to present realities: "she would have been oh perfectly happy, perfectly good, instead of which here she was forced to listen to a young man saying—and she laughed almost scornfully and yet tears were in her eyes—that he could not bear to watch cricket matches!"

The major example of a story formed by the return of its opening lines at the end is **"A Haunted House."** Here the repetition is far from exact, and the complex pattern suggests another category of form, in which a *group* of elements is returned to at the close. But I shall treat **"A Haunted House"** as a borderline case of sentence repetition. The sentence in question begins not the first but the second paragraph: "Here we left it," says one of the ghostly presences in the house. After the previously discussed cases, we should have no trouble in deferring curiosity about the reference of "it" until the final paragraph, when the same voice says, "Here we left our treasure." If this seems insufficient to designate the object of their search, the following sentences go further: the wakened sleeper exclaims, "Oh, is this *your* buried treasure? The light in the heart." To sum up the sequence: the past inhabitants of the house return to seek some treasure they have left and discover it as "their light lifts the lids" of the sleeper's eyes. The place called "here" by the searchers becomes localized as the body of the sleeper; they discover their past happiness still alive in her eyes and heart, and the sleeper recognizes her happiness as the buried treasure left by the past inhabitants. The metaphoric element by which this transfer of feeling is effected is the medium of light: the presences shine their light into the sleeper's eyes, and the latter declares the treasure to be the light in her heart.

So much is established by the subtle shifts of implication in the closing paragraph. Other strains of language and imagery considerably thicken the texture. In addition to the quoted statements of the presences and the first-person narrative of the sleeper, another being is quoted in the story: the house itself. " 'Safe, safe, safe,' the pulse of the house beat gladly." " 'Safe, safe, safe,' the pulse of the house beat softly." " 'Safe, safe, safe,' the heart of the house beats proudly." And finally: " 'Safe! safe! safe!' the pulse of the house beats wildly.'' These repetitive strands set up interweaving connections with other chains, such as the relation between the heart of the house, which beats and pulses, and the sleeper's heart, which contains the light of the presences. These are only the beginnings of a complete account of the brilliantly elaborated form of this story, but what stands out is the trend of all these patterns toward the final discovery of value in the heart or consciousness with which the story begins.

It is apparent, even from this curtailed description of **"A Haunted House,"** that we are on the verge of another sort of circular form, in which not one sentence merely but a *cluster* of elements is used to introduce a story and later to close it. Four stories, at least, fall into this category, the best known of which is the title story of Woolf's first collection, **"Monday or Tuesday."** This piece marks the closest approach in Woolf to the prose poem—if not to the condition of music—but even here form has significance, while conveying little paraphrasable content. The piece begins: "Lazy and indifferent, shaking space easily from his wings, knowing his way, the heron passes over the church beneath the sky. White and distant, absorbed in itself, endlessly the sky covers and uncovers, moves and remains." The last sentence takes up the elements of the first in the same order, although in compressed expressions: "Lazy and indifferent the heron returns; the sky veils her stars; then bares them." Between the opening and closing sentences, four short paragraphs establish a pattern suggesting a persistent search for the truth of experience: "Desiring truth . . . for ever desiring . . . for ever desiring . . . for ever desiring truth . . . and truth? . . . and truth? . . . truth?" It is to this internal sequence, as well as to the opening evocation, that the closing sentence responds. Truth here, as in the use of a similar bird symbol by Yeats, lies in the perfect equipoise of dynamic elements: over, beneath; covers, uncovers; moves and remains; veils, then bares. The finale of **"Monday or Tuesday"** comes not merely with the reverberation of a previously heard chord but by the reestablishment of a prior condition; the dynamic equilibrium broken at the beginning sets in again as language dies away at the close.

While the complex of elements returning at the end of **"Monday or Tuesday"** is a set of images, somewhat different elements are to be found giving form to **"The Summing Up," "The Shooting Party,"** and **"The Searchlight."** In **"The Summing Up,"** one of the Dalloway stories, the elements are place designations. The story begins with the movement of the protagonist and her interlocutor from the Dalloway house into the garden, from which a sense of the city beyond the garden walls is caught. In the midst of the narrative, the relation of places is altered, the conversing pair clambering up to peer over the garden wall at "the vast inattentive impersonal world" around them, and then looking back at "the dry, thick Queen Anne house" where they are being entertained. The spatial relation is changed again at the conclusion: at the point when the interlocutors turn to reenter the house from the garden, London is behind them, disturbingly: "At that moment, in some back street or public house, the usual terrible sexless, inarticulate voice rang out; a shriek, a cry." Between these three clusters of place, two images are repeatedly introduced: between the beginning and middle, a "golden shaft" is seen as running through the protagonist, and her imagination evokes a tree or tree branch dripping

gold. Between the middle and end, these images reappear as a "cloud of gold" and a "field tree" in the primeval marsh that preceded the building of London. The protagonist also sees her soul as an "aloof" and "unmated" widow bird perched on that tree, and in a coda to the final cluster of places that bird takes wing, describes wider and wider circles and becomes remote as a crow. Obviously, the imaginative construction in **"The Summing Up"** overflows beyond the form traced by its place designations, but those viewpoints of social position serve as a grid upon which the freer images of self are poised.

In **"The Shooting Party,"** the clusters that provide formal order are parts of a conventional framing device. This story of the gentry's degeneration hinges on the discovery of a sexual taint in the scion of a smug county family. The opening scene (part of the frame) reveals a woman in a railway carriage, who is designated only by the initials "M.M." on her luggage, who carries a brace of pheasants as if from a shoot, and who utters only the sound indicated by the letters "Chk." Before she reappears in the closing frame, M.M. is revealed in the course of the narrative as Milly Masters, the housekeeper and the mistress of the squire, whose illegitimate son is twice described as "the boy who cleaned the Church." The sound "Chk" is also elaborated in the body of the narrative, being twice uttered by one of the squire's spinster sisters. Before the story returns to that framing scene, the staid life of the gentry suffers an upheaval in the narrative as the squire and his hounds burst into the drawing room and thrash about wildly. But a more effective signal of the end of a class's heyday is given in the closing frame. The figure of M.M. becomes etherealized, a mist, "eyes without a body"; and her state of existence is suggested by the question, "since there is nothing that does not leave some residue, and memory is a light that dances in the mind when the reality is buried, why should not the eyes there, gleaming, moving, be the ghost of a family, of an age, of a civilization dancing over the grave?" The return of the woman at the close now carries with it the ghostly presence of the aristocracy. The entire framing cluster—including even the "Chk Chk" of the last sentence—serves as a point of repair from which to take a distant perspective on the past, on a country house, its decorous manners and decadent morals.

The last of this group of stories with returning clusters is **"The Searchlight,"** another of those which overflow their form yet gain strength from their firm underpinnings. Again a frame situation is established, this time of the Conradian type, in which a speaker in purportedly present time delivers a tale of the past; the story later returns to this narrative situation and its distant perspective on the past. (pp. 60-6)

Only two more stories need be included among those with circular forms: **"The String Quartet"** and **"The Introduction."** **"The String Quartet"** has perhaps the most elaborate and independently interesting form among Woolf's short stories, but it is constructed so clearly as an exercise in form per se that it cannot be considered among the most important tales. **"The String Quartet"** is what we may call an exercise in *imitative* form, in which Woolf's prose follows the phases of experience that make up a chamber music concert so as to resemble the music itself. First comes a sketch of the audience assembling, then a freely

Woolf with Lytton Strachey, a core participant in the Bloomsbury group, at Garsington in Oxfordshire.

imagined description of the Mozart quartet being played, then a reverie in which the listener imagines a little love story unfolding—it is not clear where, but the scene is set in a society like that in which the music was written. Abruptly, the imaginative description of the music returns, and at last the audience is described filing out. If we were to put this in the way musical themes are labelled, the form would be A-B-C-B-A. The circularity of form may be said to be concentric, with the daydream of romance in a past age forming the inner core, but never developing significant relations with the outer and middle circles.

Finally, a slight variation on the form in which a cluster of elements appears at beginning and end is offered by the Dalloway story **"The Introduction,"** in which the transition is from *middle* to end. A young lady attains a sort of initiation into society at the middle of the story, only to reach a further turn in her development at the close. The midpoint climax is couched in these terms: "all made her feel that she had come out of her chrysalis and was being proclaimed what in the long comfortable darkness of childhood she had never been . . . this butterfly with a thousand facets to its eyes, and delicate fine plumage, and difficulties and sensibilities and sadnesses innumerable: a woman." At the close of the story, these elements are reas-

sembled and their symbolic valence is reoriented: "she felt like a naked wretch who having sought shelter in some shady garden is turned out and made to understand (ah, but there was a kind of passion in it too) that there are no sanctuaries, or butterflies, and this civilisation, said Lily Everit to herself . . . depends upon me." The coming out is replaced by a turning out in nakedness from an Edenic state; the butterflies with their fine plumage are suddenly withdrawn, and the "comfortable darkness of childhood" gives way to a world without sanctuaries. Yet this series of negations is accompanied by a consciousness of connection with the ongoing life of mankind. As a family friend puts it in the story's final line, " . . . like all the Everits, Lily looked 'as if she had the weight of the world upon her shoulders.' "

Having said this much about the kinds of form observable in Virginia Woolf's short stories, what can we say about the structure of the collection as a whole? There is as yet no complete edition of the stories. The most substantial collection was arranged by Leonard Woolf in an apparently symmetrical way: six of the eight from *Monday or Tuesday,* followed by six published in magazines, concluding with six unpublished pieces. (The true figures are a bit altered by the fact that **"Moments of Being"** had been previously published, as Woolf himself suspected.) The seven pieces collected in the volume called **Mrs. Dalloway's Party** approximate a structural conception that Virginia Woolf entertained in 1922: "a short book consisting of six or seven chapters, each complete separately. Yet there must be some sort of fusion! And all must converge upon the party at the end." Clearly, no such conception can hold all her stories together—although it may do so for the Dalloway pieces—nor is there any requirement to think of the collection as a totality. But I suspect this body of prose has more structural unity than has yet been acknowledged.

When the datable stories are related to the above analysis, Woolf's performance shows a steady tendency toward circular form. By 1921, she had already written three such stories, **"A Haunted House," "Monday or Tuesday,"** and **"The String Quartet."** If the latter is merely an exercise in circular form, the other two are seminal works in the canon. From **"A Haunted House"** proceed all the tales based on a return to the opening lines of a text; from **"Monday or Tuesday"** come all the pieces which repeat a cluster of thematic or verbal elements at the close. As Woolf's explorations continue (after passing through a period of writing Dalloway stories), the quest for form reaches a point of high fulfillment in the late twenties with **"Moments of Being"** and **"The Lady in the Looking-Glass."** There follow a number of further explorations in the late thirties, none of them producing outstanding achievement.

What should be most apparent from this formal analysis is the persistence of certain kinds of meaning in close association with particular forms. The stories described as circular are those that come back to their origins, reestablish an equilibrium, or discover the nature of what is already there. They are "moments" of being not only in the temporal sense—flashes of insight at an instant of time—but also in the dialectical sense, as philosophers in the Hegelian tradition have used the term. In the dialectical moment, a being takes a turn in its development that unfolds what is potential all along. It comes into its own, as we say; it reveals itself as in itself it really is. Such a manifestation of individual selves occurs in stories like **"Moments of Being," "The Lady in the Looking-Glass,"** and **"The Summing Up."** In **"A Haunted House"** and **"The Searchlight"** the manifestation is somewhat more complicated, involving the identification of one self with another, especially with past selves. In other instances, particularly **"The Shooting Party"** and **"Monday or Tuesday,"** the revelation is not of a person but rather of an overarching condition—sociological in the one case, what we can only call metaphysical in the other.

If circular stories can be said to engage themselves entirely in what is initially given, linear forms can be described as leading beyond the given to what is scarcely known or controlled. In **"Kew Gardens,"** for example, the series of ordinary and apparently easily-known passers-by in the park ends in a final term, the voices, which is composed of known elements (the sounds of the city), yet is presented as an existence beyond the confines of the park, beyond even what is ordinarily known as life. **"The Mark on the Wall"** and **"An Unwritten Novel"** pursue something like the same course, moving from what seems to be easily grasped to what is tenuous and ultimately unknowable—even though it seems to be controlled when a name is as-

signed it (as when the mark is named a snail). The shift in Woolf's habitual practice noticed above—from the linear to the circular, broadly speaking—represents a tendency to return to the given, rather than to pursue the unknown and possibly unknowable. But it also marks a return to what has been latent all along, the meaning of the given, discovered in the act of repetition. It is in this sense that Woolf's rounded stories, like Slater's pins, can be acknowledged as having "no points." (pp. 67-70)

Avrom Fleishman, "Forms of the Woolfian Short Story," in Virginia Woolf: Revaluation and Continuity, *edited by Ralph Freedman, University of California Press, 1980, pp. 44-70.*

Selma Meyerowitz (essay date 1981)

[*In the following excerpt, Meyerowitz approaches Woolf's early story "A Society" and four later pieces— "Lappin and Lapinova," "The New Dress," "The Legacy," and "The Introduction"—as evidence of Woolf's social criticism in which she examines through female characters the effects of patriarchal society upon the individual.*]

Virginia Woolf's short stories have frequently been viewed as lyrical fiction that is experimental in form and concerned with a quest for reality. This approach, however, denies a political vision which shapes most of the short fiction just as it does Woolf's feminist essays and her novels. As in *A Room of One's Own* and *Three Guineas*, Woolf's political analysis of social experience in the short stories is presented through female characters whom she considers a society of outsiders. Because they are denied social and class privilege, women reveal the destructive nature of a classbound society and its effects on individual consciousness and interpersonal relationships.

When readers have not ignored Woolf's social criticism or political vision in the short stories, they have reacted negatively. This is clear with Woolf's story **"A Society,"** which appeared in her first volume of short fiction, **Monday or Tuesday.** Jean Guiguet, for example, commented that in **"A Society"** Woolf was extreme in her social criticism, and, as a result, the work was 'a failed venture into militant literature which Virginia Woolf had the good taste to cast aside' [see excerpt dated 1962]. Guiguet also criticised technical aspects of the work, stating that 'the general design is uncertain, the irony often clumsy'. Woolf seems to have anticipated negative public reaction to this story, for in her diary she wrote, 'And as for **"A Society"** though spirited it is too one-sided.' At this point, relatively early in her literary career, she may have been reluctant to offend her reading public; thus, according to Leonard Woolf, she decided not to republish the work.

In **"A Society,"** Virginia Woolf's sense of social criticism is developed through a feminist vision of the role of women in society. At the beginning of her story, her female characters are portrayed as conventional upper-middle-class ladies; they focus on the 'scarlet feathers and golden slippers' in a milliner's window and spend their energies 'building little towers of sugar upon the edge of the tea tray'. Their attitude towards men is also determined by the sex roles typical of their class: they admire and praise the male sex and consider marriage their highest priority, indeed, their life's goal. Yet Woolf's spirit of social iconoclasm, her desire to destroy meaningless conventions of a patriarchal, classbound society, emerges in the character of Poll who has been devoting all her time to reading, only to discover that the literature created by men is 'unutterably bad': for example, in what passes for history, 'not a word . . . seemed to be true and the style in which it was written was execrable'; similarly, poetry contains 'verbose sentimental foolery'. Woolf's female characters are now determined to judge the civilisation created by men. As they form their society for asking questions and come in contact with the institutions of society, Woolf ridicules the professional men. . . . The women investigate male-dominated social institutions and professions with the serious purpose of evaluating whether or not the achievements of men justify the continuation of the human race and having women 'sacrifice' their youth to bear sons. They begin to suspect that perhaps women should not have 'taken it for granted that it was a woman's duty to spend her youth in bearing children'.

Woolf's female characters in **"A Society"** conclude that a belief in the superiority of male intellect is a fallacy; not only does it deny women a role in social and political life, but it also distorts the male ego and the emotional and sexual relationship between men and women. They comment on the male sex:

> Soon he cannot come into a room without making us all feel uncomfortable; he condescends to every woman he meets, and dares not tell the truth even to his own wife; instead of rejoicing our eyes we have to shut them if we are to take him in our arms. True, they console themselves with stars of all shapes, ribbons of all shades, and incomes of all sizes—but what is to console us?

(pp. 238-40)

In **"A Society"**, Woolf's political vision evaluates the relationship between the individual and the social, political and economic structures of society. In addition to criticising social institutions, Woolf offers a perspective for social change. Women must assume the responsibility of re-educating themselves in order to reassess the social structure and its effects on individual life, and to examine the role of men in society. To do this, women must no longer believe in the superiority of men; instead, each women must realise that she should teach her daughter, the woman of the future, that 'there's only one thing . . . to believe in—and that is herself'.

Virginia Woolf's political understanding of sex-role divisions and social conventions and institutions is developed further in several other short stories which analyse the relationship between the social structure and individual psychology. Through her women characters, Woolf portrays a struggle to achieve fulfillment and continuity of self, either through or despite social conventions and institutions determined by the class and patriarchal structure of society. As the mental and emotional states of Woolf's characters are developed in relation to such social institutions as marriage, the family, the professions and the society world, they reveal the class nature of individual psychology and interpersonal relationships.

The women in Woolf's short stories are often portrayed as insecure, unsatisfied, and uncertain about their role in society. As a result, their attempts to establish emotional

and psychological security and social acceptance become a dominant concern. When her female characters fail to achieve fulfilment, Woolf suggests it is because their inner life is distorted by social influences, particularly class conflict, social snobbery, and the destructive nature of social institutions in a patriarchal and class society. Four short stories, **"Lappin and Lapinova"**, **"The Legacy"**, **"The New Dress"** and **"The Introduction"**, reveal the role of deception in the lives of women. Sex and class oppression cause women to deceive themselves and others, or to use deception as a protection from reality. Woolf presents the struggles of her women characters to overcome deception as a measure of the possibility for psychological and physical survival in a classbound society.

In **"Lappin and Lapinova"** and **"The Legacy"**, the conflict between the public and private self is explored through the social institution of marriage which is examined in relation to class position. Although there are some strains of sentimentality, **"Lappin and Lapinova"** comments on an intense struggle to achive self-fulfilment despite social conventions; it also reveals the futility of an escape from reality which involves retreating into the imagination. Likewise, in **"The Legacy"**, a rather typical plot involving an extramarital love relationship is transformed into a perceptive statement about the destructive effects of class and status on human values and interpersonal communication.

Rosalind of **"Lappin and Lapinova"** is clearly in rebellion against the upper-class life-style to which her husband, Ernest Thorburn, belongs. After a conventional marriage ceremony, Rosalind avoids a realistic appraisal of her husband's nature. By transforming him into a creature of her imagination, she hopes to disguise the fact that he is a typical upper-class Englishman, 'born at Portchester Terrace, educated at Rugby; now a clerk in Her Majesty's Civil Service'. This reaction is part of her inability to adjust to her new social position and role: 'Rosalind had still to get used to the fact that she was now Mrs. Ernest Thornurn. Perhaps she would never get used to the fact that she was Mrs. Ernest Anybody'. She senses a surrender of individuality in marriage; she is no longer a separate identity, but the wife of someone else. Rosalind, moreover, wishes to rebel against some English conventions, particularly 'the Albert Memorial, mahogany sideboards, steel engravings of the Prince Consort with his family—her mother-in-law's dining-room in Portchester Terrace in short'. Yet she accepts traditional class and sex roles. When Ernest's physical characteristics remind Rosalind of a pet rabbit, she transforms that image into one appropriate to Ernest's physical appearance and temperament. He is 'A hunting rabbit; a King Rabbit; a rabbit that makes laws for all the other rabbits'. Ernest thereby preserves his ruling-class status, as well as his dignity and domination. As this animal fantasy builds, it is clear that Rosalind and Ernest each embody the qualities conventionally associated with the male and female sexes respectively. . . . Rosalind's imaginary world is both destructive and nurturing: it prevents her from developing communication with Ernest; at the same time, it ensures her survival by providing a shelter from everyday reality, for 'without that world, how, Rosalind wondered, that winter could she have lived at all?' Rosalind needs fantasy to compensate for her insecurities, especially when faced with the upper-class world of Ernest's family, which makes her feel insignificant, 'an only child and an orphan at that; a mere drop among all those Thorburns'. At the fiftieth wedding anniversary of Ernest's parents, the irony underlying Rosalind's rabbit world is apparent. The sexuality of rabbits is implicitly a parallel to the 'fruitful' union of Ernest's parents, which 'produced nine other sons and daughters into the bargain, many themselves married and also fruitful'. In contrast, Rosalind's white wedding dress suggests her virginal nature and non-procreative state. (pp. 240-43)

Through fantasy, Rosalind avoids being destroyed by the Thorburn world, which she feels she can never enter as an equal.

Virginia Woolf reveals that an imaginative retreat from reality is but a feeble and temporary attempt to achieve emotional fulfilment or to create communication with others. Rosalind's fantasy rabbit world does not survive. When Ernest can no longer participate in their imaginative game, Rosalind feels her life becoming a replica of the Thorburns' pattern of living: 'A vision of her mother-in-law's dining-room came before her; and there they sat, she and Ernest, grown old, under the engravings, in front of the sideboard. It was, their golden-wedding day. She could not bear it'. Although saved from psychic destruction two years earlier when she became Mrs. Ernest Thorburn, Rosalind now faces the death of her rabbit world and the sterility of her marriage. Woolf clearly leaves no illusions alive at the end of the story, as she comments, 'that was the end of that marriage'.

Although Rosalind in **"Lappin and Lapinova"** rejects the social conventions of the class into which she marries, she cannot establish viable conventions outside that class's lifestyle. She accepts the typical role of a submissive wife, remaining sheltered from contact with the outside world and exalting her husband's status. Her position in her marriage and in society does not allow her to develop a sense of identity or the resources necessary for a continuing emotional relationship. As a result, her fantasy world proves ineffectual and destructive. Sadly, Rosalind's awakening to the truth is painful, yet Woolf implies that her fantasy retreat ensured her immaturity and fruitlessness, as well as her inability to communicate and achieve emotional fulfilment in her marriage.

"The Legacy" presents another picture of the failure of emotional commitment and communication in marriage. Angela Clandon has led a life of deception by maintaining the facade of her conventional upper-class marriage. After her death, however, Angela's diary reveals the truth to her husband, as it records the alienation which grew between them and destroyed their marriage. Again, Virginia Woolf links the destruction of personal happiness and interpersonal relationships to class status and social conventions, primarily through the characterisation of Gilbert Clandon, which develops as his wife's diary reveals her role in their marriage. Clandon seems isolated in his own world of upper-class social status and public esteem that is characteristic of a moderately successful politician, a type Virginia Woolf portrays in several of her works. Consequently, he is insensitive to what has happened to his marriage and to his wife.

Gilbert Clandon's insensitivity to others is related to upperclass snobbishness. This is first evident in his thoughts about Sissy Miller, his wife's secretary: 'She was scarcely

distinguishable from any other woman of her kind. There were thousands of Sissy Millers—drab little women in black carrying attaché cases'. His thoughts contrast with his wife's evaluation of Sissy: 'But Angela, with her genius for sympathy, had discovered all sorts of qualities in Sissy Miller. She was the soul of discretion; so silent; so trustworthy, one could tell her anything, and so on'. Clandon, prominent politician though he is, certainly lacks his wife's sensitivity to people, her 'genius for sympathy'. (pp. 243-45)

Clandon emerges as thoroughly self-centered. Unaware that he neglected his wife in his efforts for political success, he is surprised to read about Angela's regret at not having a son: 'Oddly enough he had never much regretted that himself. Life had been so full, so rich as it was. That year he had been given a minor post in the government'. For Clandon, personal fulfilment and the richness of life lay in a government position, not in personal relationships or parenthood. Moreover, he obviously had no respect for his wife's individuality, but saw her mostly as a beautiful object, of which he was proud, and as someone to minister to his needs. When Angela claimed she wanted to help others, Clandon reflected, 'Hadn't she enough to do looking after him, after her home? Still if it amused her, of course he had no objection'. Thus, Clandon cannot relate to the sections of Angela's diary which reveal her involvement in social activities: 'His own name occurred less frequently. His interest slackened. Some of the entries conveyed nothing to him'. Nevertheless, her references to BM raise his curiosity. Since BM is of the lower classes, Clandon is supercilious:

> So B.M was a man—no doubt one of those 'intellectuals' as they call themselves, who are so violent, as Angela said, and so narrow-minded. Gilbert knew the type and had no liking for this particular specimen. . . . He could see him quite distinctly—a stubby little man, with a rough beard, red tie, dressed as they always did in tweeds, who had never done an honest day's work in his life.

Clandon's thoughts reveal a typical upper-class attitude towards social reformers which associates them with violence and a lack of manners and aesthetic taste.

Clandon's attitude toward his wife is patronising. He feels Angela was intellectually immature, perhaps even unable to comprehend the complex social questions BM raised. Similarly, he cannot imagine that she was dissatisfied with their marriage or that she found emotional fulfilment with another man. His limited understanding of his wife makes his final realisation that her suicide was a rejection of him a surprise: 'She had told the truth. She had stepped off the kerb to rejoin her lover . . . to escape from him'. While his self-satisfaction and insensitivity to others make him a less than admirable character, Clandon's final understanding of the illusions he maintained about his wife and his marriage renders him somewhat pathetic.

In contrast to Clandon, Angela had overcome the emptiness of her marriage by using deception as a means to achieve freedom and pursue fulfilment outside her relationship to her husband. While social prestige and vanity have left Clandon without emotional fulfilment and have contributed to the self-destruction of others, namely Angela and BM, Angela's diary, a record of her inner life, becomes the source of truth and self-revelation for her hus-

Cover of the first edition of Woolf's short story collection Monday or Tuesday.

band—a veritable gift or legacy. Thus, through her characters in **"The Legacy"**, Woolf suggests that people can find emotional fulfilment only through intimate communication and selfless caring. The world of social conventions, embodied in upper-class status and conventional political aspirations, creates vanity, self-centredness, and insensitivity to others. Under these circumstances, a marriage relationship becomes meaningless.

Social and class discrimination again destroy emotional fulfilment in **"The New Dress"**, as seen in the character of Mabel Waring. Mabel is of the lower class, part of a family of ten 'never having money enough, always skimping and paring'. At Mrs. Dalloway's party, she thinks of 'her own drawing-room so shabby' and of her inability to dress fashionably because it is too costly. Mabel's anxiety about her appearance, her manners, and her values is provoked by her encounter with the society world of the Dalloways; however, her insecurity is more pervasive: 'At once the misery which she always tried to hide, the profound dissatisfaction—the sense that she had had, ever since she was a child, of being inferior to other people—set upon her, relentlessly, remorselessly, with an intensity which she could not beat off'. When she imagines that everyone is judging her appearance, Mabel's painful self-

consciousness turns to self-hatred. Sensing her ineffectuality, she expresses her low self-esteem through an animal image, 'We are all like flies trying to crawl over the edge of the saucer'; she also expresses a similar sense of alienation from others: 'She was a fly—but the others were dragonflies, butterflies, beautiful insects'. Her need for assurance makes her attempt to communicate with another guest, Robert Haydon, whose polite but insincere comments leave her even more disillusioned and unhappy with herself and her social interactions.

Virginia Woolf suggests that society's conventions destroy Mabel's inner resources, since she implies that there are moments when Mabel has self-confidence and experiences pleasure. (pp. 245-47)

Mabel's sense of alienation also exists because her insecurity makes her self-centered and unable to respond to others. She sees herself and another guest, Mrs Holman, as a yellow dot and a black dot, both detached; therefore, 'it was impossible that the black dot . . . should make the yellow dot, sitting solitary, self-centred, feel what the black dot was feeling, yet they pretended!' Neither Mabel nor Mrs Holman understands what the other feels, because each demands sympathy for herself: 'Ah, it was tragic, this greed, this clamour of human beings . . . for sympathy—it was tragic, could one have felt it and not merely pretended to feel it!' To Mabel, and to Virginia Woolf, who presumably uses the above comment by the narrator to imply her own view, pretence and lies are more despicable and more destructive to interpersonal communication than a self-centred demand for sympathy.

Woolf does suggest positive values in this story. Again, although Mabel feels only distress from social interactions, she can at least remember moments of spontaneous joy, either in nature, where social competition and alienation do not exist, or in everyday activities. . . . Mabel's sense of the meaning and peace of life gives her a momentary determination to reject dissatisfying social relationships and strive for a way of life which provides 'divine moments'. She decides to leave Mrs Dalloway's party, but she is again caught in the trap of social intercourse. Exclaiming, 'I have enjoyed myself' to Mr and Mrs Dalloway, she realises that she is back 'right in the saucer'. Her struggle to rise above superficial social amenities and painful social interactions is thus largely unsuccessful. Mabel cannot develop a consistently independent sense of values necessary for security. Instead, she is vulnerable to social status and social pretences.

In **"The Introduction"**, Virginia Woolf provides an alternative female character to Mabel Waring, while still focusing on the position of women in society and on aspects of male-female relationships as set against the society world and a patriarchal and hierarchical social structure. Lily Everit, a young woman in Academia, struggles to preserve her sense of self while surrounded by the guests at Mrs Dalloway's party. She desperately clings to her sole source of strength, her literary work, an 'essay on the character of Dean Swift . . . marked with three stars: First rate'. In the presence of upper-class society, however, the essay 'wobbled, began wilting . . . and all her being . . . turned to a mist of alarm, apprehension and defence. . . . This was the famous place: the world'. Thus, Mrs Dalloway, coming to introduce Lily to the other guests, seems to be 'bearing down on her', like an animal after its prey, and people seem 'to menace and mount over her, to turn everything to water'.

The social situation is awkward physically and emotionally for Lily. She senses that her movements and appearance are being observed and that she is expected to behave accordingly: 'Lily accepted the part which was now laid on her, and, naturally, overdid it a little . . . accentuating the delicacy, the artificiality of her bearing'. Lily also senses the formality of the new world she enters; it is regulated and orderly, like 'the towers of Westminster; the high and formal building; the talk; this civilisation'. This world is foreign to her and contrasts with her usual terrain, the countryside . . . By identifying Lily with a love of nature and close family relationships, Woolf indicates the contrast between the world of personal fulfilment and the world of social and professional status.

Civilisation appears to Lily to be a 'massive masculine achievement', thus indicating her awareness of the patriarchal nature of society. Similarly, she views the academic world as a masculine preserve. When she wonders what she can offer of her own to this male-dominated realm of society, she thinks of her essay. Yet her security and sense of academic accomplishment are soon challenged by Bob Brinsley: 'With his great forehead, and his look of self-assurance . . . and direct descent from Shakespeare, what could she do but lay her essay, oh and the whole of her being, on the floor as a cloak for him to trample on, as a rose for him to rifle'. Here Woolf aptly links masculine domination in intellectual and social matters with sexual oppression and dehumanisation. There is a brutal, destructive aspect to Brinsley, as if he is tearing off the wings of a fly. Lily sees herself as the fly, fighting not to let 'this terror, this suspicion of something different, get hold of her and shrivel up her wings and drive her out into loneliness'. To assert herself against the male world, Lily must risk the destruction of her wings which she would need to escape from the typical isolation of the non-professional woman who stays at home. The choices are clear: Lily can be an object of beauty, admired and protected by men—'She wanted to have her handkerchief picked up on the staircase and be a butterfly'; or she can be the source of flattery and the moral and emotional support of a man—'Why not, since this is the greatest of all worldly objects? And to worship, to adorn, to embellish was her task, her wings were for that'; or, as the last choice, she can gain independence and respect through professional, academic accomplishment, despite the domination of men.

Although Lily does assert her right to be a professional woman, her instincts have been distorted by the male supremacy inherent in a patriarchal society. . . . Male achievements, male self-assertion, and male domination of women in social, intellectual, and economic areas make Lily think of 'civilisation with horror'. Yet she is determined that the accomplishments of men must be rejected because they are destructive. It is a woman's duty to preserve the life-sustaining qualities upon which civilised instincts are based: 'This civilisation, said Lily Everit to herself . . . depends on me'.

Virginia Woolf's short stories thus portray social and interpersonal relationships as painful and unfulfilling. Through her female characters she reveals the effects of class discrimination and alienation on individual psychology. . . . As her characters attempt to overcome deception and class alienation in order to achieve fulfilment, she affirms love and social responsibility as necessary to emotional satisfaction. Class conflict, social divisions, and meaningless social institutions must be rejected for the characters in her short stories to establish personal and social survival. The commitment to social criticism and the political vision so evident in Woolf's early story **"A Society"** pervades her later short fiction which examines the effects of social and class reality on individual consciousness. (pp. 248-52)

> *Selma Meyerowitz, "What Is to Console Us? The Politics of Deception in Woolf's Short Stories," in* New Feminist Essays on Virginia Woolf, *edited by Jane Marcus, University of Nebraska Press, 1981, pp. 238-52.*

Joanne Trautmann Banks   (essay date 1985)

[*Banks contributed to the compilation of Woolf's myriad correspondences as assistant editor to Nigel Nicolson in the six-volume publication* The Letters of Virginia Woolf (1975-1980). *In the following excerpt, she offers an appreciative overview of Woolf's themes and narrative technique in her short stories.*]

[A] typical story by Virginia Woolf could be an ideal model of Frank O'Connor's definition of the genre as a "significant moment" from which past, present, and future may be viewed simultaneously.

The moment is her subject; the moment is her method. Perhaps there never was another short-story writer for whom form and content were thus merged. An excellent example is **"The Searchlight."** Its opening captures a party of sophisticated people paused on a London balcony between dinner and theater. Casually drinking coffee, smoking, and chatting, they watch an air force searchlight probing the night skies. In one burst of light, Mrs. Ivimey "sees" something. She sees the setting and action of a story told her by her great-grandfather about his youth. It seems that he lived in a lonely tower on the Yorkshire moors. One day, using his telescope, he saw a kiss between a man and a girl. He saw love, and, leaving his tower, he ran miles across the moors to find that girl, whom he would later marry. That's all: "The light . . . only falls here and there." Present time restrictions intervene: "Right you are. Friday." But with her story, Mrs. Ivimey has swept away one hundred years. She has had a glimpse of love observed, as with books and telescopes, as opposed to love embraced. Once again life has happened between the acts, between, in this case, dinner and the theater.

Like **"The Searchlight,"** almost all the other Woolf stories have at their center a philosophical theme expressed in tones reserved by many writers for sensual experience. She cares passionately about the precise nature of reality and the values of existence. She worries about philosophical dichotomies; the "knowing" versus "being" dilemma, for instance, is central to **"The Searchlight."** Woolf is likewise intrigued by the opposition of art and life, appearance and reality, subjectivity and objectivity, the self and the not-self, vision and fact. Even when she writes about social class division or, as she so often does, the man-woman confrontation, her concerns are as much philosophical as political or psychological.

Above all, Woolf investigates the imagination as a tool for knowing, unifying, and finally transcending its environment through love. For her, short stories are also "religious." They constitute a search for lasting significance in natural and human phenomena. The sea, the landscape, animals, and above all the mysterious human figures themselves, beckon to her, then depart through mists: "If I fall on my knees, if I go through the ritual, the ancient antics, it's you, unknown figures, you I adore; if I open my arms, it's you I embrace, you I draw to me—adorable world!" (**"An Unwritten Novel"**).

Her work had this philosophical and religious emphasis from the beginning. One of her first short stories, **"Monday or Tuesday,"** manages in just three hundred words to present both details and panoramas of reality while simultaneously questioning its essential qualities. The story opens far from the human activity that is always for Woolf only one component of an overlapping universe. A heron, who can afford to be "lazy and indifferent" because he knows his way instinctively, passes over the human sphere and under the sky. The sky is even more self-absorbed. Indifferent to lakes, mountains, and stars, the sky—though she "moves"—"remains." Heron and sky, male and female, are contrasted with the active world of men, women, and children, of jarring omnibuses, reflections in London shop windows, and Miss Thingummy, who sits in her office drinking her tea. Could anything be more real than Miss Thingummy?

"And is truth then a list of observable details?" the narrative consciousness seems to be asking. So many details are simply reflections of something else. So many are transient and incomparable—"squandered in separate scales." So much happens parenthetically. Though the questions are difficult, the searching long and laborious, still the mind behind this story is "for ever desiring truth." Above it all, not needing to desire but simply to be, are the heron and the sky. The gap between the two worlds is traveled—"voyaging," Woolf says, using her favored water metaphor—via the imagination. In the penultimate paragraph someone very like a conventional narrator takes shape, home from all that activity, sitting by the fire, reading her way into the reality behind the flames, smoke, and sparks—Platonic imagery for this Platonic search. The view in the last lines drifts upward from the dross of everyday activity. Visions of mosques enter the consciousness, followed—higher up—by the Indian seas, then by blue space and the stars themselves. Is this perhaps truth at last? Or is it only psychic "closeness" with the vast elements, which is all we have and all we need to have? As if in answer, the sky first covers the stars, those bright specks of near certainty, then uncovers them to our hungering gaze.

This human miracle of connectedness has happened amid the most ordinary facts of life. Realizations about the mind, the way it knows, and its involvement with the world outside itself, await us any Monday or Tuesday.

The abundance of her speculations sometimes threatens to dilute Woolf's considerable energies. A period of abstract questioning can drive her back to facts, to **"Solid Objects"** (to mention another story title), to the Miss Thingummys. There she roots happily among direct experiences. But as soon as she describes the solid objects, she brings them sensuously to life. And once she has done that, she cannot

help herself—she must daydream. So, like all of us, Woolf oscillates between experience and interpretation.

She speaks of these matters directly in **"The Mark on the Wall,"** as charming a piece of philosophy as has ever been written. Glancing up from her daily concerns one day, Woolf—for it is surely proper to identify the voice here as hers—notices a small black mark against a white wall. Is it a large nail mark? Thus begins a series of meanderings through, among other topics, the nature of fantasizing, selfhood as an infinite series of reflected phantom images, the male-induced fraudulence of social convention, and the vast ignorance behind what learned professors call factual knowledge. Life, she decides, is an accidental matter in spite of all our civilized attempts to control it. Very little sticks to us: "Why, if one wants to compare life to anything, one must liken it to being blown through the Tube at fifty miles an hour—landing at the other end without a single hairpin in one's hair! Shot out at the feet of God entirely naked!" Therefore, it is useless to get up to see just what the mark on the wall really is. What it "really" is, is just another particle of so-called solid reality, which will not connect. Staying where she sits, this pensive Woolf wants "to sink deeper and deeper, away from the surface, with its hard separate facts."

Just here she gets caught. To be sure, she opens up the world of speculation. But she does so by daring to deny the importance of long-established convention, such as which Anglican archbishop precedes which Anglican archbishop, thereby forcing Nature to protect herself. No one's thoughts must collide with Nature's reality. People must not be left dangerously adrift in solipsism. So in spite of her love of the daydream, Woolf finds she must learn what the mark on the wall is, and thereby hang onto something as definite and real as "a plank in the sea." She seeks salvation by "worshipping solidity, worshipping reality, worshipping the impersonal world which is a proof of some existence other than ours."

When Woolf turns from the speculative story to a more recognizable version of the genre, she is nonetheless often working through the same issues. **"The Introduction,"** for instance, dramatizes one of Woolf's lasting concerns, the endangered self. The theme is embodied in a shy, intellectually ambitious young woman who is introduced to an arrogant young man and learns that her role in civilization is merely to adorn him. One of several stories about people meeting and parting without significantly altering their isolation, **"The Introduction"** builds its feminist theme on the question of what is real. As Lily Everit drives to the party in a cab, she looks through the glass between her and the driver to see "her own white phantom reflected in his dark coat." Her personality, as in **"The Mark on the Wall,"** is an infinitely possible rather than definitely knowable thing. She responds to this situation, as other Woolf characters do, by calling life a series of dualisms between which one must steer the craft of one's self. "One divided life . . . into fact and into fiction, into rock and into wave." At the beginning of the story, Lily's rock is her essay on Swift, for which she has just that morning received high praise from her professor. But in the hands of the unwittingly brutal Bob Brinsley, a gem of conventional English manhood and harder, more assertively real, than her essay, she feels her own sense of reality melting away. Everything turns to water, "leaving her only the power to stand at bay." Mrs. Dalloway, a "steamer" of a woman, flings her "into a whirlpool where either she would perish or be saved." But in this whirlpool of the man-woman involvement, though there is "a kind of passion," there is no salvation. Lily has entered naked and vulnerable—like Eve, Woolf's language would urge us to remember—"in some shady garden" from which she is evicted, "a naked wretch," knowing at that moment of vision that "there are no sanctuaries."

Even in the relatively plotted stories (which Woolf wrote for money, thinking plot was what people wanted), she cannot turn her mind completely from metaphorical thinking. In **"Lappin and Lapinova"** she creates a plot that is saved from being cloying by the universality of its conceptual underpinnings. That the story is in addition romantic, sad, and filled with longing makes it among the most appealing of her short works of fiction. (pp. 57-60)

To the service of her themes, Woolf brought an astonishing array of technical skills. Some of the stories are, in the first place, so unusual as to merit, sixty years after they were written, the label "experimental." Stories like **"Monday or Tuesday"** and **"Kew Gardens"** have not so much a concealed narrator or shifting points of view as what has been called, with respect to the New Novel in France, "the experiencing mind." Frequently that mind makes the distance between observer and observed seem to disappear. Then there is the magic of what Woolf does with time. In the time it takes Fanny Wilmot in **"Moments of Being"** to search for a pin, she re-creates Julia Craye's lifetime and pinpoints her essence. Woolf also performs magic with space: in **"The String Quartet"** a piece by Mozart sends Woolf's readers racing around the sensual universe—to a pear tree on top of a mountain, to the silver fishes in the Rhone. Perhaps only with Proust is language equal to these same tasks. A further very contemporary touch in **"The String Quartet"** is the telescoped dialogue, which is like Harold Pinter's but without his overtones of absurdity, fear, and cruelty. Yet there are rich and ancient iambic rhythms to Woolf's language as well: "How lovely goodness is in those who, stepping lightly, go smiling through the world." In fact, what marks Woolf's techniques throughout her fiction is this combination of the experimental and the traditional. In a story like **"Monday or Tuesday,"** for instance, there are not true characters and only the haziest of actions. The setting floats; the conflict is intellectual. The piece is too philosophical to qualify as a traditional story, too personal and sensual to be called a traditional essay. And yet we can find our way back to Addison as one of its progenitors.

Much has been made of the visual elements in Woolf's style. She lived among painters and knew well the technique of impressionistic pointillism. She adapted it perfectly to her philosophy that reality appears to us in light-illuminated moments rather than in big slabs of uninterrupted truth. Woolf is the prose painter in such pieces as **"Blue and Green"** (published in *Monday or Tuesday,* 1921, and never reprinted), where she demonstrates that color is not static; and the beautiful **"Kew Gardens,"** the first paragraph of which is a profuse palette of primary colors and light.

Woolf on the Composition of Her Short Stories

One of these days I will write out some phases of my writer's life; and expound what I now merely say in short—After being ill and suffering every form and variety of nightmare and extravagant intensity of perception—for I used to make up poems, stories, profound and to me inspired phrases all day long as I lay in bed, and thus sketched, I think, all that I now, by the light of reason, try to put into prose (I thought of the *Lighthouse* then, and **"Kew"** and others, not in substance, but in idea)—after all this, when I came to, I was so tremblingly afraid of my own insanity that I wrote *Night and Day* [1919] mainly to prove to my own satisfaction that I could keep entirely off that dangerous ground. I wrote it, lying in bed, allowed to write only for one half hour a day. And I made myself copy from plaster casts, partly to tranquilise, partly to learn anatomy. Bad as the book is, it composed my mind, and I think taught me certain elements of composition which I should not have had the patience to learn had I been in full flush of health always. These little pieces in *Monday or* (and) *Tuesday* were written by way of diversion; they were the treats I allowed myself when I had done my exercise in the conventional style. I shall never forget the day I wrote **"The Mark on the Wall"**—all in a flash, as if flying, after being kept stone breaking for months. **"The Unwritten Novel"** was the great discovery, however. That—again in one second—showed me how I could embody all my deposit of experience in a shape that fitted it—not that I have ever reached that end; but anyhow I saw, branching out of the tunnel I made, when I discovered that method of approach, *Jacobs Room* [1922], *Mrs Dalloway* [1925] etc—How I trembled with excitement; and then Leonard came in, and I drank my milk, and concealed my excitement, and wrote I suppose another page of that interminable *Night and Day* (which some say is my best book). All this I will tell you one day—here I suppress my natural inclination to say, if dear Ethel you have the least wish to hear anymore on a subject that can't be of the least interest to you. And, I add, Green and Blue [published as **"Blue and Green"**] and the heron [**"Monday or Tuesday"**] were the wild outbursts of freedom, inarticulate, ridiculous, unprintable mere outcries.

Excerpted from a 1930 letter to Woolf's friend Ethel Smith, a composer and autobiographer, The Letters of Virginia Woolf, *Volume IV: 1929-1931, (1978).*

In other stories Woolf is more photographer than painter, very much the great-niece of the famous Victorian photographer Julia Margaret Cameron. Brilliantly, in **"The Lady in the Looking-Glass,"** she contrasts immutable mirror images with the daily world, where change is constant. How can she fit a portrait of the unknowable Isabella, now moving about in the garden, into the fixed truth the mirror seems to offer? A Platonic exercise again. If the mirror seems at first dependent upon older photographic techniques, it becomes startlingly contemporary once Isabella moves into the reflection. At this point, the scene is reminiscent of the relatively static parts of Robert Altman's film *Images,* which uses mirrors to depict the multiple phantasmagoria of personality, and of Bergman's *Persona.* (pp. 61-2)

When we have spoken of the rhythms of her language and the bond between her outer and inner eyes, we have not yet explained the beauty of Woolf's style. We must underscore the fact that her prose moves as often through sensuous images, one leading directly to another, as it does through the linear method dictated by discursive reasoning and normal chronology. She writes a lyrical short story, not a mimetic one. She needs the freedom of prose to explore the corners of her mind, but the resources of poetry to record her discoveries. She writes telescopically. She condenses and intensifies. So elliptical are some of her stories that one must explicate them as one would a poem by her friend T. S. Eliot. Her sentences, her paragraphs, are long and elegant, yet not "feminine" as she feared, but sinewy, with anatomical strength achieved through the exercise of rewriting.

Behind all Woolf's short fiction is a complex motivation. To speak of it is to add to our understanding of the genre. It can be argued that Virginia Woolf was haunted by impacted grief and ambivalence toward death; between the ages of thirteen and twenty-five, she lost first her mother and father, and then their substitutes, her half-sister and beloved brother. Art, and its handmaiden the imagination, worked wonders with her pain, but just at the point of its greatest beauty, art also "unseals . . . sorrow" (as she expresses it in **"The String Quartet"**). It may be that the short story is particularly dissatisfying in this regard. In Woolf's hands it creates an illusion of perpetual being, something of an antidote to grief. Then the moment ceases, leaving, as a residue, joy but also yearning. Along the continuum between time and eternity, the novel can mark more moments; so it was as a novelist that Woolf found her deepest pleasure.

Eventually, of course, all fictions failed to sustain her. She committed suicide by walking into a river. It was an interesting choice in that water always has dichotomous potentials in Woolf's stories. Water either unifies conflicting elements or it dissolves the self utterly (see, for instance, the discussion of **"The Introduction,"** above). Unification and dissolution: these, it seems, are the two aspects of death for Woolf.

They are invoked again in **"A Haunted House,"** and shown to be not two aspects, but one. Mysterious, elliptical, and bursting the confines of time, the story names the ultimate separation: "So fine, so rare, coolly sunk beneath the surface the beam I sought always burnt behind the glass. Death was the glass; death was between us." Death comes between the narrator and the couple who died in her house hundreds of years before. Death—the fact and the fear of it—comes between any potential "us." It is the

frightening reflection in the glass. Of the ghostly couple who haunt the house, the wife died first, we learn. The bereaved husband first went north, east, and south—his wife, in the language of folklore, having gone west. But finally he returned to their house, where the narrator encounters them, joyfully reunited in each other. The reunion occurs in a structure that seems to be both a house and a body. For the most part, the "pulse of the house" beats regularly. It says, "Safe, safe, safe . . . the treasure buried." In this state the house merges with human factors, both dead and alive. It dissolves too into natural factors—the woodthrush and the rose, the wind and the trees. Death is thereby overcome. In the midst of all the activity, however, the narrator hears the pulse stop short. Until she can find the buried treasure, she is at the mercy of death. Happily, the ghostly couple, gazing down at the sleeping narrator and her husband, see that they have fallen asleep with "love upon their lips." The pulse of the house now beats strongly its message of perpetual security. The beam, in a sense, breaks through the glass. Waking, the narrator knows that the hidden treasure is "the light in the heart." The treasure is love. The story's title is ironic, for in this story all sorts of ghosts are laid to rest for the moment. (pp. 62-4)

Joanne Trautmann Banks, "Virginia Woolf and Katherine Mansfield," in The English Short Story, 1880-1945: A Critical History, *edited by Joseph M. Flora, Twayne Publishers, 1985, pp. 57-82.*

Walter J. Slatoff   (essay date 1985)

[*In the following excerpt, Slatoff explores what he considers the unhappy nature of Woolf's fictional narrator in "An Unwritten Novel" and posits that Woolf and the narrator are distanced from society, both preferring the company of their imagined characters over real people.*]

[**"An Unwritten Novel"**] is a story that will support a wide variety of interpretation and rumination, especially about its commentary on the relations between art and life, fiction and reality. It can, after all, be viewed as a story by a real author about a fictional author who is writing a novel about a woman with whom she is sharing a train compartment, a woman who is fictional to the first author and real to the second, whose fictional re-creation of her turns out to be incorrect—and so on. With enough ingenuity one could play the mirror images against one another in a way to dazzle oneself with one's own cleverness. Those who know Virginia Woolf's essay "Mr. Bennett and Mrs. Brown" may find it hard not to relate the story to the concerns she expresses there about the problems of character portrayal. And those who know her story **"The Looking Glass"** might wish to compare the two stories, particularly in relation to the way the two narrators react to their incorrect imaginings and to the change in the second narrator's feeling about her imaginative seizure— from an impatient sense that her "quarry" concealed so much that "one must prize her open with the first tool that came to hand—the imagination" to the view that such talk of " 'prizing her open' as if she were an oyster" is "impious and absurd."

What interests me most here, however, is the spaces between all the women, the ways both authors (Virginia Woolf and her fictional narrator) have accomplished their embraces from a distance, and the ways the other person (object?) is handled and mishandled. To some extent . . . , the story is playful, both in tone and plot, in many respects a traditional comedy. It is built on error that is corrected by a sudden reversal, and both characters achieve happy unions, the woman with her son, the narrator with her unknown figures and adorable world. But it has its darker side, one that I believe is not only the product of my own less than rose colored glasses.

The woman in the carriage looks to the narrator like "the most unhappy woman in the world." She seems to move her head with "infinite weariness." And she does suffer apparently from a highly visible and unpleasant twitch. She makes a small effort to close the distance between herself and the narrator by chatting "palely and colourlessly," but then subsides with a twitch into silence, which apparently lasts until they arrive at Eastbourne.

The narrator seems even less able to close the space between herself and the other passenger. At first she folds her newspaper into a " 'shield,' impervious even to life." Before she and the woman are left alone in the carriage, the other travelers in the compartment have left one by one except for one man. As the train enters the Three Bridges station, she wonders, "Was he going to leave us? I prayed both ways—I prayed last that he might stay." She apparently has nothing to say to her companion, whose conversation seems pale and colorless, except to prod her once with the phrase "sisters-in-law" in an effort to learn the reason for her unhappiness—not with any eye to give her sympathy, to say nothing of assistance, but because, as she puts it, "If there were a reason, and if I knew the reason, the stigma was removed from life."

When the woman does not respond, she leans back in her corner, shields her eyes from the woman's eyes and in her aloneness, like artists and lonely children do, she invents imaginary beings to occupy her thoughts. By such an act, she does, in one way, people her world and reduce her isolation; but in the very act, she at the same time lengthens the distance between herself and the flesh-and-blood (though fictionally so for us) woman who actually shares her compartment. One cannot even say that her imagining has been a kind of connection with that woman or valid act of sympathy or empathy, for as the story makes so patently clear, the Minnie she has invented is not the woman who has been sitting opposite to her. At the end of the story, the narrator is elated, full of readiness for new verbal embraces (of the incorrect sort we have just witnessed?); but she is still alone. No one seems to have met *her* at the station.

Not only is the narrator's connection with her imaginary figures greater than with her traveling companion, but she has greater sympathy and concern for them. She seems far more upset by the departure of Moggridge [an imagined character in the narrator's "novel"] or even of his wife ("that unborn [child] of the mind") from her life than she does by the departure of the woman. She is able to join and cheer for the fictive Minnie Marsh when she has imagined her into confronting her sister-in-law. But when her companion, whom she had thought perhaps one of the loneliest and unhappiest women in the world, turns out to be lucky enough to have a son to laugh with and walk down the road side by side with, she seems incapable even of a moment of pleasure for her, not even a glimmer of it. All she seems capable of feeling is distress at the dissolution of her imaginary figures and momentary collapse of her fictive world. When she does cheer up, there is still no sympathetic pleasure for the woman; the excitement is about the potentiality for creating and embracing new imaginary people.

In a way what I am doing here is absurd and unfair. Her quiet withdrawal when the woman refuses to tell her story is surely far better than Miss Lonelyhearts' response when he twists the arms of the old gentleman who refuses to tell his. Far better even if one thinks of her imaginings mostly as a form of voyeurism in which she is using the woman for purposes of emotional and intellectual self-excitation. I do not really wish her to be a Scobie, determined at all costs to be her sister's keeper. I do not even think she can be accused of turning "quite leisurely away from the disaster." But, at the same time, I have no satisfactory way of explaining to myself why the narrator, the author, and I myself have been permitted to move with quite so much ease, even pleasure, from an expression of unhappiness so great it seemed to announce the most unhappy woman in the world to the adoration of unknown figures in an "adorable world." It is possible that Virginia Woolf wants the reader to worry about this, but I do not think so. At the same time, however, I am not sure that I hope she did, for much about her life and death suggests those verbal embraces helped keep her alive so long as she was able to imagine them. (pp. 215-17)

Walter J. Slatoff, "The Lonely Embraces of Artists," in his The Look of Distance: Reflections on Suffering & Sympathy in Modern Literature—Auden to Agee, Whitman to Woolf, *Ohio State University Press, 1985, pp. 199-232.*

Susan Dick   (essay date 1987)

[*Dick is an American editor and critic who has edited several studies on Woolf, including* "To the Lighthouse": The Original Holograph Draft *(1982) and* The Complete Shorter Fiction of Virginia Woolf *(1985). In the following excerpt, Dick provides background for the genesis of Woolf's short story "A Society," discussing the work as a response to novelist William Bennett's and critic Desmond MacCarthy's public assertions of male intellectual superiority, and posits that "Woolf reflects in 'A Society' with striking immediacy the historical and cultural context in which [the story] was written."*]

Virginia Woolf's short story **"A Society"** was out of print for over sixty years. Written in 1920 and published in 1921 in ***Monday or Tuesday,*** Woolf's only collection of short stories, **"A Society"** was excluded by Leonard Woolf from ***A Haunted House and Other Short Stories*** (1944), the collection he published after her death in 1941, because, he explained, she had decided not to include it in the collection of stories she had proposed bringing out in 1942. I suspect that Virginia Woolf wished not to reprint **"A So-**

ciety" primarily for three reasons. First, unlike the other seven stories in **Monday or Tuesday,** "A Society" does not reflect the innovations she was making in narrative technique. It resembles *Night and Day* (1919), the long novel that she later called her "exercise in the conventional style" far more than it does the experimental works that surround it in the collection. Secondly, in 1940, when a new collection was being discussed, she probably felt that she had explored the feminist views presented in the story far more extensively and effectively in *A Room of One's Own* (1929) and *Three Guineas* (1938) than in this early story. A third reason may be that aspect of the story which, from our perspective, contributes enormously to its interest: the extent to which Woolf reflects in **"A Society"** with striking immediacy the historical and cultural context in which it was written. (p. 51)

My interest here is in the ways that Woolf uses in **"A Society"** specific historical events and draws upon contemporary art and literature in her portrayal of the inquiry undertaken by this society of young women. The story spans one of the most important decades in the twentieth century, 1909 to 1919. World War I, which is commemorated by a silent five-year hiatus in the story, grimly clarifies the implications of their discoveries. The cultural context in which her characters live is equally important, for it provides Woolf with the motive for her story and with a rich source of allusion and humor. (p. 52)

I suspect that one reason for the immediacy with which the historical and cultural context of **"A Society"** is presented stems from its having been conceived as a response to Arnold Bennett's book *Our Women: Chapters on the Sex Discord,* which received considerable attention in the press following its publication on September 23, 1920. On September 26, Woolf noted in her diary that she was considering "making up a paper upon Women, as a counterblast to Mr. Bennett's adverse views reported in the papers." These reports must not only have angered Woolf, but depressed her as well. The paragraph in which she contemplates her "counterblast" contains a moving description of a loss of self-confidence. She has been working steadily on *Jacob's Room* for two months, she notes, and T. S. Eliot's recent visit, during which he praised *Ulysses,* has left her "listless. . . . He said nothing—but I reflected how what I'm doing is probably being better done by Mr. Joyce." The same paragraph ends with the following comment: "Perhaps at the bottom of my mind, I feel that I'm distanced by L. [eonard] in every respect." A consideration of the effects of discouragement upon the mind of the female artist, a central topic in *A Room of One's Own,* will figure obliquely in **"A Society"** as well.

If she was at all hesitant to mount her "counterblast," Desmond MacCarthy's comments on Bennett's book in the *New Statesman* of October 2 clearly provided further incentive. Writing as "Affable Hawk" in his "Books in General" feature, MacCarthy devoted nearly two columns to *Our Women.* While he found some of Bennett's generalizations superficial, he agreed wholeheartedly with Bennett's assertion that "women are inferior to men in intellectual power, especially in that kind of power which is described as creative. Certainly," MacCarthy added, "that fact stares one in the face." At the end of his review, he mentioned two other books about women: Otto Weininger's *Sex and Character* and Orlo Williams' lighthearted

and condescending *The Good Englishwoman.* His brief summary of Weininger's distasteful book included the gratuitous information that Weininger, as well as two women who read his book, committed suicide.

The following week Virginia Woolf's response to this provocative review appeared in the *New Statesman.* In her letter Woolf takes issue with Bennett's and Affable Hawk's assumption that women are intellectually inferior to men and with their further conviction that neither education nor liberty will alter this fact. How "does Affable Hawk account for the fact which stares me, and I should have thought any other impartial observer, in the face," she asks, "that the seventeenth century produced more remarkable women than the sixteenth, the eighteenth than the seventeenth, and the nineteenth than all three put together?" The comparison of the advance in intellectual power of women with that of men is, she adds, "not in the least one that inclines me to suicide. . . . " She concludes her letter by suggesting that if Affable Hawk "sincerely wishes to discover a great poetess" he should consider Sappho. "Naturally," she says, "I cannot claim to know Greek as Mr. Bennett and Affable Hawk know it, but I have often been told that Sappho was a woman, and that Plato and Aristotle placed her with Homer and Archilochus among the greatest of their poets." She challenges Bennett or Affable Hawk to name fifty male poets who are Sappho's superiors. If they can do so, she promises "as an act of that submission which is so dear to my sex, not only to buy their works but, so far as my faculties allow, to learn them by heart."

Affable Hawk's response to Woolf's letter appeared beneath it. Not surprisingly, he remained unchanged in his views. . . . (pp. 52-4)

The questions [the group of women in **"A Society"**] set out to ask invert Bennett's and Affable Hawk's assumptions, for these women want to know if *men* have produced anything of high value. In her firmly controlled letters, Woolf makes no effort to disguise her vehement disagreement with Bennett and Affable Hawk. She uses an effective combination of direct statement, sarcasm, and ironic humor to express it. This exchange obviously made her aware of the kind of reception a story that explored these ideas would be given by male reviewers. Her decision to tell **"A Society"** from the point of view of Cassandra may reflect in part a desire to conceal herself behind the voice of another. While some of the characters are blunt in their judgments of the failures of men, Cassandra tends not to impose an evaluation on her report of the society's deliberations, but rather to let her readers draw their own conclusions about the discoveries the society makes.

The probable links between **"A Society"** and *Our Women* may also help to illuminate the special qualities of this story *as a story.* Its overt didactic thrust makes it unlike any other work of fiction that Virginia Woolf wrote. In its didacticism, its playfulness, its satirical view of contemporary society, and in its use of characters who are for the most part indistinguishable from one another and whose function it is to express ideas rather than personalities, **"A Society"** has affinities with the fable and the novel of ideas. It also resembles some of Woolf's own essays in which fictional situations serve as the occasion for the discussion of ideas. In particular, the narrative method of **"A Society"** anticipates that of *A Room of One's Own,* in which we are addressed by an "I" who insists that we think of her as fictional: "call me Mary Beton, Mary Seton, Mary Carmichael or by any name you please," she says, "it is not a matter of any importance," and in which this speaker's reflections on the place of women in society grow out of particular scenes and events. However, unlike *A Room of One's Own*, **"A Society"** does tell a story, and it tells it, as we shall see, by drawing on a variety of literary conventions.

In the opening scene of **"A Society,"** a group of young women, whom Woolf might later have called "the daughters of educated men," while "sitting one day after tea," begin "as usual to praise men." The subtle irony of Cassandra's casual phrase, "as usual," strikes the note heard throughout the story. These young women are about to begin questioning the "usual" assumptions of their society. In doing this, they are unknowingly enacting the process through which, according to Susanne K. Langer, new societies evolve. "Every society meets a new idea with its own concepts, its own tacit, fundamental way of seeing things; that is to say *with its own questions,* its peculiar curiosity." The heuristic process that begins here grows out of their curiosity about the extent to which the production of "good people and good books," which they assume to be the primary aim of life, is accomplished by men.

In this opening scene, Poll, who will inherit the fortune left her by her father only after she has read all the books in the London Library, challenges their complacent praise of men. " 'Books,' she cried, rising to her feet and speaking with an intensity of desolation which I shall never forget, 'are for the most part unutterably bad!' " To prove her point, she reads them some passages of prose and then of poetry. The "verbose, sentimental foolery" of some of the verses prompts one of them to say, " 'It must have been written by a woman.' " But her assumption, it turns out, is wrong. They have, as Poll ironically observes when Shakespeare, Milton, and Shelley are held up as examples of men who wrote good books, " 'been well taught.' " Thus the premise on which Woolf bases her story is that these young women know as little about the social, political, and artistic achievements of men as most men, to judge from Arnold Bennett and Affable Hawk, know about those of women. They are just beginning to realize that their assumptions are those of the patriarchal society they have grown up in; the society they now create among themselves will both expose those assumptions and challenge them.

Having established their "society for asking questions" and having resolved to bear no children until they have found some answers, they spend the next five years investigating men's achievements in the military, law, scholarship, painting, and literature. (pp. 54-6)

The somnolent judges at the law courts, the vast and sentimental Academy pictures, Oxbridge's sterile researches into the question of Sappho's chastity, all the inventions and institutions of men, fail to convince the women that men produce anything that proves their superiority. When they reach the subject of literature they again reflect the assumptions that Poll had challenged at the outset and that Bennett had put forth in *Our Women*. One member observes, " 'no woman has ever been an artist, has she Poll?' " Poll's response echoes Woolf's first letter to Affable Hawk. " 'Jane-Austen-Charlotte-Brontë-George-

Eliot,' cried Poll, like a man crying muffins in a back street." This impressive list fails to persuade Eleanor, as it failed to persuade Affable Hawk, and she quotes "from a weekly newspaper" a statement which is almost that of Affable Hawk: "Since Sappho there has been no female of first rate. . . ." Unable to agree about the past, they now turn to contemporary writers. Although Elizabeth has also taken to disguise and spent the last five years writing reviews as a man, she cannot evaluate the popular novelists. "Do they write good books?" they ask of Wells, Bennett, Compton Mackenzie, Stephen McKenna, and Hugh Walpole.

> "Good books?" she said, looking at the ceiling. "You must remember," she began, speaking with extreme rapidity, "that fiction is the mirror of life. And you can't deny that education is of the highest importance, and that it would be extremely annoying, if you found yourself alone at Brighton late at night, not to know which was best boarding house to stay at. . . ."
>
> "But what has that got to do with it?" we asked.
>
> "Nothing—nothing—nothing whatever," she replied.
>
> "Well, tell us the truth," we bade her.

And to this insistent demand Elizabeth must finally answer, " 'Oh, the truth . . . has nothing to do with literature.' " Elizabeth's desperate defense of the usefulness of these novels as guidebooks to rooming houses in seaside resorts may be a comic allusion to Arnold Bennett's novel *Hilda Lessways,* a portion of which is set in a Brighton boarding house. Also, Elizabeth's assumption that "truth" has nothing to do with literature, an assumption undoubtedly based on all the novels written by men that she has read, will be contradicted in **"Monday or Tuesday,"** the work that follows **"A Society"** in the collection, in which the narrator is engaged in a persistent, if oblique, search for "truth."

Elizabeth's failure to provide them with conclusive evidence about the modern writers is now forgotten as the cry " 'War! War! War!' " is heard from the street. Cassandra's report is deeply ironic: " 'What war?' we cried. 'What war?' We remembered, too late, that we had never thought of sending anyone to the House of Commons. We had forgotten all about it." This comment reminds us that in 1914 women could neither vote nor stand for election to Parliament. (pp. 56-8)

A five-year break now intervenes before the second and final part of the story begins, in June 1919, on the day of the signing of the Treaty of Peace. In the scene that opens this section, Cassandra and Castalia casually look through the society's old minute books and comment on how much their ideas have changed. " 'We are agreed,' Castalia quoted, reading over my shoulder, 'that it is the object of life to produce good people and good books.' We made no comment upon *that*," Cassandra notes. In the typescript of **"A Society,"** Cassandra's reply was originally less tentative: " '*That* was a bad shot wasn't it?' " Woolf typed and then canceled. After reading out the next sentence in the minutes—"A good man is at any rate honest, passionate and unworldly"—Cassandra says, " 'What a woman's language!' " Woolf's difficulties with this comment are revealed in the typescript. She had typed " 'Nobody but a woman could have written that' I observed." Above this she wrote and then canceled " 'That is a very feminine opinion,' I observed." These variants suggest that she was trying to reflect the biases contained in the assertion without making use of derogatory female stereotypes. Cassandra's comment in the published version is ambiguous for it places the emphasis on the language as much as on the opinion it expresses. Castalia is more direct. " 'What fools we were!' " she exclaims.

Castalia had in fact played a major role in changing one of their fundamental assumptions, for she had stunned the other members of the society by breaking their vow of chastity during her researches at Oxbridge and becoming pregnant. Her action provoked an amusing debate about chastity, which Poll decided was " 'nothing but ignorance—a most discreditable state of mind. We should admit only the unchaste to our society.' " At her suggestion they made Castalia the president of the society. Now Castalia worries about her daughter Ann who, despite Castalia's efforts to prevent her, has learned to read:

> "I caught Ann only yesterday with a newspaper in her hand and she was beginning to ask me if it was 'true.' Next she'll ask me whether Mr. Lloyd George is a good man, then whether Mr. Arnold Bennett is a good novelist, and finally whether I be-

Leonard and Virginia Woolf in 1939 in their home at 52 Tavistock Square, where they maintained the offices of the Hogarth Press.

lieve in God. How can I bring my daughter up to believe in nothing?" she asks.

Cassandra's suggestion (which could be taken straight out of *Our Women*) that Castalia " 'teach her to believe that a man's intellect is, and always will be, fundamentally superior to a woman's,' " seems intended to provoke Castalia's impassioned response: " 'Oh, Cassandra why do you torment me? Don't you know that our belief in man's intellect is the greatest fallacy of them all?' " Unless some way can be found, Castalia concludes, undoubtedly thinking of the war, to make men the bearers of children and thus give them an "innocent occupation . . . we shall perish beneath the fruits of their unbridled activity. . . . " (pp. 58-9)

While Cassandra and Castalia talk, they hear men in the street "crying hoarsely and wearily" that the Treaty of Peace has been signed. This passage, which associates Castalia's concern for her daughter's future and her denunciation of the fruits of men's intellect with the war and its aftermath, both foreshadows *Three Guineas* and echoes a statement Woolf makes in her first letter to Affable Hawk. "Thus," she says after outlining the obvious progress of women's achievements through the centuries, "though women have every reason to hope that the intellect of the male sex is steadily diminishing, it would be unwise, until they have more evidence than the great war and the great peace supply, to announce it as a fact." Cassandra now makes a second suggestion, which Castalia accepts. " 'Once she knows how to read,' " she says of Ann, " 'there's only one thing you can teach her to believe in— and that is herself.' " " 'Well,' " Castalia sardonically observes, " 'that would be a change.' " The story ends on an ironic note. They tell Ann, who is happily playing with her doll, that she has been chosen "President of the Society of the future—upon which she burst into tears," Cassandra adds, "poor little girl."

Cassandra's ironic tone does not disguise the serious implications of this ending. The deliberations of the original society were brought to an abrupt and premature end by the war. In now handing the society's minutes and its presidency over to her daughter, Ann, Castalia is establishing a matrilineal line of descent. Perhaps Ann and the society she forms will find a way, as the original society did not (for this was not their intention), to change their world and the men who control it.

The suggestion—and it is only that—that a matriarchal society could evolve to replace the bellicose patriarchal one is supplemented in the story by the richly allusive names Woolf gives her characters. The very range of names, from those with mythic, biblical, and literary associations, to those with more recent historical antecedents, to familiar pet names, suggests a long female tradition of which these women are a vital part. Woolf's use of allusive names contributes to her portrayal of the cultural context in which these women live and often enhances the playful, comic, even at times farcical, aspects of the story. "Be truthful," Woolf urges her audience of women in *A Room of One's Own*. "Comedy is bound to be enriched." While the characters are not developed in any detail—no descriptions of them are given—their names seem intended to function metaphorically and thus to add another level of meaning to the story. (pp. 59-60)

[One] can, given the nature of names, find allusions in all of [the characters in **"A Society"**]. Only the following four, however, seem to me to be especially suggestive within the context of Woolf's story. The first of these, Clorinda, who proposes that the women find out what the world is like before they have any children, has the name of the warlike pagan heroine in Tasso's epic poem, *Jerusalem Delivered.* The second, Judith, who proposes to dispense with prostitutes and to fertilize virgins by Act of Parliament, is the name of the biblical heroine who saved her beseiged town by entering the enemy camp disguised as a traitor and then cutting off the head of the commander, Holofernes, while he slept. Judith was celebrated for having achieved this heroic feat while also preserving her chastity. Judith is, in addition, the name Woolf gives in *A Room of One's Own* to Shakespeare's imaginary, gifted, and ill-fated sister who commits suicide after becoming pregnant with an illegitimate child. The third, Ruth, whose sarcastic observation that Sappho is a lewd invention of Professor Hobkin, whom Castalia observed in Oxbridge, is the name both of another biblical heroine and of the central character in Mrs. Gaskell's 1853 novel of that name whose trials include giving birth to an illegitimate son. And finally, the observation that men despise women too much to mind what they say is made by Jill, the name Bennett uses throughout *Our Women* (a detail Woolf would have known from Affable Hawk's column) in his exemplary domestic scenes featuring "Jack and Jill."

Significantly, none of the female characters in **"A Society"** has a surname. The surnames of two of the men questioned by the women, Lord Bunkum and Sir Harley Tightboots, recall the more ridiculous characters in Restoration comedies. Also, Sir Harley's Christian name brings to mind the famous (and for Woolf infamous) London street of doctors. (pp. 61-2)

A month before **Monday or Tuesday** was published, Woolf speculated in her diary about its critical reception. "And as for A Society," she imagined reviewers saying, "though spirited, it is too one-sided." Her prophecy was correct. Desmond MacCarthy, writing as Affable Hawk in the *New Statesman* on April 9, 1921, liked **Monday or Tuesday** on the whole, but noted that "when, as in '**A Society**,' she writes from contempt, her work is not her best" [see MacCarthy excerpt dated 1921]. Clive Bell later said (in *Dial,* December 1924) that **"A Society"** was "quite beneath her genius." However, a third critic, Harold Child, who was not a friend of Woolf's as the other two were, did see the playful side of her story. "And while the whole book is either humourous or witty," he wrote of **Monday or Tuesday** in his *TLS* review, "there is a thread of hearty, 'masculine' fun woven in with the shrewd and wicked wit of that very feminine (almost feminist) tale, '**A Society**,' which brings one to outright laughter." Child's cheerful use of sexual stereotypes is all too reminiscent of Woolf's earlier exchange with Affable Hawk. Not surprisingly, she found his review "complimentary enough, but quite unintelligent. I mean by that," she added, "they don't see that I'm after something interesting."

These hostile or condescending and imperceptive reviews invite us to consider one last name that has multiple associations, and that is "society" itself. For the title refers, as we have seen, both to the "society for asking questions"

which the women form and to the larger society which has shaped their lives. Woolf's reflections in *Three Guineas* on this second society are useful here. "The very word 'society,'" she observes, "sets tolling in memory the dismal bells of a harsh music: shall not, shall not, shall not. You shall not learn; you shall not earn; you shall not own. . . . Inevitably we look upon society, so kind to you, so harsh to us, as an ill-fitting form that distorts the truth; deforms the mind; fetters the will." This is the same society the "daughters of educated men" in **"A Society"** come, after their researches and the war, to see more clearly. And in the first sense, the society of women in Woolf's story can be seen as the ancestor of the Outsiders' Society that she proposes in *Three Guineas,* a society that will work "for our common ends—justice and equality and liberty for all men and women—outside your society," she tells her male correspondent, "not within." This may be, to return to Susanne K. Langer, the nucleus of the new society that could evolve out of the questions asked by these "outsiders." The new society will re-form, rather than cast off the old, just as Woolf in her allusive and playful story looks at the same world that men see, but sees it, as she says in *Three Guineas,* "through different eyes."

The compelling links between the societies of women envisioned in **"A Society"** and *Three Guineas* bring to mind the observation Woolf makes in *A Room of One's Own,* that "we think back through our mothers if we are women." Ann's tears at the end of the story suggest that this inheritance may not always be welcome or easy; but it contains, as all of Woolf's feminist writings prophesy, unlimited potential for good. (pp. 62-3)

Susan Dick, " 'What Fools We Were!': Virginia Woolf's 'A Society'," in Twentieth Century Literature, *Vol. 33, No. 1, Spring, 1987, pp. 51-66.*

John Oakland (essay date 1987)

[*In the following excerpt, Oakland examines "Kew Gardens," revealing a progression of formal and thematic patterns in which "random individual activity has been given coherence, order, and optimism."*]

[It] is salutary to re-examine, against a background of Woolf's literary principles, what is actually being said in ["**Kew Gardens**"], as well as how it is being said. For **"Kew Gardens"** is more than atmosphere, insubstantial impressionism or an experiment. Arguably, it is not an expression of meaningless life but, on the contrary, reveals a harmonious, organic optimism. The choice of such a short piece for close reading is appropriate, since it is perhaps more central to Woolf's fiction than has been generally accepted, and contains in embryo many of the issues of form, theme, content, character, plot and action which occupied her in all her work.

While these are, unfortunately, loaded terms in contemporary criticism, they are all symbiotically subsumed in Woolf's design under 'form', to include both technical and thematic concerns. So that theme was not merely the subject matter of a story, but more appropriately the essential significance of the total work revealed through its organisation. Although it has been frequently argued that Woolf's fiction lacks the traditional ideas of plot, action

and character, **"Kew Gardens"** can be very adequately analysed in these terms, while accepting that here they are
minimal and couched in special ways. Indeed, Woolf's
creative method is perhaps more conventional than has
been granted, and within it the old categories still operate.

Woolf herself was conscious of their inherent value in her
attempts to organise all the various aspects of form. Writing of the proposed composition of *Jacob's Room* (1922)
in words which reflect the already completed **"Kew Gardens"**, she remarks that:

> I'm a great deal happier . . . today than I was yes-
> terday having this afternoon arrived at some idea
> of a new form for a new novel. Suppose that one
> thing should open out of another—as in an unwrit-
> ten novel—only not for 10 pages, but 200 or so—
> doesn't that give the looseness and lightness that I
> want; doesn't that get closer and yet keep form and
> speed, and enclose everything, everything? . . . but
> conceive (?) **"Mark on the Wall,"** "K.G." [**"Kew
> Gardens"**], and **"Unwritten Novel"** taking hands
> and dancing in unity. What the unity shall be I have
> yet to discover; the theme is a blank to me; but I
> see immense possibilities in the form I hit upon
> more or less by chance two weeks ago.

These views show that Woolf did deliberately work in
terms of theme and form, that she was concerned to show
one thing opening out of another in good narrative fashion, and that this creative process should demonstrate a
thematic unity in the work, culminating in a final resolution. (pp. 264-65)

Woolf's search for a fictional form which would allow her
to communicate her particular view of life and the modern
consciousness was mainly expressed in her famous comments about the conventions of Edwardian literature. Life
was not 'a series of gig-lamps symmetrically arranged', but
a 'luminous halo' allowing the mind to receive 'an incessant shower of innumerable atoms', each differing in intensity, quality and duration, which created a particular identification at a specific moment in time. Once glimpsed, this
fleeting impression passes to be replaced by a succession
of others. While such views may seem inadequate psychology and involve a too passive conception of perception,
they do nevertheless reflect the framework in which
Woolf's fiction is set.

Although this emphasis upon the fragmented temporary
rendered by impressions and associations superficially
suggests passivity, many of Woolf's characters, even in a
short piece like **"Kew Gardens,"** do respond to stimuli and
assert themselves. Such reactions are part of a movement
towards a unified meaning, and also have an identifying
quality in the presentation of character over a period of
time. Terms such as space, perception, time, relativity and
subjectivity have been frequently used by critics to identify
Woolf's immediate fictional world, with a warning that
the vision is only transient. But **"Kew Gardens"** invites us
beyond the surface impressions to a larger, growing reality. It is significant that Woolf was very aware of December
1910 (the first London Exhibition of Post-Impressionist
Paintings) as being the date for a new consciousness. The
Exhibition proclaimed that the earlier Impressionism was
dead, and that Post-Impressionism would rescue the object from mere light and air by concentrating upon firmer
pictorial construction and interconnected form. In its

translation to fiction, this emphasis obviously implied
both an organic structure and a thematic centre beyond
impressions. These were the means to the end, not ends
in themselves, so that painting's representation in space
would be echoed in fiction's arrangment over time. (pp.
265-66)

[Woolf's] fiction initially focuses upon the characters' interior responses to associations. Implicit in this process,
as it is actually conveyed in works such as **"Kew Gardens,"** is both an acceptance of the temporariness and
fragmentation of the initial impressions, but also, in a
time-lapse continuum, a realisation of a continuing character identification composed collectively of these moments and the reactions to them, so that a wider version
of life and selfhood is promoted.

The initial impressions constitute the primary texture of
experience and awareness. The organisational function
then creates formal coherence and harmonious themes out
of the moments. **"Kew Gardens"** is structured to present
a series of points of view, authorial comment and descriptions, progressing from one experience to another by interlocking devices of association. The various stages of the
story appear to be very consciously planned in a formal
and thematic attempt to create order despite (or because
of) the fluid nature of the initial impressions.

In this process, the presentation of character through an
examination of individual consciousness is central to
Woolf's design. The characters in **"Kew Gardens"** may be
sketchy, but the story demonstrates that even the minimal
is composed of revelation in action, and that the apparently ordinary has significance. The characters do confront
experience in their individual ways, and are engaged in the
problems of choice, self-awareness and self-definition that
such a confrontation forces. There is enough information
in the character-presentation for the reader to analyse personality and theme. Surfaces are penetrated to reveal a
newer view of the characters' realities, as well as suggesting, in the unfolding plot, a shared experience and fate.

For, although Woolf is clearly the third person omniscient
narrator who reveals as much (or as little) as she wishes,
there is beyond her no one dominant character in terms
of point of view. Rather, the individual characters after
their various exposures (together with the narrator) make
up a collective theme-voice, which is progressively expanded through the episodes. The story additionally focuses on the natural background and non-human creatures to such an extent that they anthropomorphically become characters with lives and points of view of their own.
The snail, insects, butterflies, water-drops, flowers, buses,
an aeroplane, a thrush and the final voices are included
within an all-embracing thematic perspective. The cumulative theme-voice of **"Kew Gardens"** is composed of descriptions, fragmented conversations and interior monologues which all generalise character in a dramatically creative way that eventually leads to the universality of the
voices in the final paragraph.

This technique demonstrates the major process of **"Kew
Gardens,"** that of the gradual fusion of the human and the
non-human into an organic whole. Formally and thematically, one thing opens out of another and all experience is
fused into one reality. This theme, as some critics have
suggested, indicates that behind the diversity of people

and things there lies an essential oneness. More importantly for Woolf's later work, such an awareness represents
the kind of organicism which would be examined at greater length in *Jacob's Room, Mrs. Dalloway* (1925) and *The
Waves* (1931). . . . This particular kind of organicism,
however, does not so much indicate pantheism with its
postulation of a God, but rather a non-specific form of vi-
talism which, in spite of its vagueness, is nevertheless illustrated as the main thrust of **"Kew Gardens."**

While the initial revelations of the characters are shown
in fragmented isolation, the episodic structure demonstrates the growing commonality of these experiences and
develops significant patterns in the movement towards fusion. All the events share common elements such as the
flower bed and Kew Gardens, but also references to relationships, restrictions, desires, purpose, introspection,
consciousness and unconsciousness. From these roots rise
larger interconnected themes such as the nature and perception of time, memory and space, death, the quality of
understanding, the nature of love and personal relationships, the attraction and mystery of the unknown, linear
and lateral movement, and the urge to freedom beyond re-
straints. All the characters, human and non-human, share
to some degree in aspects of these various concerns.

There is nothing in the text to suggest that this qualitative
movement towards unity is anything but harmonious and
optimistic, and the tone is joyful rather than despairing.
The story does not show the meaninglessness and horror
of life, but a progress towards meaning, in much the same
way as the snail, far from being victimised, demonstrates
purpose and achievement. Each revelatory experience is
part of and contributes to a unified reality, and the fusing
processes, particularly that of human with non-human,
break down differentiation in the establishment of interrelated harmonies. (pp. 266-68)

The story's associational structures, changing and deepening in each episode, provide constant transitions from the
natural to the human and back again The catalysts for the
individual revelations in this linear progression are the
flower bed and Kew Gardens itself. All these experiences
and movements occur between the first and last paragraphs which form the 'book-ends' or the lyrical prose-
poetry of the events.

The description of the flower bed in the first paragraph,
with its erotic stalk imagery, references to 'heart-shaped
or tongue-shaped leaves', and the 'throats' of the flowers,
immediately connects the human and the natural worlds.
Within the latter there is an active aggressiveness of a
quasi-human type, with the conditioning influences of the
summer breeze, sun and light upon petals, the earth, peb-
bles, leaves and raindrops. The snail is similarly coloured
by the setting, and operates within the natural world in
terms of the problems it faces from lateral and linear
choices of movement. (p. 268)

The shifting mixture of a linear plot and lateral experiences, together with the circling of the dragonfly in this
episode and the continuing struggles of the snail, bring together, both formally and thematically, the two worlds.
Such descriptions do not serve merely for decorative or experimental effect, but indicate very conscious designs. Significantly, the fluctuating themes of purpose, introspection, consciousness and unconsciousness are also intro-

*Cover design by Vanessa Bell for Woolf's posthumously pub-
lished volume* The Haunted House, and Other Stories.

duced at this stage. For, while Simon strolls carelessly and
Eleanor bears on with greater determination, he ' . . .
kept this distance in front of the woman purposely, though
perhaps unconsciously, for he wished to go on with his
thoughts'.

In spite of its brevity, much happens to Simon and Eleanor
in this first human episode. They connect the past with the
present through associations of love and relationships,
which are additionally reflected by natural objects such as
the dragonfly and the waterlilies, by humans such as Lily
and the old grey-haired woman, and by inanimate objects
such as the silver shoe buckle and shoes. Fusion of these
elements is natural for Simon since ' . . . the whole of her
seemed to be in her shoe. And my love, my desire, were
in the dragonfly . . . '. Furthermore, the dragonfly in its
refusal to settle and confirm Lily's choice, maintains a
sense of perennial flux, just as Eleanor's marking the time
of the kiss with her watch is a continuous present and a
universal referent, ' . . . the mother of all my kisses in my
life'. Similarly, for Eleanor, past and present are joined in
common experiences and in the collection of other human
beings in Kew Gardens. 'Doesn't one always think of the
past, in a garden with men and women lying under the
trees? Aren't they one's past, all that remains of it, those

men and women, those ghosts lying under the trees . . . one's happiness, one's reality"? Such time and space references scattered throughout the story have structural and thematic parts to play in the unfolding theme of fusion, and are not simply superfluous. The consciousness of past and present, the dead and the living, in this first episode becomes more confused as the story progresses, when similar processes are repeated by other characters. This illustrates not only the gradual blurring sense of objective reality as against the power of association, but also the movements towards a fusion of elements in time and space.

The human interlude of Simon and Eleanor eventually shifts again into the natural world, as they walk past the flower bed ' . . . now walking four abreast, and soon diminished in size among the trees and looked half-transparent as the sunlight and shade swam over their backs in large trembling irregular patches'. The family's earlier haphazard progress has become almost military, and the irregularity passes to the natural world, under whose conditioning the human characters now fall in partial fusion. Their reduction in size and significance illustrates the joining of the two worlds, and also invites comparison with the snail's scene, to which the transition structure now returns.

In this episode, the snail is a link between human and natural, and possesses a linear identity which is different to that of 'the singular high stepping angular green insect', which is able to change direction at will. The snail is again briefly, like the family earlier, stained by the flowers before moving on, significantly now appearing to have a definite goal in front of it. It is faced by obstacles in its movement until its attempts are interrupted by the human. 'Before he had decided whether to circumvent the arched tent of a dead leaf or to breast it there came past the bed the feet of other human beings'. This episode illustrates not the snail's victim-status but its gradual immersion in the two worlds, its purposive manoeuvres, and its discovered possibility of choice between lateral and linear progression. (pp. 269-70)

[The] final paragraph of the story shows the apparent fusion of all in the common experience of Kew Gardens. The natural and the human worlds coincide in a unity which resolves all previous tentative approaches and haphazard movements. 'Thus one couple after another with much the same irregular and aimless movement passed the flower-bed and were enveloped in layer after layer of green blue vapour, in which at first their bodies had substance and a dash of colour, but later both substance and colour dissolved in the green-blue atmosphere'. Under the influence of the heat the irregular movements of the thrush and butterflies are conditioned into more orderly patterns, and eventually all the colours of the human and natural worlds are unified. 'Yellow and black, pink and snow white, shapes of all these colours, men, women, and children were spotted for a second upon the horizon, and then, seeing the breadth of yellow that lay upon the grass they wavered and sought shade beneath the trees, dissolving like drops of water in the yellow and green atmosphere, staining it faintly with red and blue'.

From this immersion voices rise, expressing contentment, desire and freshness of surprise, reaching beyond the purely material. But Kew Gardens is now only a microcosm of this process, for the fusing image is also applied to the adjacent city of London and its buses, ' . . . like a vast nest of Chinese boxes all of wrought steel turning ceaselessly one within another the city murmured; on the top of which the voices cried aloud and the petals of myriads of flowers flashed their colours into the air'. Beyond, ' . . . in the drone of the aeroplane the voice of the summer sky murmured its fierce soul', so that all the elements of the story, animate and inanimate, have been fused, and their sounds stretch beyond the earth to a further universal fusion and identification.

The Chinese box reference demonstrates precisely the main theme of **"Kew Gardens"** by showing the interconnection of objects, or a complex of boxes within boxes, the opening of which are presumably infinite. The story's progressive uncoverings have illustrated a greater reality and fusion at each step, so that, formally and thematically, random individual activity has been given coherence, order and optimism. (pp. 272-73)

John Oakland, "Virginia Woolf's 'Kew Gardens'," in English Studies, *Netherlands, Vol. 68, No. 3, June, 1987, pp. 264-73.*

Susan Dick (essay date 1989)

[*In the following excerpt, Dick analyzes the stories "The Lady in the Looking-Glass: A Reflection," "The Fascination of the Pool," and "Three Pictures" in relation to some of Woolf's longer works to explore her preoccupation with the elusive nature of storytelling.*]

In the final section of *The Waves,* Bernard, the vociferous story-teller, confronts the realization that "life is not susceptible perhaps to the treatment we give it when we try to tell it." In all of her fiction Virginia Woolf, like Bernard, is engaged in the process of "telling life." For Woolf, "life" means especially our perception of ourselves and of the world around us. The process of telling life involves the creation of stories that capture the multiple and elusive forms that life takes, and the challenging of these stories through insights, such as Bernard's, into their limitations. "I must tell you a story," he says to his silent dinner companion, "and there are so many . . . and none of them are true."

Woolf's sense of the resistance of life to a conventional telling persists from the beginning of her career to the end. "But she is trammelled by the limitations of the novel form," she wrote in a 1905 notice for the *Guardian* of Eleanor G. Hayden's *Rose of Lone Farm,* "and is at her best when she describes what she has seen and forgets the necessity of telling a story." (p. 162)

The tension between the need to tell stories, which as Peter Brooks has observed is central to our lives ("We live immersed in narrative," he writes, "recounting and reassessing the meaning of our past actions, anticipating the outcome of our future projects, situating ourselves at the intersection of several stories not yet completed"), and the recognition of the limitations of the stories we tell, of the elements of life that resist narration, is one of the dominant rhythms in *The Waves.* My interest in the discussion that follows is in the ways that Woolf explores some of the implications of this tension in three short fictions which she wrote immediately before she began the first draft of *The Waves:* **"The Lady in the Looking-Glass: A Reflec-**

tion," "The Fascination of the Pool," and "Three Pictures." In each of these works, the narrator attempts to tell herself the story of the scene she observes and in each that scene resists such a telling. These three works of short fiction are not only interesting in themselves, but when read within the context of her more familiar longer fictions (*The Waves* in particular), they can deepend our understanding of Woolf's special contribution to "the critique of story" which is a central preoccupation of many modern writers.

Before I turn to these three works, I would like to comment briefly on the relationship in the late twenties between Woolf's long and her short fiction. In September of 1926, when Woolf was about to finish *To the Lighthouse,* she noted in her diary, "As usual, side stories are sprouting in great variety as I wind this up: a book of characters; the whole string being pulled out from some simple sentence, like Clara Pater's, 'Don't you find that Barker's pins have no points to them?' " Clara Pater's statement is only slightly changed in the opening paragraph of **"Moments of Being: 'Slater's Pins Have No Points,' "** the narrative that grew out of her simple observation: " 'Slater's pins have no points—don't you always find that?' said Miss Craye, turning round as the rose fell out of Fanny Wilmot's dress, and Fanny stooped with her ears full of the music, to look for the pin on the floor." Miss Craye's unexpected comment gives Fanny an "extraordinary shock" and thus initiates the heuristic process of enquiry that makes up the narrative. As in **"An Unwritten Novel,"** the narrative traces the attempt of one character to tell herself the story of another. Fanny's role is also very like Lily Briscoe's in the first and third sections of *To the Lighthouse.* Like Lily, who attempts through her immediate impressions, her memories, and through imagined scenes to comprehend Mrs. Ramsay and the life that surrounds her, Fanny calls upon the same resources in her attempt to answer the question that Miss Craye's statement prompts: "What need had she of pins?"

"Moments of Being: 'Slater's Pins Have No Points' " was finished during the summer of 1927, and published in *Forum* in January of 1928. **"The Lady in the Looking-Glass"** was written in May of 1929. During the two-year interval that separates these works, Woolf conceived and wrote *Orlando* and *A Room of One's Own* and she gave a great deal of thought to *The Waves,* which by her account she began "seriously" in September of 1929. While **"Slater's Pins"** grew directly out of the writing of *To the Lighthouse,* Woolf's later short fictions, beginning with **"The Lady in the Looking-Glass,"** tend to be related less simply to her longer fictions. A reflection she made in her diary in March of 1927 illuminates the impulse behind many of these later short works. After recording "the conception last night between 12 & one of a new book," she writes: "For the truth is I feel the need of an escapade after these serious poetic experimental books whose form is always so closely considered. I want to kick up my heels & be off. I want to embody all those innumerable little ideas & tiny stories which flash into my mind at all seasons." In July of 1933, she wrote in the margin at this point, "Orlando leading to The Waves." In November of 1928, with *Orlando* finished and *The Waves* not yet begun, Woolf reflected again in a related passage on the impulses directing her writing.

Well but Orlando was the outcome of a perfectly definite, indeed overmastering impulse. I want fun. I want fantasy. I want (& this was serious) to give things their caricature value. . . . My notion is that there are offices to be discharged by talent for the relief of genius: meaning that one has the play side; the gift when it is mere gift, unapplied gift; & the gift when it is serious, going to business. And one relieves the other. . . .

I rather think the upshot will be books that relieve other books: a variety of styles & subjects: for after all, that is my temperament, I think.

It was through the writing of short fiction as well as long that Woolf would fulfil these prophecies. (pp. 162-64)

Woolf's desire to explore the potentialities of "caricature," to ignore, as John Graham has put it, "the complexity of the total object" by isolating only particular features of it, can be related not only to her movement away from the psychological novel, but also to her growing recognition in the late twenties of the importance in her work of what in "A Sketch of the Past" she would call "scene making." "I can make up situations," she wrote in her diary on 5 October 1927, "but I cannot make up plots. That is: if I pass the lame girl, I can without knowing I do it, instantly make up a scene: (now I cant think of one). This is the germ of such fictitious gift as I have." (pp. 164-65)

A similar attempt to solidify a vision into words lies behind the first short fiction I wish to discuss, **"The Lady in the Looking-Glass: A Reflection."** Two weeks after recording the graveyard scene and the death of the flying princess, Woolf reflected in her diary on the possibility of writing "outlines" of her friends which could form "the memoirs of one's own times during peoples lifetimes. . . . it should be," she added, "truthful; but fantastic." After naming the people she would include, she reflected, "How many little stories come into my head! For instance: Ethel Sands not looking at her letters. What this implies. One might write a book of short significant separate scenes. She did not open her letters." The first draft of **"The Lady in the Looking-Glass"** ends with the line, "Isabella did not open her letters." (p. 165)

Like **"An Unwritten Novel"** and " **'Slater's Pins Have No Points,' "** **"The Lady in the Looking-Glass"** presents one character's attempt to tell herself the story of another. The variations Woolf works on this familiar situation reflect some of the questions she was asking herself as she prepared to write *The Waves.*

One of these variations concerns the narrator. Although she speaks in the first person, she refers to herself (as she will again in **"The Fascination of the Pool"** and **"Three Pictures"**) as "one" rather than "I." "One could not help looking, that summer afternoon," she says in the opening paragraph, "in the long glass that hung outside in the hall." The use of the impersonal pronoun both distances the narrator from us and enhances her anonymity by subtly implying that she speaks as anyone, not as a distinct "I" and not as Virginia Woolf. The playful comments of the narrator of *A Room of One's Own* (who insists that she not be mistaken for Woolf) on the intrusive "I" that dominates the "new novel by Mr. A." may be associated with Woolf's avoidance of the egoistic "I" in these short works. (pp. 165-66)

A second variation concerns the function of the setting. The narrator of each of these three narratives, like that of **"An Unwritten Novel,"** is a stationary observer whose subject is close at hand. In **"An Unwritten Novel,"** as in **"Slater's Pins," "The Mark on the Wall," "Sympathy,"** and many other earlier works, the setting provides the narrative-present to which the narrator or narrating character's attention periodically returns after her excursions into remembered or imagined scenes. In these three later narratives, however, the setting is an integral part of the narrator's enquiry. In **"The Lady in the Looking-Glass,"** the looking-glass hanging in the hall, Isabella Tyson's house, furniture, and garden all appear, to the narrator's enquiring mind, to reflect their owner.

The narrator opens on a cautionary note—"People should not leave looking-glasses hanging in their rooms any more than they should leave open cheque books or letters confessing some hideous crime"—which she repeats at the end. She then illustrates the contrast between the mirror, a reflector of the scene around it, and the mind, a shaper of that scene, by recalling what she saw one summer afternoon as she sat alone in Isabella Tyson's drawing-room. As if to stress her anonymity, she claims that what she saw cannot be seen when "someone is looking": a room filled with "nocturnal creatures" who "came pirouetting across the floor, stepping delicately with high-lifted feet and spread tails and pecking allusive beaks as if they had been cranes or flocks of elegant flamingoes whose pink was faded, or peacocks whose trains were veined with silver." Like the fantastic scene that springs to life on Nurse Lugton's curtain (in Woolf's children's story of that name) once she falls asleep and then becomes fixed and inanimate when she awakes, the pirouetting creatures in the narrator's vision of the dining-room are contrasted to the still scene framed by the looking-glass in the hall. "It was a strange contrast," she observes, "all changing here, all stillness there." The narrative that follows this initial contrast between the fixed and changing scenes is the narrator's recreation of her attempt to "catch and turn into words" Isabella Tyson's "profounder state of being." The "reflection" in the title thus refers to the images the narrator sees in the looking-glass, to the process of her vision and, because like **"The Mark on the Wall"** this is a retrospective narrative, to her memory of that process.

The narrator begins her enquiry by playfully comparing Isabella Tyson to the convolvulus she imagines her to be cutting at the bottom of the garden. She quickly decides, however, that such comparisons are "cruel," for they come "between one's eyes and the truth." In rejecting her analogy, she initiates the process of continual revision to which she will subject her thoughts. She recalls here Lily Briscoe, who wanted to capture in her painting a perception of "the thing itself before it has been made anything," and anticipates Rhoda [in *The Waves*], who will ask, " 'Like' and 'like' and 'like'—but what is the thing that lies beneath the semblance of the thing?" Rejecting similes, the narrator next turns to facts, only to discover that the facts of Isabella Tyson's life do not reveal this truth either, nor does her room, although it may have the potential to do so. "Under the stress of thinking about Isabella," she recalls, "her room became more shadowy and symbolic; the corners seemed darker, the legs of chairs and tables more spindly and hieroglyphic."

This promising vision of the room as a text to be read is complicated unexpectedly by some letters dropped by the postman on the hall table. These interrupt the narrator's train of thought by destroying the fixed scene reflected in the looking-glass. She again asserts the mind's ability to order the world around it by accommodating these to her vision. "And, whether it was fancy or not," she says, "they seemed to have become not merely a handful of casual letters but to be tablets graven with eternal truth—if one could read them, one would know everything there was to know about Isabella, yes, and about life, too."

Since she cannot read these letters, any more than she can read Isabella's room, she will try to discover this "eternal truth" by using "the first tool that came to hand—the imagination." Again envisioning Isabella in the garden, the narrator decides that "she must be happy. She was rich; she was distinguished; she had many friends. . . . Avenues of pleasure radiated this way and that from where she stood with her scissors raised to cut the trembling branches while the lacy clouds veiled her face." The narrator is elaborating this vision of her friend's rich life when Isabella, like her letters before her, suddenly appears in the looking-glass. As the narrator looks at Isabella's reflection, she suddenly sees "the thing itself," or so she believes. The mirror, which had been a passive reflector before, now seems to unveil the true Isabella.

> At once the looking-glass began to pour over her a light that seemed to fix her; that seemed like some acid to bite off the unessential and superficial and to leave only the truth. It was an enthralling spectacle. Everything dropped from her—clouds, dress, basket, diamond—all that one had called the creeper and convolvulus. Here was the hard wall beneath. Here was the woman herself. She stood naked in that pitiless light. And there was nothing. Isabella was perfectly empty. She had no thoughts. She had no friends. She cared for nobody. As for her letters, they were all bills. Look, as she stood there, old and angular, veined and lined, with her high nose and her wrinkled neck, she did not even trouble to open them.

The definitive tone the narrator adopts as she describes this pitiless unveiling has led some readers to accept this final vision of Isabella Tyson as the "truth." But to interpret the passage in this way is to overlook the initial repetition of "seemed," and to forget that the "enthralling spectacle" so vividly described is itself yet another reading of the reflected scene. The narrator looks at Isabella Tyson in the mirror and believes that what she sees there is the reverse image of the character she had created in her mind: Isabella has no thoughts, friends, or affections. Her life, unlike her room, is empty.

It is possible, of course, that Woolf meant the sudden reversal at the end to be a comic revelation in which overstatement and exaggeration play their parts in the exploratory presentation of character as caricature. Yet the stark vision seen in the looking-glass is so chilling that it goes beyond comedy and anticipates the far more profound vision of "the world seen without a self" which Bernard describes near the end of *The Waves*. The light cast from the mirror has an effect similar to that of the eclipse: "The scene beneath me withered," Bernard recalls. "It was like the eclipse when the sun went out and left the earth, flourishing in full summer foliage, withered, brittle, false."

Under the influence of this vision, everything in Bernard's life, including his friends, was reduced to a " 'dust dance. . . . I, carrying a notebook, making phrases, had recorded mere changes; a shadow, I had been sedulous to take note of shadows' ". Both instances record a sudden disillusionment, a failure of belief in the story being told, which takes the form of an absence of meaning. Thus while Isabella Tyson acts as the catalyst for the narrator's final vision of her as "perfectly empty," she is not its real subject. The narrator has attempted to tell herself the story of her friend's life and she has decided in the end, as Bernard does in a more profound way, that there is no story to tell.

Woolf's narrator concludes with this negative vision and, as we have seen, repeats as her final line the warning with which she began. The mirroring of the beginning in the ending, a device Woolf had used in **"Slater's Pins"** and would use again in **"The Fascination of the Pool"** and **"Three Pictures,"** has the effect of bringing the narrative to a firm conclusion while simultaneously taking the reader's mind back to its opening and initiating the heuristic process again. Thus a subtle cyclical pattern is suggested which works in counterpoint to the closure imposed by the stark final vision [see Fleishman excerpt dated 1980]. (pp. 166-69)

I would like to return for a moment to Woolf's diary entry of 28 May 1929. After noting that she was writing a "little sketch" every morning to amuse herself, she added, "I am not saying, I might say, that these sketches have any relevance. I am not trying to tell a story. Yet perhaps it might be done in that way. A mind thinking. They might be islands of light—islands in the stream that I am trying to convey: life itself going on." Like **"The Lady in the Looking-Glass," "The Fascination of the Pool,"** which she typed, if not wrote, on 29 May, traces "a mind thinking." Instead of thinking about another person and trying to tell that person's story, however, the anonymous "one" of the second sketch is thinking about "life itself going on" as she sits looking at a pool and listening to the voices of the figures who rise to its surface.

The pool functions as both a mirror and a window. Initially the narrator's attention is caught by the reflection of a sign in the surface of the pool. As she watches this, she becomes aware of something else. "But if one sat down among the rushes and watched the pool—pools have some curious fascination, one knows not what—the red and black letters and the white paper seemed to lie very thinly on the surface, while beneath went on some profound under-water life like the brooding, the ruminating of a mind." The figures who appear near the surface of the water and briefly speak confirm the narrator's belief that the pool contains "in a liquid state" the thoughts of the many people who must have come to it "asking it some question, as one did oneself this summer evening." The speakers evoke a series of brief scenes from the past as each describes the occasion when he or she visited the pool. These adumbrate stories which the narrator makes no attempt to tell. One voice remains suggestively anonymous and faceless, and only its words, "Alas, alas," are audible.

The narrator does not say what questions she has asked at the pool, but her effort to hear what more the voice who says "alas," whom she refers to in a cancelled passage as

"the seer," will say implies that it is a question that will remain unanswered. "All the voices slipped gently away to the side of the pool," she observes, "to listen to the voice which so sad it seemed—it must surely know the reason of all this. For they all wished to know." Not only does that voice offer no explanation for "all this," but the narrator now becomes aware that beneath it "There was always another face, another voice." This voice remains inaudible.

The narrator uses a metaphor which Bernard too will use to describe her failure to hear what this voice says and thus to obtain, as she believes, an inclusive vision. "For though there are moments when a spoon seems about to lift all of us," she observes, "and our thoughts and longings and questions and confessions and disillusions into the light of day, somehow the spoon always slips beneath and we flow back again over the edge into the pool." After describing the "rushing stream of broken dreams, nursery rhymes, street cries," and other debris of the inner life that give the lie to our pretense that life is an "orderly and military progress," Bernard adds, "There is nothing one can fish up in a spoon; nothing one can call an event."

This passage is only one example of the "relevance" of **"The Fascination of the Pool"** to *The Waves,* despite Woolf's claim to the contrary. In the early pages of the first draft of *The Waves,* Woolf was looking for a way to tell "the story of the world from the beginning. I am not

In the upstairs sitting room in Monks House at Rodmell, the country home Virginia and Leonard purchased to escape from their busy life in London.

concerned with the single life," she wrote, "but with lives together. I . . . am trying to find, in the folds of the past . . . such fragments as time having broken the . . . perfect vessel . . . still keeps safe." The "lonely mind" that attempts to make a whole out of these fragments seems closely related to the narrator in the sketch as well as to the pool, which contains fragments of the past in the form of faces and voices and which she describes as the "ruminating mind . . . The water, always a deeply resonant symbol in Woolf's work, contains not only the past, but the present and the future as well.

Like **"The Lady in the Looking-Glass"** and many of Woolf's other short fictions, **"The Fascination of the Pool"** is given an internal rhythm by the narrator's shifts of attention. The reflection of the sign on the surface of the pool, which initiates her train of thought, is mentioned in the middle of the narrative—"A girl; we used to come down from the farm (the placard of its sale was reflected on the top of the water)"—and again at the end. These brief references to the surface reflection, like the intrusions of movement into the still scene in the looking-glass in the previous narrative, punctuate and check the narrator's expanding vision. Both narratives end soon after the narrator has encountered an obstacle to that vision and both close with a passage that mirrors the opening. As we shall see, Woolf will experiment with a similar narrative pattern in the third sketch.

It seems likely that **"Three Pictures,"** which according to Leonard Woolf was written in June of 1929, is another of the sketches Woolf wrote while she was planning *The Waves.* Like the two preceding sketches, this one also opens by drawing the reader's attention to an act of perception: "One could not help looking . . . " (**"The Lady in the Looking-Glass"**); "one could not see to the bottom of it" (**"The Fascination of the Pool"**); "It is impossible that one should not see pictures . . . " (**"Three Pictures"**). Further, the narrator of **"Three Pictures,"** like the narrators of the previous two sketches, uses a variant of the mirror/window motif as she enacts in a retrospective narrative her attempt to tell the story of the scene she perceives.

The division of **"Three Pictures"** into three distinct sections recalls the three-part structure of **"In the Orchard."** In this later work, however, the three scenes occur serially, rather than simultaneously; further, each succeeding scene challenges the one that went before it. Thus the process of vision and revision animates and shapes the progress of this narrative as it does **"The Lady in the Looking-Glass."**

According to the narrator, two assumptions underlie the story-telling impulse, which in this sketch takes the form of "scene making." The first is that we all impose a confining "frame" on people whose lives are distant from our own which prevents us from seeing the other except as a picture. The second assumption, which, she says, follows naturally from the first, is that we "are quite wrong in our judgments no doubt, but that is inevitable." After offering this pessimistic assessment of our ability to perceive others clearly, the narrator presents "The First Picture," a scene she glimpsed at the turn of the road, composed and framed in her mind as a picture, and grandly named "The Sailor's Homecoming." Her memory of this touching scene of a young man's happy reunion with his wife and friends be-

came a source of comfort. "There was something wholesome and satisfactory in the sight of such happiness," she recalls, "life seemed sweeter and more enviable than before." She extends the picture into narrative by imagining further scenes of domestic bliss: "The imagination supplied other pictures springing from that first one, a picture of the sailor cutting firewood, drawing water; and they talked about China; and the girl set his present on the chimney piece where everyone who came could see it."

The movement of **"Three Pictures"** recalls that of "Time Passes," the middle section of *To the Lighthouse,* in which a vision of the natural world as harmonious and benign is juxtaposed to events that challenge that vision: the deaths of the three Ramsays, the dull thud of exploding bombs, the chaos of unreason that boils beneath the surface calm. The cry that awakens the narrator in "The Second Picture" recalls both the "ominous sounds" in "Time Passes" and the "terrible sexless inarticulate voice" that rings out at the end of Woolf's earlier story, **"A Summing Up."** This cry, like the earlier one, seems beyond interpretation, a sound for which no analogy exists. "There was nothing to connect it with," the narrator of **"Three Pictures"** recalls, "No picture of any sort came to interpret it, to make it intelligible to the mind." This may be a nightmare variant of the other "voice" which the narrator of **"The Fascination of the Pool"** senses but cannot hear. The emptiness that follows the cry is finally filled by the "second picture," an "obscure human form, almost without shape, raising a gigantic arm in vain against some overwhelming iniquity," a vision which again recalls "Time Passes" and which originates in no scene, but, like the life-stories of Isabella Tyson, exists only in the narrator's imagination.

Like a dream that infiltrates one's day, the memory of this cry now alters the narrator's perception of the scene around her and challenges the comforting lesson of the first picture. "This goodness, this safety were only on the surface," she acknowledges. To escape from these thoughts, she tells over to herself the scene of the sailor's homecoming, "so that one picture after another of happiness and satisfaction might be laid over that unrest, that hideous cry, until it was crushed and silenced by their pressure out of existence."

While in this complacent state of mind she comes upon the third picture, a man digging a grave while his wife and children picnic nearby. The narrator does not interpret the scene as Woolf did when she recorded its original (as "A graveyard scene") in her diary: "They were having tea," she wrote, "& dressed in their reds & blue looked more like a picture, by Millais, or some other Victorian, of life & death, youth & the grave, than any real sight. It was quite unconscious; yet the most deliberate picture making; hence, unreal, sentimental, overdone." Since she assumes that Mrs. Avery and her children had not posed themselves beside the grave, her final comments must refer to her own reading of the scene. Ironically, the scene contributes too much to its own telling. When she recreates this picture in her narrative, she suggests that her narrator sees it as she did, but that, unlike Woolf, she is pleased by its overt symbolism.

The irony here is at the narrator's expense, for her discovery that the grave being dug so picturesquely is for the sailor whose homecoming she has made talismanic, will force a new reading of the scene. This sudden inversion of a story of happiness and security recalls that at the close of **"The Lady in the Looking-Glass."** In this sketch, however, the narrator ends her narration before she revises her story. Indeed, her final exclamation—"What a picture it made!"—hands the task of interpretation over to the reader. This abrupt ending, which may strike us as glib, as one of the "smart endings" Woolf noted her dissatisfaction with, enables her to withdraw her narrator from the scene and to let its meaning emerge from its narrative context, rather than be imposed upon it by the narrator. Her silence in the face of this third picture may indicate a new distrust of interpretation, a recognition of the limitations of story-telling which again foreshadows Bernard's discovery of this in *The Waves*.

The failure of the narrator of each of these short fictions to tell herself the story of the scene she observes becomes the story that she tells. The reader's attention is focused finally not on Isabella Tyson, the shadowy figures in the pool, or the sailor's homecoming—the materials of conventional stories—but on the narrator's attempt to shape those materials into a story and on the silence which accompanies her failure to do so.

In the works that follow these three sketches and *The Waves*, Woolf would continue to explore the role of the story-teller. I would like to close by quoting some reflections she makes on this subject in the earlier typescript draft of her last book, *Between the Acts*. In this early version of the description of the empty dining-room at Pointz Hall, she is drawing a distinction between the novelist, who "all agree, must tell a story," and the "nameless spirit . . . who is not 'we' nor 'I,' nor the novelist either." It is this spirit who notes the silence and the emptiness of the dining-room. "What name is to be given to that which notes that a room is empty?" the narrator asks. This nameless spirit, whom near the end of the passage she calls "this being," is the narrator who has escaped the limitations imposed on the novelist: "this spirit is not concerned to follow lovers to the altar, nor to cut chapter from chapter; and write as novelists do 'The End' with a flourish; since there is no end." (pp. 170-74)

While the narrators of the three short fictions I have been discussing are cast in the role of story-tellers, they also have some affinities with the other narrator Woolf experiments with in "Time Passes" and the interludes in *The Waves*, and describes in the *Pointz Hall* passage. In her ability to see the fantastic scene which she claims is enacted in Isabella's room only when there is no one there to see it, the narrator of **"The Lady in the Looking-Glass"** resembles the narrator of "Time Passes" and the "nameless spirit" of the *Pointz Hall* passage. The voice the narrator of **"The Fascination of the Pool"** strains to hear but cannot foreshadows even more closely this mysterious "being" who is "nameless, yet partakes of all things named." The elusive "third voice" heard in *Between the Acts* and described in "A Sketch of the Past" as one of the "things we have no words for" seems also to be closely related to this earlier figure. Finally, the pictures the narrator of **"Three Pictures"** makes out of the scenes she encounters are (as she predicted they would be) as false to life as are the chapters and flourishing closing words "The End" that novelists use to shape their stories. "But if there are no stories," Bernard wonders, "what end can there be or what beginning?"

There *are* stories, of course, as Bernard also acknowledges, for we live in the sequences of time and know our lives, however, haphazardly, as a medley of stories. What Woolf continually draws to our attention, however, as these three short fictions illustrate, is the fictive nature of these stories, the processes by which we tell them to ourselves, and the presence beyond their beginnings and endings of "another voice." This voice eludes such a telling, but in privileged moments we may be able to hear it speak. (p. 175)

> *Susan Dick, "'I Am Not Trying to Tell a Story': Three Short Fictions by Virginia Woolf," in* English Studies in Canada, *Vol. XV, No. 2, June, 1989, pp. 162-77.*

FURTHER READING

Barzilai, Shuli. "Virginia Woolf's Pursuit of Truth: 'Monday or Tuesday,' 'Moments of Being,' and 'The Lady in the Looking-Glass'." *The Journal of Narrative Technique* 18, No. 3 (Fall 1988): 199-210
  Explores ways in which Woolf attempted to impart truth through the act of composition and the delineation of character from multiple perspectives.

Bell, Quentin. *Virginia Woolf: A Biography.* New York: Harcourt Brace Jovanovich, 1972, 314 p.
  Standard biography written by Woolf's nephew.

Bishop, Edward L. "Pursuing 'It' through 'Kew Gardens'." *Studies in Short Fiction* 19, No. 3 (Summer 1982): 269-75.
  Analyzes Woolf's evocative use of language and atmosphere in "Kew Gardens."

Daiches, David. *Virginia Woolf.* Norfolk, Conn.: New Direction Books, 1942, 169 p.
  Appreciative critical biography.

de Araujo, Victor. "'A Haunted House'—the Shattered Glass." *Studies in Short Fiction* III, No. 2 (Winter 1966): 157-64.
  Examines "A Haunted House" as an "allegory of the creative imagination" in which insight and truth are best revealed through the unconscious.

DeSalvo, Louise. *Virginia Woolf: The Impact of Childhood Sexual Abuse on Her Life and Work.* Boston: Beacon Press, 1989, 372 p.
  Study of Woolf's life and work within the context of Victorian society, illuminating the darker side of Woolf's childhood during which she endured sexual abuse.

Fox, Stephen D. "'An Unwritten Novel' and a Hidden Protagonist." *Virginia Woolf Quarterly* 1, No. 4 (Summer 1973): 69-77.
  Posits that the protagonist in Woolf's short story "An Unwritten Novel" is the narrator.

Gorsky, Susan Rubinow. *Virginia Woolf.* Rev. ed. Boston: Twayne Publishers, 1989, 150 p.
  Critical biography. Gorsky writes in her introduction:

"This book provides a unified introduction to Virginia Woolf as human being, literary and social theoretician representative of modernism, and especially fiction writer."

Hafley, James. "Virginia Woolf's Narrators and the Art of 'Life Itself'." In *Virginia Woolf: Revaluation and Continuity,* edited by Ralph Freedman, pp. 29-43. Berkeley and Los Angeles: University of California Press, 1980.
Discusses narrative voice in Woolf's writings, focusing on stories collected in *Monday or Tuesday.*

Kenney, Susan M., and Kenney, Edwin J., Jr. "Virginia Woolf and the Art of Madness." *The Massachusetts Review,* XXIII, No. 1 (Spring 1982): 161-85.
Draws upon Woolf's autobiographical essays, letters, and diaries as well as Leonard Woolf's autobiography to discern a reciprocal nature between Woolf's madness and her artistic vision.

Rice, Thomas Jackson. *Virginia Woolf: A Guide to Research.* New York: Garland Publishing, 1984, 258 p.
Extensive annotated bibliography.

Rosenthal, Michael. "Jacob's Room." In his *Virginia Woolf,* pp. 75-86. New York: Columbia University Press, 1979.
In a chapter mainly devoted to discussion of Woolf's novel *Jacob's Room,* Rosenthal emphasizes the importance of "The Mark on the Wall," "Kew Gardens," and "An Unwritten Novel" as experimental stories that freed Woolf from Edwardian conventions.

Saunders, Judith P. "Mortal Stain: Literary Allusion and Female Sexuality in 'Mrs. Dalloway in Bond Street'." *Studies in Short Fiction* 15, No. 2 (Spring 1978): 139-44.
Maintains that allusions to Shelley's *Adonais* in Woolf's short story "Mrs. Dalloway in Bond Street" "serve as organizing metaphor and running refrain in [the protagonist's] elegy for her living, female self."

Appendix:

Select Bibliography of General Sources on Short Fiction

BOOKS OF CRITICISM

Allen, Walter. *The Short Story in English.* New York: Oxford University Press, 1981, 413 p.

Aycock, Wendell M., ed. *The Teller and the Tale: Aspects of the Short Story* (Proceedings of the Comparative Literature Symposium, Texas Tech University, Volume XIII). Lubbock: Texas Tech Press, 1982, 156 p.

Bates, H. E. *The Modern Short Story: A Critical Survey.* Boston: Writer, 1941, 231 p.

Bayley, John. *The Short Story: Henry James to Elizabeth Bowen.* Great Britain: The Harvester Press Limited, 1988, 197 p.

Bennett, E. K. *A History of the German Novelle: From Goethe to Thomas Mann.* Cambridge: At the University Press, 1934, 296 p.

Bone, Robert. *Down Home: A History of Afro-American Short Fiction from Its Beginning to the End of the Harlem Renaissance.* Rev. ed. New York: Columbia University Press, 1988, 350 p.

Bruck, Peter. *The Black American Short Story in the Twentieth Century: A Collection of Critical Essays.* Amsterdam: B. R. Grüner Publishing Co., 1977, 209 p.

Burnett, Whit, and Burnett, Hallie. *The Modern Short Story in the Making.* New York: Hawthorn Books, 1964, 405 p.

Canby, Henry Seidel. *The Short Story in English.* New York: Henry Holt and Co., 1909, 386 p.

Current-García, Eugene. *The American Short Story before 1850: A Critical History.* Twayne's Critical History of the Short Story, edited by William Peden. Boston: Twayne Publishers, 1985, 168 p.

Flora, Joseph M., ed. *The English Short Story, 1880-1945: A Critical History.* Twayne's Critical History of the Short Story, edited by William Peden. Boston: Twayne Publishers, 1985, 215 p.

Foster, David William. *Studies in the Contemporary Spanish-American Short Story.* Columbia, Mo.: University of Missouri Press, 1979, 126 p.

George, Albert J. *Short Fiction in France, 1800-1850.* Syracuse, N.Y.: Syracuse University Press, 1964, 245 p.

Gerlach, John. *Toward an End: Closure and Structure in the American Short Story.* University, Ala.: The University of Alabama Press, 1985, 193 p.

Hankin, Cherry, ed. *Critical Essays on the New Zealand Short Story.* Auckland: Heinemann Publishers, 1982, 186 p.

Hanson, Clare, ed. *Re-Reading the Short Story.* London: MacMillan Press, 1989, 137 p.

Harris, Wendell V. *British Short Fiction in the Nineteenth Century.* Detroit: Wayne State University Press, 1979, 209 p.

Kilroy, James F., ed. *The Irish Short Story: A Critical History.* Twayne's Critical History of the Short Story, edited by William Peden. Boston: Twayne Publishers, 1984, 251 p.

Lee, A. Robert. *The Nineteenth-Century American Short Story.* Totowa, N. J.: Vision / Barnes & Noble, 1986, 196 p.

Leibowitz, Judith. *Narrative Purpose in the Novella.* The Hague: Mouton, 1974, 137 p.

Lohafer, Susan. *Coming to Terms with the Short Story.* Baton Rouge: Louisiana State University Press, 1983, 171 p.

Lohafer, Susan, and Clarey, Jo Ellyn. *Short Story Theory at a Crossroads.* Baton Rouge: Louisiana State University Press, 1989, 352 p.

Mann, Susan Garland. *The Short Story Cycle: A Genre Companion and Reference Guide.* New York: Greenwood Press, 1989, 228 p.

Matthews, Brander. *The Philosophy of the Short Story.* New York: Longmans, Green and Co., 1901, 83 p.

May, Charles E., ed. *Short Story Theories.* Athens, Oh.: Ohio University Press, 1976, 251 p.

McClave, Heather, ed. *Women Writers of the Short Story: A Collection of Critical Essays.* Englewood Cliffs, N. J.: Prentice-Hall, 1980, 171 p.

Moser, Charles, ed. *The Russian Short Story: A Critical History.* Twayne's Critical History of the Short Story, edited by William Peden. Boston: Twayne Publishers, 1986, 232 p.

New, W. H. *Dreams of Speech and Violence: The Art of the Short Story in Canada and New Zealand.* Toronto: The University of Toronto Press, 1987, 302 p.

Newman, Frances. *The Short Story's Mutations: From Petronius to Paul Morand.* New York: B. W. Huebsch, 1925, 332 p.

O'Connor, Frank. *The Lonely Voice: A Study of the Short Story.* Cleveland: World Publishing Co., 1963, 220 p.

O'Faolain, Sean. *The Short Story.* New York: Devin-Adair Co., 1951, 370 p.

Orel, Harold. *The Victorian Short Story: Development and Triumph of a Literary Genre.* Cambridge: Cambridge University Press, 1986, 213 p.

O'Toole, L. Michael. *Structure, Style and Interpretation in the Russian Short Story.* New Haven: Yale University Press, 1982, 272 p.

Pattee, Fred Lewis. *The Development of the American Short Story: An Historical Survey.* New York: Harper and Brothers Publishers, 1923, 388 p.

Peden, Margaret Sayers, ed. *The Latin American Short Story: A Critical History.* Twayne's Critical History of the Short Story, edited by William Peden. Boston: Twayne Publishers, 1983, 160 p.

Peden, William. *The American Short Story: Continuity and Change, 1940-1975.* Rev. ed. Boston: Houghton Mifflin Co., 1975, 215 p.

Reid, Ian. *The Short Story.* The Critical Idiom, edited by John D. Jump. London: Methuen and Co., 1977, 76 p.

Rhode, Robert D. *Setting in the American Short Story of Local Color, 1865-1900.* The Hague: Mouton, 1975, 189 p.

Rohrberger, Mary. *Hawthorne and the Modern Short Story: A Study in Genre.* The Hague: Mouton and Co., 1966, 148 p.

Shaw, Valerie, *The Short Story: A Critical Introduction.* London: Longman, 1983, 294 p.

Stevick, Philip, ed. *The American Short Story, 1900-1945: A Critical History.* Twayne's Critical History of the Short Story, edited by William Peden, Boston: Twayne Publishers, 1984, 209 p.

Summers, Hollis, ed. *Discussion of the Short Story.* Boston: D. C. Heath and Co., 1963, 118 p.

Vannatta, Dennis, ed. *The English Short Story, 1945-1980: A Critical History.* Twayne's Critical History of the Short Story, edited by William Peden. Boston: Twayne Publishers, 1985, 206 p.

Voss, Arthur. *The American Short Story: A Critical Survey.* Norman, Okla.: University of Oklahoma Press, 1973, 399 p.

Ward, Alfred C. *Aspects of the Modern Short Story: English and American.* London: University of London Press, 1924, 307 p.

Weaver, Gordon, ed. *The American Short Story, 1945-1980: A Critical History.* Twayne's Critical History of the Short Story, edited by William Peden. Boston: Twayne Publishers, 1983, 150 p.

West, Ray B., Jr. *The Short Story in America, 1900-1950.* Chicago: Henry Regnery Co., 1952, 147 p.

Williams, Blanche Colton. *Our Short Story Writers.* New York: Moffat, Yard and Co., 1920, 357 p.

Wright, Austin McGiffert. *The American Short Story in the Twenties.* Chicago: University of Chicago Press, 1961, 425 p.

CRITICAL ANTHOLOGIES

Atkinson, W. Patterson, ed. *The Short-Story.* Boston: Allyn and Bacon, 1923, 317 p.

Baldwin, Charles Sears, ed. *American Short Stories.* New York: Longmans, Green and Co., 1904, 333 p.

Current-García, Eugene, and Patrick, Walton R., eds. *American Short Stories: 1820 to the Present.* Key Editions, edited by John C. Gerber. Chicago: Scott, Foresman and Co., 1952, 633 p.

Fagin, N. Bryllion, ed. *America through the Short Story.* Boston: Little, Brown, and Co., 1936, 508 p.

Frakes, James R., and Traschen, Isadore, eds. *Short Fiction: A Critical Collection.* Prentice-Hall English Literature Series, edited by Maynard Mack. Englewood Cliffs, N.J.: Prentice-Hall, 1959, 459 p.

Gordon, Caroline, and Tate, Allen, eds. *The House of Fiction: An Anthology of the Short Story with Commentary.* Rev. ed. New York: Charles Scribner's Sons, 1960, 469 p.

Greet, T. Y., et. al. *The Worlds of Fiction: Stories in Context.* Boston: Houghton Mifflin Co., 1964, 429 p.

Gullason, Thomas A., and Caspar, Leonard, eds. *The World of Short Fiction: An International Collection.* New York: Harper and Row, 1962, 548 p.

Havighurst, Walter, ed. *Masters of the Modern Short Story.* New York: Harcourt, Brace and Co., 1945, 538 p.

Litz, A. Walton, ed. *Major American Short Stories.* New York: Oxford University Press, 1975, 823 p.

Matthews, Brander, ed. *The Short-Story: Specimens Illustrating Its Development.* New York: American Book Co., 1907, 399 p.

Menton, Seymour, ed. *The Spanish American Short Story: A Critical Anthology.* Berkeley and Los Angeles: University of California Press, 1980, 496 p.

Mzamane, Mbulelo Vizikhungo, ed. *Hungry Flames, and Other Black South African Short Stories.* Longman African Classics. Essex: Longman, 1986, 162 p.

Schorer, Mark, ed. *The Short Story: A Critical Anthology.* Rev. ed. Prentice-Hall English Literature Series, edited by Maynard Mack. Englewood Cliffs, N. J.: Prentice-Hall, 1967, 459 p.

Simpson, Claude M., ed. *The Local Colorists: American Short Stories, 1857-1900.* New York: Harper and Brothers Publishers, 1960, 340 p.

Stanton, Robert, ed. *The Short Story and the Reader.* New York: Henry Holt and Co., 1960, 557 p.

West, Ray B., Jr., ed. *American Short Stories.* New York: Thomas Y. Crowell Co., 1959, 267 p.

Short Story Criticism

Indexes

Literary Criticism Series
Cumulative Author Index

SSC Cumulative Nationality Index

SSC Cumulative Title Index

This Index Includes References to Entries in These Gale Series

Contemporary Literary Criticism presents excerpts of criticism on the works of novelists, poets, dramatists, short story writers, scriptwriters, and other creative writers who are now living or who have died since 1960.

Twentieth-Century Literary Criticism contains critical excerpts by the most significant commentators on poets, novelists, short story writers, dramatists, and philosophers who died between 1900 and 1960.

Nineteenth-Century Literature Criticism offers significant passages from criticism on authors who died between 1800 and 1899.

Literature Criticism from 1400 to 1800 compiles significant passages from the most noteworthy criticism on authors of the fifteenth through eighteenth centuries.

Classical and Medieval Literature Criticism offers excerpts of criticism on the works of world authors from classical antiquity through the fourteenth century.

Short Story Criticism compiles excerpts of criticism on short fiction by writers of all eras and nationalities.

Poetry Criticism presents excerpts of criticism on the works of poets from all eras, movements, and nationalities.

Children's Literature Review includes excerpts from reviews, criticism, and commentary on works of authors and illustrators who create books for children.

Contemporary Authors Series encompasses five related series. *Contemporary Authors* provides biographical and bibliographical information on more than 97,000 writers of fiction and nonfiction. *Contemporary Authors New Revision Series* provides completely updated information on authors covered in *CA*. *Contemporary Authors Permanent Series* consists of listings for deceased and inactive authors. *Contemporary Authors Autobiography Series* presents specially commissioned autobiographies by leading contemporary writers. *Contemporary Authors Bibliographical Series* contains primary and secondary bibliographies as well as analytical bibliographical essays by authorities on major modern authors.

Dictionary of Literary Biography encompasses four related series. *Dictionary of Literary Biography* furnishes illustrated overviews of authors' lives and works. *Dictionary of Literary Biography Documentary Series* illuminates the careers of major figures through a selection of literary documents, including letters, interviews, and photographs. *Dictionary of Literary Biography Yearbook* summarizes the past year's literary activity and includes updated entries on individual authors. *Concise Dictionary of American Literary Biography* comprises six volumes of revised and updated sketches on major American authors that were originally presented in *Dictionary of Literary Biography*.

Something about the Author Series encompasses three related series. *Something about the Author* contains well-illustrated biographical sketches on juvenile and young adult authors and illustrators from all eras. *Something about the Author Autobiography Series* presents specially commissioned autobiographies by prominent authors and illustrators of books for children and young adults. *Authors & Artists for Young Adults* provides high school and junior high school students with profiles of their favorite creative artists.

Yesterday's Authors of Books for Children contains heavily illustrated entries on children's writers who died before 1961. Complete in two volumes.

Literary Criticism Series
Cumulative Author Index

This index lists all author entries in the Gale Literary Criticism Series and includes cross-references to other Gale sources. References in the index are identified as follows:

Aiken, Conrad (Potter)
      1889-1973 . . . . **CLC 1, 3, 5, 10, 52**
   See also CANR 4; CA 5-8R;
      obituary CA 45-48; SATA 3, 30; DLB 9,
      45

Aiken, Joan (Delano)   1924- . . . . **CLC 35**
   See also CLR 1; CANR 4; CA 9-12R;
      SAAS 1; SATA 2, 30

Ainsworth, William Harrison
      1805-1882 . . . . **NCLC 13**
   See also SATA 24; DLB 21

Ajar, Emile   1914-1980
   See Gary, Romain

Akhmadulina, Bella (Akhatovna)
      1937- . . . . **CLC 53**
   See also CA 65-68

Akhmatova, Anna   1888-1966. . . . **CLC 11, 25**
   See also CAP 1; CA 19-20;
      obituary CA 25-28R

Aksakov, Sergei Timofeyvich
      1791-1859 . . . . **NCLC 2**

Aksenov, Vassily (Pavlovich)   1932-
   See Aksyonov, Vasily (Pavlovich)

Aksyonov, Vasily (Pavlovich)
      1932- . . . . **CLC 22, 37**
   See also CANR 12; CA 53-56

Akutagawa Ryunosuke
      1892-1927 . . . . **TCLC 16**
   See also CA 117

Alain-Fournier   1886-1914 . . . . **TCLC 6**
   See also Fournier, Henri Alban
   See also DLB 65

Alarcon, Pedro Antonio de
      1833-1891 . . . . **NCLC 1**

Alas (y Urena), Leopoldo (Enrique Garcia)
      1852-1901 . . . . **TCLC 29**
   See also CA 113

Albee, Edward (Franklin III)
      1928- . . . **CLC 1, 2, 3, 5, 9, 11, 13, 25, 53**
   See also CANR 8; CA 5-8R; DLB 7;
      CDALB 1941-1968

Alberti, Rafael   1902- . . . . **CLC 7**
   See also CA 85-88

Alcott, Amos Bronson   1799-1888 . . **NCLC 1**
   See also DLB 1

Alcott, Louisa May   1832-1888 . . . . **NCLC 6**
   See also CLR 1; YABC 1; DLB 1, 42;
      CDALB 1865-1917

Aldanov, Mark   1887-1957 . . . . **TCLC 23**
   See also CA 118

Aldington, Richard   1892-1962 . . . . . . **CLC 49**
   See also CA 85-88; DLB 20, 36

Aldiss, Brian W(ilson)
      1925- . . . . **CLC 5, 14, 40**
   See also CAAS 2; CANR 5; CA 5-8R;
      SATA 34; DLB 14

Alegria, Fernando   1918- . . . . **CLC 57**
   See also CANR 5; CA 11-12R

Aleixandre, Vicente   1898-1984 . . . **CLC 9, 36**
   See also CANR 26; CA 85-88;
      obituary CA 114

Alepoudelis, Odysseus   1911-
   See Elytis, Odysseus

Aleshkovsky, Yuz   1929- . . . . **CLC 44**
   See also CA 121

Alexander, Lloyd (Chudley)   1924- . . **CLC 35**
   See also CLR 1, 5; CANR 1; CA 1-4R;
      SATA 3, 49; DLB 52

Alger, Horatio, Jr.   1832-1899 . . . . . **NCLC 8**
   See also SATA 16; DLB 42

Algren, Nelson   1909-1981 . . . . **CLC 4, 10, 33**
   See also CANR 20; CA 13-16R;
      obituary CA 103; DLB 9; DLB-Y 81, 82;
      CDALB 1941-1968

Alighieri, Dante   1265-1321 . . . . **CMLC 3**

Allard, Janet   1975- . . . . **CLC 59**

Allen, Edward   1948- . . . . **CLC 59**

Allen, Roland   1939-
   See Ayckbourn, Alan

Allen, Woody   1935- . . . . **CLC 16, 52**
   See also CANR 27; CA 33-36R; DLB 44

Allende, Isabel   1942- . . . . **CLC 39, 57**
   See also CA 125

Allingham, Margery (Louise)
      1904-1966 . . . . **CLC 19**
   See also CANR 4; CA 5-8R;
      obituary CA 25-28R

Allingham, William   1824-1889 . . . **NCLC 25**
   See also DLB 35

Allston, Washington   1779-1843 . . . . **NCLC 2**
   See also DLB 1

Almedingen, E. M.   1898-1971 . . . . . . **CLC 12**
   See also Almedingen, Martha Edith von
   See also SATA 3

Almedingen, Martha Edith von   1898-1971
   See Almedingen, E. M.
   See also CANR 1; CA 1-4R

Alonso, Damaso   1898- . . . . **CLC 14**
   See also CA 110

Alta   1942- . . . . **CLC 19**
   See also CA 57-60

Alter, Robert B(ernard)   1935- . . . . . **CLC 34**
   See also CANR 1; CA 49-52

Alther, Lisa   1944- . . . . **CLC 7, 41**
   See also CANR 12; CA 65-68

Altman, Robert   1925- . . . . **CLC 16**
   See also CA 73-76

Alvarez, A(lfred)   1929- . . . . **CLC 5, 13**
   See also CANR 3; CA 1-4R; DLB 14, 40

Alvarez, Alejandro Rodriguez   1903-1965
   See Casona, Alejandro
   See also obituary CA 93-96

Amado, Jorge   1912- . . . . **CLC 13, 40**
   See also CA 77-80

Ambler, Eric   1909- . . . . **CLC 4, 6, 9**
   See also CANR 7; CA 9-12R

Amichai, Yehuda   1924- . . . . . . **CLC 9, 22, 57**
   See also CA 85-88

Amiel, Henri Frederic   1821-1881 . . **NCLC 4**

Amis, Kingsley (William)
      1922- . . . . . . **CLC 1, 2, 3, 5, 8, 13, 40, 44**
   See also CANR 8; CA 9-12R; DLB 15, 27

Amis, Martin   1949- . . . . **CLC 4, 9, 38, 62**
   See also CANR 8, 28; CA 65-68; DLB 14

Ammons, A(rchie) R(andolph)
      1926- . . . . **CLC 2, 3, 5, 8, 9, 25, 57**
   See also CANR 6; CA 9-12R; DLB 5

Anand, Mulk Raj   1905- . . . . **CLC 23**
   See also CA 65-68

Anaya, Rudolfo A(lfonso)   1937- . . . . **CLC 23**
   See also CAAS 4; CANR 1; CA 45-48

Andersen, Hans Christian
      1805-1875 . . . . **NCLC 7; SSC 6**
   See also CLR 6; YABC 1, 1

Anderson, Jessica (Margaret Queale)
      19??- . . . . **CLC 37**
   See also CANR 4; CA 9-12R

Anderson, Jon (Victor)   1940- . . . . **CLC 9**
   See also CANR 20; CA 25-28R

Anderson, Lindsay   1923- . . . . **CLC 20**

Anderson, Maxwell   1888-1959 . . . . . **TCLC 2**
   See also CA 105; DLB 7

Anderson, Poul (William)   1926- . . . . **CLC 15**
   See also CAAS 2; CANR 2, 15; CA 1-4R;
      SATA 39; DLB 8

Anderson, Robert (Woodruff)
      1917- . . . . **CLC 23**
   See also CA 21-24R; DLB 7

Anderson, Roberta Joan   1943-
   See Mitchell, Joni

Anderson, Sherwood
      1876-1941 . . . . . . **TCLC 1, 10, 24; SSC 1**
   See also CAAS 3; CA 104, 121; DLB 4, 9;
      DLB-DS 1

Andrade, Carlos Drummond de
      1902-1987 . . . . **CLC 18**
   See also CA 123

Andrewes, Lancelot   1555-1626 . . . . **LC 5**

Andrews, Cicily Fairfield   1892-1983
   See West, Rebecca

Andreyev, Leonid (Nikolaevich)
      1871-1919 . . . . **TCLC 3**
   See also CA 104

Andrezel, Pierre   1885-1962
   See Dinesen, Isak; Blixen, Karen
      (Christentze Dinesen)

Andric, Ivo   1892-1975 . . . . **CLC 8**
   See also CA 81-84; obituary CA 57-60

Angelique, Pierre   1897-1962
   See Bataille, Georges

Angell, Roger   1920- . . . . **CLC 26**
   See also CANR 13; CA 57-60

Angelou, Maya   1928- . . . . **CLC 12, 35**
   See also CANR 19; CA 65-68; SATA 49;
      DLB 38

Annensky, Innokenty   1856-1909 . . . **TCLC 14**
   See also CA 110

Anouilh, Jean (Marie Lucien Pierre)
      1910-1987 . . . . . . **CLC 1, 3, 8, 13, 40, 50**
   See also CA 17-20R; obituary CA 123

Anthony, Florence   1947-
   See Ai

Anthony (Jacob), Piers   1934- . . . . . . **CLC 35**
   See also Jacob, Piers A(nthony)
      D(illingham)
   See also DLB 8

Antoninus, Brother   1912-
   See Everson, William (Oliver)

Antonioni, Michelangelo   1912- . . . . . **CLC 20**
   See also CA 73-76

Author Index

Bragg, Melvyn 1939- . . . . **CLC 10**
See also CANR 10; CA 57-60; DLB 14

Braine, John (Gerard)
1922-1986 . . . . **CLC 1, 3, 41**
See also CANR 1; CA 1-4R;
obituary CA 120; DLB 15; DLB-Y 86

Brammer, Billy Lee 1930?-1978
See Brammer, William

Brammer, William 1930?-1978 . . . . . **CLC 31**
See also obituary CA 77-80

Brancati, Vitaliano 1907-1954 . . . . . **TCLC 12**
See also CA 109

Brancato, Robin F(idler) 1936- . . . . . **CLC 35**
See also CANR 11; CA 69-72; SATA 23

Brand, Millen 1906-1980 . . . . **CLC 7**
See also CA 21-24R; obituary CA 97-100

Branden, Barbara 19??- . . . . **CLC 44**

Brandes, Georg (Morris Cohen)
1842-1927 . . . . **TCLC 10**
See also CA 105

Brandys, Kazimierz 1916- . . . . **CLC 62**

Branley, Franklyn M(ansfield)
1915- . . . . **CLC 21**
See also CLR 13; CANR 14; CA 33-36R;
SATA 4

Brathwaite, Edward 1930- . . . . **CLC 11**
See also CANR 11; CA 25-28R; DLB 53

Brautigan, Richard (Gary)
1935-1984 . . . . **CLC 1, 3, 5, 9, 12, 34, 42**
See also CA 53-56; obituary CA 113;
DLB 2, 5; DLB-Y 80, 84

Brecht, (Eugen) Bertolt (Friedrich)
1898-1956 . . . . **TCLC 1, 6, 13, 35**
See also CA 104; DLB 56

Bremer, Fredrika 1801-1865 . . . . . **NCLC 11**

Brennan, Christopher John
1870-1932 . . . . **TCLC 17**
See also CA 117

Brennan, Maeve 1917- . . . . **CLC 5**
See also CA 81-84

Brentano, Clemens (Maria)
1778-1842 . . . . **NCLC 1**

Brenton, Howard 1942- . . . . **CLC 31**
See also CA 69-72; DLB 13

Breslin, James 1930-
See Breslin, Jimmy
See also CA 73-76

Breslin, Jimmy 1930- . . . . **CLC 4, 43**
See also Breslin, James

Bresson, Robert 1907- . . . . **CLC 16**
See also CA 110

Breton, Andre 1896-1966 . . . **CLC 2, 9, 15, 54**
See also CAP 2; CA 19-20;
obituary CA 25-28R; DLB 65

Breytenbach, Breyten 1939- . . . . . **CLC 23, 37**
See also CA 113

Bridgers, Sue Ellen 1942- . . . . **CLC 26**
See also CANR 11; CA 65-68; SAAS 1;
SATA 22; DLB 52

Bridges, Robert 1844-1930 . . . . **TCLC 1**
See also CA 104; DLB 19

Bridie, James 1888-1951 . . . . **TCLC 3**
See also Mavor, Osborne Henry
See also DLB 10

Brin, David 1950- . . . . **CLC 34**
See also CANR 24; CA 102

Brink, Andre (Philippus)
1935- . . . . **CLC 18, 36**
See also CA 104

Brinsmead, H(esba) F(ay) 1922- . . . . **CLC 21**
See also CANR 10; CA 21-24R; SAAS 5;
SATA 18

Brittain, Vera (Mary) 1893?-1970 . . . **CLC 23**
See also CAP 1; CA 15-16;
obituary CA 25-28R

Broch, Hermann 1886-1951 . . . . **TCLC 20**
See also CA 117

Brock, Rose 1923-
See Hansen, Joseph

Brodkey, Harold 1930- . . . . **CLC 56**
See also CA 111

Brodsky, Iosif Alexandrovich 1940-
See Brodsky, Joseph (Alexandrovich)
See also CA 41-44R

Brodsky, Joseph (Alexandrovich)
1940- . . . . **CLC 4, 6, 13, 36, 50**
See also Brodsky, Iosif Alexandrovich

Brodsky, Michael (Mark) 1948- . . . . **CLC 19**
See also CANR 18; CA 102

Bromell, Henry 1947- . . . . **CLC 5**
See also CANR 9; CA 53-56

Bromfield, Louis (Brucker)
1896-1956 . . . . **TCLC 11**
See also CA 107; DLB 4, 9

Broner, E(sther) M(asserman)
1930- . . . . **CLC 19**
See also CANR 8, 25; CA 17-20R; DLB 28

Bronk, William 1918- . . . . **CLC 10**
See also CANR 23; CA 89-92

Bronte, Anne 1820-1849 . . . . **NCLC 4**
See also DLB 21

Bronte, Charlotte 1816-1855 . . . . **NCLC 3, 8**
See also DLB 21

Bronte, (Jane) Emily 1818-1848 . . **NCLC 16**
See also DLB 21, 32

Brooke, Frances 1724-1789 . . . . **LC 6**
See also DLB 39

Brooke, Henry 1703?-1783 . . . . **LC 1**
See also DLB 39

Brooke, Rupert (Chawner)
1887-1915 . . . . **TCLC 2, 7**
See also CA 104; DLB 19

Brooke-Rose, Christine 1926- . . . . . . **CLC 40**
See also CA 13-16R; DLB 14

Brookner, Anita 1928- . . . . . . **CLC 32, 34, 51**
See also CA 114, 120; DLB-Y 87

Brooks, Cleanth 1906- . . . . **CLC 24**
See also CA 17-20R; DLB 63

Brooks, Gwendolyn
1917- . . . . **CLC 1, 2, 4, 5, 15, 49**
See also CANR 1; CA 1-4R; SATA 6;
DLB 5, 76; CDALB 1941-1968

Brooks, Mel 1926- . . . . **CLC 12**
See also Kaminsky, Melvin
See also CA 65-68; DLB 26

Brooks, Peter 1938- . . . . **CLC 34**
See also CANR 1; CA 45-48

Brooks, Van Wyck 1886-1963 . . . . . . **CLC 29**
See also CANR 6; CA 1-4R; DLB 45, 63

Brophy, Brigid (Antonia)
1929- . . . . **CLC 6, 11, 29**
See also CAAS 4; CANR 25; CA 5-8R;
DLB 14

Brosman, Catharine Savage 1934- . . . . **CLC 9**
See also CANR 21; CA 61-64

Broughton, T(homas) Alan 1936- . . . **CLC 19**
See also CANR 2, 23; CA 45-48

Broumas, Olga 1949- . . . . **CLC 10**
See also CANR 20; CA 85-88

Brown, Charles Brockden
1771-1810 . . . . **NCLC 22**
See also DLB 37, 59, 73;
CDALB 1640-1865

Brown, Christy 1932-1981 . . . . **CLC 63**
See also CA 105; obituary CA 104

Brown, Claude 1937- . . . . **CLC 30**
See also CA 73-76

Brown, Dee (Alexander) 1908- . . **CLC 18, 47**
See also CAAS 6; CANR 11; CA 13-16R;
SATA 5; DLB-Y 80

Brown, George Douglas 1869-1902
See Douglas, George

Brown, George Mackay 1921- . . . **CLC 5, 28**
See also CAAS 6; CANR 12; CA 21-24R;
SATA 35; DLB 14, 27

Brown, Rita Mae 1944- . . . . **CLC 18, 43**
See also CANR 2, 11; CA 45-48

Brown, Rosellen 1939- . . . . **CLC 32**
See also CANR 14; CA 77-80

Brown, Sterling A(llen)
1901-1989 . . . . **CLC 1, 23, 59**
See also CANR 26; CA 85-88;
obituary CA 27; DLB 48, 51, 63

Brown, William Wells
1816?-1884 . . . . **NCLC 2**
See also DLB 3, 50

Browne, Jackson 1950- . . . . **CLC 21**
See also CA 120

Browning, Elizabeth Barrett
1806-1861 . . . . **NCLC 1, 16**
See also DLB 32

Browning, Robert 1812-1889 . . . . . **NCLC 19**
See also YABC 1; DLB 32

Browning, Tod 1882-1962 . . . . **CLC 16**
See also obituary CA 117

Bruccoli, Matthew J(oseph) 1931- . . **CLC 34**
See also CANR 7; CA 9-12R

Bruce, Lenny 1925-1966 . . . . **CLC 21**
See also Schneider, Leonard Alfred

Brunner, John (Kilian Houston)
1934- . . . . **CLC 8, 10**
See also CANR 2; CA 1-4R

Brutus, Dennis 1924- . . . . **CLC 43**
See also CANR 2; CA 49-52

Bryan, C(ourtlandt) D(ixon) B(arnes)
1936- . . . . **CLC 29**
See also CANR 13; CA 73-76

Bryant, William Cullen
1794-1878 . . . . **NCLC 6**
See also DLB 3, 43, 59; CDALB 1640-1865

Bryusov, Valery (Yakovlevich)
    1873-1924 . . . . TCLC 10
    See also CA 107

Buchanan, George 1506-1582 . . . . LC 4

Buchheim, Lothar-Gunther 1918- . . . . CLC 6
    See also CA 85-88

Buchner, (Karl) Georg
    1813-1837 . . . . NCLC 26

Buchwald, Art(hur) 1925- . . . . CLC 33
    See also CANR 21; CA 5-8R; SATA 10

Buck, Pearl S(ydenstricker)
    1892-1973 . . . . CLC 7, 11, 18
    See also CANR 1; CA 1-4R;
    obituary CA 41-44R; SATA 1, 25; DLB 9

Buckler, Ernest 1908-1984 . . . . CLC 13
    See also CAP 1; CA 11-12;
    obituary CA 114; SATA 47

Buckley, Vincent (Thomas)
    1925-1988 . . . . CLC 57
    See also CA 101

Buckley, William F(rank), Jr.
    1925- . . . . CLC 7, 18, 37
    See also CANR 1, 24; CA 1-4R; DLB-Y 80

Buechner, (Carl) Frederick
    1926- . . . . CLC 2, 4, 6, 9
    See also CANR 11; CA 13-16R; DLB-Y 80

Buell, John (Edward) 1927- . . . . CLC 10
    See also CA 1-4R; DLB 53

Buero Vallejo, Antonio 1916- . . . CLC 15, 46
    See also CANR 24; CA 106

Bukowski, Charles 1920- . . . . CLC 2, 5, 9, 41
    See also CA 17-20R; DLB 5

Bulgakov, Mikhail (Afanas'evich)
    1891-1940 . . . . TCLC 2, 16
    See also CA 105

Bullins, Ed 1935- . . . . CLC 1, 5, 7
    See also CANR 24; CA 49-52; DLB 7, 38

Bulwer-Lytton, (Lord) Edward (George Earle
    Lytton) 1803-1873 . . . . NCLC 1
    See also Lytton, Edward Bulwer
    See also DLB 21

Bunin, Ivan (Alexeyevich)
    1870-1953 . . . . TCLC 6; SSC 5
    See also CA 104

Bunting, Basil 1900-1985 . . . . CLC 10, 39, 47
    See also CANR 7; CA 53-56;
    obituary CA 115; DLB 20

Bunuel, Luis 1900-1983 . . . . CLC 16
    See also CA 101; obituary CA 110

Bunyan, John 1628-1688 . . . . LC 4
    See also DLB 39

Burgess (Wilson, John) Anthony
    1917- . . . . . CLC 1, 2, 4, 5, 8, 10, 13, 15,
                                          22, 40, 62
    See also Wilson, John (Anthony) Burgess
    See also DLB 14

Burke, Edmund 1729-1797 . . . . LC 7

Burke, Kenneth (Duva) 1897- . . . . CLC 2, 24
    See also CA 5-8R; DLB 45, 63

Burney, Fanny 1752-1840 . . . . NCLC 12
    See also DLB 39

Burns, Robert 1759-1796 . . . . LC 3

Burns, Tex 1908?-
    See L'Amour, Louis (Dearborn)

Burnshaw, Stanley 1906- . . . . . CLC 3, 13, 44
    See also CA 9-12R; DLB 48

Burr, Anne 1937- . . . . CLC 6
    See also CA 25-28R

Burroughs, Edgar Rice
    1875-1950 . . . . TCLC 2, 32
    See also CA 104; SATA 41; DLB 8

Burroughs, William S(eward)
    1914- . . . . CLC 1, 2, 5, 15, 22, 42
    See also CANR 20; CA 9-12R; DLB 2, 8,
    16; DLB-Y 81

Busch, Frederick 1941- . . . CLC 7, 10, 18, 47
    See also CAAS 1; CA 33-36R; DLB 6

Bush, Ronald 19??- . . . . CLC 34

Butler, Octavia E(stelle) 1947- . . . . . CLC 38
    See also CANR 12, 24; CA 73-76; DLB 33

Butler, Samuel 1835-1902 . . . . . . TCLC 1, 33
    See also CA 104; DLB 18, 57

Butor, Michel (Marie Francois)
    1926- . . . . CLC 1, 3, 8, 11, 15
    See also CA 9-12R

Buzo, Alexander 1944- . . . . CLC 61
    See also CANR 17; CA 97-100

Buzzati, Dino 1906-1972 . . . . CLC 36
    See also obituary CA 33-36R

Byars, Betsy 1928- . . . . CLC 35
    See also CLR 1, 16; CANR 18; CA 33-36R;
    SAAS 1; SATA 4, 46; DLB 52

Byatt, A(ntonia) S(usan Drabble)
    1936- . . . . CLC 19
    See also CANR 13; CA 13-16R; DLB 14

Byrne, David 1953?- . . . . CLC 26

Byrne, John Keyes 1926-
    See Leonard, Hugh
    See also CA 102

Byron, George Gordon (Noel), Lord Byron
    1788-1824 . . . . NCLC 2, 12

Caballero, Fernan 1796-1877 . . . . . NCLC 10

Cabell, James Branch 1879-1958 . . . TCLC 6
    See also CA 105; DLB 9

Cable, George Washington
    1844-1925 . . . . TCLC 4; SSC 4
    See also CA 104; DLB 12, 74

Cabrera Infante, G(uillermo)
    1929- . . . . CLC 5, 25, 45
    See also CA 85-88

Cage, John (Milton, Jr.) 1912- . . . . . CLC 41
    See also CANR 9; CA 13-16R

Cain, G. 1929-
    See Cabrera Infante, G(uillermo)

Cain, James M(allahan)
    1892-1977 . . . . CLC 3, 11, 28
    See also CANR 8; CA 17-20R;
    obituary CA 73-76

Caldwell, Erskine (Preston)
    1903-1987 . . . . CLC 1, 8, 14, 50, 60
    See also CAAS 1; CANR 2; CA 1-4R;
    obituary CA 121; DLB 9

Caldwell, (Janet Miriam) Taylor (Holland)
    1900-1985 . . . . CLC 2, 28, 39
    See also CANR 5; CA 5-8R;
    obituary CA 116

Calhoun, John Caldwell
    1782-1850 . . . . NCLC 15
    See also DLB 3

Calisher, Hortense 1911- . . . . CLC 2, 4, 8, 38
    See also CANR 1, 22; CA 1-4R; DLB 2

Callaghan, Morley (Edward)
    1903- . . . . CLC 3, 14, 41
    See also CA 9-12R; DLB 68

Calvino, Italo
    1923-1985 . . . . CLC 5, 8, 11, 22, 33, 39;
                                                  SSC 3
    See also CANR 23; CA 85-88;
    obituary CA 116

Cameron, Carey 1952- . . . . CLC 59

Cameron, Peter 1959- . . . . CLC 44
    See also CA 125

Campana, Dino 1885-1932 . . . . TCLC 20
    See also CA 117

Campbell, John W(ood), Jr.
    1910-1971 . . . . CLC 32
    See also CAP 2; CA 21-22;
    obituary CA 29-32R; DLB 8

Campbell, (John) Ramsey 1946- . . . . CLC 42
    See also CANR 7; CA 57-60

Campbell, (Ignatius) Roy (Dunnachie)
    1901-1957 . . . . TCLC 5
    See also CA 104; DLB 20

Campbell, Thomas 1777-1844 . . . . NCLC 19

Campbell, (William) Wilfred
    1861-1918 . . . . TCLC 9
    See also CA 106

Camus, Albert
    1913-1960 . . . CLC 1, 2, 4, 9, 11, 14, 32,
                                                     63
    See also CA 89-92; DLB 72

Canby, Vincent 1924- . . . . CLC 13
    See also CA 81-84

Canetti, Elias 1905- . . . . CLC 3, 14, 25
    See also CANR 23; CA 21-24R

Canin, Ethan 1960- . . . . CLC 55

Cape, Judith 1916-
    See Page, P(atricia) K(athleen)

Capek, Karel 1890-1938 . . . . TCLC 6, 37
    See also CA 104

Capote, Truman
    1924-1984 . . . . . CLC 1, 3, 8, 13, 19, 34,
                                          38, 58; SSC 2
    See also CANR 18; CA 5-8R;
    obituary CA 113; DLB 2; DLB-Y 80, 84;
    CDALB 1941-1968

Capra, Frank 1897- . . . . CLC 16
    See also CA 61-64

Caputo, Philip 1941- . . . . CLC 32
    See also CA 73-76

Card, Orson Scott 1951- . . . . CLC 44, 47, 50
    See also CA 102

Cardenal, Ernesto 1925- . . . . CLC 31
    See also CANR 2; CA 49-52

Carducci, Giosue 1835-1907 . . . . . . TCLC 32

Carew, Thomas 1595?-1640 . . . . LC 13

Carey, Ernestine Gilbreth 1908- . . . . CLC 17
    See also CA 5-8R; SATA 2

Carey, Peter 1943- . . . . CLC 40, 55
    See also CA 123, 127

Carleton, William 1794-1869 ..... NCLC 3

Carlisle, Henry (Coffin) 1926- ...... CLC 33
See also CANR 15; CA 13-16R

Carlson, Ron(ald F.) 1947- .... CLC 54
See also CA 105

Carlyle, Thomas 1795-1881 ...... NCLC 22
See also DLB 55

Carman, (William) Bliss
1861-1929 .... TCLC 7
See also CA 104

Carpenter, Don(ald Richard)
1931- .... CLC 41
See also CANR 1; CA 45-48

Carpentier (y Valmont), Alejo
1904-1980 .... CLC 8, 11, 38
See also CANR 11; CA 65-68;
obituary CA 97-100

Carr, Emily 1871-1945 .... TCLC 32
See also DLB 68

Carr, John Dickson 1906-1977 ...... CLC 3
See also CANR 3; CA 49-52;
obituary CA 69-72

Carr, Virginia Spencer 1929- .... CLC 34
See also CA 61-64

Carrier, Roch 1937- .... CLC 13
See also DLB 53

Carroll, James (P.) 1943- .... CLC 38
See also CA 81-84

Carroll, Jim 1951- .... CLC 35
See also CA 45-48

Carroll, Lewis 1832-1898 .... NCLC 2
See also Dodgson, Charles Lutwidge
See also CLR 2; DLB 18

Carroll, Paul Vincent 1900-1968 .... CLC 10
See also CA 9-12R; obituary CA 25-28R;
DLB 10

Carruth, Hayden 1921- .... CLC 4, 7, 10, 18
See also CANR 4; CA 9-12R; SATA 47;
DLB 5

Carter, Angela (Olive) 1940- ..... CLC 5, 41
See also CANR 12; CA 53-56; DLB 14

Carver, Raymond
1938-1988 .... CLC 22, 36, 53, 55
See also CANR 17; CA 33-36R;
obituary CA 126; DLB-Y 84, 88

Cary, (Arthur) Joyce (Lunel)
1888-1957 .... TCLC 1, 29
See also CA 104; DLB 15

Casanova de Seingalt, Giovanni Jacopo
1725-1798 .... LC 13

Casares, Adolfo Bioy 1914-
See Bioy Casares, Adolfo

Casely-Hayford, J(oseph) E(phraim)
1866-1930 .... TCLC 24
See also CA 123

Casey, John 1880-1964
See O'Casey, Sean

Casey, John 1939- .... CLC 59
See also CANR 23; CA 69-72

Casey, Michael 1947- .... CLC 2
See also CA 65-68; DLB 5

Casey, Warren 1935- .... CLC 12
See also Jacobs, Jim and Casey, Warren
See also CA 101

Casona, Alejandro 1903-1965 ...... CLC 49
See also Alvarez, Alejandro Rodriguez

Cassavetes, John 1929- .... CLC 20
See also CA 85-88

Cassill, R(onald) V(erlin) 1919- ... CLC 4, 23
See also CAAS 1; CANR 7; CA 9-12R;
DLB 6

Cassity, (Allen) Turner 1929- .... CLC 6, 42
See also CANR 11; CA 17-20R

Castaneda, Carlos 1935?- .... CLC 12
See also CA 25-28R

Castelvetro, Lodovico 1505-1571 ..... LC 12

Castiglione, Baldassare 1478-1529 ... LC 12

Castro, Rosalia de 1837-1885 ..... NCLC 3

Cather, Willa (Sibert)
1873-1947 ...... TCLC 1, 11, 31; SSC 2
See also CA 104; SATA 30; DLB 9, 54;
DLB-DS 1; CDALB 1865-1917

Catton, (Charles) Bruce
1899-1978 .... CLC 35
See also CANR 7; CA 5-8R;
obituary CA 81-84; SATA 2;
obituary SATA 24; DLB 17

Cauldwell, Frank 1923-
See King, Francis (Henry)

Caunitz, William 1935- .... CLC 34

Causley, Charles (Stanley) 1917- ..... CLC 7
See also CANR 5; CA 9-12R; SATA 3;
DLB 27

Caute, (John) David 1936- .... CLC 29
See also CAAS 4; CANR 1; CA 1-4R;
DLB 14

Cavafy, C(onstantine) P(eter)
1863-1933 .... TCLC 2, 7
See also CA 104

Cavanna, Betty 1909- .... CLC 12
See also CANR 6; CA 9-12R; SATA 1, 30

Cayrol, Jean 1911- .... CLC 11
See also CA 89-92

Cela, Camilo Jose 1916- ..... CLC 4, 13, 59
See also CAAS 10; CANR 21; CA 21-24R

Celan, Paul 1920-1970 ...... CLC 10, 19, 53
See also Antschel, Paul
See also DLB 69

Celine, Louis-Ferdinand
1894-1961 ..... CLC 1, 3, 4, 7, 9, 15, 47
See also Destouches,
Louis-Ferdinand-Auguste
See also DLB 72

Cellini, Benvenuto 1500-1571 .... LC 7

Cendrars, Blaise 1887-1961 .... CLC 18
See also Sauser-Hall, Frederic

Cernuda, Luis (y Bidon)
1902-1963 .... CLC 54
See also CA 89-92

Cervantes (Saavedra), Miguel de
1547-1616 .... LC 6

Cesaire, Aime (Fernand) 1913- .. CLC 19, 32
See also CANR 24; CA 65-68

Chabon, Michael 1965?- .... CLC 55

Chabrol, Claude 1930- .... CLC 16
See also CA 110

Challans, Mary 1905-1983
See Renault, Mary
See also CA 81-84; obituary CA 111;
SATA 23; obituary SATA 36

Chambers, Aidan 1934- .... CLC 35
See also CANR 12; CA 25-28R; SATA 1

Chambers, James 1948-
See Cliff, Jimmy

Chandler, Raymond 1888-1959 ... TCLC 1, 7
See also CA 104

Channing, William Ellery
1780-1842 .... NCLC 17
See also DLB 1, 59

Chaplin, Charles (Spencer)
1889-1977 .... CLC 16
See also CA 81-84; obituary CA 73-76;
DLB 44

Chapman, Graham 1941?- .... CLC 21
See also Monty Python
See also CA 116

Chapman, John Jay 1862-1933 ..... TCLC 7
See also CA 104

Chappell, Fred 1936- .... CLC 40
See also CAAS 4; CANR 8; CA 5-8R;
DLB 6

Char, Rene (Emile)
1907-1988 .... CLC 9, 11, 14, 55
See also CA 13-16R; obituary CA 124

Charles I 1600-1649 .... LC 13

Charyn, Jerome 1937- .... CLC 5, 8, 18
See also CAAS 1; CANR 7; CA 5-8R;
DLB-Y 83

Chase, Mary Ellen 1887-1973 .... CLC 2
See also CAP 1; CA 15-16;
obituary CA 41-44R; SATA 10

Chateaubriand, Francois Rene de
1768-1848 .... NCLC 3

Chatterji, Bankim Chandra
1838-1894 .... NCLC 19

Chatterji, Saratchandra
1876-1938 .... TCLC 13
See also CA 109

Chatterton, Thomas 1752-1770 ...... LC 3

Chatwin, (Charles) Bruce
1940-1989 .... CLC 28, 57, 59
See also CA 85-88,; obituary CA 127

Chayefsky, Paddy 1923-1981 ...... CLC 23
See also CA 9-12R; obituary CA 104;
DLB 7, 44; DLB-Y 81

Chayefsky, Sidney 1923-1981
See Chayefsky, Paddy
See also CANR 18

Chedid, Andree 1920- .... CLC 47

Cheever, John
1912-1982 ..... CLC 3, 7, 8, 11, 15, 25;
SSC 1
See also CANR 5; CA 5-8R;
obituary CA 106; CABS 1; DLB 2;
DLB-Y 80, 82; CDALB 1941-1968

Cheever, Susan 1943- .... CLC 18, 48
See also CA 103; DLB-Y 82

Chekhov, Anton (Pavlovich)
1860-1904 ...... TCLC 3, 10, 31; SSC 2
See also CA 104, 124

Cunningham, Julia (Woolfolk)
1916- .... CLC 12
See also CANR 4, 19; CA 9-12R; SAAS 2;
SATA 1, 26

Cunningham, Michael 1952- .... CLC 34

Currie, Ellen 19??- .... CLC 44

Dabrowska, Maria (Szumska)
1889-1965 .... CLC 15
See also CA 106

Dabydeen, David 1956?- .... CLC 34
See also CA 106

Dacey, Philip 1939- .... CLC 51
See also CANR 14; CA 37-40R

Dagerman, Stig (Halvard)
1923-1954 .... TCLC 17
See also CA 117

Dahl, Roald 1916-............ CLC 1, 6, 18
See also CLR 1, 7; CANR 6; CA 1-4R;
SATA 1, 26

Dahlberg, Edward 1900-1977... CLC 1, 7, 14
See also CA 9-12R; obituary CA 69-72;
DLB 48

Daly, Elizabeth 1878-1967........ CLC 52
See also CAP 2; CA 23-24;
obituary CA 25-28R

Daly, Maureen 1921-............. CLC 17
See also McGivern, Maureen Daly
See also SAAS 1; SATA 2

Daniken, Erich von 1935-
See Von Daniken, Erich

Dannay, Frederic 1905-1982
See Queen, Ellery
See also CANR 1; CA 1-4R;
obituary CA 107

D'Annunzio, Gabriele 1863-1938.... TCLC 6
See also CA 104

Dante (Alighieri)
See Alighieri, Dante

Danziger, Paula 1944- .... CLC 21
See also CLR 20; CA 112, 115; SATA 30,
36

Dario, Ruben 1867-1916 .... TCLC 4
See also Sarmiento, Felix Ruben Garcia
See also CA 104

Darley, George 1795-1846....... NCLC 2

Daryush, Elizabeth 1887-1977.... CLC 6, 19
See also CANR 3; CA 49-52; DLB 20

Daudet, (Louis Marie) Alphonse
1840-1897 .... NCLC 1

Daumal, Rene 1908-1944........ TCLC 14
See also CA 114

Davenport, Guy (Mattison, Jr.)
1927- .... CLC 6, 14, 38
See also CANR 23; CA 33-36R

Davidson, Donald (Grady)
1893-1968 .... CLC 2, 13, 19
See also CANR 4; CA 5-8R;
obituary CA 25-28R; DLB 45

Davidson, John 1857-1909....... TCLC 24
See also CA 118; DLB 19

Davidson, Sara 1943-............. CLC 9
See also CA 81-84

Davie, Donald (Alfred)
1922- .... CLC 5, 8, 10, 31
See also CAAS 3; CANR 1; CA 1-4R;
DLB 27

Davies, Ray(mond Douglas) 1944- .. CLC 21
See also CA 116

Davies, Rhys 1903-1978.......... CLC 23
See also CANR 4; CA 9-12R;
obituary CA 81-84

Davies, (William) Robertson
1913- .... CLC 2, 7, 13, 25, 42
See also CANR 17; CA 33-36R; DLB 68

Davies, W(illiam) H(enry)
1871-1940 .... TCLC 5
See also CA 104; DLB 19

Davis, H(arold) L(enoir)
1896-1960 .... CLC 49
See also obituary CA 89-92; DLB 9

Davis, Rebecca (Blaine) Harding
1831-1910 .... TCLC 6
See also CA 104; DLB 74

Davis, Richard Harding
1864-1916 .... TCLC 24
See also CA 114; DLB 12, 23

Davison, Frank Dalby 1893-1970... CLC 15
See also obituary CA 116

Davison, Peter 1928-............. CLC 28
See also CAAS 4; CANR 3; CA 9-12R;
DLB 5

Davys, Mary 1674-1732........... LC 1
See also DLB 39

Dawson, Fielding 1930-........... CLC 6
See also CA 85-88

Day, Clarence (Shepard, Jr.)
1874-1935 .... TCLC 25
See also CA 108; DLB 11

Day, Thomas 1748-1789 .... LC 1
See also YABC 1; DLB 39

Day Lewis, C(ecil)
1904-1972 .... CLC 1, 6, 10
See also CAP 1; CA 15-16;
obituary CA 33-36R; DLB 15, 20

Dazai Osamu 1909-1948 .... TCLC 11
See also Tsushima Shuji

De Crayencour, Marguerite 1903-1987
See Yourcenar, Marguerite

Deer, Sandra 1940-.............. CLC 45

Defoe, Daniel 1660?-1731 .... LC 1
See also SATA 22; DLB 39

De Hartog, Jan 1914-............. CLC 19
See also CANR 1; CA 1-4R

Deighton, Len 1929-....... CLC 4, 7, 22, 46
See also Deighton, Leonard Cyril

Deighton, Leonard Cyril 1929-
See Deighton, Len
See also CANR 19; CA 9-12R

De la Mare, Walter (John)
1873-1956 .... TCLC 4
See also CLR 23; CA 110; SATA 16;
DLB 19

Delaney, Shelagh 1939- .... CLC 29
See also CA 17-20R; DLB 13

Delany, Mary (Granville Pendarves)
1700-1788 .... LC 12

Delany, Samuel R(ay, Jr.)
1942- .... CLC 8, 14, 38
See also CA 81-84; DLB 8, 33

De la Roche, Mazo 1885-1961 ..... CLC 14
See also CA 85-88; DLB 68

Delbanco, Nicholas (Franklin)
1942- .... CLC 6, 13
See also CAAS 2; CA 17-20R; DLB 6

del Castillo, Michel 1933-......... CLC 38
See also CA 109

Deledda, Grazia 1871-1936 .... TCLC 23
See also CA 123

Delibes (Setien), Miguel 1920- ... CLC 8, 18
See also CANR 1; CA 45-48

DeLillo, Don
1936- .... CLC 8, 10, 13, 27, 39, 54
See also CANR 21; CA 81-84; DLB 6

De Lisser, H(erbert) G(eorge)
1878-1944 .... TCLC 12
See also CA 109

Deloria, Vine (Victor), Jr. 1933-.... CLC 21
See also CANR 5, 20; CA 53-56; SATA 21

Del Vecchio, John M(ichael)
1947- .... CLC 29
See also CA 110

de Man, Paul 1919-1983 .... CLC 55
See also obituary CA 111; DLB 67

De Marinis, Rick 1934-........... CLC 54
See also CANR 9, 25; CA 57-60

Demby, William 1922-............ CLC 53
See also CA 81-84; DLB 33

Denby, Edwin (Orr) 1903-1983..... CLC 48
See also obituary CA 110

Dennis, John 1657-1734........... LC 11

Dennis, Nigel (Forbes) 1912-........ CLC 8
See also CA 25-28R; DLB 13, 15

De Palma, Brian 1940-........... CLC 20
See also CA 109

De Quincey, Thomas 1785-1859 ... NCLC 4

Deren, Eleanora 1908-1961
See Deren, Maya
See also obituary CA 111

Deren, Maya 1908-1961........... CLC 16
See also Deren, Eleanora

Derleth, August (William)
1909-1971 .... CLC 31
See also CANR 4; CA 1-4R;
obituary CA 29-32R; SATA 5; DLB 9

Derrida, Jacques 1930-........... CLC 24
See also CA 124

Desai, Anita 1937- .... CLC 19, 37
See also CA 81-84

De Saint-Luc, Jean 1909-1981
See Glassco, John

De Sica, Vittorio 1902-1974 .... CLC 20
See also obituary CA 117

Desnos, Robert 1900-1945........ TCLC 22
See also CA 121

Destouches, Louis-Ferdinand-Auguste
1894-1961
See Celine, Louis-Ferdinand
See also CA 85-88

Heat Moon, William Least   1939-... **CLC 29**

Hebert, Anne   1916- .... **CLC 4, 13, 29**
See also CA 85-88; DLB 68

Hecht, Anthony (Evan)
1923- .... **CLC 8, 13, 19**
See also CANR 6; CA 9-12R; DLB 5

Hecht, Ben   1894-1964 .... **CLC 8**
See also CA 85-88; DLB 7, 9, 25, 26, 28

Hedayat, Sadeq   1903-1951....... **TCLC 21**
See also CA 120

Heidegger, Martin   1889-1976 ...... **CLC 24**
See also CA 81-84; obituary CA 65-68

Heidenstam, (Karl Gustaf) Verner von
1859-1940 .... **TCLC 5**
See also CA 104

Heifner, Jack   1946- .... **CLC 11**
See also CA 105

Heijermans, Herman   1864-1924 ... **TCLC 24**
See also CA 123

Heilbrun, Carolyn G(old)   1926-..... **CLC 25**
See also CANR 1; CA 45-48

Heine, Harry   1797-1856
See Heine, Heinrich

Heine, Heinrich   1797-1856 .... **NCLC 4**

Heinemann, Larry C(urtiss)   1944- .. **CLC 50**
See also CA 110

Heiney, Donald (William)   1921-
See Harris, MacDonald
See also CANR 3; CA 1-4R

Heinlein, Robert A(nson)
1907-1988 ...... **CLC 1, 3, 8, 14, 26, 55**
See also CANR 1, 20; CA 1-4R;
obituary CA 125; SATA 9; DLB 8

Heller, Joseph
1923- .... **CLC 1, 3, 5, 8, 11, 36, 63**
See also CANR 8; CA 5-8R; CABS 1;
DLB 2, 28; DLB-Y 80

Hellman, Lillian (Florence)
1905?-1984..... **CLC 2, 4, 8, 14, 18, 34,
44, 52**
See also CA 13-16R; obituary CA 112;
DLB 7; DLB-Y 84

Helprin, Mark   1947- ..... **CLC 7, 10, 22, 32**
See also CA 81-84; DLB-Y 85

Hemans, Felicia   1793-1835 ...... **NCLC 29**

Hemingway, Ernest (Miller)
1899-1961 ...   **CLC 1, 3, 6, 8, 10, 13, 19,
30, 34, 39, 41, 44, 50, 61; SSC 1**
See also CA 77-80; DLB 4, 9; DLB-Y 81,
87; DLB-DS 1

Hempel, Amy   1951- .... **CLC 39**
See also CA 118

Henley, Beth   1952-............... **CLC 23**
See also Henley, Elizabeth Becker
See also DLB-Y 86

Henley, Elizabeth Becker   1952-
See Henley, Beth
See also CA 107

Henley, William Ernest
1849-1903 .... **TCLC 8**
See also CA 105; DLB 19

Hennissart, Martha
See Lathen, Emma
See also CA 85-88

Henry, O.   1862-1910 ... **TCLC 1, 19; SSC 5**
See also Porter, William Sydney
See also YABC 2; CA 104; DLB 12, 78, 79;
CDALB 1865-1917

Henry VIII   1491-1547 .... **LC 10**

Hentoff, Nat(han Irving)   1925-..... **CLC 26**
See also CLR 1; CAAS 6; CANR 5;
CA 1-4R; SATA 27, 42

Heppenstall, (John) Rayner
1911-1981 .... **CLC 10**
See also CA 1-4R; obituary CA 103

Herbert, Frank (Patrick)
1920-1986 .... **CLC 12, 23, 35, 44**
See also CANR 5; CA 53-56;
obituary CA 118; SATA 9, 37, 47; DLB 8

Herbert, Zbigniew   1924- .... **CLC 9, 43**
See also CA 89-92

Herbst, Josephine   1897-1969....... **CLC 34**
See also CA 5-8R; obituary CA 25-28R;
DLB 9

Herder, Johann Gottfried von
1744-1803 .... **NCLC 8**

Hergesheimer, Joseph
1880-1954 .... **TCLC 11**
See also CA 109; DLB 9

Herlagnez, Pablo de   1844-1896
See Verlaine, Paul (Marie)

Herlihy, James Leo   1927-.......... **CLC 6**
See also CANR 2; CA 1-4R

Hermogenes   fl.c. 175-............. **CMLC 6**

Hernandez, Jose   1834-1886...... **NCLC 17**

Herrick, Robert   1591-1674 .... **LC 13**

Herriot, James   1916-.............. **CLC 12**
See also Wight, James Alfred

Herrmann, Dorothy   1941-.......... **CLC 44**
See also CA 107

Hersey, John (Richard)
1914- .... **CLC 1, 2, 7, 9, 40**
See also CA 17-20R; SATA 25; DLB 6

Herzen, Aleksandr Ivanovich
1812-1870 .... **NCLC 10**

Herzl, Theodor   1860-1904 .... **TCLC 36**

Herzog, Werner   1942-............. **CLC 16**
See also CA 89-92

Hesiod   c. 8th Century B.C.- ...... **CMLC 5**

Hesse, Hermann
1877-1962 ..... **CLC 1, 2, 3, 6, 11, 17, 25**
See also CAP 2; CA 17-18; SATA 50;
DLB 66

Heyen, William   1940- .... **CLC 13, 18**
See also CA 33-36R; DLB 5

Heyerdahl, Thor   1914-............. **CLC 26**
See also CANR 5, 22; CA 5-8R; SATA 2,
52

Heym, Georg (Theodor Franz Arthur)
1887-1912 .... **TCLC 9**
See also CA 106

Heym, Stefan   1913-.............. **CLC 41**
See also CANR 4; CA 9-12R; DLB 69

Heyse, Paul (Johann Ludwig von)
1830-1914 .... **TCLC 8**
See also CA 104

Hibbert, Eleanor (Burford)   1906-..... **CLC 7**
See also CANR 9; CA 17-20R; SATA 2

Higgins, George V(incent)
1939- .... **CLC 4, 7, 10, 18**
See also CAAS 5; CANR 17; CA 77-80;
DLB 2; DLB-Y 81

Higginson, Thomas Wentworth
1823-1911 .... **TCLC 36**
See also DLB 1, 64

Highsmith, (Mary) Patricia
1921-................ **CLC 2, 4, 14, 42**
See also CANR 1, 20; CA 1-4R

Highwater, Jamake   1942- .... **CLC 12**
See also CAAS 7; CANR 10; CA 65-68;
SATA 30, 32; DLB 52; DLB-Y 85

Hikmet (Ran), Nazim   1902-1963.... **CLC 40**
See also obituary CA 93-96

Hildesheimer, Wolfgang   1916- ..... **CLC 49**
See also CA 101; DLB 69

Hill, Geoffrey (William)
1932- .... **CLC 5, 8, 18, 45**
See also CANR 21; CA 81-84; DLB 40

Hill, George Roy   1922-........... **CLC 26**
See also CA 110

Hill, Susan B.   1942-................ **CLC 4**
See also CA 33-36R; DLB 14

Hillerman, Tony   1925-............. **CLC 62**
See also CANR 21; CA 29-32R; SATA 6

Hilliard, Noel (Harvey)   1929-....... **CLC 15**
See also CANR 7; CA 9-12R

Hilton, James   1900-1954............ **TCLC 21**
See also CA 108; SATA 34; DLB 34

Himes, Chester (Bomar)
1909-1984 .... **CLC 2, 4, 7, 18, 58**
See also CANR 22; CA 25-28R;
obituary CA 114; DLB 2, 76

Hinde, Thomas   1926-........... **CLC 6, 11**
See also Chitty, (Sir) Thomas Willes

Hine, (William) Daryl   1936-........ **CLC 15**
See also CANR 1, 20; CA 1-4R; DLB 60

Hinton, S(usan) E(loise)   1950- ..... **CLC 30**
See also CLR 3, 23; CA 81-84; SATA 19

Hippius (Merezhkovsky), Zinaida
(Nikolayevna)   1869-1945...... **TCLC 9**
See also Gippius, Zinaida (Nikolayevna)

Hiraoka, Kimitake   1925-1970
See Mishima, Yukio
See also CA 97-100; obituary CA 29-32R

Hirsch, Edward (Mark)   1950-... **CLC 31, 50**
See also CANR 20; CA 104

Hitchcock, (Sir) Alfred (Joseph)
1899-1980 .... **CLC 16**
See also obituary CA 97-100; SATA 27;
obituary SATA 24

Hoagland, Edward   1932-.......... **CLC 28**
See also CANR 2; CA 1-4R; SATA 51;
DLB 6

Hoban, Russell C(onwell)   1925- ... **CLC 7, 25**
See also CLR 3; CANR 23; CA 5-8R;
SATA 1, 40; DLB 52

Hobson, Laura Z(ametkin)
1900-1986 .... **CLC 7, 25**
See also CA 17-20R; obituary CA 118;
SATA 52; DLB 28

Author Index

Lynn, Kenneth S(chuyler) 1923- .... **CLC 50**
See also CANR 3; CA 1-4R

Lytle, Andrew (Nelson) 1902- ...... **CLC 22**
See also CA 9-12R; DLB 6

Lyttelton, George 1709-1773 .... **LC 10**

Lytton, Edward Bulwer 1803-1873
See Bulwer-Lytton, (Lord) Edward (George Earle Lytton)
See also SATA 23

Maas, Peter 1929- .... **CLC 29**
See also CA 93-96

Macaulay, (Dame Emile) Rose
1881-1958 .... **TCLC 7**
See also CA 104; DLB 36

MacBeth, George (Mann)
1932- .... **CLC 2, 5, 9**
See also CA 25-28R; SATA 4; DLB 40

MacCaig, Norman (Alexander)
1910- .... **CLC 36**
See also CANR 3; CA 9-12R; DLB 27

MacCarthy, Desmond 1877-1952 .. **TCLC 36**

MacDermot, Thomas H. 1870-1933
See Redcam, Tom

MacDiarmid, Hugh
1892-1978 .... **CLC 2, 4, 11, 19, 63**
See also Grieve, C(hristopher) M(urray)
See also DLB 20

Macdonald, Cynthia 1928- ...... **CLC 13, 19**
See also CANR 4; CA 49-52

MacDonald, George 1824-1905 ..... **TCLC 9**
See also CA 106; SATA 33; DLB 18

MacDonald, John D(ann)
1916-1986 .... **CLC 3, 27, 44**
See also CANR 1, 19; CA 1-4R;
obituary CA 121; DLB 8; DLB-Y 86

Macdonald, (John) Ross
1915-1983 ...... **CLC 1, 2, 3, 14, 34, 41**
See also Millar, Kenneth

MacEwen, Gwendolyn (Margaret)
1941-1987 .... **CLC 13, 55**
See also CANR 7, 22; CA 9-12R;
obituary CA 124; SATA 50; DLB 53

Machado (y Ruiz), Antonio
1875-1939 .... **TCLC 3**
See also CA 104

Machado de Assis, (Joaquim Maria)
1839-1908 .... **TCLC 10**
See also CA 107

Machen, Arthur (Llewellyn Jones)
1863-1947 .... **TCLC 4**
See also CA 104; DLB 36

Machiavelli, Niccolo 1469-1527 ...... **LC 8**

MacInnes, Colin 1914-1976 ...... **CLC 4, 23**
See also CA 69-72; obituary CA 65-68;
DLB 14

MacInnes, Helen (Clark)
1907-1985 .... **CLC 27, 39**
See also CANR 1; CA 1-4R;
obituary CA 65-68, 117; SATA 22, 44

Macintosh, Elizabeth 1897-1952
See Tey, Josephine
See also CA 110

Mackenzie, (Edward Montague) Compton
1883-1972 .... **CLC 18**
See also CAP 2; CA 21-22;
obituary CA 37-40R; DLB 34

Mac Laverty, Bernard 1942- .... **CLC 31**
See also CA 116, 118

MacLean, Alistair (Stuart)
1922-1987 .... **CLC 3, 13, 50, 63**
See also CANR 28; CA 57-60;
obituary CA 121; SATA 23, 50

MacLeish, Archibald
1892-1982 .... **CLC 3, 8, 14**
See also CA 9-12R; obituary CA 106;
DLB 4, 7, 45; DLB-Y 82

MacLennan, (John) Hugh
1907- .... **CLC 2, 14**
See also CA 5-8R

MacLeod, Alistair 1936- .... **CLC 56**
See also CA 123; DLB 60

Macleod, Fiona 1855-1905
See Sharp, William

MacNeice, (Frederick) Louis
1907-1963 .... **CLC 1, 4, 10, 53**
See also CA 85-88; DLB 10, 20

Macpherson, (Jean) Jay 1931- ...... **CLC 14**
See also CA 5-8R; DLB 53

MacShane, Frank 1927- .... **CLC 39**
See also CANR 3; CA 11-12R

Macumber, Mari 1896-1966
See Sandoz, Mari (Susette)

Madach, Imre 1823-1864 .... **NCLC 19**

Madden, (Jerry) David 1933- .... **CLC 5, 15**
See also CAAS 3; CANR 4; CA 1-4R;
DLB 6

Madhubuti, Haki R. 1942- .... **CLC 6**
See also Lee, Don L.
See also CANR 24; CA 73-76; DLB 5, 41

Maeterlinck, Maurice 1862-1949 ... **TCLC 3**
See also CA 104

Mafouz, Naguib 1912-
See Mahfuz, Najib

Maginn, William 1794-1842 .... **NCLC 8**

Mahapatra, Jayanta 1928- .... **CLC 33**
See also CANR 15; CA 73-76

Mahfuz Najib 1912- .... **CLC 52, 55**
See also DLB-Y 88

Mahon, Derek 1941- .... **CLC 27**
See also CA 113; DLB 40

Mailer, Norman
1923- ...... **CLC 1, 2, 3, 4, 5, 8, 11, 14, 28, 39**
See also CA 9-12R; CABS 1; DLB 2, 16,
28; DLB-Y 80, 83; DLB-DS 3

Maillet, Antonine 1929- .... **CLC 54**
See also CA 115, 120; DLB 60

Mais, Roger 1905-1955 .... **TCLC 8**
See also CA 105

Maitland, Sara (Louise) 1950- ...... **CLC 49**
See also CANR 13; CA 69-72

Major, Clarence 1936- .... **CLC 3, 19, 48**
See also CAAS 6; CANR 13; CA 21-24R;
DLB 33

Major, Kevin 1949- .... **CLC 26**
See also CLR 11; CANR 21; CA 97-100;
SATA 32; DLB 60

Malamud, Bernard
1914-1986 ..... **CLC 1, 2, 3, 5, 8, 9, 11, 18, 27, 44**
See also CA 5-8R; obituary CA 118;
CABS 1; DLB 2, 28; DLB-Y 80, 86;
CDALB 1941-1968

Malherbe, Francois de 1555-1628 ..... **LC 5**

Mallarme, Stephane 1842-1898 .... **NCLC 4**

Mallet-Joris, Francoise 1930- ...... **CLC 11**
See also CANR 17; CA 65-68

Maloff, Saul 1922- .... **CLC 5**
See also CA 33-36R

Malone, Louis 1907-1963
See MacNeice, (Frederick) Louis

Malone, Michael (Christopher)
1942- .... **CLC 43**
See also CANR 14; CA 77-80

Malory, (Sir) Thomas ?-1471 .... **LC 11**
See also SATA 33

Malouf, David 1934- .... **CLC 28**

Malraux, (Georges-) Andre
1901-1976 ...... **CLC 1, 4, 9, 13, 15, 57**
See also CAP 2; CA 21-24;
obituary CA 69-72; DLB 72

Malzberg, Barry N. 1939- .... **CLC 7**
See also CAAS 4; CANR 16; CA 61-64;
DLB 8

Mamet, David (Alan)
1947-1987 .... **CLC 9, 15, 34, 46**
See also CANR 15; CA 81-84, 124; DLB 7

Mamoulian, Rouben 1898- .... **CLC 16**
See also CA 25-28R

Mandelstam, Osip (Emilievich)
1891?-1938? .... **TCLC 2, 6**
See also CA 104

Mander, Jane 1877-1949 .... **TCLC 31**

Mandiargues, Andre Pieyre de
1909- .... **CLC 41**
See also CA 103

Mangan, James Clarence
1803-1849 .... **NCLC 27**

Manley, (Mary) Delariviere
1672?-1724 .... **LC 1**
See also DLB 39

Mann, (Luiz) Heinrich 1871-1950 ... **TCLC 9**
See also CA 106; DLB 66

Mann, Thomas
1875-1955 ...... **TCLC 2, 8, 14, 21, 35; SSC 5**
See also CA 104, 128; DLB 66

Manning, Frederic 1882-1935 ..... **TCLC 25**

Manning, Olivia 1915-1980 ...... **CLC 5, 19**
See also CA 5-8R; obituary CA 101

Mano, D. Keith 1942- .... **CLC 2, 10**
See also CAAS 6; CANR 26; CA 25-28R;
DLB 6

Mansfield, Katherine
1888-1923 .... **TCLC 2, 8, 39**
See also CA 104

Manso, Peter 1940- .... **CLC 39**
See also CA 29-32R

Manzoni, Alessandro 1785-1873 .. **NCLC 29**

Mapu, Abraham (ben Jekutiel)
1808-1867 .... **NCLC 18**

Marat, Jean Paul 1743-1793 .... **LC 10**

Marcel, Gabriel (Honore)
1889-1973 .... **CLC 15**
See also CA 102; obituary CA 45-48

Marchbanks, Samuel 1913-
See Davies, (William) Robertson

Marie de l'Incarnation 1599-1672 .... **LC 10**

Marinetti, F(ilippo) T(ommaso)
1876-1944 .... **TCLC 10**
See also CA 107

Marivaux, Pierre Carlet de Chamblain de
(1688-1763) .... **LC 4**

Markandaya, Kamala 1924- ...... **CLC 8, 38**
See also Taylor, Kamala (Purnaiya)

Markfield, Wallace (Arthur) 1926- ... **CLC 8**
See also CAAS 3; CA 69-72; DLB 2, 28

Markham, Robert 1922-
See Amis, Kingsley (William)

Marks, J. 1942-
See Highwater, Jamake

Marley, Bob 1945-1981 .... **CLC 17**
See also Marley, Robert Nesta

Marley, Robert Nesta 1945-1981
See Marley, Bob
See also CA 107; obituary CA 103

Marmontel, Jean-Francois
1723-1799 .... **LC 2**

Marquand, John P(hillips)
1893-1960 .... **CLC 2, 10**
See also CA 85-88; DLB 9

Marquez, Gabriel Garcia 1928-
See Garcia Marquez, Gabriel

Marquis, Don(ald Robert Perry)
1878-1937 .... **TCLC 7**
See also CA 104; DLB 11, 25

Marryat, Frederick 1792-1848 .... **NCLC 3**
See also DLB 21

Marsh, (Dame Edith) Ngaio
1899-1982 .... **CLC 7, 53**
See also CANR 6; CA 9-12R; DLB 77

Marshall, Garry 1935?- .... **CLC 17**
See also CA 111

Marshall, Paule 1929- ..... **CLC 27; SSC 3**
See also CANR 25; CA 77-80; DLB 33

Marsten, Richard 1926-
See Hunter, Evan

Martin, Steve 1945?- .... **CLC 30**
See also CA 97-100

Martin du Gard, Roger
1881-1958 .... **TCLC 24**
See also CA 118

Martineau, Harriet 1802-1876 .... **NCLC 26**
See also YABC 2; DLB 21, 55

Martinez Ruiz, Jose 1874-1967
See Azorin
See also CA 93-96

Martinez Sierra, Gregorio
1881-1947 .... **TCLC 6**
See also CA 104, 115

Martinez Sierra, Maria (de la O'LeJarraga)
1880?-1974 .... **TCLC 6**
See also obituary CA 115

Martinson, Harry (Edmund)
1904-1978 .... **CLC 14**
See also CA 77-80

Marvell, Andrew 1621-1678 .... **LC 4**

Marx, Karl (Heinrich)
1818-1883 .... **NCLC 17**

Masaoka Shiki 1867-1902 .... **TCLC 18**

Masefield, John (Edward)
1878-1967 .... **CLC 11, 47**
See also CAP 2; CA 19-20;
obituary CA 25-28R; SATA 19; DLB 10, 19

Maso, Carole 19??- .... **CLC 44**

Mason, Bobbie Ann
1940- .... **CLC 28, 43; SSC 4**
See also CANR 11; CA 53-56; SAAS 1;
DLB-Y 87

Mason, Nick 1945- .... **CLC 35**
See also Pink Floyd

Mason, Tally 1909-1971
See Derleth, August (William)

Masters, Edgar Lee
1868?-1950 .... **TCLC 2, 25; PC 1**
See also CA 104; DLB 54;
CDALB 1865-1917

Masters, Hilary 1928- .... **CLC 48**
See also CANR 13; CA 25-28R

Mastrosimone, William 19??- ...... **CLC 36**

Matheson, Richard (Burton)
1926- .... **CLC 37**
See also CA 97-100; DLB 8, 44

Mathews, Harry 1930- .... **CLC 6, 52**
See also CAAS 6; CANR 18; CA 21-24R

Mathias, Roland (Glyn) 1915- ..... **CLC 45**
See also CANR 19; CA 97-100; DLB 27

Matthews, Greg 1949- .... **CLC 45**

Matthews, William 1942- .... **CLC 40**
See also CANR 12; CA 29-32R; DLB 5

Matthias, John (Edward) 1941- ...... **CLC 9**
See also CA 33-36R

Matthiessen, Peter 1927- ... **CLC 5, 7, 11, 32**
See also CANR 21; CA 9-12R; SATA 27;
DLB 6

Maturin, Charles Robert
1780?-1824 .... **NCLC 6**

Matute, Ana Maria 1925- .... **CLC 11**
See also CA 89-92

Maugham, W(illiam) Somerset
1874-1965 .... **CLC 1, 11, 15**
See also CA 5-8R; obituary CA 25-28R;
DLB 10, 36

Maupassant, (Henri Rene Albert) Guy de
1850-1893 .... **NCLC 1; SSC 1**

Mauriac, Claude 1914- .... **CLC 9**
See also CA 89-92

Mauriac, Francois (Charles)
1885-1970 .... **CLC 4, 9, 56**
See also CAP 2; CA 25-28; DLB 65

Mavor, Osborne Henry 1888-1951
See Bridie, James
See also CA 104

Maxwell, William (Keepers, Jr.)
1908- .... **CLC 19**
See also CA 93-96; DLB-Y 80

May, Elaine 1932- .... **CLC 16**
See also CA 124; DLB 44

Mayakovsky, Vladimir (Vladimirovich)
1893-1930 .... **TCLC 4, 18**
See also CA 104

Maynard, Joyce 1953- .... **CLC 23**
See also CA 111

Mayne, William (James Carter)
1928- .... **CLC 12**
See also CA 9-12R; SATA 6

Mayo, Jim 1908?-
See L'Amour, Louis (Dearborn)

Maysles, Albert 1926- and **Maysles, David**
1926- .... **CLC 16**

Maysles, Albert 1926-
See Maysles, Albert and Maysles, David
See also CA 29-32R

Maysles, David 1932-
See Maysles, Albert and Maysles, David

Mazer, Norma Fox 1931- .... **CLC 26**
See also CLR 23; CANR 12; CA 69-72;
SAAS 1; SATA 24

McAuley, James (Phillip)
1917-1976 .... **CLC 45**
See also CA 97-100

McBain, Ed 1926-
See Hunter, Evan

McBrien, William 1930- .... **CLC 44**
See also CA 107

McCaffrey, Anne 1926- .... **CLC 17**
See also CANR 15; CA 25-28R; SATA 8;
DLB 8

McCarthy, Cormac 1933- .... **CLC 4, 57**
See also CANR 10; CA 13-16R; DLB 6

McCarthy, Mary (Therese)
1912-1989- ... **CLC 1, 3, 5, 14, 24, 39, 59**
See also CANR 16; CA 5-8R; DLB 2;
DLB-Y 81

McCartney, (James) Paul
1942- .... **CLC 12, 35**

McCauley, Stephen 19??- .... **CLC 50**

McClure, Michael 1932- .... **CLC 6, 10**
See also CANR 17; CA 21-24R; DLB 16

McCorkle, Jill (Collins) 1958- ...... **CLC 51**
See also CA 121; DLB-Y 87

McCourt, James 1941- .... **CLC 5**
See also CA 57-60

McCoy, Horace 1897-1955 .... **TCLC 28**
See also CA 108; DLB 9

McCrae, John 1872-1918 .... **TCLC 12**
See also CA 109

McCullers, (Lula) Carson (Smith)
1917-1967 .... **CLC 1, 4, 10, 12, 48**
See also CANR 18; CA 5-8R;
obituary CA 25-28R; CABS 1; SATA 27;
DLB 2, 7; CDALB 1941-1968

McCullough, Colleen 1938?- .... **CLC 27**
See also CANR 17; CA 81-84

McElroy, Joseph (Prince)
1930- .... **CLC 5, 47**
See also CA 17-20R

McEwan, Ian (Russell) 1948- . . . . . . CLC 13
See also CANR 14; CA 61-64; DLB 14

McFadden, David 1940- . . . . CLC 48
See also CA 104; DLB 60

McGahern, John 1934- . . . . CLC 5, 9, 48
See also CA 17-20R; DLB 14

McGinley, Patrick 1937- . . . . CLC 41
See also CA 120

McGinley, Phyllis 1905-1978 . . . . . . CLC 14
See also CANR 19; CA 9-12R;
obituary CA 77-80; SATA 2, 44;
obituary SATA 24; DLB 11, 48

McGinniss, Joe 1942- . . . . CLC 32
See also CA 25-28R

McGivern, Maureen Daly 1921-
See Daly, Maureen
See also CA 9-12R

McGrath, Patrick 1950- . . . . CLC 55

McGrath, Thomas 1916- . . . . . . CLC 28, 59
See also CANR 6; CA 9-12R, 130;
SATA 41

McGuane, Thomas (Francis III)
1939- . . . . CLC 3, 7, 18
See also CANR 5; CA 49-52; DLB 2;
DLB-Y 80

McGuckian, Medbh 1950- . . . . CLC 48
See also DLB 40

McHale, Tom 1941-1982 . . . . CLC 3, 5
See also CA 77-80; obituary CA 106

McIlvanney, William 1936- . . . . CLC 42
See also CA 25-28R; DLB 14

McIlwraith, Maureen Mollie Hunter 1922-
See Hunter, Mollie
See also CA 29-32R; SATA 2

McInerney, Jay 1955- . . . . CLC 34
See also CA 116, 123

McIntyre, Vonda N(eel) 1948- . . . . . CLC 18
See also CANR 17; CA 81-84

McKay, Claude 1890-1948 . . . . TCLC 7
See also CA 104; DLB 4, 45

McKuen, Rod 1933- . . . . CLC 1, 3
See also CA 41-44R

McLuhan, (Herbert) Marshall
1911-1980 . . . . CLC 37
See also CANR 12; CA 9-12R;
obituary CA 102

McManus, Declan Patrick 1955-
See Costello, Elvis

McMillan, Terry 1951- . . . . CLC 50, 61

McMurtry, Larry (Jeff)
1936- . . . . CLC 2, 3, 7, 11, 27, 44
See also CANR 19; CA 5-8R; DLB 2;
DLB-Y 80, 87

McNally, Terrence 1939- . . . . . . CLC 4, 7, 41
See also CANR 2; CA 45-48; DLB 7

McPhee, John 1931- . . . . CLC 36
See also CANR 20; CA 65-68

McPherson, James Alan 1943- . . . . . CLC 19
See also CANR 24; CA 25-28R; DLB 38

McPherson, William 1939- . . . . CLC 34
See also CA 57-60

McSweeney, Kerry 19??- . . . . CLC 34

Mead, Margaret 1901-1978 . . . . CLC 37
See also CANR 4; CA 1-4R;
obituary CA 81-84; SATA 20

Meaker, M. J. 1927-
See Kerr, M. E.; Meaker, Marijane

Meaker, Marijane 1927-
See Kerr, M. E.
See also CA 107; SATA 20

Medoff, Mark (Howard) 1940- . . . CLC 6, 23
See also CANR 5; CA 53-56; DLB 7

Megged, Aharon 1920- . . . . CLC 9
See also CANR 1; CA 49-52

Mehta, Ved (Parkash) 1934- . . . . CLC 37
See also CANR 2, 23; CA 1-4R

Mellor, John 1953?-
See The Clash

Meltzer, Milton 1915- . . . . CLC 26 13
See also CA 13-16R; SAAS 1; SATA 1, 50;
DLB 61

Melville, Herman
1819-1891 . . . . . . NCLC 3, 12, 29; SSC 1
See also SATA 59; DLB 3, 74;
CDALB 1640-1865

Membreno, Alejandro 1972- . . . . CLC 59

Mencken, H(enry) L(ouis)
1880-1956 . . . . TCLC 13
See also CA 105; DLB 11, 29, 63

Mercer, David 1928-1980 . . . . CLC 5
See also CA 9-12R; obituary CA 102;
DLB 13

Meredith, George 1828-1909 . . . . . . TCLC 17
See also CA 117; DLB 18, 35, 57

Meredith, William (Morris)
1919- . . . . CLC 4, 13, 22, 55
See also CANR 6; CA 9-12R; DLB 5

Merezhkovsky, Dmitri
1865-1941 . . . . TCLC 29

Merimee, Prosper
1803-1870 . . . . NCLC 6; SSC 7

Merkin, Daphne 1954- . . . . CLC 44
See also CANR 123

Merrill, James (Ingram)
1926- . . . . CLC 2, 3, 6, 8, 13, 18, 34
See also CANR 10; CA 13-16R; DLB 5;
DLB-Y 85

Merton, Thomas (James)
1915-1968 . . . . CLC 1, 3, 11, 34
See also CANR 22; CA 5-8R;
obituary CA 25-28R; DLB 48; DLB-Y 81

Merwin, W(illiam) S(tanley)
1927- . . . . . . CLC 1, 2, 3, 5, 8, 13, 18, 45
See also CANR 15; CA 13-16R; DLB 5

Metcalf, John 1938- . . . . CLC 37
See also CA 113; DLB 60

Mew, Charlotte (Mary)
1870-1928 . . . . TCLC 8
See also CA 105; DLB 19

Mewshaw, Michael 1943- . . . . CLC 9
See also CANR 7; CA 53-56; DLB-Y 80

Meyer-Meyrink, Gustav 1868-1932
See Meyrink, Gustav
See also CA 117

Meyers, Jeffrey 1939- . . . . CLC 39
See also CA 73-76

Meynell, Alice (Christiana Gertrude
Thompson) 1847-1922 . . . . TCLC 6
See also CA 104; DLB 19

Meyrink, Gustav 1868-1932 . . . . . . TCLC 21
See also Meyer-Meyrink, Gustav

Michaels, Leonard 1933- . . . . CLC 6, 25
See also CANR 21; CA 61-64

Michaux, Henri 1899-1984 . . . . . . CLC 8, 19
See also CA 85-88; obituary CA 114

Michelangelo 1475-1564 . . . . LC 12

Michener, James A(lbert)
1907- . . . . CLC 1, 5, 11, 29, 60
See also CANR 21; CA 5-8R; DLB 6

Mickiewicz, Adam 1798-1855 . . . . . NCLC 3

Middleton, Christopher 1926- . . . . . CLC 13
See also CA 13-16R; DLB 40

Middleton, Stanley 1919- . . . . CLC 7, 38
See also CANR 21; CA 25-28R; DLB 14

Migueis, Jose Rodrigues 1901- . . . . . CLC 10

Mikszath, Kalman 1847-1910 . . . . . TCLC 31

Miles, Josephine (Louise)
1911-1985 . . . . CLC 1, 2, 14, 34, 39
See also CANR 2; CA 1-4R;
obituary CA 116; DLB 48

Mill, John Stuart 1806-1873 . . . . . NCLC 11

Millar, Kenneth 1915-1983 . . . . CLC 14
See also Macdonald, Ross
See also CANR 16; CA 9-12R;
obituary CA 110; DLB 2; DLB-Y 83

Millay, Edna St. Vincent
1892-1950 . . . . TCLC 4
See also CA 104; DLB 45

Miller, Arthur
1915- . . . . CLC 1, 2, 6, 10, 15, 26, 47
See also CANR 2; CA 1-4R; DLB 7;
CDALB 1941-1968

Miller, Henry (Valentine)
1891-1980 . . . . CLC 1, 2, 4, 9, 14, 43
See also CA 9-12R; obituary CA 97-100;
DLB 4, 9; DLB-Y 80

Miller, Jason 1939?- . . . . CLC 2
See also CA 73-76; DLB 7

Miller, Sue 19??- . . . . CLC 44

Miller, Walter M(ichael), Jr.
1923- . . . . CLC 4, 30
See also CA 85-88; DLB 8

Millhauser, Steven 1943- . . . . CLC 21, 54
See also CA 108, 110, 111; DLB 2

Millin, Sarah Gertrude 1889-1968 . . CLC 49
See also CA 102; obituary CA 93-96

Milne, A(lan) A(lexander)
1882-1956 . . . . TCLC 6
See also CLR 1; YABC 1; CA 104; DLB 10

Milner, Ron(ald) 1938- . . . . CLC 56
See also CANR 24; CA 73-76; DLB 38

Milosz Czeslaw
1911- . . . . CLC 5, 11, 22, 31, 56
See also CANR 23; CA 81-84

Milton, John 1608-1674 . . . . LC 9

Miner, Valerie (Jane) 1947- . . . . CLC 40
See also CA 97-100

Minot, Susan 1956- . . . . CLC 44

Minus, Ed 1938- . . . . CLC 39

Author Index

Mujica Lainez, Manuel
1910-1984 . . . . **CLC 31**
See also CA 81-84; obituary CA 112

Mukherjee, Bharati 1940- . . . . **CLC 53**
See also CA 107; DLB 60

Muldoon, Paul 1951- . . . . **CLC 32**
See also CA 113; DLB 40

Mulisch, Harry (Kurt Victor)
1927- . . . . **CLC 42**
See also CANR 6; CA 9-12R

Mull, Martin 1943- . . . . **CLC 17**
See also CA 105

Munford, Robert 1737?-1783 . . . . **LC 5**
See also DLB 31

Munro, Alice (Laidlaw)
1931- . . . . **CLC 6, 10, 19, 50; SSC 3**
See also CA 33-36R; SATA 29; DLB 53

Munro, H(ector) H(ugh) 1870-1916
See Saki
See also CA 104; DLB 34

Murasaki, Lady c. 11th century- . . . **CMLC 1**

Murdoch, (Jean) Iris
1919- . . . . . . **CLC 1, 2, 3, 4, 6, 8, 11, 15,**
22, 31, 51
See also CANR 8; CA 13-16R; DLB 14

Murphy, Richard 1927- . . . . **CLC 41**
See also CA 29-32R; DLB 40

Murphy, Sylvia 19??- . . . . **CLC 34**

Murphy, Thomas (Bernard) 1935- . . . **CLC 51**
See also CA 101

Murray, Les(lie) A(llan) 1938- . . . . . **CLC 40**
See also CANR 11; CA 21-24R

Murry, John Middleton
1889-1957 . . . . **TCLC 16**
See also CA 118

Musgrave, Susan 1951- . . . . **CLC 13, 54**
See also CA 69-72

Musil, Robert (Edler von)
1880-1942 . . . . **TCLC 12**
See also CA 109

Musset, (Louis Charles) Alfred de
1810-1857 . . . . **NCLC 7**

Myers, Walter Dean 1937- . . . . **CLC 35**
See also CLR 4, 16; CANR 20; CA 33-36R;
SAAS 2; SATA 27, 41; DLB 33

Nabokov, Vladimir (Vladimirovich)
1899-1977 . . . . **CLC 1, 2, 3, 6, 8, 11, 15,**
23, 44, 46
See also CANR 20; CA 5-8R;
obituary CA 69-72; DLB 2; DLB-Y 80;
DLB-DS 3; CDALB 1941-1968

Nagy, Laszlo 1925-1978 . . . . **CLC 7**
See also obituary CA 112

Naipaul, Shiva(dhar Srinivasa)
1945-1985 . . . . **CLC 32, 39**
See also CA 110, 112; obituary CA 116;
DLB-Y 85

Naipaul, V(idiadhar) S(urajprasad)
1932- . . . . **CLC 4, 7, 9, 13, 18, 37**
See also CANR 1; CA 1-4R; DLB-Y 85

Nakos, Ioulia 1899?-
See Nakos, Lilika

Nakos, Lilika 1899?- . . . . **CLC 29**

Nakou, Lilika 1899?-
See Nakos, Lilika

Narayan, R(asipuram) K(rishnaswami)
1906- . . . . **CLC 7, 28, 47**
See also CA 81-84

Nash, (Frediric) Ogden 1902-1971 . . **CLC 23**
See also CAP 1; CA 13-14;
obituary CA 29-32R; SATA 2, 46;
DLB 11

Nathan, George Jean 1882-1958 . . . **TCLC 18**
See also CA 114

Natsume, Kinnosuke 1867-1916
See Natsume, Soseki
See also CA 104

Natsume, Soseki 1867-1916 . . . . . **TCLC 2, 10**
See also Natsume, Kinnosuke

Natti, (Mary) Lee 1919-
See Kingman, (Mary) Lee
See also CANR 2; CA 7-8R

Naylor, Gloria 1950- . . . . **CLC 28, 52**
See also CANR 27; CA 107

Neff, Debra 1972- . . . . **CLC 59**

Neihardt, John G(neisenau)
1881-1973 . . . . **CLC 32**
See also CAP 1; CA 13-14; DLB 9, 54

Nekrasov, Nikolai Alekseevich
1821-1878 . . . . **NCLC 11**

Nelligan, Emile 1879-1941 . . . . **TCLC 14**
See also CA 114

Nelson, Willie 1933- . . . . **CLC 17**
See also CA 107

Nemerov, Howard 1920- . . . . **CLC 2, 6, 9, 36**
See also CANR 1; CA 1-4R; CABS 2;
DLB 5, 6; DLB-Y 83

Neruda, Pablo
1904-1973 . . . . . **CLC 1, 2, 5, 7, 9, 28, 62**
See also CAP 2; CA 19-20;
obituary CA 45-48

Nerval, Gerard de 1808-1855 . . . . . . **NCLC 1**

Nervo, (Jose) Amado (Ruiz de)
1870-1919 . . . . **TCLC 11**
See also CA 109

Neufeld, John (Arthur) 1938- . . . . . . **CLC 17**
See also CANR 11; CA 25-28R; SAAS 3;
SATA 6

Neville, Emily Cheney 1919- . . . . **CLC 12**
See also CANR 3; CA 5-8R; SAAS 2;
SATA 1

Newbound, Bernard Slade 1930-
See Slade, Bernard
See also CA 81-84

Newby, P(ercy) H(oward)
1918- . . . . **CLC 2, 13**
See also CA 5-8R; DLB 15

Newlove, Donald 1928- . . . . **CLC 6**
See also CANR 25; CA 29-32R

Newlove, John (Herbert) 1938- . . . . . **CLC 14**
See also CANR 9, 25; CA 21-24R

Newman, Charles 1938- . . . . **CLC 2, 8**
See also CA 21-24R

Newman, Edwin (Harold) 1919- . . . . **CLC 14**
See also CANR 5; CA 69-72

Newton, Suzanne 1936- . . . . **CLC 35**
See also CANR 14; CA 41-44R; SATA 5

Ngema, Mbongeni 1955- . . . . **CLC 57**

Ngugi, James (Thiong'o)
1938- . . . . **CLC 3, 7, 13, 36**
See also Ngugi wa Thiong'o; Wa Thiong'o,
Ngugi
See also CA 81-84

Ngugi wa Thiong'o 1938- . . . **CLC 3, 7, 13, 36**
See also Ngugi, James (Thiong'o); Wa
Thiong'o, Ngugi

Nichol, B(arrie) P(hillip) 1944- . . . . . **CLC 18**
See also CA 53-56; DLB 53

Nichols, John (Treadwell) 1940- . . . . **CLC 38**
See also CAAS 2; CANR 6; CA 9-12R;
DLB-Y 82

Nichols, Peter (Richard) 1927- . . . **CLC 5, 36**
See also CA 104; DLB 13

Nicolas, F.R.E. 1927-
See Freeling, Nicolas

Niedecker, Lorine 1903-1970 . . . . **CLC 10, 42**
See also CAP 2; CA 25-28; DLB 48

Nietzsche, Friedrich (Wilhelm)
1844-1900 . . . . **TCLC 10, 18**
See also CA 107

Nievo, Ippolito 1831-1861 . . . . **NCLC 22**

Nightingale, Anne Redmon 1943-
See Redmon (Nightingale), Anne
See also CA 103

Nin, Anais
1903-1977 . . . . . . **CLC 1, 4, 8, 11, 14, 60**
See also CANR 22; CA 13-16R;
obituary CA 69-72; DLB 2, 4

Nissenson, Hugh 1933- . . . . **CLC 4, 9**
See also CA 17-20R; DLB 28

Niven, Larry 1938- . . . . **CLC 8**
See also Niven, Laurence Van Cott
See also DLB 8

Niven, Laurence Van Cott 1938-
See Niven, Larry
See also CANR 14; CA 21-24R

Nixon, Agnes Eckhardt 1927- . . . . . . **CLC 21**
See also CA 110

Nkosi, Lewis 1936- . . . . **CLC 45**
See also CA 65-68

Nodier, (Jean) Charles (Emmanuel)
1780-1844 . . . . **NCLC 19**

Nolan, Christopher 1965- . . . . **CLC 58**
See also CA 111

Nordhoff, Charles 1887-1947 . . . . . . **TCLC 23**
See also CA 108; SATA 23; DLB 9

Norman, Marsha 1947- . . . . **CLC 28**
See also CA 105; DLB-Y 84

Norris, (Benjamin) Frank(lin)
1870-1902 . . . . **TCLC 24**
See also CA 110; DLB 12, 71;
CDALB 1865-1917

Norris, Leslie 1921- . . . . **CLC 14**
See also CANR 14; CAP 1; CA 11-12;
DLB 27

North, Andrew 1912-
See Norton, Andre

North, Christopher 1785-1854
See Wilson, John

Author Index

Proust, Marcel 1871-1922 . . **TCLC 7, 13, 33**
See also CA 104, 120; DLB 65

Pryor, Richard 1940- . . . . **CLC 26**
See also CA 122

Przybyszewski, Stanislaw
1868-1927 . . . . **TCLC 36**
See also DLB 66

Puig, Manuel 1932- . . . . **CLC 3, 5, 10, 28**
See also CANR 2; CA 45-48

Purdy, A(lfred) W(ellington)
1918- . . . . **CLC 3, 6, 14, 50**
See also CA 81-84

Purdy, James (Amos)
1923- . . . . **CLC 2, 4, 10, 28, 52**
See also CAAS 1; CANR 19; CA 33-36R;
DLB 2

Pushkin, Alexander (Sergeyevich)
1799-1837 . . . . **NCLC 3, 27**

P'u Sung-ling 1640-1715 . . . . **LC 3**

Puzo, Mario 1920- . . . . **CLC 1, 2, 6, 36**
See also CANR 4; CA 65-68; DLB 6

Pym, Barbara (Mary Crampton)
1913-1980 . . . . **CLC 13, 19, 37**
See also CANR 13; CAP 1; CA 13-14;
obituary CA 97-100; DLB 14; DLB-Y 87

Pynchon, Thomas (Ruggles, Jr.)
1937- . . . . . **CLC 2, 3, 6, 9, 11, 18, 33, 62**
See also CANR 22; CA 17-20R; DLB 2

Quasimodo, Salvatore 1901-1968 . . . **CLC 10**
See also CAP 1; CA 15-16;
obituary CA 25-28R

Queen, Ellery 1905-1982 . . . . **CLC 3, 11**
See also Dannay, Frederic; Lee, Manfred
B(ennington)

Queneau, Raymond
1903-1976 . . . . **CLC 2, 5, 10, 42**
See also CA 77-80; obituary CA 69-72;
DLB 72

Quin, Ann (Marie) 1936-1973 . . . . **CLC 6**
See also CA 9-12R; obituary CA 45-48;
DLB 14

Quinn, Simon 1942-
See Smith, Martin Cruz
See also CANR 6, 23; CA 85-88

Quiroga, Horacio (Sylvestre)
1878-1937 . . . . **TCLC 20**
See also CA 117

Quoirez, Francoise 1935-
See Sagan, Francoise
See also CANR 6; CA 49-52

Rabe, David (William) 1940- . . . **CLC 4, 8, 33**
See also CA 85-88; DLB 7

Rabelais, Francois 1494?-1553 . . . . **LC 5**

Rabinovitch, Sholem 1859-1916
See Aleichem, Sholom
See also CA 104

Rachen, Kurt von 1911-1986
See Hubbard, L(afayette) Ron(ald)

Radcliffe, Ann (Ward) 1764-1823 . . **NCLC 6**
See also DLB 39

Radiguet, Raymond 1903-1923 . . . . **TCLC 29**

Radnoti, Miklos 1909-1944 . . . . **TCLC 16**
See also CA 118

Rado, James 1939- . . . . **CLC 17**
See also CA 105

Radomski, James 1932-
See Rado, James

Radvanyi, Netty Reiling 1900-1983
See Seghers, Anna
See also CA 85-88; obituary CA 110

Rae, Ben 1935-
See Griffiths, Trevor

Raeburn, John 1941- . . . . **CLC 34**
See also CA 57-60

Ragni, Gerome 1942- . . . . **CLC 17**
See also CA 105

Rahv, Philip 1908-1973 . . . . **CLC 24**
See also Greenberg, Ivan

Raine, Craig 1944- . . . . **CLC 32**
See also CA 108; DLB 40

Raine, Kathleen (Jessie) 1908- . . . **CLC 7, 45**
See also CA 85-88; DLB 20

Rainis, Janis 1865-1929 . . . . **TCLC 29**

Rakosi, Carl 1903- . . . . **CLC 47**
See also Rawley, Callman
See also CAAS 5

Ramos, Graciliano 1892-1953 . . . . . **TCLC 32**

Rampersad, Arnold 19??- . . . . **CLC 44**

Ramuz, Charles-Ferdinand
1878-1947 . . . . **TCLC 33**

Rand, Ayn 1905-1982 . . . . **CLC 3, 30, 44**
See also CA 13-16R; obituary CA 105

Randall, Dudley (Felker) 1914- . . . . . . **CLC 1**
See also CANR 23; CA 25-28R; DLB 41

Ransom, John Crowe
1888-1974 . . . . **CLC 2, 4, 5, 11, 24**
See also CANR 6; CA 5-8R;
obituary CA 49-52; DLB 45, 63

Rao, Raja 1909- . . . . **CLC 25, 56**
See also CA 73-76

Raphael, Frederic (Michael)
1931- . . . . **CLC 2, 14**
See also CANR 1; CA 1-4R; DLB 14

Rathbone, Julian 1935- . . . . **CLC 41**
See also CA 101

Rattigan, Terence (Mervyn)
1911-1977 . . . . **CLC 7**
See also CA 85-88; obituary CA 73-76;
DLB 13

Ratushinskaya, Irina 1954- . . . . **CLC 54**

Raven, Simon (Arthur Noel)
1927- . . . . **CLC 14**
See also CA 81-84

Rawley, Callman 1903-
See Rakosi, Carl
See also CANR 12; CA 21-24R

Rawlings, Marjorie Kinnan
1896-1953 . . . . **TCLC 4**
See also YABC 1; CA 104; DLB 9, 22

Ray, Satyajit 1921- . . . . **CLC 16**
See also CA 114

Read, Herbert (Edward) 1893-1968 . . **CLC 4**
See also CA 85-88; obituary CA 25-28R;
DLB 20

Read, Piers Paul 1941- . . . . . . **CLC 4, 10, 25**
See also CA 21-24R; SATA 21; DLB 14

Reade, Charles 1814-1884 . . . . **NCLC 2**
See also DLB 21

Reade, Hamish 1936-
See Gray, Simon (James Holliday)

Reading, Peter 1946- . . . . **CLC 47**
See also CA 103; DLB 40

Reaney, James 1926- . . . . **CLC 13**
See also CA 41-44R; SATA 43; DLB 68

Rebreanu, Liviu 1885-1944 . . . . **TCLC 28**

Rechy, John (Francisco)
1934- . . . . **CLC 1, 7, 14, 18**
See also CAAS 4; CANR 6; CA 5-8R;
DLB-Y 82

Redcam, Tom 1870-1933 . . . . **TCLC 25**

Redgrove, Peter (William)
1932- . . . . **CLC 6, 41**
See also CANR 3; CA 1-4R; DLB 40

Redmon (Nightingale), Anne
1943- . . . . **CLC 22**
See also Nightingale, Anne Redmon
See also DLB-Y 86

Reed, Ishmael
1938- . . . . **CLC 2, 3, 5, 6, 13, 32, 60**
See also CANR 25; CA 21-24R; DLB 2, 5,
33

Reed, John (Silas) 1887-1920 . . . . . . **TCLC 9**
See also CA 106

Reed, Lou 1944- . . . . **CLC 21**

Reeve, Clara 1729-1807 . . . . **NCLC 19**
See also DLB 39

Reid, Christopher 1949- . . . . **CLC 33**
See also DLB 40

Reid Banks, Lynne 1929-
See Banks, Lynne Reid
See also CANR 6, 22; CA 1-4R; SATA 22

Reiner, Max 1900-
See Caldwell, (Janet Miriam) Taylor
(Holland)

Reizenstein, Elmer Leopold 1892-1967
See Rice, Elmer

Remark, Erich Paul 1898-1970
See Remarque, Erich Maria

Remarque, Erich Maria
1898-1970 . . . . **CLC 21**
See also CA 77-80; obituary CA 29-32R;
DLB 56

Remizov, Alexey (Mikhailovich)
1877-1957 . . . . **TCLC 27**
See also CA 125

Renan, Joseph Ernest
1823-1892 . . . . **NCLC 26**

Renard, Jules 1864-1910 . . . . **TCLC 17**
See also CA 117

Renault, Mary 1905-1983 . . . . **CLC 3, 11, 17**
See also Challans, Mary
See also DLB-Y 83

Rendell, Ruth 1930- . . . . **CLC 28, 48**
See also Vine, Barbara
See also CA 109

Renoir, Jean 1894-1979 . . . . **CLC 20**
See also obituary CA 85-88

Resnais, Alain 1922- . . . . **CLC 16**

Reverdy, Pierre 1899-1960 . . . . **CLC 53**
See also CA 97-100; obituary CA 89-92

Rexroth, Kenneth
1905-1982 ...... **CLC 1, 2, 6, 11, 22, 49**
See also CANR 14; CA 5-8R;
obituary CA 107; DLB 16, 48; DLB-Y 82;
CDALB 1941-1968

Reyes, Alfonso 1889-1959 .... **TCLC 33**

Reyes y Basoalto, Ricardo Eliecer Neftali
1904-1973
See Neruda, Pablo

Reymont, Wladyslaw Stanislaw
1867-1925 .... **TCLC 5**
See also CA 104

Reynolds, Jonathan 1942?- ...... **CLC 6, 38**
See also CA 65-68

Reynolds, Michael (Shane) 1937- ... **CLC 44**
See also CANR 9; CA 65-68

Reynolds, (Sir) Joshua 1723-1792.... **LC 15**

Reznikoff, Charles 1894-1976 .... **CLC 9**
See also CAP 2; CA 33-36;
obituary CA 61-64; DLB 28, 45

Rezzori, Gregor von 1914-........ **CLC 25**
See also CA 122

Rhys, Jean
1890-1979 ...... **CLC 2, 4, 6, 14, 19, 51**
See also CA 25-28R; obituary CA 85-88;
DLB 36

Ribeiro, Darcy 1922- .... **CLC 34**
See also CA 33-36R

Ribeiro, Joao Ubaldo (Osorio Pimentel)
1941- .... **CLC 10**
See also CA 81-84

Ribman, Ronald (Burt) 1932- .... **CLC 7**
See also CA 21-24R

Rice, Anne 1941- .... **CLC 41**
See also CANR 12; CA 65-68

Rice, Elmer 1892-1967.......... **CLC 7, 49**
See also CAP 2; CA 21-22;
obituary CA 25-28R; DLB 4, 7

Rice, Tim 1944- .... **CLC 21**
See also CA 103

Rich, Adrienne (Cecile)
1929- .... **CLC 3, 6, 7, 11, 18, 36**
See also CANR 20; CA 9-12R; DLB 5, 67

Richard, Keith 1943- .... **CLC 17**
See also CA 107

Richards, David Adam 1950-...... **CLC 59**
See also CA 93-96; DLB 53

Richards, I(vor) A(rmstrong)
1893-1979 .... **CLC 14, 24**
See also CA 41-44R; obituary CA 89-92;
DLB 27

Richards, Keith 1943-
See Richard, Keith
See also CA 107

Richardson, Dorothy (Miller)
1873-1957 .... **TCLC 3**
See also CA 104; DLB 36

Richardson, Ethel 1870-1946
See Richardson, Henry Handel
See also CA 105

Richardson, Henry Handel
1870-1946 .... **TCLC 4**
See also Richardson, Ethel

Richardson, Samuel 1689-1761 ...... **LC 1**
See also DLB 39

Richler, Mordecai
1931- .... **CLC 3, 5, 9, 13, 18, 46**
See also CA 65-68; SATA 27, 44; DLB 53

Richter, Conrad (Michael)
1890-1968 .... **CLC 30**
See also CA 5-8R; obituary CA 25-28R;
SATA 3; DLB 9

Richter, Johann Paul Friedrich 1763-1825
See Jean Paul

Riding, Laura 1901- .... **CLC 3, 7**
See also Jackson, Laura (Riding)

Riefenstahl, Berta Helene Amalia
1902- .... **CLC 16**
See also Riefenstahl, Leni
See also CA 108

Riefenstahl, Leni 1902- .... **CLC 16**
See also Riefenstahl, Berta Helene Amalia
See also CA 108

Rilke, Rainer Maria
1875-1926 .... **TCLC 1, 6, 19**
See also CA 104

Rimbaud, (Jean Nicolas) Arthur
1854-1891 .... **NCLC 4**

Ringwood, Gwen(dolyn Margaret) Pharis
1910-1984 .... **CLC 48**
See also obituary CA 112

Rio, Michel 19??-................. **CLC 43**

Ritsos, Yannis 1909-......... **CLC 6, 13, 31**
See also CA 77-80

Ritter, Erika 1948?- .... **CLC 52**

Rivera, Jose Eustasio 1889-1928... **TCLC 35**

Rivers, Conrad Kent 1933-1968...... **CLC 1**
See also CA 85-88; DLB 41

Rizal, Jose 1861-1896.......... **NCLC 27**

Roa Bastos, Augusto 1917- .... **CLC 45**

Robbe-Grillet, Alain
1922- ...... **CLC 1, 2, 4, 6, 8, 10, 14, 43**
See also CA 9-12R

Robbins, Harold 1916-............ **CLC 5**
See also CANR 26; CA 73-76

Robbins, Thomas Eugene 1936-
See Robbins, Tom
See also CA 81-84

Robbins, Tom 1936-............ **CLC 9, 32**
See also Robbins, Thomas Eugene
See also DLB-Y 80

Robbins, Trina 1938- .... **CLC 21**

Roberts, (Sir) Charles G(eorge) D(ouglas)
1860-1943 .... **TCLC 8**
See also CA 105; SATA 29

Roberts, Kate 1891-1985 .... **CLC 15**
See also CA 107; obituary CA 116

Roberts, Keith (John Kingston)
1935- .... **CLC 14**
See also CA 25-28R

Roberts, Kenneth 1885-1957 ...... **TCLC 23**
See also CA 109; DLB 9

Roberts, Michele (B.) 1949-........ **CLC 48**
See also CA 115

Robinson, Edwin Arlington
1869-1935 .... **TCLC 5; PC 1**
See also CA 104; DLB 54;
CDALB 1865-1917

Robinson, Henry Crabb
1775-1867 .... **NCLC 15**

Robinson, Jill 1936-.............. **CLC 10**
See also CA 102

Robinson, Kim Stanley 19??-....... **CLC 34**
See also CA 126

Robinson, Marilynne 1944-....... **CLC 25**
See also CA 116

Robinson, Smokey 1940-.......... **CLC 21**

Robinson, William 1940-
See Robinson, Smokey
See also CA 116

Robison, Mary 1949-............. **CLC 42**
See also CA 113, 116

Roddenberry, Gene 1921-.......... **CLC 17**
See also CANR 110

Rodgers, Mary 1931-............. **CLC 12**
See also CLR 20; CANR 8; CA 49-52;
SATA 8

Rodgers, W(illiam) R(obert)
1909-1969 .... **CLC 7**
See also CA 85-88; DLB 20

Rodriguez, Claudio 1934-......... **CLC 10**

Roethke, Theodore (Huebner)
1908-1963 ...... **CLC 1, 3, 8, 11, 19, 46**
See also CA 81-84; CABS 2; SAAS 1;
DLB 5; CDALB 1941-1968

Rogers, Sam 1943-
See Shepard, Sam

Rogers, Thomas (Hunton) 1931-.... **CLC 57**
See also CA 89-92

Rogers, Will(iam Penn Adair)
1879-1935 .... **TCLC 8**
See also CA 105; DLB 11

Rogin, Gilbert 1929-.............. **CLC 18**
See also CANR 15; CA 65-68

Rohan, Koda 1867-1947........... **TCLC 22**
See also CA 121

Rohmer, Eric 1920- .... **CLC 16**
See also Scherer, Jean-Marie Maurice

Rohmer, Sax 1883-1959.......... **TCLC 28**
See also Ward, Arthur Henry Sarsfield
See also CA 108; DLB 70

Roiphe, Anne (Richardson)
1935-...................... **CLC 3, 9**
See also CA 89-92; DLB-Y 80

Rolfe, Frederick (William Serafino Austin
Lewis Mary) 1860-1913...... **TCLC 12**
See also CA 107; DLB 34

Rolland, Romain 1866-1944....... **TCLC 23**
See also CA 118

Rolvaag, O(le) E(dvart)
1876-1931 .... **TCLC 17**
See also CA 117; DLB 9

Romains, Jules 1885-1972.......... **CLC 7**
See also CA 85-88

Romero, Jose Ruben 1890-1952 ... **TCLC 14**
See also CA 114

Ronsard, Pierre de 1524-1585........ **LC 6**

Silverstein, Alvin 1933- . . . . **CLC 17**
See also CANR 2; CA 49-52; SATA 8

Silverstein, Virginia B(arbara Opshelor)
1937- . . . . **CLC 17**
See also CANR 2; CA 49-52; SATA 8

Simak, Clifford D(onald)
1904-1988 . . . . **CLC 1, 55**
See also CANR 1; CA 1-4R;
obituary CA 125; DLB 8

Simenon, Georges (Jacques Christian)
1903-1989 . . . . **CLC 1, 2, 3, 8, 18, 47**
See also CA 85-88; DLB 72

Simenon, Paul 1956?-
See The Clash

Simic, Charles 1938- . . . . . . **CLC 6, 9, 22, 49**
See also CAAS 4; CANR 12; CA 29-32R

Simmons, Charles (Paul) 1924- . . . . . **CLC 57**
See also CA 89-92

Simmons, Dan 1948- . . . . **CLC 44**

Simmons, James (Stewart Alexander)
1933- . . . . **CLC 43**
See also CA 105; DLB 40

Simms, William Gilmore
1806-1870 . . . . **NCLC 3**
See also DLB 3, 30

Simon, Carly 1945- . . . . **CLC 26**
See also CA 105

Simon, Claude (Henri Eugene)
1913- . . . . **CLC 4, 9, 15, 39**
See also CA 89-92

Simon, (Marvin) Neil
1927- . . . . **CLC 6, 11, 31, 39**
See also CA 21-24R; DLB 7

Simon, Paul 1941- . . . . **CLC 17**
See also CA 116

Simonon, Paul 1956?-
See The Clash

Simpson, Louis (Aston Marantz)
1923- . . . . **CLC 4, 7, 9, 32**
See also CAAS 4; CANR 1; CA 1-4R;
DLB 5

Simpson, Mona (Elizabeth) 1957- . . . **CLC 44**
See also CA 122

Simpson, N(orman) F(rederick)
1919- . . . . **CLC 29**
See also CA 11-14R; DLB 13

Sinclair, Andrew (Annandale)
1935- . . . . **CLC 2, 14**
See also CAAS 5; CANR 14; CA 9-12R;
DLB 14

Sinclair, Mary Amelia St. Clair 1865?-1946
See Sinclair, May
See also CA 104

Sinclair, May 1865?-1946 . . . . . . **TCLC 3, 11**
See also Sinclair, Mary Amelia St. Clair
See also DLB 36

Sinclair, Upton (Beall)
1878-1968 . . . . **CLC 1, 11, 15, 63**
See also CANR 7; CA 5-8R;
obituary CA 25-28R; SATA 9; DLB 9

Singer, Isaac Bashevis
1904- . . . . **CLC 1, 3, 6, 9, 11, 15, 23, 38;**
SSC 3
See also CLR 1; CANR 1; CA 1-4R;
SATA 3, 27; DLB 6, 28, 52;
CDALB 1941-1968

Singer, Israel Joshua 1893-1944 . . . **TCLC 33**

Singh, Khushwant 1915- . . . . **CLC 11**
See also CANR 6; CA 9-12R

Sinyavsky, Andrei (Donatevich)
1925- . . . . **CLC 8**
See also CA 85-88

Sirin, V.
See Nabokov, Vladimir (Vladimirovich)

Sissman, L(ouis) E(dward)
1928-1976 . . . . **CLC 9, 18**
See also CANR 13; CA 21-24R;
obituary CA 65-68; DLB 5

Sisson, C(harles) H(ubert) 1914- . . . . . **CLC 8**
See also CAAS 3; CANR 3; CA 1-4R;
DLB 27

Sitwell, (Dame) Edith 1887-1964 . . . **CLC 2, 9**
See also CA 9-12R; DLB 20

Sjoewall, Maj 1935-
See Wahloo, Per
See also CA 61-64, 65-68

Sjowall, Maj 1935-
See Wahloo, Per

Skelton, Robin 1925- . . . . **CLC 13**
See also CAAS 5; CA 5-8R; DLB 27, 53

Skolimowski, Jerzy 1938- . . . . **CLC 20**

Skolimowski, Yurek 1938-
See Skolimowski, Jerzy

Skram, Amalie (Bertha)
1847-1905 . . . . **TCLC 25**

Skrine, Mary Nesta 1904-
See Keane, Molly

Skvorecky, Josef (Vaclav)
1924- . . . . **CLC 15, 39**
See also CAAS 1; CANR 10; CA 61-64

Slade, Bernard 1930- . . . . **CLC 11, 46**
See also Newbound, Bernard Slade
See also DLB 53

Slaughter, Carolyn 1946- . . . . **CLC 56**
See also CA 85-88

Slaughter, Frank G(ill) 1908- . . . . . . **CLC 29**
See also CANR 5; CA 5-8R

Slavitt, David (R.) 1935- . . . . **CLC 5, 14**
See also CAAS 3; CA 21-24R; DLB 5, 6

Slesinger, Tess 1905-1945 . . . . **TCLC 10**
See also CA 107

Slessor, Kenneth 1901-1971 . . . . **CLC 14**
See also CA 102; obituary CA 89-92

Slowacki, Juliusz 1809-1849 . . . . . **NCLC 15**

Smart, Christopher 1722-1771 . . . . **LC 3**

Smart, Elizabeth 1913-1986 . . . . **CLC 54**
See also CA 81-84; obituary CA 118

Smiley, Jane (Graves) 1949- . . . . **CLC 53**
See also CA 104

Smith, A(rthur) J(ames) M(arshall)
1902-1980 . . . . **CLC 15**
See also CANR 4; CA 1-4R;
obituary CA 102

Smith, Betty (Wehner) 1896-1972 . . . **CLC 19**
See also CA 5-8R; obituary CA 33-36R;
SATA 6; DLB-Y 82

Smith, Cecil Lewis Troughton 1899-1966
See Forester, C(ecil) S(cott)

Smith, Charlotte (Turner)
1749-1806 . . . . **NCLC 23**
See also DLB 39

Smith, Clark Ashton 1893-1961 . . . . **CLC 43**

Smith, Dave 1942- . . . . **CLC 22, 42**
See also Smith, David (Jeddie)
See also CAAS 7; CANR 1; DLB 5

Smith, David (Jeddie) 1942-
See Smith, Dave
See also CANR 1; CA 49-52

Smith, Florence Margaret 1902-1971
See Smith, Stevie
See also CAP 2; CA 17-18;
obituary CA 29-32R

Smith, John 1580?-1631 . . . . **LC 9**
See also DLB 24, 30

Smith, Lee 1944- . . . . **CLC 25**
See also CA 114, 119; DLB-Y 83

Smith, Martin Cruz 1942- . . . . **CLC 25**
See also CANR 6; CA 85-88

Smith, Martin William 1942-
See Smith, Martin Cruz

Smith, Mary-Ann Tirone 1944- . . . . . **CLC 39**
See also CA 118

Smith, Patti 1946- . . . . **CLC 12**
See also CA 93-96

Smith, Pauline (Urmson)
1882-1959 . . . . **TCLC 25**
See also CA 29-32R; SATA 27

Smith, Rosamond 1938-
See Oates, Joyce Carol

Smith, Sara Mahala Redway 1900-1972
See Benson, Sally

Smith, Stevie 1902-1971 . . . . **CLC 3, 8, 25, 44**
See also Smith, Florence Margaret
See also DLB 20

Smith, Wilbur (Addison) 1933- . . . . . **CLC 33**
See also CANR 7; CA 13-16R

Smith, William Jay 1918- . . . . **CLC 6**
See also CA 5-8R; SATA 2; DLB 5

Smollett, Tobias (George) 1721-1771 . . **LC 2**
See also DLB 39

Snodgrass, W(illiam) D(e Witt)
1926- . . . . **CLC 2, 6, 10, 18**
See also CANR 6; CA 1-4R; DLB 5

Snow, C(harles) P(ercy)
1905-1980 . . . . **CLC 1, 4, 6, 9, 13, 19**
See also CA 5-8R; obituary CA 101;
DLB 15

Snyder, Gary (Sherman)
1930- . . . . **CLC 1, 2, 5, 9, 32**
See also CA 17-20R; DLB 5, 16

Snyder, Zilpha Keatley 1927- . . . . . . **CLC 17**
See also CA 9-12R; SAAS 2; SATA 1, 28

Sobol, Joshua 19??- . . . . **CLC 60**

Soderberg. Hjalmar 1869-1941 . . . . **TCLC 39**

Sodergran, Edith 1892-1923 . . . . . . **TCLC 31**

SSC Cumulative Nationality Index

AMERICAN
Anderson, Sherwood 1
Barnes, Djuna 3
Barthelme, Donald 2
Bowles, Paul 3
Boyle, Kay 5
Cable, George Washington 4
Capote, Truman 2
Cather, Willa 2
Cheever, John 1
Chesnutt, Charles Waddell 7
Crane, Stephen 7
Faulkner, William 1
Fitzgerald, F. Scott 6
Freeman, Mary Wilkins 1
Gardner, John 7
Hawthorne, Nathaniel 3
Hemingway, Ernest 1
Henry, O. 5
Hughes, Langston 6
Hurston, Zora Neale 4
Irving, Washington 2
Jewett, Sarah Orne 6
London, Jack 4
Marshall, Paule 3
Mason, Bobbie Ann 4
Melville, Herman 1
Oates, Joyce Carol 6
O'Connor, Flannery 1
Parker, Dorothy 2
Poe, Edgar Allan 1
Porter, Katherine Anne 4
Powers, J. F. 4
Salinger, J. D. 2
Singer, Isaac Bashevis 3
Thurber, James 1
Toomer, Jean 1
Twain, Mark 6
Walker, Alice 5

Warren, Robert Penn 4
Welty, Eudora 1
Wharton, Edith 6
Wright, Richard 2

ARGENTINIAN
Borges, Jorge Luis 4
Cortazar, Julio 7

AUSTRIAN
Kafka, Franz 5

CANADIAN
Atwood, Margaret 2
Gallant, Mavis 5
Laurence, Margaret 7
Munro, Alice 3

CUBAN
Calvino, Italo 3

CZECHOSLOVAKIAN
Kafka, Franz 5

DANISH
Andersen, Hans Christian 6
Dinesen, Isak 7

ENGLISH
Ballard, J. G. 1
Bowen, Elizabeth 3
Chesterton, G. K. 1
Clarke, Arthur C. 3
Hardy, Thomas 2
Kipling, Rudyard 5
Lawrence, D. H. 4
Lessing, Doris (Newbold Jones) 6
Lovecraft, H. P. 3
Wells, H. G. 6

Wodehouse, P. G. 2
Woolf, Virginia 7

FRENCH
Balzac, Honore de 5
Maupassant, Guy de 1
Merimee, Prosper 7

GERMAN
Kafka, Franz 5
Mann, Thomas 5

IRISH
Bowen, Elizabeth 3
Joyce, James 3
Lavin, Mary 4
O'Connor, Frank 5
O'Flaherty, Liam 6

ITALIAN
Calvino, Italo 3

JAPANESE
Mishima, Yukio 4

RUSSIAN
Bunin, Ivan 5
Chekhov, Anton 2
Dostoevski, Fedor 2
Gogol, Nikolai 4
Turgenev, Ivan 7

WELSH
Thomas, Dylan 3

SSC Cumulative Title Index

"The History of the Hardcomes" (Hardy) 2:215

"The Hitch-Hikers" (Welty) 1:466, 468, 481, 487-88, 494

"The Hobo and the Fairy" (London) 4:255

"Hoboes That Pass in the Night" (London) 4:291

"Hog Pawn" (Faulkner) 1:178

"Holding Her Down" (London) 4:291

"The Hole in the Wall" (Chesterton) 1:122

"Holiday" (Porter) 4:347, 349-50, 355

"The Hollow of the Three Hills" (Hawthorne) 3:154, 157, 180-81

"The Holy Door" (O'Connor) 5:365, 367, 371, 384, 390

"The Holy Six" (Thomas) 3:399, 407-08

"Homage to Isaac Babel" (Lessing) 6:196-99, 214

"Homage to Switzerland" (Hemingway) 1:211

"Hombre de la esquina rosada" ("Hombres de las orillas"; "Streetcorner Man"; "The Pink Corner Man") (Borges) 4:10, 14-16

"El hombre en el umbral" ("The Man on the Threshold") (Borges) 4:4, 40-1

"Hombres de las orillas" (Borges)
See "Hombre de la esquina rosada"

"Home" (Boyle) 5:57

"Home" (Hughes) 6:109, 118-19, 121-22, 133

A Home for the Highland Cattle (Lessing) 6:189-91, 195-96

Home Truths: Selected Canadian Stories (Gallant) 5:138, 141, 143-44, 147

"Homecoming" (Kafka)
See "Heimkehr"

"Un homme d'affaires" (Balzac) 5:32

"The Honest Quack" (Chesterton) 1:133

"An Honest Soul" (Freeman) 1:198, 201

"An Honest Thief" (Dostoevski) 2:166, 171, 193

"The Honey Tree" (Jewett) 6:156, 158

"Honorine" (Balzac) 5:18, 31, 33

"The Honour of Israel Gow" (Chesterton) 1:134, 137

"Hood's Isle and the Hermit Oberlus" (Melville)
See "The Encantadas; or, The Enchanted Isles"

"The Hook" (O'Flaherty) 6:264, 269

"Hop-Frog" (Poe) 1:408

"Hopeless" (Atwood) 2:20

"Le horla" (Maupassant) 1:259, 262, 265, 269, 273, 283-84, 286-88

"The Horror at Red Hook" (Lovecraft) 3:258, 262, 289

"The Horror in the Museum" (Lovecraft) 3:279

"The Horse-Dealer's Daughter" (Lawrence) 4:202-03, 231-33, 235-36, 240

"The Horse-Stealers" (Chekhov) 2:130

Horses and Men (Anderson) 1:23, 25, 27, 30, 46, 50

"The Horse's Ha" (Thomas) 3:409

"A Horse's Name" (Chekhov) 2:130

"Horses of the Night" (Laurence) 7:255, 259, 262-63, 270

"A Horse's Tale" (Twain) 6:303

"Horses—One Dash" ("One Dash—Horses") (Crane) 7:104, 106, 108, 125-26, 149, 153-54

"Horsie" (Parker) 2:273-75, 280, 283-84

"A Host of Furious Fancies" (Ballard) 1:79

"Hot and Cold Blood" (Fitzgerald) 6:46

"Hot-Foot Hannibal" (Chesnutt) 7:7, 10-11, 40

"Hotel behind the Lines" (Boyle) 5:74

"The Hound" (Faulkner) 1:177

"The Hound" (Lovecraft) 3:258, 262, 274, 276, 282

"The Hours after Noon" (Bowles) 3:64-6, 80, 82

"The House of Asterión" (Borges)
See "La casa de Asterión"

"House of Flowers" (Capote) 2:67, 69, 72, 75

The House of Pride, and Other Tales of Hawaii (London) 4:268-69, 283

"The House of the Dead Hand" (Wharton) 6:428

"The House Surgeon" (Kipling) 5:272, 275, 284-85

"House Taken Over" (Cortázar)
See "Casa tomada"

"The House That Johnny Built" (O'Connor) 5:363, 371

"The House with a Mezzanine" (Chekhov)
See "An Artist's Story"

"The House with an Attic" (Chekhov)
See "An Artist's Story"

"The House with the Maisonette" (Chekhov)
See "An Artist's Story"

"The Housebreaker of Shady Hill" (Cheever) 1:111

The Housebreaker of Shady Hill, and Other Stories (Cheever) 1:89-92, 95, 100

"The Household" (Irving) 2:265

"How a Good Man Went Wrong" (Chesnutt) 7:14

"How Dasdy Came Through" (Chesnutt) 7:13

"How I Finally Lost My Heart" (Lessing) 6:197, 200-01, 206, 220

"How I Write My Songs" (Barthelme) 2:52

"How Many Midnights" (Bowles) 3:60, 69, 72, 79

"How Much Shall We Bet?" (Calvino) 3:104

"How to Write a *Blackwood* Article" (Poe) 1:405

"Howe's Masquerade" (Hawthorne) 3:154, 187

"The Human Being and the Dinosaur" (Thurber) 1:426, 430

The Human Comedy (Balzac)
See *Comédie humaine*

"Human Habitation" (Bowen) 3:55

"A Humble Romance" (Freeman) 1:196

A Humble Romance, and Other Stories (Freeman) 1:191, 194-95, 197, 201

"A Humorous Southern Story" (Chesnutt) 7:13

"The Hunchback in the Park" (Thomas) 3:400

A Hundred Camels in the Courtyard (Bowles) 3:68

Hunger (Lessing) 6:190, 192-93, 195-97

"A Hunger-Artist" (Kafka)
See "Ein Hungerkünstler"

Ein Hungerkünstler (Kafka) 5:237

"Ein Hungerkünstler" ("A Hunger-Artist") (Kafka) 5:207-09, 220, 225, 237-40

"The Hungry" (Mann) 5:319, 322-23, 330

The Hungry Ghosts (Oates) 6:241, 243

"The Hunter Gracchus" (Kafka) 5:210

"The Hunter's Waking Thoughts" (Gallant) 5:151

"The Huntsman" (Chekhov) 2:155

"Hurricane Hazel" (Atwood) 2:21-3

"The Husband" (Bowles) 3:80

"The Hyena" (Bowles) 3:64-5, 68, 80

"Hygeia at the Solito" (Henry) 5:182

"The Hypothesis of Failure" (Henry) 5:184

"I and My Chimney" (Melville) 1:298, 304, 322, 326-27

"I Live on Your Visits" (Parker) 2:283

I nostri antenati (*Our Ancestors*) (Calvino) 3:91-2, 106, 117

I racconti (Calvino) 3:96-7, 116

"I Remember Babylon" (Clarke) 3:131

"I Want to Know Why" (Anderson) 1:20, 23, 27, 35, 37-8, 40, 48-9, 62

"Ib and Christine" (Andersen) 6:14

"Ibn Hakkan al-Bokhari, Dead in His Labrynth" (Borges) 4:30, 35

"The Ice Maiden" (Andersen) 6:12, 19, 26, 34-5, 37

"The Ice Palace" (Fitzgerald) 6:57-8, 88, 96-7, 100, 103

"The Ice Wagon Going Down the Street" (Gallant) 5:139, 144

"Iconography" (Atwood) 2:15, 20

"Ida" (Bunin) 5:106-07, 116-20

"The Idol of the Cyclades" (Cortázar)
See "Ídolo de las Cícladas"

"Ídolo de las Cícladas" ("The Idol of the Cyclades") (Cortázar) 7:57-8, 69-70, 76, 78

"An Idyll of North Carolina Sand-Hill Life" (Chesnutt) 7:14

"Une idylle" (Maupassant) 1:256, 270

"If I Forget Thee, O Earth'" (Clarke) 3:124, 126, 143

"If I Should Open My Mouth" (Bowles) 3:64, 68-9, 80, 83, 85

"Ignat" (Bunin) 5:100

"The Illuminated Man" (Ballard) 1:69

"An Illusion in Red and White" (Crane) 7:

"L'illustre Gaudissart" ("Gaudissart"; "The Illustrious Gaudissart") (Balzac) 5:18, 26

"The Illustrious Gaudissart" (Balzac)
See "L'illustre Gaudissart"

"I'm a Fool" (Anderson) 1:23, 25, 27, 30, 37-8, 40, 48-50

The Image, and Other Stories (Singer) 3:384-86

"Images" (Munro) 3:326, 338, 343-44

"An Imaginative Woman" (Hardy) 2:215, 220, 223, 225

"The Immortals" (Borges)
See "El inmortal"

"Impertinent Daughters" (Lessing) 6:215

"The Impossible Man" (Ballard) 1:75-7

"The Impossible Marriage" (O'Connor) 5:372, 374

"The Impresario" (Singer) 3:389

"In a Café" (Lavin) 4:183, 185, 189

"In a Far Country" (London) 4:264, 267-68, 279, 281-82, 284-86, 290

"In a Public Place" (Oates) 6:237

"In a Strange Town" (Anderson) 1:50

"In a Thousand Years' Time" (Andersen) 6:30

"In Another Country" (Hemingway) 1:209, 230-32, 234

"In Autumn" (Bunin) 5:114

"In der Strafkolonie" ("In the Penal Colony") (Kafka) 5:218, 223-224, 229-30, 235-36, 240, 249-52

"In Exile" (Chekhov) 2:157

"One Friday Morning" (Hughes) **6**:111-12, 119, 121

"One Good Time" (Freeman) **1**:198

"One Interne" (Fitzgerald) **6**:47-8

"One is a Wanderer" (Thurber) **1**:417, 420, 425, 427, 435

"The £1,000,000 Bank-Note" (Twain) **6**:303, 328-30

"One of Them" (Powers) **4**:375-76

"One Off the Short List" (Lessing) **6**:197, 199, 200, 203-08, 214, 218

"One Reader Writes" (Hemingway) **1**:211

"One Summer" (Lavin) **4**:173, 183

"One Sunday Morning" (Boyle) **5**:64

"One Thousand Dollars" (Henry) **5**:184

"One Trip Abroad" (Fitzgerald) **6**:61, 100, 104

"One Warm Saturday" (Thomas) **3**:394-95, 398, 403, 410-12

"Only a Subaltern" (Kipling) **5**:272

"The Only Rose" (Jewett) **6**:169

"An Only Son" (Jewett) **6**:152-53

"Onnagata" (Mishima) **4**:313, 315, 318, 322-23

"The Open Boat" (Crane) **7**:100-01, 103-04, 107-13, 116-18, 120, 140, 142-43, 145, 148-49, 151-53

The Open Boat and Other Tales of Adventure (Crane) **7**:102, 104

"The Oracle of the Dog" (Chesterton) **1**:133-34, 136

"The Orchards" (Thomas) **3**:396, 399-402, 407-08

"The Ordeal" (Fitzgerald) **6**:58

"Orientation of Cats" (Cortázar) **7**:69, 71

"The Origin of the Birds" (Calvino) **3**:108-10

"The Origin of the Hatchet Story" (Chesnutt) **7**:14-15

"Orphan's Progress" (Gallant) **5**:138

"Orpheus and His Lute" (O'Connor) **5**:377, 382

"Oscar" (Barnes) **3**:2-4

"Otchayanny" ("A Desperate Character") (Turgenev) **7**:337, 362-63

"The Other Death" (Borges) **4**:35, 37, 42-4

"The Other Gods" (Lovecraft) **3**:274

"The Other Man" (Kipling) **5**:274

"The Other Paris" (Gallant) **5**:125-26, 148

The Other Side of the Sky (Clarke) **3**:125, 131-32

"The Other Two" (Wharton) **6**:421, 424-26

"The Other Woman" (Anderson) **1**:30

"Others' Dreams" (Oates) **6**:234

"El otro cielo" (Cortázar) **7**:55, 57, 59, 61-2

"The Ottawa Valley" (Munro) **3**:337

Our Ancestors (Calvino)
　See *I nostri antenati*

"Our Demeanor at Wakes" (Cortázar)
　See "Conducta en los velorios"

"Our Exploits at West Poley" (Hardy) **2**:214, 216, 221

"Our Friend Judith" (Lessing) **6**:201-02, 218-20

"Our Lady of the Easy Death of Alferce" (Oates) **6**:237

"Our Wall" (Oates) **6**:255

"Out of Nowhere into Nothing" (Anderson) **1**:21, 27, 30, 39, 46-7, 53

"Out of Season" (Hemingway) **1**:245

"Out of the Eons" (Lovecraft) **3**:279

"Out of the Sun" (Clarke) **3**:132, 135-36

"The Outcasts" (O'Flaherty) **6**:262, 264, 284

"Outside the Cabinet-Maker's" (Fitzgerald) **6**:51

"Outside the Ministry" (Lessing) **6**:199

"The Outsider" (Lovecraft) **3**:258, 260, 262, 264, 274

"The Oval Portrait" (Poe) **1**:392

"The Overcoat" ("The Cloak") (Gogol) **4**:82-3, 87-91, 93, 106-08, 110-11, 113-17, 127, 129-30

Overhead in a Balloon: Stories of Paris (Gallant) **5**:147

"The Overloaded Man" (Ballard) **1**:74-7

The Overloaded Man (Ballard) **1**:73

Overnight to Many Distant Cities (Barthelme) **2**:50-1, 56

"The Overtone" (Lawrence) **4**:238-39

"Ovsianko the Freeholder" (Turgenev)
　See "The Freeholder Ovsyanikov"

"The Pace of Youth" (Crane) **7**:149

"The Page" (Atwood) **2**:15, 17

"Pages from Cold Point" (Bowles) **3**:59, 61-2, 66, 69, 73, 76-7, 85

"Pain maudit" (Maupassant) **1**:263

"A Painful Case" (Joyce) **3**:203, 205, 209-11, 234-35, 246, 249

"The Painted Woman" (O'Flaherty) **6**:262, 264

"The Painter's Adventure" (Irving) **2**:262

"A Pair" (Singer) **3**:377, 384

"La paix du ménage" (Balzac) **5**:5, 29, 31

Pale Horse, Pale Rider (Porter) **4**:327, 329, 331-35, 339-41, 347, 349, 361, 364-65

Pale Horse, Pale Rider: Three Short Novels (Porter) **4**:327-28, 331, 339

"La panchina" (Calvino) **3**:97

"Pantaloon in Black" (Faulkner) **1**:148, 174, 183

"Le Papa de Simon" (Maupassant) **1**:261, 271

"The Paradise of Bachelors and the Tartarus of Maids" ("The Tartarus of Maids") (Melville) **1**:298, 303-05, 323

The Paradoxes of Mr. Pond (Chesterton) **1**:125, 139

"The Paragon" (O'Connor) **5**:371-72

"Paraguay" (Barthelme) **2**:35, 38, 41

"Le parapluie" (Maupassant) **1**:286

"Parker's Back" (O'Connor) **1**:344-45, 357, 359, 368-70

"The Parrot" (Bowen) **3**:37, 55

"The Parrot" (Singer) **3**:358

"The Parshley Celebration" (Jewett) **6**:156

Parti-colored Stories (Chekhov) **2**:130

"Une partie de campagne" (Maupassant) **1**:260-61

"La partie de trictrac" ("The Game of Backgammon") (Mérimée) **7**:280, 283, 287-91

"The Parting" (O'Flaherty) **6**:265, 281, 286, 288

"The Partridge Festival" (O'Connor) **1**:356

"The Party" (Barthelme) **2**:39, 55

"The Party" (Chekhov)
　See "The Name-Day Party"

"La parure" ("The Necklace") (Maupassant) **1**:273, 278, 280, 284, 286, 288

"Los paso en las huellas" (Cortázar) **7**:62

"The Passenger's Story" (Twain) **6**:337

"Passer-By" (Clarke) **3**:134

"Passing" (Hughes)
　See "Who's Passing for Who?"

"The Passing of Ambrose" (Wodehouse) **2**:356

"The Passing of Black Eagle" (Henry) **5**:158

"The Passing of Grandison" (Chesnutt) **7**:16, 19, 22-3, 25-6

"The Passion" (Barnes) **3**:5, 24-7

"Une passion" (Maupassant) **1**:274

"Une passion dans le désert" ("A Passion in the Desert") (Balzac) **5**:12-14, 31

"A Passion in the Desert" (Balzac)
　See "Une passion dans le désert"

"Passions" (Singer) **3**:378

Passions, and Other Stories (Singer) **3**:376-77, 381, 384

"Past One at Rooney's" (Henry) **5**:198

"Pastor Dowe at Tacaté" (Bowles) **3**:59, 61-3, 66-7, 69, 79

"The Pastor of Six Mile Bush" (Lavin) **4**:169

"Pastoral" (Anderson) **1**:52

"Pastoral Care" (Gardner) **7**:217, 219-22, 229, 232

"Pat Hobby's Christmas Wish" (Fitzgerald) **6**:69-70

"Patent Pending" (Clarke) **3**:133-34

"The Patented Gate and the Mean Hamburger" (Warren) **4**:387, 390, 394, 396, 399

"A Patient Waiter" (Freeman) **1**:201

"The Patriarch" (O'Connor) **5**:393-94

"Patricia, Edith, and Arnold" (Thomas) **3**:402, 405, 410, 412

"Patricide" (Oates) **6**:237

"The Patriot Son" (Lavin) **4**:167, 172, 183

The Patriot Son, and Other Stories (Lavin) **4**:165

"A Patriotic Short" (Fitzgerald) **6**:70-1

"Patriotism" (Mishima) **4**:313-15, 317-23

"La patronne" (Maupassant) **1**:256

"Paul's Case" (Cather) **2**:90-1, 94, 103, 113, 118, 121-22

"The Peace of Utrecht" (Munro) **3**:321, 326

"The Peacelike Mongoose" (Thurber) **1**:426

"The Peaches" (Thomas) **3**:394, 396, 402, 404-05, 410-12

"The Pearl" (Dinesen) **7**:165, 167-68, 198

"The Pearl" (Mishima) **4**:313, 317-18, 322

"The Pearl of Love" (Wells) **6**:376

"The Peasant Marey" (Dostoevski) **2**:166

"Peasant Women" (Chekhov) **2**:155

"Peasants" (Chekhov) **2**:126, 131, 156

"Peasants" (O'Connor) **5**:371, 377-78, 389, 394-95, 398

"Pecheneg" (Chekhov) **2**:155

"Pedro Salvadores" (Borges) **4**:14-17

"The Pegnitz Junction" (Gallant) **5**:124, 127, 132-34, 143

The Pegnitz Junction (Gallant) **5**:124, 127, 130-32

"The Pelican" (Wharton) **6**:413, 423, 428-29

"Pen and Inkstand" (Andersen) **6**:7

"The Pendulum" (Henry) **5**:158-59, 163, 188

"Un pequeño paraíso" ("A Small Paradise") (Cortázar) **7**:93

"Le père" (Maupassant) **1**:275

"Le père amable" (Maupassant) **1**:259, 284

"Père Raphaël" (Cable) **4**:51, 77-9

"Pereval" (Bunin) **5**:98

"A Perfect Day for Bananafish" (Salinger) **2**:290-93, 295, 297-99, 303, 305, 308, 312, 314, 318

"The Perfect Life" (Fitzgerald) **6**:47, 49

"The Perfect Murder" (Barnes) **3**:13

Title Index